Programming ColdFusion MX

Other resources from O'Reilly

Related titles

ActionScript for Flash MX: The Definitive Guide
ActionScript for Flash MX Pocket Guide
ActionScript Cookbook
Flash Cookbook
Flash Remoting MX: The Definitive Guide
Programming Flash Communication Server

oreilly.com

oreilly.com is more than a complete catalog of O'Reilly books. You'll also find links to news, events, articles, weblogs, sample chapters, and code examples.

oreillynet.com is the essential portal for developers interested in open and emerging technologies, including new platforms, programming languages, and operating systems.

Conferences

O'Reilly & Associates brings diverse innovators together to nurture the ideas that spark revolutionary industries. We specialize in documenting the latest tools and systems, translating the innovator's knowledge into useful skills for those in the trenches. Visit *conferences.oreilly.com* for our upcoming events.

Safari Bookshelf (*safari.oreilly.com*) is the premier online reference library for programmers and IT professionals. Conduct searches across more than 1,000 books. Subscribers can zero in on answers to time-critical questions in a matter of seconds. Read the books on your Bookshelf from cover to cover or simply flip to the page you need. Try it today with a free trial.

SECOND EDITION

Programming ColdFusion MX

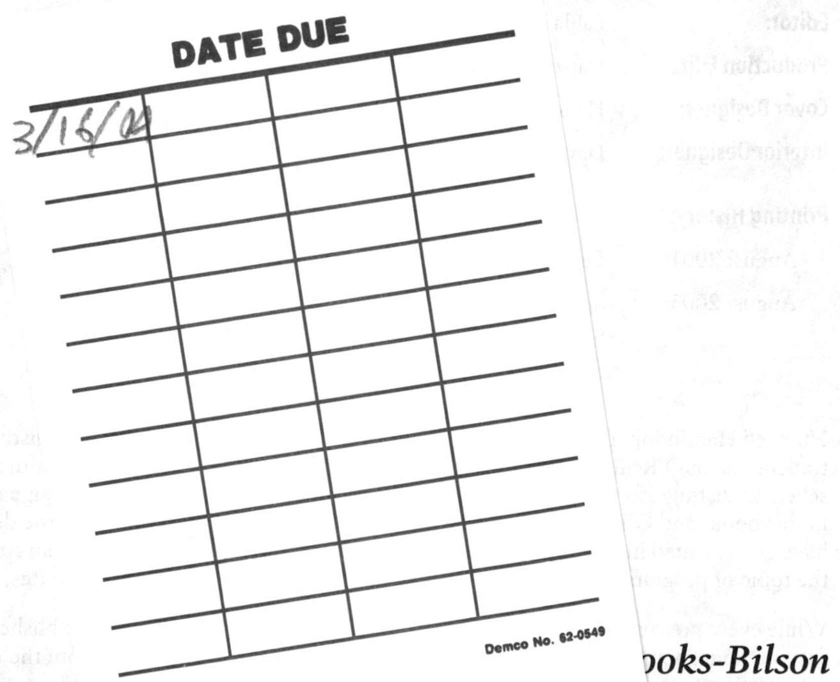

ooks-Bilson

O'REILLY®

Beijing · Cambridge · Farnham · Köln · Paris · Sebastopol · Taipei · Tokyo

Programming ColdFusion MX, Second Edition
by Rob Brooks-Bilson

Printed in the United States of America.

Published by O'Reilly & Associates, Inc., 1005 Gravenstein Highway North, Sebastopol, CA 95472.

O'Reilly & Associates books may be purchased for educational, business, or sales promotional use. Online editions are also available for most titles (*safari.oreilly.com*). For more information, contact our corporate/institutional sales department: (800) 998-9938 or *corporate@oreilly.com*.

Editor:	Paula Ferguson
Production Editor:	Darren Kelly
Cover Designer:	Hanna Dyer
Interior Designer:	David Futato

Printing History:

August 2001:	First Edition.
August 2003:	Second Edition.

ISBN: 0-596-00380-3
[M]

Table of Contents

Preface

I first started using ColdFusion in early 1996. I had been hired by a company to build and manage their external web site and their intranet. Both started as completely static sites, with a few Perl scripts thrown in to handle such tasks as emailing HTML form submissions. But it was only a matter of time before I was asked to add some dynamic content—the request was to "web enable" our corporate address book, which was stored in a Microsoft Access database. My first reaction was to develop the application in Perl. At the time, however, building an application like this in NT Perl (all of our web servers were NT-based) wasn't feasible, so I began looking for other solutions.

I first tried a product called DB Web, from a company named Aspect Software that had just been acquired by Microsoft. After a bit of experimentation, I realized that DB Web wasn't what I was looking for. It was more of a tool for querying data from Microsoft Access databases (it wrote Visual Basic code on the back end) than a real application development platform. (As a side note, Microsoft stopped supporting DB Web shortly after I evaluated it and rereleased it as Active Server Pages (ASP) a few months later.)

Frustrated, I decided to look into another product I had been hearing about on a web development discussion list. The product was Allaire's ColdFusion (Cold Fusion at the time), a rapid application development platform for creating and deploying dynamic server-based web applications.* Within hours of downloading the trial version of the software, I had created a proof-of-concept for the corporate address book application.

Looking back, it is almost funny to imagine that I fell in love with a language that had just over 30 language elements in Version 1.5. At the time, though, ColdFusion had enough power to handle any Internet programming task thrown my way. And as the tasks have become more complex, ColdFusion has kept pace. Today, those initial 30

* In March 2001, Allaire and Macromedia merged, with the combined company using the Macromedia name.

language elements have proliferated to over 355. Each new release of ColdFusion contains features and functionality that seem to show up just as I find myself needing or wanting them.

What's New in ColdFusion MX

ColdFusion MX represents perhaps the single most revolutionary release of ColdFusion yet. The application server itself was completely rewritten in Java. All previous versions of ColdFusion were written in C++. The shift to Java has allowed ColdFusion MX to take advantage of the J2EE framework and all it has to offer in terms of standards, functionality, and scalability. So much has changed since ColdFusion 5 that it would be redundant to list it all here. I've decided to highlight the major enhancements instead:

- Because ColdFusion code now compiles to Java, execution of most code is now significantly faster than in previous versions of ColdFusion.
- There is tighter integration between ColdFusion and JSPs, servlets, EJBs, and Java objects than ever before.
- Enhanced support for both internationalization and localization has been added, and ColdFusion MX now supports Unicode.
- ColdFusion's query of query feature has been greatly enhanced to support a wider array of options.
- ColdFusion MX uses JDBC (although it can still use ODBC) for database connectivity. In many cases, this eliminates the need to install separate client libraries on the server.
- Regular-expression support has been greatly enhanced in ColdFusion MX. Regular expressions are now "Perl compatible."
- User-defined functions have been enhanced in ColdFusion MX. In addition to CFScript-based user-defined functions, you can now create them using CFML tags.
- The introduction of ColdFusion Components (CFCs) has added object-oriented techniques to ColdFusion.
- Working with XML is easier than ever, thanks to several new tags and functions in ColdFusion MX.
- Producing and consuming web services couldn't be easier. In most cases, a single tag attribute is all that's necessary to publish a CFC as a web service. Consuming web services can be as simple as providing a URL to a single CFML tag.
- The graphing and charting capabilities of ColdFusion have been improved. ColdFusion 5 used Macromedia's Generator as the underlying graphing engine. ColdFusion MX takes advantage of an underlying Java engine that offers far more options for chart and graph generation.

- Application-level security has been greatly enhanced with a built-in roles-based security mechanism.
- Enhanced debugging and logging capabilities have been added.
- The need for locking access to shared scope variables, an often-misunderstood practice in previous versions of ColdFusion, has been greatly reduced.
- Major enhancements to the `cfmail` tag in ColdFusion MX 6.1 including the ability to send upward of 1 million messages an hour (in ColdFusion Enterprise), create multi-part mail messages, specify backup mail servers (ColdFusion Enterprise), and spawn multiple mail threads.
- Enhancements to the `cfhttp` tag in ColdFusion MX 6.1 to support additional HTTP operations beyond get and post.
- ColdFusion MX is integrated more tightly with Macromedia's other MX products, especially Dreamweaver MX and Flash MX. With regard to Flash MX, ColdFusion MX supports a new technology called Flash Remoting, a Macromedia technology for tying a Flash front end with ColdFusion on the server. Flash Remoting opens up a whole new category of applications known as Rich Internet Applications (RIAs) that go beyond what's currently possible with HTML/DHTML front ends.

Because there is so much new functionality in ColdFusion MX, as well as significant changes between ColdFusion 5 and MX, I've gone to great lengths to highlight the differences throughout the book.

Readers of the First Edition

If I was fortunate enough to have you as a reader of the first edition of this book (*Programming ColdFusion*), you'll be interested to know that the second edition has been completely revised and updated for ColdFusion MX 6.1. Just about every chapter has been rewritten, several of them completely. Many of the changes are the direct result of reader feedback. Four new chapters were added to deal with totally new topics introduced in ColdFusion MX. Additionally, the majority of examples used throughout the book have also been rewritten to reflect new and improved coding techniques and practices.

It's worth noting that many of the changes to ColdFusion from Version 5 to MX are significant and simple to spot, while others are subtle and easy to overlook. Wherever possible, I try to point out the differences between the two versions.

Audience

This book is for anyone who is interested in learning more about ColdFusion MX, but it is especially aimed at web developers who are designing and building web applications with ColdFusion. I hope this book will help you become proficient with ColdFusion and that you find ColdFusion as powerful, easy to program with, and productive as I do.

If you are a beginning web developer, without any programming experience, you may find that the book moves quite quickly through the basics of ColdFusion. Before you start to learn ColdFusion, you should have some experience with web page creation, including a solid understanding of HTML. After that, if you focus on the examples provided in the early chapters and do a lot of experimenting with the code while you are reading, you should be able to learn ColdFusion with this book.

For intermediate developers who already have some web programming experience, this book is the perfect place to learn ColdFusion and get up to speed quickly. You'll learn about the ColdFusion Markup Language (CFML), which is ColdFusion's tag-based language for embedding dynamic content in web pages. This book provides examples that use CFML to implement all the standard web tasks, such as processing form data, performing database queries, and handling session data, so you should be up and running with ColdFusion in no time.

And if you are an advanced ColdFusion developer, you'll find this book loaded with strategies, hints, tips, and tricks that you can apply to your own projects. I've tried to include all the useful ColdFusion tidbits that I've discovered over the years, so that you can benefit from my experience. The book also includes reference material on all CFML tags and functions, so that you can have this information at your fingertips while you are programming.

Organization

This book is divided into 28 chapters and 4 appendixes, as follows:

Chapter 1, *Introducing ColdFusion*
: Introduces the book and gives a high-level overview of the components that make up the ColdFusion development platform.

Chapter 2, *ColdFusion Basics*
: Gets you started using ColdFusion and covers such topics as datatypes, variables, expressions, conditional processing, and looping.

Chapter 3, *Passing Data Between Templates*
: Looks at passing data between templates using HTML forms and hyperlinks.

Chapter 4, *Database Basics*
: Gets you started using ColdFusion to query databases. Provides an overview of Structured Query Language (SQL) and demonstrates its use within ColdFusion applications.

Chapter 5, *Maintaining Database Records*
: Covers techniques for adding, updating, and deleting database records.

Chapter 6, *Complex Datatypes*
: Looks at the complex datatypes available in ColdFusion: lists, arrays, structures, and query objects.

Chapter 7, *Maintaining State*
: Investigates methods for maintaining state in ColdFusion applications.

Chapter 8, *Security*
: Covers the basics of application security and discusses several methods and models for securing your ColdFusion applications.

Chapter 9, *Error and Exception Handling*
: Explains several techniques for implementing error and exception handling within your ColdFusion applications.

Chapter 10, *Dynamic Form Controls*
: Gives an overview of the dynamic form controls provided by ColdFusion as an extension to standard HTML form controls.

Chapter 11, *Advanced Database Techniques*
: Covers several advanced techniques for querying and displaying data as well as advanced SQL topics.

Chapter 12, *Manipulating Files and Directories*
: Deals with techniques for manipulating files and directories on both local and remote servers. Also covers executing programs from the command line.

Chapter 13, *Working with Email*
: Shows how to use ColdFusion to send email through SMTP servers and how to retrieve messages from POP3 servers. A working example of a web-based mail client is included.

Chapter 14, *Interacting with Other Web Servers Using HTTP*
: Demonstrates how to interact with other web servers via the HTTP GET and POST methods using ColdFusion.

Chapter 15, *Interfacing with LDAP-Enabled Directories*
: Gives a general overview of the Lightweight Directory Access Protocol (LDAP) and shows how to use ColdFusion to interface with LDAP-enabled directories.

Chapter 16, *Working with the Verity Search Interface*
: Explains how ColdFusion interacts with a bundled version of Verity's VDK, K2 Server, and Spider engines to index and search both file- and query-based content.

Chapter 17, *Graphing and Charting*
: Shows how to use ColdFusion's built-in server-side graphing and charting capabilities to produce dynamic charts and graphs.

Chapter 18, *Regular Expressions in ColdFusion*
: Introduces regular expressions and demonstrates ways to integrate them into your ColdFusion applications.

Chapter 19, *Scripting*
: Provides an overview of CFScript, a server-side scripting language modeled after JavaScript that can be used in place of some of ColdFusion's tag-based language constructs.

Chapter 20, *User-Defined Functions*
: Shows how to create user-defined functions (UDFs) using both CFML tags and CFScript.

Chapter 21, *Creating Custom Tags*
: Shows how to extend the core capabilities of the ColdFusion language through reusable components called Custom Tags.

Chapter 22, *ColdFusion Components*
: Covers ColdFusion Components (CFCs), a framework for using concepts and techniques of object-oriented programming for building your applications.

Chapter 23, *XML and WDDX*
: Covers XML and the Web Distributed Data Exchange (WDDX), an XML-based technology for sharing data across disparate platforms and programming languages.

Chapter 24, *Web Services*
: Discuses web services and shows how to use ColdFusion MX to both produce and consume them.

Chapter 25, *Working with the System Registry*
: Explains how the Windows version of ColdFusion MX can be used to read and write to the system registry.

Chapter 26, *Using the ColdFusion Scheduler*
: Explains how to schedule one-time and recurring tasks using ColdFusion's built-in scheduler.

Chapter 27, *Interacting with COM, CORBA, and Java*
: Covers the basics of using ColdFusion to interact with COM, CORBA, and Java.

Chapter 28, *Flash Remoting*
: Gives a general overview of Rich Internet Applications and how to create them by pairing Macromedia Flash and ColdFusion MX via Flash Remoting.

Appendix A, *Tag Reference*
: A complete CFML tag reference that includes several previously undocumented tags.

Appendix B, *Function Reference*
: A complete CFML function reference that contains numerous previously undocumented functions. The function reference includes a working example for each function wherever possible.

Appendix C, *Example Database Tables*
: Contains the schema and sample data for all database tables used in the book's examples.

Appendix D, *ColdFusion Resources*
: Provides a comprehensive listing of free ColdFusion resources available over the Internet. These resources include user groups, e-zines, support forums, and other community-minded resources.

Conventions Used in This Book

The following typographical conventions are used throughout this book:

Italic
: Used for commands, URLs, filenames, file extensions, command-line utilities, directory and folder names, and UNC pathnames, as well as new terms where they are defined.

`Constant width`
: Used for anything that appears in a ColdFusion template, including CFML and HTML tags and attributes, variables, and functions. Also used for code listings.

`Constant-width italic`
: Used as general placeholders to indicate that an item should be replaced by some actual value in your own program.

Comments and Questions

Please address comments and questions concerning this book to the publisher:

O'Reilly & Associates, Inc.
1005 Gravenstein Highway North
Sebastopol, CA 95472
(800) 998-9938 (in the United States or Canada)
(707) 829-0515 (international/local)
(707) 829-0104 (fax)

There is a web page for this book, which lists errata, examples, or any additional information. You can access this page at:

http://www.oreilly.com/catalog/coldfusion2

To comment or ask technical questions about this book, send email to:

bookquestions@oreilly.com

For more information about books, conferences, software, Resource Centers, and the O'Reilly Network, see the O'Reilly web site at:

http://www.oreilly.com

Acknowledgments

While it is impossible to individually acknowledge everyone who had a hand in getting this book from an idea to the printed work you now hold in your hand, I would like to recognize and thank a few of these special people.

First, my thanks go out to the technical reviewers for this edition, Brendan O'Hara, Elishia Olsen, Steve Rittler, Scott Varga, and Ray West. I can't begin to describe how helpful they have been. This edition also benefited from comments and suggestions from Selene Bainum, Artur Bakhtriger, Michael Dinowitz, Elias Jo, and Amy Wong, my technical reviewers from the first edition.

I'd also like to thank the engineers, support staff, and product managers at Macromedia for their hard work and dedication to making ColdFusion what it is. Without access to your knowledge and insight, writing this book would not have been possible.

My editors at O'Reilly, Paula Ferguson (first and second edition) and Laura Lewin (first edition), also deserve recognition. Without their editorial skill and ability to help me focus in on the important aspects of the book, you wouldn't be reading this. Finally, I'd like to thank the production staff at O'Reilly for their hard work in getting the book to print.

And finally, my wife Persephone, for all things at all times.

CHAPTER 1

Introducing ColdFusion

In 1989, two chemists, Martin Fleischmann and Stanley Pons, claimed that their research had uncovered a phenomenon that promised to solve the world's energy problems. What they claimed to have accomplished was nothing short of astonishing: that they had achieved nuclear fusion at room temperature. They called their discovery cold fusion. Unfortunately, the scientific community at large dismissed their findings because no one was ever able to reproduce the results claimed in the original experiment. Oh wait, wrong book...

What Is ColdFusion?

In 1995, J.J. and Jeremy Allaire introduced a product they believed would revolutionize application development for the Web. They too called their creation ColdFusion. The two brothers formed the Allaire Corporation and began selling ColdFusion. Unlike its infamous namesake, ColdFusion has delivered on the promises put forth by its creators. In 2001, Macromedia acquired Allaire, and along with it, ColdFusion. ColdFusion MX represents the second ColdFusion product release under the Macromedia banner.

According to Macromedia's marketing materials, ColdFusion is "the rapid server scripting environment for creating rich internet applications." Internet applications exist as a collection of pages, also known as templates, which work together to allow users to perform such tasks as reading email, buying books, or tracking packages. Internet applications often act as the front-end to back-end services, such as legacy applications and databases, and can be accessed through various means such as web browsers, cell phones, and other Internet-enabled devices. Some examples of web sites and applications built using ColdFusion include Autobytel.com's application for researching and purchasing a car (*http://www.autobytel.com/*), Williams-Sonoma's storefront application (*http://www.williams-sonoma.com/*), and the online reservation system at the Broadmoor Hotel's web site (*http://www.broadmoor.com/*).

One key aspect of an Internet application is that it is dynamic; it is not just a static collection of pages. The benefits of dynamically driven design are obvious. If you think of it in practical terms, which would you rather do each time a new press release has to be added to your web site? Would you rather the marketing department send you the text for the new press release so you can convert it to an HTML page, upload the page to your server, then go add a link to the menu of available press releases? Or, would you rather provide an online form to the marketing department so they can enter the text from the press release themselves and store it in a database that can then be queried to dynamically build the press release menu and associated pages? ColdFusion allows you to create just this kind of application.

Of course, there are a lot of different technologies you can use to create dynamic applications, from open source technologies such as Perl/CGI scripts or PHP, to such commercial options as JavaServer Pages and Java servlets or Microsoft's Active Server Pages. With all these choices, why use ColdFusion MX?

One reason has to do with ease of development. Unlike most of the other technologies I mentioned, you don't have to be a hard-core programmer to get started with ColdFusion. This doesn't, however, mean that ColdFusion isn't powerful. Quite the contrary. ColdFusion makes it simple to do common tasks, such as processing form data and querying a database. But when you need to perform more complex operations, such as transaction processing and personalization, ColdFusion makes that possible too.

ColdFusion is also designed for rapid application development (RAD). ColdFusion abstracts complex, low-level programming tasks, such as establishing connectivity with a mail server or querying a database, with simple HTML-like tags. The result is an application development cycle that is second to none.

Another advantage of ColdFusion is that it is available for a broad range of popular operating systems and web servers. ColdFusion can be run on Windows 98/ME/NT 4/2000/XP/Server 2003, Linux, Solaris, HP-UX, and the AIX operating system. Additionally, the developer version of ColdFusion MX Enterprise can be deployed on Mac OS X when the J2EE configuration is used. ColdFusion works in conjunction with several popular web servers including Microsoft IIS, Netscape Enterprise Server, iPlanet Enterprise Server, Apache, and ColdFusion MX's standalone web server. In general, you can migrate ColdFusion applications between different operating systems, web servers, and databases, for instance, when you upgrade your databases for scalability purposes. There are, however, some minor incompatibilities between platforms (i.e., there is no COM support in the Unix/Linux version of ColdFusion). Although minor for the most part, these differences are explained in relevant sections of this book.

ColdFusion MX is also an integral part of Macromedia's overall MX product line, which includes Dreamweaver MX for authoring, Fireworks MX for web graphics, and Flash MX for developing rich user interfaces for Internet applications. As Macromedia's cornerstone server product, ColdFusion MX is tightly integrated with the rest of the MX products.

ColdFusion is a mature, robust product; the current version as of this writing is ColdFusion MX 6.1. When ColdFusion was released in 1995, it provided simple database and SMTP mail connectivity and supported basic output formatting. Each successive release of ColdFusion has added features and functionality. Today, ColdFusion contains over 90 tags and 265 functions for handling almost any task imaginable. Add to that scalability features such as load balancing and failover to handle high-traffic sites, and it is easy to see why ColdFusion is so popular among developers and administrators alike.

There is a vibrant community of ColdFusion users who are active both in shaping the future direction of the product and in supporting others who use it. A number of ColdFusion-related conferences are held each year by both Macromedia and members of the developer community. Macromedia also runs several web-based forums and Usenet-style newsgroups, where developers can post and answer questions related to ColdFusion development (*http://webforums.macromedia.com/coldfusion/*). The forums are monitored by Macromedia support engineers as well as a volunteer group known as Team Macromedia. In addition, Macromedia sponsors a number of user groups around the world. Known as CFUGs (ColdFusion User Groups) and MMUGs (Macromedia User Groups), these groups provide a place for ColdFusion developers to get together and share information on a variety of ColdFusion-related topics. Finally, there are a number of web sites devoted to furthering the ColdFusion community. For a complete list of community resources, see Appendix D.

ColdFusion Architecture

There are several components that make up the ColdFusion MX environment, from which you can develop ColdFusion applications. As I mentioned earlier, a ColdFusion MX application is simply a collection of templates (pages) that work together to allow a user to perform a task. By template, I mean a file that contains a combination of hard-coded HTML (or other structure/layout code) along with sections of ColdFusion code that replace otherwise static sections of content with "dynamic" content pulled from a database or other data source. These templates don't exist in a vacuum, however. To get a better idea of how a ColdFusion application is constructed, you need to understand the components that make up the ColdFusion environment:

ColdFusion MX Application Server

TheColdFusion Application Server processes all the CFML code in the templates passed to it by the web server. It then returns the dynamically generated results to the web server, so that the output can be sent to the user's browser. The ColdFusion Application Server integrates with a number of popular web servers via native APIs and is also capable of running with ColdFusion MX's standalone web server (recommended for development only). Once the ColdFusion Application Server is set up, it works silently in the background, so we won't be talking much about it in this book.

Integrated Development Environment (IDE)

DreamweaverMX is the Integrated Development Environment (IDE) designed for the ColdFusion MX Application Server. Dreamweaver MX provides developers with a visual environment for developing, testing, debugging, and deploying ColdFusion MX applications. Although ColdFusion MX applications can be written using any text editor capable of saving ASCII output, Dreamweaver MX offers many advantages that make it worth considering. Prior to the introduction of Dreamweaver MX, many ColdFusion developers used an IDE called ColdFusion Studio (later HomeSite +). Many of the features from Studio were merged into the Dreamweaver MX IDE; however, a large number of ColdFusion developers continue to use ColdFusion Studio as their IDE of choice. This book doesn't concern itself with the method you use to create your ColdFusion MX applications, so these tools aren't given much coverage.

ColdFusion Markup Language (CFML) pages and components

The ColdFusion Markup Language (CFML) is the language that you use to create ColdFusion applications. CFML is a tag-based language, just like HTML. You use it in conjunction with HTML and other client-side technologies, such as JavaScript and CSS (Cascading Style Sheets), to create the templates that make up a ColdFusion application. CFML is used to determine *what* to display, while the technologies such as HTML and CSS specify *how* to display it, an important distinction. This book covers all the CFML tags and functions supported by ColdFusion.

Web server

The web server funnels browser requests for CFML templates through the ColdFusion MX Application Server. The web server is also responsible for passing the output returned by the ColdFusion MX Application Server back to the browser. As I already mentioned, ColdFusion works the same way on all supported web servers, so your choice of web server isn't important (as far as interoperability with ColdFusion is concerned) and won't affect your programming.

ColdFusion Administrator

The ColdFusion Administrator is actually a ColdFusion application for configuring and administering the ColdFusion Application Server. The ColdFusion Administrator handles everything from registering and setting up data sources to logging and security. This is a book for programmers, so it doesn't cover configuration and administration. For more information on configuring and administering the ColdFusion Application Server, you need to consult the documentation that comes with your edition of ColdFusion.

Data sources

ColdFusion is capable of interacting with a number of external data sources, including databases (via JDBC and ODBC), Verity collections, LDAP directories, POP3 and SMTP mail servers, SOAP-based web services, FTP servers, and other HTTP servers. This allows you to create ColdFusion applications that send and receive email, transfer files with FTP, query directory servers, and request content from other web servers. This book includes chapters that show how to use ColdFusion to interact with all of the data sources I just mentioned.

Objects

ColdFusion can interact with various external objects, including ColdFusion Components (CFCs), COM/DCOM objects, CORBA objects, and Java objects (including Enterprise JavaBeans components). This allows your ColdFusion applications to interact with third-party components as well as back-end systems written in other languages, which makes ColdFusion an excellent choice for acting as the "glue" that ties together all sorts of disparate systems into a cohesive application.

Extensions

CFML is extensible via custom extensions written in a variety of languages, such as C++, Java, and even CFML. By writing an extension, you can include functionality not natively available in the core ColdFusion language. For example, ColdFusion can't natively connect to a NNTP news server, but if you are skilled in C++ or Java, you can easily build a CFX extension to support such a connection. Creating custom tags using CFML is covered in Chapter 21. Custom extensions are beyond the scope of this book, however, so for more information on developing your own custom extensions using C++ or Java, you need to consult the documentation that came with your edition of ColdFusion.

Flash Remoting

One of the benefits of Macromedia's tight integration between all of the products in their MX line is the ability to easily have ColdFusion MX applications exchange data with Macromedia Flash MX applications via a mechanism known as Flash Remoting. This opens up all sorts of possibilities for creating Flash front-ends that interact with ColdFusion in the middle tier for data access, processing, etc.

Now that you understand the components that comprise the ColdFusion environment, let's look at how ColdFusion processes a typical browser-based request:

1. A web browser makes a request to a web server for a template with a *.cfm* or *.cfc* extension (or another custom configured extension).
2. The web server receives the request and forwards it to the ColdFusion MX Application Server.

3. The ColdFusion MX Application Server parses the CFML template and processes the tags and functions accordingly, interacting with other services, such as data sources or mail servers, as necessary.
4. The ColdFusion MX Application Server combines its dynamic output with the static HTML and CSS (and JavaScript, if any) in the template and passes the whole page back to the web server.
5. The web server passes the dynamically generated content back to the client machine's web browser.

This entire process is illustrated in Figure 1-1.

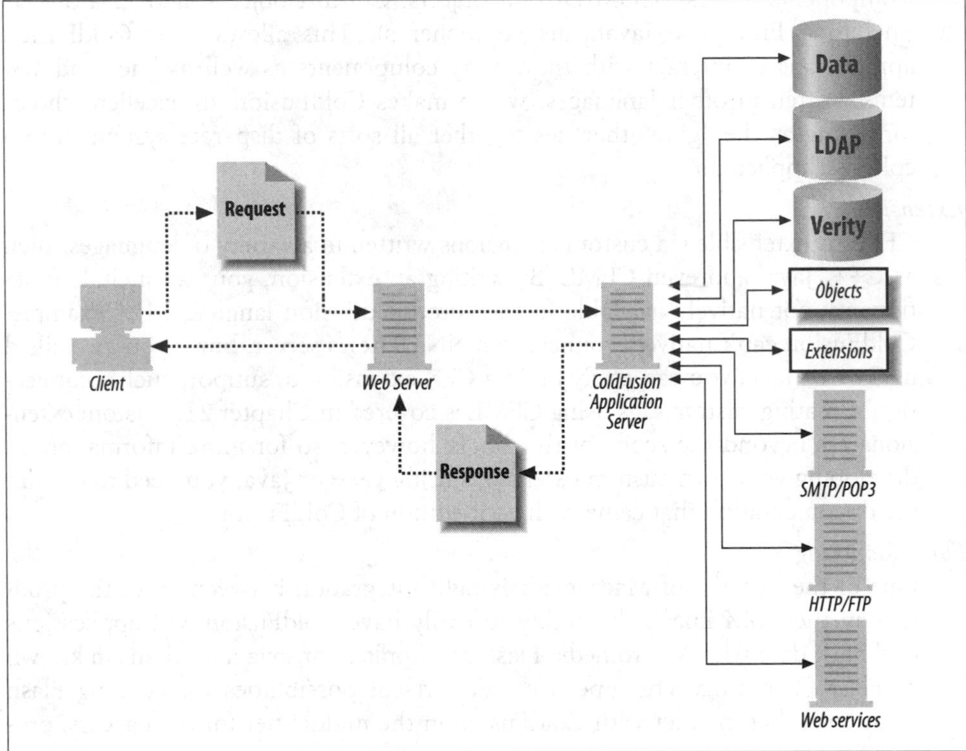

Figure 1-1. How ColdFusion requests are processed

Getting Started with ColdFusion

Obviously, to use this book, you need access to a ColdFusion MX server. If your company is already developing web applications with ColdFusion, the server should already be available to you. Or, if you are developing for a remote server, you should be all set. In either case, you just need to know where to put your templates; check with your system administrator or webmaster.

If you don't have access to a ColdFusion server, your first step is to pick an edition of ColdFusion. There are currently four editions of ColdFusion available to support the needs of various sized projects and organizations; all of them are available at Macromedia's web site, *http://www.macromedia.com* (as of this writing, the latest release is ColdFusion MX 6.1):

ColdFusion MX Standard (Windows and Linux only)
: Formerly called ColdFusion MX Professional (through ColdFusion MX 6.0), the standard edition is designed for departmental and small group use. It contains access to all CFML language features, a 125KB document limit on Verity searches, and database drivers for MS Access (Windows only), MS SQL Server, and MySQL. Email handling in ColdFusion MX 6.1 Standard has been improved as well. The underlying engine is now capable of generating approximately 33KB emails per hour, an improvement over previous versions.

*ColdFusion MX Enterprise (Windows, Linux, Solaris, HP-UX, and AIX)**
: Contains all the functionality of ColdFusion MX Standard and adds server clustering, additional Type IV JDBC database drivers for most popular databases, a 250KB document limit on Verity searches, the ability to host JSP pages, servlets, EJBs, and import JSP tag libraries, as well as additional security, management, deployment, and performance features for hosting large-scale applications. Email handling in ColdFusion MX 6.1 Enterprise has be greatly improved. The engine is capable of generating approximately 1 million messages per hour, and contains additional features such as multi-threading, connection pooling, and the ability to use backup mail servers. ColdFusion MX Enterprise can be installed in one of two configurations:

  Server Configuration
  : Installs a single instance of ColdFusion MX Enterprise (or Developer) with an embedded J2EE server. This is the equivalent to a "standard" or "standalone" installation of ColdFusion from previous versions.

  J2EE Configuration
  : Installs one or more instances of ColdFusion MX Enterprise (or Developer) on top of an included licensed copy of Macromedia JRun, or on a third-party J2EE application server such as IBM WebSphere, BEA Weblogic, or Sun One. This allows you to write and deploy ColdFusion MX applications that leverage the underlying architecture of popular J2EE application servers. For a complete list of supported J2EE application servers, see Macromedia's web site.

* In ColdFusion MX 6.0, an additional version of ColdFusion MX known as ColdFusion MX for J2EE was available. In ColdFusion MX 6.1, this option has been rolled into a single product edition known as ColdFusion MX Enterprise.

ColdFusion Developer Edition (Windows, Linux, Solaris, HP-UX, and AIX for Server or J2EE configuration; Mac OS X for J2EE configuration only)

This is a for development-only version of ColdFusion MX Enterprise (Server or J2EE configuration) that limits access to the IP address of the development machine and one additional IP address per session. Additionally, it sets the document limit for Verity searches to 10k. ColdFusion MX Developer Edition allows you to build and test applications without having to purchase a full ColdFusion MX Enterprise license. The trial version of ColdFusion Enterprise automatically becomes the developer version once the 30-day trial period expires.

Hardware requirements for running ColdFusion vary depending on your platform and the edition of ColdFusion you want to run. You should make sure the machine on which you plan to run the ColdFusion Application Server can meet the demands you might place on it. ColdFusion generally requires a system with 250 to 400 MB of hard disk space and between 128 and 512 MB of RAM, depending on the platform and whether the server is for development or production. Memory requirements are only a guideline. In general, the more physical RAM available to ColdFusion, the better it will perform, because many tasks performed by web applications are memory-intensive, such as intensive database queries, Verity indexing/searching, caching, and integration with other third-party resources. For the most up-to date system requirements, please refer to the documentation that came with your edition of ColdFusion, or visit *http://www.macromedia.com/software/coldfusion/productinfo/system_reqs/*.

If you work in an organization with an IT department, you should be able to get them to install and configure ColdFusion. Otherwise, you'll have to perform these tasks yourself. Because ColdFusion is available for multiple platforms, installation procedures vary. For specific instructions on installing and configuring the ColdFusion Application Server, see the documentation provided with your edition of ColdFusion, or visit the Macromedia ColdFusion Support Center at *http://www.macromedia.com/support/coldfusion/installation.html*.

Once you have a working ColdFusion installation, you're ready to start programming. In the next chapter, we'll dive in and learn about ColdFusion basics. For this material to make sense, though, you need to have some basic experience with web page creation and, in particular, HTML. If you don't have any experience with HTML, you should spend some time learning basic HTML before you try to learn ColdFusion. For this, I recommend *HTML & XHTML: The Definitive Guide*, by Chuck Musciano and Bill Kennedy (O'Reilly & Associates). If you are planning to use ColdFusion to interact with a database, you may also find it helpful to have a general understanding of relational databases and SQL (Structured Query Language). For more information on SQL, see *SQL in a Nutshell*, by Kevin Kline with Daniel Kline, Ph.D. (O'Reilly).

CHAPTER 2
ColdFusion Basics

Part of what makes developing web applications with ColdFusion so easy is the simplicity of the ColdFusion Markup Language (CFML). Because CFML is a tag-based language like HTML, it is simple to write and easy to understand. All ColdFusion code is written inside tags or within the boundaries of paired tags (just like HTML). There are over 90 tags and 265 functions in the CFML language that you can use to accomplish virtually any task. ColdFusion tags wrap complex functionality, such as database connectivity and data manipulation, into simple tags that can be invoked with a minimum of coding. CFML functions offer even more power, as they provide access to common operations, such as string manipulation and mathematical functions, that aren't possible using HTML alone.

Because CFML is a programming language, we need to start with some basics about the language. In this chapter, I cover how to create and save ColdFusion applications, as well as the major aspects of the language, such as datatypes, variables, expressions, conditional processing, and more.

Getting Started

To write a ColdFusion application, you can use virtually any text editor or an HTML authoring tool that allows you to directly edit the code. As we discussed in Chapter 1, a ColdFusion application is a collection of web pages, also called templates or pages that work together to allow a user to perform a task. When you create a CFML template, you typically embed the CFML code within standard HTML (although it is also possible to create files that contain only CFML, as you'll see later in the chapter). A ColdFusion application can be as simple as a single page. Consider the following example, which outputs the current date to the browser:

```
<html>
<head>
  <title>CFML Example</title>
</head>
```

```
<body>

<cfoutput>
<h2>Today's date is #DateFormat(Now( ),'mm/dd/yyyy')#</h2>
</cfoutput>

</body>
</html>
```

At first glance, this template looks just like an HTML template. If you look closer, however, you'll see embedded CFML code right in the middle of the template. The code here uses a single tag (`<cfoutput>`) and two functions (`DateFormat( )` and `Now( )`) to output the current date to the browser. We'll get to what this tag and the functions do in a bit. For now, we're just concerned with running the template and understanding how CFML and HTML coexist.

Saving CFML Templates

To execute this template, you need to save the file on the machine that is running your web server and the ColdFusion Application Server. You can either type in this example and save it to a file or you can copy the file from the book's example archive (available at *http://www.oreilly.com/catalog/coldfusion/*). You should put the file in a directory accessible under the root directory of your particular web server. For example, if the root directory for your web server is *c:\inetpub\wwwroot*, you can create a subdirectory two levels down such as *c:\inetpub\wwwroot\examples\chapter2* and save the template there as *2-1.cfm*. Now if you use your web browser to view this file (*http://127.0.0.1/examples/chapter2/2-1.cfm*), you'll see the web page displayed in Figure 2-1.

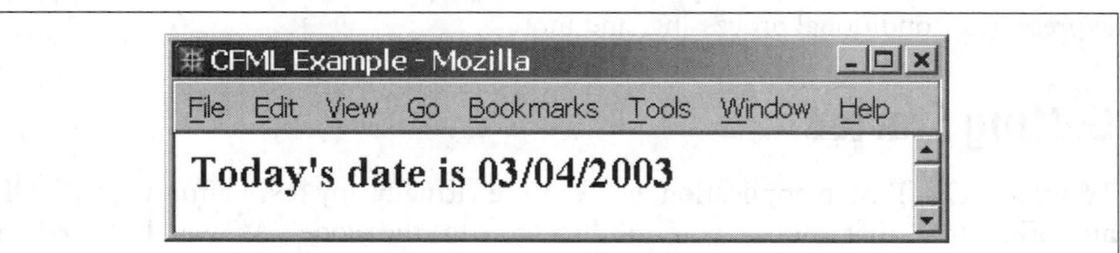

Figure 2-1. Calling a CFML template from your web browser

By default, CFML files need to have the extension *.cfm* in order for your web server to know to send the files to the ColdFusion engine for processing. It is possible to use an extension other than *.cfm*, as long as you configure your web server to associate the new extension with the ColdFusion engine.

When you save your CFML template, you should follow the conventions set forth by your web server for saving HTML templates. For example, in Windows environments, filenames are case insensitive. On Unix, however, filenames are case sensitive. These differences are important to remember when coding your applications, especially if you ever need to port your application from a Windows to a Unix environment.

Tag Syntax

CFML tags are written in the same manner as HTML tags. Most CFML tags have a start tag (written as `<cf*TagName*>`) and an end tag (written as `</cf*TagName*>`). All CFML tags begin with the letters "cf". In keeping with XML conventions, any CFML tag that doesn't have or require an end tag may optionally be written with a trailing forward slash, as in `<cf*TagName*/>`. CFML tags are not case sensitive (`<cfoutput>` and `<cfoutput>` both work). However, if you are trying to code to a standard such as XHTML, you should use all lowercase tags, as I do in this book.

Most CFML tags accept one or more attributes that affect the tag's behavior, just like HTML tags. A tag's attributes allow you to pass values to the tag for processing. Tags can accept both required and optional attributes. To get a better idea of how attributes affect a tag's behavior, consider the following example, in which we call the `<cfmail>` tag (used to send email messages via SMTP):

```
<!--- Call the cfmail tag --->
<cfmail from="webmaster@example.com"
        to="you@example.com"
        subject="Test Message"
        server="127.0.0.1">
This is a test message
</cfmail>

<h2>Message Sent</h2>
```

In this example, we pass four attributes to the `cfmail` tag. The `from`, `to`, and `subject` attributes are all required attributes; they specify what you'd expect about the email message. `server` is an optional attribute that specifies the server name or IP address of the mail server ColdFusion should use to send SMTP mail. Specifying a value here overrides any value set in the ColdFusion Administrator. Several other optional attributes can be passed to the `cfmail` tag to further affect its behavior. You need to pass optional parameters only if you wish to use a value other than the default. (The `cfmail` tag is discussed in detail in Chapter 12.)

Attributes can accept both literal values and expressions. Literal values are generally surrounded by double quotes, although this isn't necessary when referring to numeric values, Boolean values, or expressions. In the interest of style and consistency, however, I suggest that you surround all attribute values with double quotes. Because ColdFusion is a weakly typed language, you can pass numeric values inside quotes without causing any problems.

Attributes aren't the only way for CFML tags to get data. Many CFML tags can act on any content that appears between its start and end tags. These tags are often referred to as container tags. If you look at the previous example, you'll notice that the text "This is a test message" appears between the `<cfmail>` and `</cfmail>` tags. In the case of the `cfmail` tag, any text appearing within the `cfmail` block is used by the tag as the message body. Other container tags make different use of the text placed between the tag pairs.

Comments

One final thing to note about the previous example is its use of comments. Commenting your code is an essential part of application development. Including quality comments in your code is important for a number of reasons:

- It allows you to remember what a particular section of code does long after you have forgotten about the application.
- It helps break up sections of code into more readable chunks.
- It helps other developers understand your development style in the event they inherit your application.

There are two types of comments that can be used in your CFML templates: HTML-style comments and CFML comments. The standard HTML-style comment takes the form:

```
<!--This is a comment-->

<!-- This is a comment too. -->

<!-- So is this
     it is just on two lines -->
```

Notice that each comment begins with `<!--` and ends with `-->`. HTML comments contain two dashes and may or may not have a space between the dash and the comment text.

CFML comments differ from HTML comments in four ways. First, CFML comments contain three dashes, as opposed to the two dashes in HTML comments:

```
<!--- This is a CFML comment --->

<!--- This is a multi-line
      CFML comment --->
```

The second difference is that CFML comments must have a space between the opening and closing comment marker and the comment text. Failure to include these spaces can result in incorrectly parsed code and produce undesirable results when a template is executed.

The third difference between CFML comments and regular HTML comments is that CFML comments aren't displayed in the HTML code generated by ColdFusion. If you display the HTML code generated by ColdFusion by using your browser's "View Source" function, you won't see any CFML comments you wrote in the source code.

You will, however, see any HTML comments you made. For this reason, you should write your comments as CFML comments when you want to comment your code but you don't want to let visitors to your site view the comments.

The final difference is a new feature in ColdFusion MX. CFML comments can now be placed within tags, functions, and pound signs (discussed later). All of the following examples are valid CFML comments in ColdFusion MX:

```
<cfset x = 1 <!--- I am valid --->>
<cfset y = DateFormat(Now( ), 'mm/dd/yyyy' <!--- I'm valid too --->)>
<cfset z = (1 + 2<!--- still valid --->)>
<cf_mytag var="x" <!--- I'm valid too --->>
<cfoutput>
#y<!---I'm valid as well, although this looks weird--->#
</cfoutput>
```

Datatypes

ColdFusion supports a number of datatypes for use in building expressions. These datatypes can be broken into four categories: simple, complex, binary, and object. The simple datatypes are made up of Booleans, strings, numbers (both integer and floating point), and date/time objects:

Boolean
: ColdFusion uses the Boolean datatype to store the value generated by a logical operation. Boolean values are stored as either `true` or `false`. In numeric operations, Boolean values evaluate to `1` for `true` and `0` for `false`. When dealing with strings, Boolean values are set to `Yes` for `true` and `No` for `false`. Note that no quotes are necessary to delimit Boolean values, nor are Boolean values case sensitive.

Strings
: ColdFusion stores text values in strings delimited by a set of single or double quotes. For example, `"This is a string."` and `'So is this!'` are both strings. `"1000"` and `'1000'` are also strings so long as the numbers are delimited by a set of quotes. The empty string can be written as either `''` or `""`. There are certain special characters that must be escaped within strings. These special characters are the single quote ('), double quote ("), and pound sign (#). These characters may be escaped by doubling up on them as in the following examples:

```
<cfset String1 = "This is a ""good"" use of escaped double quotes">
<cfset String2 = "This is a ''good'' use of escaped single quotes">
<cfset String3 = "What is the ##1 team in the league?">
```

As we'll discuss in the next section, `<cfset>` is a CFML tag you use to set a variable to a particular value.

Numbers

ColdFusion supports both floating-point (decimal) and integer (whole number) values. Numbers don't need to be delimited by quotes when referenced within expressions. The range for floating-point values in ColdFusion is 10^{300} (1 followed by 300 zeros) with up to 12 significant digits. The range for integer values is –2,147,483,648 to 2,147,483,647. ColdFusion automatically converts numbers outside this range to floating-point values.

Most ColdFusion functions can perform calculations accurate to 12 decimal places. Numbers may be represented as either regular numbers or in scientific notation. ColdFusion formats numbers in scientific notation as *x*E*y* (*x**10*y*) where *x* is a positive real number in the range 1–10, and *y* is an integer. So, 100,000 equals 1.0E5 or $1*10^5$ while .001 equals 1.0E-3 or $1*10^{-3}$.

Date/time objects

ColdFusion allows you to specify date and time values separately or combined. Dates must range from 100 A.D. to 9999 A.D. and can be written as:

```
8/15/02
08/15/2002
2002-08-15
August 15, 2002
Aug 15, 2002
Aug. 15, 2002
```

ColdFusion MX uses the underlying Java Runtime Environment (JRE) as well as the current locale to determine how to process two-digit years. For most locales, two-digit years are processed relative to the current century. Based on this, two digit years are interpreted to within 80 years before the current date and 20 years after. There are a few exceptions to this. The following locales interpret two digit years to within 72 years before the current date and 28 years after: English (Australian), English (New Zealand), German (Austrian), German (Standard), German (Swiss), Portuguese (Brazilian), Portuguese (Standard), Swedish.

Times are accurate to the second and can be written as:

```
7pm
07:00pm
7:00pm
19:00:00
```

Combined date/time objects can be written as any combination of the previous dates and times.

Complex datatypes include query objects, lists, arrays, structures, and XML document objects:

Lists

Lists are a special type of string that contains delimited elements. For example, `"a,b,c,d,e,f,g"` is a list where `"a"`, `"b"`, `"c"`, `"d"`, `"e"`, `"f"`, and `"g"` are considered the list elements while the comma (,) is considered the delimiter. Lists are covered in Chapter 6.

Arrays

Arrays are objects that can store indexed values. Each value stored in an array is referred to as an element of the array. Each element has an integer assigned to it that marks its position within the array. This number is referred to as the element's index. Array elements can store any ColdFusion datatype including additional arrays.

ColdFusion supports one-dimensional (think of this as a single column of data or a list), two-dimensional (think of this as a spreadsheet with rows and columns), and three-dimensional (think of this as a cube of data) arrays. Additional dimensions can be created dynamically by nesting multidimensional arrays (creating an array of arrays). Arrays are discussed in Chapter 6.

Structures

Structures are objects that allow you to store and manipulate key/value pairs. Structures are similar to one-dimensional arrays except elements are referenced via an alphanumeric "key" (string) as opposed to a numeric index within the array. Structures offer an advantage over arrays in certain situations by allowing you to reference groups of related information by key as opposed to by numeric index. This feature allows structures to also be used as associative arrays. Structures are covered in Chapter 6.

Query objects

Query objects are special ColdFusion data structures that hold record sets. Record sets are most often returned by database query operations. In addition, several CFML tags return query objects upon completion. Query objects are similar in structure to two-dimensional arrays and are made up of rows and columns (like a spreadsheet). Query objects are discussed in Chapter 4.

XML document objects

XML document objects are a special datatype ColdFusion uses to represent XML data. XML document objects are very similar to structures containing nested arrays and structures that represent the DOM (Document Object Model) of the XML data. XML document objects can be easily manipulated using most of ColdFusion's structure and array functions as well as the new XML functions introduced in ColdFusion MX. XML is discussed in Chapter 23.

The binary datatype is used to store raw data, usually from files. Binary data in its raw format generally isn't very useful as it isn't human readable. However, it may be desirable to manipulate it in various ways such as reading or writing values. In versions of ColdFusion prior to MX, binary data couldn't be directly manipulated using CFML functions. It first had to be converted to Base64 using the `ToBase64()` function. Base64 is an encoding scheme that uses printable characters to represent binary data. Base64 is typically used to encode binary data before it is sent via email or stored in a database. In ColdFusion MX, binary data is stored as a byte array that can easily be manipulated with ColdFusion's array and string functions. For more information on working with binary data, see Chapter 12.

Object datatypes include COM (Windows 95, 98, NT, and 2000 only), CORBA, Java, ColdFusion Components (CFCs), and web services objects. Regardless of the type of object invoked, objects usually consist of methods and properties that can be accessed by ColdFusion. Objects are a fairly advanced topic and are covered in Chapters 22 and 27. CFMLprovides a number of functions for dynamically determining the datatype of a variable: `IsArray()`, `IsBinary()`, `IsBoolean()`, `IsDate()`, `IsNumeric()`, `IsNumericDate()`, `IsObject()`, `IsQuery()`, `IsSimpleValue()`, `IsStruct()`, and `IsXmlDoc()`. Additionally, several functions exist specifically for manipulating data specific to each particular datatype. These functions are discussed throughout the book and can be found in Appendix B.

Variables

A *variable* is a name associated with a data value; it is common to say that a variable stores or contains a value. Variables allow you to store and manipulate data in your applications; they are called variables because the values they represent can change throughout the life of an application. In ColdFusion, you don't have to explicitly declare your variables, as you do in a language such as C++. Additionally, ColdFusion variables are typeless, meaning that you can assign a value of any datatype (string, numeric, Boolean, object, etc.) to any variable.

Variable Names

The following rules and guidelines apply to variable names in CFML:

- Variable names must begin with a letter, an underscore, or the Unicode currency symbol ($) and can contain only letters, numbers, underscores, and Unicode currency symbols. Variable names can't contain spaces. For example, `Test`, `MyVariable`, `My_variable`, `MyVariable1`, and `MyDescriptive_var2` are all valid ColdFusion variables, while `4C`, `My Variable`, `Phone#`, and `A/P` aren't. Note that the addition of the Unicode currency symbol is new in ColdFusion MX.
- In ColdFusion MX, you cannot use compound variable names delimited with a period, such as `Employee.Name`. In previous versions of ColdFusion, compound variable names were allowed. In ColdFusion MX, the same syntax is used to automatically create a structure with a specific key and assign a value to that key. For example, `<cfset Employee.Name="Pere Money">` creates a structure named `Employee` and assigns "Pere Money" to a key called `Name`. There are two exceptions to this rule: cookie names and client variable names may contain periods.
- Avoid using variable names that are the same as ColdFusion variable scopes, scope structures, return values, tag names, function names, operators, or SQL keywords.

- Avoid using variable names that end in `_date`, `_eurodate`, `_float`, `_integer`, `_range`, `_required`, or `_time`, as these are reserved suffixes for server-side form validation variables and can cause naming conflicts.
- ColdFusion variable names aren't case sensitive. In the interest of good style and readability, however, you should keep the case of your variable names consistent.
- Always try to use descriptive names for your variables. It might seem like a pain, but you will be grateful when it comes time to debug or add a new feature.
- If your application interacts with a database, you can make your code clearer by using ColdFusion variable names that match the corresponding fields in the database.

Assigning Values to Variables

The `<cfset>` tag assigns a value to a variable in ColdFusion. The variable name is followed by an equal sign and the value or expression you want to assign to the variable. For example:

```
<cfset x = 1>
<cfset y = x+2>
<cfset Name = "Rob">
<cfset x = Name>
<cfset Authenticated = true>
<cfset TheDate = DateFormat(Now(),'mm/dd/yyyy')>
```

You can set only one variable in each `cfset` tag. Note that the `cfset` tag doesn't have a closing tag.

Variable Scope

ColdFusion supports a number of different variable scopes, where *scope* refers to the context in which the variable exists within an application. The scope encompasses where the variable came from (such as a form field, a URL, etc.), how it can be used, and how long it persists. As we'll discuss shortly, when you refer to a variable in your code, you can use just the variable's simple name (*MyVar*) or its fully scoped name (*scope*.*MyVar*). The variable scopes available in ColdFusion are as follows:

Local
: By default, all variables created using the `cfset` and `cfparam` tags are local variables. (We haven't discussed the `cfparam` tag yet; we'll get to it shortly.) Local variables are accessible only on the page on which they are created and can be referenced by their simple names or as `variables.`*`variable_name`*.

Form
: Form variables are passed from HTML forms or ColdFusion Java forms to other ColdFusion templates. Data is passed when a user fills out a form and submits it. Both the form field name and associated data are passed from the form to the

ColdFusion template specified in the form's action attribute. Form field variables can be referenced as form.*field_name*. By default, a variable called form.FieldNames is always available within the form scope; it contains a comma-delimited list of all field names posted from a form.

URL

URL variables contain parameters passed to ColdFusion templates via URLs. For example, consider the following hypertext link:

```
http://www.example.com/view_news.cfm?ArticleID=5&ViewMode=public
```

Clicking on this link causes a ColdFusion template named *view_news.cfm* to execute. Two variables, ArticleID and ViewMode, with the values 5 and public, respectively, are available to the *view_news.cfm* template. To refer to the variables in the *view_mode.cfm* template, you can use the syntax URL.ArticleID and URL.ViewMode.

Query

The query scope references variables within a ColdFusion query object. For example, to reference a field called Name from a query called Employees, you use the following syntax: Employees.Name. Three predefined variables are always available for any query object:

```
queryname.ColumnList
queryname.CurrentRow
queryname.RecordCount
```

The query scope is covered in detail in Chapter 4.

File

File variables are automatically created by ColdFusion when you use the <cffile> tag to upload a file. These variables are referenced as cffile.*variable_name*. File variables are covered in detail in Chapter 12. For a complete list of available file variables, see the <cffile> tag in Appendix A.*

CGI

CGI variables are read-only variables that report specific information about the server and browser environments in use. CGI variables are accessible in all ColdFusion templates; the available variables vary depend on the combination of server and browser software being used. CGI variables take the form CGI.*variable_name*. A list of some of the most common CGI variables is shown in Table 2-1.

Table 2-1. Common CGI variables

AUTH_PASSWORD	HTTP_HOST
AUTH_TYPE	HTTP_USER_AGENT

* Prior to Version 4.5, the file scope was prefixed using the File prefix. This prefix was deprecated in ColdFusion 5.0.

Table 2-1. Common CGI variables (continued)

AUTH_USER	HTTPS
CERT_COOKIE	HTTPS_KEYSIZE
CERT_FLAGS	HTTPS_SECRETKEYSIZE
CERT_ISSUER	HTTPS_SERVER_ISSUER
CERT_KEYSIZE	HTTPS_SERVER_SUBJECTS
CERT_SECRETKEYSIZE	PATH_INFO
CERT_SERIALNUMBER	PATH_TRANSLATED
CERT_SERVER_ISSUER	QUERY_STRING
CERT_SERVER_SUBJECT	REMOTE_ADDR
CERT_SUBJECT	REMOTE_HOST
CF_TEMPLATE_PATH	REMOTE_USER
CONTENT_LENGTH	REQUEST_METHOD
CONTENT_TYPE	SCRIPT_NAME
GATEWAY_INTERFACE	SERVER_NAME
HTTP_ACCEPT	SERVER_PORT
HTTP_ACCEPT_CHARSET	SERVER_PORT_SECURE
HTTP_ACCEPT_ENCODING	SERVER_PROTOCOL
HTTP_ACCEPT_LANGUAGE	SERVER_SOFTWARE
HTTP_CONNECTION	WEB_SERVER_API
HTTP_COOKIE	

It is also possible to obtain a list of the CGI variables available for your particular configuration by turning on debugging in the ColdFusion Administrator. Once you have done this (provided you have access to the ColdFusion Administrator), simply execute any CFML template on your server. A list of all accessible CGI variables should appear at the bottom of the page.

Server

Server variables store data associated with the server on which ColdFusion is running. Server variables are available to all ColdFusion applications and persist until the ColdFusion Application Server is stopped. You can create your own server variables or reference the following predefined ones:

```
server.COLDFUSION.APPSERVER
server.COLDFUSION.PRODUCTNAME
server.COLDFUSION.PRODUCTVERSION
server.COLDFUSION.PRODUCTLEVEL
server.COLDFUSION.ROOTDIR
server.COLDFUSION.SERIALNUMBER
server.COLDFUSION.SUPPORTEDLOCALES
server.COLDFUSION.EXPIRATION
server.OS.ARCH
server.OS.NAME
```

```
server.OS.ADDITIONALINFORMATION
server.OS.VERSION
server.OS.BUILDNUMBER
```

Server variables must always be referenced using the server prefix as in `server.`*`variable_name`*. Server variables are discussed in detail in Chapter 7.

Cookie

Cookie variables hold the values of HTTP cookies retrieved from a user's web browser. Cookies are a unique type of persistent variable that are stored on the client machine and sent to the ColdFusion server each time a page is requested. Cookies are covered in Chapter 7.

Application

Application variables define application-wide settings such as default directories and data source names. Application variables are usually defined in the *Application.cfm* file. Application variables are available to all clients, or users, accessing the named application and are often referred to as global variables. Application variables must always be referenced using the `application` prefix, as in `application.`*`variable_name`*. By default, a single predefined application variable is available:

```
application.ApplicationName
```

Application variables and the `cfapplication` tag are discussed in detail in Chapter 7.

Session

Session variables are persistent variables that store information for a specific session. Session variables are held in the server's memory and persist for a finite amount of time. Each session is unique to a user and can be referenced across ColdFusion templates. Session variables are often used for shopping carts and user authentication systems. Session variables must be specifically set and referenced as `session.`*`variable_name`*. In order to use session variables, they must be turned on in both the ColdFusion administrator and within an *Application.cfm* template for the application. By default, the following predefined session variables are available:

```
session.cfid
session.cftoken
session.sessionid
session.urltoken
```

Session variables as well as the *Application.cfm* template are discussed in detail in Chapter 7.

Client

Client variables store values associated with a particular user, just like session variables. Most often they are used to maintain state across a server cluster as a user navigates from page to page throughout an application. What makes client variables different from session variables is that they can persist across multiple sessions. That is, client variables are stored by the ColdFusion server and can be retrieved during subsequent visits. For example, an application might use a client variable to remember things such as the last time a user visited your site or their font size/color preferences. By default, client variables are stored in the system registry, but they can also be stored in a cookie or a database. When creating client variables, the variable name must always be referenced using the `client` prefix, as in `client.`*`variable_name`*. This is optional when reading client variables. In addition to the client variables you create in an application, there are several read-only client variables ColdFusion creates automatically:

```
client.cfid
client.cftoken
client.hitcount
client.lastvisit
client.timecreated
client.urltoken
```

Client variables are discussed in Chapter 7.

Attributes
The attributes scope is unique to ColdFusion custom tags. It allows you to refer to attributes passed from the calling template to the custom tag. Caller variables must always be referenced using the `attributes` prefix as in `attributes.`*`variable_name`*. Custom tags and attribute variables are discussed in detail in Chapter 21.

Caller
The caller scope is also unique to ColdFusion custom tags; it passes a value from a custom tag back to its calling template. Caller variables must always be referenced using the `caller` prefix as in `caller.`*`variable_name`*. Caller variables are discussed in Chapter 21.

ThisTag
The ThisTag scope is unique to custom tags as well and is generally used with paired custom tags, or for intertag communication. Variables in the ThisTag scope must always be referenced with the `thistag` prefix, as in `thistag.`*`variable_name`*. There are four variables that are automatically created by ColdFusion:

```
thistag.executionMode
thistag.HasEndTag
thistag.GeneratedContent
thistag.AssocAttribs[index]  (only when child tag is associated with base tag)
```

For more information on the ThisTag scope, see Chapter 21.

Request
Request variables offer a way to store data in a structure that can be passed to nested custom tags. Because variables in the request scope are available to all templates in a request, they are often set in an application's *Application.cfm* template and used in lieu of application variables. Request variables must always be referenced using the `request` prefix as in `request.`*`variable_name`*. Request variables are discussed in Chapter 21.

Arguments

The arguments scope is used to reference arguments passed to user-defined functions (UDFs) and ColdFusion Components (CFCs) methods. The arguments scope differs from other variable scopes in that it can be accessed as both a scope structure and a scope array. Arguments should always be referenced as `arguments.`*`variable_name`* or `arguments[`*`array_index`*`]`. Arguments are discussed in Chapters 20 and 22.

Function

This scope is only available within UDFs and CFC methods and is used to declare variables local to the function. It differs from all other variable scopes in two ways. The first is that there's no prefix for the function scope. Once a function variable has been initialized, it is referred to just like any other unscoped variable. The second difference is that function variables must be initialized using the `var` attribute of the `cfset` tag as in this example:

```
<cfset var x=10> <!--- Assigns 10 to a function variable named x --->
```

The function scope is discussed in Chapters 20 and 22.

Super

The super scope is unique to CFCs that use inheritance. Super is not actually used to scope variables, but instead is used to scope component methods. The super scope contains all the methods that the current component extends, which is useful in situations where a component and the component it extends have like-named methods. In this case, super lets you reference a method in the parent object, as opposed to the like-named method in the child object that you called.

This

The this scope is unique to CFCs and is functionally equivalent to the this scope in JavaScript and ActionScript. Variables in the this scope are available to all methods within a CFC, to any pages they include, and to the page that calls the CFC. Within a CFC, you refer to variables in the this scope using the `this` prefix: `this.varName`. Outside the CFC, you use the component name to reference variables in the this scope: `myComponent.varName`.

Flash

The flash scope is used in conjunction with Macromedia's Flash Remoting technology to reference values passed to ColdFusion from a Flash movie. Variables in this scope must always be referenced with the `flash` prefix. For more information on Flash Remoting, see Chapter 28.

Most variable scopes can be accessed via like-named ColdFusion structures. These scope structures are `application`, `arguments`, `attributes`, `caller`, `CGI`, `cookie`, `client`, `file`, `form`, `local`, `request`, `server`, `session`, `this`, `thistag`, and `URL`. These structures contain all the variable names and associated values for the particular scope and can be manipulated using any of the structure functions listed in Appendix B.

In addition to the previously mentioned variable types, many CFML tags return variables known as *return values* or *return variables*. These variables are usually prefixed with the name of the tag generating them. For example, the `<cfhttp>` tag returns several variables, such as `cfhttp.FileContent` and `cfhttp.MimeType`, depending on the action you have it perform.

The ColdFusion environment also defines some variables automatically in different scopes. For example, when form data is passed to a ColdFusion template, form variables are automatically created for all the form fields. The same holds true for URL parameters passed to a ColdFusion template.

To get a better understanding of how these variable scopes relate to one another, consider the relationships depicted in Figure 2-2.

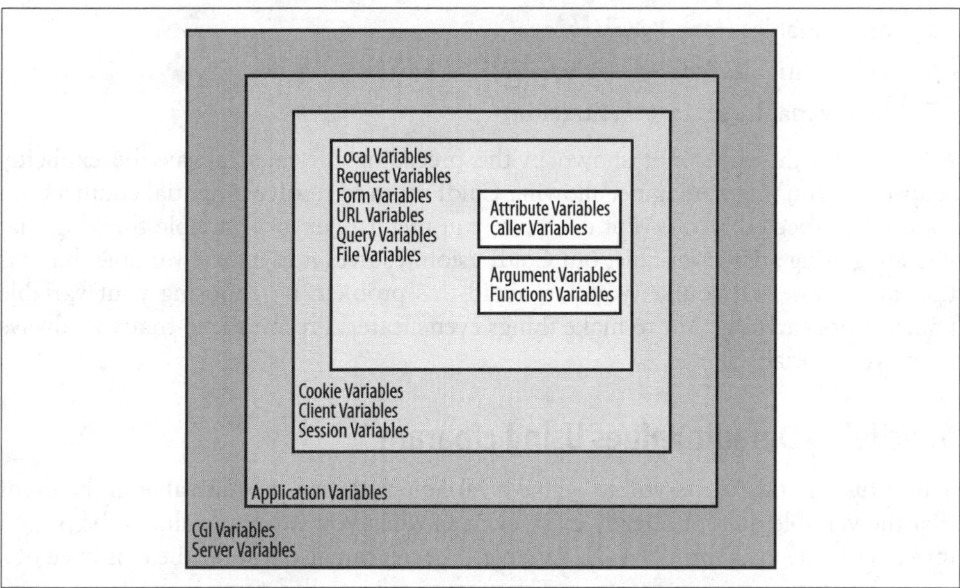

Figure 2-2. Variable scope relationships

When you refer to a variable in your code, you can refer to it using just the variable's simple name (*MyVar*) or its fully scoped name (*scope.MyVar*). Referencing a variable using its fully scoped name is called *scoping* the variable. Because ColdFusion supports different variable scopes, the potential exists for having like-named variables of different scopes within an application. ColdFusion allows you to deal with this potential conflict in two ways.

One way to handle potential variable conflicts is to always provide the variable scope when referencing a variable. For example, a URL variable should be referenced as `URL.MyVariable`, while a form variable should be referenced as `form.MyVariable`. Using the variable scope has two additional benefits. First, by identifying the variable scope right along with the variable, it makes your code more readable. When you look through your code, you know in exactly what context a particular variable is used. The second benefit has to do with performance. When ColdFusion encounters a scoped variable, it is able to process the code faster because it doesn't have to take time to determine the variable's scope.

The second way to deal with potential variable conflicts is to let ColdFusion handle them. When the ColdFusion server encounters an unscoped variable, it attempts to evaluate it in a specific order:

1. Local variables (`variables.MyVariable`)
2. CGI variables (`CGI.MyVariable`)
3. File variables (`cffile.MyVariable`)
4. URL variables (`URL.MyVariable`)
5. Form variables (`form.MyVariable`)
6. Cookie variables (`cookie.MyVariable`)
7. Client variables (`client.MyVariable`)

All variables in scopes not shown in the preceding list must always be explicitly scoped. As you might imagine, allowing ColdFusion to resolve potential conflicts can lead to unexpected results. For example, you might refer to a variable thinking that you are getting a URL variable, but ColdFusion resolves it to a local variable that has the same name. Of course, you can avoid this problem by choosing your variable names more carefully. But to make things even clearer, I recommend that you always scope your variables.

Specifying Default Values Using cfparam

The `<cfparam>` tag allows you to define a variable and set a default value in the event that the variable doesn't already exist, such as when you expect a value to be passed into a template via a form or URL variable. The tag can also test for the existence of a variable as well as test its datatype. The `cfparam` tag is called using the following syntax:

```
<cfparam name="parameter_name"
         type="data_type"
         default="value">
```

The `name` attribute specifies the name of the variable to create. `type` is optional and is used to specify the datatype the variable must be to be considered valid. Possible options are `Any`, `Array`, `Binary`, `Boolean`, `Date`, `GUID`, `Numeric`, `Query`, `String`, `Struct`, `UUID`, and `VariableName`. The default value for `type` is `Any`. `VariableName` is a special option; it checks to make sure the variable you are checking contains a value that is a valid variable name according to the naming conventions we covered earlier. The final attribute, `default`, assigns a default value or expression to the variable if it doesn't exist or has no value already assigned. The `cfparam` tag can be used in three ways:

Test for a required variable
: Use the `name` attribute to specify the name of the variable to test for. If the variable doesn't exist, ColdFusion throws an error.

Test for a required variable of a specific datatype
: Use the `name` attribute to specify the name of the variable and the `type` attribute to specify the required datatype for the value assigned to the variable. If the variable doesn't exist or contains a value of the wrong datatype, ColdFusion throws an error.

Test for an optional variable and assign a default value
: Use the `name` attribute to specify the name of the variable and the `default` attribute to specify a value assigned to the variable in the event it doesn't exist.

The following example demonstrates how the `cfparam` tag can assign a default value to a variable in the event it doesn't already exist:

```
<cfparam name="URL.RecordID" default="12">
```

In this case, the `cfparam` tag assigns a default value of 12 to a URL variable called `RecordID` in the event that the variable doesn't already exist in the template. Using `cfparam` lets you define a default value to use in the event that the URL variable isn't passed (for whatever reason) so that ColdFusion doesn't throw an error.

Expressions

Expressions are the building blocks of the CFML language. In its most basic form, an expression is nothing more than a single element such as `1`, `test`, `MyVar`, or `Chr(54)`. Compound expressions let you to evaluate data that is acted upon by operators. For example, `1*10` is a mathematical expression that evaluates to `10`. The values `1` and `10` are both data, while the asterisk (*) is considered an operator. On the other end of the spectrum, expressions can be complex, consisting of one or more subexpressions:

```
<cfset x = 1+(10 mod (3 * (11 - acos(-1))))>
```

Operators

Operators allow you to perform calculations and make comparisons between expressions. In other words, they allow you to combine simple expressions to form ones that are more complex. For example, `<cfset x = 10*(3+2)>` uses the asterisk (*) as an operator to multiply 10 by the sum of another expression that uses the plus (+) operator to add 3 and 2. There are four types of operators available in ColdFusion:

Arithmetic
: Performs arithmetic operations such as sign changes, addition, subtraction, etc., on numeric values.

Comparison
: Compares two values and returns a Boolean `true`/`false`.

String
: There is only one string operator in the CFML language. The ampersand (&) concatenates strings.

Boolean
: Also known as logical operators, Boolean operators perform connective and negation operations and return Boolean `true`/`false` values.

Table 2-2 lists the operators available in ColdFusion by order of precedence (P).

Table 2-2. ColdFusion operators

Operator	Operation	Type	P
Unary +, unary -	Sign change	Arithmetic	1
^	Raise to a power	Arithmetic	2
*, /	Multiplication, division	Arithmetic	3
\	Integer division	Arithmetic	4
mod	Remainder	Arithmetic	5
+, -	Addition, subtraction	Arithmetic	6
&	Concatenation	String	7
is (equal, eq), is not (not equal, neq), contains, does not contain, greater than (gt), greater than or equal to (gte), less than (lt), less than or equal to (lte)	Equality Inequality Contains substring Doesn't contain > >= < <=	Comparison	8
not	Logical NOT	Boolean	9
and	Logical AND	Boolean	10
or	Logical OR	Boolean	11
xor	Logical XOR	Boolean	12
eqv	Equivalence	Boolean	13
imp	Implication	Boolean	14

Functions

Functions are a type of operator that let you perform a predefined action on a piece of data. CFML functions encapsulate a set of operations that would otherwise require a substantial amount of programming. ColdFusion comes with several hundred predefined functions. In addition, as of ColdFusion 5.0, you can create your own user-defined functions. Most functions take input in the form of parameters. Functions can stand alone or be nested.

Many functions accept a single argument:

```
<cfset MyCharacter = Chr(76)>
```

String arguments may be delimited by single or double quotes:

```
<cfset String1 = Reverse('Hello')>
<cfset String2 = Reverse("Hello")>
```

Functions can also accept variables as arguments:

```
<cfset x = -1>
<cfset absx = abs(x)>
```

There are a few functions that take no arguments:

```
<cfset TheTime = Now( )>
<cfset x = CreateUUID( )>
```

Some functions require more than one argument. Multiple arguments are separated with a comma:

```
<cfset x = Compare(1234, 4321)>
```

Other functions contain both required and optional arguments. If no value is supplied for an optional argument, a default is used instead:

```
<cfset MyList = "Monday;Tuesday;Wednesday;Thursday;Friday;Saturday;Sunday">
<cfset Length = ListLen(MyList, ';')>
```

In this example, the second argument passed to the `ListLen( )` function is optional. It specifies the delimiter that separates elements of the list. If no delimiter is specified, the function uses the default, a comma (,).

Function calls can also be nested within other function calls. Consider this example where the `Now( )` function is nested within the `DateFormat( )` function:

```
<cfset TodaysDate = DateFormat(Now( ),'mm/dd/yyyy')>
```

Regardless of an expression's complexity, they all have one thing in common: functions always return a value. This value can be of any ColdFusion datatype (Boolean, string, numeric, date/time, list, array, structure, query object, or component object) and can be output to the browser or included as part of another expression. There are over 265 functions in the CFML language. For a complete list, see Appendix B. For more information on creating your own functions, see Chapter 20.

Writing Output

To output the contents or results of a ColdFusion expression, you use the `<cfoutput>` tag. `cfoutput` is a paired tag, which means that it has both start and end tags. `cfoutput` tells ColdFusion to parse any text found between the tag pairs for variables and expressions that need to be evaluated. We'll use the cfoutput tag in a variety of ways throughout the book; it is one of the most commonly used CFML tags. For now, let's focus on how the cfoutput tag outputs simple variable values.

The following example creates a number of variables using cfset tags and then outputs the values of the variables within cfoutput tags:

```
<!--- Assign values to variables --->
<cfset x = 1>
<cfset y = x+2>
<cfset Name = "Rob">
<cfset z = Name>
<cfset Authenticated = true>
<cfset TheDate = DateFormat(Now( ),'mm/dd/yyyy')>

<!--- Output the variable values --->
<h2>Writing Output</h2>
<cfoutput>
x = #x#<br>
y = #y#<br>
Name = #Name#<br>
z = #z#<br>
TheDate = #TheDate#<br>
Authenticated = #Authenticated#<br>
</cfoutput>
```

Executing this template causes the value assigned to each variable to be output to the browser, as shown in Figure 2-3. Note the use of pound signs (#) in this example. ColdFusion uses pound signs to separate expressions from literal text. When ColdFusion encounters an expression surrounded by pound signs, it attempts to evaluate it.

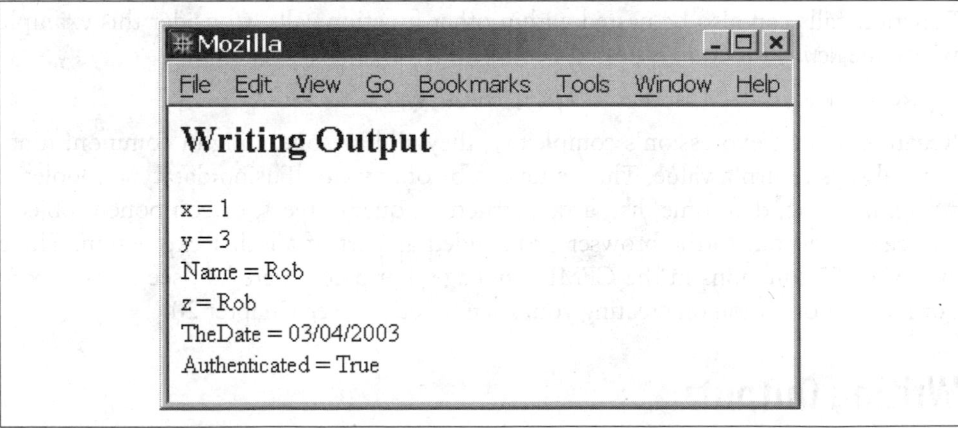

Figure 2-3. Writing output using the cfoutput tag

The most common usage of pound signs occurs when evaluating expressions within cfoutput tags. Use pound signs around variable names when you want to substitute the variable's value within your output:

```
<cfoutput>
Hello #Name#, how are you today?
</cfoutput>
```

When you have multiple variables, each variable should be delimited by its own set of pound signs:

```
<cfoutput>
Hello #FirstName# #LastName#, how are you today?
</cfoutput>
```

In addition, expressions also need to be delimited by pound signs:

```
<cfoutput>
The absolute value of -1 is #abs(-1)#.
</cfoutput>
```

In ColdFusion MX, you can evaluate compound expressions directly between pound signs:

```
<cfoutput>
10*10 = #10*10#<br>
1+5+abs(-4) = #(1+5+abs(-4))#
</cfoutput>
```

In older versions of ColdFusion, you need to evaluate a compound expression using the cfset tag to perform the evaluation:

```
<cfset x=10*10>

<cfoutput>
10*10 = #x#
</cfoutput>
```

There's also the Evaluate( ) function, but you should rarely need to use this. Additionally, it can be slower than alternative methods of expression evaluation:

```
<cfoutput>
10*10 = #Evaluate(10*10)#
</cfoutput>
```

This doesn't mean that it is always necessary to delimit your expressions with pound signs, though. The following guidelines should help you understand when it is necessary to use pound signs in your expressions and when it isn't. As a rule, you should try to use pound signs only when necessary, for both aesthetic and performance reasons; unnecessary pound signs add to the time it takes ColdFusion to parse a template.

Using Pound Signs Within Expressions

For the most part, you don't need to use pound signs within ColdFusion expressions. For example, the following expressions, although valid, use pound signs unnecessarily:

```
<cfset #x# = 1>
<cfset x = #abs(-1)#>
<cfset x = #DateFormat(#Now( )#,'mm/dd/yyyy')#>
```

Because the ColdFusion parser must take time to parse all text within a tag or function, it is much more efficient (not to mention readable) to write the expressions as:

```
<cfset x = 1>
<cfset x = abs(-1)>
<cfset x = DateFormat(Now( ),'mm/dd/yyyy')>
```

There are a few instances, however, where it is necessary to use pound signs within a ColdFusion function or tag.

Including an expression within a string

You need to use pound signs when you include an expression within a string:

```
<cfset MyNewString = "Hello #Name#, how are you today?">
```

Alternately, you can achieve the same results via concatenation:

```
<cfset MyNewString = "Hello" & " " & Name & ", how are you today?">
```

In this case, you don't need to use pound signs around the variable name, nor is it necessary to delimit the variable using quotation marks.

Including expressions within tag attributes

You need to use pound signs within tag attributes when the value being passed is contained in a variable or expression:

```
<cfmail to=#DistributionList#
        from="webmaster@mycompany.com"
        subject="Hello #Name#">
Greetings!
</cfmail>
```

It isn't necessary (although I encourage it) to delimit the variable name `DistributionList` with quotes. The same code can also be written as:

```
<cfmail to="#DistributionList#"
        from="webmaster@mycompany.com"
        subject="Hello #Name#">
Greetings!
</cfmail>
```

It is worth noting that CFML custom tags can have complex datatypes, such as queries, arrays, and structures, passed to them via tag attributes. These datatypes are passed the same way as simple values—with their variable names escaped by pound signs. This example assumes that `#TheItems#` is a query object:

```
<cf_mytag name="orders"
          items="#TheItems#">
```

Nested Pound Signs

There are rare occasions where it may appear necessary to nest pound signs within other pound signs. While there is never a situation where this is absolutely a requirement (there is always a workaround), certain complex expressions involving string manipulation can be created using nested pound signs:

```
<cfset List1="a,b,c,d">
<cfset List2="1,2,3,4">

<cfoutput>
The combined list: #List1#,#List2#<br>
The fourth element: #ListGetAt("#List1#,#List2#", 4)#
</cfoutput>
```

While this code is allowable, it is preferable to write it as:

```
<cfset List1="a,b,c,d">
<cfset List2="1,2,3,4">
<cfset CombinedList = ListAppend(List1, List2)>

<cfoutput>
The combined list: #CombinedList#<br>
The fourth element: #ListGetAt(CombinedList, 4)#
</cfoutput>
```

Escaping Pound Signs

There are occasions where you will find it necessary or desirable to use pound signs as plain text within your CFML. In these instances, pound signs can be escaped by doubling them up:

```
<cfoutput>
<tr>
  <td bgcolor="##FFFFCC">My phone ## is #MyPhoneNumber#</td>
</tr>
</cfoutput>
```

Notice that both the pound sign used for the color's hex value and the pound sign for the telephone number abbreviation are escaped. Using a single pound sign in either case results in ColdFusion throwing an exception.

Conditional Processing

Conditional processing makes it possible to implement flow control and decision making within your ColdFusion templates. ColdFusion provides three techniques for applying conditional processing in your programs: if/elseif/else functionality with the <cfif>, <cfelseif>, and <cfelse> tags; a C-style switch statement with the <cfswitch>, <cfcase>, and <cfdefaultcase> tags; and the IIF( ) function for inline conditionals.

cfif, cfelseif, and cfelse

If/elseif/else processing allows you to add logical decision-making and flow control to your ColdFusion applications, so you can evaluate an expression and take different actions based upon the results. Basic if/elseif/else processing takes the following form:

```
<cfif expression>
   HTML and CFML...
<cfelseif expression>
   HTML and CFML...
<cfelse>
   HTML and CFML...
</cfif>
```

The cfif statement can evaluate any expression capable of returning a Boolean value. If the statement evaluates true, ColdFusion processes the code associated with the cfif statement. The cfelseif statement provides an alternate expression in the event that the expression in the cfif statement evaluates false. Any number of cfelseif statements can provide additional decision-making options. The cfelse statement provides a default option in the event that both the cfif statement and any cfelseif statements all evaluate false. The following example uses if/elseif/else logic to evaluate a URL variable called Action:

```
<cfif URL.Action IS "Add">
   <cfinclude template="AddRecord.cfm">
<cfelseif URL.Action IS "Edit">
   <cfinclude template="EditRecord.cfm">
<cfelseif URL.Action IS "Delete">
   <cfinclude template="DeleteRecord.cfm">
<cfelse>
   You have chosen an invalid action!
</cfif>
```

Depending on the value of Action, one of three additional templates is called via a <cfinclude> tag (which we'll discuss shortly). If the value of the URL variable doesn't match one of the values in the cfif or cfelseif statements, a default message contained within the cfelse tag is displayed.

The following rules can be applied to if/elseif/else statements:

- cfif/cfelseif/cfelse statements can be nested.
- Multiple cfelseif statements can be used within a single cfif block.
- cfif statements can contain more than one expression to evaluate, as in:

  ```
  <cfif IsDefined('MyVar') and MyVar is "a">
  ```

- Compound `cfif` statements that contain multiple expressions separated by operators such as `and` and `or` are processed using short-circuit Boolean evaluation. This means that ColdFusion stops processing the `<cfif>` statement once an expression evaluates `true`.
- Consider using `cfswitch/cfcase` to speed up performance when possible.

cfswitch, cfcase, and cfdefaultcase

In addition to standard if/elseif/else decision-making using `cfif`, `cfelseif`, and `cfelse` tags, ColdFusion also supports switch/case processing. Switch/case is often used in place of lengthy if/elseif/else statements for both readability and performance reasons. Whenever possible, switch/case should be used in place of if/elseif/else processing as it provides better overall performance. The syntax used for switch/case processing is as follows:

```
<cfswitch expression="expression">
     <cfcase value="value_or_list_of_values" delimiters="delimiter">
          HTML and CFML...
     </cfcase>
     <cfcase value="value_or_list_of_values" delimiters="delimiter">
          HTML and CFML...
     </cfcase>
     ...
     <cfdefaultcase>
          HTML and CFML...
     </cfdefaultcase>
</cfswitch>
```

The `cfswitch` tag sets the expression to be evaluated. `cfcase` statements allow you to specify individual values or delimited lists of values that can result from the expression evaluated by the `cfswitch` statement. If the expression contained in the `cfswitch` statement evaluates to a value contained in one of the `cfcase` statements, then the corresponding code is executed. The `cfdefaultcase` tag allows you to specify a default action to take in the event that no `cfcase` value matches the result of the expression from the `cfswitch` tag. The same example used in the section on if/elseif/else processing can be easily rewritten using switch/case logic as follows:

```
<cfswitch expression="Url.Action">
  <cfcase value="Add">
     <cfinclude template="AddRecord.cfm">
  </cfcase>
  <cfcase value="Edit">
     <cfinclude template="EditRecord.cfm">
  </cfcase>
  <cfcase value="Delete">
     <cfinclude template="DeleteRecord.cfm">
  </cfcase>
  <cfdefaultcase>
     You have chosen an invalid action!
  </cfdefaultcase>
</cfswitch>
```

cfswitch/cfcase can be used to reduce the amount of code necessary to evaluate certain types of conditions. Consider the following example in which a number of cfif statements are used to evaluate the current month and determine the corresponding season:

```
<!--- Sets TheMonth to the current month --->
<cfset TheMonth=MonthAsString(Month(Now( )))>

<cfoutput>
<cfif TheMonth IS "December">
  #TheMonth# is in the winter.
<cfelseif TheMonth IS "January">
  #TheMonth# is in the winter.
<cfelseif TheMonth IS "February">
  #TheMonth# is in the winter.
<cfelseif TheMonth IS "March">
  #TheMonth# is in the spring.
<cfelseif TheMonth IS "April">
  #TheMonth# is in the spring.
<cfelseif TheMonth IS "May">
  #TheMonth# is in the spring.
<cfelseif TheMonth IS "June">
  #TheMonth# is in the summer.
<cfelseif TheMonth IS "July">
  #TheMonth# is in the summer.
<cfelseif TheMonth IS "August">
  #TheMonth# is in the summer.
<cfelseif TheMonth IS "September">
  #TheMonth# is in the fall.
<cfelseif TheMonth IS "October">
  #TheMonth# is in the fall.
<cfelseif TheMonth IS "November">
  #TheMonth# is in the fall.
</cfif>
</cfoutput>
```

As you can see, each month of the year requires its own cfif statement to determine whether it is the same as the current month. While this code is perfectly acceptable, it is redundant. We can use switch/case processing to handle the same task using considerably less code:

```
<!--- Sets TheMonth to the current month --->
<cfset TheMonth=MonthAsString(Month(Now( )))>

<cfoutput>
<cfswitch expression="#TheMonth#">
   <cfcase value="December,January,February" delimiters=",">
      #TheMonth# is in the winter.
   </cfcase>
   <cfcase value="March,April,May" delimiters=",">
      #TheMonth# is in the spring.
   </cfcase>
   <cfcase value="June,July,August" delimiters=",">
```

```
        #TheMonth# is in the summer.
    </cfcase>
    <cfdefaultcase>
        #TheMonth# is in the fall.
    </cfdefaultcase>
</cfswitch>
</cfoutput>
```

IIF

IIF( ) is a ColdFusion function that evaluates a condition inline and, depending on the results, outputs one of two expressions. The function takes the form:

```
IIF(Condition, Expression_A, Expression_B)
```

If *Condition* evaluates true, *Expression_A* is processed and *Expression_B* is ignored. If, however, *Condition* evaluates false, *Expression_B* is processed, and *Expression_A* is ignored.

Consider the following example that uses IIF( ) to evaluate the current day of the week. If the day of the week is Wednesday, the message Today is Wednesday! is displayed. If the current day isn't Wednesday, the message Today is not Wednesday, it is ___ is displayed:

```
<html>
<head>
    <title>IIF/DE Example</title>
</head>

<body>
<cfoutput>
#IIF(DayOfWeek(Now( )) IS 4, DE("Today is <B>Wednesday</B>!"), DE("Today is not
     Wednesday, it is <B>#DayOfWeekAsString(DayOfWeek(Now( )))#</B>"))#
</cfoutput>
</body>
</html>
```

The DE( ) function, which stands for delay evaluation, is used with the IIF( ) function to allow you to pass it a string without having the string evaluated. This is necessary in the case of the second expression in the IIF( ) function (the third parameter): it keeps ColdFusion from evaluating the third parameter when the IIF( ) function is initially evaluated.

Looping

Looping allows you to repeat specific blocks of code (both HTML and CFML) within your CFML templates. ColdFusion supports a variety of looping constructs with the <cfloop> tag, including index (for) loops, conditional (while) loops, collection loops, list loops, and query loops. For now, we are just going to cover basic index and conditional loops. Query loops are covered in Chapter 4, while collection and list loops are covered in Chapter 6.

Index Loops

Also known as a for loop, an index loop repeats a number of times specified as a range of values:

```
<cfloop index="index_name" from="number" to="number" step="increment">
  HTML and CFML...
</cfloop>
```

The index attribute of the loop specifies a variable name to hold the value corresponding to the current iteration of the loop. The from attribute initializes the starting value for the loop. The to attribute refers to the value at which iteration should stop. step specifies the increment value for each iteration of the loop. step may be either a positive or a negative number. Here is an example that uses an index loop to output all the numbers between 10 and 100 in increments of 10, with each number on its own line:

```
<h2>Calling the loop...</h2>

<cfoutput>
<cfloop index="i" from="10" to="100" step="10">
  #i#<br>
</cfloop>
</cfoutput>

<h2>We are now outside of the loop</h2>
```

Here, index is set to i. Since we want to begin the count at 10, we assign that value to the from attribute. The to attribute is set to 100 because that is where we want the loop to stop iterating. In order to get the loop to increment by multiples of 10, the step attribute is set to 10. Executing the template results in the output shown in Figure 2-4.

We can easily modify this example to output all of the numbers between 1 and 100 by changing the from attribute to 1 and the to attribute to 100:

```
<h2>Calling the loop...</h2>

<cfoutput>
<cfloop index="i" from="1" to="100">
  #i#<br>
</cfloop>
</cfoutput>

<h2>We are now outside of the loop</h2>
```

Likewise, we can output the numbers from 1 to 100 in reverse order (100 to 1) simply by changing the from attribute to 100, the to attribute to 1, and the step attribute to -1:

```
<h2>Calling the loop...</h2>

<cfoutput>
<cfloop index="i" from="100" to="1" step="-1">
```

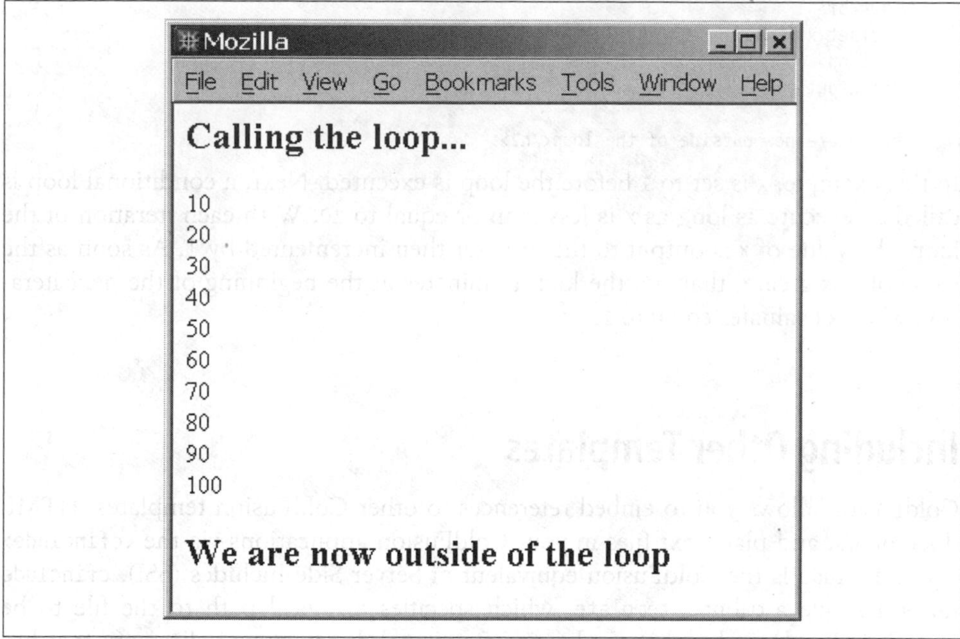

Figure 2-4. Use an index loop to output the numbers between 10 and 100 in multiples of 10

```
   #i#<br>
</cfloop>
</cfoutput>

<h2>We are now outside of the loop</h2>
```

Conditional Loops

Also known as a `while` loop, a conditional loop repeats while a specified condition is `true`. In order to work, the condition being tested must change with each iteration of the loop until the condition evaluates to `false`. Conditional loops allow you to keep repeating a chunk of code as long as the specified condition is still `true`:

```
<cfloop condition="expression">
   HTML and CFML...
</cfloop>
```

The `condition` attribute may contain any valid expression that evaluates to `true`. The following example uses a conditional loop to update the value of `x` as long as `x` remains less than or equal to `10`:

```
<cfset x=1>

<h2>Calling the loop...</h2>

<cfoutput>
<cfloop condition="x lte 10">
```

```
    #x#<br>
    <cfset x = x+1>
  </cfloop>
  </cfoutput>

  <h2>We are now outside of the loop</h2>
```

In this example, `x` is set to `1` before the loop is executed. Next, a conditional loop is called to execute as long as `x` is less than or equal to `10`. With each iteration of the loop, the value of `x` is output to the browser then incremented by 1. As soon as the value of `x` is greater than `10`, the loop terminates at the beginning of the next iteration when `x` evaluates equal to `10`.

Including Other Templates

ColdFusion allows you to embed references to other ColdFusion templates, HTML documents, and plain-text files in your ColdFusion applications via the `<cfinclude>` tag. `cfinclude` is the ColdFusion equivalent of Server Side Includes (SSI). `cfinclude` takes a single attribute, `template`, which specifies a logical path to the file to be included. The logical path must be either a virtual directory or a directory that has been explicitly mapped in the ColdFusion Administrator:

```
<cfinclude template="MyIncludedFile.cfm">
```

Or:

```
<cfinclude template="/MyDirectory/MyIncludedFile.txt">
```

Including files allows you to use repetitive code without having to cut and paste it into your template every time you want to use it. A good example of this is header and footer files that contain things such as site navigation, legal notices, and copyright information. By including header and footer files with each of your templates, you can make changes to the header or footer once and have that change instantly available to every template that includes the files. To understand how this works, consider the following ColdFusion template that includes both a header and footer file:

```
<!--- Set the title for the page --->
<cfset Title="My Page">

<!--- Include the header for the page --->
<cfinclude template="_header.cfm">

<h2>Hello World!</h2>
I'm just some regular text.

<!--- Include the footer --->
<cfinclude template="_footer.cfm">
```

You can save this template under any name you want. For this example, I saved the template as *mypage.cfm*. The template works by assigning a title for the page to a variable appropriately named `Title`. Next, a template called *_header.cfm* is included using the `cfinclude` tag. I use the underscore as the first character of any include files so that I can differentiate include files from other templates. The next part of the template constitutes the body of the page. In this example, we just output some simple text. The last line of code in the template uses another `cfinclude` tag to include the footer for the page.

The code for the header template follows. The header sets the title for the page based on the value of the `Title` variable set in the *mypage.cfm* template. The header also sets the background color for the page as well as other display characteristics for various page elements. Be sure to save the template as *_header.cfm* in the same directory as the previous template.

```
<html>
<head>
  <cfoutput><title>#Title#</title></cfoutput>
  <style>
    body {
      background: #C0C0C0;
      font-family: Arial;
      font-size: 10pt;
      text-align: center;
      }
    h2 {
      font-family: Arial;
      font-size: 16pt;
      }
  </style>
</head>

<body>
```

The footer file is even simpler. If contains a copyright notice to display at the end of each template that calls it. The footer template should be saved as *_footer.cfm* in the same directory as the previous two templates.

```
<hr width="400" noshade>
<cfoutput>
<div align="Center">Copyright 1998-#Year(now())#My company, Inc. All Rights
Reserved.</div>
</cfoutput>
</body>
</html>
```

When the *mypage.cfm* template is requested by a web browser, ColdFusion dynamically assembles the page from the *mypage.cfm*, *_header.cfm*, and *_footer.cfm* templates and returns it as a single page to the browser. This is shown in Figure 2-5.

Figure 2-5. Using the cfinclude tag to include a header and footer

Included CFML templates have access to all the variables available to the calling CFML template. Because of this, you should make sure your include templates don't unintentionally contain variable names that exist in your calling template as it is possible for one template to overwrite the variables referenced in the other.

CHAPTER 3

Passing Data Between Templates

While web applications might seem to be all about individual web pages, it is the passing of data between pages that is key to making an application work. You need to be able to pass data between ColdFusion templates for any form of interactivity. For example, if the user fills out an online form requesting additional information about a product, your application needs a mechanism for passing the data entered in the form fields to another page (or itself) that is capable of taking that data and acting on it. Likewise, if the user clicks on a hyperlink that initiates a parameter-driven query, the application needs a way to pass the parameters that make up the choice to the next template in the application for processing.

There are three methods for passing data between application templates in ColdFusion. You can pass data in the form of URL parameters, by posting it as form-field variables, or via persistent variables. This section covers the first two methods of passing data between application templates. The use of persistent variables is covered at length in Chapter 7.

Passing Parameters Via URL

One way to pass data from one template to the next is through hyperlinks containing special URL parameters. The HTTP specification allows you to append parameters to the end of a URL in the format:

```
filename.cfm?param1=value1&param2=value2&param3=value3
```

The question mark immediately following the extension of the template in the URL specifies the beginning point for appending URL parameters. Each URL parameter consists of a parameter name followed by an equal sign, then the value assigned to the parameter. You can append more than one URL parameter to a URL by delimiting them with ampersands. Note that no spaces may appear in the URL string unless they are escaped first (see "Dealing with Special Characters").

When you click on a hyperlink containing one or more URL parameters, those parameters are automatically sent to the template specified in the URL of the link and thus are available to the template as URL variables. The following example illustrates how URL variables are passed from template to template in ColdFusion. The first template, shown in Example 3-1, creates several ColdFusion variables and appends them and their associated values to a URL.

Example 3-1. Creating URL parameters

```
<!--- Set variables to be passed to another template --->
<cfset x=1>
<cfset color="green">
<cfset Pass = True>

<h2>Passing Data via URL Parameters</h2>

<!--- Create a hyperlink containing URL parameters --->
<cfoutput>
<a href="receiveurlparameters.cfm?x=#x#&color=#color#&pass=#pass#">Click
this link to pass the URL parameters</a>
</cfoutput>
```

Executing this template results in a page that contains a single hyperlink. If you move your mouse over the hyperlink and look in the status window of your browser, you should see a URL that looks like this:

```
http://myserver.com/receiveurlparameters.cfm?x=1&color=green&Pass=True
```

As you can see, the URL contains the parameters you appended in the original code. Clicking on the hyperlink requests the template in Example 3-2, called *receiveurlparameters.cfm*, and passes along the URL parameters.

Example 3-2. Receiving URL parameters

```
<h2>URL Parameters from the Previous Template</h2>
<cfoutput>
x: #URL.x#<br>
Color: #URL.Color#<br>
Pass: #URL.Pass#
</cfoutput>
```

receiveurlparameters.cfm does nothing more than output the value associated with each URL parameter; you can see the results in Figure 3-1. Notice that each reference to a URL parameter is scoped by the URL prefix. Although this isn't required, it is the preferred method for referring to variables passed to a template via a URL.

If you pass more than one URL parameter with the same name, ColdFusion creates a single URL variable that contains a comma-delimited list of values from those passed in the URL. For example, if the URL looks like this:

```
myfile.cfm?a=1&a=2&a=3
```

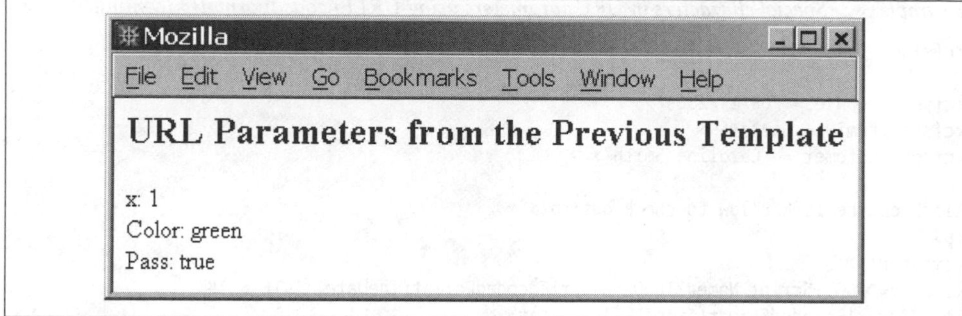

Figure 3-1. Passing data via URL parameters

And you output the URL variable `a`, ColdFusion returns "1,2,3":

```
<cfoutput>
#URL.a#
</cfoutput>
```

This is a new behavior in ColdFusion MX. In previous versions, ColdFusion simply returned the value for the last duplicate-named URL parameter passed.

Dealing with Special Characters

There are certain special characters, such as spaces, symbols, and other nonalphanumeric characters, that don't lend themselves to being passed via URL. The `URLEncodedFormat( )` function is used to encode strings that would otherwise cause errors or truncate the URL when passed as URL parameters. `URLEncodedFormat( )` replaces nonalphanumeric characters with their equivalent hexadecimal escape sequences. When a URL-encoded parameter is passed to another template, ColdFusion automatically decodes any URL-escaped strings it encounters. You can also specify an optional Java character set for the string encoding. Depending on the server's JRE, options typically include `UTF-8`, `UTF-16`, `UTF-16BE`, `UTF-16LE`, `US-ASCII`, and `ISO-8859-1`. The following template, called *encodedurl.cfm*, illustrates this point. This template, shown in Example 3-3, takes three variables, encodes them using the `URLEncodedFormat( )` function, and appends them to the URL of a hyperlink. Clicking on the hyperlink causes the template to call itself, passing the URL parameters to the template.

Example 3-3. Special characters in URL parameters using URLEncodedFormat()

```
<cfif IsDefined('URL.TheDate')>
<h2>Decoded URL Parameters</h2>

<cfoutput>
TheDate: #URL.TheDate#<br>
ItemID: #URL.ItemID#<br>
Customer: #URL.Customer#
</cfoutput>
```

Example 3-3. Special characters in URL parameters using URLEncodedFormat() (continued)

```
<cfelse>

<cfset TheDate = "08/15/2003">
<cfset ItemID = "123456">
<cfset Customer = "Caroline Smith">

Click on the link below to check out:<br>
<p>
<cfoutput>
<a href="#CGI.Script_Name#?TheDate=#UrlEncodedFormat(TheDate, 'UTF-8')#&
ItemID=#UrlEncodedFormat(ItemID, 'UTF-8')#&
Customer=#UrlEncodedFormat(Customer, 'UTF-8')#">
Check-out
</a>
</cfoutput>
</cfif>
```

If you execute this template and move your mouse over the hyperlink, you should see a URL that looks like this (assuming you named your template *encodedurl.cfm*):

```
encodedurl.cfm?TheDate=08%2F15%2F2002&ItemID=123456&Customer=Caroline%20Smith
```

Clicking on the link causes the template to call itself. This is done by having the link point to the CGI variable `Script_Name`. `Script_Name` is a special CGI variable that returns the name of the current template and is useful for building self-referencing hyperlinks and HTML forms that post to themselves. The `cfif` statement at the beginning of the template checks for the existence of a URL variable called `TheDate`. If it exists in the URL (which it should), all the URL variables passed in are output to the browser. The results of clicking on the hyperlink are shown in Figure 3-2.

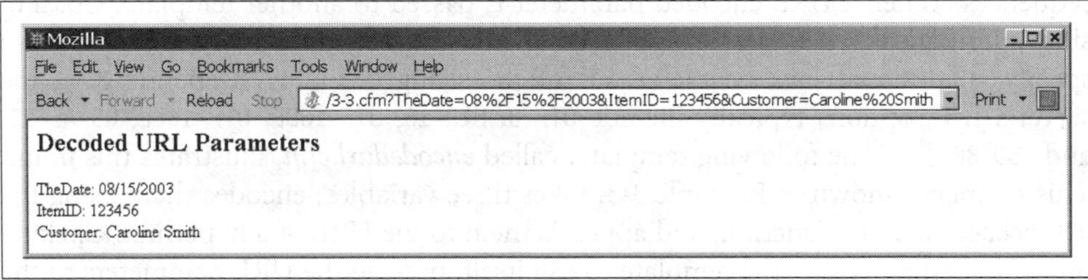

Figure 3-2. Automatically decoding encoded URL parameters

If for some reason you ever find yourself in the situation where you must manually decode an encoded URL parameter, ColdFusion has a `URLDecode( )` function to handle the task. `URLDecode( )` takes a single parameter, the encoded string to be decoded. Example 3-4 demonstrates how to use the `URLDecode( )` function.

Example 3-4. Manually decoding an encoded URL parameter using URLDecode()

```
<cfset MyString="Why is the sky blue?">
<cfset EncodedString=URLEncodedFormat(MyString)>
```

Example 3-4. Manually decoding an encoded URL parameter using URLDecode() (continued)

```
<cfset DecodedString=URLDecode(EncodedString)>

<cfoutput>
Original String: #MyString#<br>
URL Encoded: #EncodedString#<br>
Decoded: #DecodedString#
</cfoutput>
```

In this example, a variable called `MyString` is assigned a value, then encoded using the `URLEncodedFormat( )` function. The resulting encoded value is assigned to a variable called `EncodedString`. Next, `EncodedString` is decoded using the `URLDecode( )` function, and the resulting string is assigned to a variable called `DecodedString`. A `cfoutput` block then outputs the original string, the encoded version, and the decoded version for comparison, as shown in Figure 3-3.

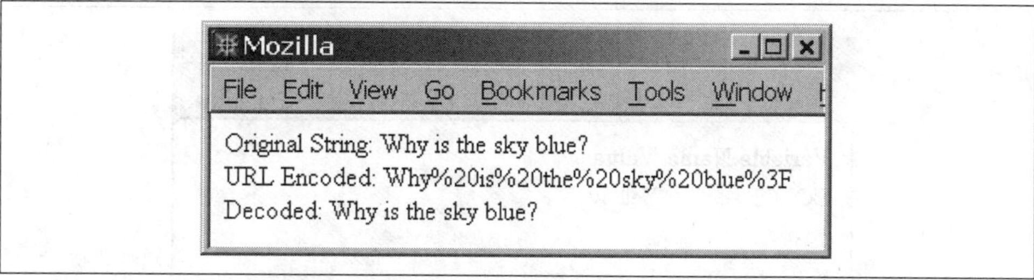

Figure 3-3. Manually decoding an encoded string using URLDecode()

Obtaining a List of All Available URL Parameters

You can obtain a list of all URL variables that have been passed to a given template without knowing the names of any of the parameters. This is useful in situations such as debugging where you want to view all the URL parameters that have been passed to a given page. URL variables have a ColdFusion structure associated with them that contains a list of all URL variable names and values available to the current template. This structure is appropriately named `URL`. To obtain a list of all URL variables within a given template, you can use the code shown in Example 3-5.

Example 3-5. Accessing the URL structure to obtain a list of URL variables

```
<!--- This simulates URL variables being passed into the template --->
<cfset URL.x=1>
<cfset URL.y=2>
<cfset URL.Color="Yellow">

<table>
  <tr>
    <th>Variable Name</th>
    <th>Value</th>
  </tr>
```

Example 3-5. Accessing the URL structure to obtain a list of URL variables (continued)

```
<!--- Loop over the URL structure and output all of the variable names
      and their associated values --->
<cfloop collection="#URL#" item="VarName">
  <cfoutput>
  <tr>
    <td>#VarName#</td>
    <td>#URL[VarName]#</td>
  </tr>
  </cfoutput>
</cfloop>
</table>
```

This template uses a collection loop to iterate over the URL structure. Each variable name and its associated value are output in an HTML table. Executing this template results in the output shown in Figure 3-4.

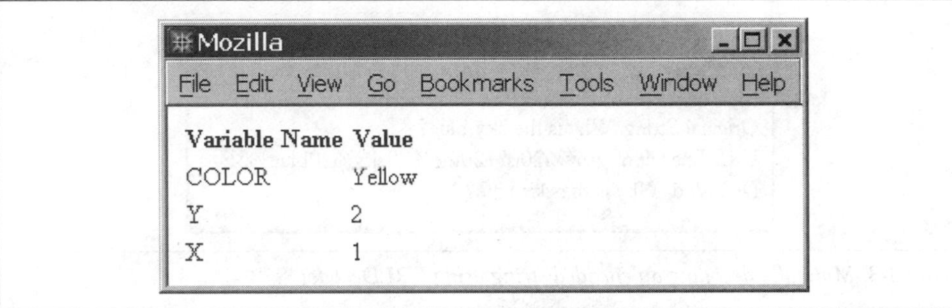

Figure 3-4. Outputting the contents of the URL structure

For more information about working with structures, including how to use a collection loop, see Chapter 6.

Passing Data Using Forms

Another method for passing data from template to template involves sending the data via the HTTP Post method as form-field data. When you create an HTML form that posts to another ColdFusion template, each form field is automatically available as a form variable within the template specified in the `action` attribute of the `form` tag. Within the receiving template, each form field can be referenced by prefixing the field name with `form`, as in `form.*MyField*`. To see just how this works, let's look at an example. The *contactform.cfm* template, shown in Example 3-6, creates a simple HTML form that collects basic contact information and posts it to the *displaycontactinfo.cfm* template, shown in Example 3-7.

Example 3-6. Template for collecting and posting contact information

```
<html>
<head>
  <title>Passing Variables via Form Fields</title>
</head>

<body>

<h2>Employee Contact Information</h2>
<form action="displaycontactinfo.cfm" method="post">

<table>
  <tr>
    <td>Name:</td>
    <td><input type="text" name="Name" size="25" maxlength="50"></td>
  </tr>
  <tr>
    <td>Title:</td>
    <td><input type="text" name="Title" size="25" maxlength="50"></td>
  </tr>
  <tr>
    <td>Department:</td>
    <td><input type="text" name="Department" size="25" maxlength="50"></td>
  </tr>
  <tr>
    <td>E-mail:</td>
    <td><input type="text" name="Email" size="25" maxlength="255"></td>
  </tr>
  <tr>
    <td>Phone Ext.:</td>
    <td><input type="text" name="PhoneExt" size="6" maxlength="4"></td>
  </tr>
  <tr>
    <td colspan="2"><input type="submit" name="submit" value="submit"></td>
  </tr>
</table>
</form>

</body>
</html>
```

Filling in the form fields (Figure 3-5) and clicking on the "submit" button posts the form-field information to the *displaycontactinfo.cfm* template shown in Example 3-7.

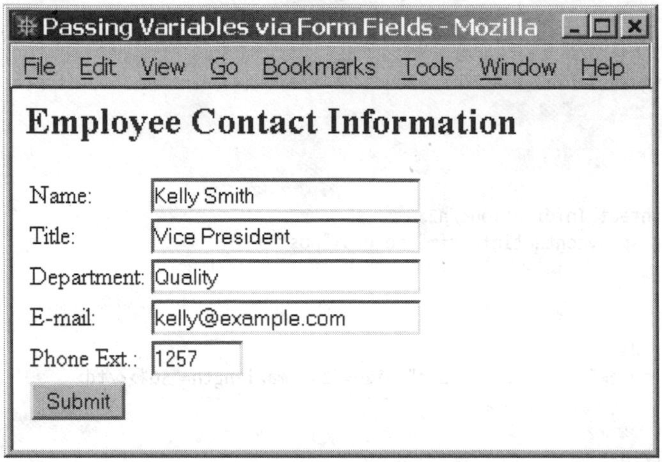

Figure 3-5. HTML form for collecting employee contact information

Example 3-7. Displaying submitted form-field values

```
<cfoutput>
Name: #form.Name#<br>
Title: #form.Title#<br>
Department: #form.Department#<br>
E-mail: #form.Email#<br>
Phone Ext.: #form.PhoneExt#
</cfoutput>
```

Once the form in Example 3-6 is submitted, the template in Example 3-7 outputs the contents of each form field in an HTML table. Each form variable name corresponds to the form-field name from the template in Example 3-6. Note that the output is wrapped in a set of `cfoutput` tags, since we need to output the values of the form variables. The results are shown in Figure 3-6.

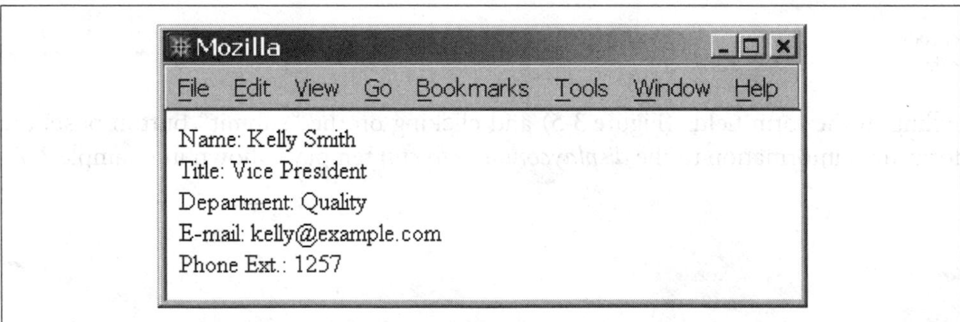

Figure 3-6. Displaying form-field values

Handling Specific Types of Form Fields

Most form fields in HTML are handled as you saw in the previous examples. One key aspect of this is that you have to define a name attribute for each field in your form. When the user submits the form, the value of each form field is available to the processing template in a form variable of the same name.

Thus, with a text input field (<input type="text">), the processing template has access to a form variable with the same name as the form field that contains the text the user entered in the input field. This is also true of password fields (<input type="password">), file fields (<input type="file">, single selection lists or drop-down boxes (<select> and <option> tags), text areas (<textarea> tags), and submit buttons (<input type="submit">).

You should note with submit buttons that the value attribute of the tag controls what text is displayed on the button as well as what value is passed to the processing template. Another feature is that submit buttons allow you to check from the processing template whether or not a particular submit button was pressed. This allows you to build forms with more than one submit button for handling different tasks. For example, consider a form with the following submit buttons:

```
<input type="submit" name="Add" value="Add Record">
<input type="submit" name="Edit" value="Edit Record">
<input type="submit" name="Delete" value="Delete Record">
```

In your processing template, you can easily test to see what action the user wants to perform by checking for the existence of a form variable corresponding to a specific button name:

```
<cfif IsDefined('form.Add')>
  Add record code goes here...
<cfelseif IsDefined('form.Edit')>
  Edit record code goes here...
<cfelseif IsDefined('form.Delete')>
  Delete record code goes here...
<cfelse>
  Default code goes here...
</cfif>
```

Some form fields are a bit more complicated than the ones we just covered, so we'll discuss them in more detail.

Multiple selection lists

A multiple selection list is a special type of form field that allows you to choose one or more options from a list of possible choices. They are actually the same as single selection lists (drop-down boxes) except they contain an additional attribute, multiple, that indicates the control should allow more than one item to be selected. Additionally, multiple selection lists generally display more than one item from the list within their window. The number of items to display is specified by the `size` attribute.

Multiple items may be chosen by holding down the Control key and clicking on each item you wish to choose. When a form containing a multiple selection list is submitted, a single form-field parameter that matches the name given to the selection list is passed to the template specified by the form. This parameter contains a comma-delimited list of the values the user selected in the multiple selection box. The *multipleselect.cfm* template in Example 3-8 shows how a form passes values from a multiple select list. For simplicity, the form posts to itself using the self-posting technique covered earlier in the chapter.

Example 3-8. Passing form-field values from a multiple select list

```
<h2>Multiple Selection List Example</h2>
<cfoutput>
<form action="#CGI.Script_Name#" method="Post">
</cfoutput>
<table>
  <tr>
    <th>Colors:</th>
  <td><select name="Colors" size="5" multiple>
        <option value="Red" selected>Red</option>
        <option value="Yellow">Yellow</option>
        <option value="Pink">Pink</option>
        <option value="Green">Green</option>
        <option value="Purple">Purple</option>
        <option value="Orange">Orange</option>
        <option value="Blue">Blue</option>
      </select></td>
    <td><input type="submit" name="submit" value="submit"></td>
  </tr>
  <tr>
    <td colspan="3">Use the ctrl key to select multiple colors</td>
  </tr>
</table>
</form>

<!--- If the page has been submitted to itself, output the values passed
      by the form --->
<cfif IsDefined('form.Submit')>
<hr>
<cfoutput>
You selected: <b>#form.Colors#</b>
</cfoutput>
</cfif>
```

The template creates an HTML form that contains a multiple selection list and a submit button. The multiple selection list displays seven colors (anyone remember Captain Noah?) from which to select. As I mentioned, the form submits to itself. When this occurs, the last section of code in the template uses a `cfif` statement to determine whether a variable called form.Submit exists. If it does, we know that the template is calling itself, and the selected colors are output to the browser. Figure 3-7 shows both multiple selection lists, both before and after a selection is made. Since we are just outputting the values, we don't have to do anything special with the form.Colors variable. But if we needed to get at the individual values, we could do that by manipulating the list, as described in Chapter 6.

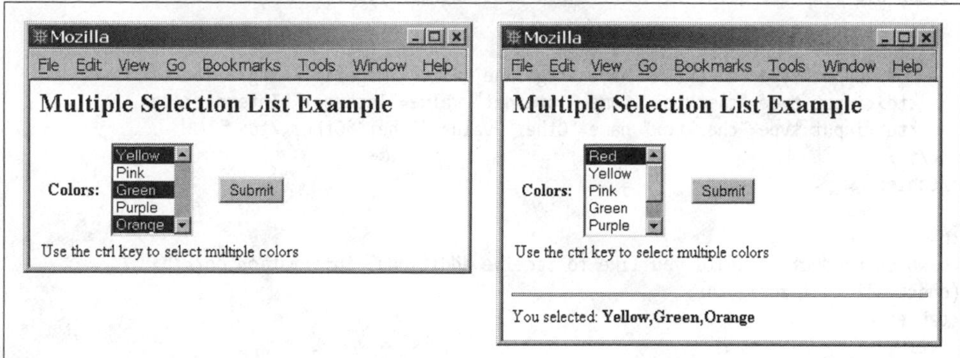

Figure 3-7. Handling a multiple selection list

Checkboxes and radio buttons

Checkboxes (<input type="checkbox">) and radio buttons (<input type="radio">) differ from other form controls in how they pass data from one template to the next. Both checkboxes and radio buttons use the name attribute to specify the name of the form field to pass to the processing template. Additionally, a value for the form field must be specified using the value attribute. Unlike the other types of form fields we've discussed, both radio buttons and checkboxes must be checked at the time the form is submitted for the form fields to be passed to the processing template. In other words, if a user doesn't check any boxes or buttons associated with a particular form-field name, that form field isn't passed to the processing template and is therefore not available as a form variable. This is an extremely important point because attempting to reference a variable that doesn't exist causes ColdFusion to throw an error. To get a better idea of how ColdFusion handles data passed by radio button and checkboxes, look at the *checkboxradio.cfm* template shown in Example 3-9.

Example 3-9. Passing form-field values from radio buttons and checkboxes

```
<html>
<head>
  <title>Passing Checkbox and Radio Button Values</title>
</head>

<body>
```

Example 3-9. Passing form-field values from radio buttons and checkboxes (continued)

```
<h2>Checkbox and Radio Button Example</h2>

<cfoutput>
<form action="#CGI.Script_Name#" method="Post">
</cfoutput>

<b>How did you hear about us?</b> (check all that apply)<br>
<table>
  <tr>
    <td><input type="checkbox" name="Magazine" value="Magazine">Magazine</td>
    <td><input type="checkbox" name="Internet" value="Internet">Internet</td>
    <td><input type="checkbox" name="Other" value="Other">Other</td>
  </tr>
</table>

<p>
<b>Which product(s) would you like to receive additional information on?</b>
(check all that apply)<br>
<table>
  <tr>
    <td><input type="checkbox" name="Products" value="Widgets">Widgets</td>
    <td><input type="checkbox" name="Products" value="Thingies">Thingies</td>
    <td><input type="checkbox" name="Products" value="Stuff">Stuff</td>
  </tr>
  <tr>
    <td><input type="checkbox" name="Products" value="Gadgets">Gadgets</td>
    <td><input type="checkbox" name="Products"
               value="Whatchamacallits">Whatchamacallits</td>
    <td><input type="checkbox" name="Products" value="Junk">Junk</td>
  </tr>
</table>

<p>
<b>Would you like to be added to our mailing list?</b>
<input type="radio" name="MailingList" value="Yes" checked>Yes
<input type="radio" name="MailingList" value="No">No
<p>
<input type="submit" name="submit" value="submit">
</form>

<!--- If the page has been submitted to itself, output the values passed
      by the form --->

<!--- Check to see if each of the "how did you hear about us" values was
      passed in.  This is an example of how not to code your
      checkboxes --->
<cfif IsDefined('form.Submit')>
<hr>
<cfoutput>
<cfif IsDefined('form.Magazine') or IsDefined('form.Internet') or
      IsDefined('form.Other')>
```

Example 3-9. Passing form-field values from radio buttons and checkboxes (continued)

```
<b>How you heard about us:</b>
   <cfif IsDefined('form.Magazine')>
   #form.Magazine#
   </cfif>
   <cfif IsDefined('form.Internet')>
   #form.Internet#
   </cfif>
   <cfif IsDefined('form.Other')>
   #form.Other#
   </cfif>
<br>
</cfif>

<!--- If any products were checked, output them.  This is the proper way to
      code a checkbox --->
<cfif IsDefined('form.Products')>
<b>Products:</b> #Products#<br>
<cfelse>
<b>Products:</b> No Products Selected<br>
</cfif>

<!--- Output the mailing list value from the radio button --->
<b>Mailing List:</b> #MailingList#
</cfoutput>
</cfif>

</body>
</html>
```

This template creates an HTML form that contains three questions the user is asked to answer using both checkbox and radio button form controls. The form is shown in Figure 3-8.

The first section of the form asks how the user heard about the fictitious company providing the form. The user may check any boxes that apply. If you look at the code that created this section, you'll notice that each checkbox has its own name and associated value. When the form is submitted, a form-field variable is created only for each checkbox that was selected. This is an example of how *not* to code checkboxes. We'll talk about why in just a moment.

But first, let's look at the second section. Here we have another set of checkboxes that specify products the user is interested in receiving additional information about. If you look at the code here, you'll notice that each checkbox control has the same name but a different value. Using this technique for coding checkboxes is the preferred method, as it passes a single form variable that contains all the checked values in a comma-delimited list. Thus, simply by examining the list elements, it's easy to see if a particular checkbox was checked. This is in contrast to the first method I described, where you have no programmatic way of knowing which checkboxes are

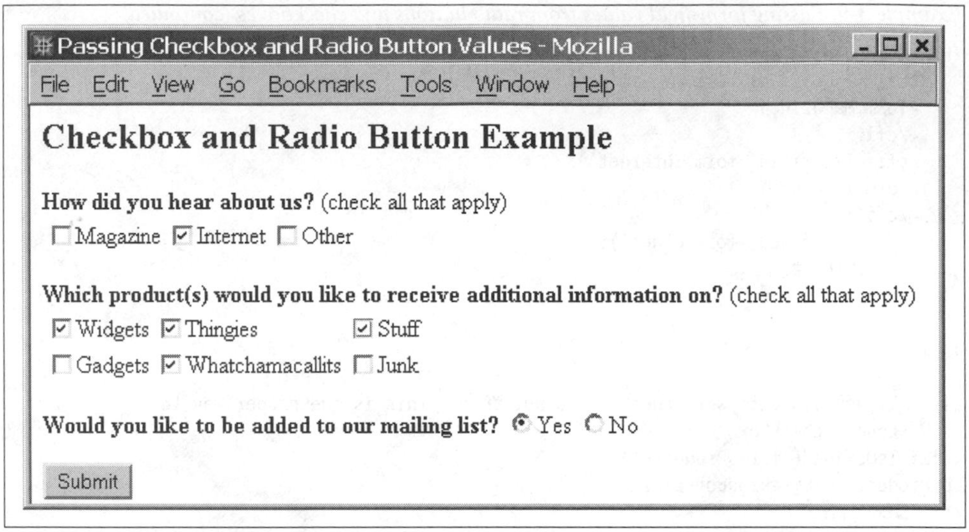

Figure 3-8. HTML form containing checkboxes and radio buttons

checked except by using an individual `IsDefined()` statement for each form-field variable that *could* be passed.

The third section of the form asks users to indicate whether they wish to subscribe to a mailing list. The yes/no choice is coded using two radio button controls. Each radio button has the same name but a different value (`Yes` and `No` respectively). This allows you to force a choice between one or the other option. This also guarantees that when the form is submitted, the form variable associated with the radio button will exist and will contain a value.

When the user presses the submit button, the form template posts all the form-field data back to itself. The code in the second half of the template determines what form variables were passed in, so that you can output the user's choices. The results can be seen in Figure 3-9.

Using Hidden Form Fields

Hidden form fields allow you to pass form-field parameters without having to create an associated input control. This lets you pass data from one template to another without having to display that data on the page containing your HTML form. Hidden form fields are often used to pass session information, such as a username, a primary key value, or client state information, between templates. As far as ColdFusion is concerned, data passed via hidden form fields is treated exactly the same as data passed using a text field. The processing template has a form variable with the same name and value as the hidden form field. Consider a scenario where a time stamp is generated when a user requests a particular form. In order to pass the value of the

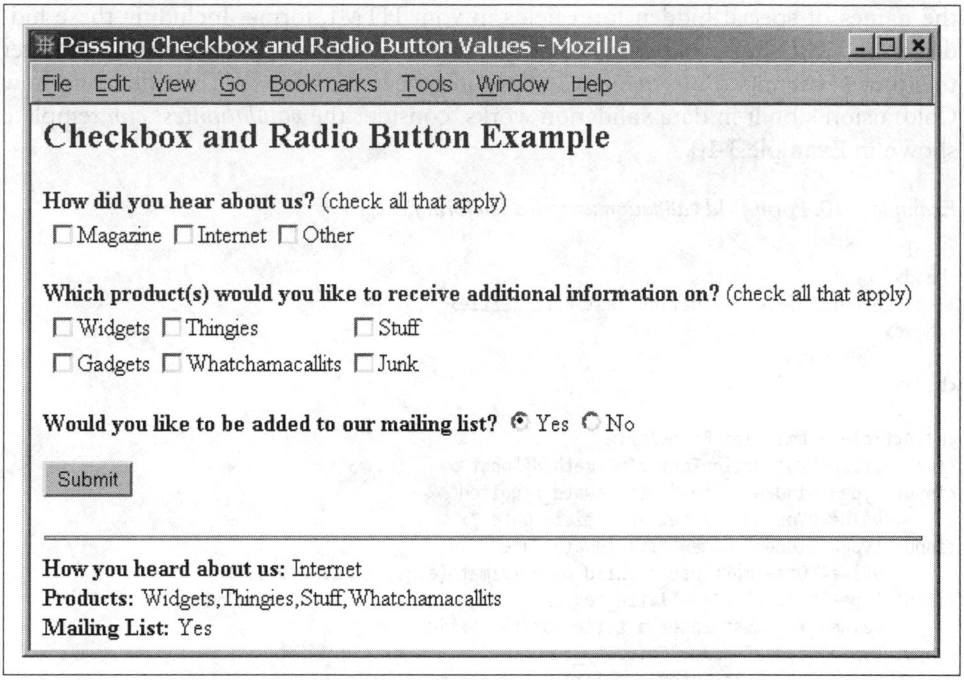

Figure 3-9. Displaying posted radio button and checkbox values

time stamp without having to display it as a visible form field, you use a hidden form field as in the following code:

```
<form name="MyForm" action="Process.cfm" method="Post">
<cfoutput>
<input type="hidden" name="TimeStamp" value="#Now()#">
</cfoutput>

Name: <input type="text" name="Name"><br>
Age: <input type="text" name="Age"><br>
<input type="submit" name="submit" value="submit">
</form>
```

Note that although the data being passed via hidden form fields isn't immediately visible on the page containing the HTML form, all hidden form fields and their associated values can easily be seen by viewing the template source from within your web browser. Because hidden form-field data is stored as plain text, you should never use this mechanism to pass sensitive data such as passwords or credit-card numbers.

Automatically Validating Form-Field Data

HTML forms don't contain a built-in mechanism for making fields required or for validating the data entered in form fields. ColdFusion allows you to make form fields required and perform certain data-validation checks by appending certain suffixes to the names of special hidden form fields in your HTML forms. Including these hidden form fields causes ColdFusion to perform a server-side check of the data after the form is submitted but before ColdFusion processes the data. To understand how ColdFusion's built-in data validation works, consider the *validationtest.cfm* template shown in Example 3-10.

Example 3-10. Form-field validation using hidden form fields

```
<html>
<head>
  <title>Form Field Validation Test Form</title>
</head>

<body>

<h2>Article Submission Form</h2>
<form action="ValidationTest.cfm" method="post">
<input type="hidden" name="ArticleDate_required"
       value="You must enter an Article Date.">
<input type="hidden" name="ArticleDate_date"
       value="Date must use a valid date format (e.g., 11/11/2002).">
<input type="hidden" name="Title_required"
       value="You must enter a title for the article.">
<input type="hidden" name="Priority_required"
       value="You must enter a priority for the article.">
<input type="hidden" name="Priority_range" value="Min=1 Max=100">

<table>
  <tr>
    <td>Date:</td>
    <td><input type="text" name="ArticleDate" size="12" maxlength="10"></td>
  </tr>
  <tr>
    <td>Title:</td>
    <td><input type="text" name="Title" size="50" maxlength="255"></td>
  </tr>
  <tr>
    <td>Article:</td>
    <td><textarea COLS="43" ROWS="5" name="Article"></textarea></td>
  </tr>
  <tr>
    <td>Priority (1-100):</td>
    <td><input type="text" name="Priority" size="4" maxlength="3"></td>
  </tr>
  <tr>
    <td colspan="2"><input type="submit" name="submit" value="submit"></td>
  </tr>
</table>
</form>

</body>
</html>
```

This HTML form contains four fields, named `ArticleDate`, `Title`, `Article`, and `Priority`. If you look at the code immediately following the `form` tag, you'll notice a number of hidden form fields. Each of these hidden form fields is responsible for a specific type of validation for a single form field. A suffix specifying what type of validation to perform is appended to the name of the form field specified in the `name` attribute. The supported validation suffixes are:

`_required`
: Makes the form field a required field.

`_date`
: Checks to see that the form field contains a date. Automatically converts the date to ODBC date format.

`_eurodate`
: Checks to see that the form field contains a European-formatted date. Automatically converts the date to ODBC date format.

`_time`
: Checks to see that the form field contains a time. Automatically converts the time to ODBC time format.

`_integer`
: Checks to see that the form field contains a number. If the number isn't an integer, it is automatically rounded to the nearest integer.

`_float`
: Checks to see that the form field contains a number.

`_range`
: Checks to see that the form field contains a numeric value in the range specified by the `value="Min=x Max=y"` attribute of the `input` tag.

The `value` attribute of each hidden field specifies a message to display in the event that a validation rule is broken. To see how the validation violation messages are displayed, try submitting the form without filling in any form fields. You should see output similar to that shown in Figure 3-10.

To see some of the other validation error messages, try entering bogus values in the form fields and submit the form. Notice that the validation screen is entirely generated by ColdFusion. The only aspect you have any control over is the bullet point message generated for each incomplete or invalid form-field entry. Each message may be set in the `value` attribute of the hidden form field used to specify the validation rule.

To prevent variable name conflicts, you should avoid choosing variable names that end in `_date`, `_eurodate`, `_float`, `_integer`, `_range`, `_required`, or `_time` as they are reserved suffixes for server-side form validation.

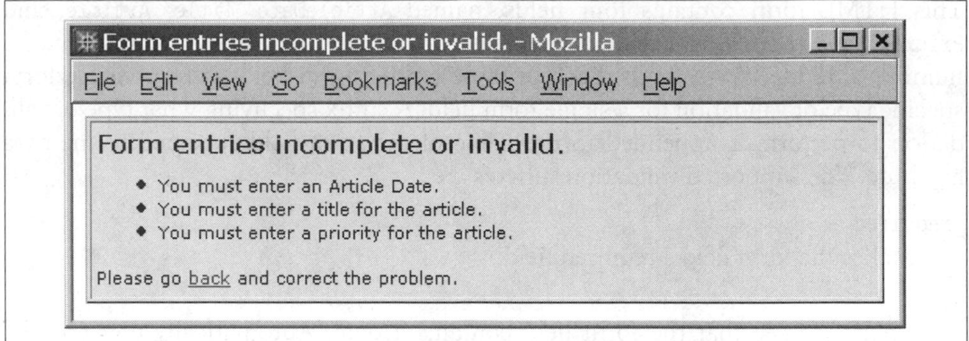

Figure 3-10. Error messages displayed when validation rules are violated

Manually Validating Form-Field Data

The automatic form-field validation provided by ColdFusion is nice, but it obviously doesn't cover every situation in which you might like to validate form data on the server side, such as ensuring a phone number has the correct number of digits and is formatted correctly. In cases like this, it is necessary to manually create a validation routine at the beginning of the template that accepts the form-field data. If you wanted to build a routine for validating a phone number to ensure it contained the proper number of digits and was formatted correctly, you could use code like that shown in Example 3-11.

Example 3-11. Manual form-field validation

```
<!--- Create a form field called form.Phone.  Normally, this would be
      passed in by a form. --->
<cfset form.Phone = "302-555 1212">

<!--- Strip all non numeric values from the string --->
<cfset form.Phone = ReReplace(form.Phone, "[^0-9]", "", "ALL")>

<!--- A standard U.S. phone number has 10 digits.  If there are more or
      less, assign "invalid" to the string.  Otherwise, reformat the phone
      number using (xxx)xxx-xxxx as the mask.  --->
<cfif Len(form.Phone) EQ 10>
  <cfset form.Phone = ReReplace(form.Phone,
         '([0-9]{3})([0-9]{3})([0-9]{4})','(\1)\2-\3')>
<cfelse>
  <cfset form.Phone = "Invalid">
</cfif>

<!--- Output the phone number --->
<cfoutput>
#form.Phone#
</cfoutput>
```

In order to show how to validate a form field, this example sets a form-field value called `form.Phone` at the beginning of the template. Normally, all form fields are passed to the template by a submitted form. The validation is performed in two steps. First, the `ReReplace( )` function is used to remove any nonnumeric values contained in `form.Phone`. `ReReplace( )` uses a regular expression to specify the data to be removed. Regular expressions are covered in Chapter 18.

The second step uses a bit of conditional logic along with the `Len( )` function to check the number of characters remaining in the `form.Phone` field. If there are exactly 10 digits in the field (the number of digits in a U.S. phone number), the `ReReplace( )` function is used with a different regular expression to reformat the digits so they conform to the mask *(xxx)xxx-xxxx*. If the number of digits in `form.Phone` isn't 10, we know the string contained in the form variable doesn't contain enough digits to be a valid phone number, so the value `Invalid` is assigned to `form.Phone` instead. If this were an actual application, you could include additional code to act appropriately if the phone number was determined to be invalid.

Obtaining a List of All Available Form Variables

There are two methods you can use to obtain a list of all form variables that have been passed to a given template. Just like with URL variables, form variables also have a special ColdFusion structure named `form` that contains each form-field name and its associated value. To obtain a list of all form variables within the `form` structure, you can use the code shown in Example 3-12.

Example 3-12. Obtaining a list of all form variables passed to a template

```
<table>
<tr>
  <th>Variable Name</th>
  <th>Value</th>
</tr>

<!--- Loop over the form structure and output all of the variable
      names and their associated values --->
<cfloop collection="#form#" item="VarName">
<cfoutput>
<tr>
  <td>#VarName#</td>
  <td>#form[VarName]#</td>
</tr>
</cfoutput>
</cfloop>
</table>
```

This template uses a collection loop to loop over the `form` structure. Each variable name and its associated value are output in an HTML table. For more information about working with structures, see Chapter 6.

The second method for obtaining a list of every form variable passed to a template involves a special form variable called `form.FieldNames`. This variable is automatically available to any ColdFusion template and contains a comma-delimited list of form-field names that have been posted to the current template. If the form-field variables were manually created and not created as the result of a form post, the `form.FieldNames` variable does not exist. Example 3-13 shows how to access the `form.FieldNames` variable and the value associated with each form field.

Example 3-13. Obtaining a list of form fields using form.FieldNames

```
<cfoutput>
<b>Field Names:</b> #form.FieldNames#
<p>
<b>Field Values:</b><br>
<cfloop index="TheField" list="#form.FieldNames#">
#TheField# = #form[TheField]#<br>
</cfloop>
</cfoutput>
```

In this example, the list of field names is output on a single line. Next, a list loop loops over the list of field names and outputs each one along with its associated value. The value for each form field is obtained by referencing its key in the `form` structure.

Note that the special validation form fields (i.e., ones that have names that end with `_date`, `_time`, etc.) aren't present in the `form.FieldNames` variable. They are, however, present in the `form` structure.

Dealing with Nonexistent Parameters

The final thing to consider when passing data between templates is how to check for and handle missing parameters. When dealing with data passed via URL or form field, it is entirely possible that an application template won't receive a parameter it is expecting. You should build mechanisms into your application templates to account for this possibility. As always, there are a few ways you can go about this.

The first method involves using the `cfparam` tag to assign a default value to any parameters expected by your application template. That way, if an expected parameter isn't passed, a default value is automatically assigned, and the application can continue processing. If you remember, the `cfparam` tag was covered earlier in Chapter 2. Additional information on the `cfparam` tag can be found in Appendix A.

The `cfparam` tag is great for assigning a default value if one doesn't exist; however, it doesn't allow you to display an error message or perform an alternate action if an expected variable doesn't exist. The next method uses the `IsDefined()` function to check for the existence of a variable before allowing processing of the template to continue. If the expected variable exists, the template is processed. If not, an error message is written to the browser. For example, if you have a template that is expecting a URL parameter named ArticleID to be passed in, you can use the following code to output an error message if the parameter isn't present:

```
<!--- If the parameter is present, output it to the screen --->
<cfif IsDefined('URL.ArticleID')>
<cfoutput>
The article ID is: #URL.ArticleID#
</cfoutput>

Additional program code...

<!--- Otherwise, output an error message --->
<cfelse>
A required parameter, <b>ArticleID</b> was not supplied!
</cfif>
```

In this example, the IsDefined( ) function checks for the existence of a URL parameter called ArticleID. If it is present, its value is output to the browser, and any additional program code for the page is executed. If the parameter isn't present, an error message to that effect is written to the browser.

This technique can be extended to check additional properties of a parameter. For example, say your application template expects a parameter called ArticleID as in our previous example. Now let's say that ArticleID must contain a value, and that value must be numeric. We can easily test for these conditions using the following code:

```
<cfif not IsDefined('URL.ArticleID') or not IsNumeric(URL.ArticleID)>
  A required parameter, <b>ArticleID</b> was not supplied or the supplied value
  was not numeric.
<cfelse>
  <!--- If If the parameter is present, output it to the screen --->
  <cfoutput>
  The article ID is: #URL.ArticleID#
  </cfoutput>
</cfif>
```

This time, we added another condition to the initial cfif statement to check to make sure that the value passed in is numeric. The IsNumeric( ) function determines whether the value associated with the ArticleID parameter is a numeric value. Note that quotation marks aren't used around the variable name within the IsNumeric( ) function. If ArticleID doesn't contain a value, or the value is any datatype other than numeric, a message to that effect is output to the browser. If the ArticleID parameter does exist and it does contain a numeric value, the value of ArticleID is written to the browser.

CHAPTER 4
Database Basics

Many people begin their relationship with ColdFusion out of a need to provide web-based access to data stored in a database. This might be as simple as wanting to output the contents of a single database table as an HTML table or as sophisticated as a multipage report generated from several related tables in a database. Whatever your requirements, the methods for querying the data from the database and outputting the results to a user's web browser using ColdFusion remain the same.

ColdFusion doesn't stop with allowing you to query data from a database. Using ColdFusion, you can perform a wide range of database operations including adding, updating, and deleting records; adding new columns to existing tables; and creating, altering, and dropping existing tables. In this chapter, we cover the basics you need to know in order to use ColdFusion to interact with a database. Included in the discussion are configuring data sources, an introduction to SQL, and techniques for retrieving and displaying data.

Configuring Data Sources

In ColdFusion, the term *data source* refers to a connection between ColdFusion and an information source, such as a database, LDAP server, flat file, etc. This chapter focuses on connecting with one specific type of data source: databases. Before you can use ColdFusion to interact with a database, the database has to be set up as a data source that the ColdFusion server can recognize. Unlike previous version of ColdFusion, which used ODBC, OLEDB, and native drivers to connect to databases, ColdFusion MX handles all database connections via JDBC (Java Database Connectivity). There are currently four distinct types of JDBC drivers, appropriately named type 1, 2, 3, and 4. Each JDBC type works in a slightly different way:

JDBC to ODBC Bridge (Type 1)
: JDBC calls are translated to appropriate ODBC calls and sent through an ODBC driver.

Native-API Partly Java Technology–Enabled Driver (Type 2)
: A JDBC call is converted to a client-specific API call.

Net-Protocol Fully Java Technology–Enabled Driver (Type 3)
: A JDBC call is first translated to an independent net protocol, then to a database-specific call.

Native-Protocol Fully Java Technology–Enabled Driver (Type 4)
: A JDBC call is converted to the network protocol used by the specific database.

ColdFusion MX comes with JDBC drivers for connecting to several popular databases. Depending on the version of ColdFusion MX you have, drivers may include MS Access, MS SQL Server, Oracle, various flavors of DB2, Informix, MySQL, and Sybase. Additionally, you may connect to almost any other database for which you have a third-party JDBC driver or an ODBC driver (through a JDBC Type 3 socket connection). ColdFusion MX ships with Type 2, Type 3, and Type 4 JDBC drivers. For more information on JDBC driver types, see the book *Administering and Configuring ColdFusion MX* that comes with the ColdFusion documentation, or visit Sun's web site at *http://java.sun.com/products/jdbc/driverdesc.html*.

Regardless of the method you choose for connecting your data source to ColdFusion, one thing remains the same. You must register the data source with the ColdFusion Administrator in order to take advantage of ColdFusion's database management and security features. Registering the data-source name also tells ColdFusion which database to associate with a particular data-source name.

You should note that not all databases and connection methods are supported across all editions of ColdFusion. For the most up-to-date listing of supported database drivers, see the *Administering and Configuring ColdFusion MX* book (part of the ColdFusion documentation) for your edition of ColdFusion.

Configuring a Data Source in the ColdFusion Administrator

To add a new data source via the ColdFusion Administrator, follow these steps:

1. Open the ColdFusion Administrator in your browser.
2. Click on the Datasources link under the Data & Services section.
3. Enter a name for your data source. The name you choose is up to you, but it should be something meaningful. Names can only contain letters, numbers, underscores, Unicode currency symbols, and spaces. Be sure not to use any ColdFusion tag, function, variable name, or other reserved word as your data source name.
4. Choose your driver/provider type from the drop-down list of available types. If you are attempting to set up a connection via a third party JDBC driver, choose Other. If you want to setup a connection through an ODBC driver, choose ODBC Socket.

5. After you have provided a name for the data source and chosen the driver/connection type, click the Add button. This takes you to a driver-specific page for the driver or connection type you chose.
6. Depending on the driver/connection type you chose, this page lets you enter information about the data source you want to add such as its name, location (if it is a file-based database such as MS Access), username, password, and server/port (hostname or IP address) if it is an enterprise-level database such as SQL Server, Oracle, or DB2. For more information on various configuration options, see the *Administering and Configuring ColdFusion MX* book.
7. After you have finished entering the basic setup information, click on the Show Advanced Settings button in the lower right corner of the page. This takes you to a new page where you can enter information about how ColdFusion MX should access the database and the actions it should be allowed to perform.*
8. Once you have finished configuring any advanced settings, click the Submit button in the middle of the page. ColdFusion will attempt to register your data source and verify the connectivity. If verification fails, a message that lists likely causes for the problem is displayed. If you can connect to the data source successfully, you will be returned to the main data source configuration page. You should see the word "OK" to the right of the data source you just created (under the Status column).

Once you have successfully created and verified the connection to your data source, you are ready to begin using it in your ColdFusion applications.

Additional Resources

In the event you run into trouble trying to get a data source setup, consult the documentation that came with ColdFusion. Additionally, there are a number of Macromedia Servers Knowledge Base TechNotes that may help you troubleshoot the problem. These can be found at *http://www.macromedia.com/v1/support/knowledgebase/searchform.cfm*.

Introducing cfquery

The `cfquery` tag is the main tag used by ColdFusion to interact with databases. Using `cfquery`, you can pass any Structured Query Language (SQL) statement to a data source registered with the ColdFusion Administrator. The content of your SQL state-

* If you are adding a data source for a Microsoft Access database, and you wish to be able to retrieve data from Memo fields, you'll need to check the box labeled "Enable long text retrieval (CLOB)". This box is unchecked by default.

ments determines what action is performed against the data source. The next section provides a quick primer on SQL.

The cfquery tag works by establishing a connection with the specified data source, passing a series of SQL commands, and returning query variables that contain information about the operation. The basic syntax for using the cfquery tag is as follows:

```
<cfquery name="query_name"
         datasource="datasource_name">
SQL statements
</cfquery>
```

Each attribute in the opening cfquery tag specifies information about the data source and how ColdFusion should access it. The name attribute assigns a name to the query. Valid query names must begin with a letter and can contain only letters, numbers, and underscore characters. name is required when passing an SQL SELECT statement and is optional for all other SQL operations.* The datasource attribute is required in all circumstances except when dbtype is Query (covered later in Chapter 11) and specifies the name of the data source (as it appears in the ColdFusion Administrator) to connect to when executing the query. There are a number of additional attributes that can be used with the cfquery tag. For a complete list, see its tag reference in Appendix A.

A Quick SQL Primer

Before we go any further, a quick primer on SQL is in order. If you are already an SQL guru, feel free to skip this section. If, however, you are new to SQL, this section quickly covers the basic elements that go into creating an SQL statement. This primer is by no means a substitute for a thorough lesson on SQL. You may want to consult additional SQL references before proceeding, as a good understanding of SQL is an essential element in ColdFusion application design. One of the surest ways to bottleneck your applications is with poorly written SQL. Additionally, SQL is implemented in slightly different ways across various RDBMS platforms. For this reason, it is important to consult the documentation specific to your database to understand these differences.

With the disclaimer out of the way, let's move on and look at the elements that go into creating an SQL statement for use in a cfquery tag. If you don't completely understand everything we are about to cover, don't worry. Every aspect (and more) of the SQL we cover in the primer is covered in more detail throughout this and the next chapter.

* Although the name attribute is required only for SQL SELECT statements, you may wish to use it with all your queries. It makes debugging easier, especially for templates that contain multiple queries, because it allows you to identify each query by name in the debug output.

Most database transactions in a web application can be grouped into one of four categories: selecting, inserting, updating, and deleting data. Not surprisingly, there are four commands in SQL that handle theses tasks. They are `SELECT`, `INSERT`, `UPDATE`, and `DELETE`, respectively:

`SELECT`
: Retrieves data from a data source

`INSERT`
: Inserts new data in a data source

`UPDATE`
: Updates existing data in a data source

`DELETE`
: Deletes data from a data source

Once you have determined the type of operation you want to perform, the next step is to refine the SQL statement by adding various clauses and operators. Depending on the action you want to perform, the syntax of the SQL statement varies. Here are some common SQL clauses:

`FROM`
: The table name or names you want to perform the `SELECT` or `DELETE` action against

`INTO`
: Specifies the table name and column names you want to `INSERT` data into

`VALUES`
: The values to add to the columns specified in `INTO` when adding data with an `INSERT`

`SET`
: Specifies the column names you wish to `UPDATE` with new values

`WHERE`
: Specifies one or more conditions governing what data is returned by a `SELECT`, what data is changed by a `UPDATE`, or what data is deleted by a `DELETE`

`ORDER BY`
: Determines the sort order for records returned by a `SELECT`

`group BY`
: Groups related data in a `SELECT`. Frequently used along with aggregate functions (discussed later in the chapter)

`HAVING`
: Generally used in place of a `WHERE` clause when using the `group BY` clause

`JOIN`
: Used along with a `SELECT` statement to retrieve data from two or more related tables

`UNION`
: Combines the results of two record sets returned by a `SELECT` statement into a single record set, provided both record sets have the same number of columns, and those columns are of compatible or convertible datatypes

SQL provides a number of operators, such as `AND`, `=`, and `OR`, that can be used to construct compound, conditional, and comparison statements. Some of the more popular operators are shown in Table 4-1.

Table 4-1. Common SQL operators

Operator	Description
`=`	Equal to
`<>`	Not equal to
`<`	Less than
`>`	Greater than
`<=`	Less than or equal to
`>=`	Greater than or equal to
`+`	Plus (addition)
`-`	Minus (subtraction)
`/`	Divided by (division)
`*`	Multiplied by (multiplication)
`AND`	Both conditions must be `True`
`OR`	One or the other condition must be `True`
`NOT`	Ignores a condition
`IS [NOT] NULL`	Value is [not] null
`IN`	Value is in a list of values
`BETWEEN`	Value is in the range between one value and another
`LIKE`	Value is like a wildcarded value; wildcards are % (string) and _ (character)
`EXISTS`	Used only with subqueries; tests for a nonempty record set

Now we can look at some SQL examples. Here's how to select all the fields from a database table:

```
SELECT *
FROM TableName
```

Here's how to select specific fields from a table where a certain field must meet a specific condition:

```
SELECT Field1, Field2
FROM TableName
WHERE Field1 = value
```

This example shows how to select fields from two different tables:

```
SELECT TableName1.Field1, TableName2.Field1
FROM TableName1, TableName2
```

This example selects two fields from a table and orders the result set by the value of *Field1* in ascending order:

```
SELECT Field1, Field2
FROM TableName
WHERE Field1 = Value1 AND Field2 = Value2
ORDER BY Field1 ASC
```

To perform the same query but have the result set ordered in descending order use this code:

```
SELECT Field1, Field2
FROM TableName
WHERE Field1 = Value1 OR Field1 = Value2
ORDER BY Field1 DESC
```

To insert a record into a table, use the INSERT clause with the INTO and VALUES operators:

```
INSERT INTO TableName(Field1, Field2, Field3)
VALUES('value1', value2, 'value3')
```

If you want to update an existing row, you can do so on a field-by-field basis using the UPDATE clause along with the SET and WHERE operators:

```
UPDATE TableName
SET Field1 = 'value1',
    Field2 = value2,
    Field3 = 'value3'
WHERE Fieldx = valuex
```

This code deletes a single row of data from a table:

```
DELETE FROM TableName
WHERE Field = value
```

If you want to delete multiple rows in one operation, use the IN operator like this:

```
DELETE FROM TableName
WHERE field IN (field1,field2,fieldx)
```

String values passed using the IN operator must be surrounded by single quotes. Additionally, many databases have a limit of 1000 items in a single IN list.

Now you should be primed and ready to jump into embedding SQL statements within the cfquery tag. The next section looks at using the cfquery tag in conjunction with SQL to retrieve data from a database and display the results in the browser.

Retrieving and Displaying Data

When you query records from a database, the results (known as a record set) are returned in a special ColdFusion data type called a *query object*. A query object stores the records within it in rows and columns—just like a spreadsheet. Throughout this book, I'll use the terms record and row interchangeably. Column name and field are also used interchangeably. Before we get into the specifics of querying databases and working with query objects, we need to create a database with some sample data to work with.

Creating the Example Database

The majority of examples in this chapter (and throughout the book) use a data source called `ProgrammingCF` that contains several database tables including one called `EmployeeDirectory`. The schema and sample data for this database are listed in Appendix C. For simplicity, I've chosen to use a Microsoft Access database for all the examples; you can download the sample Access database from O'Reilly's catalog page for this book (*http://www.oreilly.com/catalog/coldfusion2/*). Of course, you can use any database you choose. To get started, you need to create a new database and save it as `ProgrammingCF`. Next, create a new table and add the fields shown in Table 4-2.

Table 4-2. Employee directory table within the ProgrammingCF database

Field name	Field type	Max length
`ID` (primary key)	AutoNumber	N/A
`Name`	Text	255
`Title`	Text	255
`Department`	Text	255
`Email`	Text	255
`PhoneExt`	Number (long int)	N/A
`Salary`	Number (double, two decimal places)	N/A
`Picture`	Memo	N/A

In this example, `ID` is an AutoNumber field designated as the primary key for the table. A primary key is a single field or concatenation of fields that uniquely identifies a record. In Microsoft Access, AutoNumber is a special field type that automatically assigns a sequentially incremental number when a record is inserted into the table.* If you aren't using Access as your database, and your database doesn't have the equivalent of the AutoNumber field, consider using ColdFusion's `CreateUUID()` function to generate a universally unique identifier (UUID) to use as the primary key value for your record. UUIDs are 35-character representations of 128-bit strings

* Because portability from one database platform to another may be an issue, it's not desirable to use an AutoNumber field as a table's primary key value. The examples in this book use AutoNumber fields for primary key values as a matter of convenience.

where each character is a hexadecimal value in the range 0–9 and A–F.* UUIDs are guaranteed to be unique:

```
<!--- Create a UUID and output it to the browser --->
<cfset MyPrimaryKeyValue = CreateUUID( )>
<cfoutput>
ID: #MyPrimaryKeyValue#
</cfoutput>
```

When you finish adding the fields, go ahead and save the table as `EmployeeDirectory`. Now it is time to populate the `EmployeeDirectory` table with data. Table 4-3 contains a short listing of records. For the complete list, see Appendix C.

Table 4-3. Employee directory database table containing employee contact information

ID	Name	Title	Department	Email	Phone-ext	Salary
1	Pere Money	President	Executive Mgmt	*pere@example.com*	1234	400K
2	Greg Corcoran	Director	Marketing	*greg@example.com*	1237	960K
3	Mark Edward	VP	Sales	*mark@example.com*	1208	155K

Once you finish entering all the records, save the database to a directory on your ColdFusion server. If you have downloaded the sample Access database, you need to make sure that it resides on the same machine as your ColdFusion server or on a network share available to the server. Before you can begin using the database, you need to register it as a data source with the ColdFusion Administrator. Be sure to register the data-source name as `ProgrammingCF`.

Retrieving Data from a Data Source

The `cfquery` tag can retrieve data from a data source by passing an SQL `SELECT` statement to the data source. The `SELECT` statement specifies what data to retrieve from the data source. For example, if you want to retrieve all records from the `EmployeeDirectory` table in the `ProgrammingCF` data source, you can use a `cfquery` tag with a `SELECT` statement like this:

```
<cfquery name="GetEmployeeInfo" datasource="ProgrammingCF">
  SELECT *
  FROM EmployeeDirectory
</cfquery>
```

* UUIDs are guaranteed to be unique and are assigned randomly on most operating systems. Note that the format that ColdFusion uses for UUIDs is not the same format used by Microsoft and DCE's GUID (Globally Unique Identifier). ColdFusion UUIDs follow the format xxxxxxxx-xxxx-xxxx-xxxxxxxxxxxxxxxx (35 characters), whereas Microsoft/DCE GUIDs are formatted as xxxxxxxx-xxxx-xxxx-xxxxxx-xxxxxxxxxx (36 characters—note the additional dash). If you need a UUID/GUID that follows the Microsoft/DCE format, see the `CreateGUID( )` user defined function available at *http://www.cflib.org*.

This SELECT statement uses a wildcard (*) to retrieve all records from the EmployeeDirectory table in the ProgrammingCF data source.

Alternately, if you want to retrieve data from only a few columns as opposed to all columns (don't confuse this with all rows), you can modify the SELECT statement like this:

```
<cfquery name="GetEmployeeInfo" datasource="ProgrammingCF">
  SELECT Name, Title
  FROM EmployeeDirectory
</cfquery>
```

This query retrieves only the Name and Title columns from each row of the database. This type of query is used when you need only a subset of the data stored in a data source. Retrieving only the data you need as opposed to the entire table contents improves the overall performance of your queries. It is much more efficient for a database to send a small subset of data back to ColdFusion as opposed to an entire table, especially when you need only a small portion of the larger data set to begin with.

In general, it is not advisable to retrieve data using SELECT *. From a database standpoint, selecting all fields using a wildcard creates a performance hit, especially on larger record sets, because the database has to do extra work to determine what fields to return. If you really do need all the fields from a particular table returned in your result set, still consider specifying them individually by name, because it saves the database from having to construct the list.

You can further refine the SELECT statement to return only a limited number of rows of data based on a condition. This is done by including the condition using the WHERE keyword. The idea at work here is to return the smallest record set you need. The more specific the data returned by a query is to your needs, the less work you need to have the ColdFusion server do to process it. Executing the following cfquery returns just the names and email addresses of employees in the IT department:

```
<cfquery name="GetEmployeeInfo" datasource="ProgrammingCF">
  SELECT Name, Title
  FROM EmployeeDirectory
  WHERE Department = 'IT'
</cfquery>
```

Note the use of the single quotes around the value 'IT' in the WHERE clause. String values must always be enclosed in single quotes. Numeric, Boolean, and date values may be specified without quotes.

You can extend this one step further, providing a dynamic value for the condition in the WHERE clause:

```
<cfquery name="GetEmployeeInfo" datasource="ProgrammingCF">
  SELECT Name, Title
  FROM EmployeeDirectory
  WHERE Department = '#Form.Department#'
</cfquery>
```

This example retrieves the name and title of each employee in the department specified by a form variable called `Department`. Using this type of technique allows you to build dynamic SQL statements that return different results depending on form or URL input. Dynamic SQL is discussed in Chapter 11.

Outputting Query Results

Once you have data stored in a query object, the next step is to display it using the `cfoutput` tag. The `cfoutput` tag allows you to display data contained in a query object by referencing the query name in the `query` attribute. Example 4-1 queries the `EmployeeDirectory` of the `ProgrammingCF` data source and outputs the results to the browser using `cfoutput`.

Example 4-1. Outputting the results of a query in an HTML table

```
<!--- Retrieve all records from the database --->
<cfquery name="GetEmployeeInfo" datasource="ProgrammingCF">
  SELECT ID, Name, Title, Department, Email, PhoneExt, Salary
  FROM EmployeeDirectory
</cfquery>

<html>
<head>
  <title>Outputting query results</title>
  <style type="text/css">
    th {
      background-color : #888888;
      font-weight : bold;
      text-align : center;
    }
    td {
      background-color : #C0C0C0;
    }
  </style>
</head>

<body>
<h2>Employee Records</h2>
<!--- Create an HTML table for outputting the query results.  This section
      creates the first row of the table - used to hold the column
      headers --->
<table cellpadding="3" cellspacing="1">
  <tr>
    <th>ID</th>
    <th>Name</th>
    <th>Title</th>
    <th>Department</th>
    <th>E-mail</th>
    <th>Phone Extension</th>
    <th>Salary</th>
  </tr>
```

Example 4-1. Outputting the results of a query in an HTML table (continued)

```
  <!--- The cfoutput tag is used in conjunction with the query attribute to
        loop over each row of data in the result set.  During each iteration
        of the loop, a table row is dynamically created and populated with the
        query data from the current row. --->
  <cfoutput query="GetEmployeeInfo">
  <tr>
    <td>#ID#</td>
    <td>#Name#</td>
    <td>#Title#</td>
    <td>#Department#</td>
    <td><a href="Mailto:#Email#">#Email#</a></td>
    <td>#PhoneExt#</td>
    <td>#Salary#</td>
  </tr>
  </cfoutput>
</table>
</body>
</html>
```

In this example, the `cfquery` tag executes a `SELECT` statement against the `EmployeeDirectory` table of the `ProgrammingCF` data source. The query retrieves all the columns for all the records stored in the table. The template then creates an HTML table and generates column headings using a series of HTML `<th>` tags.

Next, the `cfoutput` tag is used in conjunction with the `query` attribute to loop over each row of data in the result set. With each iteration of the loop, a table row is dynamically created and populated with the query data from the current row.

Obtaining Additional Query Information

Whenever you perform a query using ColdFusion, four variables are automatically created that contain information about the `cfquery` operation and the result set it returned, if any. Here are the four variables:

`cfquery.ExecutionTime`
: The amount of time in milliseconds it takes the query to execute.

`queryname``.ColumnList`
: Comma-delimited list of the query column names from the database. The list is returned in alphabetical order, not in the order specified in the `SELECT` statement used to generate the result set. Additionally, all column names are returned in uppercase.

`queryname``.CurrentRow`
: The current row of the query that is being processed by `cfoutput`.

`queryname``.RecordCount`
: The total number of records returned by the query.

These variables can be used in countless ways and are used heavily throughout this book for such things as knowing how many records were returned by a particular query and breaking the display of query result sets into manageable chunks.

Sorting Query Results

When you use a basic SQL SELECT statement to retrieve records from a database, those records are returned in the order in which they are stored. If you want to change the order in which the records are displayed (which you probably do), you need to use an ORDER BY clause, as shown in Example 4-2.

Example 4-2. Sorting query results using the SQL ORDER clause

```
<cfquery name="GetEmployeeInfo" datasource="ProgrammingCF">
  SELECT Name, Title, Department, Email, PhoneExt
  FROM EmployeeDirectory
  ORDER BY Name ASC
</cfquery>

<html>
<head>
  <title>Sorting Query Results Using the SQL ORDER Clause</title>
  <style type="text/css">
    th {
      background-color : #888888;
      font-weight : bold;
      text-align : center;
    }
    td {
      background-color : #C0C0C0;
    }
  </style>
</head>

<body>
<table cellpadding="3" cellspacing="1">
  <tr>
    <th>Name</th>
    <th>Title</th>
    <th>Department</th>
    <th>E-mail</th>
    <th>Phone Extension</th>
  </tr>
  <cfoutput query="GetEmployeeInfo">
  <tr>
    <td>#Name#</td>
    <td>#Title#</td>
    <td>#Department#</td>
    <td><a href="Mailto:#Email#">#Email#</a></td>
    <td>#PhoneExt#</td>
  </tr>
```

Example 4-2. Sorting query results using the SQL ORDER clause (continued)

```
  </cfoutput>
</table>
</body>
</html>
```

The `ORDER BY` clause specifies which column or columns to use in ordering the query results. Sorting can be either `ASC` (ascending) or `DESC` (descending). Example 4-2 sorts the result set by `name` column, in ascending order. The output is shown in Figure 4-1.

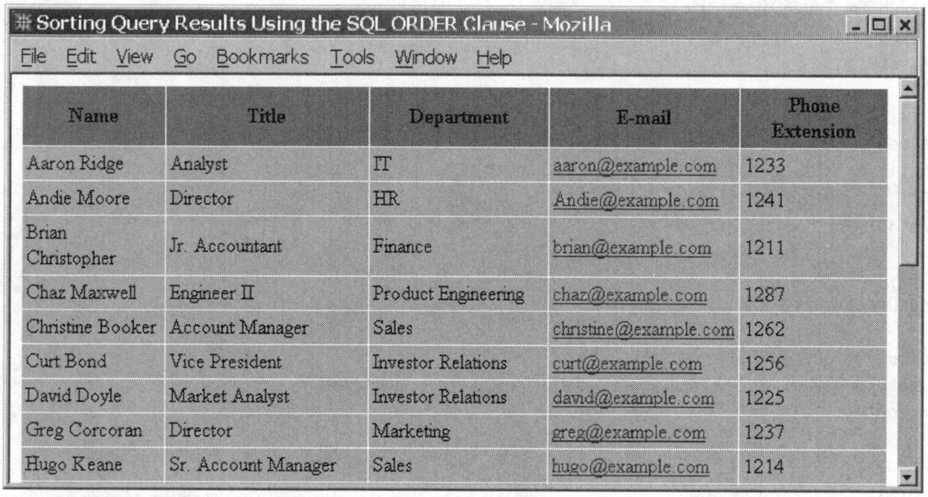

Sorting Query Results Using the SQL ORDER Clause - Mozilla

File Edit View Go Bookmarks Tools Window Help

Name	Title	Department	E-mail	Phone Extension
Aaron Ridge	Analyst	IT	aaron@example.com	1233
Andie Moore	Director	HR	Andie@example.com	1241
Brian Christopher	Jr. Accountant	Finance	brian@example.com	1211
Chaz Maxwell	Engineer II	Product Engineering	chaz@example.com	1287
Christine Booker	Account Manager	Sales	christine@example.com	1262
Curt Bond	Vice President	Investor Relations	curt@example.com	1256
David Doyle	Market Analyst	Investor Relations	david@example.com	1225
Greg Corcoran	Director	Marketing	greg@example.com	1237
Hugo Keane	Sr. Account Manager	Sales	hugo@example.com	1214

Figure 4-1. Sorting a result set using the ORDER BY clause

Multicolumn sorts can be performed by specifying a comma-delimited list of column names and sort orders for the `ORDER BY` clause as in:

```
<cfquery name="GetEmployeeInfo" datasource="ProgrammingCF">
  SELECT Name, Title, Department, Email, PhoneExt
  FROM EmployeeDirectory
  ORDER BY Title ASC, Name ASC
</cfquery>
```

Grouping Output

The `cfoutput` tag has an attribute called `group` that lets you to group output from your record sets before displaying it to the browser. There are two ways to use the `group` attribute of the `cfoutput` tag. The first method uses `group` to remove any duplicate rows from the query result set.* This is useful in situations where the result set

* Don't confuse the group attribute of the cfoutput tag with the SQL group BY keyword, because they perform entirely different functions. The SQL group BY keyword is discussed in Chapter 11.

you return from a query contains duplicate rows of data but you want to display only unique records.

Example 4-3 demonstrates what happens when you query a table containing duplicate values and output the results without using the group attribute of the cfoutput tag.

Example 4-3. Failing to use the group attribute results in duplicate values in the output

```
<cfquery name="GetDepartment" datasource="ProgrammingCF">
  SELECT Department
  FROM EmployeeDirectory
  ORDER BY Department
</cfquery>

<html>
<head>
  <title>Failing to Use the group Attribute Results in Duplicate Values in the
        Output </title>
</head>

<body>
<h2>Departments:</h2>

<cfoutput query="GetDepartment">
#Department#<br>
</cfoutput>

</body>
</html>
```

As you can see in Figure 4-2, executing the template results in many of the same values being output more than once.

This is easy enough to fix. To remove the duplicates from the output, all you have to do is modify the line of code containing the cfoutput tag to read like this:

```
<cfoutput query="GetDepartment" group="Department" groupcasesensitive="No">
```

Adding group="Department" to the cfoutput tag tells ColdFusion to discard any duplicate values in the result set and output only unique values. The groupcasesensitive attribute indicates whether grouping should be case insensitive or case sensitive. This attribute is optional and defaults to Yes. For our example, set groupcasesensitive to No in case someone enters the name of a department using the wrong case. The difference in output is shown in Figure 4-3.

It is important to note that using group to remove duplicates from the result set does so *after* the result set is returned from the database. You should consider how this might affect the performance of your application if you want to return only a few records from a large record set that contains numerous duplicate values. In such a case, you should use SQL to remove the duplicates.

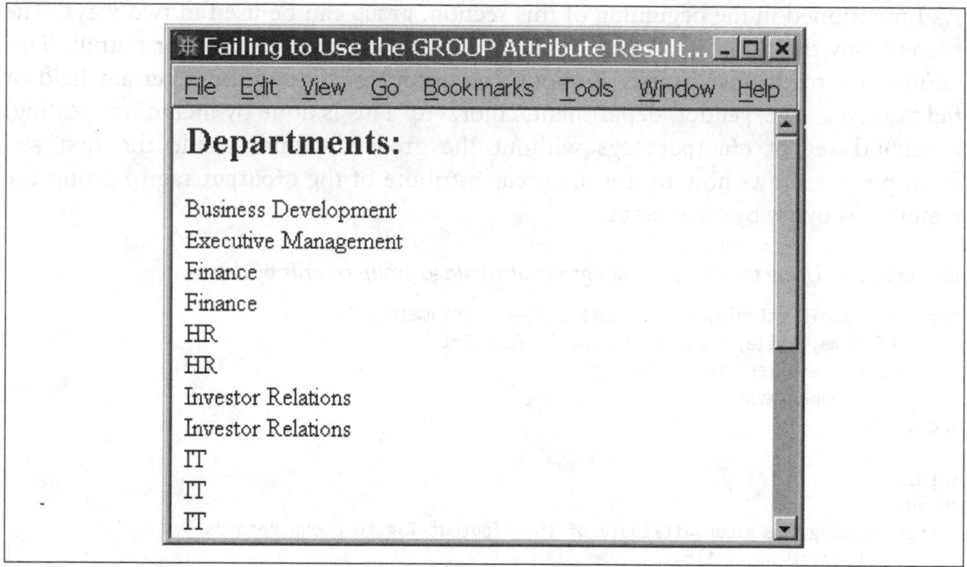

Figure 4-2. Duplicate records are displayed because group wasn't used

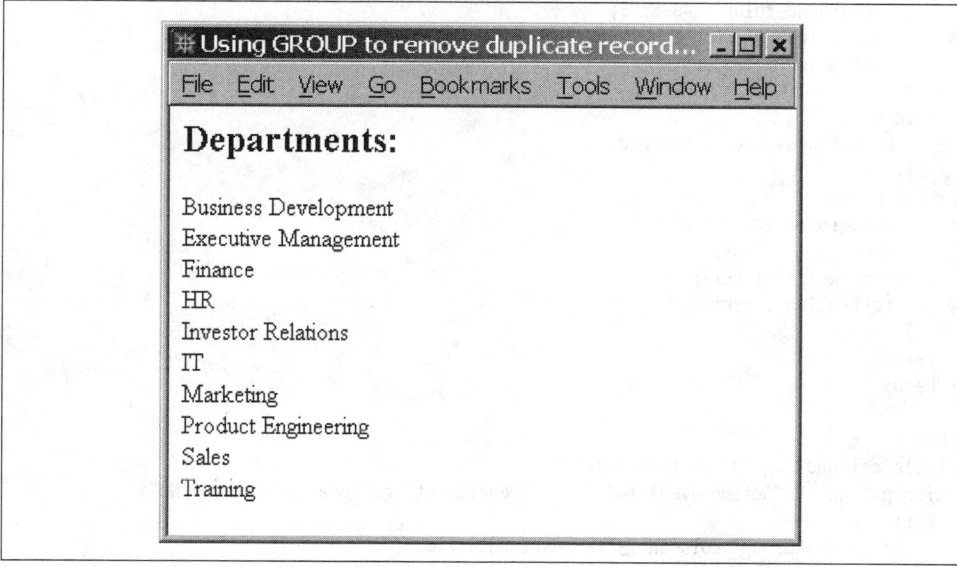

Figure 4-3. Using group to remove duplicate records

If you look at the code in Example 4-3, you'll notice that we included `ORDER BY Department` in our SQL statement. It is necessary to sort the result set by the column being grouped. To see what happens if you don't include the `ORDER BY` clause, remove it from the query and execute the template.

As I mentioned in the beginning of this section, group can be used in two ways. The second way the group attribute can be used is to group like records for output. This allows you to do such things as group the output of a query by a certain field or fields such as age, gender, department, color, etc. This is done by including (nesting) a second set of `cfoutput` tags without the group attribute inside the first set. Example 4-4 shows how to use the group attribute of the `cfoutput` tag to group the results of a query by `Department`.

Example 4-4. Using the cfoutput tag's group attribute to group records by department

```
<cfquery name="GetEmployeeInfo" datasource="ProgrammingCF">
  SELECT Name, Title, Department, Email, PhoneExt
  FROM EmployeeDirectory
  ORDER BY Department
</cfquery>

<html>
<head>
  <title>Using the group Attribute of the cfoutput Tag to Group Records by
        Department</title>
  <style type="text/css">
    th {
      background-color : #888888;
      font-weight : bold;
      text-align : center;
    }
    td {
      background-color : #C0C0C0;
    }
    td.Group {
      background-color : #FFFFFF;
      font-size : 14pt;
      font-weight : bold;
      text-align : center;
    }
  </style>
</head>

<body>
<table cellpadding="3" cellspacing="1">
<cfoutput query="GetEmployeeInfo" group="Department" groupcasesensitive="No">
  <tr>
    <td class="Group" colspan="5">#Department#</td>
  </tr>
  <tr>
    <th>Name</th>
    <th>Title</th>
    <th>Department</th>
    <th>E-mail</th>
    <th>Phone Extension</th>
  </tr>
  <cfoutput>
```

Example 4-4. Using the cfoutput tag's group attribute to group records by department (continued)

```
  <tr>
    <td>#Name#</td>
    <td>#Title#</td>
    <td>#Department#</td>
    <td><a href="Mailto:#Email#">#Email#</a></td>
    <td>#PhoneExt#</td>
  </tr>
  </cfoutput>
  <tr>
    <td class="Group" colspan="5"> </td>
  </tr>
</cfoutput>
</table>
```

The group attribute of the cfquery tag lets you group your query's result set by the specified column. In this case, we want to group the query results by Department. It is necessary to use the ORDER BY clause to order the result set by the column being grouped. Failing to do so results in unwanted output. Notice the second set of cfoutput tags nested within the pair declaring the group. This creates an outer and inner loop for looping over the result set and grouping the output appropriately. Nested cfoutput tags may be used only when the outermost cfoutput tag has a value specified for the query and group attributes. If you attempt to nest cfoutput tags without using these attributes in the outermost tag, ColdFusion throws an error. Additionally, if you omit the nested cfoutput, the nested grouping doesn't occur, and you end up removing any duplicate records from the result set (just like our previous example). Executing the template results in the output shown in Figure 4-4.

It is entirely possible to group data several levels deep. Doing so requires nesting several sets of cfoutput tags using the following general syntax:

```
<cfoutput query="query_name" group="column">
HTML and CFML...
  <cfoutput group="different_column">
  HTML and CFML...
    <cfoutput>
    HTML and CFML...
    </cfoutput>
  </cfoutput>
</cfoutput>
```

When ColdFusion encounters nested cfoutput tags, it executes successive levels of nested loops to group the query result set. In general, there are a few rules you need to keep in mind when working with nested cfoutput tags:

- The outermost cfoutput tag must have the query and group attributes defined.
- The innermost cfoutput tag can't have any attributes specified.
- All other cfoutput tags may have only the group attribute specified.

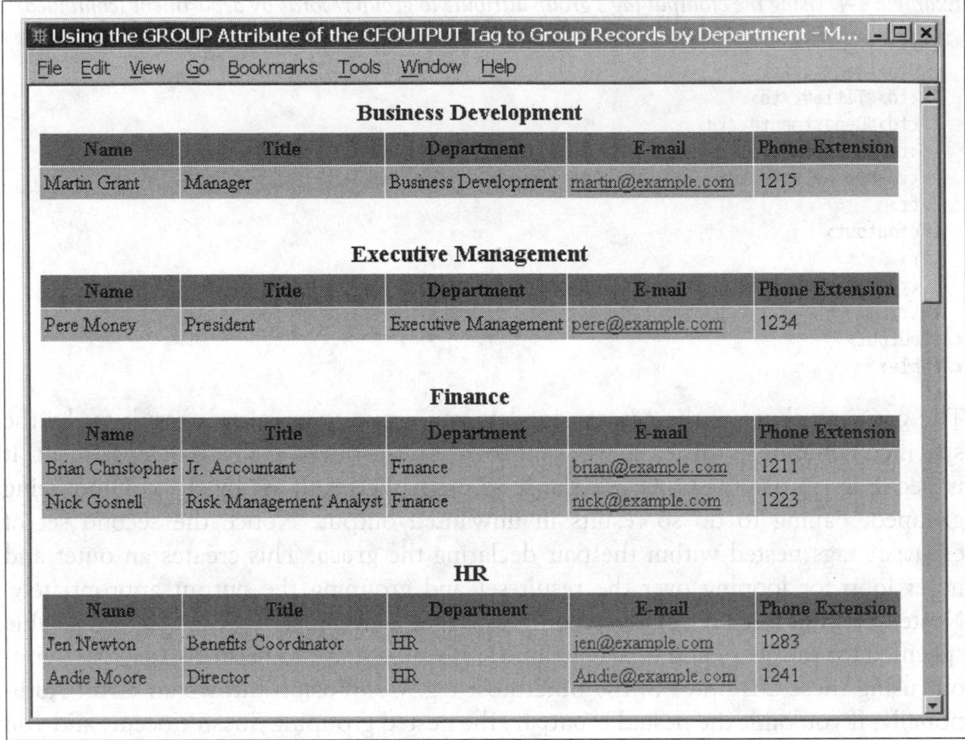

Figure 4-4. Using cfoutput to group query results

Looping Over a Query Result Set

As I mentioned briefly in Chapter 2, a query loop (`cfloop` tag with the `query` attribute) performs essentially the same job as using a `cfoutput` tag with the `query` attribute. A query loop iterates over each row in a query object. Optionally, a start row and end row within the query may be specified:

```
<cfloop query="query_name"
        startrow="row_number"
        endrow="row_number">
...
</cfloop>
```

The query attribute specifies the name of a valid ColdFusion query object. `startrow` is optional and may be used to specify the row within the query object where the loop should begin. `endrow` is also optional and specifies the last row within a query object that should be included within the loop.

The query loop may be used instead of the `query` attribute of the `cfoutput` tag to display the contents of a query:

```
<cfquery name="GetEmployeeInfo" datasource="ProgrammingCF">
  SELECT Name, Title
```

```
  FROM EmployeeDirectory
</cfquery>

<cfloop query="GetEmployeeInfo">
  <cfoutput>#Name#, #Title#<br></cfoutput>
</cfloop>
```

Using a query loop allows you to work around limitations inherent in the cfoutput tag such as the inability to nest additional output queries within a cfoutput block. For example, the following code produces an error in ColdFusion because you can't nest cfoutput tags without using the group attribute:

```
<cfquery name="MyQuery1" datasource="MyDSN">
  SELECT *
  FROM MyTable
  WHERE Field = Value
</cfquery>

<cfoutput query="MyQuery1">
  <cfquery name="MyQuery2" datasource="MyDSN">
    SELECT *
    FROM MyTable
    WHERE Field = Value
  </cfquery>

  <cfoutput query="MyQuery2">
    Additional processing and output code here...
  </cfoutput>
</cfoutput>
```

You can get around this limitation by using a query loop within the cfoutput block:

```
<cfquery name="MyQuery1" datasource="MyDSN">
  SELECT *
  FROM MyTable
  WHERE Field = Value
</cfquery>

<cfoutput query="MyQuery1">
  <cfquery name="MyQuery2" datasource="MyDSN">
    SELECT *
    FROM MyTable
    WHERE Field = Value
  </cfquery>

  <cfloop query="MyQuery2">
    Additional processing and output code here...
  </cfloop>
</cfoutput>
```

Additionally, you can use the query loop to output a section of a record set by dynamically defining the start row and end row of the query object to loop over:

```
<cfset TheStart = 3>
<cfset TheEnd = 5>
```

```
<cfquery name="GetEmployeeInfo" datasource="ProgrammingCF">
  SELECT Name, Title
  FROM EmployeeDirectory
</cfquery>

<cfloop query="GetEmployeeInfo" startrow="#TheStart#" endrow="#TheEnd#">
  <cfoutput>#Name#, #Title#<br></cfoutput>
</cfloop>
```

This technique can be used to create a next/previous record browser in which a predetermined number of rows from a query result set are displayed on the page. This allows users to browse a set number of records at a time while moving forward and backward through the record set. Next/previous browsing is discussed in detail in Chapter 11.

Formatting Techniques

Once you have query data in the form of a result set, you might want to massage it a bit before outputting it to the browser or to a file. ColdFusion provides several built-in functions for formatting a variety of datatypes. This section covers some of the more popular functions for formatting strings, HTML code, numbers, currency, dates, times, and Boolean values. For more information on all the functions covered in this section, see Appendix B.

Formatting Plain-Text Strings

ColdFusion provides functions for formatting text strings: `ParagraphFormat( )`, `Wrap( )`, `Ucase( )`, `Lcase( )`, `JSStringFormat( )`, and `XMLFormat( )`. Each function is covered in the sections that follow.

Using ParagraphFormat

`ParagraphFormat( )`takes a string and formats it so that single newline characters are replaced with a space, and double newline characters are replaced with HTML `<p>` tags. This function is most often used to display data that has been entered into a `Textarea` HTML form field. The following example shows how the `ParagraphFormat( )` function handles single and double newline characters:

```
<cfset MyText="This is my block of text.
It has both single newline characters in it like this paragraph, and double
newline characters like in the next paragraph.

This is the paragraph with the double newline characters.">

<form>
<cfoutput>
<textarea cols="50" rows="10" name="TheText" wrap="Virtual">
#ParagraphFormat(MyText)#
```

```
</textarea>
</cfoutput>
</form>
```

Wrapping text

As of ColdFusion MX 6.1, you can wrap a block of text with the `Wrap()` function so that no line exceeds a specified number of characters. `Wrap()` takes two required arguments and one optional argument:

```
wrap(string, limit [,strip])
```

`string` represents the string you want to wrap, *`limit`* specifies the maximum number of characters to allow per line in *`string`*, and *`strip`* indicates whether to remove all existing line breaks before wrapping the string. If a line is longer than the specified number of characters, an attempt is made to break the line by inserting a line break at the nearest whitespace character (space, tab, etc) before the character limit. If *`string`* contains no whitespace characters before the maximum number of characters per line, a line break is inserted at the maximum line length. `Wrap()` uses operating system specific line breaks. On Windows, it uses a carriage return and newline character. On Unix/Linux, it uses a newline. Here is an example that wraps a string at 80 characters:

```
<cfset myString="This is a string that is so long, I probably would like to
break it up.  What do you think about that?  Is it a good idea?">

<cfoutput>
<pre>#Wrap(myString, 80, False)#</pre>
</cfoutput>
```

Changing case

You can change the case of an entire string using the `Ucase( )` and `Lcase( )` functions. `Ucase( )` converts a string to all uppercase characters, while `Lcase( )` converts a string to all lowercase characters. The following example demonstrates both functions:

```
<cfset MyString = "This Is A Mixed Case String!">

<h3>UCase/LCase</h3>
<cfoutput>
Original String: #MyString#<br>
After UCase: #UCase(MyString)#<br>
After LCase: #LCase(MyString)#
</cfoutput>
```

Making strings JavaScript-safe

On occasion, you may need to retrieve a string from a database for use in a JavaScript function within your application. The `JSStringFormat( )` function can be used to make the string safe for use in JavaScript statements by automatically escaping special characters that normally cause a problem, such as double quotes, single quotes, and the newline character (\). The following example returns a string that has been formatted for use in a JavaScript statement:

```
<cfset MyString="""Escape double quotes"". Escape the \ character. 'Escape
    single quotes'">

<cfset SafeString=JSStringFormat(MyString)>

<cfoutput>
<b>Original String:</b> #MyString#<br>
<b>JavaScript Safe String:</b> #SafeString#
</cfoutput>
```

Making strings safe for XML

You can make a string safe to use with XML by using the `XMLFormat()` function. `XMLFormat()` takes a string as its only parameter and returns it in a format that is safe to use with XML by escaping the following special characters:

- Ampersand (&)
- Double quotation mark (")
- Greater-than sign (>)
- Less-than sign (<)
- Single quotation mark (')

The following example takes a string and makes it safe to use with XML:

```
<cfset MyString="Here's an example of the XMLFormat function: 5+5<20">

<cfoutput>
#XMLFormat(MyString)#
</cfoutput>

<p>
<i>View the page source to see the escaped text.</i>
```

Formatting HTML

In order to display literal HTML or CFML code, it is necessary to escape certain special characters so that they don't cause the browser to interpret the code contained inside them. For example, if you have a string that contains `Hello <b>World!</b>`, and you want to display the HTML code contained in the string without having it execute, you need to escape the < and > characters. ColdFusion provides you with two functions to do this: `HTMLCodeFormat()` and `HTMLEditFormat()`.

HTMLCodeFormat

The `HTMLCodeFormat()` function returns a string enclosed in `<pre>` and `</pre>` tags with all carriage returns removed and special characters (< > " &) escaped. The function takes two parameters, a string to format and optionally, the HTML version to use for the character escape sequences. Valid entries for the HTML version are shown in Table 4-4.

Table 4-4. HTML versions

Value	Description
-1	Current HTML version
2.0	HTML v2.0 (default)
3.2	HTML v3.0

The following example demonstrates the `HTMLCodeFormat( )` function:

```
<cfset MyString="<h3>This is an example of the HTMLCodeFormat function.</h3>
View the source of this document to see the escaping of the HTML characters.">

<cfoutput>
#HTMLCodeFormat(MyString, "3.2")#
</cfoutput>
```

HTMLEditFormat

The `HTMLEditFormat( )` function is almost identical in functionality to `HTMLCodeFormat( )`. The only difference is that it doesn't add `<pre></pre>` tags to the output returned by the function. The following example demonstrates the `HTMLEditFormat( )` function:

```
<cfset MyString="<h3>This is an example of the HTMLEditFormat function.</h3>
View the source of this document to see the escaping of the HTML characters.">

<cfoutput>
#HTMLEditFormat(MyString, "3.2")#
</cfoutput>
```

Formatting Numbers

ColdFusion provides three functions for formatting numbers: `DecimalFormat( )`, `NumberFormat( )`, and `LSNumberFormat( )`. These functions can format numbers in a variety of ways, as described in the following sections.

Formatting decimal numbers

The `DecimalFormat( )` function takes a number and returns it formatted to two decimal places, with thousands separators. The following example formats a variety of numbers using `DecimalFormat( )`:

```
<cfoutput>
1:  #DecimalFormat(1)#<br>
10: #DecimalFormat(10)#<br>
100: #DecimalFormat(100)#<br>
1000: #DecimalFormat(1000)#<br>
```

```
10000: #DecimalFormat(10000)#<br>
100000: #DecimalFormat(100000)#<br>
1000000: #DecimalFormat(1000000)#<br>
</cfoutput>
```

General number formatting

The `NumberFormat()` function handles general number formatting in ColdFusion. `NumberFormat()` allows you to format numbers using a variety of masks. The function accepts two parameters, the number you wish to format and a mask to specify the formatting, in the form `NumberFormat(Number, 'mask')`. If no mask is supplied, `NumberFormat()` returns the number formatted with thousands separators. If for any reason ColdFusion is not able to format the number with the supplied mask, the original value is returned unformatted. Valid entries for the mask are listed in Table 4-5.

Table 4-5. Mask Values for NumberFormat()

Mask	Description
- (underscore)	Optional digit placeholder
9	Optional digit placeholder; same as _ but better for showing decimal places
.	Decimal point location
	Forces padding with zeros
( )	Surrounds negative numbers in parentheses
+	Places a plus sign in front of positive numbers and a minus sign in front of negative numbers
- (hyphen)	Places a space in front of positive numbers and a minus sign in front of negative numbers
,	Separates thousands with commas
L	Left-justifies the number within the width of the mask
C	Centers the number within the width of the mask
$	Places a dollar sign in front of the number
^	Separates left from right formatting

The following example shows the `NumberFormat()` function applied to various numbers:

```
<!--- Assign a number to a variable to be used throughout the example --->
<cfset MyNumber = 1000.99>

<h3>Formatting Numeric Values using NumberFormat</h3>

<cfoutput>
<b>MyNumber = #MyNumber#</b>
<p>
NumberFormat(MyNumber, '____'): #NumberFormat(MyNumber, '____')#<br>
NumberFormat(MyNumber, '9999.99'): #NumberFormat(MyNumber, '9999.99')#<br>
NumberFormat(MyNumber, '09999.9900'): #NumberFormat(MyNumber, '09999.9900')#<br>
NumberFormat(-MyNumber, '(9999.99)'): #NumberFormat(-MyNumber, '(9999.99)')#<br>
NumberFormat(MyNumber, '+9999.99'): #NumberFormat(MyNumber, '+9999.99')#<br>
```

```
NumberFormat(-MyNumber, '+9999.99'): #NumberFormat(-MyNumber, '+9999.99')#<br>
NumberFormat(MyNumber, '-9999.99'): #NumberFormat(MyNumber, '-9999.99')#<br>
NumberFormat(-MyNumber, '-9999.99'): #NumberFormat(-MyNumber, '-9999.99')#<br>
NumberFormat(MyNumber, '$9,999.99'): #NumberFormat(MyNumber, '$9,999.99')#<br>
NumberFormat(MyNumber, 'L999,999.99'): #NumberFormat(MyNumber, 'L999,999.99')#<br>
NumberFormat(MyNumber, 'C999,999.99'): #NumberFormat(MyNumber, 'C999,999.99')#<br>
NumberFormat(MyNumber, 'C_____(^___)'): #NumberFormat(MyNumber, 'C_____(^___)')#
</cfoutput>
```

Locale-specific number formatting

In addition to general number formatting using the NumberFormat( ) function, ColdFusion provides another function for formatting numbers in a format that is locale-specific. Locale-specific formatting allows you to format numbers for a specific language or dialect (often country-specific). For example, in many European countries, the period (.) is used as a thousands separator instead of the comma (,) as in the United States. The LSNumberFormat( ) function behaves the same as the NumberFormat( ) function (using the same masks), but it takes into account the formatting used by the default locale. If no formatting mask is supplied, LSNumberFormat( ) returns the number as an integer.

The following example loops through each locale supported by ColdFusion and applies a variety of different number masks for each locale:

```
<h3>Formatting Locale Specific Numeric Values using LSNumberFormat</h3>

<!--- Loop over each locale.  The list of locales is obtained from the server
      variable Server.ColdFusion.SupportedLocales --->
<cfloop index="locale" list="#Server.Coldfusion.SupportedLocales#">
<!--- This causes the CF server to assume the locale specified by the current
      iteration of the loop --->
<cfset SetLocale(locale)>

<cfoutput>
<p>
<b>#locale#</b><br>
LSNumberFormat(1000.99, '____'): #LSNumberFormat(1000.99, '____')#<br>
LSNumberFormat(1000.99, '9999.99'): #LSNumberFormat(1000.99, '9999.99')#<br>
LSNumberFormat(1000.99, '09999.9900'): #LSNumberFormat(1000.99, '09999.9900')#<br>
LSNumberFormat(-1000.99, '(9999.99)'): #LSNumberFormat(-1000.99, '(9999.99)')#<br>
LSNumberFormat(1000.99, '+9999.99'): #LSNumberFormat(1000.99, '+9999.99')#<br>
LSNumberFormat(-1000.99, '+9999.99'): #LSNumberFormat(-1000.99, '+9999.99')#<br>
LSNumberFormat(1000.99, '-9999.99'): #LSNumberFormat(1000.99, '-9999.99')#<br>
LSNumberFormat(-1000.99, '-9999.99'): #LSNumberFormat(-1000.99, '-9999.99')#<br>
LSNumberFormat(1000.99, '$9,999.99'): #LSNumberFormat(1000.99, '$9,999.99')#<br>
LSNumberFormat(1000.99, 'L999,999.99'):
  #LSNumberFormat(1000.99, 'L999,999.99')#<br>
LSNumberFormat(1000.99, 'C999,999.99'):
  #LSNumberFormat(1000.99,'C999,999.99')#<br>
LSNumberFormat(1000.99, 'C____(^___)'):
  #LSNumberFormat(1000.99, 'C____(^___)')#<br>
</cfoutput>
</cfloop>
```

Formatting Currency Values

Numeric values can be automatically formatted as currency values with the help of three ColdFusion functions: `DollarFormat()`, `LSCurrencyFormat()`, and `LSEuroCurrencyFormat()`.

Formatting dollars

The `DollarFormat()` function returns a number formatted as U.S. dollars. The returned number is formatted to two decimal places with a dollar sign and thousands separators. If the number is negative, it is returned in parentheses. The following example formats a variety of numbers using `DollarFormat()`:

```
<cfoutput>
-1000: #DollarFormat(-1000)#<br>
-100: #DollarFormat(-100)#<br>
-10: #DollarFormat(-10)#<br>
-1: #DollarFormat(-1)#<br>
1:  #DollarFormat(1)#<br>
10: #DollarFormat(10)#<br>
100: #DollarFormat(100)#<br>
1000: #DollarFormat(1000)#<br>
10000: #DollarFormat(10000)#<br>
100000: #DollarFormat(100000)#<br>
1000000: #DollarFormat(1000000)#<br>
</cfoutput>
```

Locale-specific currency formatting

In addition to U.S. dollar formatting using the `DollarFormat()` function, ColdFusion provides another function for formatting currency values specific to a particular locale. The `LSCurrencyFormat()` function behaves the same as the `DollarFormat()` function, but it takes into account the currency conventions used by the default locale. The function takes two parameters, a numeric value and an optional locale-specific convention. Table 4-6 lists the valid values for the convention.

Table 4-6. Locale-specific conventions for LSCurrencyFormat()

Value	Description
`None`	Returns the amount
`Local`	Returns the currency amount with locale-specific currency formatting; the default
`International`	Returns the currency value with its corresponding three-letter international currency prefix

The following example loops through each locale supported by ColdFusion and applies each type of currency mask to a currency value for each locale:

```
<h3>Formatting Locale Specific Currency Values using LSCurrencyFormat</h3>

<!--- Loop over each locale.  The list of locales is obtained from the server
      variable Server.ColdFusion.SupportedLocales --->
```

```
<cfloop index="locale" list="#Server.Coldfusion.SupportedLocales#">
<!--- This causes the CF server to assume the locale specified by the current
      iteration of the loop --->
<cfset SetLocale(locale)>

<cfoutput>
<p>
<b>#locale#</b><br>
None: #LSCurrencyFormat(1000000.99, "None")#<br>
Local: #LSCurrencyFormat(1000000.99, "Local")#<br>
International: #LSCurrencyFormat(1000000.99, "International")#<br>
</cfoutput>
</cfloop>
```

Locale-specific currency formatting with the euro

The final currency formatting function, `LSEuroCurrencyFormat( )`, is the same as the `LSCurrencyFormat( )` function except it returns the formatted currency with the euro symbol for locales using the euro. The following example displays euro currency formats for each locale:

```
<h3>Formatting Locale Specific Currency Values with the Euro using
    LSCurrencyFormat</h3>

<!--- Loop over each locale. The list of locales is obtained from the server
      variable Server.ColdFusion.SupportedLocales --->
<cfloop index="locale" list="#Server.Coldfusion.SupportedLocales#">
<!--- This causes the CF server to assume the locale specified by the current
      iteration of the loop --->
<cfset SetLocale(locale)>

<cfoutput>
<p>
<b>#locale#</b><br>
None: #LSEuroCurrencyFormat(1000000.99, "None")#<br>
Local: #LSEuroCurrencyFormat(1000000.99, "Local")#<br>
International: #LSEuroCurrencyFormat(1000000.99, "International")#<br>
</cfoutput>
</cfloop>
```

Formatting Boolean Values

ColdFusion uses the Boolean datatype to store the value generated by a logical operation. Boolean values are stored as either `true` or `false`. In numeric operations, Boolean values evaluate to `1` for `true` and `0` for `false`. When dealing with strings, Boolean values are set to `Yes` for `true` and `No` for `false`. Because most users are used to seeing the results of a Boolean operation as either `Yes` or `No`, ColdFusion has a function called `YesNoFormat( )` you can use to automatically convert any Boolean value to its equivalent `Yes/No` format (all nonzero values are returned as `Yes`, while a zero value is returned as No). The following example demonstrates this by applying the YesNoFormat( ) function to a variety of Boolean values:

```
<h3>Formatting Boolean Values using YesNoFormat</h3>

<cfoutput>
-1: #YesNoFormat(-1)#<br>
-1.123: #YesNoFormat(-1.123)#<br>
-0.123: #YesNoFormat(-0.123)#<br>
0: #YesNoFormat(0)#<br>
0.123: #YesNoFormat(0.123)#<br>
1: #YesNoFormat(1)#<br>
1.123: #YesNoFormat(1.123)#
</cfoutput>
```

Formatting Dates and Times

Depending on the database you use, date and time values returned as part of a query result set can come in a variety of formats. ColdFusion affords a lot of flexibility in formatting date and time values before you output them to the browser.

General date formatting

General date formatting is handled by the DateFormat( ) function. DateFormat( ) allows you to format dates using a variety of masks. The function accepts two parameters, the date you wish to format and a mask to specify the formatting in the format DateFormat(*date*, "*mask*"). If no mask is supplied, DateFormat( ) defaults to *dd-mmm-yy*. Valid entries for the date mask are shown in Table 4-7.

Table 4-7. Mask values for DateFormat()

Mask	Description
d	Day of the month as a number with no leading zero for single-digit days
dd	Day of the month as a number with a leading zero for single-digit days
ddd	Three-letter abbreviation for day of the week
dddd	Full name of the day of the week
gg	Period/era; this mask is currently ignored
m	Month as a number with no leading zero for single-digit months
mm	Month as a number with a leading zero for single-digit months
mmm	Three-letter abbreviation for the month
mmmm	Full name of the month
y	Last two digits of year with no leading zero for years less than 10
yy	Last two digits of year with a leading zero for years less than 10
yyyy	Four-digit year
gg	Period/era
short	Java Short date format

Table 4-7. Mask values for DateFormat() (continued)

Mask	Description
medium	Java Medium date format
long	Java Long date format
full	Java Full date format

You should note that DateFormat( ) supports U.S. date formats only. To use locale-specific date formats, see the LSDateFormat( ) function in the next section. For more information on how ColdFusion handles dates, see Chapter 2.

The following example demonstrates the DateFormat( ) function utilizing a variety of different date masks:

```
<cfset TheDate = Now( )>

<cfoutput>
TheDate = #DateFormat(TheDate, 'mm/dd/yyyy')#
<p>
m/d/yy: #DateFormat(TheDate, 'm/d/yy')#<br>
mm/dd/yy: #DateFormat(TheDate, 'mm/dd/yy')#<br>
mm/dd/yyyy: #DateFormat(TheDate, 'mm/dd/yyyy')#<br>
dd/mm/yyyy gg: #DateFormat(TheDate, 'dd/mm/yyyy gg')#<br>
dd mmm yy: #DateFormat(TheDate, 'dd mmm yy')#<br>
dddd mmmm dd, yyyy: #DateFormat(TheDate, 'dddd mmmm dd, yyyy')#<br>
<p>
And these formats are new in ColdFusion MX:<br>
short: #DateFormat(TheDate, 'short')#<br>
medium: #DateFormat(TheDate, 'medium')#<br>
long: #DateFormat(TheDate, 'long')#<br>
full: #DateFormat(TheDate, 'full')#<br>
</cfoutput>
```

Locale-specific date formatting

In addition to U.S. date formatting using the DateFormat( ) function, ColdFusion provides another function for formatting dates specific to a particular locale. The LSDateFormat( ) function behaves the same as the DateFormat( ) function, but it takes into account the formatting used by the default locale. If no formatting mask is supplied, LSDateFormat( ) uses the locale-specific default.

The following example loops through each locale supported by ColdFusion and applies a number of different date masks to the current date for each locale:

```
<h3>Formatting Locale Specific Date Values using LSDateFormat</h3>

<!--- Loop over each locale.  The list of locales is obtained from the server
      variable Server.ColdFusion.SupportedLocales --->
<cfloop index="locale" list="#Server.Coldfusion.SupportedLocales#">
<!--- This causes the CF server to assume the locale specified by the current
      iteration of the loop --->
<cfset SetLocale(locale)>
```

```
<!--- Output formatted dates using a variety of masks --->
<cfoutput>
<p>
<b>#locale#</b><br>
#LSDateFormat(Now( ))#<br>
#LSDateFormat(Now( ), "d/m/yy")#<br>
#LSDateFormat(Now( ), "d-mmm-yyyy")#<br>
#LSDateFormat(Now( ), "dd mmm yy")#<br>
#LSDateFormat(Now( ), "dddd, mmmm dd, yyyy")#<br>
#LSDateFormat(Now( ), "mm/dd/yyyy")#<br>
#LSDateFormat(Now( ), "mmmm d, yyyy")#<br>
#LSDateFormat(Now( ), "mmm-dd-yyyy")#<br>
</cfoutput>
</cfloop>
```

General time formatting

You can format times in ColdFusion using the `TimeFormat( )` function. `TimeFormat( )` is similar to the `DateFormat( )` function in that it allows you to use a mask to control the formatting. The function accepts two parameters, the time you wish to format and a mask to specify the formatting in the format `TimeFormat(`*`time`*`, "`*`mask`*`")`. If no mask is specified, the default `hh:mm tt` is used. Valid mask values are shown in Table 4-8.

Table 4-8. Mask values for TimeFormat()

Mask	Description
h	Hours based on a 12-hour clock with no leading zeros for single-digit hours
hh	Hours based on a 12-hour clock with leading zeros for single-digit hours
H	Hours based on a 24-hour clock with no leading zeros for single-digit hours
HH	Hours based on a 24-hour clock with leading zeros for single-digit hours
m	Minutes with no leading zero for single-digit minutes
mm	Minutes with a leading zero for single-digit minutes
s	Seconds with no leading zero for single-digit seconds
ss	Seconds with a leading zero for single-digit seconds
l	Milliseconds with no leading zeros for single or double-digit milliseconds
t	Single character meridian, either A or p
tt	Multicharacter meridian, either AM or PM
short	Java Short time format
medium	Java Medium time format
long	Java Long time format
full	Java Full time format

The following example demonstrates the `TimeFormat( )` function using a number of time masks:

```
<cfset TheTime = Now( )>

<cfoutput>
TheTime = #TimeFormat(TheTime,'hh:mm:ss tt')#<p>

TimeFormat(TheTime, 'h:m:s'): #TimeFormat(TheTime, 'h:m:s')#<br>
TimeFormat(TheTime, 'h:m:s t'): #TimeFormat(TheTime, 'h:m:s t')#<br>
TimeFormat(TheTime, 'hh:mm:ss'): #TimeFormat(TheTime, 'hh:mm:ss')#<br>
TimeFormat(TheTime, 'hh:mm:ss tt'): #TimeFormat(TheTime, 'hh:mm:ss tt')#<br>
TimeFormat(TheTime, 'H:M:ss'): #TimeFormat(TheTime, 'H:M:s')#<br>
TimeFormat(TheTime, 'HH:MM:ss'): #TimeFormat(TheTime, 'HH:MM:ss')#<br>
<p>
And these formats are new in ColdFusion MX:<br>
short: #TimeFormat(TheTime, 'short')#<br>
medium: #TimeFormat(TheTime, 'medium')#<br>
long: #TimeFormat(TheTime, 'long')#<br>
full: #TimeFormat(TheTime, 'full')#<br>
</cfoutput>
```

Locale-specific time formatting

In addition to U.S. time formatting using the `TimeFormat()` function, ColdFusion provides another function for formatting dates specific to a particular locale. The `LSTimeFormat()` function behaves the same as the `TimeFormat()` function, but it takes into account the formatting used by the default locale. If no formatting mask is supplied, `LSTimeFormat()` uses the locale-specific default. The following example loops through each locale supported by ColdFusion and applies a number of different time masks to the current time for each locale:

```
<cfset theTime = Now()>

<cfloop index="locale" list="#Server.Coldfusion.SupportedLocales#">
  <cfset SetLocale(locale)>
  <cfoutput>
    <p><b>#locale#</b><br>
    TheTime = #LSTimeFormat(TheTime)#<br>
    LSTimeFormat(TheTime, 'h:m:s'): #LSTimeFormat(TheTime, 'h:m:s')#<br>
    LSTimeFormat(TheTime, 'h:m:s t'): #LSTimeFormat(TheTime,
              'h:m:s t')#<br>
    LSTimeFormat(TheTime, 'hh:mm:ss'): #LSTimeFormat(TheTime,
              'hh:mm:ss')#<br>
    LSTimeFormat(TheTime, 'hh:mm:ss tt'):
      #LSTimeFormat(TheTime, 'hh:mm:ss tt')#<br>
    LSTimeFormat(TheTime, 'H:M:ss'): #LSTimeFormat(TheTime, 'H:M:s')#<br>
    LSTimeFormat(TheTime, 'HH:MM:ss'): #LSTimeFormat(TheTime,
              'HH:MM:ss')#<br>
    <p>
    And these formats are new in ColdFusion MX:<br>
    short: #LSTimeFormat(TheTime, 'short')#<br>
    medium: #LSTimeFormat(TheTime, 'medium')#<br>
    long: #LSTimeFormat(TheTime, 'long')#<br>
    full: #LSTimeFormat(TheTime, 'full')#<br>
  </cfoutput>
</cfloop>
```

CHAPTER 5
Maintaining Database Records

Now that we've covered the basics of retrieving records from a database, let's focus our attention on techniques you can use to add new records, update existing records, and delete unwanted records from a database. These techniques come into play when your web application needs to go beyond simply displaying information from a database. For example, with our employee directory application, we can add the ability to insert new employees into the directory, update employee information, and delete employee records.

Inserting Records

Inserting a new record into a database table is a two-step process. The first step involves creating a template with an input form that collects the information you want to insert. The second step in the process takes the form-field data and inserts it into the database table. The code for this process can be broken up into two templates, but it is possible to use a single template (with conditional code, as described in Chapter 3) that posts to itself if you desire. With the introduction of ColdFusion Components (CFCs) in ColdFusion MX, several more advanced options exist for architecting this type of functionality. CFCs are covered in Chapter 22. For now, we'll focus on the first two techniques,

Inputting Data Via Forms

The most popular method for collecting data to insert into a database is via an HTML form. When creating your input form, you should name your form fields the same as their equivalent database fields (or stored procedure parameters if you are using stored procedures, which are covered in Chapter 11). This avoids any confusion when writing SQL statements or code that manipulates data.

Example 5-1 shows the *insertform.cfm* template, which creates an HTML form for inputting a new employee record in the `EmployeeDirectory` table of the `ProgrammingCF` database.

Example 5-1. HTML input form for inserting a record into a database

```
<html>
<head>
    <title>Data Input Form</title>
</head>

<body>

<h2>Add a New User</h2>
<form action="insert.cfm" method="post">
<!--- Data validation --->
<input type="hidden" name="Name_Required" value="Name is a required field">
<input type="hidden" name="Title_Required"
       value="Title is a required field">
<input type="hidden" name="Department_Required"
       value="Department is a required field">
<input type="hidden" name="Email_Required"
       value="E-mail is a required field">
<input type="hidden" name="PhoneExt_Required"
       value="Phone Ext. is a required field">
<input type="hidden" name="Salary_Required"
       value="Salary is a required field">
<input type="hidden" name="PhoneExt_Integer"
       value="Phone Ext. is a numeric field">
<input type="hidden" name="Salary_Float" value="Salary is a numeric field">

<table>
  <tr>
    <td>Name:</td>
    <td><input type="text" name="Name" size="20" maxlength="80"></td>
  </tr>
  <tr>
    <td>Title:</td>
    <td><input type="text" name="Title" size="20" maxlength="80"></td>
  </tr>
  <tr>
    <td>Department:</td>
    <td><input type="text" name="Department" size="20" maxlength="80"></td>
  </tr>
  <tr>
    <td>E-mail:</td>
    <td><input type="text" name="Email" size="20" maxlength="80"></td>
  </tr>
  <tr>
    <td>Phone Ext::</td>
    <td><input type="text" name="PhoneExt" size="5" maxlength="4"></td>
  </tr>
  <tr>
```

Example 5-1. HTML input form for inserting a record into a database (continued)

```
    <td>Salary:</td>
    <td><input type="text" name="Salary" size="20" maxlength="12"></td>
  </tr>
</table>
<input type="submit" value="submit">
</form>
</body>
</html>
```

The input form uses the HTTP POST method to post the form-field data to a template called *insert.cfm*. We're going to look at three different implementations of this template, in Examples 5-2, 5-3, and 5-4. The input form also uses several hidden fields to set up server-side validation rules for the form fields. The form itself is shown in Figure 5-1.

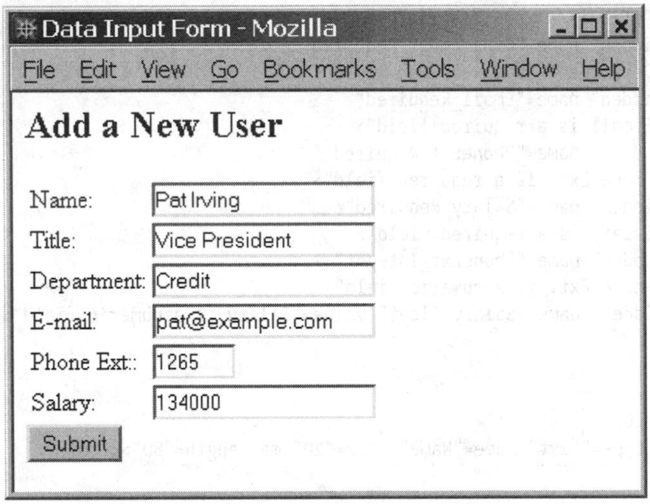

Figure 5-1. HTML form for inserting a new employee record

Inserting Form-Field Data

When you have form-field data to be inserted into a database, you have numerous options for how to do the actual insert. You can use the `cfquery` tag and write your own SQL `INSERT` statement, you can use the `cfinsert` tag to handle the insert without writing a single line of SQL, or you can use a stored procedure. We'll cover the first two methods here. Stored procedures are discussed in Chapter 11.

Inserting a record using cfquery

The `cfquery` tag lets you insert a record into a table using an SQL `INSERT` statement. This method gives you the most flexibility and power in inserting records.

Example 5-2 demonstrates using the cfquery tag to insert a new record into the database. The template receives its input from the form shown in Example 5-1. In order for the example to work, the template in Example 5-2 must be saved as *insert.cfm* in the same directory as the template in Example 5-1.

Example 5-2. Using cfquery to insert data into a data source

```
<!--- Insert the record into the EmployeeDirectory table. --->
<cflock name="InsertNewRecord" type="exclusive" timeout="30">
<cftransaction>
<cfquery name="AddRecord" datasource="ProgrammingCF">
         INSERT INTO EmployeeDirectory(Name, Title, Department, Email,
                     PhoneExt, Salary)
         VALUES('#form.Name#', '#form.Title#', '#form.Department#',
               '#form.Email#', #form.PhoneExt#, #form.Salary#)
</cfquery>

<!--- This query retrieves the primary key value of the record we
      just inserted. --->
<cfquery name="GetPK" datasource="ProgrammingCF">
         SELECT Max(ID) AS MaxID
         FROM EmployeeDirectory
</cfquery>
</cftransaction>
</cflock>

<!--- This query uses the value returned by the GetPK query to lookup
      the full record we inserted. --->
<cfquery name="GetRecord" datasource="ProgrammingCF">
         SELECT ID, Name, Title, Department, Email, PhoneExt, Salary
         FROM EmployeeDirectory
         WHERE ID = #GetPK.MaxID#
</cfquery>

<html>
<head>
  <title>cfquery Insert</title>
  <style type="text/css">
    th {
      background-color : #888888;
    }
    td {
      background-color : #C0C0C0;
    }
  </style>
</head>

<body>

<h2>Record Inserted!</h2>

<h3>Here are the record details...</h3>
```

Example 5-2. Using cfquery to insert data into a data source (continued)

```
<table cellpadding="3" cellspacing="0">
  <tr>
    <th>ID</th>
    <th>Name</th>
    <th>Title</th>
    <th>Department</th>
    <th>E-mail</th>
    <th>Phone Extension</th>
    <th>Salary</th>
  </tr>

<!--- Output the record --->
<cfoutput query="GetRecord">
  <tr>
    <td>#ID#</td>
    <td>#Name#</td>
    <td>#Title#</td>
    <td>#Department#</td>
    <td><a href="Mailto:#Email#">#Email#</a></td>
    <td>#PhoneExt#</td>
    <td>#DollarFormat(Salary)#</td>
  </tr>
</cfoutput>
</table>

</body>
</html>
```

If you fill out the form in Example 5-1 and submit it to this template, a new record containing all the information from the form is inserted into the `EmployeeDirectory` table. The `INSERT` statement is used within the `cfquery` tag to insert a record into the database. The `INTO` clause controls what fields to insert data into by specifying them as a comma-delimited list. `VALUES` specifies the data to insert into each field specified by the `INTO` clause. Note that numeric values aren't enclosed in single quotes in the `VALUES` clause.

Notice that we are inserting the employee name, title, etc., but not the ID. That's because the ID is specified as an AutoNumber field in our Access database. If you are using a database that doesn't support AutoNumber fields, you can use the `CreateUUID( )` function here to generate a unique value on the fly. If you do this, be sure to include the ID field in the `INSERT INTO` clause and the UUID value in the `VALUES` clause.

After the record is inserted, another `cfquery` is run to extract the primary key value for the record we just inserted, so that we can look up the record we just inserted. This query uses a `SELECT` statement containing a special clause, known as an aggregate function, to obtain the maximum value in the `ID` column. (Aggregate functions are discussed in Chapter 11.) Because we use an AutoNumber field that automatically increments by one each time a new record is inserted into the database, the value returned by our query is the primary key value for the record we just inserted.

The `cflock` tag ensures that the code it wraps is accessible by only one request at a time. The `cftransaction` tag groups the queries into a single transaction. The combination of these two techniques prevents you from retrieving the primary key value of another user's record in the event they insert a new record right after you do and before you retrieve the `MAX ID` value. The `cflock` tag is covered in Chapter 7, while the `cftransaction` tag is covered in Chapter 11.

Once we know the primary key value for the record we inserted, we execute yet another `cfquery` tag to `SELECT` the record from the `EmployeeDirectory` table whose `ID` field contains the primary key value returned by our second query. The template finishes by outputting all the values stored in the record we just inserted in a neatly formatted HTML table. The results are seen in Figure 5-2.

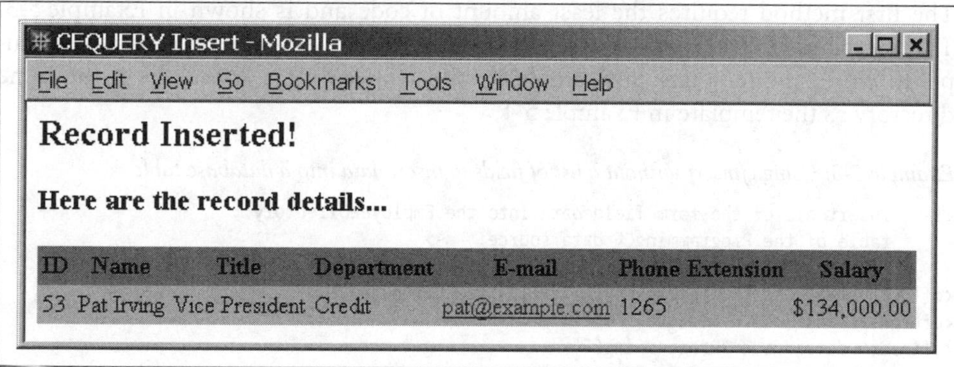

Figure 5-2. Inserting a record into a table using cfquery

Inserting a record using cfinsert

If you don't want to concern yourself with the SQL necessary to insert a record into a database, ColdFusion provides a tag called `cfinsert` that does most of the work for you. The tag takes most of the parameters the `cfquery` tag takes but doesn't require you to include any SQL inside the tag. The basic syntax for using the `cfinsert` tag is as follows:

```
<cfinsert datasource="datasource_name"
          tablename="table_name"
          formfields="formfield1, formfield2, ...">
```

The three attributes for the `cfinsert` tag are:

`datasource`
: The name of the data source to connect to when performing the insert. Required.

`tablename`
: The name of the table to insert the data into. Required. It should be noted that Oracle database drivers require the table name to be in all uppercase. In addition, Sybase database drivers use a case-sensitive table name.

`formfields`
: A comma-delimited list of form fields to insert. Optional. If no form fields are supplied, ColdFusion uses all the form fields passed from the form.

Several additional attributes are available for use with the `cfinsert` tag. For a complete list, see Appendix A.

There are two ways to use the `cfinsert` tag. You can use the tag to insert values for every form field passed to the template containing the tag, or you can supply a comma-delimited list of form fields (using the `formfields` attribute) you want to insert.

The first method requires the least amount of code and is shown in Example 5-3. This template receives its input from the form in Example 5-1. In order for the example to work, the template in Example 5-3 must be saved as *insert.cfm* in the same directory as the template in Example 5-1.

Example 5-3. Using cfinsert without a list of fields to insert data into a database table

```
<!--- Insert all of the form field data into the EmployeeDirectory
      table of the ProgrammingCF data source. --->

<cflock name="InsertNewRecord" type="exclusive" timeout="30">
<cftransaction>
<cfinsert datasource="ProgrammingCF"
          tablename="EmployeeDirectory">

<!--- This query retrieves the primary key value of the record we
      just inserted. --->
<cfquery name="GetPK" datasource="ProgrammingCF">
      SELECT Max(ID) AS MaxID
      FROM EmployeeDirectory
</cfquery>
</cftransaction>
</cflock>

<!--- This query uses the value returned by the GetPK query to lookup
      the full record we inserted. --->
<cfquery name="GetRecord" datasource="ProgrammingCF">
         SELECT ID, Name, Title, Department, Email, PhoneExt, Salary
         FROM EmployeeDirectory
         WHERE ID = #GetPK.MaxID#
</cfquery>

<html>
<head>
  <title>cfinsert Insert</title>
```

Example 5-3. Using cfinsert without a list of fields to insert data into a database table (continued)

```
  <style type="text/css">
    th {
      background-color : #888888;
    }
    td {
      background-color : #C0C0C0;
    }
  </style>
</head>

<body>

<h2>Record Inserted using cfinsert without Field Names!</h2>

<h3>Here are the record details...</h3>

<table cellpadding="3" cellspacing="0">
  <tr>
    <th>ID</th>
    <th>Name</th>
    <th>Title</th>
    <th>Department</th>
    <th>E-mail</th>
    <th>Phone Extension</th>
    <th>Salary</th>
  </tr>

<!--- Output the record --->
<cfoutput query="GetRecord">
  <tr>
    <td>#ID#</td>
    <td>#Name#</td>
    <td>#Title#</td>
    <td>#Department#</td>
    <td><a href="Mailto:#Email#">#Email#</a></td>
    <td>#PhoneExt#</td>
    <td>#DollarFormat(Salary)#</td>
  </tr>
</cfoutput>
</table>

</body>
</html>
```

When the form in Example 5-1 posts to this template, the `cfinsert` tag attempts to take every form field passed in and inserts it into the `EmployeeDirectory` table. This method works well when you have a corresponding database field for each form field. If, however, there are form fields that don't have corresponding database fields, ColdFusion throws an error. Once the record has been inserted, the template uses the same code from Example 5-3 to retrieve the record we just inserted and display it in the browser. As with our first implementation of *insert.cfm*, the value for the employee ID is inserted automatically by Access. This version also uses `cflock` and `cftransaction` to protect against collisions between multiple requests. If you look at the output from this template, you should notice that it looks identical to that shown in Example 5-2 (minus the title, of course).

The second method for inserting a new record using the `cfinsert` tag requires one more line of code but allows you to specify which form fields should be inserted into the database. This lets you make sure that only the form fields you want inserted into the table are inserted. The code for this template is shown in Example 5-4. As in the previous examples, this template receives its input from the form in Example 5-1. In order for the example to work, the template in Example 5-4 must be saved as *insert.cfm* in the same directory as the template in Example 5-1.

Example 5-4. Inserting a record using the cfinsert tag with field names specified

```
<!--- Insert the data from the specified form fields into the
      EmployeeDirectory table of the ProgrammingCF data source. --->

<cflock name="InsertNewRecord" type="exclusive" timeout="30">
<cftransaction>
<cfinsert datasource="ProgrammingCF"
          tablename="EmployeeDirectory"
          formfields="Name,Title,Email">

<!--- This query retrieves the primary key value of the record we
      just inserted. --->
<cfquery name="GetPK" datasource="ProgrammingCF">
         SELECT Max(ID) AS MaxID
         FROM EmployeeDirectory
</cfquery>
</cftransaction>
</cflock>

<!--- This query uses the value returned by the GetPK query to lookup
      the full record we inserted. --->
<cfquery name="GetRecord" datasource="ProgrammingCF">
         SELECT ID, Name, Title, Department, Email, PhoneExt, Salary
         FROM EmployeeDirectory
         WHERE ID = #GetPK.MaxID#
</cfquery>

<html>
<head>
  <title>cfinsert Insert</title>
  <style type="text/css">
    th {
      background-color : #888888;
    }
    td {
      background-color : #C0C0C0;
    }
  </style>
```

Example 5-4. Inserting a record using the cfinsert tag with field names specified (continued)

```
</head>

<body>

<h2>Record Inserted using cfinsert with Specific Field Names!</h2>

<h3>Here are the record details...</h3>

<table cellpadding="3" cellspacing="0">
  <tr>
    <th>ID</th>
    <th>Name</th>
    <th>Title</th>
    <th>Department</th>
    <th>E-mail</th>
    <th>Phone Extension</th>
    <th>Salary</th>
  </tr>

<!--- Output the record --->
<cfoutput query="GetRecord">
  <tr>
    <td>#ID#</td>
    <td>#Name#</td>
    <td>#Title#</td>
    <td>#Department#</td>
    <td><a href="Mailto:#Email#">#Email#</a></td>
    <td>#PhoneExt#</td>
    <td>#DollarFormat(Salary)#</td>
  </tr>
</cfoutput>
</table>

</body>
</html>
```

Using the form in Example 5-1 to post to this template, the `cfinsert` tag inserts only the `Name`, `Title`, and `Email` form fields into the `EmployeeDirectory` table. Once the record has been inserted, the template uses the same code from Example 5-3 to retrieve the record we just inserted and display it in the browser. The results are shown in Figure 5-3. Notice that the `Department` and `PhoneExt` fields contain no values, and the `Salary` field contains a zero.

Updating Existing Records

Updating a database record is a three-step process that involves a bit more work that just inserting a new record. The first step in the process is to identify the record to be updated; there are two ways to handle this task. Next, an HTML form containing the editable fields needs to be created. This form must be prepopulated with the data

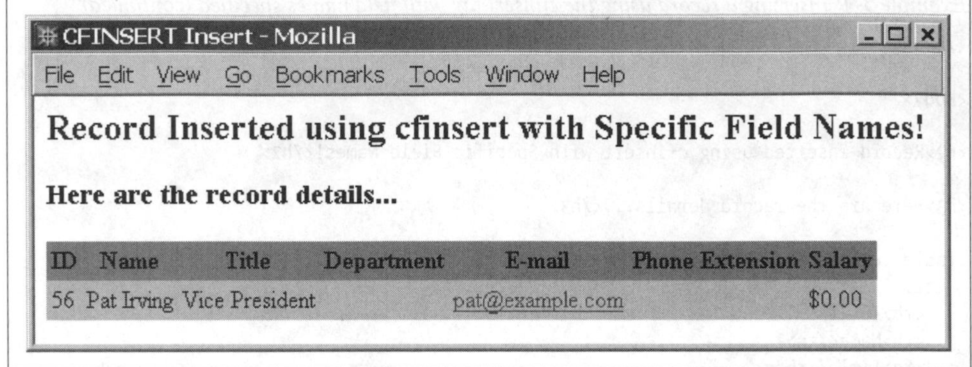

Figure 5-3. Inserting specific fields using cfinsert

from the record to be edited. Finally, you need another template to take the updated form-field data and update the appropriate record in the database.

Choosing a Record to Update

Before you can make an update to a record, you need some sort of interface that allows you to choose the record you wish to modify. There are two general approaches to this interface. The first approach involves a URL-based technique for selecting the record to modify. The second approach utilizes a forms-based technique to achieve the same goal. Both approaches begin by querying a data source (in our case, the `EmployeeDirectory` table of the `ProgrammingCF` data source) to retrieve a list of all the records from the database. Usually, you need to retrieve only the primary key value and a distinguishing field or two. A primary key is necessary to ensure that you update only the record you intend to update. In many cases, the primary key is a single field that contains a unique value such as an auto-increment number or a UUID (Universally Unique Identifier—see `CreateUUID( )` in Appendix B for more information). In some cases, the primary key may be made up of a concatenation of more than one field. In our example, we retrieve the `ID` field (primary key) and the `Name` field from the `EmployeeDirectory` table. It is from this point forward that the two approaches differ.

The first approach uses the information returned by the query to generate an HTML table listing each employee from the database. The code for this template, *updatemenu_hyperlink.cfm*, is shown in Example 5-5.

Example 5-5. URL-based menu for selecting a record to update

```
<!--- Query the database for all employee names and their associated
    IDs (the primary key value) --->
<cfquery name="GetEmployees" datasource="ProgrammingCF">
      SELECT ID, Name
      FROM EmployeeDirectory
      ORDER BY Name
```

Example 5-5. URL-based menu for selecting a record to update (continued)

```
</cfquery>

<html>
<head>
  <title>Employee Update Menu</title>
  <style type="text/css">
    th {
      background-color : #C0C0C0;
    }
    td {
      background-color : #E7E7E7;
    }
  </style>
</head>
<body>
<div align="Center">
<h3>Employee Profiles</h3>
<table border="1">
  <tr>
    <th>Employee</th>
    <th>Action</th>
  </tr>
<!--- Output a table containing each employee's name.  Create dynamic
      links to edit and delete templates.  Pass the ID
      associated with each record in the URL of the link --->
<cfoutput query="GetEmployees">
  <tr>
    <td>#Name#</td>
    <td><a href="updateform.cfm?ID=#ID#">Update</a> |
      <a href="updateform.cfm?ID=#ID#&Action=Delete">Delete</a></td>
  </tr>
</cfoutput>
  <tr>
    <td COLSPAN="2" align="Center"><a href="insertform.cfm">Add</a> a
      new record</td>
  </tr>
</table>
</div>
</body>
</html>
```

Executing this template generates an HTML table that contains each employee's name in the left column, as shown in Figure 5-4. The right column contains two hyperlinks, one labeled Update and the other labeled Delete. Each of the Update hyperlinks contains a link to a template called *updateform.cfm*. Appended to each URL is a URL parameter called `ID` that contains the `ID` associated with the employee as returned by the `GetEmployees` query. Clicking on any of the "Update" links calls the *updateform.cfm* template, shown later in Example 5-7, and passes the `ID` associated with the employee so that the record can be retrieved for editing. If a "Delete" link is clicked on, the same *updateform.cfm* template is called, but this time, a URL parameter called Action with a value of Delete is passed so that the *updateform.cfm* template knows that the user want to delete a record and what record to delete. At the bottom of the template is a hyperlink that points to the *insertform.cfm* template from Example 5-1. Clicking on this link takes the user to the template for inserting a new record into the database.

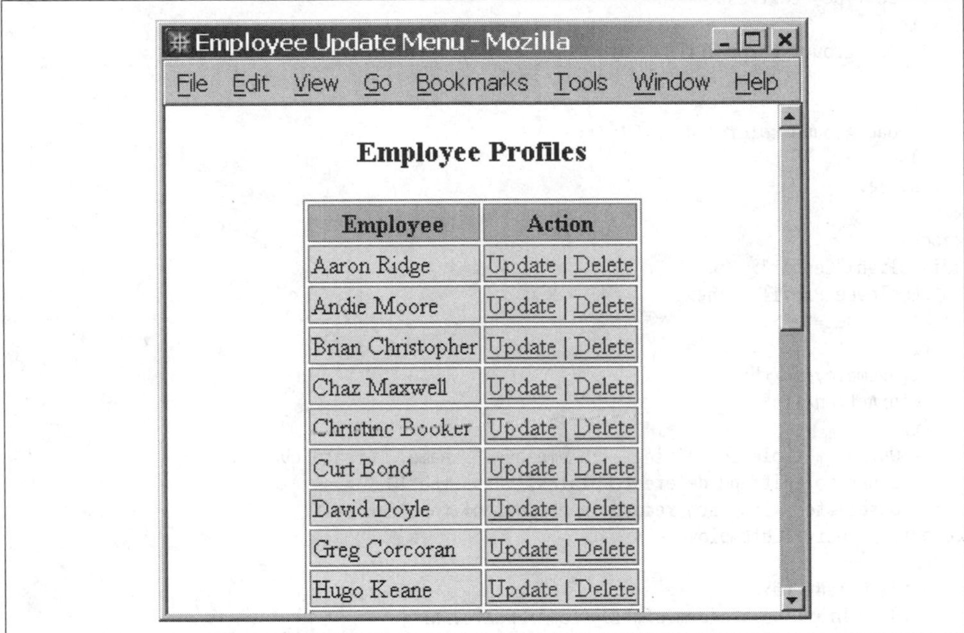

Figure 5-4. Hyperlink-based menu for selecting a record to update/delete

One drawback to the URL method becomes evident when the user needs to make a selection from a large number of records. It becomes highly inefficient to display hundreds or thousands of employees in an HTML table and realistically expect the user to scroll through all of them.

In this scenario, it is more efficient to use the second approach, which involves building a select list to display the names of all the employees. While the user still has to scroll through the list of names, the scrolling is confined to the select list, keeping the main body of the page in view at all times. Building the select list as opposed to an entire HTML table is also a lot easier on the client's machine, as it takes far less code and thus less system memory.* Using a select list also changes the way the ID field associated with the user's record is passed to the next template. Instead of passing

* You should note that there are limitations on how much information you can put into a select box. Although there is no hard limit, I'd recommend against putting more than a few thousand items (if that) into a single select box. If you have that many records, it probably makes more sense to change your interface to allow for the selection of records in smaller batches.

the ID value in a URL, the value is submitted as a form-field value. The code for the select box method, *updatemenu_form.cfm*, is shown in Example 5-6.

Example 5-6. Form-based menu for selecting a record to update/delete

```
<!--- Query the database for all employee names and their associated Ids
      (the primary key value --->
<cfquery name="GetEmployees" datasource="ProgrammingCF">
         SELECT ID, Name
         FROM EmployeeDirectory
         ORDER BY Name
</cfquery>

<html>
<head>
  <title>Employee Update Menu</title>
</head>

<body>

<div align="Center">
<h3>Employee Profiles</h3>

<table border="3" cellpadding="5" cellspacing="0" bgcolor="#cOcOcO">
  <form action="updateform.cfm" method="post">
  <tr>
    <td rowspan="3">
     <!--- Generate a dynamic select list based on the GetEmployees
           query --->
     <select name="ID" size="5">
      <cfoutput query="GetEmployees">
        <option value="#ID#" <cfif GetEmployees.CurrentRow eq 1>selected
        </cfif>>#Name#</option>
      </cfoutput>
    </select>
    </td>
    <td><input type="submit" name="Update" value="Update Record"></td>
  </tr>
  <tr>
    <td><input type="submit" name="Delete" value="Delete Record "></td>
  </tr>
  </form>
  <tr>
  <form action="insertform.cfm" method="post">
    <td><input type="submit" Name="Insert" value="  Add Record  "></td>
  </form>
  </tr>
</table>
</div>

</body>
</html>
```

This template illustrates a new technique we haven't covered yet: how to generate a select box containing data pulled from a query. The technique works by querying a data source and retrieving a record set. In this case, we queried the `EmployeeDirectory` table of the `ProgrammingCF` data source and returned a record set containing employee names (`name`) and their associated employee IDs (`ID`). The dynamic select box is generated within the form by using a `cfoutput` statement to loop over the contents of the `GetEmployees` query, building the `option` list for the `SELECT` statement from the record set. Each `option value` is populated with the value of an `ID` from the record set while the actual value displayed in the select box is derived from the corresponding `name`. The result is a menu of employee names the user can use to select an employee record to update, as shown in Figure 5-5.

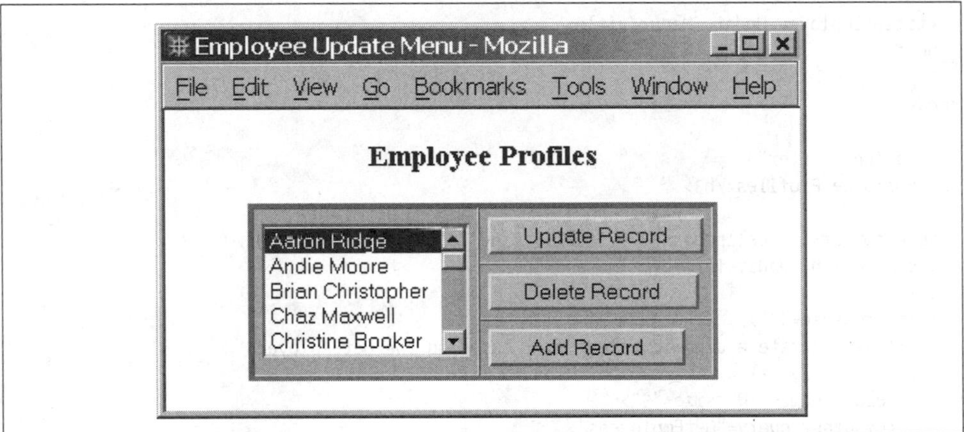

Figure 5-5. Dynamically generated select box for choosing an employee record to update

Note the `cfif` statement that builds the `option` tags for the `SELECT` statement. It makes sure the first option is always selected. This prevents a user from clicking the Update Record or Delete Record buttons without first choosing a record to update or delete. This piece of code eliminates the need for a hidden form field to make a selection from the menu required.

Highlighting an employee name and clicking on the Update Record or Delete Record button posts the `ID` value to a template called *updateform.cfm* (Example 5-7). Clicking on the Add Record button calls the *insertform.cfm* template from Example 5-1.

Dynamically Populating Update Forms

Once the user has selected a record to update, the next step for our application is to query the database and retrieve all the fields associated with the chosen record. This data is then used to populate the appropriate fields in an HTML form. As is often the case, our update form is identical to the form that inserts a new record. Our update template can also delete a record if the appropriate parameters are passed to the template by the record selection menu. Example 5-7 shows the *updateform.cfm* template for populating the update form with the record information retrieved from the database.

Example 5-7. Dynamically populating the update form

```
<!--- Check to see if we're dealing with a delete operation --->
<cfif (IsDefined('form.Delete') and Trim(form.Delete) eq "Delete Record")
   or (IsDefined('URL.Action') and URL.Action eq "Delete")>
  <cfquery name="DeleteRecord" datasource="ProgrammingCF">
          DELETE FROM EmployeeDirectory
          WHERE ID = #ID#
  </cfquery>
  <h2>Record Deleted Successfully</h2>

<cfelse>

<!--- Retrieve the record specified by the ID value passed into the
      template by form or url variable --->
<cfquery name="GetRecord" datasource="ProgrammingCF">
         SELECT ID, Name, Title, Department, Email, PhoneExt, Salary
         FROM EmployeeDirectory
         WHERE ID = #ID#
</cfquery>

<html>
<head>
    <title>Record Update Form</title>
</head>

<body>

<h2>Edit an Existing User</h2>
<form action="update.cfm" method="post">
<!--- Include the primary key value for this record so we know which
      record to update without SQL UPDATE (or cfupdate) statement in
      the next template --->
<cfoutput>
<input type="hidden" name="ID" value="#GetRecord.ID#">
</cfoutput>

<!--- Data validation --->
<input type="Hidden" name="Name_Required"
       value="Name is a required field">
<input type="Hidden" name="Title_Required"
       value="Title is a required field">
<input type="Hidden" name="Department_Required"
       value="Department is a required field">
<input type="Hidden" name="Email_Required"
       value="E-mail is a required field">
<input type="Hidden" name="PhoneExt_Required"
       value="Phone Ext. is a required field">
<input type="Hidden" name="Salary_Required"
       value="Salary is a required field">
```

Example 5-7. Dynamically populating the update form (continued)

```
<input type="Hidden" name="PhoneExt_Integer"
       value="Phone Ext. is a numeric field">
<input type="Hidden" name="Salary_Float"
       value="Salary is a numeric field">

<!--- Populate the form with the user's record --->
<cfoutput>
<table>
  <tr>
    <td>Name:</td>
    <td><input type="text" name="Name" value="#GetRecord.Name#"
               size="20" maxlength="80"></td>
  </tr>
  <tr>
    <td>Title:</td>
    <td><input type="text" name="Title" value="#GetRecord.Title#"
               size="20" maxlength="80"></td>
  </tr>
  <tr>
    <td>Department:</td>
    <td><input type="text" name="Department" value="#GetRecord.Department#"
               size="20" maxlength="80"></td>
  </tr>
  <tr>
    <td>E-mail:</td>
    <td><input type="text" name="Email"
               value="#GetRecord.Email#" size="20" maxlength="80"></td>
  </tr>
  <tr>
    <td>Phone Ext:</td>
    <td><input type="text" name="PhoneExt" value="#GetRecord.PhoneExt#"
               size="5" maxlength="4"></td>
  </tr>
  <tr>
    <td>Salary:</td>
    <td><input type="text" name="Salary" value="#GetRecord.Salary#"
               size="20" maxlength="12"></td>
  </tr>
</table>
</cfoutput>

<input type="submit" value="submit">
</form>

</body>
</html>
</cfif>
```

As you can see, this template isn't all that different from the template we used to insert new employee profiles into our database. There are, however, a few important distinctions.

First, the template checks to see if a URL or form variable was passed to the template indicating a record should be deleted. If so, the appropriate record is deleted using an SQL DELETE statement. This code is included to show you how to create a template for adding, updating, and deleting records from a single administrative interface. We'll cover deleting records later in this chapter. For now, let's concentrate on updating an existing record.

Once we determine that we aren't dealing with a delete operation, we can proceed with the update operation. Because we are going to update a specific record, we need a way to tell ColdFusion exactly what record to update. This is done by specifying the primary key value for the record in a hidden form field. The hidden form field that passes the value must have the same name as the primary key field in the database. If the primary key field isn't specified, ColdFusion throws an error. In this case, we specify the value using the ID form field. Another difference is that in the case of our update form, we populate each HTML form field with data from the employee's record so that it can be modified. In this example, all the fields in our form are text boxes. All you need to do to populate a text box with a value from a query is include a value attribute containing the variable name from the query in the input tag:

```
<input type="text" name="Name" value="#GetRecord.Name#>
```

It is important to note a couple of things here. First, populating form fields requires they be enclosed in a cfoutput block. Second, because you aren't using the query attribute of the cfoutput tag, you must scope your variables with the name of the query that retrieves the record. In this example, all query variables are scoped with GetRecord:

```
<cfoutput>
#GetRecord.Name#
</cfoutput>
```

Figure 5-6 shows the form populated with an employee record from the database.

Performing the Database Update

When the user submits the form for the record that is being updated in the database, you have two options for doing the actual update. You can use the cfquery tag and write your own SQL UPDATE statement, or you can use the cfupdate tag to handle the update without writing a single line of SQL. We'll use our update template (Example 5-7) to post the employee record to a template called *update.cfm*. We're going to look at three different implementations of this template, in Examples 5-8, 5-9, and 5-10.

Updating a record using cfquery

The cfquery tag offers the most power and flexibility when it comes to updating a database record. The cfquery tag allows you to write your own SQL UPDATE statement, giving you full control over how the update takes place. Example 5-8 demonstrates

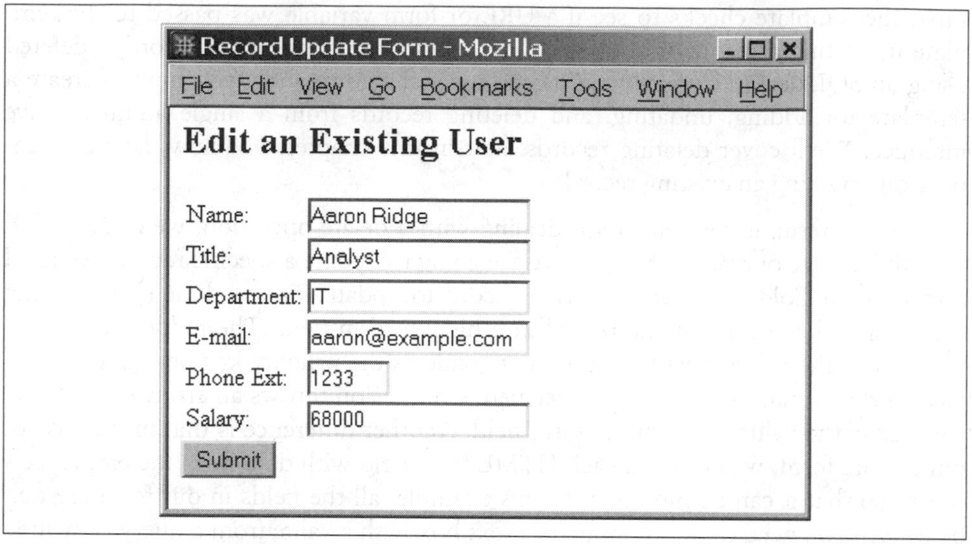

Figure 5-6. The populated employee update form

using the cfquery tag to update an existing record with form-field data passed in by the template in Example 5-7. In order for the example to work, the template in Example 5-8 must be saved as *update.cfm* in the same directory as the template in Example 5-7.

Example 5-8. Using cfquery to update a database record

```
<!--- Update the record specified by the ID field.  Note that numeric
      values are not enclosed in single quotes in the SET clause. --->
<cfquery name="UpdateRecord" datasource="ProgrammingCF">
  UPDATE EmployeeDirectory
  SET Name = '#form.Name#',
      Title = '#form.Title#',
      Department = '#form.Department#',
      Email = '#form.Email#',
      PhoneExt = #form.PhoneExt#,
      Salary = #form.Salary#
  WHERE ID = #form.ID#
</cfquery>

<!--- Retrieve the record we just updated --->
<cfquery name="GetRecord" datasource="ProgrammingCF">
  SELECT ID, Name, Title, Department, Email, PhoneExt, Salary
  FROM EmployeeDirectory
  WHERE ID = #form.ID#
</cfquery>

<html>
<head>
  <title>cfquery Update</title>
  <style type="text/css">
```

Example 5-8. Using cfquery to update a database record (continued)

```
    th {
      background-color : #888888;
    }
    td {
      background-color : #C0C0C0;
    }
  </style>
</head>

<body>

<h2>Record updated using cfquery!</h2>

<h3>Here are the record details...</h3>

<table cellpadding="3" cellspacing="0">
  <tr>
    <th>ID</th>
    <th>Name</th>
    <th>Title</th>
    <th>Department</th>
    <th>E-mail</th>
    <th>Phone Extension</th>
    <th>Salary</th>
  </tr>

<!--- Output the record --->
<cfoutput query="GetRecord">
  <tr>
    <td>#ID#</td>
    <td>#Name#</td>
    <td>#Title#</td>
    <td>#Department#</td>
    <td><a href="Mailto:#Email#">#Email#</a></td>
    <td>#PhoneExt#</td>
    <td>#Salary#</td>
  </tr>
</cfoutput>
</table>

</body>
</html>
```

Submitting the form from Example 5-7 posts to the template in Example 5-8 and updates the record in the database using the SQL `UPDATE` statement. Each field to be updated is specified as part of the `SET` clause. Multiple fields are separated by a comma. Note that numeric fields don't need to be surrounded by single quotes. The `WHERE` clause specifies the `ID` of the record we want to update.

After the record is updated, another `cfquery` is run to retrieve the record we just updated. Because we already have the `ID` value for the record, it only takes a single query to retrieve the record. The template finishes by outputting all the values stored in the record we just updated in a neatly formatted HTML table. The results are can be seen in Figure 5-7.

Figure 5-7. Updating an existing record using cfquery

Updating a record using cfupdate

The `cfupdate` tag lets you update a record in a table without having to write an SQL `UPDATE` statement. The tag looks and functions almost identically to the `cfinsert` tag and uses the following basic syntax:

```
<cfupdate datasource="datasource_name"
          tablename="table_name"
          formfields="field_names">
```

The attributes for the `cfupdate` tag are:

`datasource`
: The name of the data source to connect to when performing the update. Required.

`tablename`
: The name of the table to perform the update on. Required. It should be noted that Oracle database drivers require the table name to be in all uppercase. In addition, Sybase database drivers use a case-sensitive table name.

`formfields`
: A comma-delimited list of form fields to update. Optional. If no form fields are supplied, ColdFusion attempts to update the database using all the form fields passed from the form. If the form field names do not match the database field names, ColdFusion throws an exception.

Several additional attributes are available for use with the `cfupdate` tag. For a complete list, see Appendix A.

Just as with the `cfinsert` tag, there are two ways to use the `cfupdate` tag to update a record. You can use the tag to update values for every form field passed to the template containing the tag, or you can supply a comma-delimited list of form fields you want to update. Regardless of the method you use, it is important to make sure the primary key value for the record is passed to the `cfupdate` statement as a hidden form field. The hidden form field that passes the value must have the same name as the primary key field in the database. If the primary key field isn't specified, ColdFusion throws an error.

The first method requires only a few lines of code and is shown in Example 5-9. This template receives its input from the form in Example 5-7. In order for the example to work, the template in Example 5-9 must be saved as *update.cfm* in the same directory as the template in Example 5-7.

Example 5-9. Updating a record with cfupdate

```
<!--- Update all of the form fields passed in the EmployeeDirectory
      table of the ProgrammingCF data source. --->
<cfupdate datasource="ProgrammingCF"
          tablename="EmployeeDirectory">

<!--- This query uses the form.ID value to lookup the full record
      we just updated. --->
<cfquery name="GetRecord" datasource="ProgrammingCF">
         SELECT ID, Name, Title, Department, Email, PhoneExt, Salary
         FROM EmployeeDirectory
         WHERE ID = #form.ID#
</cfquery>

<html>
<head>
  <title>cfupdate Update</title>
  <style type="text/css">
    th {
      background-color : #888888;
    }
    td {
      background-color : #C0C0C0;
    }
  </style>
</head>

<body>

<h2>Record updated using cfupdate without Field Names!</h2>

<h3>Here are the record details...</h3>

<table cellpadding="3" cellspacing="0">
  <tr>
    <th>ID</th>
    <th>Name</th>
```

Example 5-9. Updating a record with cfupdate (continued)

```
    <th>Title</th>
    <th>Department</th>
    <th>E-mail</th>
    <th>Phone Extension</th>
    <th>Salary</th>
  </tr>

<!--- Output the record --->
<cfoutput query="GetRecord">
  <tr>
    <td>#ID#</td>
    <td>#Name#</td>
    <td>#Title#</td>
    <td>#Department#</td>
    <td><a href="Mailto:#Email#">#Email#</a></td>
    <td>#PhoneExt#</td>
    <td>#Salary#</td>
  </tr>
</cfoutput>
</table>

</body>
</html>
```

When the form in Example 5-7 posts to this template, the `cfupdate` tag attempts to take every form field passed and updates the equivalent field in the `EmployeeDirectory` table. This method works only when you have a corresponding database field for each form field. If, however, there are form fields that don't have corresponding database fields, ColdFusion throws an error. Once the record has been updated, the template uses the same code from Example 5-8 to retrieve the record we just inserted and display it in the browser. If you look at the output from this template, you should notice that it looks identical to that shown in Example 5-8 (minus the title, of course).

The second method for using the `cfupdate` tag involves passing one additional attribute that allows you to specify which form fields should be updated in the database. This ensures that only the form fields you want are updated. The code for this template is shown in Example 5-10. As in the previous examples, this template receives its input from the form in Example 5-7. In order for the example to work, the template in Example 5-10 must be saved as *update.cfm* in the same directory as the template in Example 5-7.

Example 5-10. Updating specific form fields using cfupdate

```
<!--- Update the specified form fields in the EmployeeDirectory
      table of the ProgrammingCF data source. --->
<cfupdate datasource="ProgrammingCF"
          tablename="EmployeeDirectory"
          formfields="Name,Title,Email">
```

Example 5-10. Updating specific form fields using cfupdate (continued)

```
<!--- This query uses the form.ID value to lookup the full record
      we just updated. --->
<cfquery name="GetRecord" datasource="ProgrammingCF">
         SELECT ID, Name, Title, Department, Email, PhoneExt, Salary
         FROM EmployeeDirectory
         WHERE ID = #form.ID#
</cfquery>

<html>
<head>
    <title>cfupdate Update</title>
  <style type="text/css">
    th {
      background-color : #888888;
    }
    td {
      background-color : #C0C0C0;
    }
  </style>
</head>

<body>

<h2>Record updated using cfupdate with Specific Field Names!</h2>

<h3>Here are the record details...</h3>

<table cellpadding="3" cellspacing="0">
  <tr>
    <th>ID</th>
    <th>Name</th>
    <th>Title</th>
    <th>Department</th>
    <th>E-mail</th>
    <th>Phone Extension</th>
    <th>Salary</th>
  </tr>

<!--- Output the record --->
<cfoutput query="GetRecord">
  <tr>
    <td>#ID#</td>
    <td>#Name#</td>
    <td>#Title#</td>
    <td>#Department#</td>
    <td><a href="Mailto:#Email#">#Email#</a></td>
    <td>#PhoneExt#</td>
    <td>#Salary#</td>
  </tr>
</cfoutput>
</table>
```

Example 5-10. Updating specific form fields using cfupdate (continued)

```
</body>
</html>
```

Using the form in Example 5-7 to post to this template, the `cfupdate` tag updates only the `Name`, `Title`, and `Email` fields in the `EmployeeDirectory` table with the data from `form.Name`, `form.Title`, and `form.Email`. Once the record has been updated, the template uses the same code from Example 5-9 to retrieve the record we just updated and display it in the browser. Notice that even though we were able to make changes to all the fields in the update form, only the `Name`, `Title`, and `Email` fields contain updated values.

Dynamically Populating Additional Form-Field Types

In Example 5-7, we dynamically populated several text boxes with data pulled from a query object. It is also possible to dynamically populate other form-field types using techniques that vary from form-field type to form-field type.

Populating text areas

Populating a text area with data from a query is a little different from populating a text box. In the case of the text area, there is no `value` attribute. Instead, the query variable is placed between the text area tags as shown in Example 5-11.

Example 5-11. Dynamically populating a text area

```
<cfquery name="GetName" datasource="ProgrammingCF">
         SELECT Name
         FROM EmployeeDirectory
         Where ID=1
</cfquery>

<h2>Populating a Text Area</h2>
<form>
Name:<br>

<!--- Output the employee's name in a text area.  Generally, text areas are
      used to store large blocks of text. --->
<cfoutput>
<textarea cols="50" rows="5" name="Department"
          wrap="virtual">#GetName.Name#</textarea>
</cfoutput>
</form>
```

This example queries the `EmployeeDirectory` table of the `ProgrammingCF` database and returns the `Name` of the employee whose `ID` is `1`. This value is then output inside a text area. The results are shown in Figure 5-8. In general, text areas are used with large blocks of text. The `Name` column was used here for illustrative purposes only.

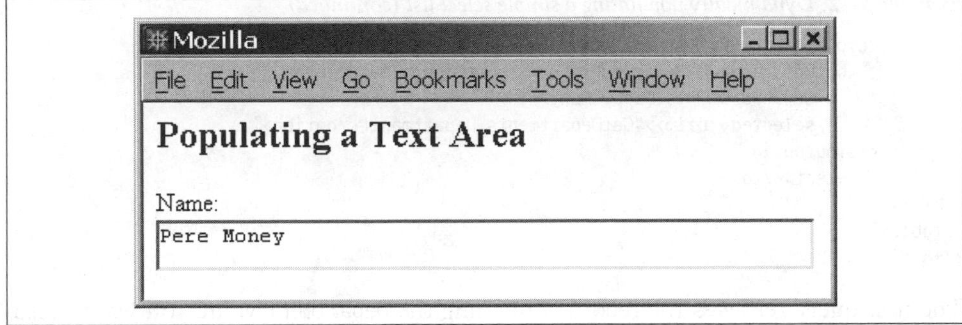

Figure 5-8. Dynamically populating a text area

Populating select lists

Select lists are a bit trickier to handle than the other form-field types we have covered so far. In order to dynamically generate a simple select list and automatically select the option that matches a value from a database record, you need to run two queries, as shown in Example 5-12.

Example 5-12. Dynamically populating a simple select list

```
<!--- Retrieve a specific employee record --->
<cfquery name="GetRecord" datasource="ProgrammingCF">
        SELECT Name, Department
        FROM EmployeeDirectory
        WHERE ID=1
</cfquery>

<!--- Retrieve a unique list of departments from the Department column
      of the EmployeeDirectory using the DISTINCT operator --->
<cfquery name="GetDepartments" datasource="ProgrammingCF">
        SELECT DISTINCT Department
        FROM EmployeeDirectory
        ORDER BY Department
</cfquery>

<h2>Populating a Select List</h2>
<form>
<table>
  <tr>
    <td>Name:</td>
    <td><cfoutput>#GetRecord.Name#</cfoutput></td>
  </tr>
  <tr>
    <td>Department:</td>
    <td><select name="Department">
        <!--- Dynamically generate the department list from the
              GetDepartments query.  Use a cfif statement to determine if
              the current option tag is equal to the Department value
              retrieved as part of the employee record. If so, add the
              selected attribute to the option tag --->
```

Example 5-12. Dynamically populating a simple select list (continued)

```
        <cfoutput query="GetDepartments">
          <option value="#Department#"<cfif GetRecord.Department eq
              GetDepartments.Department>
              selected</cfif>>#GetDepartments.Department#</option>
        </cfoutput>
        </select></td>
  </tr>
</table>
</form>
```

The first query retrieves the record containing the Department value you want preselected in the select list. In this example, we retrieve the Name and Department for the employee whose ID is 1. The second query retrieves a list of unique department names from the database. The unique list is obtained by using the DISTINCT operator in the query. DISTINCT is discussed in Chapter 11. Once both queries have been run, the select list is dynamically generated using the GetDepartments query. With each option tag generated, a check is made to see if the current Department (from the GetDepartments query) matches the Department from the GetRecord query. If a match is made, that option tag has a selected attribute added. The result is a select list with the option matching the database record preselected, as shown in Figure 5-9.

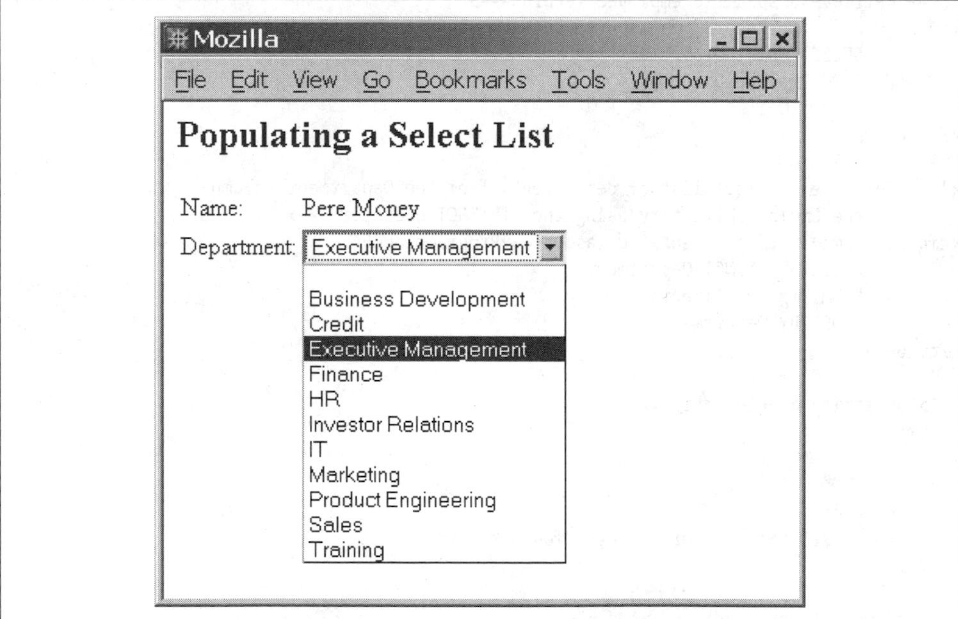

Figure 5-9. Dynamically populating a select list

The technique for dynamically populating a multiple select list is a little different from the technique we used for the simple select list. In this scenario, we want to dynamically generate a select list, but instead of having one option selected, we want to have multiple items selected based on a record retrieved from the database. Let's look at an example in which we want to build a prepopulated multiple select list that contains a list of all employees in our `EmployeeDirectory` table. To make things interesting, we'll preselect only those employees belonging to the IT department. Example 5-13 shows the code.

Example 5-13. Dynamically populating a multiple select list

```
<!--- Retrieve a list of all employees who are in the IT department --->
<cfquery name="GetITEmployees" datasource="ProgrammingCF">
        SELECT Name
        FROM EmployeeDirectory
        WHERE Department = 'IT'
</cfquery>

<!--- Retrieve all the employee from the EmployeeDirectory table --->
<cfquery name="GetAllEmployees" datasource="ProgrammingCF">
        SELECT ID, Name
        FROM EmployeeDirectory
        ORDER BY Name
</cfquery>

<!-- The ValueList function is used to build a comma-delimited list of
     values from a query column --->
<cfset EmployeeList = ValueList(GetITEmployees.Name)>

<h2>Populating a Multiple Select Box</h2>
<form>
<table>
  <tr>
    <td><b>Department:</b></td>
    <td>IT</td>
  </tr>

  <!--- Generate the options for the multiple select list.  If the option
        being generated matches a value from the list of IT employees,
        make that option a selected option. --->
  <tr>
    <td valign="top"><b>Name:</b></td>
    <td><select name="Employees" size="10" multiple>
        <cfoutput query="GetAllEmployees">
        <option value="#GetAllEmployees.ID#" <cfif ListFind(EmployeeList,
    GetAllEmployees.Name)>selected</cfif>>#GetAllEmployees.Name#
        </cfoutput>
        </select></td>
  </tr>
</table>
</form>
```

In this example, we use two queries to populate the multiple select list. The first query retrieves a list of all employees in the IT department. The second query retrieves a list of all employees (their `ID` and `Name`) in the database. Next, the `ValueList( )` function is used to build a comma-delimited list of values from the `Name` column of the `GetITEmployees` query. The list is assigned to a variable called `EmployeeList`. The next section of the template dynamically generates a multiple select list using the results of the `GetAllEmployees` query. With each `option` tag generated, the `ListFind( )` function is used to see if the current `Name` is in the `EmployeeList` list. If so, that `option` tag has a `selected` attribute added. The result is a multiple select list with the options matching the database record preselected, as shown in Figure 5-10.

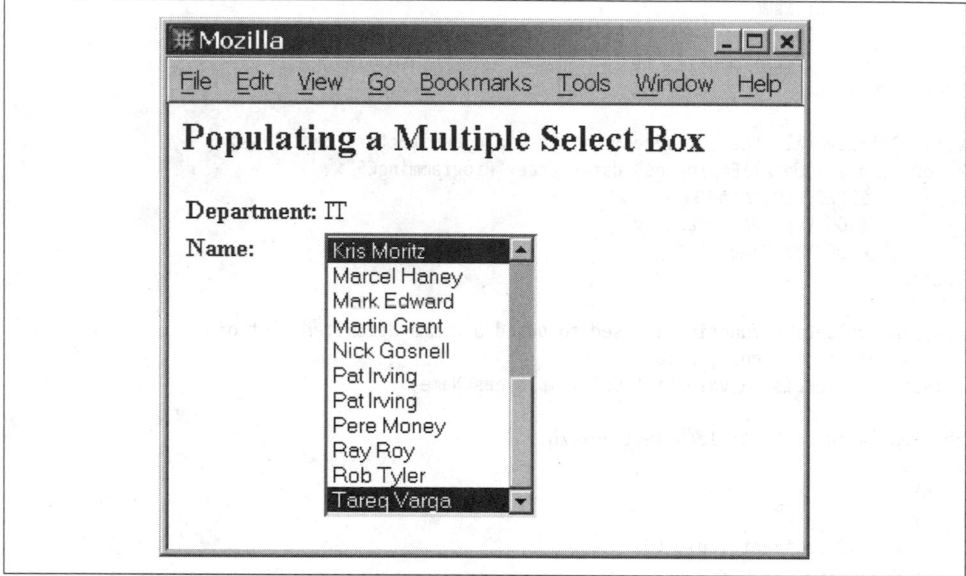

Figure 5-10. Dynamically populating a multiple select list

Generating and selecting multiple checkboxes

Checkboxes are similar to multiple select lists in that they are typically used to select one or more options from a list of choices. Dynamically generating checkboxes and automatically checking the ones that match entries in a database record is similar to the technique we used to generate the multiple select list. In fact, we'll use the same scenario to generate a checkbox for each employee in the `EmployeeDirectory` table and to automatically place a check in the box of each employee belonging to the IT department. The code to accomplish this is shown in Example 5-14.

Example 5-14. Generating and selecting multiple checkboxes

```
<!--- Retrieve a list of all employees who are in the IT department --->
<cfquery name="GetITEmployees" datasource="ProgrammingCF">
         SELECT Name
         FROM EmployeeDirectory
```

Example 5-14. Generating and selecting multiple checkboxes (continued)

```
        WHERE Department = 'IT'
</cfquery>

<!--- Retrieve all the employee from the EmployeeDirectory table --->
<cfquery name="GetAllEmployees" datasource="ProgrammingCF">
        SELECT ID, Name
        FROM EmployeeDirectory
        ORDER BY Name
</cfquery>

<!-- The ValueList function is used to build a comma-delimited list of
     values from a query column --->
<cfset EmployeeList = ValueList(GetITEmployees.Name)>

<h2>Populating Multiple Checkboxes</h2>
<form>
<table>
  <tr>
    <td><b>Department:</b></td>
    <td>IT</td>
  </tr>

  <!--- Generate the individual checkboxes by looping over the query
        results and creating a check box for each record.  Check the
        appropriate boxes based on the cfif statement. --->
  <tr>
    <td valign="top"><b>Name:</b></td>
    <td><cfloop query="GetAllEmployees">
          <cfoutput>
          <input type="Checkbox" name="Employees"
                 value="#GetAllEmployees.ID#" <cfif ListFind(EmployeeList,
                 GetAllEmployees.Name)>
                 checked</cfif>>#GetAllEmployees.Name#<br>
          </cfoutput>
        </cfloop></td>
  </tr>
</table>
</form>
```

The first section of this template is identical in form and function to the code we used for the multiple select list example (Example 5-13). The second section of the template uses a query loop to generate a checkbox for each employee in the `GetAllEmployees` query. With each checkbox generated, the `ListFind( )` function is used to see if the current Name is in the `EmployeeList` list. If so, the `input` tag associated with the checkbox has a `checked` attribute added. The result is a list of checkboxes with the checkboxes matching the database record checked. The results are shown in Figure 5-11.

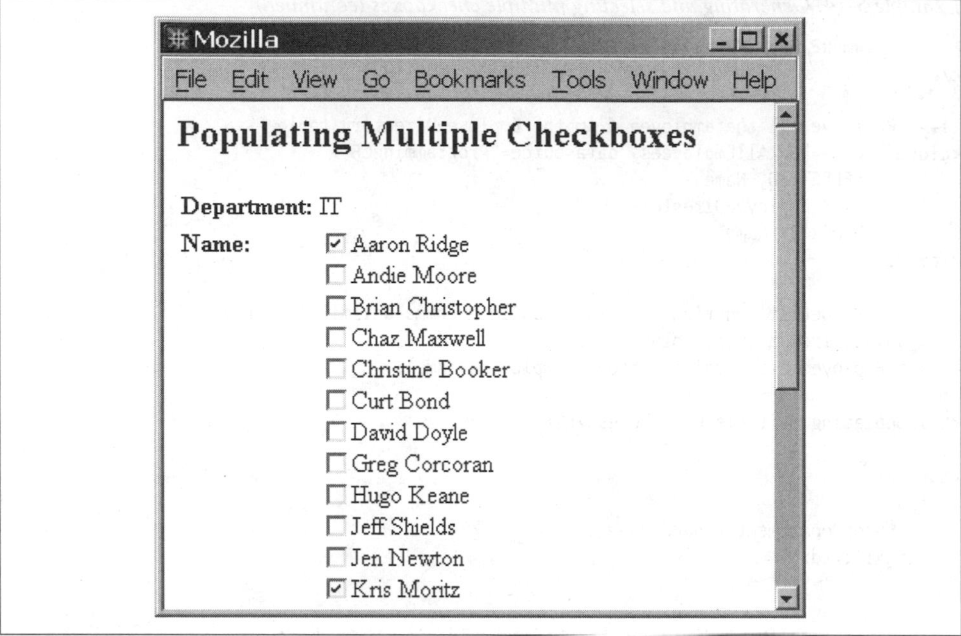

Figure 5-11. Generating and selecting multiple checkboxes

Note that checkboxes are sometimes used to represent Boolean values such as `Yes/No`, `True/False`, or `On/Off`. Although you can code checkboxes in this manner, this type of option is better represented by radio buttons.

Generating and selecting radio buttons

The final type of form field we need to cover is radio buttons. As you know, radio buttons are used to force a choice between several options. Dynamically generating radio buttons and automatically selecting the one that matches an entry in a database record is similar to the technique we used to generate the simple select list in Example 5-12.

Example 5-15 outputs the name of an employee from the `EmployeeDirectory` table and displays radio buttons that correspond to the distinct departments in the database, with the radio button that matches to the department in the database record selected.

Example 5-15. Dynamically generating radio buttons

```
<!--- Retrieve a specific employee record --->
<cfquery name="GetRecord" datasource="ProgrammingCF">
         SELECT Name, Department
         FROM EmployeeDirectory
         WHERE ID=3
</cfquery>
```

Example 5-15. Dynamically generating radio buttons (continued)

```
<!--- Retrieve a unique list of departments from the Department column of
      the EmployeeDirectory using the DISTINCT operator --->
<cfquery name="GetDepartments" datasource="ProgrammingCF">
         SELECT DISTINCT Department
         FROM EmployeeDirectory
         ORDER BY Department
</cfquery>

<h2>Populating Radio Buttons</h2>
<form>
<table>
  <tr>
    <td><b>Name:</b></td>
    <td><cfoutput>#GetRecord.Name#</cfoutput></td>
  </tr>
  <tr>
    <td valign="top"><b>Department:</b></td>
    <td><cfloop query="GetDepartments">
          <cfoutput>
          <input type="Radio" name="Department" value="#Department#" <cfif
                 GetRecord.Department eq GetDepartments.Department>checked</cfif>
                 >#Department#<br>
          </cfoutput>
        </cfloop></td>
  </tr>
</table>
</form>
```

In this example, two queries generate a radio button for each department and select the one corresponding to the department in the employee record. The first query retrieves the Name and Department associated with the record that has an ID of 3. The second query retrieves a list of unique department names from the database. The unique list is obtained by using the DISTINCT operator in the query.

The second part of the template uses a query loop to generate a radio button for each department returned by the GetDepartments query. With each radio button generated, a check is made to see if the current Department (from the GetDepartments query) matches the Department from the GetRecord query. If a match is made, the input tag associated with the radio button has a selected attribute added. The result is a list of radio buttons, one for each department, with the radio button matching the Department from the database record selected, as is shown in Figure 5-12.

Deleting Records

The cfquery tag can be used to delete records from a data source using the SQL DELETE clause. You can use DELETE to delete a single record or multiple records, depending on how you write the code. Once a record has been deleted, it can't be recovered, so be extremely careful when writing code that deletes records, as it is

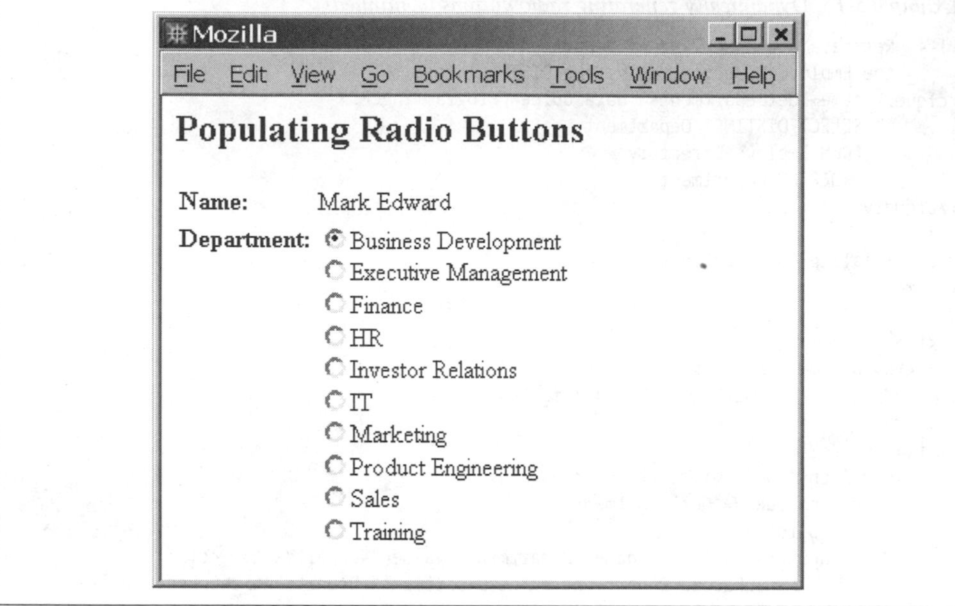

Figure 5-12. Generating and selecting radio buttons

quite easy to accidentally delete the contents of an entire table. Because of this, I recommend testing your code against a test database or a temporary table before deploying it in a live application.

Deleting a Single Record

Deleting a single record is as simple as it gets. The SQL for the delete looks something like this:

```
DELETE FROM tablename
WHERE primary_key = #primary_key#
```

We simply instruct the database to delete the record from the specified table where the primary key matches the one we supply. If there is such a record in the database, it is deleted. In this case, the primary key is a numeric value called `ID`. Primary keys don't have to be numeric values, but they do have to be unique.

If you look back at Example 5-7, you'll recall that it supports the ability to delete a record instead of populating the update form, if the appropriate parameter is passed from the record selection template. The code used to delete the record is quite simple:

```
<cfquery name="DeleteRecord" datasource="ProgrammingCF">
         DELETE FROM EmployeeDirectory
         WHERE ID = #ID#
```

To better illustrate the technique of deleting a record, let's look at a single template, *deleteform.cfm*, that allows a user to select a record from a database and then delete it. Example 5-16 shows the code.

Example 5-16. Deleting a single record from a database

```
<!--- Check to see if the form is calling itself to delete a single record.
     Note that by NOT scoping the ID variable in the WHERE clause, we
     Allow the template to accept both form and URL variables. --->
<cfif IsDefined('Delete')>
  <cfquery name="DeleteRecord" datasource="ProgrammingCF">
          DELETE FROM EmployeeDirectory
          WHERE ID = #ID#
  </cfquery>
</cfif>

<!--- Query the database for all employee names and their associated Ids
     (the primary key value --->
<cfquery name="GetEmployees" datasource="ProgrammingCF">
        SELECT ID, Name
        FROM EmployeeDirectory
        ORDER BY Name
</cfquery>

<html>
<head>
    <title>Deleting a Single Record</title>
</head>

<body>

<div align="Center">
<h3>Please select the employee you wish to delete</h3>

<form action="deleteform.cfm" method="post">
<table border="0">
  <tr>
    <td>
    <select name="ID" size="5">
      <cfoutput query="GetEmployees">
        <option value="#ID#">#Name#</option>
      </cfoutput>
    </select>
    </td>
  </tr>
  <tr>
    <td align="Center">
      <input type="submit" name="Delete" value="Delete">
    </td>
  </tr>
</table>
</form>
</div>
```

Example 5-16. Deleting a single record from a database (continued)

```
</body>
</html>
```

This template first checks to see if a variable called `Delete` has been passed in. This is done using the `IsDefined( )` function. If `Delete` does exist, a `cfquery` statement deletes the record whose primary key value (`ID`) was also passed as a form or URL variable. By not scoping the `ID` variable in the `WHERE` clause, we allow the template to accept both form and URL variables. Because `ID` is a numeric value, no quotes are needed around the variable name in the `WHERE` clause.

The next part of the template performs a `SELECT` query to return all the employee names as well as their associated `ID`s from the database. An HTML form containing a select box and a submit button is then constructed. The query object then generates an `option` tag for each record returned by the query. The `value` attribute of each `option` tag is dynamically populated with the `ID` of the corresponding record. The actual value displayed is determined by the `Name` field. The results are an HTML form with a select box containing a list of every employee from the database. A user can select a single employee from the select box and click on the submit button. The template then posts to itself. If an employee is selected, that record is deleted from the database. The form is then regenerated.

Deleting Multiple Records

The `DELETE` clause can also be used to delete more than one record at a time. There are two basic techniques for implementing this. The first technique allows you to delete a group of records having one or more common values. For example, to delete the records for all employees who work in the marketing department, use the following:

```
<cfquery name="DeleteMarketing" datasource="ProgrammingCF">
        DELETE FROM EmployeeDirectory
        WHERE Department = 'Marketing'
</cfquery>
```

Here, we specify that all records with `Marketing` as the value for `Department` should be deleted.

The second technique involves passing a comma-delimited list of primary key values in the SQL statement. The syntax is similar to what we have already covered in Example 5-16. The main difference is that instead of using a `WHERE` clause like this:

```
WHERE ID = #ID#
```

we introduce a new operator, `IN`:

```
WHERE ID IN (#ID#)
```

In this case, the value of `#ID#` is either a single value or a comma-delimited list of values. The `IN` operator tells the database that `ID` must be `IN` (as opposed to equal to a single ID) a list of passed IDs. We can get a better idea of how this works by looking at an example. If you remember from Example 5-16, we created an HTML form that allowed a user to select a single employee from the database and subsequently deleted that employee's record. We can modify that example to allow a user to select more than one employee at a time. Example 5-17 shows the *multipledelete.cfm* template that implements this functionality.

Example 5-17. Deleting multiple records from a database

```
<!--- Check to see if the form is calling itself to delete record(s) --->
<cfif IsDefined('form.Delete')>
  <cfquery name="DeleteRecord" datasource="ProgrammingCF">
          DELETE FROM EmployeeDirectory
          WHERE ID IN (#form.ID#)
  </cfquery>
</cfif>

<!--- Query the database for all employee names and their associated Ids
     (the primary key value) --->
<cfquery name="GetEmployees" datasource="ProgrammingCF">
         SELECT ID, Name
         FROM EmployeeDirectory
         ORDER BY Name
</cfquery>

<html>
<head>
    <title>Deleting Multiple Records</title>
</head>

<body>

<div align="Center">
<h3>Please select the employee(s) you wish to delete</h3>

<form action="multipledelete.cfm" method="post">
<table border="0">
  <tr>
    <td>
    <select name="ID" size="5" multiple>
      <cfoutput query="GetEmployees">
        <option value="#ID#">#Name#</option>
      </cfoutput>
    </select>
    </td>
  </tr>
  <tr>
    <td align="Center">
      <input type="submit" name="Delete" value="Delete">
    </td>
  </tr>
</table>
```

Example 5-17. Deleting multiple records from a database (continued)

```
</form>
</div>

</body>
</html>
```

There are only two areas where Example 5-16 differs from Example 5-17. The first is in the `cfquery` statement (the first one) that deletes the records selected in the form. Notice the `WHERE` clause is changed to read:

```
WHERE ID IN (#form.ID#)
```

This is what allows us to delete either a single record or multiple records passed in from the select box.

The second difference is in the code that generates the select box. If you remember, Example 5-16 allowed only a single selection. We overcome this in Example 5-17 by adding the `multiple` attribute to the `select` tag. This small change allows us to select multiple values within the select box. When the form is submitted, the values (in this case `ID`s) of the items selected are passed as a comma-delimited list. This list is stored as the form variable `form.ID`.

Asking for Confirmation Before Deleting

As you have seen, it is quite easy to delete records from a database table using a web-based frontend. This means that it is also easy to accidentally delete records with the click of a button. Because of this, you should consider including a confirmation mechanism in your application that warns users that the action they are about to take will permanently delete records from the database. This mechanism allows users to cancel the delete operation if they so desire.

You can easily make this functionality server-side and include it in the template that performs the SQL `DELETE`. However, this requires the use of several templates and actions on the part of users as they step screen by screen through the confirmation process. A better method is to use a single line of JavaScript in the same template as the HTML form you use to select the record(s) you want to delete. To include this functionality, change the `input` statement that creates the Delete button in either Example 5-16 or Example 5-17 to use the following code:

```
<input type="submit" name="Delete" value="Delete"
       onClick="return confirm('Are you sure you want to delete the
specified record(s)?')">
```

Including a JavaScript `onClick` event handler similar to the one we just described causes a JavaScript confirmation box to pop up whenever the Delete button is pressed. This confirmation box displays the message "Are you sure you want to delete the specified record(s)?" along with an OK and a Cancel button. If the OK button is clicked, the form submits, and the records are deleted. If on the other hand, the Cancel button is clicked, the form isn't submitted, and the user is free to select another record.

A Note About Referential Integrity and Cascading Deletes

Many databases have the option to enforce what's known as *referential integrity* between related tables in a database. This option keeps you from adding/updating/deleting data in one table that could cause an inconsistency in a related table. For example, if you have one table for employees and a related table that stores related data for each employee, deleting a record in the employee table could orphan one or more records in the related table. If your database is set up to enforce referential integrity for the relationship between those two tables, it will not allow the delete to be made unless both tables are deleted from.

An additional option, known as a *cascading delete*, is available in most databases. A cascading delete automatically deletes any related records from a foreign table when a related record is deleted from the primary table. For more information on these concepts, consult the documentation for your particular database.

You may also want to consider "deactivating" records as opposed to deleting them, in case you should ever need to recover the information. One way to deactivate a record is to add an additional field to your primary table (usually a Boolean/Bit field), using that field to indicate a record is inactive. That way, you can query your database as needed, selecting only records that haven't been deactivated.

CHAPTER 6

Complex Datatypes

Besides the simple datatypes covered in Chapter 2, ColdFusion supports several complex datatypes you can use to increase the complexity and functionality of your applications. These datatypes include lists, arrays, structures, query objects, and XML document objects. With the exception of XML document objects (these are covered later in Chapter 23), this chapter discusses each of these complex datatypes and provides numerous examples illustrating how they can further enhance your applications. One tool you may find especially helpful in dealing with complex datatypes is the `cfdump` tag. `cfdump` was added in ColdFusion 5.0 and enhanced in ColdFusion MX. The tag allows you to "dump" the contents of virtually any ColdFusion variable or function to the browser in a nicely formatted table. For more information on `cfdump`, see Appendix A.

Lists

A list is a special type of string that contains delimited elements. For example, "a,b,c,d,e,f,g" is a list where "a", "b", "c", "d", "e", "f", and "g" are considered the list elements while the comma (,) is considered the delimiter. Lists are commonly used to store related items in a single variable. For example, you might use a list to store all the primary key values for a group of database records you want to delete.

It should be noted that ColdFusion treats list elements containing null values as though they don't exist. For example, the list "1,2,,4" contains only three list elements (as far as ColdFusion is concerned) even though there is a null list element ",,". The concept of a null list element shouldn't be confused with a blank list element as in "1,2, ,4", which contains four list elements, the space occupying list element three being counted. To further illustrate the point, consider Example 6-1, which creates three lists using `cfset` tags and then uses the `ListLen()` function to evaluate the number of elements in each list.

Example 6-1. Creating lists and evaluating their length

```
<cfset List1 = "1,2,3,4">
<cfset List2 = "1,2,,4">
<cfset List3 = "1,2, ,4">

<cfoutput>
List1 (#List1#) contains #ListLen(List1)# elements.<br>
List2 (#List2#) contains #ListLen(List2)# elements.<br>
List3 (#List3#) contains #ListLen(List3)# elements.
</cfoutput>
```

Executing the template in Example 6-1 results in the output shown in Figure 6-1.

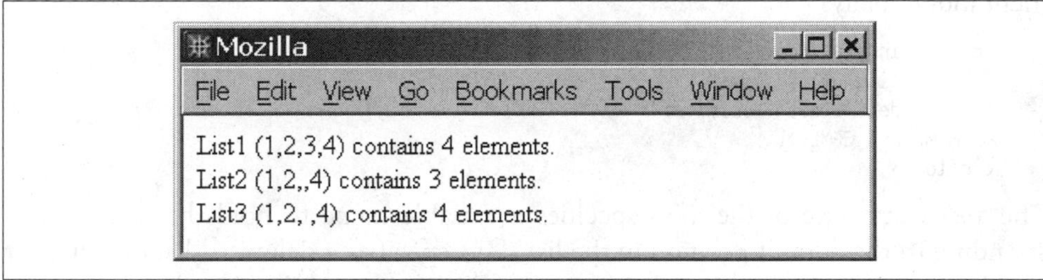

Figure 6-1. Outputting the number of elements in various lists

In the previous example, each element in the list was delimited by a comma. Although the comma is considered the default delimiter for lists in ColdFusion, it is possible to use any character or combination of characters as the delimiter. This is done by specifying the delimiter as an optional parameter in the appropriate list function:

```
<cfset List1 = "a;b;c;d">
<cfset List2 = "a|b|c|d">
<cfset List3 = "a+|+b+|+c+|+d">

<cfoutput>
List1 (#List1#) contains #ListLen(List1, ";")# elements.<br>
List2 (#List2#) contains #ListLen(List2, "|")# elements.<br>
List3 (#List3#) contains #ListLen(List3, "+|")# elements.
</cfoutput>
```

In this example, the `ListLen( )` function outputs the number of elements contained in each list. Note that each list uses a delimiter other than the comma. Because of this, it is necessary to specify the delimiter in the `ListLen( )` function. If you omit the delimiter in any of these examples, the `ListLen( )` function returns 1 for the length of the list because no commas are found.

It's also possible to use more than one delimiter within a list:

```
<cfset List1 = "a,b;c,d;">
<cfset List2 = "a,b,c|d">
```

```
<cfoutput>
List1 (#List1#) contains #ListLen(List1, ",;")# elements.<br>
List2 (#List2#) contains #ListLen(List2, ",|")# elements.
</cfoutput>
```

In this case, each list has two different delimiters. In order to be recognized by the `ListLen()` function, each delimiter has to be specified. Note that the delimiters themselves aren't separated by a delimiter.

Looping over a List

List loops iterate over the elements of a list, allowing you to manipulate each element individually:

```
<cfloop index="index_name"
        list="list_items"
        delimiters="delimiter">
   HTML and CFML...
</cfloop>
```

The `index` attribute of the loop specifies a variable name to hold the value corresponding to the current position in the list. `list` specifies a delimited list of values or variable name (including pound signs) over which to loop. The `delimiters` attribute specifies the delimiter that separates the elements of the list. The default is the comma. Example 6-2 uses a list loop to output each element of a list on a new line.

Example 6-2. Looping over a list using a list loop

```
<cfset MyList = "a,b,c,d,e,f,g,h,i,j,k,l,m,n,o,p,q,r,s,t,u,v,w,x,y,z">
<cfloop index="i"
        list="#MyList#"
        delimiters=",">

<cfoutput>
#i#<br>
</cfoutput>
</cfloop>
```

Manipulating Lists

A number of functions are available in ColdFusion to manipulate list elements. We've already looked at the `ListLen()` function. Other commonly used list functions enable you to manipulate lists in a number of ways.

To append an item to the end of an existing list, you can use the `ListAppend()` function:

```
<cfset MyList = "1,2,3,4">
<cfset MyList = ListAppend(MyList, 5)>
```

You can also prepend an item to the beginning of a list using the `ListPrepend()` function:

```
<cfset MyList = "2,3,4,5">
<cfset MyList = ListPrepend(MyList, 1)>
```

To insert an item into a specific position within a list, use the `ListInsertAt( )` function:

```
<cfset MyList = "Monday,Tuesday,Thursday,Friday">
<cfset MyList = ListInsertAt(MyList, 3, "Wednesday")>
```

Note that in ColdFusion, 1 is the first position in a list.

If you want to return the first item in a list, use the `ListFirst( )` function:

```
<cfset MyList = "1,2,3,4">
<cfoutput>
#ListFirst(MyList)#
</cfoutput>
```

Likewise, you can use the `ListLast( )` function to return the last item in a list:

```
<cfset MyList = "1,2,3,4">
<cfoutput>
#ListLast(MyList)#
</cfoutput>
```

You can output a list item occupying a specific position within a list using the `ListGetAt( )` function:

```
<cfset MyList = "1,2,3,4">
<cfoutput>
#ListGetAt(MyList, 3)#
</cfoutput>
```

For a complete listing as well as examples showing the usage of all list functions, see Appendix B. If there is an operation you need to perform on a list that isn't covered by one of ColdFusion's built in functions, chances are someone has already written a user defined function (UDF) that does the job. The Common Function Library Project at *http://www.cflib.org* contains a string library with dozens of freely available list functions you can download and use in your applications.

Arrays

An array is an object that stores indexed values. Each value stored in an array is referred to as an element of the array. Each element has an integer assigned to it that marks its position within the array. This number is referred to as the element's index. Arrays elements can store any ColdFusion datatype including additional arrays.

As previously discussed, ColdFusion supports one-dimensional (think of this as a single column of data or a list), two-dimensional (think of this as a spreadsheet with rows and columns), and three-dimensional (think of this as a cube of data) arrays. Additional dimensions can be created dynamically by nesting multidimensional arrays (creating an array of arrays). ColdFusion arrays differ slightly from traditional arrays found in other programming languages. Whereas traditional arrays are fixed in size, ColdFusion arrays are dynamic. This means that a ColdFusion array can expand or contract as elements are added and removed from the array.

Arrays can store groups of related data such as the contents of a visitor's shopping cart, student test scores, or historic stock prices. Because array elements can store any ColdFusion datatype, they are ideal for storing complex objects such as an array of query result sets or an array of structures.

Initializing an Array

Initializing an array in ColdFusion is accomplished using the `ArrayNew( )` function. This function takes a single argument that determines the number of dimensions for the array (1, 2, or 3). The following code initializes a one-dimensional array called `Grades`:

```
<cfset Grades = ArrayNew(1)>
```

If you wanted to create a two-dimensional array called `Grades`, use the following:

```
<cfset Grades = ArrayNew(2)>
```

Similarly, a three-dimensional array called `Grades` is created like this:

```
<cfset Grades = ArrayNew(3)>
```

To create an array with more than three dimensions, you must nest multidimensional arrays:

```
<cfset MyArray = ArrayNew(3)>
<cfset NestedArray = ArrayNew(3)>
<cfset MyArray[1][1][1] = NestedArray>
```

You can also initialize an array using the `cfparam` tag, as in the following:

```
<cfparam name="Grades" type="Array" value="#ArrayNew(1)#>
```

Note that you must surround the `ArrayNew( )` function with pound signs. This tells ColdFusion to evaluate the `ArrayNew( )` function as opposed to treating it as literal text.

Adding Data to an Array

Once you have initialized an array, you can populate it with data. Because ColdFusion arrays are dynamic, there is no need to predefine the size of the array. Data is added to an array using the `cfset` tag to specify the index position within the array where the data should be stored. The index position within each dimension is referenced with a set of brackets ([ ]). Unlike in many other programming languages, in ColdFusion, array indexes begin with 1. Consider the following example that populates elements in a one-, two-, and three-dimensional array:

```
<!--- This populates an element in a one-dimensional array --->
<cfset MyArray[1]  = "cat">
```

```
<!--- This populates an element in a two-dimensional array --->
<cfset MyArray[1][1] = "dog">

<!--- This populates an element in a three-dimensional array --->
<cfset MyArray[1][1][1] = "fish">
```

In a one-dimensional array, the index position refers to the element's linear position within the array (if you think of a one-dimensional array as a list of elements). In a two-dimensional array, the index positions refer to the element's x-y position (if you think of a two-dimensional array as a grid of data with an x and y axis). Because a three-dimensional array stores data in a three-dimensional cube configuration, the index position of any element is referred to by its x-y-z position within the cube.

To get a better idea of how data is stored in an array, consider Example 6-3, in which a one-dimensional array called `Grades` is initialized, populated with values, then output by looping over each element in the array. A visual representation of the array is also provided by dumping the array with the `cfdump` tag.

Example 6-3. Grades for a single student stored in a one-dimensional array

```
<cfset Grades = ArrayNew(1)>

<cfset Grades[1] = 95>
<cfset Grades[2] = 93>
<cfset Grades[3] = 87>
<cfset Grades[4] = 100>
<cfset Grades[5] = 74>

<cfloop index="Element" from="1" to="#ArrayLen(Grades)#">
  <cfoutput>
  Grade #Element#: #Grades[Element]#<br>
  </cfoutput>
</cfloop>

<cfdump var="#Grades#">
```

In this example, an index loop is used to loop over the elements in the `Grades` array. This is accomplished by setting the `to` attribute of the `cfloop` tag to the total number of elements in the array. This number is derived using the `ArrayLen( )` function. Executing this template results in the output shown in Figure 6-2.

It's just as easy to create a two-dimensional array. The next example creates a two-dimensional array called `Grades`. This array also holds student Grades, but instead of holding the Grades for a single student, the array holds multiple Grades for multiple students. Each student is represented by the first dimension of the array while each corresponding grade is represented by the second dimension. The code in Example 6-4 initializes the `Grades` array, populates it with data, and then uses a nested loop technique to output the contents to the browser, along with a visual representation of the array using the `cfdump` tag.

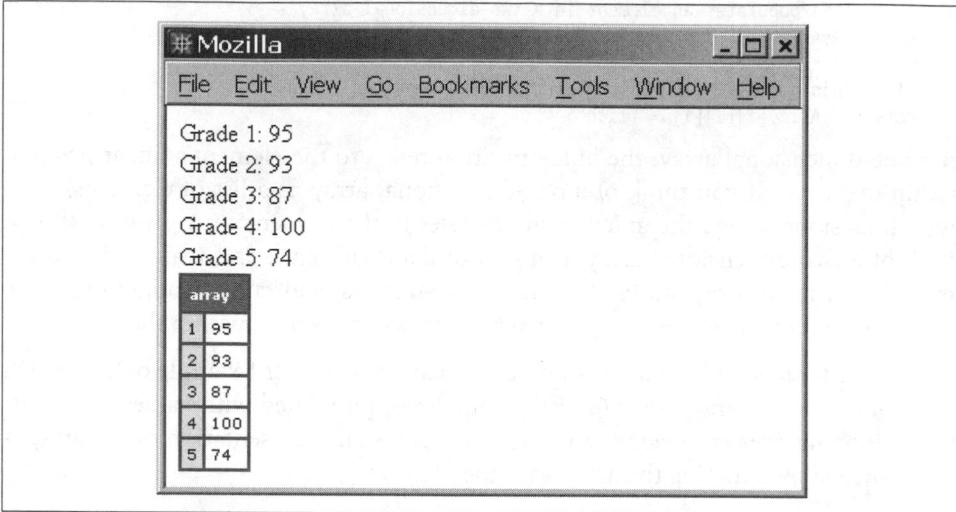

Figure 6-2. Outputting the contents of the one-dimensional Grades array

Example 6-4. Grades for more than one student stored in a two-dimensional array

```
<!--- Create a two dimensional array of student Grades.  Each student
     (represented by the first dimension) has Grades for multiple tests
     (represented by the second dimension). --->
<cfset Grades = ArrayNew(2)>

<cfset Grades[1][1] = 95>
<cfset Grades[1][2] = 93>
<cfset Grades[1][3] = 87>
<cfset Grades[2][1] = 100>
<cfset Grades[2][2] = 74>
<cfset Grades[2][3] = 86>
<cfset Grades[3][1] = 90>
<cfset Grades[3][2] = 94>
<cfset Grades[3][3] = 96>

<!--- This looping technique utilizes an outer and an inner loop (designated
      o and i respectively) for looping through each element in each
      dimension of the array --->
<cfloop index="o" from="1" to="#ArrayLen(Grades)#">
  <cfloop index="i" from="1" to="#ArrayLen(Grades[o])#">
    <cfoutput>
    Student #o#, Grade #i#: #Grades[o][i]#<br>
    </cfoutput>
  </cfloop>
</cfloop>

<cfdump var="#Grades#">
```

Executing this template results in the output shown in Figure 6-3.

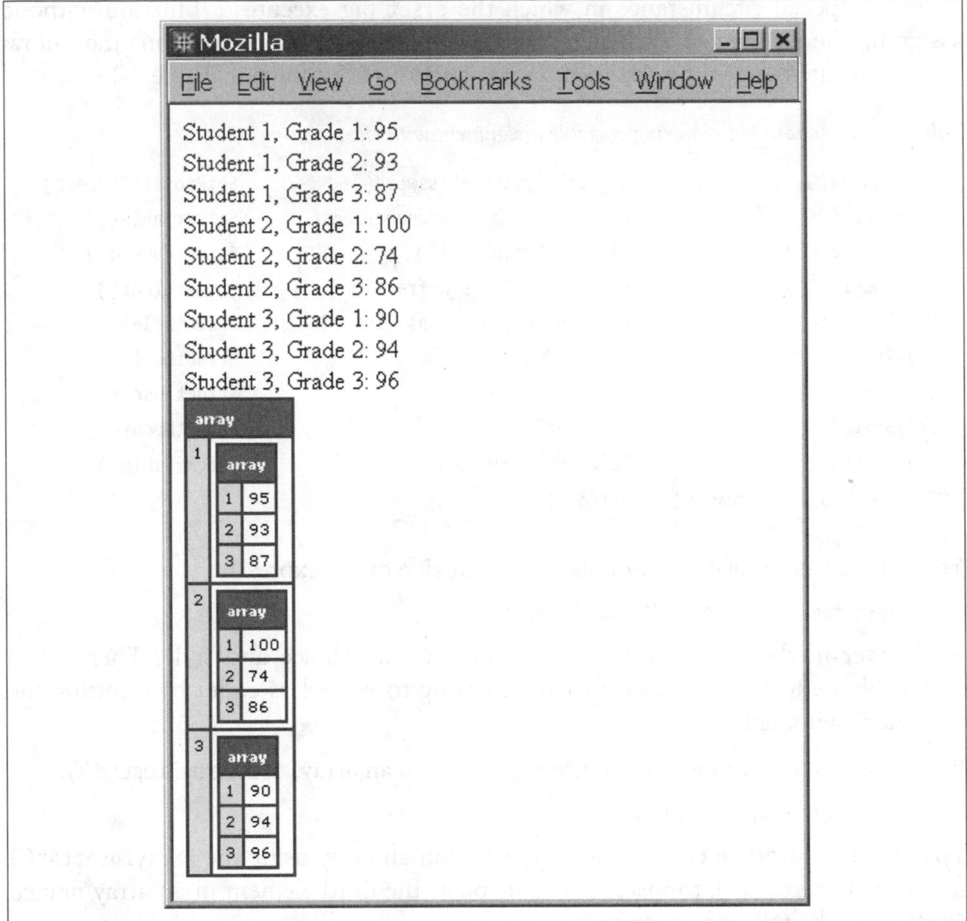

Figure 6-3. Outputting the contents of the two-dimensional Grades array

Manipulating Array Elements

A number of functions are available in ColdFusion to manipulate arrays. We've already covered the `ArrayNew()` and `ArrayLen()` functions as well as how to create array elements. There are other common array functions worth mentioning.

To append an element to the end of an existing array, use the `ArrayAppend()` function:

```
<cfset ArrayAppend(Grades, "66")>
```

You may have noticed that the `cfset` tag in the previous example doesn't assign a value to a variable:

```
<cfset ArrayAppend(Grades, "66")>
```

This is a special circumstance in which the cfset tag executes a function without assigning the results to a variable. There are only a handful of functions that allow you to execute them in this manner. These functions are shown in Table 6-1.

Table 6-1. Functions not requiring variable assignment with cfset

ArrayAppend( )	CF_SetDataSourcePassword( )	SetProfileString( )
ArrayClear( )	Cfusion_Disable_DBConnections( )	SetVariable( )
ArrayDeleteAt( )	Cfusion_SetODBCIni( )	StructAppend( )
ArrayInsertAt( )	CFusion_Settings_Refresh( )	StructClear( )
ArrayPrepend( )	CFusion_DBConnections_Flush( )	StructDelete( )
ArrayResize( )	QueryAddColumn( )	StructGet( )
ArraySet( )	QueryAddRow( )	StructInsert( )
ArraySort( )	QuerySetCell( )	StructUpdate( )
ArraySwap( )	ReleaseComObject( )	SetVariable( )
CF_SetDataSourceUsername( )	SetLocale( )	

You can just as easily use a variable on the left side of the expression:

```
<cfset temp = ArrayAppend(Grades, "66")>
```

Whichever method you use is a matter of personal choice and style. There is no noticeable performance gain (other than having to write less code) by omitting the variable assignment.

If you want to prepend a value to the beginning on an array, use ArrayPrepend( ):

```
<cfset ArrayPrepend(Grades, "66")>
```

You can also insert an element anywhere within an array using the ArrayInsertAt( ) function. For example, to insert the value 66 as the third element in an array named Grades, use the following syntax:

```
<cfset ArrayInsertAt(Grades, 66, 3)>
```

Deleting an element is just as simple and is done using the ArrayDeleteAt( ) function. For example, to delete the third element in an array named Grades, use:

```
<cfset ArrayDeleteAt(Grades, 3)>
```

Because ColdFusion arrays are dynamic, adding or deleting an element from the middle of an index results in a shift in the index position of other elements in the array.

You can remove all data from an array using ArrayClear( ):

```
<cfset ArrayClear(Grades)>
```

If you need to determine whether an array contains any data, use the ArrayIsEmpty( ) function:

```
<cfif ArrayIsEmpty(Grades)>
  There are no Grades to process
</cfelse>
```

```
    Processing Grades...
</cfif>
```

Sorting an array is done using the `ArraySort( )` function. You can specify a sort type (`Numeric`, `Text`, or `TextNoCase`) as well as a sort order (the default, `Asc`, or `Desc`):

```
<cfset SortedGrades = ArraySort(Grades, 'Numeric', 'Asc')>
```

If you are dealing with numeric elements in an array, you can find the average value using the `ArrayAvg( )` function:

```
<cfset TheAverage = ArrayAvg(Scores)>
```

You can just as easily determine the minimum value or maximum value using `ArrayMin( )` or `ArrayMax( )`:

```
<cfset MinValue = ArrayMin(Scores)>
<cfset MaxValue = ArrayMax(Scores)>
```

If you want to add the numeric values in an array, use the `ArraySum( )` function:

```
<cfset TheSum = ArraySum(Scores)>
```

For a complete listing as well as examples showing the usage of each array function, see Appendix B. Many additional array functions are available as UDFs from the Common Function Library Project at *http:/www.cflib.org*.

Structures

A structure is a ColdFusion datatype that allows you to store and manipulate key/value pairs. Structures are similar to one-dimensional arrays, except each element is referenced via an alphanumeric "key" (string) as opposed to a numeric index within the array. Structures are also commonly known as associative arrays or hashes. Structures offer an advantage over arrays in certain situations, by allowing you to reference groups of related information by key as opposed to by numeric index. Structures are useful for storing sets of related data in a single variable. For example, you can easily store an employee's contact information in a structure called `Employee`. That structure can contain keys such as `Name`, `Address`, `City`, `State`, and `Zip`. Additionally, a number of ColdFusion variable scopes are accessible as structures. For example, you can access all form variables available to a page by referencing a structure named `form`. A similar structure is also available for most other variable scopes.

Creating a Structure

Structures are created using the `StructNew( )` function. Unlike with arrays, you don't have to pass any information to this function. To create a new structure called `Employee`, you use the following code:

```
<cfset Employee = StructNew( )>
```

Just like arrays, structures can also be created using the `cfparam` tag:

```
<cfparam name="Employee" type="Struct" default="#StructNew( )#">
```

Be sure to wrap the StructNew() function with hash marks to avoid having ColdFusion treat the function as literal text.

In ColdFusion MX, you can also create a structure by using a compound variable name separated by a period. For example, the following code creates a structure named Employee, adds a key called Name, and populates the key with a value:

```
<cfset Employee.Name="Pere Money">
```

In previous versions of ColdFusion, this code would simply create a variable in the local variables scope named Employee.Name. In ColdFusion MX, compound variable names separated by a period automatically create the appropriate substructures should they not already exist. This can be used to nest structures any number of levels:

```
<cfset Company.Department.Marketing="Pat Irving">

<cfdump var="#Company#">
```

Doing a cfdump of the Company structure displays a visual representation of the nested data. If you are upgrading to ColdFusion MX from a previous version, you should run the code compatibility analyzer included in the ColdFusion Administrator to find any existing code that might pose a compatibility problem due to this change in functionality.

Populating a Structure with Data

Once you have created a structure with the StructNew() function, it is ready to be populated with key/value pairs. Structures are a unique datatype in that you can reference structure elements using three styles of notation:

Function notation
: Elements within structures can be indirectly referenced using structure functions as opposed to directly using one of the other methods of notation:

```
<cfset StructInsert(Employee, "Name", "Pere Money")>
```

Object notation
: Structure values are referenced as *object.property* where *object* is the name of the structure, and *property* is the name of the key. All references using object notation are case insensitive.

```
<cfset Employee.Name = "Pere Money">
```

Associative array notation
: You can use associative array notation to refer to structure elements much as you refer to elements within an array. The difference is that in the case of associative arrays, the indexes are strings as opposed to numbers:

```
<cfset Employee["Name"] = "Pere Money">
```

Example 6-5 uses function notation to create a structure called Employee and populate it with key/value pairs. Each key/value pair is added using the StructInsert( ) function.

Example 6-5. Populating a structure using function notation

```
<cfset Employee=StructNew( )>
<cfset StructInsert(Employee, "Name", "Pere Money")>
<cfset StructInsert(Employee, "Title", "President")>
<cfset StructInsert(Employee, "Department", "Executive Management")>
<cfset StructInsert(Employee, "Email", "pmoney@example.com")>
<cfset StructInsert(Employee, "PhoneExt", "1234")>

<cfset MyKeyList = StructKeyList(Employee)>

<table>
<tr>
  <th>Key</th><th>Value</th>
</tr>

<cfloop index="Key" list="#MyKeyList#">
  <cfoutput>
  <tr>
    <td>#Key#</td><td>#StructFind(Employee,Key)#</td>
  </tr>
  </cfoutput>
</cfloop>

</table>

<cfdump var="#Employee#">
```

In this example, once the structure has been populated, the StructKeyList( ) function generates a delimited list of all keys in the Employee structure. A list loop is then used to iterate over each key in the list. A table containing each key/value pair is dynamically generated by obtaining the key from the list and the value from the structure. The structure is also dumped using cfdump so you can get a better idea of how a structure is put together. The output from this template is shown in Figure 6-4.

Example 6-6 shows how to populate the same Employee structure with object notation.

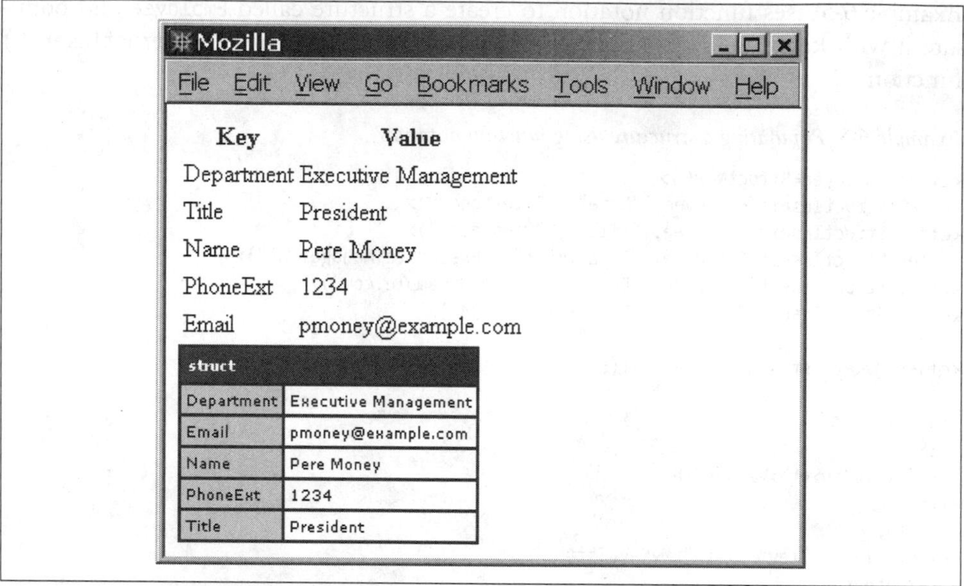

Figure 6-4. Outputting the contents of a structure using a list loop and the StructFind() function

Example 6-6. Populating a structure using object notation

```
<cfset Employee=StructNew( )>
<cfset Employee.Name="Pere Money">
<cfset Employee.Title="President">
<cfset Employee.Department="Executive Management">
<cfset Employee.Email="pmoney@example.com">
<cfset Employee.PhoneExt="1234">

<table>
  <tr>
    <th>Key</th><th>Value</th>
  </tr>

  <cfoutput>
  <tr><td>Name</td><td>#Employee.Name#</td></tr>
  <tr><td>Title</td><td>#Employee.Title#</td></tr>
  <tr><td>Department</td><td>#Employee.Department#</td></tr>
  <tr><td>Email</td><td>#Employee.Email#</td></tr>
  <tr><td>PhoneExt</td><td>#Employee.PhoneExt#</td></tr>
  </cfoutput>
</table>
```

Once the Employee structure has been populated, the contents of the structure are output by referencing each element individually using object notation. Executing the example results in the same output (minus the cfdump) as shown in Figure 6-4.

Working with the same Employee structure from our previous examples, we can use associative array notation to populate the structure with key/value pairs as in Example 6-7.

Example 6-7. Populating a structure using associative array notation

```
<cfset Employee = StructNew( )>
<cfset Employee["Name"] = "Pere Money">
<cfset Employee["Title"] = "President">
<cfset Employee["Department"] = "Executive Management">
<cfset Employee["Email"] = "pmoney@example.com">
<cfset Employee["PhoneExt"] = "1234">

<cfset MyKeyArray = StructKeyArray(Employee)>

<table>
<tr>
  <th>Key</th><th>Value</th>
</tr>
<cfloop index="position" from="1" to="#ArrayLen(MyKeyArray)#">
  <cfoutput>
  <tr>
    <td>#MyKeyArray[position]#</td>
    <td>#Employee[MyKeyArray[position]]#</td>
  </tr>
  </cfoutput>
</cfloop>
</table>
```

We use a third technique here to output the contents of the `Employee` structure. The `StructKeyArray( )` function is used to create an array called `MyKeyArray( )` that contains all the keys in the structure. An `index` loop is then used to iterate over each of the keys in the array. A table containing each key/value pair is dynamically generated by obtaining the key from the array and the value from the structure. The results, minus the `cfdump`, are the same as those shown in Figure 6-4.

Using a Collection Loop to Loop over the Contents of a Structure

Collection loops can iterate over a COM collection object or a ColdFusion structure. To better understand how collection loops allow you to loop over structures, let's look at the general syntax that codes a collection loop:

```
<cfloop collection="COM_object_or_structure"
        item="collection_or_key">
   HTML and CFML...
</cfloop>
```

The `collection` attribute specifies the name of a registered COM object or a ColdFusion structure object. `item` specifies the name of the variable that holds each item in the COM collection or structure object that is referenced by the loop. Example 6-8 uses a collection loop to output each key/value pair contained in a structure object called `Employee`.

Example 6-8. Using a collection loop to loop over a structure

```
<cfset Employee=StructNew( )>
<cfset Employee.Name="Pere Money">
<cfset Employee.Title="President">
<cfset Employee.Department="Executive Management">
<cfset Employee.Email="pmoney@example.com">
<cfset Employee.PhoneExt="1234">

<table>
<tr>
  <th>Key</th><th>Value</th>
</tr>

<cfloop collection="#Employee#" item="Key">
  <cfoutput>
  <tr>
    <td>#Key#</td><td>#Employee[Key]#</td>
  </tr>
  </cfoutput>
</cfloop>
</table>
```

Here, a `collection` loop iterates over each of the keys in the structure. The value for each key is output using the associative array notation we discussed earlier in the section. This is the preferred method for referencing unknown structure key/value pairs and should be used instead of the `StructFind( )` function as it is better performing. The output from this template is the same as shown in Figure 6-4 (minus the `cfdump`).

Creating an Array of Structures

If you look at all the structure examples we've created so far, you'll probably come to the conclusion that while structures appear to be a great way to store and reference data, their ability to store multiple sets of similar data seems limited. For example, while you can store all the information about a particular employee in a structure, you can't store information about additional employees in the same structure. You can create a separate structure for each employee, but that could get unwieldy to manage, especially if you need to pass the data to another template. The solution is to create an array of structures to hold the information about each employee. Example 6-9 shows the code to do just this.

Example 6-9. Creating an array of structures to hold employee information

```
<!--- Create an array called Employees --->
<cfset Employees = ArrayNew(1)>

<!--- Create a structure as the first array element --->
<cfset Employees[1] = StructNew( )>
<cfset Employees[1].Name = "Pere Money">
<cfset Employees[1].Title = "President">
```

Example 6-9. Creating an array of structures to hold employee information (continued)

```
<cfset Employees[1].Email = "pmoney@example.com">

<!--- Create a structure as the second array element --->
<cfset Employees[2] = StructNew( )>
<cfset Employees[2].Name = "Pat Irving">
<cfset Employees[2].Title = "Vice President">
<cfset Employees[2].Email = "pirving@example.com">

<!--- Create a structure as the third array element --->
<cfset Employees[3] = StructNew( )>
<cfset Employees[3].Name = "Ray Roy">
<cfset Employees[3].Title = "Instructor">
<cfset Employees[3].Email = "rroy@example.com">

<h2>Employees in an Array of Structures</h2>
<table>
<tr>
  <th>Name</th><th>Title</th><th>Email</th>
</tr>

<cfloop index="i" from="1" to="#ArrayLen(Employees)#">
  <cfoutput>
  <tr>
    <td>#Employees[i].Name#</td>
    <td>#Employees[i].Title#</td>
    <td>#Employees[i].Email#</td>
  </tr>
  </cfoutput>
</cfloop>
</table>

<cfdump var="#Employees#">
```

The template begins by initializing a one-dimensional array called `Employees`. Next, `cfset` tags are used to assign values to each index in the array. Instead of assigning string values, a new structure is created for each employee. The structure is then populated with the employee's name, title, and email address. Once the array of structures has been populated, an HTML table containing the information from each structure is constructed on the fly by looping over each array element. Additionally, the `cfdump` tag is used to output a visual representation of the array of structures. Executing the template results in the output shown in Figure 6-5.

Manipulating Structures

A number of functions are available in ColdFusion to manipulate structures. We've already seen the `StructInsert( )`, `StructKeyList( )`, `StructKeyArray( )`, and `StructFind( )` and functions. There are a few others worth mentioning here.

Use the `StructClear( )` function to remove all data from a structure named `Employee`:

```
<cfset StructClear(Employee)>
```

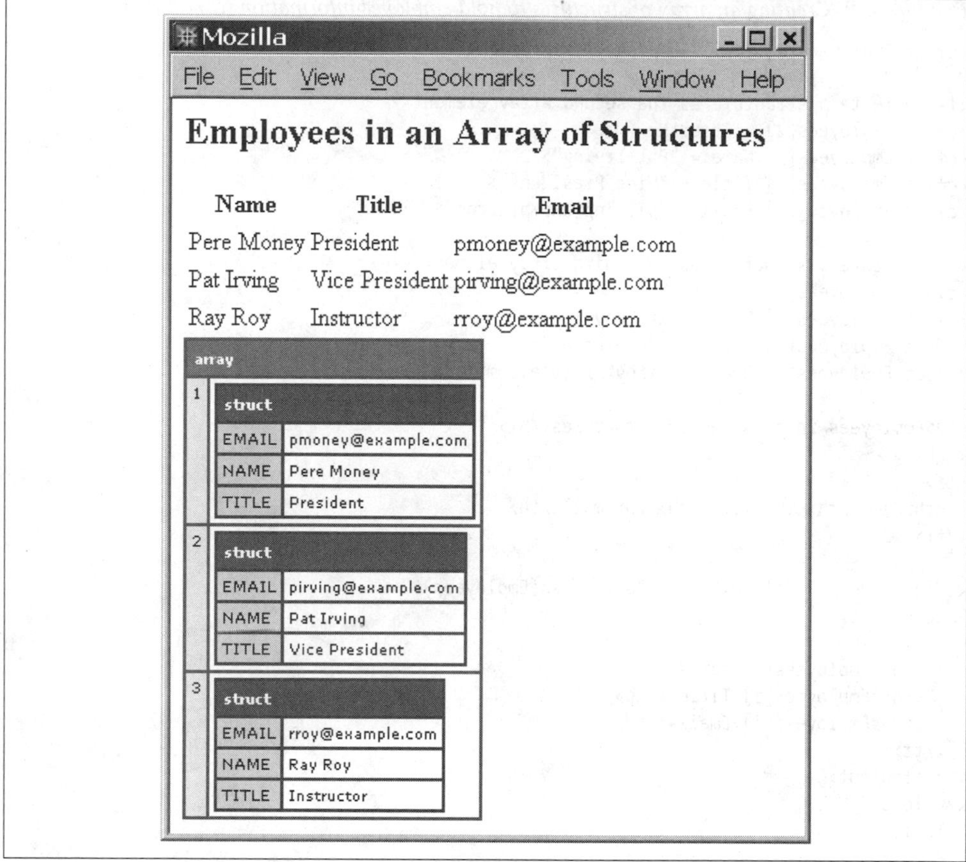

Figure 6-5. Outputting employee information from an array of structures

To delete a specific key named `Name` (and its associated value) from a structure named `Employee`, use `StructDelete( )`:

```
<cfset StructDelete(Employee, "Name")>
```

You can obtain a count of the number of key/value pairs in a structure using the `StructCount( )` function:

```
<cfset TheCount = StructCount(Employee)>
```

If you want to determine whether a given structure contains data, use `StructIsEmpty( )`:

```
<cfif StructIsEmpty(Employee)>
  The Employee structure doesn't contain any data.
<cfelse>
  The Employee structure contains data.
</cfif>
```

You can determine whether a particular key exists within a structure using the StructKeyExists() function:

```
<cfif StructKeyExists(Employee, Name)>
  <cfoutput>
  The employee's name is #Name#
  </cfoutput>
<cfelse>
  There is no name for this employee.
</cfif>
```

You can make a copy of a structure in a number of ways. The easiest way is through simple assignment:

```
<cfset Employee=StructNew()>
<cfset Employee.Name="Pere Money">
<cfset Employee.Title="President">

<cfset EmployeeCopy = Employee>

<cfdump var="#EmployeeCopy#">
```

There is one thing to be aware of, however, when it comes to copying structures. Structures (as well as query objects) are copied by reference instead of by value. Thus, any changes made to the copy of the structure result in changes to the original. The converse is also true: changes to the original result in changes to the copy. To get around this, you can use the StructCopy() function:

```
<cfset Employee=StructNew()>
<cfset Employee.Name="Pere Money">
<cfset Employee.Title="President">

<cfset EmployeeCopy = StructCopy(Employee)>

<cfdump var="#EmployeeCopy#">
```

This technique creates a copy of the structure by value as opposed to by reference. Here, changes to the copy do not result in changes to the original structure, with one exception. For nested structures or other complex values containing nested structures, the StructCopy() function should not be used. Instead, use Duplicate(). In fact, it's my preference always to use Duplicate() instead of StructCopy(), because Duplicate() always creates a copy by value regardless of the type or complexity of the variable, and it can be used with any ColdFusion datatype with the exception of COM, CORBA, and Java objects. Here's an example that uses both StructCopy() and Duplicate() to copy a nested structure:

```
<cfset Employee=StructNew()>
<cfset Employee.Name="Pere Money">
<cfset Employee.Title="President">

<cfset EmployeeCopy = Employee>

<cfdump var="#EmployeeCopy#">
```

```
<!--- Create a nested structure --->
<cfset Company=StructNew( )>
<cfset Company.Employee=StructNew( )>
<cfset Company.Employee.Name="Pere Money">
<cfset Company.Employee.Title="President">
<cfset Company.Employee.Department="Executive Management">
<cfset Company.Employee.Email="pmoney@example.com">
<cfset Company.Employee.PhoneExt="1234">

<!--- Create a copy and a duplicate of the structure --->
<cfset CompanyCopy = StructCopy(Company)>
<cfset CompanyDuplicate = Duplicate(Company)>

<cfoutput>
<b>Name:</b> #Company.Employee.Name#<br>
<b>Original Title:</b> #Company.Employee.Title#<br>
<cfset Company.Employee.Title = "CEO">
<b>Copied Title:</b> #CompanyCopy.Employee.Title#<br>
<b>Duplicate Title:</b> #CompanyDuplicate.Employee.Title#
</cfoutput>
```

Notice in this example that setting `Company.Employee.Title="CEO"` after the `Company` structure is copied (with `StructCopy( )`) results in a change to the copied structure, but not to the one copied using `Duplicate( )`.

For a complete listing as well as examples showing the usage of each structure function, see Appendix B. Additional user-defined structure functions can be downloaded from the Common Function Library Project at *http://www.cflib.org*.

Query Objects

Query objects are special ColdFusion data structures that hold record sets. Query objects are similar in structure to two-dimensional arrays and are made up of rows and columns (like a spreadsheet). There are three ways to create a query object:

- Using the `cfquery` or `cfstoredproc` tag to retrieve a record set from a data source. We haven't covered the `cfstoredproc` tag yet; we'll get to it in Chapter 11. For now, just be aware that the tag can return a record set just like the `cfquery` tag.
- Certain CFML tags such as `cfftp` and `cfhttp` return information stored in a query object.
- Query objects can be manually created using `QueryNew( )` and other associated query manipulation functions.

By this point, you should be quite familiar with the first method, in which query objects are automatically returned by the `cfquery` tag. The second method has to do with certain CFML tags returning information stored as query objects. These tags are covered in detail later in the book. We're going to focus on the third method in this section, creating and manipulating query objects using `QueryNew( )` and several other CFML functions. Creating a query in this way is useful when you want to make application-generated data available as a query object. This technique is especially useful when used within custom tags and components to return a query result set. Custom tags are covered in Chapter 21, components in Chapter 22. The query manipulation functions can also add additional data to an existing query.

To create a query object, you use the `QueryNew( )` function. `QueryNew( )` takes a single argument—a comma-delimited list of column names for the query object. If you want to create a query object called `Products` with column headers for the product name, color, price, and quantity on hand, you can use the following code:

```
<cfset Products = QueryNew("ProductName, Color, Price, Qty")>
```

Once you have created a query object, the next step is to populate it with data. This is done using various query-manipulation functions. Example 6-10 shows how to use the most popular query manipulation functions to manually create a query object, populate it with data, and output the contents to the browser.

Example 6-10. Manually creating a query object and outputting to the browser

```
<!--- Create a new query object called Products and add four column
      headers --->
<cfset Products = QueryNew("ProductName, Color, Price, Qty")>

<!--- Add three blank rows of data --->
<cfset NewRows  = QueryAddRow(Products, 3)>

<!--- Populate each blank row with data for each column --->
<cfset QuerySetCell(Products, "ProductName", "Widget", 1)>
<cfset QuerySetCell(Products, "Color", "Silver", 1)>
<cfset QuerySetCell(Products, "Price", "19.99", 1)>
<cfset QuerySetCell(Products, "Qty", "46", 1)>

<cfset QuerySetCell(Products, "ProductName", "Thingy", 2)>
<cfset QuerySetCell(Products, "Color", "Red", 2)>
<cfset QuerySetCell(Products, "Price", "34.99", 2)>
<cfset QuerySetCell(Products, "Qty", "12", 2)>

<cfset QuerySetCell(Products, "ProductName", "Sprocket", 3)>
<cfset QuerySetCell(Products, "Color", "Blue", 3)>
<cfset QuerySetCell(Products, "Price", "1.50", 3)>
<cfset QuerySetCell(Products, "Qty", "460", 3)>

<!--- Create a one-dimensional array called ShippingArray to hold shipping
      prices to be appended to the query object --->
<cfset ShippingArray = ArrayNew(1)>
<cfset ShippingArray[1] = "1.99">
<cfset ShippingArray[2] = "3.48">
<cfset ShippingArray[3] = "5.00">

<!--- Create a new column called Shipping and populate it with the data from
      the ShippingArray array --->
<cfset MyNewColumn = QueryAddColumn(Products, "Shipping", ShippingArray)>
```

Example 6-10. Manually creating a query object and outputting to the browser (continued)

```
<!--- Create a table and output the contents of the query object --->
<table>
<tr>
  <th>Product</th>
  <th>Color</th>
  <th>Price</th>
  <th>Quantity</th>
  <th>Shipping</th>
</tr>
<cfoutput query="Products">
<tr>
  <td>#ProductName#</td>
  <td>#Color#</td>
  <td>#Price#</td>
  <td>#Qty#</td>
  <td>#DollarFormat(Shipping)#</td>
</tr>
</cfoutput>
</table>

<cfdump var="#Products#">
```

In this example, the `QueryNew( )` function is used to create an empty query object named `Products` and give it four column headers, `ProductName`, `Color`, `Price`, and `Qty`. Three empty rows are then added to the query object using `QueryAddRow( )`, which takes the name of a query and an optional number of rows. If the number is omitted, one blank row is added.

Next, each row is populated with data using the `QuerySetCell( )` function to populate each individual cell in the given row with data. This function takes the name of a query, a column name, a value, and an optional row number. The cell specified by the column name and row number is set to the given value. If no row number is specified, the last row in the query is used.

After this, a one-dimensional array called `ShippingArray` is created and populated with three prices. The `QueryAddColumn( )` function is used to create a new column called `Shipping` and populate it with the contents of the `ShippingArray` array.

Finally, the `cfoutput` tag is used to output the contents of the query object in a nicely formatted HTML table. The `cfdump` tag is used to help us visualize the query object's structure. You can see the results of the outputted query in Figure 6-6.

Manipulating Query Objects

Although we've already covered the main functions available for creating, appending to, and updating query objects, you should be aware of several additional techniques for working with query objects.

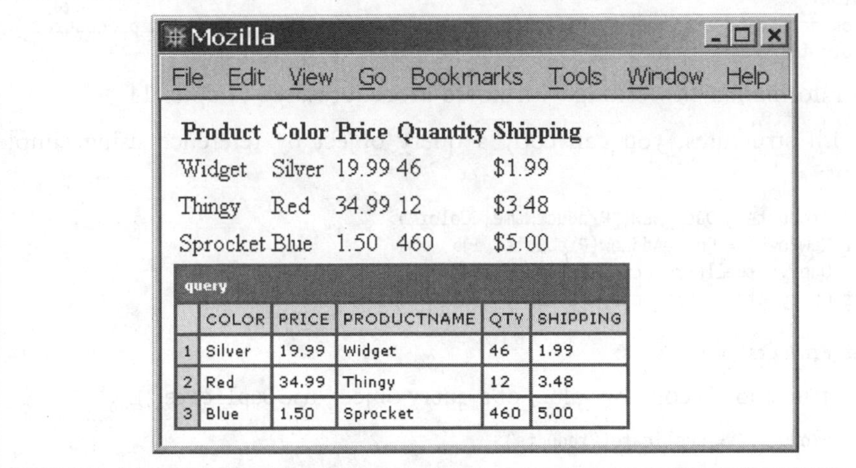

Figure 6-6. Outputting the contents of a manually created query

You can find out the total number of records in a query object by referencing *QueryName*.RecordCount:

```
<cfoutput>
There are #Products.RecordCount# products in the Products query.
</cfoutput>
```

To obtain a list of all the column names in the Products query object, use *QueryName*.ColumnList:

```
<cfoutput>
The Products query contains these columns: #Products.ColumnList#
</cfoutput>
```

You can reference the current row in a query object using *QueryName*.CurrentRow:

```
<cfloop query="Products">
  <cfoutput>Row #Products.CurrentRow#: #ProductName#</cfoutput><br>
</cfloop>
```

For query objects returned by the cfquery tag, you can get the time taken to execute the query using cfquery.ExecutionTime:

```
<cfoutput>
It took #cfquery.ExecutionTime# milliseconds to execute the query.
</cfoutput>
```

Note that this does not work for query objects manually created with the QueryNew( ) function, or with query objects returned by other tags such as cfpop and cfhttp. Attempting to reference cfquery.ExecutionTime for a query object created in any of these ways causes ColdFusion to throw an exception. If your query object is generated by calling a stored procedure via cfstoredproc, you can reference the execution time by using cfstoredproc.ExecutionTime:

```
<cfoutput>
It took #cfstoredproc.ExecutionTime# milliseconds to execute the stored procedure.
</cfoutput>
```

For more information on working with stored procedures, see Chapter 11.

Just as with structures, you can copy a query object by reference using simple assignment:

```
<cfset Products = QueryNew("ProductName, Color")>
<cfset NewRows  = QueryAddRow(Products, 1)>
<cfset QuerySetCell(Products, "ProductName", "Widget", 1)>
<cfset QuerySetCell(Products, "Color", "Silver", 1)>

<cfset Products2 = Products>
```

To make a true copy (a copy by value) of a query object, use `Duplicate( )`:

```
<cfset Products2 = Duplicate(Products)>
```

ColdFusion treats query columns like one-dimensional arrays. This means you can use array syntax to access the data in any query cell using array syntax. Consider the following query object:

```
<cfset Products = QueryNew("ProductName, Color, Price, Qty")>
<cfset NewRows  = QueryAddRow(Products, 3)>

<cfset QuerySetCell(Products, "ProductName", "Widget", 1)>
<cfset QuerySetCell(Products, "Color", "Silver", 1)>
<cfset QuerySetCell(Products, "Price", "19.99", 1)>
<cfset QuerySetCell(Products, "Qty", "46", 1)>

<cfset QuerySetCell(Products, "ProductName", "Thingy", 2)>
<cfset QuerySetCell(Products, "Color", "Red", 2)>
<cfset QuerySetCell(Products, "Price", "34.99", 2)>
<cfset QuerySetCell(Products, "Qty", "12", 2)>

<cfset QuerySetCell(Products, "ProductName", "Sprocket", 3)>
<cfset QuerySetCell(Products, "Color", "Blue", 3)>
<cfset QuerySetCell(Products, "Price", "1.50", 3)>
<cfset QuerySetCell(Products, "Qty", "460", 3)>
```

Using array syntax, you can easily refer to any query cell using the syntax *`queryName.columnName`*`[`*`row`*`]` or *`queryName`*`['`*`columnName`*`'][`*`row`*`]`. Thus, if you want to get the `ProductName` in row 3 of the query, you can do so like this:

```
<cfoutput>
#Products.ProductName[3]#
<br>-OR-<br>
#Products['ProductName'][3]#
</cfoutput>
```

You should be aware that you cannot, however, use array syntax to output all columns for a specific row. Specifying `Products.ProductName` returns the first product name in the `Products` query. Specifying `Products['ProductName']` causes ColdFusion to throw an exception.

In ColdFusion MX, you can now store any ColdFusion datatype in a query cell, including complex types such as arrays and structures. Say, for example, you have a query object that contains columns for product name, color, price, and quantity. If your products come in multiple colors, you could easily store the colors as an array within the Colors column:

```
<cfset Colors = ArrayNew(1)>
<cfset Colors[1]="Red">
<cfset Colors[2]="Silver">
<cfset Colors[3]="Blue">

<cfset Products = QueryNew("ProductName, Color, Price, Qty")>
<cfset NewRows  = QueryAddRow(Products, 3)>

<cfset QuerySetCell(Products, "ProductName", "Widget", 1)>
<cfset QuerySetCell(Products, "Color", Colors, 1)>
<cfset QuerySetCell(Products, "Price", "19.99", 1)>
<cfset QuerySetCell(Products, "Qty", "46", 1)>

<cfset QuerySetCell(Products, "ProductName", "Thingy", 2)>
<cfset QuerySetCell(Products, "Color", Colors, 2)>
<cfset QuerySetCell(Products, "Price", "34.99", 2)>
<cfset QuerySetCell(Products, "Qty", "12", 2)>

<cfset QuerySetCell(Products, "ProductName", "Sprocket", 3)>
<cfset QuerySetCell(Products, "Color", Colors, 3)>
<cfset QuerySetCell(Products, "Price", "1.50", 3)>
<cfset QuerySetCell(Products, "Qty", "460", 3)>

<cfdump var="#Products#">
```

You can get a visual representation of the data in the query object by dumping it using the cfdump tag. The results are shown in Figure 6-7.

You should be aware, however, that queries with cells containing complex datatypes cannot be used in memory queries with ColdFusion's query of query functionality. Query of query is covered in Chapter 11.

For more information on all of ColdFusion's query-manipulation functions, including the ones shown here, see Appendix B. Additional user-defined query functions can be downloaded from the Common Function Library Project at *http://www.cflib.org*.

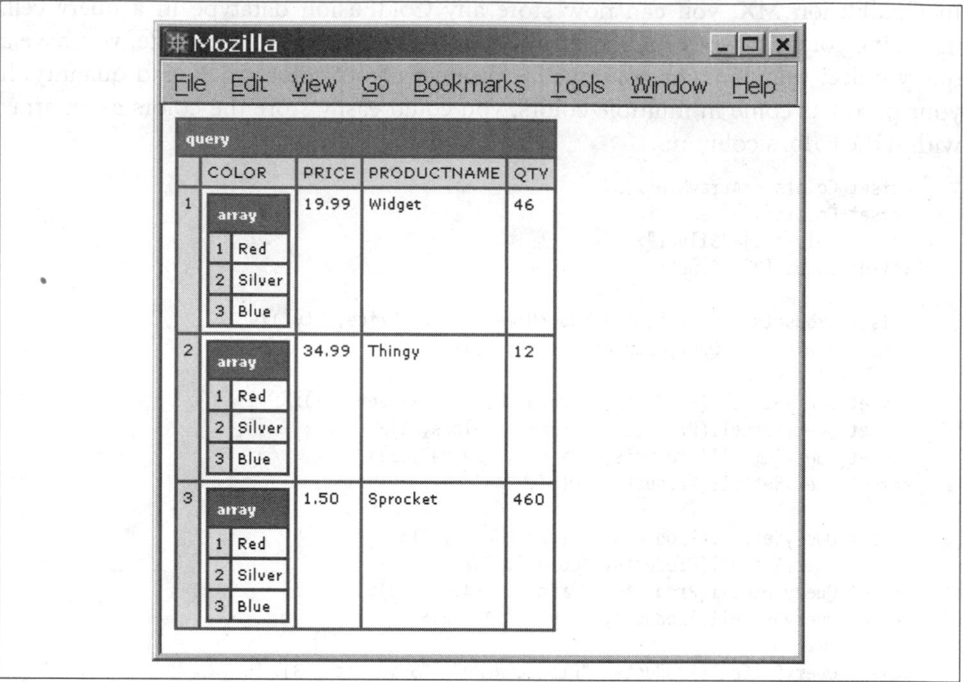

Figure 6-7. Storing an array within a query cell

CHAPTER 7

Maintaining State

By design, the Web is a stateless environment. This means that each request from a web browser to a web server is independent of every other request. While this might make for efficient use of bandwidth, it is the bane of web developers, who must be able to keep track of users as they navigate their way through an application. Without the ability to maintain state, applications have no way of knowing what information belongs to which user. To borrow a metaphor, this means that a shopping cart can't remember what items it contains, let alone which user is pushing the cart!

ColdFusion handles the stateless nature of the Web via a mechanism known as the Web Application Framework. The Web Application Framework enables you to build and manage virtually any type of application, from a simple employee directory to amazingly complex business-to-business systems and everything in between. Specifically, the Web Application Framework was devised as a means for maintaining state, setting application constants, handling errors, and managing security.

In this chapter, we'll discuss the state maintenance features of the Web Application Framework. Chapter 8 covers the security features, and Chapter 9 explores exception and error handling.

Setting Up the Web Application Framework

The first question you might be asking is, "Why do I need an application framework in the first place?" The answer is simple: the Web Application Framework allows you to group your CFML templates logically into a cohesive application or group of applications capable of maintaining state, utilizing constants, handling errors and exceptions, and enforcing security. Sound complicated? It really isn't. As usual, ColdFusion abstracts the low-level programming that would normally be required to accomplish all of the tasks I just mentioned by providing two templates that serve as the foundation for the Web Application Framework. These templates, named *Application.cfm* and *OnRequestEnd.cfm*, are responsible for setting up and controlling every aspect of the Web Application Framework.

The Application.cfm File

In order to use the Web Application Framework, you have to create a template named *Application.cfm*, a special filename reserved by ColdFusion for use in the Web Application Framework. The initial *Application.cfm* template (there can be more than one) should be placed in the root directory of your ColdFusion application. Note that the filename is spelled with a capital "A". This is especially important if you are running ColdFusion for Unix or Linux, where filenames are case sensitive.

When a CFML template is requested, ColdFusion checks to see whether there is an *Application.cfm* file in the same directory as the requested template. If so, the application template is included at the beginning of the requested template. In other words, if ColdFusion finds an *Application.cfm* file, it essentially uses `cfinclude` at the beginning of the page request to include this file. If no *Application.cfm* file is found, ColdFusion traverses up the directory tree looking for an *Application.cfm* file until it finds one.

This system allows you to specify a single *Application.cfm* file for all your ColdFusion code regardless of where the code resides in your application's directory structure, as shown in Figure 7-1.

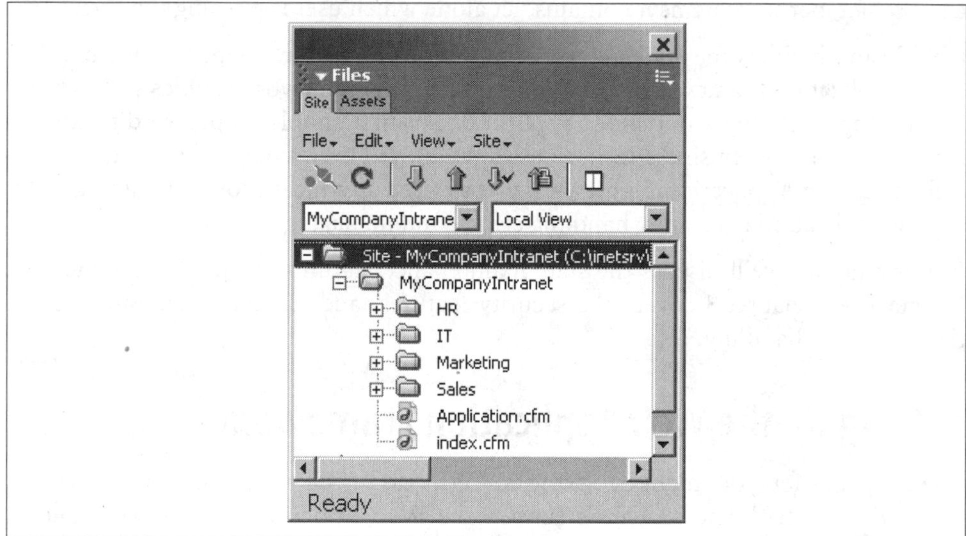

Figure 7-1. A single Application.cfm file placed in the application's root directory

It also means that you can use different *Application.cfm* files to control different segments of your application within the directory structure, as shown in Figure 7-2, because ColdFusion uses the first *Application.cfm* file it finds. (A child *Application.cfm* file does not inherit from an *Application.cfm* in a parent directory, although it is possible for one *Application.cfm* to include another via `cfinclude`.) Regardless of where you place your *Application.cfm* file or how many you have in your application's directory structure, only one *Application.cfm* file is processed per page request. Thus, if your application template includes additional templates with `cfinclude`, ColdFusion still performs just one search for an *Application.cfm* file as part of the initial request; it doesn't search for additional *Application.cfm* files for each included file.

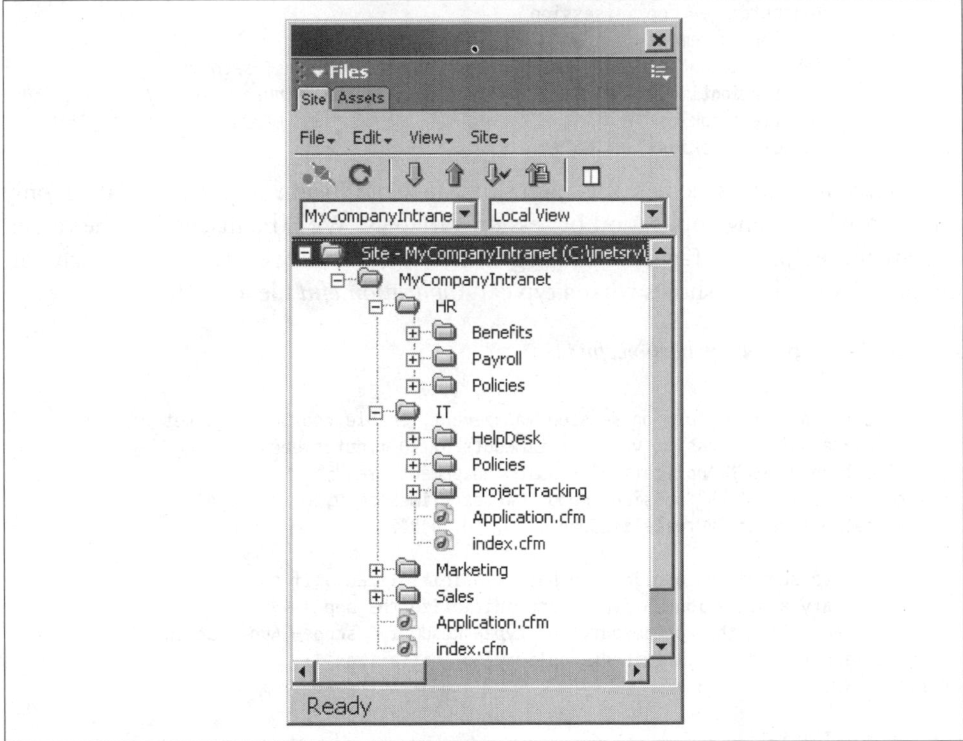

Figure 7-2. Each directory has its own Application.cfm file

Now that you understand how to create an *Application.cfm* file and where to save it, let's look at what it consists of. As I mentioned earlier, the *Application.cfm* template is used for a number of tasks within the Web Application Framework, including:

- Maintaining state by providing a means for creating application, client, and session variables
- Setting application constants, such as data-source names, source directories, and style elements
- Handling errors that occur within your application
- Providing security services such as user authentication and entitlements

At the most basic level, the *Application.cfm* template should contain a cfapplication tag. The cfapplication tag names the application and sets state management options. Here's the syntax for the cfapplication tag:

```
<cfapplication name="application_name"
        clientmanagement="Yes|No"
        clientstorage="client_storage_type"
        loginstorage="cookie|session"
        sessionmanagement="Yes|No"
        sessiontimeout="#CreateTimeSpan(days, hours, minutes, seconds)#"
        applicationtimeout="#CreateTimeSpan(days, hours, minutes, seconds)#"
        setclientcookies="Yes|No"
        setdomaincookies="Yes|No">
```

The name attribute specifies the name of the ColdFusion application. It is only required when using application or session variables. We'll be discussing the rest of the attributes of the cfapplication tag in more detail as we proceed through this chapter. Example 7-1 shows what a typical *Application.cfm* file looks like.

Example 7-1. A typical Application.cfm file

```
<cfsilent>
<!--- Set the app name, turn on session management, enable cookies, and set
      application and session variable timeouts of 30 minutes each --->
<cfapplication name="MyApplication" sessionmanagement="Yes"
   setclientcookies="Yes" sessiontimeout="#CreateTimeSpan(0, 0, 30, 0)#"
   applicationtimeout="#CreateTimeSpan(0, 0, 30, 0)#">

<!--- Check to see if the application has been initialized.  If not, set the
      necessary application variables and initialize the app --->
<cflock timeout="30" throwontimeout="No" type="ReadOnly" scope="Application">
  <cfset IsInitialized = IsDefined('application.Initialized')>
</cflock>

<cfif not IsInitialized>
  <cflock timeout="30" throwontimeout="No" type="Exclusive" scope="Application">
    <cfif not IsDefined('application.Initialized')>
      <!--- Determine whether server is beta or production and set application
            variables appropriately --->
      <cfif CGI.server_name is "beta.example.com">
        <cfset application.TheDatasource = "TestDSN">
        <cfset application.AdminEmail = "dev@example.com">
        <cfset application.UploadDirectory = "D:\uploads\">
      <cfelse>
        <cfset application.TheDatasource = "ProdDSN">
        <cfset application.AdminEmail = "webmaster@example.com">
        <cfset application.UploadDirectory = "E:\uploads\">
      </cfif>
      <!--- Set the application.initialized variable to true so that this block
            of code does not execute every time the Application.cfm file is
            called --->
      <cfset application.Initialized = true>
    </cfif>
```

Example 7-1. A typical Application.cfm file (continued)

```
  </cflock>
</cfif>
</cfsilent>
```

The OnRequestEnd.cfm File

The *OnRequestEnd.cfm* template is executed after every template request. The main purpose for this template is to allow you to include a common footer at the bottom of each requested page.

The *OnRequestEnd.cfm* template must be located in the same directory as the *Application.cfm* file used by ColdFusion. You may not have an *OnRequestEnd.cfm* template without a corresponding *Application.cfm*. It is also important to note that the "O", "R", and "E" in the filename must be capitalized. This is especially true on Linux- and Unix-based ColdFusion servers where filenames are case sensitive. If a ColdFusion template throws an error during execution, the *OnRequestEnd.cfm* template doesn't execute. Likewise, if a `cfabort` or `cfexit` tag is encountered in the calling template, the *OnRequestEnd.cfm* template isn't executed.

Using Shared Scope Variables

As I mentioned in the introduction, the Web is a stateless environment. ColdFusion addresses this problem by providing five variable scopes you can use to maintain state within your application: application, client, cookie, session, and server. These are known as shared variable scopes because the variables you set within them can exist from template to template, in spite of the stateless nature of the Web. This allows you to build applications that can share data across multiple templates without having to pass the values via form fields or URL variables.

Here's an overview of the types of shared scope variables you can use in your ColdFusion applications:

Application

Application variables define application-wide settings for your application, such as data-source names and other constants. Application variables are stored in the server's RAM and are most often defined in the *Application.cfm* template. Application variables are available to all users accessing the named application and are often referred to as global variables. Application variables must always be referenced using the `application` prefix, as in `application.`*`variable_name`*. By default, a single predefined application variable is available:

```
application.ApplicationName
```

`application.ApplicationName` returns the name of the application as defined in the `name` attribute of the `cfapplication` tag.

Client

Client variables store values associated with a particular user across multiple sessions. An application might use a client variable to remember things such as the last time a user visited a site or their font size/color preferences. By default, client variables are stored in the system registry on Windows servers or in a text file on Solaris, Linux, and HP-UX servers, but they can also be stored in a cookie or a database. Client variables are often used in conjunction with database storage for clustered ColdFusion applications. When creating client variables, the variable name must always be referenced using the `client` prefix, as in `client.`*`variable_name`*. This is optional when reading client variables. In addition to the client variables you create in an application, there are several read-only client variables that ColdFusion creates automatically:

```
client.CFID
client.CFToken
client.HitCount
client.LastVisit
client.TimeCreated
client.URLToken
```

Cookie

Cookie variables hold the values of HTTP cookies retrieved from a user's web browser. Cookies are a unique type of shared scope variable that are stored on the client machine and sent to the ColdFusion server each time a page is requested. By default, ColdFusion uses cookies to store the `CFID` and `CFToken` values associated with client and session variable management. Additional uses for cookies typically include storing a unique identifier (such as a user ID or UUID) for a particular user that is used by each page request to determine what content to deliver to the user.

Session

Session variables are shared scope variables that store information for a specific user session. Session variables are held in the server's memory and exist for a finite amount of time (as specified in the *Application.cfm* template or in the ColdFusion Administrator). Each session is unique to a user and can be referenced across all ColdFusion templates in a given application. Session variables are often used for things like shopping carts and user authentication systems. Session variables must be specifically set and must be referenced as `session.`*`variable_name`*. By default, the following predefined session variables are available:

```
session.CFID
session.CFToken
session.SessionID
session.URLToken
```

Server

Server variables, as their name implies, store data associated with the server on which ColdFusion is running. Server variables are stored in the server's RAM and are available to all ColdFusion applications and users. Additionally, server variables exist until the ColdFusion Application Server is stopped. Server variables are often used in multiplatform ColdFusion applications where the application behaves differently depending on what platform the code is running on. You can create your own server variables using `cfset` or `cfparam`, or you can reference the following predefined ones:

```
server.ColdFusion.Appserver (MX Only)
server.ColdFusion.ProductName
server.ColdFusion.ProductVersion
server.ColdFusion.ProductLevel
server.ColdFusion.RootDir (MX Only)
server.ColdFusion.SerialNumber
server.ColdFusion.SupportedLocales
server.ColdFusion.Expiration
server.OS.AdditionalInformation
server.OS.Arch (MX Only)
server.OS.BuildNumber
server.OS.Name
server.OS.Version
```

Server variables must always be referenced using the server prefix, as in `server.`*`variable_name`*. Because server variables exist until the ColdFusion server is stopped, you should try to limit the number of server variables you create, as the memory consumption required might negatively affect performance.

Locking

Before we can discuss the details of the different kinds of shared scope variables in ColdFusion, we need to spend a little time talking about a concept known as *locking*. Because ColdFusion is a multithreaded application server, it is possible for multiple threads to attempt to access the same variable at the same time. For application, session, and server variables, this can be a problem. In versions of ColdFusion prior to MX, this could lead to server instability and crashes due to memory collisions. In ColdFusion MX, the underlying Java architecture for managing shared scopes is thread safe. This means you no longer have to worry about memory collisions when two threads attempt to access the same shared scope variable at the same time. You do, however, have to worry about a situation known as a *race condition*.

A race condition occurs when two or more threads try to access the same data at relatively the same time. This can result in unexpected behavior, as the actual timing of each read/write may not happen in the desired order. A common example of this is two threads that try to access the same file at the same time. If thread A tries to write to the file at the same time that thread B is trying to read from it, there is no way of knowing whether thread B is reading the old data, the new data, or a corrupted version of the data. This same concept can be applied to shared scope variables as well. It's easy to imagine a situation in which the value stored in a session, application, or server variable could be misrepresented if a race condition occurred.

Fortunately, ColdFusion's locking mechanism can prevent race conditions. When I talk about locking, what I'm really referring to is ColdFusion's ability to manage concurrent access to specific chunks of code. Locking can be broken down into two types, exclusive and read-only. *Exclusive locking* means that ColdFusion single-threads access to a particular chunk of code; only one thread at a time is allowed to access code that has been exclusively locked. Any other threads that attempt to access an exclusively locked block of code are queued until the initial request completes. Exclusive locks should be used when writing to application, session, and server variables in order to prevent race conditions. They should also be used when writing to nonthread-safe objects or when using file-manipulation tags such as `cffile`, `cfindex`, and `cfcollection`. Because exclusive locks single-thread concurrent requests, they have a negative impact on performance. For this reason, it is important to use them sparingly.

The other type of lock you can use is a *read-only lock*. When you place a read-only lock around a particular piece of code, ColdFusion doesn't automatically single-thread access to that code. Instead, it prevents an exclusive lock from being placed on the code while it is being read from. In other words, if you have a read-only lock placed around a chunk of code that reads a shared scope variable, multiple threads can read the variable's value, but a concurrent request to write to the variable isn't processed until the read operations complete. Conversely, if an exclusive lock is already in effect, a read-only lock waits until the exclusive lock is released before proceeding. Because of this, read-only locks don't generally result in degraded performance. Read-only locks should be used any time you read data from a shared scope variable or perform a file-based operation in which the potential exists for concurrent write access by another thread. For clarity and consistency, all examples in this book use locking when dealing with application, session, and server variables.

Now that you understand the why of locking, let's discuss the how. ColdFusion allows you to deal with locking via the `cflock` tag. The `cflock` tag provides a programmatic means or protecting access to shared scope variables as well as other blocks of code. `cflock` should be used when reading and writing application, session, and server variables within your ColdFusion applications. `cflock` can also be used to lock access to non-thread-safe objects (such as CFX tags, covered in Chapter 21, and COM objects, covered in Chapter 27) and to file-manipulation operations (`cffile`, `cfdirectory`, `cfcollection`, and `cfindex`) that could result in multiple threads attempting to access an already open file.

The `cflock` tag uses different attribute combinations depending on the context it is used in. The tag usage and syntax can be divided into three categories based on these combinations: locking shared scope variables at the scope level, locking shared scope variables using named locks, and locking access to blocks of code (such as file and object access) using named locks.

Locking shared scope variables at the scope level

The most common use for the cflock tag is for locking access to shared persistent scope variables (application, session, and server variables). As we already discussed, you should lock access to all reads and writes of these types of variables. The following example demonstrates one way to lock application, session, or server variables using scope-level locking:

```
<cflock scope="Session" type="Exclusive" timeout="30" throwontimeout="Yes">
  <cfset session.Username="pmoney">
  <cfset session.AccessLevel=5>
</cflock>

<cflock scope="Session" type="ReadOnly" timeout="30" throwontimeout="Yes">
  <cfoutput>
  Username: #session.Username#<br>
  Access Level: #session.AccessLevel#
  </cfoutput>
</cflock>
```

The first thing you'll notice is that the example uses two sets of cflock tags. We'll get to the reason for this in just a moment. For now, look at the first cflock tag used. The scope attribute references the scope of the variable you are attempting to lock access to. Possible values are Application, Server, and Session. In this case, we are locking access to a session variable, so we set scope to Session.

The next attribute, type, specifies the type of lock to employ. Possible entries are ReadOnly or Exclusive. ReadOnly allows more than one read request to access the block of code within the cflock tag at a time. This option should be used when reading application, session, and server variables. This is the faster of the two options. Exclusive allows only one request at a time to access the block of code within the cflock tag. This option should be used when writing data to persistent variables, as is the case with the first cflock tag in our example.

The timeout attribute specifies the time in seconds that ColdFusion should wait when attempting to obtain an exclusive lock before timing out. It is a required attribute. throwontimeout indicates how ColdFusion should behave in the event that a cflock request times out. If set to Yes and a timeout occurs, ColdFusion throws an error that can be caught with cftry/cfcatch (which are discussed in more detail in Chapter 9). If No, the template continues execution after skipping the code within the cflock tag. The throwontimeout attribute is optional and defaults to Yes.

Locking shared scope variable access using named locks

Using scope-level locking to lock access to shared scope variables is an easy way to ensure access to shared scope variables. This convenience does come with a performance cost, though. When you use a shared scope lock, you tell ColdFusion to use a single lock for all scope-locked code that accesses the specified scope. For session variables, this means that access is locked for a particular user's session (not all sessions). For application variables, access is locked for the entire named application. Using a scoped lock for server variables effectively locks access for the entire server. An exclusive lock to an entire scope means that no other threads can access that scope until the exclusive lock is released. This can negatively affect performance, especially under load, as multiple threads have to queue while waiting for the exclusive lock to be released.

A better solution is to use named locks to lock access to shared scope variables. Named locks give you finer control over how and when code is locked. It offers better overall performance than scoped locks, but it comes at the cost of convenience. When you use named locks, you must make sure you use the same lock name for all code that accesses a particular variable. To illustrate this, we can rewrite the code we used in our scope-level locking example to use a named lock instead:

```
<cflock name="AccessLevel" type="Exclusive" timeout="30" throwontimeout="Yes">
  <cfset session.Username="pmoney">
  <cfset session.AccessLevel=5>
</cflock>

<cflock name="AccessLevel" type="ReadOnly" timeout="30" throwontimeout="Yes">
  <cfoutput>
  Username: #session.Username#<br>
  Access Level: #session.AccessLevel#
  </cfoutput>
</cflock>
```

As you can see, we used the same lock name for both read and write access to the `session.Username` and `session.AccessLevel` variables. We must lock access to these variables using the same lock name throughout our application.

Locking access to nonthread-safe objects and file operations

Besides locking access to shared scope variables, the `cflock` tag can also be used to lock access to nonthread-safe objects and file-manipulation operations such as `cffile`, `cfcollection`, and `cfindex`. In each of these instances, the `name` attribute should specify a name for the lock. All locks for code accessing the same object or file should have the same name in order to be effective. Failure to use the same lock name opens the possibility for data corruption as locks to the same variable, object, or file without the same name aren't able to synchronize.

In the case of nonthread-safe objects, locking is important to guard against potential data corruption resulting from concurrent access. Since these objects aren't designed to handle concurrent access from multiple threads, all access to them should be exclusively locked. For example, to lock access to a nonthread-safe CFX tag called `cfx_mytag`, use the following code:

```
<cflock name="cfx_mytag_Lock" type="Exclusive" timeout="10" throwontimeout="Yes">
  <cfx_mytag SomeAttribute="Some value">
</cflock>
```

File-manipulation operations should be locked to prevent multiple threads from concurrently trying to read/write to the same file because of the possibility of data corruption. If there is a possibility that a particular file can be written to by multiple threads concurrently, you need to place read locks around all code that reads the file and exclusive locks on all operations that write to the file. You should be sure to keep lock naming (both read-only and exclusive) consistent across your applications. The most common file-manipulation operations that require locking are `cffile`, `cfdirectory`, `cfcollection`, and `cfindex`. Additionally, you may want to lock calls to `cfhttp` and `cfftp` depending on how you use these tags. Locking examples for each tag are given in the chapters dealing with the specific tags.

Additional locking considerations

Now that we've talked about the basics of locking in ColdFusion, let's turn our attention to a few scenarios that developers inevitably run into. The first scenario involves a situation where you need to both read and write to a shared scope variable in a block of code. Let's say we have a situation in which we need to evaluate whether or not an application variable called `application.Initialized` exists. If the variable doesn't exist, two application variables are written to. For example:

```
<cfif not IsDefined(application.Initialized')>
  <cfset application.TheDatasource = "MyDatasource">
  <cfset application.DefaultDir = "c:\temp">
</cfif>
```

Based on what we discussed earlier, it is obvious that you'll need to place a read-only lock on the code that evaluates `application.Initialized` and an exclusive lock around the code that writes to the two other application variables. One way to do this is to place a single exclusive lock around the entire operation:

```
<cflock name="Globals_Lock" type="Exclusive" timeout="30" throwontimeout="No">
<cfif not IsDefined('application.Initialized')>
  <cfset application.TheDatasource = "MyDatasource">
  <cfset application.DefaultDir = "c:\temp">
</cfif>
</cflock>
```

Using an exclusive lock forces ColdFusion to single-thread access to this particular piece of code each time it is requested. Normally, you won't experience very much of a performance hit by single threading such a basic operation. However, in the case of a more complex operation, such as a long running query, you run a greater risk of queued requests timing out while waiting to obtain an exclusive lock. To get around this problem, you can use another technique that involves making a local copy of the shared scope variable in the request scope, thus allowing you to avoid the excessive use of read locks:

```
<cflock name="Globals_Lock" type="Readonly" timeout="30">
  <cfset request.Initialized = IsDefined('application.Initialized')>
</cflock>
```

```
<cfif not request.Initialized>
  <cflock name="Globals_Lock" type="Exclusive" timeout="30">
    <cfif not IsDefined('application.Initialized')>
      <cfset application.TheDatasource = "MyDatasource">
      <cfset application.DefaultDir = "c:\temp">
      <cfset application.Initialized = true>
    </cfif>
  </cflock>
</cfif>
```

Another situation where you can use this technique is with code that appears to need nested locks in order to lock differently scoped variables, such as:

```
<cfquery name="GetRecord" datasource="#application.dsn#"
         username="#application.dbusername#"
         password="#application.dbpassword#">
    SELECT * FROM MyTable WHERE Name = '#session.Name#'
</cfquery>
```

As you can see, this example presents a bit of a challenge. Because the query uses both application and session variables, you can't place a single scope-level lock on the entire operation. The solution seems to call for nested locks, as follows:

```
<cflock scope="Session" type="Readonly" timeout="10">
  <cflock scope="Application" type="Readonly" timeout="10">
    <cfquery name="GetRecord" datasource="#application.dsn#"
             username="#application.dbusername#"
             password="#application.dbpassword#">
      SELECT * FROM MyTable WHERE Name = '#session.Name#'
    </cfquery>
  </cflock>
</cflock>
```

While this solution does indeed work, it isn't recommended, for a number of reasons. First, you really don't want to place a lock around an operation such as a query, as the time it takes to complete the query can be rather long compared to other typically locked operations, such as variable reads and writes. Second, nesting locks can lead to a problem known as a *deadlock*, where no request can access a locked piece of code, resulting in a timeout. Deadlocks occur when you have inconsistencies in how nested locks are implemented. As a rule, it is recommended you always follow this sequence when nesting locks:

1. Lock the session scope.
2. Lock the application scope.
3. Lock the server scope.

Strict adherence to these guidelines helps ensure you don't unintentionally create a potential deadlock in your application.

The preferred way to solve the problem from the previous example is to copy both the application and the session variables to the request scope, eliminating both the need to place a lock around the query operation and the need for nested locks:

```
<cflock name="DSN_Lock" timeout="30" throwontimeout="No" type="Readonly">
  <cfset request.dsn = application.dsn>
  <cfset request.dbUsername = application.dbusername>
  <cfset request.dbPassword = application.dbpassword>
</cflock>

<cflock name="DSN_Lock" timeout="30" throwontimeout="No" type="Readonly">
    <cfset request.Name = session.Name>
</cflock>

<cfquery name="GetRecord" datasource="#request.dsn#"
         username="#request.dbusername#" password="#request.dbpassword#">
    SELECT * FROM MyTable WHERE Name = '#request.Name#'
</cfquery>
```

An even simpler solution here is simply to use the request scope for all of your application's constants. You can easily set the request variables in your *Application.cfm* template. Even though they are set each time a page is requested, the overhead is minimal, and it may be worth not having to mess with locks and scope copying.

There is one exception to these techniques you need to be aware of. If you want to copy a structure to a different variable scope such as the request scope, you can't do it using the `cfset` tag alone. This is because structures aren't really copied to the new scope. Instead, a pointer is created in the new scope that points to the variable in the old scope. Because of this, any time you reference the variable in the new scope, you are actually referencing the original variable. This means you can't simply move a variable containing a structure to the request scope to avoid having to lock access to that variable.

In order to copy a structure without creating a pointer to it, you need to use the `Duplicate( )` function. Consider a structure named `Grades` that is stored as a session variable. If you attempt to assign `session.Grades` to the request scope using the `cfset` tag, you end up with a pointer to the variable in the session scope:

```
<cfset request.Grades = session.Grades>
```

Instead, to create a true copy of the `Grades` structure, you need to use the `Duplicate( )` function:

```
<cflock name="Grades_Lock" type="ReadOnly" timeout="10">
  <cfset request.Grades = Duplicate(session.Grades)>
</cflock>
```

Copying a structure using the `Duplicate( )` function ensures you have a true copy of the structure, not a pointer.

One final scenario worth mentioning is known as write once, read many. This is common when dealing with shared scope variables that you write to once, but read from many times. The writing usually takes place in an *Application.cfm* template when the variables are first assigned values. After that, they are not updated again. They are, however, frequently read from in other application templates. In this scenario, you only need to lock the write to the variables with an exclusive lock, but you do not need to lock any reads from the variables. This scenario is most common when dealing with application variables.

Application Variables

You can think of application variables as global variables within a ColdFusion application, because they are available to all templates within an application without regard to user sessions. Application variables typically define application-wide settings such as default directories and data-source names. Any ColdFusion datatype may be assigned to an application variable. Application variables are most often set in the *Application.cfm* file. Like session and server variables, application variables exist in the server's RAM and have a set timeout period. This timeout period can be set using the `applicationtimeout` attribute of the `cfapplication` tag. The following example shows how to set application variables within the *Application.cfm* file:

```
<cfsilent>
<cfapplication name="MyApplication"
  applicationtimeout="#CreateTimeSpan(0, 2, 0, 0)#">

<cflock scope="Application" type="Readonly" timeout="30">
  <cfset request.Initialized = IsDefined('application.Initialized')>
</cflock>

<cfif not request.Initialized>
  <cflock scope="Application" type="Exclusive" timeout="30">
    <cfif not IsDefined('application.Initialized')>
      <cfset application.TheDatasource = "MyDatasource">
      <cfset application.AdminEmail = "webmaster@mydomain.com">
      <cfset application.BGColor = "##FFFFCC">
      <cfset application.Initialized = true>
    </cfif>
  </cflock>
</cfif>
</cfsilent>
```

In this example, the `cfsilent` tag suppresses any output that might be generated by the tags within the *Application.cfm* file. This is because ColdFusion has a tendency to generate unnecessary whitespace in the output returned to the browser, resulting in pages that take longer to download. Suppressing the whitespace results in smaller files that, in turn, translate into faster downloads.

The `cfapplication` tag simply sets the application name and a timeout for any application variables used in the application. In this case, we set the timeout for application variables to two hours. This is done using the `CreateTimeSpan( )` function. `CreateTimeSpan( )` allows us to specify a date/time object that can be added to and subtracted from other date/time objects. The `CreateTimeSpan( )` function creates the date/time object from a comma-delimited list of four values: *`days`*, *`hours`*, *`minutes`*, and *`seconds`*. Next, we test for the existence of a variable called `application.Initialized` and store the result (either `true` or `false`) in a request scope variable called request.Initialized. This is done to make locking the code easier. The next block of code starts with a cfif statement that checks to see if an application variable named request.Initialized is false. If it is, the code within the cfif tags is executed. (You'll see the importance of this in just a second.) If not, the block of code is skipped.

If request.Initialized is false, four application variables are set using the cfset tag. Before these variables can be set, however, write access must first be locked. This is accomplished using the cflock tag. The scope attribute is set to Application since we want to lock access while we set application variables. Because we are writing values to application variables, we set the type attribute to Exclusive. This ensures that no one else can access these application variables while we assign them values. The timeout attribute is required and specifies the time in seconds that ColdFusion should wait when attempting to obtain an exclusive lock before timing out. Note the use of a second check for the existence of application.Initialized. This is done to guard against the possibility that two requests for the *Application.cfm* template at the same moment could cause a race condition.

The first application variable we set is called application.TheDatasource; it contains the name of the data source used throughout the application. Setting the data-source name here allows us to insert the variable name into cfquery statements as opposed to the actual data-source name. This makes it easy to change the data-source name at a later point. Instead of having to open every template within your application to change the hardcoded data-source name, all you have to do is open the *Application.cfm* file and change the name of the data source you assigned to the application. TheDatasource variable.

The next two application variables, application.AdminEmail and application. BGColor, store an administrator's email address and a default background color for the web site. Again, the value here isn't in the one-to-one substitution but in the ability to change any of these values once and have the changes reflected across your application.

The final application variable we set, application.Initialized, is used as a control variable to indicate whether the application variables within the *Application.cfm* file have already been set. Because the *Application.cfm* file is called with each request for a CFML template, it is important that we have a way to determine whether application variables have already been set. Resetting the application variables every time the *Application.cfm* file is called is a waste of resources and processing time, as application variables need to be set only once within an application. The solution is to set an application variable called application.Initialized to true the first time the *Application.cfm* file is called. Once this variable has been created, it is easy to check whether it exists each time *Application.cfm* is executed. If the variable exists, there is no need to set the application variables. If the variable doesn't exist, we know that the application variables haven't been set yet, and we can execute the appropriate code to set them.

You should note that application variables shouldn't be used within a clustered environment, as they are stored in the RAM of a single ColdFusion server and may not be available to other servers within the cluster. The exception to this is in the case of session-aware or "sticky" clusters. We'll talk more about session-aware clusters later in the chapter.

Because application variables are stored in a structure object called `application`, you can manipulate application variables using structure functions. For example, to delete an application variable (e.g., for debugging purposes) called `application.Datasource`, you can use the `StructDelete( )` function:

```
<cflock scope="Application" type="Exclusive" timeout="60" throwontimeout="No">
  <cfset StructDelete(application,"Datasource")>
</cflock>
```

Client Variables

Client variables store values associated with a particular client or, to use the more common term, user. Most often, they are used to maintain state as a user navigates from page to page throughout an application. What makes client variables different from session variables is that they can live across multiple sessions. That is, client variables are stored by the ColdFusion server and can be retrieved during subsequent visits by the user. By default, client variables are stored in the system registry on Windows servers or in a text file on Unix, Linux, and HP-UX servers, but they can also be stored in a cookie or a database.* Client variables are commonly used to store things such as user preferences for highly personalized applications. These preferences often include background and text colors as well as font faces and sizes. Client variables can also be used in place of session variables in clustered environments where it is essential to maintain state in the event that a user is redirected from one server to another. In order to use client variables, you have to enable them using the `cfapplication` tag within your application's *Application.cfm* file:

```
<cfsilent>
  <cfapplication name="MyApplication" clientmanagement="Yes"
       setclientcookies="Yes" clientstorage="Registry">
</cfsilent>
```

In this example, there are four attributes for the `cfapplication` tag to consider. The `name` attribute specifies the name to associate with the application and all its shared

* In versions of ColdFusion prior to MX, Unix, Linux, and HP-UX versions of ColdFusion stored client variables in a "pseudo-registry." In ColdFusion MX, this is no longer the case. On these platforms, client variables are stored in a text file. For performance reasons, using the "registry" setting to store client variables is not recommended on these platforms.

scope variables. The `clientmanagement` attribute must be set to `Yes` in order to use client variables. `setclientcookies` determines whether to save the `CFID` and `CFToken` values as HTTP cookies on the user's machine. If you set this attribute to `No`, you must be sure to manually pass the `CFID` and `CFToken` values from template to template. Techniques for doing this are described later in this section. The final attribute, `clientstorage`, determines which method to use for storing the client variables. Possible options include `Registry` (the default), `Database`, and `Cookie`. Each of these methods will be described in detail shortly.

Besides the client variables you create yourself, ColdFusion creates several client variables automatically:

`client.CFID`
: An incremental ID number created by the ColdFusion Application Server for each client accessing the server.

`client.CFToken`
: A random token that combines with the `CFID` to form a unique identifier for each client visiting your site.

`client.HitCount`
: An integer that represents the number of times a client has visited the web site.

`client.LastVisit`
: The time and date of a client's last visit to the web site.

`client.TimeCreated`
: The time and date that the `CFID` and `CFToken` were created.

`client.URLToken`
: A concatenation of the `CFID` and `CFToken` values that can be appended to a URL when cookies aren't used for client variable storage.

By default, ColdFusion MX uses an eight-digit random number for the value of `CFToken`. Although sufficient for most purposes, this method doesn't guarantee a unique `CFToken` value. You can guarantee a unique `CFToken` value by making a small configuration change in the ColdFusion Administrator. In the Settings section, simply check the box labeled "Use UUID for cftoken."

Making this change causes ColdFusion to generate a `CFToken` consisting of a random 16-digit hexadecimal number prepended to a UUID (Universal Unique Identifier). To understand how this all looks, consider the following UUID generated by ColdFusion:

```
777A3190-6D65-11D4-BC6B00105A16C3AD
```

If the same UUID were used in generating a `CFToken` value, it might look something like this:

```
003cdf23ce012fdb-777a3190-6d65-11d4-bc6b-00105a16c3ad
```

Like all shared scope variables in ColdFusion MX, client variables are stored in a named structure called `client`. You can manipulate this structure just as you would any other. You can also obtain a list of all currently available client variables (excluding the system-generated ones) using the `GetClientVariablesList( )` function:

```
<cfoutput>
Client Variables available within this application: #GetClientVariablesList( )#
</cfoutput>
```

Client-variable storage options

ColdFusion offers three options for client-variable storage: the system registry, browser cookies, or an external data source. A default storage mechanism can be set within the ColdFusion Administrator. Figure 7-3 shows the ColdFusion Administrator page for managing client-variable storage options.

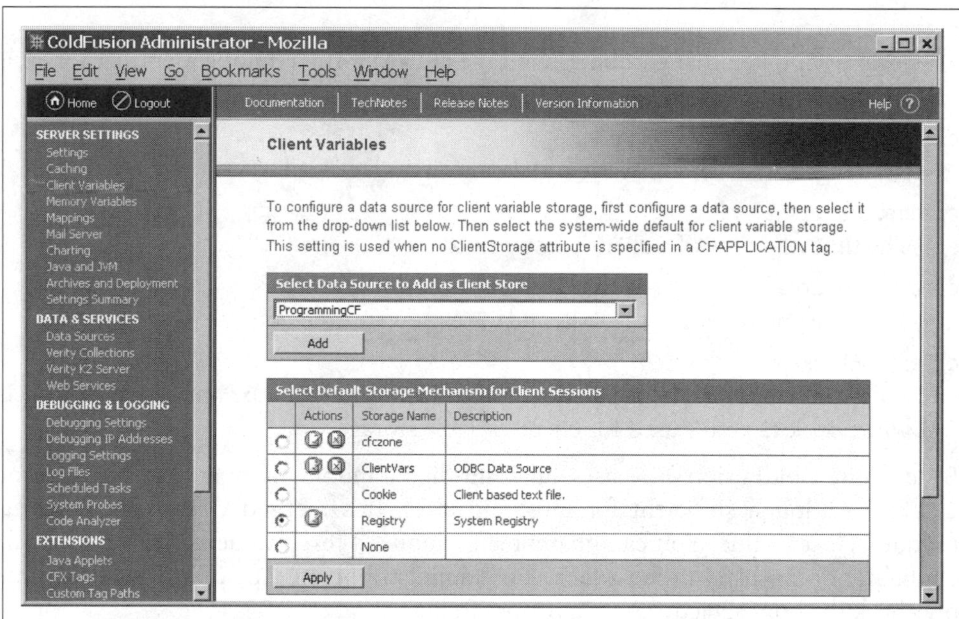

Figure 7-3. Managing client-variable storage options within the ColdFusion Administrator

You can override the default client-variable storage mechanism set in the ColdFusion Administrator by using the `clientstorage` attribute of the `cfapplication` tag to specify the method you wish to use. You should note that you can access client variables only for the storage method specified for a particular application, even if you have client variables stored in another storage type. To help you decide which client-variable storage option is right for you, here are some pros and cons of each of the three storage methods:

System registry (default)

Setting `clientstorage` to `Registry` stores all client variables in the system registry on Windows servers, or in a text file on Unix, Linux, and HP-UX servers. This method is the easiest to implement and offers relatively good performance on Windows but sub-par performance on the other platforms. Additionally, size limitations of the system registry can affect scalability. Also, client variables stored in the registry can't be used in a clustered environment. Client variables stored in the registry are automatically purged after 10 days of inactivity by the client. This 10-day period can be modified using the ColdFusion Administrator.

Cookie

Specifying `Cookie` for `clientstorage` causes client variables to be stored in browser cookies. This storage mechanism places the responsibility for variable storage on the client as opposed to the server. If you choose to store client variables in cookies, ColdFusion stores any client variables you set in a special cookie. This cookie is named `cfclient_`*appname*, where *appname* is the name of your application as specified in the *Application.cfm* template. Additionally, ColdFusion stores the automatically created client variables `HitCount`, `LastVisited`, and `TimeCreated` in a special cookie called `CFGlobals`.

While this may seem like the ideal situation from a performance standpoint, there are a number of potential problems with this storage method. First, you can't set client variables for users that can't or choose not to accept cookies. The second issue is that ColdFusion limits the amount of data set as a cookie to 4 KB. In addition, many browsers have a 20-cookie-per-host limit. This means that only 20 cookies can be set by your server at any one time. If the 20-cookie limit is reached, any new cookies that are added automatically overwrite older cookies. Because ColdFusion automatically uses three of these cookies (`CFID`, `CFToken`, `CFGlobals`) to store read-only client information, only 17 cookies are available per host. The default timeout for cookies is 38 years.

External data source

Setting `clientstorage` to `External` stores client variables in an external data source, which allows you to keep your client data in a platform-independent format. It also allows you to use client variables within a clustered environment. However, using an external data source to store client variables can negatively impact performance because each read or write of a client variable requires a database transaction. If you choose to use an external data source to store your client variables, ColdFusion can automatically create the necessary database tables for you. It is recommended that whatever data source you use be dedicated to the storage and retrieval of client variables. The default timeout for client variables stored in an external database is 90 days. This timeout period can be modified using the ColdFusion Administrator.

Creating an external data source for client variable storage

If you decide to use an external data source to store your client variables, you need to create the necessary database tables and register the data source with the ColdFusion Administrator. You may manually create the tables, or you can have ColdFusion create them for you. Whichever method you choose, the first step is to register the data source with the ColdFusion Administrator. To do this, you need to go to the Data Sources section of the ColdFusion Administrator and register the data source. The second step is to access the Client Variables section of the ColdFusion Administrator, as shown in Figure 7-3. To add a new data source for storing client variables, highlight the data-source name in the drop-down box and click the Add button. You will then be presented with three options for configuring your data source. These choices can be seen in Figure 7-4.

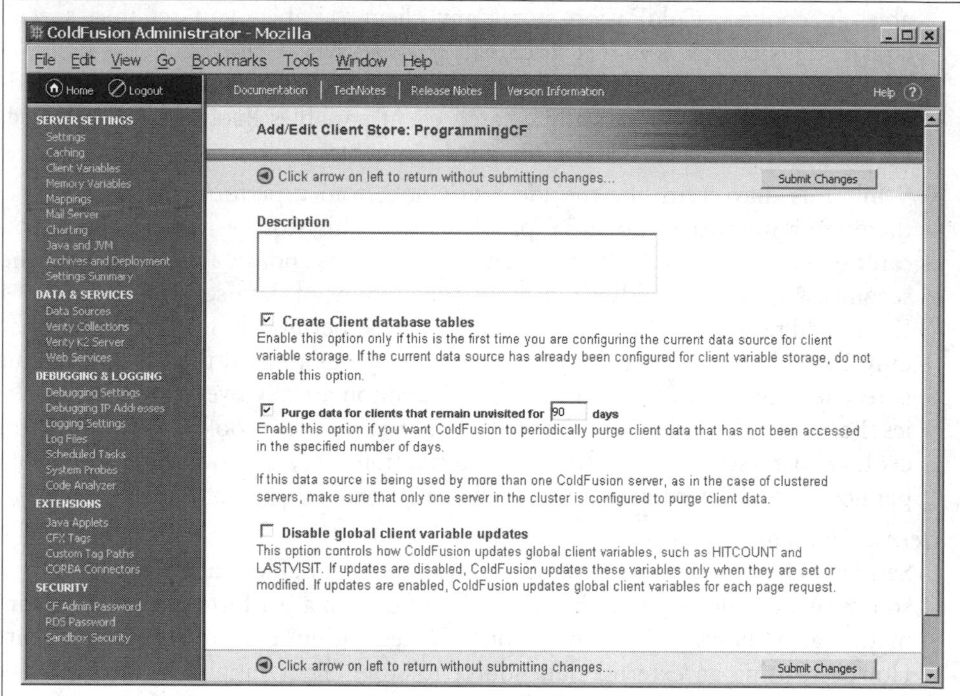

Figure 7-4. Configuring an external data source to store client variables

At this time, you need to decide whether you want to manually create the database tables necessary to store client variables or let ColdFusion create the tables for you. The preferred method is to let ColdFusion create the tables for you. However, depending on your database platform and the level of access you are allowed to the database, it may be necessary to manually create the necessary tables. If you choose to manually create the tables, you need to create two tables, as shown in Tables 7-1 and 7-2.

Table 7-1. CDATA table

Field name	Datatype	Max length
CFID	Text	64
APP	Text	64
DATA	Memo	N/A

Table 7-2. CGLOBAL table

Field name	Datatype	Max length
CFID	Text	64
DATA	Memo	N/A
LVISIT	Date	N/A

Note that the datatypes listed in Tables 7-1 and 7-2 are Microsoft Access datatypes. Depending on the database you use to store your client variables, you may need to use different datatypes (i.e., `Memo` is a datatype specific to MS Access). Additionally, if you use Access, you need to modify the `DATA` field in the `CDATA` table to allow zero-length strings. This is necessary to avoid errors in the event you attempt to delete all application-defined client variables associated with a particular user.

If you don't want to create the tables yourself, you can have ColdFusion do it for you automatically. To have ColdFusion create the tables for you, simply check the box labeled "Create Client Database Tables."

The other two choices on the screen allow you to determine how often ColdFusion automatically purges client variables and how often it should update the global (read-only) client variables. Purging client variables is an important function for two reasons. First, it keeps your database from accumulating unnecessary and irrelevant data. The second reason is that you usually want to expire data associated with a particular client after some predetermined period of inactivity. For example, say you run a public web site that allows users to customize certain aspects of the site to their own liking. If you use client variables to keep track of these preferences, you probably want to delete the preferences of visitors that haven't visited your site for a predetermined amount of time. You can specify the amount of time in days before ColdFusion purges inactive client variables by checking the box labeled "Purge data for clients that remain unvisited for x days" and specifying the number of days in the text box.

The "Disable Global Client Variable Updates" option allows you to indicate whether ColdFusion should update global client variables such as `HitCount`, `LastVisited`, and `TimeCreated` each time a ColdFusion template is requested or only when the variables are set or updated. If the box is checked (the default), global client variables are updated only when they are set or updated, not with each page request.

Using client variables without cookies

By default, the CFID and CFToken variables for each user are stored as cookies on the user's hard drive. In order to make your application work with users who can't or don't accept cookies, you must pass the CFID and CFToken values via URL to each template within your application. To pass CFID and CFToken from template to template, all you need to do is append the URLToken variable to each URL that you use in your application. For example, to pass the CFID and CFToken along in a form, you can use the following code:

```
<cfoutput>
<form name="MyForm" action="MyTemplate.cfm?#Client.URLToken#" method="Post">
</cfoutput>
```

If you want to pass the CFID and CFToken using standard hyperlinks, the code looks like this:

```
<cfoutput>
<a href="mytemplate.cfm?#client.URLToken#">MyTemplate</a>
</cfoutput>
```

It is important to remember that after users who do not accept cookies leave your site, their client variables are effectively abandoned, because when they return, ColdFusion has no way of determining who they are (unless they return via a bookmark that has their CFID and CFToken values in it).

You can also automatically determine whether a particular client accepts cookies by using the URLSessionFormat( ) function. If the client does not accept cookies, URLSessionFormat( ) appends appropriate client identification parameters (CFID, CFToken, jsessionid) to the end of the specified URL. Otherwise, the URL is returned as is. This function provides similar functionality to the addtoken attribute of the cflocation tag. However, URLSessionFormat( ) is more powerful and versatile in that it appends identification information only in the event a client does not support cookies. Additionally, URLSessionFormat( ) can be used anywhere a URL is coded, whereas cflocation is used only to redirect a user to another location. Here's an example that uses URLSessionFormat( ) to create a link that passes identification parameters only if the user's browser doesn't support cookies:

```
<cfoutput>
<a href="#URLSessionFormat("checkout.cfm")#">Check Out</a>
</cfoutput>
```

Storing complex datatypes in client variables

Because client variables must be stored in a physical medium such as the system registry, a database field, or a cookie, it isn't possible to assign complex datatypes such as arrays, structures, or query objects to them. There is a workaround, however. Using the cfwddx tag, you can serialize a complex datatype and assign the resulting WDDX packet to a client variable. For more information on using WDDX to serialize and deserialize complex datatypes, see Chapter 23.

Client variables and clustering

In order to effectively use client variables within a clustered environment, you need to have ColdFusion store them in an external data source or as cookies. By storing the client variables in either fashion, they become accessible from any server in your cluster.

If you choose to store your client variables in an external data source, you should be sure to set the `setdomaincookies` attribute to `Yes` in the `cfapplication` tag of your *Application.cfm* template. Setting this attribute to `Yes` causes ColdFusion to create a new cookie variable at the domain level called `CFMagic`. `CFMagic` tells ColdFusion that cookies have been set at the domain level and contains the values of the `CFID` and `CFToken` cookies. Existing host-level cookies are automatically compared to the values stored in `CFMagic` and migrated to domain-level cookies if the values don't match.

There are a few additional considerations when configuring your clustered servers to use client variables. First, if you want to have ColdFusion automatically purge client variables stored in a data source after a set period of inactivity, you need to make sure that this option is set on only one of the ColdFusion servers in your cluster. To enable or disable this option, click on the name of the data source in the Variables section of the ColdFusion Administrator, and check or uncheck the box labeled "Purge data for clients that remain unvisited for x days."

The second consideration has to do with setting up the external data source for each of your clustered servers. If you want ColdFusion to automatically create the database tables for you, you need to make sure to check this option in the ColdFusion Administrator during the setup of the first server only. If you attempt to have ColdFusion create tables for the same data source more than once, the ColdFusion Administrator generates a database error.

Deleting client variables

Several scenarios exist in which you might find it necessary to delete one or more client variables, such as a login application in a clustered environment. There are different techniques you can use to delete client variables depending on the number and type you want to delete. To delete a single client variable, use the `DeleteClientVariable( )` function:

```
<cfset DeleteClientVariable("MyClientVar")>
```

You can also use the `StructDelete( )` function:

```
<cfset StructDelete(MyStruct, "MyClientVar")>
```

If you want to delete all client variables for the current user associated with your application, you can use a list loop to loop over the contents of the list of client variables returned by the `GetClientVariableList( )` function, deleting each variable one at a time:

```
<!--- Loop over the list of client variables, deleting them one by one --->
<cfloop index="i" list="#GetClientVariablesList( )#">
```

```
  <cfset DeleteClientVariable(i)>
</cfloop>
```

Note that the DeleteClientVariable( ) function can't be used to delete any of the automatically created client variables such as CFID, CFToken, and HitCount.

You can also use a loop to delete all of a user's client variables, including the automatically generated ones. Do this using a collection loop:

```
<cfloop collection="#client#" item="i">
  <cfset StructDelete(client, i)>
</cfloop>
```

This can also be accomplished using the StructClear( ) function:

```
<cfset StructClear(client)>
```

You can "delete" all of a user's client variables by expiring the CFID, CFToken, and CFGlobals cookies for that user. To do this, set the expiration for each cookie to Now:

```
<cfcookie name="CFID" expires="Now">
<cfcookie name="CFToken" expires="Now">
<cfcookie name="CFGlobals" expires="Now">
```

Cookies

As I mentioned earlier in the chapter, cookies are a unique type of shared scope variable in that they are stored on the client machine and sent to the ColdFusion server each time a page is requested. Cookies are available to every ColdFusion template provided they exist and are set within the domain from which they are being requested. Cookies typically store identifying information about a user, such as a user ID or other unique value. Because cookies exist as plain text on a user's system, they should never be used to store sensitive information, such as passwords or credit-card numbers. Cookies can be both set and read by ColdFusion. All cookie operations are performed using the cfcookie tag.

Setting cookies

ColdFusion allows you to set cookies via the cfcookie tag. Before you decide to use cookies in your application, please keep in mind the following considerations:

- You can't set cookies for users that can't or choose not to accept them. This has the potential to limit the audience for your application.
- ColdFusion limits the amount of data set in a cookie to 4 KB.
- Some browsers have a 20-cookie-per-host limit. As more cookies are added, older ones are pushed out.

The following example sets a cookie called UserID on the client's browser:

```
<cfcookie name="UserID" value="123456" path="/MyPath;/MyOtherPath"
domain=".example.com" expires="Never" secure="No">
```

The name attribute is required and specifies the name for the cookie. value refers to the value you want to set for the cookie. Cookie names may contain any printable ASCII characters with the exception of commas, semicolons, and whitespace. The path attribute is also optional and specifies which URL(s) the cookie applies to. Multiple paths are separated by semicolons. If you specify values for path, you also have to use the domain attribute. domain lists domains for which the cookie can be read or written. Entries must always start with a dot. Multiple domains can be specified provided they are separated by semicolons. The expires attribute allows you to set an expiration for the cookie. You have a lot of flexibility here. You can specify the expiration as an integer, a specific date, Never, or Now. Specifying an integer for expires causes the cookie to expire in that number of days. For example, setting expires="14" causes the cookie to expire 14 days from when it is set. Likewise, setting expires="1/1/2099" causes the cookie to expire on January 1, 2099. Setting expires="Never" causes the cookie to exist forever, while setting expires="Now" causes the cookie to expire immediately. Omitting the expires attribute altogether causes the cookie to be set as an in-memory-session-only cookie. This means that the cookie is never written to the user's hard drive and automatically expires when the browser is closed. The final attribute, secure, indicates whether the cookie must be transmitted securely via SSL. This attribute is optional and defaults to No.

Retrieving cookies

To retrieve a cookie, all you have to do is reference it by name using the cookie variable scope. The following example shows you how to retrieve the value of the UserID cookie that we set in the previous example:

```
<cfoutput>
The Value of the UserID cookie is: #Cookie.UserID#
</cfoutput>
```

You can see a list of all cookies and their associated values by turning on debugging for the current template and viewing the list of CGI variables available, or by referencing the cookie structure.

Deleting cookies

To delete a cookie, simply set the expires attribute of the cfcookie tag to Now, as in the following example:

```
<cfcookie name="UserID" expires="Now">
```

Setting the expires attribute to Now causes the cookie to expire and therefore deletes it from the user's system.

Session Variables

Session variables are shared scope variables that store information for a specific user session. Session variables are held in the server's memory and exist for a finite amount of time. Each session variable is unique to a user and can be referenced across all ColdFusion templates within an application. Session variables must be specifically set and are scoped as `session.variable_name`. Any ColdFusion datatype may be assigned to a session variable. Session variables are commonly used in applications where information about a particular user needs to accompany the user from page to page for the duration of the visit to the site or application. Session variables are commonly used to store information such as authentication information, shopping cart contents, and other data specific to an individual user.

Session management in ColdFusion MX can be broken into two categories: ColdFusion session management and J2EE session management. In ColdFusion session management mode, session variables are accessible only by CFML pages and CFCs. J2EE session management lets you share your session variables with JSP templates and Java servlets in addition to CFML templates and CFCs. J2EE session management also offers additional benefits not found in the standard ColdFusion session management:

- J2EE session variables automatically expire when a user closes his or her browser.
- J2EE session variables can be made to persist after server restarts provided the underlying J2EE server is configured for this.

In order to use either type of session variables, they must be enabled both in the ColdFusion Administrator and within an *Application.cfm* template for the application. Additionally, J2EE session variables must be explicitly enabled in the ColdFusion Administrator. You do this by checking "Use J2EE Session Variables" in the Memory Variables section. This example shows how to enable session variables within the *Application.cfm* file:

```
<cfsilent>
  <cfapplication name="MyApplication" sessionmanagement="Yes"
       setclientcookies="Yes"
       sessiontimeout="#CREATETIMESPAN(0, 0, 30, 0)#">
</cfsilent>
```

In this case, the `cfapplication` tag turns on session variables by setting the `sessionmanagement` attribute to `Yes`. `setclientcookies` determines whether to save the `CFID` and `CFToken` values as HTTP cookies on the user's machine. Since the `CFID` and `CFToken` values are used by both session and client variables, it is important to note that the value you specify for `setclientcookies` affects both session and client management. If you set this attribute to `No`, you must be sure to manually pass the `CFID` and `CFToken` values from template to template. Techniques for doing this are described later in this section. The `sessiontimeout` attribute sets the timeout for any session variables used in the application. In this case, the timeout for session variables is set to 30 minutes using the `CreateTimeSpan( )` function.

Besides the session variables you create throughout your application, ColdFusion automatically creates the following session variables whenever ColdFusion session management is enabled:

`session.CFID`
: An incremental ID number created by the ColdFusion Application Server for each client accessing the server.

`session.CFToken`
: A random token that combines with the `CFID` to form a unique identifier for each client visiting your site.

`session.SessionID`
: A concatenation of the application name (as specified in the Name attribute of the `cfapplication` tag), the `CFID`, and the `CFToken`. `SessionID` is used to uniquely identify each session within an application.

`session.URLToken`
: A concatenation of the `CFID` and `CFToken` values that can be appended to a URL when cookies aren't used for session variable storage.

If you are using J2EE session management instead of ColdFusion session management, ColdFusion only sets two default variables:

`session.SessionID`
: The J2EE session ID (maps to a special variable called `jsessionid`) assigned for the user's session.

`session.URLToken`
: A string containing `jsessionid=`*`sessionID`* where *`sessionID`* is the J2EE session ID for the current session. If client variable management is also enabled, or a domain-level cookie exists for the domain, `session.URLToken` may also contain values for `CFID` and `CFToken` even though the J2EE session management doesn't use them.

There is a structure object associated with session variables that contains a list of all available session-variable names within a given application. This structure is appropriately named `session` and can be manipulated just like any other structure object.

Using session variables without cookies

As with client variables, by default the `CFID` and `CFToken` variables for each ColdFusion session are stored on the client's hard drive. For J2EE session variables, the `jsessionid` variable is stored as a nonpersistent cookie. In order to make your application work with users who can't or don't accept cookies, you must pass the `CFID` and `CFToken` or `jsessionid` values via URL to each template within your application. To pass these variables and their associated values from template to template, all you need to do is append the URLToken variable to each URL you use in your application. For example, to pass the CFID and CFToken or jsessionid along in a form, you can use the following code:

```
<cflock name="URLToken_Lock" type="ReadOnly" timeout="60">
<cfoutput>
<form name="MyForm" action="mytemplate.cfm?#session.URLToken#" method="Post">
</cfoutput>
</cflock>
...
</form>
```

If you prefer, you can also pass the values of CFID and CFToken as hidden form fields as opposed to URL parameters:

```
<form name="MyForm" action="mytemplate.cfm" method="Post">
<cflock name="SessionID_Lock" type="ReadOnly" timeout="60">
<cfoutput>
<input type="Hidden" name="CFID" value="#session.CFID#">
<input type="Hidden" name="CFToken" value="#session.CFToken#">
</cfoutput>
</cflock>
...
</form>
```

To pass the J2EE SessionID as a hidden form field, use this code instead:

```
<input type="Hidden" name="SessionID" value="#session.SessionID#">
```

If you want to pass the CFID and CFToken or jsessionid using standard hyperlinks, the code looks like this:

```
<cflock name="URLToken_Lock" type="ReadOnly" timeout="60" throwontimeout="No" >
<cfoutput>
<a href="mytemplate.cfm?#session.URLToken#">MyTemplate</a>
</cfoutput>
</cflock>
```

As with client variables, you can also use the URLSessionFormat( ) function with session variables to determine whether a particular client accepts cookies, and you can automatically append the CFID/CFToken and/or jsessionid values to the URL string if necessary:

```
<cfoutput>
<a href="#URLSessionFormat("checkout.cfm")#">Check Out</a>
</cfoutput>
```

Deleting session variables

Sometimes, you may find it necessary to delete one or more session variables, such as when a user logs out of an application. Because session variables are stored in a structure object called session, you can delete individual session variables using the structure function StructDelete( ). For example, to delete a session variable called session.Username, you can use the StructDelete( ) function as shown in the following example:

```
<cflock Name="Session_Lock" type="Exclusive" timeout="60" throwontimeout="No" >
  <cfset StructDelete(session,"Username")>
</cflock>
```

Remember that you should use cflock whenever you read or write a session variable. In this example, we set the lock type to Exclusive because we are writing to a session variable.

You can also delete all the session variables contained within the current session (without expiring the session) by looping through the session structure and individually deleting each variable. It is necessary to loop through the structure, excluding the preset session variables CFID, CFToken, SessionID, and URLToken, because ColdFusion sets these variables only at the start of the session:

```
<cflock scope="Session" type="Exclusive" timeout="60" throwontimeout="No" >
<cfloop collection="#session#" item="Key">
  <cfif not ListFindNoCase('CFID,CFToken,SessionID,URLToken', Key)>
    <cfset StructDelete(session, Key)>
  </cfif>
</cfloop>
</cflock>
```

The same code can be used if you are using J2EE session management even though there are no CFID and CFToken values in the session scope.

You can take things one step further and terminate a user's session using the StructClear( ) function:

```
<cflock scope="Session" type="Exclusive" timeout="60" throwontimeout="No" >
  <cfset StructClear(session)>
</cflock>
```

Using StructClear( ) deletes all session variables, including the CFID and CFToken variables, effectively terminating the user's session. You should note that while using StructClear( ) clears all session variables from the session structure, it doesn't delete the session structure itself.

Session variables and clustering

Because session variables are stored in the ColdFusion server's RAM, they can't be shared across multiple servers in a clustered environment. Many clustering products (including Macromedia's ClusterCATS, part of the ColdFusion Enterprise Server) offer "sticky" or session-aware load-balancing options. This type of load balancing allows you to use memory-resident variables (session, application, and server) in your applications by ensuring that a user isn't bumped from the server they are originally routed to regardless of the amount of load on the server. In the event that a server fails in a session-aware cluster, all memory-resident variables on that server are lost, resulting in a loss of all active user sessions. For more information on using ClusterCATS, see the Macromedia documentation.

You may have additional clustering options for session variables if you are using J2EE sessions. Many J2EE servers, including Macromedia's JRun 4, allow you to configure the application server to retain `jsessionid` values in the event a server goes down and is restarted. For more information, consult the documentation for your particular application server and version of ColdFusion for J2EE.

Server Variables

Server variables are the final type of shared scope variable in ColdFusion. Server variables store data associated with the server on which ColdFusion is running. Server variables are stored in the ColdFusion server's RAM and are available to all ColdFusion applications and users. Server variables exist until the ColdFusion Application Server is stopped. You can create your own server variables using the `cfset` and `cfparam` tags, or you can reference the following predefined ones:

`server.ColdFusion.Appserver`
: Name of the underlying J2EE application server that ColdFusion sits on top of. For standalone versions of ColdFusion MX, the value is JRun 4. New as of ColdFusion MX.

`server.ColdFusion.Expiration`
: Date (in ODBC date format) on which the ColdFusion server expires. Applies only to trial versions of ColdFusion.

`server.ColdFusion.ProductLevel`
: The level of the ColdFusion product running on the server (Developer, Professional, Enterprise, etc.).

`server.ColdFusion.ProductName`
: The name of the ColdFusion product running on the server.

`server.ColdFusion.ProductVersion`
: The version number of the ColdFusion product running on the server.

`server.ColdFusion.RootDir`
: The full path to the directory where ColdFusion MX is installed; new as of ColdFusion MX.

`server.ColdFusion.SerialNumber`
: The serial number registered to the ColdFusion server.

`server.ColdFusion.SupportedLocales`
: A comma-delimited list of locales supported by the server.

`server.OS.AdditionalInformation`
: Any additional information specified by the operating system on the ColdFusion server, such as service packs installed, etc.

`server.OS.Arch`
: The processor architecture of the underlying server; new as of ColdFusion MX.

`server.OS.BuildNumber`
: The build number of the operating system installed on the ColdFusion server.

`server.OS.Name`
: The name of the operating system installed on the ColdFusion server.

`server.OS.Version`
: The version number of the operating system running on the ColdFusion server.

Server variables are often used in multiplatform ColdFusion applications in which the applications behave differently depending on what platform the code is running on.

When you read or write a server variable, it is important to consider using the `cflock` tag to guard against problems arising from race conditions. Remember to set the `type` of lock to `ReadOnly` when reading server variables and `Exclusive` when writing them. The following example writes several server variables, then displays them:

```
<cflock scope="Server" type="Exclusive" timeout="60" throwontimeout="No" >
  <cfset server.Location = "West Chester">
  <cfset server.Function = "B2B Applications">
</cflock>

<cflock scope="Server" type="ReadOnly" timeout="60" throwontimeout="No" >
  <cfoutput>
  This server is located in #server.Location#<br>
  This server is used for #server.Function#
  </cfoutput>
</cflock>
```

Typically, server variables aren't used within a clustered environment unless "sticky" or session-aware load balancing is used. Another possible use is when the server variables are written to once and an initialization flag is provided (similar to the method used in the *Application.cfm* template covered earlier in the chapter), because they are exclusive to the server on which they are created.

Browser Redirection

At times, you may wish to redirect a user's browser to a location other than the current template. This is generally handled using the `cflocation` tag. The following example creates a drop-down box listing several web sites. Choosing one of the sites and clicking the Go button posts the form to itself and uses the `cflocation` tag to redirect the user to the selected web site.

```
<cfif IsDefined(form.Go')>
  <cflocation URL="http://#form.Goto#" addtoken="No">
</cfif>
```

```
<h2>Please choose a location:</h2>
<cfoutput>
<form action="#CGI.Script_Name#" method="Post">
</cfoutput>
  <select name="Goto">
    <option value="www.macromedia.com" Selected>Macromedia</option>
    <option value="www.yahoo.com">Yahoo</option>
    <option value="www.amkor.com">Amkor</option>
  </select>
<input type="Submit" name="Go" value="Go">
</form>
```

The URL attribute specifies an absolute or relative path to the page you want to redirect the user's browser to. addtoken is an optional attribute and indicates whether to append client variable information (CFID and CFToken values) to the end of the URL specified in the URL attribute. In order to use the addtoken attribute, clientmanagement must be turned on in the *Application.cfm* file. The default value for addtoken is Yes.

You can also redirect to a different page using the cfheader tag:

```
<cfheader name="Refresh" value="0; URL=http://www.example.com/mytemplate.cfm">
```

This code uses the cfheader tag to generate a custom HTTP header with a Refresh element that contains the number of seconds to wait before refreshing the page, as well as the URL of the page to retrieve when the refresh occurs. Another alternative is to send an HTTP 302 status code that tells the browser that the document has moved and provides the new location (most browsers will automatically redirect to the new location):

```
<cfheader name="Location" value=" http://www.example.com/mytemplate.cfm ">
<cfheader statuscode="302" statustext="Document Moved">
```

Portal Example

Because state management is such an important part of web application development, I think it's appropriate to end the chapter with an example application that showcases the material we've just covered. I've opted to create a portal application that allows a registered visitor to create a personalized home page from a list of prebuilt modules, as it is simple enough to allow me to demonstrate a number of techniques. Figure 7-5 shows an overview of how the portal application is put together, including relationships between the various templates. The application uses all the shared variable scopes we discussed with the exception of the server scope. We'll cover all of the templates used in the application except for *login.cfm*. This template is discussed in Chapter 8 (you should go ahead and grab it now, though, and save it in the same directory as the rest of the templates in the portal example).

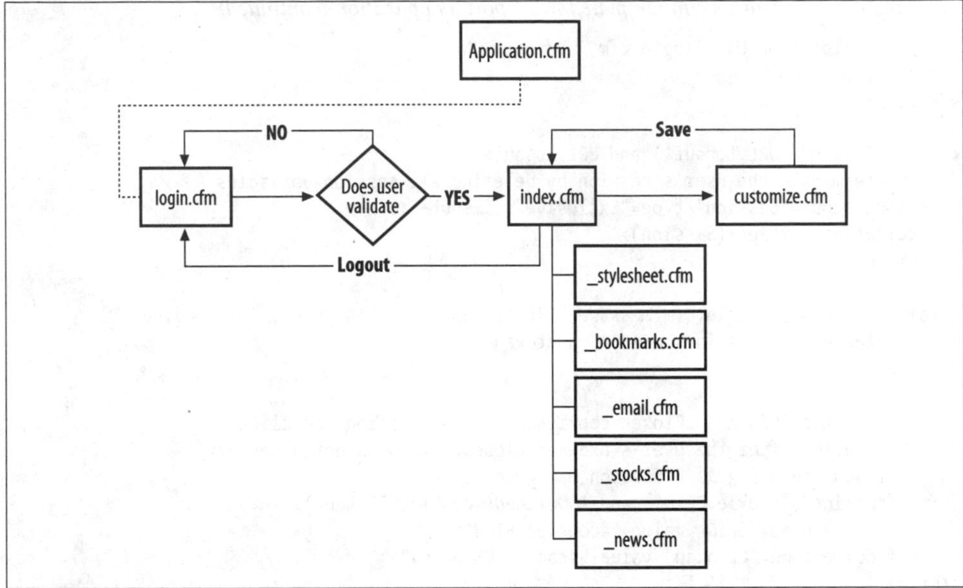

Figure 7-5. Application flow for the portal example

Web Application Framework

The *Application.cfm* template shown in Example 7-2 has four functions in the portal application: it turns on client and session management, handles authentication, logs the user out when appropriate, and initializes application and client variables. This template, along with all others in this example, should be saved in a directory called */programmingcf/examples/7/portal* off of the web root directory.

Example 7-2. Application.cfm template for the portal application

```
<cfsilent>
<cfapplication name="MyPortal" clientmanagement="Yes"
   sessionmanagement="Yes" setclientcookies="Yes"
   sessiontimeout="#CreateTimeSpan(0, 0, 30, 0)#"
   applicationtimeout="#CreateTimeSpan(0, 0, 30, 0)#"
   clientstorage="Registry">

<!--- Set the default session state to false, meaning that by default,
      users are not logged into the application --->
<cflock name="sLogin_Lock" type="Exclusive" timeout="10">
  <cfparam name="session.LoggedIn" default="false">
</cflock>

<!--- If the user isn't logged in or they aren't currently on the login
      page, send them to the login page --->
<cflock name="sLogin_Lock" type="ReadOnly" timeout="10">
  <cfif (not session.LoggedIn) and (CGI.script_name is
        not "/programmingcf/examples/7/portal/login.cfm")>
```

Example 7-2. Application.cfm template for the portal application (continued)

```
        <cflocation URL="login.cfm" addtoken="No">
  </cfif>
</cflock>

<cfif IsDefined('URL.Logout') and URL.Logout>
  <!--- Terminate the user's session by deleting all session variables --->
  <cflock scope="Session" type="Exclusive" timeout="10">
    <cfset StructClear(Session)>
  </cflock>

  <cflocation URL="login.cfm?Message=#URLEncodedFormat("Thank you for logging
  out. Please visit again soon!")#" addtoken="No">
</cfif>

<!--- Reset the CFID and CFToken cookies to expire session and client
      variables after the user's browser closes.  This is not necessary
      if you are using J2EE Session Management. --->
<cfif IsDefined("cookie.CFID") and IsDefined("cookie.CFToken")>
    <cfcookie name="CFID" value="#cookie.CFID#">
    <cfcookie name="CFToken" value="#cookie.CFToken#">
</cfif>

<!--- Check to see if the application has been initialized.  If not, set the
      necessary application variables and initialize the app --->
<cflock timeout="30" throwontimeout="No" type="ReadOnly" scope="Application">
  <cfset IsInitialized = IsDefined('application.Initialized')>
</cflock>

<cfif not IsInitialized>
  <cflock type="Exclusive" scope="Application" timeout="10">
    <cfif not IsDefined('application.Initialized')>
      <cfset application.DSN = "ProgrammingCF">
      <cfset application.AdminEmail = "webmaster@example.com">
      <cfset application.Initialized = true>
    </cfif>
  </cflock>
</cfif>

<!--- Set default values for client variables --->
<cfparam name="client.Email" default="Yes">
<cfparam name="client.Stocks" default="Yes">
<cfparam name="client.News" default="Yes">
<cfparam name="client.Bookmarks" default="Yes">
<cfparam name="client.BGColor" default="FFFFFF">
<cfparam name="client.FontFace" default="Arial">
<cfparam name="client.HeaderFontColor" default="000000">
<cfparam name="client.HeaderBGColor" default="6666FF">
<cfparam name="client.FontColor" default="000000">
</cfsilent>
```

The first task in *Application.cfm* is to turn on both client and session management for the application. For simplicity, the application uses the system registry to store client variables, but you can use any storage option you choose. Both application and session variables are set to time out after 30 minutes. Additionally, client cookies are enabled.

Because the *Application.cfm* template is invoked each time a template is requested, it is well suited to handle authentication for the portal. Although we'll be discussing the entire login process in Chapter 8, it is important to understand that the *Application.cfm* template prescreens all user requests to see whether a user is logged into the application. It does this by checking for a session variable called `session.LoggedIn`. If this variable exists and is set to `true`, the requested template is sent to the user. If the variable isn't present or is set to `false` (as it is by default), the user is rerouted to the *login.cfm* template via a `cflocation` tag.

The third function of this *Application.cfm* template is to log a user out if she has clicked on the Logout link on the main portal page. This is done by checking to see whether a URL variable called `URL.Logout` is present and set to `true`. If so, the `session` structure is cleared using `StructClear( )`. Because this is where the `session.CFID`, `session.CFToken`, and `session.LoggedIn` values associated with the user's session are stored, clearing these values terminates the user's session. The user is then automatically rerouted back to the login screen.

The next chunk of code expires a user's session in the event the browser is closed. This is done so that in a shared environment, another user can't simply open the previous user's browser and start using the application. The technique used to accomplish this involves resetting the `CFID` and `CFToken` cookies so that they are never written to the user's system. This in effect terminates a user's session. You should note that this technique works only if the `CFID` and `CFToken` values aren't passed via URL. This code is not necessary if J2EE session management is used, as the cookie set by J2EE session management is not a persistent cookie.

The next function of this *Application.cfm* template checks for the existence of an application variable called `application.Initialized`. If it doesn't exist (which it won't the first time a CFML template is invoked), ColdFusion responds by setting a number of constants for the application. After the constants are set, `application.Initialized` is set to `true` so the next time the *Application.cfm* template is called, it isn't necessary to set all the constants again (since you only need to set application variables once).

The final section of code in the template sets default values for the client variables used by the application. These client variables define the look and feel for the portal and specify what types of content should be displayed. Because these values are stored in client variables, they are specific to individual users. This allows you to provide a personalized portal experience for each user.

Main Template

When a user successfully logs in to the application via the *login.cfm* template (discussed in Chapter 8), two session variables are set, `session.LoggedIn` (set to `true`) and `session.FullName` (set to the full name of the user who logged in). The user is then redirected to the *index.cfm* template shown in Example 7-3. The *index.cfm* template is the main template for the portal. It displays all the user's content and contains links to customize the portal, remove specific content modules, and log out of the portal.

Example 7-3. The main application template, index.cfm

```
<html>
  <head>
    <title>My Portal</title>
    <cfinclude template="_stylesheet.cfm">
  </head>
<body>
<cfoutput><h1>Welcome #ListFirst(session.FullName, " ")#</h1></cfoutput>
<table width="100%" border="0" cellpadding="0" cellspacing="5">
  <tr>
    <cfoutput>
    <td class="CustomizeLink"><a href="customize.cfm">Customize</a></td>
    <td class="CustomizeLink" align="Right"><a
        href="index.cfm?logout=true">Logout</a></td>
    </cfoutput>
  </tr>
  <tr>
    <td width="19%" valign="Top">
      <table width="100%" border="0" cellspacing="0" cellpadding="5">
        <cfif client.Email>
          <cfinclude template="_email.cfm">
        </cfif>
        <cfif client.Stocks>
          <cfinclude template="_stock.cfm">
        </cfif>
      </table>
    </td>
    <td width="81%" valign="Top">
      <table width="100%" border="0" cellspacing="0" cellpadding="5">
        <cfif client.News>
          <cfinclude template="_news.cfm">
        </cfif>
        <cfif client.Bookmarks>
          <cfinclude template="_bookmarks.cfm">
        </cfif>
      </table>
    </td>
  </tr>
</table>
<hr>
<cfoutput>
```

Example 7-3. The main application template, index.cfm (continued)

```
<div class="Footer">Please email questions or concerns to <a href="mailto:
 #application.AdminEmail#">#application.AdminEmail#</a>.</div>
</cfoutput>
</body>
</html>
```

The *index.cfm* template begins by using a `cfinclude` tag to include an inline stylesheet for the application. The stylesheet defines such things as the font face and size for various sections of the portal. These attributes are dynamically populated based on values stored in the various client variables specified at the beginning of the template. The code for the stylesheet (*_stylesheet.cfm*) is shown in Example 7-4.

Example 7-4. _stylesheet.cfm template for defining the stylesheet for the portal

```
<style type="text/css">
  <!--
  <cfoutput>
  body {background-color: ###client.BGColor#; font-family: #client.FontFace#;
        font-size: 10pt; color: ###client.FontColor#}
  h1 {font-family: #client.FontFace#; font-size: 16pt; font-weight: bold}
  .Message {font-family: #client.FontFace#; font-weight: bold; color: red;}
  .SectionHeader {font-family: #client.FontFace#; font-size: 12pt;
                  font-weight: bold; background-color: ###client.HeaderBGColor#;
                  color: ###client.HeaderFontColor#}
  .LeftTableBody {font-family: #client.FontFace#; font-size: 9pt;
                  font-weight: normal; background-color: ##CCCCCC;
                  color: ###client.FontColor#}
  .TableRemove {font-family: #client.FontFace#; font-size: 8pt;
                text-decoration: underline;
                background-color: ###client.HeaderBGColor#; text-align: right;
                color: ###client.FontColor#}
  .ListItems {font-family: #client.FontFace#; font-size: 10pt;
              list-style-type: circle; color: ###client.FontColor#}
  .CustomizeLink {font-family: #client.FontFace#; font-size: 8pt;
                  text-decoration: underline; color: ###client.FontColor#}
  .Ticker {font-family: #client.FontFace#; font-size: 9pt; font-weight: bold}
  .Quote {font-family: #client.FontFace#; font-size: 9pt}
  .Footer {font-family: #client.FontFace#; font-size: 8pt}
  </cfoutput>
  -->
</style>
```

The rest of the *index.cfm* template displays the various types of content the user has specified for inclusion in the portal. By default, all content is displayed the first time the user logs into the application. This is accomplished by setting defaults for all the client variables in the beginning of the template. Each type of content (email, stock quotes, news, and bookmarks) is pulled into the template via `cfinclude` tags. This allows the design of the portal to remain modular and makes editing any of the individual content modules easy. The code for the various content modules is shown in

Example 7-5 (*_email.cfm*), Example 7-6 (*_stock.cfm*), Example 7-7 (*_news.cfm*), and Example 7-8 (*_bookmarks.cfm*). Figure 7-6 shows how the portal looks the first time a user logs in.

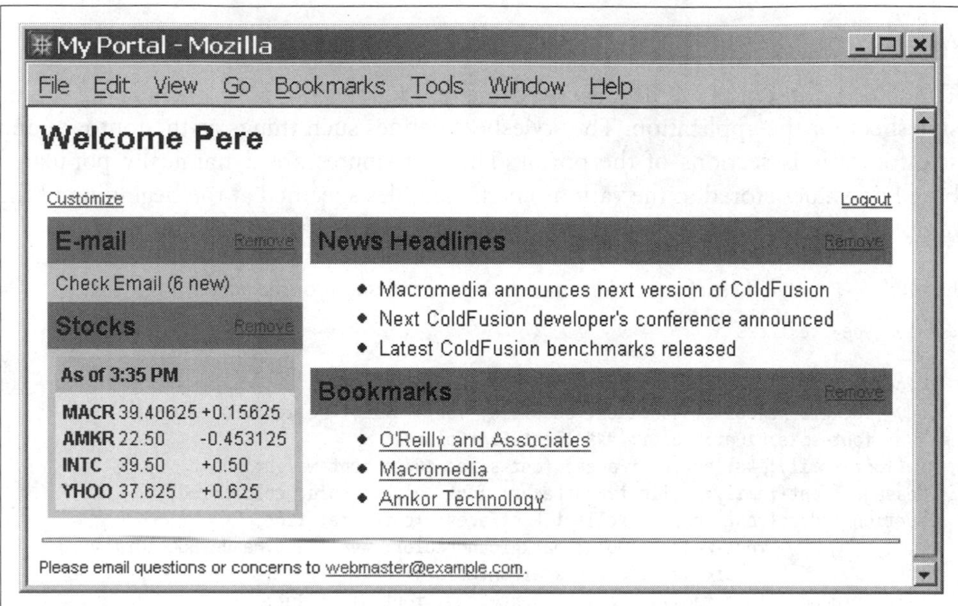

Figure 7-6. Displaying the portal the first time a user logs in

Example 7-5. _email.cfm template for the email module

```
<tr>
  <td class="SectionHeader">E-mail</td>
  <td class="TableRemove">
    <cfoutput>
      <a href="customize.cfm?section=email&action=remove">Remove</a>
    </cfoutput></td>
</tr>
<tr>
  <td class="LeftTableBody" colspan="2">Check Email (6 new)</td>
</tr>
```

Example 7-6. _stock.cfm template for displaying stock quotes

```
<tr>
  <td bgcolor="#CCCC66" class="SectionHeader">Stocks</td>
  <td class="TableRemove">
    <cfoutput>
      <a href="customize.cfm?section=stocks&action=remove">Remove</a>
    </cfoutput>
  </td>
</tr>
<tr bgcolor="#CCCCCC">
  <td class="LeftTableBody" colspan="2">
```

Example 7-6. _stock.cfm template for displaying stock quotes (continued)

```
  <table border="0" cellpadding="4" cellspacing="0" width="100%"
         bgcolor="#EEEEEE">
  <tr bgcolor="#C0C0C0">
    <td width="100%" class="Ticker">As of 3:35 PM</td>
  </tr>
  <tr>
    <td>
    <table width="100%" cellspacing="0" cellpadding="1">
      <tr>
        <td class="Ticker">MACR</td><td class="Quote">39.40625</td>
        <td class="Quote">+0.15625</td>
      </tr>
      <tr>
        <td class="Ticker">AMKR</td><td class="Quote">22.50</td>
        <td class="Quote">-0.453125</td>
      </tr>
      <tr>
        <td class="Ticker">INTC</td><td class="Quote">39.50</td>
        <td class="Quote">+0.50</td>
      </tr>
      <tr>
        <td class="Ticker">YHOO</td><td class="Quote">37.625</td>
        <td class="Quote">+0.625</td>
      </tr>
    </table>
    </td>
  </tr>
  </table>
  </td>
</tr>
```

Example 7-7. _news.cfm template for displaying news headlines

```
<tr>
  <td class="SectionHeader">News Headlines</td>
  <td class="TableRemove">
    <cfoutput>
      <a href="customize.cfm?section=news&action=remove">Remove</a>
    </cfoutput>
  </td>
</tr>
<tr>
  <td colspan="2">
    <ul>
      <li><span class="ListItems">Macromedia announces next version of
          ColdFusion</span></li>
      <li><span class="ListItems">Next ColdFusion developer's
          conference announced</span></li>
      <li><span class="ListItems">Latest ColdFusion benchmarks
          released</span></li>
    </ul>
  </td>
</tr>
```

Example 7-8. _bookmarks.cfm template for displaying links to other sites

```
<tr>
  <td class="SectionHeader">Bookmarks</td>
  <td class="TableRemove">
    <cfoutput>
      <a href="customize.cfm?section=bookmarks&action=remove">Remove</a>
    </cfoutput>
  </td>
</tr>
<tr>
  <td colspan="2">
    <ul>
      <li><span class="ListItems"><a
          href="http://www.oreilly.com">O'Reilly and Associates</a></span></li>
      <li><span class="ListItems"><a
          href="http://www.macromedia.com">Macromedia</a></span></li>
      <li><span class="ListItems"><a
          href="http://www.amkor.com">Amkor Technology</a></span></li>
    </ul>
  </td>
</tr>
```

Customization

From the main page of the portal (*index.cfm*), a user can customize the portal by clicking on the Customize link in the upper left corner of the screen. Clicking this link takes the user to the *customize.cfm* template. Example 7-9 contains the code for the *customize.cfm* template.

Example 7-9. customize.cfm template customizes the portal's look/feel, content

```
<cfif CGI.request_method is "Post">
  <h1>Saving Changes...</h1>
  <cfparam name="form.Email" default="No">
  <cfparam name="form.Stocks" default="No">
  <cfparam name="form.News" default="No">
  <cfparam name="form.Bookmarks" default="No">

  <cfset client.BGColor = form.BGColor>
  <cfset client.FontFace = form.FontFace>
  <cfset client.FontColor = form.FontColor>
  <cfset client.HeaderBGColor = form.HeaderBGColor>
  <cfset client.HeaderFontColor = form.HeaderFontColor>
  <cfset client.Email = form.Email>
  <cfset client.Stocks = form.Stocks>
  <cfset client.News = form.News>
  <cfset client.Bookmarks = form.Bookmarks>
  <cflocation URL="index.cfm" addtoken="No">
<cfelse>
  <cfif IsDefined('URL.Action') and URL.Action is "Remove">
    <cfswitch expression="#Section#">
      <cfcase value="Email">
```

Example 7-9. customize.cfm template customizes the portal's look/feel, content (continued)

```
        <cfset client.Email = "No">
      </cfcase>
      <cfcase value="Stocks">
        <cfset client.Stocks = "No">
      </cfcase>
      <cfcase value="News">
        <cfset client.News = "No">
      </cfcase>
      <cfcase value="Bookmarks">
        <cfset client.Bookmarks = "No">
      </cfcase>
    </cfswitch>

    <cflocation URL="index.cfm" addtoken="No">
  <cfelse>
    <h1>Customize Your Portal</h2>
    <cfoutput>
    <form action="#CGI.script_name#" method="Post">
    <table>
    <tr>
      <td>Background color:</td>
      <td><input type="Text" name="BGColor" size="6" maxlength="6"
       value="#client.BGColor#"></td>
    </tr>
    <tr>
      <td>Font face:</td>
      <td><select name="FontFace">
            <option value="Arial" <cfif client.FontFace eq
          "Arial">selected</cfif>>Arial</option>
            <option value="Helvetica" <cfif client.FontFace eq
          "Helvetica">selected</cfif>>Helvetica</option>
            <option value="Sans-serif" <cfif client.FontFace eq
          "Sans-serif">selected</cfif>>Sans-Serif</option>
            <option value="Comic Sans MS" <cfif client.FontFace eq
          "Comic Sans MS">selected</cfif>>Comic Sans MS</option>
          </select></td>
    </tr>
    <tr>
      <td>Header font color:</td>
      <td><input type="Text" name="HeaderFontColor" size="6" maxlength="6"
               value="#client.HeaderFontColor#"></td>
    </tr>
    <tr>
      <td>Header background color:</td>
      <td><input type="Text" name="HeaderBGColor" size="6" maxlength="6"
       value="#client.HeaderBGColor#"></td>
    </tr>
    <tr>
      <td>Font color:</td>
      <td><input type="Text" name="FontColor" size="6" maxlength="6"
               value="#client.FontColor#"></td>
    </tr>
```

Example 7-9. customize.cfm template customizes the portal's look/feel, content (continued)

```
    </cfoutput>
    <tr>
      <td colspan="2">Content:</td>
    </tr>
    <tr>
      <td colspan="2">
      <table>
        <tr>
          <td><input type="Checkbox" name="Email"
               value="Yes" <cfif client.Email>checked</cfif>>Email</td>
          <td><input type="Checkbox" name="News"
               value="Yes" <cfif client.News>checked</cfif>>News</td>
        </tr>
        <tr>
          <td><input type="Checkbox" name="Stocks"
               value="Yes" <cfif client.Stocks>checked</cfif>>Stocks</td>
          <td><input type="Checkbox" name="Bookmarks"
               value="Yes" <cfif client.Bookmarks>checked</cfif>>Bookmarks</td>
        </tr>
      </table>
      </td>
    </tr>
    <tr>
      <td colspan="2"><input type="Submit" name="Customize" value="Save"></td>
    </tr>
    </table>
    </form>
  </cfif>
</cfif>
```

The *customize.cfm* template checks to see whether it was called via a POST (form post) or a GET (hyperlink) method because the template has three functions. The first function, called via hyperlink from the main portal page, is to generate a form that allows the user to customize the portal. The second function is to process the customizations set by the user (the template is a self-posting form). The third function of the template is to remove a content module from the user's main portal page when a Remove link is clicked on the main portal page.

Figure 7-7 shows the HTML form that lets the user change the background color, font face, font color, header background color, and header font color for the portal. Additionally, checkboxes are provided next to the name of each available content module. Unchecking a box removes the specified module from the user's portal display, while checking a box adds the specified module. All the values used to populate this page come from the client variables associated with the user. Clicking on the Save button at the bottom of the page self-posts the changes, and the user's client variables are updated with the new values.

If the user came to the template by clicking on one of the Remove links on the *index.cfm* page, the client variable controlling the display of that particular content mod-

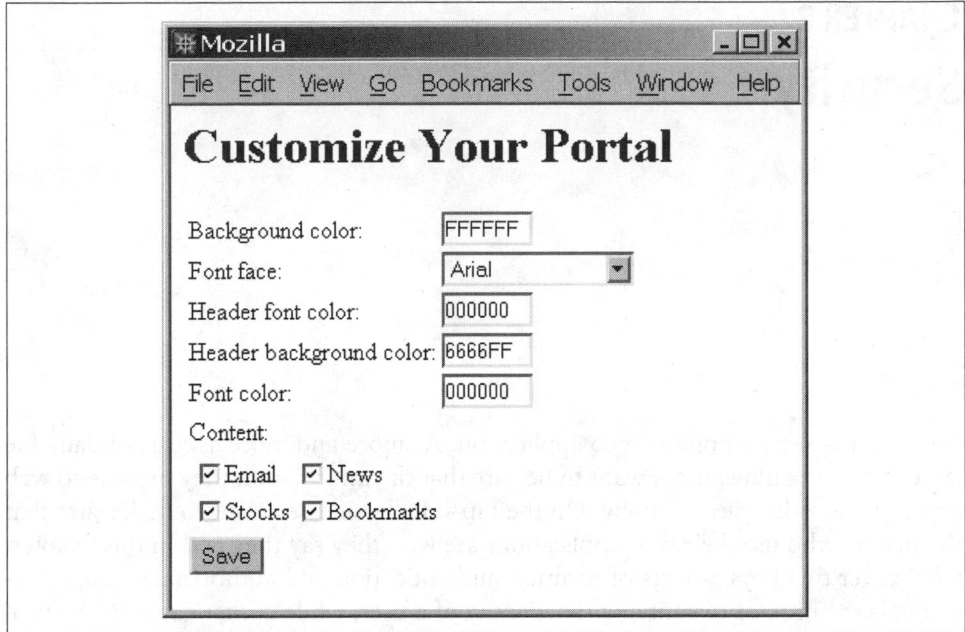

Figure 7-7. Customizing the portal

ule is set to `No`, so that it is no longer displayed. Regardless of how the user arrived, once the template has finished executing, the user is sent back to the *index.cfm* template via a `cflocation` tag.

CHAPTER 8
Security

Security is a key part of any web application. As more and more aspects of daily life are conducted online, users want to be sure that the information they provide to web applications is handled securely. On the flip side, businesses want to make sure that the people who use their web applications are who they say they are. In this chapter, we'll cover two keys aspects of security: authentication and authorization. *Authentication* is the process of verifying the identity of a user, while *authorization* is the process of limiting access to resources to particular users.

In this chapter, we'll look at two approaches to application security. The first approach uses a combination of database tables and application code to manage authentication and user entitlements, in effect implementing security from scratch. Because the *Application.cfm* template is automatically invoked with each page request, it is the ideal place to handle security tasks in your ColdFusion applications. The second approach uses ColdFusion MX's new security tags and functions for authenticating users and authorizing access to resources. Each method has its pros and cons, which will be discussed.

Note that there is Sandbox Security within ColdFusion, but it has a different purpose than the application-level security we'll be discussing in this chapter. Sandbox Security is configurable only from within the ColdFusion Administrator and is used to control access to various ColdFusion resources such as CFML templates, tags, functions, data sources, etc. For more information on Sandbox Security, refer to the Macromedia documentation specific to your flavor of ColdFusion MX.

Security Basics

Before we dive into the different security techniques, let's look at some general dos and don'ts to consider when designing and implementing a security solution for your ColdFusion applications:

- Don't base security solely on a user's IP address. IP addresses are easily spoofed and can often change during a user's session (especially in the case of AOL users because of the way AOL's network works). Additionally, dialup users most likely won't have the same IP address the next time they dial in and use your application because most ISPs use DHCP.
- Do use SSL wherever necessary to encrypt the session between the server and the browser. Because SSL is handled at the web-server level and not by ColdFusion, you need to consult the documentation for your particular web server to determine how to set it up.
- Do require users to choose passwords that aren't easily guessed or found in the dictionary. If possible, require users to choose a password that contains a combination of letters, numbers, and possibly symbols. One way to handle this is by automatically assigning passwords to users. If you let users choose their own passwords, you can still ensure they contain certain characters by using ColdFusion `ReFind( )` function (described in Chapter 18).
- Do include error and exception handling in your applications to prevent users from receiving server and application information when an error or exception occurs. These concepts are covered in Chapter 9.
- Don't store passwords as clear text if you store them in a database or LDAP directory. Use the `Hash( )` function or some other method to obfuscate the password before storing it.
- Don't pass usernames and passwords from template to template in URLs or as hidden form fields because this increases the potential for compromise. Use session variables to store and pass usernames and passwords from template to template, because they are stored in the ColdFusion server's memory and expire when a user's session expires.

Implementing Security from Scratch

As I mentioned in the introduction, it is entirely possible and quite easy to build a robust security model using nothing more than a simple database table and a small bit of CFML code. Consider the portal example we created at the end of Chapter 7. This application is the perfect candidate for implementing security from scratch.

If you refer back to Chapter 7 for a moment, to Figure 7-5, you'll remember that we said security for the portal could be handled by two templates: *Application.cfm* and *login.cfm*. Both authentication and authorization functions are handled by these templates. If you look at Figure 8-1, you'll see the basic flow of the authentication/authorization process. Note that this view differs slightly from the one in Chapter 7 due to the addition of a new template that handles user registration. Don't worry about this template for the time being; we'll get to it soon enough.

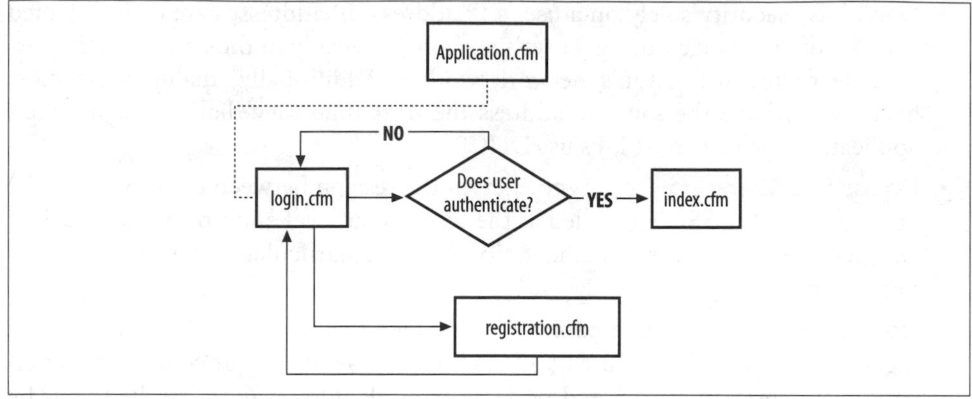

Figure 8-1. Security scheme for the portal application

Creating a Simple Security Table in the Database

The first step to building security into the portal application is to create a database to store username, password, and role information. Table 8-1 shows the schema for a single table called `Users` that will store our profile and security information.

Table 8-1. Setup for the user security table

Field name	Field type	Max length
`Username` (primary key)	`Text`	`50`
`Salt`	`Text`	`12`
`Password`	`Text`	`50`
`FullName`	`Text`	`255`
`Roles`	`Text`	`255`

The field names should be self-descriptive. In our table, `Username` holds an individual's username, and the `Password` field stores the user's password. Because it isn't a good idea to store passwords as plain text in the database, we'll be storing salted hashes (a type of one-way encryption) of the passwords instead. The `Salt` and `Password` fields are used in combination to make this possible. We'll cover how this works later in the chapter. We decided to include a field called `FullName` to store the full name of the user associated with the `Username` and `Password`. The `Roles` field stores a comma-delimited list of roles the user is assigned.* This table is about as bare bones as you can get. You could easily expand it to include all sorts of additional profiling information such as the user's address, phone number, email address, etc.

* Roles are stored as a comma-delimited list here as a matter of convenience and simplicity. In a real-world situation, where you could have numerous roles, it would probably be more appropriate to add two additional tables, one to store roles, and another to act as a lookup table matching usernames to roles.

Setting Up the Application.cfm Template

Now that we have a security table, we need an *Application.cfm* template to serve as the foundation for our security model. In Chapter 7, we designed an *Application.cfm* template to handle security for our portal application. We are going to use the same *Application.cfm* template here, with one minor modification. Example 8-1 shows the modified code for our *Application.cfm* template.

Example 8-1. Application.cfm file for setting up application security

```
<cfsilent>
<cfapplication name="MyPortal" clientmanagement="Yes"
   sessionmanagement="Yes" setclientcookies="Yes"
   sessiontimeout="#CreateTimeSpan(0, 0, 30, 0)#"
   applicationtimeout="#CreateTimeSpan(0, 0, 30, 0)#"
   clientstorage="Registry">

<!--- Set the default session state to false, meaning that by default,
      users are not logged into the application --->
<cflock name="sLogin_Lock" type="Exclusive" timeout="10">
  <cfparam name="session.LoggedIn" default="false">
</cflock>

<!--- If the user isn't logged in or they aren't currently on the login
      page or registration page, send them to the login page --->
<cflock name="sLogin_Lock" type="ReadOnly" timeout="10">
  <cfif (not session.LoggedIn) and
      (CGI.script_name is not "/programmingcf/examples/7/portal/login.cfm") and
      (CGI.script_name is not "/programmingcf/examples/7/portal/registration.cfm")>
        <cflocation URL="login.cfm" addtoken="No">
  </cfif>
</cflock>

<cfif IsDefined('URL.Logout') and URL.Logout>
  <!--- Terminate the user's session by deleting all session variables --->
  <cflock scope="session" type="Exclusive" timeout="10">
    <cfset StructClear(session)>
  </cflock>

  <cflocation URL="Login.cfm?Message=#URLEncodedFormat("Thank you for logging
  out. Please visit again soon!")#" addtoken="No">
</cfif>

<!--- Reset the CFID and CFToken cookies to expire session and client
      variables after the user's browser closes.  This is not necessary
      if you are using J2EE session Management. --->
<cfif IsDefined("cookie.CFID") and IsDefined("cookie.CFToken")>
    <cfcookie name="CFID" value="#cookie.CFID#">
    <cfcookie name="CFToken" value="#cookie.CFToken#">
</cfif>

<!--- Check to see if the application has been initialized.  If not, set the
      necessary application variables and initialize the app --->
```

Example 8-1. Application.cfm file for setting up application security (continued)

```
<cflock timeout="30" throwontimeout="No" type="ReadOnly" scope="Application">
  <cfset IsInitialized = IsDefined('application.Initialized')>
</cflock>

<cfif not IsInitialized>
  <cflock type="Exclusive" scope="Application" timeout="10">
    <cfif not IsDefined('application.Initialized')>
      <cfset application.DSN = "ProgrammingCF">
      <cfset application.AdminEmail = "webmaster@example.com">
      <cfset application.Initialized = true>
    </cfif>
  </cflock>
</cfif>

<!--- Set default values for client variables --->
<cfparam name="client.Email" default="Yes">
<cfparam name="client.Stocks" default="Yes">
<cfparam name="client.News" default="Yes">
<cfparam name="client.Bookmarks" default="Yes">
<cfparam name="client.BGColor" default="FFFFFF">
<cfparam name="client.FontFace" default="Arial">
<cfparam name="client.HeaderFontColor" default="000000">
<cfparam name="client.HeaderBGColor" default="6666FF">
<cfparam name="client.FontColor" default="000000">
</cfsilent>
```

Once we name the application and set up session and application variable management, the next thing to do is make sure all users are logged out by default. This is accomplished by creating a session variable called `session.LoggedIn` and setting it to `false`. This ensures that any user request to a template governed by the *Application.cfm* template from a user who isn't yet logged in will be treated as such. The next bit of code says that if `session.LoggedIn` is `false`, and the user isn't currently in one of the login, validation, registration, or registration-processing templates, the user isn't logged in and should be redirected to the login screen. The addition of the registration form and registration-processing template to the list of templates exempt from the login requirement is the only difference between this *Application.cfm* template and the one from Chapter 7. This is the most important part of this type of security model, as it determines who is logged in and who isn't and responds appropriately. If `session.LoggedIn` is `true`, we know that the user has successfully logged in.

The next action taken by the *Application.cfm* template is to take the `CFID` and `CFTOKEN` cookies set by ColdFusion and reset them to their current values. Doing this changes the expiration date of the cookies used by ColdFusion to maintain session state so that they expire as soon as the user closes his or her browser. This prevents the potentially negative consequences of a user's session persisting after they have closed their browser.

The final section of this *Application.cfm* template checks for the existence of an application variable called `Application.Initialized`. If it doesn't exist (which it won't the first time a CFML template is invoked), ColdFusion responds by setting a number of constants for the application. After the constants are set, `Application.Initialized` is set to `true` so the next time the *Application.cfm* template is called, it isn't necessary to set all the constants again (since you only need to set application variables once).

Creating Login and Registration Screens

The portal application is designed so that an anonymous user (a user who is not authenticated) attempting to access the portal is automatically redirected to a login screen, unless the user is already on the login screen or registering to become a user of the portal. A template containing a self-posting form handles the login process. The form collects the user's username and password and posts the data to itself for processing. Because this is a portal application, it's appropriate to allow users who aren't yet registered with the site to enroll themselves. To do this, a link to a registration form (*registration.cfm*) is provided. Example 8-2 shows the code for the *login.cfm* template.

Example 8-2. login.cfm template for authenticating users

```
<cfif CGI.request_method is "Post">
  <cfquery name="ValidateUser" datasource="#application.DSN#">
      SELECT FullName, Salt, Password
      FROM Users
      WHERE Username = <cfqueryparam value="#form.UserName#"
                                     cfsqltype="CF_SQL_VARCHAR"
                                     maxlength="255">
   </cfquery>

  <!--- If the login is successful, log the user in.  Otherwise, redirect
        them back to the login.cfm page --->
  <cfif (ValidateUser.RecordCount eq 1) and
        (ValidateUser.Password is Hash(ValidateUser.Salt & form.Password))>
     <!--- Set session.LoggedIn to true, logging the user in --->
     <cflock name="sLogin_Lock" timeout="30" type="Exclusive">
       <cfset session.LoggedIn = true>
       <cfset session.FullName = ValidateUser.FullName>
     </cflock>
     <!--- If save username box is checked, set cookie --->
     <cfif IsDefined('form.SaveUsername')>
       <cfcookie name="Username" value="#form.Username#">
     </cfif>
     <!--- Redirect the user to the index.cfm page of our application  --->
     <cflocation URL="index.cfm" addtoken="No">
  <cfelse>
     <!--- Redirect the user back to the login page and display the error
           message --->
     <cflocation URL="login.cfm?Message=#UrlEncodedFormat("Invalid Login.
                 Please Try Again")#&username=#form.Username#" addtoken="No">
  </cfif>
```

Example 8-2. login.cfm template for authenticating users (continued)

```
<cfelse>
  <cfparam name="form.Username" default="">

  <cfif IsDefined('cookie.Username')>
    <cfset form.Username = cookie.Username>
  </cfif>

  <!--- If there was an invalid login, reuse the username --->
  <cfif IsDefined('URL.Username')>
    <cfset form.Username = URL.Username>
  </cfif>

  <div align="center">
  <h2>Portal Login</h2>
  <cfif IsDefined('URL.Message')>
    <cfoutput><span style="Message">#Trim(URL.Message)#</span></cfoutput>
    <p>
  </cfif>

  <cfoutput>
  <form name="ValidateUser" action="#CGI.script_name#" method="Post">
  </cfoutput>
  <input type="hidden" name="Username_required"
        value="You must supply a username">
  <input type="hidden" name="Password_required"
        value="You must supply a password">
  <table border="0">
  <tr>
    <td>Username:</td>
    <td>
      <cfoutput>
        <input type="Text" name="Username" size="15"
               maxlength="255" value="#form.Username#">
      </cfoutput>
    </td>
  </tr>
  <tr>
    <td>Password:</td>
    <td><input type="Password" name="Password" size="15" "maxlength="255"></td>
  </tr>
  <tr>
    <td colspan="2">
      <input type="Checkbox" name="SaveUsername"
             value="Yes">Remember my username for future logins</td>
  </tr>
  <tr>
    <td colspan="2" align="Center">
      <input type="Submit" name="Submit" value="Submit">
    </td>
  </tr>
  </table>
  </form>
```

Example 8-2. login.cfm template for authenticating users (continued)

```
  *This site is for registered users.  If you are not currently a member,
  you may <a href="registration.cfm">register here</a>.
  </div>
</cfif>
```

This template creates a simple login screen that allows the user to enter a username and password (Figure 8-2). The password field uses the HTML password form control so that the user's password is obfuscated as it is typed.

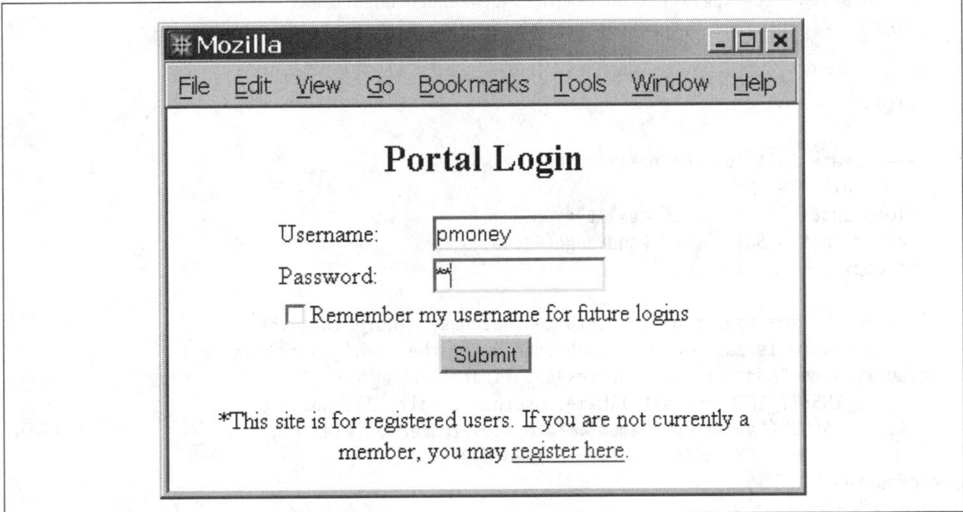

Figure 8-2. login.cfm template for logging in to the portal

When this form is submitted, the information is posted to the *login.cfm* template for processing (we'll discuss the authentication process in the next section, when we discuss authenticating users). If the user doesn't yet have an account, however, and wishes to register for one, he may do so by clicking on the "register here" link at the bottom of the page. Doing so takes the user to the registration form, *registration.cfm*, shown in Example 8-3.

Example 8-3. registration.cfm template for enrolling users

```
<cfif CGI.request_method is "Post">
  <!--- Check to see that passwords match in case the user had JavaScript
        disabled --->
  <cfif form.Password neq form.Password2>
    The passwords you entered on the registration screen do not match.  Please
    hit your browser's back button and try again.
    <cfabort>
  </cfif>

  <!--- Check to make sure the username (the primary key) doesn't already
        exist. If it does, make the user go back and enter a different
```

Example 8-3. registration.cfm template for enrolling users (continued)

```
       username --->
  <cfquery name="CheckPK" datasource="#application.DSN#">
      SELECT Username
      FROM Users
      WHERE Username = <cfqueryparam value="#form.UserName#"
                                     cfsqltype="CF_SQL_VARCHAR"
                                     maxlength="255">
  </cfquery>
  <cfif CheckPK.RecordCount GT 0>
    <cflocation URL="Registration.cfm?Message=#URLEncodedFormat("The
                username you chose already exists, please choose a different
                username.")#&FullName=#URLEncodedFormat(form.FullName)#"
                addtoken="No">
  </cfif>

  <!--- Create Salt for the password hash --->
  <cfset Salt="">
  <cfloop index="i" from="1" to="12">
    <cfset Salt = Salt & chr(RandRange(65,90))>
  </cfloop>

  <!--- Insert the user profile, into the database.  Note that the
        password is salted and then hashed using the Hash( ) function --->
  <cfquery name="AddUser" datasource="#application.DSN#">
          INSERT INTO Users(FullName, Username, Salt, Password)
          VALUES('#form.FullName#', '#form.Username#', '#Salt#',
                 '#Hash(Salt & form.Password)#')
  </cfquery>

  <cflocation URL="login.cfm?Message=#URLEncodedFormat("Profile successfully
                   created. Please login below")#" addtoken="No">
<cfelse>
  <cfparam name="form.FullName" default="">

  <!--- Function that ensures passwords match and that they aren't blank --->
  <script language="JavaScript">
  function formCheck( )
  {
    if (document.PortalRegistration.Password.value !=
      document.PortalRegistration.Password2.value) {
        alert("The passwords you entered do not match.  Please reenter them.");
        document.PortalRegistration.Password.value = '';
        document.PortalRegistration.Password2.value = '';
        return false;
    }
    if (document.PortalRegistration.Password.value == "" ||
      document.PortalRegistration.Password2.value == "") {
        alert("You can not leave either password field blank.");
        return false;
    }
  }
  </script>
```

Example 8-3. registration.cfm template for enrolling users (continued)

```
  <div align="Center">
  <h2>Portal Account Registration</h2>
  <cfif IsDefined('URL.Message')>
    <cfoutput><span style="Message">#URL.Message#</span></cfoutput>
    <p>
  </cfif>

  <cfoutput>
  <form name="PortalRegistration" action="#CGI.script_name#" method="POST"
        onSubmit="return formCheck( )">
   </cfoutput>
  <input type="hidden" name="FullName_required"
        value="You must supply a Name for the user">
  <input type="hidden" name="Username_required"
        value="You must supply a username">
  <input type="hidden" name="Password_required"
        value="You must supply a password">

  <table border=0>
  <tr>
    <td>Full Name:</td>
    <td><cfoutput><input type="Text" name="FullName" size="15" maxlength="255"
                        value="#form.FullName#"></cfoutput>
    </td>
  </tr>
  <tr>
    <td>Username:</td>
    <td>
      <input type="Text" name="Username" size="15" maxlength="50">
    </td>
  </tr>
  <tr>
    <td>Password:</td>
    <td>
      <input type="Password" name="Password" size="15" maxlength="50">
    </td>
  </tr>
  <tr>
    <td>Confirm Password:</td>
    <td>
      <input type="Password" name="Password2" size="15" maxlength="50">
    </td>
  </tr>
  <tr>
    <td colspan="2" align="Center">
      <input type="Submit" name="Submit" value="Submit">
    </td>
  </tr>
  </table>
  </form>
  </div>
</cfif>
```

This template creates a self-posting form that takes four inputs: Full Name, Username, Password, and Confirm Password (Figure 8-3). The reason for two password fields is to ensure that the person entering the password gets it right (since the password is obfuscated by asterisks when it is typed).

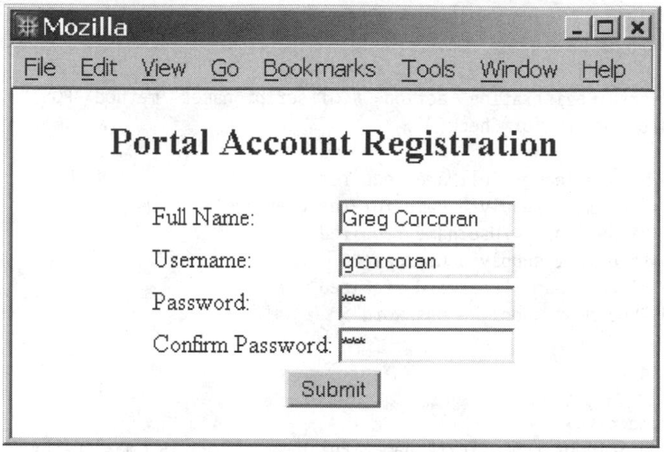

Figure 8-3. registration.cfm template for the portal application

When the form is submitted, a JavaScript `onSubmit` event handler is invoked from the `form` tag. This event handler calls a short JavaScript function called `formCheck( )` at the beginning of our template. Note that JavaScript is case sensitive, so it is important to reference field names and other functions with the proper case. The `formCheck( )` function checks to see that the values entered for `Password` and Confirm Password (`Password2`) are the same and that they aren't blank. If either test fails, a JavaScript alert box pops up letting the user know. After the user clicks the OK button, the function clears the Password and Confirm Password fields and returns the user to the form so that he can reenter the password. If both passwords match, the form information is submitted back to the *registration.cfm* template.

The form processing code in the template has two functions. The first is to ensure that the passwords passed from the entry form match. Even though this task was handled by our JavaScript function in the entry form, there are instances where a user's browser doesn't support JavaScript or has it disabled. In case of this, we provide a server-side check by checking to see if `Form.Password` and `Form.Password2` are the same. If they aren't, a message is displayed to the user telling him to hit the back button on his browser and reenter the passwords, and processing of the template is halted.

If the passwords do match, a `cfquery` is executed to insert the information from the form into the database. Before the password is inserted, a randomly generated 12-character string called a salt is generated and concatenated with the `form.Password` value. The resulting “salted” string is then hashed using ColdFusion’s `Hash()` function. The `Hash()` function encrypts a string one way using the MD5 hash algorithm. The resulting string is a 32-character hexadecimal representation of the original string. Because the MD5 algorithm is a one-way hash, there is no way to decrypt the encrypted string. This makes it ideal for storing passwords in database tables, where you wouldn’t want anyone to be able to open a table and view a list of user passwords. You should note, though, that using hashes makes it impossible to implement a system for recovering a lost or forgotten password. When dealing with hashes, you’ll need to reset a user’s password should he forget it.

Salting the password before hashing it makes it virtually impossible to launch a successful dictionary-style attack against the hashed password values stored in the database, because an attacker would have to try all of the possible salt values for each hash value in their dictionary. In our example, we use a 12-character string consisting of uppercase letters from A to Z. This means there are 26^{12} possible salt combinations for each password!

Let’s go ahead and add two records to the database using the form we just created. Use the data supplied in Table 8-2.

Table 8-2. User profile information to enter for security table

Username	Password	FullName
gcorcoran	dog	Greg Corcoran
pmoney	cat	Pere Money

Once you have entered the data, open up your database and look at the data you just entered. Notice that each `Password` field is populated with a 32-character string (as shown in Table 8-3). These strings are the hashed versions of the passwords you initially entered. Note that the `Salt` and `Password` values shown in Table 8-3 will differ from what you see in your database table due to the fact that the `Salt` is randomly generated. We’ll cover how to validate a password entered by a user on the login screen against the hashed value stored in the database in a few moments.

Table 8-3. User profile as it appears in the database after having the passwords salted and hashed

Username	Salt	Password	FullName
gcorcoran	TLQKYTPRJKSW	CAFC92F41D23D58CEA80E0EA3061F71B	Greg Corcoran
pmoney	LUMLATYEFUHR	3CD608EBCB054FD49079A18CD9680432	Pere Money

Authenticating Users

Once a user is registered for our portal, the next step is to allow him to log in to the system. You’ve already seen the login form from Example 8-2. When a user enters a username and password in the login form and clicks the submit button, the information is self-posted back to the *login.cfm* template.

The form processing code in Example 8-2 queries the `Users` table of the database using the username posted by the login form in Example 8-2 as parameters for the `WHERE` clause. Because the password stored in the database is a salted hash of the user's password, we need a way to make sure the password entered in the login form matches the password stored in the database. This is done by looking up the salt value for the username entered in the login form, concatenating it with the password entered in the login form, hashing the concatenated string, and then comparing it with the hashed value stored in the database. If a record was found for the username entered in the login form, and the salted, hashed password matches the value stored in the database, we consider this a valid login and set the session variable `session.LoggedIn` to `true`.

Next, a check is performed to see whether the user checked the "Remember my username for future logins" box. If so, her username (`form.Username`) is stored in a cookie called `Username`. The user is then redirected to our portal's *index.cfm* template (Example 7-3 in Chapter 7). If no records are found, `ValidateUser.RecordCount` evaluates to `0`. At this point, we know that the username/password combination is invalid, so we redirect the user back to the login page where the message "Invalid Login. Please Try Again" is displayed along with the login form. As a courtesy to users, the `Username` box is populated with the username originally submitted by the form. This is accomplished by passing the `Username` back as a URL variable.

As you can see, it really wasn't much work to add basic security features to our portal application. We simply made a database table to hold our user profiles and created a few simple CFML templates to handle the authentication and authorization functions required for the application.

Securing Non-CFML Files

The security model we used in our portal application works well for controlling access to CFML templates, but what about other types of files, such as HTML templates, Microsoft Word documents, or Adobe PDF files? The problem is that if you place any file type other than a CFML template in a directory under the control of the security model, the user can still access the file by entering its URL, because the *Application.cfm* template is included only for CFML templates. Because these files aren't parsed by ColdFusion, they aren't subject to the control of our security model. So, how can you secure non-CFML files while still using the security model?

The trick is to store the files you want to secure in a directory above your web root directory where they can't be accessed by a URL. For example, if your web root directory is *c:\inetsrv\wwwroot*, you can store the files you wish to secure in *c:\inetsrv*, *c:\inetsrv\securedfiles*, *c:\securedfiles*, or any other directory above *c:\inetsrv\wwwroot*, keeping the files inaccessible via URL provided you don't create a virtual directory to any of those directories.

Since files stored above the web root are inaccessible via URL, you need to use another method to retrieve them. This is where the `cfcontent` tag comes in. The `cfcontent` tag sends content (in this case a file) of a specified MIME type to the browser. This allows you to grab the file from its location above the web root and send it to the user's browser. The `cfcontent` tag accepts the following attributes:

```
<cfcontent type="MIME_type"
           file="filename"
           reset="Yes|No"
           deletefile="Yes|No">
```

The `type` attribute is required and specifies the MIME type or character set of the content to be sent to the browser. `file` is optional and specifies the name of the file being sent to the browser. The `reset` attribute is another optional attribute and accepts a `Yes`/`No` value. Specifying `Yes` results in the suppression of any output preceding the call to the `cfcontent` tag, while `No` preserves the output. The `reset` attribute is ignored if a value is specified for `file`. The default is `Yes`. The final attribute, `deletefile`, is also optional and determines whether to delete the file after it has been sent to the browser. `deletefile` is valid only if a file is specified in the `file` attribute. The default is `No`.

To demonstrate how the `cfcontent` tag can retrieve secured files, look at the code in Example 8-4. The template creates three hyperlinks, one for a Word document, one for a PDF file, and one for an HTML file.

Example 8-4. Displaying a menu of secured files

```
<!--- You may use other files here.  Simply change the file name and MIME
      type to match the file you wish to use --->
<cfset File1 = "MyDocument.doc">
<cfset MIME1 = "application/msword">
<cfset File2 = "MyPDF.pdf">
<cfset MIME2 = "application/pdf">
<cfset File3 = "MyHTML.htm">
<cfset MIME3 = "text/html; charset=utf-8">

<h2>Secure File Download</h2>
<cfoutput>
<table>
<tr>
  <td><a href="display.cfm?Filename=#URLEncodedFormat(File1)#&
MIMEType=#URLEncodedFormat(MIME1)#">Word Document</a></td>
</tr>
<tr>
  <td><a href="display.cfm?Filename=#URLEncodedFormat(File2)#&
MIMEType=#URLEncodedFormat(MIME2)#">PDF Document</a></td>
</tr>
<tr>
```

Example 8-4. Displaying a menu of secured files (continued)

```
  <td><a href="display.cfm?Filename=#URLEncodedFormat(File3)#&
MIMEType=#URLEncodedFormat(MIME3)#">HTML File</a></td>
</tr>
</table>
</cfoutput>
```

Although the list in this example is static, you can imagine how to easily pull the information used to construct the list from a database. This allows you to basically control who sees what file. Each link points to a template called *display.cfm*, shown in Example 8-5. Two URL parameters are appended to each link. The first parameter, `Filename`, specifies the filename (including extension) of the file you want to download or display. The second URL parameter is `MIMEType` and specifies the MIME type of the file. You'll see why this is important in a moment. For now, look at the output generated by the template, shown in Figure 8-4.

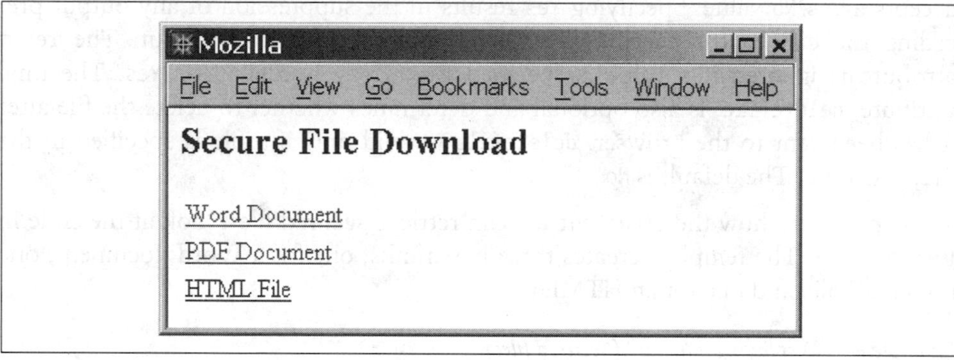

Figure 8-4. Displaying links to secured files

Clicking on any of the links generated by Example 8-4 passes the associated URL parameters to the *display.cfm* template in Example 8-5.

Example 8-5. Displaying secured files using cfcontent

```
<!--- Check to make sure the filename and mime type were passed in
      before processing --->
<cfif IsDefined('URL.MIMEType') and IsDefined('URL.FileName')>
  <!--- send the specified file to the browser.  You will need to store
        your files in a directory called c:\SecuredFiles for this
        example to work.  If you wish to use a different directory,
        change the directory name In the file attribute of the cfcontent
        tag. --->
  <cfcontent type="#URL.MIMEType#"
             file="c:\SecuredFiles\#URL.Filename#">
<cfelse>
  <h2>The specified file does not exist</h2>
</cfif>
```

When the *display.cfm* template receives the `Filename` and `MIMEType` URL parameters, it uses them to dynamically populate the `type` and `file` attributes of the `cfcontent` tag. If the user clicks on the hyperlink to the Word document, the `cfcontent` tag retrieves the Word document and returns it to the browser. If the user has Word associated with the web browser, Word should launch automatically and display the document. If not, a Save As dialog box should pop up, allowing the user to save the Word document to his system. If the user clicks on the hyperlink to the Adobe PDF document and has the Adobe Acrobat reader installed on the system, the PDF file should automatically display in the browser. If Acrobat reader isn't installed, the same Save As dialog box appears. Finally, if the user clicks on the link to the HTML file, the `cfcontent` tag retrieves it and displays it directly in the browser.

The technique presented here isn't the only way to use the `cfcontent` tag to serve secured files. Instead of passing the filename and MIME type in the URL, you could pass a file ID (such as a UUID) and use it to look up a database record containing the filename and MIME type as well as any additional information such as the directory on the server where the file is stored. Regardless of the technique you use, it is important to make sure you control access to the template(s) used to retrieve the secured files.

Levels of Access

The security model we've been discussing is great for granting and denying access to an application based on a user login. If a user is granted access, she is given access to the entire application and all its functionality. There are instances, however, where you might want to grant different levels of access to an application depending on who the user is. This can be handled easily in the security model we just described with the introduction of a few additional lines of code and the `Roles` field we created in our Users database table. In each template of your application, include a bit of logic to check the user's `session.Roles` against the role required for access to the page or section of code.

Taking Advantage of ColdFusion MX's New Security Framework

Before we get into the new security framework in ColdFusion MX, it's important that we cover a few important changes from previous versions of ColdFusion. In versions prior to MX, ColdFusion supported a set of Advanced Security services that integrated with an OEM version of Netegrity's popular SiteMinder (Version 3.51 for ColdFusion 4.5.x and Version 4.11 for ColdFusion 5.0) security product for providing granular control within ColdFusion applications. Advanced Security was a bear to use and a nightmare to administer, to say the least. Macromedia dropped the

Advanced Security services in ColdFusion MX in favor of a simpler system that uses Java as the underlying service.

This system makes uses of several new tags and functions to provide authentication and authorization functionality in your applications. Additionally, the new system is roles based, meaning that group-level permissions are inherent in its design. To get an idea of just how this new system works and how it differs from the security framework we built in the previous section, let's rework our portal application to make use of ColdFusion MX's built-in security framework. We'll start by rewriting the authentication piece of the portal.

Authenticating Users

ColdFusion MX supports two different types of authentication, application-based and HTTP (web server)–based. We'll cover both methods in this chapter, but I'd like to start out with a discussion of application-based authentication as it's the method that ColdFusion MX's security framework was primarily designed around.

Application-based authentication

In the previous section, we used a session-based mechanism for authenticating and authorizing portal users. With ColdFusion MX's security framework, a session-based model is no longer necessary. Instead, two tags, `cflogin` and `cfloginuser`, are used to authenticate a user and log that person into the system. Most commonly, these tags are used in an *Application.cfm* template to provide the security framework for an entire application. As such, let's rewrite the *Application.cfm* template for our portal application to use these new tags. The code for our new *Application.cfm* template can be seen in Example 8-6.

Example 8-6. Application.cfm template for implementing advanced security

```
<cfapplication name="MyPortal" clientmanagement="Yes"
   sessionmanagement="Yes" setclientcookies="Yes"
   sessiontimeout="#CreateTimeSpan(0, 0, 30, 0)#"
   applicationtimeout="#CreateTimeSpan(0, 0, 30, 0)#"
   clientstorage="Registry" loginstorage="Session">

<!--- Check to see if the application has been initialized.  If not, set the
      necessary application variables and initialize the app --->
<cflock timeout="30" throwontimeout="No" type="ReadOnly" scope="Application">
  <cfset IsInitialized = IsDefined('application.Initialized')>
</cflock>

<cfif not IsInitialized>
  <cflock type="Exclusive" scope="Application" timeout="10">
    <cfif not IsDefined('application.Initialized')>
      <cfset application.DSN = "ProgrammingCF">
      <cfset application.AdminEmail = "webmaster@example.com">
      <cfset application.Initialized = true>
```

Example 8-6. Application.cfm template for implementing advanced security (continued)

```
    </cfif>
  </cflock>
</cfif>

<!--- set default values for client variables --->
<cfparam name="client.Email" default="Yes">
<cfparam name="client.Stocks" default="Yes">
<cfparam name="client.News" default="Yes">
<cfparam name="client.Bookmarks" default="Yes">
<cfparam name="client.BGColor" default="FFFFFF">
<cfparam name="client.FontFace" default="Arial">
<cfparam name="client.HeaderFontColor" default="000000">
<cfparam name="client.HeaderBGColor" default="6666FF">
<cfparam name="client.FontColor" default="000000">

<!--- If the user clicked the logout link, log them out --->
<cfif IsDefined("URL.Logout")>
  <!--- Log out the user --->
  <cflogout>

  <cfset URL.Message="Thank you for logging out. Please visit again soon!">
</cfif>

<cflogin idletimeout="1800" applicationtoken="MyPortal"
         cookiedomain="example.com">
  <!--- If the cflogin structure does not exist, send the user to the login
        form. --->
  <cfif not IsDefined("cflogin")>
    <cfinclude template="login.cfm">
    <cfabort>
  <!--- Validate the user and assign roles --->
  <cfelse>
    <!--- If for some reason username or password is blank, send the user back
          to the login form. --->
    <cfif cflogin.Name is "" or cflogin.Password is "">
      <cfset URL.Message = "You must enter text in both the Username and Password
                             fields">
      <cfinclude template="login.cfm">
      <cfabort>
    <!--- Perform the user validation --->
    <cfelse>
      <cfquery name="ValidateUser" datasource="#application.DSN#">
          SELECT FullName, Salt, Password, Roles
          FROM Users
          WHERE Username = <cfqueryparam value="#cflogin.Name#"
                                         cfsqltype="CF_SQL_VARCHAR"
                                         maxlength="255">
      </cfquery>

      <!--- If the username and salted hashed password match, the user is
            authenticated and their role(s) assigned --->
      <cfif (ValidateUser.RecordCount) and
            (ValidateUser.Password is Hash(ValidateUser.Salt & cflogin.Password))>
```

Example 8-6. Application.cfm template for implementing advanced security (continued)

```
        <!--- If the user has no assigned roles, assign them to the generic
              "user" role. --->
        <cfif ValidateUser.Roles is "">
          <cfset ValidateUser.Roles = "User">
        </cfif>

        <cfloginuser name="#cflogin.Name#" password="#cflogin.Password#"
                     roles="#ValidateUser.Roles#">
        <cflock name="sLogin_Lock" timeout="30" type="Exclusive">
          <cfset session.FullName = ValidateUser.FullName>
        </cflock>

        <!--- If save username box is checked, set cookie --->
        <cfif IsDefined('form.SaveUsername')>
          <cfcookie name="Username" value="#cflogin.Name#">
        </cfif>
      <cfelse>
        <cfset URL.Message = "Invalid Login.  Please Try Again">
        <cfinclude template="login.cfm">
        <cfabort>
      </cfif>
    </cfif>
  </cfif>
</cflogin>
```

This *Application.cfm* template differs from the one we previously created for our portal application (Example 8-1) in a number of ways. The `cfapplication` tag establishes an application called `MyPortal`. Session and client management are enabled, and session and application timeouts of 30 minutes are set. Application and client variable defaults are set just as they were in our first portal example.

The optional `loginstorage` attribute is new in ColdFusion MX 6.1. It specifies whether login information associated with the `cflogin` scope should be stored in a cookie or session variable. If the attribute is set to `session`, the login is tied directly to a user's ColdFusion session and it remains active for as long as the session exists. If it is set to `cookie` (the default), the `cflogin` scope is stored in a cookie, and the session timeout is not tied to the user's ColdFusion session. In this case, we tie the `cflogin` scope to the session scope.

Next, a check for a URL variable called `URL.Logout` is made. If the variable exists, we know that the user clicked on the logout link in the portal application, so we need to log that person out. In our session-based application, we simply cleared the contents of the `session` structure, which essentially deleted the user's session, causing him to be logged out of the system. In our new security framework, however, we aren't using session variables to determine whether a user is logged in or not, so we need a different way to log a person out. Here's where the `cflogout` tag comes into play. `cflogout` is a new tag in ColdFusion MX. Its sole purpose is to log a user out of ColdFusion MX's security framework. If a `cflogout` tag is not used, a user is automatically logged out when his ColdFusion session times out or when his cflogin "session" ends as defined by the idletimeout attribute in the cflogin tag, which we'll cover in just a moment. After the user is logged out, we still clear the session structure, because session variables are used to store the user's full name.

The next part of the *Application.cfm* template is where the actual user authentication is performed. The first thing you should notice is the cflogin tag. cflogin is new in ColdFusion MX and acts as a container for ColdFusion MX's built-in security framework. The cflogin tag provides a facility for authenticating users against a database, an LDAP directory, or another authentication store. The body of the tag gets executed only if the user is not logged in. Code to authenticate the user, such as a database or cfldap query, is executed within the cflogin tags. A cfloginuser tag is used to establish the user's identity and any roles he might have. In this case, we're going to use the same database query we used in the first portal application, only with a slight twist.

Notice that the cflogin tag has three attributes, idletimeout, applicationtoken, and cookiedomain. All three attributes are optional. idletimeout specifies the number of seconds of idle time (no page interactivity) ColdFusion should wait before logging the user off. The default is 1,800 (30 minutes). When the cflogin tag is used in conjunction with the cfloginuser tag and the loginstorage attribute of the cfapplication tag is set to cookie, an in-memory cookie identifying the security session is set. When the user closes his browser, this cookie is automatically destroyed, effectively logging the user out within the context of the ColdFusion MX security framework. If loginstorage is set to session, the lesser of the idletimeout value set in cfloginuser or the session timeout period set in the cfapplication tag (or ColdFusion Administrator) is used to determine the timeout value for the session. This behavior is new in ColdFusion MX 6.1; in ColdFusion MX 6.0, the cflogin scope can only be tied to a cookie and not to the session scope. The applicationtoken attribute specifies a unique identifier for the application that the security framework should apply to. The default is the application name as specified in the name attribute of the cfapplication tag. The final attribute, cookiedomain, specifies the domain for which the security framework cookie can be read and written. Entries must always start with a dot. For example, cookiedomain=".oreilly.com" is a valid entry. Multiple entries should be separated by semicolons. The default is no domain restrictions.

The first thing that happens within the cflogin container in our code is a check for the existence of a structure called cflogin. This structure exists only if HTTP Basic, HTTP Digest, or NTLM Authentication is used, or if form or URL variables named j_username and j_password are used to pass the username and password, respectively, to the cflogin tag. If so, a special scope structure named cflogin is available that contains the following key/value pairs:

cflogin.Username
: The username passed via HTTP Basic, HTTP Digest, or NTLM Authentication or a j_username form or URL variable.

`cflogin.Password`
: The password passed via HTTP Basic Authentication or a `j_password` form or URL variable. Both HTTP Digest and NTLM Authentication do not usually supply the password. If you use either of these methods, `cflogin.Password` usually contains an empty string.

In order to take advantage of the `cflogin` scope, you must either use HTTP Basic, HTTP Digest, or NTLM Authentication (via your web server) or name the username and password fields in your login form `j_username` and `j_password` as I'll show you in just a moment. For now, the important thing to note in our example is the check for the `cflogin` structure. If it doesn't exist, we know than no username and password has been passed via our login form, so we redirect the user to a login form using the `cflocation` tag.

If the `cflogin` structure does exist, we know that someone is trying to log in and has submitted a username and password via our login form. If this is the case, we execute a `cfquery` to look up the user in the database. We use the same salted, hashed password check we used in the first portal security example to handle our user authentication. If the user doesn't check out, he is sent back to the login form with a message to try again. If the user does authenticate, the `cfloginuser` tag is used to identify the user to the ColdFusion MX security framework and to assign him access roles. `cfloginuser` takes three required attributes: `name` for the username of the user, `password` for the user's password, and `roles` for a comma-delimited list of roles for the user. Be sure that there are no spaces between commas and list elements; otherwise, ColdFusion processes them as part of the list element.

In our example, the `Name` and `Password` values stored in the `cflogin` structure are used to populate the like-named attributes of the `cfloginuser` tag. The user's roles are pulled from the `Roles` field in the `Users` table in our database. If the user doesn't have any roles assigned in the database, our *Application.cfm* template sets a default role of `User`. Finally, a session variable is set that contains the user's full name as pulled from the database. This completes our revised *Application.cfm* template.

With that out of the way, let's take a look at Example 8-7, which contains the new login form for our portal. You can replace the existing *login.cfm* template with this new version.

Example 8-7. Replacement login.cfm template

```
<cfparam name="form.j_username" default="">

<cfif IsDefined('cookie.Username')>
  <cfset form.j_username = cookie.Username>
</cfif>

<div align="center">
<h2>Portal Login</h2>
<cfif IsDefined('URL.Message')>
```

Example 8-7. Replacement login.cfm template (continued)

```
  <cfoutput><span style="Message">#Trim(URL.Message)#</span></cfoutput>
  <p>
</cfif>

<cfoutput>
<form name="ValidateUser" action="index.cfm" method="Post">
</cfoutput>
<input type="hidden" name="j_username_required"
       value="You must supply a username">
<input type="hidden" name="j_password_required"
       value="You must supply a password">
<table border="0">
<tr>
  <td>Username:</td>
  <td>
    <cfoutput>
      <input type="Text" name="j_username" size="15"
             maxlength="255" value="#form.j_username#">
    </cfoutput>
  </td>
</tr>
<tr>
  <td>Password:</td>
  <td><input type="Password" name="j_password" size="15" "maxlength="255"></td>
</tr>
<tr>
  <td colspan="2">
    <input type="Checkbox" name="SaveUsername"
           value="Yes">Remember my username for future logins</td>
</tr>
<tr>
  <td colspan="2" align="Center">
    <input type="Submit" name="Submit" value="Submit">
  </td>
</tr>
</table>
</form>
*This site is for registered users.  If you are not currently a member,
you may <a href="registration.cfm">register here</a>.
</div>
```

Because we are handling the actual authentication process in our *Application.cfm* template, it isn't necessary to code any of that logic into our login form. All the login form needs to do now is provide a place for the user to enter his username and password and submit the page. Note that the username and password fields are named j_username and j_password respectively. This is necessary to make use of the cflogin structure in the *Application.cfm* template.

The *Application.cfm* template handles all the form processing. The login form posts to the portal's *index.cfm* page. This allows us to route the user to the main portal page upon successful login, as the *Application.cfm* template with the authentication check runs before the *index.cfm* template executes. If the user authenticates successfully, *index.cfm* is allowed to run. If authentication fails, *index.cfm* never runs, and the user is sent back to the login form. With the *Application.cfm* and *login.cfm* templates rewritten, you can go ahead and test them out to see how they handle the authentication tasks for the portal. When you are finished, we'll look at how we can use this framework to control access to specific pages or sections of code based on user roles.

HTTP authentication

As I mentioned earlier in the chapter, ColdFusion MX also supports HTTP-based authentication in addition to, or combined with, application-based authentication. HTTP authentication is a standardized authentication method supported by most web servers on the market. It's an HTTP-based mechanism for prompting a user for username and password information and supplying those credentials to each requested page via a standard HTTP header. HTTP authentication can easily be used in concert with ColdFusion MX's security framework to provide the login prompt instead of using a standard HTML form.

In order to make use of HTTP authentication, you use the `cfheader` tag to pass two standard HTTP headers to the user's browser. The first header should specify a 401 status code (Unauthorized); the second should pass the header `WWW-Authenticate: Basic realm="`*`My Realm`*`"`. This causes the browser to pop up a standard HTTP username/password dialog box. When submitted, the information entered in the dialog box is automatically passed to the `cflogin` structure and is available as `cflogin.Username` and `cflogin.Password`, respectively. You should note that when using HTTP Basic Authentication, username and password values are Base64 encoded and passed in the clear. This means that the values can easily be intercepted and converted back to string values with a minimum of effort. If you require an additional level of security, consider using HTTP Digest or NTLM Authentication, as those methods pass password values as a one-way hash. Additionally, consider using SSL in order to further secure the communication between a user's browser and your server. Example 8-8 shows how we can once again rewrite our portal's *login.cfm* template to use HTTP authentication instead of the HTML form we used in previous examples.

Example 8-8. Using HTTP authentication with ColdFusion MX

```
<cfheader statuscode="401">
<cfheader name="WWW-Authenticate" value="Basic realm=""MyPortal""">
<h3>You are not authorized to access the portal</h3>
```

The code in this example sends the two headers we described earlier to the user's browser, causing the authentication popup box to appear. Entering an invalid username and/or password causes the "You are not authorized to access the portal" message to appear.

Technically, you should also modify the *Application.cfm* and *index.cfm* templates if you are going to use this authentication method. These templates should be modified to remove the code for logging out a user. This is necessary because of how the HTTP authentication mechanism works. Once a successful login is made, the username and password information are cached and automatically passed along in the HTTP header for each subsequent page the user requests. Using the `cflogout` tag removes the login credentials from the `cflogin` scope, but the next time the user requests a page, his username and password will be passed along in the HTTP header, and the user will automatically be logged back into the system! The only way to reliably log out when HTTP authentication is used is to close the browser (the `idletimeout` attribute in the `cflogin` tag has no effect either). For this reason alone, I tend to shy away from using HTTP authentication in favor of using a standard HTML login form.

Role-Based Permissions

Besides authenticating users, ColdFusion MX's security framework allows you to grant and deny access to individual users based on roles you assign to them. You can think of roles as having the same purpose as groups. In other words, you can assign a user a role such as "user" or "administrator," then grant or deny access to portions of your application based on these roles. Roles are assigned to users using the `cfloginuser` tag's `roles` attribute. As I mentioned earlier, users can be assigned a single role, or they can be assigned multiple roles by providing a comma-delimited list to the `roles` attribute. It's important to note that roles are case sensitive as well. Also, if you are providing a list of roles for a user, you need to make sure there are no spaces between each role and the comma used to delimit the list. Failing to do this will cause you problems, as ColdFusion interprets those spaces as part of the role name. The granularity of this type of security framework lets you be as relaxed or as strict with security as you need to be.

Earlier in the chapter, we created a field called `Roles` in our `Users` table. It's time to populate that field for our two user records. Table 8-4 shows the roles you should add to the two user records stored in the table.

Table 8-4. Adding roles to the Users table

Username	Roles
Pmoney	Administrator,User
Gcorcoran	User

With the roles added to the database, let's look at how we can take advantage of these roles to secure application functionality in ColdFusion MX. Two new functions are available to make writing your authorization code easier: `GetAuthUser( )` and `IsUserInRole( )`. `GetAuthUser( )` simply returns the name of the currently authorized user as was provided to the `cfloginuser` tag. If no user is currently authorized, the function returns an empty string. `IsUserInRole( )`, on the other hand, is used to determine whether a particular user's role(s) match the role(s) you pass to the function. This allows you to grant or deny access to particular sections of code based on a user's role(s). For example, going back to our portal application, it's easy to create an administrator's widget and include it only if a user has "Administrator" as one of his roles. Example 8-9 shows a modified *index.cfm* template that uses the `GetAuthUser( )` function to display the user's username and the `IsUserInRole( )` function to determine whether the current user should see the administration widget.

Example 8-9. Using GetAuthUser() and IsUserInRole()

```
<html>
  <head>
    <title>My Portal</title>
    <cfinclude template="_stylesheet.cfm">
  </head>
<body>
<cfoutput>
<h1>Welcome #ListFirst(session.FullName, " ")# (#GetAuthUser( )#)</h1>
</cfoutput>
<table width="100%" border="0" cellpadding="0" cellspacing="5">
  <tr>
    <cfoutput>
    <td class="CustomizeLink"><a href="Customize.cfm">Customize</a></td>
    <td class="CustomizeLink" align="Right"><a
        href="index.cfm?logout=true">Logout</a></td>
    </cfoutput>
  </tr>
  <tr>
    <td width="19%" valign="Top">
      <table width="100%" border="0" cellspacing="0" cellpadding="5">
        <!--- If a user is an Administrator, show them the admin widget --->
        <cfif IsUserInRole("Administrator")>
          <cfinclude template="_admin.cfm">
        </cfif>
        <cfif client.Email>
          <cfinclude template="_email.cfm">
        </cfif>
        <cfif client.Stocks>
          <cfinclude template="_stock.cfm">
        </cfif>
      </table>
    </td>
    <td width="81%" valign="Top">
      <table width="100%" border="0" cellspacing="0" cellpadding="5">
        <cfif client.News>
          <cfinclude template="_news.cfm">
        </cfif>
        <cfif client.Bookmarks>
          <cfinclude template="_bookmarks.cfm">
        </cfif>
```

Example 8-9. Using GetAuthUser() and IsUserInRole() (continued)

```
      </table>
    </td>
  </tr>
</table>
<hr>
<cfoutput>
<div class="Footer">Please email questions or concerns to <a href="mailto:
 #application.AdminEmail#">#application.AdminEmail#</a>.</div>
</cfoutput>
</body>
</html>
```

The code for the administration widget is shown in Example 8-10. The first thing you should notice is that we use a second `IsUserInRole( )` function around all of the code. Although this may seem redundant, it's done because the administration widget is a simple included file. If we didn't have this second check, any logged-in user, regardless of her role, could simply type the URL to the administrator widget into her browser and execute the code. This is, of course, only one way to do things. There are other ways (many of them superior to this method) to build a portal-type application. The techniques shown here are meant only to provide an example of how to authorize access to functionality, as opposed to being an endorsement for any particular type of development practice.

Example 8-10. Secured administrator widget

```
<cfif IsUserInRole("Administrator")>
<tr>
  <td class="SectionHeader" colspan="2">Administration</td>
</tr>
<tr>
  <td class="LeftTableBody" colspan="2">
    <ul>
      <li><span class="ListItems"><a
          href="/admin/user.cfm">User Management</a></span></li>
      <li><span class="ListItems"><a
          href="/admin/roles.cfm">Roles Management</a></span></li>
      <li><span class="ListItems"><a
          href="/admin/content.cfm">Content Management</a></span></li>
    </ul>
  </td>
</tr>
</cfif>
```

You should note that passing more than one role to the `IsUserInRole( )` function means a user must possess at least those roles (not any single role) to be authorized. Thus, `IsUserInRole("Editor,Writer")` returns `true` only if the authenticated user has both the "Editor" and "Writer" roles.

CHAPTER 9

Error and Exception Handling

Structured exception handling lets you gracefully catch and handle exceptions that occur in your ColdFusion applications. Exceptions can include anything from a page timeout or a missing file to a database error or a problem with an external object. Using the techniques discussed in this chapter, you can build extremely robust exception-handling capabilities into your ColdFusion applications.

There are a number of different levels at which you can handle exceptions and errors in a ColdFusion application. At the most basic level, you can use the `cftry` and `cfcatch` tags in a template, to test for and trap exceptions right where they occur. With the `cfthrow` tag, you can also define, throw, and catch custom exceptions in your application.

Of course, catching every exception when it occurs can become quite tedious, so ColdFusion provides a couple of different mechanisms for handling exceptions at a higher level. With the `cferror` tag, you can define generic error handlers for different kinds of errors. The `cferror` tag is normally used in the *Application.cfm* template, so that error handling occurs in the context of the Web Application Framework. This ability to provide "catch all" error handling for an application is quite convenient and powerful.

In addition, a site administrator can set up error and exception handling at the server level, using the ColdFusion Administrator. We'll cover all these different techniques for error and exception handling in this chapter.

Basic Exception Handling

Exception handling allows you to test for and trap exceptions when they happen, so that your applications can respond to problems appropriately, as opposed to just throwing an error or invoking a separate error-handling template. With exception handling, it is usually possible to allow your application to continue functioning despite the fact that an exception has occurred.

Basic exception handling in ColdFusion uses two tags, cftry and cfcatch. These tags allow you to identify potentially problematic areas of your application code and deal with anticipated exceptions where they are most likely to occur. The basic syntax for using cftry/cfcatch is:

```
<cftry>
Potentially problematic code...

  <cfcatch type="exception_type">
  Code to implement in the event the exception is caught...
  </cfcatch>

  <cfcatch type="exception_type">
  ...
  </cfcatch>

</cftry>
```

The cftry/cfcatch syntax is straightforward. First, you wrap the section of code for which you wish to provide exception handling by a set of cftry tags. Immediately following the potentially problematic code, you use one or more cfcatch blocks to test for various types of exceptions. This means that you can protect individual sections of your code from more than one exception at a time. Within a cfcatch block, you can include any HTML and CFML you want, including cfcatch variables (which we'll cover in just a few moments). It is also possible to nest additional cftry/cfcatch tags within a cfcatch block for.

Let's consider an example. Say you have an application that uses the cfhttp tag to retrieve data from a text file that is generated and stored on your server on a regular basis. There is a chance that your application might attempt to access the text file at the same time that the file is being updated, resulting in an error. To prevent this, you can wrap your cfhttp call with cftry/cfcatch tags to catch any problems that might come up when trying to access the text file. If an exception does occur, you can handle it by displaying a page that tells the user that the file is in the process of being updated and to try back again in a few minutes. Example 9-1 illustrates this technique.

Example 9-1. cftry/cfcatch block for handling any exception generated by a cfhttp call

```
<!--- Attempt to use the cfhttp tag to retrieve the stock quotes file --->
<cftry>

<cfhttp URL="http://www.example.com/myfile.txt" method="Get"
        columns="Ticker, Time, Price" delimiter=","
        resolveurl="False" throwonerror="Yes">

  <!--- Catch any exceptions and let the user know the file is being updated --->
  <cfcatch type="Any">
    <h2>Stock quotes are currently being updated.  Please check back again in a
    few minutes...</h2>
```

Example 9-1. cftry/cfcatch block for handling any exception generated by a cfhttp call (continued)

```
  </cfcatch>
</cftry>
```

The cfcatch tag takes a single attribute called type, which specifies the type of exception to watch for. Possible values for type include the following:

Any
: Catches any unexpected exceptions. In versions of ColdFusion prior to MX, this exception type had to be coded as the last cfcatch within a cftry block if more than one cfcatch was used. As of ColdFusion MX, this is no longer true. You can code your cfcatch blocks in any order you want. If an exception occurs, ColdFusion MX automatically chooses the most appropriate cfcatch type.

Application
: Catches application-level exceptions, which are defined using the Application type in the cfthrow tag. This type is covered in detail in the next section.

CustomType
: Catches developer-specified exceptions as defined with the cfthrow tag. This type is covered in detail in the next section.

Database
: Catches exceptions raised when interacting with data sources.

Expression
: Catches exceptions that occur when the evaluation of an expression results in an error.

Lock
: Catches exceptions associated with the cflock tag, such as timeouts, etc.

MissingInclude
: Catches exceptions that occur when an included template isn't found. This exception type covers exceptions thrown by the cfinclude, cfmodule, and cferror tags.

Object
: Catches exceptions associated with external objects, such as COM/DCOM, CORBA, and Java objects.

SearchEngine
: Catches exceptions thrown by the cfcollection, cfindex, and cfsearch tags associated with the Verity search engine. This type is new in ColdFusion MX.

Security
: Catches exceptions that result when authentication fails within the ColdFusion security framework.

Template
: Catches general application errors associated with ColdFusion templates.

Besides the values already listed for the type attribute, ColdFusion also supports a number of additional structured exception types. These exception types are generated by very specific conditions, such as request timeouts or by exceptions encountered as the result of a call to various ColdFusion tags. These exceptions types are listed under cftry in Appendix A.

Additionally, as of ColdFusion MX, you can now specify Java exception classes in the type attribute. This gives you even more granular control over error handling, as every exception thrown by ColdFusion belongs to one of these classes. An exception's class can be viewed by turning debugging on in the ColdFusion Administrator and looking at the first line in the stack trace of the error output. As an additional benefit of this type of exception handling, you can use it to handle exceptions thrown by non-CFML Java objects.

As I already mentioned, you can refer to several cfcatch variables inside a cfcatch block. These variables are automatically generated whenever an exception is trapped by a cfcatch block; they are stored in a read-only structure called cfcatch. The cfcatch variables are available to use within the trapping cfcatch block only and can perform any number of tasks, such as evaluating additional processing options, writing log entries, and providing custom error or informational messages to users. Additionally, any valid HTML, CFML, or JavaScript can be used within a cfcatch block in conjunction with the cfcatch return variables. The following variables are available regardless of the exception type raised:

`cfcatch.Type`
: The type of exception that occurred.

`cfcatch.Message`
: The error message generated by the exception, if any.

`cfcatch.Detail`
: A detailed error message generated by the CFML interpreter.

`cfcatch.RootCause`
: Returns a Java object containing the Java servlet exception generated by the JVM as the exception's root cause. This variable is new in ColdFusion MX.

`cfcatch.TagContext`
: The name and position of each tag in the tag stack, as well as the full pathnames of the files containing the tags as an array of structures. Each structure in the TagContext array contains the following:

  `type`
  : The type of page generating the exception. type always returns "CFML". This key is new in ColdFusion MX.

  `ID`
  : The name of the tag within the stack where the exception occurred. If the exception occurs within cfscript tags, ID returns "??".

`template`
: The full path to the template containing the tag.

`line`
: The line number within the template where the tag was found.

`column`
: No longer supported in ColdFusion MX. This key is still available for backward compatibility with previous versions of ColdFusion, but it always returns 0. In previous versions of ColdFusion, `column` returned the column number within the template where the tag was found

`raw_trace`
: The raw Java stack trace for the exception. This key is new in ColdFusion MX.

  In versions of ColdFusion prior to MX, CFML Stack Trace must be enabled in the Debugging section of the ColdFusion Administrator in order to populate this variable. If this option isn't enabled, ColdFusion returns a zero-length array for `cfcatch.TagContext`.

In addition to these variables, there are some `cfcatch` variables that are available only for specific exception types. These variables are detailed under `cftry` in Appendix A.

The next three examples step through the process of trapping different types of exceptions and offer different strategies for handling them. Example 9-2 generates an exception by attempting to use an undefined variable (`y`) in an expression. Because the `type` of exception it's set to catch is `Any`, the `cfcatch` tag that handles the exception is an example of a general exception handler.

Example 9-2. Using cftry/cfcatch to catch unexpected exceptions

```
<cftry>
  <cfset x=y+1>

  <cfcatch type="Any">
    <cfdump var="#cfcatch#">
  </cfcatch>
</cftry>
```

The `cfcatch` block in this template is set to catch any type of exception that occurs (`type` is `Any`). Generally, you should trap for specific types of exceptions before implementing a `cfcatch` tag to handle `Any` exceptions. As a matter of style, and to make code easier to debug, setting `type` to `Any` should be done as the last `cfcatch` tag in a multi `cfcatch` scenario. I've used it alone in this example mainly for illustrative purposes.

If we execute the template in Example 9-2, it generates a nicely formatted table that contains all the `cfcatch` error variables and their associated values. The table is created using the `cfdump` tag to dump the `cfcatch` structure (remember that the `cfcatch` variables are all stored in a special read-only structure called `cfcatch`). Using `cfdump` provides us with a simple way to quickly view the nested contents of the cfcatch structure.

Example 9-3 takes a different approach to exception handling. It attempts to include a template called *mybogusheader.cfm* at the beginning of the template via cfinclude. The cfinclude tag is wrapped in a cftry block. A cfcatch tag with type set to MissingInclude is used to deal with the exception generated in the event that the included file doesn't exist (which it doesn't).

Example 9-3. Handling a missing include and notifying the site administrator of the problem

```
<cftry>
<cfinclude template="mybogusheader.cfm">

<cfcatch type="MissingInclude">
Error loading header template.  Notifying site administrator...

<cfmail to="siteadministrator@example.com"
        from="webmaster@example.com"
        subject="Missing Header Template">
Site Administrator,

The following template: #cfcatch.MissingFileName# seems to be missing from the
Web site.  Please investigate as soon as possible.

Regards,

The Webmaster
</cfmail>
</cfcatch>
</cftry>

<center>
<h2>Hello World!</h2>
</center>
```

When this template is invoked, the cfcatch is triggered, and an email message is automatically generated (via cfmail) and sent to the site administrator informing her of the error. The name of the missing template is included in the email. Although executing the template in Example 9-3 generates an exception, the template can still continue processing (thanks to the cftry/cfcatch handlers).

As I mentioned earlier, it is possible to use more than one cfcatch tag within a single cftry block. Example 9-4 illustrates this point by providing two different types of exception handling for the same piece of code.

Example 9-4. Anticipating multiple exception types with cftry/cfcatch

```
<cftry>

<!--- Set the default log file write status to successful --->
<cfparam name="LogFileStatus" default="Log entry successful.">
```

Example 9-4. Anticipating multiple exception types with cftry/cfcatch (continued)

```
<h2>Attempting to write a log file entry...</h2>

<!--- Lock the cffile call so that only one call can be attempted at a time.
      If you want to purposely generate an exception for the second cfcatch
      tag to catch, change the directory in the file attribute of the cffile
      tag to a directory that does not exist on your server. --->
<cflock timeout="30" throwontimeout="Yes" type="Exclusive">

<!--- Write an entry to the log file --->
<cffile action="Append" file="c:\temp\logfile.txt"
        output="This is a test entry" addnewline="Yes">
</cflock>

<!--- Catch lock exceptions --->
<cfcatch type="Lock">
  <cfset LogFileStatus = "There was a problem obtaining a file lock.  Log
         entry <b>not</b> written.">
</cfcatch>

<!-- Catch any other type of exception that might occur --->
<cfcatch type="Any">
  <cfset LogFileStatus = "An unknown exception occurred.  Log entry <b>not</b>
         written.">
</cfcatch>
</cftry>

<p>
<cfoutput>
Processing Complete:  #LogFileStatus#
</cfoutput>
```

This template uses the `cffile` tag to attempt to write a simple log file entry. The `cffile` tag is wrapped by a `cflock` tag so that the log file can be accessed only one process at a time. Failing to use the `cflock` tag can result in a file-access error or corruption of the log file. The call to the `cffile` tag is also wrapped by a `cftry` tag and two `cfcatch` tags. The first `cfcatch` tag catches exceptions related to the `cflock` tag we used around our `cffile` call. This is done by specifying `Lock` for the `type` attribute of this `cfcatch` tag. Any exceptions resulting from the lock (such as a timeout) are handled by this tag. If an exception is generated, the value of `LogFileStatus` is set to "There was a problem obtaining a file lock. Log entry not written".

A second `cfcatch` tag is used as a backup to catch any unforeseen exceptions. This is facilitated by setting the `type` attribute of the second `cfcatch` tag to `Any`. If any exception not caught by the first `cfcatch` tag is thrown, this `cfcatch` tag handles it by setting the value of `LogFileStatus` to "An unknown exception occurred. Log entry not written". Once the `cftry/cfcatch` section has completed, a message containing the value of `LogFileStatus` is output to the browser.

Custom Exception Handling

In the previous section, we covered the basics of using cftry/cfcatch to handle predefined types of exceptions that might occur within a ColdFusion application. While these general exception types can handle any type of exception, they do so in a generic, one-size-fits-all manner. Fortunately, ColdFusion also allows you to specify custom exception types that can be caught with the same cftry/cfcatch techniques we already covered.

As I mentioned in the previous section, the cfcatch tag can accept a custom exception type for its type attribute. That custom exception type is defined using the cfthrow tag. The cfthrow tag generates a custom exception type that can be caught by a cfcatch tag when the type attribute is set to Application, Any, or the custom type you specified in the cfthrow tag. In other words, when something goes wrong in your application, and you need to generate a custom exception, use cfthrow. The general syntax for using cfthrow is as follows:

```
<cfthrow type="custom_exception_type"
         message="error_message"
         detail="detailed_event_description"
         errorcode="error_code"
         extendedinfo="extended_information"
         object="name">
```

The cfthrow tag accepts the following optional attributes:

type
: Specifies a name for the exception type. You may give the exception type a custom name or use the predefined type Application.

message
: Message describing the event that triggered the exception.

detail
: Specifies additional information about the exception.

errorcode
: A custom error code (numeric) you want to make available.

extendedinfo
: Specifies additional information regarding the error you want made available.

object
: Used to throw a Java exception from a CFML page. *name* specifies the name of the object throwing the exception. This must be the same as the name attribute of the cfobject tag. If the object attribute is used, all other attributes are ignored.

When you have CFML code that can possibly generate a custom exception with the cfthrow tag, you obviously want to use a cfcatch block to test for the custom exception. This is done by setting the type attribute of the cfcatch tag to the name specified in the type attribute of the cfthrow tag or by setting it to Application (the default).

You can name custom exception types in a hierarchical manner, so that you can reference groups of custom exception types with a single cfcatch tag. ColdFusion uses pattern matching to search from the most specific to the least specific name. Consider the following cfthrow tag:

```
<cfthrow type="MyApp.RequiredParameters.MyVar">
```

Any of the three following cfcatch tags can catch the exception:

```
<cfcatch type="MyApp.RequiredParameters.MyVar ">
<cfcatch type="MyApp.RequiredParameters">
<cfcatch type="MyApp">
```

Note that this behavior results in a potential backward compatibility problem with versions of ColdFusion prior to 4.5. In these older versions, a custom exception coded as:

```
<cfthrow type="MyApp.RequiredParameters.MyVar">
```

can be caught only by an identically named cfcatch tag, as in:

```
<cfcatch type="MyApp.RequiredParameters.MyVar">
```

but not by these:

```
<cfcatch type="MyApp.RequiredParameters">
<cfcatch type-"MyApp">
```

This behavior can be manually overridden in versions of ColdFusion prior to MX by including the cfsetting tag in your *Application.cfm* template with the catchexceptionsbypattern attribute set to No, as in:

```
<cfapplication name="MyApplication">
<cfsetting catchexceptionsbypattern="No">
```

Note that the catchexceptionsbypattern attribute is not supported in ColdFusion MX.

Now that we've covered the basics of how the cfthrow tag works in conjunction with cftry/cfcatch, let's look at an example that ties everything together. Example 9-5 uses the cfthrow tag to define a custom exception to throw in the event that a variable called form.MyVar doesn't exist.

Example 9-5. Trapping a custom exception type using cfthrow

```
<style type="text/css">
  th {
    background-color : #0000FF;
    font-weight : bold;
    color : #FFFFFF;
    text-align : center;
  }
  td {
    background-color : #C0C0C0;
  }
  td.TagStack {
```

Example 9-5. Trapping a custom exception type using cfthrow (continued)

```
    background-color : #D3D3D3;
  }
</style>

<cftry>
  <!--- see if the form variable MyVar exists.  If not, throw a custom
        exception --->
  <cfif not IsDefined('form.MyVar')>
      <cfthrow type="MyApp.RequiredParameters.MissingMyVar"
               message="The form variable MyVar does not exist!"
               detail="This variable must be present for this template to
                       function"
               errorcode="10"
               extendedinfo="This is all the information available.">
  </cfif>

  <!--- catch the custom exception --->
  <cfcatch type="MyApp.RequiredParameters.MissingMyVar">
    <h2>Ooops - your variable (form.MyVar) was not found!  Diagnostic
        information is shown below:</h2>

    <br>
    <h3>cfcatch Exception Information</h3>
    <table border="0">
    <tr>
      <th>Variable</th>
      <th>Value</th>
    </tr>

    <cfoutput>
    <tr>
      <td>cfcatch.Type</td><td>#cfcatch.Type#</td>
    </tr>
    <tr>
      <td>cfcatch.Message</td><td>#cfcatch.Message#</td>
    </tr>
    <tr>
      <td>cfcatch.Detail</td><td>#cfcatch.Detail#</td>
    </tr>
    <tr>
      <td>cfcatch.TagContext</td>
      <td>
        <table border="0">
        <tr>
          <th colspan="3">Tag Stack</th>
        </tr>
        <tr>
          <th>Tag</th>
          <th>Position</th>
          <th>Template</th>
        </tr>
```

Example 9-5. Trapping a custom exception type using cfthrow (continued)

```
        <cfloop index="element" from="1" to="#ArrayLen(cfcatch.TagContext)#">
          <cfset TheStack = #cfcatch.TagContext[element]#>
          <tr>
            <td class="TagStack">#TheStack["ID"]#</td>
            <td class="TagStack">(#TheStack["Line"]#:#TheStack["Column"]#)</td>
            <td class="TagStack">#TheStack["Template"]#</td>
          </tr>
        </cfloop>
        </table>
      </td>
    </tr>
    <tr>
      <td>cfcatch.ErrorCode</td><td>#cfcatch.ErrorCode#</td>
    </tr>
    <tr>
      <td>cfcatch.ExtendedInfo</td><td>#cfcatch.ExtendedInfo#</td>
    </tr>
    </cfoutput>
    </table>
  </cfcatch>
</cftry>
```

In this example, a `cfif` statement is used within a `cftry` block to check for the existence of a form variable called `form.MyVar`. If the form variable doesn't exist (which it doesn't), a `cfthrow` tag generates a custom exception. The tag uses several attributes to identify the exception and provide detailed error information. After the exception has been defined with the `cfthrow` tag, a `cfcatch` block tests for the custom exception. Notice the `type` attribute of the `cfcatch` tag is set to the same name as specified in the `type` attribute of the `cfthrow` tag. The `cfcatch` block catches the error and writes a table out to the browser containing the information related to the exception.

When `cfthrow` is used in conjunction with the `cftry` and `cfcatch` tags, a number of variables are made available when an exception is thrown. If these variables look familiar, it is because they are. The variables are the same as those available for a regular `cfcatch` tag, except that most of the values are provided by the `cfthrow` tag as opposed to the CFML interpreter:

`cfcatch.Type`
: The type of exception that occurred.

`cfcatch.Message`
: The error message specified in the `message` attribute of the `cfthrow` tag, if any.

`cfcatch.Detail`
: A detailed error message generated by the CFML interpreter.

`cfcatch.TagContext`
: The name and position of each tag in the tag stack as well as the full pathnames of the files containing the tags. In versions of ColdFusion prior to MX, CFML

Stack Trace must be enabled in the Debugging section of the ColdFusion Administrator in order to populate this variable.

`cfcatch.ErrorCode`
: The contents of the `ErrorCode` attribute, if any, from the `cfthrow` tag.

`cfcatch.ExtendedInfo`
: The contents of the `ExtendedInfo` attribute, if any, from the `cfthrow` tag.

Rethrowing Exceptions

Now that we've discussed the framework for building robust error- and exception-handling capabilities into your ColdFusion applications, let's look at a technique you can use to create more advanced exception-handling systems for your applications. On occasion, it may be desirable to rethrow an exception that can't be handled adequately by a `cfcatch` tag. For example, you may have a `cfcatch` block that catches an error that it isn't explicitly designed to handle. In this case, it's desirable to rethrow the exception so that a more qualified error handler can deal with the exception. This can be accomplished using the `cfrethrow` tag. The `cfrethrow` tag is used within a `cfcatch` block to rethrow the active exception while preserving the `cfcatch.Type` and `cfcatch.TagContext` return variables. This lets you build an additional level of decision making into your exception-handling routines.

To get a better idea of how the `cfrethrow` tag can be used, consider an example in which you want to provide a backup data source to use in the event that a query to your main data source fails. This type of functionality is highly desirable in cases where your entire database is refreshed (i.e., in the case of an extract file) or when you use a file-based database such as MS Access or FoxPro where updating the database often means overwriting the production version with a new version. It is also a good idea when you just want to provide redundancy, as you would in any sort of e-commerce or mission-critical application that requires 100% uptime.

Example 9-6 shows how to create this type of functionality using nested `cftry`/`cfcatch` tags and the `cfrethrow` tag.

Example 9-6. Using cfrethrow

```
<html>
<head>
  <title>Using cfrethrow</title>
  <style type="text/css">
    th {
      background-color : #0000FF;
      font-weight : bold;
      color : #FFFFFF;
      text-align : center;
    }
    td {
      background-color : #C0C0C0;
```

Example 9-6. Using cfrethrow (continued)

```
    }
    td.TagStack {
      background-color : #D3D3D3;
    }
  </style>
</head>

<body>
<cftry>

<!--- Try to query the first database.  Note that the query points to a bogus
      table, so it will fail. --->
<cftry>
<cfquery name="GetData" datasource="ProgrammingCF">
   SELECT * FROM BogusTable
</cfquery>

<!--- Catch any database errors resulting from the attempt to query the first
      database. --->
<cfcatch type="database">
  <h3>First data source failed.  Attempting to use alternate...</h3>

  <!--- Write out a table containing all cfcatch variables except for
        tagcontext and raw_trace --->
  <cfset MyKeyArray = StructKeyArray(cfcatch)>
  <table border="0">
    <tr>
      <th>Name</th><th>Value</th>
    </tr>
  <cfloop index="position" from="1" to="#ArrayLen(MyKeyArray)#">
    <cfoutput>
    <cfif IsSimpleValue(cfcatch[MyKeyArray[position]])>
    <tr>
      <td>#MyKeyArray[position]#</td>
      <td>#cfcatch[MyKeyArray[position]]# </td>
    </tr>
    </cfif>
    </cfoutput>
  </cfloop>
  </table>

  <cftry>
  <!--- Try querying the second database.  Note that this also points to a
        bogus data source, so it will fail.  We do this to illustrate the use
        of the cfrethrow tag. --->
  <cfquery name="GetData" datasource="ProgrammingCF">
     SELECT * FROM EmployeeDirectory
  </cfquery>

  <!--- If there is a problem with the second database, rethrow the exception
        so that it can be handled by the general cfcatch handler --->
  <cfcatch type="database">
```

Example 9-6. Using cfrethrow (continued)

```
    <h3>Alternate data source failed.  Rethrowing exception...</h3>

    <cfset MyKeyArray = StructKeyArray(cfcatch)>
    <table border="0">
    <tr>
      <th>Name</th><th>Value</th>
    </tr>
    <cfloop index="position" from="1" to="#ArrayLen(MyKeyArray)#">
      <cfoutput>
      <cfif IsSimpleValue(cfcatch[MyKeyArray[position]])>
      <tr>
        <td>#MyKeyArray[position]#</td>
        <td>#cfcatch[MyKeyArray[position]]# </td>
      </tr>
      </cfif>
      </cfoutput>
    </cfloop>
    </table>
    <!--- This is where the exception is rethrown --->
    <cfrethrow>
  </cfcatch>
  </cftry>
</cfcatch>
</cftry>

<!--- Catch any exception not already planned for.  Write out a table containing
      all cfcatch variables except for tagcontext and raw_trace --->
<cfcatch type="Any">
  <h3>Unexpected exception caught.  Detailed information follows:</h3>

  <cfset MyKeyArray = StructKeyArray(cfcatch)>
  <table border="0">
  <tr>
    <th>Name</th><th>Value</th>
  </tr>
  <cfloop index="position" from="1" to="#ArrayLen(MyKeyArray)#">
    <cfoutput>
    <cfif IsSimpleValue(cfcatch[MyKeyArray[position]])>
    <tr>
      <td>#MyKeyArray[position]#</td>
      <td>#cfcatch[MyKeyArray[position]]# </td>
    </tr>
    </cfif>
    </cfoutput>
  </cfloop>
  </table>
</cfcatch>
</cftry>
</body>
</html>
```

The template works by attempting to query the primary data source. If an exception is thrown, an attempt is made to query a backup data source. If an exception occurs while trying to query the backup data source, the `cfrethrow` tag rethrows the exception, which can then be caught by a general `cfcatch` tag with `type` set to `Any`. To get a better idea of what is happening, consider the following pseudocode:

```
try {
   query database
}
catch(database){
  output exception information
  try{
      query alternate database
  }
  catch(database){
    output exception information
    rethrow exception
  }
}
catch(any){
  output exception information
}
```

For illustrative purposes, each time an exception is detected in Example 9-6, all the associated `cfcatch` variables are written to the browser so that you can see what is happening.

Error Handling Within the Web-Application Framework

While `cftry` and `cfcatch` provide a granular means of handling errors and exceptions within your applications, they can be cumbersome to code. Trying to identify all the potential trouble spots in your applications where `cftry`/`cfcatch` code should be placed only compounds the problem. Fortunately, ColdFusion provides a way to handle errors at a more general level. By including ColdFusion's `cferror` tag within your application's *Application.cfm* template, you can implement application-specific "catch all" error handlers.

Although the `cferror` tag can be used in other templates besides *Application.cfm*, it makes the most sense to use it in this template. The `cferror` tag is generally placed directly below the `cfapplication` tag:

```
<cfapplication name="MyApplication">

<!--- Implement error handling --->
<cferror type="Exception" template="exception_handler.cfm"
         exception="Any" mailto="webmaster@example.com">
```

The cferror tag can implement one of four types of error handling, depending on the value specified in the type attribute. The template attribute is also required; it specifies the relative path to a custom error template to execute in the event that an error or exception occurs. Depending on the value specified in the type attribute, different options are available to the error-handling template. Here are the values for type and the corresponding options that are available in the error template:

Exception
: Handles a specific exception type as specified in the exception attribute of the cferror tag. Any ColdFusion tags may be used in the exception-handling template. Exception-handling templates may also be invoked by specifying a Site-wide Error Handler within the Server Settings section of the ColdFusion Administrator.

Monitor
: This type is no longer supported in ColdFusion MX. In ColdFusion 5, setting type to Monitor sets up an exception monitor for the exception type specified in the exception attribute of the cferror tag. Used to monitor and debug ColdFusion applications. With this type of exception handling, ColdFusion invokes the specified error-handling template before processing any cftry/cfcatch error handling that may be in the executing template.

Request *(default)*
: Handles any errors generated during a template request. Only certain error variables are available to the error-handling page. No other CFML tags may be used in the template.

Validation
: Handles form-field validation errors that occur when a form is submitted. This type is useful only when the cferror tag is included within an *Appplication.cfm* template. Only certain error variables are available to the error-handling page. No other CFML tags or functions may be used in the template.

If you set the type attribute to Exception, you should specify the type of exception that the cferror tag should watch for in the exception attribute. You may specify the same exception types as for the cfcatch tag: Any (the default), Application, *CustomType*, Database, Expression, Lock, MissingInclude, Object, SearchEngine, Security, and Template. And just as with the cfcatch tag, the cferror tag also supports a number of additional structured exception types. These exception types are listed under cftry in Appendix A.

The final attribute, mailto, is optional and provides the email address of the person who should be notified if an error occurs. The value of mailto is available to the custom error handler specified in the template attribute.

Depending on the type of error handling you implement in your application, ColdFusion makes several variables available to the template specified in the template

attribute that can be referenced within a cfoutput block. These variables can be referenced individually or as key/value pairs within a ColdFusion structure called error.*
For Exception and Request error handling, the available variables are:

error.Browser
: The browser in use when the error occurred

error.DateTime
: The date and time when the error occurred

error.Diagnostics
: A detailed error message provided by the ColdFusion server

error.HTTPReferer
: The page that contains the link to the template where the error occurred

error.MailTo
: The email address specified in the mailto attribute of the cferror tag

error.RemoteAddress
: The IP address of the remote client

error.QueryString
: The URL query string, if any, from the client's request

error.Template
: The page that was in the process of executing when the error occurred

Additionally, if type is set to Exception, the following variables are available:

error.Message
: Abbreviated error message thrown by the ColdFusion server. The detailed message is available in error.Diagnostics.

error.RootCause
: Returns a Java object containing the Java servlet exception generated by the JVM as the exception's root cause. This variable is new in ColdFusion MX.

error.TagContext
: The name and position of each tag in the tag stack as well as the full pathnames of the files containing the tags as an array of structures. Each structure in the TagContext array contains the following elements:

    type
    : Type of page generating the exception. type always returns "CFML". This key is new in ColdFusion MX.

* You can use the cferror prefix instead of the error prefix if you have type set to Exception, as in cferror.Browser or cferror.Template. The cferror prefix may be more intuitive to use as it matches the cferror tag name and makes identifying variable names and scopes easier. Just like error, cferror can also be referenced as a structure.

`ID`
: The name of the tag within the stack where the exception occurred. If the exception occurs within `cfscript` tags, `ID` returns "??".

`template`
: The full path to the template containing the tag.

`line`
: The line number within the template where the tag was found.

`column`
: No longer supported in ColdFusion MX. This key is still available for backward compatibility with previous versions of ColdFusion, but it always returns 0. In previous versions of ColdFusion, `column` returned the column number within the template where the tag was found.

`raw_trace`
: The raw Java stack trace for the exception. This key is new in ColdFusion MX.

In versions of ColdFusion prior to MX, CFML Stack Trace must be enabled in the Debugging section of the ColdFusion Administrator in order to populate this variable. If this option isn't enabled, ColdFusion returns a zero-length array for `error.TagContext`.

`error.Type`
: The exception type thrown by the server

You can also use any of the `cfcatch` return variables available to the exception specified in the `exception` attribute of the `cferror` tag. The variables are discussed in the section on `cftry/cfcatch`.

When `type` is set to `Validation`, the following variables are available:

`error.ValidationHeader`
: Predefined header text for the validation error page

`error.InvalidFields`
: An HTML unordered (`<ul>`) list of validation errors

`error.ValidationFooter`
: Predefined footer text for the validation error page

`error.MailTo`
: In versions of ColdFusion prior to MX, the email address specified in the `mailto` attribute of the `cferror` tag

Now that we've covered what the `cferror` tag can do, let's look at some specific examples of how it can be used. We'll discuss each type of exception handling and provide examples.

Form Validation Errors

Validation errors occur when you use ColdFusion's built-in form-field validation routines to handle form submissions. As you may recall from Chapter 3, ColdFusion allows you to embed special hidden form fields within your HTML forms for validating user input. To refresh your memory, here are the built-in validation suffixes: `_required`, `_date`, `_eurodate`, `_time`, `_integer`, `_float`, and `_range`.

Under normal circumstances, if a validation rule is violated, ColdFusion displays a generic error page that lets the user know that the input violated a validation rule. While this is a handy feature, the generic page displayed by ColdFusion leaves something to be desired. There is no way to customize the generic error page displayed when a validation rule is violated. By using the `cferror` tag with `type` set to `Validation`, however, you can overcome this limitation (to a degree). Although you can place the `cferror` tag directly in the page responsible for processing the form post, it makes more sense to place it in your *Application.cfm* template, as you generally want to apply this type of error handling to an entire application as opposed to a single form. The following examples show how to set up a custom validation handler for your application. To begin, we need to create an *Application.cfm* template with the code for calling the validation error handler. This code is shown in Example 9-7.

Example 9-7. Application.cfm file with cferror tag set to handle validation errors

```
<cfapplication name="MyApplication">

<!--- Handle any form field validation errors --->
<cferror type="Validation" template="validationhandler.cfm"
        mailto="webmaster@example.com">
```

All that's necessary to set up the custom validation handler is a single `cferror` tag. `type` is set to `Validation` so that any validation errors are handled by the template specified by the tag. The `template` attribute specifies the relative path to a ColdFusion template to invoke in the event a validation error occurs. In this case, we want to invoke a template called *validationhandler.cfm* that resides in the same directory as our *Application.cfm* template. The final attribute, `mailto`, is optional and provides the email address of the person who should be notified if an error occurs. The value of `mailto` is available to the custom error handler specified in the `template` attribute.

With the *Application.cfm* template all set up, let's look at the *validationhandler.cfm* template our `cferror` tag calls when a validation error occurs. The code for this template is shown in Example 9-8.

Example 9-8. validationhandler.cfm template for custom handling of validation errors

```
<html>
<head>
```

Example 9-8. validationhandler.cfm template for custom handling of validation errors (continued)

```
  <title>Validation Error Handler</title>
</head>

<body>

<div align="Center">
<h2>Validation Handler</h2>

<table border="1" cellpadding="10">
  <tr>
    <td>
    #error.ValidationHeader#<br>
    #error.InvalidFields#<br>
    #error.ValidationFooter#
    <p>
    Please send any questions or comments to
    <a href="mailto:webmaster@example.com">webmaster@example.com</a>
    </td>
  </tr>
</table>
</div>
</body>
</html>
```

As I already mentioned, only the variables passed by the `cferror` tag can be referenced in the *validationhandler.cfm* template. It isn't necessary to use a `cfoutput` tag. No additional CFML tags or functions may be used. For our template, I chose to add a background color and create a centered table for holding the rest of our content. A header displaying "Form Entries Incomplete or Invalid. One or more problems exist with the data you have entered" is automatically placed on the page by the `error.ValidationHeader` variable. If you want to preset a different header, simply omit this variable and supply your own text. Next, an unordered (bulleted) list of validation errors is presented within the table using the `error.InvalidFields` variable. The bullets are automatically created by ColdFusion and can't be modified. The footer "Use the Back button on your web browser to return to the previous page and correct the listed problems" is automatically included by referencing `error.ValidationFooter`.

Now that we have our *Application.cfm* and *validationhandler.cfm* templates set up, we need to create a template to test them. The code for the form that tests the validation error handler is shown in Example 9-9. This template should be called *validationtest.cfm* and placed in the same directory as the other templates for this example.

Example 9-9. HTML form for testing custom validation error handling

```
<h2>Article Submission Form</h2>
<form action="validationtest.cfm" method="Post">
<input type="hidden" name="ArticleDate_date" value="You must supply a valid date
      format (ex. 11/11/2000).">
```

Example 9-9. HTML form for testing custom validation error handling (continued)

```
<input type="hidden" name="Title_required" value="You must enter a title for the
      article.">
<input type="hidden" name="Priority_required" value="You must enter a priority
      for the article.">
<input type="hidden" name="Priority_range" value="Min=1 Max=100">

<table>
  <tr>
    <td>Date:</td>
    <td><input type="text" name="ArticleDate" size="12" maxlength="10"></td>
  </tr>
  <tr>
    <td>Title:</td>
    <td><input type="text" name="Title" size="50" maxlength="255"></td>
  </tr>
  <tr>
    <td>Article:</td>
    <td><textarea cols="43" rows="5" name="Article"></textarea></td>
  </tr>
  <tr>
    <td>Priority (1-100):</td>
    <td><input type="text" name="Priority" size="4" maxlength="3"></td>
  </tr>
  <tr>
    <td colspan="2"><input type="submit" name="submit" value="submit"></td>
  </tr>
</table>
</form>
```

Note the four hidden form fields declared after the `form` tag. These form fields use some of the built-in form validation suffixes. These suffixes apply validation rules to the form fields listed in each `name` attribute. When the form is submitted, ColdFusion checks the values supplied for each form field against the validation rules defined by each hidden form field. If any rules are violated, the `cferror` tag in the *Application.cfm* template invokes the *validationhandler.cfm* template, displaying the custom error message to the user. An example of this can be seen in Figure 9-1.

Request Errors

Setting `type` to `Request` allows you to handle any application-related errors that occur during a page request. If you are going to use the `cferror` tag to catch `Request` errors, you have two options. First, you can include the `cferror` tag at the beginning of every template for which you want to provide error handling. While this option works fine, it is a pain to have to put the code (or a `cfinclude` to the code) at the beginning of each CFML template. A more logical solution is to place the `cferror` tag in your *Application.cfm* template to provide error checking for your entire application. Example 9-10 shows the fragment of an *Application.cfm* template that sets up `Request` error handling.

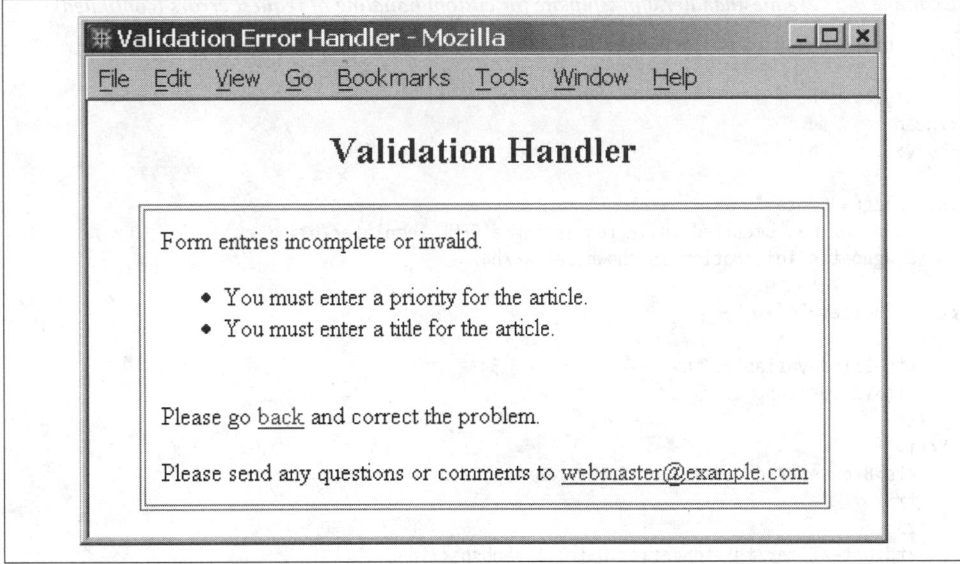

Figure 9-1. Custom validation error page invoked when a validation rule is violated

Example 9-10. cferror tag set to handle request errors

```
<cfapplication name="MyApplication">

<!--- Handle Request Errors --->
<cferror type="Request" template="requesthandler.cfm"
        mailto="webmaster@example.com">
```

All you have to do to set up a custom-request error handler is place a single `cferror` tag inside your *Application.cfm* template. `type` is set to `Request` so that any application errors are handled by the *requesthandler.cfm* template specified by the `template` attribute. As before, specify the `mailto` attribute to set an email address for notification about any errors.

With the *Application.cfm* template taken care of, let's focus our attention on the *requesthandler.cfm* template our `cferror` tag calls when a request error occurs. The code for this template is shown in Example 9-11.

Example 9-11. requesthandler.cfm template for custom handling of request errors

```
<html>
<head>
  <title>Custom Handling of Request Errors</title>
  <style type="text/css">
    th {
      background-color : #0000FF;
      font-weight : bold;
      color : #FFFFFF;
      text-align : center;
    }
    td {
```

Example 9-11. requesthandler.cfm template for custom handling of request errors (continued)

```
      background-color : #C0C0C0;
    }
  </style>
</head>
<body>

<div align="Center">
<h3>An error has occurred while requesting a CFML template</h3>
<h4>Diagnostic information is shown below</h4>

<table border="0">
  <tr>
    <th>Error Variable</th>
    <th>Value</th>
  </tr>
  <tr>
    <td>Browser</td><td>#error.Browser# </td>
  </tr>
  <tr>
    <td>Date/Time</td><td>#error.DateTime# </td>
  </tr>
  <tr>
    <td>Diagnostics</td><td>#error.Diagnostics# </td>
  </tr>
  <tr>
    <td>HTTP Referer</td><td>#error.HTTPReferer# </td>
  </tr>
  <tr>
    <td>Mailto</td><td>#error.MailTo# </td>
  </tr>
  <tr>
    <td>Remote Address</td><td>#error.RemoteAddress# </td>
  </tr>
  <tr>
    <td>Query String</td><td>#error.QueryString# </td>
  </tr>
  <tr>
    <td>Template</td><td>#error.Template# </td>
  </tr>
</table>
</div>
</body>
</html>
```

The *requesthandler.cfm* template creates a custom page for reporting details of the request error to the user. Only the variables passed by the `cferror` tag can be referenced in the *requesthandler.cfm* template. It isn't necessary to reference the error variables within a `cfoutput` block. Just like `Validation` handling, no additional CFML tags or functions may be used within the template. The actual details of the error are output in a nicely formatted table with the error variables in the left column and their values in the right column.

Now that we've created our *Application.cfm* and *requesthandler.cfm* templates, let's test them. Here's some code that tests our templates:

```
<!--- Try to cfinclude a template that does not exist --->
<cfinclude template="nonexistanttemplate.cfm?ID=123">
```

Executing this template causes the `cferror` tag in our *Application.cfm* template to invoke the *requesthandler.cfm* template (because of the `cfinclude` call to a nonexistent template). The results of this can be seen in Figure 9-2.

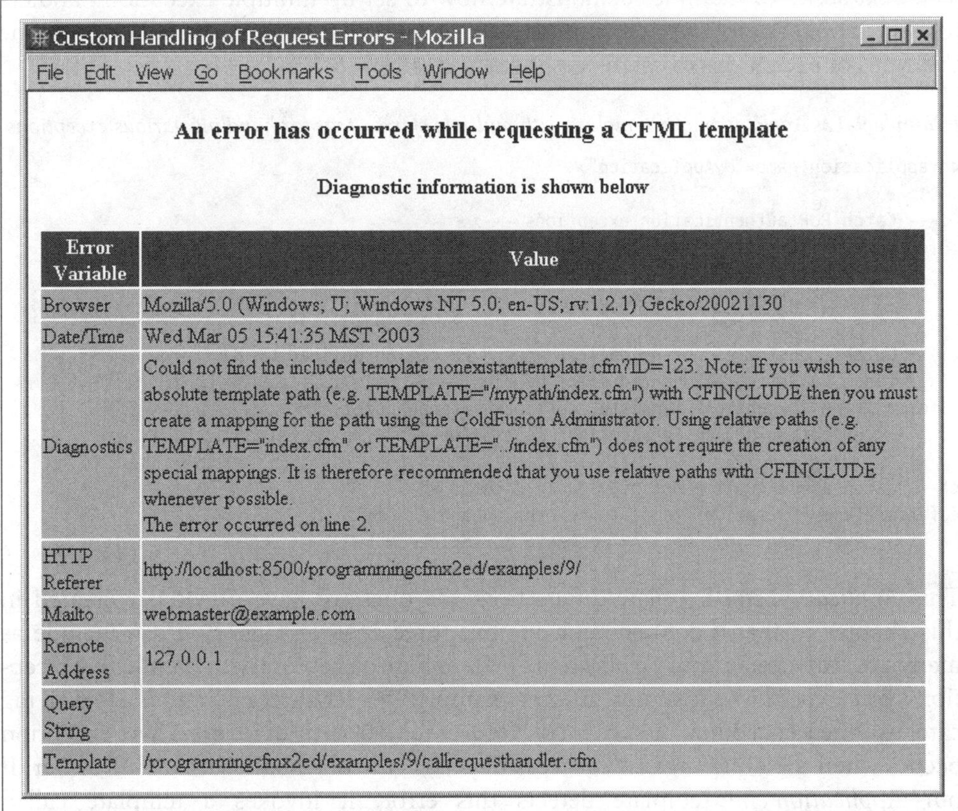

Figure 9-2. Custom request error handler

Specific Exceptions

The `cferror` tag can catch specific exceptions at either the application or template level when `type` is set to `Exception`. `Exception` handling differs from `Request` handling in three important ways. First, using `Exception` allows you to specify an exception to trigger the `cferror` response. If `type` is set to `Request`, ColdFusion responds to *any* error or exception by invoking the `cferror` tag.

The second difference has to do with the information the `cferror` tag makes available to the error-handling template specified in the `template` attribute. In addition to the error variables available to a Request handler, an Exception handler also has access to all the error variables available to the cfcatch tag.

The third difference is perhaps the most significant. Unlike the template specified by the cferror tag when type is Request, the template specified when type is Exception has access to all CFML tags and functions. This gives you the ability to code much more sophisticated and customized error handlers than using the Request type because you can include any ColdFusion tags (such as cfmail) or functions you wish.

The next series of examples demonstrate how to set up multiple exception handlers for your application. The first step is to create an *Application.cfm* template to define the types of exceptions to catch, as shown in Example 9-12.

Example 9-12. Application.cfm template with multiple cferror tags for handling various exceptions

```
<cfapplication name="MyApplication">

<!--- Catch POP authentication exceptions --->
<cferror type="Exception" template="exceptionhandler.cfm"
         exception="COM.Allaire.ColdFusion.POPAuthFailure"
         mailto="webmaster@example.com">

<!--- Catch a custom exception called MyApp.MyException defined by a cfthrow
      tag.  Call a more advanced error handler --->
<cferror type="Exception" template="customexceptionhandler.cfm"
         exception="MyApp.MyException" mailto="webmaster@example.com">

<!--- Catch any exception not previously covered --->
<cferror type="Exception" template="exceptionhandler.cfm"
         exception="Any" mailto="webmaster@example.com">
```

This *Application.cfm* template differs from the ones we have previously created in this chapter in that it contains not one but three cferror tags. You can include as many cferror tags in your *Application.cfm* template as necessary to handle the exceptions you expect to encounter. In this example, we set three. The first cferror tag catches the exception COM.Allaire.ColdFusion.POPAuthFailure. This exception occurs when the cfpop tag can't successfully authenticate a user with a POP server. If our *Application.cfm* template detects this error, it invokes a template called *exceptionhandler.cfm*, shown in Example 9-13.

The second cferror tag catches a custom exception called MyApp.MyException that is defined using the cfthrow tag. If the exception is detected, a template called *customexceptionhandler.cfm* is invoked to handle the error, as shown in Example 9-14.

The third and final cferror tag catches any exceptions not handled by our other two cferror tags. By setting the type attribute to Any, we effectively create a backup exception handler for dealing with unforeseen exceptions. This type of error handler should always be included as the last cferror tag in your *Application.cfm* template. If an exception occurs that isn't caught by either specific exception handler, the *exceptionhandler.cfm* template (the same template used by our first cferror tag) is invoked to deal with the exception.

Let's turn our attention now to the two exception-handling templates we just mentioned, *exceptionhandler.cfm* and *customexceptionhandler.cfm*. The *exceptionhandler.cfm* template is used by both the first and third `cferror` tags in our *Application.cfm* template to handle a `COM.Allaire.ColdFusion.POPAuth-Failure` exception as well as any exception other than a custom one called `MyApp.MyException` (the second `cferror` tag). The code for the *exceptionhandler.cfm* template is shown in Example 9-13.

Example 9-13. Displaying exception error variables

```
<h3>Generic Exception Handler</h3>
<cfdump var="#cferror#">
```

The *exceptionhandler.cfm* template generates a table containing all the error variables and their associated values by the `cfdump` tag. This allows you to easily see the nested hierarchy of the `cferror.RootCause` and `cferror.TagContext` values. The output of this template is in Figure 9-3.

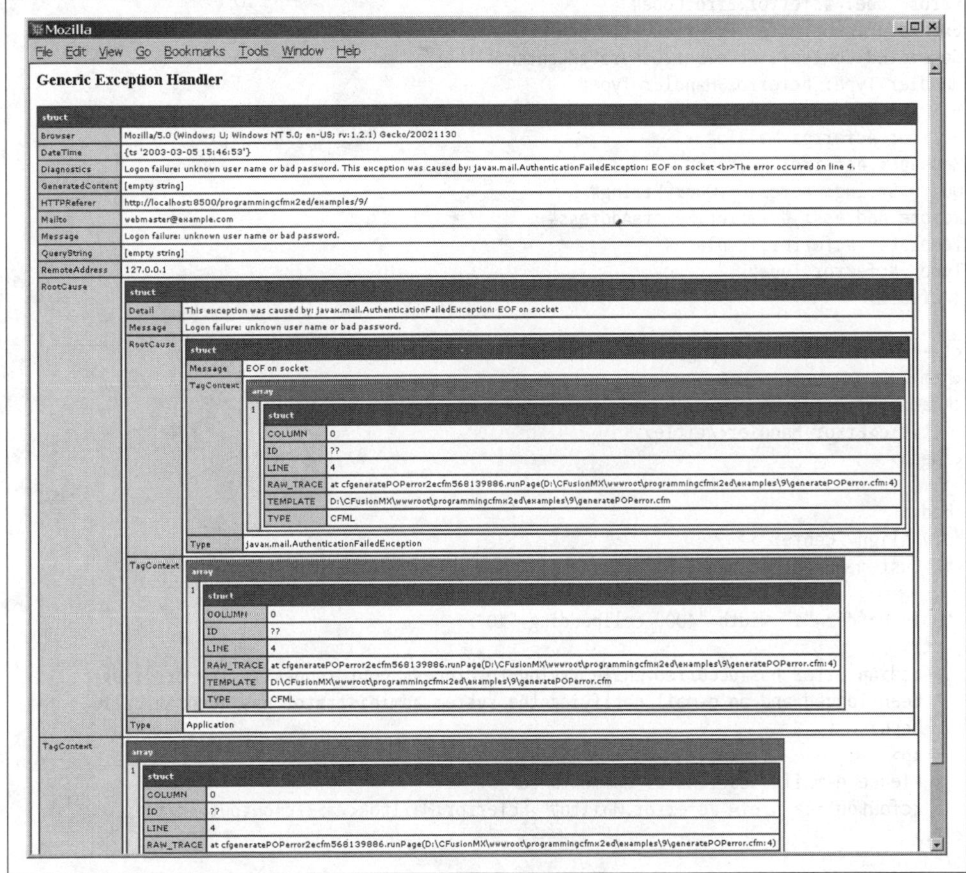

Figure 9-3. Handling a POP authentication exception with cferror

The next example we have to look at is the *customexceptionhandler.cfm* template. This template highlights the level of customization you can achieve using the cferror tag. Unlike the Request and Validation examples given earlier, this type of exception handler has access to the full range of CFML tags and functions. The code for the *customexceptionhandler.cfm* template is shown in Example 9-14.

Example 9-14. Emailing error information to the site administrator

```
<!--- Email the administrative contact and let them know that an exception
      occurred.  Include the details in the message. --->
<cfmail to="#cferror.MailTo#" from="webmaster@example.com"
        subject="Application Exception Encountered">
An exception occurred with one of our applications.  Details follow:

Browser: #cferror.Browser#
DateTime: #cferror.DateTime#
Detail: #cferror.Detail#
Diagnostics: #cferror.Diagnostics#
Error Code: #cferror.ErrorCode#
Extended Info: #cferror.ExtendedInfo#
Generated Content: #cferror.GeneratedContent#
Handler Type: #cferror.Handler_Type#
HTTPREFERER: #cferror.HTTPReferer#
Mailto: #cferror.MailTo#
Message: #cferror.Message#
Query String: #cferror.QueryString#
Remote Address: #cferror.RemoteAddress#
Template: #cferror.Template#
Type: #cferror.Type#
</cfmail>

<!--- Display an error page to the user --->
<html>
<head>
  <title>Error Handler</title>
</head>

<body>
<div align="Center">
<h2>Custom Exception Handler</h2>

<table border="1" width="400" cellpadding="10">
  <tr>
    <td>An error has occurred while trying to process your request.  The error has
    been logged and an e-mail notifying the system administrator has automatically
    been sent.
    <p>
    Please e-mail questions or comments to
    <cfoutput><a href="#cferror.Mailto#">#cferror.Mailto#</a></cfoutput>.</td>
</tr>
</table>
</div>
</body>
</html>
```

The *customexceptionhandler.cfm* template uses the exception information it receives from the cferror tag to generate an email (using cfmail) that is automatically sent to the contact specified in the mailto attribute of the cferror tag. This email contains information about the exception (from the Error variables) such as the time and date the error occurred, diagnostic information, and the template executing when the exception happened. A message is also displayed to the user telling him that an error has occurred and that an email message has been sent to the site administrator.

Now let's look at some templates for generating exceptions that can be caught by the cferror tags in our *Application.cfm* template. Here's some code that generates a POP authentication exception; in order to use this example, you must change the server attribute to the name of a valid POP server:

```
<!--- make sure to change the server attribute to a valid POP server.  Be sure
      to use a username and password you know to be invalid --->
<cfpop action="GetHeaderOnly" name="test" server="my.popserver.com"
       username="test" password="test">
```

Executing this template causes the first cferror tag in our *Application.cfm* template to invoke the *exceptionhandler.cfm* template (Example 9-13). The results can be seen in Figure 9-3.

Here's a template that generates a custom exception called MyApp.MyException (defined using the cfthrow tag) if a variable called form.MyVar doesn't exist:

```
<cfif not IsDefined('form.MyVar')>
<cfthrow message="<h2>My variable does not exist!</h2>"
         type="MyApp.MyException" detail="Here are the details:"
         errorcode="100"
         extendedinfo="No extended information is available.">
</cfif>
```

When this template is executed, ColdFusion checks for the existence of a form variable called form.MyVar. If the variable doesn't exist (which it doesn't in this example), a custom exception named MyApp.MyException is generated using the cfthrow tag. Once the exception is thrown, the cferror tag in our *Application.cfm* template invokes the *customexceptionhandler.cfm* template from Example 9-14.

Our final example causes a database exception to occur, triggering the third cferror tag in our *Application.cfm* template:

```
<!--- perform a bogus query --->
<cfquery name="Test" datasource="ProgrammingCF">
  SELECT * FROM BogusTable
</cfquery>
```

As you may recall, the third cferror tag has its type attribute set to Any so it can handle any exceptions not caught by the first two cferror tags. Since our database exception isn't handled by either of the first two cferror tags, it is automatically caught by the final one.

Monitors (ColdFusion 5 Only)

In ColdFusion 5, when ColdFusion's CFML interpreter first detects an exception, it searches for an exception monitor to invoke before it starts looking for cfcatch blocks or other cferror tags to handle the exception. Exception monitors are useful for monitoring and debugging exception handling within ColdFusion applications. To create a monitor, you simply place a cferror tag with the type attribute set to Monitor in your *Application.cfm* template. If an exception occurs, and a monitor is found, the template specified in the template attribute of the cferror tag is executed. Once the template has finished executing, the exception is rethrown to allow any additional error and exception handling code to deal with the exception. Because of this, it is necessary to have additional cftry/cfcatch or cferror tags in place to handle the rethrown exception. Exception monitors are most often used to log errors to a log file, while still allowing other cferror tags or cfcatch blocks to deal with the actual exception.

Example 9-15 shows an *Application.cfm* template that creates a basic exception monitor to write all available exception information to a log file in the event an exception occurs.

Example 9-15. Application.cfm template containing cferror code for invoking an exception monitor

```
<cfapplication name="MyApplication">

<!--- Call an exception monitor for any type of exception --->
<cferror type="Monitor" template="monitorhandler.cfm" exception="Any"
         mailto="webmaster@example.com">

<!--- After the exception monitor has finished executing, this cferror tag will
      execute.  It calls the ExceptionHandler.cfm template from Example 9-13 --->
<cferror type="Exception" template="exceptionhandler.cfm" exception="Any"
         mailto="webmaster@example.com">
```

This *Application.cfm* template contains two cferror tags. The first cferror tag makes the call to the *monitorhandler.cfm* template in the event that any exception occurs. This is done by setting the type attribute to Monitor and the exception attribute to Any.

Because of the way that the Monitor exception type works, it is necessary to include a second cferror tag with the type attribute set to Exception and the exception attribute set to Any. This is because ColdFusion automatically rethrows the original exception after the *monitorhandler.cfm* template has finished executing. Because of this, we need a second cferror tag to handle the rethrown exception. If the second cferror isn't there, the exception is rethrown, an error is written out to the browser, and all processing halts.

With the *Application.cfm* template set up, it's time to move to the *monitorhandler.cfm* template we specified in the template attribute of our first cferror tag. This template is used to write an entry in a log file called *monitorlog.txt* each time it is invoked by the cferror tag. The code for *monitorhandler.cfm* is shown in Example 9-16.

Example 9-16. Writing exception information to a log file with cffile

```
<!--- Basic exception monitor for writing a log file with cffile --->

<!--- Initialize a variable to hold the log entry --->
<cfset TheException = "">

<!--- Loop over the error structure and build the log entry --->
<cfloop collection=#Error# item="Message">
  <cfif IsSimpleValue(Error[Message])>
    <cfset TheException = ListAppend(TheException, Error[message], "|")>
  </cfif>
</cfloop>

<!--- Write the exception info in the log file --->
<cflock timeout="60" throwontimeout="Yes" type="Exclusive">
<cffile action="append" file="c:\temp\Monitor_log.txt"
        output="#TheException#" addnewline="Yes">
</cflock>
```

Once invoked, the *monitorhandler.cfm* template initializes a variable called TheException. The template then loops over the Error structure, appending each value to TheException and delimiting values with the pipe (|) character. The pipe is used as a delimiter because we know that it is unlikely to show up as a character in any of the error variable values. Each value is tested with the IsSimpleValue( ) function before it is appended to the list. If the value isn't a simple value, we know it is part of the cferror.TagContext variable, and we omit it from the log file (for simplicity's sake). Finally, the cffile tag is used to write the contents of our exception string (TheException) to a file called *monitorlog.txt*. A newline character is added at the end of each entry so that the next time an entry is written, it begins on a new line. The cflock tag is used around the cffile tag so that no two exceptions can write to the *monitorlog.txt* file at the same time.

Our exception monitor example wouldn't be complete without a template to test everything out. The following code causes a database exception by attempting to query a nonexistent data source:

```
<cfquery name="test" datasource="asd">
  SELECT * FROM Test
</cfquery>
```

Executing this template causes the first cferror tag to invoke the *monitorhandler.cfm* template and write the exception information to the log file. After that is complete, the exception is rethrown and caught by the second cferror tag in our *Application.cfm* template. That cferror tag calls the *exceptionhandler.cfm* template from Example 9-13.

Exception Logging

When handling exceptions, you might find it desirable to write relevant information to a log file. You can do this using the cffile tag, or you can make it easy on yourself and use ColdFusion's cflog tag. cflog allows you to log messages to ColdFusion's default *Application.log*, to *Scheduler.log*, or to a custom log file that you specify. Example 9-17 shows a simple example that writes some of the contents of the error scope to a log file called *exceptionlog.txt* using the cflog tag.

Example 9-17. Writing exception information to a log file with cflog

```
<!--- Basic exception handler for writing a log file with cflog.  Name this
      template exceptionlogger.cfm --->

<!--- Initialize a variable to hold the log message --->
<cfset TheException = "">

<!--- Loop over the error structure and build the log entry --->
<cfloop collection="#error#" item="Message">
  <cfif IsSimpleValue(error[Message])>
    <cfset TheException = ListAppend(TheException, error[message], "|")>
  </cfif>
</cfloop>

<!--- Write the exception info in the log file --->
<cflog text = "#TheException#"
       file = "exceptionlog"
       type = "Error"
       application = "Yes">
```

When this exception handler is invoked, it builds the message to add to the log file by looping over the error scope and concatenating all of the simple values into a list separated by pipe characters. The cflog tag is then used to write the message to a log file. The log files generated by cflog follow a standard format. The first line of each log file contains a comma-delimited list of column headers qualified with double quotes that looks like this:

```
"Severity","ThreadID","Date","Time","Application","Message"
```

When an entry is made to the log file, the values that are written to each column are also qualified with double quotes and delimited with commas. Some column values are based on the values specified for the various attributes of the cflog tag. text is the only required attribute and specifies the message to be written to the file. Here, we use the exception string (TheException). The file attribute specifies the name of the log file (without the extension) you want to write the log entry to. You must specify the name of a file with a *.log* extension. If the file doesn't exist, ColdFusion automatically creates it in the default log file directory specified in the Logging section of the ColdFusion Administrator. In this case, we are going to write our log entry to a log file called *exception.log*.

If you don't want to write your entry to a custom log file, you may omit the `file` attribute and use the `log` attribute instead (not shown in the example). The `log` attribute specifies one of two standard ColdFusion log files to write the entry to:

`Application`
: The entry is written to the *Application.log* file. This file is automatically created by ColdFusion and is used to log application-specific messages.

`Scheduler`
: The entry is written to the *Scheduler.log* file. This file is used by ColdFusion to log execution information concerning scheduled tasks.

The `type` attribute lets you assign a severity level to the log entry. Possible entries are `Information` (the default), `Warning`, `Error`, and `Fatal`. Specifying `Yes` (the default) for the `application` attribute writes the application name to the log file if a name is specified in a `cfapplication` tag for the application. The `ThreadID`, `Date`, and `Time` columns are all automatically populated by ColdFusion when a log entry is made. `ThreadID` corresponds to the ID of the service thread responsible for logging the message in the log entry. Service threads typically handle a particular page request from request through completion before moving to the next queued request. Logging thread IDs can be useful (especially to Macromedia technical support) for identifying server activity patterns. `date` and `time` correspond to the system date and time, respectively, when the log entry was made. To test this example, change the third `cferror` tag in the *Application.cfm* template from Example 9-12 to the following:

```
<!--- Call the exception logger --->
<cferror type="Exception" template="exceptionlogger.cfm"
         exception="Any" mailto="webmaster@example.com">
```

For more information on the `cflog` tag, see Appendix A.

Server-Wide Error Handling

ColdFusion provides site administrators with a way to handle errors and exceptions at the server level. Via the ColdFusion Administrator, you can designate a template to handle requests for CFML templates that don't exist on the server. You can also specify an additional template that is invoked when an error or exception occurs anywhere within your ColdFusion application.

Missing Template Handler

Within the Settings section of the ColdFusion Administrator, there is a place for you to specify a Missing Template Handler. This template is called if a requested ColdFusion template can't be found on the server, allowing you to avoid the dreaded "404 Object Not Found" error that otherwise results. Note that the Missing Template Handler isn't invoked for template types other than CFML. In other words, requests for missing HTML templates are handled by the web server, not ColdFusion. When setting the Missing Template Handler, you should provide the relative path (in ColdFusion MX) such as */MissingTemplateHandler.cfm* or the physical path (in ColdFusion 5) such as *d:\inetpub\errorhandlers\MissingTemplateHandler.cfm* to the template's location on your ColdFusion server. If you are using ColdFusion MX, the relative path is relative to your web root directory.*

If the template you are calling attempts to call another template that doesn't exist, such as a custom tag call, `cfmodule`, or `cfinclude`, ColdFusion generates a `MissingInclude` exception but doesn't invoke the Missing Template Handler. This exception can be trapped by placing the following code in the *Application.cfm* template of your application:

```
<cferror type="Exception" exception="MissingInclude"
         template="missing_include_handler.cfm">
```

Site-wide Error Handler

There are times when you might want to display a generic error page in the event that an unforeseen error occurs somewhere in your application. The Site-wide Error Handler setting, again in the Settings section of the ColdFusion Administrator, lets you specify a ColdFusion template to invoke in the event that an error occurs within any of your ColdFusion applications. This feature is useful in situations where you have applications that don't contain their own internal error and exception handling or where you want to provide a backup error handler.

Using the Site-wide Error Handler is equivalent to placing the following code in your *Application.cfm* file:

```
<cferror type="Exception" exception="Any" template="error_handler.cfm">
```

Note, however, that using a Site-wide Error Handler overrides the use of any instances of the `cferror` tag when the `type` attribute of `cferror` is set to `Exception`.

When setting the Site-wide Error Handler, you should provide the relative path (ColdFusion MX) or physical path (ColdFusion 5) to the template's location on your ColdFusion server.

* Storing an error handler in a directory relative to the web root means that the error-handling template itself is accessible via URL. For security reasons, it makes more sense to store your error-handling templates in a directory that cannot be directly accessed. In order to make a directory above your web root accessible, you'll need to first create a mapping for the directory in the ColdFusion Administrator

CHAPTER 10

Dynamic Form Controls

Anyone who has ever worked with HTML forms knows their importance. Forms are the basis for much of the interaction between users and web applications. Yet, for all of their benefits, HTML forms leave a lot to be desired from a development standpoint. For starters, HTML forms are all alike—from a data-gathering perspective and from a user-interface perspective. A text box is a text box is a text box. Nothing you can do can change that. With regular HTML forms, you are limited to a standard set of input types, each identical in style and function to those used by every other HTML developer. Sure, you can make your forms unique, but the form controls themselves are completely devoid of customization. The second limitation (if you want to call it that) of HTML form controls is the lack of data-validation capabilities. HTML form controls do nothing more than gather data and post it to another template for processing. Sure, you can write JavaScript routines to validate each form field individually, but do you really want to? This is where ColdFusion comes in.

ColdFusion includes a set of tags for extending the capabilities of regular HTML forms. These tags provide additional functionality to forms such as data validation, new data views, and new input types. Not only can you customize the appearance of many of the form controls, but there are several additional ColdFusion form controls, including Java applet-based tree, grid, and slider controls. The following list details the form controls available under `cfform`:

`cfinput`
: Creates text boxes, password entry boxes, radio buttons, and checkboxes with optional JavaScript validation routines. Not a Java applet.

`cftextinput`
: Java applet-based text box. Allows more formatting options than a standard text box.

`cfselect`
: Creates drop-down lists from query results with optional JavaScript validation routines. Not a Java applet.

`cfslider`
: Java applet-based slider control for selecting a value from a range of numeric values.

`cfgrid`
: Java applet-based grid control for displaying, entering, and editing tabular data.

`cftree`
: Java applet-based tree control for displaying and selecting hierarchical data.

`cfapplet`
: Allows you to use custom Java controls as if they were native ColdFusion tags.

Version 5.0 of ColdFusion introduced a number of significant architectural, behavioral, functional, and cosmetic changes to the various `cfform` controls. The most significant change had to do with the architecture of the controls themselves. Different versions of different web browsers each have a different Java Runtime Environment (JRE), making it impossible to guarantee that the pre–ColdFusion 5.0 applets will run as intended on all browser version/JRE combinations. Because of this, all the Java applet-based `cfform` controls (`cftextinput`, `cfgrid`, `cfslider`, and `cftree`) were rewritten for ColdFusion 5.0 and further enhanced in ColdFusion MX. The new versions of the controls require the Sun Java web browser plugin, which allows the applets to function across the widest possible spectrum of browsers. When a user requests a page containing any of the new applet controls, ColdFusion automatically attempts to send and install the Java plugin if it isn't already present on the user's system. Depending on what browser the user has and the version they are running, installation can be completely seamless, or it can require a few additional steps on the part of the user.

The requirement that users download and install a plugin in order to use Java-based `cfform` controls is worth considering when designing your applications. While this may not be a concern for intranet applications, where a company may have strict control over what software users have installed, it may present a barrier to Internet/extranet users who are unwilling or unable to download and install the plugin.

Combining HTML and CFML Form Controls

The `cfform` tag enables you to create dynamic forms using controls that include such HTML controls as input boxes, drop-down boxes, and radio buttons, as well as a number of specialized Java applet-based controls, such as trees, grids, and sliders. Forms created using the `cfform` tag are coded in the same manner as regular HTML forms. In fact, the `cfform` tag allows you to mix standard HTML and CFML form controls in the same form.

The following example creates a form using `cfform` and places a standard HTML submit button on the page:

```
<cfform action="MyFormProcessor.cfm" name="MyForm"
        enctype="application/x-www-form-urlencoded">

  <input type="submit" name="submit" value="submit">

</cfform>
```

The `cfform` tag has many of the same attributes as the HTML `form` tag. The `action` attribute is required and specifies where the form should be submitted upon completion. `name` is optional and specifies a name for the form. You should specify a value for `name` if you plan to reference the form later in your application. In previous versions of ColdFusion, the `cfform` tag used an attribute called `enablecab` to make Java-based form controls available to Microsoft Internet Explorer users as Microsoft cabinet files. In Version 5.0, the `enablecab` attribute was deprecated and made nonfunctional. In its place, two new optional attributes have been added to the `cfform` tag to enhance performance of the Java-based `cfform` controls:

`codebase="`*`url`*`"`
: Specifies the URL to a downloadable JRE plugin for MS Internet Explorer. The default URL is */CFIDE/classes/cf-j2re-win.cab*.

`archive="`*`url`*`"`
: Specifies the URL to a downloadable Java archive file containing Java-based `cfform` controls. The default URL is */CFIDE/classes/CFJava2.jar*.

The `enctype` attribute is also optional and specifies the MIME type for data being submitted via the POST method. The default `enctype` is `application/x-www-form-urlencoded`. If, however, you plan to allow file uploads via your form, you must specify `multipart/form-data` for the `enctype`. For more information on uploading files via forms, see Chapter 12.

There are several additional attributes, all optional and available to the `cfform` tag, that aren't shown in the example. For instance, the `target` attribute allows you to specify the name of a frame or window for the target template to be opened in. Another attribute, `onsubmit`, allows you to designate a JavaScript function that should be executed after validation occurs but before the form is submitted. This is useful in situations where you want to use JavaScript to clean up or reformat data before submitting it. Another useful optional attribute, `passthrough`, allows you to pass any additional HTML attributes that aren't directly supported by the `cfform` tag. For example, you can pass an additional parameter called `MyParameter` with a value of `Yes` by adding the following code to your `cfform` tag:

```
passthrough="MyParameter=""Yes"""
```

Note that in order to pass quoted values through `cfform`, you must escape the quotation marks by doubling up on them.

Basic Input Controls

The cfinput tag closely resembles the HTML input tag and can be used for creating text boxes, password entry boxes, radio buttons, and checkboxes. At the most basic level, the cfinput tag behaves exactly like the HTML input tag. Consider the following HTML input tags:

```
<input type="text" name="MyText" size="10" maxlength="10" value="MyValue">
<input type="password" name="MyPassword" size="10" maxlength="10">
<input type="radio" name="MyRadioButton" value="MyValue" checked>
<input type="checkbox" name="MyCheckbox" value="MyValue" checked>
```

Here are the equivalent cfinput tags:

```
<cfinput type="text" name="MyText" size="10" maxlength="10" value="MyValue">
<cfinput type="password" name="MyPassword" size="10" maxlength="10">
<cfinput type="radio" name="MyRadioButton" value="MyValue" checked>
<cfinput type="checkbox" name="MyCheckbox" value="MyValue" checked>
```

As you can see, the tags are virtually identical. What sets a cfinput tag apart from its HTML counterpart is built-in data validation. The cfinput tag can require input for a given form field as well as validate the data against a predefined or custom validation routine. Example 10-1 demonstrates how to use the cfinput tag to require data entry for various input types.

Example 10-1. Creating a form with cfform and cfinput

```
<cfif IsDefined('form.FieldNames')>
  <h3>You submitted:</h3>
  <cfloop index="Field" list="#form.Fieldnames#">
    <cfoutput><b>#Field#</b>: #form[Field]#<br></cfoutput>
  </cfloop>
  <hr noshade>
</cfif>

<cfform action="#CGI.Script_Name#"name="MyForm"
        enctype="application/x-www-form-urlencoded">
<table>
<tr>
  <td>Name:</td>
  <td><cfinput type="text" name="Name" required="Yes"
       message="You must enter your name." size="10" maxlength="10">
  </td>
</tr>
<tr>
  <td>Password:</td>
  <td><cfinput type="password" name="password" required="Yes"
       message="You must enter your password." size="10" maxlength="10">
  </td>
</tr>
</table>

<table>
```

Example 10-1. Creating a form with cfform and cfinput (continued)

```
<tr>
  <td>Do you like programming with ColdFusion?</td>
  <td><cfinput type="radio" name="LikeCF" value="Yes" checked="Yes">Yes <cfinput
      type="radio" name="LikeCF" value="No">No
  </td>
</tr>
<tr>
  <td colspan="2">Which database(s) do you use?</td>
</tr>
<tr>
  <td colspan="2"><cfinput type="checkbox" name="Access" value="Yes">Access<br>
          <cfinput type="checkbox" name="DB2" value="Yes">DB2<br>
          <cfinput type="checkbox" name="Informix" value="Yes">Informix<br>
          <cfinput type="checkbox" name="Oracle" value="Yes">Oracle<br>
          <cfinput type="checkbox" name="SQL_Server" value="Yes">SQL Server
  </td>
</tr>
</table>

<p>
<input type="submit" name="submit" value="submit">
</cfform>
```

Example 10-1 starts by using a `cfif` statement to see if a form variable called `form.FieldNames` was passed to the template. `form.FieldNames` is a special ColdFusion variable that is automatically created whenever a ColdFusion template receives information via an HTTP POST operation. `form.FieldNames` contains a comma-delimited list of all the field names passed from the form making the POST to the ColdFusion template. If the variable `form.FieldNames` exists, the template loops through the list of field names and outputs each field name from the list as well as the value it contains. This technique allows you to submit the form to itself and display the results without knowing what form fields were passed. You could just as easily reference the special `form` scope structure that contains all available form fields. However, because this variable always exists, even when it contains no form fields, it's easier to check for the existence of `form.FieldNames`.

The form itself is set up using the `cfform` tag. The first `cfinput` tag collects a user's name. The `required` attribute indicates whether or not to require that data be entered before the form can be successfully submitted. In this case, we set `required` to `Yes`. The `message` attribute contains the text to display in a JavaScript alert box in the event that a user submits the form without filling in a required field. You can use the `required` and `message` attributes with any of the `cfinput` controls.

Besides the attributes already mentioned, there are two additional attributes available to the `cfinput` tag worth mentioning. These attributes are `onerror` and `passthrough`. `onerror` allows you to designate the name of a JavaScript function that is executed if validation fails for any reason. You can use `passthrough` to pass any additional HTML attributes that aren't directly supported by the `cfinput` tag.

Data Validation

One of the big benefits of using `cfform` over standard HTML forms is the built-in data validation that is available. Both the `cfinput` and `cftextinput` tags have an attribute called `validate` that accepts any of the following values:

`CreditCard`
: Validates the form-field data using the mod10 algorithm. A credit-card number can be entered as a single value or with dashes or spaces and must be between 12 and 16 digits in length. ColdFusion automatically strips dashes and spaces before validating.

`Date`
: Requires the form-field value to be in the U.S. date format *mm/dd/yyyy*.

`EuroDate`
: Requires the form-field value to be in the European date format *dd/mm/yyyy*.

`Float`
: Requires the form-field value to be a floating-point number.

`Integer`
: Requires the form-field value to be an integer.

`Regular_Expression`
: Validates the form-field data against a JavaScript regular expression specified in the tag's `pattern` attribute.

`Social_Security_Number`
: Requires the form-field value to be a U.S. social security number in the format *xxx-xx-xxxx* or *xxx xx xxxx*.

`Telephone`
: Requires the form-field value to be a U.S. telephone number formatted either *xxx-xxx-xxxx* or *xxx xxx xxxx*. The area code and exchange are required to begin with a number in the range of 1–9.

`Time`
: Requires that the form-field value be entered as a valid time using the format *hh:mm:ss*.

`ZipCode`
: Requires that the form-field value be entered as a five- or nine-digit U.S. ZIP code using the format *xxxxx*, *xxxxx-xxxx*, or *xxxxx xxxx*.

Example 10-2 demonstrates the `cfinput` tag along with some of the predefined data validation settings we just discussed.

Example 10-2. Using predefined data validation with cfinput

```
<cfif IsDefined('form.FieldNames')>
  <h3>You submitted:</h3>
  <cfloop index="Field" list="#form.FieldNames#">
```

Example 10-2. Using predefined data validation with cfinput (continued)

```
    <cfoutput><b>#Field#</b>: #form[Field]#<br></cfoutput>
  </cfloop>
  <hr noshade>
</cfif>

<cfform action="#CGI.Script_Name#" name="MyForm"
        enctype="application/x-www-form-urlencoded">
<table>
<tr>
  <td>Date:</td>
  <td><cfinput type="text" name="MyDate" validate="Date" required="Yes"
      message="You must enter a valid Date."  size="10" maxlength="10"></td>
</tr>
<tr>
  <td>EuroDate:</td>
  <td><cfinput type="text" name="MyEuroDate" validate="Eurodate"
      message="You must enter a valid EuroDate." size="10" maxlength="10"></td>
</tr>
<tr>
  <td>Time:</td>
  <td><cfinput type="text" name="MyTime" validate="Time"
      message="You must enter a valid Time." size="10" maxlength="10"></td>
</tr>
<tr>
  <td>Float:</td>
  <td><cfinput type="text" name="MyFloat" validate="Float"
      message="You must enter a valid floating point number." size="10"
      maxlength="255"></td>
</tr>
<tr>
  <td>Integer (range 1-100):</td>
  <td><cfinput type="text" name="MyInteger" validate="Integer" range="1,100"
      message="You must enter a valid integer between 1 and 100."  size="10"
      maxlength="255"></td>
</tr>
<tr>
  <td>Phone Number:</td>
  <td><cfinput type="text" name="MyPhone" validate="Telephone"
      message="You must enter a valid phone number (xxx-xxx-xxxx, xxx xxx xxxx)."
      size="15" maxlength="25"></td>
</tr>
<tr>
  <td>Zip code:</td>
  <td><cfinput type="text" name="MyZip" validate="Zipcode"
      message="You must enter a valid zip code (xxxxx, xxxxx-xxxx, xxxxx xxxx)."
      size="15" maxlength="15"></td>
</tr>
<tr>
  <td>Credit Card Number:</td>
  <td><cfinput type="text" name="MyCreditCard" validate="CreditCard"
      message="You must enter a valid credit card number." size="10"
      maxlength="255"></td>
```

Example 10-2. Using predefined data validation with cfinput (continued)

```
</tr>
<tr>
  <td>Social Security Number:</td>
  <td><cfinput type="text" name="MySSN" validate="Social_Security_Number"
    message="You must enter a valid SSN (xxx-xx-xxxx, xxx xx xxxx)."
    size="13" maxlength="11"></td>
</tr>
</table>

<p>
<input type="submit" name="submit" value="submit">
</cfform>
```

Each `cfinput` tag in Example 10-3 performs a different type of validation against the data it accepts. The type of validation performed is determined by the value specified by the `validate` attribute. `message` specifies a message to display in a JavaScript alert box in the event that validation for a particular field fails. You can set an additional attribute, `range`, with the Integer validation type. `range` allows you to specify a range of acceptable values for the form field. `range` is specified as `range(m,n)` where *m* is the beginning value in the range, and *n* is the ending value.

In addition to the `validate` attribute, the `cfinput` and `cftextinput` tags as well as the `cfgrid`, `cfslider`, and `cftree` tags support an additional attribute for data validation. The `onvalidate` attribute allows you to designate your own JavaScript validation function that should be executed before the form is submitted. You don't need to know all the ins and outs of JavaScript to use the `onvalidate` function (although it sure helps!). Example 10-3 demonstrates how to use `onvalidate` to call a custom JavaScript function.

Example 10-3. Using onvalidate

```
<script language="JavaScript">
  <!--
  function PasswordCheck( ) {
    if (document.MyForm.Password.value != document.MyForm.Password2.value)
      return false;
    else
      return true;
  }
  //-->
</script>

<cfif IsDefined('form.Fieldnames')>
  <h3>You submitted:</h3>
  <cfloop index="Field" list="#form.Fieldnames#">
    <cfoutput><b>#Field#</b>: #form[Field]#<br></cfoutput>
  </cfloop>
  <hr noshade>
</cfif>
```

Example 10-3. Using onvalidate (continued)

```
<!--- Submit the form to itself --->
<cfform action="#CGI.SrciptName#" name="MyForm"
      enctype="application/x-www-form-urlencoded">
<table>
<tr>
  <td>User Name:</td>
  <td><cfinput type="text" name="MyTime" required="Yes"
      message="You must enter a User Name." size="10" maxlength="10"></td>
</tr>

<tr>
  <td>Password:</td>
  <td><cfinput type="password" name="password" required="Yes"
      message="You must enter a Password." size="10" maxlength="10"></td>
</tr>
<tr>
  <td>Confirm:</td>
  <td><cfinput type="password" name="Password2"
      message="Passwords don't match, please re-enter them and submit again."
      onvalidate="PasswordCheck" size="10" maxlength="10"></td>
</tr>
</table>

<p>
<input type="submit" name="submit" value="submit">
</cfform>
```

What happens in Example 10-3 is straightforward. We define a JavaScript function called `PasswordCheck` at the beginning of the template. It contains the JavaScript code to be called by the password confirmation field (the last `cfinput` statement in the template). The second section of the code is a conditional block of code that executes only if the template is called via a POST operation. The code loops through any form fields passed to the template and outputs them along with their corresponding values.

The third section of code is the `cfform` section. This section of code creates a form with three text-input fields and a submit button. The fields allow a user to enter a username, a password of his choice, and a confirmation of that password. When the user submits the form, the first `cfinput` tag automatically checks to see that a value has been entered. If not, a JavaScript alert box is displayed along with the text in the `message` attribute of the tag. Next, the `Password` field is evaluated to ensure that a value has been entered. If one hasn't, a similar JavaScript alert box is displayed. Finally, the `cfinput` tag containing the `Password2` field calls the `PasswordCheck` JavaScript function via the `onvalidate` attribute. The `PasswordCheck` function evaluates the value of `Password1` against `Password2`. If they are equal, the form is submitted. If, however, the values aren't equal, a JavaScript alert is displayed along with the text from the `message` attribute of the `cfinput` tag. The form can't successfully be submitted until all the validation conditions have been met.

When ColdFusion calls out to a custom JavaScript function via the onvalidate attribute, the form object, input object, and input object value are all automatically passed to the specified JavaScript function. The JavaScript function should return true if the validation is successful and false if it fails. Using the onvalidate attribute overrides any options specified in the validate attribute.

Data Validation with JavaScript Regular Expressions

ColdFusion 5.0 added JavaScript regular expressions as a means for validating data entered in cfinput and cftextinput tags. Regular expressions allow you to specify patterns to match data input against. For example, you can write regular expressions to validate things such as valid email address formats, string lengths, file-naming conventions, and anything else that follows a pattern. To use a JavaScript regular expression as a validation mechanism in your cfinput or cftextinput tags, you need to do two things. First, you must specify Regular_Expression in the validate attribute of your tag. Regular_Expression lets ColdFusion know you want to use a JavaScript regular expression to validate the input for the form control.

The second thing you need to do is specify the JavaScript regular expression you want to validate against. This done using a new attribute called pattern. The pattern attribute accepts any combination of characters comprising a valid JavaScript regular expression. There are, however, a few rules that you need to be aware of:

- You shouldn't enter the forward slashes (/) normally used to surround a JavaScript regular expression as ColdFusion does this behind the scenes for you.
- ColdFusion variables and expressions can dynamically construct the regular expression as they are evaluated before the regular expression validates the form-field input.

Although there are similarities between JavaScript regular expressions and those native to ColdFusion (covered in Chapter 18), enough of a difference exists to warrant separate coverage. However, a thorough discussion of JavaScript regular expressions is beyond the scope of this book, so I recommend consulting the following resources to learn more:

JavaScript: The Definitive Guide by David Flanagan (O'Reilly)
    Chapter 10, Pattern Matching with Regular Expressions

Developing ColdFusion MX Applications with CFML (ColdFusion documentation)
    Chapter 27, Building Dynamic Forms

Netscape JavaScript Guide
    http://developer.netscape.com/docs/manuals/communicator/jsguide/regexp.htm

CNet's Builder.com
    http://www.builder.com/Programming/Kahn/050698/

For those already familiar with JavaScript regular expressions, Example 10-4 shows how to use this feature to perform a few simple validation tasks.

Example 10-4. Using JavaScript regular expressions to validate form input

```
<cfform action="#CGI.Script_Name#" name="MyForm" preservedata="Yes"
       enctype="application/x-www-form-urlencoded">
<table>
  <tr>
    <td>Employee ID:</td>
    <td><cfinput type="text" name="Name" required="Yes"
               message="You must enter your 5 digit employee ID."
               validate="Regular_Expression" pattern="^\d{5}$"></td>
  </tr>
  <!--- Note that there should not be a line break in the message attribute.
        Having one causes the validation not to work. --->
  <tr>
    <td>Password:</td>
    <td><cfinput type="password" name="Password" required="Yes"
          message="Password must be at least 8 characters, consisting of letters,
numbers, and underscores only."
          validate="Regular_Expression" pattern="^\w{8,}$"></td>
  </tr>
  <tr>
    <td>E-mail:</td>
    <td><cfinput type="text" name="Email" required="Yes"
            message="You must enter your e-mail address."
            validate="Regular_Expression"
            pattern="^[A-Za-z0-9_\.\-]+@([A-Za-z0-9_\.\-]+\.)+[A-Za-z]{2,4}$">
    </td>
  </tr>
</table>
<p>
<input type="submit" name="submit" value="submit">
</cfform>
```

The form in this example expects three inputs: a five-digit employee number, a password at least eight characters long that is made up of letters, numbers, and underscores only, and a correctly formatted (notice I didn't say valid) email address.

To validate that the user has entered exactly five digits and nothing else, the first `cfinput` tag uses this regular expression:

```
^\d{5}$
```

The ^ character anchors the expression to the beginning of the string while `\d` matches any single digit from 0–9. The `{5}` tells the regular expression to match the last group of characters (in this case, a single digit) five times. Finally, the $ character anchors the regular expression to the end of the string.

The next `cfinput` tag uses a similar regular expression to make sure the form input is at least eight characters long and contains only letters, digits, and underscores:

```
^\w{8,}$
```

In this case, the ^ and $ characters perform the same job as in the previous example. The `\w` tells the regular expression to match any single letter, digit, or underscore character. Adding the comma to the repetition character makes the regular expression match eight *or more* occurrences of the last group of characters.

The final cfinput tag uses a slightly more complicated regular expression to ensure that a correctly formatted email address is entered:

```
^[A-Za-z0-9_\.\-]+@([A-Za-z0-9_\.\-]+\.)+[A-Za-z]{2,4}$
```

This regular expression also uses the ^ and $ characters for the same purpose as the previous two regular expressions. The [A-Za-z0-9_\.\-]+@ means that the regular expression should match one or more letters (regardless of case), digits, underscores, periods, or dashes followed by an @ character. The next part, ([A-Za-z0-9_\.\-]+\.)+ matches one or more sets of letters (again, regardless of case), digits, underscores, periods, or dashes followed by a period. The final part of the regular expression matches a string containing at least two letters (regardless of case) but not more than four. This allows the user to enter email addresses such as *me@example.com* and *me.oh.my@my.example.ru*. While this regular expression doesn't prevent people from entering invalid email addresses, it does cut down on the number of accidental formatting mistakes.

Textual Input

The cftextinput tag offers a Java control for accepting basic text input. Although it provides the same basic functionality as the cfinput and HTML input tags, cftextinput differs in that it allows you to specify a number of attributes affecting the look of both the text box and the data entered into it. Consider Example 10-5, in which two cftextinput tags are used to solicit information from a user.

Example 10-5. Creating a form using cfform and cftextinput

```
<!--- Check to see if form field data is being passed and if so, display it --->
<cfif IsDefined('form.Fieldnames')>
  <h3>You submitted:</h3>
  <cfoutput>
  MyName:  #form.MyName#<br>
  PhoneNumber: #form.PhoneNumber#
  </cfoutput>
  <hr noshade>
</cfif>

<cfform action="#CGI.Script_Name#" enablecab="Yes" name="MyForm"
        enctype="application/x-www-form-urlencoded">
<table>
<tr>
  <td>Name:</td>
  <td><cftextinput name="MyName" align="AbsMiddle"
                   height="25" width="250" bgcolor="##C0C0C0"
                   font="Arial" fontsize="14" bold="Yes" italic="No"
                   textcolor="##000000" maxlength="255" required="Yes"
                   message="You must enter your name"></td>
```

Example 10-5. Creating a form using cfform and cftextinput (continued)

```
</tr>
<tr>
  <td>Phone Number:</td>
  <td><cftextinput name="PhoneNumber" value="xxx-xxx-xxxx"
                   align="AbsMiddle" height="25" width="100"
                   bgcolor="##COCOCO" font="Arial" fontsize="14" bold="Yes"
                   italic="Yes" textcolor="##000000" maxlength="12"
                   required="Yes" validate="telephone"
                   message="You must enter your phone number as xxx-xxx-xxxx">
  </td>
</tr>
<tr>
  <td colspan="2"><input type="submit" name="submit" value="submit"></td>
</tr>
</table>
</cfform>
```

Example 10-5 uses two `cftextinput` tags that solicit information from a user, as shown in Figure 10-1. The first tag creates a text box for a user to enter his name. The second collects a user's phone number. In both cases, the `name` attribute is required to name the form field. The `value` attribute is optional, and you can use it to specify a default value to appear in the text box. In the case of the text box called `PhoneNumber`, a default value of *xxx-xxx-xxxx* is used. You can specify the positioning of the text-input box by using the `align` attribute. Possible values are `top`, `texttop`, `bottom`, `absbottom`, `baseline`, `middle`, `AbsMiddle`, `left`, and `right`. The height and width of the text boxes is set using the `height` and `width` attributes, respectively. You can specify a background color for the control by entering the color name or appropriate hex color code in the `bgcolor` attribute. If you specify a hex value, you must escape the pound sign, or ColdFusion will throw an error.

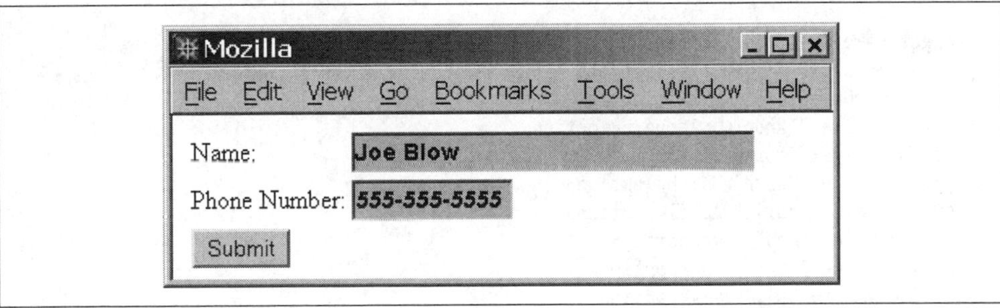

Figure 10-1. cfform using cftextinput

One nice feature of the `cftextinput` control that isn't available in regular HTML forms is the ability to control font characteristics with the form control itself. The `font` attribute specifies the font to use when representing the text entered in the form control. The size of the font is controlled by the `fontsize` attribute. Bold and italic effects may be used by indicating `Yes` or `No` within the `bold` and `italic` attributes.

Text color is specified using the `textcolor` attribute and may be entered as the color name or as a valid hex color value.

You can specify a maximum number of characters that can be entered in the text control with the `maxlength` attribute. This prevents users from entering more data in the form than your corresponding database field allows. Setting the `required` attribute to `Yes` makes the text-box field a required form field. As shown in Figure 10-1, in the case of the `PhoneNumber` field, additional validation is performed by setting the `validate` field to `"Telephone"`. This requires any value entered for `PhoneNumber` to follow the U.S. telephone format before the form can be submitted. The `message` attribute is used when the `required` attribute is set to `Yes`; the `validate` attribute is used to require a specific type of validation be performed. You specify a text message to display in the event that validation fails for the given field.

A Selection Control

The `cfselect` tag extends the functionality provided by the HTML `select` tag by including data validation as well as a mechanism for quickly and easily building dynamic drop-down boxes from query results. Example 10-6 shows a simple use of `cfselect` with static option values.

Example 10-6. Using cfselect with static option values

```
<cfif IsDefined('form.Selectbox')>
  <cfoutput>You submitted <b>#form.Selectbox#</b>.</cfoutput>
  <hr noshade>
</cfif>

<cfform action="#CGI.Script_Name#" name="MyForm"
enctype="application/x-www-form-urlencoded">

<cfselect name="Selectbox" size="5"
          message="You must select at least one item from the selection box."
          required="Yes" multiple="Yes">
   <option value="January">January</option>
   <option value="February">February</option>
   <option value="March">March</option>
   <option value="April">April</option>
   <option value="May">May</option>
   <option value="June">June</option>
   <option value="July">July</option>
   <option value="August">August</option>
   <option value="September">September</option>
   <option value="October">October</option>
   <option value="November">November</option>
   <option value="December">December</option>
</cfselect>
<p>
<input type="submit" name="submit" value="Submit Form">
</cfform>
```

In Example 10-6, a drop-down box is created within a cfform using the cfselect tag. We specify the name of the select-box field using the name attribute. Setting the size to 5 creates a select box five rows high. Note that size must be set to at least 2 for the required validation to work. The multiple attribute allows the user to select multiple values from the select box. By setting the required attribute to Yes, we can require the user to select at least one value from the list. The message attribute specifies a message to appear in a JavaScript alert box should the user fail to choose at least one option. In the case of this example, all option values for the select box are hardcoded.

While the data-validation capabilities of cfselect are a good reason to use the tag, the real benefit of cfselect becomes evident when you use it to dynamically populate the options of a select box with the results of a query. By adding a few additional attributes to the cfselect tag, it is possible to generate all the option tags necessary for the select list dynamically. Example 10-7 shows the basic syntax for populating the cfselect tag with the results of a query.

Example 10-7. Populating a cfselect box with dynamic values from a query

```
<cfif IsDefined('form.Selectbox')>
  <cfoutput>You submitted <b>#form.Selectbox#</b>.</cfoutput>
  <hr noshade>
</cfif>

<cfquery name="GetPeople" datasource="ProgrammingCF">
  SELECT ID,Name
  FROM EmployeeDirectory
</cfquery>

<cfform action="#CGI.Script_Name#" name="MyForm"
        enctype="application/x-www-form-urlencoded">

<cfselect name="Selectbox" size="5"
          message="You must select at least one item from the selection box."
          query="GetPeople" value="ID" display="Name"
          selected="Pere Money" required="Yes" multiple="Yes">
</cfselect>
<p>
<input type="submit" name="submit" value="Submit Form">
</cfform>
```

In Example 10-7, the cfselect tag takes on four additional attributes: query, value, display, and selected. The query attribute specifies the name of the query to use to populate the tag. In this case, we used GetPeople. The value attribute determines which field from the query to use to fill in the option values. For this example, we use the ID field, which happens to be the primary key for the table. The next attribute, display, allows us to choose an alternate field from the query to display in the select box itself. We chose the name field in this case. The final new attribute, selected, allows us to supply a value that is selected automatically when the template is called. In this example, we chose Pere Money, a value known to be in the database under the name column.

Sliders

The `cfslider` tag is a Java slider control you can embed in your applications. It offers an efficient and user-friendly way to select a value from a range of numeric values. Possible uses include volume controls, time lines, and dollar amounts. The control works by allowing users to drag the slider bar to the left to decrease the value or to the right to increase the value. The slider control is shown in Figure 10-2.

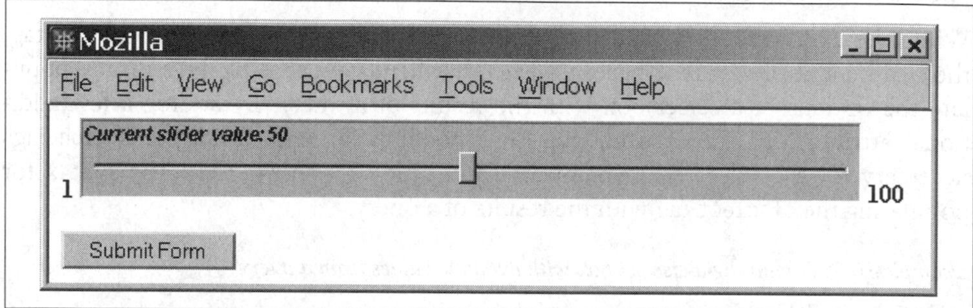

Figure 10-2. A horizontal slider control

To better illustrate how the `cfslider` control works, consider Example 10-8.

Example 10-8. Using the cfslider control

```
<cfif IsDefined('form.Slider')>
  <cfoutput>You submitted a slider value of <b>#form.Slider#</b>.</cfoutput>
  <hr noshade>
</cfif>


<cfform action="#CGI.Script_Name#" method="POST" name="MyForm"
        enctype="application/x-www-form-urlencoded">
<b>1</b> <cfslider name="Slider" label="Current slider value:  %value%"
                   refreshlabel="Yes" range="1,100" value="50" scale="1"
                   align="Baseline" height="50" width="500"
                   font="Arial" fontsize="14" bold="Yes" italic="Yes"
                   textcolor="##000000" bgcolor="##FFFFFF"
                   notsupported="<b>Your web browser must support Java to view
                   ColdFusion Java Applets</b>"><b>100</b>
<p>
<input type="submit" name="submit" value="Submit Form">
</cfform>
```

The `cfslider` tag accepts several parameters that determine how to display the slider control. The `name` attribute specifies a name for the form field. `label` is used to display a label for the slider control as well as the current value associated with the slider's position. By default, the value associated with the slider's current position is shown to the right of the `label` text. `refreshlabel` indicates whether the value specified in `label` should be refreshed as the slider control is moved from one side to the other. You can specify the beginning and ending values for the slider control by the range attribute. A default value for the slider control can be specified with the value attribute. The scale attribute allows you to specify an increment value for the slider control. When choosing a scale, be sure to pick a number that corresponds with the values you specified in range. For example, it doesn't make sense to have a range of 1–100 with a scale of 7. align determines how to position the slider control. Possible values are Top, TextTop, Bottom, AbsBottom, Baseline, Middle, AbsMiddle, Left, and Right. The height and width attributes specify a size in pixels for the slider control.

The font attribute specifies the font to use for the slider label. The size of the font is controlled by the fontsize attribute. You can use bold and italic effects by indicating Yes or No within the bold and italic attributes. You can specify text color with the textcolor attribute by entering the color name or a valid hex color value (remember the pound sign). A background color may be specified for the control by entering the color name or appropriate hex color code in the bgcolor attribute. The final attribute, notsupported, specifies a text message to display in the event that the browser accessing the form containing the slider control doesn't support Java.

Several additional attributes were added to the cfslider tag in ColdFusion 5 that affect both the look and feel of the control and its functionality. One of the most significant additions is an attribute named vertical that allows you to specify whether the control should slide vertically as opposed to horizontally. The default is No. Example 10-9 shows the code to generate a vertical slider control. The slider is shown in Figure 10-3.

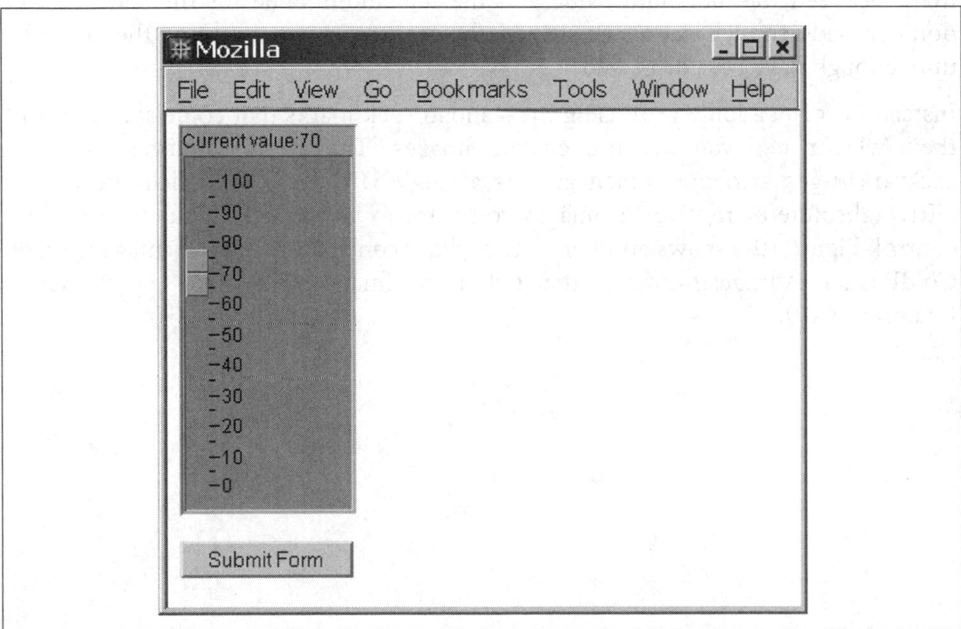

Figure 10-3. Vertical slider control with major and minor tick marks and tick mark labels

Example 10-9. Creating a vertical slider

```
<cfform action="#CGI.Script_Name#" name="MyForm" preservedata="Yes"
        enctype="application/x-www-form-urlencoded">
  <cfslider name="Slider" label="Current value:  %value%"
            refreshlabel="Yes" range="0,100" scale="10"
            value="50" align="Top" height="250" width="115"
            vertical="Yes" lookandfeel="Motif" tickmarkmajor="Yes"
            tickmarkminor="Yes" tickmarklabels="Yes">
<p>
<input type="submit" name="submit" value="Submit Form">
</cfform>
```

In this example, the `vertical` attribute tells ColdFusion to create a vertical slider. The `lookandfeel` attribute specifies an overall look and feel for the slider control. Options are `Windows` (the default), `Metal`, and `Motif`. For this example, the `cfslider` control is sporting a `Motif` look. Setting `tickmarkmajor` to `Yes` causes a large tick mark to display at every increment value along the axis of the slider control. In this case, the major tick marks are at every 10 places along the slider. The `tickmarkminor` attribute determines whether to display smaller tick marks between the major tick marks along the slider control. For this example, we set it to `Yes`. The final attribute is `tickmarklabels`. It indicates whether to display labels next to each major tick mark. If `Yes`, the numeric value corresponding to the tick mark is displayed. Instead of numeric values, you may choose to display string values instead. This is done by specifying a string or comma delimited list of string values, one for each major tick mark between the minimum value and the maximum value for the slider. If you don't provide enough tick mark strings, the `cfslider` control repeats the last value until enough have been displayed.

Instead of (or in addition to) using the standard tick marks that come standard with the `cfslider` tag, you can use custom images. This is accomplished with the `tickmarkimages` attribute, which accepts a single URL or comma-delimited list of URLs (absolute or relative) to images you want to use as tick marks for the slider control. Figure 10-4 shows another vertical slider control that uses an image from the ColdFusion Administrator as the tick-mark image. The code is shown in Example 10-10.

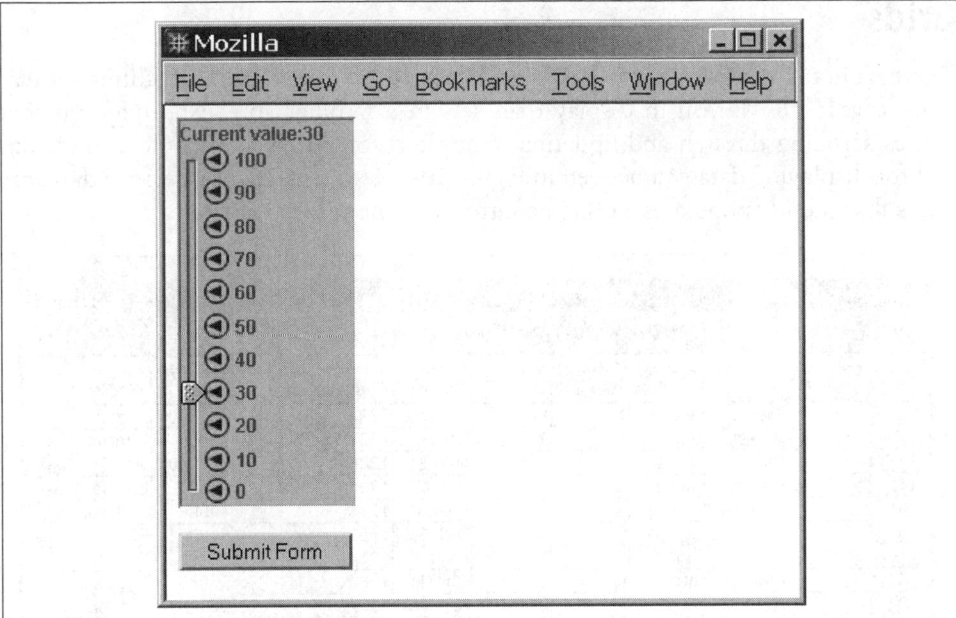

Figure 10-4. Using an image as a tick mark

Example 10-10. Specifying an image to use as a tick mark

```
<cfform action="#CGI.Script_Name#" name="MyForm" preservedata="Yes"
        enctype="application/x-www-form-urlencoded">
  <cfslider name="Slider" label="Current value:  %value%"
            refreshlabel="Yes" range="0,100" scale="10" value="50"
            align="Top" height="250" width="115" vertical="Yes"
            lookandfeel="Metal" tickmarklabels="Yes"
            tickmarkimages="/cfide/administrator/images/back.gif">
<p>
<input type="submit" name="submit" value="Submit Form">
</cfform>
```

Here you'll notice that we still include the `tickmarklabels` attribute, giving us the numeric value corresponding to each of our custom tick-mark images. The images are specified by providing the URL to the image in the `tickmarkimages` attribute. For this example, I chose an image from the ColdFusion Administrator that just happens to line up nicely on the slider control.

Grids

The cfgrid tag provides a Java-based grid control for displaying and editing tabular data. cfgrid allows you to display data sets in a familiar spreadsheet format that makes scrolling through and updating multiple records easy. A sample cfgrid control for displaying data can be seen in Figure 10-5. Example 10-11 queries a database and subsequently populates a cfgrid control with the record set data.

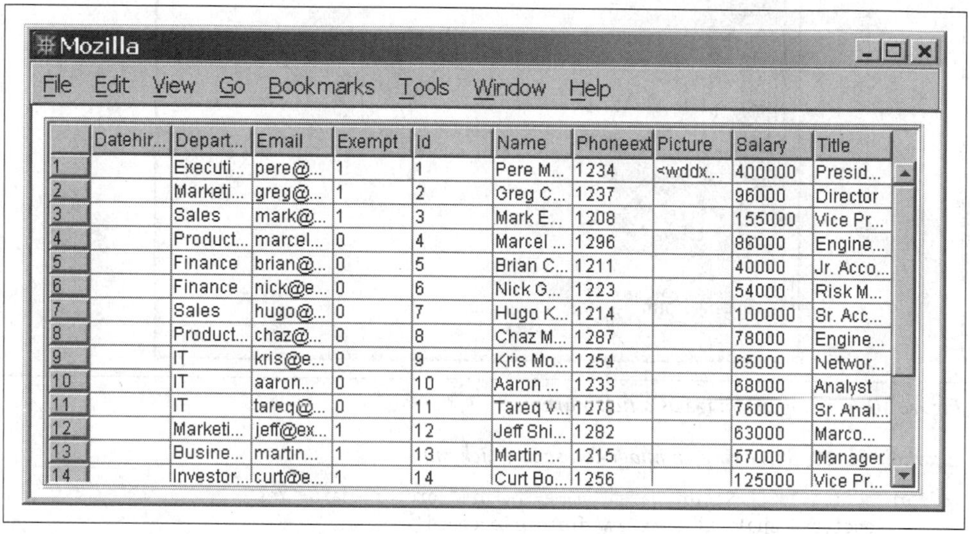

Figure 10-5. The cfgrid control

Example 10-11. Creating a basic grid control

```
<cfquery name="GetPeople" datasource="ProgrammingCF">
  SELECT *
  FROM EmployeeDirectory
</cfquery>

<cfform action="#CGI.Script_Name#" name="MyForm"
        enctype="application/x-www-form-urlencoded">
  <cfgrid name="MyGrid" width="600" height="250" autowidth="Yes"
          query="GetPeople" selectmode="Browse"
          notsupported="<b>Your web browser must support Java to view
                        ColdFusion Java Applets</b>">
  </cfgrid>
</cfform>
```

The name attribute specifies the name of the grid control. height and width specify the height and width (in pixels) for the grid's display area. autowidth indicates whether the grid should adjust the width of each column automatically so that all columns appear within the grid without having to scroll horizontally. The default is No. hspace and vspace specify the amount of padding in pixels above, below, to the left, and to the right of the grid control; we're allowing the grid to use its default values of 0 pixels for both. The align attribute determines the grid's alignment on the page. Possible values are Left, Right, Top, TextTop, Bottom, AbsBottom, Baseline, Middle, and AbsMiddle. We're relying on the default value of Baseline. The query attribute specifies the name of a query that should be used to populate the grid with data. selectmode determines the selection mode to use for items in the grid. Valid entries are:

Browse *(default)*
: Allows browsing of data only

Edit
: Allows editing of data

Single
: Confines selections to a single cell

Column
: Selections automatically include the entire column

Row
: Selections automatically include the entire row

In Example 10-11, we set the selection mode to Browse, preventing users from selecting or editing data displayed in the grid. The last attribute in this example, notsupported, specifies a text message to display in the event that the browser accessing the grid control doesn't support Java.

Before we continue, there are several behaviors in the cfgrid control you should be aware of:

- The user may rearrange the order in which columns are displayed by clicking on a column header and dragging it left or right.
- The user may sort the grid data by double-clicking the column header of the column you wish to sort by. The first time the user sorts, the data is sorted in ascending order. Double-clicking again resorts the data in descending order.
- When selectmode is Edit, Row, Column, or Single, clicking once on a noneditable cell causes the background color of that cell (or row or column) to turn pink with a yellow border. Clicking once on an editable cell turns the background color of the cell white with a yellow border.
- To edit the contents of an editable cell, the user can double click on it. Pressing the Enter key or clicking on a different cell finishes the editing.

Now that you see how simple it is to display query data using the grid control, let's look at some formatting options that are available to the grid control. These formatting options allow you to tailor the display of text within the grid and include both font and positioning options. Example 10-12 takes the same grid we built in Example 10-11 and adds formatting. You can see the results in Figure 10-6.

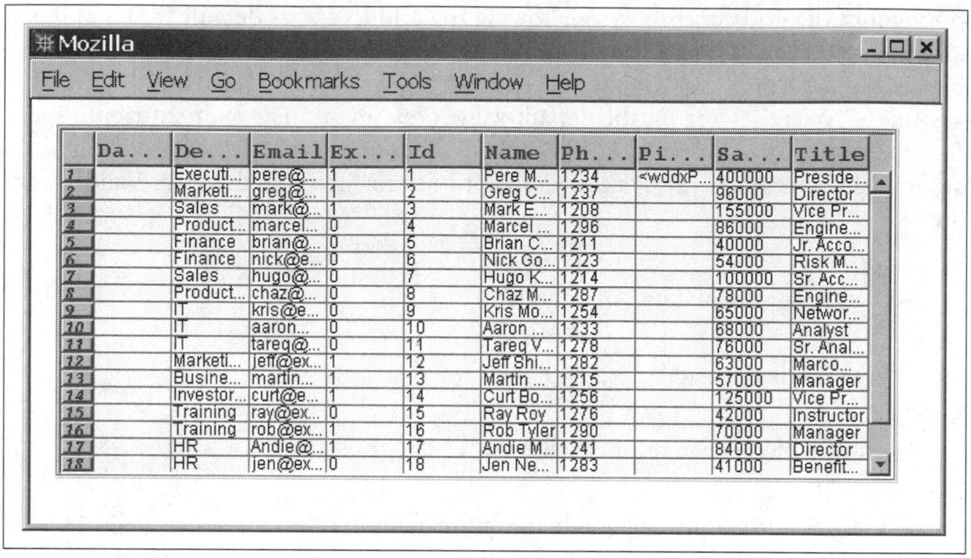

Mozilla

File Edit View Go Bookmarks Tools Window Help

	Da...	De...	Email	Ex...	Id	Name	Ph...	Pi...	Sa...	Title
1		Executi...	pere@...	1	1	Pere M...	1234	<wddxP...	400000	Preside...
2		Marketi...	greg@...	1	2	Greg C...	1237		96000	Director
3		Sales	mark@...	1	3	Mark E...	1208		155000	Vice Pr...
4		Product...	marcel...	0	4	Marcel ...	1296		86000	Engine...
5		Finance	brian@...	0	5	Brian C...	1211		40000	Jr. Acco...
6		Finance	nick@e...	0	6	Nick Go...	1223		54000	Risk M...
7		Sales	hugo@...	0	7	Hugo K...	1214		100000	Sr. Acc...
8		Product...	chaz@...	0	8	Chaz M...	1287		78000	Engine...
9		IT	kris@e...	0	9	Kris Mo...	1254		65000	Networ...
10		IT	aaron...	0	10	Aaron ...	1233		68000	Analyst
11		IT	tareq@...	0	11	Tareq V...	1278		76000	Sr. Anal...
12		Marketi...	jeff@ex...	1	12	Jeff Shi...	1282		63000	Marco...
13		Busine...	martin...	1	13	Martin ...	1215		57000	Manager
14		Investor...	curt@e...	1	14	Curt Bo...	1256		125000	Vice Pr...
15		Training	ray@ex...	0	15	Ray Roy	1276		42000	Instructor
16		Training	rob@ex...	1	16	Rob Tyler	1290		70000	Manager
17		HR	Andie@...	1	17	Andie M...	1241		84000	Director
18		HR	jen@ex...	0	18	Jen Ne...	1283		41000	Benefit...

Figure 10-6. Result of adding additional formatting to a cfgrid

Example 10-12. Using the cfgrid control to present query data

```
<cfquery name="GetPeople" datasource="ProgrammingCF">
  SELECT *
  FROM EmployeeDirectory
</cfquery>

<cfform action="#CGI.Script_Name#" name="MyForm"
        enctype="application/x-www-form-urlencoded">
  <cfgrid name="MyGrid" height="250" width="600" autowidth="Yes" hspace="10"
          vspace="10" query="GetPeople" font="Arial" textcolor="##000000"
          fontsize="12" bold="No" italic="No" griddataalign="Left"
          gridlines="Yes" rowheight="12" rowheaders="Yes"
          rowheadertextcolor="##0000FF" rowheaderalign="Left"
          rowheaderitalic="Yes" rowheaderbold="Yes" rowheaderfont="Courier"
          rowheaderfontsize="12" colheaders="Yes" colheadertextcolor="##0000FF"
          colheaderalign="Left" colheaderitalic="No" colheaderbold="Yes"
          colheaderfont="Courier" colheaderfontsize="16" bgcolor="##FFFFCC"
          selectmode="Browse"
          notsupported="<b>Your web browser must support Java to view
                        ColdFusion Java Applets.</b>">
  </cfgrid>
</cfform>
```

As you can see, we have introduced several new attributes to the `cfgrid` tag. Each attribute controls a different aspect of the grid's display properties. Many attributes have names that are fairly self-explanatory, so I'm not going to explain each one. One group of attributes control how row headings appear, while another group controls the column headings. The `griddataalign` attribute specifies alignment for the grid data. Choices are `Left`, `Right`, or `Center`. The default value is `Left`. The `gridlines` attribute indicates whether or not to add row and column lines to the grid. The default value is Yes. For a complete listing of all attributes available to the cfgrid tag, see Appendix A.

Customizing Column Data

You can get even more control of the data displayed within the grid by using a child tag of cfgrid called cfgridcolumn. cfgridcolumn allows you to specify individual column data and formatting options. Example 10-13 shows cfgridcolumn used in the most basic context.

Example 10-13. Populating a cfgrid using cfgridcolumn

```
<cfquery name="GetPeople" datasource="ProgrammingCF">
  SELECT Name, Title, Department
  FROM EmployeeDirectory
</cfquery>

<cfform action="#CGI.Script_Name#" name="MyForm"
       enctype="application/x-www-form-urlencoded">
  <cfgrid name="MyGrid" autowidth="Yes" width="600" height="250"
          query="GetPeople" griddataalign="Left" gridlines="Yes"
          rowheight="12" rowheaders="Yes" colheaders="Yes"
          bgcolor="##FFFFCC" selectmode="Browse"
          notsupported="<b>Your web browser must support Java to view
                        ColdFusion Java Applets.</b>">
      <cfgridcolumn name="Name" header="Full Name">
      <cfgridcolumn name="Title" header="Title">
      <cfgridcolumn name="Department" header="Department">
  </cfgrid>
</cfform>
```

In Example 10-13, rather than let the cfgrid tag determine which columns of data to display, we leave that task up to the cfgridcolumn tag. In Example 10-12, all the columns present in the database were displayed in the grid. In Example 10-13, only the Name, Title, and Department columns are present. The name attribute of each cfgridcolumn tag determines which query column to display. The actual column header that appears in the grid is specified in the header attribute. If header is omitted, ColdFusion uses the column name from the database.

We can specify additional formatting options for each grid column by including other attributes within the cfgridcolumn tags. Example 10-14 shows how to apply this additional formatting.

Example 10-14. Formatting individual columns with cfgridcolumn

```
<cfquery name="GetPeople" datasource="ProgrammingCF">
  SELECT Name, Title, Department
  FROM EmployeeDirectory
</cfquery>
```

Example 10-14. Formatting individual columns with cfgridcolumn (continued)

```
<cfform action="#CGI.Script_Name#" name="MyForm"
        enctype="application/x-www-form-urlencoded">
  <cfgrid name="MyGrid" autowidth="Yes" width="600" height="250"
          query="GetPeople" griddataalign="Left" gridlines="Yes"
          rowheight="12" rowheaders="Yes" colheaders="Yes"
          bgcolor="##FFFFCC" selectmode="Browse"
          notsupported="<b>Your web browser must support Java to view
                        ColdFusion Java Applets</b>">
     <cfgridcolumn name="Name" header="Full Name" headertextcolor="##0000FF"
                   headerfont="Arial" headerfontsize="14" headeritalic="Yes"
                   headerbold="Yes" headeralign="Left" width="125"
                   font="Arial" fontsize="12" italic="No" bold="No"
                   dataalign="left" select="No" display="Yes"
                   type="String_NoCase">

     <cfgridcolumn name="Title" header="Title" headerfont="Arial"
                   headerfontsize="14" headeritalic="Yes" headerbold="Yes"
                   headeralign="Left" font="Arial" fontsize="12" italic="No"
                   bold="No" dataalign="left" select="No" display="Yes"
                   type="String_NoCase">

     <cfgridcolumn name="Department" header="Department" headerfont="Arial"
                   headerfontsize="14" headeritalic="Yes" headerbold="Yes"
                   headeralign="left" font="Arial" fontsize="12" italic="No"
                   bold="No" dataalign="Left" select="No" display="Yes"
                   type="String_NoCase">
  </cfgrid>
</cfform>
```

Note that all the formatting attributes used with the `cfgridcolumn` tag are optional. Most of these attributes do exactly what their names imply and are used to control the appearance of column headers and column data. A few attributes require further explanation. `select` indicates whether or not to allow users to select column data to be edited. `select` is ignored when the `selectmode` attribute of the `cfgrid` tag is set to `Row` or `Browse`. The `select` attribute indicates whether or not to display the column in the grid. The default is `Yes`. Finally, the `type` attribute specifies the type of column data to display. Choices for this attribute are:

`Image`
: Specifies an image corresponding to the column value to display. You may specify a path to your own image or use one of the images supplied with ColdFusion by referencing the image name. Valid options are `CD`, `Computer`, `Document`, `Element`, `Folder`, `Floppy`, `Fixed`, and `Remote`. If the image is larger than the cell in which it is being displayed, the image is automatically cropped to fit within the cell.

`Numeric`
: Allows data in the grid to be sorted by the user as numeric data, rather than as text.

`String_NoCase`
: Allows data in the grid to be sorted by the user as case-insensitive text rather than case-sensitive, which is the default.

`Boolean`
: Places a checkbox in the grid column. Useful in situations where you want to represent Boolean data in a grid column. If the grid column containing the checkbox is editable, the checkbox may be checked and unchecked; otherwise it is read-only. New as of ColdFusion 5.0.

A few additional attributes aren't used in Example 10-14 but are worth mentioning here. The `href` attribute specifies a URL to associate with the grid item. The URL can be absolute or relative. You can specify the name of a frame or window in which the template specified in the `href` attribute should be opened using the `target` attribute. You may apply a mask to numeric values using the `numberformat` attribute. For valid options, see the `NumberFormat()` function in Appendix B. `hrefkey` specifies the name of a query column to use as the `Key` when a query is used to populate the grid. For a complete list of all attributes associated with the `cfgridcolumn` tag, see Appendix A.

Figure 10-7 shows some of the different effects you can achieve using the `cfgrid` control.

	Name	Title	Department	E-mail	Salary
1	Pere Money	President	Executive Manage...	pere@example.c...	$400,000
2	Greg Corcoran	Director	Marketing	greg@example.c...	$96,000
3	Mark Edward	Vice President	Sales	mark@example.c...	$155,000
4	Marcel Haney	Engineer I	Product Engineeri...	marcel@example...	$86,000
5	Brian Christopher	Jr. Accountant	Finance	brian@example.c...	$40,000
6	Nick Gosnell	Risk Managemen...	Finance	nick@example.com	$54,000
7	Hugo Keane	Sr. Account Mana...	Sales	hugo@example.c...	$100,000
8	Chaz Maxwell	Engineer II	Product Engineeri...	chaz@example.c...	$78,000
9	Kris Moritz	Network Manager	IT	kris@example.com	$65,000
10	Aaron Ridge	Analyst	IT	aaron@example....	$68,000
11	Tareq Varga	Sr. Analyst	IT	tareq@example.c...	$76,000
12	Jeff Shields	Marcom Manager	Marketing	jeff@example.com	$63,000
13	Martin Grant	Manager	Business Develo...	martin@example....	$57,000
14	Curt Bond	Vice President	Investor Relations	curt@example.com	$125,000
15	Ray Roy	Instructor	Training	ray@example.com	$42,000
16	Rob Tyler	Manager	Training	rob@example.com	$70,000
17	Andie Moore	Director	HR	Andie@example.c...	$84,000
18	Jen Newton	Benefits Coordina...	HR	jen@example.com	$41,000

Figure 10-7. cfgrid with embedded hyperlinks and a numberformat mask

Specifying Row Data

`cfgridrow` is another child tag of `cfgrid` you can use to populate a grid with query data. You can opt for `cfgridrow` instead of the `query` attribute in the `cfgrid` tag. When you do use the `query` attribute in the `cfgrid` tag, the `cfgridrow` tag is ignored. Example 10-15 illustrates this technique.

Example 10-15. Using cfgridrow

```
<cfquery name="GetPeople" datasource="ProgrammingCF">
  SELECT *
  FROM EmployeeDirectory
</cfquery>

<cfform action="#CGI.Script_Name#" name="MyForm"
        enctype="application/x-www-form-urlencoded">
  <cfgrid name="MyGrid" autowidth="Yes" width="600" height="250"
          griddataalign="Left" gridlines="Yes" rowheight="12" rowheaders="Yes"
          colheaders="Yes" bgcolor="##FFFFCC" selectmode="Browse"
          notsupported="<b>Your web browser must support Java to view
                        ColdFusion Java Applets.</b>">

    <cfgridcolumn name="Name" header="Name">
    <cfgridcolumn name="Title" header="Title">
    <cfgridcolumn name="Department" header="Department">
    <cfgridcolumn name="Email" header="E-mail">
    <cfgridcolumn name="PhoneExt" header="Extension">

    <cfloop query="GetPeople">
      <cfgridrow DATA="#Name#,#Title#,#Department#,#Email#,#PhoneExt#">
    </cfloop>
  </cfgrid>
</cfform>
```

Example 10-15 differs only slightly from our previous examples. In this example, we leave out the query attribute in the cfgrid tag, and we make use of the cfgridrow tag instead. Column headers are still defined using the cfgridcolumn tag. The actual column data is output using the cfgridrow tag. The query must be looped over so that each row of data from the query can be output. If you want to perform any additional formatting or further massage the data, you can use this method of populating the grid.

Creating Updateable Grids

You can also use the cfgrid tag to build updateable grids for adding, editing, and deleting individual cells and records. Creating an editable grid is an easy way to allow your users to quickly make database additions and updates. Making a grid editable is simply a matter of setting the selectmode attribute of the cfgrid tag to Edit.

Updating a grid using cfgridupdate

The simplest way to update the data contained in a data source is via the cfgridupdate tag.* This tag takes all the data posted from a cfgrid control and auto-

* There is a bug with the cfgridupdate tag in both ColdFusion MX 6.0 and 6.1 that causes an error when cfgridupdate attempts to insert a new record into a database containing an auto-increment field for its primary key. This may or may not be addressed in a future updater. For now, the recommended work-around is to use the technique outlined in the section "Updating a Grid using cfquery."

matically makes the necessary updates to the data source. Example 10-16 demonstrates how to create an editable grid that updates the data source using the cfgridupdate tag.

Example 10-16. Creating an updateable grid using cfgridupdate

```
<!--- If the grid has been changed, update it --->
<cfif IsDefined('form.MyGrid.rowstatus.action')>
   <cfgridupdate grid="MyGrid" datasource="ProgrammingCF"
                 tablename="EmployeeDirectory" keyonly="No">
</cfif>

<cfquery name="GetPeople" datasource="ProgrammingCF">
  SELECT *
  FROM EmployeeDirectory
</cfquery>

<cfform action="#CGI.Script_Name#" name="MyForm"
        enctype="application/x-www-form-urlencoded">
  <cfgrid name="MyGrid" autowidth="Yes" width="600" height="250"
          query="GetPeople" insert="Yes" delete="Yes" sort="Yes" font="Arial"
          bold="No" italic="No" appendkey="No" highlighthref="No"
          griddataalign="Left" gridlines="Yes" rowheaders="Yes"
          rowheaderalign="Left" rowheaderitalic="No" rowheaderbold="No"
          colheaders="Yes" colheaderalign="Left" colheaderitalic="No"
          colheaderbold="No" selectcolor="Red" selectmode="Edit"
          picturebar="No" insertbutton="Add New Record" deletebutton="Delete"
          sortascendingbutton="Sort ASC" sortdescendingbutton="Sort DESC"
          notsupported="<b>Your web browser must support Java to view
                        ColdFusion Java Applets.</b>">

    <cfgridcolumn name="ID" header="ID" dataalign="Left" bold="No" italic="No"
                  select="No" display="No" headerbold="No" headeritalic="No">

    <cfgridcolumn name="Name" header="Name" headeralign="Left" dataalign="Left"
                  bold="Yes" italic="No" select="Yes" display="Yes"
                  headerbold="No" headeritalic="Yes">

    <cfgridcolumn name="Title" header="Title" headeralign="Left"
                  dataalign="Left" bold="No" italic="No" select="Yes"
                  display="Yes" headerbold="No" headeritalic="No">

    <cfgridcolumn name="Department" header="Department" headeralign="Left"
                  dataalign="Left" font="Times" bold="No" italic="No"
                  select="Yes" display="Yes" headerbold="No" headeritalic="No">

    <cfgridcolumn name="Email" header="E-mail" headeralign="Left"
                  dataalign="Left" bold="No" italic="No" select="Yes"
                  display="Yes" headerbold="No" headeritalic="No">

    <cfgridcolumn name="PhoneExt" header="Phone ext." headeralign="Left"
                  dataalign="Left" bold="No" italic="No" select="Yes"
                  display="Yes" headerbold="No" headeritalic="No">
```

Example 10-16. Creating an updateable grid using cfgridupdate (continued)

```
  </cfgrid>
  <br>
<input type="submit" name="submit" value="Submit Changes">
</cfform>
```

In Example 10-16, the `cfgridupdate` tag takes the information submitted by the form and makes the necessary updates to the data source. The `grid` attribute specifies the name of the `cfgrid` control supplying the data for the update. The data source to update is specified using the `datasource` attribute. The database table within the data source that is to be updated is specified using the `tablename` attribute. Setting `keyonly` to `No` causes the `WHERE` clause of the SQL statement that ColdFusion generates to contain both the key values as well as the original values from any changed cells within the grid. The default for `keyonly` is `Yes`.

In addition to the attributes already mentioned, the `cfgridupdate` tag also accepts a number of optional attributes that allow you to specify more detailed information about the database being used. See Appendix A for more details.

Updating a grid using cfquery

Using `cfgridupdate` isn't the only way to update your data source with data from a `cfgrid` control. You can also use the `cfquery` tag to handle updates. When an editable grid (with `selectmode` set to `Edit`) is submitted, three one-dimensional arrays are returned containing information about the changes to the data:

`form.`*`gridname`*`.`*`columnname`*`[`*`RowIndex`*`]`
: Contains the new value of an edited grid cell

`form.`*`gridname`*`.Original.`*`columnname`*`[`*`RowIndex`*`]`
: Contains the original value of the edited grid cell

`form.`*`gridname`*`.RowStatus.Action[`*`RowIndex`*`]`
: Contains the type of edit made to the grid cell: `I` for insert, `U` for update, and `D` for delete

To update your data source using `cfquery`, you can loop through the arrays passed by the `cfgrid` tag and generate the necessary `cfquery` tags to insert, update, and delete data as necessary. This technique is shown in Example 10-17.

Example 10-17. Updating a grid using cfquery

```
<!--- Check to see if data was added, updated, or deleted from the grid --->
<cfif IsDefined('form.MyGrid.rowstatus.action')>

<!--- Loop over each instance of a grid action --->
<cfloop index="i" from="1" TO="#ArrayLen(form.MyGrid.rowstatus.action)#">

  <!--- If the action is Insert, insert a new record --->
  <cfif form.MyGrid.rowstatus.action[i] is "I">
```

Example 10-17. Updating a grid using cfquery (continued)

```
    <cfquery name="InsertNewEmployee" datasource="ProgrammingCF">
      INSERT INTO EmployeeDirectory (Name, Title, Department, Email, PhoneExt)
      values ('#form.MyGrid.Name[i]#', '#form.MyGrid.Title[i]#',
              '#form.MyGrid.Department[i]#', '#form.MyGrid.Email[i]#',
               #form.MyGrid.PhoneExt[i]#)
    </cfquery>

    <!--- If the action is Update, update the record --->
  <cfelseif form.MyGrid.rowstatus.action[i] is "U">
    <cfquery name="UpdateExistingEmployee" datasource="ProgrammingCF">
      UPDATE EmployeeDirectory
      SET Name='#form.MyGrid.Name[i]#',
          Title='#form.MyGrid.Title[i]#',
          Department='#form.MyGrid.Department[i]#',
          Email='#form.MyGrid.Email[i]#',
          PhoneExt=#form.MyGrid.PhoneExt[i]#
      WHERE ID=#form.MyGrid.original.ID[i]#
    </cfquery>

  <!--- If the action is Delete, Delete the record --->
  <cfelseif form.MyGrid.rowstatus.action[i] is "D">
    <cfquery name="DeleteExistingEmployee" datasource="ProgrammingCF">
      DELETE FROM EmployeeDirectory
      WHERE ID=#form.MyGrid.original.ID[i]#
    </cfquery>
  </cfif>
</cfloop>
</cfif>

<!--- Create/recreate the grid from a query --->
<cfquery name="GetPeople" datasource="ProgrammingCF">
  SELECT *
  FROM EmployeeDirectory
</cfquery>

<cfform action="#CGI.Script_Name#" name="MyForm"
        enctype="application/x-www-form-urlencoded">

  <cfgrid name="MyGrid" autowidth="Yes" width="600" height="250"
          query="GetPeople" insert="Yes" delete="Yes" sort="Yes" font="Arial"
          bold="No" italic="No" appendkey="No" highlighthref="No"
          griddataalign="Left" gridlines="Yes" rowheaders="Yes"
          rowheaderalign="Left" rowheaderitalic="No" rowheaderbold="No"
          colheaders="Yes" colheaderalign="Left" colheaderitalic="No"
          colheaderbold="No" selectcolor="Red" selectmode="Edit" picturebar="No"
          insertbutton="Add New Record" deletebutton="Delete"
          sortascendingbutton="Sort ASC" sortdescendingbutton="Sort DESC">

    <!--- Hide the ID (primary key) field, but make the value available for
          updates and deletes. --->
    <cfgridcolumn name="ID" display="No" headeritalic="No">
```

Example 10-17. Updating a grid using cfquery (continued)

```
    <cfgridcolumn name="Name" header="Name" headeralign="Left" dataalign="Left"
                  bold="Yes" italic="No" select="Yes" display="Yes"
                  headerbold="No" headeritalic="Yes">

    <cfgridcolumn name="Title" header="Title" headeralign="Left"
                  dataalign="Left" bold="No" italic="No" select="Yes"
                  display="Yes" headerbold="No" headeritalic="No">

    <cfgridcolumn name="Department" header="Department" headeralign="Left"
                  dataalign="Left" font="Times" bold="No" italic="No"
                  select="Yes" display="Yes" headerbold="No" headeritalic="No">

    <cfgridcolumn name="Email" header="E-mail" headeralign="Left"
                  dataalign="Left" bold="No" italic="No" select="Yes"
                  display="Yes" headerbold="No" headeritalic="No">

    <cfgridcolumn name="PhoneExt" header="Phone ext." headeralign="Left"
                  dataalign="Left" bold="No" italic="No" select="Yes"
                  display="Yes" headerbold="No" headeritalic="No">
</cfgrid>
<br>
<input type="submit" name="submit" value="Submit Changes">
</cfform>
```

In Example 10-17, the form data submitted by the `cfgrid` control comes across in three one-dimensional arrays:

```
form.MyGrid.RowStatus.Action[i]

form.MyGrid.ID[i]
form.MyGrid.Name[i]
form.MyGrid.Title[i]
form.MyGrid.Department[i]
form.MyGrid.Email[i]
form.MyGrid.PhoneExt[i]

form.MyGrid.Original.ID[i]
form.MyGrid.Original.Name[i]
form.MyGrid.Original.Title[i]
form.MyGrid.Original.Department[i]
form.MyGrid.Original.Email[i]
form.MyGrid.Original.PhoneExt[i]
```

Each cell's data from the grid is represented in an index of the array, specified by *`i`* in the code. The arrays then dynamically generate the SQL necessary to update the database. The template loops over each element in the `form.MyGrid.RowStatus.Action` array. For each iteration of the loop, ColdFusion checks to see if the `Action` is set to `I` for insert, `U` for Update, or `D` for delete. Depending on the `Action` value, ColdFusion performs the corresponding query action (add, update, or delete) using the value stored in the appropriate array index of the other two arrays. When all of the query actions have been performed, the grid control is redrawn using the updated data from the database.

Advanced editable grid controls

The `cfgridcolumn` tag has several advanced attributes you can use to enhance individual columns of data within your grids. These advanced attributes are `textcolor`, `bgcolor`, `values`, `valuesdisplay`, and `valuesdelimiter`. In addition to these attributes, the `type` attribute now accepts an additional value called `Boolean`. Rather than explain each new attribute and value individually, let's look at an example that utilizes all of them. Example 10-18 creates a grid that provides just such an example.

Example 10-18. Grid showing advanced cfgridcolumn attributes and values

```
<!--- If the grid has been changed, update it --->
<cfif IsDefined('form.MyGrid.rowstatus.action')>
   <cfgridupdate grid="MyGrid" datasource="ProgrammingCF"
                 tablename="EmployeeDirectory" keyonly="No">
</cfif>

<cfquery name="GetPeople" datasource="ProgrammingCF">
  SELECT *
  FROM EmployeeDirectory
  ORDER BY Name
</cfquery>

<cfquery name="GetDepartments" datasource="ProgrammingCF">
  SELECT DISTINCT Department
  FROM EmployeeDirectory
</cfquery>

<cfform action="#CGI.Script_Name#" name="MyForm"
        enctype="application/x-www-form-urlencoded">

  <cfgrid name="MyGrid" width="600" height="250" autowidth="Yes" query="GetPeople"
        selectmode="Edit" insert="No" delete="No">

    <cfgridcolumn name="ID" display="No">
    <!--- If the employee is the president, change the
          text color to blue. Otherwise, leave it alone --->
    <cfgridcolumn name="Name" bold="Yes" headertextcolor="Blue"
                  textcolor="(C2 eq President ? blue : black)"
                  bgcolor="LightGray">

    <cfgridcolumn name="Title" textcolor="(CX eq President ? blue : black)"
                  headertextcolor="Blue">

    <!--- Here's where we create a dropdown list of departments --->
    <cfgridcolumn name="Department" headertextcolor="Blue"
                  values="#ValueList(GetDepartments.Department)#"
                  valuesdisplay="Off" valuesdelimiter=",">
```

Example 10-18. Grid showing advanced cfgridcolumn attributes and values (continued)

```
    <cfgridcolumn name="Email" header="E-mail" headertextcolor="Blue">
    <cfgridcolumn name="PhoneExt" header="Phone ext." headertextcolor="Blue">

     <!--- Use a checkbox to represent Boolean values --->
    <cfgridcolumn name="Exempt" headertextcolor="Blue" type="Boolean">
  </cfgrid>
<br>
<input type="submit" name="submit" value="Submit Changes">
</cfform>
```

This example creates an updateable grid loosely based on the one we created in Example 10-16. There are, however, some significant differences. Before you run this template, you'll have to add a new field to the `EmployeeDirectory` table in the `ProgrammingCF` database. Call the new field `Exempt`, and make it a `Yes/No` (Boolean) data type. This new field is necessary to demonstrate one of the advanced features of `cfgridcolumn`. Don't worry about populating the new column with data just yet; we'll get to that in just a moment.

The next advanced attribute you should see in the first `cfgridcolumn` tag is `textcolor`. This attribute lets you specify the text color for all data in the column. It follows the same color-name rules as the `headertextcolor` attribute. Instead of a color, you can specify an expression that returns a color based on its evaluation, as we do in this example. The expression uses the following format:

```
( CX|Cn gt|lt|eq string ? color_true : color_false)
```

`CX` represents the current column while `Cn` specifies a specific column where *n* is the index position of the column (only displayed columns are available). Operator can be `gt`, `lt`, or `eq` for both string and numeric comparisons. The `?` separates the expression from the values you wish to return. *`color_true`* is the color to return in the event the expression evaluates `true` while *`color_false`* is the color to return if the expression evaluates `false`. Colors are specified using a color name or hex code (without the pound signs). The two return values are separated with a colon. Note that whitespace is ignored within the expression except for within *`string`*. In our example, we use the expression `(C2 eq President ? blue : black)`. What this says is if the value in the corresponding row in column 2 (`Title`) equals `President`, make the text color for this item blue; otherwise, leave it as black.

The final attribute in our first `cfgridcolumn` tag is `bgcolor`. `bgcolor` specifies a background color for all the cells in the column or, like `textcolor`, an expression that returns a color based on its evaluation. For color choices, see the `textcolor` attribute.

If you look at the fourth `cfgridcolumn` tag, the one for the Department column, you'll notice three new attributes, `values`, `valuesdisplay`, and `valuesdelimiter`. These attributes place a drop-down box for each cell in the column provided the grid is an editable grid (which ours is). The `values` attribute accepts a delimited list of values, a range of numeric values, or `Off`. It determines the actual value to pass when the form containing the grid is submitted. For a delimited list of values, the default delimiter is the comma. To specify a range of numeric values, use the format *`n-m`* where *`n`* is the minimum value in the range, and *`m`* is the maximum value. The default is `Off`. In our example, we use the results of the `GetDepartments` query to generate a list of unique department names. The `ValueList( )` function converts the values in the query to a comma-delimited list of values. The `valuesdisplay` attribute allows you to provide a delimited list or range of values to display in lieu of the values specified in `values`. This works like the HTML `select` control in that it allows you to display one set of values in the drop-down box while associating them with different values behind the scenes. The `valuesdisplay` attribute may also be set to `Off`. If you want to use a delimiter other than the default comma with the `values` and `valuesdisplay` lists, you can specify it using the `valuesdelimiter` attribute.

The final new feature of the `cfgridcolumn` tag is demonstrated in the tag that displays the new `Exempt` field we created. Setting the `type` attribute to `Boolean` causes the grid to display a checkbox representing the Boolean value in the grid column. Because the grid is editable, you can check and uncheck the box. If the grid isn't editable, the checkbox is read-only. Figure 10-8 shows the grid with all of the new features visible. Changing any values in the grid and clicking the Submit Changes button updates the database with the edited data. For more information on any of the attributes covered in this example, see Appendix A.

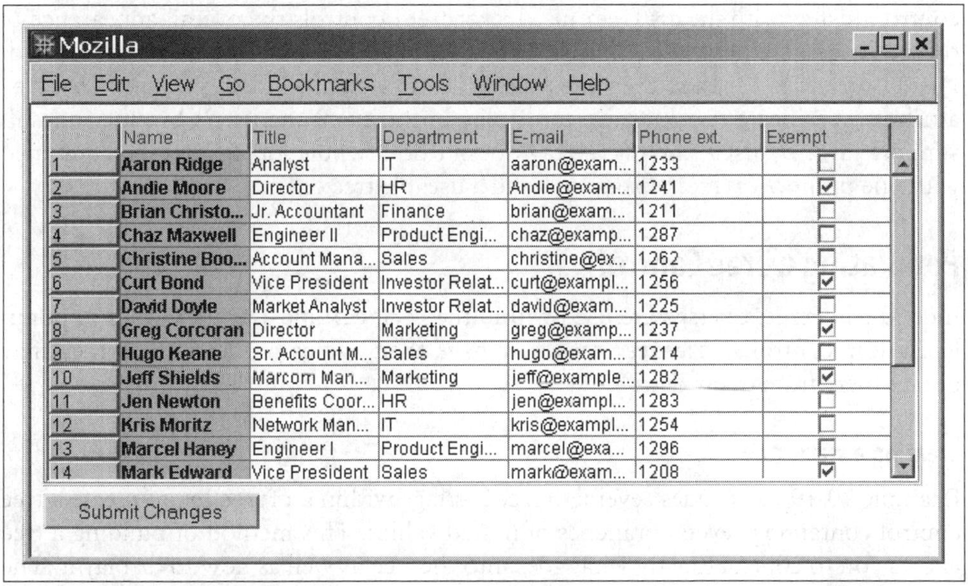

Mozilla

File Edit View Go Bookmarks Tools Window Help

	Name	Title	Department	E-mail	Phone ext.	Exempt
1	Aaron Ridge	Analyst	IT	aaron@exam...	1233	☐
2	Andie Moore	Director	HR	Andie@exam...	1241	☑
3	Brian Christo...	Jr. Accountant	Finance	brian@exam...	1211	☐
4	Chaz Maxwell	Engineer II	Product Engi...	chaz@examp...	1287	☐
5	Christine Boo...	Account Mana...	Sales	christine@ex...	1262	☐
6	Curt Bond	Vice President	Investor Relat...	curt@exampl...	1256	☑
7	David Doyle	Market Analyst	Investor Relat...	david@exam...	1225	☐
8	Greg Corcoran	Director	Marketing	greg@examp...	1237	☑
9	Hugo Keane	Sr. Account M...	Sales	hugo@exam...	1214	☐
10	Jeff Shields	Marcom Man...	Marketing	jeff@example...	1282	☑
11	Jen Newton	Benefits Coor...	HR	jen@exampl...	1283	☐
12	Kris Moritz	Network Man...	IT	kris@exampl...	1254	☐
13	Marcel Haney	Engineer I	Product Engi...	marcel@exa...	1296	☐
14	Mark Edward	Vice President	Sales	mark@exam...	1208	☑

Submit Changes

Figure 10-8. Advanced cfgridcolumn display controls

Trees

You can use the cftree tag to create a Java-based tree control within your cfform. Tree controls are useful in a number of data display and selection scenarios. Because they allow the user to expand and collapse branches, tree controls are particularly well suited for displaying large amounts of hierarchical data in a relatively small amount of screen space. You can build tree controls using the cftree tag, plus multiple cftreeitem tags for defining the individual branches. The following example uses the cftree tag to create the display area for a tree control:

```
<cfform action="#CGI.Script_Name#" name="MyForm"
        enctype="application/x-www-form-urlencoded">
  <cftree name="MyTree" height="200" width="300" border="Yes"
          hscroll="Yes" vscroll="Yes" lookandfeel="Windows"
          notsupported="<b>Your web browser must support Java to view
                        ColdFusion Java Applets</b>">
  </cftree>
</cfform>
```

This example does nothing more than create an empty shell for the tree control. The name attribute specifies a name for the tree control. The height and width attributes specify the height and width in pixels for the tree control. border indicates whether to include a border around the tree control. The default is Yes. hscroll and vscroll each indicate whether or not to allow users to scroll horizontally and vertically, respectively, in the event the tree takes up more space than the boundaries of the control. Just as with the cfslider tag, lookandfeel controls the overall appearance of the tree control. Choices are Windows, Motif, and Metal. If no value is specified, ColdFusion first tries Windows, then uses the platform default. Finally, the notsupported attribute specifies a text message to display in the event the user's browser doesn't support Java. By itself, the cftree tag doesn't do a whole lot. It must be combined with one or more cftreeitem tags to build a useable tree control.

Populating a Tree Control

Individual cftreeitem tags are used within the <cftree> and </cftree> tags to populate a tree control. cftreeitem tags may have their values hardcoded, or they may obtain them from query data.

Creating a static tree

Example 10-19 hard codes several cftreeitemtags within a cftree tag to create a tree control containing several branches of nested values. This method of building a tree allows you to control exactly what goes into the tree as well as how to display it. The results can be seen in Figure 10-9.

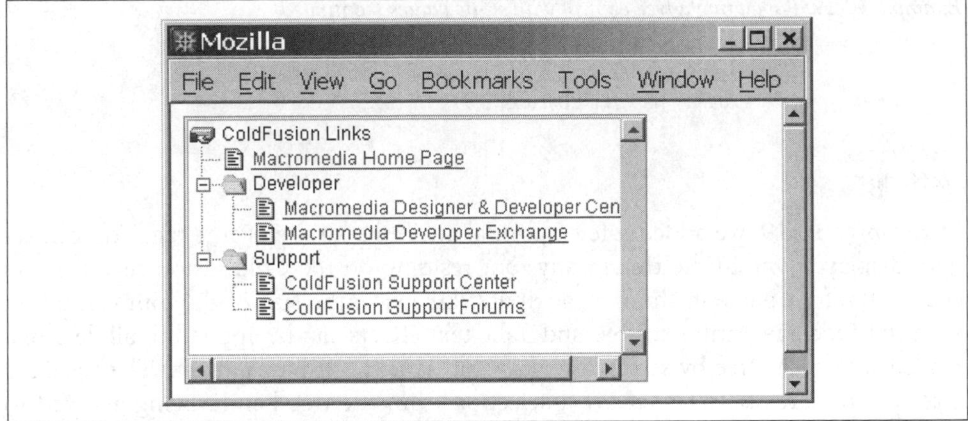

Figure 10-9. cftree control built with hardcoded cftreeitem tags

Example 10-19. Populating a tree control with static values

```
<cfform action="#CGI.Script_Name#" name="MyForm"
        enctype="application/x-www-form-urlencoded">
  <cftree name="MyTree" height="200" width="300" font="Arial" fontsize="12"
          bold="No" italic="No" border="Yes" hscroll="Yes" vscroll="Yes"
          required="Yes" message="You must select an item from the tree."
          highlighthref="Yes" completepath="Yes" appendkey="No"
          notsupported="<b>Your web browser must support Java to view
                        ColdFusion Java Applets</b>">

   <cftreeitem value="ColdFusion Links" parent="MyTree" expand="Yes"
               img="Fixed">

    <cftreeitem value="Macromedia Home Page" parent="ColdFusion Links"
                href="http://www.macromedia.com" expand="No" img="Document">

    <cftreeitem value="Developer" parent="ColdFusion Links" expand="No">

     <cftreeitem value="Macromedia Designer & Developer Center"
                 parent="Developer"
                 href="http://www.macromedia.com/desdev/"
                 expand="No" img="Document">

     <cftreeitem value="Macromedia Developer Exchange" parent="Developer"
                 href="http://devex.macromedia.com/developer/gallery/"
                 expand="No" img="Document">

    <cftreeitem value="Support" parent="ColdFusion Links" expand="No">

     <cftreeitem value="ColdFusion Support Center" parent="Support"
                 href="http://www.macromedia.com/support/coldfusion/"
                 expand="No" img="Document">
```

Example 10-19. Populating a tree control with static values (continued)

```
        <cftreeitem value="ColdFusion Support Forums" parent="Support"
                    href="http://webforums.macromedia.com/coldfusion/"
                    expand="No" img="Document">

  </cftree>
</cfform>
```

In Example 10-19, we added a few optional attributes to the cftree tag. You can set data displayed within the tree to any font residing on the ColdFusion server if you specify the font name in the font attribute. Likewise, the size of the font can be set with the fontsize attribute. Bold and italic text effects can be applied to all data displayed within the tree by setting the bold and italic attributes to Yes. The required attribute requires a user to make a selection from the tree before being allowed to submit the form to the ColdFusion server. message specifies the text message to display if the form is submitted without making a selection from the tree. The highlighthref attribute indicates whether to highlight URLs specified in the href attribute of associated cftreeitem tags. Setting the completepath attribute to Yes tells ColdFusion to pass the root level of the Path form variable (form.TreeName.Path) when the cfform containing the cftree is submitted. Although we specify Yes in this example, the attribute isn't used as we don't include a button to submit the form containing the tree control. The final attribute in the cftree tag, appendkey, indicates whether to append the cftreeitemkey variable to the end of the value of a selected cftreeitem.

You can build the tree itself by nesting a series of cftreeitem tags. The cftreeitem tag accepts several attributes for defining its position within the tree. The value attribute specifies a value to be associated with the tree item. The parent attribute allows you to specify the name of another tree item to use as the parent for the current tree item. The value you specify for parent should match the value attribute of the tree item you wish to use as the parent. The href attribute allows you to specify a hyperlink (URL or mailto) to associate with the tree item. You can indicate whether to expand a particular tree branch via the expand attribute. If expand is omitted, it is automatically set to Yes. Another optional attribute, img, allows you to specify an image to display alongside the tree item. You may specify a path to your own image or use one of the images supplied with ColdFusion by referencing the image name. Valid options for img are CD, Computer, Document, Element, Folder, Floppy, Fixed, and Remote. The default image is Folder.

Dynamically populating a tree control with query data

The cftree control can also be populated dynamically from a database query. The big advantage to populating a tree from a query instead of hardcoding it is in the amount of code you use. Using a query to populate the tree requires a minimum amount of CFML to get the job done. Example 10-20 shows how to populate a cftree control using the results of a cfquery. The results can be seen in Figure 10-10.

Figure 10-10. Dynamically populating a tree with query data

Example 10-20. Populating cftree with dynamic values from a query

```
<cfquery name="GetEmployeeInfo" datasource="ProgrammingCF">
  SELECT Name
  FROM EmployeeDirectory
  ORDER BY Name
</cfquery>

<cfform action="#CGI.Script_Name#" name="MyForm"
        enctype="application/x-www-form-urlencoded">

  <cftree name="MyTree" height="300" width="300" border="Yes"
          hscroll="Yes" vscroll="Yes"
          notsupported="<b>Your web browser must support Java to view ColdFusion
                       Java Applets</b>">

    <cftreeitem query="GetEmployeeInfo" value="Name" queryasroot="Employees"
                img="Fixed, Folder" expand="Yes">
  </cftree>
</cfform>
```

Example 10-20 creates a tree control with the `cftree` tag and then populates the tree with a single `cftreeitem` tag. The `query` attribute allows us to specify the name of a query to use to populate the tree. In this case, we used `GetEmployeeInfo`, referring to the query we executed at the top of the template. Setting `value` to `Name` populates the tree with the name of each employee. `queryasroot` lets us specify a title to appear as the root of the tree. queryasroot accepts Yes or No as possible values—indicating whether or not to use the value specified in query as the title for the root. Besides Yes|No, queryasroot also allows you to specify an arbitrary string you want to be used as the title for the query root. Therefore, in Example 10-20, we set queryasroot to Employees as it is a little more aesthetically pleasing than using GetEmployeeInfo. The next attribute, img, lets us specify a comma-delimited list of image types to use when building our tree. Setting img equal to Fixed, Folder results in the Fixed image being used for the root level and the Folder image being used for all branches off the root. Finally, expand is set to Yes, resulting in every level of the tree (all two of them in this case) being fully expanded in the display.

There is another technique for generating a tree from a query that uses cfloop to let you specify additional sublevels within your tree. Let's say you want to take the tree we built in Example 10-21 and expand it to include each employee's title, department, hyperlinked email address, and phone extension as sub-branches below each employee within the tree. The most obvious way to do this is to pull the data used to populate the cftreeitem tags from a query. What isn't so obvious, however, is the fact that you can't use the same technique we used in Example 10-21 to build the tree. This is because the technique used in that example is only capable of producing a tree with a single parent/child relationship. The way around this is to use cfloop to loop over the query data and build the appropriate cftreeitem tags with each iteration of the loop. This technique is shown in Example 10-21.

Example 10-21. Populating a cftree using cfloop

```
<cfquery name="GetEmployeeInfo" datasource="ProgrammingCF">
  SELECT *
  FROM EmployeeDirectory
</cfquery>

<cfform action="#CGI.Script_Name#" name="MyForm"
        enctype="application/x-www-form-urlencoded">

  <cftree name="MyTree" height="300" width="300" border="Yes" hscroll="Yes"
          vscroll="Yes" highlighthref="Yes"
          notsupported="<b>Your web browser must support Java to view
                        ColdFusion Java Applets</b>">

    <cftreeitem value="Employees" expand="Yes" img="Fixed">
    <cfloop query="GetEmployeeInfo">
      <cftreeitem value="#Name#" parent="Employees" expand="No">
      <cftreeitem value="#Title#" parent="#Name#" img="document" expand="No">
      <cftreeitem value="#Department#" parent="#Name#" img="document"
                  expand="No">
      <cftreeitem value="#Email#" display="#Email#" parent="#Name#"
                  img="Document" href="mailto:#Email#" expand="No">
      <cftreeitem value="ext: #PhoneExt#" parent="#Name#" img="Document">
    </cfloop>
  </cftree>
</cfform>
```

After the query is run, the shell for the tree is built with the cftree tag. Next, we specify the root level for the tree using a static cftreeitem tag. For this example, we set the root to Employees. The next step involves using a cfloop to loop over the query results from the GetEmployeeInfo query. For each record in the query, a series of cftreeitem tags are created. The first cftreeitem tag anchors the tree item to the root of the tree. This is done by setting the parent attribute to Employees—the name of our root tree item. Each of the rest of the cftreeitem tags are populated with values from the current query row. The second to last cftreeitem uses a new attribute, href, to specify a hyperlink to display within the tree control. In order to use this feature, the highlighthref attribute of the cftree tag must be set to Yes. In our example, we want to use this tree item to display the employee's email address as a mailto link. We do this by setting href to mailto:#Email#. The output of this template can be seen in Figure 10-11.

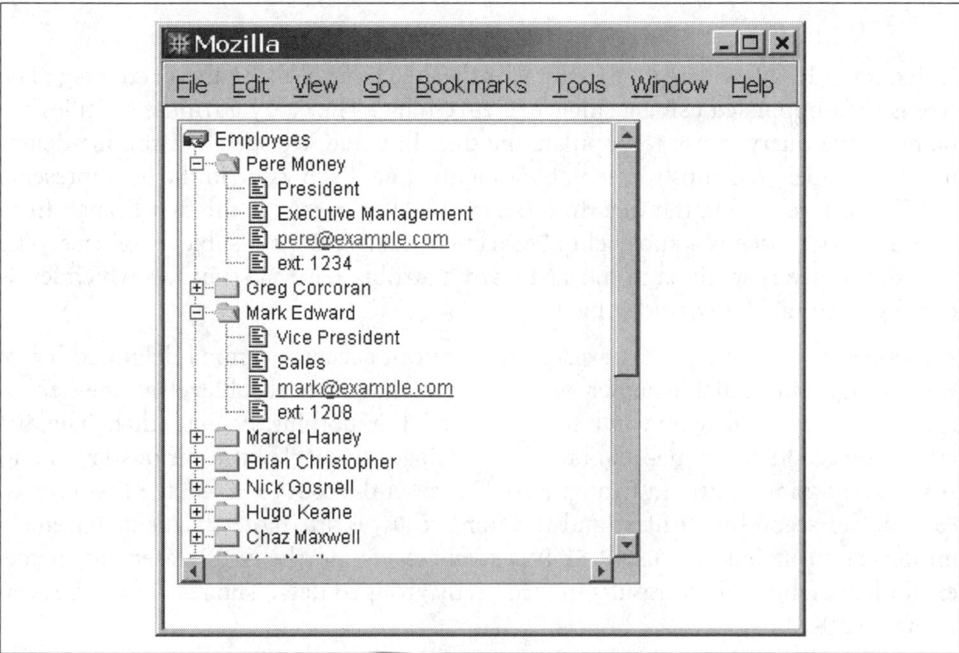

Figure 10-11. Populating a tree control from query data

Another method for populating the cftree control is to specify the tree items as a comma-delimited list of values. In this scenario, the information that populates the tree is queried from a database. A cftreeitem tag then populates the tree control. Instead of coding a cftreeitem tag for each sublevel in the tree, multiple values are specified within the value, expand, and img attributes. This technique is shown in Example 10-22.

Example 10-22. Specifying multiple tree items using a comma-delimited list

```
<cfquery name="GetEmployeeInfo" datasource="ProgrammingCF">
  SELECT Department, Name, Title
  FROM EmployeeDirectory
  ORDER BY Department
</cfquery>

<cfform action="#CGI.Script_Name#" name="MyForm"
        enctype="application/x-www-form-urlencoded">

  <cftree name="MyTree" height="300" width="300" font="Arial" bold="No"
          italic="No" border="Yes" hscroll="Yes" vscroll="Yes"
          highlighthref="Yes">
    <cftreeitem query="GetEmployeeInfo" value="Department,Name,Title"
                queryasroot="Org Chart" expand="Yes,No"
                img="Fixed,Folder,Folder,Document">
  </cftree>
</cfform>
```

In Example 10-22, we create the shell for the tree control using the `cftree` tag. The tree is then populated using a single `cftreeitem` tag. The `query` attribute specifies the name of the query to use to populate the tree. In `value`, we specify a comma-delimited list of query columns to use in building the tree. Each value in the list represents a different level within the tree. In our example, `Department` is the first branch from the main root. `Name` is a sublevel of `Department`, and `Title` is a sublevel of `Name`. The root of the tree is specified in the `queryasroot` attribute. `expand` specifies which levels of the tree should be expanded by default.

Although undocumented, the `expand` attribute can accept a comma-delimited list of `Yes/No` values indicating whether or not to expand additional sublevels in the tree. In this case, we opted to expand the root level but nothing beyond that. The `img` attribute accepts a comma-delimited list of images to display the various levels and sublevels within the tree. In Example 10-22, we set the root to `Fixed`, the first level to `Folder`, the second to `Folder`, and the third to `Document`. Note that it is extremely important to include the `ORDER BY Department` clause in the SQL statement in this example. Failing to do so results in incorrectly grouped data. The results can be seen in Figure 10-12.

Submitting a Tree Selection

Up to this point in the chapter, we have built tree controls that only display data. Because the `cftree` tag is used within the context of `cfform`, the tree control can also select and submit data. When you submit a `cfform` containing a `cftree` control, two variables are made available to the template being posted to:

`form.`*`TreeName`*`.Node`
: Returns the node selected by the user from the tree.

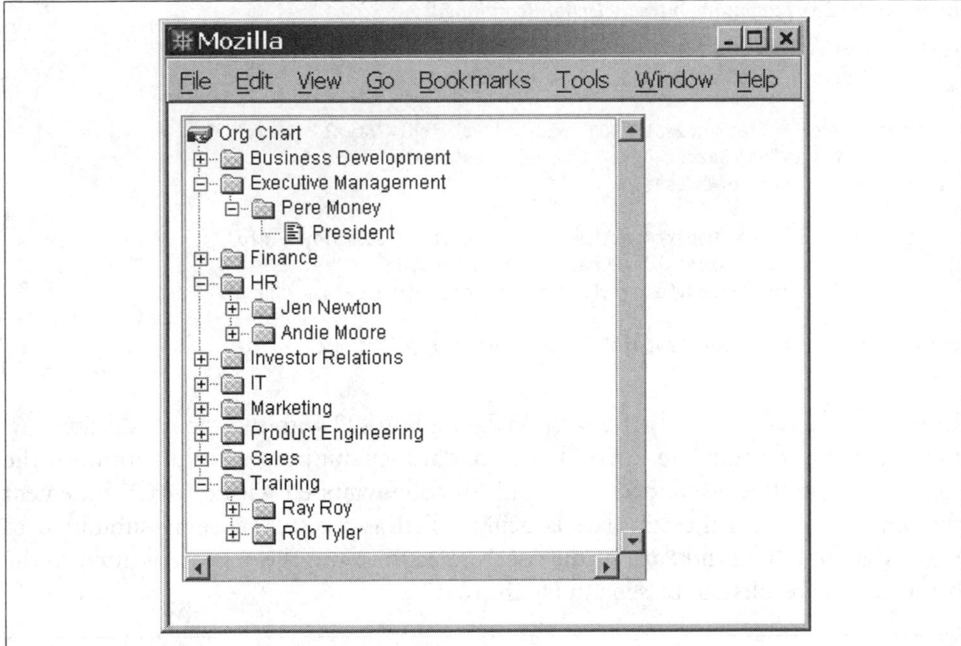

Figure 10-12. Building a multilevel tree using delimited data

form.*TreeName*.Path
: If the completepath attribute of the cftree tag is set to Yes, form.*TreeName*.Path returns the user's selection specified as root\node1\noden\value. Otherwise, form.*TreeName*.Path returns the path from the first node. The delimiter can be changed by specifying a value for the delimiter attribute.

An example demonstrating what happens when you submit a form containing a cftree is shown in Example 10-23.

Example 10-23. Submitting a tree selection

```
<cfif IsDefined('form.Submit')>
  <cfoutput>
  <h3>You chose:</h3>
  Node: #form.MyTree.Node#<br>
  Path: #form.MyTree.Path#<br>
  </cfoutput>
</cfif>

<cfquery name="GetEmployeeInfo" datasource="ProgrammingCF">
  SELECT Department, Name, Title
  FROM EmployeeDirectory
  ORDER BY Department
</cfquery>
```

Example 10-23. Submitting a tree selection (continued)

```
<cfform action="#CGI.Script_Name#" name="MyForm"
        enctype="application/x-www-form-urlencoded">

  <cftree name="MyTree" height="300" width="300" font="Arial" bold="No"
          italic="No" border="Yes" hscroll="Yes" vscroll="Yes"
          highlighthref="Yes">

    <cftreeitem value="Department,Name,Title" query="GetEmployeeInfo"
                queryasroot="Org Chart" expand="Yes,No"
                img="Fixed,Folder,Folder,Document" parent="Org Chart">
  </cftree>
<input type="submit" name="submit" value="submit">
</cfform>
```

Example 10-23 is essentially the same as Example 10-22 with two small additions. At the bottom of the template, we added a standard submit button for the form. At the top of the template, we added a short bit of code wrapped within a `cfif` statement that checks to see if the template is being called as a result of being submitted to itself. If so, the `Node` and `Path` of the user's selection from the tree are written to the browser. The results can be seen in Figure 10-13.

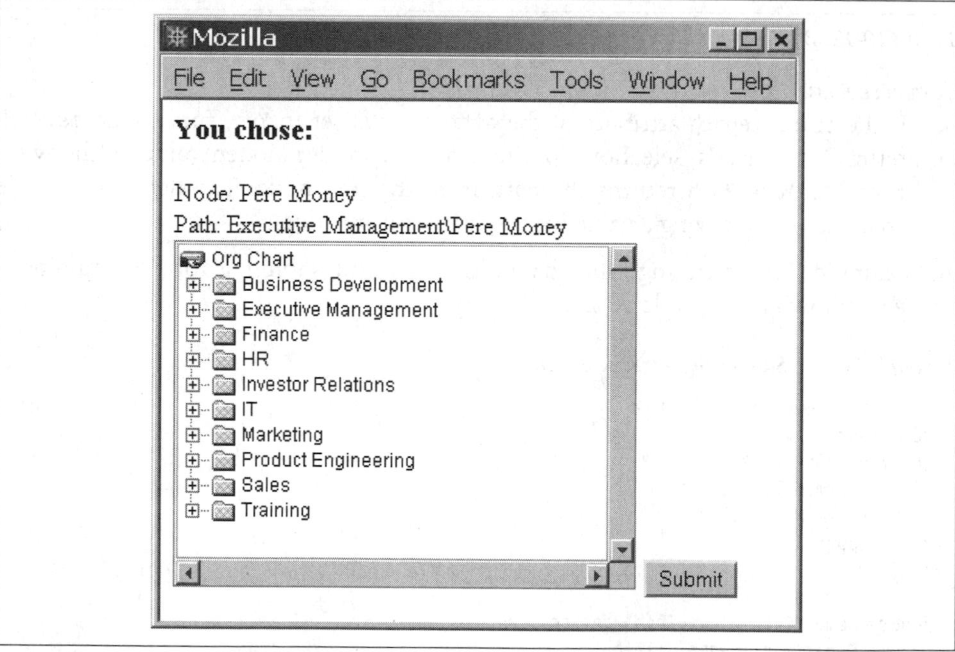

Figure 10-13. Processing the results of a cftree form submission

Creating a Tree Via Recursion

Tree controls are the perfect way to represent nested levels of data. In many cases, you might not know in advance how many sub branches the tree contains. The key to handling this in your applications is a technique known as recursion. *Recursion* is the ability to traverse all the relationships within a tree. All trees can be represented as a series of parent/child relationships. If you start at the root of the tree, each branch off of the main branch can be thought of as a child of the root. Conversely, the root is the parent to all the main branches. Now, if you look at each of the branches growing off the root, they may or may not have child branches. This pattern can potentially repeat itself for any number of sub-branches within a tree.

Modeling this pattern in a database is a straightforward process that can be accomplished with a single table. Table 10-1 shows the structure necessary to build a database table for storing all data required to build a tree of infinite sublevels.

Table 10-1. Database design for a parent/child tree

Field name	Field type	Max length
`ItemID` (primary key)	`AutoNumber`	N/A
`ParentItemID`	`Numeric`	N/A
`ItemName`	`Text`	255
`LinkURL`	`Text`	255

The model shown in Table 10-1 is generic enough that it can be used to build a tree for practically any type of data that can be grouped in multiple levels. Let's populate the database with categories and hyperlinks so that we can build a tree containing categorized hyperlinks—similar to the bookmarks concept seen in web browsers (see Table C-6 in Appendix C).

Each record in the database has a unique number assigned to it in the `ItemID` field, which ensures that no two items are identical. The parent-child relationship is established using the `ParentItemID` field. You can create a top-level tree branch by setting `ParentItemID` to `0`. You can then create child branches off these top-level branches by setting their `ParentItemID` values to an appropriate `ItemID`. This process is repeated for *n* number of branches and sub branches within the tree.

Now that we have described the setup and expected output of the application, let's look at the actual code necessary to build it. The code consists of two templates. The first template (shown in Example 10-24) displays any selected items from the tree and creates the shell for the tree control and calls the custom tag (shown in Example 10-25) that populates it.

Example 10-24. Setting up the tree control and calling the recursion custom tag

```
<cfif IsDefined('form.Submit')>
  <cfoutput>
  <h3>You chose:</h3>
  Node: #form.Links.Node#<br>
  Path: #form.Links.Path#<br>
  </cfoutput>
</cfif>

<cfform action="#CGI.Script_Name#" name="MyForm"
        enctype="application/x-www-form-urlencoded">

  <cftree name="Links" height="350" width="300"hspace="0" vspace="6"
          hscroll="Yes" vscroll="Yes" border="Yes" required="Yes"
          appendkey="No" message="You must choose a category or item from the
                                  tree.">

    <!--- Insert the root level tree item --->
    <cftreeitem value="0" parent="0" display="Links" expand="Yes"
                img="Computer">

    <!--- Call the recursion tag to generate the rest of the tree --->
    <cf_recurse>

  </cftree>
<br>
<input type="submit" name="submit" value="submit">
</cfform>
```

Example 10-24 begins with a `cfif` statement that checks to see if the form is submitting data to itself. If so, the user's tree selection is written to the browser. Next, a tree control is created with the `cftree` tag. The root level of the tree is then created using a static `cftreeitem` tag. The value of the node is set to `0`. The actual value displayed is configured by setting `value` to `Links`. Once the root level has been established, a call to the `cf_recurse` custom tag is made. We'll cover the specifics of building custom tags later in Chapter 21. For now, all you need to know is that the custom tag is responsible for the recursion algorithms necessary to build the rest of the tree.

The custom tag should be named *recurse.cfm* and saved in the same directory as Example 10-24 or in the Custom Tags directory (usually *\mx_root\CustomTags*). The code for the `cf_recurse` tag is shown in Example 10-25.

Example 10-25. Recursion custom tag for creating individual tree items

```
<!--- Check to see if a ParentItemID was passed in.  If so, this is a recursive
      call to this tag, so we set the ParentItemID to the value passed in.  If
      ParentItemID does not exist, this is a request for a top level tree item,
      so we set the ParentItemID to 0. --->
<cfparam name="attributes.ParentItemID" default="0">

<!--- Get the info for each parent item for the current level.  Items directly
```

Example 10-25. Recursion custom tag for creating individual tree items (continued)

```
    under the root have a ParentItemID of 0.  This info is passed in with each
    iteration of this tag.  By default, the ParentItemID is set to 0. --->
<cfquery name="GetParents" datasource="ProgrammingCF">
  SELECT ItemID, ParentItemID, ItemName, LinkURL
  FROM Links WHERE ParentItemID = #attributes.ParentItemID#
  ORDER BY ItemName
</cfquery>

<!--- Loop through the GetParents query and create a tree item for each
    parent --->
<cfloop query="GetParents">
  <!--- If the parent is a category, set image to Folder.  If it is a link,
      set the image to Document --->
  <cfif LinkURL is "">
    <cfset Image="Folder">
  <cfelse>
    <cfset Image="Document">
  </cfif>

  <!--- Create the tree item --->
  <cftreeitem value="#ItemID#" parent="#attributes.ParentItemID#"
             display="#ItemName#" href="#LinkURL#" img="#Image#" expand="No">

  <!--- Find children of the current parent --->
  <cfquery name="GetChildren" datasource="ProgrammingCF">
    SELECT ItemID, ParentItemID, ItemName, LinkURL
    FROM links
    WHERE ParentItemID = #GetParents.ItemID#
  </cfquery>

  <!---  If there is a child for the parent, call the recurse tag again, but
        this time make the parentitemid equal to the itemid of the current
        child item. This is what recursion is all about. --->
  <cfif GetChildren.RecordCount gt 0 >
    <cf_recurse
       parentitemid="#GetParents.ItemID#">
  </cfif>
</cfloop>
```

Example 10-25 begins by checking to see if an attribute called `attributes.ParentItemID` was passed to the custom tag. This is done using the `cfparam` tag. If `attributes.ParentItemID` doesn't exist, we know that this is the first time the tag is being called, and `attributes.ParentItemID` is initialized and assigned a value of zero (0)—the value we assigned to the root level of the tree. The next action taken by the tag is to kick off a query that gets all items in the database associated with the level specified by the `ParentItemID` value. Items directly under the root have a `ParentItemID` of zero (0). Once this is accomplished, the query results are looped over using a `cfloop`, which allows us to work with the query data one row at a time. First the `LinkURL` field from each row of the query is checked to see if it is empty. If so, we know that the item in question isn't a hyperlink. We thus set a local variable called

Image to Folder. If LinkURL isn't empty, we know that the item is a hyperlink, and we set the Image to Document. Next, a cftreeitem tag is created for each record. The img attribute is populated with the image specified in the Image variable we set a moment ago. After the initial cftreeitem tag is created, another query is run to determine if the current item (parent) has any child items. If there are child items associated with the parent, the custom tag calls itself and passes the child item's ItemID as the parentitemid attribute and the process of setting up the parent tree item and stepping through all its child items begins again. This is what recursion is all about. The pattern continues until there are no more parent/child relationships in the database. The results of this example are shown in Figure 10-14.

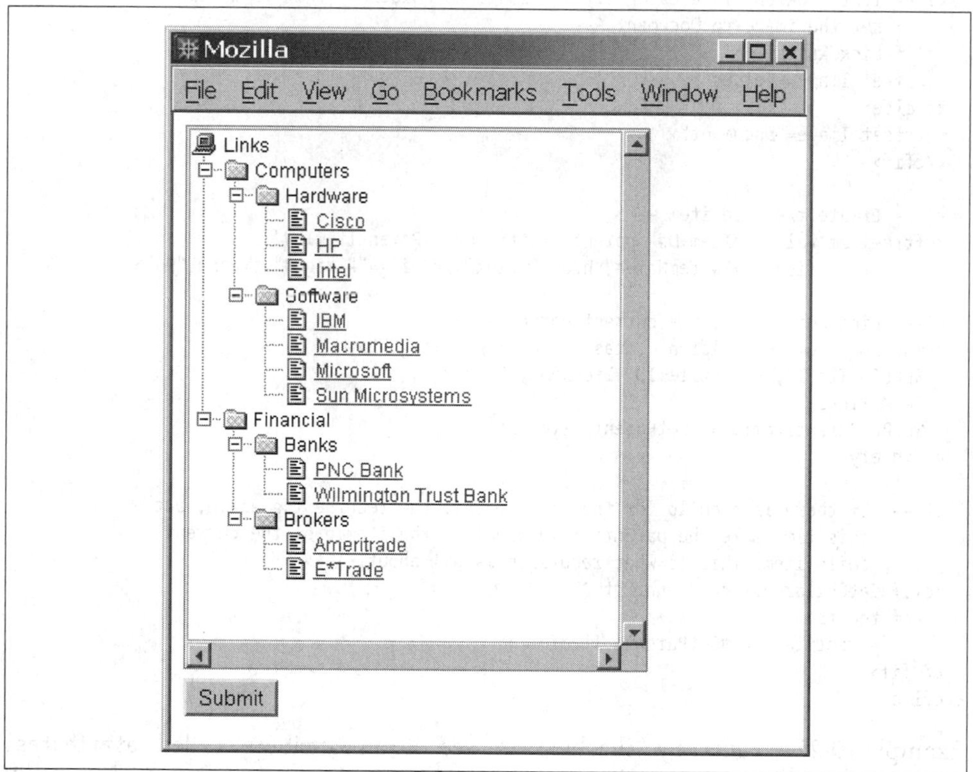

Figure 10-14. Using recursion to display hyperlinks

Preserving Input

In ColdFusion 5.0, a new attribute called preservedata was added to the cfform tag. Setting preservedata to Yes causes ColdFusion to retain and display data submitted from a cfinput, cftextinput, cfslider, or cftree control when a form is submitted to itself or to another page with like-named cfform controls. The exact effect of the preservedata attribute depends on the type of form control you use in your cfform.

For cfinput and cftextinput controls, setting preservedata to Yes allows you to display the data entered by the user after the form has been submitted without any additional coding. For cfslider controls, the slider is set automatically to the position from the previous form post. For cftree controls, the tree expands automatically to the branch containing the previously selected item. For preservedata to work with a tree control, the completepath attribute of the cftree tag must be set to Yes.

Example 10-26 shows how the preservedata attribute works with each type of form control it is compatible with. Using CGI.Script_Name for the action attribute of the cfform tag causes the form to post to itself, regardless of the filename you use to save the file.

Example 10-26. Using the preservedata attribute of cfform

```
<cfform action="#CGI.Script_Name#" name="MyForm" preservedata="Yes"
       enctype="application/x-www-form-urlencoded">
<table>
  <tr>
    <td>cfinput (text):</td>
    <td><cfinput type="text" name="teex" size="10" maxlength="10"></td>
  </tr>
  <tr>
    <td>cfinput (password):</td>
    <td><cfinput type="password" name="password" size="10" maxlength="10"></td>
  </tr>
  <tr>
    <td>cfinput (radio)</td>
    <td><cfinput type="radio" name="radio" value="Yes" checked="Yes">Yes
        <cfinput type="radio" name="radio" value="No">No</td>
  </tr>
  <tr>
    <td>cfinput (checkbox)</td>
    <td><cfinput type="checkbox" name="checkbox" value="1">One<br>
        <cfinput type="checkbox" name="checkbox" value="2">Two<br>
        <cfinput type="checkbox" name="checkbox" value="3">Three</td>
  </tr>
  <tr>
    <td>cftextinput:</td>
    <td><cftextinput name="textinput" height="25" bgcolor="##COCOCO"
                   textcolor="##000000" maxlength="255"></td>
  </tr>
  <tr>
    <td>cfslider</td>
    <td><b>1</b> <cfslider name="Slider" label="Current slider value:  %value%"
                          refreshlabel="Yes" range="1,100" value="50"
                          scale="1" align="Absmiddle" height="50"
                          width="200"><b>100</b></td>
  </tr>
  <tr>
    <td>cftree</td>
    <td><cftree name="Tree" height="150" width="250" completepath="Yes">
          <cftreeitem value="ColdFusion Links" parent="MyTree" img="Fixed"
                     expand="Yes">
```

Example 10-26. Using the preservedata attribute of cfform (continued)

```
          <cftreeitem value="Executive" parent="ColdFusion Links" expand="No">
            <cftreeitem value="Macromedia Home Page" parent="Executive"
                        img="Document">
          <cftreeitem value="Developer" parent="ColdFusion Links" expand="No">
            <cftreeitem value="Macromedia Designer & Developer Center"
                        parent="Developer"
                        img="Document">
            <cftreeitem value="Macromedia Developer Exchange"
                        parent="Developer" img="Document">
      </cftree></td>
  </tr>
  <tr>
    <td colspan="2"><input type="submit" name="submit"></td>
  </tr>
</table>
</cfform>
```

For a complete list of the attributes available in the `cfform` tag, see Appendix A.

Custom Controls

The `cfapplet` tag allows you to use custom Java controls within your ColdFusion pages as if they were native ColdFusion tags, like `cftree` and `cfgrid`. Although it isn't required that you use `cfapplet` within a `cfform` block, this is generally where the tag is used the most. For example, you might have a Java applet called Menu that acts as an expandable/collapsible menu you'd like to use in a ColdFusion application. In order to call a custom Java applet, it first has to be registered with the ColdFusion Administrator (Figure 10-15).

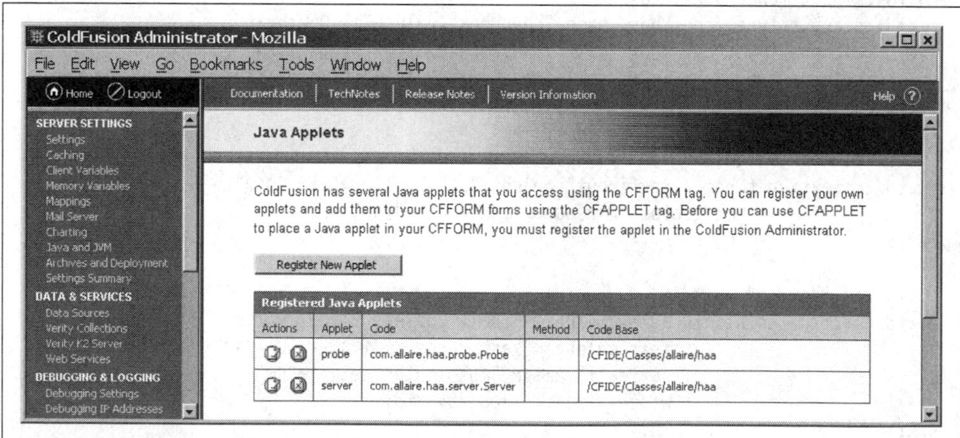

Figure 10-15. The applets section of the ColdFusion Administrator

To register a custom Java applet, you need to complete the following steps:

1. Open the ColdFusion Administrator, and click on the Java Applets link.
2. Click the Register New Applet button.
3. Enter information into the applet registration page, which is shown in Figure 10-16. When you are finished filling in the form, click the Submit Changes button to save your selection.

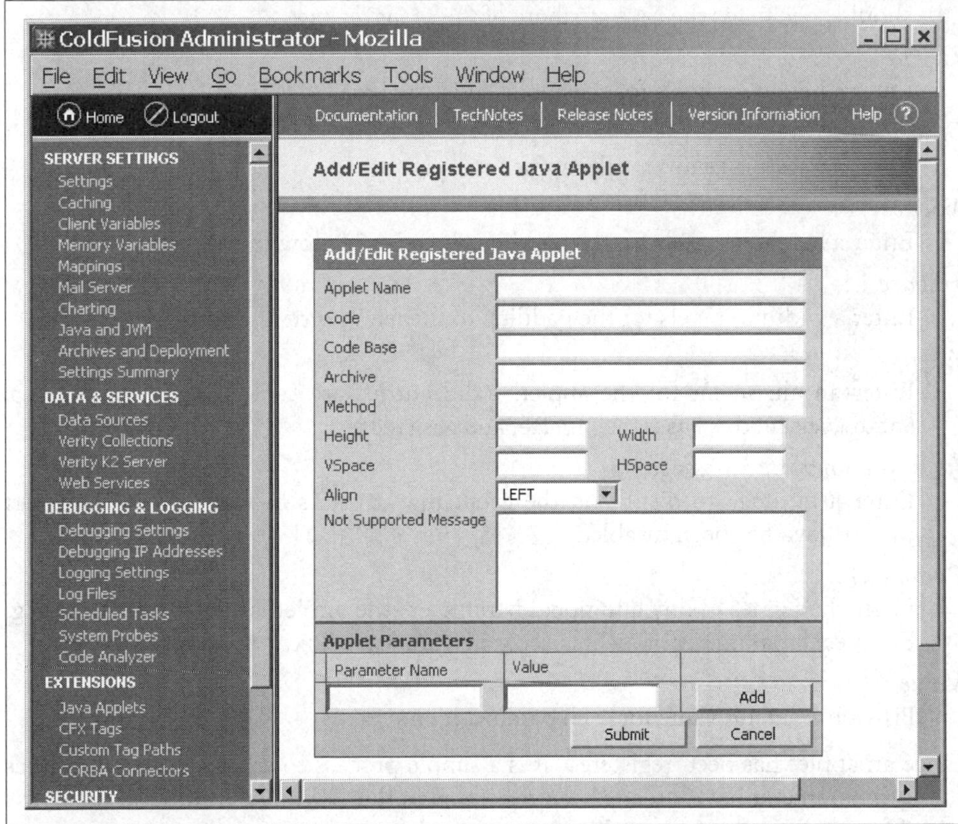

Figure 10-16. The applet registration page of the ColdFusion Administrator

The following list explains each option on the registration page:

Applet Name
: Enter a name for your Java control.

Code
: Enter the name of your Java *.class* file. You don't need to list the *.class* extension. (e.g., *myapplet*).

Codebase
: Enter the base URL to the Java applet. (e.g., *http://www.myserver.com/javaor/java*).

Archive
: Enter the location of a compressed file (*.jar*) relative to the `Codebase`. This is an optional attribute and is currently supported only by Netscape browsers.

Method
: If your Java applet provides a method that returns a string value, enter the name of that method here. The value you specify for Method is also the value you should specify for the `name` attribute of the `cfapplet` tag.

Height
: Enter a height in pixels for the applet's display area.

Width
: Enter a width in pixels for the applet's display area.

VSpace
: Enter a height in pixels for the padding above and below the applet.

HSpace
: Enter a width in pixels for the padding to the left and right of the applet.

Align
: Enter an alignment for the applet. Valid entries are `Left`, `Right`, `Top`, `TextTop`, `Bottom`, `AbsBottom`, `Baseline`, `Middle`, and `AbsMiddle`.

Java Not Supported Message
: Enter a message to display in the event that a user's browser doesn't support Java or Java has been disabled.

Parameter
: Enter the names of any additional parameters the applet is capable of accepting. Enter each parameter name in a separate `Parameter` box.

Value
: Provide a default value for each parameter entered.

Once an applet has been registered, it is a simple process to call it. As default values for each parameter have already been registered in the ColdFusion Administrator, it's possible to call the tag with nothing more than the following code line:

```
<cfapplet appletsource="Menu" name="MyFormFieldName">
```

The `cfapplet` tag has only two required attributes: `appletsource` and `name`. `appletsource` refers to the applet's registered name as entered in the ColdFusion Administrator, while `name` specifies the name to use for the form field. If a `method` was specified for the applet in the ColdFusion Administrator, it should match the value specified for `name` in the `cfapplet` tag.

Besides the two required attributes, the `cfapplet` tag also accepts a number of optional attributes. These optional attributes correspond to the information entered in the ColdFusion Administrator. Because default values have already been specified for each attribute, if you include any of the optional attributes in the `cfapplet` tag, you will overwrite the default value listed in the ColdFusion Administrator. For example, if you registered the Menu applet we previously described, you can call the applet and specify values for all the default parameters using a single cfapplet tag:

```
<cfapplet appletsource="vslider" name="MySlider"
          height="250" width="100" hspace="10" vspace="10"
          align="middle" notsupported="You need Java to see my applet!"
          fontface="Arial" fontsize="12" fontcolor="Black" bgcolor="LightGray">
```

For more information on the cfapplet tag, see Appendix A.

CHAPTER 11

Advanced Database Techniques

This chapter attempts to strengthen the concepts we have already covered while adding several advanced techniques to your bag of ColdFusion tricks. These techniques include advanced ways to display query results, query-caching strategies, and advanced SQL topics. The advanced display techniques we'll cover allow you to enhance the way you display dynamically generated data beyond simple HTML table dumps. Taking advantage of ColdFusion's query-caching abilities allows you to shave precious processing time off your frequently run queries. The advanced SQL topics cover the essentials necessary for building dynamic, highly scalable applications.

Display Techniques

This section focuses on techniques you can use to enhance the display of dynamic data. Some of these techniques include displaying limited record sets, creating dynamic HTML tables with alternating row colors, working with various multicolumn output displays, and browsing records with next/previous. You will also learn several methods for controlling whitespace in dynamic pages in order to optimize page-download times.

Flushing Page Output

A complaint often heard regarding web applications is the amount of time it takes to return data to a user once a page is requested, be it by a form submission or a URL the user clicks on. Often this is due to the large amount of data a particular operation must sift through and return to the user. In situations such as this, it is often desirable to present the user with a "Please Wait" message while their request processes or to provide incremental amounts of data as results from a large query result set become available. ColdFusion lets you handle these tasks with a new tag introduced in Version 5.0 called `cfflush`. The `cfflush` tag provides a means to send incremental amounts of data from your ColdFusion server to a user's browser as they become available.

The first time a cfflush tag is encountered on a page, it sends all the HTTP headers for the request along with any generated content up to the position in the template where the tag is encountered. Successive cfflush tags return any content generated since the previous flush. Because of this, cfflush is usually used within loops or output queries to send results back to the browser in incremental chunks. The following example shows the cfflush tag used to incrementally return the results of a database query:

```
<h1>Outputting Query Results</h1>
Please be patient as this may take a few moments...
<p>
<!--- Flush the output up to this point --->
<cfflush>

<cfquery name="GetEmployees" datasource="ProgrammingCF">
  SELECT *
  FROM EmployeeDirectory
</cfquery>

<cfset Stall=0>
<cfloop query="GetEmployees">
  <!--- Flush the rest of the output as it is generated in chunks of 100
        bytes --->
  <cfflush interval="100">
  <!--- Use this loop to exaggerate the processing time --->
  <cfloop index="i" from="1" to="3500">
    <cfset Stall = Stall+1>
  </cfloop>

  <cfoutput>
  #Name#<br>
  </cfoutput>
</cfloop>
```

If you run this example, you'll notice all of the content before the first cfflush tag is output almost immediately. After that, the next cfflush tag is used in a loop and specifies that the rest of the content generated by the page should be sent to the browser in chunks of 100 bytes. This is achieved by setting the interval attribute of cfflush to 100. The code in the example contains an index loop that essentially ties up processing time for 3,500 iterations between the output of each name returned by the query. This results in an artificially inflated amount of time required to output the query results, which is perfect to demonstrate how the cfflush tag incrementally sends data back to the browser in chunks as it becomes available. This is done because the EmployeeDirectory table doesn't contain enough records to effectively demonstrate the cfflush tag.

Once a cfflush tag has been used in a template, you can't use any other CFML tags that write to the HTTP header; doing so causes ColdFusion to throw an error because the header has already been sent to the browser. These tags include cfcontent, cfcookie, cfform, cfheader, cfhtmlhead, and cflocation. In addition, attempting to set a variable in the cookie scope with the cfset tag results in an error. This is because cookies are passed from the server to the browser in the HTTP header.

Displaying Limited Record Sets

You may decide that for a given application, it's more effective not to display the contents of an entire record set. For these applications, you can use two additional optional attributes of the cfoutput tag to display a subset of the full record set returned by a query:

startrow
: Specifies what query row to begin outputting from

maxrows
: Specifies the maximum number of rows to output

Example 11-1 uses the startrow and maxrows attributes of the cfoutput tag to output a subset of a full record set.

Example 11-1. Displaying a limited record set using cfoutput

```
<cfquery name="GetEmployeeInfo" datasource="ProgrammingCF">
  SELECT Name, Title, Department, Email, PhoneExt
  FROM EmployeeDirectory
</cfquery>

<html>
<head>
  <title>Displaying a Limited Record Set Using cfoutput</title>
  <style type="text/css">
    th {
      background-color : #888888;
      font-weight : bold;
      text-align : center;
    }
    td {
      background-color : #C0C0C0;
    }
  </style>
</head>

<body>
<!--- Display the total number of records returned by the query --->
<h2>Displaying a Limited Record Set</h2>
<cfoutput>
<h3>#GetEmployeeInfo.RecordCount# total records - Displaying records 6-10</h3>
</cfoutput>

<!--- Output rows 6-10 of the query result set --->
<table cellpadding="3" cellspacing="1">
  <tr>
```

Example 11-1. Displaying a limited record set using cfoutput (continued)

```
    <th>Record Number</th>
    <th>Name</th>
    <th>Title</th>
    <th>Department</th>
    <th>E-mail</th>
    <th>Phone Extension</th>
  </tr>
  <cfoutput query="GetEmployeeInfo" startrow="6" maxrows="5">
  <tr>
    <td>#CurrentRow#</td>
    <td>#Name#</td>
    <td>#Title#</td>
    <td>#Department#</td>
    <td><a href="Mailto:#Email#">#Email#</a></td>
    <td>#PhoneExt#</td>
  </tr>
  </cfoutput>
</table>
</body>
</html>
```

In Example 11-1, a query is performed against the `EmployeeDirectory` table. Setting the `startrow` attribute to `6` and the `maxrows` attribute to `5` results in records 6 to 10 of the query result set getting output to the browser.

Alternating Row Color in HTML Tables

Another popular way to display tabular data is to alternate the background color of the rows being displayed. The technique is easy to implement and offers an attractive way to display tabular data so that it stands out. Example 11-2 generates an HTML table of alternating row color from a database query. The results can be seen in Figure 11-1.

Alternating Row Color in HTML Tables with CSS - Mozilla

File Edit View Go Bookmarks Tools Window Help

Name	Title	Department	E-mail	Phone Extension
Pere Money	President	Executive Management	pere@example.com	1234
Greg Corcoran	Director	Marketing	greg@example.com	1237
Mark Edward	Vice President	Sales	mark@example.com	1208
Marcel Haney	Engineer I	Product Engineering	marcel@example.com	1296
Brian Christopher	Jr. Accountant	Finance	brian@example.com	1211
Nick Gosnell	Risk Management Analyst	Finance	nick@example.com	1223
Hugo Keane	Sr. Account Manager	Sales	hugo@example.com	1214

Figure 11-1. A dynamically generated table with alternating row colors

Example 11-2. Alternating row color in HTML tables with CSS

```
<cfquery name="GetEmployeeInfo" datasource="ProgrammingCF">
  SELECT Name, Title, Department, Email, PhoneExt
  FROM EmployeeDirectory
</cfquery>

<html>
<head>
  <title>Alternating Row Color in HTML Tables with CSS</title>
  <style type="text/css">
    th {
      background-color : #888888;
      font-weight : bold;
      text-align : center;
    }
    tr.Odd {
      background-color : #E6E6E6;
    }
    tr.Even {
      background-color : #C0C0C0;
    }
  </style>
</head>

<body>
<table cellpadding="3" cellspacing="1">
  <tr>
     <th>Name</th>
     <th>Title</th>
     <th>Department</th>
     <th>E-mail</th>
     <th>Phone Extension</th>
  </tr>

  <cfoutput query="GetEmployeeInfo">
  <tr class="#IIF(GetEmployeeInfo.CurrentRow mod 2, DE('Odd'), DE('Even'))#">
     <td>#Name#</td>
     <td>#Title#</td>
     <td>#Department#</td>
     <td><a href="Mailto:#Email#">#Email#</a></td>
     <td>#PhoneExt#</td>
  </tr>
  </cfoutput>
</table>
</body>
</html>
```

We alternate the row color by using the `IIF()` and `DE()` functions along with the `mod` operator to determine whether the row number for the current record is odd or even. Depending on the outcome of the evaluation, one color or the other is used as the background color for the current row. Using Cascading Style Sheets (CSS) makes changing the colors easy.

Multicolumn Output

Another popular formatting technique involves outputting a query result set in more than one column, similar to how a newspaper story is printed. There are several techniques you can use to achieve multicolumn output. Two of the more popular methods are covered in the following sections.

Sorting multicolumn output from left to right

One technique for outputting a result set in more than one column involves sorting the results from left to right, then top to bottom. You can see the technique for sorting multicolumn output from left to right in Example 11-3.

Example 11-3. Sorting multicolumn output from left to right

```
<!--- Retrieve a list of employee names from the employeedirectory table --->
<cfquery name="GetEmployeeInfo" datasource="ProgrammingCF">
  SELECT Name
  FROM EmployeeDirectory
  ORDER BY Name
</cfquery>

<!--- Initialize the StartNewRow variable as true --->
<cfset StartNewRow = true>

<h2>Two column output sorted left to right</h2>

<!--- The cfprocessingdirective tag suppresses extra whitespace as much as possible.
      To remove the max amount of whitespace, remove these comments as
      well. --->
<table border="1">
<cfprocessingdirective suppresswhitespace="Yes">
<cfoutput query="GetEmployeeInfo">
<!--- Add a tr if we are supposed to start a new row.  Otherwise, continue
      adding tds --->
<cfif StartNewRow ><tr></cfif>
  <td>#Name#</td>
<!--- Set StartNewRow to the opposite of its currnet true/false value --->
<cfset StartNewRow = not(StartNewRow)>
<!--- If StartNewRow is true, add a /tr to close the row --->
<cfif StartNewRow>
  </tr>
</cfif>
</cfoutput>
</cfprocessingdirective>
</table>
```

After the query is performed, a variable called `StartNewRow` is initialized and set to `true`. `cfprocessingdirective` helps limit the amount of whitespace created by ColdFusion during the generation of the table. Using this tag helps reduce the overall size of the file generated by ColdFusion and sent to the browser. The `cfoutput` tag loops over the result set specified in the query attribute. If the value of StartNewRow is still true, a <tr> tag is dynamically inserted, beginning a new row in the table. Next, we output an employee name in a table cell using <td>#Name#</td>. The value of StartNewRow is then set to the opposite of its current value (either false or true). A cfif statement determines the value of StartNewRow. If StartNewRow evaluates true, a </tr> tag is dynamically inserted into the table, ending the current row. If StartNewRow is false, another <td>#Name#</td> is inserted into the table, adding another employee name to the current row. This process continues until there are no more rows of data in the result set for the cfoutput tag to loop over. The two-column output generated by this example is shown in Figure 11-2. The table border is intentionally set to one so you can see that each name is contained within its own table cell.

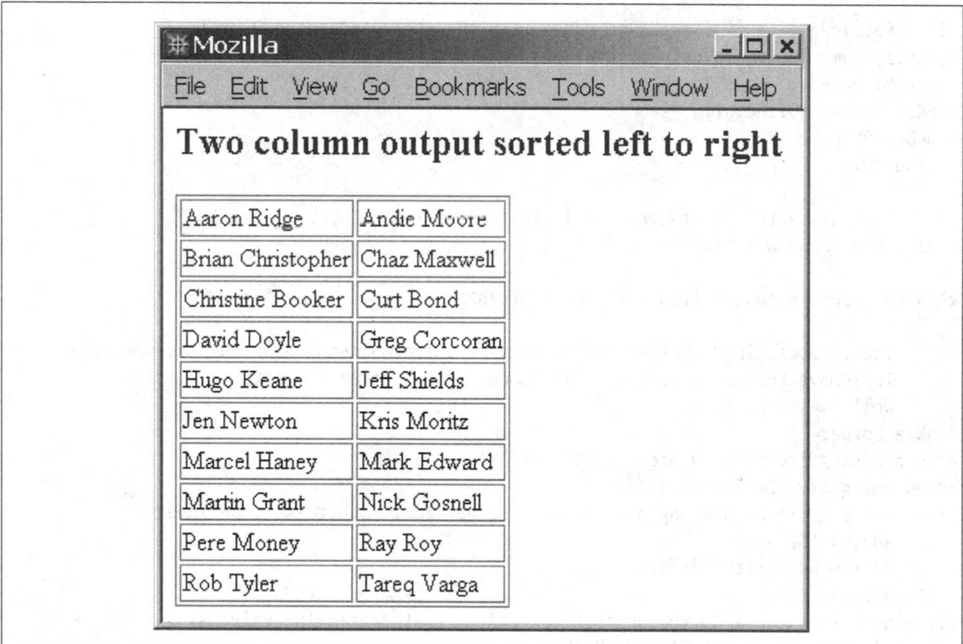

Figure 11-2. Multicolumn result set display sorted left to right

Sorting multicolumn output from top to bottom

It is also possible to sort multicolumn output from top to bottom, then left to right, as opposed to the sequence in the previous section. In this example, we also specify the number of columns to display on the page. Example 11-4 shows how to sort multicolumn output from top to bottom.

Example 11-4. Sorting multicolumn output from top to bottom

```
<!--- Thanks to Sean Clairmont for helping to refine the original code --->
<!--- Query the employeedirectory table for a list of employee names --->
```

Example 11-4. Sorting multicolumn output from top to bottom (continued)

```
<cfquery name="GetEmployeeInfo" datasource="ProgrammingCF">
  SELECT Name,Email
  FROM EmployeeDirectory
  ORDER BY Name
</cfquery>

<!--- Columns sets the total number of output columns. --->
<cfset Columns = 3>
<cfset CurrentColumn = 0>
<cfset RowCompleted = 0>
<!--- Set the total number of rows equal to the number of records divided by
      the number of columns. --->
<cfset Rows=Int(GetEmployeeInfo.RecordCount/Columns)>
<!--- Set a variable to hold the number of columns with extra records --->
<cfset OddColumns = GetEmployeeInfo.RecordCount mod Columns>
<!--- If there are columns with extra records, increase the number of rows by
      one --->
<cfif OddColumns neq 0>
  <cfset Rows = Rows+1>
</cfif>
<cfset Increment = Int(GetEmployeeInfo.RecordCount/Columns)+1>

<h2>Multicolumn Query Output Sorted Top to Bottom</h2>

<table border=0>
<cfprocessingdirective suppresswhitespace="Yes">
<!--- Create a loop that iterates a number of times equal to the total number
      of output rows needed --->
<cfloop from="1" to="#Rows#" index="Row">
  <cfset LeftOverIncrement = 0>
  <tr>
  <!--- Create an inner loop for handling each column --->
  <cfloop index="Column" from="1" to="#Columns#">
    <cfif Column gt (OddColumns + 1) >
      <cfset LeftOverIncrement = LeftOverIncrement+1>
    </cfif>
    <!--- Set the current row and column --->
    <cfset CurrentRow = (Row + (Increment * CurrentColumn) - LeftOverIncrement)>
    <cfif CurrentColumn eq (Columns-1)>
      <cfset CurrentColumn = 0>
    <cfelse>
      <cfset CurrentColumn = (CurrentColumn+1)>
    </cfif>
    <!--- Output the current row --->
    <cfoutput>
    <td><cfif (Row lt Increment or OddColumns gt 0) and (CurrentRow lte
              GetEmployeeInfo.Recordcount)>#GetEmployeeInfo.name[CurrentRow]#
      <cfelse> </cfif></td>
    </cfoutput>

    <cfif Row eq Increment>
      <cfset RowCompleted = RowCompleted+1>
```

Example 11-4. Sorting multicolumn output from top to bottom (continued)

```
    </cfif>
    <cfif RowCompleted is OddColumns>
      <cfset OddColumns = 0>
    </cfif>
  </cfloop>
  </tr>
</cfloop>
</cfprocessingdirective>
</table>
```

Before the individual columns are created and populated with data, a number of variables are initialized. You specify the number of columns to display the result set using the `Columns` variable. You may display the result set using any number of columns you desire, up to the total number of records returned. If you specify a number greater than the total number of records returned by the query, ColdFusion throws an exception. In Example 11-4, we display the result set in three columns.

We set the next variable, `CurrentColumn`, to specify a starting point for our output. `RowCompleted` is created and assigned an initial value of 0. We'll get back to the purpose for this variable in a moment. `Rows` is set to the total number of rows containing a record for each column. This is calculated by taking the total number of records and dividing it by the number of columns we want to use to display the output. The next variable we initialize is `OddColumns`. If a remainder is present when we calculate `Rows`, we use `OddColumns` to store the value. The value is important in determining how many cells need to be populated with data in the last row of the table. The final variable we initialize is `Increment`. `Increment` is used in the calculation that determines the index position of the next record to be output. Its initial value is set by adding 1 to the integer value of the total number of records divided by the number of columns to be output.

Once all of the variables have been initialized, an HTML table is started. A loop generates the appropriate number of rows for the table based on the value of the `Rows` variable. A second loop iterates over each column in the current row and populates it with the appropriate value from the query. After each table cell is built, the index position in the `Rows` loop is compared to the `Increment` value. If they are the same, the value of the `RowCompleted` variable is incremented by 1. This only happens in the last row of data generated for the table. Next, the value of `RowCompleted` is compared to the value of `OddColumns`. If they are the same, we set the value of `OddColumns` to 0. When the number of records is evenly divisible by the number of desired columns, `OddColumns` is always 0. Otherwise, it is 0 only for odd cells within the last row.

Next/Previous Record Browsing

One question of great concern to most ColdFusion developers is how to implement next/previous record browsing in ColdFusion. When building web applications with

ColdFusion, you will inevitably create an application that queries a database and returns a record set with too many rows to display in a single browser window. To display thousands of rows of data in the browser at once is an unrealistic task, for a number of reasons. Sending thousands of rows of data to the browser eats up a lot of bandwidth. And no one likes to sit around waiting for a browser to download and render a 1 MB web page when the probability of the end user reading through thousands of rows of data is slim. So, what are our options? The solution is to break up the record sets returned to the browser into manageable chunks that allow the user to browse through the query results one chunk at a time. This type of interface is known as next/previous record browsing.

Implementing next/previous record browsing in ColdFusion might seem tricky at first glance. However, thanks to ColdFusion's query caching and the partial record set display capabilities we just covered, implementing a next/previous solution is a lot simpler than you might think.

The template in Example 11-5 shows how to build a next/previous record browser that can easily be modified to work with any query. The larger the query, the more benefit to this type of interface.

Example 11-5. Creating a next/previous record browser

```
<!--- StartRow is the default starting row for the output.
      DisplayRows determines how many records to display at a time --->
<cfparam name="StartRow" default="1">
<cfparam name="DisplayRows" default="4">

<!--- Query the EmployeeDirectory table. Cache the result set for 15 minutes. --->
<cfquery name="GetEmployeeInfo" datasource="ProgrammingCF"
        cachedwithin="#CreateTimeSpan(0,0,15,0)#">
  SELECT Name,  Title, Department, Email, PhoneExt
  FROM EmployeeDirectory
</cfquery>

<!--- Set a variable to hold the record number of the last
      record to output on the current page. --->
<cfset ToRow = StartRow + (DisplayRows - 1)>
<cfif ToRow gt GetEmployeeInfo.RecordCount>
    <cfset ToRow = GetEmployeeInfo.RecordCount>
</cfif>

<html>
<head>
  <title>Next/Previous Record Browsing</title>
  <style type="text/css">
    th {
      background-color : #888888;
      font-weight : bold;
      text-align : center;
    }
    td {
```

Example 11-5. Creating a next/previous record browser (continued)

```
      background-color : #C0C0C0;
    }
  </style>
</head>
<body>

<!--- Output the range of records displayed on the page as well as the total
      number of records in the result set --->
<cfoutput>
<h4>Displaying records #StartRow# - #ToRow# from the
#GetEmployeeInfo.RecordCount# total records in the database.</h4>
</cfoutput>

<!--- Create the header for the table --->
<table cellpadding="3" cellspacing="1">
  <tr>
    <th>Name</th>
    <th>Title</th>
    <th>Department</th>
    <th>E-mail</th>
    <th>Phone Extension</th>
  </tr>
  <!--- Dynamically create the rest of the table and output the number of
        records specified in the DisplayRows variable --->
  <cfoutput query="GetEmployeeInfo" startrow="#StartRow#"
            maxrows="#DisplayRows#">
  <tr>
    <td>#Name#</td>
    <td>#Title#</td>
    <td>#Department#</td>
    <td><a href="Mailto:#Email#">#Email#</a></td>
    <td>#PhoneExt#</td>
  </tr>
  </cfoutput>
</table>

<!--- Update the values for the next and previous rows to be returned --->
<cfset Next = StartRow + DisplayRows>
<cfset Previous = StartRow - DisplayRows>

<!--- Create a previous records link if the records being displayed aren't the
      first set --->
<cfoutput>
<cfif Previous GTE 1>
   <a href="#CGI.Script_Name#?StartRow=#Previous#"><b>Previous #DisplayRows#
      Records</b></a>
<cfelse>
Previous Records
</cfif>

<b>|</b>
```

Example 11-5. Creating a next/previous record browser (continued)

```
<!--- Create a next records link if there are more records in the record set
      that haven't yet been displayed. --->
<cfif Next lte GetEmployeeInfo.RecordCount>
    <a href="#CGI.Script_Name#?StartRow=#Next#"><b>Next
    <cfif (GetEmployeeInfo.RecordCount - Next) lt DisplayRows>
      #Evaluate((GetEmployeeInfo.RecordCount - Next)+1)#
    <cfelse>
      #DisplayRows#
    </cfif>  Records</b></a>
<cfelse>
Next Records
</cfif>
</cfoutput>
</body>
</html>
```

The first thing Example 11-5 does is initialize two variables. `StartRow` specifies the starting row for the record set being displayed. The default value is set to `1`. `DisplayRows` specifies the number of rows of data to display per page. We set `DisplayRows` to `4`. Next, a query is run to retrieve all the records from the `EmployeeDirectory` table. The query is then cached for 15 minutes using the `cachedwithin` attribute of the `cfquery` tag. If you feel your users will use the record browser for more or less than 15 minutes on average, feel free to change this value.

Note that every cached query in ColdFusion takes up some of the server's memory. Depending on the amount of RAM on your server and the number of cached queries you allow (configurable in the ColdFusion Administrator), you may run into memory issues when dealing with cached queries. If you plan to use cached queries extensively, you should add additional RAM to your server so it can handle the anticipated load.

Next we set a variable called `ToRow` to hold the record number of the last record to be output on the current page. If `ToRow` is greater than the total number of records in the result set, it is set equal to the total number of records.

The next part of the template uses the `cfoutput` tag to output the first chunk of records to the browser. The `startrow` and `maxrows` attributes determine the starting row and number of rows to output, respectively. These values are dynamically populated by the `StartRow` and `DisplayRows` variables we set in the beginning of the template. The results are shown in Figure 11-3. If you turn on debugging in the ColdFusion Administrator, you should be able to see that the query is being cached.

The final section of Example 11-5 calculates the starting and previous row number for the next or previous batch of records to output. Depending on how many records have already been displayed, appropriate `Next` and `Previous` links are created for the user to click on to retrieve the next or previous set of records.* Clicking on one of the

* This example can easily be modified to use HTML form buttons. If you prefer to use buttons instead of links, simply pass the `StartRow` value as a hidden form field and have the form post to itself.

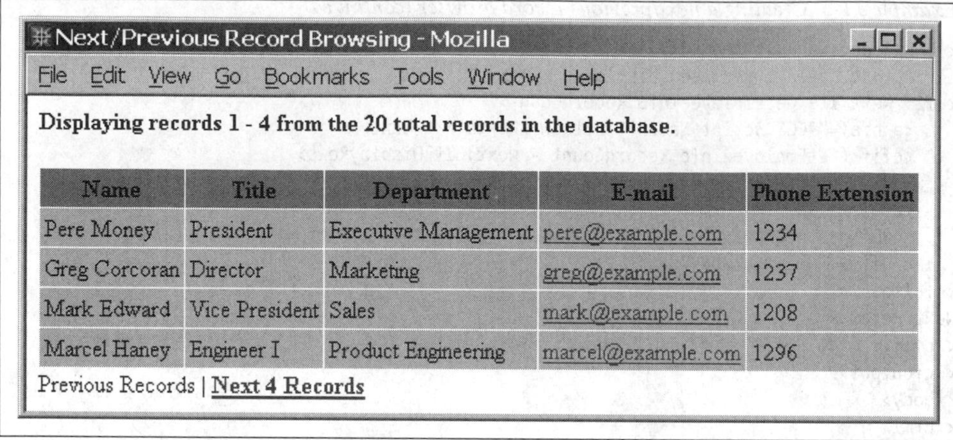

Figure 11-3. Implementing a next/previous record browser

`Next` or `Previous` links causes the template to call itself (the template self-references by linking to the CGI variable `CGI.Script_Name`) and pass the starting row number for the next/previous chunk of records as a URL variable. When the template calls itself, instead of performing a fresh query and potentially wasting a lot of time waiting for the database to generate and return a record set, the template uses the cached query and returns the next set of records almost instantaneously! If it weren't for the cached query, you would have to query the database for the full record set every time you clicked on a `Next` or `Previous` link. It doesn't take much to imagine the enormous amount of wasted overhead just to display a few records at a time.

Controlling Whitespace

If you have ever looked at the HTML generated by a ColdFusion template (by viewing the source within your web browser), you may have noticed a lot of extraneous whitespace. Though whitespace in the HTML won't affect the display of your page, it can affect the overall file size of the page that is sent to the browser. File size can have a considerable impact on the time it takes for a page generated by ColdFusion to download.

When a CFML template is requested by a web browser, the web server that fulfills the request first passes the CFML template to the ColdFusion Application Server. Before the ColdFusion Application Server can process the instructions in the CFML template, the language processor within the application server must parse the CFML template and compile it to Java byte-code that can be executed by the application server. It is during the conversion of CFML and HTML code into byte-code that the extraneous whitespace is generated. The specifics of how this all happens aren't important for our purposes. What is important is realizing that there are several techniques you can use to suppress whitespace in the pages generated by your ColdFusion application.

Optimizing output

The cfsetting tag is a sort of "catch-all" tag when it comes to optimizing output. There are three different functions currently handled by the tag: controlling whitespace, enabling/disabling the display of debug information, and overriding ColdFusion's default page timeout value. To accomplish these tasks, the cfsetting tag has three attributes:*

```
<cfsetting enablecfoutputonly="Yes|No"
           showdebugoutput="Yes|No"
           requesttimeout="seconds">
```

The first attribute, enablecfoutputonly, suppresses all HTML output, including whitespace, within a cfsetting block. When enablecfoutputonly is set to Yes, only HTML code generated within a cfoutput block is output to the browser:

```
<cfsetting enablecfoutputonly="Yes">


<cfoutput>
You should be able to see this...
</cfoutput>
But not this...
<cfsetting enablecfoutputonly="No">
Of course you can see this!
```

When the enablecfoutputonly attribute is used, cfsetting tags must occur in matched pairs, where the first tag turns on the output suppression (Yes) and the second tag turns it off (No). cfsetting tags may be nested any number of levels as long as there are always matching tag pairs.

The second attribute you can use with the cfsetting tag is showdebugoutput. This optional attribute takes a Yes/No value that indicates whether to suppress debugging information normally output to ColdFusion templates when debugging is turned on in the ColdFusion Administrator. The default value for showdebugoutput is Yes. You don't need to use paired cfsetting tags with the showdebugoutput attribute unless you are using it in combination with an enablecfoutputonly attribute.

The third attribute, requesttimeout, is new in ColdFusion MX and specifies the number of seconds ColdFusion should wait for the page to process before marking the thread as unresponsive and timing out the request. This attribute is designed to replace the technique used in previous versions of ColdFusion whereby RequestTimeout=*x* was passed as part of the query string to a ColdFusion template in order to specify how long the page should run before timing out. If the requesttimeout attribute is used, it overrides the value set in the ColdFusion Administrator. If you

* In versions of ColdFusion prior to MX, the requesttimeout attribute did not exist. Additionally, there was another attribute that is no longer available in MX, CATCHEXCEPTIONSBYPATTERN. This attribute took a Yes|No value indicating whether to override structured exception handling.

have older code that uses the URL parameter RequestTimeOut, you can avoid having to recode all of your templates by placing the following code at the beginning of your *Application.cfm* template:

```
<cfif IsDefined('URL.RequestTimeOut')>
    <cfsetting requesttimeout = "#URL.RequestTimeout#">
</cfif>
```

This code checks to see if a URL.RequestTimeOut exists, and if it does, its value is assigned to the requesttimeout attribute of the cfsetting tag. If you don't have an *Application.cfm* template, you can create one and save it in your application's root directory. For more information on *Application.cfm* files, see Chapter 7.

Suppressing output

The cfsilent tag suppresses all output produced between cfsilent tag pairs. cfsilent can suppress generated whitespace in *Application.cfm* templates as well as in instances where your template does a lot of looping but doesn't produce any output. cfsilent is similar to the cfsetting tag except that it doesn't allow any content to be generated. The following code shows how the tag can be used with a typical loop to suppress whitespace:

```
<cfsilent>
<cfloop index="i" from="1" to="1000">
  <cfset i = i+1>
</cfloop>
</cfsilent>

<cfoutput>
#i#
</cfoutput>
```

If you execute this template and view the source in your web browser, notice that the number 1001 appears at the top of the page. If you remove the cfsilent tags, rerun the template, and view the source again, notice that an awful lot of whitespace appears at the top of the page, resulting in the need to scroll considerably to reach the number 1001 in the source code.

Although it may appear to make more sense to use the cfsetting tag instead of cfsilent, the cfsilent tag is better at eliminating whitespace than cfsetting and should be used when output generation isn't a factor.

Suppressing whitespace

The cfprocessingdirective tag has two purposes. First, it can be used to specify a compiler processing option via the suppresswhitespace attribute to suppress all whitespace produced by ColdFusion within the cfprocessingdirective tag pairs. In ColdFusion MX, a new attribute called pageencoding was added, allowing you to specify a character encoding to use to read the page. cfprocessingdirective tags must occur in matched pairs (i.e., have an end tag) when used to suppress whitespace (this is not necessary if you are only setting the page encoding) and may also be nested. cfprocessingdirective settings don't apply to templates called via cfimport, cfobject, cfinvoke, cfinclude, or cfmodule or as custom tags. Macromedia recommends using either the suppresswhitespace attribute or the pageencoding attribute within a single cfprocessingdirective tag, but not both at the same time. The syntax for using the cfprocessingdirective tag to suppress whitespace is as follows:

```
<cfprocessingdirective suppresswhitespace="yes/no">
...CFML...
</cfprocessingdirective>
```

In this case, the suppresswhitespace attribute is required and indicates whether ColdFusion should suppress all whitespace between cfprocessingdirective tag pairs. The ColdFusion Administrator contains an option in the Settings section that allows you to enable this suppression of whitespace by default. If this option is enabled, it may be overridden by setting a cfprocessingdirective tag pair to No within a CFML template.

For more information on using cfprocessingdirective to set the character encoding for a page, see the Formatting Techniques section in Chapter 4.

Drilldown Queries

A drilldown query (sometimes referred to as master-detail) is one that starts by retrieving and displaying a relatively broad or general result set. Then, hyperlinks from one or more columns in the result set are used to call another template that performs a query based on URL parameters passed by the hyperlinks. This process is designed to narrow the number of records returned until a desired level of granularity is achieved, hence the name drilldown query.

For drilldown queries, you usually need two templates, but it is possible to use as many as you want to achieve the level of granularity you need. In a two-template drilldown application, the first template queries a data source and displays a summary (usually just a few fields) of every record in the data source meeting the user's criteria. Hyperlinks from some of the fields in these results pass the primary key values of records to the second template. The second template then performs a query using the primary key value passed in via URL in the WHERE clause of the SELECT statement. The results (usually the full record) are then output to the browser. Example 11-6 demonstrates how a two-template drilldown query works by querying the EmployeeDirectory table and generating an HTML table containing the Name, Title, and Department of each employee.

Example 11-6. Initial screen listing partial information about each record

```
<!--- Retrieve a list of all employees in the EmployeeDirectory table --->
<cfquery name="GetEmployeeList" datasource="ProgrammingCF">
  SELECT ID, Name, Title, Department
```

Example 11-6. Initial screen listing partial information about each record (continued)

```
  FROM EmployeeDirectory
</cfquery>

<html>
<head>
  <title>Drilldown Example - Master</title>
  <style type="text/css">
    th {
      background-color : #888888;
      font-weight : bold;
      text-align : center;
    }
    td {
      background-color : #C0C0C0;
    }
  </style>
</head>

<body>

<h2>Drilldown Query Example</h2>
Click on an employee's name to retrieve the full employee record as well
as a list of all incentive awards granted to the employee.
<p>
<table cellpadding="3" cellspacing="1">
  <tr>
    <th>Name</th>
    <th>Title</th>
    <th>Department</th>
  </tr>

  <!--- Dynamically build an HTML table containing the list of employees from
        the GetEmployeeList query.  Create a hyperlink for the Name field
        that points to a template called DrillDown.cfm and pass the value
        of the ID field as a query parameter, identifying the record --->
  <cfoutput query="GetEmployeeList">
  <tr>
    <td><a href="drilldown.cfm?ID=#ID#">#Name#</a></td>
    <td>#Title#</td>
    <td>#Department#</td>
  </tr>
  </cfoutput>
</table>
</body>
</html>
```

Example 11-6 queries the EmployeeDirectory table and returns a result set containing the Name, Title, and Department of every employee in the table. The result set dynamically generates an HTML table with a row for each record. Each name is displayed as a hyperlink that points to a template called *drilldown.cfm* (shown in Example 11-7). Clicking on any one of the names calls the *drilldown.cfm* template and passes the ID value (the primary key) associated with the name as a URL parameter so that the *drilldown.cfm* template knows which record to drill down on. The initial results screen is shown in Figure 11-4.

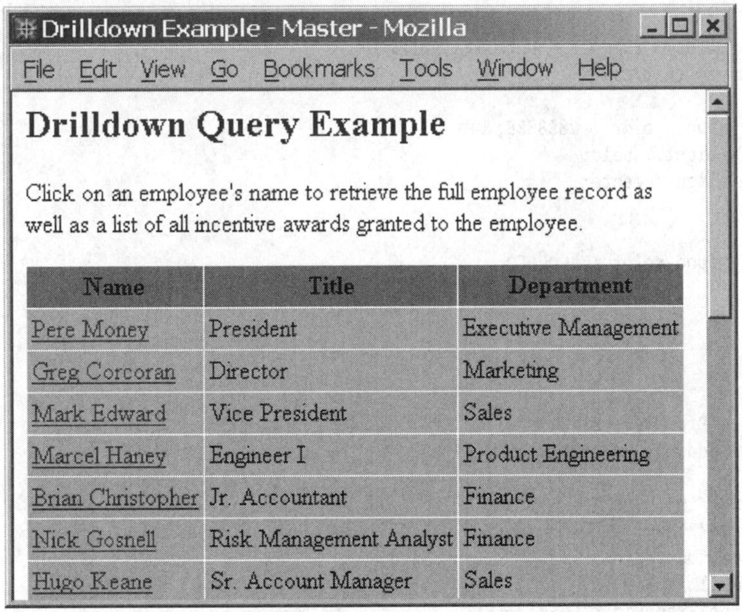

Figure 11-4. Initial results screen with hyperlink to drilldown template

When the *drilldown.cfm* template in Example 11-7 is called, the first thing it does is execute a query to retrieve all the fields in the record whose ID matches the value specified by the URL.ID parameter. These values could also be passed by form field, but for our example we'll do it this way. Just for fun, a second query is made to the IncentiveAwards table to retrieve any awards the employee has been granted.

Example 11-7. Drilldown screen for displaying detail information

```
<!--- Retrieve the full record of the employee whose ID was passed in
      as a URL parameter. --->
<cfquery name="GetEmployeeRecord" datasource="ProgrammingCF">
  SELECT Name, Title, Department, Email, PhoneExt, Salary
  FROM EmployeeDirectory
  WHERE ID = #URL.ID#
</cfquery>

<!--- Query the IncentiveAwards table and retrieve all records for
      for the ID passed in as a URL parameter.  This query can return
      0 or more records --->
<cfquery name="GetIncentiveAwards" datasource="ProgrammingCF">
  SELECT DateAwarded, Category, Amount
  FROM IncentiveAwards
```

Example 11-7. Drilldown screen for displaying detail information (continued)

```
  WHERE ID = #URL.ID#
</cfquery>

<html>
<head>
  <title>Drilldown Example - Detail</title>
  <style type="text/css">
    th {
      background-color : #888888;
      font-weight : bold;
      text-align : center;
    }
    td {
      background-color : #C0C0C0;
    }
  </style>
</head>

<body>
<h2>Employee Profile</h2>
<table cellpadding="3" cellspacing="1">
  <tr>
    <th>Name</th>
    <th>Title</th>
    <th>Department</th>
    <th>E-mail</th>
    <th>Phone Extension</th>
    <th>Salary</th>
  </tr>
  <!--- Generate an HTML table containing the employee record from the
        GetEmployeeRecord query. --->
  <cfoutput>
  <tr>
    <td>#GetEmployeeRecord.Name#</td>
    <td>#GetEmployeeRecord.Title#</td>
    <td>#GetEmployeeRecord.Department#</td>
    <td><a href="Mailto:#GetEmployeeRecord.Email#">
        #GetEmployeeRecord.Email#</a></td>
    <td>#GetEmployeeRecord.PhoneExt#</td>
    <td>#GetEmployeeRecord.Salary#</td>
  </tr>
  </cfoutput>
</table>

<h3>Incentive Awards</h3>
<!--- Only display the table if 1 or more awards are found in the database --->
<cfif GetIncentiveAwards.RecordCount gt 0>
  <table cellpadding="3" cellspacing="1">
    <tr>
      <th>Date Awarded</th>
      <th>Incentive Type</th>
      <th>Amount</th>
```

Example 11-7. Drilldown screen for displaying detail information (continued)

```
    </tr>

    <!--- Generate an HTML table listing the awards granted the employee --->
    <cfoutput query="GetIncentiveAwards">
    <tr>
      <td>#DateFormat(DateAwarded, 'mm/dd/yyyy')#</td>
      <td>#Category#</td>
      <td>#DollarFormat(Amount)#</td>
    </tr>
    </cfoutput>
  </table>
<cfelse>
  No incentive awards granted.
</cfif>
</body>
</html>
```

Next, two HTML tables are generated from the query results. The first table contains all the information about the employee stored in the `EmployeeDirectory` table. The second table lists any awards the employee has earned. If no awards are found for the employee, a message to that effect is output in lieu of the table. The results of the *drilldown.cfm* template are shown in Figure 11-5.

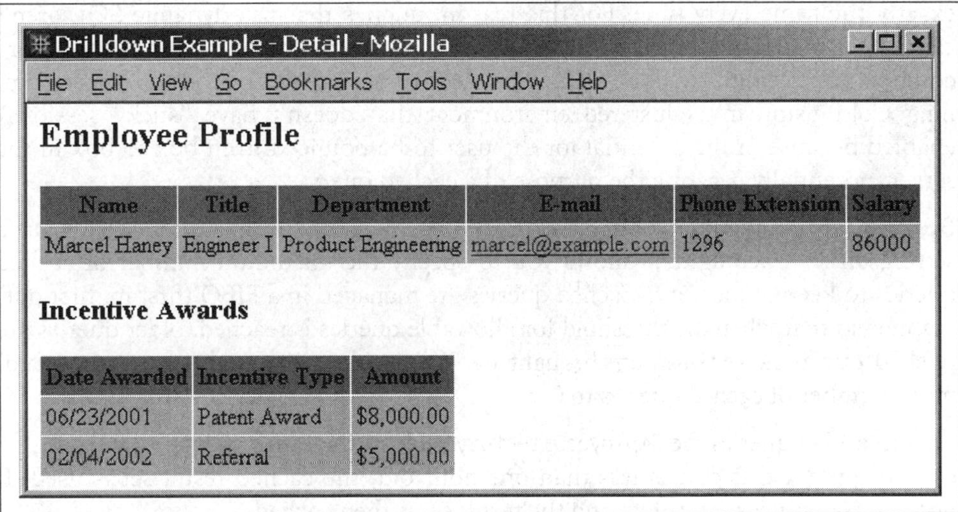

Figure 11-5. Drilldown template displaying entire employee record

Query Caching

If you want to squeeze every last bit of performance out of your ColdFusion applications (and who doesn't?), you might want to consider query caching. Query caching allows you to retrieve query result sets from memory as opposed to requiring a round trip to the database. This can significantly reduce the amount of time it takes to return a result set in your application. Query caching is implemented using the `cfquery` tag and one of two optional attributes:

`cachedafter`
: Specifies a date for using cached query data. Cached query data is used only if the date of the original query is after the date specified in `cachedafter`.

`cachedwithin`
: Specifies a time span (using the `CreateTimeSpan( )` function) for using cached query data.

Query caching is especially useful in situations where you repeatedly execute the same query to obtain a result set that remains static for a known period of time. Some examples of queries that are candidates for caching include:

- A query that retrieves a "what's new" list that is updated once a day
- A query that retrieves a company's closing stock price on a heavily trafficked intranet site that is updated once a day
- A query that retrieves a list of users to use in an administration application

Regardless of the type of query you want to cache, one guideline is absolute: the `cfquery` statement (including the SQL) that references the cached data must be exactly the same every time. For this reason, queries that use dynamic SQL aren't candidates for caching, unless you can create a cached query for every possible query combination. Additionally, you may not want to use cached queries if you are running ColdFusion in a clustered environment that doesn't have "sticky sessions" enabled because of the potential for the user to be bounced from box to box in the server, potentially negating the purpose of a cached query.

Because cached queries take up server memory, the ColdFusion Administrator has a setting under Caching that allows you to specify the maximum number of cached queries to keep in memory. Cached queries are managed in a FIFO (first in, first out) manner so that when the threshold for allowable queries is reached, older queries are pushed out as newer ones are brought in. To disable query caching, set the maximum number of cached queries to 0.

Example 11-8 queries the `EmployeeDirectory` table of the `ProgrammingCF` database. If a cached query exists that is less than one hour old, the cached result set is used. If not, a live query is performed, and the result set is then cached.

Example 11-8. Using cachedwithin to cache a query

```
<!--- Query the employeedirectory table.  If a cached result set that is less
      than 1 hour old, use it.  Otherwise, perform a new query and cache the
      result set. --->
<cfquery name="GetEmployeeInfo" datasource="ProgrammingCF"
         cachedwithin="#CreateTimeSpan(0,1,0,0)#">
  SELECT Name, Title, Department, Email, PhoneExt
```

Example 11-8. Using cachedwithin to cache a query (continued)

```
  FROM EmployeeDirectory
</cfquery>

<html>
<head>
  <title>Using cachedwithin to Cache a Query</title>
  <style type="text/css">
    th {
      background-color : #888888;
      font-weight : bold;
      text-align : center;
    }
    td {
      background-color : #C0C0C0;
    }
  </style>
</head>

<body>
<!--- Output the result set.  If you have debugging turned on, you will be able
      to see whether the query was live or cached --->
<table cellpadding="3" cellspacing="0">
  <tr>
    <th>Name</th>
    <th>Title</th>
    <th>Department</th>
    <th>E-mail</th>
    <th>Phone Extension</th>
  </tr>
  <cfoutput query="GetEmployeeInfo">
  <tr>
    <td>#Name#</td>
    <td>#Title#</td>
    <td>#Department#</td>
    <td><a href="Mailto:#Email#">#Email#</a></td>
    <td>#PhoneExt#</td>
  </tr>
  </cfoutput>
</table>
</body>
</html>
```

The cachedwithin attribute of the cfquery tag handles all the caching. Use the CreateTimeSpan( ) function to specify the amount of time the cached query should persist. In our example, we set the cached query to persist for one hour. Every time the query is called, the ColdFusion checks to see if the time associated with the cached query is more than one hour older than the time associated with the current request. If not, the cached data is used. If, however, it is older, a new query is run, the results are cached, and the timer is refreshed.

We can easily rewrite this example to use `cachedafter` instead of `cachedwithin`. Instead of providing a time span for the cached query, `cachedafter` provides a date after which all queries should be cached:

```
<cfquery name="GetEmployeeInfo" datasource="ProgrammingCF"
         cachedafter="06/15/2003">
```

Persistent queries created with `cachedafter` don't expire automatically as do those created with `cachedwithin`.

To see the difference between a normal query and a cached query, run the template in Example 11-8 (make sure debugging is turned on in the ColdFusion Administrator). The first time you run the template, you will see a processing time associated with the query of approximately 30 milliseconds. This is to be expected, as the query wasn't actually cached until after you executed it for the first time. If you hit the reload button on your browser and refresh the page, you should see something different (as shown in Figure 11-6).

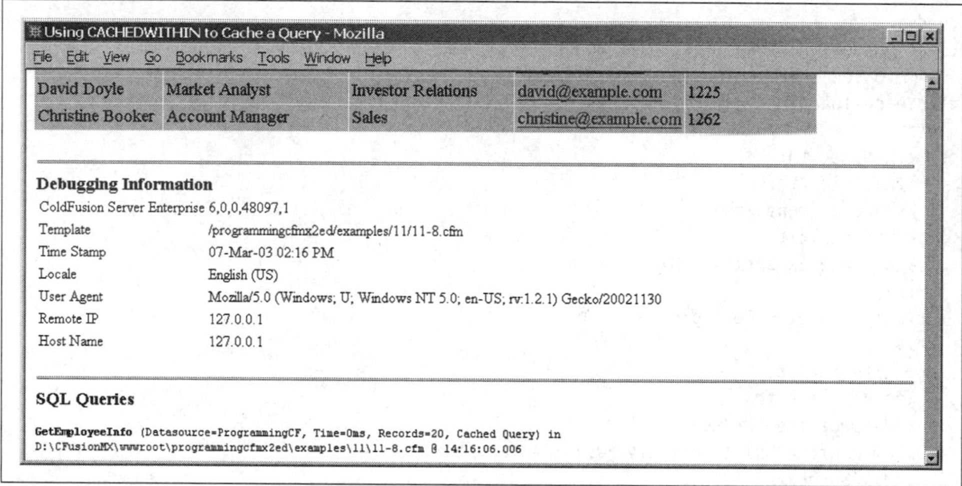

Figure 11-6. Reloading the template retrieves cached data

This time, the words "Cached Query" should appear where the processing time for the query was previously displayed. This lets you know that the query you just ran came from the cache and not from the data source.

One final thing to note: if you use the `cfqueryparam` tag to bind query parameters (discussed later in the chapter), you can't cache the query using the techniques we just discussed. You should keep this in mind as it isn't well documented in any of the ColdFusion documentation.

Advanced SQL

This section moves beyond the basic database manipulation techniques we discussed in earlier chapters. Here, we'll cover methods for creating dynamic SQL, creating and modifying database tables using SQL, using aggregate and scalar functions, performing table unions and joins, and several other database-manipulation techniques. These are the kinds of operations that allow you to interact with databases at a higher level. Most advanced applications such as shopping carts, threaded discussion lists, and business-to-business applications use one or more of the techniques described in this section.

Dynamic SQL

An extremely powerful feature of ColdFusion is the ability to generate dynamic SQL queries based on a variety of inputs. In Chapter 3, you learned how to pass a single dynamic value in an SQL statement:

```
SELECT Name, Title, Department
FROM EmployeeDirectory
WHERE ID = #ID#
```

We extend this concept a bit in Example 11-9 to allow for completely dynamic SQL in the `WHERE` clause of a SQL statement.

Example 11-9. HTML form for searching database records

```
<!--- Query the EmployeeDirectory table for a list of departments --->
<cfquery name="GetDepartments" datasource="ProgrammingCF">
  SELECT DISTINCT Department
  FROM EmployeeDirectory
  ORDER BY Department
</cfquery>

<h2>Locate a User</h2>
<form action="search.cfm" method="post">
<table>
  <tr>
    <td>Name:</td>
    <td><input type="text" name="Name" size="20" maxlength="80"></td>
  </tr>
  <tr>
    <td>Title:</td>
    <td><input type="text" name="Title" size="20" maxlength="80"></td>
  </tr>
  <tr>
    <td>Department:</td>
    <td><select name="Department" size="5" multiple>
        <cfoutput query="GetDepartments">
          <option value="#Department#">#Department#</option>
        </cfoutput>
        </select>
```

Example 11-9. HTML form for searching database records (continued)

```
  </tr>
</table>
<input type="submit" value="Submit">
</form>
```

Example 11-9 generates an HTML form for the user to specify search criteria when constructing a dynamic SQL statement to retrieve matching records from the `EmployeeDirectory` table. The form contains a field where the user can enter a name, another for title, and a multiple select list where he can choose one or more departments to narrow down the search. The list of department names in the multiple select list is obtained by performing a query using the `DISTINCT` keyword against the `Department` column in the `EmployeeDirectory` table. The `DISTINCT` keyword is covered in more detail later in this chapter. Note that the variable name in the `value` attribute of the `option` tag is enclosed in a set of single quotes. Because we'll be passing the values from the `Department` field as a delimited list of text values, it is necessary to enclose each value in the list in single quotes. If the values were numeric, this wouldn't be necessary.

Once you fill out and submit the search form, the search criteria are posted to the *search.cfm* template shown in Example 11-10.

Example 11-10. Searching database records using dynamically generated SQL

```
<!--- Set a default of "" for form.Department since the parameter isn't
      passed if no department is selected --->
<cfparam name="form.Department" default="">

<!--- Query the EmployeeDirectory table with an SQL statement dynamically
      generated by the parameters passed in as form field values. --->
<cfquery name="GetRecords" datasource="ProgrammingCF">
  SELECT Name, Title, Department, Email, PhoneExt, Salary
  FROM EmployeeDirectory
  WHERE 0=0
<!--- If a value is passed for Name, use the SQL LIKE command and the %
      wildcard to include a wildcarded search for the Name, including it
      in the SQL statement using the and operator. --->
<cfif Len(form.Name)>
   and Name LIKE '%#form.Name#%'
</cfif>

<!--- If a value is passed for Title, use the SQL LIKE command and the %
      wildcard to include a wildcarded search for the Title, including it
      in the SQL statement using the and operator. --->
<cfif Len(form.Title)>
   and Title LIKE '%#form.Title#%'
</cfif>

<!--- If the value passed for Department is "", omit the and statement
      for Department, removing Department as a criteria.  If Department
```

Example 11-10. Searching database records using dynamically generated SQL (continued)

```
     contains any values other than "", use those values to construct
     the dynamic and for Department. --->
<cfif Len(form.Department)>
   and Department IN (#ListQualify(form.Department, "'")#)
</cfif>
</cfquery>

<html>
<head>
  <title>Searching Database Records Using Dynamically Generated SQL</title>
  <style type="text/css">
    b {
      font-weight : bold;
    }
    th {
      background-color : #888888;
      font-weight : bold;
      text-align : center;
    }
    td {
      background-color : #C0C0C0;
    }
  </style>
</head>

<cfoutput>
<b>#GetRecords.RecordCount# records matched your search criteria:</b><br>
  Name like: #form.Name#<br>
  Title like: #form.Title#<br>
  Department: #form.Department#
</cfoutput>

<p>
<table cellpadding="3" cellspacing="1">
  <tr>
    <th>Name</th>
    <th>Title</th>
    <th>Department</th>
    <th>E-mail</th>
    <th>Phone Extension</th>
    <th>Salary</th>
  </tr>
  <!--- Generate an HTML table containing all of the records matching the
        search criteria --->
  <cfoutput query="GetRecords">
  <tr>
    <td>#Name#</td>
    <td>#Title#</td>
    <td>#Department#</td>
    <td><a href="Mailto:#Email#">#Email#</a></td>
    <td>#PhoneExt#</td>
    <td>#Salary#</td>
```

Example 11-10. Searching database records using dynamically generated SQL (continued)

```
  </tr>
</cfoutput>
</table>
```

Example 11-10 queries the EmployeeDirectory table with a dynamically generated SQL statement. The exact contents of the SQL statement may vary depending on the form-field values passed into the template. Note that the WHERE 0=0 clause is necessary in the cfquery tag, in order to build the dynamic WHERE statement. 0=0 is another way of saying true and provides the initial condition to which to attach any dynamically generated and statements. If no search parameters are passed, the 0=0 prevents ColdFusion from throwing an error.

cfif statements evaluate the form-field values and generate the necessary SQL. If values are passed for Name and Title, the SQL LIKE clause adds wildcarded searches to the WHERE statement. Note how the wildcard appears both before and after the values we are searching for. This allows the value to appear anywhere in the field being searched. If we wanted to match only the beginning of a field, we could remove the trailing wildcard. For example, to match only names that begin with the letter "p", the SQL would need to look like WHERE Name = 'p%'. Finally, we have to deal with the Department. Because the Department form control is a multiple selection list that passes a delimited list of string values, we have to use the ListQualify( ) function to delimit the values we passed in with single quotation marks, so they can be used in the IN statement. Once we've built up the query, it is a simple matter to output the results to the browser.

Note that in general, it is preferable not to use the SQL LIKE operator to perform wildcard searches of fields that contain large amounts of text because of the amount of database overhead associated with full-text searching. SQL (as a query language) was never meant to handle full-text searching (there are very few operators that facilitate text searches). For serious full-text indexing and searching, consider the Verity search interface included with ColdFusion and discussed in more detail in Chapter 16. Additionally, some databases such as MS SQL Server (7.0 and up) contain extensions to the database to facilitate full-text searching. Consult your database documentation for more information on how full-text searching is handled by your database.

Creating and Modifying Tables

It is possible to use SQL to handle such tasks as creating a new table, creating a new table and populating it with data from an existing table, modifying the design of a table, and deleting a table. These options are especially useful for developers working remotely without physical access to their data sources. Four SQL commands are available to facilitate these tasks: CREATE TABLE, SELECT INTO, ALTER TABLE, and DROP TABLE. The descriptions and examples given in this section are meant to provide a general overview of each function. Actual implementation and syntax varies from database to database. Consult your database documentation for specific information on how your particular database handles each function.

Creating new tables

The CREATE TABLE statement creates a new database table in the specified data source. Example 11-11 creates a new table called EmployeeDirectory2 with the same structure as the EmployeeDirectory table referred to throughout this book.

Example 11-11. Creating a new table in Microsoft Access using CREATE TABLE

```
<!--- Create the EmployeeDirectory table --->
<cfquery name="CreateTable" datasource="ProgrammingCF">
  CREATE TABLE EmployeeDirectory2 (
                ID counter,
                Name varchar(255),
                Title varchar(255),
                Department varchar(255),
                Email varchar(255),
                PhoneExt integer,
                Salary numeric,
          CONSTRAINT ID PRIMARY KEY (ID)
  )
</cfquery>

Employee Directory table created.
```

Each column you wish to add to the newly created table takes the syntax:

```
column_name data_type[(length)] [constraint]
```

Datatypes vary depending on the database you are using. Some of the more common datatypes are Bit, Byte, Char, Character, Dec, Date, DateTime, Decimal, Float, Int, Integer, Long, Memo, Numeric, Real, Short, SmallInt, Text, Time, TimeStamp, TinyInt, and Varchar. Constraints also vary from database to database. Some common constraints are CHECK, DEFAULT, FOREIGN KEY, IDENTITY, INDEX, PRIMARY KEY, [NOT] NULL, and UNIQUE.

Populating new tables with existing data

The SELECT INTO statement creates a new database table and populates it with data from an existing table. Example 11-12 demonstrates the SELECT INTO statement by selecting the name, title, email address, and phone extension for each employee in the EmployeeDirectory table who belongs to the IT department. The resulting record set is then used to populate a new table called ITDirectory.

Example 11-12. Using SELECT INTO to create a copy of a table

```
<!--- Select the name, title, email, and phone ext for each employee in
      the EmployeeDirectory table that belongs to the IT department and
```

Example 11-12. Using SELECT INTO to create a copy of a table (continued)

```
     use it to populate a new table called ITDirectory --->
<cfquery name="MakeITDirectory" datasource="ProgrammingCF">
  SELECT Name, Title, Email, PhoneExt
  INTO ITDirectory
  FROM EmployeeDirectory
  WHERE Department = 'IT'
</cfquery>

<!--- Retrieve all of the records from the ITDirectory table we just
      created --->
<cfquery name="GetEmployees" datasource="ProgrammingCF">
  SELECT Name, Title, Email, PhoneExt
  FROM ITDirectory
  ORDER BY Name
</cfquery>

<html>
<head>
  <title>Using SELECT INTO to Create a Copy of a Table</title>
  <style type="text/css">
    th {
      background-color : #888888;
      font-weight : bold;
      text-align : center;
    }
    td {
      background-color : #C0C0C0;
    }
  </style>
</head>

<body>
<h2>ITDirectorty table successfully created and populated with data:</h2>

<table cellpadding="3" cellspacing="1">
  <tr>
    <th>Name</th>
    <th>Title</th>
    <th>E-mail</th>
    <th>Phone Ext.</th>
  </tr>

  <!--- Dynamically generate a table containing all of the records returned
        by the query --->
  <cfoutput query="GetEmployees">
  <tr>
    <td>#Name#</td>
    <td>#Title#</td>
    <td>#Email#</td>
    <td>#PhoneExt#</td>
  </tr>
  </cfoutput>
```

Example 11-12. Using SELECT INTO to create a copy of a table (continued)

```
</table>
</body>
</html>
```

Altering table design

The ALTER TABLE statement alters the design of an existing database table. You can use ALTER TABLE to add, modify the properties of, or delete a column from a specified table. The syntax for using ALTER TABLE is similar to the syntax used by CREATE TABLE as shown in the following code fragments:

```
<!--- Add new column called DateHired to the Employee Directory Table --->
<cfquery name="AddDateHired" datasource="ProgrammingCF">
  ALTER TABLE EmployeeDirectory
    ADD COLUMN DateHired Varchar(8)
</cfquery>

<!--- Modify the datatype of the DateHired column from varchar to date --->
<cfquery name="AlterDateHired" datasource="ProgrammingCF">
  ALTER TABLE EmployeeDirectory
    ALTER COLUMN DateHired Date
</cfquery>

<!--- Drop (remove) the DateHired column from the table --->
<cfquery name="RemoveDateHired" datasource="ProgrammingCF">
  ALTER TABLE EmployeeDirectory
    DROP COLUMN DateHired
</cfquery>

Column added, altered, and deleted!
```

As you can see, you can perform three different actions with ALTER TABLE. You can choose to ADD, ALTER, or DROP a particular column to/from your table. Some databases let you use an additional clause called DROP CONSTRAINT to remove a named constraint from your schema.

Deleting tables

The DROP TABLE statement deletes an existing table (including all data) from a database:

```
<cfquery name="DropITDirectory" datasource="ProgrammingCF">
  DROP TABLE ITDirectory
</cfquery>
```

You should exercise caution when using the DROP TABLE statement. Once a table has been dropped, it is permanently deleted from the database. Before we go on, you should also note that DROP TABLE, ALTER TABLE, and CREATE TABLE can be used with stored procedures, triggers, views, and any other objects supported by your database.

Retrieving Unique Values

The DISTINCT keyword is used in a SELECT statement to retrieve all unique values stored in a specified column. Any duplicate values in the specified column are discarded. For example, if you want to retrieve all the unique department names stored in the Departments column of the EmployeeDirectory table, you can use the DISTINCT keyword:

```
<!--- Query the employeedirectory table for a list of departments --->
<cfquery name="GetDepartment" datasource="ProgrammingCF">
  SELECT DISTINCT Department
  FROM EmployeeDirectory
  ORDER BY Department
</cfquery>
```

Using Column Aliases

Aliases allow you to provide an alternate name to reference a particular query column. Aliases have three general uses:

- In situations where the field names used in a database aren't descriptive
- To deal with nonsupported column names, such as those that contain spaces or special characters
- With scalar and aggregate functions (covered later in this chapter)

To create an alias for a field name you use the AS operator in a SELECT statement:

```
SELECT ItmN AS ItemNumber
FROM MyTable
```

You specify the original name of the column to retrieve, in this case ItmN, followed by the AS operator and the alias name, ItemNumber.

To get a better idea of how an alias works, consider the code in Example 11-13.

Example 11-13. Creating aliases for query column names

```
<!--- Retrieve all records from the database.  Provide aliases for some of the
      field names.  Note that the Name field (not the alias) is used in the SORT
      BY clause. --->
<cfquery name="GetEmployeeInfo" datasource="ProgrammingCF">
  SELECT Name AS EmployeeName, Title, Department,
         Email AS EmailAddress, PhoneExt AS PhoneExtension
  FROM EmployeeDirectory
  ORDER BY Name
</cfquery>

<html>
<head>
  <title>Creating Aliases for Query Column Names</title>
  <style type="text/css">
    th {
```

Example 11-13. Creating aliases for query column names (continued)

```
      background-color : #888888;
      font-weight : bold;
      text-align : center;
    }
    td {
      background-color : #C0C0C0;
    }
  </style>
</head>

<body>
<h3>Using Column Aliases</h3>
<!--- Create an HTML table for outputting the query results.  This section
      creates the first row of the table - used to hold the column
      headers --->
<table cellpadding="3" cellspacing="1">
  <tr>
    <th>Employee Name</th>
    <th>Title</th>
    <th>Department</th>
    <th>E-mail Address</th>
    <th>Phone Extension</th>
  </tr>

  <!--- Output the query results. Use the new field names to refer to the
        aliases column names. --->
  <cfoutput query="GetEmployeeInfo">
  <tr>
   <td>#EmployeeName#</td>
   <td>#Title#</td>
   <td>#Department#</td>
   <td><a href="Mailto:#EmailAddress#">#EmailAddress#</a></td>
   <td>#PhoneExtension#</td>
  </tr>
</cfoutput>
</table>
</body>
</html>
```

Example 11-13 queries the `EmployeeDirectory` table of the `ProgrammingCF` data source and assigns aliases for the `Name`, `Email`, and `PhoneExt` fields. Next, an HTML table is dynamically generated from the query results. The aliased column names are used in place of the original column names to generate the output.

To escape nonsupported column names (such as those containing spaces, characters, and especially pound signs), you can use the back quote (`) character. In this case, the SQL `AS` keyword is used to alias column name as in the following example:

```
SELECT `Item Number` AS ItemNumber
FROM MyTable
```

You can also use the back quote (`) character to escape field names containing pound signs. To keep ColdFusion from throwing an error, be sure to escape the pound sign by doubling it up as in this example:

```
SELECT `Item ##` AS ItemNumber
FROM MyTable
```

Depending on the database you are working with, you may need to use a character or characters other than the back quote to identify special fields. If you get an error using the back quote, try surrounding the field name in square brackets as in `[Item Number]`, brackets with single or double quotation marks, `["Item Number"]`, or parentheses with double quotation marks (`"Item Number"`).

Scalar Functions

Scalar functions let you format record-set data at the database level before it is returned to your ColdFusion application. These functions can be grouped into one of several categories including string, math, date/time, system, and type conversion. Many scalar functions have equivalent functions in ColdFusion (even identical names for some). For example, the scalar function `Left( )` is the same as the `Left( )` function in ColdFusion. Because support for these functions varies from driver to driver and from database to database, it is important that you consult your database and database driver's documentation for a list of supported scalar functions.

At this point, you may be asking yourself why bother using scalar functions in your SQL statements when you can just code the functions in CFML. There is an inherent advantage to using scalar functions on the database side, as opposed to waiting until the data has been transferred. If you think in terms of performance, it makes sense to let the database handle any data manipulation and formatting so that ColdFusion is free to process other tasks. To illustrate the point, let's consider two examples.

The following example retrieves all the article titles from a table called `News`, then outputs the first 50 characters using the CFML `Left( )` function:

```
<cfquery name="GetTitles" datasource="ProgrammingCF">
  SELECT Title
  FROM News
</cfquery>

<cfoutput query="GetTitles">
#Left(Title, 50)#<br>
</cfoutput>
```

Now look at the same example using the scalar function `Left( )` instead:

```
<cfquery name="GetTitle" datasource="ProgrammingCF">
  SELECT {fn Left(Title, 50)} As ShortTitle
  FROM News
</cfquery>
```

```
<cfoutput query="GetTitle">
#ShortTitle#<br>
</cfoutput>
```

In this case, using the `Left()` scalar function saves processing time and memory on the ColdFusion server, since the result set returned by the query contains only the first 50 characters of each title as opposed to the entire title as in the previous example. Note the use of `{fn ...}` around the scalar `Left()` function. While this notation isn't always necessary (it depends on your database driver), I recommend you use it (if it's supported) to help visually separate scalar functions from CFML functions in your code and avoid any confusion. This scenario obviously shows just a simple example of how to use scalar functions to improve performance. It all comes down to one thing—returning the minimum amount of data possible in the most useful format.

Aggregate Functions

You can use aggregate functions to summarize data within a database. Aggregate functions are most often used to create reports that answer such questions as the following: How many employees are in each department? How many widgets were sold in the month of March? Can you break down widget sales by region? What was the date of the first press release issued by the company? What is the average employee salary?

Here are the aggregate functions commonly associated with most databases. Consult your database's documentation for implementation-specific aggregate functions that may be available:

`NIN(Fieldname)`
: Returns the minimum value (numeric, date, or character) in a column.

`MAX(fieldname)`
: Returns the maximum value (numeric, date, or character) in a column.

`AVG(Fieldname)`
: Returns the average value in a column of numeric values.

`SUM(Fieldname)`
: Returns the sum of all values in a column of numeric values.

`COUNT(Fieldname)`
: Returns the number of rows for a given column name that don't contain null values. To count the number of unique row values for a given column, use the `DISTINCT` keyword as in `COUNT(DISTINCT Fieldname)`.

`COUNT(*)`
: Returns the total number of rows in a table. If you use a `WHERE` clause, this function provides the number of rows returned in the result set.

Although ColdFusion has its own functions that can provide the same functionality as the aggregate functions, you should let the database handle calculations whenever possible. From a performance standpoint, databases are optimized to manipulate data whereas ColdFusion is less so. For this reason alone, it makes sense to offload as much processing as you can from ColdFusion to your database. To see how simple aggregate functions can make life easier, consider the following code, which uses the `COUNT(*)` function to retrieve the total number of records in the `EmployeeDirectory` table:

```
<!--- Retrieve a count of the total number of records in the EmployeeDirectory
      table of the database.  You should use COUNT(*) as opposed to COUNT for
      this operation as it is faster.  --->
<cfquery name="GetTotalRecords" datasource="ProgrammingCF">
  SELECT Count(*) AS TotalRecords
  FROM EmployeeDirectory
</cfquery>

<h3>Using COUNT(*)</h3>
<cfoutput>
Total Records in the EmployeeDirectory Table: #GetTotalRecords.TotalRecords#
</cfoutput>
```

Of course, you can do the same thing by querying an arbitrary column using the `cfquery` tag, then using the *`queryname`*`.RecordCount` variable to output the total number of records retrieved by the query. As simple as this seems, it actually wastes a fair amount of resources. Using the `cfquery` tag to query a single field returns all the data associated with that field. So, if you query a table that happens to have one million rows of data in it, you are going to get a result set back that contains one million records. From a performance standpoint, not only will the process take forever, but your server will most likely run out of memory as ColdFusion attempts to store the entire result set. By using the `COUNT(*)` method instead, the database does all the work and returns only a single record back to ColdFusion that contains the total number of rows in the table.

You can also use aggregate functions to provide summarization on groups of related data. For example, if you want to know how many employees are in each department, you could use the `COUNT` (not `COUNT(*)`) function along with the `GROUP BY` clause to find out, as shown in Example 11-14.

Example 11-14. Counting employees in each department

```
<!--- Retrieve a count of the number of employees for each department in
      the EmployeeDirectory table of the database --->
<cfquery name="GetDepartment" datasource="ProgrammingCF">
  SELECT COUNT(Name) AS TotalEmployees, Department
  FROM EmployeeDirectory
  GROUP BY Department
</cfquery>

<html>
```

Example 11-14. Counting employees in each department (continued)

```
<head>
  <title>Counting Employees in Each Department</title>
  <style type="text/css">
    th {
      background-color : #888888;
      font-weight : bold;
      text-align : center;
    }
    td {
      background-color : #C0C0C0;
    }
  </style>
</head>

<body>
<h3>Using COUNT and GROUP BY to return the Total Number of Employees for
    each Department</h3>
<table cellpadding="3" cellspacing="1">
  <tr>
    <th>Department</th>
    <th>Total Employees</th>
  </tr>

  <cfoutput query="GetDepartment">
  <tr>
    <td>#Department#</td>
    <td>#TotalEmployees#</td>
  </tr>
  </cfoutput>
</table>
</body>
</html>
```

You can provide additional filtering of grouped data with a HAVING clause. HAVING works just like the WHERE clause except the filtering takes place after the data has been grouped. In addition, HAVING allows you to specify an aggregate function, whereas the WHERE statement doesn't. Example 11-15 modifies the code in from Example 11-14 so that only departments that have two or more employees are returned by the query.

Example 11-15. Displaying departments that have two or more employees

```
<!--- Retrieve a count of the number of employees for each department in
      the EmployeeDirectory table of the database where the total number
      of employees is greater than or equal to two. --->
<cfquery name="GetDepartment" datasource="ProgrammingCF">
  SELECT COUNT(Name) AS TotalEmployees, Department
  FROM EmployeeDirectory
  GROUP BY Department
  HAVING COUNT(Name) >= 2
</cfquery>
```

Example 11-15. Displaying departments that have two or more employees (continued)

```
<html>
<head>
  <title>Displaying Departments That Have Two or More Employees</title>
  <style type="text/css">
    th {
      background-color : #888888;
      font-weight : bold;
      text-align : center;
    }
    td {
      background-color : #C0C0C0;
    }
  </style>
</head>

<body>
<h3>Using COUNT, GROUP BY, and HAVING to return the Total Number of Employees
    for each Department where the total number of employees is greater than or
    equal to two </h3>
<table cellpadding="3" cellspacing="1">
  <tr>
    <th>Department</th>
    <th>Total Employees</th>
  </tr>

  <cfoutput query="GetDepartment">
  <tr>
    <td>#Department#</td>
    <td>#TotalEmployees#</td>
  </tr>
  </cfoutput>
</table>
</body>
</html>
```

Subqueries

As the name implies, a subquery is a query that exists within another query. Subqueries can be used inside the SELECT, INSERT, UPDATE, and DELETE queries. In the case of SELECT queries, subqueries are often used along with aggregate functions to create a summarized column from data contained in the other columns. Subqueries can also associate data from different tables (much like a join, which we'll cover shortly).

Example 11-16 uses a subquery along with an aggregate function to calculate the average salary of all employees in the EmployeeDirectory table.

Example 11-16. Using a subquery along with an aggregate function

```
<!--- Retrieve employee records from the EmpoloyeeDirectory.  Employ a
      subquery to obtain the average salary of all employees  --->
<cfquery name="GetSalaries" datasource="ProgrammingCF">
```

Example 11-16. Using a subquery along with an aggregate function (continued)

```
  SELECT Name, Title, Department,
         Salary, (SELECT AVG(Salary)
                  FROM EmployeeDirectory) AS AverageSalary
  FROM EmployeeDirectory
  ORDER BY Name
</cfquery>

<html>
<head>
  <title>Using a Subquery Along with an Aggregate Function</title>
  <style type="text/css">
    th {
      background-color : #888888;
      font-weight : bold;
      text-align : center;
    }
    td {
      background-color : #C0C0C0;
    }
    td.Total {
      background-color : #D3D3D3;
      font-weight : bold;
    }
  </style>
</head>

<body>
<h3>Average Salary Report</h3>

<table cellpadding="3" cellspacing="1">
  <tr>
    <th>Name</th>
    <th>Title</th>
    <th>Department</th>
    <th>Salary</th>
  </tr>
  <!--- Output the employee records --->
  <cfoutput query="GetSalaries">
  <tr>
    <td>#Name#</td>
    <td>#Title#</td>
    <td>#Department#</td>
    <td style="text-align: right;">#DollarFormat(Salary)#</td>
  </tr>
  </cfoutput>

  <!--- Output the average employee salary.  Note that the query attribute of
        the cfoutput tag was not used.  The query name is prepended to the
        AverageSalary salary variable --->
  <cfoutput>
  <tr>
    <td class="Total">Average Salary</td>
```

Example 11-16. Using a subquery along with an aggregate function (continued)

```
    <td class="Total" style="text-align: right;"
        colspan="3">#DollarFormat(GetSalaries.AverageSalary)#</td>
  </tr>
  </cfoutput>
</table>
</body>
</html>
```

In Example 11-16, a query is run to retrieve the `Name`, `Title`, `Department`, and `Salary` of each employee in the `EmployeeDirectory` table. A subquery is used within the `SELECT` statement to obtain the average of all salaries using the `AVG` aggregate function. Subqueries returning more than one record can be used only in the `WHERE` clause. The results are written to the browser in an HTML table that contains a listing of all the employees in the table along with their salaries. The average salary is given at the bottom of the table.

You can also include subqueries in the `WHERE` clause of a query. One way to do this is with the `EXISTS` keyword. `EXISTS` is used only with subqueries and tests for a non-empty record set (you can test for an empty record set by using `NOT EXISTS`). To see how this is useful, consider Example 11-17, in which we retrieve a list of all employees from the `EmployeeDirectory` table who have received individual incentive awards of less than $5,000 each in 2003.

Example 11-17. Using EXISTS with a subquery

```
<!--- Retrieve a list of employees who received individual incentive awards
      of less than $5000 each in 2003 --->
<cfquery name="GetSalaries" datasource="ProgrammingCF">
  SELECT ID, Name, Title, Department
  FROM EmployeeDirectory
  WHERE EXISTS
    (SELECT ID
     FROM IncentiveAwards
     WHERE IncentiveAwards.ID = EmployeeDirectory.ID
     and Amount < 5000
     and {fn YEAR(DateAwarded)} = 2003)
  ORDER BY Name
</cfquery>

<html>
<head>
  <title>Using EXISTS with a Subquery</title>
  <style type="text/css">
    th {
      background-color : #888888;
      font-weight : bold;
      text-align : center;
    }
    td {
      background-color : #C0C0C0;
    }
```

Example 11-17. Using EXISTS with a subquery (continued)

```
  </style>
</head>

<body>
<h3>Incentive Awards under $5000 Granted in 2003</h3>

<table cellpadding="3" cellspacing="1">
  <tr>
    <th>Name</th>
    <th>Title</th>
    <th>Department</th>
  </tr>

  <!--- Output the employee records --->
  <cfoutput query="GetSalaries">
  <tr>
    <td>#Name#</td>
    <td>#Title#</td>
    <td>#Department#</td>
  </tr>
  </cfoutput>
</table>
</body>
</html>
```

Example 11-17 uses a few of the advanced techniques we covered so far. In plain English, the query works by saying "select the employees from the EmployeeDirectory table where a matching record exists in the IncentiveAwards table that meets the criteria set in the subquery."

Subqueries can also be used in the WHERE clause of a SELECT query by using the equal sign (=) or the [NOT] IN operator. Use the equal sign when only one record will be returned by the subquery. If more than one record can be returned, use IN. Here are some example WHERE clauses:

```
WHERE MyField = (SELECT SomeField
                 FROM SomeTable
                 WHERE OtherField = Value)

WHERE MyField IN (SELECT SomeField
                  FROM SomeTable
                  WHERE OtherField = Value)

WHERE MyField NOT IN (SELECT SomeField
                      FROM SomeTable
                      WHERE OtherField = Value)
```

Unions

The UNION clause is used with a SELECT statement to merge result sets from two or more queries into a single result set. In order to use the UNION clause, each result set must contain the same number of columns, with each matching column being of the same datatype. Additionally, each column must have been SELECT'ed in the same order during the formation of the original result sets. Example 11-18 demonstrates how this works.

Example 11-18. Using the UNION clause to merge two result sets

```
<!--- Retrieve records from both the ITDirectory and HRDirectory tables
      and merge them using the UNION clause.  This example is somewhat
      impractical as the user's department is not stored in the
      database --->
<cfquery name="GetEmployees" datasource="ProgrammingCF">
  SELECT Name, Title, Email, PhoneExt
  FROM ITDirectory
  UNION
  SELECT Name, Title, Email, PhoneExt
  FROM HRDirectory
</cfquery>

<html>
<head>
  <title>Using the UNION Clause to Merge Two Result Sets</title>
  <style type="text/css">
    th {
      background-color : #888888;
      font-weight : bold;
      text-align : center;
    }
    td {
      background-color : #C0C0C0;
    }
  </style>
</head>

<body>
<h2>Combined IT Directory and HR Directory:</h2>

<table cellpadding="3" cellspacing="1">
  <tr>
    <th>Name</th>
    <th>Title</th>
    <th>E-mail</th>
    <th>Phone Ext.</th>
  </tr>

  <!--- Dynamically generate a table containing all of the records returned
        by the query --->
  <cfoutput query="GetEmployees">
  <tr>
    <td>#Name#</td>
    <td>#Title#</td>
    <td>#Email#</td>
    <td>#PhoneExt#</td>
```

Example 11-18. Using the UNION clause to merge two result sets (continued)

```
  </tr>
  </cfoutput>
</table>
</body>
</html>
```

In order to get Example 11-18 to work, you need to go back to the code in Example 11-12 and modify it to create a new table called `HRDirectory`. Simply substitute `HRDirectory` for `ITDirectory` in the `FROM` clause and `'HR'` for `'IT'` in the `WHERE` clause and execute the template. You should now have an `ITDirectory` and an `HRDirectory` table containing IT employees and HR employees respectively.

Once you have these two tables in your database, go ahead and execute Example 11-18. The template retrieves a list of all employees from both tables and merges the result sets using the `UNION` clause. An HTML table containing the records from the merged result set is dynamically generated.

Joins

Relational database design allows you to create database tables that maintain relationships. These relationships are usually defined in terms of primary and foreign key values. For example, in our `EmployeeDirectory` table, the `ID` value for each employee is the primary key value. The `IncentiveAwards` table contains a field named `ID` as well. The `ID` field in the `IncentiveAwards` table is known as a foreign key. Records in the `IncentiveAwards` table are related to records in the `EmployeeDirectory` table by their `ID` values. Each record in the `IncentiveAwards` table should have a corresponding record in the `EmployeeDirectory` table.

A join operation lets you select records from two or more tables where a relationship between primary key and foreign key values exists. Most joins fall into one of two categories: inner or outer joins.

Inner joins

Inner joins are the most common type of join and are used to retrieve records from two or more tables where values in the joined columns match. There are many ways to implement inner joins in SQL, and support for these methods varies from database to database. Consult your database documentation to find out which methods are supported by your database.

One common method involves using the equal sign (=) in the `WHERE` statement to join the tables by a related column, as shown in Example 11-19.

Example 11-19. Inner join performed in the WHERE statement

```
<!--- Query the EmployeeDirectory and IncentiveAwards tables and only return
      records where the ID from the EmployeeDirectory table matches the ID in
```

Example 11-19. Inner join performed in the WHERE statement (continued)

```
     the IncentiveAwards table,  The inner join is performed by the equal
     sign. --->
<cfquery name="GetEmployeeInfo" datasource="ProgrammingCF">
  SELECT EmployeeDirectory.ID, EmployeeDirectory.Name,
         IncentiveAwards.ID, IncentiveAwards.Category,
         IncentiveAwards.DateAwarded, IncentiveAwards.Amount
  FROM EmployeeDirectory, IncentiveAwards
  WHERE EmployeeDirectory.ID = IncentiveAwards.ID
</cfquery>

<html>
<head>
  <title>Inner Join Performed in the WHERE Statement</title>
  <style type="text/css">
    th {
      background-color : #888888;
      font-weight : bold;
      text-align : center;
    }
    td {
      background-color : #C0C0C0;
    }
  </style>
</head>

<body>
<h3>Incentive Awards</h3>

<table cellpadding="3" cellspacing="1">
  <tr>
    <th>Name</th>
    <th>Award Type</th>
    <th>Date Awarded</th>
    <th>Amount</th>
  </tr>

  <!--- Dynamically generate a table containing all of the records returned
        by the query --->
  <cfoutput query="GetEmployeeInfo">
  <tr>
    <td>#Name#</td>
    <td>#Category#</td>
    <td>#DateFormat(DateAwarded, 'mm/dd/yyyy')#</td>
    <td>#DollarFormat(Amount)#</td>
  </tr>
  </cfoutput>
</table>
```

Example 11-19 queries the EmployeeDirectory and IncentiveAwards tables and returns only records in which the ID value from the EmployeeDirectory table matches the ID value in the IncentiveAwards table. The inner join is performed using the equal sign in the WHERE clause. Executing this template results in the output shown in Figure 11-7.

You can also perform an inner join using INNER JOIN in the FROM clause of the SELECT statement, as shown in Example 11-20. The results of this query will mimic the results of Example 11-19 (shown in Figure 11-7).

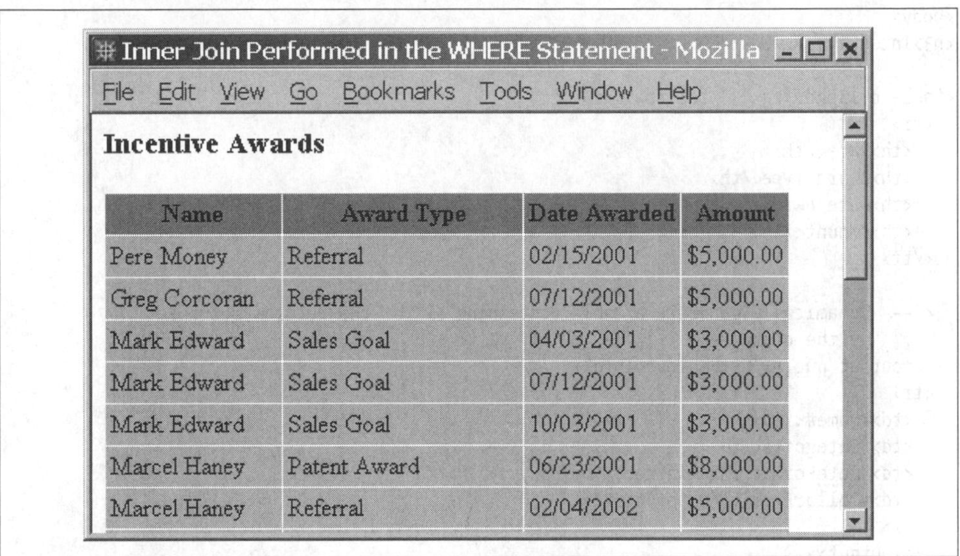

Figure 11-7. Inner join performed using the equal sign in the WHERE clause

Example 11-20. Inner join performed in the FROM statement

```
<!--- Query the EmployeeDirectory and IncentiveAwards tables and only return
      records where the ID from the EmployeeDirectory table matches the ID in
      the IncentiveAwards table.  The inner join is performed by the INNER
      JOIN operator. --->
<cfquery name="GetEmployeeInfo" datasource="ProgrammingCF">
  SELECT employee.ID, employee.Name, incentive.ID,
         incentive.Category, incentive.DateAwarded, incentive.Amount
  FROM EmployeeDirectory employee
  INNER JOIN IncentiveAwards incentive
  ON employee.ID = incentive.ID
</cfquery>

<html>
<head>
  <title>Inner Join Performed in the FROM Statement</title>
  <style type="text/css">
    th {
      background-color : #888888;
      font-weight : bold;
      text-align : center;
    }
```

Example 11-20. Inner join performed in the FROM statement (continued)

```
    td {
      background-color : #C0C0C0;
    }
  </style>
</head>

<body>
<h3>Incentive Awards</h3>

<table cellpadding="3" cellspacing="1">
  <tr>
    <th>Name</th>
    <th>Award Type</th>
    <th>Date Awarded</th>
    <th>Amount</th>
  </tr>

  <!--- Dynamically generate a table containing all of the records returned
        by the query --->
  <cfoutput query="GetEmployeeInfo">
  <tr>
    <td>#Name#</td>
    <td>#Category#</td>
    <td>#DateFormat(DateAwarded, 'mm/dd/yyyy')#</td>
    <td>#DollarFormat(Amount)#</td>
  </tr>
  </cfoutput>
</table>
</body>
</html>
```

Example 11-20 introduces another technique known as table aliasing. If you look at the first query, you'll notice that we refer to the `EmployeeDirectory` table as `employee` and the `IncentiveAwards` table as `incentive`:

```
SELECT employee.ID, employee.Name, incentive.ID,
       incentive.Category, incentive.DateAwarded, incentive.Amount
FROM EmployeeDirectory employee
INNER JOIN IncentiveAwards incentive
ON employee.ID = incentive.ID
```

SQL lets us alias table names when working with multiple tables. To create an alias for a table name, simply specify the alias immediately following the table name in the `FROM` clause.

Outer joins

Outer joins differ from inner joins in that they let you query all the records from one table even if corresponding records don't exist in the other table. There are two types of outer joins: left and right.

As its name implies, a left outer join returns all the records from the left table (as specified in the WHERE or FROM clause) and only the records from the right table where the values in the joined fields match. All empty rows from the right table are assigned NULL values.

Example 11-21 uses a left outer join in the FROM clause to query the EmployeeDirectory and IncentiveAwards tables and return all records from the left table (EmployeeDirectory) and only those from the right table (IncentiveAwards) that match ID values.

Example 11-21. Using LEFT OUTER JOIN in the FROM clause

```
<!--- Query the EmployeeDirectory and IncentiveAwards tables and return all
      records from the left table (EmployeeDirectory) and only those from
      the right table (IncentiveAwards) where the ID values are equal.  The
      left outer join is performed by the LEFT OUTER JOIN operator. --->
<cfquery name="GetEmployeeInfo" datasource="ProgrammingCF">
  SELECT employee.ID, employee.Name, incentive.ID,
         incentive.Category, incentive.DateAwarded, incentive.Amount
  FROM EmployeeDirectory employee
  LEFT OUTER JOIN IncentiveAwards incentive
  ON employee.ID = incentive.ID
</cfquery>

<html>
<head>
  <title>Using LEFT OUTER JOIN in the FROM Clause</title>
  <style type="text/css">
    th {
      background-color : #888888;
      font-weight : bold;
      text-align : center;
    }
    td {
      background-color : #COCOCO;
    }
  </style>
</head>

<body>
<h3>Incentive Awards</h3>

<table cellpadding="3" cellspacing="1">
  <tr>
    <th>Name</th>
    <th>Award Type</th>
    <th>Date Awarded</th>
    <th>Amount</th>
  </tr>

  <!--- Dynamically generate a table containing all of the records returned
        by the query.  Substitute NULL for any blanks (NULLs) returned by
        the Left Outer Join --->
```

Example 11-21. Using LEFT OUTER JOIN in the FROM clause (continued)

```
  <cfoutput query="GetEmployeeInfo">
  <tr>
    <td>#Name#</td>
    <td><cfif Category is "">NULL<cfelse>#Category#</cfif></td>
    <td><cfif DateAwarded is "">NULL<cfelse>
      #DateFormat(DateAwarded, 'mm/dd/yyyy')#</cfif></td>
    <td><cfif Amount is "">NULL<cfelse>#DollarFormat(Amount)#</cfif></td>
  </tr>
  </cfoutput>
</table>
</body>
</html>
```

Executing the template in Example 11-21 results in the output shown in Figure 11-8.

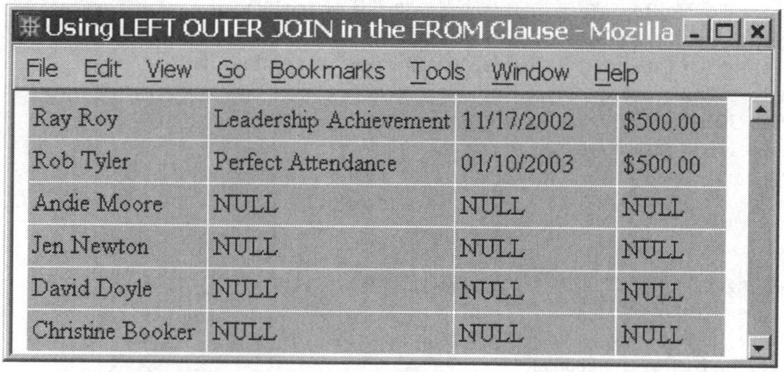
Using LEFT OUTER JOIN in the FROM Clause - Mozilla
File Edit View Go Bookmarks Tools Window Help
Ray Roy | Leadership Achievement | 11/17/2002 | $500.00
Rob Tyler | Perfect Attendance | 01/10/2003 | $500.00
Andie Moore | NULL | NULL | NULL
Jen Newton | NULL | NULL | NULL
David Doyle | NULL | NULL | NULL
Christine Booker | NULL | NULL | NULL

Figure 11-8. Results of using a left outer join in the FROM clause

A right outer join is the exact opposite of a left outer join. Right outer joins return all records from the right table and only the records from the left table where the values in the joined fields match. All empty rows from the left table are assigned `NULL` values.

Example 11-22 uses a right outer join to query the `EmployeeDirectory` and `IncentiveAwards` tables. A result set containing all records from the right table (`IncentiveAwards`) and only those from the left table (`EmployeeDirectory`) where the `ID` values are equal is returned.

Example 11-22. Using RIGHT OUTER JOIN in the FROM clause

```
<!--- Query the EmployeeDirectory and IncentiveAwards tables and return all
      records from the Right table (IncentiveAwards) and only those from
      the left table (EmployeeDirectory) where the ID values are equal.  The
      right outer join is performed by the RIGHT OUTER JOIN operator. --->
<cfquery name="GetEmployeeInfo" datasource="ProgrammingCF">
  SELECT employee.ID, employee.Name, incentive.ID,
         incentive.Category, incentive.DateAwarded, incentive.Amount
  FROM EmployeeDirectory employee
```

Example 11-22. Using RIGHT OUTER JOIN in the FROM clause (continued)

```
  RIGHT OUTER JOIN IncentiveAwards incentive
  ON employee.ID = incentive.ID
</cfquery>

<html>
<head>
  <title>Using RIGHT OUTER JOIN in the FROM Clause</title>
  <style type="text/css">
    th {
      background-color : #888888;
      font-weight : bold;
      text-align : center;
    }
    td {
      background-color : #COCOCO;
    }
  </style>
</head>

<body>
<h3>Incentive Awards</h3>

<table cellpadding="3" cellspacing="1">
  <tr>
    <th>Name</th>
    <th>Award Type</th>
    <th>Date Awarded</th>
    <th>Amount</th>
  </tr>

  <!--- Dynamically generate a table containing all of the records returned
        by the query.  Substitute NULL for any blanks (NULLs) returned by
        the Right Outer Join --->
  <cfoutput query="GetEmployeeInfo">
  <tr>
    <td><cfif Name is "">NULL<cfelse>#Name#</cfif></td>
    <td><cfif Category is "">NULL<cfelse>#Category#</cfif></td>
    <td><cfif DateAwarded is "">NULL<cfelse>#DateFormat(DateAwarded,
        'mm/dd/yyyy')#</cfif></td>
    <td><cfif Amount is "">NULL<cfelse>#DollarFormat(Amount)#</cfif></td>
  </tr>
  </cfoutput>
</table>
```

Executing the template in Example 11-22 results in the output shown in Figure 11-9.

Note that there are various shorthand techniques you can use to specify left outer joins and right outer joins in the WHERE clause. The syntax varies from database to database. Refer to your specific database's documentation for guidelines on specific syntax for outer joins.

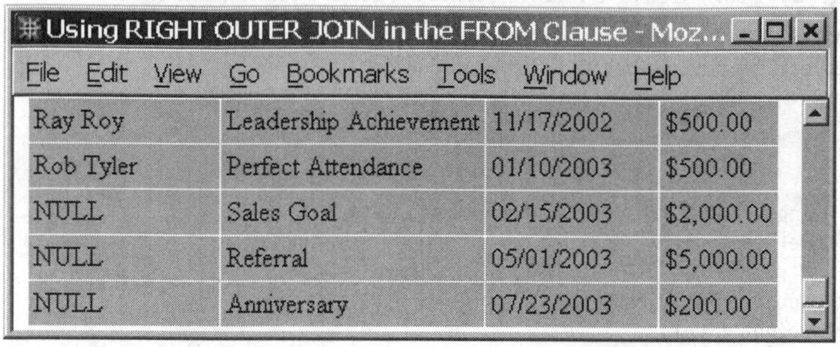

Using RIGHT OUTER JOIN in the FROM Clause - Moz...

File Edit View Go Bookmarks Tools Window Help

Ray Roy	Leadership Achievement	11/17/2002	$500.00
Rob Tyler	Perfect Attendance	01/10/2003	$500.00
NULL	Sales Goal	02/15/2003	$2,000.00
NULL	Referral	05/01/2003	$5,000.00
NULL	Anniversary	07/23/2003	$200.00

Figure 11-9. Using a right outer join in the FROM clause

There are several other types of joins that can be performed in SQL. Most of these are variations on the joins we already covered. Many are highly specialized and rarely employed. Some are exclusive to specific database platforms. For more information on joins, see your database documentation or pick up a good SQL reference book, such as *SQL in a Nutshell* by Kevin Kline and David Kline (O'Reilly).

Data Binding and Preventing Malicious Query Code

You can use the `cfqueryparam` tag to check the datatype of a query parameter and optionally validate it against a specific SQL type. This allows you to prevent arbitrary code from being passed to your queries and can also speed up performance. You can also use the `cfqueryparam` tag to update long text fields. The `cfqueryparam` tag must be nested within a `cfquery` tag and appears on the right side of the equal sign in the `WHERE` clause:

```
<cfquery name="MyQUERY" datasource="MyDatasource">
  SELECT *
  FROM MyTable
  WHERE MyValue =
        <cfqueryparam value="parameter_value"
                      cfsqltype="parameter_data_type"
                      maxlength="number"
                      scale="number_of_decimal_places"
                      separator="seperator_character"
                      list="Yes|No"
                      null="Yes|No">
</cfquery>
```

The `value` attribute is required and specifies the value that ColdFusion should pass to the right of the comparison operator in the `WHERE` clause. `cfsqltype` is also required and specifies the SQL type the parameter should be bound to. Possible entries are listed in Table 11-1. The default value for `cfsqltype` is `CF_SQL_CHAR`.

Table 11-1. Values for cfsqltype

CF_SQL_BIGINT	CF_SQL_FLOAT	CF_SQL_REFCURSOR
CF_SQL_BIT	CF_SQL_IDSTAMP	CF_SQL_SMALLINT
CF_SQL_BLOB	CF_SQL_INTEGER	CF_SQL_TIME
CF_SQL_CHAR	CF_SQL_LONGVARCHAR	CF_SQL_TIMESTAMP
CF_SQL_CLOB	CF_SQL_MONEY	CF_SQL_TINYINT
CF_SQL_DATE	CF_SQL_MONEY4	CF_SQL_VARCHAR
CF_SQL_DECIMAL	CF_SQL_NUMERIC	
CF_SQL_DOUBLE	CF_SQL_REAL	

The `maxlength` attribute specifies the maximum length of the parameter being passed and is an optional attribute. `scale` is also optional and, if you use a numeric datatype, specifies the number of decimal places for the parameter. The `separator` attribute is optional and specifies the character used to delimit the list of values when the `list` attribute is set to `Yes`. The default is the comma (`,`). The `list` attribute is optional and accepts a `Yes`/`No` value indicating whether the `value` attribute of the `cfqueryparam` tag should be treated as a list of values separated by the character specified in the `separator` attribute. If set to `Yes`, a SQL parameter is generated for each value in the list. Each list item is validated separately. If a value is specified for the `maxlength` attribute, the `maxlength` applies to each item in the list as opposed to the list as a whole. If the value passed is `NULL`, it is treated as a single `NULL` value. The default is `No`.

The final attribute is `null`. `null` is optional and specifies a `Yes`/`No` value indicating whether the value passed is a `NULL`. If `Yes`, ColdFusion ignores the `value` attribute. The default value for `null` is `No`.

If the database being used doesn't support the binding of parameters, validation is still performed with the validated parameter being written back to the string. If for any reason validation fails, ColdFusion throws an exception. The following rules determine the validation performed:

- `CF_SQL_SMALLINT`, `CF_SQL_INTEGER`, `CF_SQL_REAL`, `CF_SQL_FLOAT`, `CF_SQL_DOUBLE`, `CF_SQL_TINYINT`, `CF_SQL_MONEY`, `CF_SQL_MONEY4`, `CF_SQL_DECIMAL`, `CF_SQL_NUMERIC`, and `CF_SQL_BIGINT` can be converted to numbers.
- `CF_SQL_DATE`, `CF_SQL_TIME`, and `CF_SQL_TIMESTAMP` can be converted to a valid date format.
- If the `maxlength` attribute is used, the length of the value for the specified parameter can't exceed the specified length.

The actual SQL that is generated by the `cfqueryparam` tag is dependent on the database used. Example 11-23 uses the `cfqueryparam` tag to validate the value of a variable called `ID`. Changing the value of `ID` from numeric to a text character causes ColdFusion to throw an error.

Example 11-23. Using cfqueryparam for data binding and validation

```
<!--- Set URL.ID=1.  Normally, this value would come as a URL parameter or
      form post (then it would be form.ID) --->
<cfset URL.ID = 1>

<!--- Retrieve the full record of the employee whose ID is specified.
      Use the cfqueryparam tag to bind URL.ID to a numeric value. --->
<cfquery name="GetEmployeeRecord" datasource="ProgrammingCF">
  SELECT Name, Title, Department, Email, PhoneExt, Salary
  FROM EmployeeDirectory
  WHERE ID = <cfqueryparam value="#URL.ID#"
                           cfsqltype="CF_SQL_INTEGER">
</cfquery>

<html>
<head>
  <title>Using cfqueryparam for Data Binding and Validation</title>
  <style type="text/css">
    th {
      background-color : #888888;
      font-weight : bold;
      text-align : center;
    }
    td {
      background-color : #C0C0C0;
    }
  </style>
</head>
<body>

<h2>Employee Profile</h2>

<table cellpadding="3" cellspacing="1">
  <tr>
    <th>Name</th>
    <th>Title</th>
    <th>Department</th>
    <th>E-mail</th>
    <th>Phone Extension</th>
    <th>Salary</th>
  </tr>
<!--- Generate an HTML table containing the employee record from the
      GetEmployeeRecord query. --->
<cfoutput>
  <tr>
    <td>#GetEmployeeRecord.Name#</td>
    <td>#GetEmployeeRecord.Title#</td>
    <td>#GetEmployeeRecord.Department#</td>
    <td><a
        href="Mailto:#GetEmployeeRecord.Email#">#GetEmployeeRecord.Email#</a></td>
    <td>#GetEmployeeRecord.PhoneExt#</td>
    <td>#GetEmployeeRecord.Salary#</td>
  </tr>
```

Example 11-23. Using cfqueryparam for data binding and validation (continued)

```
</cfoutput>
</table>
</body>
</html>
```

Query of Queries

Now that you have an understanding of advanced SQL, it's time to introduce a new concept known as "query of queries" or CFSQL (ColdFusion SQL). Introduced in ColdFusion 5.0 and greatly enhanced in MX, query of queries allows you to use the `cfquery` tag to query an already existing query object using a subset of ANSI SQL 92. This feature makes it easy to program functionality previously difficult or impossible to implement in ColdFusion. Some potential uses for query of queries include:

- Manipulate query objects (sort, summarize, group, etc.) returned by other ColdFusion tags such as `cfhttp`, `cfftp`, `cfldap`, `cfpop`, `cfsearch`, or `cfstoredproc` as well as the various query functions
- Perform joins and unions between tables from different data sources
- Resorting a query result set without having to go back to the data source
- Moving entire tables into memory (Macromedia recommends no more than 50,000 rows in ColdFusion MX or 10,000 rows in ColdFusion 5), effectively speeding up query times because ColdFusion no longer has to make a round trip to the database for each query performed

Regardless of what you decide to use this feature for, you need to know what SQL constructs are available. For starters, query of queries can only be used to perform an SQL `SELECT`. This means that query of queries can be used only to select records, not `INSERT`, `UPDATE`, or `DELETE` them. This makes sense, as the purpose of query of queries is to allow you to perform a query against an already existing query object. When you perform your `SELECT`, a number of SQL keywords are available to help you construct your query. These keywords are `FROM`, `WHERE`, `ORDER BY`, `GROUP BY`, `HAVING`, and `UNION`. Query of queries does not support the `INNER JOIN` or `OUTER JOIN` statement. However, you can still perform an inner join by using the equal sign in the `WHERE` clause as was discussed in the section on joins.

A number of comparison and Boolean operators are also available: `=`, `<>`, `<`, `>`, `<=`, `>=`, `AND`, `OR`, `NOT`, `IN`, `BETWEEN`, `LIKE`, and `EXISTS`. In addition, query of queries supports several aggregate functions including `COUNT`, `SUM`, `AVG`, `MAX`, and `MIN`. You should note that query of queries doesn't support nested aggregate functions nor does it support ODBC formatted dates in comparison operations.

To perform a query of a query, you set the `dbtype` attribute of the `cfquery` tag to `Query` and reference the name of one or more existing queries in the `FROM` clause of your SQL statement. The `datasource` attribute isn't used when performing a query of a query. Example 11-24 shows a useful way to use query of a query to build an "A to Z" list of employees in the EmployeeDirectory table.

Example 11-24. Perform a query of a query

```
<cfparam name="Letter" default="A">

<cfquery name="GetAllUsers" datasource="ProgrammingCF"
         cachedwithin="#CreateTimeSpan(0,0,15,0)#">
  SELECT Name, {fn LEFT(Name, 1)} AS Initial, Email
  FROM EmployeeDirectory
  ORDER BY Name
</cfquery>

<cfquery name="GetAllInitials" dbtype="query"
         cachedwithin="#CreateTimeSpan(0,0,15,0)#">
  SELECT DISTINCT Initial
  FROM GetAllUsers
  ORDER BY Initial
</cfquery>

<cfquery name="GetSpecificLetter" dbtype="query">
  SELECT Name, Email
  FROM GetAllUsers
  WHERE Name LIKE '#Letter#%'
  ORDER BY Name
</cfquery>

<cfoutput>
<h3>#GetAllUsers.RecordCount# users in the database</h3>
<p>
<cfloop list="#ValueList(GetAllInitials.Initial)#" index="i">
<cfif i is Letter>
#i#
<cfelse>
<a href="#CGI.ScriptName#?letter=#i#">#i#</a>
</cfif>
</cfloop>
</cfoutput>
<p>
<cfoutput query="GetSpecificLetter">
#Name# (<a href="mailto:#Email#">#Email#</a>)<br>
</cfoutput>
```

In this example, the first cfquery retrieves the name, first initial, and email address of each user in the EmployeeDirectory table into a query called GetAllUsers. The results are cached for 15 minutes. The next query uses a query of a query to retrieve all of the distinct first initials from the GetAllUsers query. This information is also cached. The third query is also uses a query of a query. It retrieves all of the users from the GetAllUsers query whose first initial matches the value stored in Letter (the default is "A"). Notice that Letter is not scoped. This is to allow the value to be passed in by form post or URL. Once all of the queries have been run, the list of initials is output at the top of the page. Each letter is displayed as a hyperlink. Thanks to our second query, only those letters matching the first initial of an employee are displayed in the list. Each employee's name and email address is then listed below the A to Z list by using `cfoutput` to loop over the `GetSpecificLetter` query. Clicking on one of the letters causes the template to be rerun, pulling the employee records for the letter you clicked on. Because the first two queries are cached, the execution time for the entire page is very fast.

Calling Stored Procedures

Most enterprise-level databases (MS SQL Server, DB2, Oracle, Informix, Sybase) support creating special programs within the database called stored procedures. Stored procedures allow you to encapsulate SQL and other database-specific functions in a wrapper that can be called from external applications. There are several reasons to use stored procedures whenever possible in your applications:

- Stored procedures generally execute faster than identical code passed using the `cfquery` tag because they are precompiled on the database server.
- Stored procedures support code reuse. A single procedure needs to be created only once and can be accessed by any number of templates, even different applications and those written in other languages.
- Stored procedures allow you to encapsulate complex database manipulation routines, often utilizing database-specific functions.
- Security is enhanced by keeping all database operations encapsulated within the stored procedure. Because ColdFusion passes parameters only to the stored procedure, there is no way to execute arbitrary SQL commands.

There are two ways to call stored procedures in ColdFusion. You can use the `cfquery` tag or the `cfstoredproc` tag (generally the preferred method). Unfortunately, material on writing stored procedures is beyond the scope of this book. For more information on creating stored procedures, consult the documentation for your specific database.

Using cfstoredproc

The preferred method for calling stored procedures in ColdFusion is via the `cfstoredproc` tag. This tag takes several attributes that allow you to specify information about the data source on which you want to execute the stored procedure, as well as the stored procedure itself. The three most commonly used attributes are:

```
<cfstoredproc procedure="procedure_name"
              datasource="datasource_name"
              returncode="Yes|No">
</cfstoredproc>
```

procedure is a required attribute and specifies the name of the stored procedure on the database server that you want to execute. The datasource attribute is also required and specifies the data source that contains the stored procedure. The final attribute, returncode, is optional and accepts a Yes/No value. If set to Yes, cfstoreproc populates cfstoredproc.StatusCode with the status code returned by the stored procedure. The default value for ReturnCode is No. There are a number of additional attributes that can be used with the cfstoredproc tag. For a complete list, see Appendix A.

The cfstoredproc tag calls only the stored procedure you want to execute. You still need a way to pass values in and receive data back from the stored procedure. These functions are handled by two child tags of the cfstoredproc tag, the cfprocparam and cfprocresult tags respectively.

When a stored procedure is executed using the cfstoredproc tag, two return values are automatically created by ColdFusion. These variables are:

cfstoredproc.StatusCode
: Returned when returncode is set to Yes; contains the status code returned by the stored procedure

cfstoredproc.ExecutionCode
: The number of milliseconds it took for the stored procedure to execute

Passing parameters using cfprocparam

The cfprocparam tag specifies parameter information to send to the stored procedure named in the cfstoredproc tag. You may specify multiple cfprocparam tags within a single cfstoredproc tag. cfprocparam tags must be nested within the cfstoredproc tag and use the following syntax:

```
<cfprocparam type="In|Out|InOut"
             variable="variable_name"

             value="parameter_value"
             cfsqltype="parameter_data_type"
             maxlength="length"
             scale="decimal_places"
             null="Yes|No">
```

The type attribute is optional and specifies whether the variable being passed is an input (In), output (Out), or input/output (InOut) variable. The default type is input (In). variable is required when type is Out or InOut and specifies the name of the ColdFusion variable used to reference the value returned by the output parameter after the stored procedure is called. The value attribute is required when type is In or InOut. It specifies the value to pass to the stored procedure.

The next attribute, cfsqltype, is required and specifies the SQL type of the parameter being passed to the stored procedure. Possible values are listed back in

Table 11-1. The default value for cfsqltype is CF_SQL_CHAR. The maxlength attribute specifies the maximum length of the parameter being passed and is an optional attribute. scale is also optional and specifies the number of decimal places for the parameter should it be a numeric datatype. The final attribute is null. null is optional and specifies a Yes/No value indicating whether the value passed is a NULL. If Yes, ColdFusion ignores the value attribute. The default value for null is No.

ColdFusion MX passes values to stored procedures using positional notation. This means that cfprocparam tags must be specified in the same order as the parameters are expected by the stored procedure. Previous versions of ColdFusion allowed parameters to be passed using named notation via an attribute of the cfprocparam tag called dbvarname. Named notation is not supported in JDBC, and subsequently, the dbvarname attribute is no longer supported. If you specify a value for dbvarname, ColdFusion MX ignores it.

Specifying result sets using cfprocresult

The cfprocresult tag specifies the name for a given result set returned by the cfstoredproc tag. This allows other ColdFusion tags to reference the result set returned by the stored procedure. Because stored procedures can return more than one result set, the cfprocresult tag allows you to specify which result set to use. Because of this feature, it is possible to nest multiple cfprocresult tags within a cfstoredproc tag, provided you assign a different name for each cfprocresult set:

```
<cfprocresult name="query_name"
              resultset="1-n"
              maxrows="number">
```

The name attribute is required and specifies a name for the query result set returned by the stored procedure. resultset is an optional attribute and specifies the result set to use if the stored procedure returns more than one result set. The default value for resultset is 1. The final attribute is maxrows. maxrows is also optional and specifies the maximum number of rows to return with the result set. By default, all rows are returned.

Example 11-25 uses the cfstoredproc tag, several cfprocparam tags, and the cfprocresult tag to execute a stored procedure called sp_AddEmployee that adds a new employee record to a database.

Example 11-25. Executing a stored procedure using cfstoredproc

```
<!--- Assign blank default values for any fields not passed in --->
<cfparam name="form.Name" default="">
<cfparam name="form.Title" default="">
<cfparam name="form.Department" default="">
<cfparam name="form.Email" default="">
<cfparam name="form.PhoneExt" default="">
<cfparam name="form.Salary" default="">
```

Example 11-25. Executing a stored procedure using cfstoredproc (continued)

```
<!--- Call the sp_AddEmployee stored procedure --->
<cfstoredproc procedure="sp_AddEmployee"
              datasource="ProgrammingCF"
              returncode="Yes">
<!--- Pass each parameter.  If the field being passed contains a blank value,
      make it NULL.  Thanks to Dan Switzer for the YesNoFormat( ) tip. --->
<cfprocparam type="In" cfsqltype="CF_SQL_VARCHAR" value="#form.Name#"
             maxlength="255" null="#YesNoFormat(form.Name is "")#">
<cfprocparam type="In" cfsqltype="CF_SQL_VARCHAR" value="#form.Title#"
             maxlength="255" null="#YesNoFormat(form.Title is "")#">
<cfprocparam type="In" cfsqltype="CF_SQL_VARCHAR" value="#form.Department#"
             maxlength="255" null="#YesNoFormat(form.Department is "")#">
<cfprocparam type="In" cfsqltype="CF_SQL_VARCHAR" value="#form.Email#"
             maxlength="255" null="#YesNoFormat(form.Email is "")#">
<cfprocparam type="In" cfsqltype="CF_SQL_DECIMAL" value="#form.PhoneExt#"
             null="#YesNoFormat(form.PhoneExt is "")#">
<cfprocparam type="In" cfsqltype="CF_SQL_DECIMAL" value="#form.Salary#"
             null="#YesNoFormat(form.Salary is "")#">

<!--- Assign a query object named InsertRecord to the first result set
      returned --->
<cfprocresult name="InsertRecord" resultset="1">
</cfstoredproc>

<!--- Output status information --->
<cfif cfstoredproc.StatusCode is 1>
  <cfoutput>
  Record inserted successfully.  The employee ID assigned is: #InsertRecord.ID#
  <br>
  The stored procedure executed in #cfstoredproc.ExecutionTime# milliseconds.
  </cfoutput>
<cfelse>
  There was an error inserting the record!
</cfif>
```

In Example 11-25, if the stored procedure returns a `StatusCode` of 1, the record was inserted successfully, and you can output the ID value assigned to the newly inserted record. Returning this value is part of the stored procedure. If it returns any other `StatusCode`, an error occurred. The value of `StatusCode` is set inside of the stored procedure, allowing you to assign any status codes you intend.

Using cfquery

Prior to the introduction of the `cfstoredproc` tag in ColdFusion 4.0, the only way to call a stored procedure from ColdFusion was with the `cfquery` tag. The syntax for calling a stored procedure using `cfquery` is:

```
<cfquery name="MyQuery" datasource="MyDataSource">
  CALL MyDB.dbo.sp_mysp (#var1#, '#Var2#')
</cfquery>
```

There are several drawbacks to using the Call statement with cfquery to call stored procedures. For example, parameters must be passed in the order in which they appear in the stored procedure, and you can't specify input parameters by name or bind parameters to datatypes. There is no way to explicitly pass a NULL, and you can't specify the length for a given parameter. There is also no way to access return codes or output parameters created by the stored procedure, nor can you return multiple result sets.

Depending on your database, you may be able to use a native function to call a stored procedure with the cfquery tag. Several databases allow you to call stored procedures using the EXECUTE or EXEC keyword instead of CALL, as in:

```
<cfquery name="MyQuery" datasource="MyDataSource">
  EXECUTE MyDB.dbo.sp_mysp
   @Var = #var#,
   @Var2 = '#Var2#'
</cfquery>
```

Using a native database function for calling a stored procedure allows you to overcome some of the problems associated with using the CALL method, such as referring to input parameters by name, passing NULLs, and data binding. For example, you can use the cfqueryparam tag with a stored procedure called using cfquery with the EXECUTE statement:

```
<cfquery name="GetCustomer" datasource="dclive">
   EXECUTE MyDB.dbo.sp_mysp
   @cunu=<cfqueryparam value="1" cfsqltype="CF_SQL_INTEGER" maxlength="4">
</cfquery>
```

However, this in and of itself isn't justification for using the cfquery tag to call stored procedures. Unless you are running a version of ColdFusion prior to Version 4.0, you should consider calling your stored procedures using the cfstoredproc tag.

There is one benefit to using the cfquery method over the cfstoredproc tag and that's query caching. The cfstoredproc tag doesn't allow you to cache queries like cfquery does. Depending on your database platform, however, the stored procedure may actually cache the query on the database, making subsequent calls to the procedure execute faster. This is something you might have to weigh when deciding on which method to use. If query caching is extremely important to your application, that may be a compelling enough reason to use cfquery to execute your stored procedures.

Transaction Processing

ColdFusion provides support for database transaction processing using the cftransaction tag. The cftransaction tag lets you treat all query operations with the <cftransaction> and </cftransaction> tags as a single transaction. Changes to the database aren't committed until all queries in the transaction have executed successfully. In the event a query within the transaction fails, all previous queries are automatically rolled back. The exception to this occurs when the database itself is changed, as in the case when a table or column is created or deleted.

The `cftransaction` tag accepts two optional attributes for controlling how transactions are processed, `action` and `isolation`:

`action`
: Specifies the transaction action to take. Valid options include:

  `Begin` *(default)*
  : Specifies the beginning of the block of code to execute

  `Commit`
  : Commits a pending transaction

  `Rollback`
  : Rolls back a pending transaction

`isolation`
: Specifies the ODBC lock type to use for the transaction. The following ODBC lock types are supported: `Read_Uncommitted`, `Read_Committed`, `Repeatable_Read`, and `Serializable`.

Note that not all databases and/or database drivers support isolation levels. Many support only a subset of those listed. Refer to your particular database/driver's documentation for more information on the isolation levels supported.

Example 11-26 shows how to use the `cftransaction` tag with two queries that delete records from different tables within the same data source. You need to use the `cftransaction` tag to ensure that both queries are treated as a single transaction. If either query fails, any changes made are automatically rolled back.

Example 11-26. Simple cftransaction usage

```
<!--- Use the cftransaction tag to ensure that both queries are treated
      as a single transaction.  If either query fails, any changes made
      are automatically rolled back --->
<cftransaction>
  <!--- Delete an employee from the EmployeeDirectory table where the
        employee's ID is equal to the ID value passed in as a form var --->
  <cfquery name="DeleteEmployee" datasource="ProgrammingCF">
    DELETE FROM EmployeeDirectory
    WHERE ID = #form.ID#
  </cfquery>

  <!--- Delete any entries for the employee from the IncentiveAwards table.
        This table is described later in the chapter. --->
  <cfquery name="DeleteBonusRecords" datasource="ProgrammingCF">
    DELETE FROM IncentiveAwards
    WHERE ID = #form.ID#
  </cfquery>
</cftransaction>
```

In Example 11-25, the cftransaction tag ensures that both DELETE queries are treated as a single transaction. If either query fails, any changes made are automatically rolled back. Note that both queries are made to the same data source, but not to the same table.

A particularly useful feature of the cftransaction tag is that it can be nested to allow portions of a transaction to be committed or rolled back within the main cftransaction block as the code executes. The syntax for a nested transaction differs slightly from the syntax used to call most other tags. To commit a transaction within a nested cftransaction tag, use the following syntax:

```
<cftransaction action="Commit" />
```

Note the trailing forward slash at the end of the tag. This lets ColdFusion know you have nested the cftransaction tag and no end tag is necessary. Rolling back a transaction uses similar syntax:

```
<cftransaction action="Rollback" />
```

Using nested cftransaction tags and exception handling with cftry/cfcatch gives you full control over how queries are committed and rolled back within cftransaction blocks. This technique also lets you write to more than one database within a single cftransaction block, if each transaction is committed or rolled back prior to writing a query to the next database. Example 11-27 demonstrates how to use nested cftransaction tags to create a new table populated with data from an existing table (using SELECT INTO) and then add another record to the table.

Example 11-27. Using nested cftransaction tags with multiple queries

```
<!--- Initialize a variable called Continue to control the transaction --->
<cfset Continue = true>

<!--- Begin transaction --->
<cftransaction action="begin">
  <!--- Wrap the INSERT in a cftry block --->
  <cftry>
    <!--- Select the name, title, email, and phone ext for each employee in
          the EmployeeDirectory table that belongs to the Sales department
          and use it to populate a new table called SalesDirectory --->
    <cfquery name="MakeSalesDirectory" datasource="ProgrammingCF">
      SELECT Name, Title, Email, PhoneExt
      INTO SalesDirectory
      FROM EmployeeDirectory
      WHERE Department = 'Sales'
    </cfquery>

    <!--- If a database error occurs, rollback the transaction and set the
          Continue variable to false. --->
    <cfcatch type="Database">
      <cftransaction action="Rollback" />
      <cfset ProblemQuery = "MakeSalesDirectory">
      <cfset Continue = false>
```

Example 11-27. Using nested cftransaction tags with multiple queries (continued)

```
    </cfcatch>
  </cftry>

  <!--- If the INSERT was successful, commit the transaction and execute another
        query to insert a new record into the table we created with the last
        query. --->
  <cfif Continue>
    <cftry>
      <cftransaction action="Commit" />
        <cfquery name="InsertRecord" datasource="ProgrammingCF">
          INSERT INTO SalesDirectory(Name, Title, Email, PhoneExt)
          VALUES('Lynda Newton', 'Account Manager', 'lynda@example.com', 1261)
        </cfquery>

        <!--- If a database error occurs, rollback the transaction and set the
              Continue variable to false. --->
      <cfcatch type="Database">
        <cftransaction action="Rollback" />
        <cfset ProblemQuery = "InsertRecord">
        <cfset Continue = false>
      </cfcatch>
    </cftry>
  </cfif>

  <!--- If the record was successfully added, commit the transaction --->
  <cfif Continue>
    <cftransaction action="Commit" />
  </cfif>
</cftransaction>

<html>
<head>
  <title>Using Nested cftransaction Tags with Multiple Queries</title>
  <style type="text/css">
    th {
      background-color : #888888;
      font-weight : bold;
      text-align : center;
    }
    td {
      background-color : #C0C0C0;
    }
  </style>
</head>
<body>

<!--- If both transactions were successful, generate a table containing all
      of the records from the new table.  If not display a message letting
      the user know there was a problem. --->
<cfif Continue>
  <!--- Retrieve all of the records from the Sales Directory table we just
        created --->
```

Example 11-27. Using nested cftransaction tags with multiple queries (continued)

```
  <cfquery name="GetEmployees" datasource="ProgrammingCF">
    SELECT Name, Title, Email, PhoneExt
    FROM SalesDirectory
    ORDER BY Name
  </cfquery>

  <h2>All queries in the transaction executed successfully</h2>
  <h3>Below is the data from the new table:</h3>
  <table cellpadding="3" cellspacing="0">
    <tr>
      <th>Name</th>
      <th>Title</th>
      <th>E-mail</th>
      <th>Phone Ext.</th>
    </tr>

    <!--- Dynamically generate a table containing all of the records returned
          by the query --->
    <cfoutput query="GetEmployees">
    <tr>
      <td>#Name#</td>
      <td>#Title#</td>
      <td>#Email#</td>
      <td>#PhoneExt#</td>
    </tr>
    </cfoutput>
  </table>
<cfelse>
  <cfoutput>
  <h2>An Error has occurred.  All queries have been rolled back</h2>
  <b>The query that caused the error is: <I>#ProblemQuery#</I>.</b>
  </cfoutput>
</cfif>
</body>
</html>
```

In Example 11-27, the `Continue` variable controls the transaction. At the start of the template, this variable is initialized to `true`. As long as queries within the `cftransaction` block execute successfully, `Continue` keeps the value of `true`. Each subsequent query checks the status of this variable before executing. If at any point `Continue` is `false`, the transaction is rolled back, and no other queries with the `cftransaction` block are executed.

Executing the template in Example 11-27 results in the output shown in Figure 11-10. If you execute the template a second time, however, you should see the error message generated by the template.

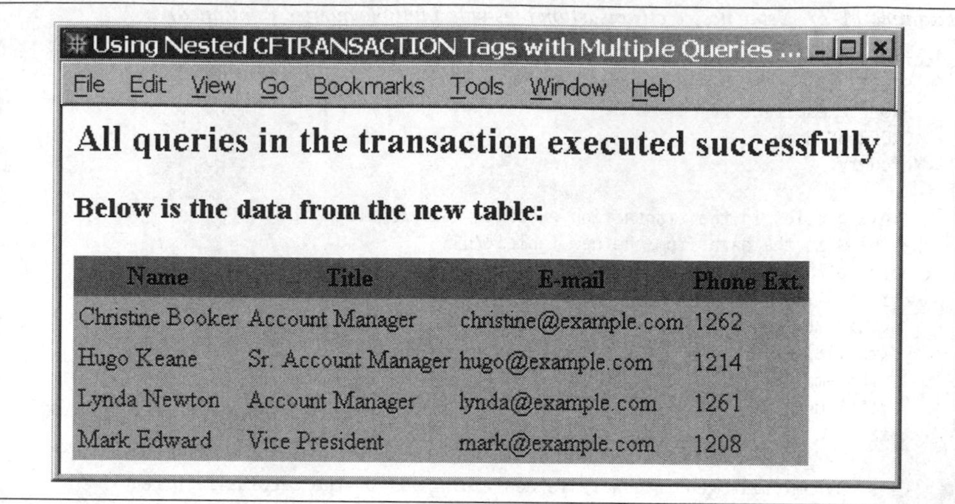

Figure 11-10. Successful completion of queries within a nested cftransaction block

CHAPTER 12

Manipulating Files and Directories

ColdFusion comes with three tags that make it possible to manipulate files and directories on both local and remote servers and an additional tag that can be used to execute command-line programs on a local ColdFusion server. These tags enable you to build sophisticated applications such as document management systems, forms capable of accepting file uploads, FTP clients, and more.

The `cfdirectory` and `cffile` tags allow you to manipulate directories and files on your local ColdFusion server, while the `cfftp` tag makes it possible to conduct file transfers between your ColdFusion server and remote FTP servers. The `cfexecute` tag lets you execute command-line programs. `cffile`, `cfdirectory`, and `cfexecute` present a potential security hazard, as these tags have direct access to the filesystem of the ColdFusion server. Therefore care should be taken with their use and deployment. Depending on the configuration of your web server and operating system, it may also be possible to upload executable code via the `cffile` tag and execute it on your server. The consequences can be potentially devastating to a system as a user could easily upload malicious code to the server and subsequently execute it. Therefore, both tags can be disabled from the ColdFusion administrator, should you decide not to make them available to developers on your server.

Working with Directories

The `cfdirectory` tag lists directory contents and creates, renames, and deletes directories on your ColdFusion application server. In an application such as a document management system, the `cfdirectory` tag allows you to do such tasks as list all the documents stored in a particular folder or build a Windows Explorer–style view of files and folders on your server. Because the `cfdirectory` tag provides direct access to your ColdFusion server's filesystem, it may represent a security concern depending on the nature of your server environment. If you wish, the tag can be disabled from the Sandbox Security section in the ColdFusion Administrator.

Listing Directory Contents

As just noted, the cfdirectory tag lists the contents of any directory on the ColdFusion server. Example 12-1 uses the cfdirectory tag to list the contents of the root directory on the C drive of the ColdFusion server.

Example 12-1. Listing a directory with cfdirectory

```
<cflock name="CLock" type="ReadOnly" timeout="30">
<cfdirectory action="List"
             directory="c:\"
             name="MyQuery"
             filter="*.*"
             sort="Type Asc, Name Asc">
</cflock>

<table border="1">
  <tr>
    <th>Name</th><th>Size</th><th>Type</th><th>Last Modified</th>
    <th>Attributes</th><th>Mode</th>
  </tr>

<cfoutput query="MyQuery">
  <tr>
    <td>#Name#</td><td>#Size#</td><td>#Type#</td><td>#DateLastModified#</td>
    <td>#Attributes#</td><td>#Mode#</td>
  </tr>
</cfoutput>
</table>
```

The first attribute, action, tells ColdFusion what cfdirectory operation to perform. In this case, we want to list the contents of a particular directory on our ColdFusion server. Valid entries for action are List, Create, Rename, and Delete. The directory attribute specifies the full path (including drive letter) to the directory that we want to list the contents of. In this case, we want to list the contents of the root directory on drive C. The name attribute specifies the name assigned to the query object returned by the cfdirectory operation. The filter attribute is optional and allows us to specify a file extension to filter the results returned. Only one file extension can be used with the filter attribute. For our example, we set the filter attribute to *.* so that all files and directories are listed. The final attribute in our example is the sort attribute. sort is an optional attribute that allows us to specify how we want to sort each query column returned by the operation. Note that the sort attribute can take a single query column or a comma-separated list. The actual direction for the sort is specified as Asc for ascending and Desc for descending.

The cflock tag places a read-only lock on the cfdirectory operation. Each individual directory you read from or write to via cfdirectory should have a unique name assigned for it in the cflock tag to keep locking consistent. This means that all read/write operations to the same directory should use the same name.

When the tag executes, a number of query columns are returned as part of the ColdFusion query object specified in the name attribute of the cfdirectory tag:

Attributes
: The attributes, if any, for the given object.

DateLastModified
: The time/date stamp that the object was last modified.

Mode
: This column applies only to the Unix and Linux versions of ColdFusion and specifies the permissions set for the file or directory. The Mode is the same as the permissions set by the Unix *chmod* command.

Name
: The name of the directory or file.

Size
: The size in bytes of the directory or file.

Type
: Dir if the object is a directory or File if it is a file.

Creating a Directory

Creating a directory using the cfdirectory tag is quick and easy to do. The following example shows the syntax for creating a directory on your ColdFusion application server:

```
<cflock name="Lock_Name" type="Exclusive" timeout="30">
  <cfdirectory action="Create"
               directory="d:\MyCreatedDirectory"
               mode="777">
</cflock>
```

Setting the action attribute to Create tells ColdFusion that you want to create a new directory. The directory to be created is referenced in the directory attribute. Note that you must specify the full path to the directory you want to create. The mode attribute is optional and is used only with the Unix and Linux versions of ColdFusion. The mode attribute allows you to set permissions the way you would with the Unix *chmod* command. For example, setting the mode equal to 777 as in our example assigns read, write, and execute permissions to the directory for everyone.

As shown in this example, we use an exclusive cflock so that only one process can access the directory at a time. This ensures that multiple operations don't step on each others' toes, potentially resulting in an error or corrupted directory.

Renaming a Directory

The cfdirectory tag can also rename an existing directory on the ColdFusion server. For example, to change the name of the directory *d:\MyOldDirectoryName* to *d:\MyNewDirectoryName*, use the cfdirectory tag as follows:

```
<cflock name="Lock_Name" type="Exclusive" timeout="30">
  <cfdirectory action="Rename"
               directory="d:\MyOldDirectoryName"
               newdirectory="MyNewDirectoryName">
</cflock>
```

Setting the action attribute to Rename lets ColdFusion know that we want to change the name of the directory specified in the directory attribute. Note that the full path, including the drive letter, is required in the directory attribute. The newdirectory parameter specifies the new name we want to use for the directory being changed. The name for the new directory doesn't require a full path. Again, note the use of cflock to exclusively lock access to the directory while it is renamed.

Deleting a Directory

The cfdirectory tag can also delete directories. The following is an example of a typical delete operation using the cfdirectory tag.

```
<cflock name="Lock_Name" type="Exclusive" timeout="30">
  <cfdirectory action="Delete"
               directory="c:\MyDirectory">
</cflock>
```

Setting the action attribute to Delete lets ColdFusion know we want to use the cfdirectory tag to delete a directory. The actual directory to delete is specified in the directory attribute. In this case, we are using the tag to delete *c:\MyDirectory*. As with the other operations that change the directory structure, we use cflock here.

Before a directory can be deleted, it must be completely empty. If you try to delete a directory that isn't empty, ColdFusion throws an error and halts processing. Therefore, it is a good idea to include code to check if a particular directory is empty before you attempt to delete it. One technique for checking to see if a directory is empty is shown here:

```
<!--- Get a list of the directory contents --->
<cflock name="TestLock" type="ReadOnly" timeout="30">
  <cfdirectory action="List"
               name="MyDirectory"
               directory="D:\test">
</cflock>

<!--- Check the record count for the query object. --->
<cfif MyDirectory.RecordCount is 0>
  <cflock name="TestLock" type="Exclusive" timeout="30">
    <cfdirectory action="Delete"
                 directory="d:\test">
```

```
  </cflock>
    Directory deleted!
  <cfelse>
    The directory wasn't empty!
  </cfif>
```

The first cfdirectory tag gets a list of the contents of *d:\test*. Next, we check to see if the directory list operation returned exactly two objects. This is done by using a cfif statement to evaluate the value stored in the RecordCount query column. If the value of RecordCount is two, we know that the directory is empty, and we use the cfdirectory tag to delete the directory by setting the action attribute to Delete. If any number other than zero is returned for the RecordCount, the directory isn't deleted, and a message is sent back to the user letting them know that the directory wasn't empty.*

Dealing with Files

The cffile tag handles all file manipulation that takes place on the local ColdFusion server. The cffile tag has three purposes. First, it makes it possible to upload files to the ColdFusion server via an HTML form. This means you can design forms that allow users to upload files from their machines directly to your ColdFusion server. This lets you create things such as web-based email clients, document management systems, and other applications that require users to upload files to your server. The second purpose of the cffile tag is to allow you to manipulate files located on your ColdFusion server. The cffile tag allows you to rename, move, copy, and delete files on the ColdFusion server. The final purpose of the cffile tag is to allow you to read, write, and append both text and binary files.

Uploading Files

Enabling file uploads is one of the more popular uses for the cffile tag. To do this, you first have to include a file input type in an HTML form. This allows a user to select a file from their system and post it along with the other form fields. When the form is submitted, the file is posted to the server/template specified in the action attribute of the form tag. The receiving template then uses a cffile tag to process the uploaded file.

You should exercise extreme caution when implementing the cffile tag's Upload action within your ColdFusion applications. Because the tag allows users to upload files directly to your ColdFusion server, you need to make sure that the security of

* In Windows versions of ColdFusion prior to MX, all directories contained two subdirectories representing the current directory and parent directory, (.) and (..) respectively. These two directories were always present in any listing returned by the cfdirectory tag. Because of this, *QueryName*.RecordCount returned 2 for an empty directory.

your server is given the proper attention. Files uploaded via the cffile tag should be written only to directories that aren't accessible via a URL. In addition, execute permissions should be turned off in the directory where files are being uploaded. These two steps help to keep executable files from being uploaded to the server and subsequently run.

Example 12-2 shows how to build a simple two-template application for uploading a file from your machine to your ColdFusion server. The first template consists of an HTML form for choosing the file to be uploaded. It can be saved as a ColdFusion template or a regular HTML file.

Example 12-2. HTML form for uploading a file

```
<html>
<head>
   <title>HTML File Upload Form</title>
</head>

<body>
<form action="Example12-2.cfm" method="POST" enctype="multipart/form-data">
<table>
  <tr>
    <td>File:</td>
    <td><input type="file" name="FileToUpload" size="25" maxlength="255"></td>
  </tr>
  <tr>
    <td colspan="2"><input type="submit" name="Submit" value="Upload"></td>
  </tr>
</table>
</form>

</body>
</html>
```

In Example 12-2, one thing you might notice right away is the use of the enctype attribute in the <form> tag. In order to upload files via HTML forms, it is necessary to specify enctype="multipart/form-data". Another feature unique to file uploads is the use of File as the input type. This input type tells the browser to allow the user to select a file from her system. You should note that not all web browsers support File as an input type. While Netscape browsers have supported file uploading since Version 2.0, Microsoft Internet Explorer didn't begin full support until Version 4.0. Other browsers may or may not support file uploading. There is no programmatic way to determine whether a particular browser supports file uploading. You need to keep this in mind when implementing file uploading in your applications.

Once the user selects a file and clicks on the submit button, the form data is passed to the ColdFusion template specified in the action attribute of the <form> tag. You should be aware that there are limitations on the size of a file that can be uploaded. File size is limited by the amount of physical memory that you have installed on the server running ColdFusion. Although there isn't an exact formula for determining the amount of memory necessary to handle file uploads, it is necessary to have more physical RAM available than the largest file size that you intend to upload. Attempting to upload a file with a file size greater than the available amount of physical RAM results in an error and causes ColdFusion to halt processing of the template.

It is possible to check the file size of a file after it has been uploaded to the web server and before it is permanently written to the filesystem, by checking the CGI environment variable `CGI.content_length`. In a file upload scenario such as ours, the `CGI.content_length` variable contains the length of the file being passed from the form template. By using a `cfif` statement, we can evaluate the length of the file after it has been uploaded to the web server, before it is written to the specified directory by ColdFusion. Because ColdFusion is a server-side language, there is no way to know the size of an uploaded file before it reaches the server. The only way to assess file size on the client machine before an upload is via a signed Java applet or ActiveX control. Another workaround would be to write a filter at the web-server level to filter incoming HTTP uploads based on file size. The technique shown here is still useful, however, as it allows you to limit the size of files accepted by your application. Example 12-3 illustrates the ColdFusion template for processing an uploaded file with code to ensure that no files over 100 KB in size are committed to the server.

Example 12-3. Uploading a file using cffile

```
<!--- Check the CGI environment variable content_length to make sure the file
      being uploaded is less than 100k in size.  If it is not, halt
      processing --->
<cfif Val(CGI.content_length) gt 100000>
The file you are attempting to upload exceeds the maximum allowable size of
100k and cannot be uploaded to this server!  Please choose a smaller file and
try again.
<cfabort>
</cfif>

<!--- Use the cffile tag to upload the file passed from the form to our
      ColdFusion server --->
<cffile action="Upload"
        filefield="FileToUpload"
        destination="c:\temp"
        nameconflict="Overwrite"
        accept="text/html,text/plain"
        attributes="Normal">

<!--- Output the results with cfdump --->
<h2>cffile Upload Results:</h2>

<cfdump var="#cffile#">
```

The first part of Example 12-3 uses a `cfif` statement to compare the number stored in the `CGI.content_length` variable to 100,000. `Val( )` is a ColdFusion function that returns a number that a particular string can be converted to. In this case, Val(CGI.content_length) returns the length in bytes of the file being uploaded via the form in Example 12-2. If the length in bytes is greater than 100,000, we know that the file is over 100 KB and we don't want to save it to our ColdFusion server. A message is written back to the browser letting the user know that the file was too big to upload, and processing of the ColdFusion template is halted before the file can be uploaded. If, however, the value of CGI.content_length is less than or equal to 100,000, the template continues processing uninterrupted.

In the next part of Example 12-3, we use the cffile tag to actually perform the file upload from the client's machine to our ColdFusion server. We set the action attribute in the cffile tag to Upload to begin the operation. In the filefield attribute, we specify the name we gave to the file upload form field from Example 12-2. The destination attribute specifies the full directory path to the location to which we want to store the uploaded file. If the full path is omitted, ColdFusion uses a path relative to the ColdFusion temp directory. To determine the location of this directory, use the getTempDirectory() function. nameconflict is used to specify how ColdFusion should proceed if the file being uploaded has the same name as a file already existing in the destination directory. There are four possible values for the nameconflict attribute:

Error
: Generates a ColdFusion error if the file already exists on the server.

MakeUnique
: Assigns a unique name to the file being uploaded if the file already exists on the server.

Overwrite
: Overwrites the file already on the server with the file being uploaded.

Skip
: Results in the uploaded file not being saved to the server. No error message is returned, however.

The accept attribute specifies a comma-separated list of MIME types the ColdFusion server should be allowed to accept. This attribute is optional and set to allow all MIME types by default. For our example, we set the accept attribute to text/html,text/plain to allow both HTML and plain-text files to be uploaded. MIME type is determined by file extension. The final attribute, attributes, is also optional and is used to specify a single attribute on Windows ColdFusion servers or a comma-separated list of attributes on non-Windows platforms for the file. Valid entries are Hidden, Normal, and ReadOnly. If Normal is specified along with other attributes, they automatically override it. If attributes is omitted, the original attributes of the file are maintained. In previous versions of ColdFusion, three additional values for attributes were supported: Archive, System, and Temporary. These values for attributes are no longer supported in ColdFusion MX.

One thing you'll notice here is that we didn't include a `cflock` tag around the `cffile` operation. In the case of file uploads, it isn't necessary to lock the `cffile` tag, as you aren't reading or writing to a file already on the ColdFusion server. ColdFusion handles the possibility of uploading a file with the same name as a file already on the server with the `nameconflict` attribute of the `cffile` tag.

Once the file has been uploaded to the server, the template in Example 12-3 displays the results of the file upload transaction using the `cfdump` tag to dump the contents of the `cffile` structure, which can be seen in Figure 12-1.

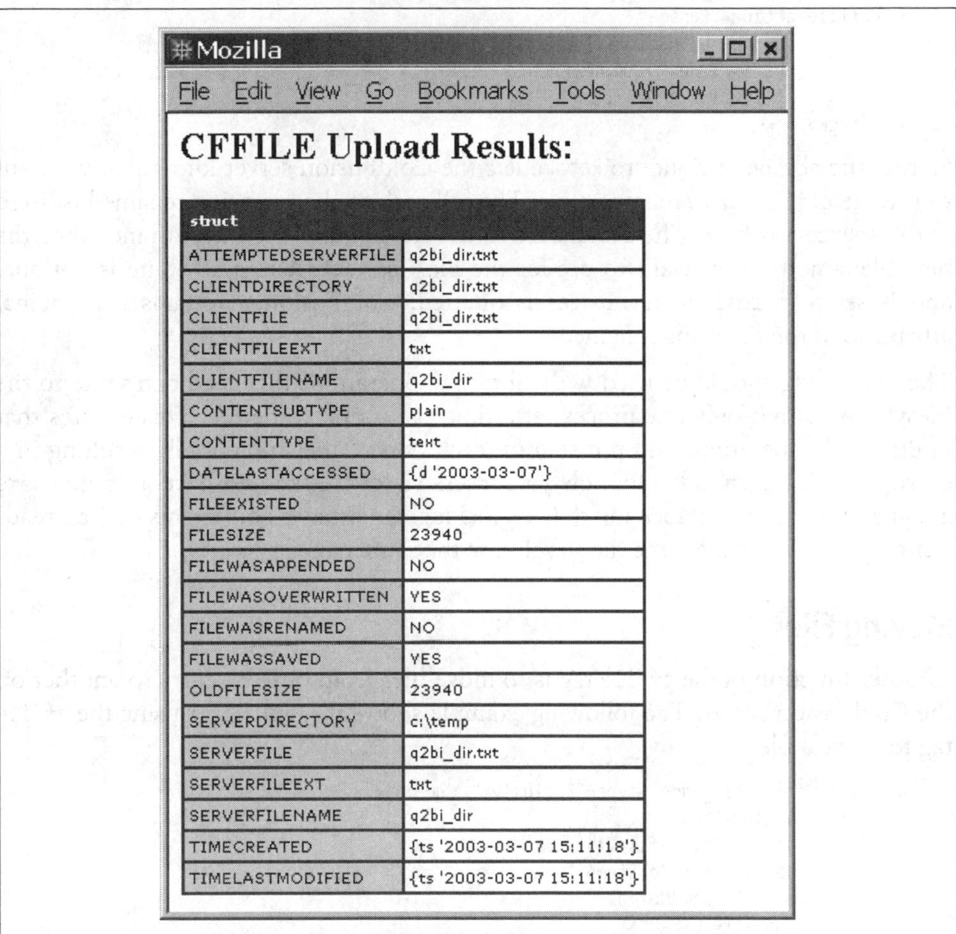

Figure 12-1. Sample output from a cffile upload operation

When the `cffile` tag is executed, a number of ColdFusion variables are created to hold information about the transaction. These variables are read-only and can be referenced using the file scope as in `cffile.VariableName`.* Most of these variables have self-explanatory names, as you can see from Example 12-3 and Figure 12-1. For more information on these variables, see the `cffile` entry in Appendix A.

Renaming Files

The `cffile` tag can also rename files already on the server. The syntax for renaming a file is as follows:

```
<cflock name="Lock_Name" type="Exclusive" timeout="30">
  <cffile action="Rename"
          source="D:\myoldfilename.txt"
          destination="D:\mynewfilename.txt"
          attributes="Normal">
</cflock>
```

Setting the `action` attribute to `Rename` lets the ColdFusion server know that we want to use the `cffile` tag to rename a file. The full path to the file being renamed is listed in the `source` attribute. The `destination` attribute contains the full path including the new filename that we want to use for the file. The `attributes` attribute is optional and is set to `Normal`. If `attributes` is omitted, ColdFusion maintains the original attributes of the file being renamed.

The `cflock` tag should be used with all `cffile` operations that read and write to the filesystem so that only one process at a time can write to the file. This ensures that multiple file operations will not step on each others' toes, potentially resulting in a corrupted file. Each individual file you access via `cffile` should have a unique `name` assigned for it in the `cflock` tag to keep locking consistent. This means that all read/write operations to the same file should use the same name.

Moving Files

Another function of the `cffile` tag is to move files from one directory to another on the ColdFusion server. The following example shows the syntax for using the `cffile` tag to move a file:

```
<cflock name="Lock_Name" type="Exclusive" timeout="30">
  <cffile action="Move"
          source="d:\myfile.txt"
          destination="d:\temp "
          attributes="Normal"
          charset="UTF-8">
</cflock>
```

* Prior to Version 4.5, the file scope was prefixed using the `file` prefix. The `file` prefix was deprecated in ColdFusion 5, and should not be used in ColdFusion MX.

This time, the action attribute is set to Move. The source attribute includes the full path to the current location of the file that we want to move. The destination attribute contains the path to the destination where we want to move the file. In previous versions of ColdFusion, it was necessary to supply a trailing slash on the destination directory. This is not necessary in ColdFusion MX. The attributes attribute is optional and is set to Normal. If attributes is omitted, ColdFusion maintains the original attributes of the file being renamed. The charset attribute is optional and new in ColdFusion MX. It lets you specify a Java character set for the contents of the file and can be used when the action attribute of the cffile tag is set to Move, Read, Write, or Append. The most common character sets are UTF-8 (the default), UTF-16, UTF-16BE, UTF-16LE, US-ASCII, and ISO-8859-1. You may use any character set supported by your JRE. Again, note the use of the cflock tag to exclusively lock access to the file while we move it.

Copying Files

The cffile tag is also capable of copying files from one directory to another. For example, to copy the file *d:\myfile.txt* to *d:\temp\myfile.txt*, you can use the following syntax within your cffile tag:

```
<cflock name="Lock_Name" type="Exclusive" timeout="30">
  <cffile action="Copy"
          source="d:\myfile.txt"
          destination="d:\temp\myfile.txt">
</cflock>
```

In this case, we set the action attribute to Copy. The source attribute specifies the full path to the file we want a copy of. The destination attribute contains the path to the directory where the file will be saved. The filename here is optional. In previous versions of ColdFusion, it was necessary to supply a trailing slash on the destination directory. This is not necessary in ColdFusion MX. attributes is optional and set to Normal for our example. If attributes is omitted, ColdFusion maintains the original attributes of the file being copied.

Deleting Files

The cffile tag can delete a tag from the server by setting the action attribute to Delete and the file attribute to the full path of the file you want to delete. For example, to delete the file *d:\myfile.txt*, use the following cffile statement:

```
<cflock name="Lock_Name" type="Exclusive" timeout="30">
  <cffile action="Delete"
          file="D:\myfile.txt">
</cflock>
```

You should exercise caution when using the cffile tag with the action attribute set to Delete, as the tag has direct access to the entire filesystem of the server. Care should also be taken to secure from unauthorized use all ColdFusion templates that perform delete functions.

Reading Text Files

The `cffile` tag can read the contents of a text file and store the data in a variable that is accessible to ColdFusion. The following example shows how to read and store the contents of a text file called *MyFile.txt* inside a ColdFusion variable called `TheFileContents`. The contents of `TheFileContents` are then output to the screen.

```
<cflock name="Lock_Name" type="ReadOnly" timeout="30">

<cffile action="Read"
        file="D:\temp\MyFile.txt"
        variable="TheFileContents"
        charset="UTF-8">
</cflock>

<cfoutput>
#TheFileContents#
</cfoutput>
```

The `action` attribute is set to `Read` so that ColdFusion knows to use the `cffile` tag to read the contents of a text file. The actual text file we want to read gets specified in the `file` attribute. For this example, we want to read the contents of a file called *MyFile.txt* that is located in *d:\temp*. Setting the `variable` attribute to `TheFileContents` causes ColdFusion to read the contents of *MyFile.txt* and store them in a variable called `TheFileContents`. The `charset` attribute is optional and lets you specify a Java character set for the contents of the file and can be used when the `action` attribute of the `cffile` tag is set to `Move`, `Read`, `Write`, or `Append`. The most common character sets are `UTF-8` (the default), `UTF-16`, `UTF-16BE`, `UTF-16LE`, `US-ASCII`, and `ISO-8859-1`. You may use any character set supported by your JRE. When a text file is read using `cffile`, a check is performed to determine whether the first character is a byte order marker (BOM). If so, ColdFusion uses this to automatically determine the character encoding for the file. If the file contains a BOM and a value is also specified for the `charset` attribute, ColdFusion throws an error. The `cfoutput` section simply writes the contents of `TheFileContents` to the screen. Note the use of the read-only `cflock` to ensure we don't try to read the file at the same moment another process is writing to it.

Reading Binary Files

ColdFusion also can read a binary file and store its contents in a variable that can be manipulated by ColdFusion. In versions of ColdFusion prior to MX, a binary file had to be converted to its Base64 representation before ColdFusion could perform any additional functions on it. Base64 is a method of encoding that takes a binary string and converts the binary data to printable characters. This is useful in situations where you want to store a binary file in a database or send it via email. In ColdFusion MX, however, binary files can now be manipulated directly.

To illustrate the differences, we'll consider two examples. The first reads a binary file and converts the object to a Base64 representation, which is then output to the screen. This technique is useful in all versions of ColdFusion, as Base64-encoded data can easily be stored in a database or emailed:

```
<cflock name="Lock_Name" type="ReadOnly" timeout="30">
  <cffile action="ReadBinary"
          file="d:\cfusionmx\wwwroot\cfide\administrator\images\cfmx.gif"
          variable="MyBinaryFile">
</cflock>
<cfset MyBase64 = ToBase64(MyBinaryFile)>

Base64 encoded binary file:<br>
<form>
<cfoutput>
<textarea cols="50" rows="25" wrap="virtual">#MyBase64#</textarea>
</cfoutput>
</form>
```

The binary file is read by setting the `action` attribute of the `cffile` tag to `ReadBinary`. The `file` attribute specifies the full path to the file to be read. The file object is stored in the ColdFusion variable specified in the `variable` attribute. Once the file has been read into memory by ColdFusion, it is converted to its Base64 representation using the `ToBase64( )` function. The results are then written out to the browser.

Example 12-4 shows how ColdFusion MX can directly manipulate binary data. In this example, we read a GIF image and output some of the metadata stored in the image file, such as its width and height.

Example 12-4. Working directly with binary data

```
<cfscript>
/**
 * Decodes a 2's complement base 10 (decimal) value into an unencoded base 10
 * value.
 *
 * @param num      2's complement you want to convert back to its original decimal
 *  value.. (Required)
 * @param bits     Number of bits in the original decimal value. (Optional)
 * @return Returns a numeric value.
 * @author Stephen Rittler (srittler@exostechnology.com)
 * @version 1, May 31, 2002
 */
function TwosCompToDec(num, bits){
  var isNegative = 0;
  var varBase10 = num;
  var varBase2 = 0;
  var varBase2Rev = "";
  var strLen=0;
```

Example 12-4. Working directly with binary data (continued)

```
  // capture whether or not the input value is negative
  if (varBase10 LT 0) {
    isNegative = 1;
    varBase10 = abs(varBase10);
  }
  // convert to base 2
  varBase2 = NumberFormat(Right(FormatBaseN(varBase10,2), bits),
                RepeatString("0", bits));
  // switch sign bit to 0
  varBase2 = "0" & Right(varBase2, (bits - 1));

  if(isNegative) {
    // if the number was negative, we have to invert the value and add one
    // invert; swap 0 for 1 and 1 for 0
    strLen = len(varBase2);
    for(i=1; i LE bits; i=i+1){
      if(Mid(varBase2, i, 1) eq 0) {
        varBase2Rev = varBase2Rev & 1;
      } else {
        varBase2Rev = varBase2Rev & 0;
      }
    }
    // convert back to base 10
    varBase10 = InputBaseN(varBase2Rev, 2);
    //add 1
    return (varBase10 + 1);
  } else {
    // if number was positive, convert straight back to base 10
    return InputBaseN(varBase2, 2);
  }
}
</cfscript>

<cffile action="ReadBinary"
        file="d:\cfusionmx\wwwroot\cfide\administrator\images\cfmx.gif"
        variable="BinFile">
<cfset Width =  TwosCompToDec((BinFile[7]) + (BinFile[8] * 256), 8)>
<cfset Height = TwosCompToDec((BinFile[9]) + (BinFile[10] * 256), 8)>

<cfoutput>
Width: #Width#<br>
Height: #Height#
</cfoutput>
```

At first glance, this example might seem a bit confusing. For now, ignore the first section of code (the stuff between the `<cfscript>`/`</cfscript>` tags). It's a user-defined function (UDF) called `TwosComplementToDec()`* that's used to manipulate the

* `TwosComplementToDec()` is an open source UDF written by Stephen Rittler (*srittler@exostechnology.com*) and available from *http://www.cflib.org*, the largest site for open source ColdFusion UDFs.

binary data read in by the `cffile` tag. Both CFScript and UDFs are advanced topics covered later on in Chapters 19 and 20. If you would like to read up on them, feel free. However, you should be able to understand what's going on in this example even without much knowledge of either.

The first thing the code does after declaring the UDF is use the `cffile` tag to read in a GIF image that's automatically installed as part of the ColdFusion MX server installation. In ColdFusion MX, a binary file is stored as a byte array that can be manipulated with any of the standard ColdFusion array functions. You should remember from Chapter 6 that unlike other languages such as Java, the first index position in a ColdFusion array is 1 instead of 0.

Once we have the file read in, we can calculate the width and height of the GIF using the values stored in the seventh, eighth, ninth, and tenth elements of the byte array. Why is that? you may be wondering. Simple. The GIF specification, available at *http://www.w3.org/Graphics/GIF/spec-gif89a.txt* among other places, states that certain information about the graphic file, such as width and height, must be stored in certain bit positions within the binary file. A simple calculation can then be used to convert the values stored in these positions within the byte array back to their original decimal (base 10) values. These values are calculated by calling the `TwosComplementToDec( )` function we declared at the beginning of the template. This function accepts two parameters: a two's complement that you want to convert back to its original decimal value and the number of bits in the original value. This conversion is necessary because of the way binary data is stored. You can read more about two's complement at a number of web sites, including *http://mathforum.org/library/drmath/view/54344.html*. Once the calculations have been performed, the height and width of the GIF image are output to the browser.

Writing Text Files

In addition to reading files, the `cffile` tag can also write files to the server. This is useful for a number of purposes, including writing log files for your applications and creating static HTML files from dynamic content. Example 12-5 shows how to create a static HTML file from the results of a `cfhttp` operation that returns the contents of a dynamically generated page.

Example 12-5. Writing a text file with cffile

```
<!--- Execute the remote cfm file via cfhttp --->
<cfhttp method="GET"
      URL="http://www.example.com/dir/file.cfm">
</cfhttp>

<!--- Write the output of the cfhttp operation to a static html file on
      the server --->
<cflock name="MyFileLock" type="Exclusive" timeout="30">
  <cffile action="write"
```

Example 12-5. Writing a text file with cffile (continued)

```
        file="d:\inetpub\wwwroot\myfile.htm"
        output="#cfhttp.FileContent#"
        attributes="Normal"
        mode="777"
        addnewline="Yes"
        charset="UTF-8">
</cflock>
```

The `cfhttp` operation executes a ColdFusion template called *file.cfm* and stores the resulting page in the `cfhttp.FileContent` variable. `cfhttp.FileContent` is automatically created by the `cfhttp` operation. This is all you need to understand about `cfhttp` for now; we'll cover this tag in more detail in Chapter 14.

The `cffile` tag then creates a text file by setting the `action` attribute to `Write`. The `file` attribute contains the filename and directory where we want to write our new text file. In this case, we are creating a text file called *myfile.htm*. The actual content to be written to the file is specified in the `output` attribute. Because we want to create a static web page from the results of the ColdFusion template we accessed with `cfhttp`, we assign `#cfhttp.FileContent#` to the `output` attribute. It is important to include the pound signs around the `cfhttp.FileContent` variable so that ColdFusion knows to treat it as a variable as opposed to literal text.

`attributes` is optional and can specify a single attribute on Windows ColdFusion servers, or a comma-delimited list of attributes on non-Windows platforms, for the newly created text file. In this case, we are making the file a `Normal` file. The `mode` attribute can define file permissions on a Unix or Linux server. In this example, the `mode` attribute is set to `777`, so that everyone has read, write, and execute permissions for the file. Setting `addnewline` to `Yes` causes ColdFusion to add a trailing newline character to the end of the `output` string. `addnewline` is an optional attribute and is set to `Yes` by default. The `charset` attribute is optional and lets you specify a Java character set for the contents of the file and can be used when the `action` attribute of the `cffile` tag is set to `Move`, `Read`, `Write`, or `Append`. The most common character sets are `UTF-8` (the default), `UTF-16`, `UTF-16BE`, `UTF-16LE`, `US-ASCII`, and `ISO-8859-1`. You may use any character set supported by your JRE.

Writing Binary Files

The `cffile` tag can also write binary files to the server. There is only one difference between writing a text file to the server and writing a binary file. The contents making up a binary file must be converted to a binary object in order to be written as a binary file. Example 12-6 illustrates the point by creating a GIF image of the letter "R" from its Base64 equivalent.

Example 12-6. Writing a binary file with cffile

```
<cfset MyBase64="R0lGODlhGQAZAPcAAP////v7+/Pz8+7u7uLi4t3d3dnZ2dXV1cTExLe3t6qqqp6e
npGRkYmJiYiIiH9/f3t7e25ubmZmZllZWVZWVlFRUURERDw8PDQ0NC8vLyIiIhUVFREREQwMDAQEBAAAA
AAAAAAAAAAAAAAAAAAAAAAAAAAAAAAAAAAAAAAAAAAAAAAAAAAAAAAAAAAAAAAAAAAAAAAAAAAAAAAAAA
AAAAAAAAAAAAAAAAAAAAAAAAAAAAAAAAAAAAAAAAAAAAAAAAAAAAAAAAAAAAAAAAAAAAAAAAAAAAAAAAA
AAAAAAAAAAAAAAAAAAAAAAAAAAAAAAAAAAAAAAAAAAAAAAAAAAAAAAAAAAAAAAAAAAAAAAAAAAAAAAAAA
AAAAAAAAAAAAAAAAAAAAAAAAAAAAAAAAAAAAAAAAAAAAAAAAAAAAAAAAAAAAAAAAAAAAAAAAAAAAAAAAA
AAAAAAAAAAAAAAAAAAAAAAAAAAAAAAAAAAAAAAAAAAAAAAAAAAAAAAAAAAAAAAAAAAAAAAAAAAAAAAAAA
AAAAAAAAAAAAAAAAAAAAAAAAAAAAAAAAAAAAAAAAAAAAAAAAAAAAAAAAAAAAAAAAAAAAAAAAAAAAAAAAA
AAAAAAAAAAAAAAAAAAAAAAAAAAAAAAAAAAAAAAAAAAAAAAAAAAAAAAAAAAAAAAAAAAAAAAAAAAAAAAAAA
AAAAAAAAAAAAAAAAAAAAAAAAAAAAAAAAAAAAAAAAAAAAAAAAAAAAAAAAAAAAAAAAAAAAAAAAAAAAAAAAA
AAAAAAAAAAAAAAAAAAAAAAAAAAAAAAAAAAAAAAAAAAAAAAAAAAAAAAAAAAAAAAAAAAAAAAAAAAAAAAAAA
AAAAAAAAAAAAAAAAAAAAAAAAAAAAAAAAAAAAAAAAAAAAAAAAAAAAAAAAAAAAAAAAAAAAAAAAAAAAAAAAA
AAAAAAAAAAAAAAAAAAAAAAAAAAAAAAAAAAAAAAAAAAAAAAAAAAAAAAAAAAAAAAAAAAAAAAAAAAAAAAAAA
AAAAACwAAAAAGQAZAEcIiwABCBxIsKDBgwQffPigAIHDBh4+YEBoUOGHAgMlLHRAsaPHjyApWlxI8sMEA
SFTqlwpkIGGlzAxUECQ0iLGgRc+cAhpE4CBDR86HKi58KbABQsrsFzKtKlTkCNLfvCQgGdRghUWWvOQ4c
EDCBYWRthaoQKHoFWJXhSYYGGGAFuNDgDagcDTu3gpBgQAOw=="">

<cfset MyBinary=ToBinary(MyBase64)>

<cflock name="MyBinaryLock" type="Exclusive" timeout="30">
  <cffile action="write"
          file="c:\temp\mybinary.gif"
          output=#MyBinary#>
</cflock>

<cflock name="MyBinaryLock" type="Exclusive" timeout="30">
  <cfcontent type="image/gif"
             file="c:\temp\mybinary.gif"
             deletefile="Yes">
</cflock>
```

The first section of this example sets a variable called `MyBase64` to the Base64 representation of a binary object (in this case, a GIF image of the letter "R"). This information could have been pulled from a database or read directly from a file. The second section of the example converts the Base64 string to a binary object using the `ToBinary()` function. Once that is done, the binary object is written out to a file using the `cffile` tag with the `output` attribute set to the value of the binary object we created. Finally, the `cfcontent` tag takes the file specified in the `file` attribute and sends it to the browser using the MIME type specified in the type attribute. Setting `deletefile` to `Yes` tells ColdFusion to delete the GIF file from the server once it has been sent to the browser. Note that a `cflock` tag is placed around the `cfcontent` tag. This is done because in this particular case, the `cfcontent` tag deletes the file it grabs after sending it to the browser.

Appending Text Files

Data can be appended to the end of an existing text file by setting the action attribute of the cffile tag to Append. The following example shows how to use the cffile tag to append additional information to a file called *MyFile.txt*:

```
<cfset MyString="This is the line to be added!">

<cflock name=" Lock_Name" type="Exclusive" timeout="30">
  <cffile action="Append"
          file="d:\temp\MyFile.txt"
          output="#MyString#"
          addnewline="Yes"
          charset="UTF-8">
</cflock>
```

The file attribute specifies the file we want to append additional information to. We use the output attribute to specify the data that we want to append to the end of the text file. The output attribute can contain text or a previously defined ColdFusion variable. In our example, we use a ColdFusion variable that has been previously defined with a cfset statement. Note the use of pound signs around the ColdFusion variable name; they are necessary in this case, to differentiate between a variable and literal text. To finish the operation off, we use the optional addnewline attribute. Setting addnewline to Yes causes ColdFusion to add a trailing new line character to the end of the output string. The charset attribute is optional and lets you specify a Java character set for the contents of the file and can be used when the action attribute of the cffile tag is set to Move, Read, Write, or Append. The most common character sets are UTF-8 (the default), UTF-16, UTF-16BE, UTF-16LE, US-ASCII, and ISO-8859-1. You may use any character set supported by your JRE.

Performing FTP Operations

As we've already discussed, the cffile tag allows you to upload files from a client machine to the ColdFusion server and perform file and directory operations on your ColdFusion server. When you need to work with files and directories on a remote server, however, you need to use the cfftp tag instead.

Connecting to a Remote Server

FTP operations using the cfftp tag begin by opening a connection to the remote FTP server. The following example shows how to connect to an anonymous FTP server using the cfftp tag:

```
<cfftp action="Open"
       server="ftp.microsoft.com"
       port="21"
       username="anonymous"
       password="YourEmailAddress@yourdomain.com"
```

```
         connection="MyConnection"
         proxyserver="MyProxyServer"
         proxybypass="127.0.0.1"
         retrycount="3"
         timeout="60"
         stoponerror="No"
         passive="No">
```

To open the connection to the remote FTP server, we set the `action` parameter of the `cfftp` tag to `Open`. There are several additional parameters available for the `action` attribute that will be discussed later in this section. The `server` attribute specifies the hostname or IP address of the remote server with which to open an FTP session. In this case, we want to connect to Microsoft's public FTP server at *ftp.microsoft.com*. The `port` attribute specifies what port the `cfftp` tag should try to connect to. This attribute is optional and defaults to the standard FTP port 21. Because Microsoft allows anonymous access to their FTP server, we set the `username` attribute to `Anonymous`. As a matter of convention and netiquette, your email address should be entered in the `password` attribute for anonymous FTP connections. We could just as easily connect to a non-anonymous FTP site by specifying an actual username and password in the `username` and `password` attributes, respectively.

The `connection` attribute is optional and set to `MyConnection`. `connection` is used to let the ColdFusion server know that the FTP connection should be cached so that we can perform batch operations without having to reestablish a new connection for each task. `agentname` is an optional attribute that allows us to declare a name for the application or entity making the FTP connection.* The `proxyserver` attribute is also optional and allows us to list the IP address or hostname of a proxy server if it is required. If this attribute is `NULL`, ColdFusion attempts to obtain proxy server information from the registry. `proxybypass` is another optional attribute and provides a list of IP addresses or hostnames that don't need to be routed through the proxy server. If the `proxybypass` attribute is `NULL`, ColdFusion attempts to obtain the proxy bypass list from the registry.

The next several attributes deal with how ColdFusion should behave if there is trouble connecting to the remote server. The `retrycount` is an optional attribute that determines the number of times the FTP operation should be attempted before an error is reported. The default number of retries is 1. The `timeout` attribute is also an optional attribute and defaults to 30 seconds. It determines the length in seconds that an operation has to execute before the request is timed out. The `stoponerror` attribute is optional and set to `No` (the default) so that the application continues to process in the event an error in the FTP operation occurs. If you set the `stoponerror` attribute to `Yes`, ColdFusion throws an error and ceases processing if an FTP opera-

* `agentname` was an attribute of the `cfftp` tag since ColdFusion 3, but was ignored in ColdFusion 5, and is no longer supported in ColdFusion MX.

tion fails. The final attribute, `passive`, specifies whether ColdFusion should initiate a passive transfer with the remote FTP server. This is an optional attribute and set to `No` by default.

If you plan to utilize the same FTP connection across multiple ColdFusion templates, you should store the connection caching information in a session variable. To do this, all you need to do is modify the `connection` attribute in your `cfftp` statement to reflect the assignment to the session variable. It is also necessary to make sure that session management is enabled for your application. Here's how we can modify our previous example to accomplish this within the context of a session:

```
<cflock scope="Session" type="Exclusive" timeout="60" throwontimeout="Yes">
<cfftp action="open"
       server="ftp.microsoft.com"
       username="anonymous"
       password="YourEmailAddress@yourdomain.com"
       connection="Session.MyConnection"
       stoponerror="No">
</cflock>
```

By establishing the cached connection as a session variable, it is possible to maintain the FTP connection across multiple ColdFusion templates. The use of `cflock` around the `cfftp` tag is necessary when reading and writing session variables, to ensure the integrity of the session. Setting the `type` attribute to `Exclusive` ensures single-threaded access when writing the session variable.

Automatically Opening a Connection

If you are only planning to perform a single FTP action, such as obtaining a directory list or downloading a file, you can combine the steps into a single `cfftp` call in which opening and closing the connection are handled automatically. For example, this code opens a connection, gets a list of all files/directories in the root directory of a remote server, then closes the connection:

```
<cfftp action="ListDir"
       server="ftp.microsoft.com"
       username="anonymous"
       password="YourEmailAddress@yourdomain.com"
       stoponerror="No"
       name="ListFiles"
       directory="/">
```

Here, instead of setting `action` to `Open`, we simply provide the action we want to perform. In this case, we want to obtain a list of all files and directories in the root folder of Microsoft's web site, so we set `action` to `ListDir`. ColdFusion knows that in order to obtain the directory list it must open an FTP connection to the server, so it does so automatically. After the directory list is obtained, the connection is automatically closed.

Closing the Connection

Before we can talk about doing anything interesting with an FTP connection, I want to discuss how you close a connection. When you are finished with all your `cfftp` operations for a cached connection, it is a good idea to close the FTP connection. You can do this by setting the `action` attribute of the `cfftp` tag to `Close`. Failing to explicitly close a cached FTP connection causes the connection to remain open until the connection times out. Depending on the server your `cfftp` operation connects to, this can take quite a while. It isn't necessary to close noncached FTP operations as the connection is automatically dropped after each operation. The following example shows how to close a cached FTP connection:

```
<cflock scope="Session" type="ReadOnly" timeout="60" throwontimeout="Yes">
<cfftp action="Close"
       connection="Session.MyConnection"
       stoponerror="Yes">
</cflock>
```

Once again, the `cfftp` operation is wrapped within a `cflock` tag to ensure exclusive reading of the session variable used to cache the FTP connection. In this case, the `type` attribute of the `cflock` tag is set to `ReadOnly`, so that more than one request can access the locked code at a time.

Setting the `action` to `Close` tells ColdFusion to close the FTP connection. The `connection` attribute specifies the exact connection we want to close. In this case, we are closing the connection from our previous example, so we use `Session.MyConnection` as the parameter. Finally, we set `stoponerror` to `Yes`. Setting this attribute to `Yes` causes ColdFusion to throw an error and halt processing in the event that an error occurs while closing the connection.

Performing File and Directory Operations

Now that we know how to open and close FTP sessions with the `cfftp` tag, it is time to move on to file and directory operations. Once a connection to a remote FTP server has been made, the `cfftp` tag can perform a variety of file and directory operations on the remote server. In the previous example, we opened a cached FTP session called `Session.MyConnection` by setting the `action` attribute to `Open`. To perform directory and file operations, all we need to do is change the value of the `action` attribute to reflect the operation we want the `cfftp` tag to perform. The following list describes the `action` parameters you have available for working with remote files and directories using the `cfftp` tag:

`ChangeDir`
: Changes the directory the `cfftp` tag has access to on the remote FTP server. Requires that you specify the directory in the `directory` attribute.

`CreateDir`
: Creates a new directory on the remote server. The `CreateDir` parameter requires the use of the `directory` attribute.

`Exists`
: Returns `Yes` if the value specified in the `item` attribute exists or `No` if it doesn't. The value for the `item` attribute can be any file, directory, or object.

`ExistsDir`
: Returns `Yes` if the value specified in the `directory` attribute exists or `No` if it doesn't.

`ExistsFile`
: Returns `Yes` if the value specified in the `remotefile` attribute exists or `No` if it doesn't.

`GetCurrentDir`
: Returns the current directory being accessed by the `cfftp` tag.

`GetCurrentURL`
: Returns the URL to the current location being accessed by the `cfftp` tag.

`GetFile`
: Gets a file from the remote server and downloads it to the ColdFusion server. Using this `action` requires that you also specify values for the `remotefile` and `localfile` attributes.

`ListDir`
: Lists the directories specified in the `name` and `directory` attributes.

`PutFile`
: Takes a file from the ColdFusion server and uploads it to the remote FTP server. Using this `action` requires that you also specify values for the `localfile` and `remotefile` attributes.

`Remove`
: Deletes a file on the remote FTP server. Using this `action` requires that you also specify values for the `server` and `item` attributes.

`Removedir`
: Deletes a directory on the remote FTP server. Using this `action` requires that you also specify a value for the `directory` attribute.

`Rename`
: Renames a file on the remote FTP server. Using this `action` requires that you also specify values for the `existing` and `new` attributes.

Obtaining a directory listing

Example 12-7 uses everything we have learned so far about the `cfftp` tag to open a connection to a remote FTP server, cache the connection, obtain a directory listing, and close the connection. Before you execute Example 12-7, make sure you have an

Application.cfm template that enables session management in the directory in which you saved the example template.

Example 12-7. Obtaining a file and directory listing from a remote FTP server

```
<!--- Open the FTP connection --->
<cflock scope="Session" type="Exclusive" timeout="60" throwontimeout="Yes">
  <cfftp action="Open"
         server="ftp.microsoft.com"
         username="anonymous"
         password="YourEmailAddress@yourdomain.com"
         connection="Session.MyConnection"
         stoponerror="No">
</cflock>

<!--- If there is an error, display it to the user and stop processing the
     template  --->
<cfif not cfftp.Succeeded>
  Connection aborted!<br>
  <cfoutput>
  Error number #cfftp.ErrorCode#: #cfftp.ErrorText#
  </cfoutput>
  <cfabort>
</cfif>

Connection opened successfully!<br>

<!--- Get a list of the files and directories in the current directory --->
<cflock scope="Session" type="ReadOnly" timeout="60" throwontimeout="Yes">
  <cfftp action="ListDir"
         stoponerror="No"
         name="ListFiles"
         directory="/"
         connection="Session.MyConnection">
</cflock>

<!--- If there is an error, display it to the user and stop processing --->
<cfif not cfftp.Succeeded>
  Connection aborted!<br>
  <cfoutput>
  Error number #cfftp.ErrorCode#: #cfftp.ErrorText#
  </cfoutput>
  <cfabort>
</cfif>

<!--- Close the ftp connection --->
<cflock scope="Session" type="ReadOnly" timeout="60" throwontimeout="Yes">
  <cfftp action="Close"
         connection="Session.MyConnection"
         stoponerror="No">
</cflock>

<!--- If there is an error, display it to the user and stop processing --->
```

Example 12-7. Obtaining a file and directory listing from a remote FTP server (continued)

```
<cfif not cfftp.Succeeded>
  Connection aborted!<br>
  <cfoutput>
  Error number #cfftp.ErrorCode#: #cfftp.ErrorText#
  </cfoutput>
  <cfabort>
<cfelse>
   Connection closed successfully!<br>
</cfif>

<style type="text/css">
  th {
    background-color : #0000FF;
    font-weight : bold;
    color : #FFFFFF;
    text-align : center;
  }
  td {
    background-color : #C0C0C0;
  }

</style>

<!--- Build a table of the directory contents --->
<p>
<h3>Directories and files at ftp.microsoft.com</h3>
<p>
<table border="0" cellspacing="1" cellpadding="3">
  <tr>
    <th>Name</th>
    <th>Path</th>
    <th>URL</th>
    <th>Length</th>
    <th>Last Modified</th>
    <th>Directory or File</th>
    <th>Attributes</th>
    <th>Mode</th>
  </tr>
<cfoutput query="ListFiles">
  <tr>
    <td>#name#</td>
    <td>#path#</td>
    <td>#url#</td>
    <td>#length#</td>
    <td>#DateFormat(lastmodified,'mm/dd/yyyy')#</td>
    <td><cfif IsDirectory>Directory<cfelse>File</cfif></td>
    <td>#Attributes#</td>
    <td>#Mode#</td>
  </tr>
</cfoutput>
</table>
```

Example 12-7 begins by opening the connection to the anonymous FTP server at *ftp.microsoft.com* and caching the connection in a session variable called `session.MyConnection`. This code follows the guidelines that were used in our previous example on opening a connection. Once the attempt to open the FTP connection has been made, we check to see if the connection was successful by checking for the existence of a special variable called `cfftp.Succeeded`. `cfftp.Succeeded` is automatically created each time a `cfftp` action is performed; it contains `true` if the operation was successful. In our case, if the FTP session is opened successfully, we allow the application to continue processing. If, however, the FTP session isn't opened successfully, an error is generated and reported back to the user in the variables `cfftp.ErrorCode` and `cfftp.ErrorText`, and processing is aborted with a `cfabort` tag. The values for `cfftp.ErrorCode` and `cfftp.ErrorText` are listed under the `cfftp` tag in Appendix A.

Now Example 12-7 uses the `cfftp` tag to get a list of the files and directories from *ftp.microsoft.com*. This is done by setting the `action` attribute to `ListDir`. Because we are using connection caching, there is no need to respecify the `server`, `username`, or `password` attributes. We set the `stoponerror` attribute to `No` so that processing of the template continues in the event an error occurs. The `name` attribute is required when the `action` attribute is set to `ListDir` and specifies a name for the ColdFusion query object created by the `ListDir action`. Another attribute that is required for `ListDir` operations is the `directory` attribute. The `directory` attribute specifies the directory from which to obtain the file and directory listing. In our case, we set the `directory` attribute to `/` to obtain a listing for the root directory at *ftp.microsoft.com*. The final attribute, `connection` is set to `MyConnection` and specifies the name of the cached connection to use for the action.

Next comes another bit of error-checking code that is identical to the code we used earlier. It is important to build in error checking like this since we set the `stoponerror` attribute to `No` to allow ColdFusion to continue processing our template in the event of an error. If the FTP operation fails for any reason, the error-checking code gives us a way to handle the error gracefully.

Now we build an HTML table that contains a list of the files and directories found in the directory specified in the `directory` attribute of the `cfftp` tag. Each row of the table is dynamically populated with information from the ColdFusion query object created by the `cfftp` operation. Query objects created by the `cfftp` tag contain the following query columns:

`Attributes`
: Returns the attributes, if any, for the given object.

`IsDirectory`
: Returns `true` if the object is a directory, `false` if it isn't.

`LastModified`
: Date that the file or directory was last modified.

`Length`
: Length in bytes of the file or directory.

`Mode`
: This column applies only to the Unix and Linux versions of ColdFusion and specifies the permissions set for the file or directory. The `Mode` is the same as the permissions set by the Unix *chmod* command.

`Name`
: The name of the file or directory.

`Path`
: Path without drive-letter designation to the file or directory.

`URL`
: URL to the file or directory.

Example 12-7 uses a `cfif` statement to evaluate the contents of the variable `IsDirectory` (note that `IsDirectory` is a variable and not a function) for each row returned by the query. If `IsDirectory` evaluates to `true`, we know the object is a directory and list it as such. If `IsDirectory` evaluates to `false`, the object is a file and is listed that way instead. Figure 12-2 shows the directory listing from Microsoft's FTP site as returned by Example 12-7.

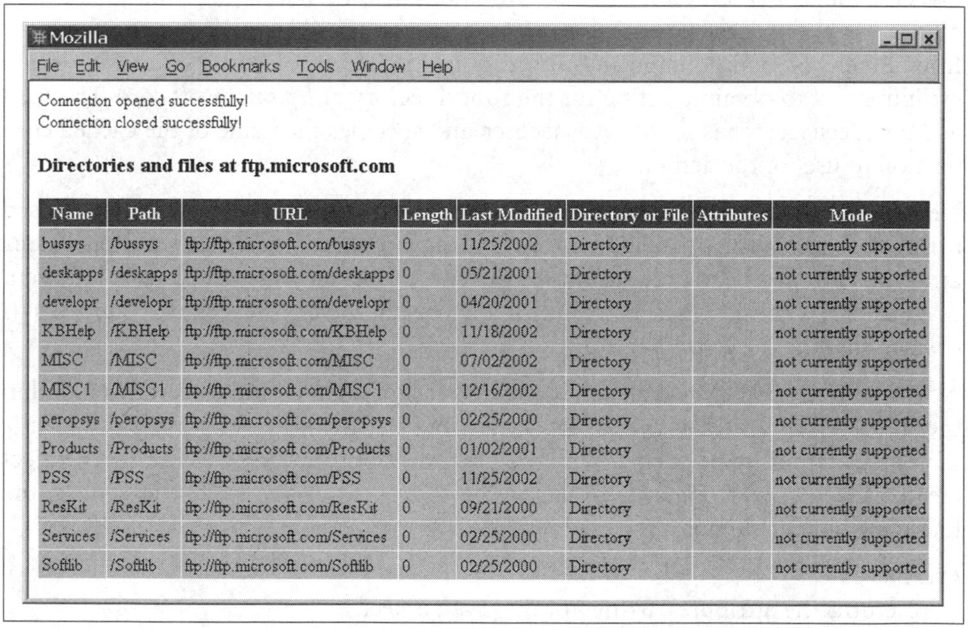

Mozilla

File Edit View Go Bookmarks Tools Window Help

Connection opened successfully!
Connection closed successfully!

Directories and files at ftp.microsoft.com

Name	Path	URL	Length	Last Modified	Directory or File	Attributes	Mode
bussys	/bussys	ftp://ftp.microsoft.com/bussys	0	11/25/2002	Directory		not currently supported
deskapps	/deskapps	ftp://ftp.microsoft.com/deskapps	0	05/21/2001	Directory		not currently supported
developr	/developr	ftp://ftp.microsoft.com/developr	0	04/20/2001	Directory		not currently supported
KBHelp	/KBHelp	ftp://ftp.microsoft.com/KBHelp	0	11/18/2002	Directory		not currently supported
MISC	/MISC	ftp://ftp.microsoft.com/MISC	0	07/02/2002	Directory		not currently supported
MISC1	/MISC1	ftp://ftp.microsoft.com/MISC1	0	12/16/2002	Directory		not currently supported
peropsys	/peropsys	ftp://ftp.microsoft.com/peropsys	0	02/25/2000	Directory		not currently supported
Products	/Products	ftp://ftp.microsoft.com/Products	0	01/02/2001	Directory		not currently supported
PSS	/PSS	ftp://ftp.microsoft.com/PSS	0	11/25/2002	Directory		not currently supported
ResKit	/ResKit	ftp://ftp.microsoft.com/ResKit	0	09/21/2000	Directory		not currently supported
Services	/Services	ftp://ftp.microsoft.com/Services	0	02/25/2000	Directory		not currently supported
Softlib	/Softlib	ftp://ftp.microsoft.com/Softlib	0	02/25/2000	Directory		not currently supported

Figure 12-2. Directory listing from ftp.microsoft.com using cfftp tag

The rest of the code in Example 12-7 closes our cached FTP connection the same way we did in our earlier example on closing connections. As with our other FTP operations, we also perform some error checking after closing the connection.

Uploading files

Example 12-8 shows how to upload a file to a remote FTP server using the `cfftp` tag. For this example to work, it is necessary to have access to an FTP server that is capable of accepting file uploads. Although the example uses 127.0.0.1 (the local host) as the FTP server, you can change this attribute to any FTP server you have write access to.

Example 12-8. Uploading a file to a remote server with cfftp

```
<!--- Open the FTP connection --->
<cflock scope="Session" type="Exclusive" timeout="60" throwontimeout="Yes">

<cfftp action="Open"
       username="myusername"
       connection="MyConnection"
       password="mypassword"
       server="127.0.0.1"
       stoponerror="Yes">
</cflock>

<p><b>Connection opened</b>

<!--- Take the file from the ColdFusion server and upload it via FTP to the
      remote machine.  put the file in a directory off the root directory
      called incoming. --->
<cflock scope="Session" type="ReadOnly" timeout="60" throwontimeout="Yes">
<cfftp action="PutFile"
       transfermode="Auto"
       stoponerror="No"
       localfile="d:\temp\myfile.txt"
       remotefile="\incoming\myfile.txt"
       connection="MyConnection">
</cflock>

<p>
<cfif cfftp.Succeeded>
   <b>File successfully uploaded!</b>
<cfelse>
    <b>The following error occurred while attempting to upload your file:</b><br>
    <cfoutput>
    <b><i>Error number #cfftp.ErrorCode#: #cfftp.ErrorText#</i></b>
    </cfoutput>
</cfif>

<!--- Close the ftp connection --->
<cflock scope="Session" type="ReadOnly" timeout="60" throwontimeout="Yes">
```

Example 12-8. Uploading a file to a remote server with cfftp (continued)

```
<cfftp action="Close"
       connection="MyConnection"
       stoponerror="Yes">
</cflock>

<p><b>Connection closed</b>
```

As you would expect, this example uses a `cfftp` tag to open an FTP session and caches the connection as `MyConnection`. Once the connection is opened, we use another `cfftp` tag to carry out the file upload from the ColdFusion server to the FTP server. This is done by setting the `action` attribute of the `cfftp` tag to `PutFile`. `transfermode` specifies the FTP transfer mode to use when retrieving the file from the FTP server. Valid options are `Text`, `Binary`, and `Auto`. In this case, we set `transfermode` to `Auto`. `stoponerror` is set to `No` so that ColdFusion continues to process the template in the event an error occurs.

`localfile` is a required attribute for a `PutFile` operation and specifies the file on the local ColdFusion server we want to upload to our FTP server. The full path to the file on the ColdFusion server should be used. In this case, the file we want to upload gets referenced as *d:\temp\myfile.txt*. The next attribute, `remotefile` is also a required attribute for a `PutFile` operation and determines the location to save the uploaded file on the remote FTP server. Setting the `remotefile` attribute to *\incoming\myfile.txt* results in ColdFusion uploading the file and saving it as *myfile.txt* in *\incoming* on the FTP server. The `connection` attribute is set to `MyConnection`, the cached connection we defined at the beginning of the code.

After the `cfftp` upload completes, a `cfif` tag evaluates the status of the transaction. If it is successful, a message is written to the browser informing the user. If the upload isn't successful, an error code and error message are written back to the browser. Finally, another `cfftp` tag closes the cached FTP connection.

Downloading files

The `cfftp` tag can also download files from remote servers to your ColdFusion server. Example 12-9 uses the `cfftp` tag to download a file called *disclaimer.txt* from Microsoft's anonymous FTP server. This is a powerful feature in that it allows your ColdFusion applications to download data files from remote FTP servers that would otherwise require a manual download using a standard FTP client.

Example 12-9. Downloading a file from a remote server with cfftp

```
<!--- Open the FTP connection --->
<cflock scope="Session" type="Exclusive" timeout="60" throwontimeout="Yes">

<cfftp action="Open"
       username="anonymous"
       connection="MyConnection"
```

Example 12-9. Downloading a file from a remote server with cfftp (continued)

```
        password="username@domain.com"
        server="ftp.microsoft.com"
        stoponerror="Yes">
</cflock>

<p><b>Connection opened</b>

<!--- Get the file called disclaimer.txt from the root directory of the
      Microsoft FTP site and download it to a temp directory on the
      ColdFusion server --->
<cflock scope="Session" type="ReadOnly" timeout="60" throwontimeout="Yes">

<cfftp action="GetFile"
        transfermode="Auto"
        stoponerror="No"
        remotefile="disclaimer.txt"
        localfile="d:\temp\disclaimer.txt"
        connection="MyConnection">
</cflock>

<p>
<cfif cfftp.Succeeded>
    <b>File successfully downloaded!</b>
<cfelse>
    <b>The following error occurred while attempting to download the file:</b><br>
    <cfoutput>
    <b><i>Error number #cfftp.ErrorCode#: #cfftp.ErrorText#</i></b>
    </cfoutput>
</cfif>

<!--- Close the ftp connection --->
<cflock scope="Session" type="ReadOnly" timeout="60" throwontimeout="Yes">

<cfftp action="Close"
        connection="MyConnection"
        stoponerror="Yes">
</cflock>

<p><b>Connection closed</b>
```

As before, this example uses the `cfftp` tag to open an FTP connection to Microsoft's FTP server and caches the connection. Once the connection has been opened and verified, we perform the actual file transfer from Microsoft's FTP server to our local ColdFusion server. This is done by setting the `action` attribute of the `cfftp` tag to `GetFile`. `transfermode` specifies the FTP transfer mode to use when retrieving the file from the FTP server. Valid options are `Text`, `Binary`, and `Auto`. In this case, we set `transfermode` to `Auto`. We also set the `stoponerror` attribute to `No` so that ColdFusion continues to process the template in the event that an error occurs.

The remotefile attribute specifies the filename, including the path, of the file we want to download from the remote FTP server. In our case, we want the *disclaimer.txt* file located in the root directory of Microsoft's FTP server. If we wanted to download a file from a directory other than the root directory, we would have to specify the path to the file as part of the remotefile attribute. The localfile attribute specifies the filename, including the path, where you want to save the downloaded file on your ColdFusion server. For our example, we'll save the file as *disclaimer.txt* to a directory on our *D* drive called *temp*. The final attribute for our cfftp operation is the connection attribute. The connection attribute is set to MyConnection, the name we assigned to our cached connection in the previous cfftp operation.

Deleting files

Another common task that can be performed with the cfftp tag is deleting files that exist on a remote FTP server. To do this, you first have to make sure that you have write access to the files you want to delete on the remote FTP server. Assuming that you have write access, you can use cfftp to perform the delete, as shown in Example 12-10.

Example 12-10. Using cfftp to delete a file on a remote server

```
<!--- Open the FTP connection --->
<cflock scope="Session" type="Exclusive" timeout="60" throwontimeout="Yes">

<cfftp action="Open"
       username="myusername"
       connection="MyConnection"
       password="mypassword"
       server="127.0.0.1"
       stoponerror="Yes">
</cflock>

<p><b>Connection opened</b>

<!--- Remove the file called myfile.txt from the incoming directory on the
      remote FTP server --->
<cflock scope="Session" type="ReadOnly" timeout="60" throwontimeout="Yes">

<cfftp action="Remove"
       stoponerror="No"
       item="/incoming/myfile.txt"
       connection="MyConnection">
</cflock>

<p>
<cfif cfftp.Succeeded>
   <b>File successfully removed!</b>
<cfelse>
   <b>The following error occurred while attempting to remove your file:</b><br>
```

Example 12-10. Using cfftp to delete a file on a remote server (continued)

```
    <cfoutput>
    <b><i>Error number #cfftp.ErrorCode#: #cfftp.ErrorText#</i></b>
    </cfoutput>
</cfif>

<!--- Close the ftp connection --->
<cflock scope="Session" type="ReadOnly" timeout="60" throwontimeout="Yes">

<cfftp action="Close"
       connection="MyConnection"
       stoponerror="Yes">
</cflock>

<p><b>Connection closed</b>
```

This template starts by opening the FTP session with the remote server and caching the connection. Since the `stoponerror` attribute of the `cfftp` tag is set to `Yes`, ColdFusion throws an error and halts processing if the connection fails.

Next comes the `cfftp` tag that deletes the remote file. This is accomplished by setting the `action` attribute to `Remove`. The file we want to delete is specified in the `item` attribute by referencing the full path and filename. We set the `connection` attribute to `MyConnection` because we are using a cached FTP connection. Once the `cfftp` tag has executed, we use a `cfif` statement to evaluate whether or not the file was deleted successfully. If it wasn't, an error code and message are output to the screen before the FTP connection is closed in section three.

You should note that the `cfftp` tag can delete both files and directories. To delete a directory instead of a file, specify `Removedir` for the `action` parameter and provide the directory you want to delete using the `directory` attribute. You don't need to use the `item` attribute when deleting a directory.

Executing Command-Line Programs

You can use the `cfexecute` tag to execute command-line programs residing on the same machine as the ColdFusion Application Server. This tag allows you to call external programs, such as batch utilities, from within your ColdFusion application. The following syntax calls an external program using `cfexecute`:

```
<cfexecute name="path_to_program_to_execute"
           arguments="argument_string"
           variable="variable_name"
           outputfile="path_to_output_file"
           timeout="timeout_in_seconds">
</cfexecute>
```

The name attribute is required and specifies the full path, including filename, to the file you want to execute. Depending on the program you are attempting to execute, you may be able to specify just the program name without the full path. arguments allows you to specify any optional arguments you want to pass to the external program. arguments can be either a string or an array and adheres to the following conventions:

String
: On Windows platforms, the entire string is passed to the Windows process control subsystem for processing.

  On Unix and Linux systems, the string is tokenized into an array of strings, delimited by spaces. If spaces occur in the array elements, they are escaped by double quotes.

Array
: On Windows platforms, the elements of the array are concatenated into a space-delimited string of tokens, which is then passed to the Windows process control subsystem for processing.

  On Unix and Linux systems, the elements of the array are copied into an array of exec( ) arguments.

The next attribute, variable, is optional and specifies a variable name to hold any output generated by the executed program. This attribute is new in ColdFusion MX 6.1. If you would rather save any output to a file instead of a variable, use the optional outputfile parameter to specify the path to an output file. If a relative path is used, it is relative to the ColdFusion temp directory. If both the variable and outputfile attributes are omitted, the output is returned to the browser. The final attribute, timeout, is also optional and specifies the time in seconds ColdFusion should wait before timing out the call to the external program. Setting the timeout attribute to 0 equates to a nonblocking execution mode. This causes ColdFusion to spawn a thread for the process and immediately return without waiting for the process to end. By contrast, setting the timeout attribute to an arbitrarily high value equates to a blocking execution mode. The default value for timeout is 0.

Note that there shouldn't be any HTML or CFML appearing between the start and end of the cfexecute tags. As a result, you can refer to the cfexecute tag using the following shorthand notation instead of including an explicit end tag:

```
<cfexecute name="c:\example.exe"/>
```

If for some reason an exception is thrown while attempting to execute the cfexecute tag, the following rules apply:

- If the application specified in the name attribute can't be found, an "Application File Not Found" exception is thrown.

- If the ColdFusion user trying to execute the application doesn't have permission to do so, a security exception is thrown.
- If a value is specified for outputfile and the file can't be opened, an "Output File Cannot be Opened" exception is thrown.

Example 12-11 demonstrates how to use the cfexecute tag to run the *ipconfig.exe* program on a Windows server.

Example 12-11. Using cfexecute to run ipconfig.exe

```
<!--- Execute the windows ipconfig.exe program.  Write the results to a
      variable called ipconfig and display in the browser. --->
<cftry>
  <cfexecute name="ipconfig.exe" arguments="/all"
             variable="ipconfig" timeout="30"/>
  <cfcatch type="Any">
    There was an error trying to execute the program specified in the
    cfexecute tag. Details follow:
    <p>
    <cfoutput>
    Type: #cfcatch.Type#<br>
    Message: #cfcatch.Message#<br>
    Details: #cfcatch.Detail#
    </cfoutput>
    <cfabort>
  </cfcatch>
</cftry>

<cfoutput>
<pre>#ipconfig#</pre>
</cfoutput>
```

Example 12-11 uses the cfexecute tag to execute the *ipconfig.exe* utility on a Windows system. The /All switch is passed along with the request using the arguments attribute. The output generated by the *ipconfig* program is written to a variable named ipconfig. The contents of the variable are then output using the cfoutput tag. The HTML pre tags preserve whitespace formatting for the output.

If any errors or exceptions are thrown during the execution of the cfexecute tag, they are caught using the cftry/cfcatch tags in the code. Executing the code in Example 12-11 results in output similar to that shown in Figure 12-3.

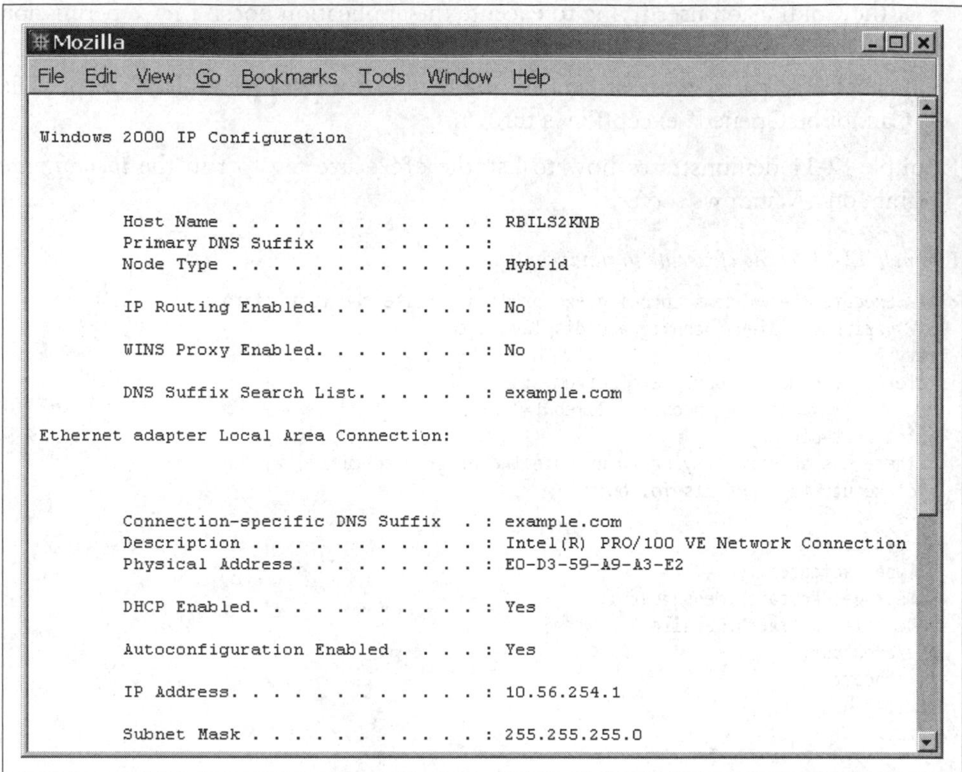

Figure 12-3. Executing the ipconfig.exe utility using cfexecute

CHAPTER 13
Working with Email

It's no wonder that email is considered one of the Internet's "killer applications." The ability to send and receive text messages as well as binary file attachments to locations around the globe has revolutionized the way we communicate. ColdFusion wouldn't be a complete development platform without a way to tap the power of email. As such, several tags are provided for working with email, three for sending messages (`cfmail`, `cfmailparam`, and `cfmailpart`) and another for retrieving messages (`cfpop`).

There are lots of ways to integrate email into your ColdFusion applications. For example, you can allow users to enter feedback about your web site via an HTML form and have the feedback automatically emailed to the appropriate people. You can send email confirmation message to users, such as a registration confirmation when the user signs up for an account or an order confirmation after the user places an order with your e-commerce application. You can also allow users to sign up to receive periodic information via email, such as announcements of new products.

Sending Email

ColdFusion uses the `cfmail` tag to send email messages using an Internet standard known as Simple Mail Transport Protocol (SMTP). In order for ColdFusion to send email, an SMTP server must be specified in the ColdFusion Administrator under the Mail option. If you don't have access to the ColdFusion Administrator, the `cfmail` tag provides an optional attribute, `server`, where you can provide a hostname or IP address to your SMTP server. The following example shows how to use the `cfmail` tag to send a simple email message. The example assumes that you are using the SMTP server specified in the ColdFusion Administrator.

```
<cfmail to="postmaster@example.com"
        from="webmaster@example.com"
        cc="administrator@example.com"
        bcc="postmaster@example.com"
        replyto="system@example.com"
```

```
          failto="bounced@example.com"
          subject="ColdFusion can send email!"
          mailerid="My Email Engine"
          server="mail.example.com,mail2.example.com"
          username="pmoney"
          password="cat"
          spoolenable="Yes"
          timeout="900"
          charset="UTF-8"
          wraptext="72">
I just wanted to let you know that ColdFusion MX is now sending email!  Isn't this
the greatest thing?

-Webmaster
</cfmail>
```

The first attribute in the cfmail tag is to, which you use to specify the addressee of the email. The to attribute is required and can accept a single email address or a comma-separated list of email addresses. In ColdFusion MX, email addresses must not contain spaces. If an email address containing a space is encountered, the cfmail tag throws an exception. Email address may be specified using any of the following formats:

pmoney@example.com
<pmoney@example.com>
pmoney@example.com (Pere Money)
"Pere Money" <pmoney@example.com>
Pere Money <pmoney@example.com>

The from attribute is also required and contains the sender's email address or other string. The cc attribute is optional and can add additional email recipients. Like the to attribute, the cc attribute can also accept a comma-separated list of email addresses. bcc stands for blind carbon copy and specifies an optional comma-delimited list of recipients that should also receive the email but whose email addresses shouldn't appear in the email's header. The replyto and failto attributes are both optional and are new in ColdFusion MX 6.1. replyto specifies an email address or comma-delimited list of email addresses to which a mail client should send replies to the message. failto provides an email address to which mail servers should send delivery failure messages. The subject attribute is required and contains the subject for our email message.

The mailerid attribute specifies a mailer ID to pass along in the X-Mailer SMTP header. The X-Mailer header identifies the program generating the SMTP message. If mailerid is not specified, it defaults to ColdFusion MX Application Server. server allows you to pass a server address or comma-delimited list of server addresses (ColdFusion MX 6.1 Enterprise only) ColdFusion should use to send SMTP mail. If more than one address is specified, ColdFusion attempts to connect to the first mail server in the list. If that fails, it attempts to connect to the second server, etc. Cold-

Fusion will not attempt to connect to a mail server if it was previously unavailable within the previous 60 seconds. This behavior is new in the Enterprise version of ColdFusion MX 6.1. If you specify multiple server addresses in ColdFusion MX 6.1 Standard, only the first server address is tried. Specifying a value for server overrides any values set in the ColdFusion Administrator. Additionally, you may prepend a username and password and/or append a port number to the server address (*username:password@servername:port*) if desired. If you specify a port number in this way, it overrides any value set in the ColdFusion Administrator. You must set a server value either in the ColdFusion Administrator or the `cfmail` tag; otherwise, ColdFusion throws an error.

The `username` and `password` attributes are also new in ColdFusion MX 6.1. They allow you to pass a username and password to your SMTP server should it require they be provided for authentication. Setting `spoolenable` to `Yes` tells ColdFusion to save a copy of the message to disk until it can be sent. Setting `spoolenable` to `No` causes the messages to queue in memory until they can be sent. Although this option may be faster than writing the messages to disk, it is not fault-tolerant, meaning if the ColdFusion server goes down before the messages can be sent, they are lost. The default value for `spoolenable` is `Yes`.

The `timeout` attribute provides an optional number of seconds that ColdFusion should wait for the `cfmail` operation to execute before timing out the connection to the SMTP server. Specifying a value for timeout overrides the default timeout value you set in the ColdFusion Administrator.

The final two attributes are optional and are both new in ColdFusion MX 6.1. `charset` lets you specify the character set to use in encoding the message. The most common character sets are `UTF-8`, `UTF-16`, `UTF-16BE`, `UTF-16LE`, `US-ASCII`, and `ISO-8859-1`. You may use any character set supported by your JRE. The default is the character encoding specified in the Mail section of the Server Settings area in the ColdFusion Administrator. By default, this is set to `UTF-8`. `wraptext` specifies the maximum number of characters to allow per line in the mail message. If a line is longer than the specified number of characters, an attempt is made to break the line by inserting a line break at the nearest whitespace character (space, tab, etc) before the character limit. If the line contains no whitespace characters before the maximum number of characters per line, a line break is inserted at the maximum line length. The default is no text wrapping.

The space between the start and end `cfmail` tags is where the email message goes. Unlike the space between most HTML and CFML tags, the area between the start and end `cfmail` tags is sensitive to whitespace. This means that ColdFusion interprets carriage returns and spaces between text as they are typed.

If you don't have access to the SMTP mail server specified in the ColdFusion Administrator or just want to send the email via a different SMTP server than the default, you can specify the server and associated port within the `cfmail` tag as shown here:

```
<cfmail to="postmaster@example.com"
        from="webmaster@example.com"
        cc="administrator@example.com"
        bcc="postmaster@example.com"
        subject="ColdFusion can send email!"
        timeout="900"
        server="127.0.0.1"
        port="25">
I just wanted to let you know that ColdFusion is now sending email!

-Webmaster
</cfmail>
```

In this example, the server attribute is set to the IP address of the SMTP server we want to use to send our message. The value for server can be either the IP address or the hostname of the SMTP server. The port attribute is optional and tells the cfmail tag what port the SMTP server is listening on for incoming requests. The default port is 25.

Note that when a ColdFusion application creates an email message using the cfmail tag, the ColdFusion server doesn't send it right away (unless spoolenable is set to Yes). Instead, a temporary file is created and stored in a spool directory on the ColdFusion server. ColdFusion then pipes the messages from the spool directory to the SMTP server as a background process. ColdFusion looks for new messages in the spool directory at an interval that can be set in the Mail section of the ColdFusion Administrator. The default is every 60 seconds.

In ColdFusion MX 6.1, ColdFusion's mail engine was totally overhauled. As such, several new options to improve performance were added to the ColdFusion Administrator. Among these are backup mail servers, the ability to keep a connection to the mail server open between messages, and the ability to specify multiple threads for sending messages. To learn more about these features, consult your Macromedia ColdFusion MX documentation or see the ColdFusion MX 6.1 release notes.

Sending HTML Mail

In addition to the standard text-based email messages, ColdFusion can also send HTML-formatted email messages. HTML-formatted messages are readable by many popular email clients and allow you to embed HTML formatting tags within the body of the message, as shown in the following example:

```
<cfmail to="postmaster@example.com"
        from="webmaster@example.com"
        subject="ColdFusion can send HTML email too!"
        type="HTML">
<center>
  <h2>This is an HTML formatted email message</h2>
</center>
<hr>
```

```
I just wanted to let you know that
<a href="http://www.example.com">ColdFusion</a> is now sending HTML
Formatted email!

-Webmaster
</cfmail>
```

The type attribute specifies the MIME type of the message. You can specify `text` (text/plain), `plain` (text/plain), `html` (text/html), or any valid MIME type you wish. The default is text/plain. In this example, setting the type attribute to `HTML` tells ColdFusion to format the email message using HTML. An entry is made in the header of the email to let email clients know that the incoming message is formatted using HTML. In order to view the email message correctly, the recipient of the message must be using an email client capable of reading HTML email, such as Netscape Communicator or Microsoft Outlook.

Sending Multi-Part Messages

ColdFusion MX 6.1 adds the capability to send multi-part messages via the new `cfmailpart` tag. Multi-part messages are typically used to send multiple versions of the same message. For example, it may be desirable to send both a plain text and an HTML version of a message. To specify multiple parts, use one `cfmailpart` tag pair for each part. If you send a multi-part message using `cfmailpart`, all message contents must appear within `cfmailpart` tags. Any content outside the tag body is ignored. Here's an example that sends both a plain text and HTML version of the same message:

```
<cfmail to="foo@bar.com"
        from="webmaster@example.com"
        subject="ColdFusion MX 6.1 can send multi-part email messages!"
        server="127.0.0.1">
<cfmailpart type="text" charset="UTF-8" wraptext="72">
This is a text formatted email message

I just wanted to let you know that
<a href="http://www.example.com">ColdFusion</a> is now sending multi-part email!

-Webmaster
</cfmailpart>

<cfmailpart type="html" charset="UTF-8" wraptext="72">
<center>
<h2>This is an HTML formatted email message</h2>
</center>
<hr>
I just wanted to let you know that
<a href="http://www.example.com">ColdFusion</a> is now sending multi-part email!
<p>
-Webmaster
```

```
</p>
</cfmailpart>
</cfmail>
```

The type attribute of each cfmailpart is optional. It specifies the MIME type of the message part. You can specify text (text/plain), plain (text/plain), html (text/html), or any valid MIME type you wish. charset servers the same purpose as it does in the cfmail tag, except it applies only to the specific message part. If charset is not specified, the value used by the cfmail tag is used instead. wraptext also serves the same purpose as in the cfmail tag, again, applying just to the specific message part.

Emailing Form Contents

One of the most popular uses of the cfmail tag is for emailing the contents of an HTML form once it has been submitted. Although the practical applications of this feature are virtually unlimited, the technique for sending the message is simple. A typical scenario involves emailing the contents of a feedback form to the appropriate department or person within a company. The following example shows how this is accomplished using two templates. The first template, shown in Example 13-1, contains the feedback form.

Example 13-1. HTML feedback form

```
<html>
<head>
  <title>Feedback form</title>
</head>

<body>
<h2>Feedback form</h2>
<form action="Example13-2.cfm" method="post">
Name: <input type="text" name="Name" size="15" maxlength="255"><br>
Email: <input type="text" name="Email" size="15" maxlength="255">
<p>
Who should recieve this feedback?<br>
<select name="SendTo">
   <option value="marketing@example.com" selected>Marketing</option>
   <option value="sales@example.com">Sales</option>
   <option value="customerservice@example.com">Customer Service</option>
</select>
<p>
Comments:<br>
<textarea cols="40" rows="4" name="Comments" wrap="Virtual"></textarea>
<br>
<input type="submit" name="Submit" value="Send">
</form>
</body>
</html>
```

The template in Example 13-1 is a basic HTML form that collects a user's name, email address, comments, and the department they would like the email sent to.

Once the information is collected and the form is submitted, the template shown in Example 13-2 takes over.

Example 13-2. Generating an email from an HTML form submission

```
<cfmail from="webmaster@example.com"
        to="#form.SendTo#"
        subject="Feedback form">
The following information was submitted via our feedback form:

Name: #form.Name#
Email: #form.Email#
Comments:
#form.Comments#
</cfmail>

<html>
<head>
  <title>Feedback form Processor</title>
</head>

<body>
<h2>The feedback form has been processed successfully!</h2>
The following information was submitted:<br>
<cfoutput>
To:  #form.SendTo#<br>
Name: #form.Name#<br>
Email: #form.Email#<br>
Comments:<br>
#form.Comments#
</cfoutput>

</body>
</html>
```

Example 13-2 takes the information posted from the form in Example 13-1 and uses it to generate an email. The `cfmail` `to` attribute is populated with the `SendTo` form field value passed from the feedback form. The body of the message is created by referencing the rest of the form fields from the feedback form. The values entered in the feedback form are also output to the browser so that you can see what values were passed.

Adding Query Results to Email

Another feature of the `cfmail` tag is the ability to include query results in `cfmail` generated email messages. Say you want to send an email to your HR department that contains a listing of the contact information for each employee in the company. You can use ColdFusion to query the database and then use the `cfmail` tag to generate an email message containing the query results in the body of the message, as shown in Example 13-3.

Example 13-3. Including query results in an email message

```
<cfquery name="GetMailingList" datasource="ProgrammingCF">
         SELECT Name, Title, Email, PhoneExt, Department
         FROM EmployeeDirectory Order BY Name
</cfquery>

<cfmail query="GetMailingList"
        to="hr@example.com"
        from="webmaster@example.com"
        subject="Employee Contact Listings"
        timeout="900"
        type="HTML">
Here is the employee contact information you requested:
<p>
<table border="1">
<tr>
  <th>Name</th><th>Title</th><th>Department</th><th>Email</th>
  <th>Phone Ext.</th>
</tr>
<cfoutput>
<tr>
  <td>#Name#</td><td>#Title#</td><td>#Department#</td><td>#Email#</td>
  <td>#PhoneExt#</td>
</tr>
</cfoutput>
</table>
<p>
Best regards,
<p>
The Webmaster
</cfmail>
```

As you can see in Example 13-3, including the query results in the message body is simple. The only real difference between using a query result set in an email message and outputting the result set to a browser is that you don't have to specify a query attribute in the `cfoutput` tag because it is already specified within the `cfmail` tag.

Including Grouped Query Results

On occasion, you may want to group query results in the body of your email message. For example, you need to send an email message to a contact in your human-resources department listing every employee in your employee database. You can list them in alphabetical order by creating a simple `cfquery` that orders the results by the employee's name. But you may want to list all the current employees grouped by department. This process gets a little more complicated.

Example 13-4 demonstrates how to query the `EmployeeDirectory` table of the database and then output each employee record to the browser. The query results are grouped by department using the `group` attribute of the `cfoutput` tag. Notice the nesting of the second `cfoutput` tag within the `cfoutput` tag that accompanies the `query` attribute.

Example 13-4. Grouping data using cfoutput

```
<cfquery name="GetMailingList" datasource="ProgrammingCF">
       SELECT Department, Name, Title, Email, PhoneExt
       FROM EmployeeDirectory Order BY Department
</cfquery>

<cfoutput query="GetMailingList" group="Department">
<h3>#Department#</h3>

<cfoutput>
#Name#<br>
#Title#<br>
#Email#<br>
x#PhoneExt#<p>
</cfoutput>
</cfoutput>
```

Now that you see how to group the query results using the `group` attribute of the `cfoutput` tag, let's apply the same logic to an email message generated by the `cfmail` tag. The syntax for grouping within a `cfmail` message is slightly different from the syntax used in the previous example. Example 13-5 shows the syntax for grouping within a `cfmail` generated message.

Example 13-5. Grouping query results within a cfmail message

```
<cfquery name="GetMailingList" datasource="ProgrammingCF">
        SELECT Department, Name, Title, Email, PhoneExt
        FROM EmployeeDirectory Order BY Department
</cfquery>

<cfmail query="GetMailingList"
       group="Department"
       to="you@example.com"
       from="me@example.com"
       subject="Employees grouped by department">
#Department#
====================
<cfoutput>
#Name#
#Title#
#Email#
x#PhoneExt#

</cfoutput>
</cfmail>

<h2>The message has been sent...</h2>
```

The first part of this template simply queries the `EmployeeDirectory` table and stores the results in a query object called `GetMailingList`. Next, the `cfmail` tag is used to construct the actual message to be sent. The first `cfoutput` tag sets the outermost loop for the output. This loop iterates for each unique value contained in the column specified in group. In this case, the loop iterates for each unique department. The second step sets the innermost loop for the output. This loop iterates for each employee within the current group. The results are added to the message until the entire query object has been output.

Sending Customized Email to Multiple Recipients

The real power of the cfmail tag lies in its ability to send email to multiple recipients based on information from a ColdFusion query object, which in effect allows you to send customized email messages to multiple recipients using very few lines of code. With this technique, you can perform such tasks as mail merges and mass emailings (not spam, of course!). Example 13-6 shows the basic method for sending out multiple emails with information pulled from a query.

Example 13-6. Sending email to multiple recipients based on a query

```
<!--- Query the sample database for all of the names and email addresses of
      people stored in the recipients table --->
<cfquery name="GetMailingList" datasource="ProgrammingCF">
         SELECT Email, Name FROM EmployeeDirectory
</cfquery>

<!--- Use the cfmail tag in conjunction with the above query to email a
      personalized message to each person in the database --->
<cfmail query="GetMailingList"
        to="#email#"
        from="webmaster@example.com"
        subject="Hello!"
        timeout="900">
#Name#,

We just wanted to let you know that a new page on the wonderful widget has
been added to our web site.  To visit the new page, point your browser here:

http://www.example.com/widget.cfm

Best regards,

The Webmaster
</cfmail>
```

Example 13-6 uses a standard cfquery to select the Name and Email fields from the database. The name of the query is then specified in the query attribute of the cfmail tag. By specifying the Email variable from the query in the to attribute of the cfmail tag, ColdFusion sends a message to the email address listed in each row of the record set returned by the query. Each recipient receives a copy of the message addressed specifically to that recipient, with no other recipients appearing in the to header. The body for each email message can be personalized with the name of the recipient if you reference the Name variable from the query. Additional fields from the database can also be added depending on your requirements.

Sending File Attachments

ColdFusion can send file attachments via email. Files are attached to a message using the cfmailparam tag nested within the cfmail tag. The following example shows the proper syntax to get this done:

```
<cfmail to="webmaster@example.com"
        from="rbils@example.com"
        subject="Test cfmail file attachments">
This is a test. There should be two file attachments included in this email.

-Rob

<cfmailparam file="d:\myfile.txt" type="text">
<cfmailparam file="d:\mydoc.doc" type="application/msword">
</cfmail>
```

The cfmailparam tag uses the file attribute to specify the full path (on your ColdFusion server) to the file you'd like to attach to your email message. type is a new optional attribute in ColdFusion MX 6.1. It lets you set the MIME type of the file attachment. You can specify text (text/plain), plain (text/plain), html (text/html), or any valid MIME type you wish. To specify more than one file to attach, use one cfmailparam tag for each file.

There are two additional items related to message attachments you should be aware of. First, to attach a file to a cfmail-generated message, the file must reside on the local ColdFusion server or on a network drive accessible from that server. If you are building an application such as a web-based email client that allows users to attach files to their messages, the attachment must first be uploaded to the ColdFusion server with the cffile tag before it can be included as an attachment. There will be more on this technique later on in this chapter. The second issue is that ColdFusion does not make a copy of any file attachments before sending them. If you attach a file to a mail message, you must wait until after the message is sent before deleting the file. If ColdFusion tries to send a message with an attachment and it cannot find the attachment, an exception is raised and the message is not sent.

Specifying Additional Header Information

The cfmailparam tag also lets you specify additional SMTP header information not natively supplied by the cfmail tag. The following example uses the cfmailparam tag to append a delivery Importance value to the message header generated by the cfmail tag:

```
<cfmail to="webmaster@example.com"
        from="rbils@example.com"
        subject="cfmail Test">
```

```
    <cfmailparam name="Importance" value="High">
    This email specifies additional header information!

    -Rob
    </cfmail>
```

In this case, the `cfmailparam` tag uses the `name` attribute to specify the name for the header entry. The `value` attribute passes the actual value for the header entry. Multiple header entries can be made using multiple `cfmailparam` tags.

Dealing with Undeliverable Email

Every now and then, something goes wrong when ColdFusion attempts to send an email. Problems can range from a missing email address in the `to` attribute, to a problem connecting to the SMTP server. Regardless of the cause of the problem, ColdFusion deals with undeliverable email in a consistent and simple manner. All undeliverable email messages are written to temporary files with a *.cfmail* extension and saved to a folder on the ColdFusion server called *\undelivr*.* The *\undelivr* folder is usually located in *\cfusionmx\mail\undelivr*.

To resend a message that has been moved to the *\undelivr* folder, the temporary file must be moved back to the *\spool* folder, which is usually located in *\cfusionmx\mail\spool*. This can be done manually or via ColdFusion. Obviously, using ColdFusion to monitor the *\undelivr* directory for undelivered mail is more convenient than manually checking the directory every time an email is generated. To do this, you need to create a template that scans the *\undelivr* folder and schedule it to run at set intervals. Example 13-7 contains a template you can use to scan your *\undelivr* folder and move any files found back to the *\spool* folder so that attempts can be made to resend them. Using the Scheduler within the ColdFusion Administrator, the template can be set to run at predetermined intervals.

Example 13-7. CFML template for dealing with undeliverable mail

```
<!--- Get the mail root directory --->
<cfset MailRoot="#server.ColdFusion.RootDir#\mail">

<!--- set the date trigger to 7, one week --->
<cfset DateTrigger=7>

<!--- Read all of the files from the undeliverable directory for processing --->
<cfdirectory action="List"
             directory="#MailRoot#\undelivr"
```

* There's a bug in the ColdFusion MX release (fixed in Updater 2) that causes the mail spool to append "Undelievered_" to the beginning of a mail message each time an attempt to send it fails. This can results in very long filenames if an automated attempt (such as this program) is made to resend the file unsuccessfully. Also, note the extra "e" in the word "Undelievered_". It's not a typo here; it's a bug in the pre–Updater 2 release of ColdFusion MX.

Example 13-7. CFML template for dealing with undeliverable mail (continued)

```
          name="Undeliverables"
          filter="*.cfmail">

<cfif Undeliverables.RecordCount eq 0>
  <cfset FilesMoved = 0>
  <cfset FilesDeleted = 0>
  <cfset UndeliveredMail = QueryNew("FileName, FileSize, LastMod, Status")>
  <cfset QueryAddRow(UndeliveredMail)>
  <cfset QuerySetCell(UndeliveredMail, "FileName", "N/A", 1)>
  <cfset QuerySetCell(UndeliveredMail, "FileSize", "N/A", 1)>
  <cfset QuerySetCell(UndeliveredMail, "LastMod", "N/A", 1)>
  <cfset QuerySetCell(UndeliveredMail, "Status", "N/A", 1)>
<cfelse>
  <!--- Set Constants --->
  <cfset FilesMoved = 0>
  <cfset FilesDeleted = 0>
  <cfset UndeliveredMail=QueryNew("FileName, FileSize, LastMod, Status")>
  <cfset QueryAddRow(UndeliveredMail, Undeliverables.RecordCount)>

  <cfloop Query="Undeliverables">
    <!--- if the last modified date of the file in the undelivr directory is
          older than the date trigger, or if the file size is 0, delete it.
          Otherwise, move the file to the spool directory to be resent. --->
    <cfif (DateDiff("y", DateLastModified, Now( )) gt DateTrigger)
           or (Size eq 0)>
      <cffile action="Delete"
              file="#MailRoot#\undelivr\#Name#">
      <cfset QuerySetCell(UndeliveredMail, "FileName", Name,
             Undeliverables.CurrentRow)>
      <cfset QuerySetCell(UndeliveredMail, "FileSize", Size,
             Undeliverables.CurrentRow)>
      <cfset QuerySetCell(UndeliveredMail, "LastMod", DateLastModified,
             Undeliverables.CurrentRow)>
     <cfset QuerySetCell(UndeliveredMail, "Status", "Deleted",
             Undeliverables.CurrentRow)>
      <cfset FilesDeleted = FilesDeleted + 1>
    <cfelse>
      <!--- There's a bug in the CF MX release (fixed in Updater 2) that causes the
            mail spool to append Undelievered_ to the beginning of a mail
            message each time an attempt to send it fails.  This can results in
            very long file names if an automated attempt (such as this program)
            is made to resend the file unsuccessfully.  Also, note the extra "e"
            in the word "Undelievered_" - it's not a typo here, it's a bug in
            the pre updater 2 release of CF MX --->
      <!--- Strip out Undelievered_ from the filename in case CFMX Updater 2 or
      later isn't installed --->
      <cffile action="Move"
              source="#MailRoot#\undelivr\#Name#"
              destination="#MailRoot#\spool\#ReplaceNoCase(Name, "Undelievered_",
                "", "All")#">
      <cfset QuerySetCell(UndeliveredMail, "FileName", Name,
             Undeliverables.CurrentRow)>
```

Example 13-7. CFML template for dealing with undeliverable mail (continued)

```
      <cfset QuerySetCell(UndeliveredMail, "FileSize", Size,
             Undeliverables.CurrentRow)>
      <cfset QuerySetCell(UndeliveredMail, "LastMod", DateLastModified,
             Undeliverables.CurrentRow)>
      <cfset QuerySetCell(UndeliveredMail, "Status", "Moved",
             Undeliverables.CurrentRow)>
      <cfset FilesMoved = FilesMoved+1>
    </cfif>
  </cfloop>
</cfif>

<cfif FilesMoved gte 1 or FilesDeleted gte 1>
<cfmail query="UndeliveredMail"
        to="webmaster@example.com"
        from="webmaster@example.com"
        subject="Undeliverable Mail Report for Server #CGI.Server_Name#">
Total Files Moved: #FilesMoved#
Total Files Deleted: #FilesDeleted#

These are the files affected:
<cfoutput>
#Status#: #FileName# (#filesize# bytes, #DateFormat(LastMod,'mm/dd/yyyy')#)
</cfoutput>
</cfmail>
</cfif>

<h2>Task Completed<h2>
```

This template works by setting a variable called `DateTrigger` to specify the number of days ColdFusion should attempt to move the file back into the *spool* directory before deleting it. Next, the `cfdirectory` tag obtains a list of all undeliverable mail files in the *undelivr* directory. This is done by setting the `filter` attribute to `"*.cfmail"`. If files exist in the directory, their last-modified dates are compared to the number of days specified in the `DateTrigger`. If the file is older than the specified number of days, it is deleted. If not, the file is moved back to the *spool* directory so ColdFusion can attempt to send it again. Finally, an email is sent out listing the number of files deleted and the number moved as well as the names of the files affected along with other identifying information.

Retrieving Messages

You have seen that ColdFusion can send email via the `cfmail` tag. In addition to sending email, ColdFusion can also retrieve email messages using the Post Office Protocol (POP3) via the `cfpop` tag. Using this tag, ColdFusion can retrieve message headers, message contents including multi-part messages (this is new in ColdFusion MX 6.1), and file attachments. In essence, this allows you to use ColdFusion to create a web-based email system, like Yahoo! Mail or Hotmail. The `cfpop` tag can also create applications such as auto-responders and mailing-list managers.

Retrieving Message Headers

The cfpop tag can retrieve just the header portion of email messages stored on a POP server. This is useful when you want to retrieve summary information such as the message title for more than one message. Retrieving just the message headers allows you to avoid the overhead associated with retrieving the entire contents of each message you retrieve. In the context of a web-based email client, this technique is used to build a list of messages in a user's mailbox. You can retrieve the headers for a group of messages by setting the action attribute of the cfpop tag to GetHeaderOnly as shown in Example 13-8.

Example 13-8. Retrieving message headers

```
<cfpop action="getheaderonly" name="GetMessageHeaders"
       server="wcpamh01.amkor.com" port="110" timeout="600"
       username="rbils" password="leb##sggy"
       startrow="1" maxrows="100">
<html>
<head>
  <title>Example 13-8: Retrieving Message Headers</title>
  <style type="text/css">
    th {
      background-color : #0000FF;
      font-weight : bold;
      color : #FFFFFF;
      text-align : center;
    }
    td {
      background-color : #C0C0C0;
    }
  </style>
</head>

<body>

<cfoutput>
   <h3>Retrieved #GetMessageHeaders.RecordCount# messages from the server</h3>
</cfoutput>

<table border="0" cellpadding="5" cellspacing="1">
<tr>
   <th>From</th><th>Date</th><th>Subject</th>
</tr>

<!--- Output the message header contents --->
<cfoutput query="GetMessageHeaders">
<tr>
   <td>#HTMLEditFormat(From)#</td>
   <td>#DateFormat(ParseDateTime(Date),'mm/dd/yyyy')#
       #TimeFormat(ParseDateTime(Date),'hh:mm:ss tt')#</td>
   <td>#HTMLEditFormat(Subject)#</td>
```

Example 13-8. Retrieving message headers (continued)

```
</tr>
</cfoutput>
</table>
</body>
</html>
```

Example 13-8 calls the cfpop tag and sets the action attribute to GetHeaderOnly. This tells ColdFusion to retrieve only message headers from the POP server. Message headers contain information such as who the message is from, the time and date it was sent, and the subject of the message. The name attribute specifies the name to give the query object created to hold the header information. In this example, we'll call our query GetMessageHeaders. The server attribute is set to the hostname or IP address of the POP server you want to retrieve messages from. port is an optional attribute that specifies the port the POP server listens on for requests. The default port is 110. timeout specifies an amount of time in seconds that you want ColdFusion to wait while processing a request before timing out the connection to the POP server. This attribute is optional and defaults to 60 seconds.

The username and password attributes send the username and password to the POP server you want to retrieve messages from. The remote POP server authenticates access and determines which messages should be returned to the ColdFusion application. Both startrow and maxrows are optional attributes. startrow tells ColdFusion where to start retrieving messages from. maxrows specifies the maximum number of messages to return starting from the row specified in startrow. In this example, we've instructed ColdFusion to retrieve the first 100 messages from the server. If these attributes are both omitted, ColdFusion retrieves all messages. For more information on all of the attributes available when action="GetHeaderOnly", see the cfpop tag in Appendix A.

After the cfpop tag executes (assuming no errors occur), the message headers retrieved from the POP server are output to the browser as a simple HTML table. Note the use of the HTMLEditFormat( ) function on the From and Subject query columns. This function is used to escape any HTML that might be in these fields so that they render properly in the browser. Only a subset of the available return variables are used in our example. See the cfpop tag in Appendix A for the complete list of variables returned when retrieving message headers.

Retrieving Message Contents

Besides retrieving message headers, the cfpop tag can also retrieve the rest of a message's content, such as the body text and any attachments included with the message. In the context of a web-based email system, this functionality allows you to display an email message and build links to any file attachments. To retrieve everything associated with a particular message, set the action attribute of the cfpop tag to GetAll as in Example 13-9.

Example 13-9. Retrieving a complete message

```
<cfpop action="GetAll" name="GetMessage" messagenumber="1"
       server="popserver.example.com"
       timeout="600" username="username" password="password">

<html>
<head>
  <title>Example 13-9: Retrieving a Complete Message</title>
  <style type="text/css">
    th {
      font-weight : bold;
      color : #0000FF;
      text-align : left;
    }
  </style>
</head>

<body>
<cfoutput>
<table>
  <tr>
    <th>From:</th>
    <td>#HTMLEditFormat(GetMessage.From)# on #HTMLEditFormat(GetMessage.Date)#</td>
  </tr>
  <tr>
    <th>To:</th>
    <td>#HTMLEditFormat(GetMessage.To)#</td>
  </tr>
  <tr>
    <th>Cc:</th>
    <td>#HTMLEditFormat(GetMessage.Cc)#</td>
  </tr>
  <tr>
    <th>Subject:</th>
    <td>#HTMLEditFormat(GetMessage.Subject)#</td>
  </tr>
</table>
<p>
#HTMLCodeFormat(GetMessage.Body)# <br>
</cfoutput>
</body>
</html>
```

In Example 13-9, the action attribute of the cfpop tag is set to GetAll, which lets ColdFusion know that we want to retrieve an entire message as opposed to just the message header. The name attribute lets us specify a name for the query object that will hold the contents of the retrieved message. Because we are retrieving the full contents of a single message, we need to specify the actual message to retrieve using the messagenumber attribute.* In Example 13-9, we hardcode the value for messagenumber, setting it to 1, so that it retrieves the first message stored in the user's account. If you wish to retrieve a full message in an application, the value assigned to messagenumber is dynamic, most likely passed in via URL. We'll look at how this is done at the end of the chapter when we cover how to build a web-based mail client.

If you look at the output section in Example 13-9, you can see that we used the same output variables as were used in our previous example with one exception. In this case, we displayed the body of the message using the variable Body. The HTMLCodeFormat( ) function escapes any HTML that might be contained in the message body while wrapping the contents in HTML <pre>/</pre> tags to preserve the messages layout. This is generally a good idea if you want to keep HTML tags embedded in the message body from being rendered by the browser. It is also a good way to avoid potential security exploits from malicious code embedded within a message.

Dealing with Attachments

When you retrieve the contents of a message with the action attribute set to GetAll, ColdFusion allows you to use an optional attribute, attachmentpath, to specify a path where any attachments retrieved should be stored. ColdFusion creates two additional variables to store the filenames as they are retrieved from the POP server and written to the ColdFusion server, respectively:

queryname.Attachments
: Returns a tab-delimited list of the original filenames of all attached files

queryname.AttachmentFiles
: Returns a tab-delimited list of the names of the attachment files as they were written to the directory specified in the attachmentpath attribute of the cfpop tag

Now that you know what variables are offered for dealing with file attachments, let's look at how to use them. Example 13-10 uses the cfpop tag to retrieve an email message along with any attached files.

Example 13-10. Retrieving multiple attachments with cfpop

```
<!--- Set a variable called tab to the chr value of tab --->
<cfset Tab = Chr(9)>

<!--- Set the message number to retrieve to 1.  This is used as an example only.
      in an actual application, the message number to retrieve would most likely
```

* As an alternative to the messagenumber attribute, ColdFusion offers an optional attribute called UID. The UID attribute allows you to specify the unique identifier (UID) assigned to a mail message (or comma-delimited list of UIDs) as opposed to the message number. UID can be used instead of the messagenumber attribute in cases where the specified POP server doesn't support message numbers (as in the case of the Mercury POP server).

Example 13-10. Retrieving multiple attachments with cfpop (continued)

```
     be passed in as a URL variable from a hyperlinked message header --->
<cfset Message = 1>

<!--- Set the attachment path for the retrieved attachments. --->
<cfset AttachmentPath = "d:\cfusionmx\wwwroot\programmingcf\13">

<!--- Retrieve the message from the POP server --->
<cfpop action="GetAll" name="GetMessage" messagenumber="#Message#"
       server="popserver.example.com"
       timeout="600" username="username" password="password"
       attachmentpath="#AttachmentPath#"
       generateuniquefilenames="yes">

<!--- Output the message header info as well as the body --->
<html>
<head>
  <title>Example 13-10: Retrieving Multiple Attachments with cfpop</title>
  <style type="text/css">
    th {
      font-weight : bold;
      color : #0000FF;
      text-align : left;
    }
  </style>
</head>

<body>

<cfoutput>
<table>
  <tr>
    <th>From:</th>
    <td>#HTMLEditFormat(GetMessage.From)# on #HTMLEditFormat(GetMessage.Date)#</td>
  </tr>
  <tr>
    <th>To:</th>
    <td>#HTMLEditFormat(GetMessage.To)#</td>
  </tr>
  <tr>
    <th>Cc:</th>
    <td>#HTMLEditFormat(GetMessage.Cc)#</td>
  </tr>
  <tr>
    <th>Subject:</th>
    <td>#HTMLEditFormat(GetMessage.Subject)#</td>
  </tr>
</table>
<p>
#HTMLCodeFormat(GetMessage.Body)# <br>

<!--- If there are file attachments, display them and provide links to the
      attachments --->
```

Example 13-10. Retrieving multiple attachments with cfpop (continued)

```
<cfif GetMessage.Attachments is not "">
  <p>
  Attachments:<br>
  <cfloop from="1" to="#ListLen(GetMessage.Attachments,Tab)#"
          index="TheAttachment">
    <a href="#GetFileFromPath(ListGetAt(GetMessage.AttachmentFiles,
       TheAttachment,tab))#">#ListGetAt(GetMessage.Attachments, TheAttachment,
       tab)#</a><br>
  </cfloop>
</cfif>
</cfoutput>
```

The first thing we do in Example 13-10 is create a variable called `Tab` and set it equal to `Chr(9)`, the ASCII value for the tab character. This allows us to represent the tab as a delimiter without having to actually include a hard tab in our code. This might seem like a trivial step, but it solves a problem that often occurs when trying to include tabs in programming code. Depending on the editor you use to write your code and the platform you develop on, the tab character may not be preserved when you save your code. Using `Chr(9)` instead of a hard tab eliminates the possibility of this occurring. The next step involves creating a variable called `Message` that holds the message number to be retrieved. Please note that this is used as an example only. In an actual application, the message number to retrieve would most likely be passed in as a URL variable from a hyperlinked message header. We'll cover this technique later in the chapter when we build a complete POP mail client.

The third step is to create a variable called `AttachmentPath`, to specify the location on your ColdFusion server where file attachments should be stored after they are retrieved from the POP server. It is important that this path be within your web server's root directory, so that it can be viewed/downloaded without having to call a separate template to retrieve the file(s).

Once all the constants have been defined, the next step is to use the `cfpop` tag to retrieve the message, including attachments, from the POP server. To do this, you need to include a new attribute within the tag. The `attachmentpath` attribute specifies a location on the ColdFusion server where any attachments retrieved from the POP server should be stored. In our example, we set this attribute to the value of the `AttachmentPath` variable we defined at the beginning of the template. A second new attribute, `generateuniquefilenames`, is set to `Yes`, causing ColdFusion to automatically generate unique filenames for any attachment retrieved from the POP server so that any name conflicts can be avoided. Generated names are guaranteed to be unique within the directory specified in `attachmentpath`.

Once the message and associated attachments have been retrieved, the message header and body are output to the browser. Next, a `cfif` statement determines if there are any attachments associated with the message. If there are, the `Attachments` variable is looped over, and a link to each file attachment in the list is provided.

Deleting Messages

The cfpop tag can delete unwanted messages from the POP server. Deleting messages is a simple process and takes only a few short lines of code:

```
<cfpop action="Delete"
       messagenumber="1,2,6,9"
       server="popserver.example.com"
       timeout="600"
       username="username"
       password="password">
```

In this case, we set the action attribute of the cfpop tag to Delete. messagenumber specifies the message number or comma-delimited list of message numbers to delete.* Message numbers are usually passed to the tag via a URL or form variable. We'll cover this technique in more detail in the next section. The POP server to delete the message from is specified using the server attribute. An optional timeout value for the operation can be set with the timeout attribute. The username and password attributes are required and specify which account on the POP server the message(s) should be deleted from. You should note that once a message has been deleted from the POP server, message numbers are automatically reassigned. This isn't true of UIDs, which are unique and persist for the life of each message.

Building a Web-Based Email Client

Now that you have a feel for how the cfmail and cfpop tags work, let's take a look at a more complex example that showcases most features of both tags. In our example, we shall build a basic web-based email client. Before beginning, let's outline the functionality and features we'll need for the application. Remember, this is a *basic* email client with bare-bones functionality. We'll need:

- A login screen for users to enter POP server, SMTP server, email address, username, and password
- A method for passing login information from template to template (in a *relatively* secure manner) without using persistent variables
- An Inbox for listing all emails belonging to the user on the POP server with next/previous functionality
- The ability to read a message and download any associated file attachments
- The ability to forward a message to other recipients, including file attachments
- The ability to reply to a message
- The ability to create a new message and attach a file to that message
- The ability to delete messages from the POP server

* You can use the UID attribute in place of the messagenumber attribute to specify message(s) to delete.

With the list of requirements for the application defined, let's map out exactly how the application should flow. The application consists of three templates for handling all POP client functions. The first template, named *login.cfm*, gathers login information for the POP server and posts to the *inbox.cfm* template. The *inbox.cfm* template creates the user's inbox. The inbox consists of a list of the email messages in the user's mailbox. It is here that a user can choose what message to read, delete a message, or create a new message. The *action.cfm* template handles the bulk of the mail client's functionality. It is responsible for reading, creating, forwarding, replying to, and deleting messages.

Now that we have the basic flow of the application, let's look at the templates. Example 13-11 shows *login.cfm*, the user login screen for the application.

Example 13-11. Email client login screen

```
<html>
  <head>
    <title>ColdFusion Mail Client - Login</title>
  </head>
<body>

<h2>Email Login</h2>
<form action="inbox.cfm" method="post">
<table>
  <tr>
    <td>Your email address:</td>
    <td><input type="text" name="EmailAddress" size="30" maxlength="255"></td>
  </tr>
  <tr>
    <td>POP server:</td>
    <td><input type="text" name="POPServer" size="30" maxlength="255"></td>
  </tr>
  <tr>
    <td>SMTP Server:</td>
    <td><input type="text" name="SMTPServer" size="30" maxlength="255"></td>
  </tr>
  <tr>
    <td>Username:</td>
    <td><input type="text" name="UserName" size="30" maxlength="255"></td>
  </tr>
  <tr>
    <td>Password:</td>
    <td><input type="password" name="Password" size="30" maxlength="255"></td>
  </tr>
  <tr>
    <td colspan="2"><input type="submit" name="Submit" value="Submit"></td>
  </tr>
</table>
</form>

</body>
</html>
```

There isn't much to the login screen. It is just a simple HTML form that gathers the user's email address, POP and SMTP server addresses, username, and password. The results are then sent to the next template, *inbox.cfm*, shown in Example 13-12.

Example 13-12. inbox.cfm for the mail client

```
<!--- Initialize constants --->
<cfparam name="NumDisplayMessages" default=10>
<cfparam name="CurrentMessageNumber" default=1>

<!--- If the Password is sent encrypted by URL, decrypt it --->
<cfif IsDefined('URL.Password')>
  <cfset Password = Decrypt(URL.Password,"z815$98")>
</cfif>

<!--- Create a url parameter string. Encrypt the password.  This is not strong
      encryption --->
<cfset Parameters = "EmailAddress=#URLEncodedFormat(EmailAddress)#&PopServer=
#URLEncodedFormat(PopServer)#&SMTPServer=#URLEncodedFormat(SMTPServer)#&Username=
#URLEncodedFormat(Username)#&Password=#URLEncodedFormat(Encrypt(Password,"z815$98"))#">

<!--- Retrieve and display all message headers, 10 at a time.  The number
      displayed per screen can be increased here by increasing the value of the
      NumDisplayMessages variable --->
<cfpop action="GetHeaderOnly" name="GetMessageHeaders" server="#popserver#"
       timeout="600" username="#username#" password="#password#"
       startrow="#CurrentMessageNumber#" maxrows="#NumDisplayMessages#">

<html>
<head>
  <title>Email Client - Inbox</title>
  <style type="text/css">
    body {
      background-color : #C0C0C0;
    }
    th {
      background-color : #0000FF;
      font-weight : bold;
      color : #FFFFFF;
      text-align : center;
    }
    td {
      background-color : #C0C0C0;
      font-size : 10pt;
    }
    td.Main {
      background-color : #FFFFFF;
    }
    .Nav {
      background-color : #C0C0C0;
      font-weight: bold;
    }
  </style>
```

Example 13-12. inbox.cfm for the mail client (continued)

```
</head>
<body>

<div align="Center">
<table border="1" cellpadding="5" cellspacing="1">
  <tr>
    <td class="Main">
      <table border="1" cellpadding="5" cellspacing="0">
        <tr>
          <!--- allow the user to refresh the page or create a new message --->
          <cfoutput>
          <td class="Nav"><a href="inbox.cfm?#Parameters#">Refresh</a></td>
          <td class="Nav"><a href="action.cfm?action=create&#Parameters#">Create
                      Message</a></td>
          </cfoutput>
        </tr>
      </table>

  <div align="Center">
  <h2>Email Client - Inbox</h2>
  </div>

  <!--- Create next/previous buttons as necessary for the messages displayed in
        the inbox.  If you want to display more than 10 messages at a time, you
        need to increase the value in the constants section. --->
  <cfoutput>
  <cfif (CurrentMessageNumber - NumDisplayMessages) gte 0>
  <a href="inbox.cfm?CurrentMessageNumber=#(CurrentMessageNumber
  - 10)#&#Parameters#">Previous</a> |
  </cfif>

  <cfif GetMessageHeaders.RecordCount eq NumDisplayMessages>
  <a href="Inbox.cfm?CurrentMessageNumber=#(CurrentMessageNumber
  + NumDisplayMessages)#&#Parameters#">Next</a>
  </cfif>
  </cfoutput>

  <!--- If there are messages to be displayed, do so and make the page a form so
        that multiple messages can be deleted. --->
  <cfif GetMessageHeaders.RecordCount gt 0>
    <cfoutput>
    <form action="action.cfm?action=delete&#Parameters#" method="Post">
    </cfoutput>
    <input type="submit" value="Delete">
    <table border="0" cellpadding="5" cellspacing="1">
      <tr>
        <th> </th><th>From</th><th>Date</th><th>Subject</th>
      </tr>

      <!--- Output the message headers --->
      <cfoutput query="GetMessageHeaders">
      <tr>
```

Example 13-12. inbox.cfm for the mail client (continued)

```
        <td><input type="Checkbox" name="Message" value="#MessageNumber#"></td>
           <!--- Link the message to the action.cfm page where the full message
                 can be retrieved --->
        <td><a href="action.cfm?action=read&#Parameters#&message=#MessageNumber#">
           #From#</a></td>
           <!--- This date is not formatted because some mail messages contain
                 non standard date formats that cause ColdFusion to throw an
                 error when attempting to format them --->
        <td>#DateFormat(ParseDateTime(Date), 'mm/dd/yyyy')#
           #TimeFormat(ParseDateTime(Date), 'hh:mm tt')#</td>
        <td>#Subject#</td>
      </tr>
      </cfoutput>
    </table>
    <input type="submit" value="Delete">
    </form>

  <!--- If no messages are found, let the user know --->
  <cfelse>
    <h3>No messages found...</h3>
  </cfif>
    </td>
  </tr>
</table>
</div>
</body>
</html>
```

The first thing that Example 13-12 does is initialize a few constants to be used throughout the template. These constants make it easy to customize the application without having to replace multiple instances of the same value. After the constants are initialized, the template checks to see if a user's POP account password has been passed in via an encrypted URL variable. If it has, ColdFusion decrypts the password using the key `z815$98` (this is arbitrary and can be changed to anything you want provided it is used consistently throughout the application) so that it can be used by the application. Next, a variable called `Parameters` is created to hold all the URL parameters that will be passed from template to template throughout the application. The URL parameters contain the user's email address, POP server, SMTP server, username, and encrypted password.

The next section of Example 13-12 retrieves a list of the message headers from the user's POP account using the `cfpop` tag with the `action` attribute set to `GetHeaderOnly`. Only the first 10 message headers are retrieved by setting the `startrow` and `maxrows` attributes to 1 and 10, respectively. These values are set in the constants section of the template. This is also how next/previous functionality is enabled. After the first 10 message headers are retrieved, next/previous links are automatically created that recalculate the values for `startrow` and `maxrows`. Clicking on one of the next/previous links causes the *inbox.cfm* template to be reloaded with the attribute values necessary to grab the next/previous set of message headers.

Once the messages have been retrieved, the inbox page is dynamically assembled and output to the browser, as shown in Figure 13-1. The message headers are listed in table format with the From part of the header displayed as a hyperlink. The From addresses are linked to the next template in the application, *action.cfm*, shown in Example 13-13. The links pass several variables as URL parameters. These variables contain all the user's login information, as well as the message number to be retrieved and the action to be performed by the *action.cfm* template. The inbox template also adds a checkbox next to each message header displayed, which allows users to select multiple messages to be deleted at one time, a very useful feature for web-based mail clients.

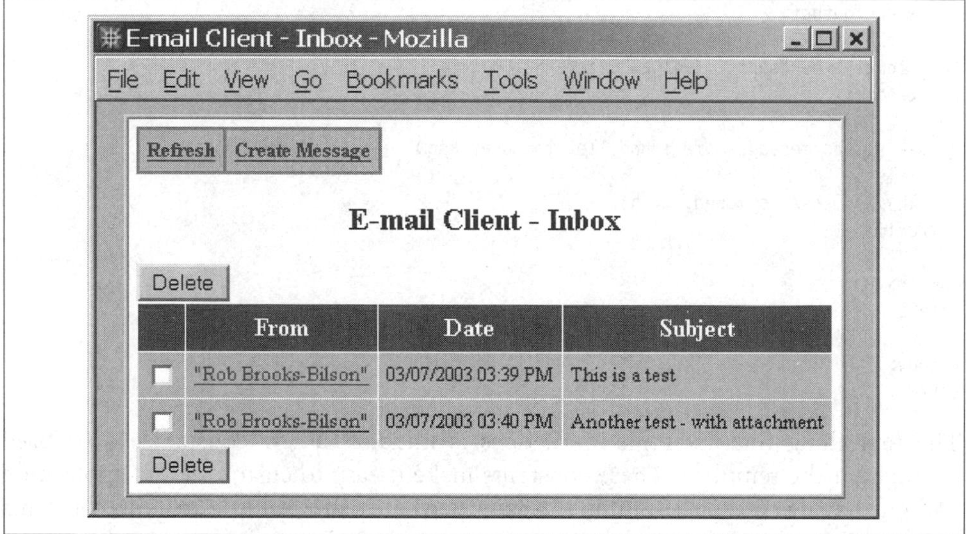

Figure 13-1. Inbox page generated by inbox.cfm

The *action.cfm* template (shown in Example 13-13) performs the majority of the tasks available in the application. This template is responsible for, displaying message contents, creating, forwarding, replying to, and deleting messages.

Example 13-13. action.cfm file for the POP mail client

```
<!--- Initialize constants --->
<cfparam name="Action" default="Invalid"> <!--- Sets default action --->
<cfparam name="ReSubject" default=""> <!--- Default Re: subject --->
<cfparam name="Message" default="0"> <!--- Default message number for delete --->
<!--- Set the attachment path to the same directory where the application
      resides. --->
<cfset TheAttachmentPath = GetDirectoryFromPath(GetCurrentTemplatePath( ))>
<cfset Tab = Chr(9)> <!--- Sets a tab character --->

<!--- If the Password is sent encrypted by URL, decrypt it --->
<cfif IsDefined('URL.Password')>
```

Example 13-13. action.cfm file for the POP mail client (continued)

```
   <cfset Password = Decrypt(URL.Password,"z815$98")>
</cfif>

<!--- Create a url parameter string containing the user's email address, POP
      server, SMTP server, username, and password. Encrypt the password using
      the encrypt( ) function.  This is not strong encryption --->
<cfset Parameters = "EmailAddress=#URLEncodedFormat(EmailAddress)#&PopServer=
#URLEncodedFormat(PopServer)#&SMTPServer=#URLEncodedFormat(SMTPServer)#&Username=
#URLEncodedFormat(Username)#&Password=#URLEncodedFormat(Encrypt(Password,"z815$98"))#">

<html>
<head>
  <title>Pop Client</title>
  <style type="text/css">
    body {
      background-color : #COCOCO;
    }
    th {
      font-weight : bold;
      color : #0000FF;
      text-align : left;
    }
    .Attachments {
      color : #0000FF;
    }
    .Nav {
      background-color : #COCOCO;
      font-weight: bold;
    }
  </style>
</head>
<body>

<div align="Center">
<table border="1"  cellpadding="5">
  <tr>
    <td style="background-color : #FFFFFF;">
      <cfswitch expression="#Action#">

      <!--- Read a message --->
      <cfcase value="Read">
        <cfpop action="GetAll" name="GetMessages" messagenumber="#Message#"
               server="#Popserver#" timeout="600" username="#Username#"
               password="#Password#" attachmentpath="#TheAttachmentPath#"
               generateuniquefilenames="Yes">

        <!--- Output action options --->
        <table border="1" cellpadding="5" cellspacing="0">
          <tr>
            <cfoutput>
            <td class="Nav"><a href="inbox.cfm?#Parameters#">Inbox</a></td>
            <td class="Nav">
```

Example 13-13. action.cfm file for the POP mail client (continued)

```
          <a href="action.cfm?action=create&#Parameters#">Create Message</a></td>
        <td class="Nav">
          <a href="action.cfm?action=reply&message=#URL.Message#&#Parameters#">
            Reply</a></td>
        <td class="Nav">
          <a href="action.cfm?action=forward&message=#URL.Message#&#Parameters#">
            Forward</a></td>
        <td class="Nav">
          <a href="action.cfm?action=delete&message=#URL.Message#&#Parameters#">
            Delete</a></td>
        </cfoutput>
      </tr>
    </table>

    <cfoutput query="GetMessages">
    <hr noshade>
    <p>
    <table>
      <tr>
        <th>From:</th>
        <td>#HTMLEditFormat(GetMessages.From)# on
            #HTMLEditFormat(GetMessages.Date)#</td>
      </tr>
      <tr>
        <th>To:</th>
        <td>#HTMLEditFormat(GetMessages.To)#</td>
      </tr>
      <tr>
        <th>Cc:</th>
        <td>#HTMLEditFormat(GetMessages.Cc)#</td>
      </tr>
      <tr>
        <th>Subject:</th>
        <td>#HTMLEditFormat(GetMessages.Subject)#</td>
      </tr>
    </table>
    <p>
    #HTMLCodeFormat(Trim(GetMessages.Body))# <br>
    <!--- If there are attachments, display links to them --->
    <cfif GetMessages.Attachments is not "">
      Attachments:<br>
      <cfloop from="1" to="#ListLen(GetMessages.Attachments, Tab)#"
              index="TheAttachment">
        <a href="#GetFileFromPath(ListGetAt(GetMessagesAttachmentFiles,
           TheAttachment, Tab))#">#ListGetAt(GetMessagesAttachments,
           TheAttachment, Tab)#</a><br>
      </cfloop>
    </cfif>
    </cfoutput>
  </cfcase>

  <!--- Reply to, forward, or create a message --->
```

Example 13-13. action.cfm file for the POP mail client (continued)

```
<cfcase value="Reply,Forward,Create">
  <table border="1" cellpadding="5" cellspacing="0">
    <tr>
      <cfoutput>
      <td class="Nav"><a href="inbox.cfm?#Parameters#">Inbox</a></td>
      </cfoutput>
    </tr>
  </table>
  <cfif Action is "Reply" or Action is "Forward">
    <cfpop action="GetAll" name="GetMessage" messagenumber="#Message#"
           server="#Popserver#" timeout="600" username="#Username#"
           password="#Password#" attachmentpath="#TheAttachmentPath#"
           generateuniquefilenames="yes">

    <!--- Preface the subject with Re: --->
    <cfif FindNoCase("Re:", Left(Trim(GetMessage.Subject), 3)) is 0>
      <cfset ReSubject = "Re: " & Trim(GetMessage.Subject)>
    <cfelse>
      <cfset ReSubject = Trim(GetMessage.Subject)>
    </cfif>
  </cfif>

  <cfoutput>
  <form action="action.cfm?action=send&#Parameters#" method="POST"
        enctype="multipart/form-data">
  <cfif IsDefined('GetMessage.Attachments')>
    <!--- Include the attachment info --->
    <input type="hidden" name="ForwardedAttachmentFiles"
           value="#GetMessage.AttachmentFiles#">
    <input type="hidden" name="ForwardedAttachments"
           value="#GetMessage.Attachments#">
  </cfif>
  </cfoutput>
  <input type="Submit" value="Send">
  <cfoutput>
  <table>
    <tr>
      <th>To:</th>
      <td><input type="text" name="To" value="<cfif Action is
          "Reply">#HTMLEditFormat(Trim(GetMessage.From))#</cfif>"
          size="50"></td>
    </tr>
    <tr>
      <th>Cc:</th>
      <td><input type="text" name="Cc" size="50"></td>
    </tr>
    <tr>
      <th>Bcc:</th>
      <td><input type="text" name="Bcc" size="50"></td>
    </tr>
    <tr>
      <th>Subject:</th>
```

Example 13-13. action.cfm file for the POP mail client (continued)

```
          <td><input type="text" name="Subject" value="<cfif Action is not
             "Create">#HTMLEditFormat(ReSubject)#</cfif>" size="50"></td>
        </tr>
      </table>

      <p>
      <textarea name="Body" cols="70" rows="15" wrap="Virtual"><cfif Action is
        not "Create">#Chr(10)##Chr(13)#>>#GetMessage.Body#</cfif></textarea></p>
      </cfoutput>

      <!--- If forwarding, include attachments --->
      <cfif Action is "Forward" and GetMessage.Attachments is not "">
        <span class="Attachments" style="font-weight : bold;">Current File
          Attachments:</span><br>
        <cfoutput>
        <span class="Attachments">
        <cfloop from="1"
                to="#ListLen(GetMessage.Attachments, Tab)#"
                index="TheAttachment">
          #ListGetAt(GetMessage.Attachments, TheAttachment, Tab)#<br>
        </cfloop></span>
        </cfoutput>
      </cfif>
      <p>
      <span class="Attachments" style="font-weight : bold;">File
        Attachment:</span><br>
      <input type="File" name="Attachment">
      <p>
      <input type="Submit" value="Send">
      </form>
    </cfcase>

    <!--- Delete a message.  --->
    <cfcase value="Delete">
      <cfpop action="Delete" messagenumber="#Message#" server="#popserver#"
             timeout="600" username="#username#" password="#password#">
      <cflocation URL="inbox.cfm?#Parameters#">
    </cfcase>

    <!--- Send the message --->
    <cfcase value="Send">
      <!--- Check to see if there is an attachment to upload before sending --->
      <cfif IsDefined('form.Attachment') and form.Attachment is not "">
        <cffile action="Upload" filefield="Attachment"
                destination="#TheAttachmentPath#"
                nameconflict="MakeUnique">
      </cfif>

<!--- Send the message --->
<cfmail to="#form.To#"
        from="#EmailAddress#"
        subject="#form.Subject#"
```

Example 13-13. action.cfm file for the POP mail client (continued)

```
        cc="#form.cc#"
        bcc="#form.bcc#"
        server="#SMTPServer#"
        timeout="600">
#form.Body#
<!--- Include the new attachment if necessary --->
<cfif IsDefined('form.Attachment') and form.Attachment is not "">
  <cfmailparam file="#TheAttachmentPath#\#cffile.ServerFile#">
</cfif>

<!--- Include any forwarded attachments if necessary --->
<cfif IsDefined('ForwardedAttachments')>
  <cfloop from="1" to="#ListLen(ForwardedAttachments, Tab)#"
          index="TheAttachment">
    <cfmailparam file="#ListGetAt(ForwardedAttachmentFiles, TheAttachment, Tab)#">
  </cfloop>
</cfif>
</cfmail>
        <cflocation URL="Inbox.cfm?#Parameters#">
      </cfcase>

      <!--- No Action selected.  Redirect back to inbox --->
      <cfdefaultcase>
        <cflocation URL="Inbox.cfm?#Parameters#">
      </cfdefaultcase>
      </cfswitch>
    </td>
  </tr>
</table>
</div>
</body>
</html>
```

Example 13-13 begins in much the same way as Example 13-12. First, constants are assigned for the entire template. If an encrypted password is received, it is unencrypted. Next, a variable called `Parameters` is created to hold all the URL parameters that will be passed from template to template throughout the application. The URL parameters contain the user's email address, POP server, SMTP server, username, and encrypted password.

After these preliminary steps, the template evaluates the `Action` variable passed from the previous template (either *inbox.cfm* or the *action.cfm* template calling itself) and performs the appropriate action. Possible actions for the *action.cfm* template are:

`Action="Read"`
: If `Action` is set to `Read`, the `cfpop` tag retrieves the entire message including attachments. The message number to retrieve is supplied from the *Inbox.cfm* template as a URL variable. If there are file attachments associated with the message, they are displayed by looping through the contents of the `Attachments` and `AttachmentFiles` variables and creating hyperlinks to the actual files. A menu is

generated at the top of the page allowing the user to create a new message, reply to, forward, or delete the message being read, or return to the inbox.

`Action="Create"`
: When the `Action` is set to `Create`, the template displays a form for creating a mail message. The form allows you to specify values for `To`, `Cc`, `Bcc`, `Subject`, `Body`, and a single file attachment.

`Action="Reply"`
: If `Action` is set to `Reply`, the template displays a form for creating a new message with the `To` field already populated with the email address of the sender of the original message. In addition, the body of the original message is included in the body of the new message.

`Action="Forward"`
: Forwarding a message works exactly like replying to a message, except that the `To` field isn't automatically populated. Additionally, any file attachments included with the original message are automatically sent along with the message that is forwarded.

`Action="Delete"`
: If `Action` is set to `Delete`, the template permanently deletes one or more messages from the POP server. Messages are selected for deletion from the inbox page (one message or multiple messages) or from the "Read Message" page.

`Action="Send"`
: If `Action` is set to `Send`, ColdFusion physically sends the message that was created, replied to, or forwarded. If a file attachment is specified, it is uploaded from the client machine to the ColdFusion server, so that it can be sent along with the message. File attachments associated with forwarded messages are also included.

Moving Beyond a Basic Email Client

As I mentioned earlier, the email client we just built is designed to showcase the functionality of the `cfpop` and `cfmail` tags. It is by no means a feature-rich email client, nor is it architected in the most efficient and secure manner. Here are some general ideas for improving the application, should you desire to do so:

- Architect the application using ColdFusion Components (CFCs). This approach makes it easier to segment functionality as well as maintain code. For more information on CFCs, see Chapter 22.
- Instead of passing configuration and security information around in the URL, store these values in a persistent variable scope such as the client or session scope.
- Currently, operations such as replying to and forwarding a message require another round trip to the POP server to retrieve the message a second time to

populate the forward/reply screen. This functionality could be changed so that clicking the forward or reply link when reading a message uses JavaScript to perform a form post with hidden form fields containing the message data. That way, on the forward/reply screen, a second call to the POP server wouldn't be necessary.

- Build in additional functionality to handle things like message folders, message priority, displaying read vs. unread messages, etc.
- Add SSL functionality for more secure transmission of data between the client and the server.
- Include the ability to maintain a name and address book for selecting message recipients.
- Attach personalized email signatures to the end of outgoing messages.
- Allow users to attach multiple file attachments to each outbound message.
- Add exception handling to deal with problems connecting to the POP/SMTP server and other unforeseen exceptions.

CHAPTER 14
Interacting with Other Web Servers Using HTTP

One of ColdFusion's most powerful features is its ability to interact with other web servers via the cfhttp tag. cfhttp allows a ColdFusion application to perform standard HTTP operations (Delete, Get, Head, Options, Post, Put, and Trace) on remote servers. Using cfhttp, you can perform a wide range of functions, such as retrieving text and binary files, reading the contents of delimited text files into query objects, and posting information such as form-field data or XML to forms and applications on remote servers. Some of the more common uses include generating static HTML pages from dynamic data, gathering content such as news articles and press releases from remote sites, automatic form submissions, and intelligent agents capable of interacting with remote services such as stock quote and news feeds. For example, you can use cfhttp to write an agent that can gather information related to a particular company from various services including news sources, search engines, and financial service providers. The information gathered by the agent can be presented to users in any number of ways such as in an email, on a personalized web page, or even in an alphanumeric message sent to a pager. The uses for the cfhttp tag are limited only by your imagination.

Because cfhttp has the ability to grab content from remote sites, questions of copyright, trademark, and intellectual property infringement can come up. It is important to remember that much of what is out on the Internet is protected by copyright. When using cfhttp to gather information from remote sites, you should have a clear understanding of what is protected and what is considered to be under public domain. When in doubt, consider contacting the publisher of the information for permission.

Retrieving Information

cfhttp uses the HTTP GET method to initiate a one-way request for information from a remote server. The transaction mimics the one that a standard web browser uses to request a web page. The only difference is that in the case of cfhttp, the requested page is stored in a ColdFusion variable or in a query object, as opposed to being displayed in the user's browser. Let's look at the different ways in which you can use `cfhttp` to request information from a remote server.

Saving Information to a Variable

In its most simplistic form, `cfhttp` can grab an entire file (either plain text or HTML) and store it in a single variable called `cfhttp.FileContent`. You can access and manipulate the information stored in `cfhttp.FileContent` as you can with any other ColdFusion variable. `cfhttp.FileContent` is only one return variable made available by the `cfhttp` tag. All `cfhttp` operations return a structure called `cfhttp` that contains information returned by the target server. Depending on the HTTP operation performed (as defined by the `method` attribute) as well as the response returned by the target server, the `cfhttp` structure may or may not contain values for the following keys:

`cfhttp.charset`
: Character encoding specified by the response Content-Type header.

`cfhttp.errorDetail`
: In the event of a connection failure, contains details related to the failure. If no failure occurs, this key contains an empty string.

`cfhttp.fileContent`
: Contains the response body resulting from an HTTP operation. If the response is saved as a file, `cfhttp.fileContent` is blank.

`cfhttp.header`
: A string that contains the complete HTTP header in raw form. Contains the same information as `cfhttp.responseHeader`.

`cfhttp.mimeType`
: MIME type of the response as specified by the Content-Type header.

`cfhttp.responseHeader`
: A ColdFusion structure that contains the names and values from the HTTP response header. If a particular key appears only once in the header, it is stored as a simple value within the structure. If a key appears more than once, it is stored as an array within the structure. In ColdFusion MX 6.0, keys that appeared more than once in the response header were stored as a structure within the `cfhttp.responseHeader` structure. This is important to note for backward compatibility.

`cfhttp.statusCode`
: Returns the HTTP status code and associated message relating to the status of the HTTP operation.

cfhttp.text
: Boolean indicating whether the response body Content-Type is text. For a list of the rules used to determine whether the response body is text, see the getasbinary attribute.

The following example illustrates how to use cfhttp to retrieve a remote web page and store it as a variable:

```
<cfhttp method="Get"
        getasbinary="No"
        proxyserver="myproxy.example.com"
        proxyport="80"
        proxyuser="pmoney"
        proxypasswrod="cat"
        URL="http://www.yahoo.com/"
        port="80"
        resolveurl="Yes"
        redirect="Yes"
        useragent="Mozilla/4.0 (compatible; MSIE 6.0; Windows NT 5.0)"
        charset="UTF-8"
        multipart="No"
        timeout="180"
        throwonerror="Yes" />

<cfoutput>
#cfhttp.FileContent#
</cfoutput>
```

The first cfhttp attribute you see is the required method attribute. This specifies the type of HTTP operation to perform. Options are Delete, Get, Head, Options, Post, Put, and Trace. Delete, Head, Options, Put, and Trace are new in ColdFusion MX 6.1. For more information on each of these methods, see Appendix A. getasbinary is a new optional attribute in ColdFusion MX 6.1. It indicates whether to convert the response body returned by a cfhttp operation to the ColdFusion binary data type. If Yes, ColdFusion converts the response body to the binary data type. If No (the default), a response body not recognized by ColdFusion as text is automatically converted to a ColdFusion object. If Auto, a response body not recognized as text is automatically converted to the binary data type. ColdFusion recognizes a response body as text if it meets one or more of the following criteria:

- The header doesn't specify a content type
- The content type starts with "text" or "message"
- The content type is set as "application/octet-stream"

If you must pass through a proxy server for Internet access, the hostname or IP address of that server may be specified in the proxyserver attribute. If the proxy server uses a port other than 80, specify the port number using the proxyport attribute. Likewise, if the proxy server requires a username and password for authentication, you may specify them using the proxyuser and proxypassword attributes, respectively. Both proxyuser and proxypassword are new in ColdFusion MX 6.1. If you don't use a proxy server, don't include this attribute.

The next attribute, URL, is also required; it specifies the full URL, including the protocol (*http://* or *https://*) and host name or IP address of the remote web page you are accessing. Additionally, you may append a port number to the URL (e.g., *http://www.myserver.com:8080/*). In this case, we've used cfhttp to retrieve the home page from Yahoo!'s web site. The port attribute specifies what port the cfhttp tag should try to connect to. This attribute is optional and defaults to the standard HTTP port 80. If used in conjunction with the resolveurl attribute, the port number is automatically appended to all resolved URLs. The port attribute is ignored if a port number is specified in the URL attribute.

Setting the resolveurl attribute to Yes specifies that any partial or relative URLs embedded in the retrieved document are fully resolved, so that all links in the document remain valid. If you want to resolve a URL that doesn't end in a filename (such as *http://www.example.com*), and you set the resolveurl attribute to Yes, you need to supply a trailing forward slash (*http://www.example.com/*) for the URL attribute in order for certain URLs (such as those in img tags) to resolve properly. Since we are outputting the retrieved page to the screen using cfoutput, it is important that all the links function properly.

redirect is an optional attribute that indicates whether or not to allow a cfhttp request to be automatically redirected. If set to No, the cfhttp request fails upon encountering a redirect. If throwonerror is set to Yes, the error code and message associated with the error are written to the cfhttp.StatusCode variable. The cfhttp tag can follow as many as four redirections per request. If this limit is exceeded, ColdFusion treats the next redirect as if the redirect is set to No. The useragent attribute specifies the user agent to pass in the HTTP request header when cfhttp makes a request to a remote web server. In this example, we set useragent to Mozilla/4.0 (compatible; MSIE 6.0; Windows NT 5.0) so that the request appears to the remote web server as if it originated from an Internet Explorer 6.0 browser running on Windows 2000. This feature is especially useful when the information you are trying to retrieve varies depending on the browser making the request.

multipart is a new optional Boolean attribute in ColdFusion MX 6.1. If Yes, ColdFusion sends all form field data (set using the cfhttpparam tag which we'll cover soon) as non-URL encoded multipart form data (Content-Type=multipart/form-data). Additionally, the request's charset is sent along in each Content-Type description, and each form field must be encoded using the same charset. If No, form field data is sent as Content-Type=application/x-www-form-urlencoded unless file type data is also included, in which case all parts are sent using Content-Type=multipart/form-data. The default is No. The charset attribute is optional and new in ColdFusion MX. It lets you specify a Java character set for the file or URL the cfhttp tag is getting or posting. The most common character sets are UTF-8 (the default), UTF-16, UTF-16BE,

UTF-16LE, US-ASCII, and ISO-8859-1. You may use any character set supported by your JRE.

Another optional attribute, timeout,* specifies a timeout in seconds for the cfhttp operation. If a cfsetting requesttimeout value is used in conjunction with the template employing the cfhttp tag, and the timeout attribute of the cfhttp tag is used, ColdFusion uses the lesser of the two values. If, however, no URL timeout value is passed, no cfhttp timeout attribute is used, and no default timeout value is set in the ColdFusion Administrator, ColdFusion will wait indefinitely for the cfhttp tag to process. Because each instance of the cfhttp tag being processed requires a thread of its own, this can have serious performance consequences. Depending on your server and ColdFusion configuration, the potential to hang the server exists if the cfhttp tag utilizes all available threads on the system.

Finally, the throwonerror attribute specifies whether ColdFusion should generate an exception that can be caught with cftry/cfcatch tags should an error occur when executing the cfhttp request. throwonerror is optional and defaults to No. If the throwonerror attribute is set to No, you can still use the cfhttp.StatusCode return variable to detect and handle any errors raised by the operation. cfhttp.StatusCode returns an HTTP 1.1 status code along with a descriptive message. There are 37 status codes detailed in the HTTP 1.1 specification outlined in RFC-2068. For a list of the status codes, see the listing for the cfhttp tag in Appendix A. The complete text of RFC 2068 is available at *http://www.w3.org/Protocols/rfc2068/rfc2068*. In order to get detailed information in the event the cfhttp tag throws an exception, throwonerror must be set to Yes. More information on error and exception handling can be found in Chapter 9.

The use of the closing </cfhttp> tag is only required when cfhttp is used in conjunction with one or more cfhttpparam tags. In the interest of good style and to be compatible with XML standards, however, it is a good idea to use the closing shorthand syntax for cfhttp Get operations:

```
<cfhttp method="Get" URL="www.example.com" />
```

Saving Information to a File

You may opt to save a retrieved file directly to the local filesystem. By adding the path and file attributes to the previous example, we can store the page we retrieved from Yahoo!'s web site right on the hard drive of our ColdFusion server:

```
<cfhttp method="Get" URL="http://www.yahoo.com/"
    file="index.htm" path="c:\temp" />
```

* In ColdFusion MX, the timeout attribute is not functional with versions of the SUN JDK prior to Version 1.4.0.

Note that the resolveurl attribute is intentionally left out. Setting the file and path attributes causes the resolveurl attribute to be ignored. When retrieving a file, ColdFusion uses an additional variable, cfhttp.MimeType, to contain the MIME type of the downloaded file. This is especially useful when downloading a file with an unknown MIME type.

You can also use cfhttp to retrieve binary files from a remote server. Here's how to use cfhttp to retrieve a binary file, in this case a GIF file from the local ColdFusion server:

```
<cfhttp method="Get"
    URL="http://localhost/cfide/administrator/images/cfmx.gif"
    path="c:\temp" />

<cfoutput>
The MIME type of the downloaded file is #cfhttp.MimeType#
</cfoutput>
```

After the file is downloaded, its MIME type is returned to the screen via cfoutput. Note that the file attribute has been left out this time. By default, cfhttp uses the filename from the URL if no file attribute is specified. To save the file under a different name from the default, simply add the new name using the file attribute.

Retrieving HTTP Header Information

The cfhttp tag returns the response header associated with all HTTP operations. The HTTP response header is returned as a ColdFusion structure called cfhttp.ResponseHeader. The exact contents of the cfhttp.ResponseHeader structure vary depending on the web server in use where the page is requested. If a particular key appears only once in the header, it is stored as a simple value within the structure. If a key appears more than once, it is stored as an array within the structure.* Other special header keys, such as the Set-Cookie header, are also stored as structures regardless of the number of times they appear in the header. Another variable, cfhttp.Header, is also returned and contains the raw HTTP response header as a string as opposed to a structure. Example 14-1 illustrates a method for requesting a remote web page and outputting all the data in the HTTP response header without knowing the specific keys in the cfhttp.ResponseHeader structure.

Example 14-1. Outputting the HTTP response header

```
<cfhttp URL="http://www.macromedia.com" method="Head">

<table border="1" cellspacing="0" cellpadding="5">
  <tr>
```

* In ColdFusion MX 6.0, keys that appeared more than once in the response header were stored as a structure within the cfhttp.ResponseHeader structure. This is important to note for backward compatibility.

Example 14-1. Outputting the HTTP response header (continued)

```
    <th>Key</th><th>Value</th>
  </tr>

<cfloop collection="#cfhttp.ResponseHeader#" item="Key">
  <cfset Value = cfhttp.ResponseHeader[Key]>

  <cfif IsStruct(Value)>
    <cfloop collection="#cfhttp.ResponseHeader[Key]#" item="i">
      <cfoutput>
      <tr>
        <td>#key#</td><td>#value[i]#</td>
      </tr>
      </cfoutput>
    </cfloop>
  <cfelse>
  <cfoutput>
  <tr>
    <td>#Key#</td><td>#value#</td>
  </tr>
  </cfoutput>
  </cfif>
</cfloop>
</table>
```

In this example, the cfhttp tag retrieves the header for the home page of Macromedia's web site using the cfhttp Head method. The Head method is useful because it allows you to retrieve the header without having to bring back the entire content of the page. The cfhttp.ResponseHeader is then looped over using the cfloop tag. Each value in the structure is then evaluated to determine whether it is a string or a structure. If the value is a string, it is output directly to the browser. If, however, the value is a structure (as is the case for the Set-Cookie key in the response header obtained from Macromedia's web site), the elements of the structure must be looped over individually and output one at a time. You can also get a good visual representation of the contents of the cfhttp.ResponseHeader structure by dumping it out with cfdump:

```
<cfhttp URL="http://www.macromedia.com" method="Head">
<cfdump var="#cfhttp.ResponseHeader#">
```

Creating Query Objects from Text Files

One of the most useful features of the cfhttp tag is its ability to construct a query object from data contained in a delimited text file. This essentially allows you to use any delimited text file accessible via a URL as a "pseudo" ColdFusion data source; in other words, you don't need a database driver. I say a "pseudo" data source because although a query object can be built from a delimited text file using cfhttp, the cfhttp tag itself can't execute a ColdFusion query against the text file.

There are a number of different scenarios for having `cfhttp` import the contents of a delimited text file into a query object. Some of the more common ones include working with flat files, interfacing with legacy systems, and handling news and stock feeds. For instance, say that the Human Resources department of a particular company uses an outdated personnel program that stores personnel data as a comma-delimited text file on the server. As your company is serious about web-enabling all your legacy data, your boss decides that a contact list application needs to be built that queries the Human Resources personnel database and displays the results as a web page. Using `cfhttp`, you can construct a small program to read in the contents of the text file and dynamically generate a nicely formatted web page listing all the employees and their contact information.

Here's a typical comma-delimited text file with column headers:

```
Name,Title,Department,Extension
Joe Smith,Lead Salesperson,Sales,5515
Nancy Jones,Liaison,Marketing,5596
Tom White,Mechanical Engineer I,Engineering,5525
Jen Brown,Collection Specialist,Billing,5543
```

Getting `cfhttp` to import the contents of such a delimited text file into a query object is easy. The following example shows the proper syntax for building a query object from the data:

```
<cfhttp URL="http://127.0.0.1/programmingcf/14/myfile.txt"
    method="get" name="MyQuery" delimiter="," textqualifier="">
</cfhttp>

<table>
  <tr>
    <th>Name</th><th>Title</th><th>Department</th><th>Extension</th>
  </tr>
<cfoutput query="MyQuery">
  <tr>
    <td>#Name#</td><td>#Title#</td><td>#Department#</td><td>#Extension#</td>
  </tr>
</cfoutput>
</table>
```

We use the `name` attribute to specify the name of the query. Note that this attribute tells `cfhttp` to construct a query object. We set the `delimiter` attribute to a comma, since we are dealing with a comma-delimited text file. Because no text qualifier is used in the text file, the `textqualifier` attribute is set to `""`. A text qualifier is sometimes used in a delimited text file to mark the beginning and end of a column. The default value for the `textqualifier` attribute is the quotation mark ("). Because the quotation mark is a reserved character, if you code it directly in the `textqualifier` attribute it must be escaped as `textqualifier=""""`.

By default, `cfhttp` uses the values found in the first row of a delimited text file as column headers. These headers are used as column names for the query unless alternate names are specified with the `columns` attribute. To ensure that all column headers remain unique within a given query, ColdFusion automatically adds an underscore character (_) to any duplicate column header it finds in the delimited text file. For example, if two column headers called `Name` are found, ColdFusion leaves the first one alone and adds an underscore to the second one, making it `Name_`. In ColdFusion MX, the column names specified in the first row of data do not need to be enclosed in double quotation marks, even if the rest of the column data in the text file is.

Once we have the data stored as a query object, displaying the data is only a matter of using the variables in a `cfoutput` tag. Our example displays the data stored in the query as an HTML table. Note that the column headers used in the `<th>` tags are arbitrary and must be created manually.

In addition to creating a ColdFusion query, the `cfhttp` operation creates a number of other variables that give information about the query object itself:

queryname`.ColumnList`
: A comma-delimited list of column headers for the query

queryname`.CurrentRow`
: The current row of the query that is being processed by `cfoutput`

queryname`.RecordCount`
: The total number of records returned by the query

If for some reason you decide you don't like the column headers that accompany the delimited text file, you can change them with the `columns` attribute. You can use any value as a column header, provided it begins with a letter and contain only letters, numbers, and the underscore character. You must be careful to use the same number of column headers as there are columns in the delimited text file. Failure to do so causes `cfhttp` to return an error.

Because you may not always know the column names being used in a text file, ColdFusion provides a variable called *queryname*`.ColumnList` that holds all the column headers contained in a specified query. As always, you access this variable through the query name:

```
#queryname.ColumnList#
```

With access to the column names, it is fairly easy to construct a single ColdFusion template that can use `cfhttp` to retrieve the contents of any delimited text file that contains column headers and output the results to the screen. All this can be accomplished without knowing anything other than the location of the text file and the delimiter used, as illustrated in Example 14-2.

Example 14-2. Displaying the contents of any comma-delimited text file with cfhttp

```
<!--- Use cfhttp GET to grab the delimited text file.  Assume that the comma
      is the delimiter and there is no text qualifier --->
<cfhttp method="Get"
```

Example 14-2. Displaying the contents of any comma-delimited text file with cfhttp (continued)

```
    URL="http://127.0.0.1/programmingcf/14/myfile.txt"
    name="MyQuery" delimiter="," textqualifier="">

<html>
<head>
  <title>Example 14-2: Displaying the Contents of Any Comma-Delimited Text File
       with cfhttp</title>
  <style type="text/css">
    th {
      background-color : #888888;
      font-weight : bold;
      text-align : center;
    }
    td {
      background-color : #C0C0C0;
    }
  </style>
</head>
<body>
<!--- Build an HTML table with the column headers parsed from the first line
      of the delimited text file --->
<table border="0" cellpadding="3">
  <tr>
<!--- Dynamically build the column headers by looping through the column
      headers returned in the MyQuery.ColumnList variable --->
<cfloop index="ThePosition" from="1" to="#ListLen(MyQuery.ColumnList)#">
  <cfoutput>
    <th>#ListGetAt(MyQuery.ColumnList, ThePosition)#</th>
  </cfoutput>
</cfloop>
  </tr>

<!--- Dynamically build the columns and rows to be output by looping over the
      column names listed in the MyQuery.ColumnList variable.  The values
      contained in the column headers are extracted using array notation. --->
<cfloop query="MyQuery">
  <tr>
  <cfloop index="ListElement" list="#MyQuery.ColumnList#">
    <cfset ColumnValue = MyQuery[ListElement]>
    <td><cfoutput>#ColumnValue#</cfoutput></td>
  </cfloop>
  </tr>
</cfloop>
</table>
</body>
</html>
```

This template uses the `cfhttp` tag to grab a text file called *textfile.txt* and store its contents in a query called `MyQuery`. To obtain the column names, we use a list loop to loop over `MyQuery.ColumnList` and output each column name as a cell in the first row of an HTML table. Remember that `ColumnList` is a special variable created by

ColdFusion that contains a list of all columns in a given query object. Once we have the column names, all that is left is to dump the contents of the query object into the HTML table. This is done by looping over the column names listed in the `MyQuery.ColumnList` variable. The values contained in the column headers are extracted using array notation. Executing the template in Example 14-2 results in the output shown in Figure 14-1.

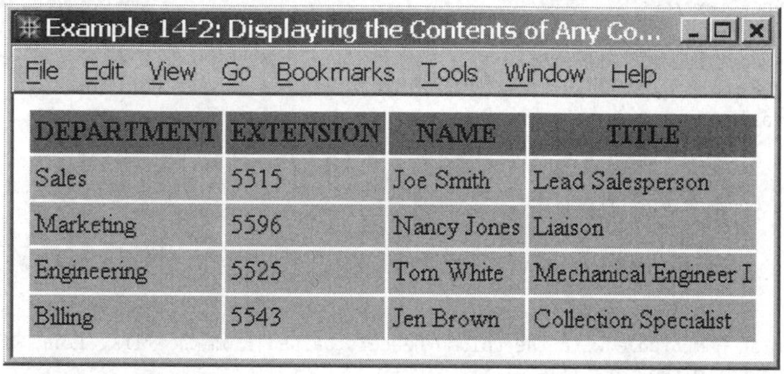

Example 14-2: Displaying the Contents of Any Co...

File Edit View Go Bookmarks Tools Window Help

DEPARTMENT	EXTENSION	NAME	TITLE
Sales	5515	Joe Smith	Lead Salesperson
Marketing	5596	Nancy Jones	Liaison
Engineering	5525	Tom White	Mechanical Engineer I
Billing	5543	Jen Brown	Collection Specialist

Figure 14-1. Using cfhttp to display the contents of a comma-delimited text file

There may be cases where the text file you retrieve with `cfhttp` does not contain column headers in the first row of the file. If you find yourself in this situation, use the `cfhttp` tag's optional `firstrowasheaders` attribute to tell the `cfhttp` tag not to treat the first row of the file as data. If the attribute is set to `No` (the default is `Yes`) and `columns` is not specified, the first row of the text file is treated as data, and column names are automatically generated using the convention `column_1`, `column_2`, ..., `column_n`.* If `firstrowasheaders` is set to `No` and `columns` is specified, ColdFusion uses the values passed in `columns` as the column headers for the query and treats the first row in the text file as data. This functionality is new in ColdFusion MX. For a real world example of how this is useful, take a look at Example 14-3.

Example 14-3. Handling delimited text files without column headers

```
<!--- Use cfhttp to get the delimited text file from Yahoo's web site.  Note
      that the material at yahoo.com is copyrighted. Also note there are no
      line breaks in any of the attribute values in the cfhttp tag. --->
<cfhttp method="Get"
  URL="http://quote.yahoo.com/d/quotes.csv?s=yhoo+amkr+macr&f=sl1d1t1c1ohgv&e=.csv"
  name="MyQuery"
  columns="Symbol,Last_Traded_Price,Last_Traded_Date,Last_Traded_Time,
Change,Opening_Price,Days_High,Days_Low,Volume"
```

* Due to a bug in the initial release of ColdFusion MX, specifying `firstrowasheaders="No"` and omitting the `columns` attribute causes ColdFusion to treat the first row of data in the text file as column headers (just as if the attribute was set to `Yes`). This issue has been fixed in ColdFusion MX 6.1.

Example 14-3. Handling delimited text files without column headers (continued)

```
    delimiter=","
    firstrowasheaders="No">

<html>
<head>
  <title>Example 14-3: Handling Delimited Text Files Without Column
        Headers</title>
  <style type="text/css">
    th {
      background-color : #FFCC99;
      font-weight : bold;
      text-align : center;
    }
    td {
      background-color : #EFD6C6;
    }
  </style>
</head>
<body>
<!--- Build an HTML table with the results from the query --->
<div align="center">
<h2>Stock Quotes From Yahoo</h2>
<table border="1" cellpadding="3">
  <tr>
    <th>Symbol</th><th>Price</th><th>Change</th><th>Time</th><th>Date</th>
    <th>Open</th><th>High</th><th>Low</th><th>Volume</th>
  </tr>
<cfoutput query="MyQuery">
  <tr>
    <td>#Symbol#</td><td>#Last_Traded_Price#</td><td>#Change#</td>
    <td>#Last_Traded_Time#</td><td>#Last_Traded_Date#</td><td>#Opening_Price#</td>
    <td>#Days_High#</td><td>#Days_Low#</td><td>#Volume#</td>
  </tr>
</cfoutput>
</table>
</div>
</body>
</html>
```

The code in this example works by calling a special CGI program on Yahoo!'s web site via URL that returns a delimited text file containing stock quotes. The quotes returned are determined by the ticker symbols that are passed in the URL. The delimited text file returned by the CGI program is converted to a query object by the `cfhttp` tag. Because the first line of the text file doesn't contain any column headers, we specify some using the `columns` attribute and setting `firstrowasheaders` to `No`. Additionally, because the text file uses double quotes to distinguish text from numeric values, we don't need to explicitly set a value for the `textqualifier` attribute since it defaults to double quotes. Once the contents of the text file are stored in a query object, an HTML table is dynamically constructed by outputting the contents of the query.

Passing Parameters

With a cfhttp GET operation, you can pass URL parameters to a remote page that you are attempting to retrieve. This means you can retrieve a page that is dynamically generated from a script based on the parameters passed to it, such as a search page. Here's an example that shows the use of cfhttp to retrieve the results page from a search for "ColdFusion" on Yahoo!'s web site:

```
<cfhttp URL="http://search.yahoo.com/bin/search?p=ColdFusion"
    method="Get" resolveurl="Yes">
</cfhttp>

<cfoutput>
#cfhttp.FileContent#
</cfoutput>
```

Note the URL we are using. It contains the parameters needed to perform the search. Normally, searches on the Yahoo! web site are performed by filling out and submitting an HTML form. The HTML form uses an HTTP GET operation to pass the search criteria as URL parameters to a CGI script. The script returns a dynamically generated HTML page that contains the search results. By passing the search criteria in the URL for our cfhttp operation, we can completely bypass the search form. Of course, to do this, you need to understand exactly what parameters a remote page is expecting and in what form.

Parsing Data

As shown in the previous examples, cfhttp is great for importing the contents of a text file into a query object and allowing for output of results to the screen. This process is useful if you want to dump the results of the file into another database or output the results to a simple HTML table. But what if the data you import requires a little cleaning up beforehand? Take, for example, the following delimited text file containing employee information for a fictitious company:

```
Name,Title,Department,Extension,JobCode
Joe Smith,Lead Salesperson,Sales,5515,A:001
Nancy Jones,Liaison,Marketing,5596,b:003
Tom White,Mechanical Engineer I,Engineering,5525,A:002
Jen Brown,Collection Specialist,Billing,5543,C:004
Mike Johnson,Security Guard,Security,5512,E:012
```

Note that this text file is very similar to the one we used earlier, but there is an added field called JobCode. This new field is used for a number of purposes within the company, including classifying an employee's position. Suppose that we want to use cfhttp to put the contents of this text file into a query object. Nothing tricky needed; it's just a simple cfhttp GET operation.

Once we have the contents of the file in a query object, however, we will want to append an additional column of data called Status and populate it based on each employee's job code. Because the data is already contained within a query, there is no simple way to make the additions. We can wait until the results are output and make the additions inside the cfoutput section, but that will work only if the data is output to the screen and not if you want to save the results of the query to another database. Making additions or changes within the query is the most efficient method. Example 14-4 details a method for inserting additional information into an existing query. In this case, we append an additional column, Status, to the query. This column is populated with data based on the value of the JobCode column.

Example 14-4. Parsing the contents of a cfhttp query

```
<!--- Use cfhttp GET to grab the delimited text file --->
<cfhttp method="Get"
    URL="http://127.0.0.1/programmingcf/14/hrdata.txt"
    name="MyQuery"
    delimiter=","
    textqualifier="">
</cfhttp>

<!--- Create a one-dimensional array called StatusArray to hold the
      status value to be appended to the query object --->
<cfset StatusArray = ArrayNew(1)>

<!--- Loop over the query object checking the first letter of the jobcode.
      Assign a value to the StatusArray depending on the jobcode. --->
<cfloop query="MyQuery">
  <cfswitch expression="#Left(MyQuery.JobCode, 1)#">
    <cfcase value="A,b">
      <cfset StatusArray[CurrentRow]="Exempt">
    </cfcase>
    <cfcase value="C">
      <cfset StatusArray[CurrentRow]="Non-exempt">
    </cfcase>
    <cfcase value="D">
      <cfset StatusArray[CurrentRow]="Temporary">
    </cfcase>
    <cfdefaultcase>
      <cfset StatusArray[CurrentRow]="Other">
    </cfdefaultcase>
  </cfswitch>
</cfloop>

<!--- Create a new column called Status and populate it with the data from
      the StatusArray. --->
<cfset MyNewColumn = QueryAddColumn(MyQuery, "Status", StatusArray)>

<html>
<head>
  <title>Example 14-4: Parsing the Contents of a cfhttp Query</title>
  <style type="text/css">
    th {
      background-color : #8A8A8A;
```

Example 14-4. Parsing the contents of a cfhttp query (continued)

```
        font-weight : bold;
        text-align : center;
      }
      td {
        background-color : #C0C0C0;
      }
    </style>
  </head>
  <body>

  <!--- Output the results of the modified query to an HTML table. --->
  <table border="0" cellpadding="3">
    <tr>
      <th>Name</th>
      <th>Title</th>
      <th>Department</th>
      <th>Extension</th>
      <th>Job Code</th>
      <th>Status</th>
    </tr>
  <cfoutput query="MyQuery">
    <tr>
      <td>#Name#</td>
      <td>#Title#</td>
      <td>#Department#</td>
      <td>#Extension#</td>
      <td>#JobCode#</td>
      <td>#Status#</td>
    </tr>
  </cfoutput>
  </table>
  </body>
  </html>
```

This template uses `cfhttp` to grab a delimited text file and store its contents in a query object called `MyQuery`. Next a one-dimensional array called `StatusArray` is created to hold the status value we are going to append to each record in the query. The actual status value is assigned by looping over `MyQuery` and evaluating the first character of the `JobCode` column for each row. A status is then assigned for each row based on `JobCode` and written to the `StatusArray` array. Once the loop has completed, the values in the array are appended to the `MyQuery` query object using the `QueryAddColumn( )` function. Finally, an HTML table containing the appended `Status` column is produced.

Generating Static HTML Pages

Another popular use for `cfhttp` is to generate static HTML pages from dynamic content. As useful as dynamically generated pages are, there are still times when using static HTML pages makes more sense, because static pages load faster than dynamic pages. Dynamic pages require more processing overhead, because each request must be passed to the ColdFusion Application Server in addition to the web server. This doesn't include the added time it takes to process all the CFML code contained in each template. The differences in load time between static and dynamic pages becomes clear.

Yet, it isn't practical or even desirable to convert every page in a site to a static page. There are some amazing things that can be done with dynamic pages that just can't be re-created with static HTML pages. How do you decide which pages in a site or application should be static and which dynamic? There is no simple answer, but there are some useful guidelines to help you decide:

- Data that is infrequently refreshed is a prime candidate for static page material. For instance, if you have a ColdFusion template that outputs a table of sales figures that change only once per month, it makes more sense to have the page exist as a static page. Why tie up your server with the additional overhead of running the exact same query over and over only to return the same result set each time? It's much simpler to write a small ColdFusion template that performs the query and outputs the results to a static page. The template can even be scheduled to run on an automated basis via the ColdFusion Administrator. This completely eliminates the need for any further administrator involvement.
- Queries that take a long time to process are another candidate for static page generation. If there is one thing that drives users nuts, it is having to wait long periods of time while a query executes or a page loads. Creating static pages from ColdFusion templates that contain unusually long queries, long execution times, or complex CFML code is a service to your users that should definitely be considered.
- Making your site more visible to search engines is the third reason to consider generating static pages from your ColdFusion templates. While many of the popular search engines on the Web can now index ColdFusion pages, some still have problems following links that contain URL parameters. If search-engine exposure is a high priority for your site, you should consider making at least some of your pages static.

Creating a static HTML page from dynamic content is easy. Say your company web site has a dynamically generated press release page that gets its data from a small database residing on the server (in this case, Microsoft Access). The CFML template shown in Example 14-5 is used to query the database for a list of press release titles for the current year. Note that `ArticleID` is the primary key for the table. The other two field names are self-explanatory. Example 14-5 also queries the database for a list of previous years' press releases. Each time a user on the Internet requests this page with their web browser, both queries must be run against the database, and a results page must be dynamically constructed before it can be sent back to the user.

This process has the potential to tie up a lot of the server's processing time. Because the query is the same each and every time this page is accessed, it is a perfect candidate for a static page.

Example 14-5. Listing press-release headers in a database

```
<cfsetting showdebugoutput="No">
<!--- Assign the current year to the variable whichyear --->
<cfparam name="WhichYear" default="#Year(Now( ))#">

<!--- Query the database for all articles from the current year --->
<cfquery name="GetTitles" DATASOURCE="ProgrammingCF">
  SELECT ArticleID,Title,DatePosted
  FROM News
  WHERE {fn YEAR(DatePosted)} = #CreateODBCDate(WhichYear)#
  ORDER BY DatePosted
</cfquery>

<!--- Query the database for all years besides the current year --->
<cfquery name="GetArchiveDates" DATASOURCE="ProgrammingCF">
  SELECT DISTINCT {fn YEAR(DatePosted)} AS PreviousYears
  FROM News
  WHERE {fn YEAR(DatePosted)} <> #CreateODBCDate(WhichYear)#
</cfquery>

<html>
<head>
  <title>Company Press Releases</title>
</head>
<body>

<div align="Center">
<cfoutput><h2>Press Releases for #WhichYear#</h2></cfoutput>

<!--- Output all of the article headers from the selected year.  Make the
      headers links to another template which displays the entire article from
      the database --->
<cfif GetTitles.RecordCount gt 0>
  <table cellspacing="0" cellpadding="3" border="0">
  <cfoutput query="GetTitles">
    <tr>
     <td valign="center">#DateFormat(DatePosted,'mm/dd/yyyy')#  </td>
     <td valign="top"><a href="shownews.cfm?ArticleID=#ArticleID#">#Title#</a></td>
    </tr>
  </cfoutput>
  </table>
<cfelse>
  <h3>There are no press releases for this year</h3>
</cfif>
<!--- List other years available for display.  If another year is chosen, it
      reloads the page with the press releases from that particular year --->
<p>
<b>Other Years</b>
```

Example 14-5. Listing press-release headers in a database (continued)

```
<br>
<cfoutput query="GetArchiveDates">
   <a href="#CGI.Script_Name#?WhichYear=#PreviousYears#">#PreviousYears#</a>
</cfoutput>
</div>
</body>
</html>
```

The actual process of creating a static page from the output of a CFML template is easily achieved using cfhttp. Example 14-6 shows the code necessary to create a static HTML page from the output of any CFML page. This template can be manually run once a day, included as part of an application for adding new press releases to the database, or scheduled to run via the Scheduler in the ColdFusion Administrator.

Example 14-6. Creating a static HTML page from the content

```
<cfhttp method="Get"
        URL="http://localhost/programmingcf/14/14-5.cfm"
        resolveurl="yes">
</cfhttp>

<!--- Write the file grabbed by cfhttp to a new html file on the server --->
<cffile action="write"
        file="c:\inetpub\wwwroot\press_releases\index.htm"
        output="#cfhttp.FileContent#">
Completed
```

It is worth noting that you need to turn off debugging options before attempting to create static pages from ColdFusion templates residing on your local server. Having debug information turned on will cause your static pages to contain all the debug information at the bottom of every page—not a pretty sight. In Example 14-5, we turn off debugging for the template using the cfsetting tag. The option to display debug information can also be turned off site-wide from in the ColdFusion Administrator.

Posting Information

Besides allowing you to retrieve information, you can also post information to remote web sites with cfhttp. By setting the method attribute to Post, you can use cfhttp to pass information such as files, URLs, CGI variables, cookies, and form fields to other web applications, such as a ColdFusion page or CGI program, on a remote server. cfhttp post operations are considered two-way transactions because they pass variables to remote applications, which usually process the input and return data.

When performing cfhttp post operations, you have to specify an additional tag, cfhttpparam, for each value you are passing in the transaction. In other words, if you are using cfhttp to post two form-field variables to a remote form, you need to use two cfhttpparam tags in conjunction with the cfhttp tag. By specifying the variable type in each cfhttpparam tag, ColdFusion allows you to interact with applications that require multipart form data, such as cookies, text, and file fields, in the same operation. Note that cfhttpparam tags are always nested within a cfhttp tag. Here is the syntax for using the cfhttpparam tag:

```
<cfhttpparam name="name"
             type="transaction_type"
             value="variable_value"
             encoded="Yes|No"
             mimetype="MIME_type[and_charset]"
             file="filename">
```

The type attribute specifies the type of information you are passing to the remote application. Possible values are:

`Body`
: Body of an HTTP request. Only one cfhttpparam tag with type="Body" can be used per cfhttp request. Additionally, no other cfhttpparam tags with a type of File, Formfield, or XML may be used in the same request when type="Body". Body cannot be used when the method attribute of cfhttp is set to Trace. This option is new in ColdFusion MX 6.1.

`CGI`
: Sends a variable as a URL encoded HTTP header.

`Cookie`
: Cookie data to send as an HTTP header. The value is automatically URL encoded.

`File`
: Sends the contents of the specified file without URL encoding. File may only be used when the cfhttp method attribute is set to Post or Put.

`Formfield`
: Form field to send. By default, ColdFusion URL encodes the form field value. Formfield is only used when the method attribute of cfhttp is set to Get or Post.

`Header`
: Sends a non-URL-encoded HTTP header. This option is new in ColdFusion MX 6.1.

`URL`
: Appends a URL parameter to the query string on the URL specified in the URL attribute of the CFHTTP tag. The query string is URL encoded.

`XML`
: Sets a Content-Type header of "text/xml" for the request. Automatically sets the body of the request to the XML specified in the value attribute. The XML data is not URL encoded. Only one cfhttpparam tag with type="XML" can be used per cfhttp request. Additionally, no other cfhttpparam tags with a type of Body, File,

or Formfield may be used in the same request when type="XML". XML cannot be used when the method attribute of cfhttp is set to Trace. This option is new in ColdFusion MX.

Sending Form-Field Data

Probably the widest use for the cfhttp post method is posting form-field information to remote applications and scripts. cfhttp allows you to pass variables to an application that takes its input from an HTML form. In Example 14-7, we use cfhttp to pass information to a ColdFusion application on the Macromedia.com web site.

Example 14-7. Using cfhttp post to obtain TechNote articles

```
<cfhttp URL="http://www.macromedia.com/v1/support/KnowledgeBase/Search.cfm"
      method="Post" resolveurl="Yes">
  <cfhttpparam type="FormField" name="SearchString" value="cfhttp">
  <cfhttpparam type="FormField" name="FilterKeywords" value="330, 649, 690, 334">
</cfhttp>

<cfoutput>
#cfhttp.FileContent#
</cfoutput>
```

This application takes the information posted by cfhttp and uses it to find all articles in the Macromedia TechNote database pertaining to the cfhttp tag. The application then dynamically constructs an HTML page that contains the results of the search and passes it back to cfhttp. cfhttp stores the HTML file in the cfhttp.FileContent variable, as always, so we can use cfoutput to display the results.

Sending URL Variables

Using a type of URL allows you to post URL variables to an application that resides on a remote server. Passing a type="URL" also allows you to exploit cfhttp GET functionality in cfhttp post operations. This is done by passing URL variables in conjunction with form fields, cookies, CGI environment variables, or file variables. This technique is useful for interacting with applications that require multipart form data such as cookies and URL parameters in the same operation. Example 14-8 demonstrates how to pass URL parameters along with a cookie to a remote application. You will find here that we make a cfhttp request to Macromedia's TechNote application and pass it two URL parameters as well as two cookie parameters.

Example 14-8. Posting URL and cookie variables to the TechNote application

```
<!--- Use cfhttp to retrieve TechNote 22811 from Macromedia's web
      site.  Also pass two cookies, CFID and CFToken so the web site knows
      who the user is --->
<cfhttp URL="http://www.macromedia.com/v1/handlers/index.cfm"
       method="Post" resolveurl="yes">
```

Example 14-8. Posting URL and cookie variables to the TechNote application (continued)

```
    <cfhttpparam type="URL" name="ID" value="22811">
    <cfhttpparam type="URL" name="method" value="full">
    <cfhttpparam type="Cookie" name="CFID" value="1181774">
    <cfhttpparam type="Cookie" name="CFToken" value="2159">
</cfhttp>

<cfoutput>
#cfhttp.FileContent#
</cfoutput>
```

Note that attempting to post URL variables as parameters in the URL itself causes an error unless at least one `cfhttpparam` tag is declared within the `cfhttp` operation (of course, you can pass parameters in the URL itself if you are using the GET method, as we discussed earlier). Likewise, attempting to pass URL variables in both the URL and in a `cfhttpparam` tag causes an error.

Sending CGI Variables

Most CGI applications don't require that actual CGI environment variables be passed to them (although there are some that do). The CGI variables that are available to an application depend on the server and browser software being used for the request. As a result, the `cfhttp` tag provides a method for passing user-defined CGI environment variables to remote applications regardless of the browser or server software being used. It should be noted, however, that the CGI environment variables are read-only and thus can't be overwritten. This means that if a CGI environment variable already exists in your particular environment, its value can't be changed. A common mistake is to attempt to pass variables to a remote CGI application such as a Perl script in the form of CGI variables. More often than not, the application requires form-field variables, not CGI environment variables. You should use a type of `CGI` only when you need to pass CGI environment variables to a remote application. For example, an application might need the value of the `HTTP_USER_AGENT` variable to check what browser is being used, so that it can determine what browser-specific features to include in its output. The following example shows how to pass two CGI environment variables, `HTTP_USER_AGENT` and `REMOTE_HOST`, to a remote template for processing. While you can pass the `HTTP_USER_AGENT` value with the `useragent` attribute of the `cfhttp` tag, it can also be passed via the `cfhttpparam` tag, as shown here:

```
<cfhttp URL="http://127.0.0.1/programmingcf/14/cgi.cfm"
        method="Post" resolveurl="yes">
    <cfhttpparam type="CGI" name="HTTP_USER_AGENT" value="ColdFusion MX">
    <cfhttpparam type="CGI" name="REMOTE_HOST" value="10.32.34.21">
</cfhttp>

<cfoutput>
#cfhttp.FileContent#
</cfoutput>
```

Sending Cookies

cfhttp can also post cookies to remote sites, which is a useful feature in situations where you want your cfhttp operations to mimic those of an actual user. For example, if you have an application that uses cookies to track users, you can have your cfhttp post operation pass the value of the cookie to the remote application each time it posts information there. This enables your application to differentiate hits caused by your cfhttp operation from hits made by actual users. cfhttp can only send cookies to remote servers; there's currently no mechanism for cfhttp to receive cookies from remote servers (except in the HTTP header returned by a cfhttp request). For an example showing how to pass cookie values using cfhttpparam, refer to Example 14-8.

Sending Files

You can also use cfhttp to post files to remote web servers using the HTTP protocol. You should use this functionality when you want to send a file from your local ColdFusion server to an application located on a remote server for processing. In other words, a type of file supports moving files only from your local ColdFusion server to a remote applications. Once the file has been posted, it is up to the remote program to handle the actual processing of the file. cfhttp can't upload files from client browsers or send files to FTP servers; those operations are handled by the cffile and cfftp tags, respectively. Consider the following scenario. Imagine you have a ColdFusion application that uses an HTML form to allow users to upload files to a particular directory on the ColdFusion server. Now imagine that every week the same file must be manually uploaded to the ColdFusion server from the local development server. This menial process can easily be automated using cfhttp to send the file from the local development server to the remote ColdFusion server. The following template can be called manually or scheduled via the Scheduler in the ColdFusion Administrator:

```
<!--- Post the file to the application that processes the HTML form on the remote
      ColdFusion server --->
<cfhttp URL="http://127.0.0.1/programmingcf/14/TemplateThatProcessesFile.cfm"
      method="Post">

<!--- Picks the file from the specified directory on the server hosting this
      template --->
<cfhttpparam type="File" name="File_Variable"
             file="c:\cfusionmx\wwwroot\programmingcf\14\myfile.txt">
</cfhttp>
```

As of ColdFusion MX 6.1, you can also use the Put method to send a file to a server.

Sending XML

ColdFusion MX added a new type of data that can be posted using the cfhttpparam tag: XML. You can use the cfhttp tag in conjunction with cfhttpparam to post raw

XML in the HTTP header sent with the post. Only one cfhttpparam tag maybe used when posting XML data. XML sent in the HTTP header is not automatically URL-encoded. Here's an example that uses two templates to demonstrate how to post XML data with cfhttp. The first template, shown in Example 14-9, gets an XML news feed from Macromedia.com and posts it to a template named *xmlaccept.cfm* using the cfhttp/cfhttpparam tags.

Example 14-9. Posting XML using the cfhttp/cfhttpparam tags

```
<cfsetting showdebugoutput="No">
<cfhttp URL="http://www.macromedia.com/desdev/resources/macromedia_resources.xml"
       method="Get">

<!--- Post the XML to a second page which dumps the header --->
<cfhttp URL="http://localhost:8500/programmingcf/14/xmlaccept.cfm"
       method="Post" resolveurl="false">
  <cfhttpparam name="TheXML" type="Xml" value="#cfhttp.FileContent#">
</cfhttp>

<cfoutput>
#cfhttp.FileContent#
</cfoutput>
```

The template that Example 14-9 posts to does nothing more than dump the contents of the HTTP header using the cfdump tag:

```
<!--- Save as xmlaccept.cfm --->
<cfsetting showdebugoutput="No">
<cfdump var="#GetHTTPRequestData( )#">
```

The dumped output is displayed in the browser by outputting the contents of the cfhttp.FileContent variable (as shown in Example 14-9).

Sending Header and Body Content

In ColdFusion MX 6.1, you can send header and/or body content using cfhttp. You may send any number of custom headers using this technique. Additionally, you can send along a single message body if you wish. If you send a body along with the request, no other cfhttpparam tags with a type of File, Formfield, or XML may be used in the same request. You should also note that you can't use type="Body" when the cfhttp tag's method attribute is set to Trace. For more information on these parameter types, see the entry for the cfhttpparam tag in Appendix A.

cfhttp Considerations

While cfhttp is extremely powerful, it is worth mentioning some limitations in the various versions of ColdFusion. If you plan to make heavy use of cfhttp, you should carefully consider the issues discussed here.

JRE-Related Issues in ColdFusion MX

Depending on the JRE you are using with ColdFusion MX, there are several issues you need to be aware of that have the potential to affect your use of the `cfhttp` tag:

- The IBM JRE does not properly support SSL connections. If you need to make an SSL connection, consider using the SUN JRE instead.
- The SUN JRE does not always return a 404 status code when an attempt is made to GET or POST a nonexistent page.
- As mentioned earlier, the `timeout` attribute of the `cfhttp` tag is not supported in versions of the SUN JRE prior to version 1.4.0.

Authentication

`cfhttp` supports Basic (plain text), Digest, and NTLM Authentication. This means you can use `cfhttp` to access password-protected pages and files residing on remote servers. Authentication is performed by entering a valid username and password in the `username` and `password` attributes of the `cfhttp` tag, as shown here:

```
<cfhttp method="method"
        URL="url_to_server"
        username="username"
        password="password">
```

CHAPTER 15

Interfacing with LDAP-Enabled Directories

This chapter covers techniques for accessing both public and private Lightweight Directory Access Protocol (LDAP) servers and provides examples of searching directories, displaying results, and adding, editing, and deleting entries. You can use Cold Fusion's `cfldap` tag to access information stored in LDAP-enabled directories (including X.500 directories). LDAP is quickly becoming a standard for delivering directory-based information over the Internet. Popular uses for the `cfldap` tag include creating search interfaces for public and private user directories and creating administrative interfaces for managing LDAP directories.

LDAP Basics

LDAP, currently at Version 3, originated at the University of Michigan. LDAP is a specification that defines a standardized way for organizations to store and access directory information over TCP/IP. Information stored in an LDAP directory is arranged in a hierarchical manner as depicted in Figure 15-1.

LDAP makes it possible to create complex directories of information that can be searched quickly and easily. LDAP directories are most commonly (although by no means exclusively) used to maintain "white pages" information such as names, addresses, and telephone numbers, or organizational structures and contact information. Regardless of the information contained in an LDAP directory, the structure defined by LDAP makes it simple to find the information within the directory.

For clarity and consistency, all the examples used in this chapter assume you are using the Netscape Directory Server 6.01 and that you've installed the included sample LDAP directory for the fictitious company, *example.com*. The examples can be modified easily to work with other directory servers such as those from Lotus, Microsoft, and Novell. For more information on installing and configuring Netscape Directory Server, consult the documentation included with the program. Both the server and the documentation are available for download at *http://enterprise.netscape.com/products/identsvcs/directory.html*.

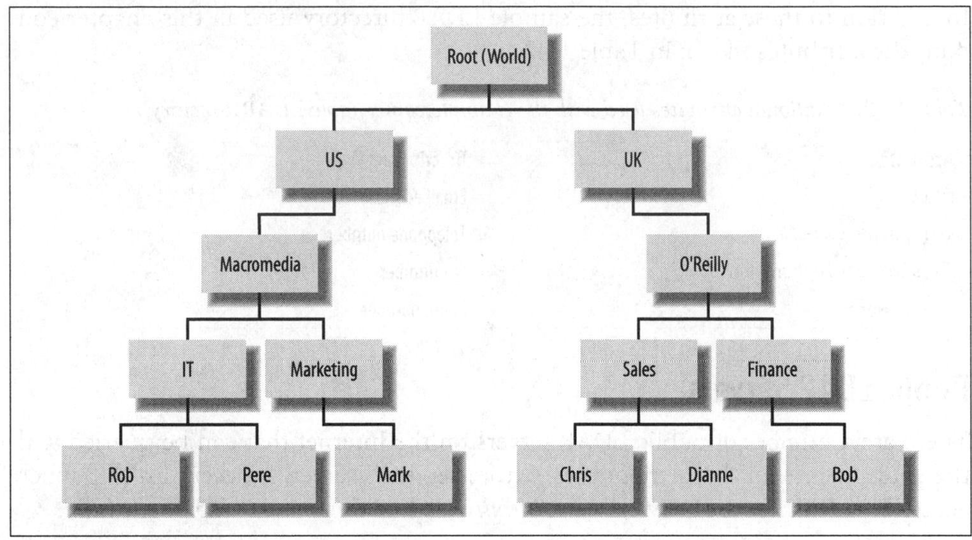

Figure 15-1. A typical LDAP structure

LDAP Attributes

To understand how an LDAP server stores information, you can think of it in database terms. The common descriptive element in a database is a field. In an LDAP directory, fields are called attributes. Although an LDAP server can be configured with any number of custom attributes, several common attributes can be found on most servers being used to store white-pages information. Table 15-1 lists the common attributes along with their descriptions.

Table 15-1. Attributes common to most LDAP directories

Attribute	Description
`c`	Country
`st`	State/province
`l`	Locality/state
`o`	Organization
`ou`	Organizational unit
`cn`	Common name (full name)
`givenname`	Given name (first name)
`sn`	Surname (last name)
`dn`	Distinguished name
`dc`	Domain component
`uid`	User ID

In addition to these attributes, the sample LDAP directory used in this chapter contains the attributes shown in Table 15-2.

Table 15-2. Additional attributes used with the example.com sample LDAP directory

Attribute	Description
`mail`	Email address
`telephonenumber`	Telephone number
`facsimiletelephonenumber`	Fax number
`roomnumber`	Room number

Public LDAP Servers

There are a number of public LDAP servers on the Internet that can be queried with the `cfldap` tag. Available attributes vary from server to server. A decent list of publicly accessible LDAP servers is available at *http://www.emailman.com/ldap/public.html*.

Before continuing, you should be thoroughly familiar with the ins and outs of LDAPv3. For more information on the protocol, associated concepts, and terminology, check out the following web sites:

OpenLDAP
    http://www.openldap.org

The Internet Engineering Task Force's (IETF) LDAP Extension (ldapext) charter and related information
    http://www.ietf.org/html.charters/ldapext-charter.html

LDAPzone.com
    http://www.ldapzone.com

Querying an LDAP Directory

The `cfldap` tag can query an LDAP directory and return the results as a ColdFusion query object. This gives you tremendous flexibility in how you use the data. The query object can be output to the browser using `cfoutput` or used to feed directory information to other functions or templates.

Performing an LDAP Query

Once you know the available attributes of a given LDAP server, you can easily perform a basic query against the directory and output the results to the browser. Example 15-1 shows how to perform a simple query against the *example.com* sample directory included with the Netscape Directory Server.

Example 15-1. Querying an LDAP directory

```
<!--- query the LDAP server for all entries where the surname of the person
      begins with 's' and their location is 'Santa Clara'.  Sort the results
      by surname and given name. --->
<cfldap action="Query"
        name="MyLDAPQuery"
        server="localhost"
        port="389"
        attributes="cn,sn,givenname,ou,mail,l"
        maxrows="100"
        start="dc=example,dc=com"
        scope="Subtree"
        filter="(&(sn=s*)(l=Santa Clara))"
        sort="sn, givenNnme"
        sortcontrol="nocase, ASC"
        timeout="90">

<html>
<head>
  <title>Example 15-1: Querying an LDAP Directory</title>
  <style type="text/css">
    th {
      background-color : #COCOCO;
      font-weight : bold;
      text-align : center;
    }
    td {
      background-color : #9999FF;
    }
  </style>
</head>

<body>
<!--- output the query results --->
<table cellspacing="3" cellspacing="1">
  <tr>
    <th>Common Name (cn)</th>
    <th>Surname (sn)</th>
    <th>Given Name (givenname)</th>
    <th>Organizational Unit (ou)</th>
    <th>Email (mail)</th>
    <th>Locality (l)</th>
  </tr>

  <cfoutput query="MyLDAPQuery">
  <tr>
    <td><cfif cn is ""> <cfelse>#cn#</cfif></td>
    <td><cfif sn is ""> <cfelse>#sn#</cfif></td>
    <td><cfif givenName is ""> <cfelse>#givenName#</cfif></td>
    <td><cfif ou is ""> <cfelse>#ou#</cfif></td>
    <td><cfif mail is ""> <cfelse>#mail#</cfif></td>
    <td><cfif l is ""> <cfelse>#l#</cfif></td>
  </tr>
```

Example 15-1. Querying an LDAP directory (continued)

```
  </cfoutput>
</table>
</body>
</html>
```

In Example 15-1, the first attribute, `action`, is required to specify what action the `cfldap` tag should perform. In this case, we want to use the tag to query an LDAP server, so we set `action` to `Query`. Other possible values for the `action` attribute are `Add`, `Modify`, `ModifyDN`, and `Delete`. Each action is covered later in this chapter. `name` is another required attribute and specifies the name of the query ColdFusion should create to hold the results of the LDAP query. The hostname or IP address of the LDAP server you want to perform the search against is specified in the required `server` attribute. Our LDAP server resides on the same machine as our ColdFusion server, so we set `server` to `localhost`. If the LDAP server you are trying to query listens on a port other than the default 389, you enter that value in the `port` attribute. If `port` isn't specified, the `cfldap` tag defaults to port 389.

`attributes` specifies a comma-delimited list of attributes to be returned by the query. Specifying a wildcard (*) returns all the attributes associated with the query. In this case, we want to retrieve the common name (`cn`), surname, (`sn`), organizational unit (`ou`), and locality (`l`) for each person listed in the directory. The maximum number of results returned by the query is set using the `maxrows` attribute. We set a limit of 100 records for our query. `filter` specifies the search criteria to use when performing the query. `filter` entries are referenced as:

```
(attribute operator value)
```

The default value for `filter` is `(objectclass=*)`. In our example, we set the `filter` attribute so that only entries having a surname (`sn`) beginning with `"s"` and a locality (`l`) of `Santa Clara` are returned. Table 15-3 lists all filter operators.

Table 15-3. Filter operators

Operator	Usage
=	Returns entries where the attribute equals the specified value. For example, searching for `sn=smith` returns entries where the surname of the person is `smith`.
~=	Returns entries where the attribute approximates the specified value. For example, searching for `sn~=smith` returns entries where the surname of the person approximates `smith`.
<=	Returns entries where the entry is equal to or comes before the value specified by the attribute. For example, searching for `st<=de` returns entries where the state equals or comes before `de`.
>=	Returns entries where the entry is equal to or comes after the value specified by the attribute. For example, searching for `st>=de` returns entries where the state equals or comes after `de`.
*	Acts as a wildcard. For example, searching for `sn=*` returns all entries that have a surname attribute, `sn=sm*` returns entries that have a surname beginning with the letters `sm`, and searching for `sn=*ith` returns entries that have a surname ending with the letters `ith`.

Table 15-3. Filter operators (continued)

Operator	Usage
&	Returns entries only when all attributes are found. For example, searching for `(&(sn=smith) (st=de))` returns only entries that contain both the surname `smith` and the state de.
|	Returns entries when any of the attributes are found. For example, searching for `(|(sn=smith) (st=de))` returns entries containing only the surname `smith`, only the state de, or both the surname `smith` and the state de.
!	Returns entries that don't contain the value specified in the attribute. For example, searching for `(!(email=*))` returns all entries that don't have an email address.

If the pattern you are trying to match with `filter` contains any of the special characters in Table 15-4, you must use an escape sequence in place of the special character.

Table 15-4. Escape sequences for the filter attribute

Special character	Escape sequence
*	\2A
(	\28
)	\29
\	\5C
NULL	\00

The next attribute, `start`, specifies the distinguished name to use as the start of the search. In Example 15-1, we use `dc=example,dc=com` to begin the search at the domain component level in our sample LDAP directory. We use the `scope` attribute to specify the scope of the search in relation to the value listed in `start`. Possible entries for `scope` include:

`OneLevel` *(default)*
: Searches one level below the entry specified in the `start` attribute

`Base`
: Searches just the entry specified in the `start` attribute

`Subtree`
: Searches the entry specified in the `start` attribute and all entries below it

`sort` is optional and specifies the attribute or comma-delimited list of attributes to use when sorting query results. In this example, the query results are sorted by the surname (`sn`) then given name (`givenname`) attributes. The `sortcontrol` attribute is also optional and specifies how the results should be sorted. If you wish to perform a case-insensitive sort, `sortcontrol` should be set to `Nocase`. Additionally, sort order may be specified as `Asc` (ascending, the default) or `Desc` (descending). Case sensitivity and sort order may be combined as in our example `sortcontrol="Nocase, Asc"`. Sorting is case sensitive by default.

The final attribute, `timeout`, is also optional and specifies the maximum amount of time in seconds that ColdFusion should wait when processing the query. If no `timeout` is specified, ColdFusion defaults to 60 seconds.

There are several additional attributes available in the `cfldap` tag that aren't covered in this example. For a complete list, see Appendix A.

Once the `cfldap` tag has finished querying the LDAP server, the results are returned in a ColdFusion query object that is subsequently output in an HTML table. The results can be seen in Figure 15-2.

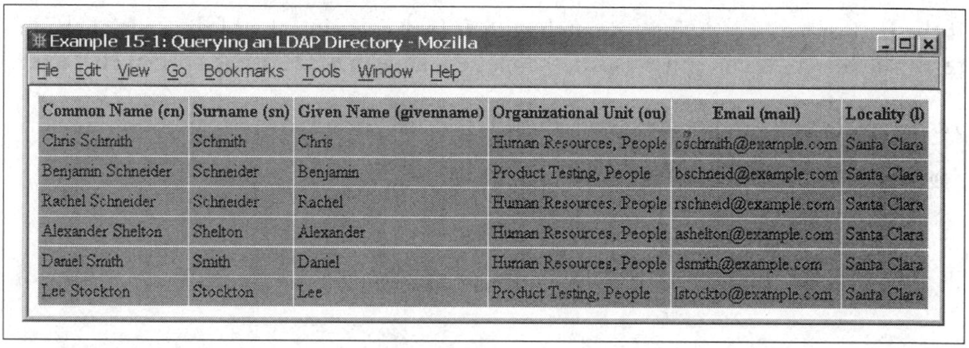
Example 15-1: Querying an LDAP Directory - Mozilla
File Edit View Go Bookmarks Tools Window Help
Common Name (cn) Surname (sn) Given Name (givenname) Organizational Unit (ou) Email (mail) Locality (l)
Chris Schmith Schmith Chris Human Resources, People cschmith@example.com Santa Clara
Benjamin Schneider Schneider Benjamin Product Testing, People bschneid@example.com Santa Clara
Rachel Schneider Schneider Rachel Human Resources, People rschneid@example.com Santa Clara
Alexander Shelton Shelton Alexander Human Resources, People ashelton@example.com Santa Clara
Daniel Smith Smith Daniel Human Resources, People dsmith@example.com Santa Clara
Lee Stockton Stockton Lee Product Testing, People lstockto@example.com Santa Clara

Figure 15-2. Outputting the results of a cfldap query

Obtaining the LDAP Server Schema

In the previous example, we knew ahead of time what attributes were available on our LDAP server. This isn't always the case. If you aren't fortunate enough to have an LDAP server administrator who can provide you with a list of available attributes, you have to query the LDAP server directly and request its schema. LDAPv3 provides a mechanism for obtaining a directory's schema via a special entry in the root `DN`. Example 15-2 shows how to obtain the schema from an LDAPv3-compliant server.

Example 15-2. Retrieving the schema from an LDAPv3-compliant server

```
<cfldap name="GetEntries"
        action="Query"
        server="localhost"
        attributes="subschemasubentry"
        scope="Base"
        start="">

<cfldap name="GetSubEntries"
        action="Query"
        server="localhost"
        attributes="dn, objectclasses, attributetypes"
        scope="Base"
        filter="objectclass=*"
```

Example 15-2. Retrieving the schema from an LDAPv3-compliant server (continued)

```
        start=#GetEntries.SubSchemaSubEntry#>

<!--- Because the comma is the delimiter in the returned lists, and the comma
      can also appear in the list elements, we change the delimiter to the
      pipe --->
<cfset GetSubEntries.ObjectClasses =
    Replace(GetSubEntries.ObjectClasses,  "),",    ")|", "All")>
<cfset GetSubEntries.AttributeTypes =
    Replace(GetSubEntries.AttributeTypes,  "),",   ")|", "All")>

<html>
<head>
  <title>Example 15-2: Retrieving the Schema from a LDAP v3 Compliant
         Server</title>
  <style type="text/css">
    th {
      background-color : #COCOCO;
      font-weight : bold;
      text-align : center;
    }
    td {
      background-color : #9999FF;
    }
  </style>
</head>

<body>

<cfoutput>
<h2>DN: #GetSubEntries.dn#</h2>
</cfoutput>

<h2>Object Classes</h2>
<table cellspacing="3" cellspacing="1">
  <tr>
    <th>Name</th>
    <th>Description</th>
    <th>Superior</th>
    <th>Must</th>
    <th>May</th>
  </tr>
<cfoutput>
<cfloop index="i" list="#GetSubEntries.ObjectClasses#" delimiters="|">
  <cfset Name=Refind("name '([^']*)'",  I,  1, "True")>
  <cfset Desc=Refind("DESC '([^']*)'",  I,  1, "True")>
  <cfset Sup=Refind("SUP ([A-Za-z0-9]*) ",  I,  1, "True")>
  <cfset Must=Refind("MUST ([A-Za-z0-9]*) ",  I,  1, "True")>
  <cfset May=Refind("MAY ([A-Za-z0-9]*) ",  I,  1, "True")>
  <tr>
  <cfif ArrayLen(Name.Pos) gt 1>
    <td>#Mid(i, name.pos[2], name.len[2])#</td>
  <cfelse>
```

Example 15-2. Retrieving the schema from an LDAPv3-compliant server (continued)

```
    <td> </td>
  </cfif>

  <cfif ArrayLen(Desc.Pos) gt 1>
    <td>#Mid(i, desc.pos[2], desc.len[2])#</td>
  <cfelse>
    <td> </td>
  </cfif>

  <cfif ArrayLen(Sup.Pos) gt 1>
    <td>#Mid(i, sup.pos[2], sup.len[2])#</td>
  <cfelse>
    <td> </td>
  </cfif>

  <cfif ArrayLen(Must.Pos) gt 1>
    <td>#Mid(i, must.pos[2], must.len[2])#</td>
  <cfelse>
    <td> </td>
  </cfif>

  <cfif ArrayLen(May.Pos) gt 1>
    <td>#Mid(i, may.pos[2], may.len[2])#</td>
  <cfelse>
    <td> </td>
  </cfif>
  </tr>
</cfloop>
</cfoutput>
</table>

<h2>Attribute Types</h2>
<table cellspacing="3" cellspacing="1">
  <tr>
    <th>Name</th>
    <th>Description</th>
    <th>Single Value?</th>
  </tr>
<cfoutput>
<cfloop index="i" list="#GetSubEntries.AttributeTypes#" delimiters="|">
  <cfset Name=Refind("NAME '([^']*)'", i, 1, "True")>
  <cfset Desc=Refind("DESC '([^']*)'", i, 1, "True")>
  <cfset SingleValue=Find("SINGLE-value", i, 1)>
  <tr>
  <cfif ArrayLen(Name.Pos) gt 1>
    <td>#Mid(i, name.pos[2], name.len[2])#</td>
  <cfelse>
    <td> </td>
  </cfif>

  <cfif ArrayLen(Desc.Pos) gt 1>
    <td>#Mid(i, Desc.Pos[2], Desc.Len[2])#</td>
```

Example 15-2. Retrieving the schema from an LDAPv3-compliant server (continued)

```
    <cfelse>
      <td> </td>
    </cfif>

    <cfif SingleValue eq 0>
      <td>No</td>
    <cfelse>
      <td>Yes</td>
    </cfif>
    </tr>
  </cfloop>
  </cfoutput>
  </table>
  </body>
  </html>
```

In Example 15-2, the `cfldap` query queries the LDAP server specified in the `server` attribute. `server` is required and accepts the IP address or hostname of the LDAP server you want to connect to. We set the `action` attribute to `Query`, letting ColdFusion know we want to use the tag to query an LDAP server. The `name` attribute sets up a query object to hold the result set of the query. In `attributes`, we specify `dn, subschemasubentry` as they are the attributes we want to retrieve. The `scope` attribute is set to `Base` so that the query searches just the entry specified by the `start` attribute. `filter` is set to the default `objectclass=*`, resulting in all entries for the attribute being returned. The final attribute, `start`, specifies the distinguished name (`DN`) to use as the start of the search. In Example 15-2, we set `start` to `""`.

We use the second instance of the `cfldap` tag to query the actual attribute values returned by the first `cfldap` call. We do this by setting the `start` attribute of the second `cfldap` tag to `#GetEntries.SubSchemaSubEntry#`. Note that in this instance, we set `attributes` to `dn, objectclasses, attributetypes`.

Both the `objectclasses` and `attributetypes` attributes return a comma-delimited list of values. If we output these directly to the browser, they would be difficult to read. A much easier-to-read representation of the schema can be had with a little extra parsing. The output code used in Example 15-2 parses out the most relevant parts of the schema and outputs them in a nicely formatted table. For the object type table, the following columns are displayed:

Name
: Name of the object class

Description
: Description for the object class

Superior
: Superior class from which the object class is derived

Must
: Any attribute types required by the object class for entries

May
: Any optional attribute types available to the object class for entries

Note that there are additional values for each object class, but for the purposes of this example, only the most relevant ones are displayed.

The attribute types table consists of the following columns:

Name
: Name of the attribute type

Description
: Description of the attribute type

Single Value
: Yes if the attribute type is a single value, No if it is multivalued

As with the object type table, the attribute type table contains only the most relevant information from the schema.

Modifying LDAP Entries

The best way to illustrate adding, updating, and deleting LDAP entries is to build an example administrative interface that can perform these tasks. The main template of the application is a template named *index.cfm*, which is shown in Example 15-3. This template contains an HTML form with a single select box control containing the common names (first and last names) of each entry in the LDAP server. Below the select box are three buttons—one for adding a new entry, one for modifying an existing entry, and one for deleting an entry.

Example 15-3. Main LDAP administration template

```
<!--- Query the ldap server for all entries --->
<cfldap action="Query" name="GetEntries" server="localhost"
       attributes="dn,cn,sn,givenName" filter="(sn>=A)"
       start="dc=example,dc=com" scope="subtree" sort="sn, givenname">

<html>
<head>
  <title>LDAP Administration</title>
</head>

<center>
<h2>LDAP Administration</h2>

<!--- If a message was passed from the action form, display it --->
<cfif IsDefined('URL.Message')>
  <cfoutput>
```

Example 15-3. Main LDAP administration template (continued)

```
  <h3 style="color: red;">#Message#</h3>
  </cfoutput>
</cfif>

<!--- Display the common name for each entry in a multi-select box.  Assign
      the DN to each option value --->
<form name="MyForm" action="Action.cfm" method="post">

<select name="dn" size="5">
    <cfoutput query="GetEntries">
    <option name="DN" value="#DN#">#CN#</option>
    </cfoutput>
</select>
<br>
<input name="submit" type="Submit" value="Add">
<input name="submit" type="Submit" value="Update">
<input name="submit" type="Submit" value="Delete Entry">
</form>
</center>
</body>
</html>
```

The *index.cfm* template dynamically populates the select box form control by using the cfldap tag to query the LDAP server specified in the server attribute. The query object designated to hold the results of the LDAP query is specified in the name attribute. Here we set name to GetEntries.

attributes takes a comma-delimited list of attributes to be returned with the query. In this case, we want to get the distinguished name (dn), common name (cn), surname (sn), and given name (givenname) for each entry. The filter attribute specifies the search criteria to use for the query. Because we want to return only names (and not blanks and groups), we set the filter to (sn>=A) so that only entries containing a surname (sn) are returned. start specifies the distinguished name to use as the beginning of the search. We set start to dc=example,dc=com because we want to search entries that fall under the example domain component. The scope attribute determines the scope of the search in relation to the value we set in scope. We set scope to SubTree because we want our search to encompass the entry specified in start as well as all the entries below it. The final attribute, sort, specifies the list of attributes to use when sorting the query results. We chose to sort our results by surname (sn), then given name (givenname) in ascending order.

When an administrator opens the *index.cfm* template in a browser window, highlights a user in the select box, or adds a new user by clicking one of the buttons at the bottom of the page, the form posts to the *action.cfm* template shown in Example 15-4.

Example 15-4. Taking the appropriate action

```
<cfparam name="form.Submit" default="Invalid">

<cfswitch expression="#form.Submit#">
  <!--- Include the add/update form --->
  <cfcase value="Add,Update">
    <cfinclude template="_addupdateform.cfm">
  </cfcase>

  <!--- Include the add/update/delete code --->
  <cfcase value="Add Entry,Update Entry,Delete Entry">
    <cfinclude template="_addupdatedelete.cfm">
  </cfcase>

  <!--- Invalid action, redirect to main menu --->
  <cfdefaultcase>
    <cflocation URL="index.cfm?Message=#URLEncodedFormat("Invalid Action")#"
      addtoken="No">
  </cfdefaultcase>
</cfswitch>
```

The *action.cfm* template in Example 15-4 uses a series of `cfcase` statements to evaluate the value of the Submit form field passed to the template. Depending on the value passed in, the template includes an appropriate CFML template to handle the requested function. If no passed parameter meets the `cfcase` criteria, a final `cfdefaultcase` statement redirects the user back to the *index.cfm* template and passes a message stating "Invalid Action." This message also displays if an administrator clicks on the Update or Delete buttons on the *index.cfm* template in Example 15-3 without choosing an entry from the select box.

Adding/Updating Entries

If the user clicks on the Add or Update button in the administration template, the *action.cfm* template includes the *_addupdateform.cfm* template, as shown in Example 15-5.

Example 15-5. _addupdateform.cfm template

```
<cfif form.Submit is "Add">
  <!--- Set default values for all form fields --->
  <cfset GetEntry=StructNew( )>
  <cfset GetEntry.dn="">
  <cfset GetEntry.givenname="">
  <cfset GetEntry.sn="">
  <cfset GetEntry.ou="">
  <cfset GetEntry.l="">
  <cfset GetEntry.telephonenumber="">
  <cfset GetEntry.mail="">
<cfelse>
  <cfif not IsDefined('form.dn')>
```

Example 15-5. _addupdateform.cfm template (continued)

```
    <cflocation URL="Index.cfm?Message=#URLEncodedFormat("You must select a
        record to update.")#" addtoken="No">
  </cfif>
  <!--- Query the ldap server for the user --->
  <cfldap name="GetEntry" action="Query" server="localhost"
          attributes="dn,cn,sn,givenName,ou,l,telephonenumber,mail"
          scope="subtree" start="dc=example,dc=com"
          filter="(#ListFirst(form.DN)#)">
</cfif>

<html>
<head>
  <title>Add/Update LDAP Entry</title>
</head>

<body>

<h2>Add/Update LDAP Entry</h2>
<form action="action.cfm" method="post">
<cfoutput>
<input type="hidden" name="dn" value="#GetEntry.dn#">

<table>
  <tr>
    <td>First Name:</td>
    <td><input type="text" name="givenName" value="#GetEntry.givenname#"
         size="15" maxlength="50"></td>
  </tr>
  <tr>
    <td>Last Name:</td>
    <td><input type="text" name="sn" size="15" value="#GetEntry.sn#"
         maxlength="50"></td>
  </tr>
  <tr>
    <td>Organizational Unit (ou):</td>
    <td><input type="text" name="ou" size="15" value="#GetEntry.ou#"
         maxlength="50"><td>
  </tr>
  <tr>
    <td>Locality:</td>
    <td><input type="text" name="l" value="#GetEntry.l#" size="15"
         maxlength="50"><td>
  </tr>
  <tr>
    <td>Phone</td>
    <td><input type="text" name="telephonenumber"
         value="#GetEntry.telephonenumber#" size="15" maxlength="50"><td>
  </tr>
  <tr>
    <td>E-mail:</td>
    <td><input type="text" name="mail" value="#GetEntry.mail#" size="25"
         maxlength="50"><td>
```

Example 15-5. _addupdateform.cfm template (continued)

```
  </tr>
  <tr>
    <td colspan="2"><input type="submit" name="Submit"
        value="#IIF(Form.Submit is 'Add',
               DE('Add'), DE('Update'))# Entry"></td>
  </tr>
</table>
</cfoutput>
</form>
</body>
</html>
```

This template is a dual-purpose form and can be used to add a new record or update an existing one. If a new record is going to be added, we want to display a blank form. However, if the form is being used to update an existing record, we want to populate the form fields with the data from the record. The technique used here allows us to combine both these functions in a single template that intelligently handles either task.

The template uses a `cfif` statement to determine whether it's being called to add a new record or to update an existing one. If it is being called to add a new record, a structure called `GetEntry` is created, and a key is added that corresponds to each form field. The value for each form field is set to blank. If the *_addupdateform.cfm* template is called as an update form, the template uses the `cfldap` tag to query the directory server for the entry matching the one the administrator selected. In order to retrieve just the record the administrator selected, the `filter` attribute is set to `uid=`*`x`*, where *`x`* is a unique identifier for the entry similar to a database's primary key. The `uid=`*`x`* string is extracted from the `form.dn` field passed from the *index.cfm* template. Because the `dn` contains three values delimited by commas, we use the `ListFirst()` function to retrieve just the first list item, which we know to be the `uid`.

Next, the template either creates a blank HTML form or one populated with the record returned by the LDAP query. The form contains fields for an entrant's given name, surname, organizational unit, locality, phone number, and email address. If the form is being used to create a new entry, the `value` attribute of each form field is populated with a corresponding value from the `GetEntry` structure. Because each of the structure keys contains a blank value, all of the form fields appear blank. Structure values are referenced by calling them as `GetEntry.`*`Fieldname`*, much the same way as the values of a query object are output (you'll see the relevance in a minute). The sample directory included with Netscape's LDAP server contains many more attributes than we use here, but I have decided to keep our application simple.

If the form is used to update an existing record, it is populated with the values from the `GetEntry` query object. The `DN` from the selected entry is assigned to a hidden form field so that it can be passed to the next template and used to identify the entry to be updated in the database.

Notice how the form outputs each value as `GetEntry.Fieldname`: it doesn't care whether `GetEntry` is a structure (for adding a new record) or a query object (for updating an existing record). This powerful technique allows us to use the same form for either purpose in a clean and elegant way. It definitely beats using a bunch of `cfif` statements to check whether a value exists before deciding whether or not to display it in the form.

The `value` attribute of the submit button that appears at the bottom of the form is dynamically generated based upon whether the form is an add form or an update form. Clicking on the button at the bottom of the page posts the form information back to the *action.cfm* template in Example 15-4. The *action.cfm* template then includes the *_addeditdelete.cfm* template. The *_addeditdelete.cfm* template takes the information posted by the form, including the value passed by the submit button, and performs either the add or the update as specified by the form (deleting an entry is covered in the next section). Example 15-6 shows the code for performing the add/update/delete of a record.

Example 15-6. Adding, updating, or deleting an LDAP entry

```
<cfswitch expression="#form.Submit#">
  <!--- Add a new entry --->
  <cfcase value="Add Entry">
    <cfldap action="Add" server="localhost"
            username="cn=Directory Manager" password="administrator"
            attributes="objectclass=top, person, organizationalPerson,
                        inetOrgPerson; cn=#form.givenname# #form.sn#;
                        givenName = #form.givenName#;
                        sn=#form.sn#; mail=#form.mail#;
                        telephonenumber=#form.Telephonenumber#; ou=#form.OU#;
                        l=#form.l#"
            DN="uid=#CreateUUID( )#, ou=People, dc=example,dc=com">

    <cfset Message=UrlEncodedFormat("Entry Successfully Added")>
  </cfcase>

  <!--- Update the entry --->
  <cfcase value="Update Entry">
    <cfldap server="localhost" action="Modify"
            username="cn=Directory Manager" password="administrator"
            attributes="objectclass=top, person, organizationalPerson,
                        inetOrgPerson; cn=#form.givenName# #form.sn#;
                        givenName = #form.givenName#;
                        sn=#form.sn#; mail=#form.mail#;
                        telephonenumber=#form.Telephonenumber#; ou=#form.ou#;
                        l=#form.l#"
            DN="#form.dn#">

    <cfset Message=UrlEncodedFormat("Entry Successfully Updated")>
  </cfcase>

  <!--- Delete the entry from the LDAP server.  Use the DN passed from the form
```

Example 15-6. Adding, updating, or deleting an LDAP entry (continued)

```
        on the Index.cfm page --->
    <cfif not IsDefined('form.dn')>
      <cflocation URL="index.cfm?Message=#URLEncodedFormat("You must select a
         record to delete.")#" addtoken="No">
    </cfif>

  <cfcase value="Delete Entry">
    <cfldap action="Delete" server="localhost" username="cn=Directory Manager"
            password="administrator" DN="#Form.DN#">

    <cfset Message=UrlEncodedFormat("Entry Successfully Deleted")>
  </cfcase>

  <cfdefaultcase>
    <cfset Message=URLEncodedFormat("Invalid Action")>
  </cfdefaultcase>
</cfswitch>

<!--- send the user back to the index page and display a message the
      appropriate message --->
<cflocation URL="index.cfm?Message=#Message#" addtoken="No">
```

If the value of `form.Submit` is "Add Entry", the template takes the information posted by the form and adds the entry to the LDAP directory using the `cfldap` tag with the `action` set to `Add`. Because our LDAP server is set up on the same machine as our ColdFusion server, we set `server` to `localhost`. If your LDAP server is on another machine, enter the hostname or IP address of that machine instead. The `username` attribute specifies the common name (`cn`) of a user with authority to add/update/delete entries. Note that you must prepend `cn=` to the username you specify. If you don't provide it, ColdFusion throws an error stating that you don't have permission to execute the action on the server. The user's password is specified with the `password` attribute.

The attributes to be added are specified as a semicolon-delimited list in `attributes`. `DN` is required and specifies the distinguished name of the entry to be added. For the sample LDAP directory, the distinguished name consists of three attribute/value pairs: `uid`, `ou`, and `o`. For new entries in this example, only user id (`uid`) is a dynamic value. `uid` is used as a unique identifier for each individual entry. You can think of the `uid` attribute as a database's primary key. Netscape's sample LDAP directory creates the `uid` as a concatenation of the first letter of the user's given name and their last name. This obviously causes problems when there are multiple users whose given names begin with the same letter. To account for this, we assign a UUID for each added user's `uid` using ColdFusion's `CreateUUID()` function to guarantee a unique value for each entry that is added. Once the entry is added, the administrator is sent back to the *index.cfm* template, and the message "Entry Successfully Added" is displayed.

If the value of form.Submit is "Update Entry", the template takes the information posted by the form, including the hidden form.DN field, and uses the cfldap tag with the action set to Modify to update the selected entry in the LDAP directory. The username attribute specifies the common name (cn) of a user with authority to update entries. The user's password is specified with the password attribute. The attributes to be updated are specified as a semicolon-delimited list in attributes. DN is required and specifies the distinguished name of the entry to be updated. Once the entry is updated, the administrator is sent back to the *index.cfm* template, and the message "Entry Successfully Updated" is displayed.

Deleting Entries

If an administrator selects an entry on the *index.cfm* page and clicks the Delete button, the *action.cfm* template includes the *_addeditdelete.cfm* template in Example 15-6. The Switch/Case logic in the template then executes the code for deleting an entry. Deleting an entry is simple once you have its DN.

Setting action to delete lets ColdFusion know to pass the DELETE command to the LDAP server specified in the server attribute. The distinguished name of the entry to be deleted is specified in DN. We take the form variable form.DN passed to this template from the *index.cfm* template. Once the entry is deleted, the user is sent back to the *index.cfm* template, and the message "Entry Successfully Deleted" is displayed.

You should note that you can delete only one entry at a time with the cfldap tag. In order to delete more than one entry (if you allow administrators to select more than one user from the main user administration screen), you have to loop over each DN and perform a separate delete.

Modifying the Distinguished Name

The cfldap tag can modify the distinguished name (DN) for a given entry by setting the action attribute to ModifyDN. Our example LDAP directory uses a distinguished name (DN) consisting of three parts:

```
uid=x, ou=People, dc=example,dc=com
```

The uid portion of the dn is known as the leaf relative distinguished name (RDN). The LDAP protocol specifies that when modifying the dn, only the leaf RDN may be modified. This means that you can only change the value of uid using the cfldap tag with the action set to ModifyDN. If you need to change any of the non-leaf RDN values (effectively moving the location of the entry in the directory), you have to delete the entry and re-create it under the correct branch.

To better understand how this works, consider Example 15-7, in which we modify the distinguished name by changing each entry's current user ID (uid) to a unique one created with ColdFusion's CreateUUID( ) function. This method of generating a uid guarantees a unique identifier (unlike concatenating strings like the user's given name and surname).

Example 15-7. Modifying the DN for each entry with a new uid

```
<!--- Query the LDAP directory for all of the user entries --->
<cfldap action="query" name="GetUsers" attributes="dn,cn"
       start="dc=example,dc=com" scope="Subtree" filter="sn>=a"
       server="localhost" timeout="90">

<!--- Output before changing the DN --->
<h3>Original list of user entries</h3>
<cfoutput query="GetUsers">
#cn#: #dn#<br>
</cfoutput>

<!--- Loop over each entry and attempt to change the DN so that the current uid
      is replaced with a UUID created by ColdFusion.  Write an error message to
      the screen for any entries that can not be updated for whatever reason --->
<h3>Modifying the DN for each entry to update the UID</h3>
<cfloop query="GetUsers">
  <cftry>
   <cfldap action="ModifyDN" server="localhost" username="cn=Directory Manager"
          password="administrator" attributes="uid=#CreateUUID( )#"
          DN="#GetUsers.DN#" timeout="90">
   <cfcatch type="any">
    <cfoutput>
    <b>Error:</b>  Couldn't modify DN for entry: #GetUsers.DN#<br>
    </cfoutput>
   </cfcatch>
  </cftry>
</cfloop>

<!--- Query the LDAP directory for all of the user entries --->
<cfldap action="query" name="GetModifiedUsers" attributes="dn,cn"
       start="dc=example,dc=com" scope="Subtree" filter="sn>=a"
       server="localhost" timeout="90">

<!--- Output the modified entries --->
<h3>Modified list of user entries</h3>
<cfoutput query="GetModifiedUsers">
#cn#: #dn#<br>
</cfoutput>
```

The template in Example 15-7 works by first querying the LDAP server for all entries under dc=example,dc=com. A table containing each entry's common name (cn) and distinguished name (DN) is output so you can see the original value for each DN.

Next, cfloop loops over each entry in the query object returned by the first call to the cfldap tag. With each iteration of the loop, another call is made to the cfldap tag with the action set to ModifyDN, so that an attempt can be made to change the DN for each entry. We want to modify the DN such that the current user id (uid) is replaced with a UUID created by ColdFusion. The `cftry/cfcatch` tags can trap any errors that occur and allow processing to continue in case of an error or exception.

Finally, a third call to `cfldap` is made to query the directory for all of the entries we just changed. Another table is generated containing each entry's common name (`cn`) and distinguished name (`DN`), so you can see the changes that were made to each `DN`.

CHAPTER 16
Working with the Verity Search Interface

There is hardly a useful web site out there that doesn't contain a mechanism for allowing users to search through the site for information they are interested in. Not to be left out, ColdFusion MX comes bundled with a set of tags that leverage Verity Developer's Kit (VDK) 2.6.1 technology* to allow you to build powerful search interfaces into your own ColdFusion applications.

This chapter covers methods for setting up and indexing searchable collections using the ColdFusion Administrator and various CFML tags. Once you are familiar with these operations, we will explore techniques for searching collections and returning search results. Additional techniques for maintaining and optimizing collections are also discussed. The chapter concludes with several advanced techniques including methods for synchronizing database and document collections and scheduling automatic indexing of your data.

In addition to the VDK 2.6.1 engine, ColdFusion MX comes with a restricted version of Verity's enterprise-level K2 server. The K2 server offers features that appeal to large-scale and clustered sites, such as simultaneous searching of distributed collections, concurrent queries, and an overall, approvimately ten-fold performance gain over VDK 2.6.1. The version of K2 server that comes with ColdFusion MX is limited to searching 250,000 documents for ColdFusion MX Enterprise and 125,000 documents for ColdFusion MX Professional. Users of Macromedia's Spectra product have a search limit of 750,000 documents. Procedures for searching collections on the K2 server are the same as for the VDK engine. There is no difference in the implementation of the `cfsearch` tag. ColdFusion uses the VDK server to search collections unless they have been specifically configured to use the K2 server. Setting up, configuring, and running the Verity K2 server is a completely separate process and beyond the scope of this chapter. For more information on administering the K2 server, consult the "Working with Verity Tools" section of the *Configuring and Administering Cold-*

* Prior to Version 5.0, ColdFusion shipped with an older version of the VDK.

Fusion MX book that comes with the Macromedia documentation for your version of ColdFusion.

Additionally, there are several command-line utilities for creating, indexing, maintaining, and troubleshooting Verity collections. Although a thorough examination of each of these tools is well beyond the scope of this chapter, they are listed here as a reference. For complete documentation, see the "Working with Verity Tools" section of the *Configuring and Administering ColdFusion MX* book that comes with the documentation for your version of ColdFusion:

mkvdk
: Utility for creating, indexing, and maintaining collections from the command line.

rcvdk
: Performs command-line searching of collections using the VDK engine.

rck2
: Performs command-line searching of collections using the K2 engine.

didump
: Utility for viewing collection word lists.

browse
: Utility for browsing the contents of document tables.

merge
: Utility for combining multiple collections into a single collection or for splitting a single collection into smaller collections. In order to merge collections, all the smaller collections must have been created with the same schema.

Verity Spider
: Creates and indexes collections by crawling filesystems. Spidering is limited to the same domain the ColdFusion server is installed on.

Creating Collections

The first step in creating a search interface for your ColdFusion application is to define a Verity collection and register it with ColdFusion. A Verity collection is actually a specialized database that stores metadata about a group of documents or a ColdFusion query object that you specify. Instead of searching through each of your documents or query objects every time a search is performed, Verity searches through the metadata stored in the collection you created. Because the metadata is highly optimized, Verity can quickly and efficiently locate your search criteria. Collections can be created and subsequently registered via the ColdFusion Administrator or created programmatically with the `cfcollection` tag or via command-line utilities such as Verity's *mkvdk* or *Spider* tools. Consult your ColdFusion documentation for more information on creating and indexing collections with Verity's command-line tools.

Creating Collections with the ColdFusion Administrator

Creating a Verity collection using the ColdFusion Administrator is a quick and painless process. The steps for creating a new collection in the ColdFusion Administrator are as follows:

1. Click on the Verity Collections link in the Data & Services section of the ColdFusion Administrator.
2. Type a unique name for the new collection in the Name text box under the Add New Verity Collections section. Names should contain only letters, numbers, and underscores. In ColdFusion MX, collection names may now contain spaces. However, I'd discourage you from using spaces in collection names in order to preserve backward compatibility with older versions of ColdFusion.
3. Enter a path on the server for the new Verity collection to be stored in. The default path for Verity collections is *\cfusionmx\verity\collections*.
4. Choose the language for the new collection. English is the default language. To create an index in a language other than English requires the Verity Search Pack. This add-on is available for download from Macromedia's web site.
5. Click the Create Collection button to create the new collection. Your new collection should appear in the Connected Local Verity Collections table.

The ColdFusion Administrator also allows you to register a Verity collection that resides on another ColdFusion server (as in a clustered environment) or a collection that was created with a tool other than ColdFusion. The steps for mapping an existing Verity collection are similar to those for creating a new collection. The only difference is that you specify the location to the existing collection in the Path text box of the Add New Verity collections form.

Note that collections created using the retail version of Verity cannot be mapped and searched using the VDK engine, regardless of whether you own a license for the retail version of Verity. To search these types of collections, you need to use the K2 server engine.

Creating Collections with the cfcollection Tag

The `cfcollection` tag allows you to create or map a Verity collection programmatically without having to use the ColdFusion Administrator. This method offers the advantage of allowing your ColdFusion applications to register their own Verity collections. It also allows developers without access to the ColdFusion Administrator to exploit all the administrative functions from within CFML templates.

To create a Verity collection using the `cfcollection` tag, all you have to do is specify a name for the collection, the path to the collection on the ColdFusion server, and the language that the information is in. The following example shows how to create a Verity collection using the `cfcollection` tag:

```
<cflock name="cfcollection_Lock" type="Exclusive" timeout="30">
  <cfcollection action="Create"
                collection="MyVerityCollection"
                path="c:\cfusionmx\verity\collections"
                language="English">
</cflock>
```

It is a good idea to use the cflock tag with all cfcollection operations so that only one process can access the collection at a time. This ensures that multiple operations don't step on each others' toes, potentially resulting in a corrupted Verity collection. Each collection you access via cfcollection should have a unique name assigned to it in the cflock tag

The first attribute, action, is required and tells the cfcollection tag what action to perform on the specified Verity collection. In this case, we are telling the cfcollection tag we want to create a new collection. Other values for the action attribute are discussed later in the chapter. The collection attribute is also required and specifies a name for the collection being created. path, another required attribute, specifies the path to the Verity collection on the server. This must be a physical path accessible by the ColdFusion server. The language attribute is optional. It determines the language to be used when creating the collection. As noted above, to specify a language other than English (the default), you must download and install the appropriate Verity Search Pack from Macromedia's web site.

The cfcollection tag also lets you register an already existing Verity collection, just as you can do with the ColdFusion Administrator. To map an already existing Verity collection, that collection must be available to the ColdFusion server via the local filesystem. The following example demonstrates how to map an existing Verity collection using the cfcollection tag:

```
<cflock name="cfcollection_Lock" type="Exclusive" timeout="30">
  <cfcollection action="Create"
                collection="MyVerityCollection"
                path="c:\cfusion\verity\collections"
                language="English">
</cflock>
```

As you can see, the syntax for mapping a collection is exactly the same as that for creating a collection from scratch. ColdFusion MX is automatically able to determine whether a collection is being created internally or maps to an external collection.

Populating Collections

The next step after creating a Verity collection is to populate it with indexed data. Populating a Verity collection is accomplished with the cfindex tag. With the cfindex tag, ColdFusion can index data from a number of sources including numerous file types and query results from any ColdFusion query. What this means is that you can use the `cfindex` tag to index everything from HTML files and word-processed documents to relational databases, LDAP directories, and POP mail accounts.

Indexing Files

The great thing about bundling Verity's search technology with ColdFusion is that you can build applications capable of searching a wide range of document types, including both text and binary formats. The Verity engine comes with the KeyView Filter Kit, allowing it to index and search over 45 popular document types, including most popular text, word processing, spreadsheet, and presentation formats. For a complete list of supported formats, see the ColdFusion MX documentation at *http://livedocs.macromedia.com*.

Note that versions of ColdFusion through 4.5.1 contain the VDK 2.4.1 engine. Because VDK 2.4.1 is an older technology, Microsoft Office 2000 documents aren't supported. ColdFusion 5.0 and MX include the newer VDK 2.6.1 as well as the Verity K2 Server. These versions of the Verity engine include support for MS Office 2000 documents. You should also be aware that, due to a limitation in the Verity engine, the Linux versions of ColdFusion through 5.0 and MX can't index Adobe PDF documents.

Indexing files with the ColdFusion Administrator

The ColdFusion Administrator provides an interface for indexing files. To follow is a quick and easy way to index a single file or group of files without having to write any code to do it:

1. Click the Index icon in the Connected Local Verity Collections table next to the collection you want to index.
2. Enter a comma-delimited list of file extensions for the Verity engine to index.
3. Enter the full directory path for the directory in which you would like the indexing to take place.
4. If you want Verity to recursively index documents below the directory you specified in the Directory Path field, check the box. Otherwise, Verity indexes only the documents contained in the Directory Path field.
5. You can add a URL to be appended to the beginning of all files indexed by the Verity server. This is useful because it allows you to easily create links to the files indexed by the Verity engine. This technique will be discussed later in this chapter.
6. If you have installed a Verity Search Pack, you can specify an alternate language for the indexing process.
7. Click on the Submit button to begin indexing your collection. The indexing time varies depending on the number, type, and size of the files being indexed.

Indexing files programmatically with cfindex

Indexing files programmatically with the cfindex tag allows you to exert more fine-grained control over your Verity collections. Suppose you have a web site consisting of nothing but HTML pages that you want to index. The following bit of code is all that is necessary to populate a Verity collection from all your HTML pages:

```
<cfindex collection="MyWebsite" type="Path" action="Refresh"
         key="c:\inetsrv\wwwroot\" urlpath="http://127.0.0.1/"
         extensions=".htm, .html" recurse="Yes">
<h2>Finished Indexing The Web Site...</h2>
```

The first thing you should notice here is that we didn't use the cflock tag to lock access to the indexing process. This is because Verity is designed to allow indexing and searching to take place simultaneously. The only time you need to use cflock with Verity is when using the cfcollection tag.

The collection attribute specifies the name of the collection (as created with the ColdFusion Administrator or the cfcollection tag) we want to populate. We set the type attribute equal to Path to let ColdFusion know we want to index a group of files located in a particular path. The type attribute is optional and defaults to Custom if none is specified. The second attribute, action, is also optional and is set to Update in our example. Setting the action attribute to Refresh purges the collection of any existing data and then repopulates it with new data.

We set the key attribute to the path where the files that we are indexing are located. In the previous example, we set key equal to the root directory of our web site. urlpath is also optional and is set to the URL path for the files on our fictitious web site. When this collection is searched using the cfsearch tag, the value specified in the urlpath attribute is added to the beginning of all filenames and returned as the URL attribute. The extensions attribute is optional and should be used when type="Path". It specifies a comma-delimited list of file extensions to be included in the indexing operation. In our example, we set the extensions attribute to *.htm* and *.html* so that only HTML files on our web site get indexed. Setting extensions="*." indexes all files without extensions. Finally, recurse is set to Yes so that our indexing operation indexes all HTML files below the path specified in the key attribute.

Note that the cfindex tag can populate only an existing Verity collection. If the collection you want to populate doesn't exist, you have to create it using the ColdFusion Administrator or the cfcollection tag. The examples throughout this chapter assume you have already created a Verity collection with the name specified in the collection attribute of the cfindex tag.

Sometimes you may need to index only a single file contained in a particular directory as opposed to the whole directory. The cfindex tag can accommodate this by setting the type attribute to File as opposed to Path. This lets ColdFusion know to index only a single file as opposed to every file in the designated path. The following example shows how to index a single file:

```
<cfindex action="Refresh" collection="MyCollection"
        key="D:\inetsrv\wwwroot\myfile.htm"
        type="File" urlpath="http://127.0.0.1">
```

As you can see from the example, the value assigned to the key attribute now contains the filename to index as well as the path to it on the server. Because the filename is specified as part of the key attribute, the extensions attribute can be omitted from the operation.

Indexing Query Results

Besides being able to index files, the Verity engine can also index the contents of any ColdFusion query object. This means that you can create collections from databases, LDAP directories, and POP mail accounts. Query objects can be indexed programmatically only via the cfindex tag. There is no means for indexing them through the ColdFusion Administrator.

Indexing database query results

Why would you want to index the contents of a relational database when you can use SQL to perform searches of the database? The answer is simple. Standard SQL just wasn't designed to efficiently handle full-text searching. Searching for text-based information using the Verity search interface is generally more powerful and faster than using standard SQL queries.*

Suppose we have a Microsoft Access database that stores news-related articles. The database consists of a single table called News that contains the fields shown in Table 16-1.

Table 16-1. News table schema

Field name	Field type	Max length
ArticleID (primary key)	AutoNumber	N/A
ArticleType	Text	255
Title	Text	255
Article	Memo	N/A
DatePosted	Date/Time	N/A

The article titles are stored in the Title field while the actual text of the articles is stored in the Article field. Let's say that we want to make the database searchable by

* Many popular database servers include extensions that allow for various types of full-text searching. The latest versions of both Oracle and MS SQL Server come with such extensions. Before using Verity to handle full-text searching of database data, you might want to explore what options may be available to you in the database itself, as having the database server perform the majority of the work required for the search frees your ColdFusion server to perform other tasks.

either the Title field or the Article field. Creating a Verity collection that contains the contents of both the Title and Article fields is easy.

There are some differences between indexing files and indexing the contents of a relational database. For starters, you aren't actually indexing the database itself but rather a subset of the data existing as a query object. In other words, you are creating your Verity collection from the results of a ColdFusion query against a data source. Example 16-1 demonstrates the method for indexing the contents of a database query object.

Example 16-1. Indexing the contents of a database query result set using cfindex

```
<!--- Query the database for each of the news items to get the ArticleID, Title,
      and Article body --->
<cfquery name="IndexNews" datasource="ProgrammingCF">
   SELECT ArticleID, Title, Article
   FROM News
</cfquery>
<!--- Index the contents of the query object using cfindex --->
<cfindex collection="News" action="Refresh" type="Custom" body="Title,Article"
         key="ArticleID" title="Title" query="IndexNews">

<h2>Finished Indexing The News Database</h2>
```

The first part of the template in Example 16-1 creates a query object containing the ArticleID, Title, and Article for each news item in the database. The second part of the template in Example 16-1 is the actual cfindex operation. This time, we change the type attribute to Custom. This lets ColdFusion know we want to index the contents of a query object as opposed to a group of files. The body attribute contains the column names from the query that we want to index and is a required attribute when type is set to Custom. In our case, we want to index both the Title and Article fields so we define them in the body attribute as a comma-delimited list. When indexing query objects, the key attribute should be set to a unique identifier, usually the primary key for the table. The key attribute differentiates records found during a cfsearch. In our example, we set the key attribute equal to the ArticleID field (primary key) from our database.

Indexing cfldap query results

LDAP directories are another candidate for indexing using ColdFusion and the Verity engine. ColdFusion can index the results of cfldap queries against both public and private LDAP directories. Although most public LDAP servers provide a web page for browser-based searching, the Verity search interface offers a more powerful and flexible way of finding and presenting the information you need for your applications. The cfindex tag makes it easy to index the results of a query performed with the cfldap tag. Example 16-2 shows how to populate a collection with the results of a cfldap query. Because the contents of LDAP directories are subject to frequent change, it may be necessary to update the collection on a regular basis to avoid inaccurate searches. Example 16-2 shows how to use `cfldap` in conjunction with `cfindex` to create a small collection from the Example.com LDAP directory we discussed in Chapter 15.

Example 16-2. Creating a collection from the results of a cfldap query

```
<!--- Use cfldap to query the example.com directory for people in Santa Clara --->
<cfldap action="Query"
        name="MyLDAPQuery"
        server="127.0.0.1"
        attributes="dn,cn,mail,l"
        start="dc=example,dc=com"
        scope="Subtree"
        filter="(&(sn=s*)(l=Santa Clara))">
<!--- Populate the ldap_test collection with the results of the cfldap
      query --->
<cfindex action="Refresh" collection="LDAP_Test" key="dn"
         type="Custom" title="cn" body="cn,mail,l" query="MyLDAPQuery">
<h2>Done Indexing the LDAP Query</h2>
```

In this case, we use `cfldap` to query the *example.com* directory for all people in the Santa Clara office. The results of the query are then added to a Verity collection. In the `cfindex` operation, we set the `action` attribute to `Refresh`. This causes ColdFusion to clear out the contents of the entire collection before repopulating it with the data from the query. Setting the `action` to `Refresh` is a good idea in situations where the data being indexed changes frequently.

Indexing cfpop query results

The `cfindex` tag can also index the contents of a POP mailbox. This is useful in situations where you want to allow users to search through the contents of a particular POP mailbox such as a mailing list or customer service request archive. Example 16-3 shows a simple template for querying and indexing the contents of a POP mailbox. To get the template to work with your POP server, all you have to do is change the values of the `server`, `username`, and `password` attributes to those of your choosing.

Example 16-3. Populating an index based on the results of a cfpop query

```
<!--- Query the POP server --->
<cfpop action="GetAll" name="GetMessages" server="127.0.0.1"
       username="username" password="password">
<!--- Populate the pop_test collection with the results of the cfpop query --->
<cfindex action="Refresh" collection="pop_test" key="Messagenumber"
         type="Custom" title="Subject" query="GetMessages" body="Body">
<h2>Done Indexing the POP Query</h2>
```

Because of the way POP servers work, message numbers tend to change frequently as messages are added or deleted from the server. In order to avoid searching through a collection that is out of sync with the data residing on the POP server, you should probably reindex your POP collection before performing each search operation against it.

Searching Collections

Once you have created and populated a Verity collection, you will naturally want to provide a means for users to search its contents. The cfsearch tag provides just such capability. Using the cfsearch tag, ColdFusion allows you to build sophisticated searching into your applications. In its simplest form, cfsearch can perform the searching operation directly against a Verity collection without the user having to enter anything for the search criteria. A popular use for this technique is in the creation of "top ten" lists of search terms. This technique is covered later in the "Advanced Techniques" section of this chapter. For now, let's take a look at a basic example that demonstrates how to use the cfsearch tag to search a Verity collection without the user having to enter the search criteria:

```
<cfsearch collection="cfdocumentation" name="MySearchQuery" type="Simple"
          criteria="Verity" language="English" external="No">
<cfoutput query="MySearchQuery">
  <a href="/cfdocs/#MySearchQuery.URL#">#MySearchQuery.Title#</a><br>
</cfoutput>
```

The collection attribute is required and specifies the name of the collection you wish to search or, in the case of externally generated collections, the full path to the collection directory. Multiple collections may be searched provided the collection names or paths are separated by commas. When specifying multiple collections, you can't mix internal and external collections, nor can you have VDK and K2 collections in the same search operation. As of ColdFusion MX, collection names may contain spaces. Entering the name of a Verity collection that doesn't exist causes ColdFusion to throw an error. name is also a required attribute and assigns a name to the query object created by the search operation.

The type attribute is optional and defines the type of search to be performed against the Verity collection. Valid types are Simple (the default) and Explicit. In this case, we set the type to Simple, which means that the search returns matches for the word the user specifies and any stemmed variations. (You will find more information on different types of searches later in this chapter.) We define exactly what we want to search for with the criteria attribute. In this example, we want to find all documents that contain the word "verity". The criteria attribute can contain single words or expressions. This attribute is explained in full detail later in the chapter. Leaving the criteria attribute blank causes all records in the Verity collection to be returned. The language attribute is optional and requires the use of the Verity Search Pack for languages other than English. It specifies which language to use in searching a particular Verity collection.

Every cfsearch operation returns a number of variables that can build various types of search result templates, as listed in Appendix A. We'll use some of these variables in upcoming examples.

Building a Search Interface

Creating a search interface for your Verity collections is most often a two- or three-template process. The first template usually contains a form that allows a user to specify their search criteria. The second template (unless the template posts to itself) takes the search criteria from the first template, uses it to search the Verity collection, and returns the results to the user in a meaningful way. In the case of a search against a file collection, the second template typically displays the filename or title of the file, the score assigned to the file, and possibly a short summary of the files contents. For searches against database collections, the second template usually displays the value placed in the title attribute, with a hyperlink to a third template that drills down to a database record identified by the key value in the hyperlink.

Searching file collections

Examples 16-4 and 16-5 illustrate the two-template approach with a search interface that searches the ColdFusion documentation that is installed as part of the standard ColdFusion installation. You'll need to create a Verity collection named cfdocumentation using one of the techniques we covered earlier in the chapter. You'll also need to populate the collection. To do so, run the following code. You may need to tweak the URL and path attributes to match your existing environment:

```
<cfindex action="Refresh"
         collection="cfdocumentation"
         key="d:\cfusionmx\wwwroot\cfdocs"
         type="Path"
         urlpath="http://localhost:8500/cfdocs"
         extensions=".cfm,.htm,.html"
         recurse="Yes">
```

The template in Example 16-4 creates a simple HTML form that allows the user to specify a string they want to search for. A checkbox is provided to allow them to optionally have the summary for each document displayed on the search results page.

Example 16-4. Verity search form for searching a document collection

```
<div align="Center">
<h2>ColdFusion MX Documentation Search</h2>
<form action="16-5.cfm" method="post">
<table border="0">
  <tr>
    <td>Search For:</td>
    <td><input type="text" name="Criteria" size="25" maxlength="255"></td>
  </tr>
```

Example 16-4. Verity search form for searching a document collection (continued)

```
  <tr>
    <td>Include Summary:</td>
    <td><input type="checkbox" name="Summary" value="Yes"></td>
 </tr>
 <tr>
   <td colspan="2" align="center">
     <input type="submit" name="Search" value="Search">
   </td>
 </tr>
</table>
</form>
</div>
```

The second template in our scenario (Example 16-5) receives the form-field data from the template in Example 16-4. It performs the actual search and outputs any matches that it finds.

Example 16-5. Verity document collection search results template

```
<!--- If no search criteria is passed, assume user wants all documents in the
      collection, so assign a wildcard (*) to the search criteria --->
<cfif form.Criteria is "">
   <cfset form.Criteria = "*">
</cfif>
<!--- Perform the search of the Verity collection(s) based on the parameters
      passed from the search criteria form.  In this case, we are searching
      the Verity collection created by ColdFusion the first time you attempt
      to search the ColdFusion documentation using the interface that ships
      with ColdFusion. --->
<cfsearch collection="cfdocumentation" name="Results"
          type="Simple" criteria="#form.Criteria#">
<html>
<head>
  <title>Example 16-5: Verity Document Collection Search Results Template</title>
  <style type="text/css">
    b {
      font-Weight: bold;
    }
    .boldRed {
      color : #FF0000;
      font-weight : bold;
    }
  </style>
</head>
<body>
<h2>Search Results</h2>
<cfoutput>
Your search for: <span class="boldRed">#form.Criteria#</span> turned up
#Results.RecordCount# documents out of #Results.RecordsSearched#
documents searched.
</cfoutput>
<!--- If no records match the search criteria, inform the user --->
```

Example 16-5. Verity document collection search results template (continued)

```
<cfif Results.RecordCount lte 0>
   <cfoutput>
   <p>Sorry.  No instances of <span class="boldRed">#form.Criteria#</span> were
   found in the specified collection(s).  Please hit the back button on your
   browser and try again.
   </cfoutput>
<!--- Otherwise, output the search results including linbks to the
      documents --->
<cfelse>
  <table border="0" cellpadding="3" cellspacing="3" width="75%">
    <tr>
      <td><b>Document Title</b></td>
      <td><b>Score</b></td>
    </tr>
    <tr>
      <td colspan="2"><hr></td>
    </tr>
     <cfoutput query="Results">
    <tr>
      <td>
        <a href="#Results.URL#"><b><cfif Results.Title is "">Untitled><cfelse>
        #Results.Title#</cfif></b></a>
      </td>
      <td>
        <span class="boldRed"><cfif Results.Score is not "">#(Results.Score
        * 100)#%</cfif></span>
      </td>
    </tr>
    <cfif IsDefined('form.Summary')>
    <tr>
      <td><div align="justify">#Results.Summary#</div></td>
      <td> </td>
    </tr>
    </cfif>
    </cfoutput>
    <tr>
      <td colspan="2"><hr></td>
    </tr>
  </table>
</cfif>
</body>
</html>
```

The template in Example 16-5 takes the search string from the form in Example 16-4 and uses it as the `criteria` in the `cfsearch` routine. Once the search has been performed, the template checks to see if there were any matches and if so, presents them to the user. The template presents the results as a table containing the document's title as a hyperlink to the actual document as well and a score for the document. The score is calculated based on Verity's internal set of rules and is returned as a number between 0 and 1. The search results are automatically sorted by score. If you wish to change the sort order, you can do so as of ColdFusion 5.0 by writing a query of a query to resort the results based on a different sort criteria. The template checks to make sure a score was returned, and if so multiplies the number returned by 100, which results in a percentage score for each match. Finally, if the user checks the summary box in the search template, a short summary of each document is included in the table. The output from Example 16-5 can be seen in Figure 16-1.

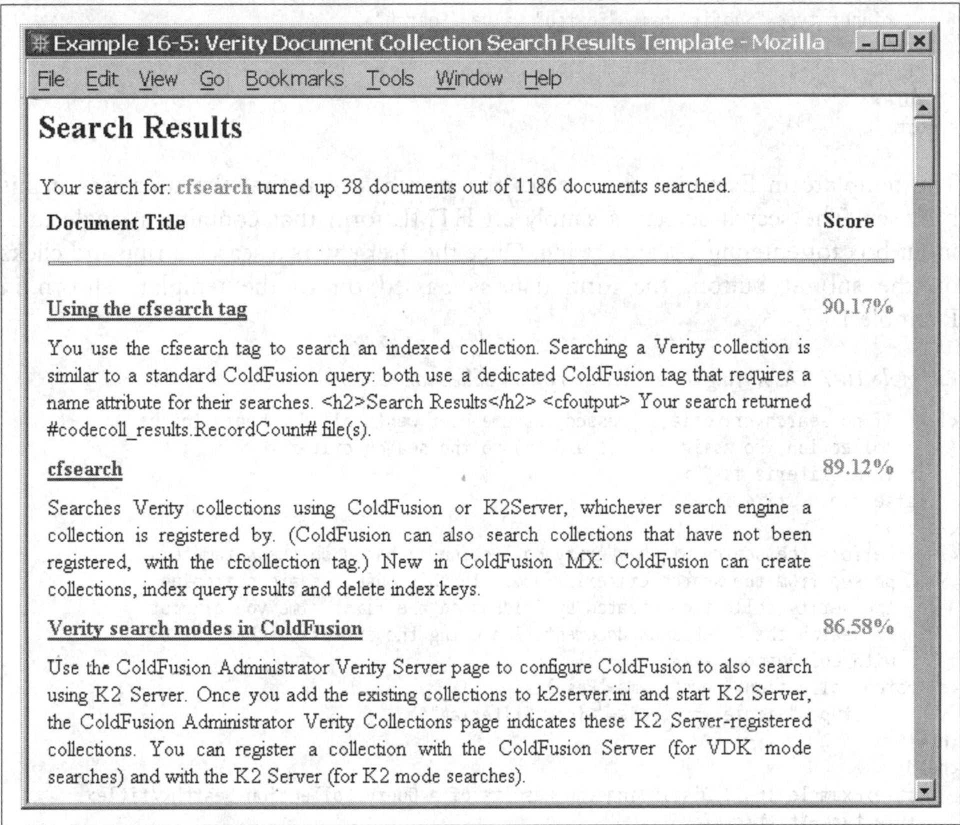

Figure 16-1. Output from a cfsearch of a document collection

Searching database collections

Searching a database collection is just as simple as searching a file collection with a few notable differences. Since we are now searching the contents of a query as opposed to a file collection, we need to change the way the search results are displayed and subsequently acted upon. This is relatively easy to do. Examples 16-6 through 16-18 show a common three-template method for displaying the results of a search against a query collection. The examples use the collection we created back in Example 16-1, which indexed data from the same sample database we have been using throughout the book.

Example 16-6. Specifying database search criteria

```
<form action="16-7.cfm" method="Post">
<table border="0">
  <tr>
    <td>Search For:</td>
    <td>
      <input type="Text" name="Criteria" size="25" maxlength="255">
      <input type="Submit" name="Search" value="Search">
    </td>
  </tr>
</table>
</form>
```

The template in Example 16-6 creates the search screen that the user sees in his browser. The search screen is simply an HTML form that contains a single text-input box for entering a search string. Once the user enters a search string and clicks on the submit button, the form data is passed on to the template shown in Example 16-7.

Example 16-7. Displaying the results of a query collection search

```
<!--- If no search criteria is passed, assume user wants all documents in the
      collection, so assign a wildcard (*) to the search criteria --->
<cfif form.Criteria is "">
   <cfset form.Criteria = "*">
</cfif>
<!--- Perform the search of the Verity collection(s) based on the parameters
      passed from the search criteria form.  In this case, we are searching
      the Verity collection created by ColdFusion the first time you attempt
      to search the ColdFusion documentation using the interface that ships
      with ColdFusion. --->
<cfsearch collection="news" name="Results"
          type="Simple" criteria="#form.Criteria#">
<html>
<head>
  <title>Example 16-7: Displaying the Results of a Query Collection Search</title>
  <style type="text/css">
    b {
      font-Weight: bold;
    }
    .boldRed {
      color : #FF0000;
      font-weight : bold;
    }
  </style>
</head>
<body>
<h2>Search Results</h2>
<cfoutput>
Your search for: <span class="boldRed">#form.Criteria#</span> turned up
#Results.RecordCount# documents out of #Results.RecordsSearched#
documents searched.
```

Example 16-7. Displaying the results of a query collection search (continued)

```
</cfoutput>
<!--- If no records match the search criteria, inform the user --->
<cfif Results.RecordCount lte 0>
   <cfoutput>
   <p>Sorry.  No instances of <span class="boldRed">#form.Criteria#</span> were
   found in the specified collection(s).  Please hit the back button on your
   browser and try again.
   </cfoutput>
<!--- Otherwise, output the search results including linbks to the
      documents --->
<cfelse>
  <table border="0" cellpadding="3" cellspacing="3" width="75%">
    <tr>
      <td><b>Title</b></td>
      <td><b>Score</b></td>
    </tr>
    <tr>
      <td colspan="2"><hr></td>
    </tr>
    <cfoutput query="Results">
    <tr>
      <td><a href="16-8.cfm?ID=#Results.Key#">#Results.Title#</a></td>
      <td>
        <cfif Results.Score is not ""><span class="boldRed">
        #(Results.Score * 100)#%</span></cfif>
      </td>
    </tr>
  </cfoutput>
    <tr>
      <td colspan="2"><hr></td>
    </tr>
  </table>
</cfif>
</body>
</html>
```

The template in Example 16-7 works the same way as the search and results template from Example 16-5, with one notable difference. Instead of returning the title of the document as a link to the actual document, the template returns the value placed in the title attribute as a hyperlink to the template in Example 16-8. A parameter called `ID` is appended to the URL in the link so that the template in Example 16-8 knows which record to drill down to.

Example 16-8. Displaying database record from search results page

```
<!--- Query the news table for the record specified by the ID
      parameter passed in the URL from the previous template --->
<cfquery name="GetRecord" datasource="ProgrammingCF">
  SELECT Title,Article
  FROM News
  WHERE ArticleID=<cfqueryparam value="#Val(URL.ID)#"
                                cfsqltype="CF_SQL_INTEGER">
```

Example 16-8. Displaying database record from search results page (continued)

```
</cfquery>
<cfoutput query="GetRecord">
<b>#Title#</b>
<p>
#Article#
</cfoutput>
```

Example 16-8 takes the value in the URL parameter (the primary key value for the record) passed to it from the template in Example 16-7 and uses it to look up the actual news article in the example database. The article itself is retrieved from the database via a `cfquery` and output to the browser using a corresponding `cfoutput` statement.

The Verity Search Language

When you search a Verity collection using the `cfsearch` tag, you specify a number of parameters, including the `criteria` used for the search. The search criteria consists of zero or more words and/or phrases. The search criteria can also include operators and modifiers to further refine the search. We'll cover all of this in the next section.

It should be noted that Verity handles case sensitivity in the following way:

- If your search string is in all lowercase characters or all uppercase characters, the search is treated as a case-insensitive search.
- If your search string consists of mixed-case characters, the search is treated as a case-sensitive search.

This default behavior can be changed via the `<case>` modifier (which is addressed in the following section) to specify the case for the search.

Simple Versus Explicit Searches

Simple searches allow you to use single words, comma-delimited lists of words, and phrases as the `criteria` for a `cfsearch`. For example, if you want to return all documents containing the word "fish", specify the word "fish" in the `criteria` attribute of the `cfsearch` tag. Similarly, entering a comma-delimited list such as "trout, bass, carp" returns all documents containing "trout", "bass", or "carp". Simple searches treat the comma as a Boolean `or`. Phrases can also be used as `criteria` in a `cfsearch`. Phrases are searched for by entering the phrase as it appears in the `criteria` attribute. For example, entering the phrase "I like fishing" returns only documents that contain that complete phrase.

By default, simple searches employ the `stem` and `many` modifiers. This means that searching for the word "fish" returns all documents containing "fish" as well as "fishes" and "fishing". `stem` is considered an evidence operator and causes the Verity engine to return documents containing derivatives of the word or words in the `criteria` attribute. The `many` modifier counts the number of times a particular search term is encountered within a record being searched. A score is then calculated based on the number of times it appears and the density of the search term within the record.

Simple searches can also use wildcards. For example, entering `con*` as the `criteria` returns all words beginning with "con" such as "construction," "condominium," and "conundrum."

Explicit searches differ from simple searches in that the Verity search engine interprets each search term as a literal. So, a search for the word "test" returns only records containing the word "test", not "tests" or "testing." In an explicit search, the `stem` and `many` modifiers must be called explicitly.

Operators

Operators apply logic and rules to a Verity search. Operators determine the criteria a record must meet before it can be considered a match. Operators can be invoked by the user when using a form-based search interface or behind the scenes when hard-coded into the application. Operators can be used in both simple and explicit searches.

With the exception of `and`, `or`, and `not`, all operators must be enclosed in angle brackets. Enclosing operators in angle brackets keeps the Verity engine from treating the operator as a literal search term. For example, to search for the word "TEST" in uppercase, it is necessary to enter the search criteria as `<case>` as opposed to `case`. The latter causes Verity to look for the word "case" as opposed to interpreting it is an operator. Operators themselves aren't case sensitive.

Order of evaluation. Like expressions, the use of operators is also governed by a set of rules for establishing an order of evaluation. By default, certain operators are given more weight when evaluating search criteria. For instance, the `and` operator is evaluated before an `or` operator. Like the order of evaluation in math, parentheses take precedence over all other factors. When nested parentheses are encountered, evaluation begins with the innermost set.

Prefix and infix notation. Excluding evidence operators, any search string that contains operators can be represented using either prefix or infix notation.

Prefix notation means that the operator being used gets specified before the search string. For example, setting the search criteria to `and (test, exam, final)` returns records only if they contain the words "test", "exam", and "final".

Infix notation requires that an operator be placed between each search term. Using the previous search criteria of "test", "exam", and "final", if you want to search for them using infix notation, you would specify `test and exam and final` or `test <and> exam <and> final` as the search criteria.

Quotation marks. Single or double quotation marks are used to search for operators as literal words. For example, to search for the word "not", it needs to be surrounded in quotes to avoid having the Verity engine interpret it as an operator. I prefer to use single quotes as they don't need to be escaped when specifying a literal criteria such as `criteria="'not'"`.

Special characters. There are several characters considered "special" by the Verity engine that must be escaped to be searched as literals. The backslash (\) is used to escape all special characters. To specify a backslash as a literal search character, it must be escaped by another backslash (\\). The following is a list of special characters that require escaping:

- At/for sign (@)
- Backslash (\)
- Backquote (')
- Comma (,)
- Double quotation mark (")
- Left and right angle bracket (<>)
- Left and right bracket ([ ])
- Left and right curly bracket ({ })
- Left and right parentheses (( ))

In addition to the backslash character, special characters can also be searched as literals if they are included within backquotes. For example, to search for "webmaster@example.com", you specify the search criteria as "'webmaster@example.com'". To search for the backquote as a literal, it must be escaped with another backquote.

Concept operators. Concept operators identify a concept in a document by linking a group of search terms using criteria specified by the operator. Records retrieved using concept operators are ranked by relevance. The following concept operators are available for use in your search criteria:

`accrue`
: Causes records to be returned when they contain at least one of the search terms specified. `accrue` differs from `or` in that ranking is based on the number of times each search term is found.

`all`
: Causes records to be returned only when all search terms are found. Same as the `and` operator except a score of 1.00 is always returned for matches.

`and`
: Causes records to be returned only when all search terms are found. For example, searching for "dog and cat" returns only records that contain both the word "dog" and the word "cat".

`any`
: Causes records to be returned when any of the search terms are found. Same as the `or` operator except a score of 1.00 is always returned for matches.

`or`
: Causes records to be returned when any one word is found. For example, searching for "cat or dog" returns records containing only "cat", only "dog", or both "cat" and "dog".

Evidence operators. Evidence operators differentiate between basic and intelligent word searches. Basic word searches look only for the particular word specified. Intelligent word searches look for additional words related to the search term based on derivatives and wildcards. Here are the evidence operators:

`soundex`
: Finds words that sound alike or have a similar structure to the specified word. `soundex` uses the AT&T standard soundex algorithm. For example, searching for "<soundex> there" typically returns records containing words such as "their" and "they're". In order to use `soundex`, you must edit the *style.prm* file located in either *c:\cfusionmx\lib\common\style\custom* or *c:\cfusionmx\lib\common\style\file*, depending on the type of collection that you are working with. Change the line that reads:

```
$define word-IDXOPTS  "Stemdex Casedex"
```

to:

```
$define word-IDXOPTS  "Stemdex Casedex Soundex"
```

Once you have done this, purge and reindex the collection. You can now perform soundex searches using the `soundex` operator.

`stem`
: Finds words that derive from the search term(s). Searching for "<stem>list" returns records containing the words "list", "lists", and "listing", etc. Simple searches employ the `stem` operator by default.

`thesaurus`
: Allows you to search for synonyms of search terms. For example, searching for "<thesaurus>run" returns records containing the word "run" as well as synonyms such as "sprint", "jog", and "dash".

`typo/N`
: Searches for words that are spelled similarly. For example, searching for "<typo>special" finds all documents with words spelled similarly to the word "special". The `/N` is optional and specifies the maximum number of spelling

errors to allow between the search word and any matched words. If no value is specified, a default of two errors is used.

`wildcard`

Returns all records matching wildcard characters used in the search criteria. The search string used with the `wildcard` operator should be enclosed in backquotes (‘). For example, searching for “<wildcard>‘test*’” returns all records containing words such as “test”, “testing”, and “tested”. Table 16-2 shows a list of all wildcard characters that can be used in your Verity searches.

Table 16-2. Wildcards

Wildcard	Description
*	The asterisk specifies zero or more alphanumeric characters in a particular search string. Asterisks are ignored inside [ ] and { } wildcard searches.
?	A question mark specifies a single alphanumeric character. For example, searching for "<wildcard>‘test?’" returns records containing "test" and "tests", but not "testing".
[ ]	Square brackets specify one of any characters appearing in a set. For example, searching for "<wildcard> ‘st[a,i,o]ck’" returns records containing "stack", "stick", and "stock".
{ }	Curly brackets specify one of a group of characters appearing in a set. For example, searching for "<wildcard>‘stock{s,ed,ing}’" returns any records containing the word "stocks", "stocked", and "stocking".
^	The caret is used with the square brackets to specify one of any character that isn't listed in the set so that a search for "<wildcard>‘st[^io]ck’" matches records containing "stack" or "stuck" but not "stick" or "stock". The caret must be the first character following the left bracket; otherwise it is matched as a literal character.
-	A hyphen is used in conjunction with square brackets and specifies a range of characters such that a search for "<wildcard>‘b[a-z]d’" returns "bad", "bed", "bid", and "bud".

It should be noted that in order to search for a wildcard character as a literal, it must be escaped. To escape a wildcard character, it must be preceded with a backslash. For example, to search for the sentence “What?”, you need to escape it as “What\?”. Asterisks must be escaped by two backslashes as in “test*”.

`word`

Used when you want to have Verity match a specific word without resorting to wildcards or stemming. For example, if you want to search for the word “why?” including the question mark (Normally a wildcard), you enter your search criteria as “<word>why?”

Proximity operators. Proximity operators are used to specify the proximal location of words within a record. Using proximity operators allows you to search for records that contain search terms within the same phrase, sentence, paragraph, or zone. Zones apply to documents created with markup languages such as XML, HTML, and SGML. Zones allow you to match search criteria to specific tags (zones) within a document. Retrieved records are ranked according to the proximity of the words specified in the search criteria. Here’s a list of the proximity operators that can be used by the Verity search engine:

`in`

Finds documents that contain the search term in a specified document zone. Document zones are specially defined areas within a document such as the title, body, or, in the case of documents containing markup language, tags, and are internally defined by Verity. For example to match XML documents containing "Pere Money" in a tag pair (zone) named "<name>", you would use "(Pere Money) <in> name" as the search criteria. To specify more than one zone for the search, surround the zones in parentheses and delimit each zone with a comma as in "(ColdFusion) <in> (title, subject)". Note that Verity finds documents matching the search criteria, and not individual nodes within a document containing markup language. For more information on customizing document zones, see the "Using Verity Search Expressions" chapter in the *Developing ColdFusion MX Applications* documentation.

`near`

Causes the Verity engine to retrieve records containing the specified search terms. Records are scored based on the proximity of the search terms. The closer the terms are, the higher the score. Records with search terms more than 1,000 words apart aren't counted in the scoring process.

`near/N`

Finds documents that contain two or more search terms within `N` number of words of each other, where `N` is an integer between 1 and 1,024. Retrieved records are scored based on their proximity. The closer the words are, the higher the assigned score. Multiple search terms can be specified as long as the same value is used for `N`. For example, to search for the words "fish" and "carp" and "bass" within 10 words of each other, set the search criteria to "fish <near/10> carp <near/10> bass" or "<near/10>(fish,carp,bass)".

`paragraph`

Tells the Verity search engine to select records that contain all the specified search terms within the same paragraph. For example, to search for records containing the words "exam" and "professor" in the same paragraph, you specify "exam <paragraph> professor" as the search criteria. You may use the `paragraph` operator to search for three or more terms provided you separate each term with a `paragraph` operator.

`phrase`

Selects records that contain the phrase specified in the search criteria. A phrase is defined as two or more words that occur in a specific order. For instance, to search for the phrase "open standards", you would use "open <phrase> standards" as the search criteria.

`sentence`

Selects records that contain all the words specified within the same sentence. So, to look for the words "ColdFusion" and "Macromedia" in the same sentence, you could use "<sentence>(ColdFusion, Macromedia)" as the search criteria.

Relational operators. Relational operators search specific document fields within Verity collections. The five Verity document fields, `title`, `key`, `url`, `custom1`, and `custom2` are referenced as `cf_title`,* `cf_key`, `cf_url`, `cf_custom1`, and `cf_custom2`, respectively.

The `many` modifier can't be used with relational operators. Records retrieved using relational operators aren't ranked by relevance. Relational operators can be broken down into two categories, text comparison operators and numeric/date relational operators.

The following operators are used for text comparisons:

`contains`
: Finds records by matching a word or phrase within a specific document field. For example, to find records that contain the word "pickle" anywhere in the `title` field of a Verity collection, you use "cf_title <contains> pickle". Likewise, you could search for a word within an HTML meta keyword tag (`meta` tags are indexed as fields as opposed to zones) by searching for "`keyword <contains> pickle`".

`ends`
: Similar to the `starts` operator except that it returns only records that have values stored in the specified document field that end in the same values specified in the search criteria. For example, searching for "cf_title <ends> ime" returns only records that have words like "time", "grime", and "lime" as the last word in the `title` field.

`matches`
: Finds records by matching the search criteria with values stored in the specified document field. In order for a record to be a match, the search term must exactly match the contents of the document field. For example, using "cf_title <matches> untitled" finds records that contain only "untitled" in the `title` field.

`starts`
: Finds records by matching the characters in your search criteria with records that have the same characters as the starting values in a specified document field. For example, searching for "cf_title <starts> el" turns up records with titles beginning with "elephant" and "elevator".

`substring`
: Finds documents that contain the search criteria as a substring of a word or phrase within a document field. For example, searching for "cf_title <substring> exam" returns records with "exams", "examination", or "I have an exam today" as the `title`.

* There was a bug in ColdFusion MX that affected the ability to search the `cf_title` field. Instead of searching `cf_title`, you needed to instead search `title` (without the `cf_` prefix). This bug was fixed in ColdFusion MX Updater 3.

Table 16-3 shows the operators that can make numeric and date comparisons.

Table 16-3. Comparison operators

Operator	Description
<	Less than
>	Greater than
=	Equals
<=	Less than or equal to
>=	Greater than or equal to

For example, to search for records that have a value stored in the key field greater than 77, use "cf_key > 77" as the search criteria.

Score operators. Score operators determine how the Verity engine calculates the score it assigns to records that match the search criteria. Documents are assigned a score as a decimal percentage between 0 and 1.000 (100%) based on the operators and modifiers applied to the search criteria. Optionally, the score can be set to display the value to four decimal places. The following is a list of the score operators available to the Verity search engine:

`complement`
: Causes the Verity engine to return the complement value for the score of a matching record. The complement value is arrived at by subtracting 1 from the matched record's original score. For example, if a search for "tea" resulted in a score of .25 being assigned to a matching document, a search for "<complement> tea" results in a score of .75. It is worth noting that the `complement` operator causes all records with a score of 0 (all records not matching the search criteria) to have a recalculated score of 1 (a perfect match!). At the same time, all documents originally having a score of 1 get their score recalculated to 0. Why exactly you would want to use this feature is beyond me, but Verity makes it available nonetheless!

`product`
: Multiplies the scores of each term found in a particular Verity record. Records with higher scoring matches score significantly higher than records with lower scoring matches. For example, a document with two terms that scored .5 and .75 respectively receives an overall score of .375, while a record with two terms scoring .25 and .5, respectively, receives an overall score of .125. Use of the `product` operator has a tendency to result in fewer overall matches being returned. This can be useful in reducing the number of matches returned when searching large collections that tend to result in a high number of matches regardless of the search terms used.

`sum`
: Adds the scores together for records matching the search criteria. For example, specifying "<sum>(tea, coffee)" results in the scores for both search terms being added together. The maximum value a score can reach using the `sum` operator is 1. Use of the `sum` operator has a tendency to return more "100 percent" matches.

`yesno`
: Forces the score of a matching search term to 1 if the term's calculated score isn't 0. For example, using the search term "<yesno> test", where a search for the term "test" normally results in a score of .50, causes Verity to force the score to 1. This means that if your search term appears anywhere in a document that is being searched, it will receive a score of 1 regardless of how many times the search term appears. The `yesno` operator can return search results without ranking them by relevance.

Modifiers. Modifiers are always combined with operators to change the behavior of operators in a predetermined way. For instance, you can use the `case` modifier with an operator to specify the case for the particular term to be matched. The following modifiers, commonly referred to as search modifiers, are available for use in your searches:

`case`
: Specifies a case-sensitive search. For example, to search for the word "Bill" in the Title field of a collection, you set the `criteria` attribute in `cfsearch` to "cf_title <contains> <case>Bill".

`many`
: Causes the Verity engine to rank results by relevance (score) based on the frequency and density of the search terms found. The `many` modifier is employed by default whenever a `Simple` search is performed. It should be noted that the `many` modifier can't be used with the concept operators `and`, `or`, and `accrue`, nor can it be used with relational operators.

`not`
: Causes the Verity engine to ignore records that contain the specified search terms. For example, searching for "space not shuttle" causes Verity to return records containing the word "space" but not the word "shuttle".

`order`
: Specifies that your search criteria be found in a specified order to be considered a match. The `order` modifier is usually used in conjunction with the `paragraph`, `sentence`, `near`, and `near/N` operators. For example, to search for records containing the words "space" and "exploration", in order and in the same paragraph, you set your search criteria to "<order> <paragraph> (space, exploration)".

Building an Advanced Search Interface

Now that we have covered all the operators and modifiers used in the Verity search language, let's look at an example that puts some of these techniques to work. To show you how easy it is to use operators and modifiers in your search interfaces, we are going to build an advanced search interface for the documentation that installs with the ColdFusion application server. In order to do this, you first have to make sure that a Verity collection for the ColdFusion documentation exists on your server. This is the same collection we created for Examples 16-4 and 16-5. If you do not already have this collection, refer to those examples for more information on setting it up.

Once you have determined that you have the necessary Verity collection on your server, it is time to build the actual search interface. In Example 16-9, we build an interface that allows a user to enter a search string. It also allows users to choose case sensitivity and decide whether to search document titles only or both document titles and contents. Example 16-9 shows the template for specifying the search criteria.

Example 16-9. Advanced search form

```
<div align="Center">
<h2>ColdFusion MX Documentation Advanced Search</h2>
<form action="16-10.cfm" method="POST">
<table>
  <tr>
    <td>Search Criteria:</td>
    <td><input type="text" name="Criteria" size="20"></td>
  </tr>
  <tr>
    <td>Search What?</td>
    <td>
      <select name="SearchIn">
        <option value="Title" selected>Title Only</option>
        <option value="Both">Title and Body</option>
      </select>
    </td>
  </tr>
  <tr>
    <td>Case Sensitive?</td>
    <td><input type="radio" name="CaseSensitive" value="Yes">Yes<br>
        <input type="radio" name="CaseSensitive" value="No" checked>No
   </td>
  </tr>
  <tr>
    <td colspan="2"><input type="Submit" name="Search1" value="Search"></td>
  </tr>
</table>
</form>
</div>
```

Now that we have the search form created, we need to pass the parameters to another template so that the actual search can be performed. This is done by posting the form-field entries from Example 16-9 to the template shown in Example 16-10 for processing.

Example 16-10. Advanced search using operators and modifiers

```
<!--- If no search string is passed, assume user wants all documents in the
      collection, so assign a wildcard (*) to the search string --->
<cfif form.Criteria is "">
   <cfset form.Criteria = "*">
</cfif>
<!--- Check to see if search is for titles only. If you are running a
      version of CFMX prior to Updater 3, there's a bug with the cf_title
      field. You'll need to change the code from cf_title to just title to
      get it to work. All other fields can be referenced with their cf_
      prefix. --->
<cfif form.SearchIn is "Title">
   <cfset form.Criteria="cf_title <contains> " & form.Criteria>
</cfif>
<!--- Check to see if search is to be case sensitive --->
<cfif not form.CaseSensitive>
   <cfset form.Criteria = Lcase(form.Criteria)>
<cfelse>
   <cfset form.Criteria = "<case> " & form.Criteria>
</cfif>
<cfsearch name="Results" type="Simple" collection="cfdocumentation"
          criteria = "#form.Criteria#">
<html>
<head>
  <title>Example 16-10: Advanced Search Using Operators and Modifiers</title>
  <style type="text/css">
    b {
      font-Weight: bold;
    }
    .boldRed {
      color : #FF0000;
      font-weight : bold;
    }
  </style>
</head>
<body>
<h2>Search Results</h2>
<cfoutput>
Your search for: <span class="boldRed">#HTMLEditFormat(form.Criteria)#</span>
turned up #Results.RecordCount# documents out of #Results.RecordsSearched#
documents searched.
</cfoutput>
<!--- If no records match the search criteria, inform the user --->
<cfif Results.RecordCount lte 0>
   <cfoutput>
   <p>Sorry.  No instances of <span
   class="boldRed">#HTMLEditFormat(form.Criteria)#</span>
```

Example 16-10. Advanced search using operators and modifiers (continued)

```
   were found in the specified collection(s).  Please hit the back button on your
   browser and try again.
   </cfoutput>
<!--- Otherwise, output the search results including linbks to the
      documents --->
<cfelse>
  <table>
    <tr>
      <td><b>Title</b></td>
      <td><b>Score</b></td>
    </tr>
    <tr>
     <td colspan="2"><hr></td>
    </tr>
    <cfoutput query="Results">
    <tr>
      <td><a href="/cfdocs/#URL#">#Title#</a></td>
      <td><cfif Score is not "">#(Score * 100)#%</cfif></td>
    </tr>
    </cfoutput>
  </table>
</cfif>
</body>
</html>
```

Example 16-10 first ensures that the user enters a value for the `form.Criteria` form variable. This is done using a `cfif` statement to check that `form.Criteria` isn't blank. If it is, a `cfset` statement assigns an asterisk (*) to `form.Criteria`. The asterisk is a wildcard character that causes the Verity engine to return all records contained in the collection being searched. Next, we need to see if the user wants to search only the document titles or both the titles and the actual contents of the files. The ColdFusion documentation is in HTML, so the titles being searched are the actual HTML titles of the files. If the user chooses to search only the document titles, a `cfset` statement adds the `<contains>` operator to `form.Criteria`:

```
<cfset form.Criteria="cf_title <contains> " & form.Criteria>
```

Earlier in the chapter, you learned that `cf_title` is a special document field in a Verity collection that contains the title of the document being indexed. In this case, `cf_title` contains the HTML title of each document in the ColdFusion documentation collection.

The third `cfif` statement checks the value of `form.CaseSensitive`. If the value is `No`, `form.Criteria` is converted to lowercase using the `Lcase()` function inside a `cfset` statement. If the value of `form.CaseSensitive` is `Yes`, a `cfset` statement inserts the `<case>` operator before the search term, making the search case sensitive.

The next part of the template in Example 16-10 performs the actual search of the Verity collection using our modified `form.Criteria` as the search criteria. After the search is run, the results are output to the user's web browser in an HTML table containing a hyperlinked title and a percentage score for each matching document.

Updating Collections

Unless your Verity collection is indexed from data that never changes, at some point in time you will need to make updates to it. Whether it is to add a new record to the collection or delete one, updating a Verity collection is an important part of keeping your searchable content current.

Adding New Records to a Collection

New records can easily be added to an existing Verity collection using one of two methods. The first method consists of purging the Verity collection of all records and repopulating it. This is done by setting the `action` attribute of the `cfindex` tag to `Refresh`. This method ensures that your Verity collections always contain the most up-to-date information. The disadvantage to this method is that it can be relatively time-consuming for larger collections because it has to completely reindex a collection just to add a single record. The following syntax shows how to use the `cfindex` tag to purge and reindex a collection:

```
<!--- Purge and repopulate a collection using the refresh property of the
      action attribute --->
<cfquery name="IndexNews" datasource="ProgrammingCF">
    SELECT ArticleID, Title, Article
    FROM News
</cfquery>
<cfindex collection="News" action="Refresh" type="Custom"
         body="Title,Article" key="ArticleID" title="Title" query="IndexNews">
```

The second method is to add the new record by appending it to the end of the collection. This is simple to do using the `cfindex` tag and offers the advantage of a relatively quick update time. By setting the `action` attribute to `Update`, ColdFusion appends the referenced record to the end of the Verity collection. The disadvantages to this technique include the possibility of duplicate entries in the collection and collection information that becomes "out of sync" with the actual information being indexed because of changes made to the database from other templates or applications. The following example illustrates the technique for appending a record to the end of a Verity collection:

```
<!--- Update the Verity collection by appending the queried record to the end
      of the collection --->
<cfquery name="IndexNews" datasource="ProgrammingCF">
    SELECT ArticleID, Title, Article
    FROM News
    WHERE ArticleID = #URL.ArticleID#
</cfquery>
<cfindex collection="News" action="Update" type="Custom" body="Title,Article"
         key="ArticleID" title="Title" query="IndexNews">
```

Deleting Records from a Collection

You can delete an individual record from a collection using the cfindex tag in conjunction with a cfquery. The following example demonstrates a method for deleting a single record from a Verity collection that was created from a database query:

```
<!---This query deletes the Article from the database where ArticleID equals the
     ArticleID value passed in as a URL parameter --->
<cfquery name="RemoveArticle" datasource="ProgrammingCF">
    DELETE *
    FROM News
    WHERE ArticleID = #URL.ArticleID#
</cfquery>
<!--- Remove the reference from the verity collection --->
<cfindex collection="News" action="Delete" key="#URL.ArticleID#">
```

Setting the action="Delete" for the cfindex operation tells ColdFusion that we want to delete a record from the Verity collection. The actual record is specified by setting the key attribute to the value that was stored during the indexing of the collection. In this case, we use URL.ArticleID as the key value. The code can easily be modified to delete more than one record from the collection simply by modifying the WHERE clause in the cfquery to return more than one record.

Maintaining Collections

Once you have your Verity collection up and running, you may be tempted to sit back and leave well enough alone. However, as with any collection of information, Verity collections require periodic maintenance to keep them running in top form. ColdFusion provides several tools for accomplishing these tasks.

Optimizing Collections

Like relational databases, the contents of a Verity collection require periodic optimization for efficiency and streamlining. Because the data in a Verity collection is updated incrementally, over time the collection can become fragmented, which can result in bloated file sizes and slow search performance. Optimization compresses the data stored in a Verity collection, reducing the overall footprint of the collection and providing for more efficient searching. ColdFusion gives you two options for optimizing your Verity collections.

The first method for optimizing a Verity collection is through the ColdFusion Administrator. To optimize a Verity collection via the ColdFusion Administrator, all you need to do is click the Optimize icon next to the desired Verity collection name in the Verity Collections section of the ColdFusion Administrator. A JavaScript confirmation box asks you if you are sure you want to do this. If you choose to continue, ColdFusion carries out the optimization. The optimization process can last from a few seconds to several minutes depending on the size and type of data being optimized.

The second method for optimizing a Verity collection is to do it programmatically with the `cfcollection` tag. To optimize a collection called `MyCollection` located in the default Verity collection location, you create a template containing the following:

```
<cflock name="cfcollection_Lock" type="Exclusive" timeout="30">
  <cfcollection action="Optimize" collection="MyCollection">
</cflock>
```

As you can see from the example, the only thing that differs in this `cfcollection` operation is that we set the `action` attribute to `Optimize`. Programmatic optimization can easily be scheduled in the ColdFusion administrator for automatic and consistent results.

Repairing Collections

Occasionally, Verity collections may become corrupt. This can happen for any number of reasons, such as an interrupted indexing or optimizing operation, and the problems are often fixable. To repair a corrupted collection using the ColdFusion Administrator, all you need to do is click the Repair icon next to the name of the Verity collection you want to repair. A JavaScript confirmation box asks you if you are sure you want to do this. If you choose to continue, ColdFusion attempts to repair the collection. The repair process can last from a few seconds to several minutes depending on the size and type of the collection being repaired.

Repairs to corrupted Verity collections can also be made programmatically by setting the `action` attribute of the `cfcollection` tag to `Repair`, as shown in the following example:

```
<cflock name="cfcollection_Lock" type="Exclusive" timeout="30">
  <cfcollection action="Repair" collection="MyCollection">
</cflock>
```

You should note that although ColdFusion is often able to repair a corrupted collection, it is usually better to delete a questionable collection and recreate it. Doing this ensures that the quality and integrity of the data in your Verity collection is up to par.

Purging Collections

Purging a Verity collection results in the removal of all data stored within a particular collection without deleting the collection itself. This is useful when you want to clear out a collection and repopulate it without having to create the collection all over again. Purging a collection before repopulating it is the best way to ensure that the contents remain as up to date as possible.

Collections can be purged from the ColdFusion Administrator or programmatically. To purge a collection from the Cold Fusion Administrator, all you have to do is click on the Purge icon next to the Verity collection name you want to purge. A JavaScript confirmation box will ask if you are sure you want to purge the collection. If you choose to continue, ColdFusion executes the purge.

To purge a collection from within a CFML template, you need to use the `cfindex` tag with the `action` attribute set to `Purge`. Setting the `action` attribute to `Purge` causes ColdFusion to clear all data in the specified collection without deleting. The following example illustrates using the `cfindex` tag to purge a collection:

```
<cflock name="cfcollection_Lock" type="Exclusive" timeout="30">
  <cfindex action="Purge" collection="MyCollection">
</cflock>
```

Deleting Collections

Deleting a Verity collection is a simple task and can be done from the ColdFusion Administrator or programmatically. To delete a Verity collection from inside the ColdFusion Administrator, simply click on the Delete icon next to the Verity collection you want to delete. A JavaScript confirmation box will ask you to confirm the operation. If you choose to continue, the Verity collection is permanently deleted from the system. If the collection was created by the ColdFusion Administrator or a `cfcollection` tag with the `action` set to `Create`, deleting the collection unregisters it and deletes all files and directories created for the collection. If the collection was created externally and mapped, the collection is simply unregistered, and all files and directories associated with the collection are left intact.

Verity collections can also be deleted programmatically using the `cfcollection` tag. To delete a collection using `cfcollection`, you need to set the `action` attribute to `Delete` and specify the collection name in the `collection` attribute like so:

```
<cflock name="cfcollection_Lock" type="Exclusive" timeout="30">
  <cfcollection action="Delete" collection="MyCollection">
</cflock>
```

Advanced Techniques

Now that you understand the basics of using the Verity search engine with ColdFusion, it is time to take a look at a couple of advanced techniques to help you get the most out of the technology. This section covers several advanced topics including how to build top-ten lists for your Internet or intranet site, custom attributes, modifying the Verity `summary` attribute, and searching database and document collections simultaneously.

Creating a Top-Ten List

A cool feature that you can add to your Internet or intranet site to help your visitors find information fast is a top-ten list. Top-ten lists are nothing more than a list of the ten most frequently searched terms on your site. The list appears as a series of links that execute a Verity search when clicked. The user need not enter a search criteria as the `cfsearch` tag is automatically populated based on the link clicked from the top-ten list.

Before you can actually start using a top-ten list on your site, you have to compile a list of the most frequently searched-for terms on the site. This is a relatively easy task requiring a simple database table, a small bit of coding, and time to allow users to add terms to the list.

The first step in creating a top-ten list is to create a database table to store all the search terms that users enter as search criteria in your search page. Start by creating a table in your database called Keywords. For this example, I used Microsoft Access, but feel free to use the database of your choice. In the Keywords table, create a field called `SearchString` and make it a text field with a maximum length of 255 characters. You may optionally create a primary key field if you wish to, though it isn't necessary. Once you have the table created, save it and exit from your database program.

The second step towards creating a top-ten list is to add a snippet of code to your search page that captures and saves the terms users enter as search criteria. Add the following snippet of code to the beginning of your search template. It is important to add it before your `cfsearch` code:

```
<cfif IsDefined('SearchString') and Searchstring is not "">
<cfquery name="AddKeyWords" datasource="ProgrammingCF">
    INSERT INTO Keywords (SearchString)
    VALUES('#SearchString#')
</cfquery>
</cfif>
```

The snippet works by first checking to make sure that a search string is passed from the search form and that it isn't blank. If these two conditions are met, the search string is saved to the Keywords table using `cfquery` to add the information.

Depending on how much traffic your site gets and how often users search, it may take anywhere from a few hours to a few weeks before your table contains enough keywords to make the top-ten list useable. Once you feel that you have a sufficient number of search strings in your database, you can implement the top-ten list, as shown in Example 16-11.

Example 16-11. Creating a top-ten list of commonly used search terms

```
<!--- Query the keywords table in the database and use aggregate functions to
      get the n most frequently used words or phrases --->
<cfquery name="GetTopTen" datasource="ProgrammingCF" maxrows="10">
```

Example 16-11. Creating a top-ten list of commonly used search terms (continued)

```
        SELECT SearchString, COUNT(SearchString) AS TheCount
        FROM keywords GROUP BY SearchString order BY COUNT(SearchString) DESC
</cfquery>
<!--- Present the output to the user.  The search terms are hyperlinks that
      run the search template and automatically pass the search criteria --->
Top 10 Search terms:
<p>
<table border="1">
  <tr>
    <th>Search term</th><th>Number of times</th>
  </tr>
<cfoutput query="GetTopTen">
  <tr>
    <td><a href="Search.cfm?SearchString=#UrlEncodedFormat(SearchString)#">
        #SearchString#</a></td>
    <td>#TheCount#</td>
  </tr>
</cfoutput>
</table>
```

The first part of the template in Example 16-11 uses `cfquery` to select the search strings from the keywords table. `COUNT` is an aggregate function in SQL that allows us to count the number of times a particular string appears in a given field. In this case, we want to get a `COUNT` for each string in our `SearchString` field. The results are then ordered by the count from highest to lowest. Using the `maxrows`* attribute of the `cfquery` tag allows us to limit the result set to the top-ten records.

The second part of the template displays the results to the browser. It takes the output of the query and displays it as an HTML table containing the search string in the left column and the number of times the string was searched in the right column.

The search string itself appears as a hyperlink. Clicking on the link results in `SearchString` being passed to your Verity search template via a URL parameter. Because `SearchString` can contain spaces, it is important to use the `URLEncodedFormat( )` function when appending its value to the URL. This allows visitors to your site to search for the most popular terms without having to know how to spell them or having to enter them correctly in a search form.

Custom Attributes

ColdFusion provides two additional user-defined attributes that can be populated with data during a `cfindex` operation and subsequently searched using `cfsearch`.

* Although this example uses the `maxrows` attribute to limit the results to the top ten matches, there might be a better way depending on your database platform. For example, if you use MS Access or SQL Server, you can use `TOP(`*n*`)` in your SQL `SELECT` statement to limit the results to the top *n* items, forgoing the `maxrows` attribute.

These two attributes, custom1 and custom2, can be populated with any data you desire provided you are indexing query-based data. The value in using the custom1 and custom2 attributes comes in being able to store additional information about a particular query object that would otherwise have to be lumped in with the body attribute. For instance, when indexing a collection of database records, you might want to expose each record's creation date to the cfsearch tag so that you can search for records that were created within a certain time frame. The custom1 and custom2 attributes allow you to gain fine-grained control over your Verity searches.

Populating the custom attributes

Populating the custom1 and custom2 attributes with data is done during a cfindex operation. Table 16-4 shows the sample database we described earlier in this chapter, populated with a few records.

Table 16-4. Populating the news table with data

ArticleID	ArticleType	Title	Article	DatePosted
1	HTML	Article 1	Body of Article 1	12/31/1997
2	TEXT	Article 2	Body of Article 2	06/12/1998
3	XML	Article 3	Body of Article 3	08/22/1999
4	HTML	Article 4	Body of Article 4	10/10/2000
5	HTML	Article 5	Body of Article 5	11/07/2000
6	HTML	Article 6	Body of Article 6	12/23/2000

In a typical cfindex operation, we use the ArticleID as the key attribute, the Title as the title attribute, and the Article as the body attribute. This exposes the title and body fields to searching, but what if we also want to search the collection based on ArticleType or DatePosted? Here is where the custom attributes come in. By populating custom1 with the ArticleType and custom2 with the DatePosted, we make both of those fields searchable in our Verity collection. Example 16-12 shows how to populate the custom1 and custom2 attributes based on our example database.

Example 16-12. Populating the custom1 and custom2 attributes

```
<!--- Query the news table for all articles --->
<cfquery name="MyQuery" datasource="ProgrammingCF">
  SELECT ArticleID,ArticleType,Title,Article,DatePosted
  FROM News
</cfquery>
<!--- Purge and populate the Verity collection with the data from the above
      query --->
<cfindex action="Refresh" collection="News" key="ArticleID" type="Custom"
         title="Title" query="MyQuery" body="Article" custom1="ArticleType"
         custom2="DatePosted">

<h2>Done Indexing the Collection</h2>
```

Note that it isn't necessary to use pound signs to enclose variable names inside the custom1 and custom2 attributes.

Searching the custom attributes

Both the custom1 and custom2 attributes are searchable via the cfsearch tag. To reference either custom attribute in a cfsearch operation, you need to include them in the criteria attribute. Because they are special attributes, they need to be referenced as cf_custom1 and cf_custom2, respectively. Example 16-13 demonstrates the use of the custom1 and custom2 attributes by searching the news collection for articles that have HTML stored in the custom1 attribute. The example outputs a table of all matching records and includes the values stored in the custom1 and custom2 fields in the table.

Example 16-13. Searching the values of custom1 and custom2

```
<!--- Search the collection for articles that are in HTML --->
<cfsearch collection="News" name="MyQuery" type="Simple"
        criteria="CF_Custom1=HTML" language="English">
<!--- Output the results --->
<table>
  <tr>
    <th>Key</th><th>Title</th><th>Custom1</th><th>Custom2</th>
  </tr>
<cfoutput query="MyQuery">
  <tr>
    <td>#Key#</td><td>#Title#</td><td>#Custom1#</td>
    <td>#DateFormat(Custom2,'mm/dd/yyyy')#</td>
  </tr>
</cfoutput>
</table>
```

Extending the usefulness of custom attributes

In case you haven't noticed, there are only two custom attributes available for you to populate with additional information. What if you have three, four, or more additional bits of information that you want to make available to your search operation? The answer lies in lists. Although you have only the custom1 and custom2 attributes at your disposal, you can squeeze quite a few additional pieces of information into these attributes by creating delimited lists of values and subsequently parsing them out when necessary.

Take our previous example in which we populated the Custom1 attribute with ArticleType and Custom2 with DatePosted. Now, suppose we add one more field to our sample database called Status. Status is a text field that contains "Public" if the article is for public viewing or "Private" if the article is for private distribution. Because there are only two custom attributes, if we want to put the value of Status as well as the values of ArticleType and DatePosted in the custom attributes, we are going to have to concatenate two of the fields into a list, as shown in Example 16-14.

Example 16-14. Template for populating a collection and including custom attributes

```
<!--- Query the News table for all articles and create a new field called
      MultipleValues as a comma delimited concatenation of ArticleType and
      Status --->
<cfquery name="MyQuery" datasource="ProgrammingCF">
  SELECT *, ArticleType & ',' & Status AS MultipleValues
  FROM News
</cfquery>
<!--- Purge and populate the Verity collection with the data from the above
      query --->
<cfindex action="Refresh" collection="News" key="ArticleID" type="custom"
         title="Title" query="MyQuery" body="Article" custom1="MultipleValues"
         custom2="DatePosted">

<h2>Done Indexing the Collection</h2>
```

Example 16-14 populates the collection with data from the query. It also populates the custom1 and custom2 fields with the values contained in the MultipleValues and DatePosted variables, respectively. Concatenating the ArticleType and Status fields from the database into a comma-separated list creates the MultipleValues variable.

The next template, shown in Example 16-15, searches the collection for any news article that has "HTML" as the ArticleType and "Public" as the Status. All articles matching those criteria are then displayed to the user. Although this template is being run as a standalone search that doesn't require any user input to run, you can easily build a front-end search form to allow users to enter their own search criteria.

Example 16-15. Searching a collection

```
<!--- Search the collection based on the criteria that custom1 must contain
      HTML and Public --->
<cfsearch collection="News" name="MyQuery" type="Explicit"
   criteria="(CF_Custom1 <contains> 'HTML' and cf_custom1 <contains> 'Public')"
   language="English">
<!--- Output the results --->
<table>
  <tr>
    <th>Key</th><th>Title</th><th>Custom1</th><th>Custom2</th>
  </tr>
<cfoutput query="MyQuery">
  <tr>
    <td>#Key#</td><td>#Title#</td><td>#Custom1#</td>
    <td>#DateFormat(Custom2,'mm/dd/yyyy')#</td>
  </tr>
</cfoutput>
</table>
```

In Example 16-15, the criteria attribute in the cfsearch tag contains the following line:

```
criteria="(CF_Custom1 <contains> 'HTML' and cf_custom1 <contains> 'Public')"
```

This line tells the cfsearch tag to look for records that contain both "HTML" and "Public" in the custom1 field.

Modifying the Verity Summary Attribute

By default, the summary variable returned during a cfsearch of a Verity collection contains the best three sentences determined by score, up to 500 characters in length. Although this is acceptable for many applications, there are times when you might wish the summary feature behaved differently. For example, you might have a collection of files that contains a short two-sentence description followed by numerous tables of data. Chances are that the summary values returned after a search of those files may contain a useless bunch of text as the summary that is built from a sampling of all the data contained in the file. In this case, it would be much more beneficial if Verity would return the first two sentences in the document as opposed to the best three sentences.

Although there is no way to accomplish this using CFML, it is possible to modify a specific Verity configuration file named *style.prm* to achieve the desired results. By default, the *style.prm* file can be found under *c:\cfusionmx\lib\common\style\custom* or *c:\cfusionmx\lib\common\style\file* depending on the type of collection that you are attempting to modify. By changing the contents of the *style.prm* file in either of these directories, all subsequent indexing operations will take into account the modifications. If you want to modify the settings for a single collection as opposed to all collections, you need to make the changes to the *style.prm* file located in the individual collection directory: either *c:\cfusionmx\verity\collections\my_collection_name\file\style* for file collections or under *c:\cfusionmx\verity\collections\my_collection_name\custom\style* for database collections.

Regardless of the type of collection you have indexed, you need to open the *style.prm* file for editing. Once you have the file opened, scroll to the bottom and find the block of code that matches the following:

```
# ---------------------------------------------------------------
# Document Summarization is enabled by uncommenting one of
# the DOC-SUMMARIES lines below.  The summarization data is
# stored in the documents table so that it might easily be
# shown when displaying the results of a search.
# See the discussions on Document Summarization in the
# Collection Building Guide for more information.
# The example below stores the best three sentences of
# the document, but not more than 500 bytes.
$define DOC-SUMMARIES   "XS MaxSents 3 MaxBytes 500"
# The example below stores the first four sentences of
# the document, but not more than 500 bytes.
#$define DOC-SUMMARIES   "LS MaxSents 4 MaxBytes 500"
# The example below stores the first 150 bytes of
# the document, with whitespace compressed.
#$define DOC-SUMMARIES   "LB MaxBytes 150"
```

As I stated earlier, by default, Verity is set to create a summary for each item indexed based on the best three sentences not to exceed 500 characters. That parameter can be modified by commenting out the line using a pound sign and uncommenting one of the other configurations listed in the example. Further combinations can be created by changing the values for `MaxSents` and `MaxBytes`.

Tweaking Verity's XML Filter

The version of the Verity engine bundled with ColdFusion has been able to index and search XML documents for some time now. However, because XML is a completely flexible tag-based markup language that lets users define their own tags, there is no standard "Title" field returned when a search is performed against a collection containing XML documents. Fortunately, it is possible to tweak Verity's XML filter a bit to allow you to make any XML tag in a well-formed XML document populate the `cf_title` or any other variable returned by the `cfsearch` tag.

To make Verity populate the `cf_title` variable with the value of an XML tag, there are a few things you need to do. First, you need to decide what tag in your XML document you want to use to populate the `cf_title` variable. For this example, let's assume your XML document (*my_xml.xml*) has a tag called `<title>` and looks something like this:

```
<?xml version="1.0"?>
 <book>
   <title>Programming ColdFusion</title>
   <author>Rob Brooks-Bilson</author>
   <publisher>O'Reilly</publisher>
 </book>
```

If you index this file, Verity is smart enough to index the content and leave out the tags, but it isn't smart enough (without a little help) to take the contents of the `<title>` tag and use it to populate the `cf_title` variable. To do this, you need to create a special text file called *style.xml* and save it in your style directory: either *c:\cfusionmx\lib\common\style\file* for all file-based collections or *c:\cfusionmx\verity\collections\my_collection_name\file\style* where *my_collection_name* is the name of the Verity collection containing the index for your XML files. The *style.xml* file should look like this:

```
<?xml version="1.0" encoding="ISO-8859-1"?>
<style.xml version="2.6.1">
  <field xmltag = "title" fieldname = "cf_title" index = "override" />
</style.xml>
```

The file tells Verity to index the contents of XML tags named <title> and place the contents in the ColdFusion variable `cf_title`, overriding the default value that is supposed to go there (in the case of XML, nothing goes there by default). Using this syntax, it is very easy to change both the XML tag that Verity indexes as well as the ColdFusion variable it places the content in. It is important to note that you must use an existing ColdFusion return variable for `cfsearch`. In other words, you can't go and make up your own variables; ColdFusion won't recognize them.

Once you save the file, you need to stop and restart your ColdFusion server and reindex your collection in order for the changes to take effect. The newly indexed collection should now return the title field from an XML document in the `cf_title` variable.

There's a lot more you can do with the *style.xml* file that isn't well documented. I don't really have the space to cover all of the ins and outs of hacking Verity here. However, so you don't feel as though I've left you hanging, here is a list of the tags (and their attributes) supported in the *style.xml* file. Note that a *style.xml* file can contain one or more of these tags:

`<field xmltag="xmltag" fieldname="fieldname" index="override" />`
: Specifies the XML tag to map to a specific field name (such as `cf_title`, `cf_custom1`, etc.). The `index` attribute is optional and can be used to tell Verity to override any existing values that might be set for the field.

`<suppress xmltag="xmltag" />`
: Suppresses indexing of any XML tags nested within the specified start and end tag.

`<ignore xmltag="xmltag" />`
: Ignores indexing the specified XML tag but indexes its content.

`<preserve xmltag="xmltag" />`
: Indexes the specified XML tag as a zone if it is preceded by an `ignore` tag.

Searching Database and Document Collections Simultaneously

Chances are, sooner or later you are going to run into a situation where you want to search the contents of both a database collection and a document collection. A common scenario involves a web site that contains dynamic pages as well as static files. On the surface, it appears as though ColdFusion and the Verity engine won't provide a way to index both types of information in a single operation. The truth is, there is an easy way to get around this apparent problem using a little creative programming.

The first step in creating an interface capable of searching both database and document collections simultaneously is to create a single collection to hold both types of data to be searched. That is, you need to create a single collection for both your database information and your documents. Example 16-16 shows how to do this in a single template. The example uses the same database used in previous examples, and it assumes that you have already created a new collection, `MyDualCollection`, using the techniques described earlier.

Example 16-16. Indexing a database query and a group of documents at the same time

```
<!--- Query the news table for all articles --->
<cfquery name="IndexArticle" datasource="ProgrammingCF">
  SELECT ArticleID,Title,Article
  FROM News
</cfquery>
<!--- Populate the database collection from the indexarticle query --->
<cfindex collection="MyDualCollection" action="Refresh" type="Custom"
         body="Title,Article" key="ArticleID" title="Title" query="IndexArticle">
<!--- Populate the documents collection --->
<cfindex action="Update" collection="MyDualCollection"
         key="D:\cfusionmx\wwwroot\programmingcf\16\dual\" type="Path"
         urlpath="http://127.0.0.1:8500/programmingcf/16/dual"
         extensions=".htm, .html, .doc, .pdf" recurse="No">
<h2>Finished Indexing</h2>
```

Once you have created and populated the collections, you need to build a search interface that can return results for both types of data at the same time. The trick here is to conditionally output different results to the user depending on which type of data each match comes from. Examples 16-17 and 16-18 show the technique for searching database and document collections simultaneously.

Example 16-17. Searching database and document collections simultaneously

```
<form action="16-18.cfm" method="Post">
Search for: <input type="Text" name="Criteria" size="31" maxlength="255">
            <input type="Submit" name="Submit" value="Search">
</form>
```

Example 16-17 creates a basic search form for passing a search string to the template in Example 16-18. The search performed in Example 16-18 differs from all of the other searches we have performed so far in that it searches both `custom` and `path` data from the same collection at the same time.

Example 16-18. Simultaneous search of a database and a document collection

```
<!--- If no search criteria is passed, assume user wants all records in the
collection, so assign a wildcard (*) to the search criteria --->
<cfif form.Criteria is "">
  <cfset form.Criteria = "*">
</cfif>
<!--- Search the collections --->
<cfsearch name="Results" collection="MyDualCollection" type="Simple"
          criteria="#form.Criteria#">
<!--- If no records match, display message --->
<cfif Results.RecordCount is 0>
  No records found matching your search criteria.

<!--- Otherwise, process search --->
<cfelse>
  <!--- Output matches to the user --->
  <cfoutput>
```

Example 16-18. Simultaneous search of a database and a document collection (continued)

```
    #Results.RecordCount# records found out of #Results.RecordsSearched# records
    searched.
  </cfoutput>

  <p>
  <table border="0" width="500">
    <tr>
      <th>Title</th><th>Score</th>
    </tr>
    <cfoutput query="Results">
    <tr>
      <td>
        <cfif IsNumeric(Results.Key)>
          <a href="Showrecord.cfm?ID=#Results.Key#">#Results.Title#</a>
        <cfelse>
          <a href="#Results.URL#">#Results.Title#</a>
        </cfif>
        <br>
        #Results.Summary#
      </td>
      <td>
        <cfif Score is not "">#(Score * 100)#%</cfif>
      </td>
    </tr>
    </cfoutput>
  </table>
</cfif>
```

As you can see, the technique used for searching both types of data at the same time is fairly straightforward. Example 16-18 uses conditional logic to determine if the value of the key attribute is numeric or not. If the value of key is numeric, the template knows that the record comes from a database (custom) collection because the value of key in the database collection is always a number. If the value of key isn't numeric, the template knows that they record comes from the document (path or file) collection. The value of key in the document collection is always the path to the file on the server.

CHAPTER 17

Graphing and Charting

Graphs and charts are a great way to visually represent data. Because of this, including business-style graphs and charts is a standard part of many of today's web applications. ColdFusion MX comes with a powerful engine that allows you to include professional-looking charts and graphs in your ColdFusion applications with relative ease. For those of you interested in the technical details, Macromedia chose to OEM WebCharts3D from GreenPoint, Inc. (*http://www.gpoint.com/WebCharts3D/*) for ColdFusion MX's charting engine.

Creating a Simple Graph

Regardless of the type of chart or graph you want to create, you need to start with the `cfchart` tag. `cfchart` acts as a container tag for setting up the chart's basic characteristics, such as height, width, and background color. The `cfchart` tag is a paired tag and must have both an opening and closing tag.

The `cfchartseries` tag determines what type of chart or graph to create for a particular series of static or dynamic data and allows you to specify attributes for the series, such as labels, color, etc. ColdFusion MX 6.1 can graph multiple data series in a single chart. The number of data series is limited only by the size of the chart.* The `cfchartseries` tag is also paired and requires an opening and closing tag. Additional static data points may be added to a chart series by nesting one or more `cfchartdata` tags inside a `cfchartseries` pair. Example 17-1 shows how to generate a bar chart from static data using all three tags just mentioned.

Example 17-1. Creating a simple graph from static data

```
<cfchart format="Flash" chartheight="400" chartwidth="400"
  foregroundcolor="##000000" backgroundcolor="##C0C0C0"
  databackgroundcolor="##0000FF" rotated="No" showborder="Yes"
  scalefrom="0" scaleto="100000" gridlines="11" showxgridlines="Yes"
```

* In ColdFusion MX 6.0, the charting engine was limited to 16 data series in a single chart.

Example 17-1. Creating a simple graph from static data (continued)

```
 showygridlines="Yes" seriesplacement="Default" font="Arial" fontsize="12"
 fontbold="Yes" fontitalic="Yes" xaxistitle="Salary" yaxistitle="Employee"
 xaxistype="scale" yaxistype="scale" sortxaxis="No"
 labelformat="Currency" showlegend="No" show3d="Yes" xoffset=".1"
 yoffset=".1" tipstyle="MouseOver" tipbgcolor="##008000">
 <cfchartseries type="bar" serieslabel="Employee Salaries"
                seriescolor="Yellow" paintstyle="Plain">
   <cfchartdata item="Greg" value="96000">
   <cfchartdata item="Nick" value="54000">
   <cfchartdata item="Jen" value="41000">
   <cfchartdata item="Christine" value="80000">
 </cfchartseries>
</cfchart>
```

The `cfchart` tag has over 30 attributes you can use in various combinations depending on the type of chart you want to generate and how you want it to look. All of these attributes are optional; the `cfchart` tag has no required attributes. In Example 17-1, I use attributes common to most of the graph formats. The remaining attributes are chart type–specific or are used for other special-case situations, such as passing parameters to drill-down templates (covered later in the chapter) or saving the chart to a variable for use in Macromedia Flash Remoting (covered in Chapter 28).

The `format` attribute determines what format to use when sending the graph to the browser. You can choose `Flash` (*.swf*), `PNG` (*.png*), or `JPG` (*.jpg*). The default format, and the one we use in this example, is `Flash`. `graphheight` and `graphwidth` specify the height and width for the graph in pixels. The default height is 240 pixels, and the default width is 320 pixels. You can specify a background color for the chart using the `backgroundcolor` attribute. Colors may be specified by one of 16 names (See Appendix A for a complete list) or hex code in the form `FFFFCC` or `##FFFFCC`. The default background color is white. The double pound signs are necessary to keep ColdFusion from throwing an error. The foreground color (`foregroundcolor`) and the background color for the data area of the chart (`databackgroundcolor`) can be set using the same color choices as the `backgroundcolor` attribute. The default foreground color is black, and the default data background color is white.

The next set of attributes determines how the data area of the chart or graph is displayed. The `rotated` attribute specifies whether the chart should be rotated 90 degrees clockwise. This is usually done to display horizontal bar charts, but it can be used with any chart type except `Pie`. The default is `No`. You can specify a border for the chart by setting the `showborder` attribute to `Yes`. The minimum and maximum values to be displayed on the vertical (y) axis are set using the `scalefrom` and `scaleto` attributes. If values aren't passed, the `scalefrom` and `scaleto` value defaults to a value determined by the graphing server, based on the minimum and maximum values in the set of data points. In this example, we scale the graph from 0 to 100,000 along the y-axis. The `gridlines` attribute allows you to specify the number of gridlines, including the axis, that should be displayed on the value axis. In order to have gridlines placed every 10,000 dollars on our graph, we set `gridlines="11"` (100,000/10,000 + 1 for the axis gridline). `showxgridlines` and `showygridlines` both act as their names imply. Setting either to `No` results in the suppression of gridlines for the specified axis. The default value for `showxgridlines` is `No`, but for `showygridlines`, it's `Yes`.

You can control the relative positions of multiple series of data using the `seriesplacement` attribute. Since we're only graphing a single data series in this example, we'll leave it set to the default value of `Default`, which automatically determines the best placement. Other options include `Stacked`, `Cluster`, and `Percent`, which we'll see later in the chapter. Display characters for all text displayed in the graph are handled by the `font`, `fontsize`, `fontbold`, and `fontitalic` attributes. Titles for the x-axis and y-axis are set using the `xaxistitle` and `yaxistitle` attributes, respectively. The `xaxistype` and `yaxistype` attributes are new in ColdFusion MX 6.1 and specify how values along these axes are handled. Options are `category` (the default for `xaxistype`) and `scale` (the default for `yaxistype`). `category` specifies that the axis values should be displayed in the order in which they are coded, while `scale` tells the charting engine to display the values according to their numeric order. If `scale` is used, all axis values must be numeric, otherwise ColdFusion throws an error. Note that `yaxistype` is currently ignored by ColdFusion, as the y-axis must always have numeric values. Optionally, you can tell ColdFusion to sort the value labels along the x-axis in alphabetical order by setting `sortxaxis` to `Yes`. The default is to leave the x-axis labels unsorted. `sortxaxis` is ignored if `xaxistype="scale"`. Note that there is not an equivalent attribute for sorting y-axis labels since these are usually the values being graphed. You can specify formatting for the axis values using the `labelformat` attribute. Valid options are `Number`, `Currency`, `Date`, and `Percent`. The default is `Number`. You can also display an optional legend for charts containing more than one data series by setting `showlegend` to `Yes` (the default value). Legend placement depends on the type of chart you create.

You can give your charts and graphs a 3-D appearance by setting the `show3d` attribute to `Yes`. `xoffset` and `yoffset` determine how many units along the horizontal and vertical axis the chart should be rotated when `show3d` is `Yes`. These attributes accept a value between –1 and 1 where –1 is 90 degrees left, 0 is no rotation, and 1 is 90 degrees right rotation. The default value for each is 0.1.

Whenever you move your mouse over a data element in a chart, a small popup window appears with details about the data point. If your chart type is set to `Flash`, you can customize certain features of the popup window. The `tipstyle` attribute specifies how the tip popup window is called. Options are `MouseDown`, `MouseOver`, and `None`. `MouseDown` displays the popup when the mouse pointer is placed over a chart element and the mouse button is pressed and held. `MouseOver` is the default and displays the popup when the mouse pointer moves over a chart element. `None` disables tip popup windows (this works for all chart formats, not just Flash). The background color for the tip popup window can be changed using the `tipbgcolor` attribute. This attribute follows the same color value rules as the `backgroundcolor` attribute. The default background color is white.

Once the chart container is set up using the cfchart tag, you can use the chchartseries tag to specify the type of chart to generate other information about the data series. Like cfchart, this is also a container tag and must contain both a start and end tag. In Example 17-1, the cfchartseries tag is used to define a bar chart. This is done by setting type="Bar". Other types are Line, Area, Pyramid, Cone, Curve, Cylinder, Step, Scatter, and Pie. The serieslabel attribute specifies a name for the data series. This name is used in the tip popup box generated for all chart types except Pie. Additionally, if the showlegend attribute of cfchart is set to Yes, the series label is also displayed in the legend for all chart types except Pie (because pie charts don't support multiple series). seriescolor specifies the color to use for all data points in the series. The same color rules apply as for the cfchart tag. The cfchartseries tag doesn't allow you to specify different colors for each data point in the series. There is, however, a workaround that I'll discuss later in the chapter. The final attribute used in this example is paintstyle. This attribute lets you specify a style for rendering each data point in the chart. Options are Plain (solid color fill), Raise (beveled appearance), Shade (gradient filling darker toward the edges), and Light (gradient filled lighter shade of color). The default is Plain. There are several other attributes available in the cfchartseries tag, many of which are covered later on in the chapter. For a complete list of all attributes, see Appendix A.

The actual data points are set up using individual cfchartdata tags, one for each data point we want to chart. Notice that the cfchartdata tags are nested inside the cfchartseries tag. Each individual data point's value is specified by the value attribute, while the label for the data point value is specified by item. Executing the code in Example 17-1 results in the chart shown in Figure 17-1.

To see how ColdFusion renders the same data as different chart types, try changing the type attribute of the cfchartseries tag to the various supported chart types. The results should be similar to the charts shown in Figure 17-2.

Working with Dates

One thing that's worth giving special mention to in this chapter is the way in which cfchart handles date values when they're on the y-axis. If you remember from Example 17-1, you can use labelformat="Date" to tell cfchart to format the values along the value axis as dates. If you try the following code, however, you'll probably notice something strange:

```
<cfchart format="Flash" labelformat="Date">
  <cfchartseries type="Scatter" serieslabel="New Years Eve Party Hosts">
    <cfchartdata item="Zack" value="12/31/1972">
    <cfchartdata item="Becky" value="12/31/1996">
    <cfchartdata item="Joe" value="12/31/1984">
    <cfchartdata item="Lynda" value="12/31/2002">
  </cfchartseries>
</cfchart>
```

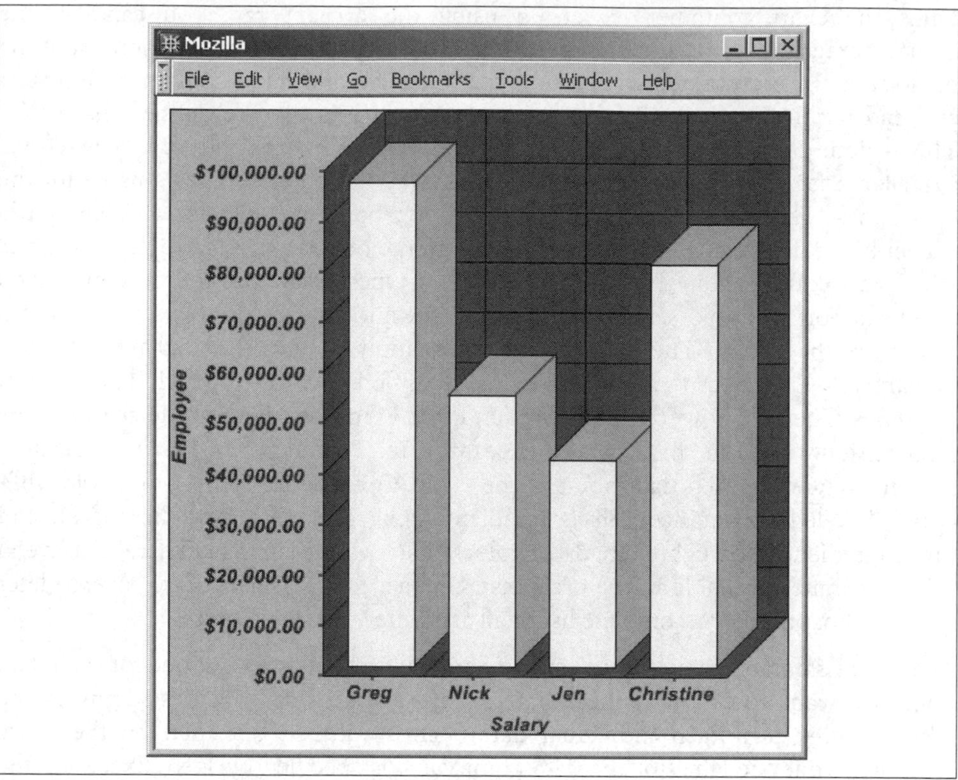

Figure 17-1. Creating a bar chart from static values

If you look at the dates on the vertical axis, you should notice that they are all 12/31/69. Additionally, if you move your mouse over any of the data points, they are also all 12/31/69. The issue here is that `cfchart` does not accept formatted dates (such as *mm/dd/yyyy*) as data-point values. If you have dates you want to plot on the y-axis of a chart, you'll have to reformat them for `cfchart`. `cfchart` expects dates passed as values be formatted in epoch seconds, adjusted for your UTC (Coordinated Universal Time) offset. What's more, the resulting number must be multiplied by 1000 (presumably to account for milliseconds?). So, how do you do all of this? The simple solution is to create a user-defined function to handle the conversion for you. This allows you to call the function repeatedly, without the need for cutting and pasting the conversion formula each time you need to perform the calculation. Example 17-2 shows the code for a user-defined function called `cfchartDateFormat()` that handles the date conversion required by `cfchart`, as well as a `cfchart` example that makes use of the function.

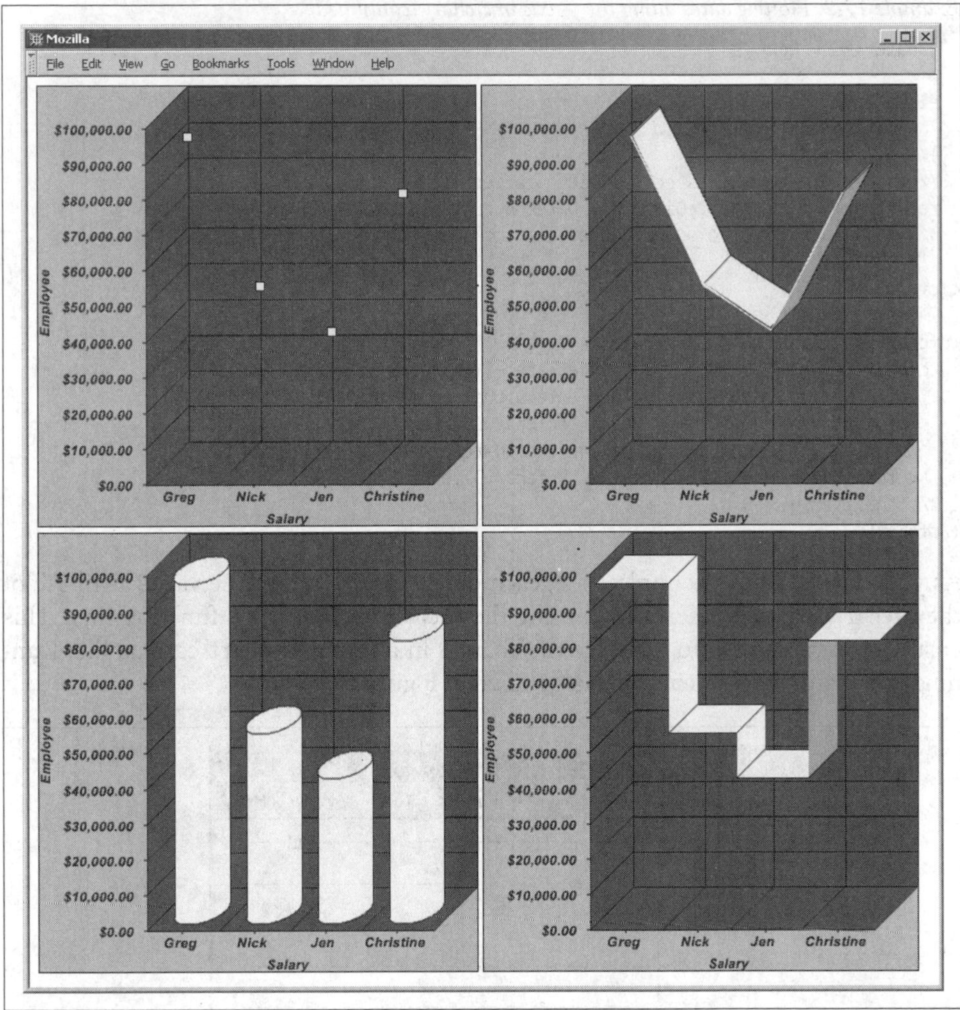

Figure 17-2. Generating various charts from the same static data

Example 17-2. Plotting dates along the y-axis in cfchart

```
<cfscript>
/**
 * Formats a date/time value for use on the y-axis in cfchart.
 *
 * @param date Date/time value you want formatted for cfchart. (Required)
 * @return Returns a numeric value.
 * @author Rob Brooks-Bilson (rbils@amkor.com)
 * @version 1, October 18, 2002
 */
function cfchartDateFormat( ) {
  var datetime = 0;
  if (ArrayLen(Arguments) eq 0) {
```

Example 17-2. Plotting dates along the y-axis in cfchart (continued)

```
    datetime = Now( );
  }
  else {
    datetime = arguments[1];
  }
  // numberFormat prevents scientific notation from breaking cfchart
  return numberFormat(DateDiff("s", DateConvert("utc2Local",
         "January 1 1970 00:00"), datetime) * 1000, '_');
}
</cfscript>

<cfchart format="Flash" labelformat="Date">
  <cfchartseries type="Scatter" serieslabel="New Years Eve Party Hosts">
    <cfchartdata item="Zack" value="#cfchartDateFormat("12/31/1972")#">
    <cfchartdata item="Becky" value="#cfchartDateFormat("12/31/1996")#">
    <cfchartdata item="Joe" value="#cfchartDateFormat("12/31/1984")#">
    <cfchartdata item="Lynda" value="#cfchartDateFormat("12/31/2002")#">
  </cfchartseries>
</cfchart>
```

As you can see in the example code, each date value placed in the `value` attribute of the `cfchartdata` tags is formatted using the `cfchartDateFormat( )` function first. This ensures the value used to generate the chart is in a format `cfchart` can handle. Running the example results in the chart shown in Figure 17-3.

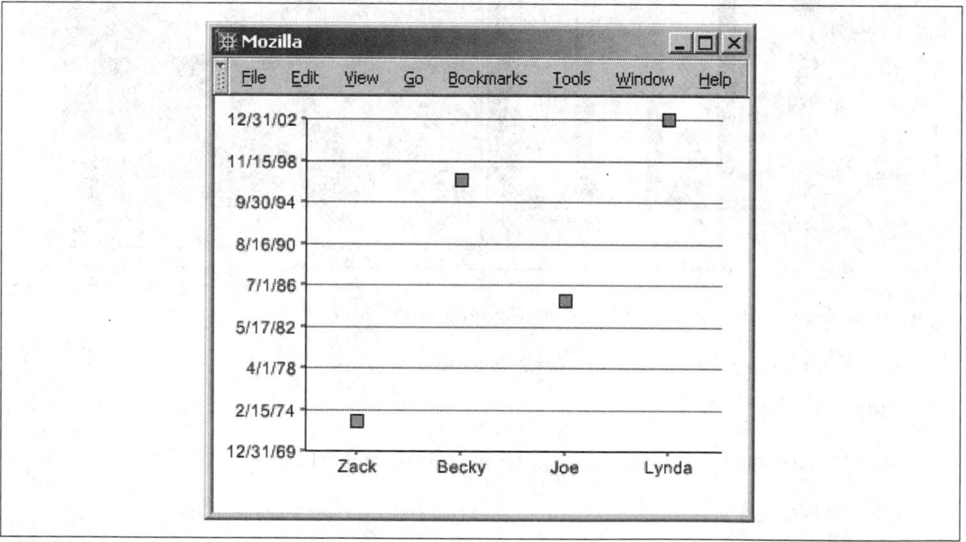

Figure 17-3. Plotting date values along the y-axis

Charting Dynamic Data

In the previous examples, you saw how simple it is to chart static values supplied by the cfchartdata tag. We'll take things one step further now and talk about charting dynamic values obtained from a query. The process is similar to what we did in the previous section. This time, however, instead of hardcoding each data point, we'll specify a query to use to populate the chart. Example 17-3 shows how to use query data to graph the average salary for each department in the EmployeeDirectory table.

Example 17-3. Charting dynamic data

```
<cfquery name="GetSalary" datasource="ProgrammingCF">
  SELECT Department, AVG(Salary) AS AvgSalary
  FROM EmployeeDirectory
  GROUP BY Department
</cfquery>

<h3>Average Salary by Department</h3>
<cfchart format="Flash" chartheight="360" chartwidth="480" scalefrom="0"
         scaleto="500000" gridlines="11" labelformat="Number"
         xaxistitle="Department" yaxistitle="Salary" rotated="Yes">
  <cfchartseries type="Bar" query="GetSalary" itemcolumn="Department"
                 valuecolumn="AvgSalary" serieslabel="Average Salary by
                               Department"
                 seriescolor="##0000FF" paintstyle="Plain" />
</cfchart>
```

The query in this example retrieves the average salary for each department in the EmployeeDirectory table using the AVG aggregate function. Two columns of data are returned, the department name (Department) and the average salary for that department (AvgSalary). This time, we're going to create a bar graph and rotate it 90 degrees clockwise, making it a horizontal bar graph. We set up the cfchart tag using some of the same attributes we used in Example 17-1. The only difference here is that we set the rotated attribute to Yes, effectively creating a horizontal instead of vertical bar chart.

With the cfchart tag set up, we can move on and define the type of chart we want to generate and specify the query data to use. Since we're creating a bar chart, we set the type attribute of the cfchartseries tag to Bar. The query attribute is required for dynamic graphs and specifies the name of the query we want to pull the data from to populate the graph. The name of the query column containing the data to graph is specified in valuecolumn. Here we use AvgSalary. itemcolumn specifies the name of the query column containing item labels that correspond to the data points from the query column specified in valuecolumn. Since we're graphing the average salary by department, we use Department as the itemcolumn. For nonrotated charts, item labels are displayed on the horizontal axis. For rotated charts, the labels appear on the vertical axis. Pie charts display item labels in an optional legend. Executing the template in Example 17-3 results in the output shown in Figure 17-4.

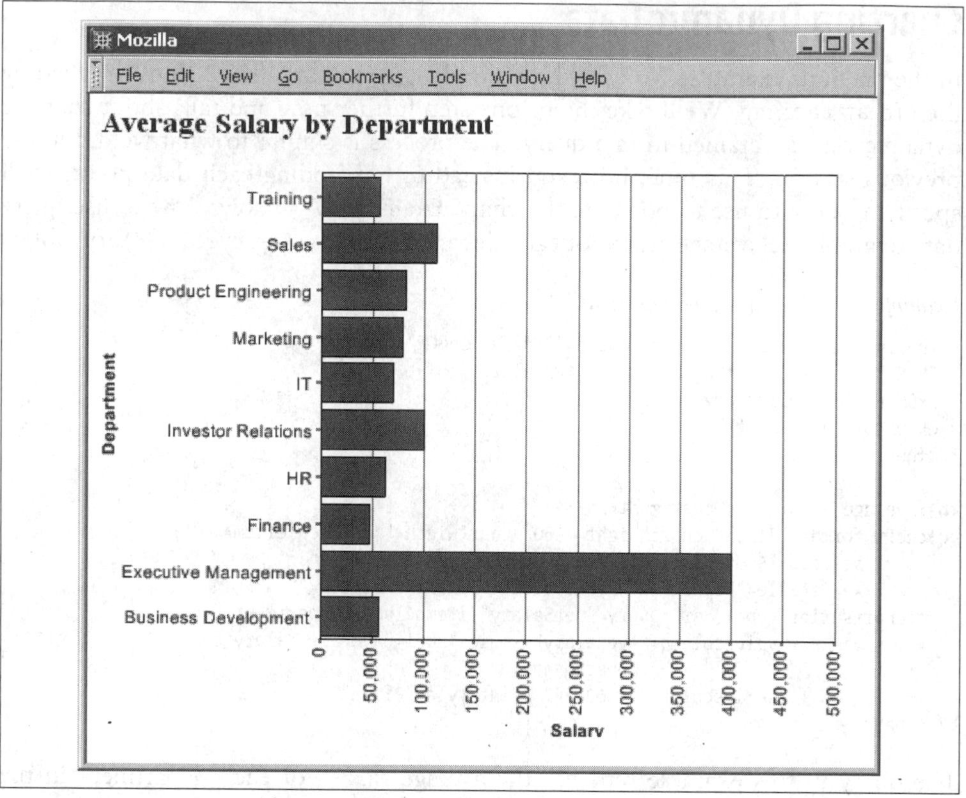

Figure 17-4. Generating a horizontal bar graph from query results

You can easily see what other charts generated using query data look like by changing the type attribute of the `cfchartseries` tag to any of the alternate values it accepts. You could also include additional static values in the example we just covered by specifying the individual data points using `cfchartdata` tags. This lets you mix both static and dynamic data in the same chart.

Charting Multiple Data Series

In ColdFusion 5, one of the biggest complaints about the `cfgraph` tag was its inability to graph more than a single series of data. For many developers looking to use ColdFusion for creating graphical representations of their data, this limitation was a disappointment. The engineers at Macromedia took this to heart when integrating ColdFusion MX's new charting engine used by `cfchart`.

As I mentioned earlier in the chapter, the `cfchart` tag is capable of graphing up to 16 different series of data in a single chart. When graphing more than one series of data, you can mix and match chart types, with one exception. If you choose to create a pie chart, it can contain only one series of data, and it's not possible to have both a pie chart and another chart type overlaid.

Consider the need to graph both the average salary in each department and the maximum salary in each department. You can write a single query to return both the average salary and the maximum salary for each department using the `AVG( )` and `MAX( )` aggregate functions discussed in Chapter 11. Example 17-4 shows the code for the query as well as the code for generating both data series.

Example 17-4. Graphing more than one data series

```
<cfquery name="GetSalary" datasource="ProgrammingCF">
  SELECT Department, AVG(Salary) AS AvgSalary, MAX(Salary) AS MaxSalary
  FROM EmployeeDirectory
  GROUP BY Department
</cfquery>

<h3>Average vs. Max Salary by Department</h3>
<cfchart format="Flash" chartheight="360" chartwidth="480" scalefrom="0"
         scaleto="500000" gridlines="11" labelformat="Currency"
         xaxistitle="Department" yaxistitle="Salary">
  <cfchartseries type="Line" query="GetSalary" itemcolumn="Department"
                 valuecolumn="AvgSalary" serieslabel="Average Salary by
                 Department" seriescolor="Blue" markerstyle="Diamond" />
  <cfchartseries type="Line" query="GetSalary" itemcolumn="Department"
                 valuecolumn="MaxSalary" serieslabel="Max Salary by Department"
                 seriescolor="Red" markerstyle="Rectangle" />
</cfchart>
```

Once the query is run, the chart container is set up using the `cfchart` tag, just as it was in all of our previous examples. The first data series is used to plot a line graph that represents the average salary for each department. This is done by setting the `type` attribute in the `cfchartseries` tag to `Line`. The color for each data point and the lines connecting them is set to `Blue` using `seriescolor`. The `markerstyle` attribute sets the style for each data point marker in 2D charts. Options are `Circle`, `Diamond`, `Letterx`, `Mcross`, `Rcross`, `Rectangle`, `Snow`, and `Triangle`. The default is `Rectangle`. In the case of the first data series, the `markerstyle` is set to `Diamond`.

The second `cfchartseries` tag is used to overlay another line chart over the first one we created. This chart plots the maximum salary for each department. This time, the data point markers are rendered as red rectangles. Using a different `markerstyle` for the second series makes it easier to identify overlapping data points (ones that have the same value).

The overall effect here is that we created a chart that represents two distinct sets of data, shown in Figure 17-5. To see how different combinations of attributes affect each data series as well as the overall chart, try changing the values of the `type` and `markerstyle` attributes.

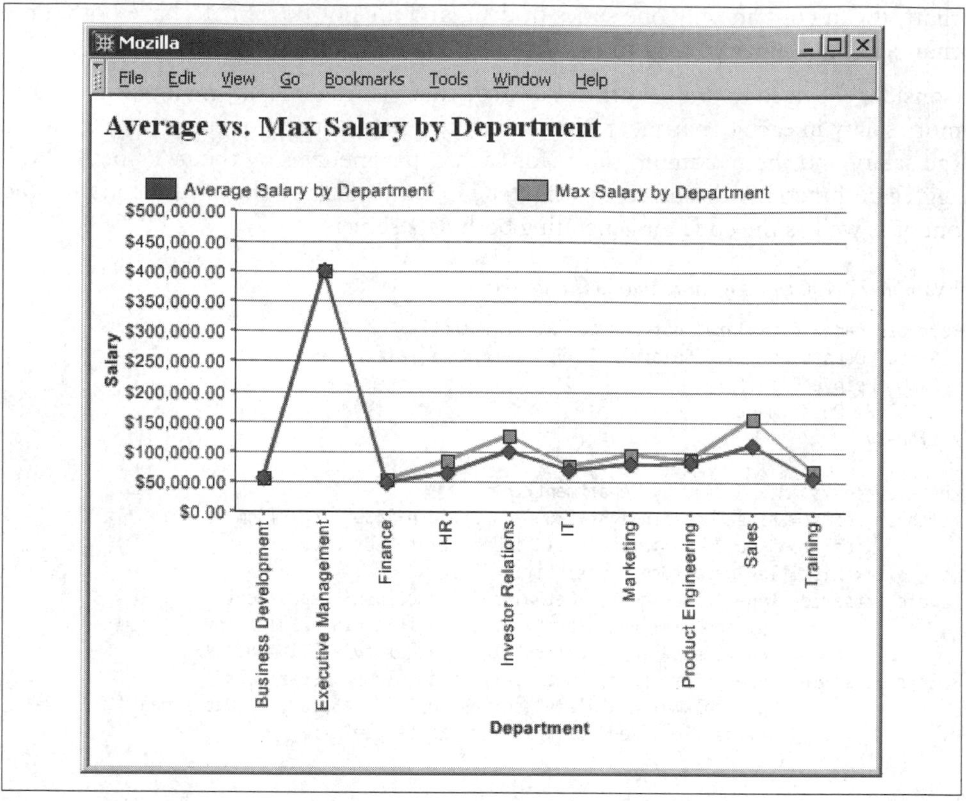

Figure 17-5. Graphing more than one series of data

Multiple Data Point Colors in a Single Series

One thing you've probably noticed is that in all of the charts we've created so far (with the exception of pie charts), all data points within a given series are the same color. This is a limitation of the `cfchart` implementation. Colors are limited to one per series when you generate a chart from query data using the `cfchartseries` tag. There is a way around this, however. Instead of using a single `cfchartseries` tag to output query data, you can use a query loop to iterate over the query data, creating a different `cfchartseries` tag for each data point to be graphed. This allows you to specify a different color for each "series". The actual data point is graphed using the `cfchartdata` tag. Example 17-5 shows how to render the same chart from Example 17-3 with different colored bars.

Example 17-5. Generating different color data points

```
<cfquery name="GetSalary" datasource="ProgrammingCF">
  SELECT Department, AVG(Salary) AS AvgSalary
  FROM EmployeeDirectory
  GROUP BY Department
```

Example 17-5. Generating different color data points (continued)

```
</cfquery>

<h3>Average Salary by Department</h3>
<cfchart format="Flash" chartheight="360" chartwidth="480" scalefrom="0"
        scaleto="500000" gridlines="11" seriesplacement="Stacked"
        labelformat="Number" xaxistitle="Department" yaxistitle="Salary"
        showlegend="No">
  <cfloop query="GetSalary">
    <cfchartseries type="Bar">
      <cfchartdata item="#Department#" value="#AvgSalary#">
    </cfchartseries>
  </cfloop>
</cfchart>
```

Note that it's necessary to specify `seriesplacement="Stacked"` in the `cfchart` tag. If you use `Default` or set it to `Cluster`, the bar chart may not appear as you would expect. Executing the code in Example 17-5 results in the chart shown in Figure 17-6.

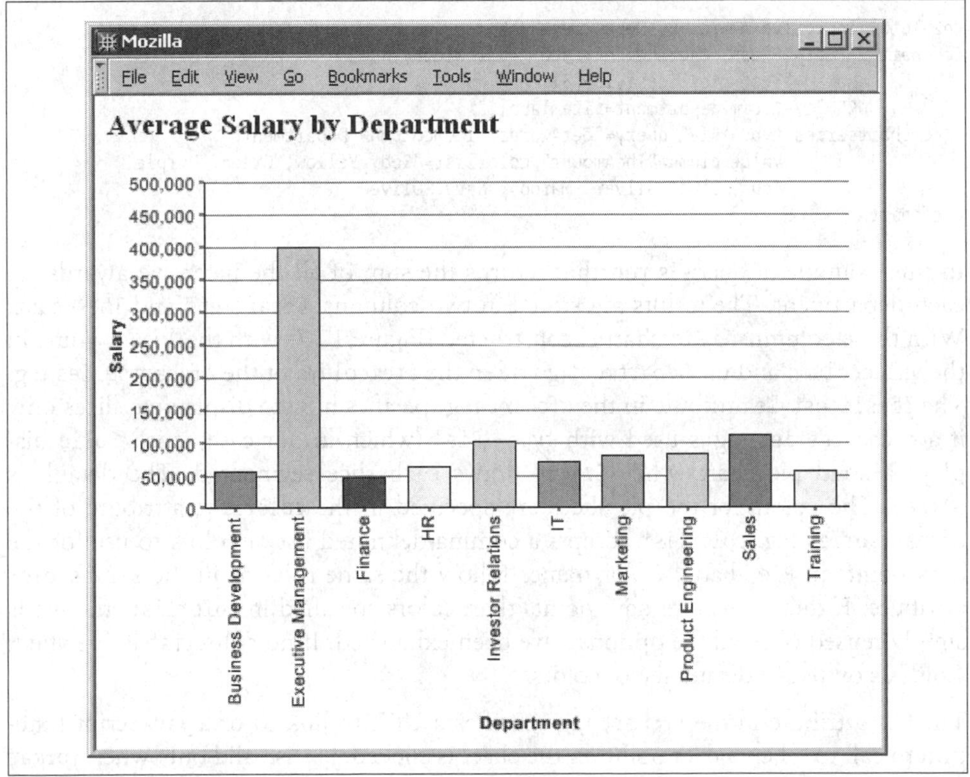

Figure 17-6. Generating a chart with more than one data point color in a series

Drilling Down on Graph Data

Another useful feature of the cfchart tag is the ability to create graphs with clickable data points that can link to other templates. This allows you to implement drill-down functionality as we did in Chapter 11, using a graph instead of an HTML table. In order to create a clickable graph, you have to set format to Flash. Examples 17-6 and 17-7 demonstrate how to create a pie chart with drill-down capabilities. The pie chart displays the total amount of incentive award dollars given out per department, and it allows you to click on any pie slice and have it drill down to that specific department's data.

Example 17-6. Pie chart displaying total incentive awards by department with drill-down capability

```
<cfquery name="GetAwards" datasource="ProgrammingCF">
  SELECT EmployeeDirectory.Department, Sum(IncentiveAwards.Amount) AS TheAmount
  FROM EmployeeDirectory, IncentiveAwards
  WHERE EmployeeDirectory.ID = IncentiveAwards.ID
  GROUP BY Department
</cfquery>

<h2>Total Incentive Awards by Department</h2>
<cfchart format="Flash" chartheight="300" chartwidth="450"
         show3d="Yes" pieslicestyle="Sliced"
         URL="17-7.cfm?department=$itemlabel$">
  <cfchartseries type="Pie" query="GetAwards" itemcolumn="Department"
                 valuecolumn="TheAmount" colorlist="Red, Yellow, Green, Purple,
                 Aqua, Blue, Silver, Maroon, Navy, Olive" />
</cfchart>
```

In this example, a query is run that returns the sum of all the incentive awards for each department. The results are stored in two columns, Department and TheAmount. With these columns, a Pie chart is constructed (Figure 17-7) with the Amount going in the valuecolumn and the Department going in the itemcolumn of the cfchartseries tag. The pieslicestyle attribute in the cfchart tag specifies how to display pie slices only if a cfchartseries tag is used with type="Pie" (which in our case, it is). Solid displays a solid pie chart, while Sliced draws each slice segmented. The default is Sliced. The colors for the pie slices are specified in the colorlist attribute of the cfchartseries tag. colorlist accepts a comma-delimited list of colors to use for the data points in Pie charts. Color names follow the same rules as in the seriescolor attribute. If there are more data points than colors specified in colorlist, the list is simply reused once all the options have been exhausted. If no colorlist is specified, ColdFusion uses a default list of colors.

The URL attribute in the cfchart tag specifies a URL to link to or a JavaScript function to call to when a data point on the chart is clicked. URL is valid only when format is Flash. There are three special variables you can use with the URL attribute to pass information about the data point to the URL or JavaScript target. These variables are $value$ (value of the data point selected), $itemlabel$ (item label associated with the

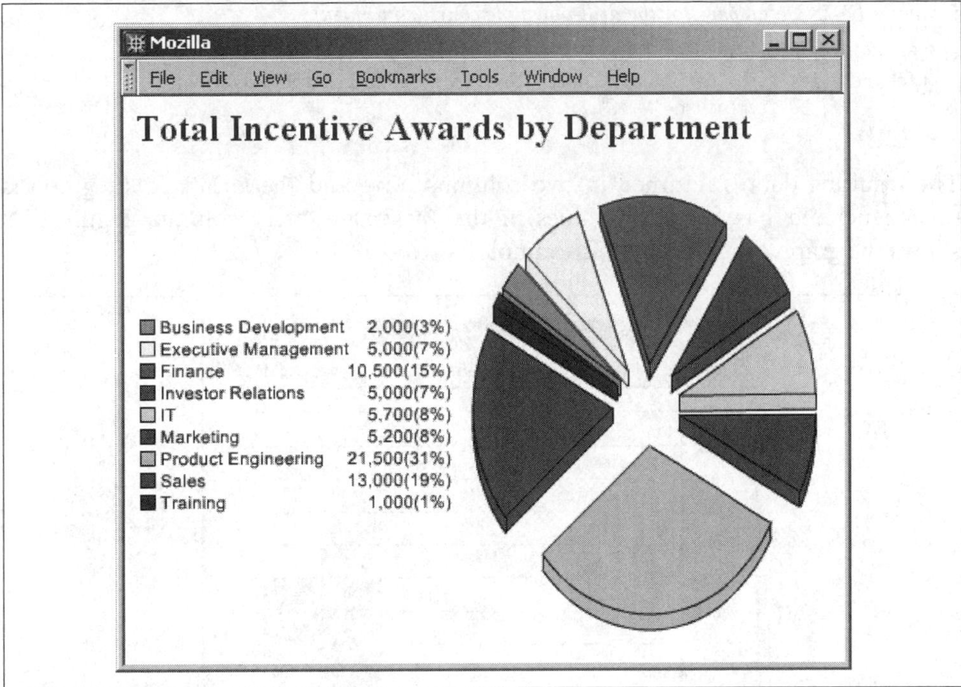

Figure 17-7. Drilling down on a pie chart

selected data point), and `$serieslabel$` (series label associated with the selected data point). In our example, the `URL` points to the template in Example 17-7. Note the `?Department=$itemlabel$` parameter appended to the end of the URL. This allows us to pass the name of the department associated with a particular data point as a URL parameter to the template in Example 17-7 for processing. Query columns whose values contain spaces and other special characters are automatically URL-encoded before being appended to the URL string.

Clicking on any of the pie wedges calls the template in Example 17-7 and passes the department name corresponding to the pie wedge as a URL parameter. The template takes the department name contained in the URL variable and uses it to retrieve the total amount of incentive awards for each employee in the department.

Example 17-7. Detail page for the drill-down pie chart

```
<!--- Retrieve all of the incentive awards for each employee in the
      department specified from the previous graph --->
<cfquery name="GetEmployeeInfo" datasource="ProgrammingCF">
         SELECT EmployeeDirectory.Name, Sum(IncentiveAwards.Amount) AS TheAmount
         FROM EmployeeDirectory, IncentiveAwards
         WHERE EmployeeDirectory.ID = IncentiveAwards.ID
         AND EmployeeDirectory.Department = '#URL.Department#'
         GROUP BY EmployeeDirectory.Name
</cfquery>
```

Example 17-7. Detail page for the drill-down pie chart (continued)

```
<cfchart gridlines="11" scalefrom="0" scaleto="10000">
  <cfchartseries type="Bar" query="GetEmployeeInfo" valuecolumn="TheAmount"
                 itemcolumn="Name" />
</cfchart>
```

The resulting data is returned in two columns, `Name` and `TheAmount`. A `Bar` graph is then generated based on the values in the `TheAmount` query column. Figure 17-8 shows the graph generated by this example.

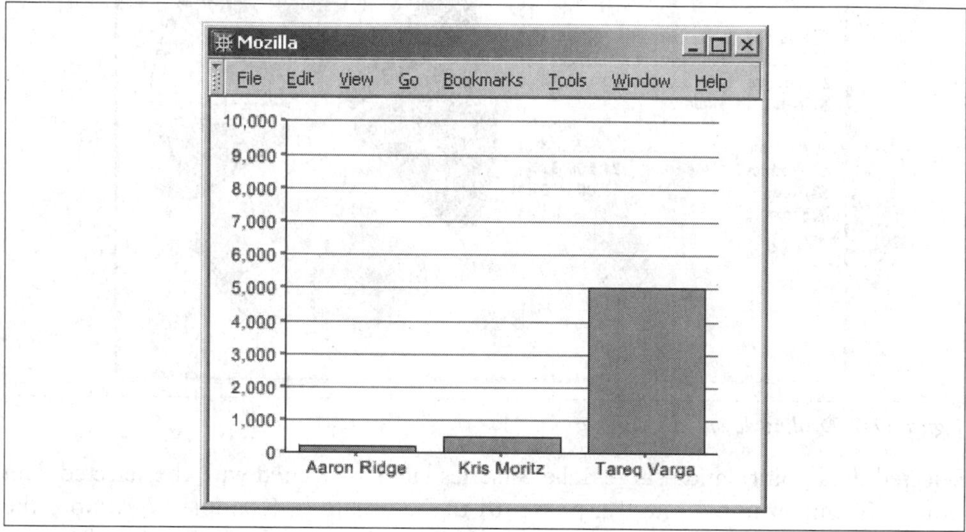

Figure 17-8. Detail page for drill-down chart

Passing Chart Parameters to JavaScript

The same technique that's used to create clickable data points for drill-down charts can also be used to call JavaScript functions when a data point is clicked. This allows you to do all sorts of things with your chart, including creating alert boxes when a data point is clicked. Example 17-8 shows you how to do this by embedding the call to a JavaScript function directly in the `URL` attribute of the `cfchart` tag; the function creates an alert box containing the data point values .

Example 17-8. Passing chart values to a JavaScript function

```
<script language="JavaScript">
<!--
  function chartAlert(Series, Item, Value){
    alert(Series + " " + Item + " = " + Value);
  }
//-->
</script>
```

Example 17-8. Passing chart values to a JavaScript function (continued)

```
<cfquery name="GetAwards" datasource="ProgrammingCF">
  SELECT EmployeeDirectory.Department, Sum(IncentiveAwards.Amount) AS TheAmount
  FROM EmployeeDirectory, IncentiveAwards
  WHERE EmployeeDirectory.ID = IncentiveAwards.ID
  GROUP BY Department
</cfquery>

<h2>Total Incentive Awards by Department</h2>
<cfchart format="Flash" chartheight="300" chartwidth="450"
         show3d="yes" pieslicestyle="Sliced"
         URL="javascript:chartAlert('$serieslabel$','$itemlabel$','$value$');">
  <cfchartseries type="Pie" query="GetAwards" itemcolumn="Department"
                 valuecolumn="TheAmount" colorlist="Red, Yellow, Green, Purple,
                 Aqua, Blue, Silver, Maroon, Navy, Olive" serieslabel="Total
                 incentive awards for" />
</cfchart>
```

This example runs a query that obtains the total dollar amount of incentive awards given for each department and draws a pie chart representing the breakout. The `URL` attribute of the `cfchart` tag is set to call a JavaScript function named `chartAlert()`, passing it the values for `$serieslabel$`, `$itemlabel$`, and `$value$`. The `chartAlert()` function pops up a JavaScript alert box that contains the values passed by the chart. The results of clicking on a pie slice are shown in Figure 17-9.

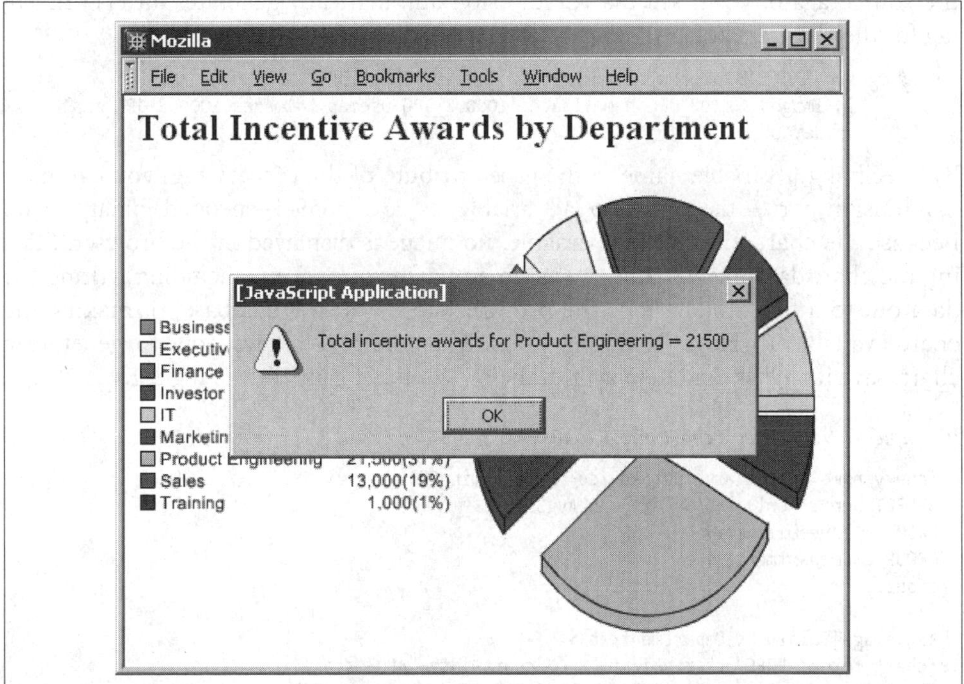

Figure 17-9. Alert box created by a JavaScript function

Saving Charts to a Variable

In all the examples we've created so far, the cfchart tag has always been used to render the chart directly to the browser. Behind the scenes, cfchart is generating a SWF, JPG, or PNG file and sending the necessary HTML code to the browser to render the file. For example, if you run the code in Example 17-1 and do a "View Source" in your web browser, you'll see that ColdFusion MX automatically generated the necessary HTML object and embed tags to display the SWF (Flash) version of the chart:

```
<object classid="clsid:D27CDB6E-AE6D-11cf-96B8-444553540000"
 codebase="http://active.macromedia.com/flash2/cabs/swflash.cab#version=4,0,2,0"
 ID=Images_100007_SWF name=Images_100007_SWF width=400 height=400>
  <param name=movie value="/CFIDE/GraphData.cfm?graphID=Images/100007.SWF">
  <param name=quality value=high>
  <param name=bgcolor value=#FFFFFF>
<embed src="/CFIDE/GraphData.cfm?graphID=Images/100007.SWF"
  quality=high bgcolor=#FFFFFF width=400 height=400 type="application/x-shockwave-
flash"
  pluginspage="http://www.macromedia.com/shockwave/download/index.cgi?P1_Prod_
Version=
ShockwaveFlash">
</embed>
</object>
```

If you change the format attribute to JPG instead of Flash, execute the code, and view the source again, you'll see that ColdFusion automatically generates an HTML img tag for the chart created by cfchart:

```
<img src="/CFIDE/GraphData.cfm?graphID=Images/100008.JPG"
     id=Images_100008_JPG name=Images_100008_JPG usemap="#Images_100008_JPG_map"
     border=0>
```

By specifying a variable name in the name attribute of the cfchart tag, you can have ColdFusion write the chart to a variable as ISO-8859-1–encoded binary data. Because the chart is stored in a variable, no image is displayed in the browser. Storing the chart data in a variable opens up a number of options, including writing the data out to a file, sending it to the browser, storing it in a database, or making the chart available to Flash Remoting users. Example 17-9 shows how to generate a chart, save it to disk, and display it in the browser using an HTML img tag.

Example 17-9. Writing a chart image to disk

```
<cfquery name="GetSalary" datasource="ProgrammingCF">
  SELECT Department, AVG(Salary) AS AvgSalary
  FROM EmployeeDirectory
  GROUP BY Department
</cfquery>

<h3>Average Salary by Department</h3>
<cfchart format="JPG" chartheight="360" chartwidth="480" scalefrom="0"
        scaleto="500000" gridlines="11" labelformat="Number"
        xaxistitle="Department" yaxistitle="Salary" name="TheChart">
```

Example 17-9. Writing a chart image to disk (continued)

```
  <cfchartseries type="Bar" query="GetSalary" itemcolumn="Department"
                 valuecolumn="AvgSalary" serieslabel="Average Salary by
                              Department"
                 seriescolor="##0000FF" paintstyle="Plain" />
</cfchart>

<cffile action="Write"
        charset="ISO-8859-1"
        file="d:\cfusionmx\wwwroot\programmingcf\17\AvgSal.jpg"
        output="#TheChart#">

<img src="/programmingcf/17/AvgSal.jpg">
```

Note that when you save a chart as a JPG or PNG file, the associated code used to generate the tip rollovers and URL drill-downs does not carry over. However, if you generate and save the chart as a SWF file, all rollovers and drill-down capabilities are preserved.

The same image we created in Example 17-9 could just as easily have been rendered straight to the browser, without the need to write it to disk first, by using the `cfcontent` tag. To see how this works, remove the `cffile` and `img` tags from Example 17-9 and insert the following code instead:

```
<cfcontent type="image/jpeg"><cfoutput>#TheChart#</cfoutput>
```

Working with the Chart Cache

When ColdFusion MX generates a chart via the `cfchart` tag, the actual image, whether it is a SWF, PNG, or JPG file, is rendered from a memory cache or a disk cache. By default, all images generated by `cfchart` are cached to disk. If you have access to the ColdFusion Administrator, you can configure exactly how the `cfchart` tag caches images that it creates. To do this, log into the ColdFusion Administrator, and choose the Charting link on the left hand side of the screen. This takes you to the Charting Settings section of the ColdFusion Administrator, shown in Figure 17-10.

In the Charting Settings section, you can set the caching mechanism via a dropdown box to either Disk (the default) or Memory. The next section allows you to specify the maximum number of images to allow in the cache at any one time. Caching images allows multiple requests that generate the same image to process much more quickly than having `cfchart` generate a new image every time someone requests the same chart. In the third section, you can set the maximum number of charts that can be processed concurrently. The higher the number, the more memory is required for the operation. The final section allows you to specify a directory location to use to store chart files if you set ColdFusion to use a disk cache. Note that the default values for all of these settings should suffice in most situations.

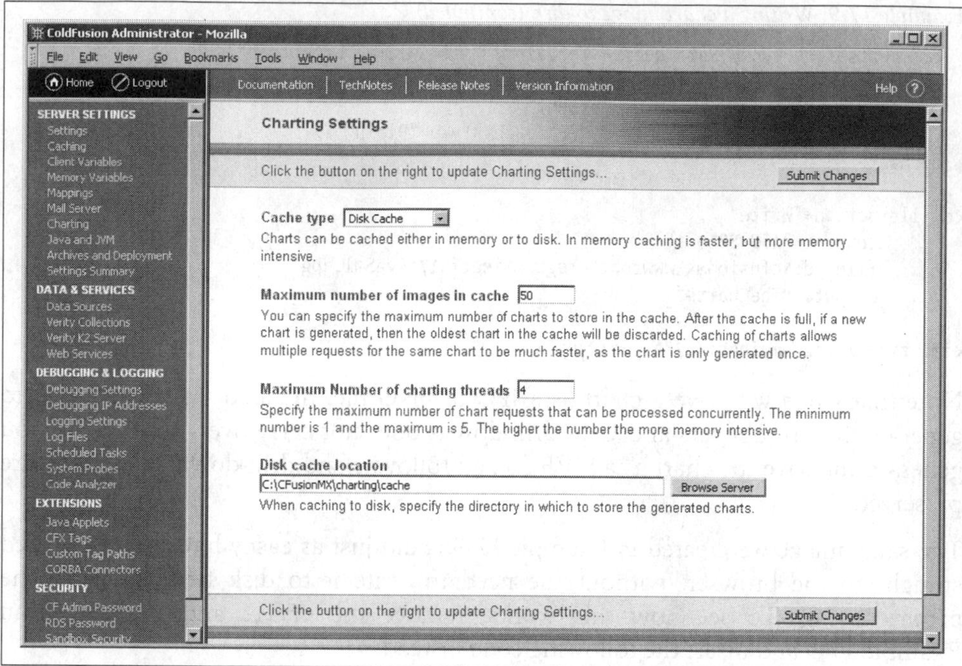

Figure 17-10. Charting Settings in the ColdFusion Administrator

CHAPTER 18
Regular Expressions in ColdFusion

Anyone who has ever worked with regular expressions knows what an indispensable tool they can be for parsing and manipulating text. Without them, text-processing operations such as search and replace can be very difficult, to say the least. Those with experience in Unix-based languages such as Perl, awk, or Tcl are probably already familiar with regular expressions, as they are used extensively in those languages. For those new to the world of regular expressions, don't worry. This chapter shows you everything you need to know to start using regular expressions in your ColdFusion applications.

ColdFusion provides you with two sets of ColdFusion functions for finding and replacing strings using regular expressions. `REFind()` and `REFindNoCase()` search for strings within blocks of text, while `REReplace()` and `REReplaceNoCase()` perform search and replace operations. Both sets of functions are extremely powerful and allow you to add a whole host of useful text-manipulation features to your ColdFusion applications.

Before we get into the mechanics of regular expressions, it is important for you to gain a basic understanding of the regular-expression language and how it is used by ColdFusion. Note that the regular-expression engine in ColdFusion MX differs significantly from the engine in all previous versions of ColdFusion. The new engine is "Perl compatible" for the most part, and it uses an underlying Java library for processing regular expressions. Because of this, if you are migrating an application from a previous version of ColdFusion to MX, be sure to read this chapter thoroughly and test your existing code with the new engine.

Regular-Expression Syntax

In their most basic form, regular expressions match characters on a one-for-one basis. Thus, you can match the first occurrence of the letter "a" in a search string as follows:

```
REFind("a", "abcdefg")
```

Likewise, you can search for the letters "can" in succession with:

```
REFind("can", "Watch the candle burn")
```

Using "can" as your regular expression matches "can", "candle", and "scan". Regular expressions that look for individual characters in this manner are said to be single-character regular expressions.

Single-character regular expressions are great when you know the exact series of characters that you want to match. But what if you don't know? What if you need to find and remove all the HTML tags in a particular block of text? You certainly don't want to have to code a regular expression for every single HTML tag. Instead, you can use what is known as a multicharacter regular expression. Multicharacter regular expressions use special characters (covered in a moment) to define ranges of characters to be matched. The following example takes the contents of a form variable (Form.MyString) and removes all HTML from it:

```
<cfset NoHTML = REReplace(Form.MyString, "<[^>]*>", "", "All")>
```

At first glance, the regular expression looks like a string of unrelated and meaningless characters. If you take the regular expression and break it down, it is easier to see what is happening. In this case, the first part of the expression, "<", matches the open angle bracket used to denote the beginning of an HTML tag. Adding "[^>]*" after the open angle bracket tells ColdFusion to match zero or more occurrences of any character other than the closed angle bracket ">". The square brackets denote a set of characters. In this case, they are used in conjunction with the caret followed by the closed angle bracket. This tells ColdFusion to exclude the closed angle bracket from the match criteria. The asterisk tells ColdFusion to match zero or more occurrences of the set contained inside the square angle brackets. The final part of the regular expression matches the closing angle bracket of an HTML tag.

Commenting Regular Expressions

Although you can use standard CFML and HTML comments above, below, and beside your regular expressions, the regular-expression language also contains a comment syntax that can be used inside the regular expression. Regular expressions allow for two types of comments: inline and end of line.

Inline comments can make it easier for you to see what's going on in otherwise complicated regular expressions. Regular expression comments in ColdFusion take the form (?##<*Your comment goes here*>). Consider the following example:

```
<cfset MyString = "The big <a href=""results.cfm"">cat</a> is fat.">
<cfset Link =
       REFindNoCase("<a [^>]*>(?##<match the href anchor>)([^<]*)(?##<match
       between href tags>)</a>(?##<match closing /a>)",
       MyString, 1 ,"true")>

<cfoutput>
```

```
#Mid(MyString, Link.Pos[2], Link.Len[2])#
</cfoutput>
```

Note the use of the escaped pound sign. Although the standard Perl-compatible commenting syntax uses a single pound sign, you must escape it by using a second pound sign or ColdFusion throws an error. You may include as many comments within your regular expression as you like.

End-of-line comments are a special case: you must use the (?x) operator discussed later in the chapter to tell ColdFusion to ignore all whitespace within the regular expression. End-of-line comments are denoted with two pound signs:

```
ReFindNoCase("(?x)
   bad\ cat      ##this is line 1
   |good\ cat    ##line 2.  Note spaces must be escaped
   ", "The cat is a good cat.")
```

Operators

There are several operators in the regular-expression language. These special characters perform functions within the regular-expression language and therefore must be escaped if you wish to search for them as literals. The following is a list of the operators along with their functions:

Dollar sign ($)
: The dollar sign anchors a regular expression to the end of a string. For example, searching for "[abc]$" matches the first occurrence of "abc" when it is at the end of a string.

Caret (^)
: The caret is used to exclude characters from being matched or to anchor a regular expression to the beginning of a string. Searching for "[^abc]" matches any characters in a string except for "a", "b", and "c". Similarly, searching for "[^0-9]" matches any characters in a string except for numbers. Searching for "^[abc]" matches "abc" only when it appears at the beginning of a string. In order for the caret to work within a set, it must be used as the first character in the set or range of characters.

Question mark (?)
: The question mark signifies zero or one matches of a regular expression within a given string. For example, searching for "ab?c" matches "ac" as well as "abc". Likewise, searching for "[ab]?c" matches "c" as well as "ac" and "bc". Using the question mark in your regular expressions essentially makes the expression optional. The question mark is a maximal, or "greedy," quantifier.

Asterisk (*)
: The asterisk is used to signify zero or more matches of a regular expression within a given string. For example, searching for "[a-z]*" matches zero or more lowercase characters in a string. Like the question mark, the asterisk effectively

makes the expression optional and is also considered a maximal or "greedy" quantifier.

Plus (+)
: The plus sign signifies one or more matches of a regular expression within a given string. For example, searching for "[a-z]+" matches one or more lowercase characters in a string. The plus sign is a maximal or "greedy" quantifier.

Parentheses (( ))
: Parentheses group segments of regular expressions together. These groups are known as subexpressions. Grouping subexpressions extends the capabilities of regular expressions by allowing you to apply special characters to the subexpressions as opposed to single characters. For example, searching for "(ab)+" matches one or more occurrences of "ab" within a string. Using parentheses to create subexpressions also enables you to take advantage of back referencing, which is covered later in the chapter.

Curly braces ({ })
: Curly braces are used to specify repeating characters to match and are considered maximal or "greedy" quantifiers. There are three ways to use curly braces:

  `{min,max}`
  : Specifies the number of times, as a range, that a regular expression should be matched, where *min* is an integer greater than or equal to zero that specifies the start of the range and *max* is a positive integer greater than or equal to *min* that specifies the end of the range. For example, searching for "(ab){1,4}" matches from one to four occurrences of "ab". Note that specifying {0,1} is the same as using the ? character.

  `{min,}`
  : Specifies that the regular expression should match at least *min* occurrences, where *min* is an integer greater than or equal to 0.

  `{n}`
  : Specifies that the regular expression should match exactly *n* occurrences, where *n* is an integer greater than or equal to 0.

Open square bracket ([)
: The open square bracket is used in conjunction with the closed square bracket (not a special character) to define a set of characters (called a character class) to be matched. For example, searching for "[abc]" matches any "a", "b", or "c" in a string. A hyphen (-) can also be used in conjunction with the square brackets to signify a range of characters to be matched, such that searching for "[a-z]" matches any single lowercase letter.

Pipe (|)
: The pipe represents a logical OR, such that searching for "tra(in|iner)" matches "train" or "trainer".

Backslash (\)

A backslash escapes special characters so they can be searched as literal characters. For example, "\+12" finds the string "+12". To search for the backslash character, it must also be escaped. For example, "c:\\" finds the string "c:\".

Period (.)

A period matches any single character, including a newline character. For example, ".am" matches both "cam" and "ham".

`(?i)`

Performs a case-insensitive comparison when used at the beginning of a regular expression in `ReFind()` or `ReReplace()`. For example, searching for "(?i)cat" will match the first instance of "cat", regardless of case.

`(?m)`

Used at the beginning of a regular expression to specify multiline mode for either the `^` or `$` character. Used with `^`, the matched string can be at the start of the search string or at the start of new lines. A new line is denoted by the linefeed character `CHR(10)`. For example, to match the word "cat" across multiple lines, you would use a regular expression like the following:

```
REFind("(?m)^cat", "the#CHR(10)#cat#CHR(10)#meows")
```

Carriage returns (`CHR(13)`) are not recognized as newline characters. When used with `$`, the matched string can be at the end of the search string or at the end of new lines.

`(?x)`

Used at the beginning of a regular expression to specify that whitespace should be ignored when performing the match, (you can allow spaces by escaping them), and to allow end-of-line comments in the regular expression. End-of-line comments are denoted with two pound signs. For example:

```
ReFindNoCase("(?x)
   bad\ cat     ##this is line 1
  |good\ cat    ##line 2.  Note spaces must be escaped
  ", "The cat is a good cat.")
```

This matches the first occurrence of either "bad cat" or "good cat".

`(?=`*`string`*`)`

Used at the beginning of a regular expression to denote a positive lookahead when searching. A positive lookahead allows you to include a subexpression in your regular expression for a match, but does not include the matched text in the result. For example, the following code searches for the string "Robert" but only returns the length of the string "Rob":

```
<cfset MyString="Is Robert a robber">
<cfset Nickname=REFind("Rob(?=ert)", MyString, 1, "Yes")>

<cfoutput>
#mid(MyString, Nickname.pos[1], Nickname.len[1])#
</cfoutput>
```

Note that because lookaheads do not capture text, their results are not included in backreferences.

`(?!string)`
: Used at the beginning of a regular expression to denote a negative lookahead when searching. A negative lookahead is similar to a positive lookahead, but it tests for the absence of a match. Like a positive lookahead, results do not include the matched text from the negative lookahead and are omitted from backreferences.

`(?:string)`
: Excludes the matched subexpression from inclusion in backreferences. For example, if you search for the string "(?:cat)", ColdFusion matches the first occurrence of "cat", but it is not available in a backreference.

To escape any special character, simply place a backslash (\) before the character. When a regular expression encounters an escaped special character, it is treated as a literal search value.

POSIX Classes

Rather than requiring use of multicharacter classes such as "[A-Za-z]" in your regular expressions, ColdFusion allows you to use Portable Operating System Interface (POSIX) character classes to make coding and reading your regular expressions easier. POSIX character classes are referenced within ColdFusion regular expressions by enclosing them inside two sets of square brackets, as in the following example:

```
<cfset NewFilename = REReplace("My Filename.doc","[[:space:]]","_","All")>
```

This example replaces all spaces in the filename with underscores and creates a variable called `NewFilename` that contains "My_Filename.doc". Here's another example:

```
<cfset NewString = REReplace("T8h3i53s i9s5 8a3 t3e2s9t.", "[[:digit:]]", "", "All")>
```

This example takes the string "T8h3i53s i9s5 8a3 t3e2s9t." and replaces all digits with a blank. The result is the string "This is a test."

The following POSIX character classes are supported by ColdFusion MX:

`[:alpha:]`
: Matches any letter regardless of the case used. Using `alpha` is the same as specifying `[A-Za-z]`.

`[:alnum:]`
: Matches any letter or number regardless of the case used. Using `alnum` is the same as specifying `[A-Za-z0-9]` or `\w`.

`[:blank:]`
: Matches a space or tab character.

`[:cntrl:]`
: Matches any character that isn't included in any of the other POSIX character classes (`alpha`, `alnum`, `digit`, `graph`, `lower`, `print`, `punct`, `space`, `upper`, `xdigit`).

`[:digit:]`
: Matches any digit. Using `digit` is the same as specifying `[0-9]` or `\d`.

`[:graph:]`
: Matches any printable character except for those listed in the `space` control set (carriage return, form feed, newline, space, or tab).

`[:lower:]`
: Matches any lowercase letter, including lowercase accented letters.

`[:print:]`
: Matches any printable character.

`[:punct:]`
: Matches any punctuation character in the following set: `! ' # $ % & ' ( ) * + , - . / : ; < = > ? @ [ / ] ^ _ { | } ~`

`[:space:]`
: Matches any carriage return, form feed, newline, space, or tab. Same as specifying `\s`.

`[:upper:]`
: Matches any uppercase letter, including accented uppercase letters.

`[:xdigit:]`
: Matches any hexadecimal digit. Using `xdigit` is the same as specifying `[0-9A-Fa-f]`.

Character Classes

Another technique you can use to make reading and writing regular expressions easier is the use of character classes. Character classes, also known as character shorthand, provide you with an easy way to abstract more complex regular expressions. Many character classes perform the same tasks as character sets or POSIX character classes. Others are unique. Note that character classes are case-sensitive. The following list represents all of the character classes supported in ColdFusion MX:

`\A`
: Similar to the `^` special character in that it is used to anchor a regular expression to the beginning of a string. However, unlike the caret, `\A` cannot be combined with `(?m)` to specify the start of a newline.

`\Z`
: Similar to the `$` operator in that it is used to anchor a regular expression to the end of a string. However, unlike the dollar sign, `\Z` cannot be combined with `(?m)` to specify the end of a newline.

\b

Matches a word boundary. A word boundary is defined as a position with an alphanumeric character on one side (\w) and a nonalphanumeric character, such as a space, on the other (\W). \b is also used to denote a backspace when used inside a set: [\b].

\b

Matches a nonword boundary. Two alphanumeric or two nonalphanumeric characters in a row indicate a nonword boundary.

\d

Matches a digit. Same as [0-9] or [[:digit:]].

\D

Matches any nondigit. Same as [^0-9] or [^[digit:]].

\ddd

Matches any 8-bit octal value in the range \000 to \377.

\xdd

Matches any hexadecimal digit. Same as [0-9A-Fa-f].

\w

Matches any alphanumeric character, including the underscore. Same as [A-Za-z0-9_]. Similar to [[:alnum:]] except \w also matches the underscore.

\W

Matches any nonalphanumeric character. Same as [^A-Za-z0-9_]. Similar to [^[:alnum:]] except \W will not match an underscore.

\f

Matches a form feed.

\n

Matches the newline character

\r

Matches a carriage return.

\s

Matches any whitespace character. Same as [[:space:]] or [\t\n\r\f].

\S

Matches any character not considered a whitespace character. Same as [^[:space:]] or [^ \t\n\r\f].

\t

Matches a tab.

Unsupported Perl Regular-Expression Conventions

Although the regular expression engine in ColdFusion MX is said to be Perl compatible, there are a few differences. There are a handful of Perl-compatible features that are not supported in ColdFusion MX:

- Lookbehind (?<=) (<?!)
- `\p\`
- `\x{hhhh}`
- `\C`
- `\N`

There are a few other minor differences between ColdFusion regular expressions and the Perl variety:

- In ColdFusion MX, the period always matches a newline character.
- Use `\n` instead of `$n` to specify the replace string in a backreference. ColdFusion automatically escapes the `$` in replacement strings.
- You don't have to escape the backslash character in replacement strings. ColdFusion does it automatically except for case-conversion characters (`\L` should be escaped as \\, etc.).
- `\Q`, `\u\L`, and `\l\U` are not supported in replacement strings.
- Embedded modifiers such as `(?i)` always operate on the entire expression, even when used inside a bracketed group.

All of these differences need to be kept in mind, especially if you are using reference material other than the ColdFusion documentation for constructing your regular expressions.

Finding Strings

To find a string in a block of text, you use the `REFind( )` or `REFindNoCase( )` functions. `REFind( )` and `REFindNoCase( )` are used when you want to know the position of the expression being searched for within a string. `REFind( )` performs a case-sensitive search; `REFindNoCase( )` performs a case-insensitive search. Regardless of the function used, they both use the same syntax:

```
REFind(RegularExpression, String [, StartPosition] [, ReturnSubExpressions])
REFindNoCase(RegularExpression, String [, StartPosition] [, ReturnSubExpressions])
```

Both the `REFind( )` and `REFindNoCase( )` functions accept the same parameters. The following example finds the first occurrence of "tom" regardless of case:

```
<cfset MyString="This is a red tomato.">
<cfset ThePosition=REFindNoCase("tom", MyString)>
```

```
<cfoutput>
The Position:  #ThePosition#
</cfoutput>
```

In this example, we use REFindNoCase( ) to find the starting position of "tom" within the string "This is a red tomato." This is done by assigning the result of the regular expression to a variable—in this case, ThePosition. The actual regular expression is embedded within the REFindNoCase( ) function. In its basic form, REFindNoCase( ) accepts two parameters, the regular expression and the string. In this example, the regular expression is simply the three characters "tom", and the string is "This is a red tomato." Upon execution, the value returned for ThePositon should be 15, as the first occurrence of "tom" begins at position 15 of the string.

Now that you see how the REFindNoCase( ) function is used, let's take a look at another example that uses REFind( ) to perform a case-sensitive search. This code finds the first case-sensitive occurrence of "Tom":

```
<cfset MyString="This is Tom's red tomato.">
<cfset ThePosition = ReFind("Tom", MyString)>

<cfoutput>
The Position:  #ThePosition#
</cfoutput>
```

The syntax for REFind( ) is the same as that for REFindNoCase( ). The only difference between the two tags is REFind( ) is case-sensitive. This time, the value of ThePosition is 9, the position at which "Tom" first occurs in MyString. If we modify the example a bit so that the regular expression is "tom" instead of "Tom", ThePosition returns 19 because the first case-sensitive occurrence of "tom" is found at position 19 (the "tom" in "tomato").

Now that you've seen the mechanics of both tags, let's take a look at some additional examples that utilize the REFind( ) and REFindNoCase( ) tags:

- Find the first occurrence of the letter "a" in the string:

  ```
  ReFind("a", "zzxxyaabbccdd")
  ```

  Returns 6 because the first occurrence of "a" is in the sixth position of the string.
- Use a case-sensitive search to find the first occurrence of any character followed by "ar":

  ```
  ReFind(".ar", "There are a lot of aardvarks around here.")
  ```

  Returns 6 because the first occurrence of any character followed by the letters "ar" is in the sixth position of the string, where a space precedes the word "are".
- Find the first case-sensitive occurrence of one or more "a" followed by one or more "b":

  ```
  ReFind("a+b+", "zzxxyaabbccdd")
  ```

  Returns 6 as "aabb" starts in the sixth position of the string.

- Find the first letter regardless of case:

  ```
  ReFind("[A-Za-z]", "1234567890asdfghjkl")
  ```

  Returns 11 because the first letter, "a", occurs in the eleventh position of the string.
- Find the first case-sensitive occurrence of "a" followed by one or more lowercase letters:

  ```
  ReFind("a[a-z]+", "Is there a doctor around here?")
  ```

  Returns 19 because the word "around", which begins in the nineteenth position, is the first occurrence of the letter "a" followed by one or more occurrences of another lowercase letter.
- Find the first occurrence of "to", "two", or "too", regardless of case:

  ```
  ReFindNoCase("(to|two|too)", "She said that he likes to rock climb.")
  ```

  Returns 24 because the word "to" occurs in the twenty-fourth position of the string.
- Find the first character in the string, regardless of case, that isn't a number:

  ```
  ReFindNoCase("[^0-9]", "50 miles to the beach!")
  ```

  Returns 3 because the first nonnumber (a space) is encountered at the third position of the string.

Both the `REFind()` and `REFindNoCase()` functions can accept two optional parameters in addition to the regular expression and the string. The first optional parameter allows you to specify a start position for the regular expression to begin its evaluation of the string. For example, to search the string "This cat is fat" for the first occurrence of "is" beginning at the fifth position, your regular expression looks like this:

```
<cfset ThePosition = ReFindNoCase("is", "This cat is fat", 5)>
```

In this case, the value returned for `ThePosition` is `10`. The regular expression begins searching for the first occurrence of "is" at the fifth position in the string, which happens to be the blank space after "This" in our example.

The second optional parameter available to the `REFind()` and `REFindNoCase()` functions allows you to specify whether to return matched subexpressions if any are found during the search. This means that if a match for your regular expression is found, ColdFusion returns a structure containing two arrays, one for the position of the first occurrence of the match and a second for the matched subexpression's length in characters. These values are stored in the keys `Pos` and `Len`, respectively. Here is an example to help illustrate the point:

```
<cfset MyString="This cat is a fat cat">
<cfset Matches = REFind("cat", MyString, 1, "true")>

<cfdump var="#Matches#">
```

```
<cfoutput>
<b>String:</b>  #MyString#<br>
<b>Regex:</b>  REFind(&quot;cat&quot;, MyString, 1, &quot;true&quot;)<br>
<b>Position:</b> #Matches.Pos[1]#<br>
<b>Length:</b> #Matches.Len[1]#
</cfoutput>
```

This example uses the `REFind( )` function to perform a case-sensitive search for "cat" in the string "This cat is a fat cat". The search begins at the first position in the string. Setting the optional `ReturnSubExpressions` parameter to `true` causes the value of `Matches` to be returned as a structure containing the keys `Pos` and `Len`. The `cfdump` tag is used to graphically illustrate the structure of arrays returned by the regular expression. The values contained in the structure are output by referencing them within a `cfoutput` section. In this example, the values output for `Pos[1]` and `Len[1]` are 6 and 3, respectively. The results are shown in Figure 18-1.

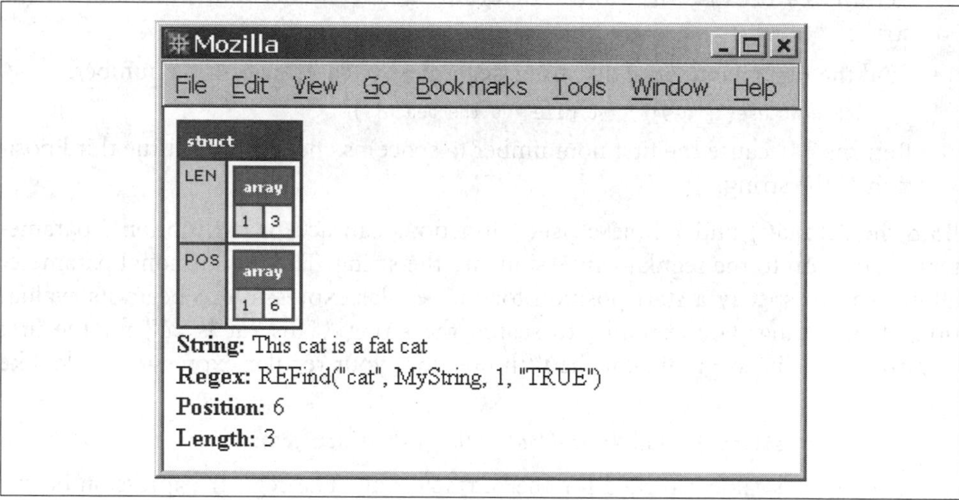

Figure 18-1. Obtaining the length and position of a matched expression

If your regular expression contains one or more subexpressions, the `Pos` and `Len` arrays contain an index for the first occurrence of each subexpression matched, in addition to the `Pos` and `Len` for the first match of the entire regular expression. For example, consider the following regular expression that looks for the first occurrence of an `<a href>/</a>` tag pair in a string, as well as the text between the tags:

```
<cfset MyString="This is a <a href=""/test/test.cfm"">test</a>.">
<cfset Matches=REFindNoCase("<a [^>]*>([[:print:]]*)</a>", MyString, 1,
       "true")>

<cfdump var="#Matches#">

<cfoutput>
#HTMLEditFormat(Mid(MyString, Matches.Pos[1], Matches.Len[1]))#<br>
#Mid(MyString, Matches.Pos[2], Matches.Len[2])#<br>
</cfoutput>
```

In this example, the regular expression contains a subexpression that matches any text between <a href>/</a> tags. Figure 18-2 shows a dump of the contents of the structure created by the `REFindNocase()` function. The output also contains the actual string values returned by the whole regular expression and the subexpression. The string values are obtained using the `Mid()` function seeded with the start position and length for the expression and sub expression.

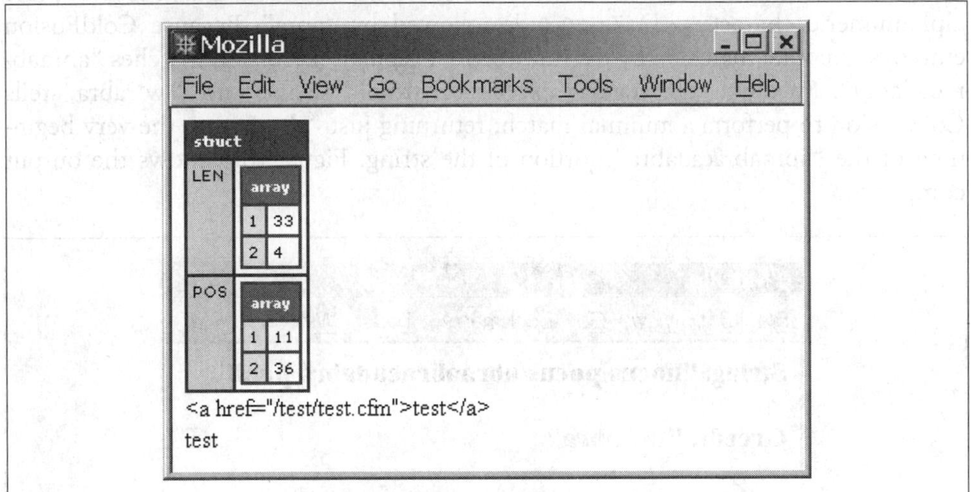

Figure 18-2. Obtaining the length and position of a matched expression

Maximal Versus Minimal Matching

By default, ColdFusion applies what is known as maximal or "greedy" matching when using the *, +, ?, {*min*,*max*}, {*min*,}, and {*n*} quantifiers. This means that ColdFusion finds the greatest number of characters possible in a search string that matches a regular expression. You can force ColdFusion to use minimal (nongreedy or "lazy") matching by appending a question mark to any of the greedy quantifiers (+?, *?, ??, {*min*,*max*}?, {*min*,}?, and {*n*}?).* Minimal matching causes ColdFusion to find the smallest number of characters in a search string that match a regular expression. To illustrate the difference between maximal and minimal matching, consider the following example:

```
<cfset MyString="hocus pocus abraabracadabra poof!">
<cfset Greedy=REFind("\w*abra", MyString, 1, "true")>
<cfset Lazy=REFind("\w*?abra", MyString, 1, "true")>

<cfoutput><h3>String: "#MyString#"</h3></cfoutput>
```

* {n}? is functionally no different than {n} and is supported for syntactic consistency.

```
<h3>Greedy: "\w*abra"</h3>
<cfoutput>#Mid(MyString, Greedy.Pos[1], Greedy.Len[1])#</cfoutput>
<cfdump var="#Greedy#">

<h3>Lazy: "\w*?abra"</h3>
<cfoutput>#Mid(MyString, Lazy.Pos[1], Lazy.Len[1])#</cfoutput>
<cfdump var="#Lazy#">
```

In this example, we use a greedy and a lazy regular expression to match zero or more alphanumeric characters (`[A-Za-z0-9_]`) followed by "abra". Because ColdFusion employs maximal matching by default, the first regular expression matches "abraabracadabra". Switching the regular expression from "\w*abra" to "\w*?abra" tells ColdFusion to perform a minimal match, returning just "abra" from the very beginning of the "abraabracadabra" portion of the string. Figure 18-3 shows the output comparison.

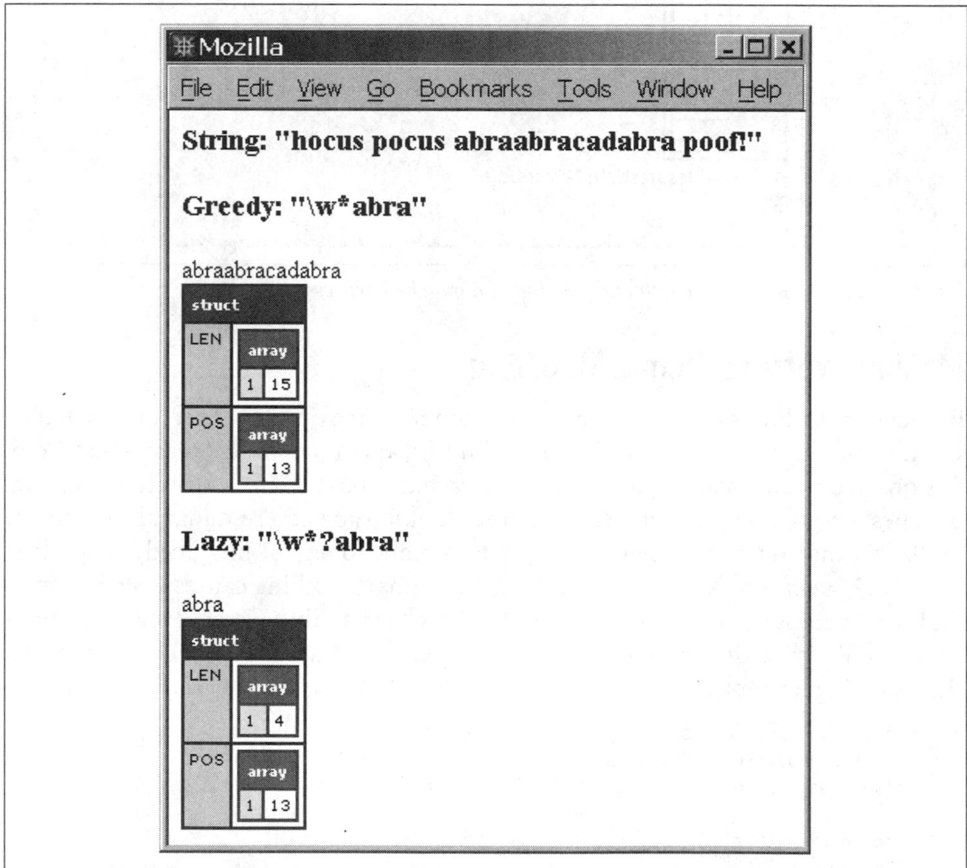

Figure 18-3. Maximal versus minimal matching

Replacing Strings

String replacement is performed with the `REReplace()` and `REReplaceNoCase()` functions. `REReplace()` performs case-sensitive search and replace functions, while `REReplaceNoCase()` is used for case-insensitive search and replace. Regardless of which tag you use, they have the same syntax:

```
REReplace(String, RegularExpression, Substring [, Scope])
REReplaceNoCase(String, RegularExpression, Substring [, Scope])
```

Both functions take three required parameters and one optional parameter. The first required parameter is the string to perform the regular expression on. The string can be either a block of text enclosed in single or double quotes or a variable that contains the text that you want to search. The second required parameter is the regular expression you want to use for your search. Any valid ColdFusion regular expression can be used. The third required parameter is the substring. The substring contains the string to replace any matches made by the regular expression. The final parameter is optional and determines the scope of the search-and-replace operation. The scope can be set to `One` or `All`. Setting the scope to `One` (the default) replaces only the first occurrence of the substring; setting it to `All` replaces all occurrences of the substring. The following two examples show the use of the `REReplace()` and `REReplaceNoCase()` functions:

- Replace all occurrences of the number 7 with the word "seven":

  ```
  REReplace("There are 7 words in this string.", "7", "Seven", "All")
  ```

- Replace all numbers with an asterisk character:

  ```
  REReplace("My Social Security number is 999-99-9999.", "[0-9]", "*", "All")
  ```

Backreferences

Backreferences allow your regular expressions to refer to previously matched subexpressions. This is useful in situations where you want your regular expression to use a match as part of the criteria for an additional regular-expression function. A commonly used scenario illustrating backreferencing involves using a regular expression to remove doubled words within a sentence. For example, suppose you have the string "I would like to go to to the park." The word "to" appears twice in a row—a common typing mistake. The regular expression to remove any doubled words from the sentence looks like this:

```
<cfset NoDupes = REReplaceNoCase("I would like to go to to the park.",
" \b([\w]+)[ ]+\1", "\1", "All")>
```

Let's break this example down so that we can get a better understanding of what is going on. We use the `REReplaceNoCase()` function to perform the search and replace without regard to case. The first parameter of the function is the string we want to perform the search and replace on. The second parameter is the actual regular expression. The "\b([\w]+)" tells ColdFusion to look for any word. Notice that this part of the regular expression is enclosed in parentheses, making it a subexpression. The next part of the regular expression "[ ]+" tells ColdFusion to look for one or more spaces. The third part of the regular expression, `\1`, is the backreference and tells ColdFusion to refer back to the first subexpression and use it as part of the search criteria. In this case, the regular expression is looking for any word followed by a space followed by the word from the first subexpression. The third parameter is the substring with which to replace the match made by the regular expression. Using `\1` as the substring tells ColdFusion to replace any doubled words with the corresponding subexpression. Using `All` as the fourth parameter tells ColdFusion to apply the search and replace to all repeated words in the string.

Let's take a look at another example of back-referencing:

```
<cfset NewString = REReplaceNoCase("<!-- This is a comment -->",
"<!--([[:print:]]*)-->", "<!--- \1 --->", "All")>
```

In this case, we use the `REReplaceNoCase()` function to search for the opening of an HTML comment tag, followed by any number of printable characters, followed by a closing HTML comment tag. Any matches are replaced by the opening of a ColdFusion comment tag, followed by the text matched by the first parenthesized subexpression (in this case "This is a comment"), followed by a closing ColdFusion comment tag. The `\1` allows us to refer to all the text matched between the `<!--` and `-->` tags.

In the previous examples, we used a single parenthesized subexpression along with a matching backreference to find and refer back to a particular string. If your regular expression contains more than one parenthesized subexpression, you can back-reference the additional subexpressions by referring to them as `\2`, `\3`, etc. To determine the numbering for your parenthesized subexpressions, simply number them from left to right across your regular expression.

It is important to note that backreferences can only refer back to parenthesized subexpressions. Attempting to refer to subexpressions not enclosed by parentheses results in an error.

Replacement String Case Conversion

There may be times when you want to change the case of backreferenced replacement text. ColdFusion lets you do this via a set of special characters that can be used in the replacement string portion of the `REReplace()` and `REReplaceNoCase()` functions:

`\l`
: Converts the subsequent character to lowercase.

`\u`
: Converts the subsequent character to uppercase.

\L
: Converts all subsequent characters to lowercase until `\E` is encountered.

\U
: Converts all subsequent characters to uppercase until `\E` is encountered.

\E
: Terminates case conversion started by `\L` or `\U`.

Let's look at an example that uses case conversion in the replacement string portion of the `REReplaceNoCase()` function. We'll use the regular expression to replace all occurrences of mixed-case HTML comments with lowercase CFML comments:

```
<cfset NewString = REReplaceNoCase("<!-- This is a comment -->",
"<!--([[:print:]]*)-->", "<!--- \L\1\E --->", "All")>
```

The first thing you'll notice is that this example is very similar to the previous one we used to demonstrate backreferences. The difference here is that we use `\L\1\E` to tell ColdFusion to convert the backreferenced part of the replacement string to lower case. The `\L` denotes the start of the text that should be lowercase, and the `\E` marks the end.

Excluding Subexpressions from Backreferences

There may be times where you find that you don't want to include a particular parenthesized subexpression in a backreference. You can instruct ColdFusion not to include a particular subexpression as a numbered backreference by placing `?:` as the first characters following the open parenthesis. Here's an example that illustrates the point:

```
<cfset NewString = REReplaceNoCase("This and that", "(this )(?:and|or)( that)",
"\1 before \2", "All")>
```

This code matches the string "this and that" or "this or that" and replaces it with "this before that". Note that the second parenthesized subexpression is not included in the numbered backreferences.

Useful Regular Expressions

Now that you have a better idea of how regular expressions work, let's take a look at how you can actually use them in your own ColdFusion applications. Here are some regular expressions that perform common search-and-replace tasks:

- Replace all characters in a string that aren't numbers, letters, or underscores with an underscore:

  ```
  <cfset NewString = REReplaceNoCase("This is a test", "\W", "_",
        "All")>
  ```

- Replace all spaces in a filename with the underscore character; this is useful in situations where you allow users to upload files to your ColdFusion server via their web browsers:

```
<cfset NewFilename = REReplace("My File Name.txt", " ", "_", "All")>
```

- Return the full directory path from a string containing a full path including filename:

```
<cfset TheDirectory = REReplaceNoCase(MyPath, "\w+\.\w+", "", "All")>
```

- Return the filename from a string containing a full path including filename:

```
<cfset TheFileName = REReplaceNoCase(MyPath, "([A-Z]:\\)|\w+\\+", "", "All")>
```

- Remove all doubled words in a string:

```
<cfset NoRepeats = REReplaceNoCase("I want to to go to the park.",
  "\b([a-z]+)[ ]+\1","\1","All")>
```

- Strip all HTML tags from a string; this is useful for removing HTML from form-field submissions:

```
<cfset NoHTML = REReplace(MyString, "<[^>]*>", "", "All")>
```

- Remove all HTML anchors in a string, leaving just the text, if any:

```
<cfset NoHTMLLinks =
  REReplaceNoCase(MyString, "<a [^>]*>([[:print:]]*)</a>","\1",'All')>
```

- Format all email addresses in a string as HTML `mailto:` links. Note that this regular expression allows for up to six characters in the domain suffix to allow for the *.museum* top-level domain:

```
<cfset MailtoLinks = REReplaceNoCase(MyString,
  "([\w\.\-]+@([\w\.\-]+\.)+[[:alpha:]]{2,6})",
  "<a href=""mailto:\1"">\1</a>", "All")>
```

- Remove all ASCII character codes, such as `"` and `•`:

```
<cfset NoASCIICodes = REReplaceNoCase(MyString,
  "&(##[0-9]{1,3}|[[:alpha:]]*[[:alnum:]]+);", "", "All")>
```

- Format a 10-digit number as a Social Security number:

```
<cfset FormattedSSN = REReplace("123456789", "([0-9]{3})([0-9]{2})([0-9]{4})",
  "\1-\2-\3")>
```

- Escape all special characters in the Verity search language:

```
<cfset EscapedSearchString =
  REReplace(SearchString, '([ ]<>\\@\`\,\(\)"\{ }\[ ])',"\\1", "All")>
```

Regular Expression Tester

Writing a regular expression is often a trial-and-error process. The process typically goes something like this:

1. Create a ColdFusion template that contains a string and a regular expression to perform the task you want.
2. Save the ColdFusion template.

3. Open your web browser, point it to the ColdFusion template, and see if the regular expression behaves as intended.
4. If the regular expression is successful, great! If not, you then have to modify the regular expression in the template and repeat Steps 2 through 4.

Some regular expressions are simple and can be worked out relatively quickly. Others, however, are more complicated and require you to repeat the trial-and-error process over and over. Constantly having to switch from the browser to the development environment can be a real pain.

With this in mind, let's look at a ColdFusion-based solution for building search-and-replace regular expressions. The template in Example 18-1, called *expressiontester.cfm*, creates a form for collecting information about the regular expression you want to test and uses the information to dynamically generate `REReplace()` or `REReplaceNoCase()` code.

Example 18-1. Regular-expression tester

```
<cfparam name="form.Operation" default="REReplace">
<cfparam name="form.MyString" default="">
<cfparam name="form.MyRegex" default="">
<cfparam name="form.MySubString" default="">
<cfparam name="form.MyScope" default="All">

<cftry>
  <cfif form.Operation is "REReplace">
    <cfset MyOutput=REReplace(form.MyString, form.MyRegex,
           form.MySubString, form.MyScope)>
  <cfelse>
    <cfset MyOutput=REReplaceNoCase(form.MyString, form.MyRegex,
           form.MySubString, form.MyScope)>
  </cfif>

  <cfcatch type="Expression">
    <cfset MyOutput="Invalid Regular Expression!">
  </cfcatch>
</cftry>

<h2>Regular Expression Builder</h2>

<cfoutput>
<form method="Post" action="#CGI.Script_Name#">
<table>
  <cfif IsDefined('form.Submit')>
  <tr>
     <td><b>Original string:</b></td>
     <td>#form.MyString#</td>
  </tr>
  <tr>
     <td colspan="2"> </td>
  </tr>
```

Example 18-1. Regular-expression tester (continued)

```
  <tr>
    <td><b>After Regex:</b></td>
    <td>#MyOutput#</td>
  </tr>
  <tr>
    <td colspan="2"> </td>
  </tr>
  <tr>
    <td><b>Your Regex:</b></td>
    <td><textarea name="Text" cols="75" rows="3"
         wrap="Virtual">#form.Operation#("#form.MyString#", "#form.MyRegex#", "#form.
MySubstring#", "#form.MyScope#")</textarea></td>
  </tr>
  </cfif>

  <tr>
    <td>String</td>
    <td><textarea name="MyString" cols="50"
                 rows="3">#form.MyString#</textarea></td>
  </tr>
  <tr>
    <td>Operation</td>
    <td><select name="Operation">
        <option value="REReplace"<cfif form.Operation is
               "REReplace"> selected</cfif>>REReplace</option>
        <option value="REReplaceNoCase"<cfif form.Operation is
               "REReplaceNoCase"> selected</cfif>>REReplaceNoCase</option>
         </select>
    </td>
  <tr>
    <td>Regex</td>
    <td><input type="text" name="MyRegex" value="#form.MyRegex#" size="52"
               maxlength="255"></td>
  </tr>
  <tr>
    <td>Substring</td>
    <td><input type="text" name="MySubstring"
               value="#form.MySubString#" size="52"
               maxlength="255"></td>
  </tr>
  <tr>
    <td>Scope</td>
    <td><select name="MyScope">
        <option value="One"<cfif form.MyScope is "One"> checked</cfif>>One</option>
        <option value="All"<cfif form.MyScope is "All"> checked</cfif>>All</option>
        </select>
    </td>
  </tr>
  <tr>
    <td colspan="2"><input type="submit" name="Submit" value="Submit"></td>
  </tr>
</table>
```

Example 18-1. Regular-expression tester (continued)

```
</form>
</cfoutput>
```

The template in Example 18-1 creates the user interface for the regular-expression tester and can be seen in Figure 18-4. The program uses an HTML form to allow the user to enter a string to perform the regular expression on. A drop-down box is used to choose whether the operation should use the `REReplace()` or `REReplaceNoCase()` function. The template also contains a text box for entering the regular expression as well as the replacement string to use. Finally, a drop-down box is used to select the `scope` attribute for the regular expression.

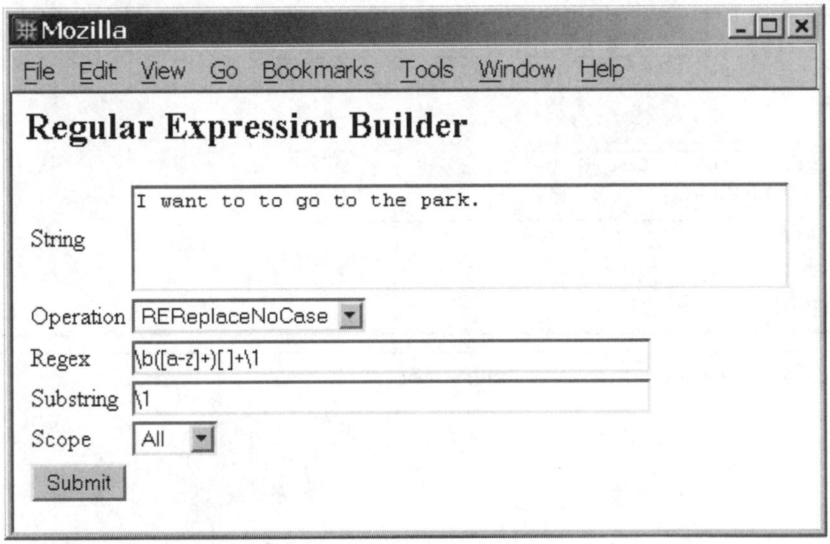

Figure 18-4. Regular-expression tester wizard

Upon submission, the data entered in the form is self-posted. The template takes the parameters from the form submission and uses them to evaluate the regular expression. The resulting output can be seen in Figure 18-5.

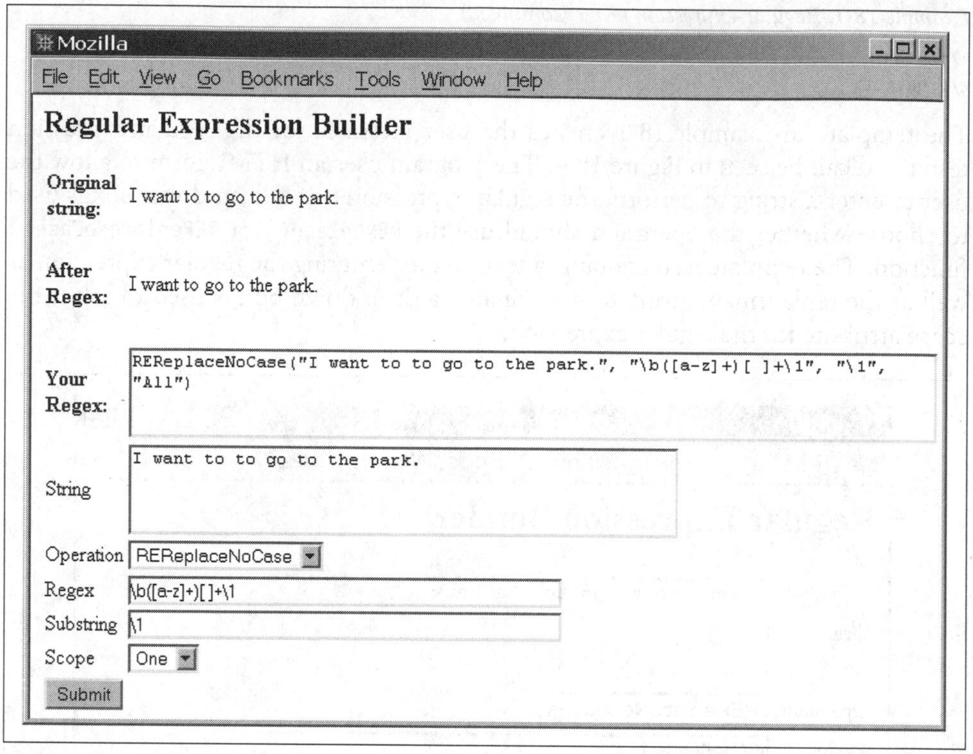

Mozilla

File Edit View Go Bookmarks Tools Window Help

Regular Expression Builder

Original string: I want to to go to the park.

After Regex: I want to go to the park.

Your Regex:

```
REReplaceNoCase("I want to to go to the park.", "\b([a-z]+)[ ]+\1", "\1",
"All")
```

String

```
I want to to go to the park.
```

Operation: REReplaceNoCase

Regex: \b([a-z]+)[ ]+\1

Substring: \1

Scope: One

Submit

Figure 18-5. Regular-expression tester result screen

CHAPTER 19

Scripting

When ColdFusion 4.0 was released, it introduced a new server-side scripting language called CFScript. CFScript is similar in appearance to JavaScript and allows you to write sections of code in your templates using a more concise format than tag-based CFML. CFScript isn't meant to replace the CFML language; it just provides you with a choice of styles for coding your pages. ColdFusion 5.0 introduced developers to user-defined function. Now, in ColdFusion MX, CFScript adds the ability to trap and handle errors with try/catch constructs. Those used to programming in JavaScript will find the CFScript constructs quite familiar. This chapter covers everything you need to know about the CFScript language, along with examples.

CFScript-based user defined functions (UDFs) were added to the ColdFusion language in Version 5. This functionality allows you to use CFScript to write custom functions that can be used just like any of ColdFusion's built-in functions. To facilitate this, three additional CFScript statements, `function`, `var`, and `return`, were added to the language. These statements are covered in detail in Chapter 20. For now, all you need to know is that they are considered reserved words in CFScript.

Scripting Syntax

The `<cfscript>` and `</cfscript>` tags are at the heart of the CFScript language. All CFScripting in a template takes place between these tags. There are a few general guidelines that will help you write your CFScripts:

- `cfscript` tag pairs can be placed anywhere in your template.
- More than one set of `cfscript` tags can be placed in your template.
- `cfscript` tags may not be nested.
- Code (including variable names) placed between `cfscript` tag pairs is case-insensitive.
- CFML tags may not be used within a `cfscript` tag block.

- CFML functions may be used within a `cfscript` block.
- CFML variables created outside a `cfscript` block are automatically available within the block.
- Not all CFML variables created inside the `cfscript` block are automatically available outside of the block.
- CFScript statements end in a semicolon.
- Curly braces ({ }) are used to group related statements.

Working with Variables

Assigning values to variables in CFScript is simple. Assignment statements take the following form:

```
variable = expression;
```

Here, *`variable`* is the name of the variable, and *`expression`* is the value you wish to assign to the variable. The semicolon marks the end of the statement. For comparison sake, consider the following example in which we assign values to a number of variables using the `cfset` tag:

```
<cfset x = 1>
<cfset y = 1+2>
<cfset MyMessage = "Hello World">
<cfset MyStructure = structNew( )>
```

The same functionality can be rewritten using CFScript syntax like so:

```
<cfscript>
 x = 1;
 y = 1+2;
 MyMessage = "Hello World";
 MyStructure = structNew( );
</cfscript>
```

As you can see, setting values within a `cfscript` block takes less code and is generally easier to read than the equivalent code done using `cfset`. Also, notice that you can use any ColdFusion functions (but not tags) that you want within a `cfscript` block.

Commenting Your Code

ColdFusion provides two conventions for commenting code within a `cfscript` block that mimic JavaScript's commenting syntax. Comments can be single-line:

```
// this is a single line comment
x = 1;
x = 1+2; //This is a comment too
```

Comments that need to span multiple lines can be written using the // syntax:

```
// This is the first line of the comment
// This is the second
```

Alternately, multiline comments can be written using paired notation like this:

```
/* This is the first line of the comment
   This is the second line
   This is the third line */
```

To keep things more readable, an asterisk is typically used at the beginning of each line between the open and close comment markers:

```
/* This is the first line of the comment
 * This is the second line
 * This is the third line
 */
```

Writing Output

You can't directly output text or variable values to the browser within a `cfscript` block. There is, however a function called `WriteOutput( )` that you can use to write directly to the page output stream. This technique can output both variable values and plain text from within a `cfscript` block. Example 19-1 demonstrates the `WriteOutput( )` function.

Example 19-1. Using the WriteOutput() function within a cfscript block

```
<h2>Using WriteOutput Within cfscript</h2>

<cfscript>
 x = 1;
 y = 2;
 MyMessage = "Hello World";

 WriteOutput("x = #x# <br>");
 WriteOutput("MyMessage = #MyMessage# <br>");
 WriteOutput(x+y);
</cfscript>
```

In this case, because there is no way to embed HTML directly within the `cfscript` block, all formatting is done by embedding the HTML code within the `WriteOutput( )` function. Executing Example 19-1 results in the output shown in Figure 19-1.

It is also possible to output the value of variables set within a `cfscript` block outside of the `cfscript` tags. This is accomplished by using a `cfoutput` block outside the `cfscript` block to handle the actual output, as shown in Example 19-2.

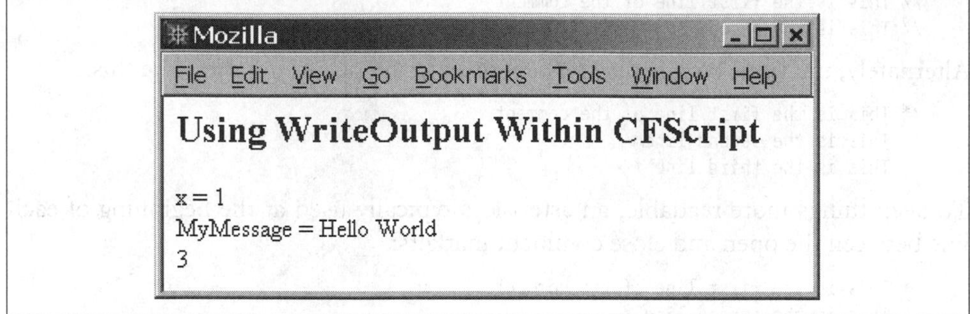

Figure 19-1. Using WriteOutput() within a CFScript block to write to the page output stream

Example 19-2. Outputting CFScript variables outside the cfscript block

```
<h2>Using cfoutput To Output Variables Created Within cfscript</h2>
<cfscript>
 x = 1;
 y = 2;
 MyMessage = "Hello World";
</cfscript>

<cfoutput>
x = #x#<br>
MyMessage = #MyMessage#<br>
#(x+y)#
</cfoutput>
```

The template in Example 19-2 generates the same output shown in Figure 19-1.

Flow Control and Looping

CFScript contains a number of statements to handle flow control and looping, as we'll discuss in this section. Note that you can't use any CFML tags within a `cfscript` block.

if/else

The `if/else` statement has the same functionality as the `cfif` and `cfelse` (and by extension, `cfelseif`) tags in regular CFML. The `if` statement can be used alone, as in:

```
if (expression)
  statement;
```

Or it can be used with the else statement, as in:

```
if(expression)
  statement;
else
  statement;
```

You can also use the else and if statements in combination to achieve the same results as the cfelseif tag:

```
if (expression)
   statement;
else if (expression)
   statement;
else
   statement;
```

To understand the differences between the cfif/cfelse tags and the ifelse statement, let's first consider an example that uses the cfif and cfelse tags. Example 19-3 assigns the current year to a variable called TheYear. The cfif and cfelse tags are then used to determine whether the current year is a leap year. The results are then written to the browser.

Example 19-3. Determining if the current year is a leap year using cfif/cfelse

```
<!--- Set a variable equal to the current year --->
<cfset TheYear=Year(Now( ))>

<!--- Check to see if the current year is a leap year. --->
<cfif IsLeapYear(TheYear)>
    <cfset ReturnOutput="is a leap year.">
<cfelse>
    <cfset ReturnOutput="is not a leap year.">
</cfif>

<cfoutput>
#TheYear# #ReturnOutput#
</cfoutput>
```

The same code can easily be rewritten using CFScript. Example 19-4 shows the ported code.

Example 19-4. Using if/else to determine if the current year is a leap year

```
<cfscript>
// set a variable equal to the current year
TheYear=Year(Now( ));

// Check to see if the current year is a leap year.
if (IsLeapYear(TheYear)){
    ReturnOutput="is a leap year.";
    }
else {
    ReturnOutput="is not a leap year.";
    }
</cfscript>

<cfoutput>
#TheYear# #ReturnOutput#
</cfoutput>
```

As you can see, the code is almost identical. The only noticeable difference is that the CFScript version uses slightly less code and may be a bit easier to read.

Note that in Example 19-4 curly braces surround the code that gets executed in the event the `if` or `else` statement evaluates `true`. Although not necessary in this example (because we are executing only a single statement in our `if` and `else` statements), it is recommended you always use the curly braces as they do become necessary when you wish to execute more than one statement within an `if` or `else` statement.

switch/case

The `switch/case` statement has the same basic functionality as do the `cfswitch`, `cfcase`, and `cfdefaultcase` tags in regular CFML. `switch/case` can simplify the coding process in situations where you would otherwise have to use multiple `ifelse` statements. To get a better idea of how `switch/case` is implemented in CFScript, let's see how it is handled in regular CFML. Example 19-5 shows how the `cfswitch`, `cfcase`, and `cfdefaultcase` tags are used.

Example 19-5. Determining what quarter of the year the current month is in

```
<!--- Assign the quarter associated with the current month to
      TheQuarter --->
<cfset TheQuarter = Quarter(Now( ))>

<!--- Evaluate the current quarter --->
<cfswitch expression="#TheQuarter#">
  <cfcase value="1">
    <cfset q="1st">
  </cfcase>

  <cfcase value="2">
    <cfset q="2nd">
  </cfcase>

  <cfcase value="3">
    <cfset q="3rd">
  </cfcase>

  <cfdefaultcase>
    <cfset q="4th">
  </cfdefaultcase>
</cfswitch>

<cfoutput>
#MonthAsString(Month(Now( )))# is in the #q# quarter of the year.
</cfoutput>
```

Example 19-6 shows the same code written using CFScript syntax.

Example 19-6. Implementing switch/case in CFScript

```
<cfscript>
// Assign the quarter associated with the current month to TheQuarter
TheQuarter = Quarter(Now( ));

// Evaluate the current quarter
switch(TheQuarter) {
  case 1: {
    q='1st';
    break;
  }
  case 2: {
    q='2nd';
    break;
  }
  case 3: {
    q='3rd';
    break;
  }
  default: {
    q='4th';
    break;
  }
}
</cfscript>

<cfoutput>
#MonthAsString(Month(Now( )))# is in the #q# quarter of the year.
</cfoutput>
```

In Example 19-6, the `switch` statement evaluates the value of `TheQuarter`. `TheQuarter` contains the quarter of the year that the current month belongs to (1, 2, 3, or 4). Each `case` statement allows you to specify an individual value that can result from the expression evaluated by the `switch` statement. Case values must be static values and can't be variables or expressions. If the expression contained in the `switch` statement evaluates to a value contained in one of the case statements, the corresponding code is executed. In this case, the text describing the quarter is assigned to the variable `q`, which is later output to the browser.

The `default` statement allows you to specify a default action to take in the event that no case value matches the result of the expression from the `switch` statement. In our example, because we didn't provide a case statement for the number `4`, the `default` statement is invoked only if the current month falls in the fourth quarter of the year.

Note that in Example 19-6, each `case` statement tests for a numeric value. You can also test for a string by enclosing it in quotation marks, such as:

```
case "myval":
```

You can also test for a Boolean value, such as

```
case true:
```

You can't, however, test for both a Boolean and a numeric value in the same `switch` statement.

The `break` statement at the end of each `case` statement is used to exit the `switch/case` statement. If you omit the `break` statements from the code, each `case` statement after the intended one will execute, regardless of whether it evaluates `true` or not. This is known as "falling through", and is generally not a desired result.

Unlike the `cfcase` tag, it isn't possible to specify a delimited list of values for a single `case` statement in CFScript. This was done to keep the behavior and syntax of the `switchcase` statement inline with its JavaScript equivalent.

for Loops

A `for` loop in CFScript is the equivalent of an index loop created by the `cfloop` tag and is used to repeat a block of code a specific number of times. Although `for` loops and index loops function identically, the syntax is a bit different. To understand the difference, look at the following index loop shown in Example 19-7.

Example 19-7. Index loop created with cfloop

```
<h2>Index Loop Using Regular CFML</h2>
<cfloop index="i" from="10" to="100" step="10">
  <cfoutput>
  #i#<br>
  </cfoutput>
</cfloop>
```

This loop loops from 10 to 100 by increments of 10. The results of each iteration are output to the browser.

Example 19-8 shows the same loop written within CFScript as a `for` loop.

Example 19-8. Creating a for loop in CFScript

```
<h2>For (Index) Loop Using cfscript</h2>
<cfscript>
for (i=10; i lte 100; i=i+10) {
    WriteOutput(i & "<br>");
    }
</cfscript>
```

In Example 19-8, the `for` statement takes three arguments, an initial expression that determines the starting value for the loop, a test expression that determines what condition is necessary for the loop to continue iterating, and an increment expression that specifies how the value in the initial expression of the loop should be incremented. In this case, the initial expression within the `for` loop sets `i=10`. The initial expression can be a variable assignment, any valid ColdFusion expression, or blank. The test expression causes the loop to iterate as long as `i` is less than or equal to `100`.

The test expression can be any valid ColdFusion expression or blank. The increment expression sets an increment value of 10 for the loop by setting i=i+10. The increment expression can be any variable assignment, valid ColdFusion expression, or blank. A for loop containing blanks for all three arguments it expects is shown in Example 19-9.

Example 19-9. for loop with blank arguments

```
<cfscript>
i=10;

for( ; ; ){
  WriteOutput(i & "<br>");
  i=i+10;
  if(i gt 100)
    break;
}
</cfscript>
```

In Example 19-9, a break statement is used to exit the loop when the value of i is greater than 100. The break statement is covered later in this chapter.

for/in Loops

for/in loops allow you to loop over ColdFusion structures and offer similar functionality to collection loops in regular CFML. Example 19-10 uses the cfloop tag to loop over the contents of a structure.

Example 19-10. Looping over a structure using cfloop

```
<cfset Stock = StructNew( )>

<cfset Stock.MACR = 30>
<cfset Stock.AMKR = 35>
<cfset Stock.YHOO = 20>

<h2>Collection Loop Using Regular CFML</h2>
<table>
<tr>
  <th>Ticker</th>
  <th>Price</th>
</tr>

<cfloop collection="#Stock#" item="Ticker">
<cfoutput>
<tr>
  <td>#Ticker#</td>
  <td>#StructFind(Stock,Ticker)#</td>
</tr>
</cfoutput>
</cfloop>
</table>
```

Example 19-11 shows the same functionality rewritten using a `for/in` loop in CFScript.

Example 19-11. Looping over a structure using a for/in loop in CFScript

```
<h2>For-In (Collection) Loop Using cfscript</h2>
<cfscript>
Stock = StructNew( );
Stock.MACR = 30;
Stock.AMKR = 35;
Stock.YHOO = 20;

WriteOutput("<table><tr><th>Ticker</th><th>Price</th></tr>");

for (Ticker in Stock) {
    WriteOutput("<tr><td>#Ticker#</td>
                     <td>#StructFind(Stock,Ticker)#</td></tr>");
    }
WriteOutput('</table>');
</cfscript>
```

Notice that in Example 19-11, the HTML table is created within the `cfscript` block by including the HTML code inside `WriteOutput( )` statements.

`for/in` loops can also be used to loop over COM collections, giving CFScript the same looping capabilities as the tag-based collection loop (`cfloop collection="`*`CollectionName`*`"`). This behavior is new in ColdFusion MX. In previous versions, for-in loops were only capable of looping over structures. To get a better understanding of what I'm talking about, consider Example 19-12, which uses the tag based `cfloop` to iterate over a COM collection, outputting a list of disk drives available to the server.

Example 19-12. Looping over a COM collection using cfloop

```
<cfobject type="COM" name="FSO" class="Scripting.FileSystemObject"
          action="Create">

<cfloop collection="#FSO.Drives#" item="i">
 <cfoutput>#i.DriveLetter#<br></cfoutput>
</cfloop>
```

Now, consider the same functionality written using CFScript. Example 19-13 shows you how it's done using a `for/in` loop.

Example 19-13. Looping over a COM collection using a for/in loop in CFScript

```
<cfscript>
  fso  = CreateObject("COM", "Scripting.FileSystemObject");

  for (i in fso.drives) {
    WriteOutput(i.DriveLetter &"<br>");
  }
</cfscript>
```

Executing either of these examples should output a list of drives on your ColdFusion server. For more information on working with COM, see Chapter 27.

while Loops

A `while` loop offers the same functionality as a conditional `cfloop`. In a `while` loop, the loop repeats while a specified condition is `true`. In order to work, the condition being tested must change with each iteration of the loop until the condition evaluates to `false`. Example 19-14 demonstrates a conditional loop written using the `cfloop` tag.

Example 19-14. Conditional loop using cfloop

```
<cfset x = 1>

<h2>Conditional (While) Loop Using Regular CFML</h2>
<cfloop condition="x lte 10">
  <cfoutput>
  #x#<br>
  </cfoutput>
  <cfset x = x+1>
</cfloop>
```

Example 19-15 shows the same code rewritten using a `while` loop in CFScript.

Example 19-15. Creating a while loop using CFScript

```
<h2>While Loop Using cfscript</h2>
<cfscript>
  x = 1;
  while (x lte 10) {
    writeoutput(x & "<br>");
    x = x+1;
  }
</cfscript>
```

In Example 19-15, while `x` is less than or equal to `10`, the loop continues to iterate. With each iteration, the value of `x` is output to the browser. Once `x` is equal to `11`, the loop stops iterating.

do/while Loops

`do/while` loops are similar in appearance to `while` loops, but the conditional statement appears at the end of the loop as opposed to the beginning. While at first glance, there appears to be no functional difference between a `do/while` loop and a plain `while` loop, a subtle difference does exist. In the case of a `while` loop, that loop may never iterate if the expression being tested evaluates `false` before the first iteration occurs. A `do/while` loop, on the other hand, is guaranteed to iterate at least once because the condition being tested appears at the end of the loop. Example 19-16 demonstrates how a do/while loop is guaranteed to iterate at least once even when the condition being tested for is false before the loop begins iterating.

Example 19-16. A do/while loop in CFScript

```
<h2>Do-While Loop Using cfscript</h2>

<cfscript>
x = 11;
do {
  WriteOutput(x & "<br>");
  x = x+1;
} while (x lte 10);
</cfscript>
```

In this case, the loop iterates once because the condition that checks to see if x is less than or equal to 10 appears at the end of the loop.

Using break Within a Loop

The break statement is used within a loop to exit the loop if a certain condition is met. It has the same functionality as the cfbreak tag.

Example 19-17 uses an index (for) loop to output the numbers between 10 and 100 in increments of 10. As soon as the loop gets to 50, the cfbreak tag causes the program to exit the loop before the number 50 can be output.

Example 19-17. Breaking out of a loop using the cfbreak tag

```
<h2>Using cfbreak Within Regular CFML</h2>
<cfloop index="i" from="10" to="100" step="10">
  <cfif i eq 50>
    <cfbreak>
  </cfif>

  <cfoutput>
  #i#<br>
  </cfoutput>
</cfloop>
```

The equivalent code written in CFScript is shown in Example 19-18.

Example 19-18. Using the break statement within a for loop in CFScript

```
<h2>Using Break Within cfscript</h2>
<cfscript>
for (i=10; i lte 100; i=i+10) {
  // this line breaks out of the loop before "50" can be output to the
  // browser
  if (i eq 50) {
     break;
  }
```

Example 19-18. Using the break statement within a for loop in CFScript (continued)

```
  WriteOutput(i & "<br>");
}
</cfscript>
```

Using continue

The `continue` statement resembles the `break` statement, but instead of breaking out of the loop altogether, `continue` allows the loop to skip over the code associated with the current iteration of the loop and pick back up with the next iteration. There is no CFML tag with equivalent functionality to the `continue` statement. Example 19-19 shows how the `continue` statement is used.

Example 19-19. Using continue within a loop to skip an iteration

```
<h2>Using Continue Within cfscript</h2>
<cfscript>
for (i=10; i lte 100; i=i+10) {
  /* This line skips the iteration of the loop that would produce "50",
   * then continues iterating.  Notice the output contains 10,20,30,40,
   * 60,70,80,90,100.
   */
  if (i eq 50) {
      continue;
  }
  WriteOutput(i & "<br>");
}
</cfscript>
```

In Example 19-19, a `for` loop outputs the number from `10` to `100` in increments of `10`. An `if` statement is used within the loop to test if the number produced by the current iteration of the loop is `50`. If `50` is encountered, the `continue` statement is executed, and that iteration of the loop is skipped.

Error and Exception Handling

New in ColdFusion MX is the ability to trap errors and exceptions within CFScript code using `try`/`catch` statements similar to the `cftry` and `cfcatch` tags described in Chapter 9. If you were writing exception-handling code using the `cftry` and `cfcatch` tags, it might look something like the code in Example 19-20.

Example 19-20. Exception handling with cftry and cfcatch

```
<cftry>
  <cfset x=y+1>

  <cfcatch type="Expression">
    <cfoutput>
    Expression Error: #cfcatch.Message#
```

Example 19-20. Exception handling with cftry and cfcatch (continued)

```
    </cfoutput>
  </cfcatch>

  <cfcatch type="Any">
    <cfoutput>
    General Error: #cfcatch.Message#
    </cfoutput>
  </cfcatch>
</cftry>
```

This code attempts to set the variable `x` equal to `y+1`. It then includes `cfcatch` code for handling `Expression` type errors, and another `cfcatch` block for catching `Any` exception that is not caught by the `Expression` type. In this case, the exception handling comes in the form of a semi-custom error message written to the browser.

The same code rewritten in CFScript is shown in Example 19-21.

Example 19-21. Exception handling with try and catch in CFScript

```
<cfscript>
try {
  x=y+1;
}

  catch("Expression" exception) {
    writeOutput("Expression Error: " & exception.Message);
  }

  catch("Any" exception) {
    writeOutput("General Error: " & exception.Message);
  }
</cfscript>
```

The CFScript equivalent `try/catch` code is slightly different than the tag-based version. In CFScript, `catch` statements do not need to be nested in the `try` code as `cfcatch` statements do in an equivalent `cftry` tag. The syntax for the `catch` code is:

```
cfcatch("ExceptionType", ErrorVar)
```

`ExceptionType` names the type of exception the `catch` block is designed to trap. The list is the same as that for the `cfcatch` tag and can be found in Chapter 9 or Appendix A. `ErrorVar` lets you specify a variable name to hold the exception structure returned should the `catch` code execute. The exception structure is identical to the `cfcatch` structure returned by the `cfcatch` tag.

Although CFScript contains equivalents for the `cftry` and `cfcatch` tags, there is no equivalent for the `cfthrow` or `cfrethrow` tags.

CHAPTER 20
User-Defined Functions

Since their introduction in ColdFusion 5.0, user-defined functions (UDFs) have become a cornerstone of the CFML language. UDFs give you the ability to create custom that can be called inline, just like other ColdFusion functions. UDFs allow you to extend ColdFusion's core set of functions with custom functions that encapsulate programming tasks not currently addressed by CFML. For example, there is no CFML function for calculating the mean (average value) of a delimited list of numeric values. Rather than writing code that uses multiple functions each time you want to calculate the mean for a given list of numbers, you can create a UDF that can be called inline in your template as often as you want.

This chapter covers everything you need to know to create your own UDFs. Included in the discussion are good practices for developing, organizing, and deploying user-defined functions. We'll also talk about advanced topics such as error- and exception-handling strategies.

In ColdFusion MX, you have two options for creating user-defined functions. You can write UDFs using the new `cffunction`, `cfargument`, and `cfreturn` tags, or you can use the older and less feature-rich CFScript-based syntax.* There are pros and cons to both options, which you should carefully consider when deciding which method to use. The major differences are shown in Table 20-1.

Table 20-1. Differences between tag- and script-based UDFs

Tag-based UDFs	Script-based UDFs
Tag syntax may be more comfortable for a broader range of developers.	Scripting syntax is more concise.
Compatible with ColdFusion MX only.	Compatible with ColdFusion 5.
Built-in argument validation.	Argument datatypes must be manually validated.

* As of ColdFusion MX, you can create UDFs using CFML tags or CFScript. In ColdFusion 5, you were limited to defining your tags using CFScript only.

Table 20-1. Differences between tag- and script-based UDFs (continued)

Tag-based UDFs	Script-based UDFs
Optional arguments may be declared.	No declaration of optional arguments; additional code is required to work around this.
Full range of CFML tags and functions can be used inside function.	No CFML tags allowed within CFScript.
Try/catch/throw exception handling.	Try/catch error handling only;[a] no throw statement in CFScript.
Access to UDF can be controlled via `roles` attribute.	No built-in security mechanism; access control has to be manually coded using `IsUserInRole( )` (see Chapter 8).

[a] This is valid only for ColdFusion MX. ColdFusion 5 does not contain try/catch functionality in CFScript.

This chapter focuses on writing user-defined functions using the tag-based syntax introduced in ColdFusion MX. Don't worry, though: we'll still cover script-based UDFs, albeit to a lesser degree.

Before we get things moving, I want to point out a few general rules related to the use of UDFs, regardless of the method you use to create them:

- UDFs can be used anywhere you use a normal CFML function: within a `cfoutput` block, within `cfset` tags, in any tag attributes, and within CFScript code.
- UDFs can be called recursively, which means that a UDF can call itself.
- UDFs can call other UDFs.
- Although it's possible to assign a UDF to a variable, it's generally not advisable to do so in the case of persistent variables (session, application, server) due to the locking issues this may present.
- UDFs referenced within custom tags must be coded inside the custom tag or assigned to a scope such as the request scope before being called by the custom tag.
- It is not necessary for a UDF to return a value.

With this in mind, let's turn our attention to what's needed to create a user-defined function.

UDF Basics

To create a tag-based UDF, you use the `cffunction` tag. Optionally, one or more `cfargument` tags can be used to define both required and optional arguments the function should expect as input. Data can be returned from the UDF using the `cfreturn` tag. Here's some code that shows the basic syntax for a tag-based UDF:

```
<cffunction name="function_name"
            output="Yes|No"
```

```
            returntype="return_type"
            roles="authorized_roles">
    <cfargument name="arg1" type="arg_type" required="Yes|No"
              default="default_val">
    <cfargument name="arg2" type="arg_type" required="Yes|No"
              default="default_val">
    ...
    additional CFML
    <cfreturn expression>
</cffunction>
```

The `cffunction` tag pair acts as a container for the UDF. The `name` attribute is required; it specifies the name for the function. There are several guidelines you should think about when deciding what to name your function, to avoid both errors and organizational problems:

1. Function names must begin with a letter, underscore, or Unicode currency symbol ($) and can contain only letters, numbers, underscores, and Unicode currency symbols.
2. UDF names cannot contain periods.
3. UDFs can't have the same name as existing CFML functions.
4. You can't have more than one UDF with a given name available on the same template.
5. When deciding on a name for your UDF, consider the naming conventions used by ColdFusion's built-in functions. For example, list functions all begin with the word "list": `ListLen( )`, `ListLast( )`, etc.

The next attribute in the `cffunction` tag is an optional Boolean attribute called `output`. If `output` is set to `Yes`, contents of the function body are processed as if surrounded by `cfoutput` tags. If the attribute is set to `No`, the function body is processed as if surrounded by `cfsilent` tags. If `output` is omitted, contents of the function body are processed as regular CFML. `returntype` is also an optional attribute. It specifies the datatype for the data returned by the function. Options for functions are `Any`, `Array`, `Binary`, `Boolean`, `Date`, `GUID`, `Numeric`, `Query`, `String`, `Struct`, `UUID`, `VariableName`, and `Void` (doesn't return a value). Although this attribute isn't required, it's a good practice to include it. If you pass a value for `returntype` that isn't in the aforementioned list of values, ColdFusion treats it as a component (CFC) name. For more information on CFCs, see Chapter 22. The final attribute, `roles`, is also optional. It specifies a comma-delimited list of roles that are allowed to access the UDF within the context of ColdFusion MX's security framework (covered in Chapter 8). This security feature is usually used when the `cffunction` tag is used to define a component method within a ColdFusion Component (CFC), but it can also be used to secure a tag-based UDF, if desired. Note that there is no built-in equivalent functionality in script based UDFs. You can approximate the same functionality, but you'll need to code it yourself using the `IsUserInRole( )` function.

Function Arguments in Tag-Based UDFs

Tag-based functions can be written to accept zero or more required arguments and any number of optional arguments. Each argument should be given a name and should be explicitly declared in the function body using a `cfargument` tag. `cfargument` has several attributes. `name` is the only required attribute. It's used to specify the name for the argument. `type` is an optional attribute for specifying the argument's type. Valid options are `Any`, `Array`, `Binary`, `Boolean`, `Date`, `GUID`, `Numeric`, `Query`, `String`, `Struct`, `UUID`, `VariableName`, and *`ComponentName`* (a valid CFC name). The default is `Any`. For information on how `GUID` differs from `UUID`, see the `CreateUUID( )` function in Appendix B. You can indicate whether the argument should be required or optional using the `required` attribute. The default is `No`. If you do decide to make an argument optional, you can supply a default value to assign to the argument in the event no argument is passed to the function when it is called. There are several other attributes for the `cfargument` tag that are specific to using the tag with CFCs. For more information on these attributes, see Appendix A.

Although it's good practice, you are not required to declare your function arguments explicitly with the `cfargument` tag. The `cfargument` tag, if used, must be the first tag to appear after the `cffunction` tag. Argument names follow the same naming conventions as the function name.

For example, to declare a function called `Mean` that accepts a single required argument called `Values`, you would code it like this:

```
<cffunction name="Mean" output="No" returntype="Numeric">
  <cfargument name="Values" type="String" required="Yes">
  ...
</cffunction>
```

Within the function body of a UDF, all arguments, both optional and required, are available via a special variable called `Arguments`. `Arguments` is special in that it exists as both a one-dimensional array and as a structure. This means that you can refer to the arguments passed into a UDF in multiple ways. Take the argument `Arg1`, for example. Within the function body, you can refer to `Arg1` several ways:

```
Arg1
Arguments.Arg1
Arguments["Arg1"]
Arguments[1]
```

The first method refers to the argument by name alone. Because arguments are automatically placed in the local function scope, it isn't necessary to prefix them unless you want to. Let's look at a full version of our `Mean( )` UDF. This UDF takes two arguments. The first is either a delimited list of numeric values or a one-dimensional array of numeric values. The second argument allows the UDF to accept an optional delimiter if the values passed in were a delimited list of values:

```
<!---
  // Mean(values [, delimiter])
  // Returns the mean (average) for an array or list of delimited values
 --->
<cffunction name="Mean" returntype="Numeric" output="No">
  <cfargument name="Values" type="Any" required="Yes">
  <cfargument name="Delimiter" type="String" required="No" default=",">

  <cfif IsArray(Values)>
    <cfreturn ArrayAvg(Values)>
  <cfelse>
    <cfreturn ArrayAvg(ListToArray(Values, Delimiter))>
  </cfif>
</cffunction>
```

Notice that the code refers to `Value` and `Delimiter` as if they were local variables.

The second and third methods refer to the arguments using structure notation. In this case, the argument name corresponds to a structure key of the same name. `Arguments` should be referred to using structure notation only when all required and optional arguments are declared using `cfargument` tags. We can easily modify our previous `Mean()` example to use structure notation to refer to the named arguments:

```
<!---
  // Mean(values [, delimiter])
  // Returns the mean (average) for an array or list of delimited values
 --->
<cffunction name="Mean" returntype="Numeric" output="No">
  <cfargument name="Values" type="Any" required="Yes">
  <cfargument name="Delimiter" type="String" default=",">

  <cfif IsArray(Arguments.Values)>
    <cfreturn ArrayAvg(Arguments.Values)>
  <cfelse>
    <cfreturn ArrayAvg(ListToArray(Arguments.Values,
              Arguments.Delimiter))>
  </cfif>
</cffunction>
```

In this case, we refer to the arguments as `Arguments.Values` and `Arguments.Delimiter`. This is the easiest syntax to use when you declare all the arguments expected by the UDF, both required and optional.

The fourth method uses array notation to refer to the argument by its index position within the array. Array notation can be used with both declared and undeclared arguments. The minimum number of elements in the `Arguments` array is always equal to the number of required arguments for a given function. For example, if a UDF takes three required arguments, the `Arguments` array contains three elements. In the event of unnamed optional arguments, each optional argument's value is added to the `Arguments` array in the order in which it is passed. In the case of named optional arguments, the array index corresponds to the order in which the arguments are declared in the function body. The following example uses a combination of structure notation (for the required argument) and array notation for an optional second argument:

```
<!---
  // Mean(values [, delimiter])
  // Returns the mean (average) for an array or list of delimited values
 --->
<cffunction name="Mean" returntype="Numeric" output="No">
  <cfargument name="Values" type="Any" required="Yes">

  <cfset Var Delimiter = ",">

  <cfif ArrayLen(Arguments) gt 1>
    <cfset Delimiter = Arguments[2]>
  </cfif>

  <cfif IsArray(Arguments.Values)>
    <cfreturn ArrayAvg(Arguments.Values)>
  <cfelse>
    <cfreturn ArrayAvg(ListToArray(Arguments.Values, Delimiter))>
  </cfif>
</cffunction>
```

Note the line of code in this example that uses `<cfset Var TheDelimiter = ",">`. Don't worry about this yet; we'll cover it in the next section.

Local Function Variables (The Function Scope)

A special variable scope called the function scope exists for variables that are local to UDFs. This scope differs slightly from the other variable scopes in ColdFusion in that there is no special prefix such as `variables` or `client` to identify the function scope. Variables within the function scope are accessible only within the UDF and can't be referenced by the template in which the UDF is called. The function scope consists of arguments passed to the function, variables created with the `Var` statement, and the `Arguments` array/structure.

Any variables available in the template calling the UDF are automatically available (and can be modified) inside the UDF. Likewise, variables created or modified within the UDF (except for those in the function scope) are available to the calling template after the function has been called. If a particular variable name exists in both the function scope and in another scope within the calling template, the function scope takes precedence within a UDF. Because of this, it's important always to scope variables outside the function scope when referencing them within a UDF.

To create a local variable within a function, you use the `Var` attribute of the `cfset` tag like this:

```
<cfset Var State = "Delaware">
<cfset Var Person = StructNew( )>
```

Var is a new attribute in ColdFusion MX and is only used when creating UDFs. There are several rules to keep in mind regarding the setting of local variables:

1. Always Var your variables. By this, I mean that you should always Var any variables that are local to a function. Failure to Var your variables will cause you untold frustration when it comes time to debug a UDF related problem.
2. All variables declared in the local function scope must be initialized with a value. You may assign an empty string ("") to the variable if you desire. Don't forget that variables created as the result of a tag operation such as cffile, cfdirectory, cfquery, etc. must also be initialized with Var.
3. Any valid expression can be assigned to the variable being declared in the local function scope.
4. There is no limit to the number of variables that can be declared in the local function scope.
5. All local functions must be declared at the beginning of the UDF, directly after any cfargument tags. Attempting to declare local function variables anywhere else within the cffunction container causes ColdFusion to throw an error.

Returning Data from a Function

As I mentioned earlier, and, you have probably figured out by now, the cfreturn tag is used to return data from a function. The cfreturn tag is optional and determines what value(s) to return when the function has finished executing.* You may specify any valid expression in the cfreturn tag. If no cfreturn tag is present, ColdFusion returns the last value encountered before the Return statement (assuming there is one):

```
<cfreturn>
<cfreturn x>
<cfreturn x-y>
<cfreturn DateFormat(MyVar, 'mm/dd/yyyy')>
```

UDFs can return any ColdFusion datatype, including complex types such as arrays, structures, and queries. The simplest form of UDF is one in which all the functionality is contained in a single cfreturn tag. To demonstrate this, consider yet another version of our UDF for calculating the mean (average) of a comma-delimited list of numeric values:

```
<!--- // Mean(values)
      // Returns the mean (average) value of a list of comma delimited
         values.
--->
<cffunction name="Mean" returntype="Numeric" output="No">
  <cfargument name="Values" type="String" required="Yes">
```

* In ColdFusion 5, the Return statement was required. This behavior is new in ColdFusion MX.

```
  <cfreturn ArrayAvg(ListToArray(Arguments.Values))>
</cffunction>
```

In this example, the first line uses the `cffunction` tag to declare a function named `Mean`. The `cfargument` tag declares a single argument called `Values`. A single `cfreturn` tag is all that's required to convert the list of values to an array using the `ListToArray( )` function and subsequently obtain the average value using the `ArrayAvg( )` function.

Calling User-Defined Functions

Regardless of whether you are dealing with a tag- or script-based UDF, you call it the same way you do any other CFML function—within a `cfoutput` block, within a `cfset` tag, in any tag attribute, and within CFScript code:

```
<cfoutput>
  #MyFunction("test", 12)#
</cfoutput>

<cfset x = MyFunction( )>

<cfmytag value="#MyFunction('test')#">

<cfscript>
  x = MyFunction(MyOtherFunction( ));
</cfscript>
```

The simplest way to call a UDF is to define it, then call it in the same template. A function defined in the template in which it is called may be defined anywhere on the page, including after it has already been referenced (ColdFusion parses the entire page before processing the instructions). If you use this method, you should define all functions at the top of the page for readability and consistency. Using one of the `Mean( )` functions we created, you can define it inline and call it like this:

```
<!--- // Mean(values [, delimiter])
      // Returns the mean (average) value of a list of delimited values.
--->
<cffunction name="Mean" returntype="Numeric" output="No">
  <cfargument name="Values" type="String" required="Yes">
  <cfargument name="Delimiter" type="String" required="No" default=",">

  <cfreturn ArrayAvg(ListToArray(Arguments.Values, Arguments.Delimiter))>
</cffunction>

<cfset MyValues="1|2|3|4|5|6|7|8|9|10">

<cfoutput>
The mean is: #Mean(MyValues, "|")#
</cfoutput>
```

Notice that when we call the `Mean()` function, we call it with two arguments. This is known as positional notation. ColdFusion expects that the arguments passed to the function be passed in the same order in which they are declared within the function body using `cfargument` tags. This is the same way that all of ColdFusion's built-in functions work.

In addition to calling a function and passing arguments via the standard positional syntax, you can also pass named arguments as key/value pairs. This means that you can call functions with syntax that looks like this:

```
<cfset MyValues="1|2|3|4|5|6|7|8|9|10">

<cfoutput>
The mean is: #Mean(values=MyValues, delimiter='|')#
</cfoutput>
```

Or like this:

```
<cfset MyValues="1|2|3|4|5|6|7|8|9|10">

<cfoutput>
The mean is: #Mean(delimiter='|', values=MyValues)#
</cfoutput>
```

Both are valid. The named argument syntax can be useful in situations where you want to vary the order in which the parameters are passed into the function (such as when you can remember the arguments a function takes, but you can't remember their order and are too lazy to look them up!). Here's a more useful example. Consider what's necessary to create a structure in ColdFusion and populate it with key/value pairs. The code typically looks something like this:

```
<cfset Person = StructNew( )>
<cfset Person.Name = "Pere Money">
<cfset Person.Title = "President">
<cfset Person.Email = "pmoney@example.com">
```

Not a huge amount of code, but imagine you needed to create a dozen or even a hundred structures like this. You can see that the amount of code you would need to write would be a real pain. This can easily be simplified with a `CreateStruct()` UDF that accepts named arguments:

```
<cffunction name="CreateStruct" returntype="Struct" output="No">
  <cfset Var MyStruct = Arguments>
  <cfreturn MyStruct>
</cffunction>
```

This UDF does nothing more than return as a structure any arguments passed to it. This allows you to both initialize and populate a structure in a single step when you call the UDF using named arguments:

```
<cfset Person = CreateStruct(Name='Pere Money', Title='President',
Email='pmoney@example.com')>

<cfdump var="#Person#">
```

This code calls the `CreateStruct()` UDF, passing it the key/value pairs for `Name`, `Title`, and `Email`. The resulting structure is assigned to a variable named `Person`. Using this technique, you can create a structure containing an arbitrary number of keys, all in a single line of code.

A Note About Datatypes

Different datatypes are passed to UDFs in different ways. Strings, numbers, date/time values, and arrays are passed by value. This means that any values passed to the UDF are actually copies of the original value. Any changes made to the value inside the UDF do not result in changes to the original value in the calling template.

Queries, structures, CFCs, and objects (e.g., COM, CORBA, and Java), on the other hand, are passed to UDFs by reference. In this case, the value passed to the UDF isn't actually the value, but rather a reference to the original value outside of the function. Because of this, any change made to a value passed by reference results in a change to the original value back in the calling template. You can avoid having the original value changed by making a copy of the variable using the `Duplicate()` function and passing the copy to the UDF. This is because the `Duplicate()` function creates an exact copy of the original variable, as opposed to a pointer back to the original.

There are certain instances where you can actually pass a variable partially by value and partially by reference. For example, in cases where you pass an array of structures to a UDF, the array is passed by value while each structure in the array is actually a reference to the original structure.

Advanced Topics

There are several advanced UDF topics worth covering here, including recursion, error and exception handling, and assigning UDFs to other variable scopes. Each of these topics covers techniques that you can use to maximize the benefit of using UDFs in your applications.

Recursion

As I mentioned in the beginning of the chapter, UDFs can be called recursively. This means that a UDF can call itself until a specific condition is met. Before you start creating recursive UDFs, there are a few things you should be aware of. First, too much recursion can be a bad thing. Recursion is both processor- and memory-intensive so recursively calling a UDF too many times has the potential to drain your server's system resources to the point where it crashes the server. The ColdFusion engineering team recommends limiting recursive calls to fewer than 800 levels. If you have a situation where you know your recursive function call has the potential to exceed 800 levels, consider using a loop instead.

Here's a classic example that uses recursion to calculate the factorial for a given number. The factorial for a positive integer is defined as the product of all of the positive integers between 1 and n. So, 5! equals 1*2*3*4*5. Written as a tag-based UDF, it looks something like this:

```
<cffunction name="Factorial">
  <cfargument name="Integer" type="Numeric" required="Yes">
  <cfif Arguments.Integer le 1>
    <cfreturn 1>
  <cfelse>
    <cfreturn Integer * Factorial(Arguments.Integer-1)>
  </cfif>
</cffunction>

<cfset n=5>

<cfoutput>
Given n=5<br>
n! is #Factorial(n)#
</cfoutput>
```

Because we have no idea what value someone may enter for n (possibly causing a stack overflow because of too many levels of recursion), we can easily rewrite the Factorial( ) UDF using a loop instead of recursion:

```
<cffunction name="Factorial">
  <cfargument name="Integer" type="Numeric" required="Yes">

  <cfset Var myFactorial = 1>

  <cfloop condition="Arguments.Integer gt 0">
    <cfset myFactorial = myFactorial*Arguments.Integer>
    <cfset Arguments.Integer = Arguments.Integer-1>
  </cfloop>

  <cfreturn myFactorial>
</cffunction>

<cfset n=5>

<cfoutput>
Given n=5<br>
n! is #Factorial(n)#
</cfoutput>
```

Error and Exception Handling

A custom function framework wouldn't be complete without a means to handle errors and exceptions that may occur both when calling and within the functions. There are several techniques you can use to deal with issues that may arise with custom functions.

First, you can use a function called IsCustomFunction( ) to determine whether a particular name is that of a UDF. IsCustomFunction( ) takes a single argument, the name you want to check. Note that the name isn't surrounded by quotes.

```
<cfif IsDefined('Mean') and IsCustomFunction(Mean)>
  Mean is a custom function!
<cfelse>
  Mean is not a custom function!
</cfif>
```

The IsDefined( ) function makes sure the name exists before testing it with IsCustomFunction( ). If you attempt to evaluate a name that doesn't exist with IsCustomFunction( ), ColdFusion throws an error.

Second, you can use cfif statements within your custom functions to deal with errors inside the function and return an error code, error message, or both in the event an error occurs. For example, if your UDF takes a single argument and expects it to be an array, you can return an error message if the value of the argument is anything other than an array:

```
<cffunction name="MyFunction" returntype="String" output="No">
  <cfset Var ErrMsg = "Error!  You must supply an array.">

  <cfif IsArray(Arguments[1])>
    <cfreturn True>
  <cfelse>
    <cfreturn ErrMsg>
  </cfif>
</cffunction>

<cfoutput>
#MyFunction("test")#
</cfoutput>
```

Of course, you could just as easily perform the same basic validation using a named argument with the type attribute set to Array:

```
<cffunction name="MyFunction" returntype="String" output="No">
  <cfargument name="Value" type="Array" required="Yes">

  <cfreturn Value>
</cffunction>

<cfoutput>
#MyFunction("test")#
</cfoutput>
```

In this case, failure to pass an array to the function causes ColdFusion to throw an error.

A third method is to use cftry/cfcatch tags within your UDF to handle errors. This functionality is new in ColdFusion MX. Using cftry/cfcatch within the UDF body allows for granular control over both expected and unexpected errors and exceptions. The following code uses cftry/cfcatch code to handle an exception (in this case, a database exception) within the UDF itself:

```
<cffunction name="getPerson">
  <cfargument name="PersonID" type="Numeric" required="Yes">

  <cftry>
    <cfquery name="Test" datasource="Bogus">
      SELECT *
      FROM MyTable
      WHERE PersonID = #Arguments.PersonID#
    </cfquery>

    <cfcatch type="Any">
      <cfreturn "Error!">
    </cfcatch>
  </cftry>
  <cfreturn Test.RecordCount>
</cffunction>

<cfoutput>
There are #GetPerson(12)# people in the database.
</cfoutput>
```

The fourth and final method is to use the cftry/cfcatch tags outside of the UDF to handle potential exceptions. A good way to do this is to use one cfcatch tag to handle Expression exceptions and a second cfcatch tag as a backup (type="Any") to catch any exceptions not caught by the first cfcatch tag:

```
<cftry>
  <cfoutput>
  #Mean( )#
  </cfoutput>

  <cfcatch type="Expression">
    Caught an exception using type="Expression"
    <cfabort>
  </cfcatch>

  <cfcatch type="Any">
    Caught an exception using type="Any"
    <cfabort>
  </cfcatch>
</cftry>
```

This is the method I prefer when working with regular CFML as it gives you more control over how you deal with an exception. This method tends to require less code than inline error handling and therefore generally offers better performance. It is also similar to the way errors and exceptions are handled within native CFML functions.

If you combine techniques three and four, you can throw a custom exception from within the UDF using the cfthrow tag, and the exception can be handled outside the UDF using the method I just described.

Assigning UDFs to Other Variable Scopes

UDFs can be assigned to other variable scopes besides the local scope they are created in. This means you can do things such as assigning a UDF to the application scope so it can be stored in the server's RAM for as long as the application scope exists. In general, I don't recommend assigning UDFs to scopes other than the request scope (I'll explain why in the next section). This especially applies to the shared scopes (application, session, and server). It doesn't really buy you a performance gain, and you may have to deal with the locking issues surrounding the use of shared scope variables if the potential for a race condition exists (see Chapter 7 for a detailed discussion on locking in ColdFusion MX). If you decide for whatever reason that you still want to do this, here's an example that assigns a UDF to the application scope:

```
<cffunction name="UpdateCount" returntype="Numeric" output="No">
  <cfargument name="CurrentCount" type="Numeric" required="Yes">
  <cfreturn Arguments.CurrentCount + 1>
</cffunction>

<!--- Copy the UDF to the Application scope --->
<cflock name="appLock" type="Exclusive" timeout="5">
  <cfset Application.UpdateCount = UpdateCount>
</cflock>

<cflock name="appLock" type="Readonly" timeout="5">
  <cfoutput>
  The updated count is is #Application.UpdateCount(3)#
  </cfoutput>
</cflock>
```

Note the use of `cflock` tags both when the UDF is assigned (written) to the application scope and later when it is output (read). The additional code required to accomplish this should be enough to dissuade you from doing so without a good reason. The one exception to assigning a UDF to another variable scope has to do with calling a UDF within a custom tag and; it is discussed in the next section.

UDFs and Custom Tags

Because UDFs exist in the local variable's scope, they are not automatically available within your custom tags. Thus, if you define or include a UDF in a template that calls a custom tag, and the custom tag tries to reference the UDF, ColdFusion will throw an error.

There are two ways around this. The first is to code the UDF within the custom tag template itself. This makes the UDF available only to the custom tag and not to the template calling it. The second option is to copy the UDF to the request scope, thereby making it available to the custom tag and any other templates that are part of the original page request. To copy a UDF to the request scope, the syntax looks like this:

```
<cffunction name="AreaCircle" returntype="Numeric" output="No">
  <cfargument name="Radius" type="Numeric" required="Yes">
  <cfreturn Pi( )*(Arguments.Radius^2)>
</cffunction>

<!--- Copy the UDF to the Request scope --->
<cfset request.AreaCircle = AreaCircle>
```

In your custom tag template, to call the AreaCircle( ) function in the request scope, you would use the following code:

```
<cfoutput>
The area of a circle with a radius
of 3 is #request.AreaCircle(3)#
</cfoutput>
```

Although both methods of dealing with UDFs within custom tags work, I prefer the first method as it allows you to keep your custom tags portable and self-contained. This is especially true if you distribute your custom tags outside of your organization. On the flip side, however, you may have to maintain multiple versions of a given UDF if that UDF is used both within your custom tag and by other pages in your application.

Function Libraries

One of the great things about UDFs is that you can have more than one in a single template. This gives you the ability to take all of the UDFs that you use in a particular application or web site and keep them in a single template, commonly referred to as a library. Depending on the number of UDFs used by your application, you may want to create one or more libraries, grouping your UDFs by functionality. The more UDFs you have, the more it may make sense to create multiple UDF libraries.

Here's an example of a small UDF library with several UDFs for calculating the area of various geometrical shapes:

```
<cffunction name="AreaCircle" returntype="Numeric" output="No">
  <cfargument name="Radius" type="Numeric" required="Yes">
  <cfreturn Pi( ) * Arguments.Radius^2>
</cffunction>

<cffunction name="AreaRectangle" returntype="Numeric" output="No">
  <cfargument name="Length" type="Numeric" required="Yes">
  <cfargument name="Width" type="Numeric" required="Yes">
  <cfreturn Arguments.Length * Arguments.Width>
</cffunction>

<cffunction name="AreaTriangle" returntype="Numeric" output="No">
  <cfargument name="Base" type="Numeric" required="Yes">
```

```
  <cfargument name="Height" type="Numeric" required="Yes">
  <cfreturn 0.5 * Arguments.Base * Arguments.Height>
</cffunction>
```

To use any of these functions in any of your templates, just `cfinclude` the template at the beginning of the page that needs them. If you save the library we just created as *_areaLib.cfm*, you call it like this:

```
<cfinclude template="_areaLib.cfm">

<cfoutput>
The area of a circle with a radius of 5 is: #AreaCircle(5)#
</cfoutput>
```

Perhaps the biggest advantage to storing your UDFs in a library has to do with code reuse and ease of management. Using a library gives you a central point from which to manage your UDFs. If you need to make a change to a particular UDF, you need to change it only in your UDF library file instead of having to track down each individual template that has the UDF coded inline.

If you find yourself frequently using `cfinclude` to include the same UDF library over and over throughout your application, you have the option of placing the `cfinclude` inside your application's *Application.cfm* template. Doing this makes all of the UDFs in your library available to all templates (except custom tags) in your application without having to place individual `cfinclude` tags in every template.

There's a common misconception that placing a bunch of UDFs in a tag library and including it within your *Application.cfm* template causes a lot of unnecessary overhead, especially in cases where only a fraction of the UDFs in the library are used in any given page. My tests show that while there is a small amount of additional overhead the first time an application page is called, all subsequent page calls incur *zero* additional overhead.

The next time you need a UDF for a particular task, you might consider checking to see whether one with the desired functionality already exists. The Common Function Library Project (*http://www.cflib.org/*) is an open-source repository of ColdFusion UDFs that you can download and use in your applications free of charge. The site is run by me and Raymond Camden, a well-known ColdFusion author and developer. The site maintains several libraries containing hundreds of functions for everything from string manipulation, statistics, and scientific calculations, to file operations and more. Because it's an open-source project, the source code for each function is available unencrypted. In addition, each function comes with documentation as well as an example showing common usage.

The site also contains several tools for working with UDFs, including the UDFDoc custom tag for autogenerating UDF documentation based on JavaDoc, a ColdFusion Studio (ColdFusion's IDE) extension for interacting with UDFs on the site from directly within Studio, and a UDF generator for automatically generating custom function libraries from the UDFs available on the site.

Because the site is a community project, submissions for new UDFs and improvements to existing UDFs from the ColdFusion community are always welcome. Each UDF submission is tested before being accepted or rejected, ensuring a high level of quality in the available code. As of this writing, there are over 600 UDFs hosted on the site, with more added all the time. For more information on the project or to download the libraries, visit *http://www.cflib.org*.

Script-Based UDFs

CFScript-based UDFs look a little different than their tag-based siblings. The first thing you should notice is that all script-based UDFs must be written within a `cfscript` tag block:

```
<cfscript>
function function_name([arg1][,arg2]...)
{
  CFScript statements
}
</cfscript>
```

Script-based UDFs begin with the `function` statement. The name of the function is defined by *`function_name`* and follows the same naming conventions as tag based UDFs. Script-based functions can be written to accept zero or more required arguments and any number of optional arguments. Each required argument must be given a name and explicitly declared in the function statement. For example, to declare a function called `Mean` that accepts a single parameter called `Values`, you would code it like this:

```
function Mean(Values)
```

Within the body of the function, you may use any CFScript statements you wish. `Var` is used to declare variables that are local to the function. Variables declared with `Var` must be defined at the top of the function, before any other CFScript statements, and they take precedence over any other variable with the same name, regardless of the variable's scope. The syntax for declaring a variable using `Var` in CFScript is:

```
Var variable = expression;
```

The `Return` statement is optional and determines what value(s) to return when the function has finished executing.* You may specify any valid expression in the `Return` statement. If no expression is given in the `Return` statement, ColdFusion returns the last value encountered before the `Return` statement (assuming there is one):

```
Return;
Return x;
Return x-y;
Return DateFormat(MyVar, 'mm/dd/yyyy');
```

* In ColdFusion 5, the `Return` statement was required. This behavior is new in ColdFusion MX.

Script-based UDFs can return any ColdFusion datatype, including complex types such as arrays, structures, and queries. The simplest form of UDF is one in which all the functionality is contained in a single `Return` statement. To demonstrate this, consider the script-based version of our `Mean( )` UDF:

```
<cfscript>
// Mean(values)
// Returns the mean (average) value of a list of comma delimited values
function Mean(Values)
{
  Return ArrayAvg(ListToArray(Arguments.Values));
}
</cfscript>
```

In this example, the first line uses the `function` statement to declare a function named `Mean` that accepts a single argument called `Values`. The body of the UDF contains a single statement. In this case, it is a `Return` statement that converts the list of values to an array using the `ListToArray( )` function and subsequently obtains the average value using the `ArrayAvg( )` function.

Because CFScript-based UDFs lack an equivalent to the `cfargument` tag, optional arguments can only be referred to by their index position and not by name. Additionally, you'll have to code the assignment of default values for optional arguments. Here's a modified version of the `Mean( )` function that accepts a delimiter as an optional argument:

```
<cfscript>
// Mean(values [, delimiter])
// Returns the mean (average) for an array or list of delimited values
function Mean(Values)
{
  Var Delimiter = ",";
  if (ArrayLen(Arguments) gt 1){
    Delimiter = Arguments[2];
  }
  if (IsArray(Values)){
    Return ArrayAvg(Arguemnts.Values);
  }
  else{
    Return ArrayAvg(ListToArray(Arguments.Values, Delimiter));
  }
}
</cfscript>
```

In this example, we've modified our `Mean( )` UDF to accept a one-dimensional array of numeric values or a delimited list of numeric values as well an optional argument called `Delimiter`. `Delimiter` allows an optional delimiter to be passed to the function in the event that the list of values is separated with a delimiter other than the comma. The argument name `Delimiter` isn't actually relevant, because all optional arguments are referred to by their index position within the `Arguments` array. I use it here just as a placeholder to make it easier to describe.

The first part of the function uses a Var statement to define a variable called TheDelimiter. The comma "," serves as the default delimiter. Remember that because we used the Var statement, TheDelimiter is available only within the Mean( ) UDF.

Since we are expecting only one required argument and one optional one, we use an if statement to determine whether there is more than one element in the Arguments array. If there is, we know the optional Delimiter argument is present, so we assign the value of Arguments[2] (the delimiter) to the function variable Delimiter.

Next another if statement is used to check whether Arguments.Values is an array. If it is, we know that an array of values, as opposed to a list of values, was passed in, so we use the ArrayAvg( ) function to calculate the mean for the values and return it using the Return statement. If Values isn't an array, we assume it is a list and use the ListToArray( ) function to convert it to an array before using the ArrayAvg( ) function to calculate the mean anda return it. The value of Delimiter is used in the ListToArray( ) function to specify the delimiter for the list.

CHAPTER 21

Creating Custom Tags

One of the most powerful features of ColdFusion is the ability to extend the core capabilities of the platform through custom tags. Custom tags allow you to encapsulate code in a neat wrapper that can then be invoked from within any CFML template. Those familiar with other programming languages can think of custom tags as similar to subroutines or procedures.

There are two varieties of custom tags: custom CFML tags (referred to as custom tags) and CFX tags. Because developing CFX tags requires C++ or Java experience, this chapter focuses on the development and use of custom tags, since they are written in CFML. A brief section at the end of the chapter discusses installing and calling CFX tags.

Getting Started

Custom tags are just like regular CFML templates and can contain any combination of CFML, HTML, JavaScript, or other markup code. What makes them different is how they are called and how they interact with the template that calls them. Custom tags allow you to pass attributes to them (just like other CFML and HTML tags), perform some sort of processing based on the attributes passed in, and can return data in the form of variables that can be used by the calling template in any number of ways. Let's first look at the benefits of custom tags.

Why Custom Tags?

Right now, you are probably wondering about the specific types of situations that might warrant the use of custom tags. Here are four reasons to use custom tags in your ColdFusion applications:

Code reuse

Custom tags give you a way to reuse frequently used code. You can create a single custom tag that can be called by any application residing on your server whenever the functionality it provides is needed. This allows you to develop your applications more quickly by reducing the amount of redundancy in your coding. It also improves development time in shared development environments where multiple developers have access to the same code base. Using custom tags, you can create a shared library of tags for handling various programming tasks that can be used by any developer on a given project.

Abstraction

Using a custom tag allows you to abstract complex code and programming logic. To understand what we mean by abstraction, consider the `cfmail` tag. The `cfmail` tag provides a simple, tag-based interface for creating and sending SMTP messages. The tag abstracts the low-level programming that is typically required to create and send an SMTP message. Like the `cfmail` tag, custom tags allow you to abstract functionality (albeit written in CFML) using the same sort of tag-based interface.

Code distribution

Custom tags provide a way to distribute your code to others. Because custom tags are self-contained, they provide an ideal framework for distributing functional code to other developers with a minimum of additional support.

Security

Custom tags can also be used to keep developers away from back-end systems and processes you might not want them to have full access to. It is possible to secure access to these back-end systems and processes by providing developers with an encrypted version of a custom tag that accesses them.

If you need any more incentive to use custom tags in your applications, consider this. As of this writing, there are over 3,000 custom tags, many of them free of charge with source code that can be downloaded from an area of Macromedia's web site called the Developer Exchange. For example, a couple of my favorite tags are ones that handle complex user interface tasks that usually require JavaScript coding, such as relating select boxes (Nate Weiss's CF_TwoselectsRelated) or moving items from one list box to another (Shlomy Gantz's CF_DoubleBox). The Developer Exchange is a central resource for collecting and distributing custom tags and other ColdFusion-based applications. The Developer Exchange can be found at *http://devex.macromedia.com/developer/gallery/*.

Custom Tags Versus Other Options

ColdFusion provides several additional ways to abstract, encapsulate, repurpose, and reuse code. With additional choices including included files (`cfinclude`), user-defined functions (UDFs), and components (CFCs), you may be wondering where custom tags fit in. In fact, with the introduction of CFCs in ColdFusion MX, you may even have heard that custom tags are dead. This couldn't be further from the truth. While it's true that much of what used to be done in custom tags can now be done more efficiently in CFCs or UDFs, custom tags still have many uses. Table 21-1 outlines some of the situations you may come across in your applications and provides very general recommendations for appropriate techniques.

Table 21-1. Code reuse matrix

Scenario	Custom tag	cfinclude	UDF	CFC
Headers and footers	Yes	Yes	No	No
Generating output	Yes	Yes	No	Yes
Calculations, string parsing, data manipulation, etc.	No	No	Yes	No
Segmenting large templates into more logical and/or manageable chunks	No	Yes	No	No
Including static code	No	Yes	No	No
Package and distribute code	Yes	No	Yes	Yes
Use recursion	Yes	No	Yes	Yes
Provide parent/child functionality	Yes	No	No	No
Need to provide start and end tag processing	Yes	No	No	No
Building web services	No	No	No	Yes

While this table is by no means exhaustive, it does provide some general guidelines for which technology may be appropriate in a given situation.

Calling Custom Tags

There is no real installation process for custom tags other than to save them on your ColdFusion server. There are, however, different locations on the server where you can save the tags that affect whether they can be called locally by a single application or shared across all applications.

To call a custom tag from within a CFML template, you simply prefix the template name of the tag with `cf_`. Therefore, if you have a custom tag saved on your server as *mytag.cfm*, you call it like this:

```
<cf_mytag>
```

When you call a custom tag from an application template, ColdFusion looks for the tag in the same directory as the calling template. For example, if your template resides in *\inetsrv\wwwroot\myapp* and tries to call a custom tag called `cf_mytag`, ColdFusion looks for the tag in the *\myapp* directory first. Saving a custom tag in the same directory as its calling template makes the tag a local tag. That is, the tag is available only to templates residing in the same directory as the application. Using the local-tag technique allows you to use custom tags in hosted environments where you might not have access to a shared custom tags directory.

The very nature of custom tags makes them ideal for sharing among multiple applications on the server. In order to facilitate this, a default custom tags directory is automatically created when you install ColdFusion on your server. This directory is *\cfusionmx\customtags* by default. Any custom tags saved in this directory or any of its subdirectories are automatically available to any applications you create on the entire server.

You can map additional shared custom tag directories from within the ColdFusion Administrator. This allows you to use directories other than the default for making your tags available to multiple applications. To add a new custom tag path in the ColdFusion Administrator, follow these simple steps:

1. Click the Custom Tag Paths link under Extensions on the main ColdFusion Administrator page.
2. Enter the full path to your directory in the text box labeled Register New Custom Tag Paths or use the Browse Server button to select a path from your ColdFusion server's filesystem.
3. Click the Add Path button when you are finished.

Note that you must start and stop the ColdFusion Application Server before the changes will take effect.

As I mentioned earlier, when a template calls a custom tag, ColdFusion starts its search for the custom tag in the same directory as the calling template. If ColdFusion can't find a tag with the name you specified, it moves its search to the default custom tags directory, and then any subdirectories. If the tag isn't found in the default custom tags directory, the search is extended to additional custom tag directories registered in the ColdFusion Administrator. These directories (and their subdirectories) are searched in the order they appear in the ColdFusion Administrator until a tag with the name you specified is found. In the event no tag is found during any of these searches, an exception is thrown.

The fact that the custom tag framework lets you store your custom tags in different locations suggests that you can have two or more different tags with the same name on your server. In the event that this happens, the order of evaluation states that ColdFusion use the first tag it encounters in its search. A method for using the `cfmodule` tag to give you greater control over invoking custom tags is discussed in the "Advanced Techniques" section later in this chapter.

Passing Data

Just like HTML and CFML tags, custom tags receive parameters via tag attributes. When you call a custom tag, you can pass parameters that automatically become available as variables within the custom tag. ColdFusion has a special variable scope called the `attributes` scope that refers to reference attributes that have been passed to a custom tag. For example, you can call a custom tag named `cf_mytag` like this:

```
<cf_mytag name="Pere Money"
          title="President">
```

Both `name` and `title` are tag attributes. Once the tag is called, these attributes and their associated values are available within the custom tag as `attributes.Name` and `attributes.Title`, respectively. Because the custom tag exists within its own scope, you must scope any variables with the `attributes` prefix in order to access them. Any ColdFusion datatype may be passed to a custom tag as an attribute. This allows you to create custom tags that can manipulate data from a variety of sources, including query objects, arrays, and structures, as well as such simple values as strings and numbers.

Let's look at a simple example that demonstrates how to pass a few attributes to a custom tag. Example 21-1 calls a custom tag called `cf_states` (Example 21-2). The tag is used to generate a select box containing U.S. state names along with their associated abbreviations. A number of attributes are passed to the tag: `selectname`, `defaultvalue`, `defaultlabel`, and `selected`.

Example 21-1. Passing attributes to the cf_states custom tag

```
<cfif IsDefined('form.Submit')>
<cfoutput>
You selected: #form.TheState#
</cfoutput>
</cfif>

<cfoutput>
<form name="MyForm" method="Post" action="#CGI.script_name#">
</cfoutput>
  State: <cf_states selectname="TheState"
                    defaultvalue="NULL"
                    defaultlabel="Please Select">
  <input type="Submit" name="Submit" value="Submit">
</form>
```

Once the `cf_states` tag is called, the attributes passed to it are automatically available as attributes variables within the tag. These variables can be manipulated in the same way that ColdFusion variables can be manipulated. In this case, they are used to specify attributes for the select box that is then output to the browser. Note that the variables are always referenced using the `attributes` scope. Failing to scope the variables results in an error. The CFML code for the cf_states tag is shown in Example 21-2. Be sure to save the template as *states.cfm*.

Example 21-2. Generating a select list of states

```
<!--- Set attribute defaults --->
<cfparam name="attributes.selectname" default="State">
<cfparam name="attributes.defaultvalue" default="">
<cfparam name="attributes.defaultlabel" default="">
<cfparam name="attributes.selected" default="#attributes.defaultvalue#">

<!--- Initialize a 2D array to hold the states --->
<cfset State = ArrayNew(2)>
<cfset State[1][1] = attributes.defaultvalue>
<cfset State[1][2] = attributes.defaultlabel>
<cfset State[2][1] = "AL"><cfset State[2][2] = "Alabama">
<cfset State[3][1] = "AK"><cfset State[3][2] = "Alaska">
<cfset State[4][1] = "AZ"><cfset State[4][2] = "Arizona">
<cfset State[5][1] = "AR"><cfset State[5][2] = "Arkansas">
<cfset State[6][1] = "CA"><cfset State[6][2] = "California">
<cfset State[7][1] = "CO"><cfset State[7][2] = "Colorado">
<cfset State[8][1] = "CT"><cfset State[8][2] = "Connecticut">
<cfset State[9][1] = "DE"><cfset State[9][2] = "Delaware">
<cfset State[10][1] = "DC"><cfset State[10][2] = "District of Columbia">
<cfset State[11][1] = "FL"><cfset State[11][2] = "Florida">
<cfset State[12][1] = "GA"><cfset State[12][2] = "Georgia">
<cfset State[13][1] = "HI"><cfset State[13][2] = "Hawaii">
<cfset State[14][1] = "ID"><cfset State[14][2] = "Idaho">
<cfset State[15][1] = "IL"><cfset State[15][2] = "Illinois">
<cfset State[16][1] = "IN"><cfset State[16][2] = "Indiana">
<cfset State[17][1] = "IA"><cfset State[17][2] = "Iowa">
<cfset State[18][1] = "KS"><cfset State[18][2] = "Kansas">
<cfset State[19][1] = "KY"><cfset State[19][2] = "Kentucky">
<cfset State[20][1] = "LA"><cfset State[20][2] = "Louisiana">
<cfset State[21][1] = "ME"><cfset State[21][2] = "Maine">
<cfset State[22][1] = "MD"><cfset State[22][2] = "Maryland">
<cfset State[23][1] = "MA"><cfset State[23][2] = "Massachusetts">
<cfset State[24][1] = "MI"><cfset State[24][2] = "Michigan">
<cfset State[25][1] = "MN"><cfset State[25][2] = "Minnesota">
<cfset State[26][1] = "MS"><cfset State[26][2] = "Mississippi">
<cfset State[27][1] = "MO"><cfset State[27][2] = "Missouri">
<cfset State[28][1] = "MT"><cfset State[28][2] = "Montana">
<cfset State[29][1] = "NE"><cfset State[29][2] = "Nebraska">
<cfset State[30][1] = "NV"><cfset State[30][2] = "Nevada">
<cfset State[31][1] = "NH"><cfset State[31][2] = "New Hampshire">
<cfset State[32][1] = "NJ"><cfset State[32][2] = "New Jersey">
<cfset State[33][1] = "NM"><cfset State[33][2] = "New Mexico">
<cfset State[34][1] = "NY"><cfset State[34][2] = "New York">
<cfset State[35][1] = "NC"><cfset State[35][2] = "North Carolina">
<cfset State[36][1] = "ND"><cfset State[36][2] = "North Dakota">
<cfset State[37][1] = "OH"><cfset State[37][2] = "Ohio">
<cfset State[38][1] = "OK"><cfset State[38][2] = "Oklahoma">
```

Example 21-2. Generating a select list of states (continued)

```
<cfset State[39][1] = "OR"><cfset State[39][2] = "Oregon">
<cfset State[40][1] = "PA"><cfset State[40][2] = "Pennsylvania">
<cfset State[41][1] = "RI"><cfset State[41][2] = "Rhode Island">
<cfset State[42][1] = "SC"><cfset State[42][2] = "South Carolina">
<cfset State[43][1] = "SD"><cfset State[43][2] = "South Dakota">
<cfset State[44][1] = "TN"><cfset State[44][2] = "Tennessee">
<cfset State[45][1] = "TX"><cfset State[45][2] = "Texas">
<cfset State[46][1] = "UT"><cfset State[46][2] = "Utah">
<cfset State[47][1] = "VT"><cfset State[47][2] = "Vermont">
<cfset State[48][1] = "VA"><cfset State[48][2] = "Virginia">
<cfset State[49][1] = "WA"><cfset State[49][2] = "Washington">
<cfset State[50][1] = "WV"><cfset State[50][2] = "West Virginia">
<cfset State[51][1] = "WI"><cfset State[51][2] = "Wisconsin">
<cfset State[52][1] = "WY"><cfset State[52][2] = "Wyoming">

<!--- Generate the select box with attributes --->
<cfoutput><select name="#attributes.selectname#"></cfoutput>
  <cfloop index="i" from="1" to="#ArrayLen(State)#">
    <cfoutput><option value="#State[i][1]#"<cfif State[i][1] is
        #attributes.selected#> selected</cfif>>#State[i][2]#</option></cfoutput>
  </cfloop>
</select>
```

The tag works by creating a two-dimensional array containing the state abbreviations in the first dimension and the full state names in the second dimension. The `selectname` attribute allows you to pass in a name to be used for the generated select box. If no value is passed in for this attribute, the default "State" is used instead. `defaultvalue` and `defaultlabel` let you pass in a default value and label, respectively, to display as the first item in the select box. In this case, we passed in "NULL" as the default value and "Please Select" as the label. Each of these attributes defaults to an empty string ("") if no value is passed. The final attribute, `selected`, lets you specify a state abbreviation (or `defaultvalue`) to act as the default selected value in the list box generated by the tag. If no value is passed for this attribute, it defaults to the value specified for `defaultvalue`.

Figure 21-1 shows the results of calling the custom tag. Note that in Example 21-2, the custom tag (as opposed to the calling template) creates the select box that is output to the browser.

Returning Data

The caller scope passes data from inside a custom tag back to the calling template. Because custom tags exist within their own scope, you must use the caller scope if you want to make variables you create within your custom tag available to the calling template.

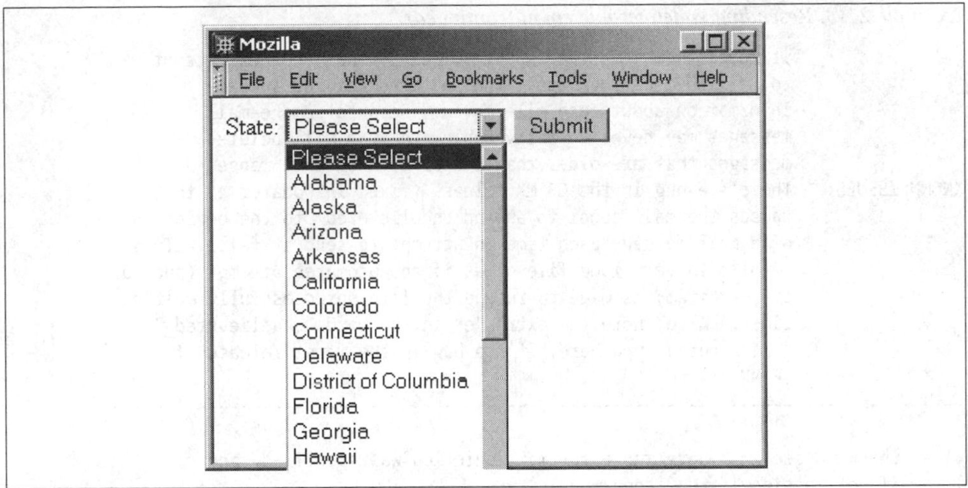

Figure 21-1. Outputting attribute values in a custom tag

Setting a caller variable is just like setting any other type of ColdFusion variable. You may assign any datatype to a variable in the caller scope. This means that you can pass both simple and complex datatypes from inside a custom tag back to the template that called it.

Let's create a quick example that demonstrates passing an attribute to a custom tag, acting on that attribute, and passing variables back using the caller scope. If you remember back to Chapter 13, you'll recall that we created a CFML file for moving undeliverable email from the *\undelivr* folder to the *\spool* folder so that an attempt could be made to resend it. That template was actually based on a custom tag I wrote (and updated over the years) for the same purpose. Having the functionality as a custom tag makes it much easier to reuse the code. Example 21-3 shows the code from Chapter 13 rewritten as a custom tag called `cf_resendundeliverablemailmx`. Be sure to save the template as *resendundeliverablemailmx.cfm* on your server

Example 21-3. Resending undeliverable email

```
<cfsilent>
<!---------------------------------------------------------------------------------
NAME:           cf_resendundeliverablemailmx
FILE:           resendundeliverablemailmx.cfm
CREATED:        03/30/1998
LAST MODIFIED:  02/10/2003
VERSION:        3.1
CF VERSION:     MX
AUTHOR:         Rob Brooks-Bilson (rbils@amkor.com)
DESCRIPTION:    This tag, when used in conjunction with the Scheduler
                in Cold Fusion MX, will scan the \undelivr directory
                of your Cold Fusion Application server for e-mail that was
                designated undeliverable.  If it finds any messages there,
```

Example 21-3. Resending undeliverable email (continued)

```
                it moves them into the \spool folder so that another attempt
                to mail them can be made.  The tag also returns summary
                information about each file moved.  Because some e-mail
                messages may never be deliverable, the tag will delete
                messages that are older than a user defined date range.
KNOWN ISSUES:   There's a bug in the CF MX release (fixed in Updater 2) that
                causes the mail spool to append Undelievered_ to the beginning
                of a mail message each time an attempt to send it fails.  This
                results in very long file names if an automated attempt (such as
                this program) is made to resend the file unsuccessfully multiple
                times.  Also, note the extra "e" in the word "Undelievered_"
                - it's not a typo here, it's a bug in the first release of
                CF MX
------------------------------------------------------------------------------->

<!--- Check to see if a date range for mail deletion was specified, and
      if not, assign it to 7 (one week) --->
<cfparam name="attributes.datetrigger" type="Numeric" default="7">

<!--- See if a query name was passed and if so, use it.  If not, assign the
      query the name "MovedQuery" --->
<cfparam name="attributes.queryname" type="VariableName" default="MovedQuery">

<!--- See if a name for the summary structure was passed.  In not, assign the
      structure the name "Summary" --->
<cfparam name="attributes.SumamryName" type="VariableName" default="Summary">

<!--- Get the mail root directory --->
<cfset MailRoot="#Server.coldfusion.rootdir#\mail">

<!--- Read all of the files from the undeliverable directory for processing --->
<cfdirectory action="List"
             directory="#MailRoot#\undelivr"
             name="Undeliverables"
             filter="*.cfmail">

<cfif Undeliverables.RecordCount eq 0>
  <cfset FilesMoved = 0>
  <cfset FilesDeleted = 0>
  <cfset UndeliveredMail = QueryNew("FileName, FileSize, LastMod, Status")>
  <cfset QueryAddRow(UndeliveredMail)>
  <cfset QuerySetCell(UndeliveredMail, "FileName", "N/A", 1)>
  <cfset QuerySetCell(UndeliveredMail, "FileSize", "N/A", 1)>
  <cfset QuerySetCell(UndeliveredMail, "LastMod", "N/A", 1)>
  <cfset QuerySetCell(UndeliveredMail, "Status", "N/A", 1)>
<cfelse>
  <!--- Set Constants --->
  <cfset FilesMoved = 0>
  <cfset FilesDeleted = 0>
  <cfset UndeliveredMail=QueryNew("FileName, FileSize, LastMod, Status")>
  <cfset QueryAddRow(UndeliveredMail, Undeliverables.RecordCount)>
```

Example 21-3. Resending undeliverable email (continued)

```
  <cfloop Query="Undeliverables">
    <!--- If the last modified date of the file in the undelivr directory is
          older than the date trigger, or if the file size is 0, delete it.
          Otherwise, move the file to the spool directory to be resent. --->
    <cfif (DateDiff("y", DateLastModified, Now( )) gt attributes.datetrigger)
           or (Size eq 0)>
      <cffile action="Delete"
              file="#MailRoot#\undelivr\#Name#">
      <cfset QuerySetCell(UndeliveredMail, "FileName", Name,
             Undeliverables.CurrentRow)>
      <cfset QuerySetCell(UndeliveredMail, "FileSize", Size,
             Undeliverables.CurrentRow)>
      <cfset QuerySetCell(UndeliveredMail, "LastMod", DateLastModified,
             Undeliverables.CurrentRow)>
     <cfset QuerySetCell(UndeliveredMail, "Status", "Deleted",
             Undeliverables.CurrentRow)>
      <cfset FilesDeleted = FilesDeleted + 1>
    <cfelse>
      <!--- Strip out Undelievered_ from the filename in case CFMX Updater 2 or
            later isn't installed --->
      <cffile action="Move"
              source="#MailRoot#\undelivr\#Name#"
              destination="#MailRoot#\spool\#ReplaceNoCase(Name, "Undelievered_",
                "", "All")#">
      <cfset QuerySetCell(UndeliveredMail, "FileName", Name,
             Undeliverables.CurrentRow)>
      <cfset QuerySetCell(UndeliveredMail, "FileSize", Size,
             Undeliverables.CurrentRow)>
      <cfset QuerySetCell(UndeliveredMail, "LastMod", DateLastModified,
             Undeliverables.CurrentRow)>
      <cfset QuerySetCell(UndeliveredMail, "Status", "Moved",
             Undeliverables.CurrentRow)>
      <cfset FilesMoved = FilesMoved+1>
    </cfif>
  </cfloop>
</cfif>

<!--- Create the summary structure --->
<cfset TempSummary = StructNew( )>
<cfset TempSummary.FilesMoved = FilesMoved>
<cfset TempSummary.FilesDeleted = FilesDeleted>

<!--- Send back the results --->
<cfset "caller.#attributes.queryname#" = UndeliveredMail>
<cfset "caller.#attributes.summaryname#" = TempSummary>
</cfsilent>
```

The `cfsilent` tag is used at the beginning and end of the custom tag. This suppresses any output, including whitespace, generated by the tag during its execution. If the tag produced any output within its body (such as error messages), you would need to use the cfsetting tag instead of cfsilent, and the output would have to be surrounded by cfoutput tags to avoid being suppressed.

The tag is designed to accept three attributes, datetrigger, queryname, and summaryname. datetrigger specifies the age (in days) an undeliverable message can be before the tag deletes it. queryname lets you pass a variable name for the query returned by the tag. The query contains information about each file that is moved or deleted, such as its filename, size, and last modified date. summaryname lets you provide a different variable name to be used to return a structure containing two keys, FilesMoved and FilesDeleted. These keys contain the number of files moved by the tag and the number deleted, respectively. Once called, the tag scans the */undelivr* folder for undeliverable email to move back to the */spool* folder. The summary variables are then populated and returned back to the calling page.

It is a good idea to get in the habit of allowing developers to specify the names of any caller variables returned by the custom tag as attributes that can be passed into the tag. This helps avoid any potential variable name conflicts between variables in the calling template and hard-coded caller variables returned by a custom tag. If a variable with the same name as a caller variable returned by a custom tag already exists in the calling template, its value is overwritten by the value in the caller variable with the same name.

As you can see in Example 21-3, instead of returning hard-coded caller variable names back to the calling template, we dynamically create them like this:

```
<cfset "caller.#attributes.queryname#" = UndeliveredMail>
<cfset "caller.#attributes.summaryname#" = TempSummary>
```

Allowing caller variable names to be specified also lets you call the same tag multiple times from a single page.

One other thing here is worth noting. Every custom tag you write (save a few of the smaller examples in this book) should have a header section that explains what the tag does, who created it, when it was last updated, what attributes it takes, and what caller variables it returns. Taking the time to add this information to your custom tags in the beginning will save you (and potentially others) a lot of time down the road when you need to look at the code behind the tag.

To test the cf_resendundeliverablemailmx custom tag, create the template shown in Example 21-4 and save it to the same directory you saved the *resendundeliverablemailmx.cfm* template to. You may name the template anything you desire.

Example 21-4. Calling the custom tag cf_resendundeliverablemailmx

```
<cfset Tab = CHR(9)>
<cfset br =  CHR(13) & CHR(10)>

<cf_resendundeliverablemailmx
```

Example 21-4. Calling the custom tag cf_resendundeliverablemailmx (continued)

```
    datetrigger="5"
    queryname="UndeliveredMail"
    summaryname="Summary">

<cfif Summary.FilesMoved gte 1 or Summary.FilesDeleted gte 1>
<cfmail query="UndeliveredMail"
        to="webmaster@example.com"
        from="webmaster@example.com"
        subject="Undeliverable Mail Report for Server #CGI.Server_Name#">
Total Files Moved: #Summary.FilesMoved#
Total Files Deleted: #Summary.FilesDeleted#

These are the files affected:

Action#Tab#Filename#Tab##Tab#FileSize#Tab#Date Modified
==============================================================
<cfoutput>
#Status# #Tab##FileName##Tab##filesize# bytes#Tab##DateFormat(LastMod)##br#
</cfoutput>
</cfmail>
</cfif>
```

This template becomes even more useful when you schedule it to run automatically on a recurring basis. To learn more about scheduling tasks in ColdFusion, see Chapter 26.

Now that you've got a general idea how the attribute and caller scopes work, let's take things one step further and examine the separation between the variables created in a calling template and those created within a custom tag. As always, an example helps illustrate the concepts.

Example 21-5 shows a template that calls a custom tag called `cf_variabledemo`, then passes it some attributes, and outputs the results returned by the tag. We include the `cfapplication` tag because this example makes use of session, client, and application variables. Normally, this tag would go in the *Application.cfm* template, but I've included it here in order to keep things simple. You also need to make sure that client and session management are enabled in the ColdFusion administrator.

Example 21-5. Calling the cf_variabledemo tag and outputting the results

```
<cfapplication name="MyApp"
               clientmanagement="Yes"
               sessionmanagement="Yes"
               setclientcookies="Yes"
               sessiontimeout="#CreateTimeSpan(0,0,10,0)#"
               applicationtimeout="#CreateTimeSpan(0,0,10,0)#">

<!--- Create a variable to hold a query object --->
<cfset QueryVariable = QueryNew("Text")>
```

Example 21-5. Calling the cf_variabledemo tag and outputting the results (continued)

```
<cfset NewRows  = QueryAddRow(QueryVariable, 1)>
<cfset QuerySetCell(QueryVariable, "Text", "I am a Query variable", 1)>

<!--- Assign values to all other variable types with the exception of CGI as
      CGI variables are read only --->
<cfset application.ApplicationVariable = "I am an Application variable">
<cfset session.SesssionVariable = "I am a Session variable">
<cfset client.ClientVariable = "I am a Client variable">
<cfset server.ServerVariable = "I am a Server variable">
<cfset variables.LocalVariable = "I am a Local variable">
<cfset form.FormVariable = "I am a Form variable">
<cfset URL.URLVariable = "I am a URL variable">
<cfcookie name="CookieVariable" value="I am a Cookie variable">
<cfset request.RequestVariable = "I am a Request variable">

<html>
<head>
    <title>Variable Demo</title>
</head>

<body>
<!--- Display all of the variable/values from the calling (this) template --->
<h2>Set in the calling template...</h2>
<cfoutput>
<table border="1">
<tr>
  <th>Variable</th><th>value</th>
</tr>
<tr>
  <td>application.ApplicationVariable</td><td>#application.ApplicationVariable#</td>
</tr>
<tr>
  <td>QueryVariable.Text</td><td>#QueryVariable.Text#</td>
</tr>
<tr>
  <td>session.SesssionVariable</td><td>#session.SesssionVariable#</td>
</tr>
<tr>
  <td>client.ClientVariable</td><td>#client.ClientVariable#</td>
</tr>
<tr>
  <td>server.ServerVariable</td><td>#server.ServerVariable#</td>
</tr>
<tr>
  <td>variables.LocalVariable</td><td>#variables.LocalVariable#</td>
</tr>
<tr>
  <td>form.FormVariable</td><td>#form.FormVariable#</td>
</tr>
<tr>
  <td>cookie.CookieVariable</td><td>#cookie.CookieVariable#</td>
</tr>
```

Example 21-5. Calling the cf_variabledemo tag and outputting the results (continued)

```
<tr>
  <td>CGI.http_user_agent</td><td>#CGI.http_user_agent#</td>
</tr>
<tr>
  <td>request.RequestVariable</td><td>#request.RequestVariable#</td>
</tr>
</table>
</cfoutput>

<!--- Call the VariableDemo custom tag and pass two attributes in.  The custom
      tag will generate some output on its own in this example. --->
<cf_variabledemo attributevariable="I am an Attribue variable"
                 outvar="CallerVariable">

<!--- Display all variables set inside of the custom tag as well as the caller
      variable returned by the tag --->
<h2>Set inside the custom tag..</h2>
<cfoutput>
<table border="1">
<tr>
  <th>Variable</th><th>value</th>
</tr>
<tr>
  <td>Application Variable:</td>
  <td><cfif IsDefined('application.Tag_ApplicationVariable')>
        #application.Tag_ApplicationVariable#
      <cfelse><b>Not Available</b></cfif>
  </td>
</tr>
<tr>
  <td>Query Variable:</td>
  <td><cfif IsDefined('Tag_QueryVariable.Text')>#Tag_QueryVariable.Text#
      <cfelse><b>Not Available</b></cfif>
  </td>
</tr>
<tr>
  <td>Session Variable:</td>
  <td><cfif IsDefined('session.Tag_SesssionVariable')>
        #session.Tag_SesssionVariable#
      <cfelse><b>Not Available</b></cfif>
  </td>
</tr>
<tr>
  <td>Client Variable:</td>
  <td><cfif IsDefined('client.Tag_ClientVariable')>#client.Tag_ClientVariable#
      <cfelse><b>Not Available</b></cfif>
  </td>
</tr>
<tr>
  <td>Server Variable:</td>
  <td><cfif IsDefined('server.Tag_ServerVariable')>#server.Tag_ServerVariable#
```

Example 21-5. Calling the cf_variabledemo tag and outputting the results (continued)

```
        <cfelse><b>Not Available</b></cfif>
    </td>
</tr>
<tr>
    <td>Local Variable:</td>
    <td><cfif IsDefined('variables.Tag_LocalVariable')>
          #variables.Tag_LocalVariable#
        <cfelse><b>Not Available</b></cfif>
    </td>
</tr>
<tr>
    <td>Form Variable:</td>
    <td><cfif IsDefined('form.Tag_FormVariable')>#form.Tag_FormVariable#
        <cfelse><b>Not Available</b></cfif>
    </td>
</tr>
<tr>
    <td>Cookie Variable:</td>
    <td><cfif IsDefined('cookie.Tag_CookieVariable')>#cookie.Tag_CookieVariable#
        <cfelse><b>Not Available</b></cfif>
    </td>
</tr>
<tr>
    <td>CGI Variable:</td>
    <td><cfif IsDefined('CGI.http_user_agent')>#CGI.http_user_agent#
        <cfelse><b>Not Available</b></cfif>
</td>
</tr>
<tr>
    <td>Request Variable:</td>
    <td><cfif IsDefined('request.Tag_RequestVariable')>
          #request.Tag_RequestVariable#
        <cfelse><b>Not Available</b></cfif>
    </td>
</tr>
<tr>
    <td>CallerVariable</td>
    <td><cfif IsDefined('CallerVariable')>#CallerVariable#
        <cfelse><b>Not Available</b></cfif>
    </td>
</tr>
</table>
</cfoutput>
</body>
</html>
```

Before the custom tag is invoked, the calling template creates a number of differently scoped variables. A table is then output (shown in Figure 21-2) containing all the values associated with these variables while in the calling template.

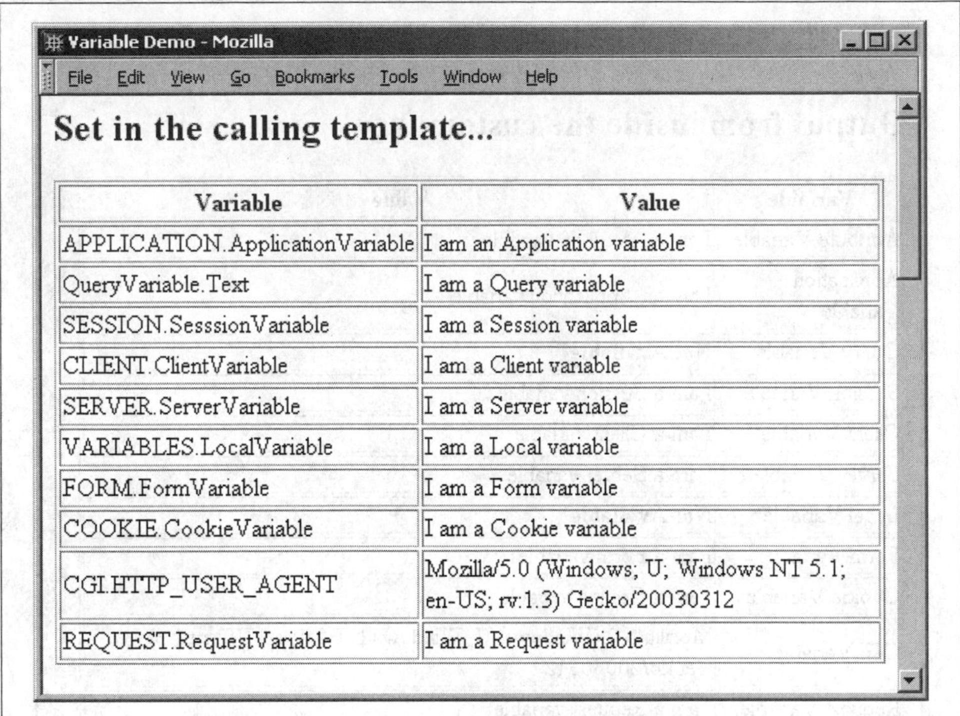

Figure 21-2. Variables set and viewable in the calling template

Next, the `cf_variabledemo` tag is called, and two attributes, `attributevariable` and `outvar`, are passed to it from the calling template. The `cf_variabledemo` tag, shown in Example 21-6, evaluates each variable that is set in the calling template and generates a table (shown in Figure 21-3) demonstrating which variables from the calling tag can be "seen" inside the custom tag.

The `cf_variabledemo` tag then creates all the previous variable types (with the exception of an attribute variable) within the space of the custom tag. A caller variable is also created and automatically passed back to the calling template. Example 21-6 shows the CFML code for `cf_variabledemo`; be sure this file is saved as *variabledemo.cfm*.

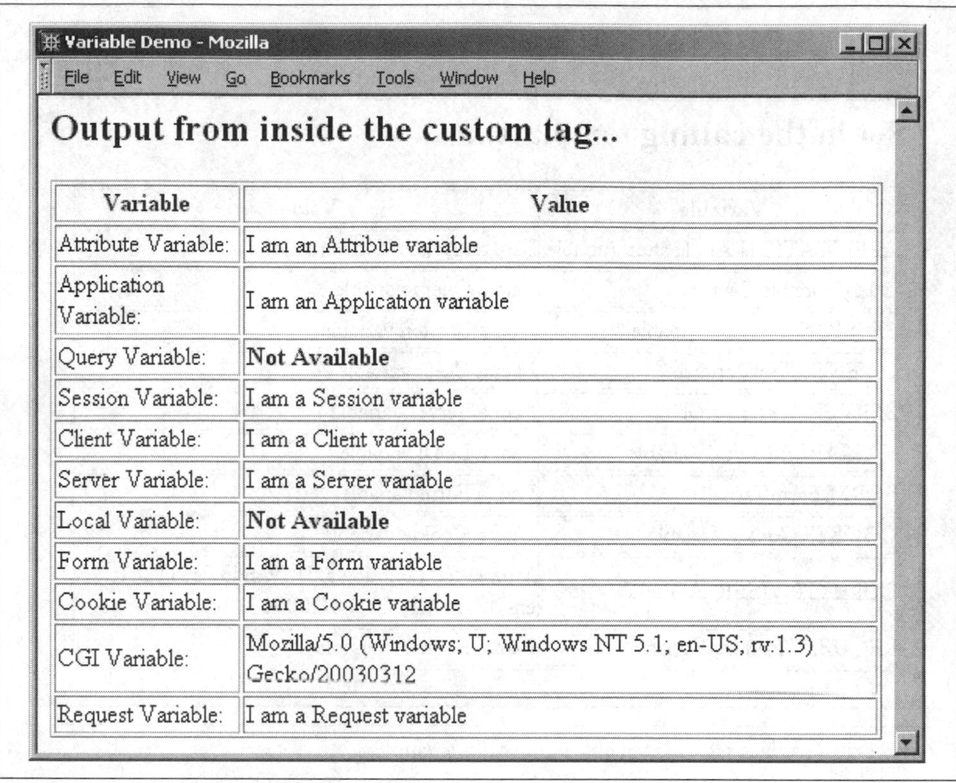

Variable	Value
Attribute Variable:	I am an Attribue variable
Application Variable:	I am an Application variable
Query Variable:	**Not Available**
Session Variable:	I am a Session variable
Client Variable:	I am a Client variable
Server Variable:	I am a Server variable
Local Variable:	**Not Available**
Form Variable:	I am a Form variable
Cookie Variable:	I am a Cookie variable
CGI Variable:	Mozilla/5.0 (Windows; U; Windows NT 5.1; en-US; rv:1.3) Gecko/20030312
Request Variable:	I am a Request variable

Figure 21-3. Variables set in the calling template and available for use by the custom tag

Example 21-6. The cf_variabledemo (variabledemo.cfm) custom tag

```
<!--- Attempt to output all of the variables set in the calling template.  If a
      variable is not accessible to the custom tag, note it.  In addition,
      output the attribute variable and set a caller and another request
      variable --->
<h2>Output from inside the custom tag...</h2>
<cfoutput>
<table border="1">
<tr>
  <th>Variable</th><th>value</th>
</tr>
<tr>
  <td>Attribute Variable:</td><td>#attributes.attributevariable#</td>
</tr>
<tr>
  <td>Application Variable:</td>
  <td><cfif IsDefined('application.ApplicationVariable')>
        #application.ApplicationVariable#
      <cfelse><b>Not Available</b></cfif>
  </td>
</tr>
<tr>
```

Example 21-6. The cf_variabledemo (variabledemo.cfm) custom tag (continued)

```
  <td>Query Variable:</td>
  <td><cfif IsDefined('QueryVariable.Text')>#QueryVariable.Text#
      <cfelse><b>Not Available</b></cfif>
  </td>
</tr>
<tr>
  <td>Session Variable:</td>
  <td><cfif IsDefined('session.SesssionVariable')>#session.SesssionVariable#
      <cfelse><b>Not Available</b></cfif>
  </td>
</tr>
<tr>
  <td>Client Variable:</td>
  <td><cfif IsDefined('client.ClientVariable')>#client.ClientVariable#
      <cfelse><b>Not Available</b></cfif>
  </td>
</tr>
<tr>
  <td>Server Variable:</td>
  <td><cfif IsDefined('server.ServerVariable')>#server.ServerVariable#
      <cfelse><b>Not Available</b></cfif>
  </td>
</tr>
<tr>
  <td>Local Variable:</td>
  <td><cfif IsDefined('variables.LocalVariable')>#variables.LocalVariable#
      <cfelse><b>Not Available</b></cfif>
  </td>
</tr>
<tr>
  <td>Form Variable:</td>
  <td><cfif IsDefined('form.FormVariable')>#form.FormVariable#
      <cfelse><b>Not Available</b></cfif>
  </td>
</tr>
<tr>
  <td>Cookie Variable:</td>
  <td><cfif IsDefined('cookie.CookieVariable')>#cookie.CookieVariable#
      <cfelse><b>Not Available</b></cfif>
  </td>
</tr>
<tr>
  <td>CGI Variable:</td>
  <td><cfif IsDefined('CGI.http_user_agent')>#CGI.http_user_agent#
      <cfelse><b>Not Available</b></cfif>
</td>
</tr>
<tr>
  <td>Request Variable:</td>
  <td><cfif IsDefined('request.RequestVariable')>#request.RequestVariable#
      <cfelse><b>Not Available</b></cfif>
  </td>
```

Example 21-6. The cf_variabledemo (variabledemo.cfm) custom tag (continued)

```
</tr>
</table>
</cfoutput>

<!--- Create a variable to hold a query object --->
<cfset Tag_QueryVariable = QueryNew("Text")>
<cfset NewRows  = QueryAddRow(Tag_QueryVariable, 1)>
<cfset temp = QuerySetCell(Tag_QueryVariable, "Text", "I am a Query
              variable", 1)>

<!--- Create variables within the scope of the custom tag to see which ones
      are available back in the calling template --->
<cfset application.Tag_ApplicationVariable = "I am an Application variable">
<cfset session.Tag_SesssionVariable = "I am a Session variable">
<cfset client.Tag_ClientVariable = "I am a Client variable">
<cfset server.Tag_ServerVariable = "I am a Server variable">
<cfset variables.Tag_LocalVariable = "I am a Local variable">
<cfset form.Tag_FormVariable = "I am a Form variable">
<cfset URL.Tag_URLVariable = "I am a URL variable">
<cfcookie name="Tag_CookieVariable" value="I am a Cookie variable">
<cfset request.Tag_RequestVariable = "I am a Request variable">

<!--- Create a Caller variable --->
<cfset "caller.#attributes.outvar#" = "I am a Caller variable">
```

Once the tag has finished processing, the calling template (shown in Example 21-5) resumes. An attempt is made to see if each of the variables set within the custom tag is now available to the calling template. Another HTML table (shown in Figure 21-4) is then generated to reveal the results.

As you can see from the results, all variables created within the calling template are available to the custom tag, with the exception of local and query variables. Conversely, the same holds true for variables created within the custom tag (with the exception of attribute variables that can't be set in the custom tag). Our examples have demonstrated the following:

- Shared scope variables (application, client, session, server, cookie) are available to both regular templates and custom tags, regardless of where they are created.
- CGI variables are available to all templates and tags because they are read-only variables created by the system.
- Form and URL variables are available to both templates and custom tags regardless of where they are created.
- Attribute variables are created in a calling template and explicitly passed to a custom tag and are available only within the custom tag.
- Caller variables are created in custom tags and are available only to the template that calls the custom tag.

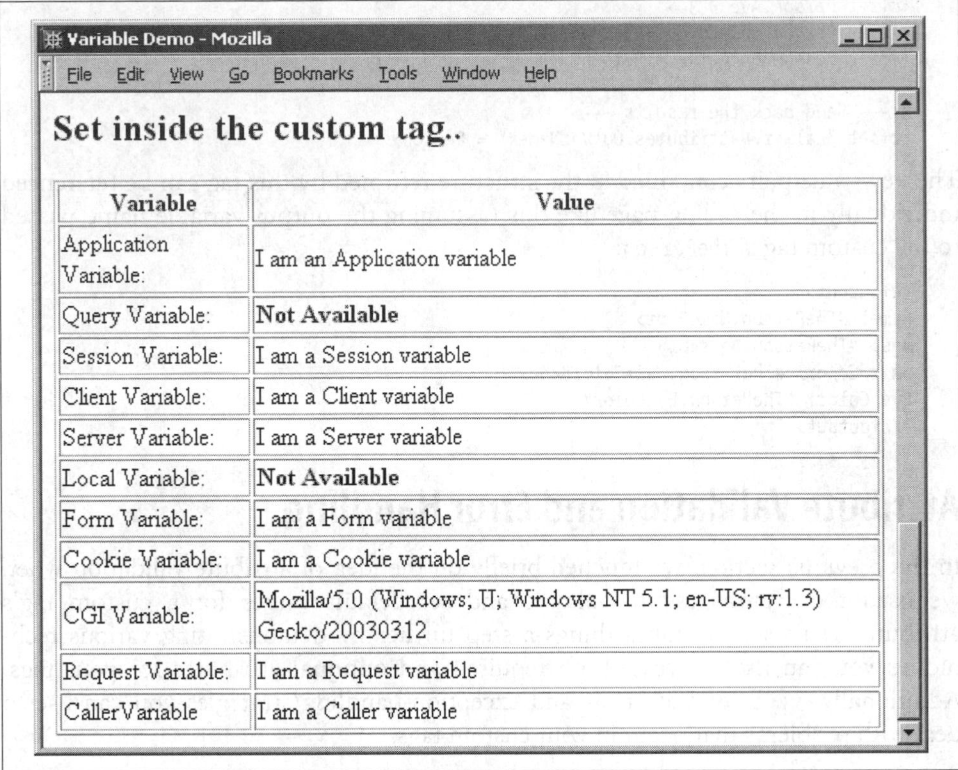

Figure 21-4. Variables set in the cf_variabledemo custom tag

- The request scope is a special variable scope that is shared by both the calling template and any custom tags for the duration of a single request.
- Local variables and query variables are available only within the templates or tags they are created in unless they are explicitly passed using a variable scope accessible to both calling templates and custom tags.

Returning Multiple Values from a Custom Tag

If your tag is designed to return multiple caller variables, you might consider returning them as a structure rather than individual variables. Returning a single structure lets you keep everything in a neat package and lets you specify the name of the caller variable (the structure) to return while still letting the tag return multiple values. For example, consider a custom tag that returns information about a person, such as their name, age, hair color, and eye color. Instead of returning four individual variables, you could return a single structure with the person's traits as keys:

```
<!--- Create the person structure --->
<cfset Person = StructNew( )>
<cfset Person.Name = "Rob">
```

```
<cfset Person.Age = 30>
<cfset Person.HairColor = "Brown">
<cfset Person.EyeColor = "Brown">

<!--- Send back the results --->
<cfset "caller.#attributes.OutVarName#" = Person>
```

The key/value pairs contained in the structure returned by this tag can be referenced individually in the calling page like this (assuming the output variable name passed to the custom tag is ThePerson:

```
<cfoutput>
Name: #ThePerson.Name#<br>
Age: #ThePerson.Age#<br>
Hair Color: #ThePerson.HairColor#<br>
Eye Color: #ThePerson.EyeColor#
</cfoutput>
```

Attribute Validation and Error Handling

In the previous section, we touched briefly on the idea of attribute validation when we used the `cfparam` tag to validate and set default values for a custom tag's attributes. This section takes things a step further by demonstrating various techniques you can use to create both required and optional attributes for your tags. Additionally, we'll look at error- and exception-handling strategies you can use to deal with problems that occur in your custom tags.

Handling Required Attributes

Depending on the type of custom tag you create, you may want or need to require certain attributes to be passed in order for the tag to do its job. Making a tag attribute required is as simple as using a `cfif` statement inside the custom tag to evaluate whether the tag exists. This is usually handled by the `IsDefined` function:

```
<cfif IsDefined('attributes.MyRequiredAttrib')>
```

If the required attribute exists, `IsDefined( )` returns `true`, and your tag can continue processing. If, however, `IsDefined( )` returns `false`, the required attribute hasn't been passed to the tag. At this point, you have a few choices:

- Assign a default value for the missing attribute and allow processing to continue. This is one of the approaches we have used in some of the examples up to this point.
- Return a message to the browser letting the user know that a required attribute wasn't passed, and abort all processing using the `cfabort` tag. This is an approach we used in some previous examples.
- Use the `cfexit` tag to exit the custom tag and continue processing the calling template. The `cfexit` tag is discussed in detail later on in this chapter.

- Throw an exception using cfthrow and let the calling template handle the exception based on the exception information provided by the tag.

The cfparam tag can also handle a required attribute that isn't passed into the custom tag by assigning a default value for the attribute:

```
<cfparam name="attributes.MyRequiredAttrib" default="MyValue">
```

If the attribute is passed to the custom tag, the cfparam tag does nothing. However, if the attribute isn't passed to the custom tag, the cfparam tag assigns the default value to the variable specified in name. The disadvantage to using the cfparam method is that you can't really take any additional action if the required attribute isn't present.

Handling Optional Attributes

In some instances, you may want to allow optional attributes to be sent to your custom tags. Optional attributes are generally handled by initializing a variable using the cfparam tag and specifying a default value in case the attribute is not passed to the tag:

```
<cfparam name="attributes.MyOptionalAttribute" type="String" default="Test">
```

You can also handle an optional attribute by checking to see if it was passed in using the IsDefined( ) function and then executing the appropriate code if it is found to exist:

```
<cfif IsDefined('attributes.MyOptionalAttribute')>
HTML and CFML...
</cfif>
```

Using this technique, if the optional attribute is passed in, it is detected, and a block of code is run related to the processing of the optional attribute. If the attribute isn't passed in, the tag ignores the code specific to the optional attribute and continues processing.

Validating Datatypes

Just because a value is passed in for a particular attribute doesn't mean it is the type of value your custom tag is expecting. For example, if you have a custom tag that expects a particular attributes value to be numeric, passing a string full of text may cause the tag to throw an error. ColdFusion provides several built-in tags and functions you can use to evaluate the type of value contained in a particular variable. For one, you can use the cfparam tag to validate a datatype:

```
<cfparam name="attributes.Age" type="Numeric">
```

This code requires an attribute called Age to be of type Numeric. If it isn't, ColdFusion will throw an error when the tag is called.

You can also use functions to validate datatypes within the custom tag body. Some of the more common functions include the following:

`IsArray(`*`value`*` [, `*`dimension`*`])`
: Returns `true` if the *`value`* specified is an array or `false` if it isn't. In addition, `IsArray` can check to see if the array is of a specified *`dimension`* (1, 2, or 3).

`IsBinary(+)`
: Returns `true` if the specified value is binary or `false` if it isn't.

`IsBoolean(`*`value`*`)`
: Returns `true` if the specified value can be converted to a Boolean or `false` if it can't.

`IsDate(`*`string`*`)`
: Returns `true` if the specified string can be converted to a valid date/time object or `false` if it can't.

`IsNumeric(`*`string`*`)`
: Returns `true` if the specified string can be converted to a number or `false` if it can't.

`IsQuery(`*`value`*`)`
: Returns `true` if the specified *`value`* is a valid ColdFusion query or `false` if it isn't.

`IsSimplevalue(`*`value`*`)`
: Returns `true` if the specified value is a number, string, Boolean, or date/time object or `false` if it isn't.

`IsStruct(`*`variable`*`)`
: Returns `true` if the specified variable is a ColdFusion structure or `false` if it isn't.

These functions are most effective when used with the `IsDefined( )` function. For example, suppose you have a custom tag that is expecting the value of an attribute named `Quantity` to be numeric. You can use the following code to make sure the `Quantity` attribute exists and its value is numeric:

```
<cfif IsDefined('attributes.Quantity') and IsNumeric(attributes.Quantity)>
  Continue processing...
<cfelse>
  You attempted to pass a non-numeric value for the attribute <b>Quantity</b>.
  <cfabort>
</cfif>
```

In order for processing to continue, `attributes.Quantity` must exist, and it must be numeric. If either condition is `false`, a message is written to the browser, and all processing (of both the custom tag and the calling template) is aborted.

Error and Exception Handling

It is generally a good idea to use some form of error and exception handling both when you build and when you call custom tags. Using the `cftry`, `cfcatch`, and cfthrow tags discussed in Chapter 9 makes it possible to include robust error- and exception-handling capabilities in your custom tags and the templates that call them.

Typically, a cfthrow tag is used inside a custom tag in an area where an error or exception is likely to occur. For example:

```
<cfif not IsDefined('attributes.MyAttrib')>
  <cfthrow message="You failed to pass a required attribute: <b>MyAttrib</b>"
           type="custom.tag.mytag">
</cfif>
```

Any template that calls the custom tag can then use cftry/cfcatch to trap the error generated by the cfthrow tag:

```
<cftry>
  <cf_mytag>

  <cfcatch type="custom.tag.mytag">
    <cfoutput>
    #cfcatch.Message#
    </cfoutput>
  </cfcatch>
</cftry>
```

Advanced Techniques

There are several advanced features of the custom tag framework you can use to greatly expand the power of custom tags. You can:

- Use two new methods to call custom tags
- Pass multiple attributes to a custom tag via a single attribute
- Create tag pairs
- Create a framework for creating nested tags
- Devise a method to halt the processing of custom tags without halting the processing of the calling template

This section covers each advanced technique and gives examples of how you can use them to extend the power of your ColdFusion applications.

Calling Custom Tags Via cfmodule

As I mentioned earlier in the chapter, the cfmodule tag provides another way to invoke custom tags. Using cfmodule to call your custom tags allows you to call tags located in directories other than the *\cfusionmx\customtags* directory or the directory the calling template resides in. cfmodule also enables you to resolve potential name conflicts among custom tags by allowing you to reference different custom tags that might have the same name but reside in different directories. The syntax for using `cfmodule` follows:

```
<cfmodule template="template"
          name="name"
          attributecollection="structure_containing_attributes"
          attribute1="value"
          attribute2="value"
          ...
          attributen="value">
[</cfmodule>]
```

The following attributes are available to the `cfmodule` tag:

`template`
: Specifies the path to the ColdFusion template to use as a custom tag. Relative paths are automatically expanded from the current page while absolute paths are expanded using the mappings defined in the ColdFusion Administrator. Optional. If a value is specified for `template`, the `name` attribute isn't used.

`name`
: Specifies the name of the custom tag you want to use. The default location for custom tag storage is *\cfusion\customtags*. Custom tags residing in this location may be referenced using dotted notation. For example, a custom tag called `mycustomtag` (*mycustomtag.cfm*) residing in the default custom tags directory (*\cfusionmx\customtags*) is referenced as `mycustomtag`. The same tag residing under a subdirectory of the `customtags` directory called *\specialtags* is referenced as `specialtags.mycustomtag`. This dotted notation may be used to reference custom tags residing in or any number of levels below the default `customtags` directory. Optional. If a value is specified for `name`, the `template` attribute isn't used.

`attributecollection`
: Specifies the name of a ColdFusion structure containing attribute names and their associated values. Optional.

`attribute`*`n`*
: Additional attributes and their associated values as required by the custom tag. Optional.

Now that you know the syntax for the `cfmodule` tag, let's look at a few examples of how to use it to call custom tags. Suppose for a moment that we have a custom tag called `cf_mytag` (*mytag.cfm*) that is located in *\cfusionmx\customtags\subtags\subsubtags*. To call this tag using `cfmodule`, we use the following code:

```
<cfmodule name="subtags.subsubtags.mytag">
```

In this scenario, the `name` attribute is used with the `cfmodule` tag to specify a subdirectory under the *\cfusionmx\customtags* directory where the custom tag resides. The path to the custom tag is specified using a special dot notation to separate the directories.

However, what if `cf_mytag` isn't stored under the *\cfusionmx\customtags* directory? This is where the `template` attribute comes in. Instead of invoking the custom tag with the `name` attribute, it is possible to use the `template` attribute to reference the tag no matter where it is located on the local filesystem. If the custom tag is located in the same directory as the calling template, it can be invoked directly as in the following example:

```
<cfmodule template="mytag.cfm">
```

If, however, the custom tag is located outside the current directory, it can be referenced using a relative path to the tag (the same way the `cfinclude` tag works). For example, the following `cfmodule` tag would call the *mytag.cfm* custom tag located two directories above the location of the calling template:

```
<cfmodule template="../../mytag.cfm">
```

If you close your `cfmodule` tag with a trailing slash or include an end tag for `cfmodule`, the tag you are calling actually executes twice, once for the start tag and once for the end tag. This is an important consideration when using `cfmodule` in this manner to call custom tags, as the custom tag must be properly coded in order to handle both calls. Techniques for handling start and end tag calls are covered later in the section entitled "Creating Tag Pairs."

Importing Custom Tags as a Tag Library

Another option for calling custom tags is to import an entire directory of them as a tag library. This allows you to organize and call your custom tags more effectively. To import a directory of custom tags, you use the `cfimport` tag:

```
<cfimport prefix="UI" taglib="/tags/ui">
```

The `prefix` attribute specifies a prefix to use for referring to imported tags. You refer to an imported tag using syntax like this:

```
<prefix:tagname>
```

Prefix names follow the same naming conventions as ColdFusion variables, with a few exceptions. First, the prefix can't be "cf", and it can't end in an underscore. Additionally, if a blank prefix ("") is specified or the `prefix` attribute is omitted altogether, the tag is referred to using only its name: `<tagname>`. `taglib` is a required attribute and is used to specify the path to the directory containing the custom tags you want to import. By default, the path is relative to the web root. To see how this works, take the `cf_states` (*states.cfm*) template we created earlier and copy it to a directory in your web root called */programmingcf/21*. Then, create and save the template shown in Example 21-7. You can save the template anywhere you desire.

Example 21-7. Importing a custom tag library

```
<cfimport prefix="UI" taglib="/programmingcf/21">

<cfif IsDefined('form.Submit')>
```

Example 21-7. Importing a custom tag library (continued)

```
<cfoutput>
You selected: #form.TheState#
</cfoutput>
</cfif>

<cfoutput>
<form name="MyForm" method="Post" action="#CGI.script_name#">
</cfoutput>
  State: <ui:states selectname="TheState"
                    defaultvalue="NULL"
                    defaultlabel="Please Select">
  <input type="Submit" name="Submit" value="Submit">
</form>
```

The `cfimport` tag imports any custom tags you have stored in the */programmingcf/21* directory and gives them a prefix of `UI` (for "user interface"). Instead of calling the custom tag as `cf_state` or with the `cfmodule` tag, we call it as `<ui:state>`. Attributes are passed just as they are for any other tag.

You can also import more than one tag library in the same namespace. This lets you pull tags from different directories together into the same library. If multiple imported tags share the same name, the first one imported is used:

```
<cfimport prefix="UI" taglib="/tags/ui/javawidgets">
<cfimport prefix="UI" taglib="/tags/ui/flashwidgets">
```

You should be aware of a few additional considerations for using the `cfimport` tag to import custom tag libraries:

- You can't place the `cfimport` tag in a file that is called by `cfinclude`.
- The `cfimport` tag can't be used within an *Application.cfm* template to include the tag library for all templates in an application.
- As with `cfmodule`, if you use an end tag for your prefixed tag call, the custom tag will execute twice: once for the start tag and once for the end tag. Be sure that your custom tag is coded to handle start and end tags.

A noteworthy cfimport bug

There's a bug in the `cfimport` tag (not fixed as of Updater 3) that causes ColdFusion to ignore ColdFusion mappings when trying to import tags from a directory that's outside the web root directory. Normally, ColdFusion allows you to create mappings for just this reason—so that you can have tags like `cfimport` get files from outside the web root without having to expose those templates via URL.

There are basically three workarounds to the mapping bug. The first is to use a web server mapping. This may or may not be desirable as it then opens your tags up to access via URL. The second option is to put the tags you want to import into the */WEB-INF* directory. I prefer not to do this because ColdFusion MX creates this directory in its own directory structure, and its location will vary depending on where you install ColdFusion MX. I'd also hate to see ColdFusion MX overwrite any of my files or directories at a later point.

The third workaround is to create the mapping in the *jrun-web.xml* file in addition to the ColdFusion Administrator:

```
<virtual-mapping>
<resource-path>/web-sys</resource-path>
<system-path>E:/inetsrv/intranet/web-sys</system-path>
</virtual-mapping>
```

That works, but it is obviously a problem for applications that need to be easily deployed to different servers and environments. Hopefully, this is something that's easy for Macromedia to fix and can be included in the next ColdFusion MX Updater.

Adaptive Tags

In the previous section, I mentioned that it's possible to leave the `prefix` attribute out of a `cfimport` call (or specify `prefix=""`). This bit of functionality lets you use the `cfimport` tag as a server-side HTML preprocessor. In other words, you can use `cfimport` to create what are known as *adaptive tags* that replace existing HTML tags with custom functionality.

To understand what I mean, let's create an adaptive tag to replace the HTML `input` tag. Our tag should have all the functionality in the existing `input` tag, and let's add in the ability to specify a new input type: `State`. Specifying `type="State"` should create a select box that contains the 50 U.S. states and the District of Columbia, just like the `cf_states` custom tag we created earlier in the chapter. Example 21-8 shows one way we could do this. Be sure to save the template as *\programmingcf\21\input.cfm*.

Example 21-8. Replacing the HTML input tag with an adaptive tag

```
<cfparam name="attributes.Type" default="Text">

<!--- Build a string with all passesed attributes --->
<cfset TheAttributes="">
<cfloop collection="#attributes#" item="i">
  <cfset TheAttributes = TheAttributes & i & "=" & """#attributes[i]#"""  & " ">
</cfloop>

<cfswitch expression="#attributes.Type#">
  <!-- If the input type is "State" --->
  <cfcase value="State">
    <cfparam name="attributes.Name" default="#attributes.Type#">
    <select name="#attributes.Name#">
      <option value="AL">Alabama</option>
      <option value="AK">Alaska</option>
      <option value="AZ">Arizona</option>
      <option value="AR">Arkansas</option>
      <option value="CA">California</option>
```

Example 21-8. Replacing the HTML input tag with an adaptive tag (continued)

```
      <option value="CO">Colorado</option>
      <option value="CT">Connecticut</option>
      <option value="DE">Delaware</option>
      <option value="DC">District of Columbia</option>
      <option value="FL">Florida</option>
      <option value="GA">Georgia</option>
      <option value="HI">Hawaii</option>
      <option value="ID">Idaho</option>
      <option value="IL">Illinois</option>
      <option value="IN">Indiana</option>
      <option value="IA">Iowa</option>
      <option value="KS">Kansas</option>
      <option value="KY">Kentucky</option>
      <option value="LA">Louisiana</option>
      <option value="ME">Maine</option>
      <option value="MD">Maryland</option>
      <option value="MA">Massachusetts</option>
      <option value="MI">Michigan</option>
      <option value="MN">Minnesota</option>
      <option value="MS">Mississippi</option>
      <option value="MO">Missouri</option>
      <option value="MT">Montana</option>
      <option value="NE">Nebraska</option>
      <option value="NV">Nevada</option>
      <option value="NH">New Hampshire</option>
      <option value="NJ">New Jersey</option>
      <option value="NM">New Mexico</option>
      <option value="NY">New York</option>
      <option value="NC">North Carolina</option>
      <option value="ND">North Dakota</option>
      <option value="OH">Ohio</option>
      <option value="OK">Oklahoma</option>
      <option value="OR">Oregon</option>
      <option value="PA">Pennsylvania</option>
      <option value="RI">Rhode Island</option>
      <option value="SC">South Carolina</option>
      <option value="SD">South Dakota</option>
      <option value="TN">Tennessee</option>
      <option value="TX">Texas</option>
      <option value="UT">Utah</option>
      <option value="VT">Vermont</option>
      <option value="VA">Virginia</option>
      <option value="WA">Washington</option>
      <option value="WV">West Virginia</option>
      <option value="WI">Wisconsin</option>
      <option value="WY">Wyoming</option>
    </select>
  </cfcase>

  <!--- All other input types --->
  <cfdefaultcase>
    <cfoutput><input #Left(TheAttributes, Len(TheAttributes)-1)#></cfoutput>
```

Example 21-8. Replacing the HTML input tag with an adaptive tag (continued)

```
  </cfdefaultcase>
</cfswitch>
```

The first thing you should know is that you have to make the filename for an adaptive tag the same as the HTML tag whose functionality you want to replace. In our example, since we want to replace the HTML `input` tag, we need to save our tag as *input.cfm*.

Our adaptive tag works by checking for an attribute called `type`. Not so coincidentally, the HTML `input` tag also has an attribute called `type`. Because our adaptive tag should behave exactly like the HTML `input` tag unless they type attribute is set to `State`, we need a way to preserve any additional attributes that might be passed to the tag. This is handled by looping over the `attributes` structure and appending each passed attribute to a temporary list variable we'll use in just a moment.

Next, a `cfswitch/cfcase` is used to evaluate the value of `type`. If it's `State`, a select box containing the 50 states and the District of Columbia is output.* Otherwise (the `cfdefaultcase`), an HTML `input` tag is returned with all of the attributes contained in the temporary list we created earlier. You can call the adaptive tag using the following code:

```
<cfimport prefix="" taglib="/programmingcf/21">

Please complete:

<form method="Post" action="<cfoutput>#CGI.Script_Name#</cfoutput>">
  State: <input type="State" name="State"><br>
  Name: <input type="Text" name="Name" width="15" maxlength="255"><br>
  <input type="Submit" name="Submit" value="Submit">
</form>
```

As you can see, by using `cfimport` to import our *input.cfm* template (saved in */programmingcf/21*) and assigning it no prefix, when the HTML `input` tag is used, ColdFusion actually uses our tag instead of the HTML `input` tag. This is the essence of adaptive tags.

Passing Attributes via Structures

The custom tag scope provides an advanced way to pass attribute information from a calling template to the custom tag. Instead of passing attributes individually, you can use a special attribute named `attributecollection` to pass in a structure containing attribute/value pairs. Example 21-9 demonstrates this by creating a structure con-

* We use a different technique here to output the 50-state select box than we did in the `cf_states` custom tag. In the latter we used a two-dimensional array to hold the state abbreviations and names, using a loop to dynamically construct the `option` tags. Example 21-8 uses a simpler but less elegant and extensible approach in which we simply hardcode each `option` tag.

taining an employee record called Employee and passing the structure to a custom tag called CF_DisplayEmployee via the attributecollection attribute.

Example 21-9. Passing attributes using attributecollection

```
<!--- Create a structure called Employee and populate it with the contact
      info for a single employee --->
<cfset Employee = StructNew( )>
<cfset Employee.Name = "Pere Money">
<cfset Employee.Title = "President">
<cfset Employee.Department = "Executive Management">
<cfset Employee.Email = "pere@mycompany.com">
<cfset Employee.PhoneExt = "1234">

<!--- Call the displayemployee custom tag.  Pass the Employee structure to
      the tag as a list of attribute/value pairs using the attributecollection
      attribute. --->
<cf_displayemployee attributecollection = "#Employee#">
```

Alternately, you can make the same tag call using the cfmodule tag in place of cf_displayemployee:

```
<cfmodule template="displayemployee.cfm"
          attributecollection="#Employee#">
```

Regardless of the method you use to call the custom tag, once the structure containing the attributes is passed to the custom tag, it is available inside the tag individually. The cf_displayemployee tag is shown in Example 21-10. Note that we don't have to reference the attribute names as part of the structure. This is what makes the attributecollection attribute so convenient.

Example 21-10. The cf_displayemployee (displayemployee.cfm) custom tag

```
<!--- Display the contents of the attributecollection attribute.  --->
<h2>Employee Detail</h2>
<cfoutput>
<table>
  <tr>
    <td>Name</td><td>#attributes.Name#</td>
  </tr>
  <tr>
    <td>Title</td><td>#attributes.Title#</td>
  </tr>
  <tr>
    <td>Department</td><td>#attributes.Department#</td>
  </tr>
  <tr>
    <td>E-mail</td><td>#attributes.Email#</td>
  </tr>
  <tr>
    <td>Phone Ext.</td><td>#attributes.PhoneExt#</td>
  </tr>
</table>
</cfoutput>
```

Note that an explicitly named attribute takes precedence over a like-named attribute contained in the structure passed by the attributecollection attribute, resulting in the value from the structure being overwritten.

Creating Tag Pairs

The next advanced feature of the custom tag framework is tag pairs. Until now, every custom tag you have created has been called something like:

```
<cf_mytag attribute="value">
```

If you look at HTML and CFML, both languages use end tags to allow you to wrap the functionality of the tag around some sort of arbitrary content. For example, in HTML, almost every tag comes in a pair. That is, each tag has a begin tag and an end tag. Take any of the heading-level tags, for example:

```
<h1>This is a heading level 1</h1>
```

Each heading-level tag contains a begin tag (<h1>) and an end tag (</h1>). Whatever content appears between the tag pairs is marked up by the tags. The same holds true for many CFML tags. Take the cfmail tag, for example:

```
<cfmail from="me@example.com"
        to="you@example.com"
        subject="Tag Pairs">
All of this content falls between the cfmail tag pairs!
</cfmail>
```

In this case, all the content between the <cfmail> and </cfmail> tags is used as the body of an email message.

The custom tag framework gives you the means to create tags like these by providing a special structure called ThisTag. It contains four key/value pairs that can be used with any custom tag to establish a tag pair:

ThisTag.AssocAttribs
: Returns an array of structures containing all the attributes of all nested tags associated with the base tag, as long as the subtags were associated using cfassociate. This variable is returned only if the cfassociate tag is used to associate a nested tag with the base tag (this is covered later in the chapter).

ThisTag.ExecutionMode
: Returns the current execution mode of the tag. ThisTag.ExecutionMode returns Start when the tag is opened, End when the tag is closed, and Inactive if subtags of the base tag are being processed.

ThisTag.GeneratedContent
: Returns any content between the start and end tags. ThisTag.GeneratedContent is a read/write variable and can therefore be written to by your application.

ThisTag.HasEndTag
: Returns true if the tag has an associated end tag and false if it doesn't.

The best way to understand how tag pairs work within the context of custom tags is to look at an example. One use for paired custom tags is something I like to call a site wrapper. A site wrapper is basically a site header and footer all wrapped into a single file. There are a couple of advantages to using a paired custom tag instead of using cfinclude to include a header and footer file. First, using a paired custom tag allows you to put all your header and footer code in a single file instead of using separate files for the header and the footer. The second advantage is that using a custom tag allows you to pass attributes to the page such as a page title and background colors, which isn't possible with includes. Here's the code used to call a basic site wrapper tag we'll call cf_sitewrapper:

```
<cf_sitewrapper>
All your page content goes here...
</cf_sitewrapper>
```

As you can imagine, this type of tag layout is extremely flexible, as it allows you to specify between the tag pairs any text or a variable containing the text. The tag can be used to wrap any page content, and it allows you to pass in a single attribute called title. As you probably guessed already, the value supplied for title is used to populate the page's HTML title tag. The code for the cf_sitewrapper tag (*sitewrapper.cfm*) is shown in Example 21-11.

Example 21-11. cf_sitewrapper custom tag

```
<cfsetting enablecfoutputonly="Yes">
<!---
NAME:           cf_sitewrapper
FILE:           sitewrapper.cfm
CREATED:        02/13/2003
LAST MODIFIED:
VERSION:        1.0
AUTHOR:         Rob Brooks-Bilson (rbils@amkor.com)
DESCRIPTION:    cf_sitewrapper is a custom CFML tag that implements a site's
                header and footer as a wrapper.
ATTRIBUTES:     Title: HTML title for the page
KNOWN ISSUES:   None
--->

<!--- Set attribute defaults --->
<cfparam name="attributes.Title" default="Example.com">

<cfif ThisTag.ExecutionMode is "Start">
  <cfif not ThisTag.HasEndTag>
    <cfabort showerror="The cf_sitewrapper tag requires an end tag.">
  </cfif>

  <cfoutput>
  <html>
  <head>
    <title>#attributes.Title#</title>
  </head>
```

Example 21-11. cf_sitewrapper custom tag (continued)

```
  <body>
  <table>
    <tr>
      <td>
        <a href="index.cfm">Home</a> |
        <a href="products.cfm">Products</a> |
        <a href="services.cfm">Services</a> |
        <a href="contact.cfm">Contact</a>
      </td>
    </tr>
    <tr>
      <td><hr noshade></td>
    </tr>
    <tr>
      <td><br>
    </cfoutput>
<cfelse>
    <cfoutput>
        <br>
      </td>
    </tr>
    <tr>
      <td><hr noshade></td>
    </tr>
    <tr>
      <td>
        Copyright #Year(Now( ))#, All Rights Reserved
      </td>
    </tr>
  </table>
</body>
</html>
</cfoutput>
</cfif>
<cfsetting enablecfoutputonly="No">
```

When a paired custom tag is called, ColdFusion actually calls the tag twice, once for the start tag and once when the end tag is encountered. Because we don't want the entire functionality of a custom tag actually to execute twice, we need a mechanism to determine when the tag is called and when it ends so that we can program the tag's functionality accordingly. To determine whether a custom tag is being called as a start tag or end tag, you can look at the value of `ThisTag.ExecutionMode`. If it is `Start` (as it would be when the opening tag is encountered), we use a `cfif` statement to evaluate `ThisTag.HasEndTag`. If it evaluates `false`, we know that no end tag is present, so an error message is written to the browser, and all processing is halted. If the value is `true`, we know that an end tag is present, and processing continues. The rest of the code that runs when `ThisTag.ExecutionMode` is `Start` writes out the header text for the page, which in this case is just a navigation bar. The HTML `title` tag is populated with the value passed in via the `title` attribute. If no `title` attribute is passed, a default value is used instead.

The actual page content (the stuff between the start and end tag of our custom tag call) outputs as soon as the end of the code in the `cfif` statement finishes. The second time the tag is called (when the end tag is detected), `ThisTag.ExecutionMode` is `End`, and the code following the `cfelse` tag executes. In this case, the code is our footer code that displays a page break and a copyright notice for the page.

To test the `cf_sitewrapper` tag, create the template shown in Example 21-12 and save it to the same directory you saved the custom tag in.

Example 21-12. Template for calling the cf_sitewrapper tag

```
<cf_sitewrapper title="Welcome to my page">
<h2>Welcome to my site</h2>

Today's date is <cfoutput>#DateFormat(Now( ),'mm/dd/yyyy')#</cfoutput>
<p>
Please feel free to look around...
</p>
</cf_sitewrapper>
```

Executing the template in Example 21-12 results in the output shown in Figure 21-5.

Figure 21-5. Providing a header and footer via custom tag

Nesting Custom Tags

Another benefit to creating tag pairs is the ability to create nested custom tags. Nested custom tags allow you to create sets of tags that can share data with one another. In CFML, a good example is the cfhttp and cfhttpparam tags. The tags can be nested as in the following example:

```
<cfhttp URL="http://127.0.0.1/foo.cfm"
        method="Post">
    <cfhttpparam type="Formfield" name="Name" value="Pere Money">
    <cfhttpparam type="Formfield" name="Title" value="President">
</cfhttp>
```

In this case, the cfhttp tag is the parent tag while the two cfhttpparam tags are considered the children. The cfhttpparam tags can pass the information contained in their attributes to the cfhttp tag so that it can be posted to another template specified by the cfhttp tag.

There are several metaphors that describe the relationships between nested custom tags. The most commonly used terms to describe the nesting relationship are ancestor/descendant, base/sub, and parent/child tags. These terms are used interchangeably throughout this section.

Another important concept to understand in ancestor/descendant tag relationships is that a single tag can be both an ancestor and a descendant. Consider the following example:

```
<cf_basetag>
    <cf_subtag>
        <cf_subsubtag>
    </cf_subtag>
</cf_basetag>
```

In this example, cf_basetag is a parent tag. cf_subtag is a child tag of cf_basetag, but it is also a parent tag of cf_subsubtag. cf_subsubtag is a child tag of both cf_subtag and cf_basetag. What is interesting about how ColdFusion handles nested-tag communication is the fact that you can have any parent or child tag pass information to any of its parent or child tags. How is this done? ColdFusion provides you with one tag and two functions that make the inter-tag communication possible.

The cfassociate tag associates a child tag with a parent by saving all the child tag's attributes to a special structure that is available to the parent tag. cfassociate takes two attributes, basetag and datacollection. basetag specifies the name of the parent tag to associate with the child tag. datacollection specifies a name for the structure used to pass all the attribute information from the child tag to the parent tag. If datacollection isn't specified, ColdFusion uses the default structure AssocAttribs.

It is also possible for a child tag to request information about its ancestors. There are two functions that facilitate this:

`GetBaseTagList()`
: Returns a comma-delimited list (in uppercase) of ancestor tag names. `GetBaseTagList` is meant for use in custom CFML tags for inter-tag data exchange. The first element in the returned list of ancestor tags is always the top-level parent tag.

`GetBaseTagData(`*`ta[,instance]`*`)`
: Returns an object containing data from the specified ancestor *`tag`*. An optional *`instance`* number may be set to specify the number of ancestor tag levels to skip through before returning data. The default value for *`instance`* is 1.

As always, the best way to explain the interaction between nested tags is with an example. In this case, we'll need to create three templates to accomplish the task. Example 21-13 through Example 21-15 show how to create a simple demonstration of how nested tags communicate and how you can use the functions and tags we just discussed to abstract the underlying complexity.

Example 21-13. Nesting custom tags

```
<h3>We start in the calling template</h3>

<!--- Call the cf_basetag custom tag and nest a number of cf_subtag tags.  Also
      call two cf_subtag tags outside the cf_basetag to demonstrate how to
      handle orphaned cf_subtag tags --->
<cf_basetag title="Colors">
   <cf_subtag title="Red">
   <cf_subtag title="Yellow">
   <cf_subtag title="Green">
   <cf_subtag title="Blue">
   <cf_subtag>
</cf_basetag>
<cf_subtag title="Orange">
<cf_subtag title="Silver">
<h3>We end up back in the calling template</h3>

<!--- If there are any orphaned cf_subtag tags, output their attributes here --->
<cfif IsDefined('request.OrphanList')>
  <cfoutput>
  <h3>There were #ListLen(request.OrphanList)# orphaned sub tags found:</h3>
  </cfoutput>
  <ul>
  <cfloop index="i" list="#request.OrphanList#">
    <cfoutput>
    <li>#i#</li>
    </cfoutput>
  </cfloop>
  </ul>
</cfif>
```

Example 21-13 shows the caller template used to call our nested tags. Executing the template results in the output shown in Figure 21-6.

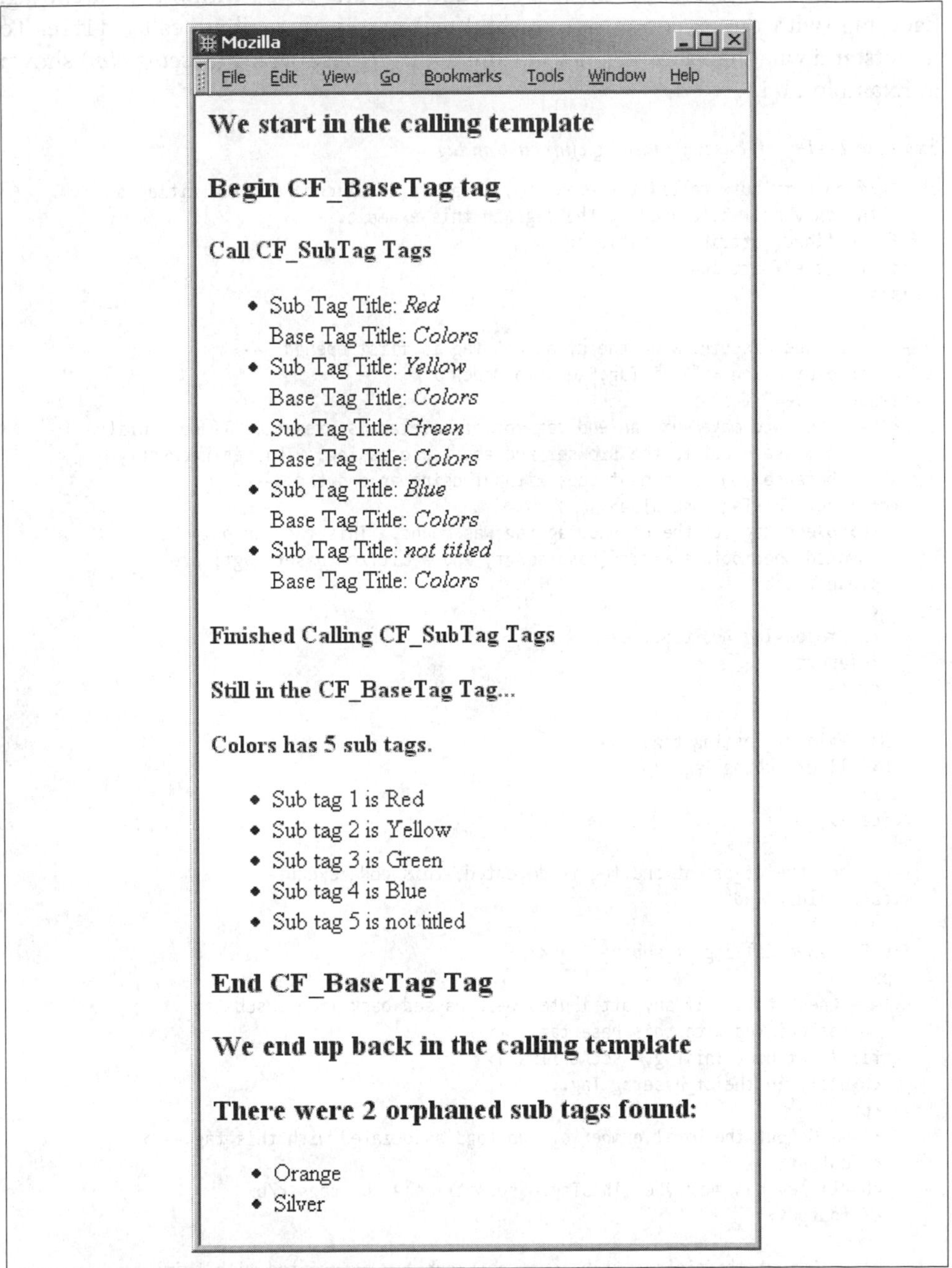

Figure 21-6. Demonstrating communication between nested custom tags

Now that you have an idea of what the output looks like, let's discuss what went on behind the scenes to make it happen. Once the template in Example 21-13 is executed, a call to cf_basetag is made. Five child tags are nested within the parent tag. Each tag (with the exception of one child tag) passes an attribute called `title`. To understand what happens next, let's examine the cf_basetag tag (*basetag.cfm*) shown in Example 21-14.

Example 21-14. cf_basetag (basetag.cfm) custom tag

```
<!--- If an attribute called title exists, create a local copy of it.  title is
      the only attribute used by the tags in this example. --->
<cfif IsDefined('attributes.title')>
  <cfset title = attributes.title>
</cfif>

<!--- This code executes when the cf_parent tag is first opened --->
<cfswitch expression = "#ThisTag.ExecutionMode#">
  <cfcase value="Start">
    <!--- Check to make sure an end tag for cf_basetag is present.  If not, write
          a message out to the browser and abort processing.  This is necessary
          because you can't nest tags without using an end tag. --->
    <cfif not ThisTag.HasEndTag>
      <b>No end tag for the cf_basetag tag was found.  This tag can only be
      invoked when both a &lt;cf_basetag&gt; and a &lt;/cf_basetag&gt; are
      present.</b>
      <p>
      <b>Processing Aborted...</b>
      <cfabort>
    </cfif>

    <h3>Begin cf_basetag tag</h3>
    <b>Call cf_subtag Tags</b>
    <ul>
  </cfcase>

  <!--- When the cf_parent end tag is detected, this code executes --->
  <cfcase value="End">
    </ul>
    <b>Finished Calling cf_subtag Tags</b>
    <p>
    <!--- Check to see if any attributes were passed back from a sub tag
          associated with this base tag --->
    <cfif IsDefined('ThisTag.AssocAttribs')>
      <b>Still in the cf_basetag Tag...</b>
      <p>
      <!--- Output the total number of sub tags associated with this tag --->
      <cfoutput>
      <b>#title# has #ArrayLen(ThisTag.AssocAttribs)# sub tags.</b>
      </cfoutput>

      <!--- Output the title attribute of each sub tag associated with this
            tag --->
```

Example 21-14. cf_basetag (basetag.cfm) custom tag (continued)

```
      <ul>
      <cfloop index="i" from="1" to="#ArrayLen(ThisTag.AssocAttribs)#">
        <cfoutput>
        <li>Sub tag #i# is #ThisTag.AssocAttribs[i].title#</li>
        </cfoutput>
      </cfloop>
      </ul>
    </cfif>

    <h3>End cf_basetag Tag</h3>
  </cfcase>
</cfswitch>
```

The tag starts by checking to see if an attribute called `title` is passed in. If so, a local variable called `title` is set. Next, `ThisTag.ExecutionMode` is checked to see if the value is `Start`. If so, the template checks to make sure an end tag for `cf_basetag` is present by evaluating the value of `ThisTag.HasEndTag`. If no end tag is found, a message is written out to the browser, and all processing of both the custom tag and the calling template is aborted. This is necessary because you can't nest tags without using an end tag. If everything up through here is okay, a message that processing of the custom tag has begun and that the subtags are being called is output to the browser.

At this point, any subtags located between the start and end tags of `cf_basetag` are processed. Let's examine what happens inside the subtags in Example 21-15. Then we'll come back to the rest of the code in `cf_basetag`.

Example 21-15. cf_subtag (subtag.cfm) custom tag

```
<!--- If no title attribute is passed with a sub tag, specify "not titled" for
      the title.  If you wanted to make title a required attribute, you could
      use IsDefined to check for its existence here.  If title wasn't passed,
      processing could be aborted or exited --->
<cfparam name="attributes.title" default="not titled">

<!--- Initialize a request variable called OrphanList.  This variable is used
      to hold a comma delimited list of orphaned cf_subtag titles in the event
      that there are any.  The request scope is used so that the list can be
      available to the calling template (or any other template) within the
      scope of this page request --->
<cfparam name="request.OrphanList" default="">

<!--- Retrieve a list of all ancestor tags --->
<cfset AncestorTags = GetBaseTagList( )>
<!--- Look for cf_basetag in the list of retrieved ancestor tags.  If it is
      found, get all of the base tag's information and assign it to a variable
      called ParentTagData.  Then, output the title for each cf_subtag as
      well as the sub tag's base tag name --->
<cfif ListFindNoCase(AncestorTags, "cf_basetag")>
   <cfoutput>
   <cfset BaseTagData = GetBaseTagData("cf_basetag")>
```

Example 21-15. cf_subtag (subtag.cfm) custom tag (continued)

```
    <li>Sub Tag Title: <I>#attributes.title#</I><br>
        Base Tag Title: <I>#BaseTagData.title#</I></li>
    </cfoutput>
    <!--- Associate this tag with the base tag (cf_basetag) --->
    <cfassociate basetag="cf_basetag">
<cfelse>
    <!--- If there are any orphaned sub tags, append their names to the
          request.OrphanList variable we initialized earlier.  This variable
          is automatically available to any template within the scope of this
          request, including the calling template --->
    <cfoutput>
    <cfset request.OrphanList = ListAppend(request.OrphanList,
           attributes.title)>
    </cfoutput>
</cfif>
```

In Example 21-15, the first thing each `cf_subtag` does is assign a default value for the `title` attribute that can be passed to the tag. If no `title` exists, `not titled` is assigned as the default.

Next, a default value of `""` is assigned to a request variable called `request.OrphanList`. This variable holds a comma-delimited list of the `title` attributes of any `cf_subtag` tags that are called outside the `cf_basetag` tag. Child tags called outside the scope of their parent tag are more commonly known as orphaned tags. The request scope is used so that the list of orphaned tags is available to any template (including and especially the calling template) within the scope of this page request.

The next part of the template calls the `GetBaseTagList()` function. The function returns a comma-delimited list of ancestor tag names for the subtag. The list is written to a variable called `AncestorTags`.

The `ListFindNoCase()` function looks for `cf_basetag` in the list of ancestor tags stored in the `AncestorTags` variable. If it is found, all the base tag's information is assigned to a variable called `BaseTagData`. Next, the `title` for each `cf_subtag` as well as the subtag's parent tag `title` is output to the browser. Finally, the subtag is associated with `cf_basetag` using the `cfassociate` tag. This lets the subtag share all of its information with the parent tag.

If `cf_basetag` isn't found in the list of ancestor tags, we know that the subtag is an orphaned tag, so we write its `title` to the `request.OrphanList` variable so that it can be passed back to the calling template.

When the last `cf_subtag` has finished processing, control is returned back to the `cf_basetag` tag. At that point, evaluating `ThisTag.GeneratedContent` returns `End`. A message is written to the browser that we have finished calling all the subtags. Next, the total number of child tags associated with the `cf_basetag` tag is output by evaluating the length of the variable `ThisTag.AssocAttribs`. If you remember from earlier, `ThisTag.AssocAttribs` is an array of structures that contain all the attribute values from each child tag. The ArrayLen( ) function returns the length of the array, which represents the number of structures returned (one for each subtag).

Next, the title of each subtag is output to the browser by looping over each structure in the ThisTag.AssocAttribs array. When the loop is finished, a message is output to the browser letting you know that the cf_basetag has finished processing. At this point, processing reverts to the calling template.

The calling template in Example 21-13 finishes up by outputting a message that processing has been passed back to it. Finally, a check is made to see if the variable request.OrphanList exists. If it does, we know that there were some orphaned tags encountered. The list is looped over, and the title from each orphaned tag is output to the browser.

Extending cf_sitewrapper with child tags

To understand how you might use child tags in a real-world application, consider the cf_sitewrapper custom tag we created earlier in the chapter. As you'll recall, cf_sitewrapper allows us to wrap any content with a standard header and footer. While this is a great way to provide a common header and footer for a site, it could be better. For instance, the navigation bar in the header portion of the cf_sitewrapper tag is hard-coded. This means that it displays the same links for every page that uses the tag. It also means that in order to add a new page to the navigation bar, you must modify the custom tag. By using child tags, however, we can rewrite the cf_sitewrapper tag to allow us to pass in the items that should appear on the navigation bar as subtags of the cf_sitewrapper tag. Here is one way to do this:

```
<cf_sitewrapper>
  <cf_sitewrapperlink linkname="Home" location="index.cfm" target="_self">
  <cf_sitewrapperlink linkname="Help" location="help.cfm" target="_self">
  ...
Page content goes here...
</cf_sitewrapper>
```

And here is another:

```
<cfmodule template="sitewrapper.cfm">
  <cfmodule template="sitewrapperlink.cfm" linkname="Home" location="index.cfm"
            target="_self" />
  <cfmodule template="sitewrapperlink.cfm" linkname="Help" location="help.cfm"
            target="_self" />
  ...
Page content goes here...
</cfmodule>
```

Using this syntax, we can pass any number of links for use in the cf_sitewrapper tag's navigation bar. The code for the cf_sitewrapperlink tag is simple:

```
<cfsilent>
<!--- Associate this tag with cf_sitewrapper as the parent --->
<cfassociate basetag="cf_sitewrapper">
```

```
<cfparam name="attributes.linkname">
<cfparam name="attributes.location">
<cfparam name="attributes.target" default="_self">
</cfsilent>
```

All the cf_sitewrapperlink tag does is associate itself with its parent tag (in this case, the cf_sitewrapper tag), and cfparam attributes for the link's linkname, location, and target. You'll see how these attributes are used in just a moment.

The bulk of the work is still done by the cf_sitewrapper tag. You'll need to modify it slightly from the one we created earlier. The new version needs to handle the data passed in by each cf_sitewrapperLink child tag, using it to construct the navigation menu dynamically. The code for the modified cf_sitewrapper tag is shown in Example 21-16.

Example 21-16. Using child tags with cf_sitewrapper

```
<cfsetting enablecfoutputonly="Yes">
<!---
NAME:           cf_sitewrapper
FILE:           sitewrapper.cfm
CREATED:        02/13/2003
LAST MODIFIED:
VERSION:        1.0
AUTHOR:         Rob Brooks-Bilson (rbils@amkor.com)
DESCRIPTION:    cf_sitewrapper is a custom CFML tag that implements a site's
                header and footer as a wrapper.
ATTRIBUTES:     Title: HTML title for the page
KNOWN ISSUES:   None
--->

<!--- Set attribute defaults --->
<cfparam name="attributes.title" default="Example.com">
<cfparam name="ThisTag.AssocAttribs" default=#ArrayNew(1)#>
<!--- Default links go here.  This is where defaults can be "hard coded".
      Multiple links should be delimited with a comma (no spaces). If
      you don't want any defaults, set Links="". --->
<cfparam name="Links" default="<a href=""index.cfm"">Home</a>">
<!--- Create a temp var to hold the page content between tag pairs --->
<cfset LocalContent = ThisTag.GeneratedContent>
<!--- Clear the generated page content --->
<cfset ThisTag.GeneratedContent = "">
<!--- Loop over the passed in links (subtags), appending them to a list --->
<cfloop from="1" to="#ArrayLen(ThisTag.AssocAttribs)#" index="i">
  <cfset Links = ListAppend(Links, "<a href=""#ThisTag.AssocAttribs[i].Location#""
  target=""#ThisTag.AssocAttribs[i].Target#"">
  #ThisTag.AssocAttribs[i].LinkName#</a>", "|")>
</cfloop>
<!--- Replace the commas in the list with pipes for cosmetics --->
<cfset Links = Replace(Links, "|", " | ", "All")>

<cfswitch expression="#ThisTag.ExecutionMode#">
  <cfcase value="Start">
```

Example 21-16. Using child tags with cf_sitewrapper (continued)

```
    <cfif not ThisTag.HasEndTag>
      <cfabort showerror="The cf_sitewrapper tag requires an end tag.">
    </cfif>
  </cfcase>

  <cfcase value="End">
    <cfoutput>
    <html>
    <head>
      <title>#attributes.title#</title>
    </head>

    <body>
    <table>
      <tr>
        <!--- Output the links passed by the child tags --->
        <td>#Links#</td>
      </tr>
      <tr>
        <td><hr noshade></td>
      </tr>
      <tr>
         <!--- Output the content between the cf_sitewrapper tags --->
        <td><br>#LocalContent#<br></td>
      </tr>
      <tr>
        <td><hr noshade></td>
      </tr>
      <tr>
        <td>
          Copyright #Year(Now( ))#, All Rights Reserved
        </td>
      </tr>
    </table>
    </body>
    </html>
    </cfoutput>
  </cfcase>
</cfswitch>
<cfsetting enablecfoutputonly="No">
```

The modified `cf_sitewrapper` tag works just like the original, with one exception. Instead of generating the navigation bar with hardcoded links, the tag uses the information from any `cf_sitewrapperlink` tags to dynamically build the navigation bar. This is done by looping over the `ThisTag.AssocAttribs` array and generating the necessary link code from the data passed in by the child tags. You can predefine any links you want to appear regardless of what's passed in by adding them to the `links` variable created with the `cfparam` tag.

To test out the new `cf_sitewrapper` tag, call the following code, which passes three links (in addition to the default hardcoded link) to the tag:

```
<cf_sitewrapper title="Welcome to my page">
  <cf_sitewrapperlink linkname="Products" location="products.cfm">
  <cf_sitewrapperlink linkname="Services" location="services.cfm">
  <cf_sitewrapperlink linkname="Contact" location="contact.cfm" target="_blank">

<h2>Welcome to my site</h2>

Today's date is <cfoutput>#DateFormat(Now( ),'mm/dd/yyyy')#</cfoutput>
<p>
Please feel free to look around...
</p>
</cf_sitewrapper>
```

Aborting Tag Processing

Sometimes, it is desirable to halt processing within a custom tag. There are many reasons why you might opt to do so, including error handling, attribute validation, and conditional processing. You can use the `cfabort` tag inside a custom tag to halt processing, but doing that terminates the processing of the calling template or tag as well. There is, however, a tag you can use that allows you to halt processing of a custom tag, exit the tag gracefully, and resume processing of the template or tag that made the original call to the custom tag. That tag is `cfexit`.

The `cfexit` tag is similar in functionality to the `cfabort` tag except that it is intended for use within custom tags. If the `cfexit` tag is used outside a custom tag, it behaves the same as the `cfabort` tag. The syntax for calling the `cfexit` tag is:

```
<cfexit method="method">
```

The tag takes a single attribute, `method`, that specifies the method to use in exiting the custom tag. Each method produces different results depending on where you locate the `cfexit` tag within your custom tag. Possible entries for `method` are:

`ExitTag` *(default)*
: When placed in the base tag, processing of the custom tag is halted, and control returns to the calling template. If placed within a block of code where `ThisTag.ExecutionMode` is `Start` or `ThisTag.ExecutionMode` is `End`, processing continues after the end tag.

`ExitTemplate`
: When placed in the base tag, processing of the custom tag is halted, and control returns to the calling template. If placed within a block of code where `ThisTag.ExecutionMode` is `Start`, processing continues from the first child tag of the calling tag. If `ThisTag.ExecutionMode` is `End`, processing continues after the end tag.

`Loop`
: Reexecutes a block of code in the currently executing custom tag (emulates a `cfloop`). This method can be used only when `ThisTag.ExecutionMode` is `End`. Using it in any other location results in an error.

The cfexit tag is most commonly used to halt the processing of a custom tag, exit the custom tag, and then resume processing of the calling template. Example 21-17 creates a custom tag called cf_exittagtest. Make sure to save the template as *exittagtest.cfm* in the directory you intend to call it from.

Example 21-17. cf_exittagtest custom tag

```
<cfif IsDefined('attributes.Name')>
   <cfset Local_Name = attributes.Name>
<cfelse>
You failed to pass a required attribute: <b>Name</b>
<cfexit method = "ExitTag">
</cfif>

<cfoutput>
Hello #attributes.Name#!
</cfoutput>
<!--- The rest of your tag goes here --->
```

The cf_exittagtest tag checks to see if an attribute called Name was passed in by the tag call. If it exists, the custom tag simply outputs the value of the attribute. If, however, the Name attribute doesn't exist, execution of the tag is halted, the tag is exited, and processing of the calling template resumes.

You can test cf_exittagtest by creating the template shown in Example 21-18. Be sure to save it in the same directory you saved the *exittagtest.cfm* template in.

Example 21-18. Template for calling the cf_exittagtest custom tag

```
<h2>Exiting a custom tag using &lt;cfexit method="Tag"&gt;</h2>
<b>This is in the Calling Template</b>
<p>
<!--- Call the ExitTagTest custom tag. --->
<cf_exittagtest>
<p>
<b>We're back to the Calling Template again</b>
```

You can also use cfexit to emulate the behavior of a conditional cfloop within the context of a custom tag. By setting the method attribute of the cfexit tag to Loop, you can have ColdFusion iterate over the same block of code in the custom tag until a specific condition is met. The template shown in Example 21-19 creates a custom tag called cf_exitlooptest (save it as *exitlooptest.cfm*) that demonstrates using the cfexit tag with the method set to Loop.

Example 21-19. cf_exitlooptest custom tag

```
<cfswitch expression = "#ThisTag.ExecutionMode#">
  <cfcase value="Start">
    <cfset Count=1>
    <b>Start Tag Execution...</b><br>
  </cfcase>
```

Example 21-19. cf_exitlooptest custom tag (continued)

```
  <cfcase value="End">
   <cfif Count lte 10>
     <cfoutput>Iteration #Count#<br></cfoutput>
     <cfset Count = Count + 1>
     <!--- This cfexit tag causes the body of the End ExecutionMode to execute
           again and again until Count=10.  When Count = 10, the tag is exited
           and processing is returned to the calling template. --->
     <cfexit method="Loop">
   </cfif>
   <b>End Tag Execution.</b>
  </cfcase>
</cfswitch>
```

The custom tag in Example 21-19 begins by checking the value of `ThisTag.ExecutionMode`. If it is `Start`, a counter variable called `Count` is set to `1`, and a message is written back to the calling template that reads "Start Tag Execution".

If `ThisTag.ExecutionMode` is `End`, a `cfif` statement evaluates the value of `Count`. If `Count` is less than or equal to 10, its value is output to the browser. The value of `Count` is then incremented by 1. Setting `method` to `Loop` reprocesses the contents of the `cfcase` statement, effectively creating a conditional loop until the value of `Count` is equal to 10. Once `Count` is greater than 10, the `cfif` statement evaluates `false`, and the custom tag returns processing control back over to the calling template.

To call the `cf_exitlooptest` tag, create the template shown in Example 21-20 and save it to the same directory you saved the *exitlooptest.cfm* template to. Note the tag is called using the syntax `<cf_exitlooptest/>`. The trailing forward slash indicates an end tag without actually having to code the opening and closing `<cf_exitlooptest>` and `</cf_exitlooptest>` tags.

Example 21-20. Template for calling the cf_exitlooptest custom tag

```
<h2>Exiting a custom tag using &lt;cfexit method="Loop"&gt;</h2>
<b>This is in the Calling Template</b>
<p>
<!--- Call the ExitLoopTest custom tag.  Note the trailing forward slash used to
      call the tag.  This indicates a start and end tag without having to write
      two lines of code --->
<cf_exitlooptest/>
<p>
<b>We're back to the Calling Template again</b>
```

Protecting Your Tags

ColdFusion comes with a command-line utility called CFEncode you can use to obfuscate the source code in your CFML templates so that it can't be easily viewed. The obfuscation process is designed to be one-way, so you should make sure you have a backup copy of any templates you wish to encode before proceeding. You should also be aware that the mechanism used to encode tags is relatively weak and has been broken in the past. For this reason, you shouldn't rely on the encoding mechanism as the sole means for protecting your source code.

To run the CFEncode utility (located in *\cfusionmx\bin* by default), simply execute it using the following syntax:

```
cfencode infile outfile [/r /q] [/h "header"] /v"2"
```

The following list explains each parameter and switch:

`infile`
: Specifies the name of the CFML template to be encoded. Optionally, you may specify a wildcarded filename if you wish to encode more than one template at a time.

`outfile`
: Specifies the full path to the output file for the encoded file. If you fail to specify an output file, the CFEncode utility overwrites the original file with the encoded version. For this reason, it is important that you always keep a backup copy of any templates you wish to encode.

`/r`
: Specifies that encoding should be recursive. This switch is used when you use a wildcard as the *`infile`* parameter, and you wish to have the CFEncode utility recurse subdirectories.

`/q`
: Specifying this optional switch turns off any warning messages usually generated by the utility.

`/h`
: Specifies a custom header to include at the beginning of the encoded file. This is an optional switch.

`/v`
: This switch allows you to use version-specific encoding. Possible values are `1` and `2`. Specifying `1` sets the encoding level at ColdFusion 3.x. Specifying `2` sets the encoding level at ColdFusion 4.0 or later. Unless you are encoding the tag to be used exclusively with ColdFusion 3.x, you should set this switch to `2`.

CFX Tags

As I mentioned in the beginning of the chapter, ColdFusion can be extended through another type of custom tag called a CFX tag. CFX tags differ from CFML custom tags in a number of ways:

- They are created in Visual C++ or Java.
- They are compiled (*.dll* for Visual C++, *.class* for Java).

- They must be registered in the ColdFusion Administrator before they can be used.
- They may or may not be cross-platform.
- They can extend the capabilities of the ColdFusion Application Server in ways that CFML tags can't by performing tasks not native to ColdFusion.
- They generally execute faster than CFML tags (because they are compiled).

Registering CFX Tags

Before a CFX tag can be used, it must be registered in the ColdFusion Administrator. The following steps outline the procedure for ColdFusion MX. If you use an earlier version, the actual registration process and screens may vary slightly. Save the tag to your ColdFusion server. The default directory for custom tags is *\cfusionmx\customtags*.

1. Under the Extensions section of the ColdFusion Administrator, click on the CFX Tags link. This takes you to the Registered CFX Tags page (shown in Figure 21-7).
2. Click the button corresponding to the type of CFX tag you wish to register. Choose C++ for tags written in C++ or choose Java for tags written in Java.
3. Depending on whether you are registering a C++ CFX tag or a Java CFX tag, follow the additional steps outlined in the appropriate following section.

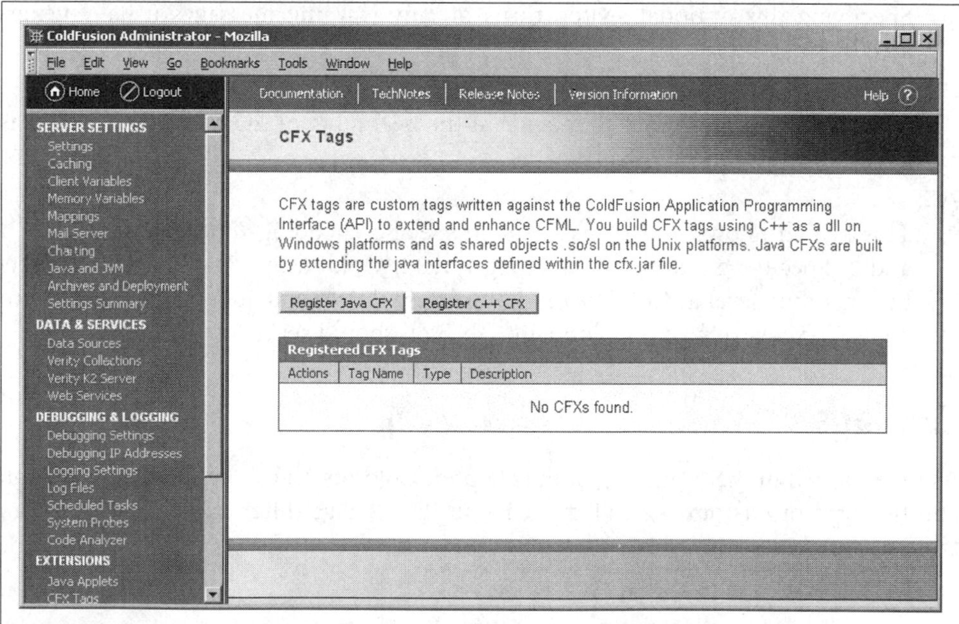

Figure 21-7. Registering a CFX tag in the ColdFusion Administrator

Registering C++ CFX tags

After clicking the Register C++ CFX button on the Registered CFX Tags page, you are taken to Add/Edit C++ CFX Tag (Figure 21-8). Here you must fill in a few details about your CFX tag before it can be registered:

1. Choose a name to register for your CFX tag. The name can be anything you want as long as it begins with `cfx_` and contains only letters, numbers, and underscores.
2. Enter the location to the CFX tag's *.dll* file on your server in the Server Library (DLL) field. If you don't know the location, you can click the Browse button to search through the local filesystem.
3. Make sure the Keep Library Loaded checkbox is checked; otherwise ColdFusion has to reload the tag into memory each time the tag is requested
4. You may enter an optional description for the tag in the Description field. The description is viewable only within the ColdFusion Administrator and generally serves as a reminder so you don't later forget what the tag is used for.
5. When you have finished adding all the setup information about the tag, click on the Submit Changes button to complete the registration process and to return to the Registered CFX Tags page.

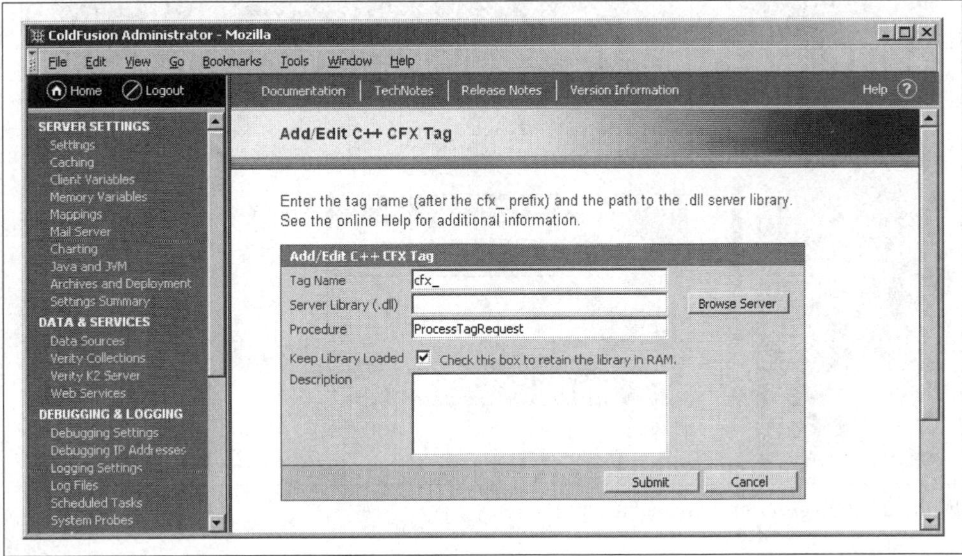

Figure 21-8. Registering a C++ CFX Tag

Registering Java CFX tags

If you choose to register a Java CFX tag from the Registered CFX Tags, you do so from the Add/Edit Java CFX Tag page shown in Figure 21-9. Here's what you need to do to register:

1. Choose a name to register for your CFX tag. The name can be anything you want as long as it begins with `cfx_` and contains only letters, numbers, and underscores.
2. In the Class Name field, enter the name of the CFX tag's Java class file. The Class Path for Java CFX tags is defined in the Java section of the ColdFusion Administrator.
3. You may enter an optional description for the tag in the Description field. The description is viewable only within the ColdFusion Administrator and generally serves as a reminder so you don't later forget what the tag is used for.
4. When you have finished adding all the setup information about the tag, click on the Submit Changes button to complete the registration process and to return to the Registered CFX Tags page.

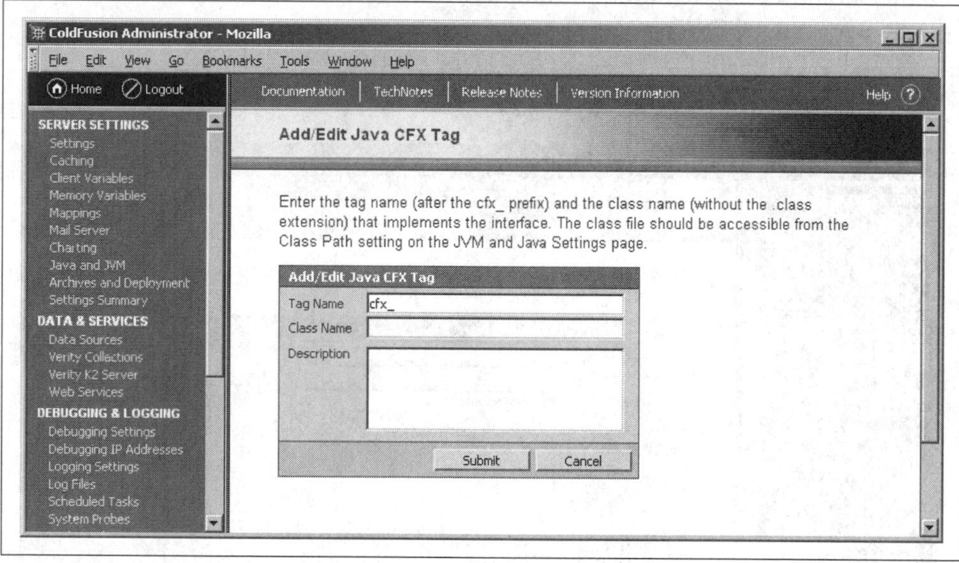

Figure 21-9. Registering a Java CFX tag

Calling CFX Tags

Calling a CFX tag is simple and follows the same basic syntax used to call a custom CFML tag:

```
<cfx_mycustomtag attribute1="value"
                 attributen="value">
```

In this example, the CFX tag is named `cfx_mycustomtag` (*mycustomtag.dll*). We differentiate calling a CFX tag from calling a regular custom tag by prefixing the call with `cfx_`.

Additional Resources

A thorough discussion on building CFX tags is well beyond the scope of this book. For more information on how you can create your own CFX tags, see the ColdFusion documentation from Macromedia.

The Macromedia Developer's Exchange (*http://devex.macromedia.com/developer/gallery/*) is a good place to look for preexisting CFX tags. At last count, there were several dozen CFX tags that were available for download free of charge as well as links to several other commercial tags.

CHAPTER 22
ColdFusion Components

ColdFusion Components (CFCs) are new in ColdFusion MX. CFCs offer an additional way to encapsulate code beyond the capabilities provided by includes, user-defined functions, and custom tags. CFCs give you a framework for leveraging object-oriented principles and techniques to better organize and reuse your code. CFCs also serve as the primary interface for web services in ColdFusion MX, as well as for integration between Flash MX and ColdFusion MX via Flash Remoting.

In previous versions of ColdFusion, if you wanted to encapsulate your code, you basically had three options. You could put your code in a separate file and `cfinclude` it, you could write it as a UDF, or you could create a custom tag. Each technique had its advantages and disadvantages, as well as appropriate usages.

A CFC-based architecture offers several advantages over previous methods for developing ColdFusion applications. Because CFCs take an object-oriented approach to ColdFusion application development, they offer a formalized, structured framework for developing application functionality. This not only tends to make your ColdFusion code easier to read, but it also generally makes your code easier to maintain.

If you are at all hesitant about object-oriented programming, don't be. A large chunk of what you need to know to work with CFCs, you already learned back in Chapter 20. In fact, user-defined functions serve as the basis for creating component methods, as you'll learn shortly.

Basic Concepts

Before we continue, I'd like to throw out a few terms from the object-oriented world that you'll see used throughout the chapter. If you are coming from an object-oriented background, you may notice that some of these concepts are implemented differently in ColdFusion than they are in other object-oriented languages, such as Java. Conversely, if you are new to object-oriented programming, you should be aware that some of the terms here have slightly different meanings or implementations outside of ColdFusion MX:

Object
: The foundation of object-oriented programming is the object. An object is an abstraction that is essentially a function containing variables and methods. Objects usually model actual entities in the real world. Using our employee directory as an example, you can model an individual employee as an object. In ColdFusion MX, we generally refer to objects as component (CFC) instances.

Class
: A class is a template that is used to create a new object (the new object is called an instance). That is, a class defines the variables and methods for all objects of a certain type. In ColdFusion MX, classes are implemented as CFCs. Individual objects are defined as instances of a particular CFC (class). For example, you may have a CFC called employee that contains variables (instance variables) and methods common to all employees. With an employee class, it's easy to create individual employee objects.

Component
: In ColdFusion, we refer to CFCs as components. In other object-oriented environments, "component" has a different meaning.

Method
: Methods are essentially functions that are part of an object. Methods allow the object to do something such as query an employee record from a database or move an employee to a different department. In ColdFusion MX, CFC methods are written exactly like tag-based UDFs—using the `cffunction` tag.

Property
: Properties are attributes of an object (instance variables). In CFCs, properties are variables you set in the this (public) scope or the variables/unnamed (private) scope. You can think of properties as defining a "has a" relationship. For example, an employee object may contain properties such as name (an employee has a name), title, email address, etc. Don't confuse this type of property with ColdFusion `cfproperty` tag. The `cfproperty` tag is used purely for declaring component metadata.

Instance
: An instance is an object of a particular class. In ColdFusion terms, you get a component instance when you call a CFC using the `cfobject` tag or the `createObject( )` function.

Constructor
: In object-oriented programming, constructors are pseudo-methods that are used to create an instance of an object. In Java, constructors are methods with the same name as the class. In ColdFusion MX, a constructor is any code contained in a CFC that is not part of a method or property. Constructor code executes in

ColdFusion MX each time an instance of the CFC is created. Because you cannot pass arguments to a CFC's constructor, use of constructors is fairly limited in ColdFusion. Most people prefer to create an `init()` method to act as the default constructor for their CFCs. I'll explain this in greater detail later in the chapter.

Inheritance
: Inheritance refers to an object's ability to automatically inherit the variables and methods of its parent (super or base) class. In ColdFusion MX, this translates to a CFC's ability to inherit all methods, variables set in the constructor area, and `cfproperty` metadata tags in another CFC (and anything that CFC inherits as well), defined as the CFC's parent.

Introspection
: Introspection is the ability for a component (or class) to examine itself. In ColdFusion MX, introspection is supported in several ways. First, both Dreamweaver MX and Flash MX have component browsers that can be used to introspect CFCs. Additionally, CFML contains a function called `getMetaData()` that can be used to return a structure containing all the properties, methods, arguments, return types, and other metadata for a given CFC.

Design patterns
: Design patterns are formalized solutions to recurring problems in object-oriented software design. CFCs allow you to make use more easily of design patterns in your ColdFusion applications. Although no books on design patterns for ColdFusion exist (yet), you can typically apply generalized patterns to ColdFusion development. For more information on design patterns, I suggest searching for "design patterns" on the Internet, or pick up the book *Design Patterns: Elements of Reusable Object-Oriented Software* by Erich Gamma, Richard Helm, Ralph Johnson, and John Vlissides (Addison-Wesley), often referred to as the Gang of Four book.

There are literally dozens of additional object-oriented concepts that I could throw around here, but for the purposes of getting started with CFCs, the aforementioned terms should get you well on your way.

Creating Components

Creating a CFC is easy. You simply define the component using the `cfcomponent` tag and save the file with a *.cfc* extension. `cfcomponent` is a paired tag that acts as a container for the CFC. Within the component, you can have any number of properties (defined by the `cfproperty` tag) and methods (each defined using a pair of `cffunction` tags). Each method can accept zero or more arguments, defined with `cfargument` tags. If a CFC returns any data, it does so with the `cfreturn` tag. Essentially, a component is a collection of related UDFs grouped within a cfcomponent container. Syntactically, a basic CFC looks like this:

```
<cfcomponent>
  <cfproperty />

  constructor code...

  <cffunction>
    <cfargument>
    CFML
    <cfreturn>
  </cffunction>

  <cffunction>
    <cfargument>
    CFML
    <cfreturn>
  </cffunction>
</cfcomponet>
```

The cfcomponent tag has four optional attributes:

displayname="*display_name*"
: Used to display a descriptive name for the component in ColdFusion MX's Component Browser or when the component is introspected using the getMetaData( ) function. These concepts are discussed later in the chapter.

hint="*text*"
: Used to display a hint describing what the component does in ColdFusion MX's Component Browser or when the component is introspected using the getMetaData( ) function.

extends="*component_name*"
: Name of a parent component from which the component should inherit methods and properties.

output="yes|no"
: Indicates whether the component's constructor code (any area within the cfcomponent container that is outside a cffunction container) allows output. If yes, expressions (surrounded with pound signs) are automatically evaluated without the need for cfoutput tags within component methods, and the method is permitted to display output. If no, ColdFusion suppresses any output within the constructor. If output is not specified, ColdFusion allows output within the constructor, but all expressions must be within cfoutput tags.

Besides the named attributes listed for the cfcomponent tag, you can pass any additional desired attributes to the tag as user-defined attributes. Although these attributes don't do anything, they are available as metadata when the component is introspected using the getMetaData( ) function. The getMetaData( ) function returns a structure containing key/value pairs for all the attributes in the cfcomponent tag.

getMetaData( ) is discussed in the section on introspection. You may use any attribute names you wish with the exception of those reserved by cfcomponent: name, displayname, hint, output, path, properties, and functions.

Example 22-1 shows a simple CFC (*employee.cfc*) that accepts a numeric ID as an argument and returns the employee record for that ID from a database table.

Example 22-1. A simple employee CFC

```
<cfcomponent displayname="Employee" hint="I'm for working with employees">
  <cffunction name="getEmployee" returnType="any" output="no" access="public">
    <cfargument name="id" type="numeric" required="true">

    <cfquery name="selectEmployee" datasource="programmingCF">
      SELECT *
      FROM employeeDirectory
      WHERE ID=#arguments.id#
    </cfquery>

    <cfreturn selectEmployee>
  </cffunction>
</cfcomponent>
```

Adding Metadata to Components

Although cfproperty is designed for use with web services authoring (see Chapter 24), it can also be used to expose additional metadata about a CFC. cfproperty tags must be positioned as the first code in a cfcomponent container. If they are not, ColdFusion throws an exception. Any metadata defined by the cfproperty tag is stored as an array of structures in the properties key of the structure returned by the getMetaData( ) function for a given component. The cfproperty tag has one required attribute and three optional ones:

name="*property_name*"
: The name of the property. name must be a static value and is required.

displayname="*display_name*"
: Used to display a descriptive name for the property in ColdFusion MX's Component Browser or when the component is introspected using the getMetaData( ) function.

hint="*text*"
: Used to display a hint describing what the property is for in ColdFusion MX's Component Browser or when the component is introspected using the getMetaData( ) function.

type="*data_type*"
: Type of property. Valid options are Any, Array, Binary, Boolean, Date, GUID, Numeric, Query, String, Struct, UUID, VariableName, and *ComponentName*. The

default is Any. For information on how GUID differs from UUID, see the createUUID( ) function in Appendix B.

Besides the named attributes listed here, you can pass any additional desired attributes to the cfproperty tag as user-defined attributes. They are then available as metadata when the component is introspected using the getMetaData( ) function. You may use any attribute names you wish with the exception of those reserved by cfproperty: name, displayname, hint, and type.

A typical use for the cfproperty tag is to include metadata for variables you set in the constructor code. Any CFML code outside a cffunction container is considered part of the constructor code and is automatically executed when the component is instantiated. Any variables set in the local (variables) scope or the this scope are automatically available to all methods in the component (we'll discuss scope shortly). For example, if you set a variables-scoped variable to hold your DSN, you could also set a cfproperty tag for it, as shown in Example 22-2.

Example 22-2. Using cfproperty to store variable metadata

```
<cfcomponent displayname="Employee" hint=" I'm for working with employees">
  <cfproperty name="dsn" type="string">
  <cfset variables.dsn="programmingCF">

  <cffunction name="getEmployee" returnType="any" output="no" access="public">
    <cfargument name="id" type="numeric" required="true">

    <cfquery name="selectEmployee" datasource="#variables.dsn#">
      SELECT *
      FROM employeeDirectory
      WHERE ID=#arguments.id#
    </cfquery>

    <cfreturn selectEmployee>
  </cffunction>
</cfcomponent>
```

Without the cfproperty tag, variables.dsn (and any other variables set in the constructor) wouldn't be visible if you introspected the CFC. We'll talk more about introspection later in the chapter.

Component Methods

Component methods are defined using the cffunction tag. cffunction is another container tag that you should be familiar with, as it's the same tag used to create user-defined functions. Optionally, one or more cfargument tags can be used to define both required and optional arguments the method should expect as input. If desired, data can be returned from the method using the cfreturn tag.

The `cffunction` tag pair acts as a container for the method. The `cffunction` tag takes one required and several optional attributes:

`name="`*`Name`*`"`
: Name for the method (required). Method names follow the same naming rules as ColdFusion variables. They must begin with a letter, underscore, or Unicode currency symbol (`$`) and can contain only letters, numbers, underscores, and Unicode currency symbols. Compound variable names such as `My.Method` are not allowed. Method names also may not begin with `CF`, `CF_`, `ColdFusion`, or `ColdFusion_`. Additionally, you may not give a method the same name as a built-in ColdFusion function.

`displayname="`*`display_name`*`"`
: Used to display a descriptive name for the method in ColdFusion MX's Component Browser or in the structure returned by the `getMetaData( )` function.

`hint="`*`text`*`"`
: Used to display a hint describing the method's purpose. The hint is displayed in ColdFusion MX's Component Browser or in the structure returned by the `getMetaData( )` function.

`returntype="`*`return_type`*`"`
: The datatype for the data returned by the method. Options are `any`, `array`, `binary`, `boolean`, `date`, `GUID`, `numeric`, `query`, `string`, `struct`, `UUID`, `variableName`, `void` (doesn't return a value), and *`componentName`* (for a custom return type). Required when component method is callable as a web service; optional otherwise.

`roles="`*`roles`*`"`
: Comma-delimited list of roles defined in the ColdFusion security framework that is authorized to invoke the component method. If `roles` is not specified, the method is accessible by anyone. Roles are discussed later in the section on security.

`access="private|package|public|remote"`
: Specifies the context within which the component method can be accessed. The default is `public`. Options are:

  `private`
  : Method is available only to the component that declares it.

  `package`
  : Method is available to the component that declares it as well as to any other component in the same package (directory). We'll cover component packages later in the chapter.

  `public`
  : Method is available to a locally executing page or other component on the server.

`remote`
: Method is available to locally executing pages, to other components on the server, via URL invocation, via form post invocation, Flash Remoting, or as a web service. This access type is required to publish the method as a web service.

`output="yes|no"`
: If `yes`, contents of the method body are processed as if surrounded by `cfoutput` tags. If `no`, the method body is processed as if surrounded by `cfsilent` tags. If `output` is omitted, contents of the method body are processed as regular CFML.

In addition to the attributes just listed, you may use any user-defined attribute names you wish with the exception of those reserved by `cffunction`: `name`, `displayname`, `hint`, `returntype`, `roles`, `access`, `output`, and `arguments`. User-defined attribute names are used for metadata purposes and are available when using the Component Browser or the `getMetaData( )` function.

Method arguments

Methods can be written to accept zero or more required arguments and any number of optional arguments. You should give each argument a name and explicitly declare it in the method body using a `cfargument` tag, just as you would do for a UDF. `cfargument` has several attributes. `name` is the only required attribute, used to specify the name for the argument. `type` is an optional attribute for specifying the argument's type; valid options are `Any`, `Array`, `Binary`, `Boolean`, `Date`, `GUID`, `Numeric`, `Query`, `String`, `Struct`, `UUID`, `VariableName`, and *`ComponentName`* (a valid CFC name). The default is `Any`. (For information on how `GUID` differs from `UUID`, see the `CreateUUID( )` function in Appendix B.) You can indicate whether the argument should be required or optional using the `required` attribute. The default is `no`. If you do decide to make an argument optional, you can supply a default value to assign to the argument in the event no argument is passed to the method when it is called.

Although it's good practice, it isn't required to declare your method arguments explicitly with the `cfargument` tag. The `cfargument` tag, if used, must be the first tag to appear after the `cffunction` tag. Argument names follow the same naming conventions as the function and argument names in UDFs. Like the `cfcomponent` tag, the `cfargument` tag also has `displayname` and `hint` attributes. Additionally, the same rules as those for adding additional user-defined metadata attributes apply.

Returning data from methods

Data is returned from a component method using the `cfreturn` tag. Just as with UDFs, the `cfreturn` tag is optional. You aren't required to return any data from a component method if you don't want to. However, if you choose not to return data from a method, you should set the `returntype` attribute of your `cffunction` tag to `void`. If you do choose to return data from your component method, the same rules that apply to UDFs apply to component methods.

Method includes

We all know that large files full of code can be come unwieldy, both to read and to manage. Fortunately, CFCs let you include the code that makes up a method body. This allows you to define your CFC as a skeleton while storing each component method as a separate CFML file that can be included in the appropriate component method body. To include a component method within a CFC, use code like that shown in Example 22-3.

Example 22-3. Including component methods

```
<cfcomponent displayname="Employee" hint=" I'm for working with employees">
  <cfproperty name="dsn" type="string">
  <cfset variables.dsn="programmingCF">

  <cffunction name="getEmployee" returnType="any" output="no" access="public">
    <cfinclude template="_methodGetEmployee">
  </cffunction>
</cfcomponent>
```

The actual method code would look like this (save it as *_methodGetEmployee*):

```
<cfargument name="id" type="numeric" required="true">

<cfquery name="selectEmployee" datasource="#variables.dsn#">
  SELECT *
  FROM employeeDirectory
  WHERE ID=#arguments.id#
</cfquery>

<cfreturn selectEmployee>
```

Variable Scope in CFCs

All ColdFusion variable scopes can be used within a CFC. Within a component, however, the behavior of various variable scopes may be different than you would expect. To avoid any potential confusion, here's a breakdown of how various variable scopes interact with the page that called them when they are used inside a CFC:

Application, CGI, Client, Cookie, Flash, Form, Request, Server, Session, URL
: Any variables placed in these scopes inside the component are automatically available to the calling page and any pages included by the CFC.

Arguments
: Variables in the arguments scope are only available within the component method they are passed to, as well as any pages included by that method. Variables in the arguments scope can be accessed either as a structure (`arguments.myVar`) or as an array (`arguments[1]`). Variables in the arguments scope do not last between method calls.

Local

Variables in the local scope are created using the `var` keyword (just like in UDFs) and are available only to the method in which they are defined and any pages included by that method. Additionally, local variables do not last beyond the life of the method call. The local variable scope differs from other variable scopes in that there is no scope prefix used for the variable. Note that if you do not define the variable with the `var` keyword, the variable exists in the variables scope, not the local scope.

Super

The super scope is unique to CFCs that use inheritance via the `extends` attribute of the `cfcomponent` tag. Super is not actually used to scope variables. Instead, it is used to scope a component method. The super scope contains all the methods that the current component extends. This is useful in situations where a component and the component it extends have like-named methods. In a situation such as this, super lets you reference a method in the parent object as opposed to the like-named method in the child object that you called.

This

The this scope is also unique to CFCs and is functionally equivalent to the this scope in JavaScript and ActionScript.* Variables in the this scope are available to the constructor code, all methods within a CFC, any pages they include, and the page that calls the CFC. Within a CFC you refer to variables in the this scope using the `this` prefix: `this.varName`. Outside the CFC, you use the component name to reference variables in the this scope: `myComponent.varName`. Note that this applies only when the CFC is instantiated as an object via the `cfobject` tag or `createObject( )` function, not when a component method is invoked using the `cfinvoke` tag, without the CFC being instantiated separately.

Variables

Variables in the variables scope are available only within the CFC. They are available to the constructor code, and to all component methods and any pages they include. They may be prefixed with the `variables` prefix or left unscoped (often called the unnamed scope). Variables in the variables scope that are set within the calling page are not automatically available within the component's variables scope. Additionally, variables in the variables scope exist as long as the component object exists. This allows them to persist between method calls.

Saving Components

CFCs differ from other CFML files in that you save them with a *.cfc* extension instead of the standard *.cfm* extension. Other than that, they share the same naming

* Because ColdFusion is built on top of Java, it is often assumed that the this scope is modeled after Java's this scope, which is not actually the case.

conventions as CFML files. Once you've created a component, you need to decide where to store it on your ColdFusion server. You have several choices:

- You can save the CFC in your web root directory or any directory below that.
- You can save the CFC in a directory above your web root directory, provided you create a mapping for the directory in the ColdFusion Administrator.
- You can save the CFC in the default custom tags directory (*c:\cfusionmx\customtags* by default) or any of its subdirectories, or in any custom tag directory defined in the ColdFusion Administrator.
- You can save the CFC in *\WEB-INF* or any subdirectory of the *\WEB-INF* directory (*c:\cfusionmx\wwwroot\WEB-INF* by default).

The location you choose to store your CFC may have an effect on how it can be called. CFCs stored in the same directory are part of a special grouping called a package. We'll talk more about packages in the section on using components.

Depending on where you store your CFC, you may or may not have to include the path when you instantiate it or invoke a method on it. Options for calling CFCs are covered later in the chapter.

Using Components

Now that you understand how to create a basic component, let's discuss how to use them in your applications. Typically, you create an instance of a component and then call a method on it, passing data in the form of arguments. The component does something based on the arguments passed and may return data to the calling page. That's component interaction in a nutshell. You have quite a bit of choice, however, in how you make it all work. There are seven basic ways in which you can call a component. These include the following:

`cfinvoke` *tag*
: Instantiates a CFC and/or invokes a method on an instantiated CFC.

`cfobject` *tag*
: Instantiates a CFC. Properties must be explicitly set, and methods explicitly called.

`createObject()` *function*
: Instantiates an object via `cfset`, `cfparam`, or `cfscript`. Properties must be explicitly set, and methods explicitly called.

URL
: Invokes a component method directly via an HTTP GET. The CFC filename is specified in the URL along with the method name as a URL parameter.

Form post
: The `Action` attribute of an HTML form or `cfform` tag posts directly to a CFC. The method to call must be specified by a form field.

Web service
: CFCs can be consumed as web services. For more information, see Chapter 24.

Flash Remoting
: Flash MX animations can call ColdFusion components via Flash Remoting. For more information, see Chapter 28.

Using cfinvoke

In an effort to make working with CFCs and methods as simple as possible, let's break each of these techniques down. Example 22-4 shows a simple CFC called employee (save it as *employee.cfc*) that we'll use to demonstrate the various ways to instantiate and call methods on a CFC. employee contains three methods: getDepartments( ), getEmployees( ), and getEmployee( ).

Example 22-4. Simple employee CFC with three methods

```
<cfcomponent>
  <cffunction name="getDepartments" access="remote" returntype="query">
    <cfquery name="qryDepartments" datasource="programmingcf">
      select distinct(department)
      from employeeDirectory
    </cfquery>

    <cfreturn qryDepartments>
  </cffunction>

  <cffunction name="getEmployees" access="remote" returntype="query">
    <cfquery name="getEmployees" datasource="programmingcf">
      select ID,Name
      from employeeDirectory
    </cfquery>

    <cfreturn getEmployees>
  </cffunction>

  <cffunction name="getEmployee" access="remote" returntype="query" output="no">
    <cfargument name="id" type="numeric" required="yes">
    <cfquery name="getEmployee" datasource="programmingcf">
      select *
      from employeeDirectory
      where id = #id#
    </cfquery>

    <cfreturn getEmployee>
  </cffunction>
</cfcomponent>
```

Here's one way to call the getDepartments( ) method of the employee CFC using the cfinvoke tag:

```
<cfinvoke component="employee"
          method="getDepartments"
          returnvariable="myDepts" />

<cfdump var="# myDepts #">
```

The component attribute is required and specifies the name of the component to instantiate or invoke a method on. If the component exists in the same directory as the page invoking it, you need only specify the component name (without the *.cfc* extension). If the component resides in a different location, you'll need to use dot notation to reference the location relative to the web root or a ColdFusion mapping. This is known as package notation. In the Java world, it's typical to create packages for storing your class files. For example, for the *example.com* company we've been using throughout the book, you might create a package off the web root called com.example (*webroot\com\example*). In the *\example* subdirectory, you would categorize your CFCs according to functionality. For example, you might have a subdirectory called *\utils* for utility CFCs, *\news* for news-related CFCs, etc. To refer to CFCs in a package, you use dot notation in the component attribute, such as com.example.utils.employee to refer to the employee CFC.

The method attribute is also required and specifies the CFC method we want to invoke. In this case, it's the getDepartments( ) method. The returnvariable attribute is optional. It specifies a variable name to hold the results of the method call to the CFC invocation. In our example, we assign the results of the call to getDepartments( ) to a variable called myDepts.

You can pass arguments to a CFC method using the argumentcollection attribute or the cfinvokeargument tag, or as an attribute of the cfinvoke tag. If more than one passed argument has the same name, ColdFusion uses the aforementioned order of precedence. Here's an example that passes an argument called id as part of the cfinvoke tag:

```
<cfinvoke component="employee"
          method="getEmployee"
          id="1"
          returnvariable="myEmployee" />

<cfdump var="#myEmployee#">
```

That same id argument could just as easily be passed using the cfinvokeargument tag, which is a child tag of cfinvoke:

```
<cfinvoke component="employee"
          method="getEmployee"

          returnvariable="myEmployee">
  <cfinvokeargument name="id" value="1">
</cfinvoke>

<cfdump var="#myEmployee#">
```

Using argumentcollection is a little different from the techniques we've just seen. It allows you to aggregate several arguments to pass as a single ColdFusion structure. Each name/value pair in the structure is considered a single argument. If your CFC method expects two arguments—name and title, respectively—you can pass them using argumentcollection like this:

```
<cfset args = structNew( )>
<cfset args.name="Pere Money">
<cfset args.title = "President">

<cfinvoke component="employee"
          method="setEmployee"
          argumentcollection="#args#" />
```

Or like this:

```
<cfset args = structNew( )>
<cfset args.name="Pere Money">
<cfset args.title = "President">

<cfset myObj = createObject("component", "employee")>
<cfset myObj.setEmployee(argumentcollection=args>
```

Using cfobject and createObject( )

Besides the cfinvoke tag, you can also create instances of CFCs using the cfobject tag or the createObject( ) function. This gives you tremendous flexibility in how you integrate CFCs into your ColdFusion applications. To create an instance of the employee CFC using the cfobject tag, your code would look like this:

```
<!--- Create an instance of the employee component --->
<cfobject name="myObj" component="employee">

<!--- Call the getEmployee( ) method on the instance --->
<cfset myEmployee = myObj.getEmployee(1)>

<cfdump var="#myEmployee#">
```

Here, the cfobject tag creates an instance of the employee component. The component attribute specifies the name of the component to instantiate. The name attribute specifies the name of a variable to store the instance of the component. Methods of the component are invoked using dot notation. In our example, we call the getEmployee( ) method, passing in a value for id (the argument the method expects). The results of the getEmployee( ) operation are assigned to myEmployee.

If you are using CFScript, you can call a CFC using the createObject( ) function:

```
<cfscript>
  myObj = createObject("component",  "employee");
  myEmployee = myObj.getEmployee(1);
</cfscript>

<cfdump var="#myEmployee#">
```

The first parameter of the createObject( ) function tells ColdFusion to create an instance of a component. The second parameter specifies the location of the CFC. The instance of the CFC is assigned to a variable called myObj. Dot notation is used to invoke the getEmployee( ) method of the component. Arguments are passed the same way as with the cfobject tag.

It's also possible to combine cfobject/createObject( ) with the cfinvoke tag. This is sometimes done when you need to invoke multiple methods on a component but only want to instantiate it once. Here's an example that creates an instance of the employee CFC and invokes two methods:

```
<cfset myObj = createObject("component",  "employee")>

<cfinvoke component="#myObj#"
          method="getEmployees"
          returnvariable="myEmployees" />

<cfloop query="myEmployees">
  <cfinvoke component="#myObj#"
            method="getEmployee"
            id="#myEmployees.id#"
            returnvariable="myEmployee" />
  <cfoutput>
  #myEmployee.Name#: #myEmployee.Title#<br>
  </cfoutput>
</cfloop>
```

Calling a CFC Method Via URL

It's also possible to invoke a CFC method directly from a browser (or other HTTP GET–style operation). To do this, you must set the access attribute of the CFC method you want to invoke to remote. For example, let's add a new method to *employee.cfc* called dumpEmployee( ):

```
<cffunction name="dumpEmployee" access="remote" output="yes" returntype="void">
  <cfargument name="id" type="numeric" required="no" default="0">
  <cfdump var="#getEmployee(arguments.id)#">
</cffunction>
```

This code dumps a call to the getEmployees( ) method within the employee CFC. Within a CFC, methods can call other methods by referencing them as if they were functions (which, of course, they are).

To call the dumpEmployee( ) method on the employee CFC from your browser, enter this URL:

http://localhost/programmingcf/22/employee.cfc?method=dumpemployee

You shouldn't see much more than an empty cfdump since the method expects an id, and if it doesn't get one, it defaults to 0 (no record has id equal to 0).

You can pass arguments to the dumpEmployee() method in the URL string as URL parameters. For example, you can pass the id argument expected by the method in the URL like this:

http://localhost/programmingcf/22/employee.cfc?method=dumpemployee&id=1

If you paste the URL into your browser, you should see output like that shown in Figure 22-1.

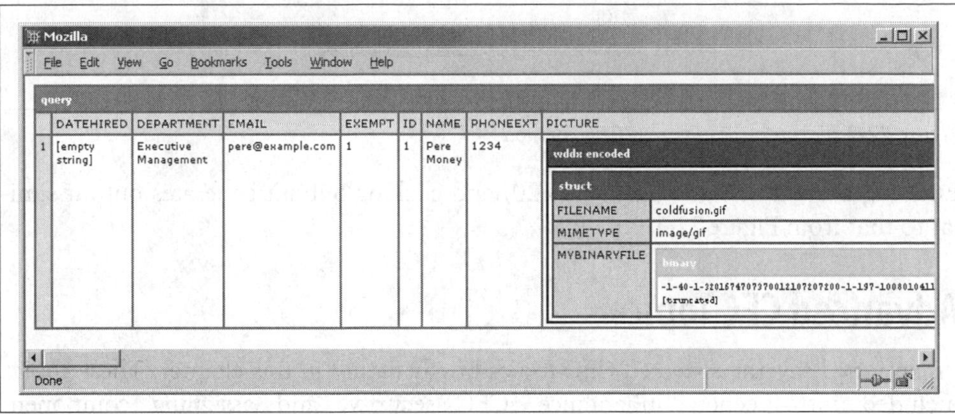

Figure 22-1. Calling a CFC method from a URL

Calling a CFC Method Via Form Post

In addition to the techniques we've discussed so far, it's also possible to invoke component methods via form post (HTTP POST). To post from a form to a component method, you specify the URL to the CFC in the action attribute of the form tag. You'll also need to post a form field called method to specify which method you want your form post to invoke. This is typically done by specifying the method as a hidden form-field value. Any additional form-field variables posted to the CFC method are treated as arguments.

On the ColdFusion side, the CFC method accepting the form post invocation must have the access attribute of its cffunction tag set to remote. We can use the same dumpEmployee() method we created in the last section to demonstrate invoking a component method via form post. All we need now is a simple HTML form that posts to our employee CFC:

```
<h2>Get Employee Record</h2>
<form action="employee.cfc" method="post">
  <input type="hidden" name="method" value="dumpemployee">
  ID: <input type="text" name="id" maxlength="2">
  <input type="submit">
</form>
```

If you save the form and open it in your browser, you'll see a screen that looks like the one shown in Figure 22-2.

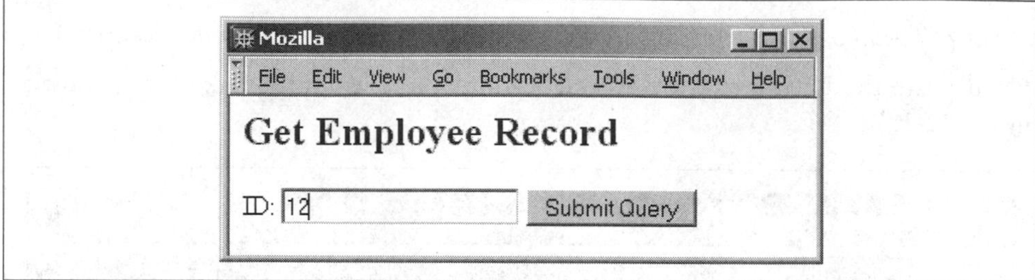

Figure 22-2. Form for posting to a CFC method

Entering a numeric value (from 1 to 20) and clicking Submit generates output similar to that from Figure 22-1.

Advanced CFC Topics

I mentioned several advanced CFC topics briefly earlier in this chapter. These topics included introspection, inheritance, CFC security, and assigning component instances to shared variable scopes. This section presents a more detailed exploration of each of these topics.

Introspection

One of the coolest features of CFCs is that they are self-documenting. All of the various tag attributes we discussed throughout the chapter, along with any user-defined attributes, are available as component metadata. This metadata exists as a ColdFusion structure that can be used for all sorts of purposes. ColdFusion MX comes with a tool called the CFC Explorer that you can use to introspect any CFC on your ColdFusion server. To use the CFC Explorer, simply fire up a browser and enter the URL to the CFC you want to introspect. You should be presented with the CFC Explorer login screen shown in Figure 22-3.

You'll need to enter the RDS password for the server to use the CFC browser Once you've entered a valid RDS password, ColdFusion MX allows you to proceed to the CFC Explorer. The CFC Explorer displays a nicely formatted screen containing the component's metadata, including the component's name, path on the server, properties, and methods. A sample CFC Explorer screen is shown in Figure 22-4.

If your ColdFusion server is used by multiple people, chances are you may not want to give everyone the RDS password for the server. The CFC Explorer and Component Browser both require this password to operate, which may put you in a bind, but fortunately there is a workaround. Simply replace the *Application.cfm* file

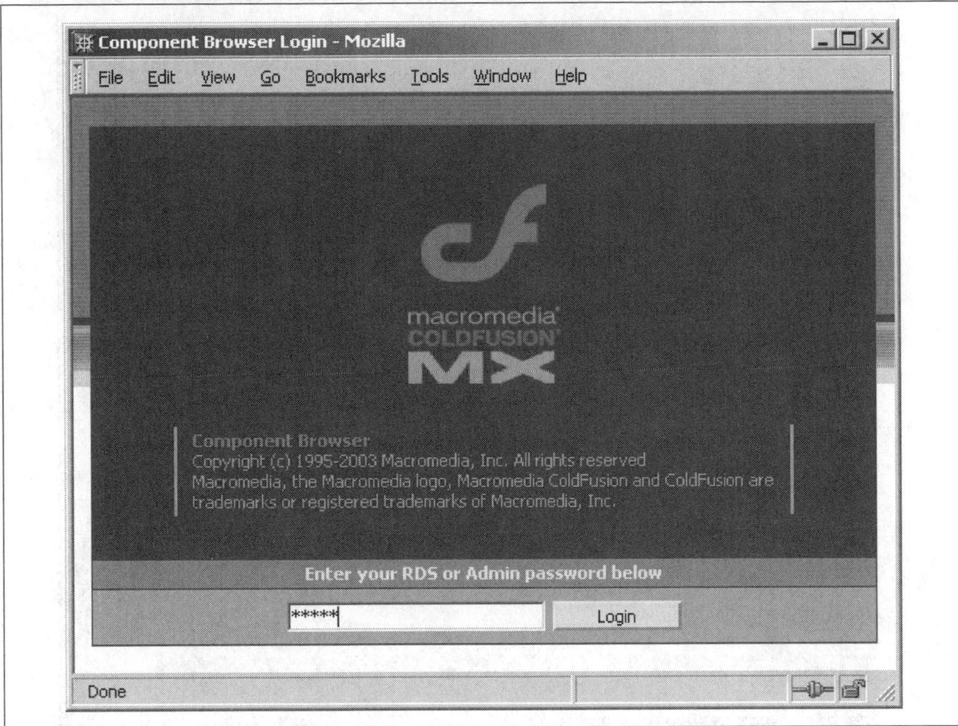

Figure 22-3. ColdFusion Administrator RDS password prompt for accessing the CFC Explorer

located in (by default) *c:\cfusionmx\wwwroot\CFIDE\componentutils* with your own *Application.cfm* file that contains customized authentication routines, and you'll be all set. Unfortunately you can't just modify the default *Appliction.cfm* file because it's encrypted. If this isn't a viable option (if you are in a shared hosting environment, for example), you may want to look into a tool called the CFCRemoteDocumenter, by Nathan Dintenfass. The CFCRemoteDocumenter is a CFML file you can include in your CFCs. It contains several methods for generating a nicely formatted page containing everything you ever wanted to know about a CFC. In fact, you might find it even more useful than the CFC Explorer that comes with ColdFusion MX. You can download a copy of the CFCRemoteDocumenter, along with documentation and examples, from Nathan's web site at *http://www.changemedia.org/cfcremotedocumenter/*.

You can use another tool included with ColdFusion MX called the Component Browser to list all packages and CFCs hosted on your server. To launch the Component Browser, open your web browser and point it to the following URL:

http://localhost/CFIDE/componentutils/componentdoc.cfm

As with the CFC Explorer, you'll be presented with a login screen where you'll need to enter the RDS password for your ColdFusion MX server before being able to pro-

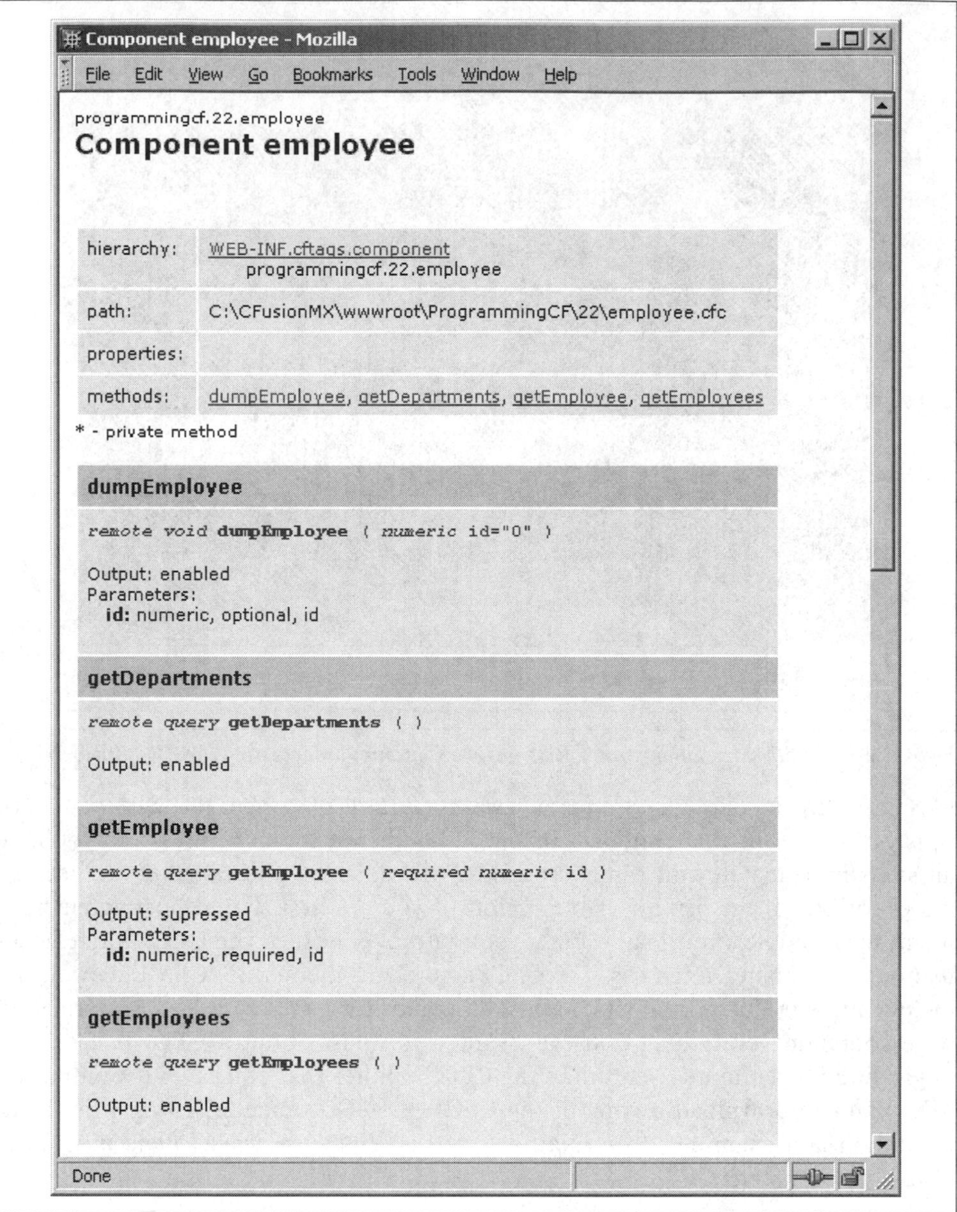

Figure 22-4. Introspecting a CFC with the CFC Explorer

ceed. Once your RDS server has been validated, you'll be presented with the Component Browser, shown in Figure 22-5.

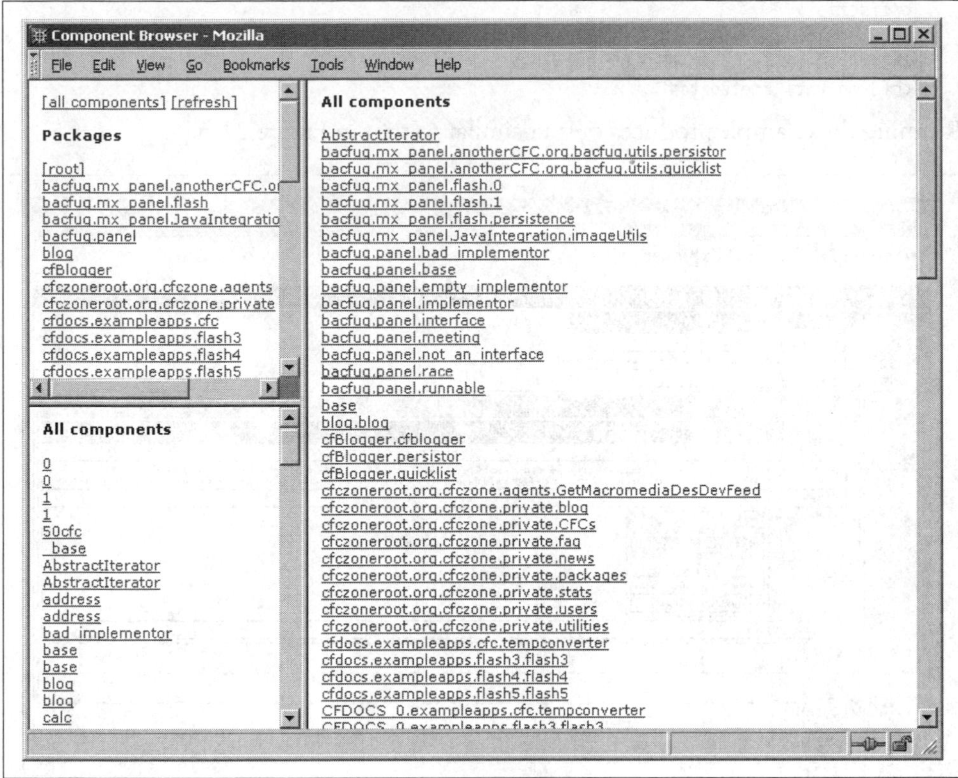

Figure 22-5. Introspecting a CFC with the ColdFusion Component Browser

Clicking on a package name in the upper left-hand frame displays a list of all CFCs in that package in the lower left-hand frame. If you click on a component name, the CFC Explorer view of that component is displayed in the main frame.

Component metadata can also be introspected programmatically using the `getMetaData()` function. When used within a CFML page, `getMetaData()` returns metadata such as properties, methods, and parameters for the specified ColdFusion Component (CFC). When used within a CFC, pass `GetMetaData()` the this scope and it returns all the metadata for the component. Metadata is returned as a structure containing various key/value pairs depending on the contents of the CFC. Values within the metadata structure may contain additional datatypes.

The best way to understand what metadata is available for a particular object is to retrieve the metadata for it and output the results to your browser with `cfdump`. Here's a piece of code that does just that for the CFC Explorer component that ships with ColdFusion MX:

```
<cfscript>
  myObj = createObject("component", "cfide.componentutils.cfcexplorer");
  metadata = getMetaData(myObj);
```

```
</cfscript>

<h2>Metadata for the CFC Explorer</h2>
<cfdump var="#metadata#">
```

Running the example produces output similar to that in Figure 22-6.

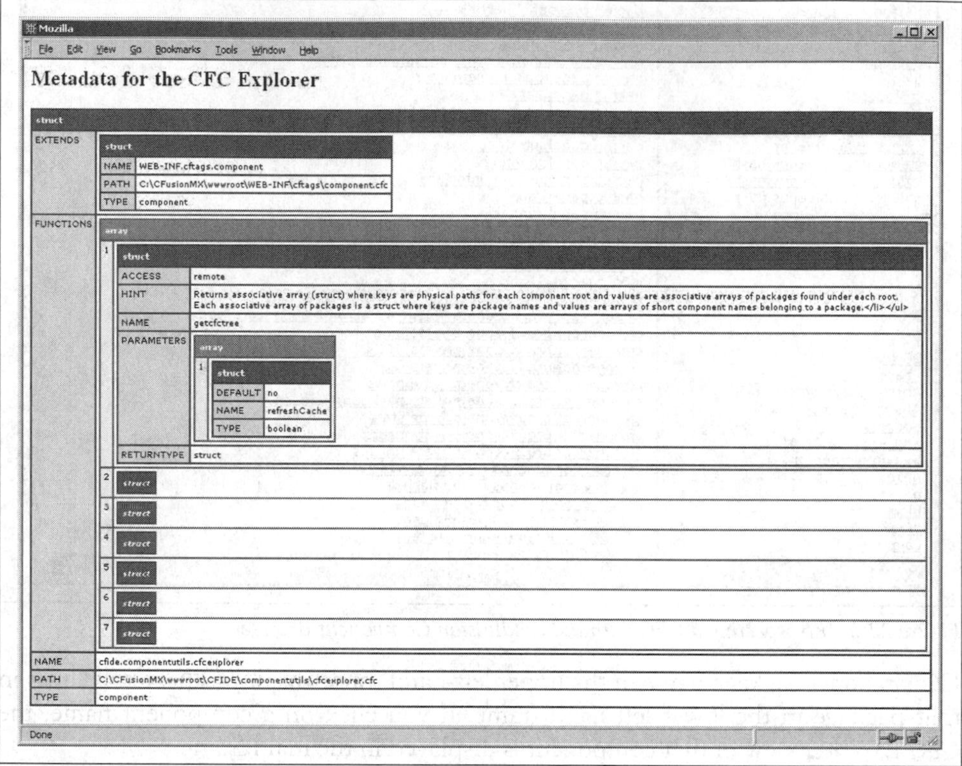

Figure 22-6. Using getMetaData() to introspect a CFC

If you are a Dreamweaver MX or Flash MX user, you can introspect CFCs from a version of the Component Browser included with those tools. For Dreamweaver MX, follow these steps:

1. Expand the Applications panel and choose the Components tab.
2. If you have not already defined a site, do so now (for more information on creating a new site, see the Dreamweaver documentation).
3. Choose CF Components from the list box in the Components tab.

   You should see a tree view of all component packages (directories containing components) on the site you defined (Figure 22-7).
4. Click on the plus sign next to a package name to list all of the components for that package.

5. To view the properties and methods for a specific component, click on the plus sign next to it.

   You can view the arguments for a method, or individual properties by clicking the plus sign next to the method name or properties label.

   To view the details for any property, method, or argument, highlight the item and click the Get Details icon (looks like a page) under the Components tab heading.

   You can drag method names from the tree view and drop them in the document window. Dreamweaver MX automatically generates the necessary CFML code to invoke the method of the component and includes code for any related arguments.

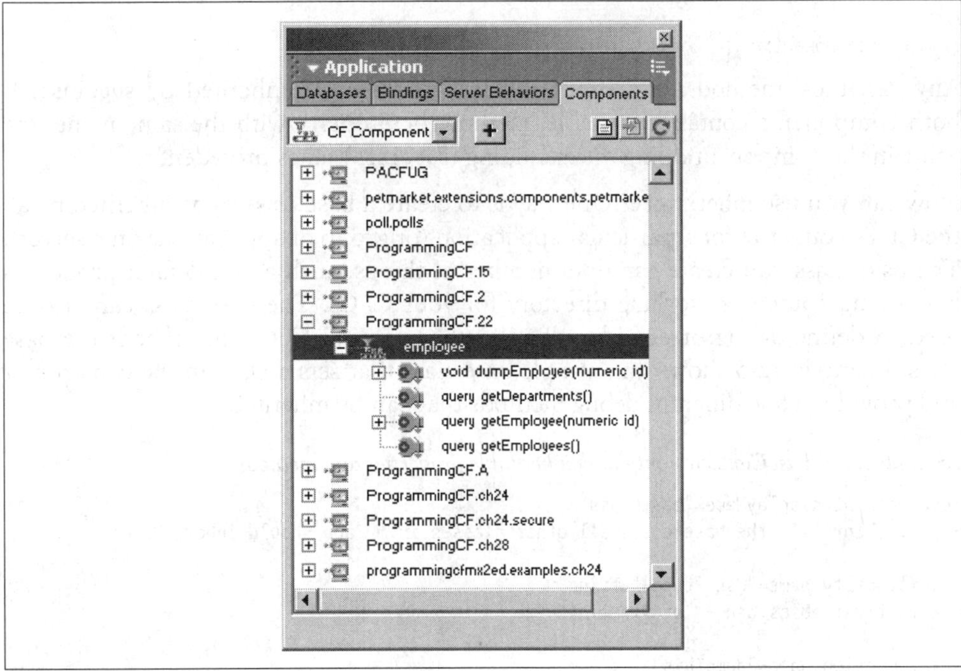

Figure 22-7. The Dreamweaver MX Component Browser

For information on using the Component Browser in Flash MX, see Chapter 28.

Inheritance

Earlier, I defined inheritance as it relates to CFCs as the ability for one component to inherit the properties and methods of another component. Inheritance is useful in situations where you have an object that contains properties or methods that are useful to other objects. Inheritance is often said to create an "is a" relationship between objects. For example, an employee CFC could inherit from a person CFC. This meets the “is a” test: an employee “is a” type of person.

CFCs support inheritance via the extends attribute of the cfcomponent tag. When one CFC extends another, it automatically inherits all the other CFC’s variables (in the constructor), properties, and methods (and the variables, properties, and methods of any CFCs it extends). If you have a property, metadata cfproperty tag, or method in the CFC doing the extending, it automatically overrides any like-named properties, metadata cfproperty tags, and methods in the inherited CFC(s). This is known as method overriding.* To avoid confusion, think of it like this: when a component (call it subclass) extends another component (call it baseclass), the code for subclass looks like this:

```
<cfcomponent extends="baseclass">
...
</cfcomponent>
```

Any variables, methods, and properties in baseclass are inherited by subclass. If both components contain a variable, method, or property with the same name, the value in the component doing the extending (subclass) takes precedence.

How can you use inheritance? One way is to create a base class to be inherited by all the CFCs you write for a particular application (or group of applications on a server). The base class you create can do a number of things, such as set default properties like a data source or working directory for your CFCs. The base class can also be used to define debug or error-handling methods for all CFCs that inherit the base class. Example 22-5 shows an example base class that sets a DSN in the constructor and provides a few different debug methods that can be inherited.

Example 22-5. baseClass.cfc containing inheritable properties and methods

```
<cfcomponent displayName="baseClass"
       hint="I'm the base class all other classes in my app should inherit">

  <cfproperty name="dsn" type="string">
  <cfset variables.dsn = "programmingCF">

  <cffunction name="dumpThis"
              access="public"
              hint="Dumps the this scope"
              output="true">
    <cfdump var="#this#" label="This Scope">
  </cffunction>
</cfcomponent>
```

* Although ColdFusion MX supports method overriding, it does not support method overloading (having a CFC with more than one method with the same name).

To use *baseClass.cfc*, you need another CFC that can inherit its properties, methods, and metadata `cfproperty` tags. Example 22-6 shows just such a CFC. It's yet another incarnation of the `employee` CFC we've used throughout the chapter.

Example 22-6. Inheriting a CFC

```
<cfcomponent extends="baseclass"
             displayname="Employee"
             hint="I'm for working with employees">
  <cffunction name="getEmployee" returnType="any" output="no" access="public">
    <cfargument name="id" type="numeric" required="true">

    <cfquery name="selectEmployee" datasource="#variables.dsn#">
      SELECT *
      FROM employeeDirectory
      WHERE ID=#arguments.id#
    </cfquery>

    <cfreturn selectEmployee>
  </cffunction>
</cfcomponent>
```

If you look at the code in Example 22-6, you'll notice that the `datasource` attribute is set to `variables.dsn`. That value isn't set in our *employee.cfc*. It's inherited from *baseclass.cfc*. To see how we can make use of the `dumpThis( )` method in the inherited `baseClass` CFC, consider the code in Example 22-7.

Example 22-7. Dumping the this scope by calling an inherited debug method

```
<cfset myObj = createObject("component", "employee")>
<!--- dump the this scope --->
<cfset myObj.dumpThis( )>
```

In this example, we create an instance of the `employee` CFC from Example 22-6. Because *employee.cfc* extends *baseclass.cfc*, it automatically has access to all of its methods. We use the `dumpThis( )` method to dump the this scope, a useful debugging tool.

When you extend an object, you may want to reference an overridden method in the parent class. As of ColdFusion MX 6.1, it's possible to do this using the super scope. Although not a true variable scope, the super scope contains all of a parent object's methods available when it is extended. Say you have a CFC called `subclass` that extends another CFC called `baseclass`, and both have a method called `getEmployee( )`. You can reference the `getEmployee( )` method in the parent object (`baseclass`) by prefixing it with `super` when calling it from the `subclass` CFC. To illustrate this, consider the following `baseClass` CFC (save it as *baseClass.cfc*):

```
<cfcomponent displayName="baseClass">
  <cffunction name="getEmployee">
    <cfreturn "I'm in the base class">
  </cffunction>
</cfcomponent>
```

The *baseClass.cfc* simply returns the string "I'm in the base class" when called. It is extended by *subClass.cfc* as follows:

```
<cfcomponent extends="baseclass">
 <cffunction name="getEmployee">
   <cfreturn "I'm in the subclass">
 </cffunction>

 <cffunction name="getTheEmployee">
   <cfreturn super.getEmployee( )>
 </cffunction>
</cfcomponent>
```

The `subClass` CFC has two methods, `getEmployee( )` and `getTheEmployee( )`. If the `cfreturn` statement returned `getEmployee( )` instead of `super.getEmployee( )`, the method would return "I'm in the subclass" when called. However, by specifying `super.getEmployee` in the `cfreturn` tag, the CFC calls the method in the `baseClass` CFC (its parent CFC). This results in the CFC returning "I'm in the base class".

To test this, save the following code as *callSuper.cfm* and launch it from your browser:

```
<cfset myObj = createObject("component", "subclass")>
<cfset myEmp = myObj.getTheEmployee( )>

<cfoutput>
#myEmp#
</cfoutput>
```

Global component inheritance with component.cfc

There may be cases where it would be useful to have one or more methods available to all of the components on your server. Ideas that come to mind are debugging methods, server-wide settings, etc. As of ColdFusion MX 6.1, you can modify a special component called *component.cfc* that all components on the server automatically extend. Out of the box, the *component.cfc* file can be found in the *\WEB-INF\cftags* directory and is completely empty. Any methods or properties you place in the file are automatically available to every CFC on your server.

Component Security

ColdFusion supports component security in two ways, at the web-server level and using ColdFusion's built-in security framework.

Securing access using HTTP Basic Authentication

At the web-server level, you can protect a web service using HTTP Basic Authentication. This is done by restricting access to the directory containing the CFC you want to expose as a web service. For more information on using HTTP Basic Authentication, see Chapter 8 and the documentation for your particular web server.

For CFCs that restrict access based on HTTP Basic Authentication, you can provide a username and password to pass along with the call to the component in the `cfinvoke` tag:

```
<cfinvoke component="addressLookup"
          returnvariable="myAddress"
          username="username"
          password="password">
  <cfinvokeargument name="userID" value="pmoney">
</cfinvoke>
```

The `username` and `password` values are Base64-encoded and passed as *`username:password`* in the authorization header to the target server.

Securing access using ColdFusion's built-in security framework

You can control access to your CFC methods at a much more granular level using ColdFusion MX's built-in security framework. This framework allows you to control access based on assigned roles at the invocation level.

Example 22-8 shows the code for a secure CFC method. The method can be invoked only by clients with an "Administrator" role.

Example 22-8. A secure CFC method

```
<cfcomponent>
  <cffunction name="returnStr" access="remote" returntype="string"
              roles="Administrator" output="false">

    <cfreturn "You have gained access">
  </cffunction>
</cfcomponent>
```

The framework for authenticating clients is the same one we discussed in Chapter 8. Using an *Application.cfm* file, we can leverage ColdFusion MX's security framework and HTTP Basic Authentication to provide a means to authenticate clients before allowing them to access a CFC method. Example 22-9 shows one way to do this.

Example 22-9. Authenticating a client for access to a CFC method

```
<cfapplication name="MySecureCFC">

<cflogin idletimeout="600">
  <cfif not isdefined("cflogin")>
    <cfheader statuscode="401">
    <cfheader name="WWW-Authenticate" value="Basic realm=""MyCFC""">
    You are noy authorized to access the CFC method.
    <cfabort>
  <cfelse>
    <cfquery name="validateUser" datasource="programmingcf">
      SELECT Roles, Salt, Password
      FROM Users
```

Example 22-9. Authenticating a client for access to a CFC method (continued)

```
    WHERE Username = <cfqueryparam value="#cflogin.name#"
                                   cfsqltype="CF_SQL_VARCHAR"
                                   maxlength="255">
  </cfquery>

  <cfif (validateUser.recordCount eq 1) and
        (validateUser.password is hash(validateUser.salt & cflogin.password))>
    <cfset userRoles = valueList(validateUser.roles)>
    <cfloginuser name="#cflogin.name#" password="#cflogin.Password#"
                 roles="#userRoles#">
  <cfelse>
    <cfheader statuscode="401">
    <cfheader name="WWW-Authenticate"
              value="Basic realm=""MyCFC""">
    You are noy authorized to access the CFC component.
    <cfabort>
  </cfif>
 </cfif>
</cflogin>
```

When a CFC method is called, a check is made to see whether there is an *Application.cfm* file that should be run first, just as there is when a CFML file is called from the browser. This lets you use the same mechanisms you are already familiar with to build a security framework for your CFC-based applications. When our *Application.cfm* file is called, a number of things happen.

First, a check is made to see whether the `cflogin` structure exists. If not, an HTTP 401 status code is sent back to the client, telling them they are not authorized to access the web service. If the `cflogin` structure does exist, we know that the call to the CFC method also included an authorization header containing (we hope) a username and password. Those values are automatically available inside the `cflogin` structure as `cflogin.name` and `cflogin.password`. A query is made to see whether the username exists in the `Users` table of our example database. If so, the salt value associated with the `cflogin.name` (from the database query) is concatenated with password provided by `cflogin.password`. The resulting string is hashed and then compared to the hashed value stored in the database. If a record was found for the username, and the salted, hashed password matches the value stored in the database, we consider this a valid login. The `cflogin` tag is then used to log the user in and assign her roles from the database. In this example, when we look up the username "pmoney," we find she is assigned the roles "Administrator, User."

The code for invoking the secure CFC method is shown in Example 22-10.

Example 22-10. Invoking a secure CFC method

```
<cfinvoke method="returnStr"
 returnvariable="retVal"
 component="ProgrammingCF.22.secure.secure.cfc "
 username="pmoney"
```

Example 22-10. Invoking a secure CFC method (continued)

```
 password="cat">
</cfinvoke>

<cfoutput>
#retVal#
</cfoutput>
```

If you run this code, you should see a message in your browser that reads "You have gained access." If you wait 30 minutes (the time specified in the `idletimeout` attribute of the `cflogin` tag) and change the username or password to a different value, you should be able to generate an authentication error if you attempt to call the web service as an unauthorized user.

Assigning Component Instances to Shared Variable Scopes

Earlier in the chapter, I mentioned that it's possible to assign a component to a shared variable scope. While you may never need to do this, there are several scenarios in which it is highly desirable. For example, if you model an entire application using CFCs, it makes sense that you would want to avoid the overhead of instantiating the various CFCs as a user navigated through the application. Likewise, if you built a multiuser blogging application, you would most likely want an instance of the blog CFC for each user. In both these cases, it makes sense to store instances of your CFCs in a shared scope. In ColdFusion MX, it's possible to assign CFC instances to the server, application, and session scopes.

To give you a better feel for how this works, we're going to rework an example from earlier in the book as a CFC-based application. In Chapter 13, we built a POP email client using a series of CFML templates. Rewriting the POP email client as a CFC-based application is a relatively straightforward process. Here are the general requirements (updated from Chapter 13):

- A login screen for users to enter their POP server, SMTP server, email address, username, and password. This data should persist across client requests in a shared variable scope. For this application, we'll store instances of the CFC in the session scope.
- In the template-based application from Chapter 13, login credentials were passed from page to page as encrypted URL variables. In our CFC example, we'll store the login credentials as variables in individual instances of `popClient` CFC.
- An Inbox with next/previous functionality for listing all emails belonging to the user on the POP server.
- The ability to read a message and download any associated file attachments.
- The ability to forward a message to other recipients, including file attachments.
- The ability to reply to a message.

- The ability to create a new message and attach a file to that message.
- The ability to delete messages from the POP server.

Given these requirements, it's relatively easy to map them to a CFC-based application. The first step is to handle the user authentication. Since this is still a basic mail client, we'll keep the functionality as simple (and at times, crude) as possible. I've chosen to use an *Application.cfm* file to handle the authentication. Example 22-11 shows the code for the *Application.cfm* file.

Example 22-11. Application.cfm for the POP email client

```
<cfapplication
   name="popClient"
   sessionmanagement="Yes"
   sessiontimeout="#createTimeSpan(0,0,30,0)#">

<!--- if a username and password are submitted from a form, consider it
      a valid "login" --->
<cfif isDefined('form.username') and isDefined('form.password')>
  <cfset session.loggedIn = "true">
  <cfset args = structNew( )>
  <cfset args.numDisplayMessages ="10">
  <cfset structAppend(args,form)>
  <!--- Instantiate the popClient CFC and cache the instance.  Notice the method
        chaining where we tack the init( ) method on --->
  <cfif not isDefined('session.popClient')>
    <cfset session.popClient =
       createObject("component","popClient").init(argumentCollection=#args#)>
  </cfif>
</cfif>

<!--- Set the default login state to false, meaning that by default,
      users are not logged into the application --->
<cfparam name="session.loggedIn" default="false">

<!--- If the user isn't logged in, give 'em the login screen --->
<cfif (not session.loggedIn)>
  <html>
    <head>
      <title>ColdFusion Mail Client - Login</title>
    </head>
  <body>

  <h2>Email Login</h2>
  <form action="index.cfm" method="post">
  <table>
    <tr>
      <td>Your e-mail address:</td>
      <td><input type="text" name="emailAddress" size="30" maxlength="255"></td>
    </tr>
    <tr>
      <td>POP server:</td>
```

Example 22-11. Application.cfm for the POP email client (continued)

```
      <td><input type="text" name="popServer" size="30" maxlength="255"></td>
    </tr>
    <tr>
      <td>SMTP Server:</td>
      <td><input type="text" name="smtpServer" size="30" maxlength="255"></td>
    </tr>
    <tr>
      <td>Username:</td>
      <td><input type="text" name="username" size="30" maxlength="255"></td>
    </tr>
    <tr>
      <td>Password:</td>
      <td><input type="password" name="password" size="30" maxlength="255"></td>
    </tr>
    <tr>
      <td colspan="2"><input type="submit" name="submit" value="Submit"></td>
    </tr>
  </table>
  </form>
  </body>
  </html>
  <cfabort>
</cfif>

<cfif isdefined('url.logout')>
  <!--- Terminate the user's session by deleting all session variables --->
  <cfset structClear(session)>
  <cflocation url="index.cfm" addtoken="no">
</cfif>
```

This *Application.cfm* file is called with every page request in the application. The first thing it does is check to see whether a username and password were passed in the form scope (from the authentication form post). If so, it automatically considers this a valid login. We aren't worried here about truly securing this application. The actual login to the POP server will serve as enough security for demonstration purposes. If `form.username` and `form.password` are both defined, `session.loggedIn` is set to `true`. This tells the *Application.cfm* file that the user is an authenticated user. Next, a structure called `args` is created. `args.numDisplayMessages` is an argument that we'll use to determine how many messages to display per page in our mail client's inbox. The form scope is then appended to the `args` structure. This is done so we can pass all of the user's login information, such as username, POP server, etc., to the CFC that controls the bulk of the application's functionality.

The next bit of code checks to see whether `session.popClient` exists. `Session.popClient` is an instance of the `popClient` CFC stored in the session scope. If it doesn't already exist, the `createObject( )` function is called to create an instance of the component and assign it to the session scope. If you look closely at the createObject( ) call, you'll notice an extra bit of code appended to the end of the call:

```
<cfset session.popClient =
createObject("component","popClient").init(argumentCollection=#args#)>
```

The addition of the .init( ) method to the end of the createObject( ) call is known as *method chaining*. The technique allows you to create an instance of an object and call a method on it at the same time. This technique requires a small amount of additional code in the init( ) method of our CFC, which we'll talk about shortly.

Next, a check is made to see whether the user is logged in. If so, they are allowed to proceed to the *index.cfm* page, the main template for the application. If they are not yet logged in, a login form is displayed.

The *Application.cfm* template contains one final bit of code. From anywhere in the application, a user can log out by clicking a Logout link or by manually appending a URL variable called logout to the URL of the application. When the *Application.cfm* file detects a URL parameter called logout, it clears the session scope using the structClear( ) function. This essentially logs a user out of the application and clears their instance of *popClient.cfc*. They are then automatically sent back to the login screen.

Once a user has authenticated and an instance of the popClient CFC has been created, the user is sent to *index.cfm*, the main (and only) CFML template of the application. The *index.cfm* file is used as the user interface for all aspects of the mail client. The code for the *index.cfm* page is shown in Example 22-12.

Example 22-12. index.cfm page for the POP mail client

```
<!--- Set the default action to refresh the inbox --->
<cfparam name="url.action" default="refresh">

<html>
<head>
  <title>E-mail Client</title>
  <style type="text/css">
    body {
      background-color : #COCOCO;
    }
    th {
      background-color : #0000FF;
      font-weight : bold;
      color : #FFFFFF;
      text-align : center;
    }
    td {
      background-color : #COCOCO;
      font-size : 10pt;
    }
    td.Main {
```

Example 22-12. index.cfm page for the POP mail client (continued)

```
      background-color : #FFFFFF;
    }
    .Attachments {
      color : #0000FF;
    }
    .Nav {
      background-color : #C0C0C0;
      font-weight: bold;
    }
  </style>
</head>

<body>
<div align="Center">
<table border="1" cellpadding="5" cellspacing="1" width="90%">
  <tr>
    <td class="Main">

<cfswitch expression="#url.action#">
  <cfdefaultcase>
    <cfparam name="url.currentMessageNumber" default="1">
    <cfset messageHeaders =
session.popClient.getMessageHeaders(currentMessageNumber=url.currentMessageNumber)>
          <table border="1" cellpadding="5" cellspacing="0">
            <tr>
              <!--- allow the user to refresh the page or create a new message --->
              <cfoutput>
              <td class="Nav"><a href="index.cfm">Refresh</a></td>
              <td class="Nav"><a href="index.cfm?action=create">Create Message</a></td>
              <td class="Nav"><a href="index.cfm?logout">Logout</a></td>
              </cfoutput>
            </tr>
          </table>

      <div align="Center">
      <h2>E-mail Client - Inbox</h2>
      </div>

      <!--- Create next/previous buttons as necessary for the messages displayed in
            the inbox.  If you want to display more than 10 messages at a time, you
            need to increase the value in the constants section. --->
      <cfoutput>
      <cfif (session.popclient.getcurrentmessagenumber() -
             session.popclient.getnumdisplaymessages()) gte 0>
      <a href=
"index.cfm?CurrentMessageNumber=#(session.popClient.getCurrentMessageNumber() -
session.popClient.getNumDisplayMessages())#">Previous</a> |
      </cfif>

      <cfif messageheaders.recordcount eq session.popclient.getnumdisplaymessages()>
      <a href=
"index.cfm?CurrentMessageNumber=#(session.popClient.getCurrentMessageNumber() +
```

Example 22-12. index.cfm page for the POP mail client (continued)

```
session.popClient.getNumDisplayMessages( ))#">Next</a>
      </cfif>
      </cfoutput>

      <!--- If there are messages to be displayed, do so and make the page a form so
            that multiple messages can be deleted. --->
      <cfif messageheaders.recordcount gt 0>
        <cfoutput>
        <form action="index.cfm?action=delete" method="Post">
        </cfoutput>
        <input type="Submit" value="Delete">
        <table border="0" cellpadding="5" cellspacing="1" width="100%">
          <tr>
            <th> </th><th>From</th><th>Date</th><th>Subject</th>
          </tr>

          <!--- Output the message headers --->
          <cfoutput query="messageHeaders">
          <tr>
            <td><input type="Checkbox" name="messageNumber" value="#messageNumber#"></td>
                <!--- Link the message to the index.cfm page where the full message
                      can be retrieved --->
            <td><a href=
                 "index.cfm?action=read&messagenumber=#messageNumber#">#From#</a></td>
                <!--- This date is not formatted because some mail messages contain
                      non standard date formats that cause ColdFusion to throw an
                      error when attempting to format them --->
            <td>#dateFormat(parseDateTime(date), 'mm/dd/yyyy')#
                #timeFormat(parseDateTime(date), 'hh:mm tt')#</td>
            <td>#subject#</td>
          </tr>
          </cfoutput>
        </table>
        <input type="submit" value="Delete">
        </form>

      <!--- If no messages are found, let the user know --->
      <cfelse>
        <h3>No messages found...</h3>
      </cfif>
        </td>
      </tr>
    </table>
    </div>
  </cfdefaultcase>

  <!--- Read a message --->
  <cfcase value="Read">
    <cfparam name="url.messageNumber" default="1">
    <cfset message = session.popclient.getMessage(messageNumber=url.messageNumber)>

    <!--- Output action options --->
```

Example 22-12. index.cfm page for the POP mail client (continued)

```
<table border="1" cellpadding="5" cellspacing="0">
  <tr>
    <cfoutput>
    <td class="Nav"><a href="index.cfm">Inbox</a></td>
    <td class="Nav"><a href="index.cfm?action=create">Create Message</a></td>
    <td class="Nav"><a href=
      "index.cfm?action=reply&messagenumber=#url.messageNumber#">Reply</a></td>
    <td class="Nav"><a href=
      "index.cfm?action=forward&messagenumber=#url.messageNumber#">Forward</a></td>
    <td class="Nav"><a href=
      "index.cfm?action=delete&messagenumber=#url.messageNumber#">Delete</a></td>
    <td class="Nav"><a href="index.cfm?logout">Logout</a></td>
    </cfoutput>
  </tr>
</table>

<cfoutput query="message">
<hr noshade>
<p>
<table width="100%">
  <tr>
    <th>From:</th>
    <td>#HTMLEditFormat(message.From)# on
        #HTMLEditFormat(message.Date)#</td>
  </tr>
  <tr>
    <th>To:</th>
    <td>#HTMLEditFormat(message.To)#</td>
  </tr>
  <tr>
    <th>Cc:</th>
    <td>#HTMLEditFormat(message.Cc)#</td>
  </tr>
  <tr>
    <th>Subject:</th>
    <td>#HTMLEditFormat(message.Subject)#</td>
  </tr>
</table>
<p>
<table width="100%">
<tr>
<td>
#HTMLCodeFormat(Trim(message.Body))# <br>
<!--- If there are attachments, display links to them --->
<cfif message.attachments is not "">
  Attachments:<br>
  <cfloop from="1" to="#ListLen(message.Attachments, chr(9))#"
          index="TheAttachment">
   <a href="#GetFileFromPath(ListGetAt(message.AttachmentFiles,
      TheAttachment, chr(9)))#">#ListGetAt(message.Attachments,
      TheAttachment, chr(9))#</a><br>
  </cfloop>
```

Example 22-12. index.cfm page for the POP mail client (continued)

```
    </cfif>
    </td>
    </tr>
    </table>
    </cfoutput>
  </cfcase>

  <!--- Reply to, forward, or create a message --->
  <cfcase value="Reply,Forward,Create">
    <table border="1" cellpadding="5" cellspacing="0">
      <tr>
        <td class="Nav"><a href="index.cfm">Inbox</a></td>
        <td class="Nav"><a href="index.cfm?logout">Logout</a></td>
      </tr>
    </table>
    <cfif action is "Reply" or action is "Forward">
    <cfparam name="url.messageNumber" default="1">
    <cfset message = session.popclient.getMessage(messageNumber=url.messageNumber)>

      <!--- Preface the subject with Re: --->
      <cfif findnocase("Re:", left(trim(message.subject), 3)) is 0>
        <cfset resubject = "Re: " & trim(message.subject)>
      <cfelse>
        <cfset resubject = trim(message.subject)>
      </cfif>
    </cfif>

    <cfoutput>
    <form action="index.cfm?action=send" method="POST"
          enctype="multipart/form-data">
    <cfif isdefined('message.attachments')>
      <!--- Include the attachment info --->
      <input type="Hidden" name="ForwardedAttachmentFiles"
             value="#message.AttachmentFiles#">
      <input type="Hidden" name="ForwardedAttachments"
             value="#message.Attachments#">
    </cfif>
    </cfoutput>
    <input type="Submit" value="Send">
    <cfoutput>
    <table>
      <tr>
        <th>To:</th>
        <td><input type="Text" name="To" value="<CFIF Action IS
          "reply">#HTMLEditFormat(Trim(message.From))#</cfif>" SIZE="50"></td>
      </tr>
      <tr>
        <th>Cc:</th>
        <td><input type="Text" name="Cc" size="50"></td>
      </tr>
      <tr>
        <th>Bcc:</th>
```

Example 22-12. index.cfm page for the POP mail client (continued)

```
        <td><input type="Text" name="Bcc" size="50"></td>
      </tr>
      <tr>
        <th>Subject:</th>
        <td><input type="TEXT" name="Subject" value="<CFIF Action IS NOT
          "create">#HTMLEditFormat(ReSubject)#</cfif>" SIZE="50"></td>
      </tr>
    </table>

    <p>
    <textarea name="Body" cols="70" rows="15" wrap="VIRTUAL"><cfif action is
      not "Create">#Chr(10)##Chr(13)#>>#message.Body#</cfif></textarea></p>
    </cfoutput>

    <!--- If forwarding, include attachments --->
    <cfif action is "Forward" and message.attachments is not "">
      <span class="Attachments" style="font-weight : bold;">Current File
        Attachments:</span><br>
      <cfoutput>
      <span class="Attachments">
      <cfloop from="1"
              to="#ListLen(message.Attachments, chr(9))#"
              index="TheAttachment">
        #ListGetAt(message.Attachments, TheAttachment, chr(9))#<br>
      </cfloop></span>
      </cfoutput>
    </cfif>
    <p>
    <span class="Attachments" style="font-weight : bold;">File
      Attachment:</span><br>
    <input type="File" name="Attachment">
    <p>
    <input type="Submit" value="Send">
    </form>
  </cfcase>

  <!--- Delete a message.  --->
  <cfcase value="Delete">
    <cfparam name="url.messageNumber" default="0">
    <cfif isDefined('form.messageNumber')>
      <cfset url.messageNumber = form.messageNumber>
    </cfif>
    <cfset message = session.popClient.deleteMessages(messageNumber=url.messageNumber)>

    <cflocation url="index.cfm" addtoken="no">
  </cfcase>

  <!--- Send the message --->
  <cfcase value="Send">
    <cfset args = structNew( )>
    <cfset args.to = form.to>
    <cfset args.subject = form.subject>
```

Example 22-12. index.cfm page for the POP mail client (continued)

```
    <cfset args.cc = form.cc>
    <cfset args.bcc = form.bcc>
    <cfset args.body = form.body>
    <!--- Check to see if there is an attachment to upload before sending --->
    <cfif isdefined('form.attachment') and form.attachment is not "">
      <!--- Note we are passing the name of the form field and not its value --->
      <cfset args.attachment = 'attachment'>
    </cfif>

    <cfif isdefined('form.forwardedAttachmentFiles') and
              form.forwardedAttachmentFiles is not "">
      <!--- Note we are passing the form field values this time --->
      <cfset args.forwardedAttachmentFiles = #forwardedAttachmentFiles#>
      <cfset args.forwardedAttachments = #forwardedAttachments#>
    </cfif>

    <!--- Upload the file --->
    <cfset session.popClient.sendMessage(argumentCollection=args)>
    <cflocation url="index.cfm" addtoken="no">
  </cfcase>
</cfswitch>
    </td>
  </tr>
</table>
</div>
</body>
</html>
```

The *index.cfm* page here combines the functionality of the *inbox.cfm* and *action.cfm* templates from Chapter 13. However, instead of placing all of the various `cfpop`, `cfmail`, and `cffile` tags (for attachment sending and viewing) inline, all of that functionality has been moved into the `popClient` CFC, leaving only display and method calls in the *index.cfm* file.

The guts of the application lie in the `popClient` CFC. This file contains all of the properties and methods used to get mail headers, get individual mail messages, deal with file attachments, etc. The code for *popClient.cfc* is shown in Example 22-13.

Example 22-13. The POP mail client's popClient.cfc

```
<cfcomponent>
  <!--- Initialize constants --->
  <cfset variables.currentMessageNumber = 1>
  <cfset variables.theAttachmentPath = getDirectoryFromPath(getCurrentTemplatePath( ))>
  <cfset variables.username = "">
  <cfset variables.password = "">
  <cfset variables.smtpServer = "">
  <cfset variables.popServer = "">
  <cfset variables.emailAddress = "">
  <cfset variables.numDisplayMessages = 0>
```

Example 22-13. The POP mail client's popClient.cfc (continued)

```
<!--- init( ) method should be called when component is instantiated.  It
      acts as the default constructor --->
<cffunction name="init" output="no" access="remote" returntype="struct">
  <cfargument name="username" type="string" required="yes">
  <cfargument name="password" type="string" required="yes">
  <cfargument name="smtpServer" type="string" required="yes">
  <cfargument name="popServer" type="string" required="yes">
  <cfargument name="emailAddress" type="string" required="yes">
  <cfargument name="numDisplayMessages" type="numeric" requierd="yes">

  <cfset variables.username = arguments.username>
  <cfset variables.password = arguments.password>
  <cfset variables.smtpServer = arguments.smtpServer>
  <cfset variables.popServer = arguments.popServer>
  <cfset variables.emailAddress = arguments.emailAddress>
  <cfset variables.numDisplayMessages = arguments.numDisplayMessages>
  <!--- Return an instance of the CFC --->
  <cfreturn this>
</cffunction>

<!--- Retrieve message headers --->
<cffunction name="getMessageHeaders" output="yes" returntype="query" access="remote"
            hint="I retrieve n message headers at a time">
  <cfargument name="currentMessageNumber" type="numeric" required="false" default="1">
  <cfset var qryMessageHeaders = "">
  <cfset variables.currentMessageNumber = arguments.currentMessageNumber>
  <cfpop action="getHeaderOnly" name="qryMessageHeaders" server="#variables.popServer#"
        timeout="600" username="#variables.username#" password="#variables.password#"
        startrow="#arguments.currentMessageNumber#"
        maxrows="#variables.numDisplayMessages#">
  <cfreturn qryMessageHeaders>
</cffunction>

<!--- Retrieve a full message --->
<cffunction name="getMessage" output="no" returntype="query" access="remote">
  <cfargument name="messageNumber" type="numeric" required="false" default="1">
  <cfset var qryGetMessage = "">
  <cfpop action="getAll" name="qryGetMessage" messagenumber="#arguments.messageNumber#"
        server="#variables.popServer#" timeout="600" username="#variables.username#"
        password="#variables.password#" attachmentpath="#variables.theAttachmentPath#"
        generateuniquefilenames="yes">
  <cfreturn qryGetMessage>
</cffunction>

<!--- Delete one or more messages --->
<cffunction name="deleteMessages" output="no" returntype="void" access="remote">
  <cfargument name="messageNumber" type="string" required="false" default="1">
  <cfpop action="delete" messagenumber="#arguments.messageNumber#"
        server="#variables.popServer#"
       timeout="600" username="#variables.username#" password="#variables.password#">
</cffunction>
```

Example 22-13. The POP mail client's popClient.cfc (continued)

```
<!--- Send a message --->
<cffunction name="sendMessage" output="yes" returntype="struct" access="remote">
  <cfargument name="to" type="string" required="yes">
  <cfargument name="subject" type="string" required="yes">
  <cfargument name="cc" type="string" required="yes">
  <cfargument name="bcc" type="string" required="yes">
  <cfargument name="attachment" required="no" type="string">
  <cfargument name="forwardedAttachmentFiles" required="no" type="string">
  <cfargument name="forwardedAttachments" required="no" type="string">

  <cfif isdefined('arguments.attachment') and arguments.attachment is not "">
    <cffile
      action="upload"
      filefield="#arguments.attachment#"
      destination="#variables.theAttachmentPath#"
      nameconflict="makeunique">
  </cfif>

  <!--- Send the message --->
  <cfmail
    from="#variables.emailAddress#"
    to="#arguments.to#"
    subject="#arguments.subject#"
    cc="#arguments.cc#"
    bcc="#arguments.bcc#"
    server="#variables.smtpServer#">
  #arguments.body#
  <!--- Include the new attachment if necessary --->

  <cfif isdefined('arguments.attachment') and arguments.attachment is not "">
    <cfmailparam file="#variables.theAttachmentPath#\#cffile.serverfile#">
  </cfif>

  <!--- Include any forwarded attachments if necessary --->
  <cfif isdefined('arguments.ForwardedAttachments')>
  <cfloop from="1" to="#ListLen(arguments.forwardedAttachments, chr(9))#"
        index="TheAttachment">
  <cfmailparam
     file="#ListGetAt(arguments.forwardedAttachmentFiles, TheAttachment, chr(9))#">
  </cfloop>
  </cfif>
  </cfmail>
  <cfreturn cffile>
</cffunction>

<!--- Get the number of messages to display at a time --->
<cffunction name="getNumDisplayMessages" output="no" returntype="numeric"
            access="remote">
  <cfreturn variables.numDisplayMessages>
</cffunction>

<!--- Get the current message number --->
```

Example 22-13. The POP mail client's popClient.cfc (continued)

```
<cffunction name="getCurrentMessageNumber" output="no" returntype="numeric"
            access="remote">
  <cfreturn variables.currentMessageNumber>
</cffunction>

<!--- Set the current message number --->
<cffunction name="setCurrentMessageNumber" output="no" returntype="void"
            access="remote">
  <cfargument name="currentMessageNumber" type="numeric" required="no" default="1">
  <cfset variables.currentMessageNumber = arguments.currentMessageNumber>
</cffunction>

<!--- Get the previous starting message number for paging back --->
<cffunction name="getPreviousMessageNumber" output="no" returntype="numeric"
            access="remote">
  <cfreturn variables.currentMessageNumber - variables.numDisplayMessages>
</cffunction>

<!--- get the next starting message number for paging forward --->
<cffunction name="getNextMessageNumber" output="no" returntype="numeric"
            access="remote">
  <cfreturn variables.currentMessageNumber + variables.numDisplayMessages>
</cffunction>
```

The `popClient` CFC is pretty well documented. However, it's worth discussing a few key sections of the code. First, the constructor area of the CFC is used to set variables that can be used throughout the life of the CFC instance. We set these in the variables scope so they would be private to the CFC (i.e., available only in the constructor and within component methods).

The second feature worth mentioning is the `init( )` method. Earlier in the chapter, we discussed the fact that the CFC's constructor area leaves a lot to be desired, as you cannot pass arguments to it. To get around this, a common technique among ColdFusion developers is to create an `init( )` method that you call when you create an instance of the component. If you remember, we created an instance of the `popClient` CFC by using the `createObject( )` function and chaining the `init( )` method on the end. If you look at the function body of the `init( )` method, you'll see that the method's main purpose is to create instance variables from the user profile information submitted in the login form. Simply placing these values in instance variables, however, is not enough. We need to return an instance of the object for things to work correctly. This is done by setting the `cfreturn` tag to return `this`. As you may recall, in addition to being a variable scope, `this` can also be used to return an instance of an object.

Just like the POP mail client we built back in Chapter 13, this application leaves a lot to be desired in terms of both functionality and robustness. Improving it would certainly make for an excellent exercise in applying many of the principles and techniques we've covered throughout the book.

CHAPTER 23

XML and WDDX

As the Internet continues to evolve, XML is playing an increasingly important role. It is often referred to as the de facto language of the Internet and indeed is worthy of this title. It seems as though everywhere you turn, XML is there. Perhaps XML's most appealing feature is its simplicity. After all, it's a plain-text format that does nothing more than describe data. What could be simpler?

This chapter is divided into two main themes, working with XML and using Web Distributed Data Exchange, or WDDX as it's commonly referred to. We're going to cover a lot of ground fairly quickly. As simple as the concept of XML is, working with it in a meaningful way is often anything but. Luckily, ColdFusion makes the tasks you are likely to encounter—creating, parsing, searching, and transforming XML—far easier than any other language I know of. As we've come to expect from ColdFusion, what are often high-level programming tasks in other languages are cleverly abstracted in ColdFusion. This does not mean they are any less powerful, just that ColdFusion makes them easier to implement. And as you know, in programming, easier to implement tends to mean faster to accomplish.

Working with XML

As I mentioned in the introduction, ColdFusion MX makes working with XML easy. With ColdFusion MX, you can easily do things such as generate your own XML, parse existing XML using native ColdFusion functions, search through XML using XPath, and transform XML using XSLT and XSL.

Because this chapter does not cover XML itself in any great detail, I recommend reading up on the topic if you aren't already familiar with it. Two excellent resources to consider are O'Reilly's *http://xml.com* web site and the O'Reilly book *Learning XML* by Erik T. Ray.

A 30-Second XML Primer

The basics of XML are simple to learn. Because you'll need a basic understanding of XML for the rest of this chapter to make any sense, I'm including what I call a 30-second XML primer to get you started. It doesn't teach you everything, but it should set you well on your way.

In its most basic form, XML is simply a tag-based markup language for describing data. Both HTML and XML are subsets of SGML (Standard Generalized Markup Language). Although similar in appearance to HTML, XML differs in that it doesn't have anything to do with how the data it describes is displayed. HTML, on the other hand, is designed to specify how data should be displayed in a hierarchical manner. Another difference between XML and HTML is that XML is extensible. In HTML, you are limited to using the tags that are officially part of the HTML specification (or are supported as browser extensions). In XML, you can create any tags you want. XML uses a document type definition (DTD) or schema to describe the content of an XML document. For more information on these concepts, I recommend visiting *http://www.w3.org/tr/REC-xml* and *http://www.w3.org/XML/Schema*, respectively.

Now that we've covered what XML is, let's look at a basic XML file describing a company and its three employees. Example 23-1 shows how the XML might look.

Example 23-1. A simple XML document

```
<?xml version="1.0" encoding="utf-8"?>
<!-- employees for Example.com -->
<company name="Example.com">
  <employee id="1">
    <name>Pere Money</name>
    <title>President</title>
  </employee>
  <employee id="2">
    <name>Aaron Ridge</name>
    <title>Analyst</title>
  </employee>
  <employee id="3">
    <name>Martin Grant</name>
    <title>Manager</title>
  </employee>
</company>
```

There are two additional concepts I should explain before we continue. The first is the concept of well-formed XML. An XML document is said to be well formed if it adheres to the rules outlined in the XML specification—mainly that all tags must contain a start and end tag (or be self-closing like `<article type="news" />`) and that proper nesting of elements is observed. By definition, all XML documents must be well formed to be considered XML. The second concept you need to understand is that of valid XML. For an XML document to be considered valid, it must first be well formed. Additionally, it must match up against a specified DTD or schema. This means that the elements in the XML document must be explicitly defined within the DTD or schema. All the examples we'll be dealing with in this chapter are considered well-formed XML.

The first line in the XML document is called the XML declaration. This is necessary for the document to be considered valid. It simply states what version of XML the document conforms to and, optionally, what character encoding is used. In this example, the XML document conforms to the 1.0 version of XML (see *http://www.w3.org/tr/REC-xml*) and is encoded using the UTF-8 character set. An XML declaration is not an element of the XML document and therefore does not require an end tag.

The second line in our XML file is a comment. In XML, comments are written just as they are in HTML. Comments may appear anywhere in an XML document except within a tag. In other words, `<employee <!-- comment -->>` is not a legal comment in XML.

The third line (the `<company>` tag) in this XML document is known as the root element of the document. The root element acts as a container for the entire document. Notice how the `<company>` tag has both a start and an end tag: in XML, all tags are required to have an associated end tag. Additionally, XML tags are case sensitive. This means that `<employee />` is not the same as `<Employee />`. Further, the case of the start and end tag of an XML element must match.

Within the root element of the document, you can nest any number of child elements (tags). In our example, we create three child elements, each called `<employee>`. These child elements are said to be siblings of each other because they are nested at the same level. All elements in XML are related to one another in various ways. Each `<employee>` element contains two child elements, `<name>` and `<title>`. In this case, `<employee>` is said to be a parent element of `<name>` and `<title>`. In XML, it's possible to nest this parent-child relationship as necessary to structure your data. Correct nesting is strictly enforced in XML.

If you look at the `<employee>` elements, you'll also notice that each has an attribute called `id` (`<employee id="x">`). Like HTML, XML tags can have one or more attributes. Unlike HTML, however, all XML tag attributes must be quoted (you can use either double or single quotes).

In XML, end-of-line characters are always represented as a single linefeed (ASCII character code 10), regardless of whether the end-of-line was coded as a combination of carriage return (ASCII character code 13) and linefeed, as in most Windows systems, or as a single linefeed, as in most UNIX systems. Additionally, when a browser interprets HTML, it ignores additional whitespace beyond a single space within an element. XML parsers, on the other hand, preserve all whitespace within an element (although you could configure them not to).

XML Document Object

The XML document object is a new datatype in ColdFusion MX. It allows ColdFusion to represent XML in a format akin to a ColdFusion structure containing nested element structures. This is a very useful way to represent XML, as it allows you to perform all sorts of operations using standard ColdFusion structure functions. Additionally, you can use ColdFusion MX's new XML document object functions to further manipulate XML.

ColdFusion is capable of referencing an XML document object in two distinct ways. The first is called the basic view. In the basic view, the document object is an object that contains a structure for the root element of the XML document. Each XML tag pair within the root element is represented as an element structure. These element structures contain the contents of the parent element and can include additional nested element structures. You can think of the basic view as a shoebox that contains additional boxes of different sizes. Some of these boxes contain items, while others contain additional boxes that may contain items or more boxes.

ColdFusion can convert any valid XML document to an XML document object using the `XmlParse( )` function. To get a better idea of how an XML document looks as an XML document object, you can use the `cfdump` tag to give you a visual representation. Example 23-2 shows the code for reading the XML file we created in Example 23-1, parsing it into an XML document object, then dumping it out using the `cfdump` tag. The results are shown in Figure 23-1. You can toggle the dump of the XML document object between short and long versions by clicking on the version name at the top of the table.

Example 23-2. Parsing an XML document into an XML document object

```
<cffile action="read"
        file="c:\cfusionmx\wwwroot\programmingcf\23\employee.xml"
        variable="theXML">

<cfset myXml = xmlParse(theXml)>

<cfdump var="#myXml#">
```

The `cffile` tag is used to read the XML file and store it in a variable called `theXml`. Next, the `xmlParse( )` function is used to convert the raw XML (stored as a string) into an XML document object. An optional parameter allows you to specify whether the original case of the XML document elements and attributes should be maintained. The default value is `No` (in our example, we omit this parameter). Note that XML encoded in character sets other than ASCII or Latin-1 must have the character set explicitly defined to ColdFusion. If you are using the `cffile` tag to read an XML file, the character set can be defined using the `charset` parameter of the `cffile` tag. If the XML file is retrieved using another method, it may be necessary to first change the encoding. No explicit encoding is required in our example.

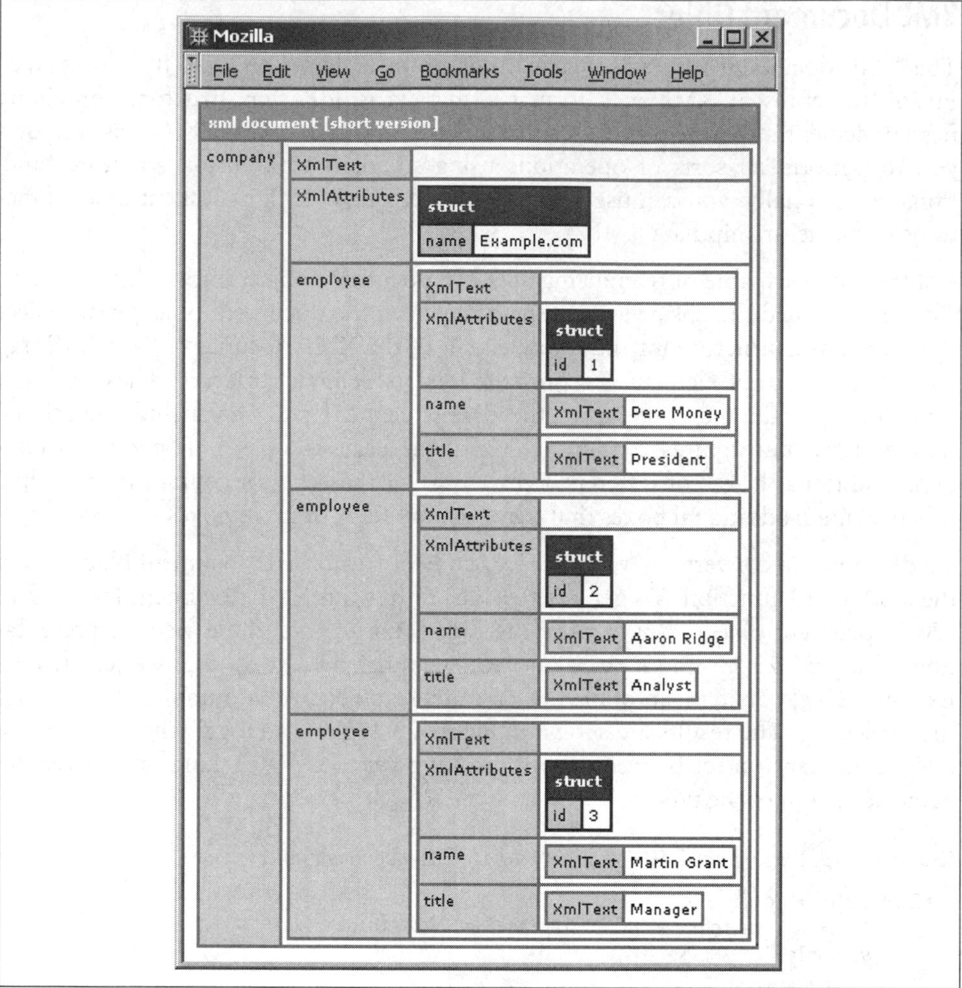

Figure 23-1. An XML document as displayed by cfdump

The final part of the code uses the `cfdump` tag to dump the contents of the XML document object. As you can see, using `cfdump` to output an XML document object is an excellent way to visualize the basic view structure of the document. The top-level document object contains three name/value pairs (only two are visible in the output produced by `cfdump`):

`XmlComment`
: String containing all comments (concatenated) outside of the root element.

`XmlRoot`
: Contains the root element of the document. In our example, this is the `<company>` tag.

`XmlDocType`
: Contains the `DocType` attribute (if any) of the document. If no `DocType` is specified in the XML document, this name/value pair does not exist. Additionally, `XmlDocType` isn't included in the output generated by the `cfdump` tag.

Within ColdFusion's XML document object, `XmlRoot` contains all of the XML elements (tags) for a given XML document. Each XML element is itself a structure that contains the following name/value pairs:

`XmlName`
: Name of the XML element (tag).

`XmlNsPrefix`
: Prefix of the corresponding namespace.

`XmlNsURI`
: URI of the namespace.

`XmlText`
: String containing all text and `CDATA` (concatenated) from within an XML element, but not its child elements.

`XmlComment`
: String containing all comments (concatenated) within the element, but not within any child elements.

`XmlAttributes`
: Structure containing all of the element's attributes as name/value pairs.

`XmlChildern`
: Array containing all of the element's child elements.

`XmlParent`
: The parent DOM node of the current element. `XmlParent` is not displayed in the output generated by `cfdump`.

`XmlNodes`
: Array containing all the `XmlNode` DOM nodes contained in the current element. `XmlNodes` is not displayed in the output generated by `cfdump`.

To access elements of the XML document object, you can use many of the structure and array functions you are already familiar with. Example 23-3 should give you a general idea of the types of things you can do with structure and array functions.

Example 23-3. Using structure and array functions to parse XML

```
<!--- Read in XML file --->
<cffile action="read"
       file="c:\cfusionmx\wwwroot\programmingcf\23\employee.xml"
       variable="theXML">

<!--- Convert XML string to XML document object --->
<cfset myXml = xmlParse(theXml)>
```

Example 23-3. Using structure and array functions to parse XML (continued)

```
<!--- Get the root element --->
<cfset theRoot = myXml.XmlRoot>

<!--- Get the number of child elements off of the root --->
<cfset numChildren = arrayLen(theRoot.XmlChildren)>

<!--- Output everything we've parsed --->
<cfoutput>
Is myXml a valid XML document object: #isXmlDoc(myXml)#<br>
The name of the root element is: #theRoot.XmlName#<br>
Is #theRoot.XmlName# really the root element? #isXmlRoot(theRoot)#<br>
Is #theRoot.XmlName# also an XML element? #isXmlElem(theRoot)#<br>
The #theRoot.XmlName# name is #theRoot.XmlAttributes["Name"]#<br>
The root element (#theRoot.XmlName#) has #numChildren# child elements:<br>
<cfloop index="i" from="1" to="#numChildren#">
   #theRoot.XmlChildren[i].XmlName#[#i#]:
  #theRoot.XmlChildren[i]["Name"].XmlText#<br>
  <!--- Loop over all attributes in the 2nd level (Employee) element --->
  <cfloop collection="#theRoot.XmlChildren[i].XmlAttributes#" item="j">
       #j#: #theRoot.XmlChildren[i].XmlAttributes[j]#<br>
  </cfloop>
</cfloop>
<br>
The index position of the 2nd occurence of "employee" is: #xmlChildPos(theRoot,
"employee", 2)#
</cfoutput>
```

At first glance, all of the dots and brackets in the code may look complicated. If we break the code down step by step, however, I think you'll see that it all makes sense. The code first reads the same XML file we've been using (Example 23-1) and converts it to an XML document object. Next, we get the root element (the structure, not the name) of the document by referencing `myXml.XmlRoot` and assign it to a variable called `theRoot`. This will save us a lot of extra typing since just about everything we reference from here on out will be at least as deep as the root level element. The next line of code gets the total number of child elements one level under the root-level element. Because `XmlChildren` is an array, we can use the `arrayLen( )` function to determine the number of child elements.

Armed with this information, outputting various details about the XML file is trivial. First, we use the `isXmlDoc( )` function to determine whether `myXML` is an XML document object. To get the actual tag name (remember, we only have the structure so far) of the root element, we reference the `theRoot.XmlName`. This gives us `company`. Next, we check to see whether `company` is really the document root using the `isDocRoot( )` function, and we use `isXmlElem( )` to determine whether it's also an XML element. Our root element also has an attribute called `name`. To get the value of the name attribute, we reference `theRoot.XmlAttributes["Name"]`. Recall that `XmlAttributes` is a structure that contains all the attributes of the referenced element. In this case, we know that the attribute we want to grab is called `name`, so we specify it using bracket notation. We could just as easily reference it using dot notation:

```
theRoot.XmlAttributes.name
```

Although many coders prefer the readability of dot notation, you have to be careful that the structure key you are referencing doesn't violate any of ColdFusion's variable naming rules. For example, `theRoot.XmlAttributes.name` is fine, but `theRoot.XmlAttributes.first-name` is not, as hyphens are not allowed in ColdFusion variable names. Because of this, you are generally better off using bracket notation when dealing with XML unless you can be absolutely sure you won't encounter tag or attribute names that violate ColdFusion's variable naming conventions.

The next section of code uses a loop to iterate over the child elements below the root. We know the number of child elements to loop over from the previous code, in which we checked the length of the `XmlChildren` array. For each child element under the root, we output the element's tag name from `XmlName` (`employee`), its index position in the `XmlChildren` array, and the value stored in `XmlText` for the `name` element under the `employee` element. A second (inner) loop is used to output the names and values of any child tags of the `employee` elements. The collection loop is just another example of the different techniques you can use to access data inside an XML document object.

Once this is completed, we use the `xmlChildPos()` function to return the index position of the second occurrence of the `employee` element within the `XmlChildren` array. The results output to the browser are shown in Figure 23-2.

For more information on using array, structure, and XML functions, including examples, see the function reference in Appendix B.

XML DOM Nodes

A second way ColdFusion can reference an XML document object is using a DOM (Document Object Model) node view. The DOM is a W3C recommendation for modeling documents. Under the covers, ColdFusion MX uses the Apache Crimson XML parser (*http://xml.apache.org/crimson/*). This means that ColdFusion MX adheres to the DOM Level 2 Core specification. You can read more about this specification and its particulars at *http://www.w3.org/tr/DOM-Level-2-Core*. In the DOM node view, XML documents are represented as a hierarchical tree of nodes. Each node in the tree consists of a node name, a node type, and a node value:

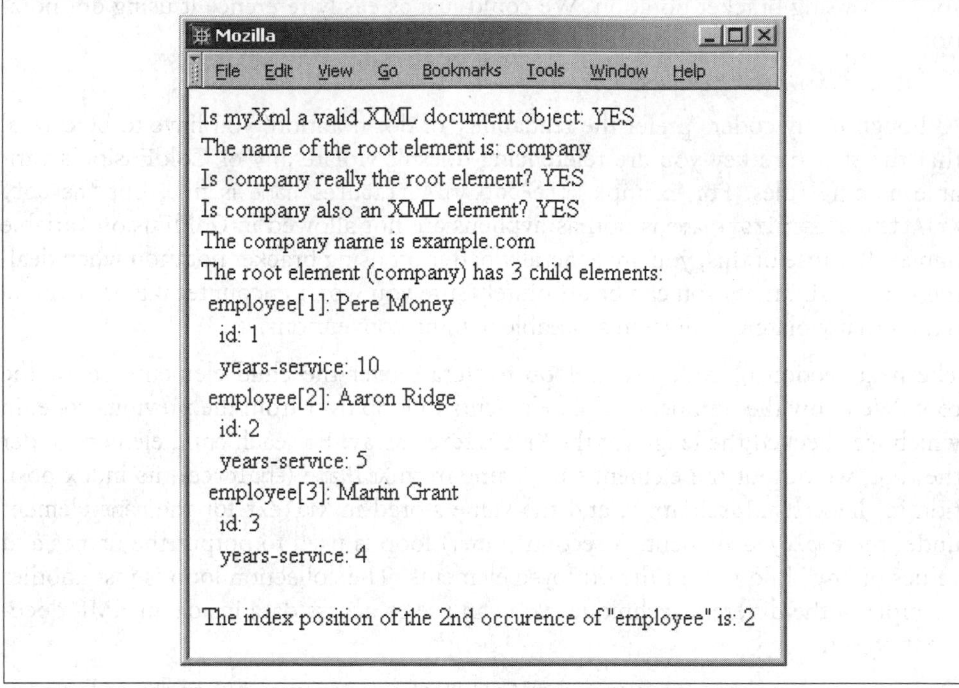

Figure 23-2. Accessing XML document object data using array and structure functions

`XmlType`*
: Type of XML DOM node. Possible return values are `CDATA`, `COMMENT`, `DOCUMENT`, `FRAGMENT`, `DOCTYPE`, `ELEMENT`, `ENTITY`, `ENTITYREF`, `NOTATION`, `PI` (processing instruction), and `Text`.

`XmlName`
: Name of the XML DOM node. For return values, see Table 23-1.

`XmlValue`
: Value stored in the XML DOM node. `XmlValue` only contains values for `CDATA`, `COMMENT`, and `Text` nodes.

Because of this, the DOM node view of an XML document gives you much more granular access to elements in the document than does the basic view.

Table 23-1 shows the possible values for `XmlType` as well as the corresponding DOM node name (`XmlName`) and the value the node contains.

* ColdFusion MX does not expose the `XmlType Attr` (attribute) as part of the DOM. To access an element's attribute(s), you must use the element's `XmlAttributes` structure.

Table 23-1. DOM XML types, names, and associated values

XmlType	XmlName	Node value
CDATA	#cdata-section	Content of the CDATA section
COMMENT	#comment	Content of the comment
DOCUMENT	#document	Empty string
FRAGMENT	#document-fragment	Empty string
DOCTYPE	Document type name	Empty string
ELEMENT	Tag name	Empty string
ENTITY	Entity name	Empty string
ENTITYREF	Name of entity referenced	Empty string
NOTATION	Notation name	Empty string
PI (processing instruction)	Entire content excluding target	Empty string
Text	#text	Content of the text node

Using the XML document from Example 23-1, we can use DOM node syntax to access data in an XML document object, as shown in Example 23-4.

Example 23-4. Accessing XML DOM nodes

```
<!--- Read in XML file --->
<cffile action="read"
        file="c:\cfusionmx\wwwroot\programmingcf\23\employee.xml"
        variable="theXML">

<!--- Convert XML string to XML document object --->
<cfset myXml = xmlParse(theXml)>

<table border="1">
  <tr>
    <th>Node</th>
    <th>XmlType</th>
    <th>XmlName</th>
    <th>XmlValue</th>
  </tr>
  <cfoutput>
  <tr>
    <td>myXml</td>
    <td>#myXml.XmlType#</td>
    <td>#myXml.XmlName#</td>
    <td>#myXml.XmlValue#</td>
  </tr>
  <tr>
    <td>myXml.XmlRoot</td>
    <td>#myXml.XmlRoot.XmlType#</td>
    <td>#myXml.XmlRoot.XmlName#</td>
    <td>#myXml.XmlRoot.XmlValue#</td>
```

Example 23-4. Accessing XML DOM nodes (continued)

```
  </tr>
  <tr>
    <td>myXml.XmlRoot.XmlNodes[2]</td>
    <td>#myXml.XmlRoot.XmlNodes[2].XmlType#</td>
    <td>#myXml.XmlRoot.XmlNodes[2].XmlName#</td>
    <td>#myXml.XmlRoot.XmlNodes[2].XmlValue#</td>
  </tr>
  </cfoutput>
</table>
```

This time around, instead of referencing each element as if it were a structure member, we reference the actual node in the XML DOM. This allows a finer degree of control over exactly what we are accessing. The code in Example 23-4 accesses three different nodes in the XML document object and outputs the `XmlType`, `XmlName`, and `XmlValue` for each. For more information on working with DOM nodes, see the web sites mentioned earlier in this section.

Generating Your Own XML

Now that you understand the structure of an XML document and its corresponding XML document object in ColdFusion, let's look at how we can generate our own XML in ColdFusion. In this section, we'll cover different methods for generating XML from scratch as well as techniques for modifying existing XML. We'll also cover sending XML to the browser and writing XML out to a file.

The easiest way to generate XML in ColdFusion MX is with the new `cfxml` tag. `cfxml` is a container tag that creates a ColdFusion XML document object from the XML and CFML code between the `<cfxml></cfxml>` tags. Any CFML code inside the container is executed, and the results are assigned to appropriate elements in the XML document object. The `cfxml` tag takes two attributes, `variable` and `casesensitive`. `variable` is a required attribute and specifies a variable name for holding the resulting XML document object. `casesensitive` is an optional Boolean attribute. It indicates whether ColdFusion should maintain the case of XML document elements and attributes. The default is `no`. Example 23-5 shows how to use the `cfxml` tag to generate XML identical to the XML file we used in Example 23-1.

Example 23-5. Generating XML using the cfxml tag

```
<cfxml variable="myXml">
  <!-- employees for example.com -->
  <company name="example.com">
    <!-- begin employee listings -->
    <employee id="1" years-service="10">
      <name>Pere Money</name>
      <title>President</title>
```

Example 23-5. Generating XML using the cfxml tag (continued)

```
    </employee>
    <employee id="2" years-service="5">
      <name>Aaron Ridge</name>
      <title>Analyst</title>
    </employee>
    <employee id="3" years-service="4">
      <name>Martin Grant</name>
      <title>Manager</title>
    </employee>
  </company>
</cfxml>
```

One thing you may notice right away is that we don't include an XML type declaration such as `<?xml version="1.0" encoding="utf-8"?>`. This is because the `cfxml` tag automatically creates it for us. If we had included the line, ColdFusion would have thrown an error.

If you run this code, what you end up with is a blank page. This is because the `cfxml` tag stores the generated XML as an XML document object (no `xmlParse( )` necessary). If you add the following `cfdump` tag to the end of Example 23-5 and run the code again, you should see output identical to that in Figure 23-1:

```
<cfdump var="#myXml#">
```

Alternatively, you could output the XML directly to the browser by using the `cfcontent` tag instead of `cfdump`. You can replace the `cfdump` tag with this code instead:

```
<cfcontent type="text/xml"><cfoutput>#toString(myXml)#</cfoutput></cfcontent>
```

Here, `cfcontent` sets the MIME type for the output stream to `text/xml`. The `toString( )` function is used to convert the XML document object to a string that can be output. If your browser is capable of displaying XML (as most modern browsers are), you should see XML that looks identical to the XML in Example 23-1.

If you don't want to output your XML to the browser, you can just as easily save it to disk using the `cffile` tag (or upload it somewhere with `cfftp`, or post it using `cfhttp`):

```
<cffile action="write" file="c:\myXml.doc" output="#toString(myXml)#">
```

It's also possible to combine static XML tags with data dynamically generated by ColdFusion. Example 23-6 shows how you can use a query result set from the `EmployeeDirectory` database table in conjunction with static XML tags to dynamically generate an XML document.

Example 23-6. Combining static and dynamically generated XML

```
<cfquery name="getEmployees" datasource="programmingcf">
  SELECT ID, Name, Title
  FROM EmployeeDirectory
</cfquery>

<cfxml variable="myXml">
  <!-- employees for example.com -->
  <company name="example.com">
    <!-- begin employee listings -->
    <cfoutput query="getEmployees">
    <employee id="#id#" years-service="#randRange(1,20)#">
      <name>#name#</name>
      <title>#title#</title>
    </employee>
    </cfoutput>
  </company>
</cfxml>

<cfcontent type="text/xml"><cfoutput>#toString(myXml)#</cfoutput></cfcontent>
```

In this template, a database query is performed to fetch the `ID`, `Name`, and `Title` of each employee in the `EmployeeDirectory` table. Next, the `cfxml` tag is used to set up the XML document object. The comments and root element of the document are hardcoded. Each child element, however, is dynamically generated by looping over the result set returned by the query.[*] The resulting XML document object is then converted to a string and output to the browser using the `cfcontent` tag. Running the example results in the output shown in Figure 23-3.

In addition to the `cfxml` tag, you can also create an XML document object using the `xmlNew( )` function. An optional Boolean parameter lets you specify whether XML document elements should maintain their case. The default is `no`. By itself, `xmlNew( )` simply creates an empty XML document object. You need to use additional structure, array, and/or XML functions to populate the XML document object. Example 23-7 shows one method of using `xmlNew( )` to create a new XML document object from a query result set.

[*] There is no `years-service` field in the `EmployeeDirectory` table. The `randRange( )` function is used to generate a random number to populate this attribute with.

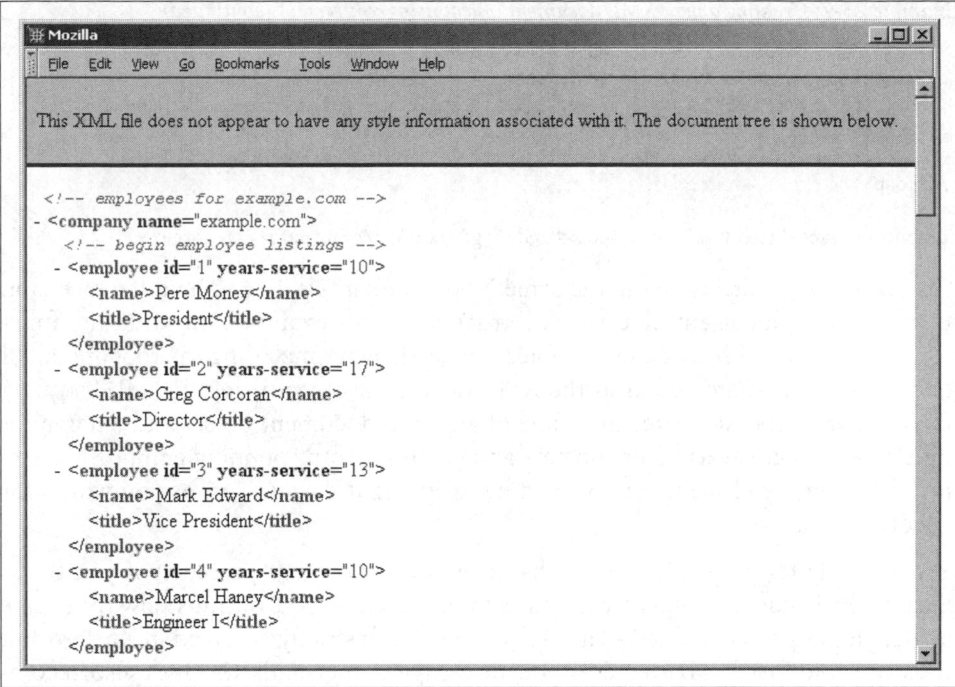

Figure 23-3. Generating XML from static and dynamic content

Example 23-7. Creating a new XML document object using xmlNew()

```
<cfquery name="getEmployees" datasource="programmingcf">
  SELECT ID, Name, Title
  FROM EmployeeDirectory
</cfquery>

<!--- create the empty XML doc object, give it a root element, and add an
      attribute called name to the root element --->
<cfset myXml = xmlNew("no")>
<cfset myXml.xmlRoot = xmlElemNew(myXml,"company")>
<cfset myXml.xmlRoot.xmlAttributes["name"] = "Example.com">

<!--- loop over the query result set, creating a child "employee" element for
      each employee in the ercord set --->
<cfloop index="i" from="1" to="#getEmployees.recordCount#">

  <!--- create a new employee element --->
  <cfset myXml.xmlRoot.xmlChildren[i] = xmlElemNew(myXml, "employee")>

    <!--- add id and years-service attributes to the employee element --->
    <cfset myXml.xmlRoot.xmlChildren[i].xmlAttributes["id"] = getEmployees.ID[i]>
    <cfset myXml.xmlRoot.xmlChildren[i].xmlAttributes["years-service"] =
          randRange(1,20)>

    <!--- add name and title (child) elements under the current employee element
```

Example 23-7. Creating a new XML document object using xmlNew() (continued)

```
        and populate them with data from the query result set --->
    <cfset myXml.xmlRoot.xmlChildren[i].name = xmlElemNew(myXml, "name")>
      <cfset myXml.xmlRoot.xmlChildren[i].name.xmlText = getEmployees.name[i]>
    <cfset myXml.xmlRoot.xmlChildren[i].title = xmlElemNew(myXml, "title")>
      <cfset myXml.xmlRoot.xmlChildren[i].title.xmlText = getEmployees.title[i]>
</cfloop>

<cfcontent type="text/xml"><cfoutput>#toString(myXml)#</cfoutput></cfcontent>
```

This example generates nearly the same XML as Example 23-6. The difference is in how the XML document object is constructed. In this example, the `xmlNew( )` function creates a new XML document object. Each element, including the root and all of its child elements, are added to the XML document object using the `xmlElemNew( )` function. `xmlElemNew( )` takes the name of an XML document object and a name for the element to create as its parameters and creates a corresponding empty XML element. The empty element is populated by assigning it a value, just as you would for any other variable.

Just like HTML, XML has special characters that can cause problems if you try to place them inside an element without escaping them first. You must always escape greater-than signs (>) and less-than signs (<) as this is strictly enforced in XML. Additionally, ColdFusion MX requires you to escape ampersands (&). It is also recommended you escape single and double quotes.

The `xmlFormat( )` function can be used to sanitize strings that may include these characters. It automatically escapes all five of the aforementioned special characters, replacing them with their corresponding entity reference (`>`, `<`, `&`, `'`, and `"`), making it safe to insert them into your XML elements. You should seriously consider using the `xmlFormat( )` function whenever creating your own XML, especially when working with dynamically generated data where you might not have control over the characters used. Using the code from Example 23-6, we can easily modify it to use `xmlFormat( )` on all of the query columns containing string values (name and title in this case):

```
<cfquery name="getEmployees" datasource="programmingcf">
  SELECT ID, Name, Title
  FROM EmployeeDirectory
</cfquery>

<cfxml variable="myXml">
  <!-- employees for example.com -->
  <company name="example.com">
    <!-- begin employee listings -->
    <cfoutput query="getEmployees">
    <employee id="#id#" years-service="#randRange(1,20)#">
      <name>#xmlFormat(name)#</name>
      <title>#xmlFormat(title)#</title>
    </employee>
```

```
    </cfoutput>
  </company>
</cfxml>

<cfcontent type="text/xml"><cfoutput>#toString(myXml)#</cfoutput></cfcontent>
```

Another option for escaping text in an XML element is to declare it as a CDATA section. A CDATA section is a special XML interface specifically designed to escape blocks of text (as opposed to individual characters) that could be confused with markup. CDATA sections are especially useful for putting snippets of code in XML elements. As per the XML specification, parsers are instructed to ignore the contents of a CDATA section when encountered. You declare a CDATA section like this:

```
<![CDATA[
Text goes here...
]]>
```

The <![CDATA[marks the start of the CDATA section and]]> ends it. It's important to note two things. First, CDATA sections cannot be nested. Second, the delimiter that marks the end of the CDATA section cannot contain any whitespace. The characters must always appear as a continuous string. Example 23-8 shows an XML file that contains two CDATA sections that contain CFML code.

Example 23-8. XML file containing CDATA sections

```
<?xml version="1.0" encoding="utf-8"?>
<library name="math">
  <udf name="areaCircle">
    <author>Rob Brooks-Bilson</author>
    <code><![CDATA[
            <cffunction name="areaCircle">
              <cfargument name="radius" type="numeric" required="true">
              <cfreturn pi()*(arguments.radius^2)>
            </cffunction>
          ]]>
    </code>
  </udf>
  <udf name="factorial">
    <author>Rob Brooks-Bilson</author>
    <code><![CDATA[
            <cffunction name="factorial">
              <cfargument name="integer" type="numeric" required="true">
              <cfset var myFactorial = 1>
              <cfloop condition="arguments.Integer gt 0">
                <cfset myFactorial = myFactorial*arguments.integer>
                <cfset arguments.integer = arguments.integer-1>
              </cfloop>
              <cfreturn myFactorial>
            </cffunction>
          ]]>
    </code>
  </udf>
</library>
```

Save this XML file as *cflib.xml*. Once you've done that, save the code shown in Example 23-9 in the same directory.

Example 23-9. Displaying XML containing CDATA

```
<cffile action="read"
        file="#expandPath("cflib.xml")#"
        variable="theXML">

<cfcontent type="text/xml"><cfoutput>#theXml#</cfoutput></cfcontent>
```

If you run this code in Internet Explorer, you should see the XML, including CDATA sections nicely formatted on the screen. Figure 23-4 shows how this should look. If you View Source in the browser, you'll see that the CFML code in the CDATA section is perfectly intact.

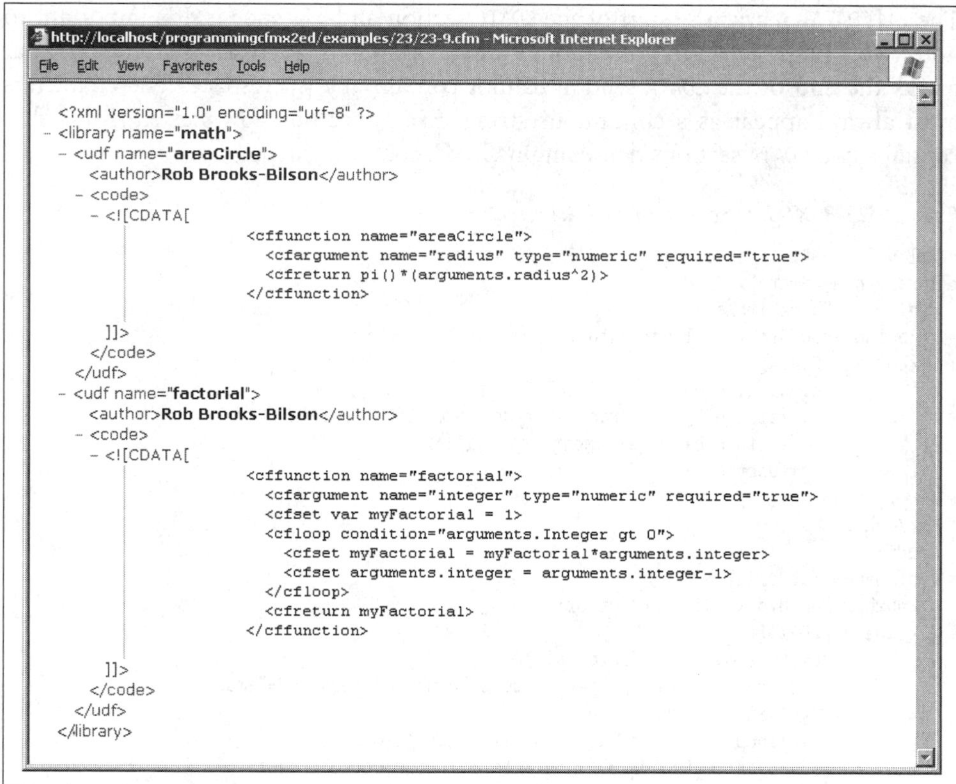

Figure 23-4. XML document containing CDATA sections as rendered in Internet Explorer

Matching XML Data with XPath

The XML Path language, or XPath, is a W3C recommendation outlining a language for addressing parts of an XML document. It was specifically designed to work with

XSLT (which we cover in the next section) as well as other XML parsers. A thorough discussion of XPath is beyond the scope of this chapter. As a result, this section assumes a working knowledge of the XPath language. If you need to brush up on XPath first, I'd suggest starting with the W3C recommendation at *http://www.w3.org/tr/xpath*. I've also found the O'Reilly *http://xml.com* web site to be a rich source of free articles and tutorials on XPath (and other XML technologies).

ColdFusion MX supports XPath as a query tool for extracting data from XML document objects via the `xmlSearch( )` function. The `xmlSearch( )` function is easy to use. It accepts two parameters, the name of an XML document object (or element of a document object) to search and the XPath expression to use. It searches the specified ColdFusion XML document object using the provided XPath expression. If a successful match is made, the function returns an array of XML document object nodes that match the search criteria.

Conceptually, XPath treats an XML document as a tree of nodes. This hierarchical relationship makes it easy to navigate the structure of an XML document using a simple path notation similar to that used to refer to directories in a file system. Take the XML document from Example 23-1. If you parse this into an XML document object, you can use the `xmlSearch( )` function along with various XPath expressions to return different portions of the document object. Table 23-2 shows you a few example expressions along with what you can expect them to return.

Table 23-2. XPath Expressions and their expected results

XPath expression	Expected result
`/`	Array containing a single index holding the entire XML document object
`/company`	Single index array containing the `company` element and its child elements
`/company/employee`	Array with three indexes; each index holds an `employee` element and its child elements

To get a better idea of how this looks, you can run this snippet of code:

```
<cffile action="read"
        file="c:\cfusionmx\wwwroot\programmingcf\23\employee.xml"
        variable="theXML">

<cfset myXml = xmlParse(theXml)>

<cfset results = xmlSearch(myXml, "/")>
<cfdump var="#results#">
<cfset results = xmlSearch(myXml, "/company")>
<cfdump var="#results#">
<cfset results = xmlSearch(myXml, "/company/employee")>
<cfdump var="#results#">
```

It applies all of the XPath expressions from Table 23-2 and dumps the results so you can see how the data structures returned by `xmlSearch( )` look.

Here's another example that goes one step further. It uses what's known as a predicate to filter a set of nodes into a new set. In this case, Example 23-10 reads in a public XML news feed from *macromedia.com*, parses it into an XML document object, uses XPath to return only the XML nodes containing articles, and outputs the results to the browser.

Example 23-10. Using XPath to query an XML document object

```
<cfhttp url="http://www.macromedia.com/devnet/resources/macromedia_resources.xml"
        method="get">

<cfset devNet = xmlParse(cfhttp.fileContent)>
<cfset searchResults =
    xmlSearch(devNet, "/macromedia_resources/resource[attribute::type='Article']")>

<h2>Available Articles</h2>
<cfloop index="i" from="1" to="#arrayLen(searchResults)#">
 <cfoutput>
 <a href="#SearchResults[i].URL.XmlText#">#SearchResults[i].Title.XmlText#</a><br>
 </cfoutput>
</cfloop>
```

The `cfhttp` tag is used to fetch an XML file containing a list of articles, tutorials, and other items on Macromedia's public DevNet site. The results are parsed into an XML document object called `devNet`. The `xmlSearch( )` function uses the XPath expression:

```
"/macromedia_resources/resource[attribute::type='Article']"
```

This matches any child elements off of the `macromedia_resources` document root that have an attribute called `type` with a value of `"Article"` (the predicate is the part in square brackets). The resulting array is looped over, and the results are output to the browser as links to the actual article. The output is shown in Figure 23-5.

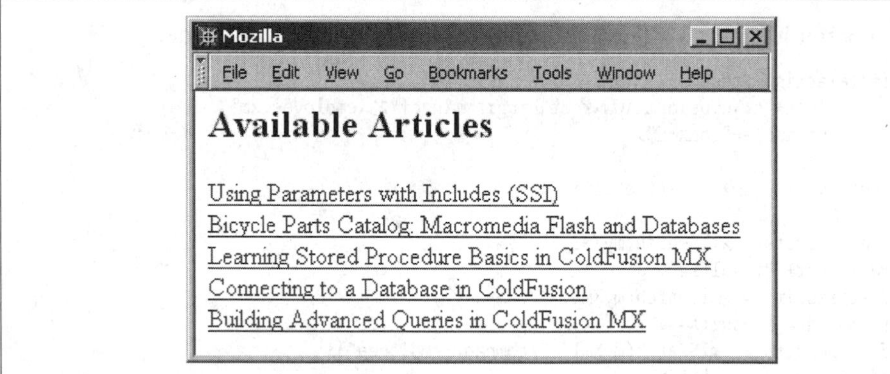

Figure 23-5. Using XPath to parse the macromedia.com DevNet XML feed

Of course, these examples only scratch the surface of what you can accomplish with XPath. The language contains several additional features such as functions and operators, as well as more advanced constructs that allow you to search and manipulate the contents of an XML file beyond your wildest dreams.

Transforming XML with XSLT

XSLT stands for Extensible Stylesheet Language Transformation. It's a W3C recommendation for rules used to transform XML data into alternate formats, such HTML, WML, and other XML vocabularies. XSLT works in conjunction with the Extensible Stylesheet Language (XSL) to perform the actual transformation. The XSL and XSLT specifications are both fairly involved, and unfortunately, it isn't possible to thoroughly cover all of the ins and outs of each in a single chapter. Before proceeding, I recommend you familiarize yourself with the concepts laid out in both specifications. For more information on XSLT and XSL, see the W3C specifications at *http://www.w3.org/tr/xslt/* and *http://www.w3.org/tr/xsl/*, respectively. Another good resource for articles and tutorials is the O'Reilly *http://xml.com* web site. I can't recommend it enough.

That said, let's again consider the XML file we created previously in Example 23-1. Suppose you wanted to create a basic HTML table displaying the name and title of each employee in the file. You could use ColdFusion to read in the XML file, parse it into an XML document object, and loop through the various nodes, constructing the table as it goes along. You could, but there's an easier, more elegant solution: use an XSL stylesheet to specify how the data should be presented, then pass it through an XSLT engine to handle the transformation.

ColdFusion MX uses the `xmlTransform( )` function to perform an XSLT transformation on an XML string or document object using an XSL stylesheet. The results are returned as a string. From the ColdFusion perspective, there's nothing to the process. You provide some XML and an XSL stylesheet, and one line of code later, ColdFusion has transformed the XML according to the instructions contained in the stylesheet. Example 23-11 shows the code to load the *employee.xml* file from Example 23-1, apply an XSL stylesheet for converting the XML into an HTML table (which we'll create in a moment), and output the results to the browser.

Example 23-11. Using xmlTransform() to perform an XSLT transformation

```
<cffile action="read"
        file="c:\cfusionmx\wwwroot\programmingcf\23\employee.xml"
        variable="MyXml">

<cffile action="read"
        file="c:\cfusionmx\wwwroot\programmingcf\23\html_employee.xsl"
        variable="MyXsl">

<cfset Transformed = xmlTransform(myXml, myXsl)>

<cfoutput>
```

Example 23-11. Using xmlTransform() to perform an XSLT transformation (continued)

```
#Transformed#
</cfoutput>
```

Example 23-12 shows a simple XSL stylesheet you can use to transform the data in the *employee.xml* file into a simple HTML table. Save the template as *html_employee.xsl*.

Example 23-12. An XSL stylesheet to transform data into an HTML table

```
<?xml version="1.0" encoding="utf-8"?>
<xsl:stylesheet
  xmlns:xsl="http://www.w3.org/1999/XSL/Transform"
  version="1.0">
  <xsl:output method="html"/>

  <xsl:template match="/company">
    <html>
      <head>
        <title>Example.com Employees</title>
      </head>
      <body>
      <table border="1">
        <tr>
          <th>Name</th>
          <th>Title</th>
        </tr>
      <xsl:apply-templates select="employee"/>
      </table>
      </body>
    </html>
  </xsl:template>

  <xsl:template match="employee">
    <tr>
      <td><xsl:value-of select="name"/></td>
      <td><xsl:value-of select="title"/></td>
    </tr>
  </xsl:template>
</xsl:stylesheet>
```

The first line in the XSL stylesheet is the same XML declaration we've used in our other XML documents. Although ignored by XSLT parsers, it's considered good form to include it. Since XSL is an XML format, it follows the same rules as other XML documents. The actual stylesheet starts with the root element on the second line. The root element in XSL is used to declare that the document is a stylesheet. In XSL, a namespace (prefix) is used to distinguish transformation instructions from other markup. The `xsl:output` element specifies how the result should be output. In this case, we specify `html`.

The next tag, `xsl:template`, defines a template rule for the node(s) matched by the XPath expression in the `match` attribute. In this example, we want to apply the template rule to the company element. The plain HTML sets up the table we want to create. Within the stylesheet, it is treated as plain text, to become part of the transformed document.

The xsl:apply-templates element is used to process the child elements of company recursively. Since there are three child elements in our XML document, the instruction generates a new table row for each of the employee child elements. The values for the cells in each row are obtained by the xsl:value-of elements.

If you run the template from Example 23-11, you should be presented with a small HTML table containing the names and titles of the three employees from the XML file, shown in Figure 23-6.

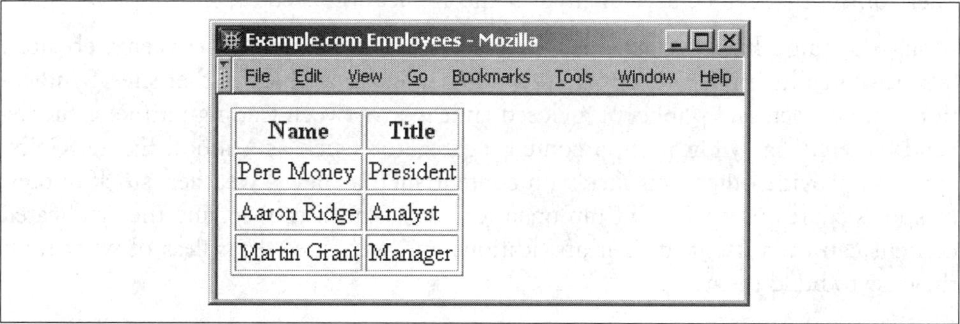

Figure 23-6. Results of using XSLT to transform XML to HTML

Using WDDX

In 1998, Macromedia (then Allaire) created an XML-based technology called the Web Distributed Data Exchange, or WDDX. WDDX is an open technology for exchanging both simple and complex datatypes using a language-independent representation of the data based on an XML 1.0–compliant DTD. It is designed to be used by any number of programming languages without regard to the platforms they are running on. A number of serialization/deserialization modules have been written for a variety of popular programming and scripting languages and are freely available. For the most up-to-date information on WDDX or to obtain the SDK, please visit *http://www.openwddx.org*.

What Can You Do with WDDX?

The first question you are probably asking is "What the heck can I do with WDDX?" Well, to put it simply, you can do a hell of a lot with it. Because WDDX allows you to represent data in a completely neutral and open format, WDDX is the perfect vehicle for sharing data between applications written in different languages. Imagine that you have an application written in Perl that performs some heavy-duty massaging on a large record set. Now suppose that you want to make the cleaned-up data available to another application within your company that is built in ColdFusion. How are you going to do that? You could write the data to a database and then query the database in ColdFusion, but what if the database isn't accessible to your ColdFusion application, say because it is behind a firewall? What then? You can save the record set as a delimited text file, then allow the ColdFusion application to grab it using `CFHTTP` or `CFFTP`, but that won't work because you need the datatypes of each field in the database to be preserved. Using WDDX, you can take the record set you created in your Perl application, convert it to the WDDX format, and send it to your ColdFusion application while preserving the datatypes of all of the data. Your ColdFusion application can then easily convert the data from the WDDX format into a query object that can be used in any way the application needs.

Along the same lines, WDDX can enable content syndication between web sites. Syndication allows one site to make selected content available to other sites. Syndication can be open and public, or a closed endeavor between trading partners, clients, vendors, etc. Via syndication, a content aggregator (such as Yahoo!, Excite, CNN, etc.) can provide other web sites with content such as news, weather, stock quotes, or sports scores using WDDX (an open format).* The sites receiving the syndicated content can then use it in their applications and web sites regardless of what tools they use to build them.

So far, we've mentioned two important ways in which you can use WDDX for server-to-server communication. But WDDX can be used for server-to-browser communication as well. If you use WDDX in conjunction with JavaScript, it is possible to create sophisticated user interfaces for browsing and manipulating data stored as WDDX.

Now that you have a better idea of what you can do with WDDX, let's look at how it works and how you can start using it within your own applications.

How Does It Work?

WDDX itself is nothing more than an XML representation of data. As such, you are probably wondering how to convert data to and from the WDDX format. The process looks something like this:

Data Serialization → WDDX Packet → Deserialization → Data

You'll notice three new terms: serialization, WDDX packet, and deserialization. *Serialization* consists of taking a chunk of data and converting it into the WDDX for-

* Increasingly, syndication of news type information (actual news headlines and stories, blogs, wikis, etc.) is being done via an XML dialect known as RSS (Really Simple Syndication). While this doesn't negate content syndication via WDDX, it certainly outpaces it. You can learn more about RSS on O'Reilly's *xml.com* web site.

mat. Data that has been converted to WDDX is referred to as a *WDDX packet*. A WDDX packet can represent a range of both simple and complex datatypes. The simple datatypes are made up of string, numeric, Boolean, null, and date/time values. Complex datatypes consist of arrays, structures, record sets (query objects in CFML), and binary data. The process of converting the contents of a WDDX packet back to their native datatype(s) is known as *deserialization*.

While this chapter primarily deals with WDDX within the context of the ColdFusion Markup Language (which has native support for WDDX), there are components available for several other languages. A COM component is available that can be used by any COM-enabled language, such as ASP, Visual Basic, Delphi, Visual C++, and PowerBuilder. Additionally, native modules now exist for Java, Perl, and PHP. Within each of these implementations (CFML, COM, Java, and Perl), support for client-side JavaScript objects capable of working with WDDX is provided. Server-side JavaScript is also supported via the COM implementation.

Show Me the WDDX!

Now that we've covered the how and why of WDDX, let's take a moment to examine the syntax of a WDDX packet. Because WDDX uses an XML DTD, a WDDX packet is just a collection of tags and data elements. The following is a WDDX packet containing a single string value:

```
<wddxPacket version='1.0'>
  <header></header>
  <data>
    <string>Programming ColdFusion</string>
  </data>
</wddxPacket>
```

All WDDX packets are considered well-formed XML in the sense that their syntax conforms to the XML 1.0 specification. Every WDDX packet must be enclosed in the `<wddxPacket></wddxPacket>` tags. The current version of the WDDX DTD is 1.0a and is specified along with the `<wddxPacket>` tag. The full WDDX DTD may be obtained by visiting *http://www.openwddx.org* and downloading the WDDX SDK. The next tag pair, `<header></header>` isn't currently used in WDDX, but it has been included in case a need for it arises in the future. The `<data></data>` tag pair marks the start and end of all serialized data within the WDDX packet. In this example, only a single string, `Programming ColdFusion`, is serialized within the packet. It is delimited appropriately using the `<string></string>` tags. Other datatypes include `<number>`, `<null>`, `<Boolean>`, `<dateTime>`, `<recordset>`, `<array>`, `<struct>`, and `<binary>`. These are covered later in the chapter.

There is no concept of whitespace in WDDX. The prior example in which we neatly indented the tag pairs of the WDDX packet and separated them with newlines is just as valid as a WDDX packet containing no whitespace at all. In fact, most WDDX packets that are created using the `cfwddx` tag contain no whitespace between the pairs of tags. Although more difficult to read, this is actually a desirable format for transporting WDDX packets, as whitespace can add to the overall bulk of the packet (eating up precious bandwidth and additional storage space).*

One of the great things about using WDDX with ColdFusion is that you don't really have to do much work to serialize and deserialize WDDX packets. ColdFusion uses the `cfwddx` tag to handle the serialization and deserialization of the data for you according to the WDDX XML DTD. The `cfwddx` tag can also be used to create JavaScript statements that instantiate equivalent JavaScript objects (more on this later). The general syntax for using the `cfwddx` tag is as follows:

```
<cfwddx action="action"
        input="data_to_be_serialized/de-serialized"
        output="variable_name_for_results"
        toplevelvariable="top_level_variable_name_for_javascript_object"
        usetimezoneinfo="Yes/No">
```

The `action` attribute is required and specifies the action to be performed by the tag. Possible values include the following:

`CFML2WDDX`
: Serializes CFML to WDDX

`WDDX2CFML`
: Deserializes WDDX to CFML

`CFML2JS`
: Serializes CFML to WDDX, then automatically deserializes it to JavaScript in a single step

`WDDX2JS`
: Deserializes WDDX to JavaScript

The `input` attribute specifies the data to be serialized/deserialized. As you might expect, `output` specifies a variable to hold the serialized/deserialized data. `output` is required when `action` is `WDDX2CFML`. For all other actions, if no value is specified for `output`, the results of the serialization/deserialization are output directly to the browser in the HTML stream. The `toplevelvariable` attribute is required when `action` is set to `CFML2JS` or `WDDX2JS`. It specifies the name of the top-level JavaScript object created when deserialization occurs.

The final attribute is `usetimezoneinfo`. This attribute is optional, can be set to `Yes` or `No`, and indicates whether to use time-zone information when serializing CFML to WDDX. If this attribute is set to `Yes`, ColdFusion calculates the hour/minute offset

* If you use ColdFusion Studio/Homesite+ as your development environment, you can open any WDDX packet residing in a file and apply the WDDX CodeSweeper (located under Tools → CodeSweeper → WDDX Sweeper) to it. The WDDX Sweeper takes an unformatted (all whitespace stripped) WDDX packet and formats it for easy readability.

for all date/time objects in the WDDX packet. If `usetimezoneinfo` is set to `No`, local time is used for all date/time objects. The default value for `usetimezoneinfo` is `Yes`.

Serializing and Deserializing Data

In CFML, the process of serializing and deserializing data is handled by the `cfwddx` tag. The following sections step through the process of using the tag to serialize and deserialize various simple and complex datatypes. Numerous examples are provided to make the concepts as clear as possible.

Serializing and deserializing simple values

The easiest types of values to work with are simple values, as simple values only consist of numbers, strings, Boolean, date/time values, and null datatypes. The process of serializing and deserializing simple values then is straightforward. Example 23-13 serializes an example of each simple datatype (`boolean`, `dateTime`, `null`, `number`, and `string`) and displays the resulting WDDX packets in an HTML table so that you can see how the structure of each packet varies depending on the datatype represented.

Example 23-13. Serializing simple datatypes to WDDX

```
<!--- serialize a boolean --->
<cfwddx action="CFML2WDDX" input="#IsDefined('y')#" output="WDDX_boolean">

<!--- serialize a dateTime --->
<cfwddx action="CFML2WDDX" input="#now( )#"
        output="WDDX_dateTime" usetimezoneinfo="Yes">

<!--- serialize a number --->
<cfwddx action="CFML2WDDX" input="#Val(123.456)#" output="WDDX_Number">

<!--- serialize a null ColdFusion style (an empty string) --->
<cfwddx action="CFML2WDDX" input="" output="WDDX_Null">

<!--- serialize a string --->
<cfwddx action="CFML2WDDX" input="I am a string!" output="WDDX_String1">

<!--- serialize a string with a newline character --->
<cfwddx action="CFML2WDDX" input="I am a string! So am I."
        output="WDDX_String2">

<!--- serialize a string with a tab --->
<cfwddx action="CFML2WDDX" input="I am a string!#CHR(9)#So am I."
        output="WDDX_String3">

<h2>Simple datatypes serialized as WDDX packets</h2>

<!--- output all of the wddx packets for the simple datatypes --->
<cfoutput>
<table border="1" cellpadding="3">
```

Example 23-13. Serializing simple datatypes to WDDX (continued)

```
<tr>
  <th>Data Type</th><th>WDDX Packet</th>
<tr>
<tr>
  <td>boolean:</td><td>#HTMLEditFormat(WDDX_boolean)#</td>
</tr>
<tr>
  <td>dateTime:</td><td>#HTMLEditFormat(WDDX_dateTime)#</td>
</tr>
<tr>
  <td>null (CFML) as an empty string</td><td>#HTMLEditFormat(WDDX_null)#</td>
</tr>
<tr>
  <td>null (COM, Java and JavaScript)</td>
  <td>&lt;wddxPacket version='1.0'&gt;&lt;header&gt;&lt;/header&gt;&lt;data&gt;
    &lt;null/&gt;&lt;/data&gt;&lt;/wddxPacket&gt;</td>
</tr>
<tr>
  <td>number</td><td>#HTMLEditFormat(WDDX_number)#</td>
</tr>
<tr>
  <td>string</td><td>#HTMLEditFormat(WDDX_String1)#</td>
</tr>
<tr>
  <td>string with newline character encoded</td>
  <td>#HTMLEditFormat(WDDX_String2)#</td>
</tr>
<tr>
  <td>string with tab encoded</td><td>#HTMLEditFormat(WDDX_String3)#</td>
</tr>
</table>
</cfoutput>
```

Figure 23-7 shows how the various simple datatypes are represented in WDDX. Each chunk of data is delimited by a set of tags declaring the datatype. Strings are delimited by `<string></string>`, numbers by `<number></number>`, and date/time objects by `<dateTime></dateTime>`. Null and Boolean values are handled slightly differently. Instead of tag pairs, null values are represented by `<null/>` while Boolean values are represented by `<boolean value='false'/>` or `<boolean value='true'/>`.*

Note that the `HTMLEditFormat()` is used with each output variable that is written to the browser. It is necessary to do this because the WDDX packets contain special characters such as < and > that must be escaped before they can be displayed by a browser. The `HTMLEditFormat()` function ensures that all special characters are

* Because some programming languages (including CFML) have no concept of null, deserialized null values are automatically converted to empty strings where appropriate.

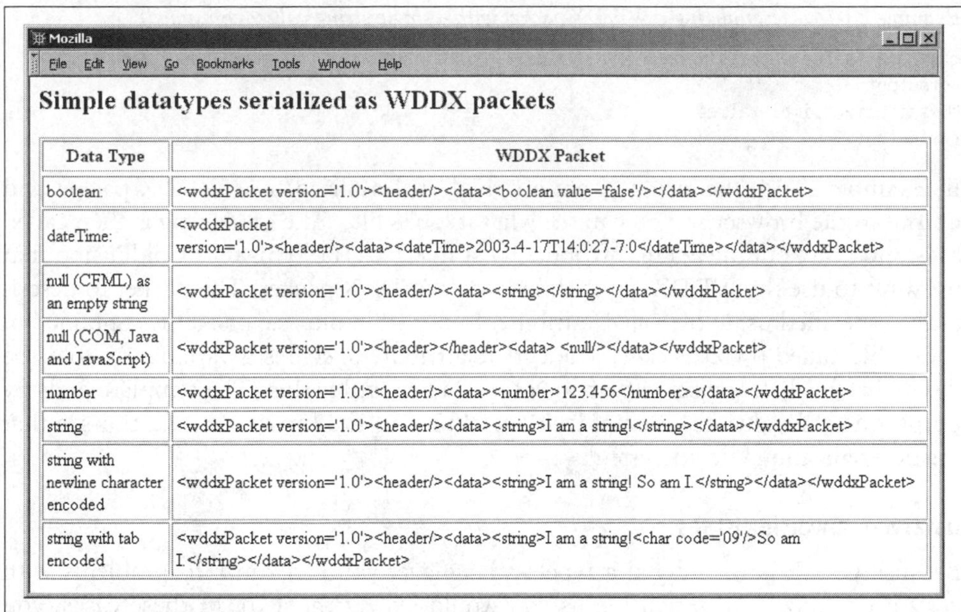

Mozilla

File Edit View Go Bookmarks Tools Window Help

Simple datatypes serialized as WDDX packets

Data Type	WDDX Packet
boolean:	<wddxPacket version='1.0'><header/><data><boolean value='false'/></data></wddxPacket>
dateTime:	<wddxPacket version='1.0'><header/><data><dateTime>2003-4-17T14:0:27-7:0</dateTime></data></wddxPacket>
null (CFML) as an empty string	<wddxPacket version='1.0'><header/><data><string></string></data></wddxPacket>
null (COM, Java and JavaScript)	<wddxPacket version='1.0'><header></header><data> <null/></data></wddxPacket>
number	<wddxPacket version='1.0'><header/><data><number>123.456</number></data></wddxPacket>
string	<wddxPacket version='1.0'><header/><data><string>I am a string!</string></data></wddxPacket>
string with newline character encoded	<wddxPacket version='1.0'><header/><data><string>I am a string! So am I.</string></data></wddxPacket>
string with tab encoded	<wddxPacket version='1.0'><header/><data><string>I am a string!<char code='09'/>So am I.</string></data></wddxPacket>

Figure 23-7. Simple values as represented by WDDX packets

escaped before the WDDX packet is displayed. This technique is especially important if you plan to pass WDDX packets between templates as `form` variables.

Now that you understand the basics of serializing simple datatypes, let's turn our attention to the deserialization process. As I mentioned earlier, deserialization is the process of taking the data stored in a WDDX packet and converting it back to its native format. Thanks to the `cfwddx` tag, deserialization involves only a single tag call. Example 23-14 demonstrates deserialization of a string stored in a WDDX packet.

Example 23-14. Deserializing a WWDX packet with a single string value

```
<!--- first we need to serialize the string into a wddx packet --->
<cfwddx action="CFML2WDDX" input="I am a string!" output="MyWDDXPacket">

<!--- output the wddx packet in a text area so you can see the entire packet --->
<h3>WDDX Packet Containing A Simple Value (string)</h3>
<form>
<cfoutput>
<textarea rows="6" cols="50" wrap="virtual">#HTMLEditFormat(MyWDDXPacket)#
</textarea>
</cfoutput>
</form>

<!--- deserialize the wddx packet containing the string.  The entire
      deserialization process is performed with this single tag call. --->
<cfwddx action="WDDX2CFML" input="#MyWDDXPacket#"
       output="DeserializedSimpleValue">
```

Example 23-14. Deserializing a WWDX packet with a single string value (continued)

```
<h3>Here Is The Deserialized Simple Value:</h3>
<cfoutput>
#DeserializedSimpleValue#
</cfoutput>
```

In Example 23-14, the string “I am a string!” is serialized to a WDDX packet and output to the browser so you can see what it looks like. The cfwddx tag is then called a second time, but the action attribute is set to WDDX2CFML. This tells ColdFusion that we want to use the WDDX tag to deserialize a WDDX packet. The packet to deserialize is specified using the input attribute. In our example, the packet is contained in a variable called MyWDDXPacket. The output attribute specifies a variable to hold the deserialized value. We set output to DeserializedSimpleValue. The template ends by outputting the value of DeserializedSimpleValue to the browser so we can see that the deserialization was successful.

Datatype conversion issues

Because CFML is considered a typeless language, you can run into problems with certain datatypes not serializing as you would expect them to. In these cases, you may need to “convert” certain values before having them properly serialized as the intended datatype by the cfwddx tag. For example, both the cfwddx calls shown in the following example serialize the date as a <string> as opposed to a <dateTime> value:

```
<cfwddx action="CFML2WDDX" input="03/03/2003"
        output="MyWDDXPacket1" usetimezoneinfo="Yes">

<cfoutput>
#HTMLEditFormat(MyWDDXPacket1)#
</cfoutput>

<cfwddx action="CFML2WDDX" input="#DateFormat('03/03/2003','mm/dd/yyyy')#"
        output="MyWDDXPacket2" usetimezoneinfo="Yes">

<cfoutput>
#HTMLEditFormat(MyWDDXPacket2)#
</cfoutput>
```

In order to get the date to serialize as a <dateTime> as opposed to a <string>, it is necessary to use a date function such as CreateDate( ), ParseDateTime( ), or Now( ) (but not CreateODBCDate( ) or DateFormat( )) before serializing the date. It is also possible to use the Now( ) function as in the following examples:

```
<!--- use the CreateDate function to create a dateTime datatype --->
<cfwddx action="CFML2WDDX" input="#CreateDate(2003,08,15)#"
        output="MyWDDXPacket1" usetimezoneinfo="Yes">

<cfoutput>
#HTMLEditFormat(MyWDDXPacket1)#
</cfoutput>
```

```
<!--- use the Now function to create a dateTime datatype --->
<cfwddx action="CFML2WDDX" input="#Now( )#"
        output="MyWDDXPacket2" usetimezoneinfo="Yes">

<p>
<cfoutput>
#HTMLEditFormat(MyWDDXPacket2)#
</cfoutput>

<!--- use the ParseDateTime function to create a dateTime datatype --->
<cfwddx action="CFML2WDDX"
        input="#ParseDateTime('Sat, 15 Aug 2003 19:00:00 +0400', 'POP')#"
        output="MyWDDXPacket3" usetimezoneinfo="Yes">

<p>
<cfoutput>
#HTMLEditFormat(MyWDDXPacket3)#
</cfoutput>
```

Because CFML is typeless, issues like this do arise with `<boolean>` and `<number>` datatypes. The following example shows one way to overcome this problem using a Boolean function (`IsDefined( )`) and the `Val( )` function, respectively:

```
<!--- using a boolean function such as IsDefined ensures a boolean datatype
      during serialization. Simply specifying "yes" or "No" for the input
      attribute will result in the value being serialized as a string. --->
<cfwddx action="CFML2WDDX" input="#IsDefined('y')#" output="MyWDDXPacket1">

<cfoutput>
#HTMLEditFormat(MyWDDXPacket1)#
</cfoutput>

<!--- use the val function to ensure that a number is serialized as a numeric
      type and not as a string --->
<cfwddx action="CFML2WDDX" input="#Val(123.456)#" output="MyWDDXPacket2">

<p>
<cfoutput>
#HTMLEditFormat(MyWDDXPacket2)#
</cfoutput>
```

Testing for well-formed WDDX

The `cfwddx` tag is capable of Deserializing only well-formed WDDX packets. If you attempt to deserialize a non–well-formed WDDX packet, ColdFusion throws an error. Because of this, you need a way to test whether a WDDX packet is well-formed. This is especially true in the case of WDDX packets retrieved from other servers over which you have no control. There are two methods for determining whether a value is a well-formed WDDX packet. The first method uses a function called `IsWDDX( )`:

```
<cfif IsWDDX(MyWDDXPacket)>
  <b>Is</b> a well-formed WDDX packet!
```

```
<cfelse>
  <b>Is not</b> a well-formed WDDX packet!
</cfif>
```

The `IsWDDX( )` function uses a validating XML parser with the WDDX DTD to determine whether a specified value is a well-formed WDDX packet. It returns `true` if the value is a well-formed WDDX packet; `false` if it isn't. For more information on `IsWDDX( )`, see Appendix B.

The second method involves an optional attribute of the `cfwddx` tag:

```
<cfwddx action="WDDX2CFML" input="#MyWDDXPacket#"
        output="DeserializedSimpleValue" validate="Yes">
```

`validate` can be set to either `Yes` or `No` and indicates whether to use a validating XML parser with the WDDX DTD to determine whether the value specified in `input` is a well-formed WDDX packet when `action` is `WDDX2CFML` or `WDDDX2JS`. If the value is a well-formed WDDX packet, deserialization takes place. If the value isn't well-formed WDDX, an exception is thrown. The `validate` parameter performs the same job as the `IsWDDX` function.

Serializing and deserializing complex datatypes

WDDX can also represent more complex datatypes than the ones we've covered so far. As such, it is possible to serialize and deserialize complex datatypes such as record sets (query objects), arrays, structures, and binary objects. Part of what makes WDDX so attractive to developers is that the process for serializing and deserializing complex datatypes is the same as it is for serializing simple values. The difference lies in how each datatype is represented within the WDDX packet. Throughout this section, we'll look at serializing and deserializing complex datatypes.

Record sets. The first complex datatype we'll cover is the record set. In ColdFusion terms, a record set is synonymous with a query object. Throughout the rest of this chapter, we'll use the terms interchangeably. With the `cfwddx` tag, it is easy to take a ColdFusion query object and serialize it to a WDDX packet. Deserializing the packet is just as simple. Example 23-15 shows just how easy it is to deserialize a packet.

Example 23-15. Serializing and deserializing a query object (record set) using cfwddx

```
<!--- get all employee records --->
<cfquery name="GetEmployeeInfo" datasource="ProgrammingCF">
   SELECT * FROM EmployeeDirectory
</cfquery>

<!--- serialize the employee records to a wddx packet --->
<cfwddx action="CFML2WDDX" input="#GetEmployeeInfo#"
        output="QueryObject" usetimezoneinfo="Yes">

<!--- output the wddx packet in a text area so you can see the entire packet --->
<h3>WDDX Packet Containing a Query Object</h3>
```

Example 23-15. Serializing and deserializing a query object (record set) using cfwddx (continued)

```
<form>
<cfoutput>
<textarea rows="15" cols="80" wrap="virtual">#HTMLEditFormat(QueryObject)#
</textarea>
</cfoutput>
</form>

<!--- deserialize the wddx packet containing the query object --->
<cfwddx action="WDDX2CFML" input="#QueryObject#"
       output="DeserializedQueryObject">

<h3>Here Is The Deserialized Query Object:</h3>
<table cellpadding="3" cellspacing="0">
<tr bgcolor="#888888">
  <th>Name</th><th>Title</th><th>Department</th><th>E-mail</th>
  <th>Phone Extension</th>
</tr>
<cfoutput query="DeserializedQueryObject">
<tr bgcolor="##C0C0C0">
  <td>#Name#</td><td>#Title#</td><td>#Department#</td>
  <td><a href="Mailto:#Email#">#Email#</a></td><td>#PhoneExt#</td>
</tr>
</cfoutput>
</table>
```

In Example 23-15, the `EmployeeDirectory` table of the `ProgrammingCF` data source is queried. The resulting record set is serialized to a WDDX packet by setting the `action` attribute of the `cfwddx` tag to `CFML2WDDX`. Setting `input` to `#GetEmployeeRecords#` tells the `cfwddx` tag to serialize the record set contained in the `GetEmployeeRecords` variable. The `output` attribute allows us to specify a variable to hold the WDDX packet created by the serialization process. We set our output variable to `QueryObject`.

Once we have the WDDX packet, it is displayed to the browser in a `textarea` form element so we can see the packet in its entirety, as shown in Figure 23-8.

In Figure 23-8, you'll notice this tag in the WDDX packet:

```
<recordset rowCount='12' fieldNames='ID,name,TITLE,DEPARTMENT,EMAIL,PHONEEXT'>
```

This line (it ends with the `</recordset>` tag) identifies the data that follows as a record set. The `rowCount` attribute defines the record set consisting of twelve records (rows). The field names (column headers) for the record set are specified by the `rowCount` attribute. The data from the record set is then included in the WDDX packet, within the `<recordset></recordset>` tags, one column at a time:

```
<field name='ID'><number>1</number><number>2</number><number>3</number>
<number>4</number><number>5</number><number>6</number><number>7</number>
<number>8</number><number>9</number><number>10</number><number>11</number>
<number>18</number></field>
```

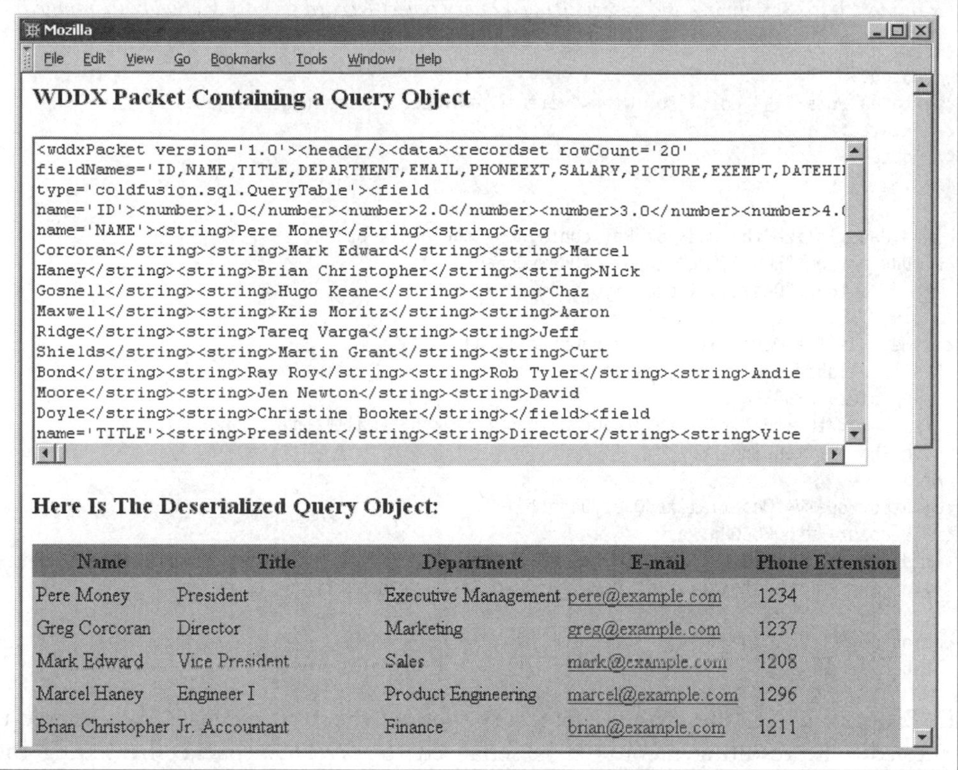

Figure 23-8. Serialization and deserialization of a record set

Each data element within the record set is marked with the appropriate tag for its datatype. Strings are marked up with `<string></string>`, numbers with `<number></number>`, etc. Only strings (including Base64-encoded binary strings), numbers, and data/time values are allowed within record sets.

The next part of the template is used to deserialize the packet we just created. This is done by calling the `cfwddx` tag and setting `action` to `WDDX2CFML`. This time, the `input` attribute is set to `QueryObject`, the variable that contains the serialized WDDX packet. The `output` attribute specifies a variable to hold the deserialized data—in this case a ColdFusion query object. We set our `output` variable to `DeserializedQueryObject`.

Once we have our query object, the next step is to output the contents to the browser. Our query object has all the same properties as any query object you would obtain using the `cfquery` tag. As such, we can create an HTML table of the values in the query object using the `cfoutput` tag, and the results are shown in Figure 23-8.

Arrays. Arrays are a complex datatype that use numeric (integer) indexes to store data of varying types. Arrays can consist of any number of dimensions but typically are limited to one, two, or three. As far as the WDDX DTD is concerned, you may nest any number of arrays to achieve the desired number of dimensions.

Example 23-16 takes a one-dimensional array that contains student grades and serializes them into a WDDX packet. The results are then output in a textarea HTML form element so you can see what the resulting packet looks like. Next, the packet is deserialized back to a one-dimensional array and the results (shown in Figure 23-9) are output to the browser.

Example 23-16. Serializing and deserializing a one-dimensional array

```
<!--- create a one-dimensional array of student grades --->
<cfset Grades = ArrayNew(1)>

<cfset Grades[1] = 95>
<cfset Grades[2] = 93>
<cfset Grades[3] = 87>
<cfset Grades[4] = 100>
<cfset Grades[5] = 74>

<!--- serialize the grades array to a wddx packet --->
<cfwddx action="CFML2WDDX" input="#Grades#" output="GradesArray">

<!--- output the wddx packet in a text area so you can see the entire packet --->
<h3>WDDX Packet Containing A One-dimensional Array</h3>
<form>
<cfoutput>
<textarea rows="6" cols="80" wrap="virtual">#HTMLEditFormat(GradesArray)#
</textarea>
</cfoutput>
</form>

<!--- deserialize the gradesarray wddx packet back to an array --->
<cfwddx action="WDDX2CFML" input="#GradesArray#" output="DeserializedArray">

<h3>Here Are The Deserialized Grades:</h3>
<cfloop index="i" from="1" to="#ArrayLen(DeserializedArray)#">
<cfoutput>
Grade #i#: #DeserializedArray[i]#<br>
</cfoutput>
</cfloop>
```

Looking at the WDDX packet shown in Figure 23-9, it is easy to see how a one-dimensional array is represented within the packet. The line:

```
<array length='5'><string>95</string><string>93</string><string>87</string>
<string>100</string><string>74</string></array>
```

defines a one-dimensional array that is five elements in length. Each element in the array (in this case, all strings) is marked up by <string></string> tags. One of the advantages to using an array is that its elements can be made up of any datatype, simple or complex, that can be represented by WDDX.

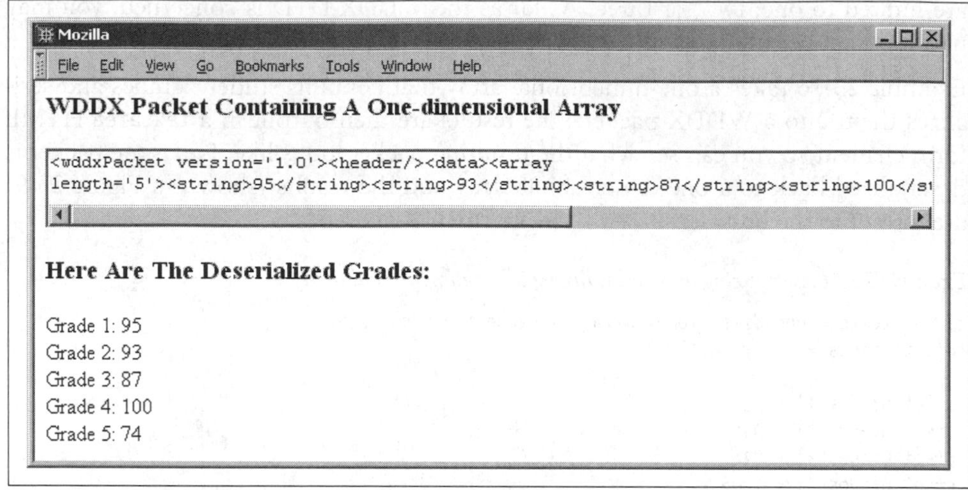

Figure 23-9. WDDX packet containing a one-dimensional array

Multidimensional arrays differ only slightly from their one-dimensional siblings in how they are represented within a WDDX packet. Consider Example 23-17, in which we create a two-dimensional array of student grades. Each student, represented by the elements in the first dimension of the array, has grades for three different tests, represented by the elements in the second dimension of the array. The array is serialized to a WDDX packet and output in a textarea element of an HTML form so that you can study the packet. After the packet is displayed, it is deserialized back into a two-dimensional array that is in turn presented to the browser, as shown in Figure 23-10.

Example 23-17. Serializing and deserializing a two-dimensional array

```
<!--- create a two dimensional array of student grades.  Each student
     (represented by the first dimension has grades for more than one test
     (represented by the second dimension). --->
<cfset Grades = ArrayNew(2)>

<cfset Grades[1][1] = 95>
<cfset Grades[1][2] = 93>
<cfset Grades[1][3] = 87>
<cfset Grades[2][1] = 100>
<cfset Grades[2][2] = 74>
<cfset Grades[2][3] = 86>
<cfset Grades[3][1] = 90>
<cfset Grades[3][2] = 94>
<cfset Grades[3][3] = 96>

<!--- serialize the grades array to a wddx packet --->
<cfwddx action="CFML2WDDX" input="#Grades#" output="GradesArray">

<!--- output the wddx packet in a text area so you can see the entire packet --->
```

Example 23-17. Serializing and deserializing a two-dimensional array (continued)

```
<h3>WDDX Packet Containing A Two-dimensional Array</h3>
<form>
<cfoutput>
<textarea rows="8" cols="80" wrap="virtual">#HTMLEditFormat(GradesArray)#
</textarea>
</cfoutput>
</form>

<!--- deserialize the gradesarray wddx packet back to an array --->
<cfwddx action="WDDX2CFML" input="#GradesArray#" output="DeserializedArray">

<h3>Here Are The Deserialized Grades:</h3>

<!--- this looping technique utilizes an outer and an inner loop (designated o
      and i respectively) for looping through each element in each dimension of
      the array --->
<cfloop index="o" FROM="1" TO="#ArrayLen(DeserializedArray)#">
  <cfloop index="i" FROM="1" TO="#ArrayLen(DeserializedArray[o])#">
    <cfoutput>
    Student #o#, Grade #i#: #DeserializedArray[o][i]#<br>
    </cfoutput>
  </cfloop>
</cfloop>
```

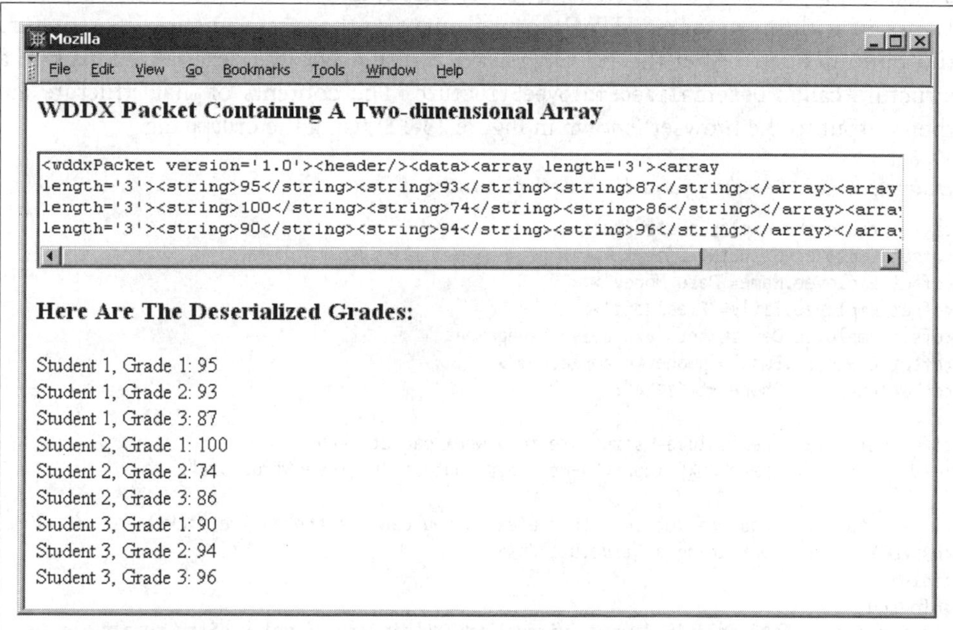

Figure 23-10. Serializing and deserializing a multidimensional array

Look at the resulting WDDX packet shown in Figure 23-10, paying particular attention to the part that reads:

```
<array length='3'><array length='3'><string>95</string><string>93</string>
<string>87</string></array><array length='3'><string>100</string>
<string>74</string><string>86</string></array><array length='3'>
<string>90</string><string>94</string><string>96</string></array></array>
```

You will notice that the WDDX packet represents multidimensional arrays as an array of arrays! This allows you to create arrays of as many dimensions as you want.

Once the WDDX packet is deserialized, outputting the contents of the two-dimensional array is just a matter of performing an outer and inner loop over the array.

Structures. Structures are similar to arrays in their architecture except that they are indexed by strings known as keys instead of integer values. Structures are also known as associative arrays, dictionaries, or maps depending on the programming language being used.

You should be careful when serializing and deserializing structures as WDDX handles them without regard to case. Because of this, if your structure contains two or more keys with the same name (regardless of case), only the last value is set when serializing or deserializing the structure. This is necessary as some programming languages with WDDX serializers/deserializers are case-insensitive.

The template in Example 23-18 creates a structure called `Employee` that contains a single employee record. The structure is serialized, and the resulting WDDX packet is output within a `textarea` HTML form element so that you can study its structure (no pun intended). After the WDDX packet is displayed, it is deserialized back to a structure called `DeserializedEmployeeStructure`. The contents of that structure are then output to the browser (shown in Figure 23-11) using the `cfdump` tag.

Example 23-18. Serializing and deserializing a structure

```
<!--- create the employee structure --->
<cfset Employee=StructNew( )>
<cfset Employee.Name="Pere Money">
<cfset Employee.Title="President">
<cfset Employee.Department="Executive Management">
<cfset Employee.Email="pmoney@example.com">
<cfset Employee.PhoneExt="1234">

<!--- serialize the employee structure to a wddx packet --->
<cfwddx action="CFML2WDDX" input="#Employee#" output="EmployeeStructure">

<!--- output the wddx packet in a text area so you can see the entire packet --->
<h3>WDDX Packet Containing a Structure</h3>
<form>
<cfoutput>
<textarea rows="10" cols="80" wrap="virtual">#HTMLEditFormat(EmployeeStructure)#
</textarea>
</cfoutput>
</form>
```

Example 23-18. Serializing and deserializing a structure (continued)

```
<!--- deserialize the wddx packet containing the structure --->
<cfwddx action="WDDX2CFML" input="#EmployeeStructure#"
        output="DeserializedEmployeeStructure">

<cfdump var="#DeserializedEmployeeStructure#">
```

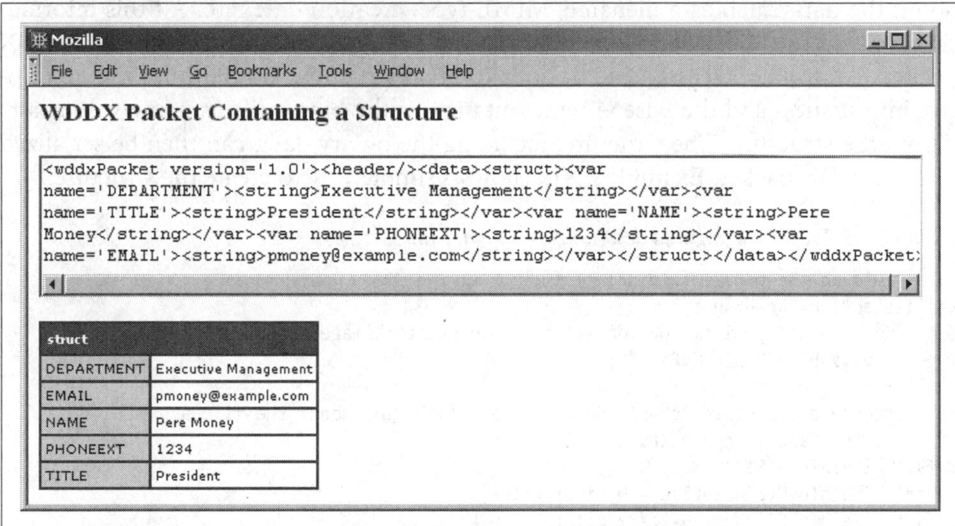

Figure 23-11. Serialization and deserialization of a structure

Looking at the WDDX packet shown in Figure 23-11, you'll notice that the structure is marked up using `<struct></struct>`:

```
<struct>
<var name='department'><string>Executive Management</string></var>
<var name='title'><string>President</string></var>
<var name='name'><string>Pere Money</string></var>
<var name='phoneext'><string>1234</string></var>
<var name='email'><string>pmoney@example.com</string></var>
</struct>
```

Each key within the structure is defined by a set of `<var></var>` tags. The value for each key is marked up within the `<var></var>` tags using the tags appropriate for the datatype. Just like arrays, you can nest structures as well as store any datatype available in WDDX.

Binary data. The ability to serialize and deserialize binary data allows you to send and receive binary files as WDDX packets. The WDDX DTD specifies that all binary data included in a WDDX packet must be Base64-encoded. All the serializers/deserializers included with the WDDX SDK as well as the `cfwddx` tag handle the encoding automatically. Future versions of WDDX may allow additional encoding schemes, but for now, only Base64 encoding is supported.

Example 23-19 demonstrates serializing and deserializing a binary file. To keep things simple, we use a GIF file, which is installed by default when you install the ColdFusion MX server. Realistically, sending just a binary file as a WDDX packet makes little sense as the deserializer has no way of knowing anything about the binary data other than its length (we'll talk about this in a few moments). When sending binary data, you'll probably want to include more descriptive information about the data, such as a filename, MIME type, creation date, etc. All this information and more (as much as you want to include) can be included in the WDDX packet. To do this, all you need to do is create a structure to hold both the descriptive information and the Base64 representation of the binary file as name/value pairs within the structure. The structure, including the binary data, can then be serialized into a WDDX packet. Example 23-19 shows a simple way to create the structure.

Example 23-19. Serializing and deserializing a binary file

```
<!--- read in the binary file using cffile --->
<cffile action="ReadBinary"
        file="c:\cfusionmx\wwwroot\cfide\administrator\images\cfmx.gif"
        variable="MyBinaryFile">

<!--- create a structure to hold descriptive information about the file as well
      as the Base64 encoded binary file --->
<cfset FileInfo = StructNew( )>
<cfset FileInfo.MyBinaryFile = MyBinaryFile>
<cfset FileInfo.FileName = "cfmx.gif">
<cfset FileInfo.MIMEType = "image/gif">

<!--- convert the structure to wddx.  The binary is automatically Base64
      encoded --->
<cfwddx action="CFML2WDDX" input="#FileInfo#" output="MyWDDX">

<!--- output the wddx packet in a text area so you can see the entire packet --->
<h3>WDDX Packet Containing Binary Representation of a GIF File</h3>
<form>
<cfoutput>
<textarea rows="15" cols="80" wrap="virtual">#HTMLEditFormat(MyWDDX)#</textarea>
</cfoutput>
</form>

<!--- deserialize the wddx packet back to a structure --->
<cfwddx action="WDDX2CFML" input="#MyWDDX#" output="myFile">

<!--- write the binary object out to a file --->
<cffile action="WRITE"
        file="c:\cfusionmx\wwwroot\cfide\administrator\images\new_#myFile.FileName#"
        output="#myFile.MyBinaryFile#">

<h3>Here Is The Deserialized Binary:</h3>
<!--- display the file to to browser.  This could be done using cfcontent as
      well, but then you wouldn't be able to see the rest of the content that
      was displayed prior to the cfcontent call --->
```

Example 23-19. Serializing and deserializing a binary file (continued)

```
<cfoutput>
FileName: #myFile.FileName#<br>
MIME Type: #myFile.MIMEType#<br>
<IMG src="/cfide/administrator/images/new_#myFile.FileName#">
</cfoutput>
```

The first task that the template in Example 23-19 performs is to read the GIF file into a binary object using the `cffile` tag's `ReadBinary action`. Next, a structure is created to hold the binary object, the file's name, and its MIME type. After that is accomplished, the `cfwddx` tag serializes the structure into a WDDX packet. During serialization, the binary object within the structure is automatically Base64-encoded. Once the WDDX packet has been created, it is displayed in the browser (Figure 23-12) so that you can see how the packet is constructed.

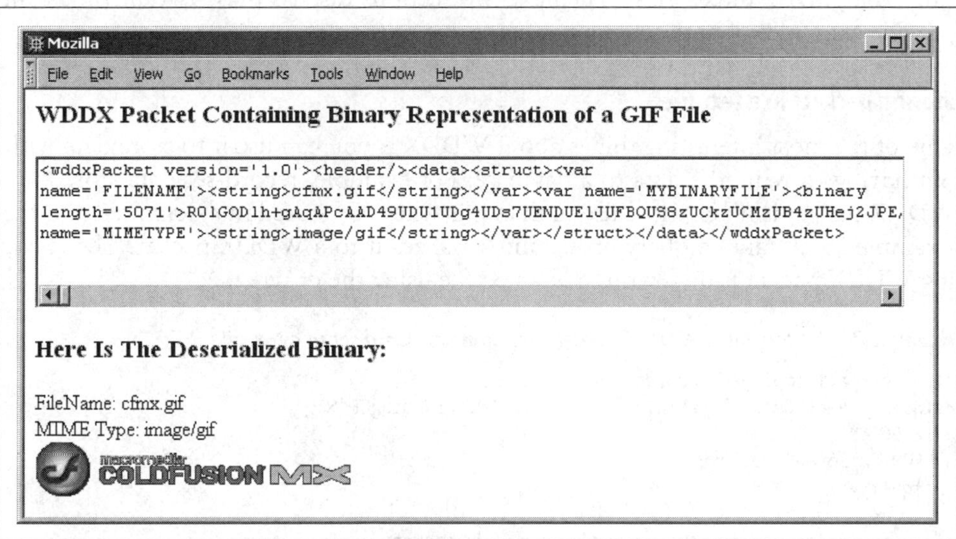

Figure 23-12. Serializing and deserializing a structure containing a binary file

There are two things worth mentioning here. The first is the `<binary length='5071'>` tag that appears near the beginning of the packet. This tag provides the deserializer with the length of the binary value being deserialized. The second important thing to notice here is that the `<binary>` datatype is nested within the `<var>` tag of a `<struct>`. As mentioned previously, complex datatypes such as arrays and structures afford a lot of flexibility and power in an incredibly simple and easy-to-use way.

After the WDDX packet has been displayed, it is deserialized back into a structure. Next, the `cffile` tag writes a copy of the GIF image back to the ColdFusion server. Finally, the filename and MIME type stored in the structure are both output along with the image itself.

If you want to include more than one binary file in your WDDX packet, all you need to do is create an array of structures with each array element containing a single structure holding the binary file and its descriptive information.

Storing WDDX Packets

So far, in this chapter, we have covered all sorts of techniques for serializing and deserializing WDDX packets. All our examples have shown the serialization and deserialization process occurring on the same page. While great for illustrative purposes, the examples have little practical application. After all, why would you want to serialize and then deserialize a packet on the same page? This leads us to the topic for this section—storing your WDDX packets so that you can refer to them later. There are two ways you can store WDDX packets: in a text file or in a database (including LDAP directories). The next two sections discuss these two methods and provide examples of both storing and retrieving packets.

Storing packets in a text file

One of the most interesting things about WDDX is you can use it to store data without having to write the data to a database. For example, record-set data stored in a WDDX packet is much more useful than it is when it's stored in a delimited text file. Example 23-20 takes a query object and serializes it to a WDDX packet. The resulting WDDX packet is then written to a text file using the `cffile` tag.

Example 23-20. Storing a WDDX packet containing a record set in a text file

```
<!--- get all employee records --->
<cfquery name="GetEmployeeInfo" datasource="ProgrammingCF">
  SELECT *
  FROM EmployeeDirectory
</cfquery>

<!--- serialize the employee records to a wddx packet --->
<cfwddx action="CFML2WDDX" input="#GetEmployeeInfo#"
        output="QueryObject" usetimezoneinfo="Yes">

<!--- store the wddx packet in a text file on the server --->
<cffile action="Write" file="c:\temp\QueryObject.txt"
        output="#QueryObject#" addnewline="No">


<!--- Let the user know the file has been written --->
<h3>The WDDX packet has been written to a text file</h3>
```

Once you have the WDDX packet saved in the text file, you need a way to retrieve the packet and deserialize it. Example 23-21 uses the `cffile` tag to read the contents of the text file into a variable that is then fed to the `cfwddx` tag and deserialized. The results are then output to the browser.

Example 23-21. Retrieving and deserializing a WDDX packet from a text file

```
<!--- store the wddx packet in a text file on the server --->
<cffile action="Read" file="c:\temp\QueryObject.txt" variable="MyWDDX">

<!--- deserialize the wddx packet containing the query object --->
<cfwddx action="WDDX2CFML" input="#MyWDDX#" output="DeserializedQueryObject">

<!--- output the results of the deserailized query object --->
<h3>Here Is The Deserialized Query Object Read From A Text File:</h3>
<table cellpadding="3" cellspacing="0">
<tr bgcolor="#888888">
  <th>Name</th><th>Title</th><th>Department</th><th>E-mail</th>
  <th>Phone Extension</th>
</tr>
<cfoutput query="DeserializedQueryObject">
<tr bgcolor="##C0C0C0">
  <td>#Name#</td><td>#Title#</td><td>#Department#</td>
  <td><a href="Mailto:#Email#">#Email#</a></td><td>#PhoneExt#</td>
</tr>
</cfoutput>
</table>
```

Storing packets in a database

There may be times when you want to store WDDX packets in a database. A classic example involves using a long text field (a memo field in MS Access) to store a WDDX packet for each record in the database, which allows you to add additional data to the database without modifying its original structure. This provides you with a mechanism for storing complex datatypes (such as arrays and structures) inside a database. Another possibility includes using WDDX to store binary files (such as GIF and JPEG images) inside a database.

Example 23-22 takes a GIF image (obtained from the sample applications that you can choose to have installed when you install ColdFusion) and stores it in a ColdFusion structure along with the filename and the file's MIME type. The structure is then serialized, and the resulting WDDX packet is saved in the `Picture` field in the `EmployeeDirectory` table used in many of our previous examples. The `Picture` field is set up as a Memo field (since our example database is an MS Access database).

Example 23-22. Serializing a binary file and storing it in a database

```
<!--- read in the binary file using cffile --->
<cffile action="ReadBinary"
        file="c:\cfusionmx\wwwroot\cfdocs\exampleapps\old\employee\images
\people\ls003081_comp.jpg"
        variable="MyBinaryFile">

<!--- create a structure to hold descriptive information about the file as well
      as the Base64 encoded binary file --->
<cfset FileInfo = StructNew()>
<cfset FileInfo.MyBinaryFile = MyBinaryFile>
```

Example 23-22. Serializing a binary file and storing it in a database (continued)

```
<cfset FileInfo.FileName = "coldfusion.gif">
<cfset FileInfo.MIMEType = "image/gif">

<!--- convert the structure to wddx.  The binary is automatically Base64
      encoded --->
<cfwddx action="CFML2WDDX" input="#FileInfo#" output="MyWDDX">

<cfquery name="SaveImage" datasource="ProgrammingCF">
  UPDATE EmployeeDirectory
  SET Picture = '#MyWDDX#'
  WHERE Name = 'Pere Money'
</cfquery>

<h3>Finished updating the database</h3>
```

If you look at the cfquery statement in Example 23-21, you'll notice that we use an UPDATE statement to add the picture to an already existing database record. In this case, we add a picture for the employee named Pere Money, so we include:

```
WHERE Name = 'Pere Money'
```

Once we have a WDDX packet stored in our database, we need a way to retrieve it and deserialize it. Example 23-23 shows how to do this.

Example 23-23. Retrieving a WDDX packet from a database and deserializing it

```
<!--- query the database and retrieve the WDDX packet --->
<cfquery name="GetEmployee" datasource="ProgrammingCF">
  SELECT *
  FROM EmployeeDirectory
  WHERE Name = 'Pere Money'
</cfquery>

<!--- deserialize the wddx packet back to a structure --->
<cfwddx action="WDDX2CFML" input="#GetEmployee.Picture#"
        output="DeserializedImage">

<!--- write the image out to a file --->
<cffile action="Write"
        file="c:\cfusionmx\wwwroot\cfdocs\images\#DeserializedImage.FileName#"
        output="#DeserializedImage.MyBinaryFile#">

<h3>From our employee directory:</h3>
<!--- display the file to to browser.  This could be done using cfcontent as
      well, but then you wouldn't be able to see the rest of the content that
      was displayed prior to the cfcontent call --->
<cfoutput query="GetEmployee">
<img src="/cfdocs/images/#DeserializedImage.FileName#" align="left">
#Name#<br>
#Title#<br>
<a href="mailto:#Email#">#Email#</a>
</cfoutput>
```

The template in Example 23-23 works by retrieving the entire record from the database using cfquery. Next, the WDDX packet contained in the Picture field is deserialized using the cfwddx tag. Because the deserialized packet contains a structure holding the binary image, the cffile tag is used to write the image to a file. After this step is complete, an HTML page is constructed, and the contents of the query are output to the browser. Using the information stored in the deserialized structure, an img tag is dynamically constructed to retrieve the saved image from the database. The image is output along with the rest of the record.

Server-to-Browser WDDX Using JavaScript

WDDX has fantastic possibilities that extend well beyond server-to-server data sharing. If you use WDDX along with client-side JavaScript, it becomes possible to offload data processing of complex datatypes to a historically underused resource—the browser. What does this mean for you as a web developer? For starters, it means that you now have the ability to easily convert complex datatypes, such as arrays, structures, and record sets from CFML, to JavaScript objects that can then be manipulated by the browser. This opens a whole range of possibilities for building more sophisticated and dynamic user interfaces to your application data. It also means you can potentially improve the performance of applications that involve heavy data browsing and editing by moving the records to the browser and using JavaScript to let the user scroll through and edit as necessary. Once all changes have been made, the data can be serialized (using Java Script) back to a WDDX packet and then posted back to the server using a hidden form field.

Passing data to JavaScript on the browser

The cfwddx tag provides two mechanisms for passing data to JavaScript on the browser. The first mechanism involves using cfwddx to serialize CFML data into a WDDX packet, then using the cfwddx tag to deserialize the WDDX packet to an equivalent JavaScript object. Example 23-24 shows how to do this by serializing a structure containing an employee record to WDDX, then deserializing the WDDX packet containing the structure to a JavaScript struct. The JavaScript code that creates the struct object is created dynamically using the cfwddx tag. The JavaScript struct is then looped over and the contents output to the browser.

Example 23-24. Generating dynamic JavaScript using the cfwddx tag

```
<!--- create an employee structure --->
<cfset Employee=StructNew( )>
<cfset Employee.Name="Pere Money">
<cfset Employee.Title="President">
<cfset Employee.Department="Executive Management">
<cfset Employee.Email="pmoney@example.com">
<cfset Employee.PhoneExt="1234">
```

Example 23-24. Generating dynamic JavaScript using the cfwddx tag (continued)

```
<!--- first we need to serialize the structure into a wddx packet --->
<cfwddx action="CFML2WDDX" input="#Employee#" output="MyWDDXPacket">

<!--- output the wddx packet in a text area so you can see the entire packet --->
<h3>WDDX Packet Containing A Simple Value (string)</h3>
<form>
<cfoutput>
<textarea rows="6" cols="50" wrap="virtual">#HTMLEditFormat(MyWDDXPacket)#
</textarea>
</cfoutput>
</form>

<h3>Deserialize it to a JavaScript variable (view the source)</h3>
<!--- deserialize the wddx packet containing the string to a JAvaScript
      variable --->
<cfwddx action="WDDX2JS" input="#MyWDDXPacket#"
        output="MyJavaScript" toplevelvariable="theEmployee">

<!--- use JavaScript to output the contents of the WDDX packet containing the
      serialized employee structure.  Note that the JavaScript code that creates
      the employee struct is created dynamically --->
<script language="JavaScript">
/** This line generates the dynamic JavaScript
  * necessary to create our "struct" object.
  */
<cfoutput>#MyJavaScript#</cfoutput>

// Loop through the employee "struct" and output each key/value
 for (i in theEmployee) {
   document.write([i] + ': ' + theEmployee[i] + '<br>');
     }
</script>
```

Looking at Example 23-24, you'll notice that the first call to the `cfwddx` tag converts the `Employee` structure to a WDDX packet. This is done by setting `action` to `CFML2WDDX`. At this point, nothing has happened that involves any JavaScript or anything else we haven't covered so far. That all changes, however, with the next call to the `cfwddx` tag. This time, we set `action` to `WDDX2JS`. The `input` attribute specifies the WDDX packet we just created. `output` holds the dynamic JavaScript that is created automatically by the `cfwddx` tag. If we were to leave out the `output` attribute, the JavaScript is output in place automatically as part of the HTML stream. Specifying a variable name for `output` allows us to decide exactly where in our template to output the dynamic JavaScript code. The final attribute, `toplevelvariable`, names the top-level JavaScript object created when the WDDX packet is deserialized to JavaScript. In Example 23-23, we set our `toplevelvariable` to `theEmployee`.

The final section of the template in Example 23-24 creates the JavaScript necessary to output the contents of the WDDX packet. First, we output the dynamic JavaScript we created in the previous section. This is done by putting the

MyJavaScript variable (specified in the output attribute) containing the JavaScript code within a set of cfoutput tags. Next, we use a simple for loop to loop over the contents of the struct object and write each key/value pair to the browser.

If you choose View Source in your browser, you will see the dynamic JavaScript code that is generated by the cfwddx tag. It should look something like this:

```
<script language="JavaScript">
/** This line generates the dynamic JavaScript
  * necessary to create our "struct" object.
  */
theEmployee = new Object( );
theEmployee["department"] = "Executive Management";
theEmployee["title"] = "President";
theEmployee["name"] = "Pere Money";
theEmployee["phoneext"] = "1234";
theEmployee["email"] = "pmoney@example.com";

// Loop through the employee "struct" and output each key/value
 for (i in theEmployee) {
   document.write([i] + ': ' + theEmployee[i] + '<br>');
     }
</script>
```

Note that the JavaScript code might not be visible in all browser versions.

Simplifying the process

As I mentioned at the beginning of this section, the cfwddx tag provides two mechanisms for passing data to JavaScript on the browser. In Example 23-24 we used a two-step process to convert a CFML structure to an equivalent JavaScript struct object. First, we used the cfwddx tag to serialize the CFML structure to a WDDX packet. Then we used the cfwddx tag a second time to deserialize the WDDX packet to a JavaScript struct object. There is a more effective way to do this. The cfwddx tag can serialize data directly from CFML to WDDX, then automatically deserialize it to JavaScript in a single step by setting action to CFML2JS, as shown in Example 23-25, which modifies the code we used in Example 23-24.

Example 23-25. Going from CFML to JavaScript in a single step

```
<!--- create an employee structure --->
<cfset Employee=StructNew( )>
<cfset Employee.Name="Pere Money">
<cfset Employee.Title="President">
<cfset Employee.Department="Executive Management">
<cfset Employee.Email="pmoney@example.com">
<cfset Employee.PhoneExt="1234">

<!--- Serialize the CFML structure to WDDX then automatically deserialize it to
      a JavaScript object.  This is all done in the background, so the WDDX
      packet is never available for viewing or use. --->
<cfwddx action="CFML2JS" input="#Employee#" output="MyJavaScript"
        toplevelvariable="theEmployee">
```

Example 23-25. Going from CFML to JavaScript in a single step (continued)

```
<h3>Create a JavaScript struct object from a CFML structure (view the source)</h3>

<!--- use JavaScript to output the contents of the WDDX packet containing the
      serialized Employee structure.  Note that the JavaScript code that creates
      the employee struct is created dynamically --->
<script language="JavaScript">
/** This line generates the dynamic JavaScript
  * necessary to create our "struct" object.
  */
<cfoutput>#MyJavaScript#</cfoutput>

// Loop through the employee "struct" and output each key/value
 for (i in theEmployee) {
   document.write([i] + ': ' + theEmployee[i] + '<br>');
     }
</script>
```

The template in Example 23-25 produces the same output as the template in Example 23-24. The difference here is that we can accomplish the task using less code. Let's hear it for efficiency!

Passing data from JavaScript to ColdFusion

In the previous sections, we discussed methods for getting simple and complex datatypes from ColdFusion to JavaScript using WDDX so that the data could be manipulated from within the browser. Now we need to look at how we can get that data back to ColdFusion from JavaScript once it is finished being manipulated. As always, the solution is close at hand.

A file called *wddx.js* is automatically installed into *\cfide\scripts* when you install the ColdFusion Application server. The *wddx.js* file contains two JavaScript objects (each with numerous functions) that can be used to manipulate WDDX data within JavaScript:

`WddxSerializer`
: The `WddxSerializer` object contains a single function, `serialize()`, that can serialize any JavaScript datatype into WDDX. Once a value or object has been serialized, the resulting WDDX is available as a JavaScript string value.

`WddxRecordset`
: The `WddxRecordset` object contains functions that can construct and manipulate WDDX record sets. Think of a record set as the same thing as a CFML query object.

To use the objects contained in the *wddx.js* template, you need to include the file from within your application code:

```
<script language="JavaScript" src="/cfide/scripts/wddx.js"></script>
```

A detailed discussion of the objects contained in the *wddx.js* file and their related functions is beyond the scope of this book. For more information, you can open the *wddx.js* file (located in *\cfide\scripts* by default when the ColdFusion server is installed) and read the detailed comments included with each function. Additional information can be found in Chapter 8, "WDDX JavaScript Objects," from the *CFML Language Reference* that comes with the ColdFusion documentation or by visiting *http://www.openwddx.org*.

Let's look at Example 23-26, in which we use the `WddxRecordset` object to convert form-field data to a WDDX record set object. The form allows you to enter information about a new employee. Once the information has been entered, you can serialize it without having to refresh the current template by clicking on the button labeled Serialize, which is shown in Figure 23-13.

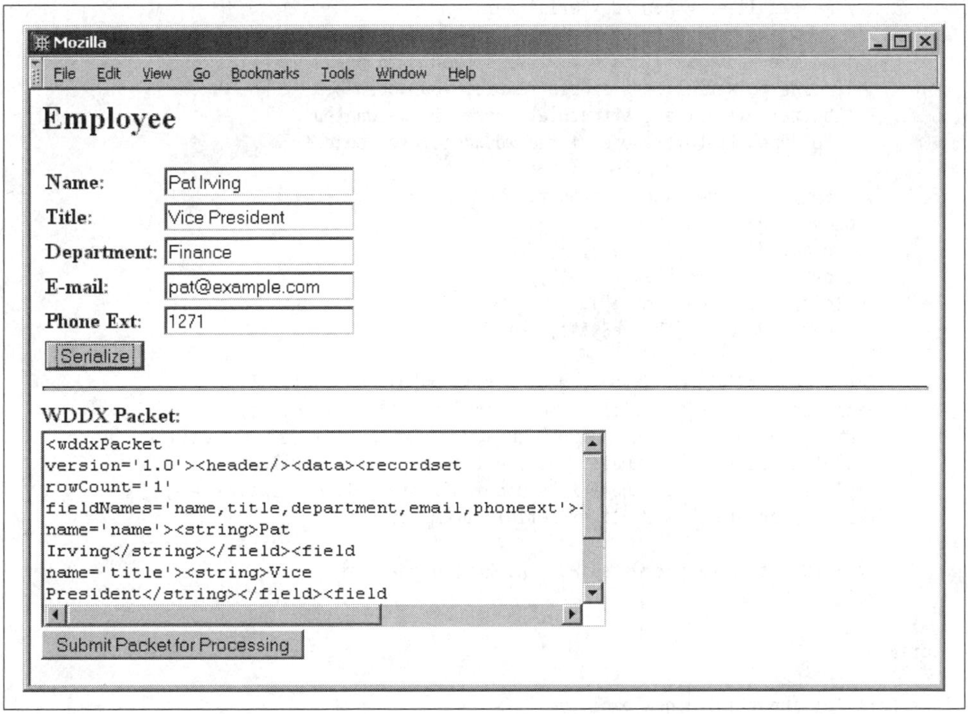

Figure 23-13. Serializing form data to WDDX using JavaScript

Once the Serialize button is clicked, the form-field information is converted to a WDDX record set object using the `WddxRecordset` object from the *wddx.js* file. The record set object is then serialized to a WDDX packet using the `WddxSerializer` object from the same file. Once the record set has been serialized, the resulting packet is placed in a `Textarea` form field called WDDX packet (shown in Figure 23-13).

Example 23-26. Serializing a record set to a WDDX packet using JavaScript

```
<h2>Employee</h2>

<!--- Include the wddx.js file containing the serialize function --->
<script language="JavaScript" src="/cfide/scripts/Wddx.js"></script>

<!--- serialize the contents of the form to a WDDX packet --->
<script language="JavaScript">
    /** this function calls the wddxSerializer object from
      * the wddx.js file to serialize the Recordset object
      * after it is created
      */
    function SerializeEmployee( ) {
        var MySerializer = new WddxSerializer;
        /** create a recordset using the wddxRecordset object
          * in the wddx.js file.  Normally, if you were only
          * going to serialize a single record, you would be
          * better off using s structure.  However, we wanted
          * to demonstrate the use of the wddxRecordset object
          */
        var Employee = new WddxRecordset;
        Employee.addColumn("Name");
        Employee.addColumn("Title");
        Employee.addColumn("Department");
        Employee.addColumn("Email");
        Employee.addColumn("PhoneExt");
        Employee.addRows(1);
        Employee.setField(0, "Name", document.forms[0].Name.value);
        Employee.setField(0, "Title", document.forms[0].Title.value);
       Employee.setField(0, "Department", document.forms[0].Department.value);
        Employee.setField(0, "Email", document.forms[0].Email.value);
        Employee.setField(0, "PhoneExt", document.forms[0].PhoneExt.value);
        var WDDXPacket = MySerializer.serialize(Employee);

        // return the newly created WDDX packet to the form
        return WDDXPacket;
    }
</script>

<!--- Form for inputting a new employee --->
<form action="DeserializeFormPost.cfm" method="Post">
<table>
<tr>
  <td><b>Name:</b></td><td><input type="Text" name="Name"></td>
</tr>
<tr>
  <td><b>Title:</b></td><td><input type="Text" name="Title"></td>
</tr>
<tr>
  <td><b>Department:</b></td><td><input type="Text" name="Department"></td>
</tr>
<tr>
  <td><b>E-mail:</b></td><td><input type="Text" name="Email"></td>
</tr>
<tr>
```

Example 23-26. Serializing a record set to a WDDX packet using JavaScript (continued)

```
  <td><b>Phone Ext:</b></td><td><input type="Text" name="PhoneExt"></td>
</tr>
<tr>
  <!--- clicking on the button calls the SerializeEmployee function that
        serializes the form contents to a WDDX packet --->
  <td colspan="2">
   <input type="Button" value="Serialize"
          onClick="this.form.WDDXPacket.value = SerializeEmployee( )"></td>
</tr>
</table>

<!--- display the WDDX packet and provide a submit button for the user to submit
      the packet to be deserialized --->
<hr>
<b>WDDX Packet:</b>
<br>
<textarea name="WDDXPacket" rows="8" cols="50" wrap="virtual"></textarea>
<br>
<input type="Submit" value="Submit Packet for Processing">
</form>
```

After serializing the form data, you can click on the "Submit Packet for Processing" button to post the serialized WDDX packet to the template in Example 23-27 to be deserialized (Figure 23-14). Example 23-27 should be saved as *deserializeformpost.cfm*.

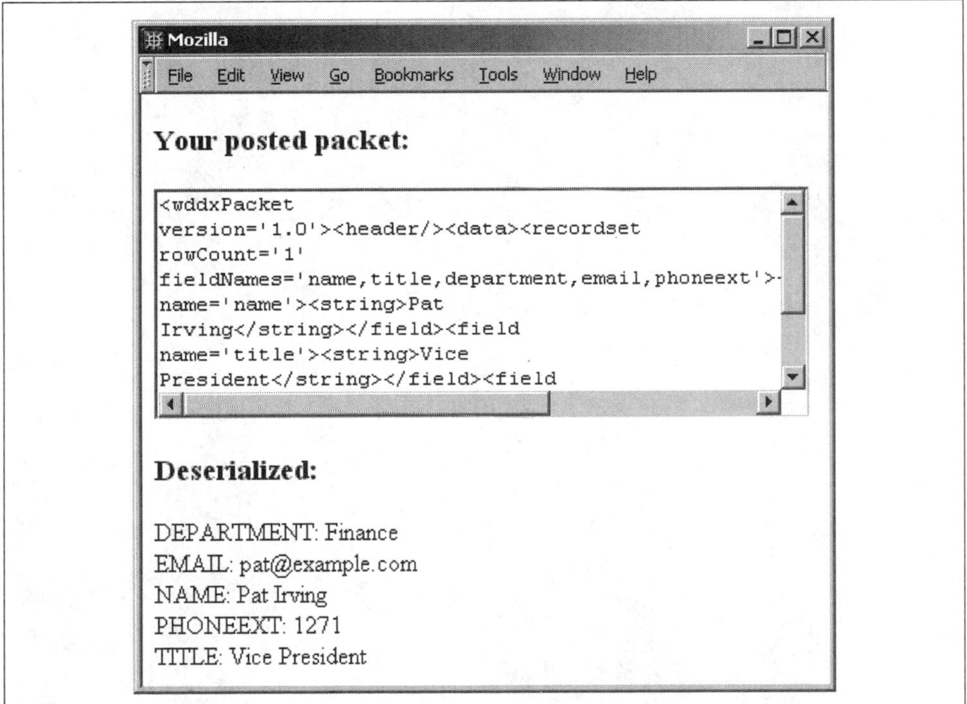

Figure 23-14. Deserializing a WDDX packet received from a form post

Example 23-27. Deserializing a posted WDDX packet with a record set

```
<form>
<h3>Your posted packet:</h3>
<cfoutput>
<textarea name="WDDXPacket" rows="8" cols="50"wrap="virtual">#HTMLEditFormat(Form.
WDDXPacket)#</textarea>
</cfoutput>
</form>

<cfwddx action="WDDX2CFML" input="#Form.WDDXPacket#" output="DeserializedPost">

<h3>Deserialized:</h3>

<!--- loop over the deserialized record set.  This technique allows you to output
      the contents of the record set without knowing any of the field names --->
<cfloop list="#DeserializedPost.ColumnList#" index="ThisField">
<cfoutput>
#ThisField#: #Evaluate("DeserializedPost." & ThisField)#<br>
</cfoutput>
</cfloop>
```

CHAPTER 24
Web Services

There's no doubt that web services are hot. It's impossible to pick up a trade publication without seeing at least half a dozen articles extolling the virtues of the web services revolution. Although still considered an immature technology, web services offer a great deal of promise in many spaces. Fully realized, the web services vision seeks to provide a global object repository where applications can be assembled from self-contained software components using relatively simple protocols and a ubiquitous transport mechanism—the Internet. In ColdFusion MX, web services are built using ColdFusion Components (CFCs).

Web services have many uses. Besides the potential to reduce the amount of code you have to write (by providing an existing web service that fits your needs), they also offer interesting possibilities for enterprise application integration, modernizing legacy applications, and providing access to data in new and interesting ways. As the idea of web services continues to evolve, so too will the ways in which they are used. For now, ColdFusion MX gives you the power to work with what's available, while at the same time maintaining the flexibility to include new pieces of the web services pie as they mature.

This chapter starts with an overview of web services. It then covers consuming web services, producing web services, and web services security.

Web Services Overview

Web services provide a new way to build loosely coupled applications from components. At a basic level, a call to a web service is similar to a remote procedure call. A client makes a request of a remote object, the object performs some action, and a response is sent back to the client. At a higher level, applications built from web services may be assembled from components local to the organization or geographically distributed across the Internet. Web services provide a framework for standardizing both the interface and transport layer for these applications. Figure 24-1 shows a basic web services architecture.

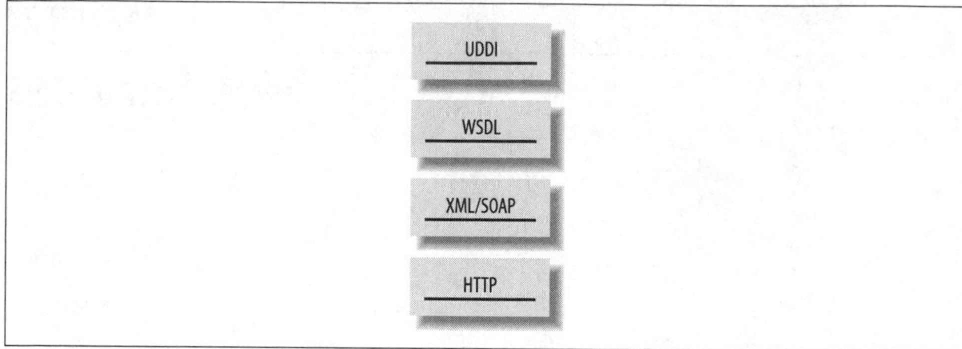

Figure 24-1. Web services architecture

Web services are really an aggregation of several technologies layered on top of common Internet protocols such as HTTP. To better understand just what web services are, as well as how they work, let's break the architecture down into its major parts. There are four main components that make up a web service:

Extensible Markup Language (XML)
: XML can be considered the foundation of the web services stack. It provides a standardized platform- and language-neutral format for exchanging data among applications. More information about XML can be found at *http://www.w3.org/XML/*. Additional information on working with XML in ColdFusion MX can be found in Chapter 22.

Web Services Description Language (WSDL)
: WSDL is an XML format for describing a web service. It describes the purpose of the web service, where and how you can access it, and what functionality (methods) it exposes. We'll be discussing various parts of the WSDL throughout the chapter.

Simple Object Access Protocol (SOAP)
: SOAP provides an XML-based messaging framework for web services. A SOAP message is essentially an XML document made up of an envelope containing an optional header and required body. Although not yet a W3C recommendation, Version 1.1 does have standing as a W3C note. You can read more about SOAP at *http://www.w3.org/TR/SOAP/*. You don't need to know SOAP to make use of web services in ColdFusion MX, as messaging is handled automatically by ColdFusion MX's underlying implementation of the Apache Axis SOAP engine.*

Universal Description, Discovery, and Integration (UDDI)
: UDDI is basically a directory service for web services. It provides a standardized interface for registering and querying web service metadata. There are currently four global public UDDI directories:

* ColdFusion MX 6.1 contains Apache Axis 1.1.

- IBM: *http://uddi.ibm.com/*
- Microsoft: *http://uddi.microsoft.com/*
- SAP: *http://uddi.sap.com/*
- NTT Communications: *http://www.ntt.com/uddi/index-e.html*

Besides global public directories, many specialized private directories exist. One of the most popular is XMethods (*http://www.xmethods.net*). It's also possible to set up your own private UDDI directory (say for use within your organization). A number of tools are available for doing this, including UDDI4J (*http://www-124.ibm.com/developerworks/oss/uddi4j/*).

ColdFusion MX does not support UDDI directly. However, it is possible to register web services you publish using ColdFusion MX with UDDI directories. Additionally, you can manually search UDDI directories for available web services you may wish to use.

As ColdFusion MX has the potential to be both a consumer and a producer of web services, it's important for you to see how this all fits together. Figure 24-2 shows how ColdFusion MX fits into the web services picture.

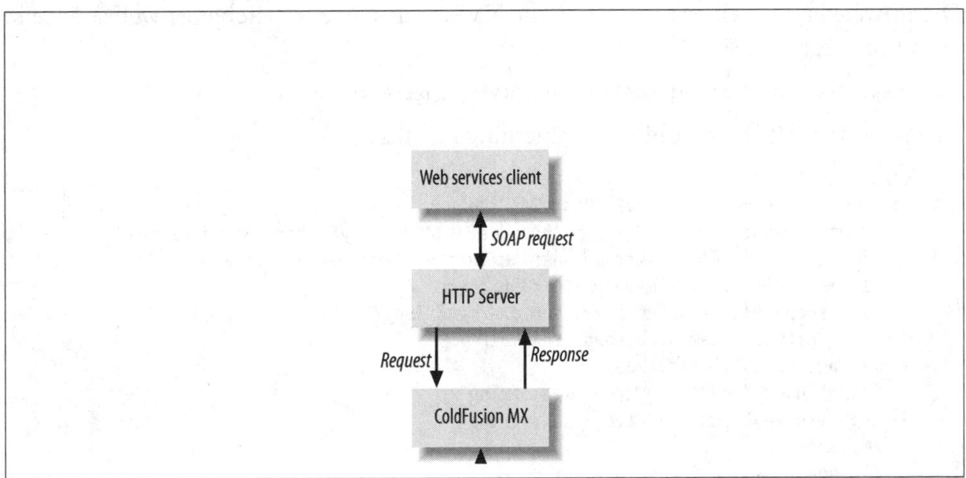

Figure 24-2. ColdFusion and web services

Consuming Web Services

When a client makes a request to a web service, it is said to be a consumer of that service. ColdFusion MX makes consuming web services simple. There are three ways to consume a web service in ColdFusion MX. You can use the `cfinvoke` tag, the `cfobject` tag, or the `createObject( )` function. It's also possible to use the `cfhttp` tag to manually consume a web service. Because of the complexity involved with that method, I'm going to limit my coverage to the first three methods.

In many cases, you don't need to know anything about the web service you want to consume other than the URL of its WSDL file. This is especially true if you use Dreamweaver MX to develop your ColdFusion MX applications. Generating the necessary CFML code to consume a web service using Dreamweaver MX is literally a point and click process:

1. Open the Components tab under the Application panel.
2. Choose Web Services from the dropdown box in the Components tab.
3. Click the plus (+) button next to the dropdown box where you selected Web Services. This opens the Add Using WSDL dialog box.
4. Enter the URL to the desired WSDL file and click OK.

Dreamweaver MX automatically generates a proxy for the web service and makes it available in the Components tab. From here, you can expand the proxy to show the web service's fields, methods, and properties as defined by the WSDL file.

If you don't use Dreamweaver MX, that's okay too. You can visually inspect a WSDL file by entering its URL into your web browser. Most modern browsers are capable of displaying the contents of a WSDL file inline. Regardless of whether you are using Dreamweaver MX, enter the URL to the XMethods currency exchange web service in your browser:

```
http://www.xmethods.net/sd/2001/CurrencyExchangeService.wsdl
```

The resulting WSDL should look something like this:

```
<?xml version="1.0"?>
<definitions name="CurrencyExchangeService"
  targetNamespace="http://www.xmethods.net/sd/CurrencyExchangeService.wsdl"
  xmlns:tns="http://www.xmethods.net/sd/CurrencyExchangeService.wsdl"
  xmlns:xsd="http://www.w3.org/2001/XMLSchema"
  xmlns:soap="http://schemas.xmlsoap.org/wsdl/soap/"
  xmlns="http://schemas.xmlsoap.org/wsdl/">
  <message name="getRateRequest">
    <part name="country1" type="xsd:string"/>
    <part name="country2" type="xsd:string"/>
  </message>
  <message name="getRateResponse">
    <part name="Result" type="xsd:float"/>
  </message>
  <portType name="CurrencyExchangePortType">
    <operation name="getRate">
      <input message="tns:getRateRequest" />
      <output message="tns:getRateResponse" />
    </operation>
  </portType>
  <binding name="CurrencyExchangeBinding"
          type="tns:CurrencyExchangePortType">
    <soap:binding style="rpc"
          transport="http://schemas.xmlsoap.org/soap/http"/>
    <operation name="getRate">
```

```
      <soap:operation soapAction=""/>
      <input>
        <soap:body use="encoded" namespace="urn:xmethods-CurrencyExchange"
              encodingStyle="http://schemas.xmlsoap.org/soap/encoding/"/>
      </input>
      <output >
        <soap:body use="encoded" namespace="urn:xmethods-CurrencyExchange"
              encodingStyle="http://schemas.xmlsoap.org/soap/encoding/"/>
      </output>
    </operation>
  </binding>
  <service name="CurrencyExchangeService">
    <documentation>Returns the exchange rate between the two
                currencies</documentation>
    <port name="CurrencyExchangePort"
          binding="tns:CurrencyExchangeBinding">
      <soap:address location="http://services.xmethods.net:80/soap"/>
    </port>
  </service>
</definitions>
```

Before we continue, I'd like to briefly cover the pieces of a WSDL file. This is especially important if you aren't using Dreamweaver MX, as you'll need to know this to determine what methods are available in the web service, what, if any, parameters they take (and their datatypes), and any values you can expect to be returned. Since a WSDL file is nothing more than an XML file, let's break it down by its elements:

`<definitions>`
: Root element of the WSDL document. This element specifies namespace definitions for the web service.

`<types>`
: Although not shown in our example WSDL, the `types` element can be used to specify datatype definitions for the exchanged messages.

`<message>`
: Message elements define the data being exchanged. Messages are typically used to define input, output, and input/output parameters.

`<part>`
: Parts describe the contents of messages. They are typically used to name parameters.

`<portType>`
: The `portType` element defines one or more operations that the web service can be called to perform. It acts as a wrapper for individual operations, just as a CFC acts as a wrapper for individual functions (methods). This element and its child elements, `operation`, `input`, and `output`, are the elements you should be most concerned with as together they tell you what the web service can do as well as what input and output parameters it has.

`<operation>`
: The `operation` element defines an operation that can be invoked within the web service. Operations are akin to functions (methods) in a CFC.

`<input>`
: Specifies an input parameter for its parent operation.

`<output>`
: Specifies an output parameter for its parent operation.

`<fault>`
: Specifies a message to be returned by its parent operation in the event an error occurs. Note that the `fault` element is not shown in our example.

`<binding>`
: Defines a protocol for accessing the specified `portType`. Protocols include HTTP GET, HTTP POST, MIME, and SOAP. Any number of bindings may be defined for a given `portType`.

`<service>`
: Defines a group of related ports.

`<documentation>`
: Optional element for specifying human-readable documentation. The documentation element may be a child element of any WSDL element.

`<port>`
: Defines an individual endpoint for a binding.

If we apply these definitions to the currency exchange web service, we can easily determine that the method we want to invoke is called `getRate()`.* It accepts two input parameters of type `string`: `country1` (currency converting from) and `country2` (currency converting to), respectively. By looking at the WSDL, we also know that we can expect the `getRate()` method to return a parameter of type `float` (the exchange rate). Based on this information, it's simple to write the ColdFusion code to call the web service and invoke the `getRate()` method, passing in the names of the country whose currency we want to convert from and the country whose currency we want to convert to.

If you are using Dreamweaver MX, you can have it write most of the code for you. Simply expand the CurrencyExchangeService web service under the Components tab, then grab the float `getRate` label and drag and drop it onto the main code editing area. Dreamweaver MX automatically creates the ColdFusion code necessary to

* One web site I can't give enough praise to is XMethods (*http://www.xmethods.net*). Besides acting as a private UDDI registry, the site has several fantastic resources, including a WSDL analyzer (*http://www.xmethods.net/ve2/Tools.po*) that allows you to enter the URL for a WSDL file for analysis. The analyzer validates the WSDL file and outputs a series of HTML pages that detail the operations and information on input and output parameters.

call the web service and invoke the getRate( ) method. The code should look like this:

```
<cfinvoke
  webservice="http://www.xmethods.net/sd/2001/CurrencyExchangeService.wsdl"
  method="getRate"
  returnvariable="aRate">
    <cfinvokeargument name="country1" value="enter_value_here"/>
    <cfinvokeargument name="country2" value="enter_value_here"/>
</cfinvoke>
```

At this point, all you need to do is replace the enter_value_here placeholders for the country1 and country2 parameters with the names of the countries you wish to use in the currency conversion (for a list of available countries, see *http://www.xmethods.net/ve2/ViewListing.po?key=uuid:D784C184-99B2-DA25-ED45-3665D11A12E5*).

If you aren't using Dreamweaver MX as your development environment, you can just as easily write the CFML code to call the web service yourself. Example 24-1 shows the code necessary to call the currency exchange web service and convert 1 USD (U.S. dollar) to euros.

Example 24-1. Calling the currency exchange web service

```
<cfinvoke
  webservice="http://www.xmethods.net/sd/2001/CurrencyExchangeService.wsdl"
  method="getRate"
  returnvariable="aRate"
  timeout="30">
    <cfinvokeargument name="country1" value="united states"/>
    <cfinvokeargument name="country2" value="euro"/>
</cfinvoke>

<cfoutput>
1 USD = #aRate# Euros
</cfoutput>
```

This code should already look somewhat familiar to you. It's basically the same code used to instantiate a CFC, but instead of using the component attribute of the cfinvoke tag as we did for instantiating a CFC, we use the webservice attribute to specify an absolute URL to the web service's WSDL file or the name of the web service if it is already registered in the ColdFusion Administrator (we'll talk about this shortly). The method attribute is also required and specifies the method in the web service we want to invoke. In this case, it's the getRate( ) method. The returnvariable attribute is optional. It specifies a variable name to hold the results of the method call to the web service invocation. In our example, we assign the results of the call to getRate( ) to a variable called aRate. The timeout attribute is new in ColdFusion MX 6.1. It is an optional attribute that lets you specify the amount of time in seconds ColdFusion should wait for a web service request to complete before timing out.

If your ColdFusion server sits behind a firewall and you must go through a proxy server to connect to external web services, you can use the following optional attributes, all new in ColdFusion MX 6.1:

`proxyserver="`*`proxy_server`*`"`
: The IP address or hostname of a proxy server or servers if required for connecting to a web service. If this attribute is omitted, ColdFusion attempts to obtain proxy server information from the JVM startup arguments (configurable from the ColdFusion Administrator).

`proxyport="`*`port`*`"`
: A port number on the proxy server specified in the `proxyserver` attribute.

`proxyuser="`*`username`*`"`
: A username, if any, required by the proxy server.

`proxypassword="`*`password`*`"`
: A password, if any, required by the proxy server.

Just as when passing arguments to a CFC, you can pass arguments to a web service's invoked method using the `argumentcollection` attribute, `cfinvokeargument` tag, or as an attribute of the `cfinvoke` tag. If more than one passed argument has the same name, ColdFusion uses the aforementioned order of precedence. In this example, we use `cfinvokeargument` tags to pass arguments to the web service. The `cfinvokeargument` tags are child tags of `cfinvoke`. Since we know that the currency exchange web service expects two input parameters, `country1` and `country2`, we use the `cfinvokeargument` tags to pass these to the web service.

Besides the `cfinvoke` tag, you can also call web services using the `cfobject` tag or the `createObject( )` function. This gives you tremendous flexibility in how you integrate web services into your ColdFusion applications. To call the currency exchange web service using the `cfobject` tag, your code would look like this:

```
<cfobject
  webservice="http://www.xmethods.net/sd/2001/CurrencyExchangeService.wsdl"
  name="ce">

<cfset aRate = ce.getRate("united states", "euro")>

<cfoutput>
1 USD = #aRate# Euros
</cfoutput>
```

Here, the `cfobject` tag calls the currency exchange web service. The `webservice` attribute specifies the absolute URL to the web service's WSDL file or the name of the web service as registered in the ColdFusion Administrator. The `name` attribute specifies the name of a variable to store the instance of the web service. Methods of the web service are invoked using dot notation. In our example, we call the `getRate( )` method, passing in values for `country1` and `country2`. The results of the `getRate( )` operation are assigned to `aRate`.

If you are using CFScript, you can call a web service using the `createObject( )` function:

```
<cfscript>
  ce = createObject("webservice",
       "http://www.xmethods.net/sd/2001/CurrencyExchangeService.wsdl");
  aRate = ce.getRate("united states", "euro");
</cfscript>

<cfoutput>
1 USD = #aRate# Euros
</cfoutput>
```

The first parameter of the `createObject( )` function tells ColdFusion to call a web service. The second parameter specifies the absolute URL to the web service's WSDL file or the name of the web service as registered in the ColdFusion Administrator. The call to the instance of the web service call is assigned to a variable called `ce`. Dot notation is used to invoke the `getRate( )` method of the web service. Arguments are passed the same way as with the `cfobject` tag.

No matter which method you choose to call the currency exchange web service, the output, shown in Figure 24-3, remains the same.

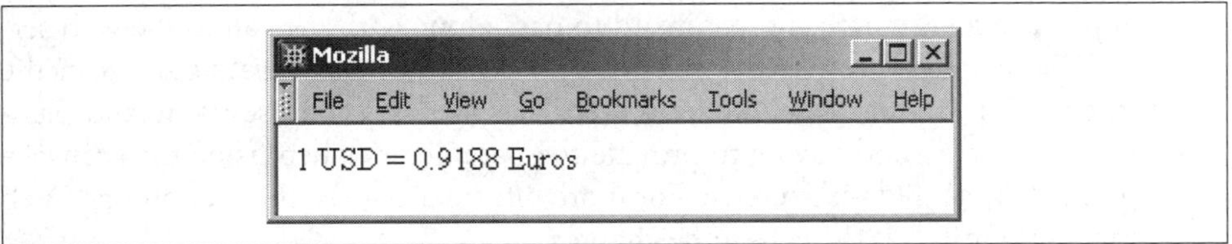

Figure 24-3. Invoking a currency converter web service from ColdFusion MX

Registering Web Services in the ColdFusion Administrator

In the previous section, I mentioned that to call a web service, you must provide either the absolute URL to the web service's WSDL file or the name of the web service as registered in the ColdFusion Administrator. All of the examples I gave used the first method. The second method consists of registering the web service with the ColdFusion Administrator and assigning it a name. This allows you to refer to frequently accessed web services using an alias, as opposed to having to remember the (often verbose) URL to the WSDL file. It also allows you to avoid having to hardcode the URL to a web service's WSDL file in your application code. By registering the URL in the ColdFusion Administrator, you merely have to update a changed URL once in the ColdFusion Administrator, as opposed to everywhere you use it within your application code.

So, how do you go about registering web services in the ColdFusion Administrator? Well, registration happens automatically, at least partially. What I mean by this is that the first time you call a web service using any of the methods we've already discussed, the web service is automatically registered in the ColdFusion Administrator. All you have to do is go in and provide a name (alias) for the web service. To do this, follow these steps:

1. Open the ColdFusion Administrator and click on the Web Services link under the Data & Services heading. You should see a table listing all web services that have already been registered with the server (Figure 24-4).
2. If you want to edit the information for an existing web service, click on the Edit icon under the Actions header, or click the name of the web service under the Web Service Name heading for the appropriate web service. This will load the web services information into the Add/Edit ColdFusion Web Service form
3. Change the name of the web service in the Web Service Name field from the URL currently displayed (it should be the URL to the WSDL file) to a more easily remembered alias. For example, in the case of the currency exchange web service from Example 24-1, an appropriate alias might be `currencyExchange`. Remember, the point is to register the web service with an easy-to-remember name that you can use in your application code to simplify the calling of web services.
4. For web services that restrict access based on HTTP Basic Authentication, you can provide a username and password to pass along with the call to the web service. These values are Base64-encoded and passed as *`username`*`:`*`password`* in the authorization header to the target server. By specifying the username and password here, you avoid having to provide the parameters when using the `cfinvoke` tag to call a secured web service. For more information, see the section on "Web Services Security" at the end of the chapter.
5. Click Update Web Service when you have finished making your changes.

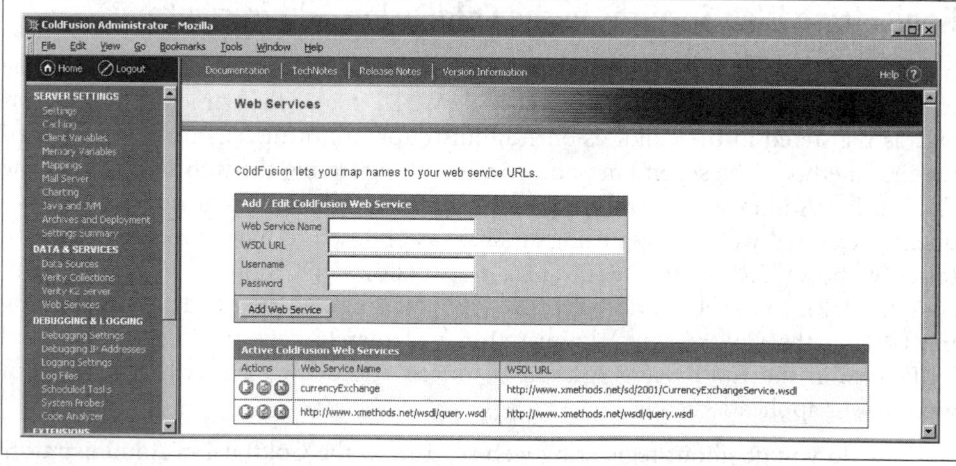

Figure 24-4. Registering a web service in the ColdFusion Administrator

Using the steps provided, it's also possible to register a new web service that hasn't yet been called from your ColdFusion server.

Once you have created an alias for your registered web service, you can use the alias instead of the full URL to the WSDL file whenever you need to consume the web service. Thus, to invoke the currency exchange web service (assuming you registered its alias as `currencyExchange`), you would use the following:

```
<cfinvoke
  webservice="currencyExchange"
  method="getRate"
  returnvariable="aRate">
    <cfinvokeargument name="country1" value="united states"/>
    <cfinvokeargument name="country2" value="euro"/>
</cfinvoke>

<cfoutput>
1 USD = #aRate# Euros
</cfoutput>
```

Consuming a ColdFusion MX Web Service

Although we haven't yet covered publishing your own web services using ColdFusion MX, it is important that we talk about how to consume them, since there are two main differences between a ColdFusion MX web service and web services created using other technologies.

The first difference is the URL to the web service's WSDL file. Because ColdFusion MX web services are really just CFCs, they generally end in a *.cfc* extension as opposed to *.wsdl*. In ColdFusion MX, you don't have to manually create a WSDL file for each of your web services (although you could) the server does it for you automatically. Whereas a typical URL to a WSDL file looks something like *http://www.example.com/myWebService.wsdl*, the equivalent URL for a ColdFusion MX–based web service looks like *http://www.example.com/myWebService.cfc?wsdl*. Note that it's the CFC and not a WSDL file that's referenced in the URL. The `?wsdl` URL parameter tells ColdFusion that you want to invoke the CFC as a web service and that it should generate the appropriate WSDL for the service. If you leave off the `?wsdl`, referencing the CFC directly, ColdFusion thinks you are trying to call the CFC directly and will attempt to invoke the CFC Explorer to show you the CFCs self-documentation.

The second difference between consuming a regular web service and one written in ColdFusion MX has to do with the datatypes of input and output parameters. Because you are using ColdFusion MX to consume a ColdFusion MX–based web service, there is no need for datatype mapping. This means that your web service can accept and return any valid ColdFusion datatype without worrying about conversion issues. While this may seem like a benefit, you need to be careful if you plan to let clients other than ColdFusion consume your web service, as it can be quite difficult for clients to handle data mapping for some of ColdFusion's datatypes.

Dealing with Complex Datatypes

All of the examples we've worked with thus far have used simple datatypes as both input and output parameters. For the most part, ColdFusion MX provides a one-to-one mapping of simple datatypes. ColdFusion strings map to strings in WSDL, Boolean to Boolean, etc. Complex datatypes are, well, a little more complex. By complex datatypes, I mean types such as arrays, structures, binary data, etc. In fact, the web services framework is designed in such a way that you can pass almost any kind of data structure, even ones you arbitrarily define.

Using ColdFusion, it's possible to pass complex datatypes as input parameters and receive complex datatypes as output parameters. Before we get into the specifics of how this is done, it's important you understand how ColdFusion automatically attempts to convert certain ColdFusion datatypes to WSDL datatypes and vice-versa when consuming web services. Table 24-1 shows the mapping between WSDL and ColdFusion datatypes.

Table 24-1. WSDL to ColdFusion datatype mapping

WSDL datatype	ColdFusion datatype
`SOAP-ENC:string`	String
`SOAP-ENC:double`	Numeric
`SOAP-ENC:boolean`	Boolean
`SOAP-ENC:Array`	Array
`xsd:base64Binary`	Binary
`xsd:dateTime`	Date/time
Complex type	Pseudo structure[a]

[a] When a web service specifies a complex type as an output parameter, ColdFusion receives it as a special type of object that can be assigned to a variable and referenced using dot notation, like a structure. However, the returned object is not a true ColdFusion structure.

Complex types as return values

Let's start by looking at another real-world example of a web service that returns a complex datatype when called. In this case, the web service is called the XMethods Query Service. It's a web service that allows you to directly query the XMethods directory. It has several methods that allow you to perform various operations. For the purposes of our example, we want to call the `getServiceSummariesByPublisher()` method. This method takes a single argument, `publisherID` of type `string`, and uses the argument to return a complex datatype containing a summary of each published web service by the specified publisher. The datatype in this case happens to be of type `SOAP-ENC:Array`, an array for all intents and purposes. What's particularly interesting about this array, though, is that each element in the array is actually a complex type defined in the WSDL as `ServiceSummary`:

```
<complexType name="ServiceSummary">
  <sequence>
    <element name="name" nillable="true" type="xsd:string"/>
    <element name="id" nillable="true" type="xsd:string"/>
    <element name="shortDescription" nillable="true" type="xsd:string"/>
    <element name="wsdlURL" nillable="true" type="xsd:string"/>
    <element name="publisherID" nillable="true" type="xsd:string"/>
  </sequence>
</complexType>
```

The `ServiceSummary` datatype is akin to a ColdFusion structure, but it does not directly map to a ColdFusion structure. It can be accessed using dot notation just like a ColdFusion structure can; however, it must be converted to a ColdFusion structure manually before it can be manipulated by the full spectrum of structure functions available in CFML. Example 24-2 shows the code for calling the `getServiceSummariesByPublisher( )` method of the XMethods Query Service for all web services published by *xmethods.net*. The results, shown in Figure 24-5, are output to the browser using the `cfdump` tag.

Example 24-2. Returning a complex datatype from a web service

```
<cfinvoke
  webservice="http://www.xmethods.net/wsdl/query.wsdl"
  method="getServiceSummariesByPublisher"
  returnvariable="aServiceSummaryArray">
    <cfinvokeargument name="publisherID" value="xmethods.net"/>
</cfinvoke>

<cfdump var="#aServiceSummaryArray#">
```

As you can see, `aServiceSummaryArray` is automatically converted from a SOAP array to a ColdFusion array, and each array element is shown as an object and not a ColdFusion structure. A quick look back at the WSDL for the complex type known as `ServiceSummary` shows that the returned "structure" contains five members: `name`, `id`, `shortDescription`, `wsdlURL`, and `publisherID`. These can be referred to using dot notation, just as you would for a ColdFusion structure, as shown in Example 24-3.

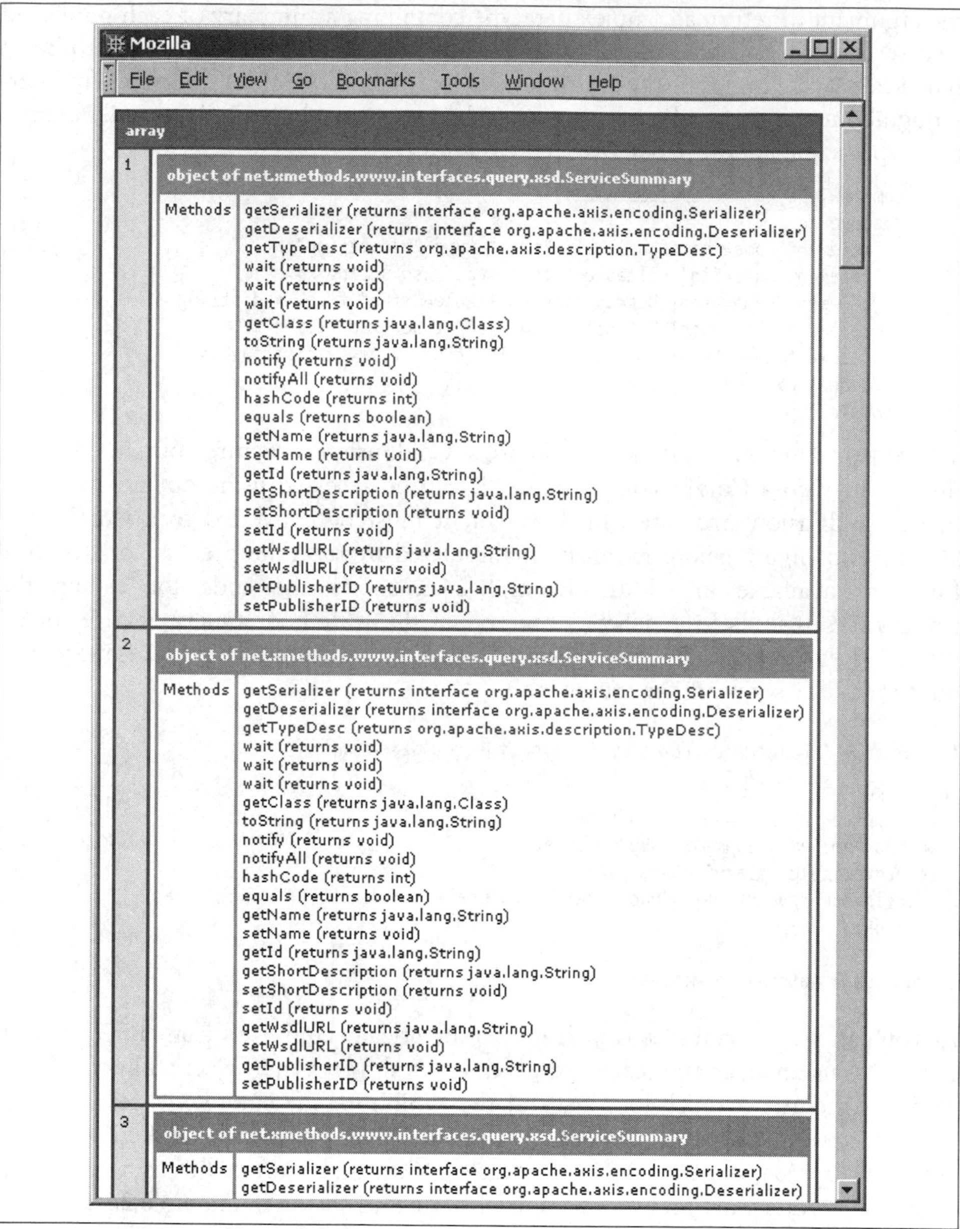

Figure 24-5. cfdump of an array of complex types returned by a web service

Example 24-3. Referencing data elements in a complex type using dot notation

```
<cfinvoke
  webservice="http://www.xmethods.net/wsdl/query.wsdl"
  method="getServiceSummariesByPublisher"
  returnvariable="aServiceSummaryArray">
```

Example 24-3. Referencing data elements in a complex type using dot notation (continued)

```
    <cfinvokeargument name="publisherID" value="xmethods.net"/>
</cfinvoke>

<table border="1">
  <tr>
    <th>Is Structure?</th>
    <th>id</th>
    <th>name</th>
    <th>publisherID</th>
    <th>shortDescription</th>
    <th>wsdlURL</th>
  </tr>
<cfloop index="i" from="1" to="10">
  <cfoutput>
  <tr>
    <td>#isStruct(aServiceSummaryArray[i])#</td>
    <td>#aServiceSummaryArray[i].id#</td>
    <td>#aServiceSummaryArray[i].name#</td>
    <td>#aServiceSummaryArray[i].publisherID#</td>
    <td>#aServiceSummaryArray[i].shortDescription#</td>
    <td>#aServiceSummaryArray[i].wsdlURL#</td>
  </tr>
  </cfoutput>
</cfloop>
</table>
```

In this example, a loop is used to iterate over the first ten elements in the aServiceSummaryArray array. A table row is generated for each ServiceSummary structure in the array. The table row contains columns corresponding to each element in the array. An additional column is used to output the results of a test (using isStruct()) to evaluate whether each ServiceSummary structure is a ColdFusion structure. Figure 24-6 shows the output. As you can see, the answer is no, ServiceSummary structures are not the same as ColdFusion structures.

It is possible to manually convert a complex type to a ColdFusion structure. Example 24-4 shows how we can convert the ServiceSummary structures contained in the aServiceSummaryArray to ColdFusion structures.

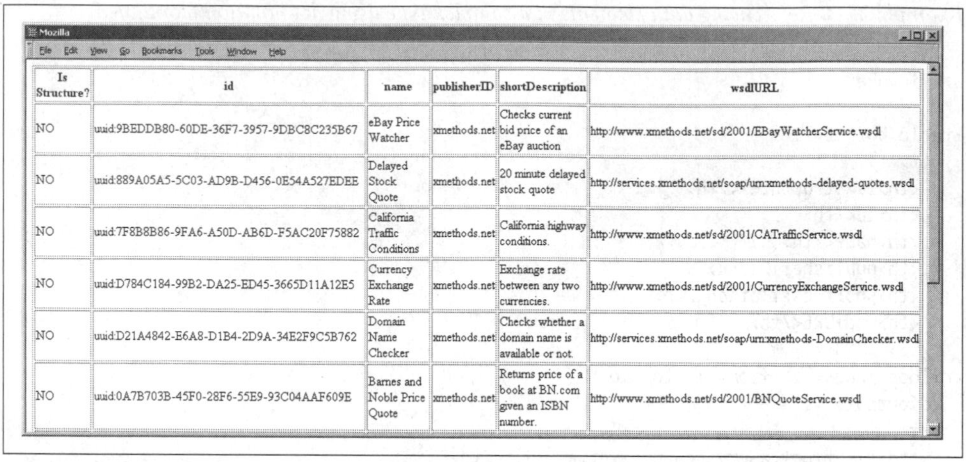

Is Structure?	id	name	publisherID	shortDescription	wsdlURL
NO	uuid:9BEDDB80-60DE-36F7-3957-9DBC8C235B67	eBay Price Watcher	xmethods.net	Checks current bid price of an eBay auction	http://www.xmethods.net/sd/2001/EBayWatcherService.wsdl
NO	uuid:889A05A5-5C03-AD9B-D456-0E54A527EDEE	Delayed Stock Quote	xmethods.net	20 minute delayed stock quote	http://services.xmethods.net/soap/urn:xmethods-delayed-quotes.wsdl
NO	uuid:7F8B8B86-9FA6-A50D-AB6D-F5AC20F75882	California Traffic Conditions	xmethods.net	California highway conditions.	http://www.xmethods.net/sd/2001/CATrafficService.wsdl
NO	uuid:D784C184-99B2-DA25-ED45-3665D11A12E5	Currency Exchange Rate	xmethods.net	Exchange rate between any two currencies.	http://www.xmethods.net/sd/2001/CurrencyExchangeService.wsdl
NO	uuid:D21A4842-E6A8-D1B4-2D9A-34E2F9C5B762	Domain Name Checker	xmethods.net	Checks whether a domain name is available or not.	http://services.xmethods.net/soap/urn:xmethods-DomainChecker.wsdl
NO	uuid:0A7B703B-45F0-28F6-55E9-93C04AAF609E	Barnes and Noble Price Quote	xmethods.net	Returns price of a book at BN.com given an ISBN number.	http://www.xmethods.net/sd/2001/BNQuoteService.wsdl

Figure 24-6. Referencing data elements in a pseudo structure using dot notation

Example 24-4. Manually converting a complex type to a ColdFusion structure

```
<cfinvoke
  webservice="http://www.xmethods.net/wsdl/query.wsdl"
  method="getServiceSummariesByPublisher"
  returnvariable="aServiceSummaryArray">
    <cfinvokeargument name="publisherID" value="xmethods.net"/>
</cfinvoke>

<cfset myArray = arrayNew(1)>

<cfloop index="i" from="1" to="10">
<cfscript>
myStruct = StructNew();
myStruct.id = aServiceSummaryArray[i].id;
myStruct.name = aServiceSummaryArray[i].name;
myStruct.publisherID = aServiceSummaryArray[i].publisherID;
myStruct.shortDescription = aServiceSummaryArray[i].shortDescription;
myStruct.wsdlURL = aServiceSummaryArray[i].wsdlURL;

MyArray[i] = myStruct;
</cfscript>
</cfloop>

<cfdump var="#myArray#">
```

Here, we create a new array (just for demonstration purposes) to mimic the original `aServiceSummaryArray` array. Next, we loop over the first ten elements (`ServiceSummary` structures) in `aServiceSummaryArray`. During each iteration, we create a new structure called `myStruct` and assign the `ServiceSummary` structure values to new ColdFusion structure keys. The resulting ColdFusion structure is then inserted into the new `myArray` array. When the loop is finished iterating, the contents of myArray are output to the browser using cfdump. The results can be seen in Figure 24-7.

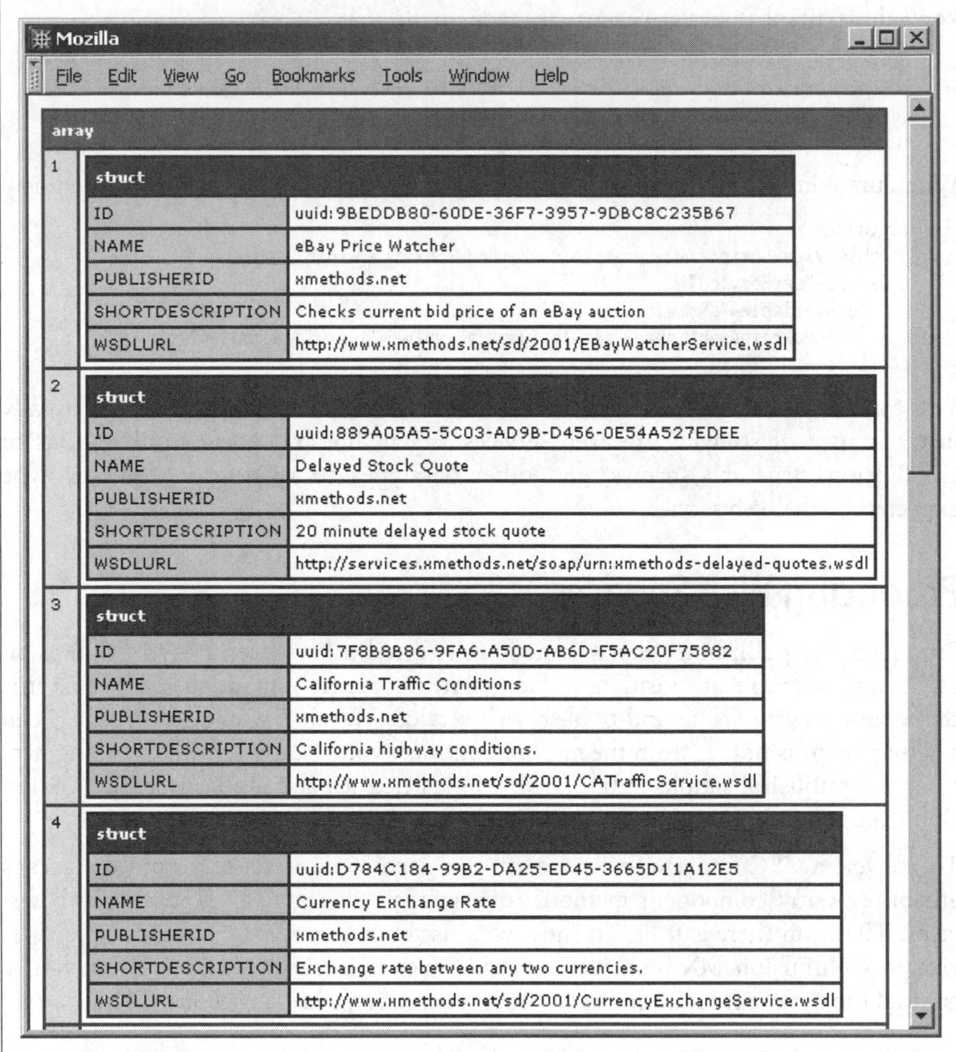

Figure 24-7. Manually converting a complex type to a ColdFusion structure

Now the contents of each ServiceSummary structure are contained in ColdFusion structures.

Complex types as input parameters

In the previous section, we discussed how to handle complex datatypes returned by a web service. Using similar techniques, we can also pass complex datatypes as input parameters to a web service.

For example, if the web service you are trying to consume expects an input parameter called serviceSummary that's defined as a complex type (and just happens to look like a ColdFusion structure), you can create a ColdFusion structure containing the key/value pairs that serviceSummary is made up of:

```
<cfset serviceSummary = structNew( )>
<cfset serviceSummary.id = "uuid:9BEDDB80-60DE-36F7-3957-9DBC8C235B67">
<cfset serviceSummary.name = "Currency Exchange Rate">
<cfset serviceSummary.publisherID = "xmethods.net">
```

When invoking our fictitious web service, we would pass the complex type like this:

```
<cfinvoke
  webservice="http://www.example.com/myBogusService.wsdl"
  method="setService"
  returnvariable="sService">
    <cfinvokeargument name="serviceSummary" value="#serviceSummary#"/>
</cfinvoke>
```

You can just as easily create even more complex data structures to pass. It's usually just a matter of studying the web services WSDL file and using combinations of ColdFusion structures, arrays, and other datatypes to model the complex type expected by the web service.

Producing Web Services

Producing (or publishing, as it's sometimes referred to) web services in ColdFusion MX is a very simple proposition. In fact, many people have made the claim that it is the easiest way to create and publish web services. While I won't go that far, I can say that claim is not far from the mark. In essence, you already know everything necessary to publish a simple web service: you learned it back in Chapter 22, ColdFusion Components.

To convert a CFC into a web service, all you need to do is set to remote the access attribute of any component methods (cffunction) you want to expose as web services. That's all there is to it. To show you just how easy it is to produce a web service in ColdFusion MX, consider the code shown in Example 24-5. After you've entered the code, save it under *webroot\programmingcf\ch24* as *helloworld.cfc*.

Example 24-5. Producing a simple web service in ColdFusion MX

```
<cfcomponent>
  <cffunction name="getMessage" access="remote" returntype="string"
              output="no">
    <cfargument name="name" type="string" required="yes">

    <cfreturn "Hello " & arguments.name &"! " & "I've been invoked as a web
      service.">
  </cffunction>
</cfcomponent>
```

After looking at this code, your first reaction was probably that it looks just like a regular CFC. That's because it *is* a regular CFC. All that really separates a CFC from a web service is setting the `access` attribute of whatever method(s) you want to expose to `remote`. There are a few additional rules for creating web services from CFCs that you need to know about:

- Every CFC method published as a web service must have a `returntype` specified. If your web service does not return a value, set `returntype="void"`.
- The `output` attribute of each `cffunction` tag should be set to `no`. Web services are not designed to output directly to a browser. They are, however, designed to return values which can then be output by the client making the call.
- Optional input parameters are not supported in web services. Therefore, if you have any `cfargument` tags with the `required` attribute set to `no`, the setting is ignored and the argument treated as required.
- Because CFCs published as web services ultimately compile to Java classes, you may not name your CFC file the same name as a Java keyword. For a list of Java keywords, see *http://java.sun.com/docs/books/tutorial/java/nutsandbolts/_keywords.html*.
- You must also be careful where you save CFC files you plan to publish as web services. Because they compile to Java classes that reference a package (location), directory names cannot begin with a digit and can contain only alphanumeric characters. If you look at Example 24-6, you'll see that we saved the CFC in a subdirectory called */ch24* instead of the usual chapter number (*/24*) as we've done throughout the book. Failure to observe this rule results in a runtime error.*

Example 24-6 calls the web service you just created, using the `cfinvoke` tag just as you have throughout the chapter.

Example 24-6. Calling a web service produced in ColdFusion MX

```
<cfinvoke
  webservice="http://localhost/programmingcf/ch24/helloworld.cfc?wsdl"
  method="getMessage"
  returnvariable="aString">
    <cfinvokeargument name="name" value="Rob"/>
</cfinvoke>

<cfoutput>
#aString#
</cfoutput>
```

Running this example results in the output shown in Figure 24-8.

* This was true in ColdFusion MX 6.0. However, in ColdFusion MX 6.1, the Macromedia engineering team made changes to ColdFusion that invalidate this rule.

Mozilla
File Edit View Go Bookmarks Tools Window Help
Hello Rob! I've been invoked as a web service.

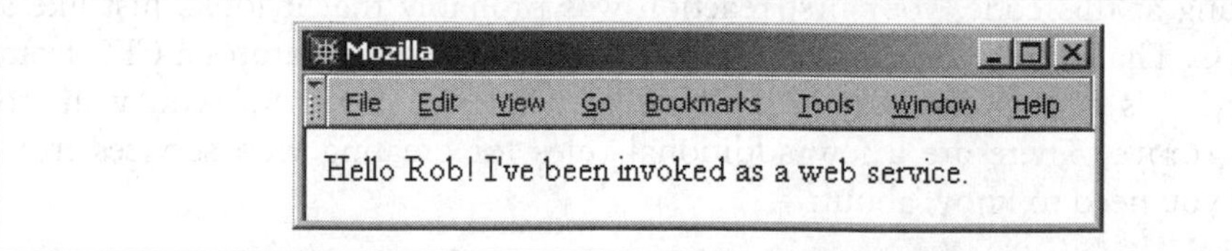

Figure 24-8. Invoking a web service produced in ColdFusion MX

Handling Datatype Mapping in ColdFusion-Produced Web Services

To see the WSDL for the web service we created in Example 24-5, point your browser to *http://localhost/programmingcf/ch24/helloworld.cfc?wsdl*. The results should look like those in Figure 24-9.

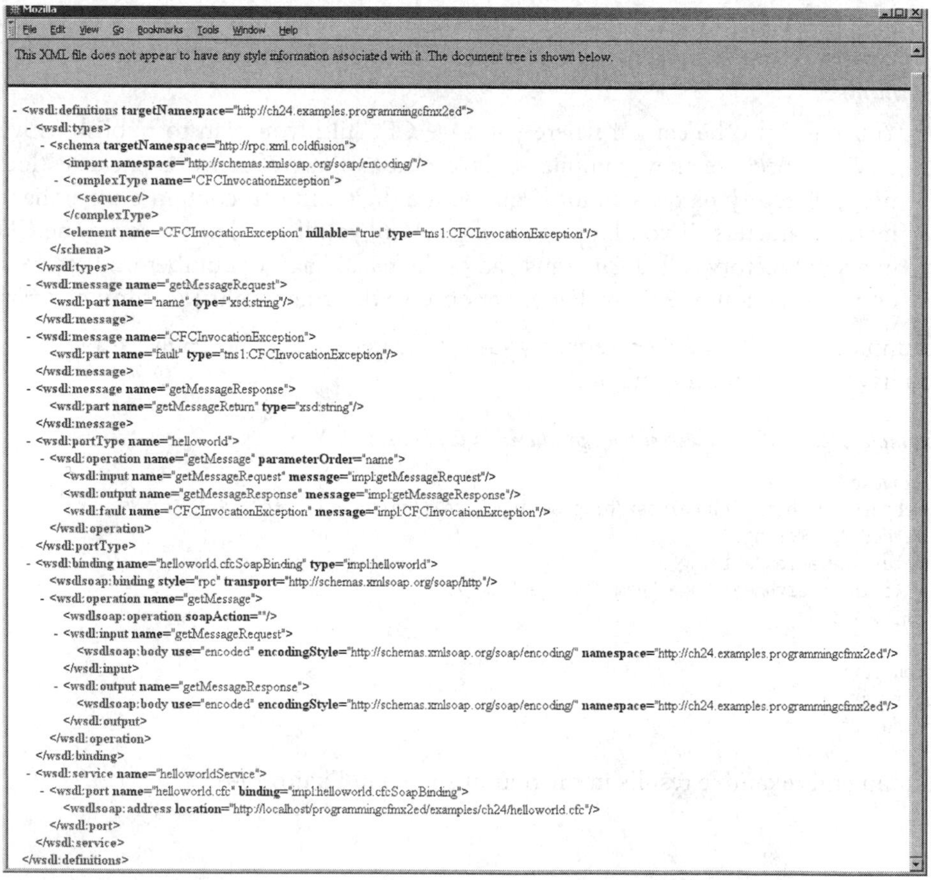

Mozilla
File Edit View Go Bookmarks Tools Window Help
This XML file does not appear to have any style information associated with it. The document tree is shown below.

```
- <wsdl:definitions targetNamespace="http://ch24.examples.programmingcfmx2ed">
  - <wsdl:types>
    - <schema targetNamespace="http://rpc.xml.coldfusion">
        <import namespace="http://schemas.xmlsoap.org/soap/encoding/"/>
      - <complexType name="CFCInvocationException">
          <sequence/>
        </complexType>
        <element name="CFCInvocationException" nillable="true" type="tns1:CFCInvocationException"/>
      </schema>
    </wsdl:types>
  - <wsdl:message name="getMessageRequest">
      <wsdl:part name="name" type="xsd:string"/>
    </wsdl:message>
  - <wsdl:message name="CFCInvocationException">
      <wsdl:part name="fault" type="tns1:CFCInvocationException"/>
    </wsdl:message>
  - <wsdl:message name="getMessageResponse">
      <wsdl:part name="getMessageReturn" type="xsd:string"/>
    </wsdl:message>
  - <wsdl:portType name="helloworld">
    - <wsdl:operation name="getMessage" parameterOrder="name">
        <wsdl:input name="getMessageRequest" message="impl:getMessageRequest"/>
        <wsdl:output name="getMessageResponse" message="impl:getMessageResponse"/>
        <wsdl:fault name="CFCInvocationException" message="impl:CFCInvocationException"/>
      </wsdl:operation>
    </wsdl:portType>
  - <wsdl:binding name="helloworld.cfcSoapBinding" type="impl:helloworld">
      <wsdlsoap:binding style="rpc" transport="http://schemas.xmlsoap.org/soap/http"/>
    - <wsdl:operation name="getMessage">
        <wsdlsoap:operation soapAction=""/>
      - <wsdl:input name="getMessageRequest">
          <wsdlsoap:body use="encoded" encodingStyle="http://schemas.xmlsoap.org/soap/encoding/" namespace="http://ch24.examples.programmingcfmx2ed"/>
        </wsdl:input>
      - <wsdl:output name="getMessageResponse">
          <wsdlsoap:body use="encoded" encodingStyle="http://schemas.xmlsoap.org/soap/encoding/" namespace="http://ch24.examples.programmingcfmx2ed"/>
        </wsdl:output>
      </wsdl:operation>
    </wsdl:binding>
  - <wsdl:service name="helloworldService">
    - <wsdl:port name="helloworld.cfc" binding="impl:helloworld.cfcSoapBinding">
        <wsdlsoap:address location="http://localhost/programmingcfmx2ed/examples/ch24/helloworld.cfc"/>
      </wsdl:port>
    </wsdl:service>
</wsdl:definitions>
```

Figure 24-9. WSDL for a ColdFusion-based web service

This WSDL file looks a little bit different than the one we saw earlier for the currency exchange service. Don't worry. The basic parts of a WSDL you learned about are still there. ColdFusion MX merely adds additional web service information that you would otherwise have to generate yourself.

One thing to note is the way in which ColdFusion datatypes are represented in the WSDL file generated by ColdFusion MX. Every ColdFusion datatype with the exception of structures and queries maps directly to a WSDL datatype, as shown in Table 24-2.

Table 24-2. ColdFusion datatype to WSDL mapping

ColdFusion datatype	WSDL datatype
String	`SOAP-ENC:string`
Numeric	`SOAP-ENC:double`
Boolean	`SOAP-ENC:boolean`
Array	`SOAP-ENC:Array`
Binary	`xsd:base64Binary`
Date	`xsd:dateTime`
Guid	`SOAP-ENC:string`
Uuid	`SOAP-ENC:string`
structure*	`Map`
query*	`QueryBean`
Any	Complex type
component definition	Complex type
void (operation returns nothing)	

When you use a ColdFusion structure as an input or output parameter, the corresponding WSDL datatype is defined as a complex type named `Map`. This is necessary because the SOAP specification currently does not have an equivalent datatype for the ColdFusion structure. Example 24-7 shows a simple ColdFusion web service that returns a structure (`Map`).

Example 24-7. Returning a structure (Map) from a ColdFusion web service

```
<cfcomponent>
  <cffunction name="getStruct" access="remote" returntype="struct"
              output="no">
    <cfset var employee = structNew( )>
    <cfset employee.name = "Pere Money">
    <cfset employee.title = "President">
    <cfset employee.department = "Executive Management">

    <cfreturn employee>
  </cffunction>
</cfcomponent>
```

The resulting WSDL file contains the `Map` mapping, as follows:

```
<complexType name="Map">
  <sequence>
    <element name="item" minOccurs="0" maxOccurs="unbounded">
      <complexType>
        <all>
          <element name="key" type="xsd:anyType"/>
          <element name="value" type="xsd:anyType"/>
        </all>
      </complexType>
    </element>
  </sequence>
</complexType>
```

This complex type represents an arbitrary number of key/value pairs. Note that keys and values can be any datatype (`xsd:anyType`).

The WSDL representation of a ColdFusion query is a little more complex. It is represented as a complex type called a `QueryBean`. A `QueryBean` is essentially an object containing a one-dimensional array of column names and a two-dimensional array containing the actual query data. Example 24-8 shows a simple ColdFusion web service that returns a query (`QueryBean`).

Example 24-8. Returning a query (QueryBean) from a ColdFusion-based web service

```
<cfcomponent>
  <cffunction name="getQuery" access="remote" returntype="query"
              output="no">
    <cfquery name="getEmployees" datasource="programmingcf">
      select *
      from employeeDirectory
    </cfquery>

    <cfreturn getEmployees>
  </cffunction>
</cfcomponent>
```

The resulting WSDL file contains the `QueryBean` mapping, as follows:

```
<complexType name="QueryBean">
  <sequence>
    <element name="columnList" nillable="true" type="impl:ArrayOf_xsd_string"/>
    <element name="data" nillable="true" type="impl:ArrayOfArrayOf_xsd_anyType"/>
  </sequence>
</complexType>

<complexType name="ArrayOf_xsd_string">
  <complexContent>
    <restriction base="soapenc:Array">
      <attribute ref="soapenc:arrayType" wsdl:arrayType="xsd:string[ ]"/>
    </restriction>
  </complexContent>
</complexType>
```

```
<complexType name="ArrayOfArrayOf_xsd_anyType">
  <complexContent>
    <restriction base="soapenc:Array">
      <attribute ref="soapenc:arrayType" wsdl:arrayType="xsd:anyType[ ][ ]"/>
    </restriction>
  </complexContent>
</complexType>
```

Creating Custom Datatypes

One of the interesting features of web services is the ability to create custom datatypes. In the XMethods Query Service example from the section on consuming web services, we dealt with a web service that returned an arbitrary datatype called `ServiceSummary`. If you recall, the WSDL for the complex type looked like this:

```
<complexType name="ServiceSummary">
  <sequence>
    <element name="name" nillable="true" type="xsd:string"/>
    <element name="id" nillable="true" type="xsd:string"/>
    <element name="shortDescription" nillable="true" type="xsd:string"/>
    <element name="wsdlURL" nillable="true" type="xsd:string"/>
    <element name="publisherID" nillable="true" type="xsd:string"/>
  </sequence>
</complexType>
```

ColdFusion MX also has a mechanism for creating arbitrary datatypes. This allows you to create your own datatypes to use as input or output parameters within your ColdFusion-based web services. To create an arbitrary datatype, you create a shell CFC for the datatype and define it using `cfproperty` tags. For example, to create a complex type called `EmployeeDetail`, you would create a CFC that looks like Example 24-9.

Example 24-9. Defining a custom datatype as a CFC

```
<cfcomponent>
  <cfproperty name="name" type="string">
  <cfproperty name="title" type="string">
  <cfproperty name="department" type="string">
  <cfproperty name="phoneExt" type="numeric">
</cfcomponent>
```

The file should be saved as *EmployeeDetail.cfc* in a directory under your web root. Once you have the *EmployeeDetail.cfc* file created, you can use it within your other CFCs as a custom datatype. It can be used as a value for the type attribute of the `cfargument` tag (as a type for an input parameter) or in the `returntype` attribute of the `cffunction` tag (as a type for an output parameter). For example, to use `EmployeeDetail` as a datatype for an input parameter, your CFC code would look like that in Example 24-10.

Example 24-10. Web service using a custom datatype as both input and output parameter

```
<cfcomponent>
  <cffunction name="addEmployee" access="remote"
              returntype="EmployeeDetail" output="no">
    <cfargument name="employee" type="EmployeeDetail" required="yes">

    <cfquery name="getEmployees" datasource="programmingcf">
      insert into employeeDirectory (name,title,department,phoneExt)
      values ('#arguments.employee.name#', '#arguments.employee.title#',
              '#arguments.employee.department#',
               #arguments.employee.phoneExt#)
    </cfquery>

    <cfreturn arguments.employee>
  </cffunction>
</cfcomponent>
```

You'll need to save this CFC as *employee.cfc*, preferably in the same directory as the *EmployeeDetail.cfc* file. When called as a web service, this CFC accepts an input parameter of type `EmployeeDetail`. It then uses the data in that data structure to perform an insert query in the `EmployeeDirectory` table of our example database. Next, the same `EmployeeDetail` data structure is returned back to the client that called the web service. The code to call the web service is shown in Example 24-11.

Example 24-11. Invoking a ColdFusion-based web service and passing in a custom datatype

```
<cfset myEmployee = structNew( )>
<cfset myEmployee.name = "Joe Blow">
<cfset myEmployee.title = "Guy Friday">
<cfset myEmployee.department = "Administrative">
<cfset myEmployee.phoneExt = "1323">

<cfinvoke
 webservice="http://localhost/programmingcf/ch24/employee.cfc?wsdl"
 method="addEmployee"
 returnvariable="aEmployeeDetail">
  <cfinvokeargument name="employee" value="#myEmployee#"/>
</cfinvoke>

<cfdump var="#aEmployeeDetail#">

<cfoutput>
#aEmployeeDetail.name#
</cfoutput>
```

The `EmployeeDetail` datatype is coded as a ColdFusion structure. The web service is invoked, and the `EmployeeDetail` datatype passed along as an input parameter. Executing the code in Example 24-11 results in the output shown in Figure 24-10. Notice that the variable `aEmployeeDetail` is a complex type, not a true ColdFusion structure.

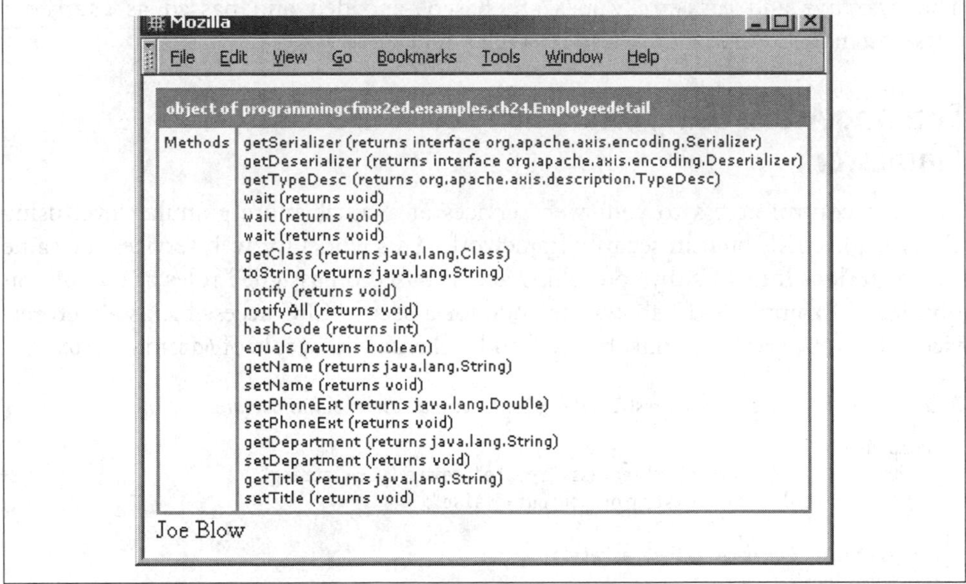

Figure 24-10. Passing and returning a custom datatype

Web Services Security

Although several competing standards for handling security within the web services framework are under development, as of this writing there is no accepted standard. That said, there are existing technologies you can use to secure access to your web services. ColdFusion supports web service security in two ways, at the web server level and using ColdFusion's built-in security framework.

Securing Access Using HTTP Basic Authentication

At the web-server level, you can protect a web service using HTTP Basic Authentication. This is done by restricting access to the directory containing the CFC you want to expose as a web service. For more information on using HTTP Basic Authentication, see Chapter 8, as well as the documentation for your particular web server.

For web services that restrict access based on HTTP Basic Authentication, you can provide a username and password to pass along with the call to the web service in the `cfinvoke` tag or by registering the web service in the ColdFusion Administrator:

```
<cfinvoke webservice="http://www.example.com/addressLookup.wsdl"
          returnvariable="myAddress"
          username="username"
          password="password">
  <cfinvokeargument name="userID" value="pmoney">
</cfinvoke>
```

The *username* and *password* values are Base64-encoded and passed as *username*:*password* in the authorization header to the target server.

Securing Access Using ColdFusion's Built-in Security Framework

You can control access to your web services at a much more granular level using ColdFusion MX's built-in security framework. This works for web services the same way as it does for CFCs, by controlling access based on assigned roles at the invocation level. Example 24-12 shows the code for a secure CFC accessible as a web service. The web service can only be invoked by clients with a role of `Administrator`.

Example 24-12. A web service restricted to clients with a role of Administrator

```
<cfcomponent>
  <cffunction name="returnStr" access="remote" returntype="string"
              roles="Administrator" output="false">

    <cfreturn "You have gained access">
  </cffunction>
</cfcomponent>
```

The framework for authenticating clients is the same one we discussed back in Chapter 8. Using an *Application.cfm* file, we can leverage ColdFusion MX's security framework and HTTP Basic Authentication to provide a means to authenticate clients before allowing them to access a web service. Example 24-13 shows one way to do this.

Example 24-13. Authenticating clients before they access a web service

```
<cfapplication name="MyWebService">

<cflogin idletimeout="600">
  <cfif not isdefined("cflogin")>
    <cfheader statuscode="401">
    <cfheader name="WWW-Authenticate" value="Basic realm=""MyWebService""">
    You are noy authorized to access the web service.
    <cfabort>
  <cfelse>
    <cfquery name="validateUser" datasource="programmingcf">
      SELECT Roles, Salt, Password
      FROM Users
      WHERE Username = <cfqueryparam value="#cflogin.name#"
                                     cfsqltype="CF_SQL_VARCHAR"
                                     maxlength="255">
    </cfquery>

    <cfif (validateUser.recordCount eq 1) and
          (validateUser.password is hash(validateUser.salt & cflogin.password))>
      <cfset userRoles = valueList(validateUser.roles)>
```

Example 24-13. Authenticating clients before they access a web service (continued)

```
      <cfloginuser name="#cflogin.name#" password="#cflogin.Password#"
                   roles="#userRoles#">
    <cfelse>
      <cfheader statuscode="401">
      <cfheader name="WWW-Authenticate"
                value="Basic realm=""MyWebService""">
      You are noy authorized to access the web service.
      <cfabort>
    </cfif>
  </cfif>
</cflogin>
```

When a client calls a ColdFusion-based web service, a check is made to see if there is an *Application.cfm* file that should be run first—just as there is when a CFML file is called from the browser. This lets you use the same mechanisms you are already familiar with to build a security framework for your CFC-based web services. When our *Application.cfm* file is called, a number of things happen.

First, a check is made to see if the `cflogin` structure exists. If not, an HTTP 401 status code is sent back to the client, telling them they are not authorized to access the web service. If the `cflogin` structure does exist, we know that the call to the web service also included an authorization header containing (hopefully) a username and password. Those values are automatically available inside the `cflogin` structure as `cflogin.name` and `cflogin.password`. A query is made to see if the username exists in the `Users` table of our example database. If so, the salt value associated with `cflogin.name` (from the database query) is concatenated with the password provided by `cflogin.password`. The resulting string is hashed and then compared to the hashed value stored in the database. If a record is found for the username, and the salted, hashed password matches the value stored in the database, we consider this a valid login. The `cflogin` tag is then used to log the user in and assign the role from the database. In this example, when we lookup the username `pmoney`, we find she is assigned the roles `Administrator, User`.

The code for invoking the secured web service is shown in Example 24-14. Note that it's necessary to create a subdirectory off the */programmingcf* directory called */ch24* instead of the */24* format we've used before. This is because directory names that begin with numbers cause ColdFusion to throw an error when dealing with web services.

Example 24-14. Invoking the secured web service

```
<cfinvoke method="returnStr"
 returnvariable="retVal"
 webservice="http://localhost/ProgrammingCF/ch24/secure/secure_ws.cfc?wsdl"
 username="pmoney"
 password="cat">
</cfinvoke>

<cfoutput>
```

Example 24-14. Invoking the secured web service (continued)

```
#retVal#
</cfoutput>
```

If you run this code, you should see a message in your browser that reads "You have gained access". If you wait 30 minutes (the time specified in the `idletimeout` attribute of the `cflogin` tag), and change the username or password to a different value, you should be able to generate an authentication error if you attempt to call the web service as an unauthorized user.

CHAPTER 25

Working with the System Registry

Anyone running ColdFusion on the Windows platform has probably encountered the system registry at one point or another. The registry is a database of sorts that contains configuration information on virtually every user and every piece of hardware and software (including ColdFusion) on your system. The registry is organized in a hierarchical fashion like that of a tree. ColdFusion provides you with a tag for working with the system registry, the `cfregistry` tag, which is capable of querying information from the registry, as well as setting new values and deleting unwanted ones.

Before we get into the specifics of manipulating registry data, let's look at how the registry is organized. There are two basic units that make up the registry, keys and values. A *key* is a logical container similar to a filesystem's directory. Like a directory that contains files and additional subdirectories, keys can contain values and/or subkeys. A registry key and the subkeys and values below it are referred to as a branch. If we were to write out the structure of a typical registry branch, it might look something like this:

```
HKEY_LOCAL_MACHINE\Software\Allaire\ColdFusion\CurrentVersion\Mail
```

This branch stores values used by ColdFusion to interface with mail servers. As you can see, the key/subkey relationship looks exactly like a directory structure might (in DOS anyway).

Values (like files) are actually a representation for name/value pairs. Values are also known as entries. The following registry branch:

```
HKEY_LOCAL_MACHINE\Software\Allaire\ColdFusion\CurrentVersion\Mail
```

contains several entries such as `BaseDirectory`, `LogEntries`, and `MailServer`. In turn, each of these entries contains a value. If you are running ColdFusion on Windows, you can use a GUI tool called the Registry Editor (which has a Windows Explorer-like interface) to view and manipulate registry keys and values.

Because the system registry contains configuration information on critical system resources, you need to be extremely careful when using the `cfregistry` tag to change or delete registry information. Always keep a current backup of your registry and limit access to the tag when possible. This is especially important for administrators using ColdFusion in a multihost environment (such as an ISP). In general, it is recommended that you disable the `cfregistry` tag from the Sandbox Security section of the ColdFusion Administrator if you don't plan to use it.

If you are running ColdFusion on a non-Windows operating system, such as Unix or Linux, the `cfregistry` tag is no longer available in ColdFusion MX. In previous versions of ColdFusion, an abbreviated version of the system registry was automatically created when you first installed ColdFusion. This scaled-down registry stored information about the configuration of your ColdFusion application server. That same information is now stored in various XML configuration files. This applies to all versions of ColdFusion on all platforms.

Getting Registry Keys and Values

The `cfregistry` tag gives you two methods for retrieving keys and values from the registry. You can set the `action` attribute to `GetAll` to retrieve all the particular keys/values associated with a particular branch, or you can set `action="Get"` to retrieve the value associated with a specific entry.

Let's consider a scenario where we want to look up information about any ODBC data sources set up on the same machine as ColdFusion. There is a registry branch we can access that contains this information. The branch is:

```
HKEY_LOCAL_MACHINE\Software\ODBC\ODBC.INI
```

It contains a list of every ODBC data source registered on the system. Each key contains several other subkeys relating to the ODBC connection. Example 25-1 shows how to perform the registry lookup.

Example 25-1. Retrieving a list of registry keys

```
<cfregistry action="GetAll" branch="HKEY_LOCAL_MACHINE\Software\ODBC\ODBC.INI"
         name="GetODBC" type="Key" sort="Entry Asc">

<h3>HKEY_LOCAL_MACHINE\Software\ODBC\ODBC.INI</h3>

<table border="1">
<tr>
  <th>Entry</th><th>Type</th><th>Value</th>
</tr>

<cfoutput query="GetODBC">
<tr>
  <td>#Entry#</td><td>#Type#</td><td>#Value#</td>
</tr>
</cfoutput>
</table>
```

In Example 25-1, we set the action attribute of the cfregistry tag to GetAll. This action results in ColdFusion retrieving all the registry keys and values that fall under the branch specified in branch. The name attribute allows us to specify a name for the query object that holds all the information we retrieve from the registry. type is an optional attribute and specifies the type of registry entry to be accessed. Possibilities include Key, DWord, String (the default), and Any. In this case, we set type to Key because we want to return only registry keys in our result set.

The final attribute, sort, is also optional and determines the sort order for the results returned from the registry. Results may be ordered by Entry, Type, and Value. Multiple sort criteria can be entered as a comma-delimited list. In addition, the sort type may be specified after each column name as either Asc (ascending) or Desc (descending). In Example 25-1, we sort the results by Entry, in ascending order.

Executing the template results in an HTML table (shown in Figure 25-1), which contains all the subkeys contained in the specified registry branch. Note that the table contains three columns, Entry, Type, and Value. These column headers match up with the three query columns returned by the cfregistry tag:

queryname.Entry
: Returns the name of the registry entry

queryname.Type
: The type of registry entry returned

queryname.Value
: The value of the registry entry if type is set to String or DWord

You should note that ColdFusion doesn't currently support the retrieval of binary values using the cfregistry tag. If you have type set to Any, and a binary value is returned, *queryname*.Type is set to "Unsupported" and *queryname*.Value returns blank.

As of ColdFusion MX, the cfregistry tag allows you to specify startrow and maxrows attributes when the action is set to GetAll and type is Key. This lets you break up potentially large result sets containing many keys in a manner that's similar to the way you can in other tags such as cfquery. To illustrate this, we can modify the code from Example 25-1 to return only the first 5 registry keys by setting startrow="1" (the default) and maxrows="5" (default is to return all remaining rows):

```
<cfregistry action="GetAll" branch="HKEY_LOCAL_MACHINE\Software\ODBC\ODBC.INI"
            name="GetODBC" type="Key" sort="Entry Asc"
            startrow="1" maxrows="5">

<h3>HKEY_LOCAL_MACHINE\Software\ODBC\ODBC.INI</h3>

<table border="1">
<tr>
  <th>Entry</th><th>Type</th><th>Value</th>
</tr>
```

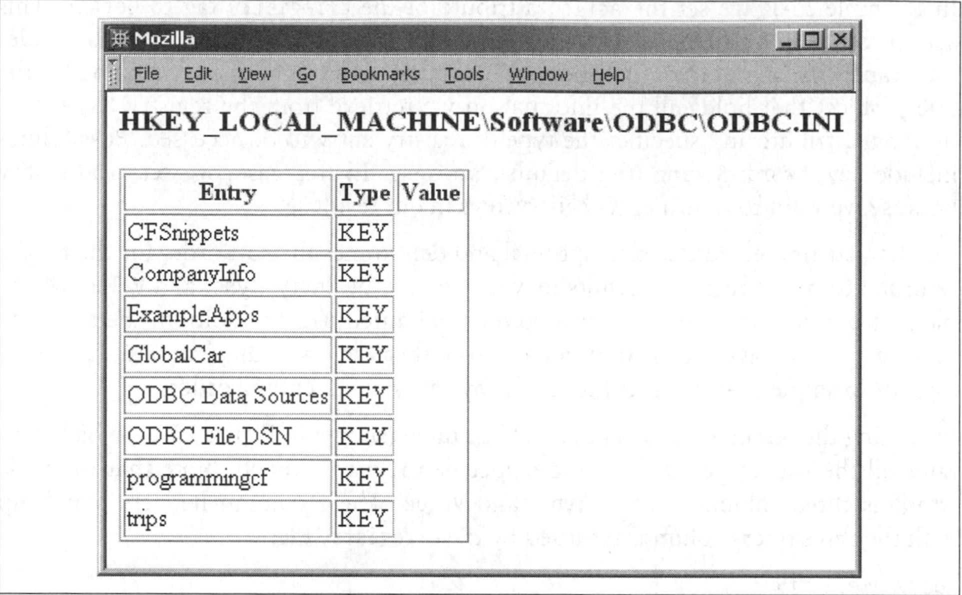

Figure 25-1. Retrieving a list of entries from the registry

```
<cfoutput query="GetODBC">
<tr>
  <td>#Entry#</td><td>#Type#</td><td>#Value#</td>
</tr>
</cfoutput>
</table>
```

Building further on Example 25-1, let's delve one level deeper in the registry. Let's look at what you get if you use `action="GetAll"` to retrieve all the subkeys from one of the keys (branches) we originally returned. We'll use the exact same code as in Example 25-1, except this time, we'll set the `branch` attribute to `HKEY_LOCAL_MACHINE\Software\ODBC\ODBC.INI\ExampleApps` and we'll set the `type` attribute to `Any`.

`ExampleApps` is the name of the sample database that installs by default when you install ColdFusion MX. If you don't have the `ExampleApps` database installed on your machine, don't worry. You can reference any valid ODBC data source you have installed on your server. The complete template for retrieving a list of registry values can be seen in Example 25-2.

Example 25-2. Retrieving a list of registry values

```
<cfregistry action="GetAll"
            branch="HKEY_LOCAL_MACHINE\Software\ODBC\ODBC.INI\ExampleApps"
            name="GetODBC" type="Any" sort="Entry Asc">

<h3>HKEY_LOCAL_MACHINE\Software\ODBC\ODBC.INI\ExampleApps</h3>

<table border="1">
```

Example 25-2. Retrieving a list of registry values (continued)

```
<tr>
  <th>Entry</th><th>Type</th><th>Value</th>
</tr>

<cfoutput query="GetODBC">
<tr>
  <td>#Entry#</td><td>#Type#</td><td>#Value#</td>
</tr>
</cfoutput>
</table>
```

If you run the template in Example 25-2, you see the output shown in Figure 25-2. Note that the table that is generated is similar to the one we created earlier in Figure 25-1, except that this time there are other values in the type column besides Key. Also, notice that the Value column now contains data for some of the entries we retrieved.

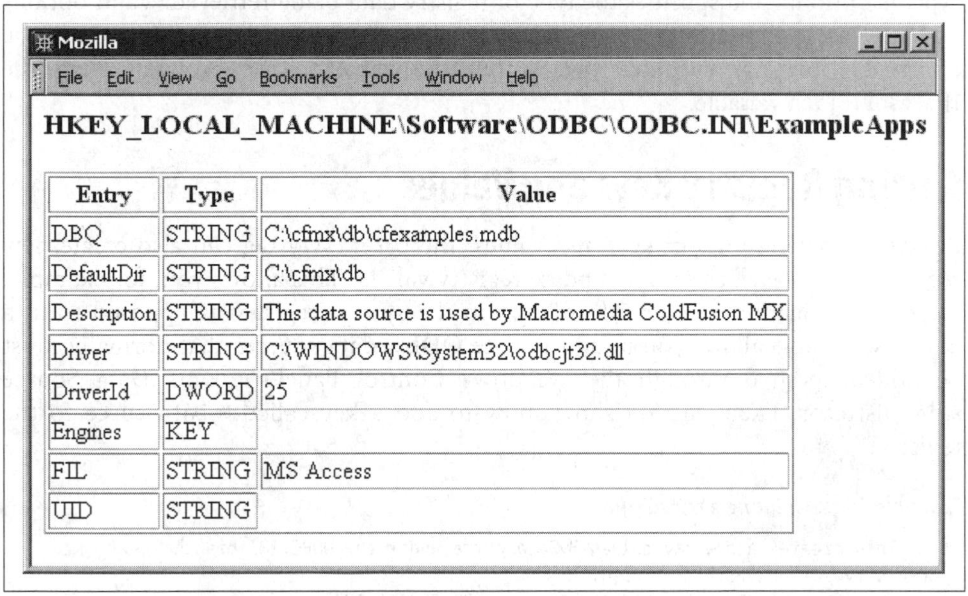

Mozilla

File Edit View Go Bookmarks Tools Window Help

HKEY_LOCAL_MACHINE\Software\ODBC\ODBC.INI\ExampleApps

Entry	Type	Value
DBQ	STRING	C:\cfmx\db\cfexamples.mdb
DefaultDir	STRING	C:\cfmx\db
Description	STRING	This data source is used by Macromedia ColdFusion MX
Driver	STRING	C:\WINDOWS\System32\odbcjt32.dll
DriverId	DWORD	25
Engines	KEY	
FIL	STRING	MS Access
UID	STRING	

Figure 25-2. Retrieving a list of entries containing values

As I mentioned earlier, cfregistry can also retrieve values for specific registry keys. For example, say you want your application to retrieve the description for the ODBC data source used in the previous example. You know the entry for Description is stored in the registry branch:

```
HKEY_LOCAL_MACHINE\Software\ODBC\ODBC.INI\ExampleApps
```

By setting the action attribute to Get, you can retrieve the value associated with the key, as shown in Example 25-3.

Example 25-3. Retrieving a specific registry value

```
<cfregistry action="Get"
      branch="HKEY_LOCAL_MACHINE\Software\ODBC\ODBC.INI\ExampleApps"
      entry="Description" variable="TheDescription" type="String">

<h3>HKEY_LOCAL_MACHINE\Software\ODBC\ODBC.INI\ExampleApps</h3>

<cfoutput>
The value of <b>Description</b> is: #TheDescription#
</cfoutput>
```

In Example 25-3, we set `action` to `Get` so that ColdFusion knows we want to retrieve a single value. The name of the registry branch containing the entry to be accessed is specified in `branch`. `entry` is required and specifies the entry in the registry we want to look up the value for. In this instance, we want to look up the value for `Description`. The `variable` attribute allows us to specify a variable name to hold the value we retrieve from the registry. We set our `variable` to `TheDescription`. The final attribute, `type`, is optional and specifies the type of registry data being retrieved. Valid options include `String` (the default), `DWord`, and `Key`. We set `type` equal to `String`. Once the `cfregistry` tag has executed, we output the value to the browser using the `TheDescription` variable.

Setting Registry Keys and Values

Besides retrieving registry keys and values, the `cfregistry` tag can also create new registry keys as well as set and update registry values. This allows you, for example, to store application-specific information in the system registry as opposed to in a database. It also allows you to add/update ODBC data sources that normally must be added/updated through the Windows Control Panel's ODBC Data Source Administrator. Example 25-4 shows how to add a key called `MyDataSource` to the registry.

Example 25-4. Creating a registry key

```
<!--- This creates a new key called MyDataSource under the ODBC.INI branch --->
<cfregistry action="Set"
        branch="HKEY_LOCAL_MACHINE\Software\ODBC\ODBC.INI"
        type="Key" entry="MyDataSource">

<!--- Query the branch so that we can show it was added --->
<cfregistry action="GatAll"
        branch="HKEY_LOCAL_MACHINE\Software\ODBC\ODBC.INI"
        name="GetDSNs" type="Any" sort="Asc">

<h3>HKEY_LOCAL_MACHINE\Software\ODBC\ODBC.INI</h3>

<table border="1">
<tr>
```

Example 25-4. Creating a registry key (continued)

```
  <th>Entry</th><th>Type</th><th>Value</th>
</tr>

<cfoutput query="GetDSNs">
<tr>
  <td>#Entry#</td><td>#Type#</td><td>#Value#</td>
</tr>
</cfoutput>
</table>
```

Example 25-4 uses the `cfregistry` tag to create a new registry key called `MyDataSource` by setting the `action` attribute to `Set`. `branch` specifies the registry branch to create the new key under. We decide to create our new key under the registry branch:

```
HKEY_LOCAL_MACHINE\Software\ODBC\ODBC.INI
```

The `type` attribute is optional and specifies the type of registry data to be set. Possible entries are `Key`, `DWord`, and `String` (the default). In Example 25-4, we set `type` to `Key`. The name of the key to create is specified by the `entry` attribute. Once the registry key has been created, we use another `cfregistry` tag to get a list of all the subkeys (including the one we just created) under `ODBC.INI`.

As I mentioned, the `cfregistry` tag can also set registry values. Example 25-5 creates an entry called `Description` and populates it with the string value "This is a test database."

Example 25-5. Setting a registry value

```
<!--- Set a string value for the Description key --->
<cfregistry action="Set"
        branch="HKEY_LOCAL_MACHINE\Software\ODBC\ODBC.INI\MyDataSource"
        entry="Description" type="String" value="This is a test database.">

<!--- Query the  key so that we can show a value was set --->
<cfregistry action="GET"
        branch="HKEY_LOCAL_MACHINE\Software\ODBC\ODBC.INI\MyDataSource"
        entry="Description" variable="GetDesc" type="String">

<h3>HKEY_LOCAL_MACHINE\Software\ODBC\ODBC.INI\MyDataSource</h3>

<cfoutput>
The value of <b>Description</b> is: <i>#GetDesc#</i>
</cfoutput>
```

In Example 25-5, the `action` is still `Set`. `branch` specifies the registry branch where we want to create our new key/value pair. The `entry` attribute is required and specifies the key or value in the registry to be set. We set `entry` to `Description`, telling ColdFusion that we want to set an entry called `Description`. `type` is an optional attribute and specifies the type of registry data to be set. Possible entries are `Key`, `DWord`, and `String` (the default). In this example, we set type to String. The actual value we want to set is specified by the value attribute. The second cfregistry call gets the value we just set and outputs it to the browser.

If you use cfregistry to set a value for an entry that already exists, ColdFusion overwrites the old value with the one you supply. Example 25-6 updates an already existing registry entry with a new value and outputs the results to the browser.

Example 25-6. Updating a registry value

```
<!--- Query the Description key so that we can show the original value --->
<cfregistry action="Get"
        branch="HKEY_LOCAL_MACHINE\Software\ODBC\ODBC.INI\MyDataSource"
        entry="Description" variable="GetOriginalDesc" type="String">

<h3>HKEY_LOCAL_MACHINE\Software\ODBC\ODBC.INI\MyDataSource</h3>

<cfoutput>
The original value of <b>Description</b>: <i>#GetOriginalDesc#</i><br>
</cfoutput>
Change the value...<br>

<!--- Set a string value for the Description key --->
<cfregistry action="Set"
        branch="HKEY_LOCAL_MACHINE\Software\ODBC\ODBC.INI\MyDataSource"
        entry="Description" type="String" value="This is an updated description.">

<!--- Query the Description key so that we can show the new value --->
<cfregistry action="Get"
        branch="HKEY_LOCAL_MACHINE\Software\ODBC\ODBC.INI\MyDataSource"
        entry="Description" variable="GetDesc" type="String">

<cfoutput>
The new value of <b>Description</b>: <i>#GetDesc#</i>
</cfoutput>
```

Deleting Registry Keys and Values

There are times when you might find it desirable to delete information from the system registry, for example, if you want to delete a data source without having to go through the ColdFusion Administrator. The cfregistry tag can delete a registry value, a single registry key or an entire registry branch by setting the action attribute to Delete. But it is extremely important to know what you are doing with regards to the registry before you use this action. You should also have a current backup of your registry before using the cfregistry tag to delete registry entries. Example 25-7 deletes an entry from the registry.

Example 25-7. Deleting a registry value

```
<cfregistry action="Delete"
         branch="HKEY_LOCAL_MACHINE\Software\ODBC\ODBC.INI\MyDataSource"
         entry="Description">

<cfregistry action="GetAll"
         branch="HKEY_LOCAL_MACHINE\Software\ODBC\ODBC.INI\MyDataSource"
         name="GetAll" type="Any" sort="Asc">

<h3>HKEY_LOCAL_MACHINE\Software\ODBC\ODBC.INI\MyDataSource</h3>

<table border="1">
<tr>
  <th>Entry</th><th>Type</th><th>Value</th>
</tr>

<cfoutput query="GetAll">
<tr>
  <td>#Entry#</td><td>#Type#</td><td>#Value#</td>
</tr>
</cfoutput>
</table>
```

In Example 25-7, we set the `action` attribute of the `cfregistry` tag to `Delete`. `branch` specifies the branch containing the entry we want to delete. The `entry` attribute specifies the name of the entry we want to delete, in this case, an entry named `Description`. Note that if the entry specified in `Entry` doesn't exist, ColdFusion returns an error.

`cfregistry` can also delete a single registry key or an entire registry branch, including all subbranches and their associated keys and values. Example 25-8 deletes all the subbranches and key/value pairs below the key:

```
HKEY_LOCAL_MACHINE\Software\ODBC\ODBC.INI\MyDataSource
```

Example 25-8. Deleting an entire registry branch

```
<cfregistry action="Delete"
     branch="HKEY_LOCAL_MACHINE\Software\ODBC\ODBC.INI\MyDataSource">

<cfregistry action="GetAll"
     branch="HKEY_LOCAL_MACHINE\Software\ODBC\ODBC.INI"
     name="GetAll" type="Any" sort="Asc">

<h3>HKEY_LOCAL_MACHINE\Software\ODBC\ODBC.INI</h3>

<table border="1">
<tr>
  <th>Entry</th><th>Type</th><th>Value</th>
</tr>

<cfoutput query="GetAll">
<tr>
```

Example 25-8. Deleting an entire registry branch (continued)

```
  <td>#Entry#</td><td>#Type#</td><td>#Value#</td>
</tr>
</cfoutput>
</table>
```

In Example 25-8, the `cfregistry` tag needs only two attributes, `action` and `branch`. As in Example 25-7, we set `action` to `Delete` to let ColdFusion know we want to delete information from the registry. The key to begin recursively deleting from is specified by `branch`. All keys, subkeys, and values in or below the specified branch are deleted. If the branch doesn't exist, ColdFusion throws an error.

CHAPTER 26

Using the ColdFusion Scheduler

The ColdFusion Scheduler allows you to incorporate a whole new level of functionality into your CFML applications. With the Scheduler, you can set up various templates to run automatically on a recurring basis. Scheduled template execution has numerous uses including automatic report generation, maintenance, and system monitoring. You can also automate so-called intelligent agents—templates that are capable of retrieving information from other sites and applications without user intervention.

The Scheduler comes standard as part of the ColdFusion Application Server and can be accessed via the ColdFusion Administrator or programmatically. Using the Scheduler, it is possible to schedule the execution of templates on a recurring basis, e.g., daily, weekly, or monthly. In addition, tasks can be set to execute at a particular time or interval or to run only a single time. Additionally, the Scheduler can automatically generate static HTML files from dynamic content.

Scheduling Tasks with the ColdFusion Administrator

The fastest way to schedule the execution of a template is through the ColdFusion Administrator. The ColdFusion Administrator provides a clean and intuitive interface for managing scheduled tasks. Using the ColdFusion Administrator interface, you can specify general settings for the Scheduler as well as add, update, and delete scheduled tasks. Scheduled tasks can also be run directly from within the ColdFusion Administrator, which makes it possible to test your scheduled tasks or execute them manually.

Logging Scheduled Tasks

Before you begin to use the Scheduler, it is important to take note of an administrative setting that impacts the logging of scheduled task execution. If you open the

ColdFusion Administrator in your browser and click on the Logging Settings link under the Debugging & Logging section, you will see a screen that allows you to set various logging options. This configuration screen is shown in Figure 26-1.

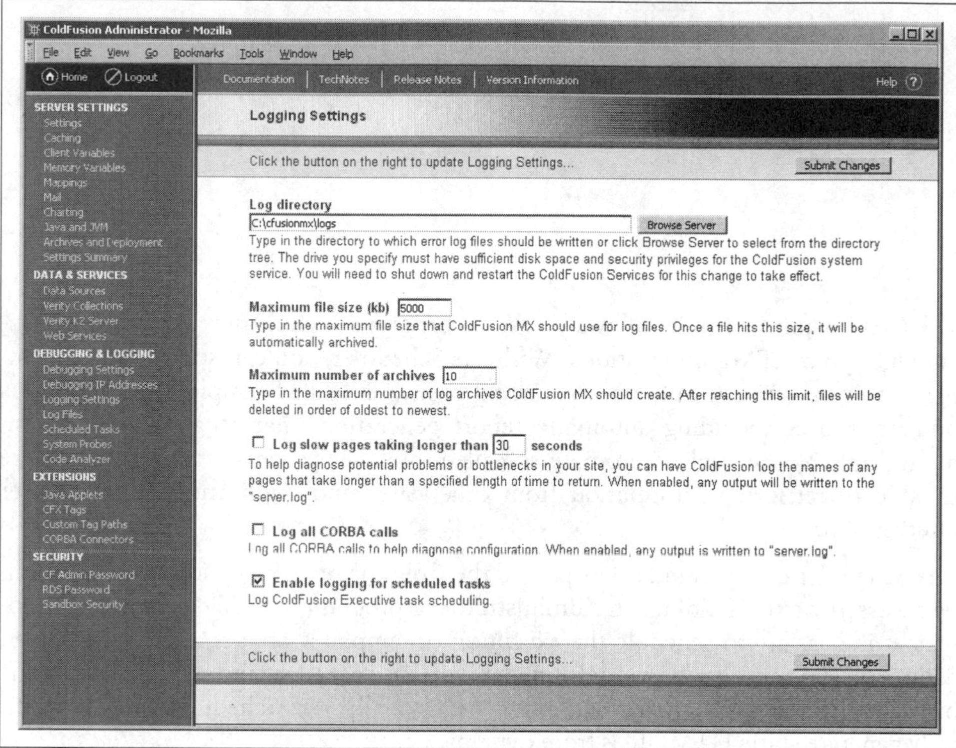

Figure 26-1. Enabling/disabling logging of scheduled tasks

Checking the "Enable logging for scheduled tasks" box causes the ColdFusion Server to write a log entry to the *scheduler.log* file each time a new task is added to the list or an existing task is modified.

Whenever a scheduled task is run, an entry is written to a log file called *scheduler.log*, regardless of whether or scheduled task logging is enabled or not. This file resides in the directory specified in the Logging Settings page under the Debugging & Logging section of the ColdFusion Administrator. Log entries vary depending on whether task execution was successful. Here's an example of what you can expect to see in the *scheduler.log* file:

```
"Information","scheduler-3","05/08/03","14:51:00",,"[test2] Executing at Thu
May 08 14:51:00 EDT 2003"
"Information","scheduler-3","05/08/03","14:51:00",,"[test2] Rescheduling for :Thu
May 08 14:52:00 EDT 2003 Now: Thu May 08 14:51:00 EDT 2003"
"Information","scheduler-3","05/08/03","14:51:00",,"[Test_badURL] Executing at
Thu May 08 14:51:00 EDT 2003"
"Information","scheduler-3","05/08/03","14:51:13",,"Error while executing task"
```

You can view the *scheduler.log* file from the Log Files section of the ColdFusion Administrator, under Debugging & Logging.

Adding a Task

To add a new task to the Scheduler, click on the Scheduled Tasks link under the Debugging & Logging section of the ColdFusion Administrator. You are then presented with a page listing all currently scheduled tasks (shown in Figure 26-2). To add a new task, click the Schedule New Task button.

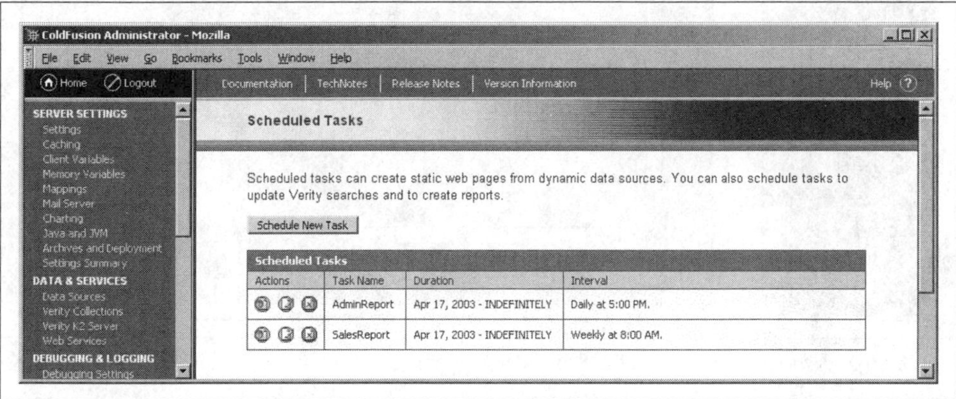

Figure 26-2. Adding a new task name to the Scheduled Tasks Menu

Submitting the form in Figure 26-2 takes you to the Add/Edit Scheduled Task page shown in Figure 26-3. This page allows you to specify all the details concerning the task you wish to schedule. The first thing you need to enter is a name for your task. The next element you need to enter is a Duration for your task. The Duration specifies a Start Date and an optional End Date corresponding with the dates you want the scheduled execution to begin and optionally end. If you want the task to remain scheduled indefinitely, omit the End Date.

The next section of the form in Figure 26-3 lets you specify an interval for your scheduled task. This interval determines how often the task is to be scheduled. You have three options:

One Time
: The scheduled task executes a single time on the Start Date you specified. The time you wish the task to execute can be specified here. After the task executes, it remains in the list of scheduled tasks, although it doesn't execute again.

Recurring
: This option allows you to specify how frequently the scheduled task should execute. Possibilities include Daily, Weekly, and Monthly. Execution begins on the

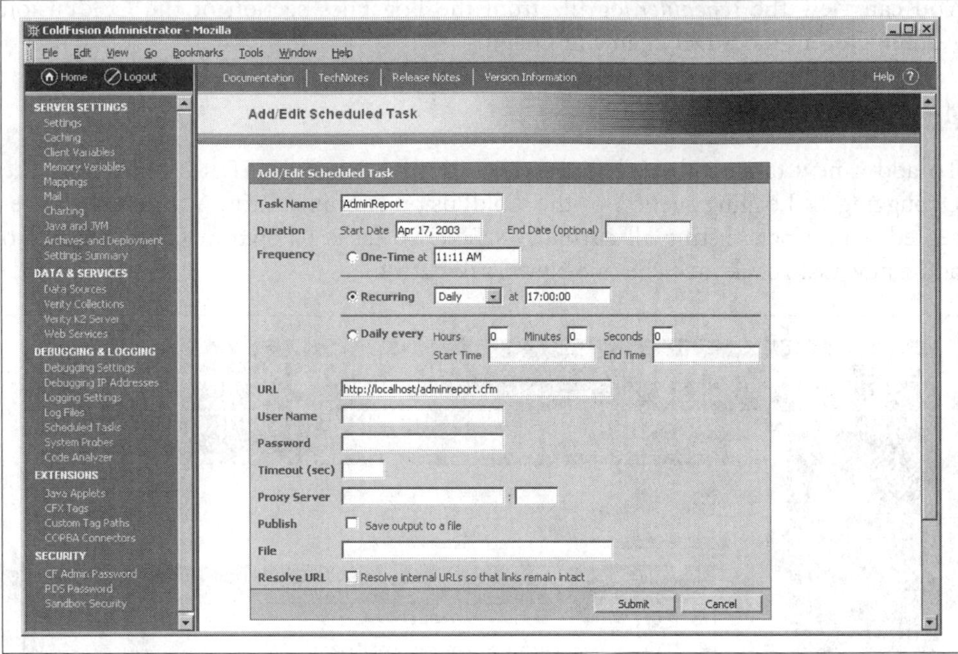

Figure 26-3. Adding a new task to the Scheduler

Start Date with the task executing at the time specified in the Daily Start Time field.

Daily every n hours/minutes/seconds
: With this option, you can schedule your task to repeat every *n* hours/minutes/seconds beginning on the Start Date. Optionally, you can specify a Daily Start Time and a Daily End Time for the task so that it executes only within the given time period each day.

The next option you can specify is URL. The value you enter for URL should be the absolute URL (*http://* or *https://*) to the template you want the scheduled task to execute. If you are attempting to execute a template over a port other than 80, make sure to specify the port in the URL attribute (*http://www.example.com:8500/*). The template can reside on any server accessible by URL. If the remote template requires authentication, you can specify a Username and Password in the appropriate fields.

You should note that the ColdFusion Scheduler uses the `cfhttp` tag behind the scenes to execute the template you specify. As such, the same issues that apply to the `cfhttp` tag also apply to tasks scheduled through the ColdFusion Scheduler.

The Timeout field is optional and lets you specify an amount of time in seconds to wait before timing out the scheduled task. This field is important because it allows you to extend the amount of time a request has to execute beyond the value set in the Server Settings section of the ColdFusion Administrator.

The next two fields are both optional. They allow you to specify the hostname or IP address of a proxy server you must pass your request through if your ColdFusion server is behind a firewall. If the template you are trying to execute sits behind a proxy server, you can specify the port number used by the proxy server as well. If a port value is specified, it is automatically appended to any resolved URLs within the executed template. This allows you to preserve links within a template that resolve to a port other than 80.

The last section of the Add/Edit Scheduled Task page gives you the option to have the output from the template you request automatically saved as a file on your ColdFusion server. This allows you to schedule tasks that call dynamically generated content and have the results saved as a static HTML template.

In order to save the output of your scheduled task, you must check the box labeled "Save output to a file". Next, enter the full path (e.g., *c:\inetsrv\wwwroot\file.htm*) to the directory where you want to save the file in the File field. You can give the file any extension you want. Checking the box next to Resolve URL results in any relative links in the output file being converted to absolute URLs. This ensures that no broken links appear in the file you create. This is especially useful when you schedule a task to retrieve dynamic content from a remote server.

Once you have finished setting up the options for your scheduled task, click the Submit button at the bottom of the page to create the task. If you decide for some reason that you don't want to create the task, click the Cancel button to return to the main Scheduled Tasks menu.

Manually Executing a Task

You can manually execute a scheduled task from within the ColdFusion Administrator. This is useful when you need to execute a scheduled task at a time other than originally scheduled, or when you want to execute a task for troubleshooting purposes. To manually execute a task from the ColdFusion Administrator, click on the Schedule Task link, then on the run icon (under the Actions column.) If the task can be executed, a page displaying a message to that effect is displayed.

Updating and Deleting Tasks

The ColdFusion Administrator provides you with a way to update existing tasks with new information and to delete tasks you no longer want or need. All editing and deleting of scheduled tasks starts by choosing a task from the Scheduled Tasks menu in the ColdFusion Administrator.

Updating a task

To edit an existing task, click on the task name link or edit icon from the Scheduled Task menu. This action takes you to a page labeled Add/Edit Scheduled Task. This is the same as the page shown in Figure 26-3, except all the information about the task is already filled in the form fields. And you can now make changes to the task information. When you are finished, click on the Submit button at the bottom of the page. If you change your mind and don't want to save the changes, click on the Cancel button.

Deleting a task

To delete a task, click on the delete icon next to the task name on the Scheduled Task menu. A JavaScript confirmation box will appear asking to you to confirm that you want to delete the task. Once you delete a task, the operation can't be undone.

Scheduling Tasks with cfschedule

Besides being able to schedule tasks with the ColdFusion Administrator, you can use the `cfschedule` tag to do it programmatically. With the `cfschedule` tag, you can add, update, delete, and run scheduled tasks. Scheduling tasks programmatically lets you add a whole new level of functionality to your applications. For example, you can create a reporting application that allows users to have automatic email delivery of their reports on a scheduled basis. With the `cfschedule` tag, it is easy to set things up so that your application automatically schedules a task for each user. And each task can automatically generate a report and email it to the user at a chosen interval.

The attributes used by the `cfschedule` tag roughly coincide with the form fields from the Add/Edit Scheduled Task page in the ColdFusion Administrator, as you can see in Appendix A.

Adding Tasks

Adding a task to the Scheduler using `cfschedule` is a lot like adding a task via the ColdFusion Administrator. The information you enter in the ColdFusion Administrator is the same information you specify for the `cfschedule` tag attributes. For example, to schedule a task called `MyTask` that calls the template located at *http://www.example.com/myscript.cfm* once a day at 1:30 p.m., you can use the following code:

```
<cfschedule action="Update" task="MyTask" operation="HTTPRequest"
            URL="http://www.example.com/myscript.cfm"
            startdate="#DateFormat(Now(),'mm/dd/yyyy')#"
            starttime="13:30:00" interval="Daily" requesttimeout="60">

<h2>Task scheduled successfully</h2>
```

The `action` attribute is required and specifies the action you want the Scheduler to perform. Possible actions are `Update`, `Delete`, and `Run`. `Update` can be used to create a new task or update an existing task. In this case, we use `Update` to create a new task.

When action attribute is set to Update, several required attributes are expected. These attributes are task, operation, URL, startdate, starttime, and interval. The task attribute allows you to specify a name for the task. The name you assign to the task is used by the ColdFusion Scheduler to uniquely identify the task—similar to how a database uses a primary key. Before adding a task using cfschedule, it is a good idea to see if a task by the same name already exists. If it does, and you try to add a new task with the same name, you will overwrite the original task. To look up a task name, you can use a simple UDF that checks the XML file ColdFusion uses to store information about scheduled tasks:

```
<cffunction name="IsScheduledTask" return="Boolean">
  <cfargument name="TaskName" required="True" type="String">
  <!--- Var local vars for the func --->
  <cfset Var TaskXML="">
  <cfset Var GetTasks="">

  <!--- Get the scheduler xml file.  It's stored as WDDX --->
  <cffile action="Read"
          file="#Server.ColdFusion.RootDir#\lib\neo-cron.xml"
          variable="TaskXML">

  <!--- Convert the WDDX to CFML - and array of structs --->
  <cfwddx action="WDDX2CFML" input="#TaskXML#" output="GetTasks">

  <!--- Search the array of structs for the name passed to the func --->
  <cfif ListContainsNoCase(StructKeyList(GetTasks[1]), Arguments.TaskName) EQ 0>
    <cfreturn False>
  <cfelse>
    <cfreturn True>
  </cfif>
</cffunction>
```

To test whether a scheduled task already exists, you simply call the IsScheduledTask( ) UDF, passing it the name of the task you want to check:

```
<cfoutput>
#IsScheduledTask("MyTaskName")#
</cfoutput>
```

The operation attribute specifies the operation the Scheduler should perform when action is Update. The only operation currently supported is HTTPRequest. URL points to the absolute URL (*http://* or *https://*) of the template to be executed when the scheduled task runs. Optionally, a port other than port 80 may be specified by using the PORT attribute. The starting date for the scheduled task is specified by startdate. In this case, we use #DateFormat(Now( ),'mm/dd/yyyy')# to indicate that the scheduled task should start on the current day. The time that the scheduled task gets executed is governed by the starttime. interval indicates how often a scheduled task should be executed. Intervals can be set in seconds or as Once, Daily, Weekly, or Monthly. The default interval is one hour (3,600 seconds). The minimum interval allowed is 1 second. Note that in previous versions of ColdFusion, the minimum value for `interval` was 60 seconds. `requesttimeout` is an optional attribute that can extend the time allowed for execution of the scheduled task beyond the default set in the ColdFusion Administrator.

There are several additional optional attributes available to the `cfschedule` tag. For more information, see Appendix A.

Let's look at a more advanced example that demonstrates the power of using the `cfschedule` tag to let your applications schedule tasks on their own. Consider a scenario in which you want to allow an administrator to schedule the automatic delivery of reports to various users within your organization. These reports can contain any sort of information. In Example 26-1, we'll send the employee a copy of their contact information.

The first step is to create a form for the administrator to select an employee and enter information on when the report should run, and how it should be delivered (either via email or published to a static HTML page).

Example 26-1. Choosing an employee and scheduling delivery of a report

```
<!--- Get all of the employees from the EmployeeDirectory table.  This query
      is used to populate the employee drop down box --->
<cfquery name="GetEmployees" datasource="ProgrammingCF">
        SELECT ID, Name FROM EmployeeDirectory
</cfquery>

<h2>Schedule Report</h2>

<form action="ScheduleTheTask.cfm" method="Post">
<table border=0 >
<tr>
  <!--- Populate the employee drop down with the query results from earlier --->
  <td><b>Employee:</b></td>
  <td><select me="Employee">
        <cfoutput query="GetEmployees">
        <option value="#ID#">#Name#</option>
        </cfoutput>
      </select>
  </td>
</tr>
<tr>
  <td><b>Task Name:</b></td>
  <td><input name="TaskName" type="text" size="20" maxlength="255"></td>
</tr>
<tr>
  <!--- Specifies the type of report to schedule --->
  <td><b>Delivery Format:</b></td>
  <td><select name="DeliveryFormat">
        <option value="Email" selected>E-mail
        <option value="HTMLPage">HTML Page</select>
```

Example 26-1. Choosing an employee and scheduling delivery of a report (continued)

```
  </td>
</tr>
<tr>
  <td><b>Start Date:</b></td>
  <td><cfoutput><input name="StartDate" type="text" value="#DateFormat(Now( ),
        'mm/dd/yy')#" size=10></cfoutput></td>
</tr>
<tr>
  <td><b>Schedule to run </b></td>
  <td><select name="Interval">
        <option value="Daily">Daily
        <option value="Weekly">Weekly
        <option value="Monthly">Monthly
      </select> at
      <cfoutput>
      <!--- Output the refresh interval in minutes --->
      <input name="StartTime" type="text" value="#TimeFormat(DateAdd("N", 15,
             Now( )),'HH:mm:ss')#" size=10> (EST)
      </cfoutput>
  </td>
</tr>
<tr>
  <td colspan="2" align="center"><input name="Create" type="submit"
      value="Schedule">
  </td>
</tr>
</table>
</form>
```

The template in Example 26-1 creates a form for the administrator to set up the scheduled task (shown in Figure 26-4). A query is performed to obtain a list of the employee names. The names are then used to dynamically populate a drop-down box in the form. The next field in the form allows the administrator to choose a delivery format for the report. Valid options here are `Email` and `HTML Page`. The rest of the fields specify a name for the scheduled task as well as the start date and frequency with which the task should run.

Once the administrator finishes filling out the form, she can click the Schedule button at the bottom of the form to schedule the task. Clicking on the button posts the form-field information to a template called *ScheduleTheTask.cfm*, shown in Example 26-2.

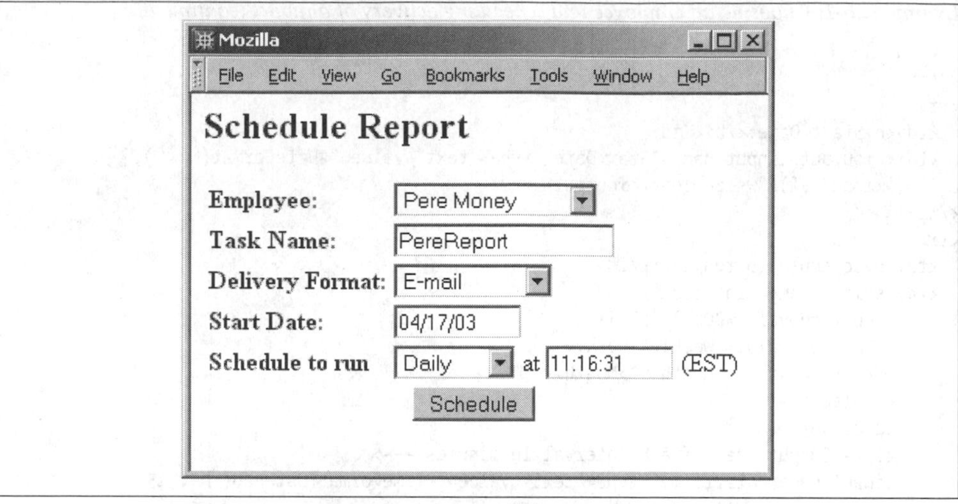

Figure 26-4. Choosing an employee and scheduling delivery of a report

Example 26-2. Scheduling the report delivery using cfschedule

```
<!--- Get the employee name associated with the ID we passed in --->
<cfquery name="GetEmployee" datasource="ProgrammingCF">
        SELECT Name
        FROM EmployeeDirectory
        WHERE ID = #form.Employee#
</cfquery>

<!--- Assign defaults in case of blanks --->
<cfparam name="form.TaskName" default="#CreateUUID( )#">
<cfparam name="form.StartDate" default="#DateFormat(Now( ),'mm/dd/yyyy')#">
<cfparam name="form.StartTime" default="#TimeFormat(Now( ),'HH:mm:ss')#">

<!--- If the delivery format is Email, schedule the task --->
<cfif form.DeliveryFormat IS "Email">
  <cfschedule action="Update" task="#form.TaskName#" operation="HTTPRequest"
     startdate="#DateFormat(form.StartDate,'mm/dd/yyyy')#"
     starttime="#TimeFormat(form.StartTime,'HH:mm:ss')#"
     URL="http://127.0.0.1/RunScheduledReport.cfm?ID=#form.Employee#&
          DeliveryFormat=#form.DeliveryFormat#"
     interval="#form.interval#" requesttimeout="60">
<!--- If the delivery format is HTML, schedule the generation of the static
      HTML file --->
<cfelse>
  <cfschedule action="Update" task="#form.TaskName#" operation="HTTPRequest"
     startdate="#DateFormat(form.StartDate,'mm/dd/yyyy')#"
     starttime="#TimeFormat(form.StartTime,'HH:mm:ss')#"
     URL="http://127.0.0.1/RunScheduledReport.cfm?ID=#form.Employee#&
          DeliveryFormat=#form.DeliveryFormat#"
     interval="#form.interval#" requesttimeout="3600"
     resolveurl="Yes" publish="Yes"
```

Example 26-2. Scheduling the report delivery using cfschedule (continued)

```
    file="#Replace(GetEmployee.Name, ' ', '_', 'All')#.htm"
    path="e:\inetsrv\wwwroot\#Replace(GetEmployee.Name, ' ', '_', 'All')#">
</cfif>

<h2>Report Successfully Scheduled</h2>
```

The template in Example 26-2 takes the form-field data posted to it and uses it to create the scheduled task. A `cfquery` is run at the beginning of the template to look up the name of the employee the task is being scheduled for. This is done because the value passed with `form.Employee` is the `ID` number (primary key from the database) of the employee as opposed to her name. (I'll show you why I did this in just a moment.)

The next part of the template assigns default values for any of the required form fields in case they are left blank. This prevents the template from throwing an error or scheduling a task that can never be executed because it is missing a start time and date. If a name for the task isn't passed, a UUID is created to serve as the name. A UUID is used because it is guaranteed to be unique.

The third part of the template uses a `cfif` statement to determine whether or not the delivery format for the report generated by the scheduled task should be an email or an HTML file. Regardless of the format, a task is scheduled using the `cfschedule` tag that runs a template called *RunScheduledReport.cfm*. Note that two URL variables are appended to the end of the URL. The first URL variable, `ID`, specifies the `ID` of the employee (see, I told you I would get to this) for whom the report should be generated. The second URL variable, `DeliveryFormat`, specifies the delivery format for the report. If `form.DeliveryFormat` is `HTMLPage`, a few additional attributes are used with the `cfschedule` tag to specify that the output generated by the *RunScheduledReport.cfm* template should be saved as a static HTML file. The filename and path for the generated file are both dynamically created using the name of the employee (with spaces stripped out). Once the task has been created, a message is output to the browser letting the administrator know that the task has been successfully added.

The template in Example 26-3 is the *RunScheduledReport.cfm* template, which is the template that is called by any scheduled task created by the two previous templates. The template takes the `ID` URL variable passed in by the scheduled task and uses it to look up the employee for whom the report is supposed to be run. It then checks the value of the `DeliveryFormat` URL variable to determine the delivery format for the report. If the delivery format is email, the `cfmail` tag sends the report to the appropriate employee. If, however, the report format is an HTML page, a table is output to the "browser." The `cfhttp` tag then writes the contents of the page to a static HTML file on the server. Note that the directory the Scheduler is supposed to write to must already exist. You could get sophisticated and have this template check to make sure the directory exists using the `cfdirectory` tag, and if not create it first, but for the purposes of this example, let's keep it simple. Once the static file has been created, an email is then sent using `cfmail` to notify the employee that her report is ready. The email contains a link to the newly created report. The *RunScheduledReport.cfm* template is shown in Example 26-3.

Example 26-3. RunScheduledReport.cfm for creating and delivering reports

```
<!--- Check the desired delivery format from URL.DeliveryFortmat and act
      accordingly --->
<cfswitch expression="#URL.DeliveryFormat#">
<cfcase value="HTMLPage">
<!--- create the page to be written as a static page. --->
<html>
<head>
 <cfoutput>
 <title>Report for #GetRecord.Name#</title>
 </cfoutput>
</head>

<body>

<cfoutput>
<h2>Employee Information for #GetRecord.Name#</h2>
</cfoutput>

<table cellpadding="3" cellspacing="0">
<tr bgcolor="#888888">
  <th>Name</th><th>Title</th><th>Department</th><th>E-mail</th>
  <th>Phone Extension</th>
</tr>
<cfoutput query="GetRecord">
<tr bgcolor="##C0C0C0">
  <td>#Name#</td><td>#Title#</td><td>#Department#</td>
  <td><a href="Mailto:#Email#">#Email#</a></td><td>#PhoneExt#</td>
</tr>
</cfoutput>
</table>
</body>
</html>

<!--- Now send an e-mail to the employee letting them know where their page
      is --->
<cfmail to="#GetRecord.Email#" from="webmaster@example.com"
        subject="Your scheduled report is ready">
#GetRecord.Name#,

Your scheduled report is now ready for viewing.  You may see it by pointing your
browser to:

http://127.0.0.1/#Replace(GetRecord.Name, ' ', '_',
'All')#/#Replace(GetRecord.Name, ' ', '_', 'All')#.htm

Best regards,
```

Example 26-3. RunScheduledReport.cfm for creating and delivering reports (continued)

```
The Webmaster
</cfmail>
</cfcase>

<!--- Or, send an e-mail report to the employee --->
<cfcase value="Email">
<cfmail TO="#GetRecord.Email#" from="webmaster@example.com"
        subject="Your scheduled report" query="GetRecord">
#Name#,

Here is your employee report:

Name: #Name#
Title: #Title#
Department: #Department#
E-mail: #Email#
Phone Ext: #PhoneExt#

Best regards,

The Webmaster
</cfmail>
</cfcase>
</cfswitch>
```

Updating Tasks

As far as the `cfschedule` tag is concerned, updating an existing task and adding a new task are the same operation. Both operations are performed by setting `action` to `Update`. To successfully update an existing task, make sure to provide the exact task name in the `task` attribute of the `cfschedule` tag. For example, if you want to take an existing task named `MyTask` and update the `interval` for the task from `Daily` to `Weekly`, all you need is the following code:

```
<cfschedule action="Update" task="MyTask" interval="Weekly">
```

The only two attributes required for an update are `action` and `task`. Beyond that, you may choose to update as few or as many attributes as you like. If you wish to change the name of the task, you have to delete it first, then re-create it under the new task name.

It is possible to pull up all the existing attributes for a record so that it is easier for a user to edit them. This can be done with a simple UDF, which retrieves the information about the scheduled task from the XML file ColdFusion uses to store scheduled task information. Examples 26-4 and 26-5 show how to update tasks programmatically.

Example 26-4. Obtaining information about a scheduled task

```
<cffunction name="GetScheduledTaskNames">
  <!--- Var local vars for the func --->
```

Example 26-4. Obtaining information about a scheduled task (continued)

```
  <cfset Var TaskXML="">
  <cfset Var GetTasks="">
  <cfset Var i=0>
  <cfset Var Task="">
  <cfset Var ListOfNames="">
  <cfset Var ReturnQuery=QueryNew("Task")>
  <!--- Get the scheduler xml file.  It's stored as WDDX --->
  <cffile action="Read"
          file="#Server.ColdFusion.RootDir#\lib\neo-cron.xml"
          variable="TaskXML">

  <!--- Convert the WDDX to CFML - and array of structs --->
  <cfwddx action="WDDX2CFML" input="#TaskXML#" output="GetTasks">

  <!--- Grab the task names --->
  <cfset ListOfNames = StructKeyList(GetTasks[1])>

  <!--- Add the appropriate number of empty rows to the query object --->
  <cfset QueryAddRow(ReturnQuery, ListLen(ListOfNames))>

  <!--- Loop over the list of task names, adding each one to the query --->
  <cfloop index="i" from="1" to="#ListLen(ListOfNames)#">
    <cfset QuerySetCell(ReturnQuery, "Task", ListGetAt(ListOfNames, i), i)>
  </cfloop>

  <cfreturn ReturnQuery>
</cffunction>

<cfset GetScheduledTasks=GetScheduledTaskNames( )>

<h2>Scheduled Tasks</h2>
<h3>Please choose a task to edit</h3>

<table border="0" cellspacing="1">
<tr>
<th bgcolor="#0000FF"><font color="#FFFFFF">Task Name</font></th>
</tr>

<!--- Output the scheduled tasks.  Create a link to the EditTask.cfm template
      and pass the name of the entry to retrieve from the XML file --->
<cfoutput query="GetScheduledTasks">
<tr>
<td bgcolor="##C0C0C0"><a href="EditTask.cfm?Task=#URLEncodedFormat(Task)#">
                        #Task#</a></td>
</tr>
</cfoutput>
</table>
```

The template in Example 26-4 uses a short UDF to retrieve the list of scheduled task names from the XML file ColdFusion uses to store scheduled task information. Once a list of all the tasks is obtained, the UDF converts the list to a query object. A table containing each task name is output to the browser. Each task name is displayed as a hypertext link with the name of the task appended to the URL as a parameter named Task. Clicking on the link passes the task name to the *EditTask.cfm* template shown in Example 26-5.

Example 26-5. EditTask.cfm template for editing a scheduled task

```
<!--- Retrieve all of the information from the entry passed in via URL --->
<cffunction name="GetScheduledTask">
  <cfargument name="TaskName" required="True" type="String">
  <!--- Var local vars for the func --->
  <cfset Var TaskXML="">
  <cfset Var GetTasks="">

  <!--- Get the scheduler xml file.  It's stored as WDDX --->
  <cffile action="Read"
          file="#Server.ColdFusion.RootDir#\lib\neo-cron.xml"
          variable="TaskXML">

  <!--- Convert the WDDX to CFML - and array of structs --->
  <cfwddx action="WDDX2CFML" input="#TaskXML#" output="GetTasks">

  <!--- Grab the structure for the task name passed to the func --->
    <cfreturn GetTasks[1][Arguments.TaskName]>
</cffunction>

<cfset GetTaskInfo =GetScheduledTask(URL.Task)>

<cfoutput>
<h2>Edit Task: #URL.Task#</h2>
</cfoutput>

<form action="UpdateTask.cfm" method="Post">
<cfoutput>
<!--- Need to pass the task name along to the next template --->
<input type="hidden" name="Task" value="#URL.Task#">
</cfoutput>

<table border="0" cellspacing="1">
<!--- Dynamically create the edit form by looping over all of the key/value
      pairs from the structure --->
<cfloop collection="#GetTaskInfo#" item="Key">
  <cfoutput>
  <tr>
    <td BGCOLOR="##COCOCO">#Key#</td>
    <td BGCOLOR="##COCOCO"><input type="text" name="#Key#"
        value="#GetTaskInfo[Key]#" size="#(Len(GetTaskInfo[Key]) + 8)#"></td>
  </tr>
  </cfoutput>
</cfloop>
  <tr>
    <td colspan="2"><input type="submit" name="Submit" value="Submit Changes"></td>
  </tr>
```

Example 26-5. EditTask.cfm template for editing a scheduled task (continued)

```
</table>
</form>
```

The *EditTask.cfm* template then takes the `Task` URL parameter passed from the *GetScheduledTasks.cfm* template in Example 26-4 and uses it to retrieve the specific record for the scheduled task that requires editing. The record is returned as a structure and contains the name of each Scheduler attribute along with its value. An HTML form containing all the Scheduler attribute names and their associated values is dynamically constructed by looping over the structure returned by the `GetScheduledTask( )` UDF. This isn't the prettiest way to construct an edit form, but it's expedient. At this point, the user can make any edits to the scheduled task they desire.

Submitting the form created by Example 26-5 posts all the task information to the *UpdateTask.cfm* template shown in Example 26-6. The *UpdateTask.cfm* template takes the information posted to it and uses it to update the scheduled task using the `cfschedule` tag.

Example 26-6. Updating a scheduled task using cfschedule

```
<!--- Set defaults so empties don't cause errors --->
<cfparam name="form.Task" default="">
<cfparam name="form.URL" default="">
<cfparam name="form.Start_Date" default="">
<cfparam name="form.Start_Time" default="">
<cfparam name="form.End_Date" default="">
<cfparam name="form.End_Time" default="">
<cfparam name="form.Username" default="">
<cfparam name="form.Password" default="">
<cfparam name="form.Interval" default="">
<cfparam name="form.Request_Time_Out" default="">
<cfparam name="form.Proxy_Server" default="">
<cfparam name="form.Resolve_URL" default="No">
<cfparam name="form.Publish" default="No">
<cfparam name="form.File" default="">
<cfparam name="form.Path" default="">
<cfparam name="form.HTTP_Port" default="80">
<cfparam name="form.HTTP_Proxy_Port" default="80">

<!--- Update the scheduled task posted by the edit form.  If this were a
      production application, we would add code before this call to validate
      that appropriate values were passed before attempting to update the
      task. --->
<cfschedule action="Update" task="#form.Task#" operation="HTTPRequest"
          URL="#form.URL#" startdate="#form.Start_Date#"
          starttime="#form.Start_Time#"
          enddate="#form.End_Date#"
          endtime="#form.End_Time#"
          username="#form.Username#" password="#form.Password#"
          interval="#form.Interval#" requesttimeout="#form.Request_Time_Out#"
```

Example 26-6. Updating a scheduled task using cfschedule (continued)

```
            proxyserver="#form.Proxy_Server#" resolveurl="#form.Resolve_URL#"
            publish="#form.Publish#" file="#form.File#" path="#form.Path#"
            port="#form.HTTP_Port#" proxyport="#form.HTTP_Proxy_Port#">

<h3>Task successfully updated</h3>
```

Deleting a Task

Deleting a task using `cfschedule` requires only two attributes, `action` and `task`. The `action` attribute should be set to `Delete`, and the `task` attribute should be set to the task name you wish to delete:

```
<!--- Delete a task named MyTask from the task list --->
<cfschedule action="Delete" task="MyTask">
```

Once you delete a task using `cfschedule`, it is permanently removed from the task list.

Running Tasks

The `cfschedule` tag can execute any scheduled task independent of the Scheduler in the ColdFusion Administrator. To do this, set the `action` attribute in the `cfschedule` tag to `Run`. Provide the name of the task to run using the `task` attribute:

```
<!--- Run a task named MyTask from the task list --->
<cfschedule action="Run"  task="MyTask">
```

When you run a task using `cfschedule`, any additional attributes specified for the task in the ColdFusion Administrator (such as Timeout, Publish, etc.) are automatically applied.

Additional Considerations

As useful as the ColdFusion Scheduler is, it does have its limitations. One of the most notable limitations of the Scheduler is that there is no built-in redundancy. That is, if a scheduled task fails to execute for whatever reason (say the server is down) the Scheduler has no way of knowing this condition and only attempts to execute the task again the next time it is scheduled for execution.

It is possible to build redundancy into your scheduled tasks, but it takes work. One solution involves creating a small database that contains a record for each entry in the Scheduler. Each time you execute a scheduled task, you `cfinclude` a file or call a custom tag that updates a field in the database with the time and date that the task should be executed next. A second template scans the database of scheduled tasks and checks to make sure none of the tasks have a time/date for next execution that is older than the current time/date. If so, you know that the task didn't execute for some reason, and you can call the `cfschedule` tag to immediately try to run that task again. The template that performs the scan should itself be scheduled to run at an interval that is appropriate for your particular needs (i.e., every 15 minutes, every 30 minutes, etc.).

CHAPTER 27

Interacting with COM, CORBA, and Java

If you had to choose a single word to describe ColdFusion, it just might be connectivity. So far, we've talked about using ColdFusion to talk to databases, LDAP servers, FTP servers, HTTP servers, SMTP servers, POP servers, Web Services, CFCs, custom tags, and the local filesystem. Well, you'll be happy to know that the list doesn't stop there. ColdFusion can also communicate with a number of other technologies including COM objects, CORBA objects, Java classes, JavaBeans, Enterprise JavaBeans, Java Servlets, JSP pages, and JSP tag libraries. This chapter discusses how to use ColdFusion to communicate with several types of external objects to expand the functionality of ColdFusion to unlimited heights.

Working with COM

The Component Object Model (COM) is a Microsoft-sponsored specification for creating distributed software components.* There are a large number of third-party COM objects, most of which can be used by ColdFusion. COM is supported only in the Windows version of ColdFusion.†

The `cfobject` tag can call COM objects located on the same machine as the ColdFusion server or on other machines connected to the network. `cfobject` can also communicate with objects residing anywhere on the network using Distributed COM (or DCOM). In order to connect to a COM object using ColdFusion, the object must first be registered. You register a COM object using the *regsvr32* command from the Windows command line, as in:

* Although COM is a widely adopted technology, Microsoft is moving away from it in favor of its newer .NET architecture. ColdFusion interacts with .NET applications primarily via SOAP-based web services, as covered in Chapter 24.

† Because ColdFusion MX is built on top of J2EE, it must use a Java-to-COM bridge bridge (J-Integra from Intrinsyc Software) to communicate with COM objects. Because of this architectural change over previous versions of ColdFusion, connecting to COM objects in ColdFusion MX may be slower than in previous versions.

```
C:\> regsvr32 myobject.dll
```

Once a COM object is registered, you can connect to it using ColdFusion. To understand how to use the `cfobject` tag to communicate with a COM object, you first need to understand the tag's syntax:

```
<cfobject type="COM"
          name="name"
          class="progID"
          action="action"
          context="context"
          server="server_name">
```

When connecting to a COM object, the `type` attribute must always be set to `COM`. The `name` attribute is required and specifies a name for the object to be used when referencing the object's attributes and methods in your code. `class` is a required attribute and specifies the program ID for the object you want to invoke. If you don't know the program ID for your object, consult the object's documentation. You can also use Microsoft's OLEView program to view any object's program ID, properties, and methods as long as the object is registered on your system. If you don't have OLEView, you can download if for free (along with instructions for use) from *http://www.microsoft.com/com/resources/oleview.asp*.

The `action` attribute is also required and has two possible values, `Create` or `Connect`. `Create` instantiates the COM object (usually a *.dll*) before assigning properties or invoking methods. `Connect` connects to a COM object (usually an *.exe*) that is already running on the server. `context` is optional and specifies the context the object is running in. Valid entries are `InProc`, `Local`, or `Remote`. `InProc` specifies an in-process server object (usually a *.dll*) running in the same process space as the ColdFusion server. `Local` specifies an out-of-process server object (usually an *.exe*) that is still running on the same server as ColdFusion, but not in the same process space. `Remote` specifies an out-of-process server object (usually an *.exe*) that is running on another machine. If `Remote` is specified, the `server` attribute is required. When no value is specified, ColdFusion uses the registry setting for the object. The final attribute, `server`, specifies a valid server.

Once an object has been instantiated, you can access the properties and methods of the object. An object's properties are similar to an HTML or CFML tag's attributes. Properties allow you to pass values to objects that can be referenced as variables inside the object. Methods are similar to CFML functions in the sense that they cause the object to perform an action and return (sometimes) a value that you can reference.

To see the properties and methods of an object, instantiate it with the `cfobject` tag, then use `cfdump`.* This example calls the Windows `Scripting.FileSystemObject` (used for interacting with the filesystem) and displays all of its properties and methods:

```
<!--- Connect to the Windows Scripting.FileSystemObject --->
<cfobject type="com" name="fso" class="Scripting.FileSystemObject"
        action="create">
<cfdump var="#fso#">
```

To set a property, you use the following syntax:

```
<cfset MyObject.MyProperty = "Value">
```

Conversely, you can read a property's value using the following syntax:

```
<cfset MyValue = MyObject.Property>
```

There are a few ways to invoke a method depending on the number and type of arguments it expects. To invoke a method that doesn't expect any arguments, use the following syntax:

```
<cfset MyVariable = MyObject.MyMethod( )>
```

Methods that require one or more arguments are said to have their arguments passed by value and are invoked like this:

```
<cfset MyVal = 123>
<cfset MyVariable = MyObject.MyMethod (MyVal, "Hello World", 1)>
```

Methods can also have their arguments passed by reference. Arguments passed by reference usually have their values changed by the method being called. In this case, `MyVal` is enclosed in double quotes and passed to `MyObject.MyMethod` by reference:

```
<cfset MyVal = 123>
<cfset MyVariable = MyObject.MyMethod("MyVal", "Hello World")>
```

Outputting the value of `MyVal` after the method is called generally results in a different value than `123`.

You should note that in versions of ColdFusion prior to MX, you can't directly access nested objects. Instead, you must access the outermost object first and work your way to the innermost object. For example, although you can directly access the object `TheObject.TheNestedObject.TheProperty` in ColdFusion MX, in previous versions such as ColdFusion 5, you can't. In order to act on `MyNestedObject.MyProperty` in older versions of ColdFusion, you need to use syntax like this:

```
<cfset MyNestedObject = TheObject.TheNestedObject>
<cfset MyProperty = MyNestedObject.TheProperty>
```

When ColdFusion makes a connection to a COM object, that connection consumes system resources, especially RAM. When ColdFusion finishes using a COM object, it doesn't immediately release the resources that the object was consuming. Because

* The ability to dump the properties and methods of COM objects was added in ColdFusion MX 6.1.

ColdFusion is built on top of Java, it uses Java's garbage collection features to deal with the cleanup of the COM connection. This often takes longer than developers would like it to.

Many COM objects have a method you can call to explicitly close the connection to the object, typically `close()` or `quit()`. While this explicitly tells ColdFusion to terminate the connection to the COM object, it does not immediately release the resources it was consuming. It still has to wait for the garbage collection to occur. You can use the `releaseComObject()` function to force ColdFusion to both terminate a connection with a COM object and immediately return any resources it was using to the server. This function is new in ColdFusion Red Sky. `releaseComObject()` should only be used once you have finished with the COM object. If you call the function while the COM object is still in use, ColdFusion throws an exception. To use the function, call it like this:

```
<cfset releaseComObject(myObject)>
```

or this:

```
<cfscript>
releaseComObject(myObject);
</cfscript>
```

Now that you have a basic understanding of how ColdFusion uses the `cfobject` tag to interact with COM objects, let's look at an example you can test on your server that demonstrates many of the concepts we just covered. Example 27-1 shows how to invoke the Microsoft Word COM object and use its methods and properties to convert a preexisting Word document to HTML. In order for this example to work, you must have Microsoft Word 97 or 2000 installed on the same server as ColdFusion. You don't need to worry about registering any COM objects as that is handled automatically when Microsoft Office is installed.

Example 27-1. Using cfobject to call the Microsoft Word COM object to convert a Word document to HTML

```
<!--- Instantiate the COM object --->
<cfobject type="COM" name="MyWord" class="Word.Application"
        action="Create" context="Local">

<!--- Turn off window visibility --->
<cfset MyWord.Visible = False>

<!--- Open the document and convert it to HTML.  You can change the
      path and filename to a document on your server --->
<cfset OriginalDoc = MyWord.Documents>
<cfset OriginalDoc.Open("d:\cfusionmx\wwwroot\programmingcf\27\test.doc")>
<cfset ConvertedDoc = MyWord.ActiveDocument>

<!--- Save the converted HTML file.  Use this line for Word 2000.
      Comment it out and use the line below for Word 97 --->
<cfset
```

Example 27-1. Using cfobject to call the Microsoft Word COM object to convert a Word document to HTML (continued)

```
  ConvertedDoc.SaveAs("d:\cfusionmx\wwwroot\programmingcf\27\test.htm",Val(8))>

<!--- Uncomment this line to use with Word 97
<cfset
  ConvertedDoc.SaveAs("d:\cfusionmx\wwwroot\programmingcf\27\test.htm",Val(10))>
--->

<!--- Close the COM connection --->
<cfset MyWord.Quit( )>
<!--- Release the COM object --->
<cfset releaseComObject(myWord)>

Conversion complete...
```

Executing the template in Example 27-1 causes the Microsoft Word COM object to open a Word document called *test.doc* (you can test this with any Word document on your server), convert it to HTML, and save it back to the server. The same example could easily be written using CFScript and the `CreateObject( )` function instead, as shown in Example 27-2.

Example 27-2. Calling the Microsoft Word COM object using CFScript notation and the CreateObject function

```
<cfscript>
// Instantiate the COM object
MyWord = CreateObject("COM","Word.Application");

// Turn off window visibility
MyWord.Visible = False;

/* Open the document and convert it to HTML.  You can change the
 * path and filename to a document on your server
 */
OriginalDoc = MyWord.Documents;
OriginalDoc.Open("d:\cfusionmx\wwwroot\programmingcf\27\test.doc");
ConvertedDoc = MyWord.ActiveDocument;

/* Save the converted HTML file.  Use this line for Word 2000.
 * Comment it out and use the line below for Word 97
 */
ConvertedDoc.SaveAs("d:\cfusionmx\wwwroot\programmingcf\27\test.htm",Val(8));

/* Uncomment this line to use with Word 97
 * ConvertedDoc.SaveAs("d:\cfusionmx\wwwroot\programmingcf\27\test.htm",Val(10));
 */

// Close the COM connection
MyWord.Quit( );
// Release the COM Object
releaseComObject(myWord);
```

Example 27-2. Calling the Microsoft Word COM object using CFScript notation and the CreateObject function (continued)

```
</cfscript>

Conversion complete...
```

In the case of the CFScript code in Example 27-2, you can't use CFML tags inside a `cfscript` block; therefore, the `CreateObject( )` function instantiates the COM object. For more information on using the `CreateObject( )` function, see Appendix B.

Calling CORBA Objects

The Common Object Request Broker Architecture (CORBA) is a specification put forth by the Object Management Group (OMG) for creating platform-neutral distributed software objects. CORBA objects can be written using any number of languages and are supported only on the Windows and Unix versions of ColdFusion. ColdFusion supports CORBA Version 2.3.

ColdFusion uses the `cfobject` tag to access CORBA objects via a piece of middleware called an Object Request Broker (ORB). Because an ORB is required to access CORBA objects, ColdFusion comes bundled with the Borland VisiBroker 4.5 ORB Java libraries. Because ColdFusion uses a connector to load the ORB, it is possible to use third-party ORBs with ColdFusion, provided they come with a ColdFusion-specific connector. You can contact Macromedia directly for connectors for several of the more popular ORB providers.

Before you can begin using CORBA with ColdFusion, you'll need to register and configure your ORB connector with the ColdFusion Administrator. This is true for third party ORB connectors as well as the VisiBroker ORB connector included with ColdFusion. For step-by-step instructions on registering and configuring an ORB connector, see the *Administering and Configuring ColdFusion MX* book that is included with the ColdFusion documentation.

Once your connector has been configured and registered, you are ready to begin using CORBA with ColdFusion. All CORBA connectivity is handled via the `cfobject` tag or the `CreateObject( )` function. When a request is made to a CORBA object by the `cfobject` tag, ColdFusion uses the ORB libraries to handle every aspect of finding the specified object, passing attributes, invoking methods, and returning results. To get a better idea of how the `cfobject` tag connects to CORBA objects, let's look at the tag's syntax:

```
<cfobject type="CORBA"
          name="name"
          context="IOR|NameService"
          class="file_or_naming_service"
          locale="-type_value_pair_1 -type_value_pair_n">
```

When you invoke a CORBA object, the type attribute must be set to CORBA. name is a required attribute and is used to specify a name for the object when referencing its attributes and methods. The context attribute specifies the context to use for accessing the CORBA object. Valid entries include:

IOR
: ColdFusion uses the Interoperable Object Reference to access the CORBA object.

NameService
: ColdFusion uses the naming service to access the CORBA object.

Depending on the value of context, the class attribute can specify one of two things. If context is IOR, class specifies the name of a file that contains the stringified version of the IOR. If context is NameService, class specifies a period-delimited naming context for the naming service. class is a required attribute.

The final attribute, locale, specifies type-value pairs of arguments to pass to init_orb( ). This feature is specific to VisiBroker ORBs and has been tested to work with the 3.2 C++ version only. Note that all type-value pairs must begin with a minus sign (-).

In CORBA, Interface Definition Language (IDL) is used to define the interface to a CORBA object. The interface describes what parameters (properties) and methods are available to the object. The methods for working with these parameters and methods is similar to the methods we used to work with COM objects. One notable difference is the ability to pass structures and arrays to parameters and methods in CORBA.

Because there is no easy way to create a CORBA object for demonstration purposes, the complexities of creating specific examples using cfobject with CORBA are beyond the scope of this book. For more information on using cfobject to call CORBA objects, refer to the ColdFusion MX documentation from Macromedia.

Integrating ColdFusion and Java

Because ColdFusion MX is built on top of J2EE, integration between ColdFusion and Java is better than ever before. ColdFusion is capable of interoperating with Java on several levels. With ColdFusion MX, you can interact with:

- Java objects, including JavaBeans and Enterprise JavaBeans (EJBs)
- Servlets and JSP pages
- JSP tags and tag libraries

Although you certainly don't have to know Java in order to make use of these capabilities, the more you understand about Java, the easier it is going to be, and the more likely you are to find new and interesting ways to extend your ColdFusion applications. The rest of this section assumes you have some knowledge of how Java works. If you don't, you may want to spend some time reading up on the fundamentals. One resource I recommend in particular (in addition to the great series of Java books O'Reilly puts out) is Bruce Eckel's *Thinking in Java, 3rd Edition*, available as a free download from *http://www.mindview.net/Books/*. While this book doesn't cover J2EE, it does do an excellent job of introducing the reader to both object-oriented programming and the Java language.

Calling Java Objects

ColdFusion has the ability to invoke Java class files, JavaBeans, and by extension Enterprise JavaBeans (EJBs), using the `cfobject` tag (or `createObject()` function). With the explosive growth of Java, this opens up a completely new realm of possibilities for your ColdFusion applications. To call a Java class file or EJB using the `cfobject` tag, you use the following syntax:

```
<cfobject type="Java"
          action="Create"
          class="Java_class"
          name="object_name">
```

The `type` attribute specifies the type of object to call. To call a Java object or EJB, `type` must be set to `Java`. `action` currently accepts only one value, `Create`. This creates the connection to the Java object or the EJB environment. The `class` attribute is required and specifies the Java object to create. You may specify the path to the object (*.class* or *.jar*) in the Class Path section of the Java and JVM area of the ColdFusion Administrator. Alternatively, you can save the *.jar* file in *web_root/WEB-INF/lib* or you can save the *.class* file in *web_root/WEB-INF/classes*. For EJBs, `class` specifies the path to the environment for the EJB. To use `cfobject` to connect to EJBs, you must have an EJB server such as JRun 4 or ColdFusion MX for J2EE (in which case the underlying J2EE application server is used).* The EJB server can reside on the same server as your ColdFusion server or on any other server accessible via the network. Additionally, the EJB you wish to invoke must be deployed appropriately. The final attribute, `name`, is also required and specifies the name to use to reference the Java object in subsequent operations.

Using the `cfobject` tag to call a Java object loads the class but doesn't automatically create an instance of the object. Once you have created the Java object with the `cfobject` tag, you can access any static methods and fields in the object. You can make an explicit call to a constructor using a special ColdFusion "method" called `init()`:

```
<cfset MyVar = MyObject.init(argument1, argument2)>
```

* The exact method for using an EJB varies depending on the EJB server you are using with ColdFusion. Because of this, the best advice I can offer you is to consult the documentation for your particular version of ColdFusion MX.

The reason I put "method" in quotes is that init( ) is not a method of the object you are calling. It is a special construct used by ColdFusion to call the new( ) method on the class constructor. In the event that your object actually has a method named init( ), a naming conflict will arise, and ColdFusion will be unable to call the init( ) method of the object.

Calling a public method within an object without first calling init( ) results in an implicit call to the default constructor. Arguments and return values may be of any valid Java datatype. When ColdFusion passes data to a Java object, the data is automatically converted to the appropriate Java datatype (when possible). Table 27-1 shows the conversion between ColdFusion datatypes and equivalent Java datatypes that takes place.

Table 27-1. Conversion from ColdFusion datatypes to Java datatypes

ColdFusion datatype	Java datatype
String or list	string, int, float, long, double, boolean, or java.util.Date (when string is a date/time value)
Date/Time	java.util.Date
Boolean	boolean
Integer	short, int, long
Real	float, double
Array	java.util.Vector unless the ColdFusion array contains data of a single datatype that can be converted to the Java array's datatype: boolean[ ], byte[ ], char[ ], double[ ], float[ ], int[ ], long[ ], Object[ ], or String[ ]
Structure	java.util.Map
Query Object	java.util.Map
ColdFusion Component (CFC)	N/A
XML Document Object	Not supported

When a Java object returns data back to ColdFusion, an attempt is made to automatically convert the Java datatype to an appropriate ColdFusion datatype. Table 27-2 shows how Java datatypes map to ColdFusion datatypes.

Table 27-2. How Java datatypes are converted to ColdFusion datatypes

Java datatype	ColdFusion datatype
boolean/Boolean	Boolean
byte/Byte	String
char/Char	String
double/Double	Real
float/Float	Real
int/Integer	Integer
long/Long	Integer

Table 27-2. How Java datatypes are converted to ColdFusion datatypes (continued)

Java datatype	ColdFusion datatype
short/Short	Integer
String	String
java.util.Date	Date/time
java.util.List	Comma-delimited list
java.util.Map	Structure
java.util.Vector	Array
byte[ ]	Array
char[ ]	Array
boolean[ ]	Array
String[ ]	Array

Just like in our COM examples, to set a property, you use the following syntax:

```
<cfset obj.myProperty = "Value">
```

You can get a property's value using the following syntax:

```
<cfset myVar = obj.myProperty>
```

To invoke a method that doesn't expect any arguments, use the following syntax:

```
<cfset myVar = obj.myMethod( )>
```

Methods that require one or more arguments can be invoked like this:

```
<cfset myVal = 5>
<cfset myVar = obj.myMethod (myVal, "Hello World")>
```

Nested objects can be called like this:

```
theObject.theNestedObject.theProperty
```

You should note that in versions of ColdFusion prior to MX, you can't directly access nested objects. Instead, you must access the outermost object first and work your way to the innermost object. In ColdFusion 5, you would need to access the previous nested object like this:

```
<cfset myNestedObject = theObject.theNestedObject>
<cfset myProperty = myNestedObject.theProperty>
```

If the Java object is a JavaBeans component, you can call `getProperty( )` and `setProperty( )` methods by referring to their property names. So, if the JavaBeans component contains a method called `getEmployeeName( )`, you could reference it like this:

```
<cfset theEmployee = myObj.EmployeeName( )>
```

It is sometimes possible to reference `getProperty( )` and `setProperty( )` methods in Java objects that have them, but aren't JavaBeans. You should take great care in doing this as many standard Java classes (and their derivatives) can't be referenced this way.

To demonstrate some of the concepts we've just covered, we need a Java object we can experiment with. Example 27-3 can be compiled using the Java compiler of your choice. It is important that the resulting class file be placed in your class path or one of the alternate locations we discussed earlier. You should save the file as *sum.java* and compile it as *sum.class*.

Example 27-3. Java code to compile to the sum.class file

```
public class sum{
  public int a;
  public int b;

  // default constructor
  public sum( ) {
    a = 0;
    b = 0;
  }

  // alternate constructor
  public sum(int x, int y) {
  a = x;
  b = y;
  }

  // getResult method for summing two numbers
  public int getResult( ) {
    return (a+b);
  }
}
```

This Java class file allows you to pass in two integer values (a and b) and call a method that returns the sum of those values.

Once you have compiled the code, you are ready to call the object. Example 27-4 shows how to call the Java object you just created using `cfobject`.

Example 27-4. Calling a Java object using cfobject

```
<!--- Load the Java class --->
<cfobject action="create" type="java" class="sum" name="add">

<!--- Call the default constructor --->
<cfset add.init( )>

<!--- Set properties --->
<cfset add.a = 5>
<cfset add.b = 10>

<!--- Call the getResult method to return the result --->
<cfset result = add.getResult( )>
```

Example 27-4. Calling a Java object using cfobject (continued)

```
<cfoutput>
#Result#
</cfoutput>
```

The example works by loading the *sum.class* file using the `cfobject` tag. The object is then assigned to a variable called `add`. The default constructor is called using the special `init( )` method. Next, two properties of the object are set, `a` and `b`, respectively. After that, the `getResult( )` method is called and the results assigned to a variable called `Result` that is then output to the browser.

Example 27-5 shows the same example written using CFScript.

Example 27-5. Calling a Java object using CFScript

```
<cfscript>
  add = createObject("Java", "sum");
  add.init( );
  add.a = 10;
  add.b = 5;
  Result = add.getResult( );
</cfscript>

<cfoutput>
#Result#
</cfoutput>
```

In this case, the `CreateObject( )` function calls the Java class file from within the `cfscript` block. `CreateObject( )` works identically to the `cfobject` tag, except that it isn't necessary to specify an `action` attribute as you would using `cfobject`.

Overloading methods

It's possible for a Java object to have more than one method (including constructors) with the same name. When you access a method like this, the JVM (Java Virtual Machine) automatically determines which method to call based on the number and datatypes of the parameters passed to the method. This is known as method overloading. ColdFusion supports method overloading when calling methods on Java objects. However, because ColdFusion is not a strongly typed language, care must be taken to explicitly cast the datatypes of the parameters passed when invoking an overloaded method. For example, if a Java object contains two methods called `getEmployee( )`, one taking an integer and the other a string, calling the method from ColdFusion could result in confusion. Consider this code:

```
<cfset employee = obj.getEmployee("123")>
```

In this example, the `getEmployee( )` method has no way of knowing whether "123" is a string or an integer. Because it is unclear what datatype is being passed, ColdFusion will throw an exception when it encounters this type of uncertainty. The

JavaCast( ) function should be used in situations such as this to cast a ColdFusion variable before it's passed to an overloaded method:

```
<cfset employee = obj.getEmployee(javaCast("int", 123))>
```

Or:

```
<cfset employee = obj.getEmployee(javaCast("string", 123))>
```

JavaCast( ) accepts two parameters, the datatype to cast to and the data. Possible datatypes are boolean, int, long, double, or string. The JavaCast( ) function can't cast complex objects, such as query objects, arrays, and structures, nor can it cast to a superclass.

If you look at the *sum.class* file we used in our previous examples, you'll notice in the comments that we declared both a default and an alternate constructor. The default constructor is called by default when ColdFusion's special init( ) method is used, or implicitly the first time a public method is called on the object when init( ) is not used. If you want to use a different constructor, you can do so via overloading. The following code loads the *sum.class* file and calls the alternate constructor by overloading the call with two int parameters cast using JavaCast( ):

```
<cfscript>
  add = createObject("Java", "sum");
  add.init(JavaCast("int", 10), JavaCast("int", 5));
  Result = add.getResult( );
</cfscript>

<cfoutput>
#Result#
</cfoutput>
```

Handling exceptions

The GetException( ) function can be used in conjunction with cftry/cfcatch tags (or try/catch in CFScript) to deal with exceptions thrown within Java objects. The function takes a single argument specifying the name of the Java object to retrieve the exception information from.

The following code calls a hypothetical Java object called MyObject. If an exception is thrown within the class, the cfcatch tag catches the exception.

```
<cfobject type="Java" action="Create" class="MyClass" name="MyObject">

<cftry>
<cfset Test = MyObject.CauseError( ) >

<cfcatch type="Any">
   <cfset MyException = GetException(MyObject)>
   <!--- call the GetErrCode and GerErrMsg methods within the exception
         object --->
   <cfset ErrorCode = MyException.GetErrCode( )
   <cfset ErrorMessage = MyException.GetErrMsg( )>
```

```
    <cfoutput>
      Error Code: #ErrorCode#<BR>
      Error Message: #ErrorMessage#
    </cfoutput>
</cfcatch>
</cftry>
```

Within the `cfcatch` block, the `GetException( )` function retrieves the Java exception object from `MyObject` and assigns it to a variable called `MyException`. Next, two methods in the object are called, `MyException.GetErrCode( )` and `MyException.GetErrMssg( )`. Each method returns a string (the error code and an error message, respectively), which is then output to the browser.

The Java API

One of the biggest potential untapped resources available to ColdFusion MX developers is the Java API itself. Since ColdFusion runs on top of J2EE, it has access to the majority of the underlying Java 2 API. This means that you can have ColdFusion use Java to perform all sorts of nifty tasks that are difficult or impossible to do with CFML alone. To get an idea of what's available, I suggest checking out the Java documentation on Sun's web site. The documentation for the JVM installed by default with ColdFusion MX is available at *http://java.sun.com/j2se/1.4.2/docs/api/index.html*. If you have upgraded your JVM, be sure to consult the documentation for your particular installation.

Because I'd hate to leave you without a usable example, let's take a look at the `java.io` package. Among other things, this package gives you access to your ColdFusion server's filesystem. The particular class we're interested in is the `File` class. This class allows you to manipulate all aspects of the server's filesystem. Say you want to get a file's size in kilobytes. You can easily do this with the `File` class:

```
<cfobject action="create" type="java" class="java.io.File" name="fileObj">
<cfset fileObj.init("d:\cfusionmx\releasenotes.htm")>
<cfset fileLen = fileObj.length( )>

<cfoutput>
d:\cfusion\releasenotes.htm is <strong>#fileLen#</strong> bytes.
</cfoutput>
```

This example loads the `java.io.File` class and assigns it to `fileObj`. Next, an alternate constructor (there are three possible constructors in this class) is called by providing the path to the file whose length we want to get (the file path is passed as a string). The `length( )` method gets the length for the file passed to the constructor. The result is then output to the browser.

Although this is a simple example, it demonstrated how easy it is to use Java objects already part of the underlying J2EE framework. All it takes is a little knowledge, not necessarily a thorough understanding of Java.

Taking advantage of the PageContext object

The `GetPageContext()` function acts as a wrapper for the Java `PageContext` object. This function returns an object containing the attributes, methods and other configuration information available to the current page. Using this object, it's possible to look up various information concerning the current page, such as scope and variable values. This function can also be useful for integrating ColdFusion with J2EE applications as it provides access to request and response objects. Additionally, `include()` and `forward()` methods are exposed, making it possible to communicate with JSP pages using the equivalent of `jsp.forward` and `jsp.include` (we'll cover this in the next section). To see the contents of the object for the current page, simply dump it using the `cfdump` tag:

```
<cfdump Var="#GetPageContext()#">
```

Method objects can be viewed by dumping them as well:

```
<cfdump Var="#GetPageContext().getRequest()">
```

This retrieves the server name from the `getRequest` method:

```
<cfdump Var="#GetPageContext().getRequest().getServerName()#">
```

Communicating with Servlets and JSP Pages

ColdFusion has always been able to invoke servlets and JSP pages by calling them through a standard URL—either as a hyperlink or via the `cfhttp` tag (Get or Post). This gave you the ability to call a servlet/JSP page, even passing it form or URL data. What it didn't give you, though, was a meaningful way to handle any data returned by the servlet or JSP page.*

ColdFusion MX changes all of this by providing a mechanism for bidirectional communication with both Java servlets and JSP pages. This means it's possible to call servlets/JSP pages from a ColdFusion page, or a ColdFusion page from a servlet or JSP page. It also means that you can share data in certain variable scopes between ColdFusion and servlets/JSP pages.

The preferred way for ColdFusion to interact with Servlets and JSP pages is through the `GetPageContext()` function. The `GetPageContext()` function acts as a wrapper for the Java `PageContext` class.† The `PageContext` class provides access to the attributes, methods, and other configuration information available to the current page. For interacting with servlets and JSP pages, we're primarily interested in two methods of

* Prior to ColdFusion MX, it was possible to communicate with servlets (but not JSP pages) bidirectionally via two tags, `cfservlet` and `cfservletparam`. These tags are no longer supported in ColdFusion MX and have been replaced by the `GetPageContext()` function. For more information on `cfservlet` and `cfservletparam`, see Appendix A.

† See *http://java.sun.com/products/servlet/2.2/javadoc/javax/servlet/jsp/PageContext.html* for more information on the Java `PageContext` class.

the PageContext class, include( ) and forward( ). Within the context of Java, these methods allow you to include a resource as part of the calling thread or forward the request to another component while preserving certain information from the calling thread. What that means for you as a ColdFusion developer is you can use these methods, exposed through ColdFusion's GetPageContext( ) function to include a servlet/JSP page in your ColdFusion page, or forward a request from a ColdFusion page to a servlet/JSP page. The syntax for including a servlet or JSP page in a CFML page looks like this:

```
GetPageContext( ).include("url_to_servlet_or_jsp_page")
```

To forward a request from a CFML page to a servlet or JSP page, the code looks like this:

```
GetPageContext( ).forward("url_to_servlet_or_jsp_page")
```

The first thing you should notice is that the syntax for using the GetPageContext( ) function is a little different than other CFML functions. I can't tell you why Macromedia decided to implement it this way, but I can tell you that the syntax more closely resembles how things are called in Java. Don't get hung up on this, however; it's easy to deal with once you've used it a few times. That said, let's look at how you can use GetPageContext( ) to include and redirect to an actual JSP page from within a ColdFusion page. We'll also look at the difference between including and forwarding. The code shown in Example 27-6 is for a simple JSP page that creates a variable of type string (remember, Java is a strongly typed language, so you have to declare a variable's type when you declare the variable) and then outputs its value to the browser. Note that JSP (and Java) is case-sensitive. Be sure to save your file as *test.jsp*.

Example 27-6. A simple JSP page

```
<%
String myString = "Look at me, I'm JSP!";
%>

<b><%= myString %></b><br>
```

Now, to include the *test.jsp* page from within a ColdFusion page, look at the code in Example 27-7.

Example 27-7. Using GetPageContext() to include a JSP page in a ColdFusion page

```
Look at me, I'm CFML<br>

<cfoutput>
#getPageContext( ).include("test.jsp")#
</cfoutput>

Look at me, I'm CFML again
```

This simple CFML page outputs some text, makes a call to include our *test.jsp* page (provided both are placed in the same directory), and outputs some additional text. JSP pages can be placed in any directory accessible via URL—the same as for your CFML files. Servlets are a little different. By default, servlets go in the */webroot/WEB-INF/classes* directory and are accessed at */servlet/servletname*. If you run the code in Example 27-7, you'll see output similar to that shown in Figure 27-1.

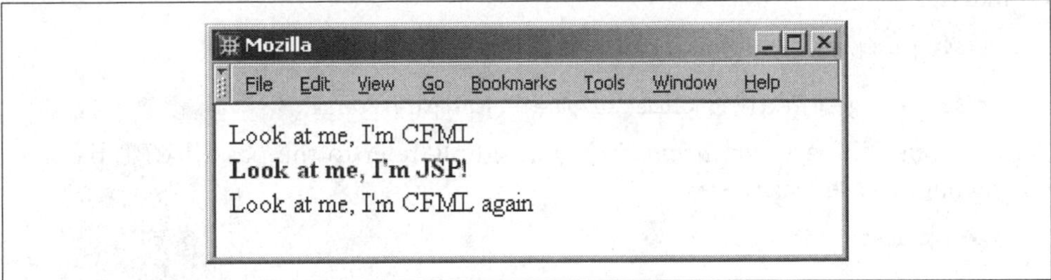

Figure 27-1. Including a JSP page from within a CFML page

To see how a forward works in contrast to an include, change the `getPageContext( )` code as follows:

```
#getPageContext( ).forward("test.jsp")#
```

Now, call the modified code from your browser. This time, you'll notice that the output is a little different. All you should see is the output generated by the JSP page. This is because the forward causes the server to redirect the page request to the JSP page provided to the function. In a CFML page that contains a forward to a JSP page, all of the CFML code before the forward gets executed. This means that if you have code that does something like insert data into a database, write out to a text file, or write a cookie, it still gets executed before the server is redirected to the servlet/JSP page. Any code in the CFML template after the forward call is made does not get executed. This is the fundamental difference between an include and a forward.

If you are working in JSP, you can easily forward to or include a CFML page using code using the `jsp:include` or `jsp:forward` directive like this:

```
<%@page import="java.util.*" %>

Look at me, I'm JSP<br>

<jsp:include page="test.cfm" />

Look at me, I'm JSP again
```

Sharing data between ColdFusion and servlets/JSP pages

Earlier, I mentioned that one of the benefits of the java `PageContext` class was the ability to share data stored in certain scopes between ColdFusion pages and servlets/JSP pages. ColdFusion and servlets/JSP are capable of sharing URL, request, application, and session scoped variables.

Passing URL variables from ColdFusion to servlets/JSP pages is easy. All you need to do is append the URL variables to the URL you provide to getPageContex().include() or getPageContext().forward(), like this:

```
<cfoutput>
#getPageContext().include("test.jsp?name=Rob")#
</cfoutput>
```

Or like this:

```
<cfset parameters = "name=Pere Money&title=President">

<cfset getPageContext().include("urlparams.jsp?#parameters#")>
```

Within your JSP page (*urlparams.jsp*), you simply refer to the passed URL parameters by name (case sensitive):

```
<%@page import="java.util.*" %>

Name: <%= request.getParameter("name")%><br>
Title: <%= request.getParameter("title")%>
```

Sharing request-scoped variables is just as easy. ColdFusion's request scope maps directly to Java's request scope. Here's a simple CFML page that sets two request scoped variables and then includes a JSP page that outputs their values:

```
<cfset request.dsn = "ProgrammingCF">
<cfset request.username = "admin">

<cfset getPageContext().include("requestscope.jsp")>
```

The corresponding JSP page (save it as *requestscope.jsp*) simply outputs the values of the two request variables set in the CFML template by accessing the getAttribute() method of the Java PageContext object and passing it the name of the request variable you want to retrieve the value for. Note that variable names for request variables are case-sensitive within your JSP code. Here's the JSP code we just discussed:

```
<%@page import="java.util.*" %>

<h2>Request Scope Variables in JSP:</h2>
request.dsn: <%= request.getAttribute("dsn")%><br>
request.username: <%= request.getAttribute("username")%>
```

Sharing application and session scoped variables between ColdFusion and servlets/JSP is a little more involved, but still straightforward. Before we start, there are a couple of considerations that need to be addressed. First, if you are going to share session data between ColdFusion and Java, you have to have J2EE session management enabled in the ColdFusion Administrator. If you need more information on J2EE session management, see Chapter 7.

Second, if you are going to share data stored in the application scope, you have two options for setting up your application on the ColdFusion side. When ColdFusion shares application-scoped data with Java servlets and JSPs, the application data is represented as an attribute of Java's ServletContext interface named by the application name (as defined by the cfapplication tag). The application scope data is stored as a hash table in the ServletContext's attribute. If you don't provide a name for your application in a cfapplication tag, your application is called an unnamed application. You are only allowed one unnamed application per ColdFusion server. If you have more than one unnamed application on your server, they all share the same application scope. This would most likely result in unwanted application behavior, as your servlet/JSP page would have access to potentially conflicting application variables from multiple applications. In the case of an unnamed application, the ColdFusion application scope maps directly to the J2EE application scope.

If you are using a named ColdFusion application to pass application or session scoped data to a servlet or JSP page, the code to do so would look something like this:

```
<!--- The cfapplication tag could also reside in an Application.cfm file -[Symbol_
Wingdings_224]
<cfapplication name="test" sessionmanagement="yes">

<cfset application.bgcolor = "Black">
<cfset session.employee = "Pere Money">

<cfset getPageContext( ).include("varscope.jsp")>
```

As you can see, there is really nothing special you need to do in your CFML code.

The JSP code you write to access the application and session scope is equally as simple:

```
<%@page import="java.util.*" %>

<h2>In JSP:</h2>
application.bgcolor: <%= ((Map)(application.getAttribute("test"))).get("bgcolor")%>
<br>
session.employee: <%= ((Map)(session.getAttribute("test"))).get("employee")%>
```

In this case, the bgcolor application variable is accessed by using the getAttribute( ) method of the test application object. The value of the employee session variable is obtained by using the getAttribute( ) method of the session object to get the named application (test) object.

The same code can easily be written to get the values from an unnamed application. Here's the CFML code to pass the application and session variables. Notice that the cfapplication tag omits the name attribute:

```
<cfapplication  sessionmanagement="yes">
<cfset application.bgcolor = "Black">
<cfset session.employee = "Pere">

<cfset getPageContext( ).include("unnamedapp.jsp")>
```

The JSP page that is included should be saved as *unnamedapp.jsp*:

```
<%@page import="java.util.*" %>

<h2>In JSP:</h2>
application.bgcolor: <%= application.getAttribute("bgcolor")%><br>
session.employee: <%= session.getAttribute("employee")%>
```

Here, the code to access the application and session variable is a little different. Since the application wasn't named in the CFML page, no named application object exists on the JSP side. In this case, ColdFusion's application and session scope map directly to Java's application and session scopes.

It's just as easy to share request, application, and session variables in a JSP page or servlet with a CFML page. The same rules for named and unnamed applications apply. The following code sets a request, application, and session variable for an unnamed application, then includes a CFML page that outputs the values:

```
<%@page import="java.util.*" %>

<% request.setAttribute("dsn", "ProgrammingCF");%>
<% application.setAttribute("bgcolor", "Red");%>
<% session.setAttribute("employee", "Pere Money");%>

<jsp:include page="varscope.cfm" />
```

The corresponding CFML page looks just like you would expect it to. Remember, though, that in this case we are sharing the variables with an unnamed application, so it's important to leave the `name` attribute out of the `cfapplication` tag:

```
<cfapplication  sessionmanagement="yes">

<h2>In CFML:</h2>
<cfoutput>
request.dsn: #request.dsn#<br>
application.bgcolor: #application.bgcolor#<br>
session.employee: #session.employee#
</cfoutput>
```

Using JSP Tags and Tag Libraries

In addition to JSP pages, ColdFusion is also capable of using JSP tags. JSP tags can be broken down into two types, native JSP tags and JSP custom tags. Native JSP tags are generally not of interest to ColdFusion developers since for the most part, they mimic the functionality already present in the CFML language. Like ColdFusion's custom tags, JSP also has a convention for extending the core JSP language known as JSP custom tags. A JSP tag can exist standalone or as part of a tag library. JSP tags and tag libraries offer JSP developers a means for encapsulating more complex Java functionality in a simpler tag-based wrapper.

You can easily make use of JSP tag libraries in ColdFusion* using the `cfimport` tag. Before you begin, however, there are a few steps you need to take for ColdFusion to use the tag library:

1. Place the *.tld* and/or JAR file in the desired directory. Although it isn't required, the default location for JSP tag libraries is in the *webroot/WEB-INF/bin* directory.
2. Make sure the path to the tag library is registered in the `CLASSPATH` field of the Java and JVM section of the ColdFusion Administrator.
3. Stop and restart the ColdFusion MX Server service.

The following example uses an open-source JSP tag library from the Apache Jakarta project called Scrape. Scrape is like a specialized version of the `cfhttp` tag. It allows you to specify a URL to grab via HTTP. What it does that `cfhttp` can't is allow you to specify a beginning and ending anchor that it will parse the document for. It then returns all content up to and optionally including the anchors you set. Using Scrape, it's possible to grab a specific chunk of content from the specified site. Here's an example that uses the Scrape JSP tag library to retrieve the list of new book titles from the O'Reilly web site. The list is then output to the browser.

```
<!--- Import the Jakarta Scrape JSP tag library.  The tag library can be found
      at http://jakarta.apache.org/taglibs/doc/scrape-doc/intro.html --->
<cfimport taglib="/WEB-INF/lib/jakarta-taglibs/scrape/taglibs-scrape.jar"
          prefix="scrp">

<!--- Grab the oreilly.com new & upcoming titles page, and scrape the list of
      new titles. --->
<scrp:page>
   <scrp:url>http://www.oreilly.com/catalog/new.html</scrp:url>
   <scrp:scrape id="newTitles" begin="<!--  New titles  -->" end="</td>"
                anchors="false"/>
</scrp:page>

<!--- Output the list of new titles --->
<cfoutput>
#newTitles#
</cfoutput>
```

The `cfimport` tag takes two attributes, `taglib` and `prefix`. `taglib` is required when using `cfimport` to import a JSP tag library. It specifies the URL to the JAR file containing the tags or to the tag library descriptor file (*.tld*) if it is not included in the JAR file. It's customary to place JSP tag libraries in the *webroot/WEB-INF/lib* directory. The `prefix` attribute is optional. It specifies a namespace to use for referring to your imported tags. You refer to an imported tag using the syntax `<prefix:tagname>`. If a blank prefix ("") is specified, or the `prefix` attribute is omitted altogether, the tag

* JSP tag libraries can only be imported in the Developer and Enterprise versions of ColdFusion MX 6.1. ColdFusion Standard does not offer support for importing JSP tag libraries.

is referred to using only its name <tagname>. This means that you could rewrite the code like this:

```
<!--- Import the Jakarta Scrape JSP tag library.  The tag library can be found
      at http://jakarta.apache.org/taglibs/doc/scrape-doc/intro.html --->
<cfimport taglib="/WEB-INF/lib/jakarta-taglibs/scrape/taglibs-scrape.jar"
          prefix="">

<!--- Grab the oreilly.com new & upcoming titles page, and scrape the list of
      new titles. --->
<page>
   <url>http://www.oreilly.com/catalog/new.html</url>
   <scrape id="newTitles" begin="<!--  New titles  -->" end="</td>"
                anchors="false"/>
</page>

<!--- Output the list of new titles --->
<cfoutput>
#newTitles#
</cfoutput>
```

For more information on Scrape, see *http://jakarta.apache.org/taglibs/doc/scrape-doc/intro.html*. You can download other JSP tag libraries from the Apache Jakarta project from *http://jakarta.apache.org/taglibs/doc/scrape-doc/intro.html*. SourceForge.net (*http://sourceforge.net*) is another good resource for open source JSP tag libraries.

CHAPTER 28
Flash Remoting

When Macromedia and Allaire merged back in 2001, hopes were high that great things would come out of the merger. After all, Macromedia had great client-side technologies and tools such as Flash and Dreamweaver, and Allaire had world-class server products such as ColdFusion and JRun. Little did anyone anticipate just how innovative the product marriage would be.

In late 2002, Macromedia launched a completely redesigned product suite, branded with the now famous MX moniker. Included in this launch was a new concept known as a Rich Internet Application (RIA). RIAs use the Flash 6 player and Flash MX on the client side, combined with the Flash Remoting gateway coupled with an application server such as ColdFusion MX, Java, ASP, or PHP, to create an entirely new class of applications. Because an RIA makes use of Flash MX on the front end, user interface options aren't limited to the confines of HTML. Further, the Flash MX player enjoys a much larger installed base than the JVMs necessary to run comparable Java applets, making it available to the majority of users out there on the Internet.

While we don't have enough room in this chapter to cover programming Flash MX in any detail, we can explore the various components of Flash Remoting as they relate to ColdFusion. Topics include a general overview of Flash MX, placing Flash movies in your ColdFusion pages, and passing data between a Flash movie and ColdFusion MX via Flash Remoting. Throughout the chapter, we'll use the terms "RIA" and "Flash Remoting application" interchangeably.

Getting Started with Flash Remoting for ColdFusion MX

You may be thinking that Flash is only an animation tool. While that used to be the primary use for Flash, with the launch of Flash MX, Flash is now a full-blown application development platform. Macromedia's vision for Flash MX is as the front end (GUI) for RIAs. RIAs are made up of several components:

Flash 6 player

The Flash 6 player provides the container in which a Flash movie runs. It can run as a web browser plug-in or as a standalone player. One of the great things about the Flash 6 player is the relative ubiquity it enjoys.*

Flash movie

A Flash movie runs inside the Flash player. It contains user interface controls and ActionScript code for controlling both the behaviors in the movie and any interactivity with ColdFusion via Flash Remoting. Flash movies are developed in the Flash MX authoring tool, compiled, and then deployed as *.swf* files.

ActionScript

ActionScript is the programming language used by Flash. ActionScript looks a lot like JavaScript. In fact, if you already know JavaScript, you should have no trouble picking up ActionScript. Within a Flash movie, ActionScript is used to control virtually all aspects of interactivity between the movie and ColdFusion and within the movie itself. There's just too much to ActionScript to even begin to cover it in this chapter. If you want an excellent reference, I recommend *ActionScript for Flash MX: The Definitive Guide* by Colin Mook (O'Reilly). It really is considered the definitive guide.

Flash Remoting

Flash Remoting acts as a bridge between a Flash movie on the client side and ColdFusion on the server side. Flash Remoting consists of two pieces. The first is a set of components that install in the Flash MX authoring environment; the components contain the ActionScript APIs and debugging services for developing Flash Remoting applications. The second piece is a communications gateway that is automatically installed as part of the ColdFusion MX server.

ColdFusion MX

ColdFusion MX provides the back-end services, such as querying a data source, interacting with a shopping cart, etc. Preferably, Flash MX interacts with CFCs running on the ColdFusion server (although it's also possible to interact with ColdFusion pages and server-side ActionScript, which we'll explore later).

To understand how these components fit together to form an RIA, consider Figure 28-1.

Now that you have a better understanding of the components involved in a Flash Remoting application, let's look at the ways in which a Flash MX front end can interact with ColdFusion on the back end. When you use Flash Remoting, you have several choices for how to write the ColdFusion code on the back end. These choices include CFML pages, CFCs, server-side ActionScript, and Java objects hosted on the

* For more information on the adoption rate of the Flash 6 player, see *http://www.macromedia.com/software/player_census/flashplayer/version_penetration.html*

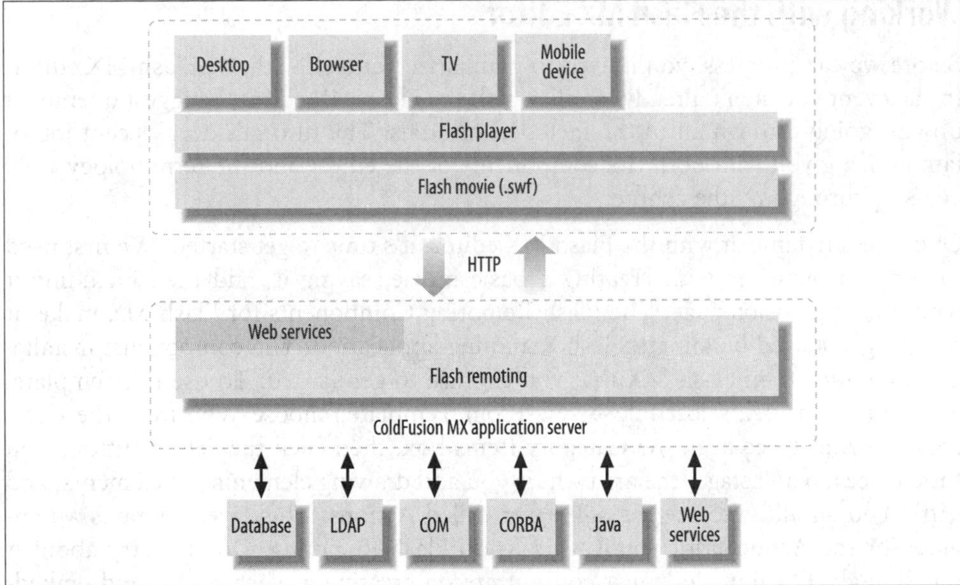

Figure 28-1. Architecture of a Rich Internet Application

ColdFusion server. We'll cover each of these to varying degrees throughout the chapter.

Setting Up Flash Remoting

I generally don't like to write about installation procedures, as they tend to be clearly explained in the documentation that ships with the product being discussed. I'm going to make an exception here because there tends to be some confusion about what needs to be installed where and how to connect it all together. I also think some general setup advice is warranted as both Flash Remoting and Flash MX are new to many ColdFusion developers.

That said, let's look at what you need in order to get going. For starters, you'll need a copy of Flash MX (the authoring environment). If you haven't already purchased Flash MX, you can download a trial copy from *http://www.macromedia.com.* Before you can develop Flash Remoting applications, you'll need to download both the Flash Remoting Components for Flash MX and the most current version of the Flash Remoting Components Updater from *http://www.macromedia.com/software/flashremoting/downloads.* These components add the ActionScript APIs used for Flash Remoting along with an excellent debugger called the NetConnection Debugger (which we'll cover later).

Once you have downloaded the Flash Remoting Components for Flash MX and Flash Remoting Components Updater, you are ready to start building Flash Remoting applications. You don't need to install anything on your ColdFusion server because the Flash Remoting gateway comes preinstalled.

Working with the Flash MX Editor

Before we can progress, you'll need to familiarize yourself with the Flash MX editor. In the event you aren't already familiar with the Flash MX editor, I suggest opening it up and going through all of the included tutorials. The tutorials do a decent job of familiarizing you with both the components of the editor and the terminology we'll be using throughout the chapter.

Once you are familiar with the Flash MX editor, it's time to get started. We first need to concern ourselves with creating a basic movie, saving it, and then including it within a ColdFusion page. The Flash Remoting Components for Flash MX make it easy to get started building a Flash Remoting application. The components install a generic template in Flash MX that you can use to get started. To use this template, open up Flash MX, select File→New From Template, choose Web from the Category box and Basic from the Category Items box, then click the Select button. You should see a blank stage (the area where you add drawing elements, UI elements, and text). You should also see a single layer called Actions. This layer contains a template for the ActionScript you'll need to do Flash Remoting. Don't worry about it yet, though. For now, let's just concentrate on creating a Flash movie and embedding it within a ColdFusion page. Here are the basic steps:

1. Select the text tool from the tools menu (it's the capital "A" icon).
2. Move your cursor onto the stage and click your mouse button. Enter something like "Flash Remoting Demo" in the area that appears on the stage (make sure you are on the Actions layer).
3. Choose File→Save to save the document (note that this is the source code and not the compiled movie). The Flash MX document saves with an extension of *.fla*. This differs from the *.swf* file used for the actual Flash movie. We'll cover this in just a moment.
4. To save the file you are working on as a Flash movie, choose File→Publish Movie. Flash MX will automatically create the Flash movie file (*.swf*) and a supporting HTML file for calling the movie in the same directory you previously saved the Flash document.

By default, when you publish a Flash MX document as a Flash movie, an HTML file is also created. This HTML file contains the code necessary to embed the Flash movie within a web page. Open the HTML file in your HTML editor. The HTML file should have the same name as the Flash movie you exported (*28-1.html*). The HTML code should look something like this:

```
<HTML>
  <HEAD>
    <meta http-equiv=Content-Type content="text/html;  charset=ISO-8859-1">
    <TITLE>28-1</TITLE>
  </HEAD>
<BODY bgcolor="#FFFFFF">
```

```
<!-- URL's used in the movie-->
<!-- text used in the movie-->
<OBJECT classid="clsid:D27CDB6E-AE6D-11cf-96B8-444553540000"
codebase="http://download.macromedia.com/pub/shockwave/cabs/flash/swflash.
cab#version=6,0,0,0"
        WIDTH="550" HEIGHT="400" id="28-1" ALIGN="">
 <PARAM NAME=movie VALUE="28-1.swf">
 <PARAM NAME=quality VALUE=high>
 <PARAM NAME=bgcolor VALUE=#FFFFFF>
 <EMBED src="28-1.swf" quality=high bgcolor=#FFFFFF  WIDTH="550"
        HEIGHT="400" NAME="test" ALIGN=""
        TYPE="application/x-shockwave-flash"
        PLUGINSPAGE="http://www.macromedia.com/go/getflashplayer"></EMBED>
</OBJECT>
</BODY>
</HTML>
```

To use the Flash movie in a ColdFusion page, just copy and paste the code contained between the `<object>/</object>` tags (be sure to include the `object` tags themselves, as well). This code tells the browser to embed the Flash movie specified by one of the `param` tags. The `embed` tag is used to ensure browser compatibility as some browsers don't recognize the `object` tag. Copy the object tag code and paste it into a new ColdFusion page now. Save the CFML page as *28-1.cfm* in the same directory as your Flash movie. If you open the ColdFusion page in your browser, you should see output similar to that in Figure 28-2. Congratulations: you just created your first Flash movie.

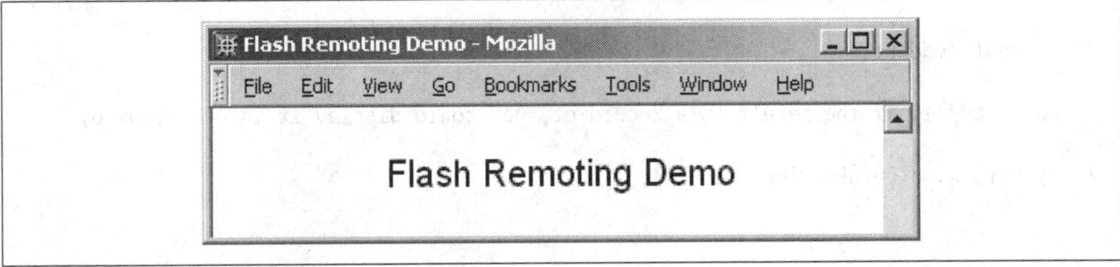

Figure 28-2. Embedding a Flash movie in a ColdFusion page

Writing ActionScript for Flash Remoting

In the previous section, we created a simple Flash movie using a predefined Flash Remoting template. We didn't actually use any of the Flash Remoting capabilities in that movie. In fact, all our example movie did was display some text on the screen—hardly what you would call a Rich Internet Application. In this section, we'll look at the ActionScript code that was created as part of the Flash Remoting template we used to create the movie in Example 28-1.

Open the example file we created earlier (*28-1.fla*) and click on the Actions layer in the Timeline panel. You should see ActionScript code like that shown in

Example 28-1 in the Actions panel of your Flash MX editor.* If the Actions panel isn't already expanded, you may need to do so (F9 is the keyboard shortcut).

Example 28-1. Generic template for creating Flash Remoting applications

```
#include "NetServices.as"

// uncomment this line when you want to use the NetConnect debugger
//#include "NetDebug.as"

// -----------------------------------------------------
// Handlers for user interaction events
// -----------------------------------------------------

// This gets called when the "aaaa" button is clicked
function aaaa_Clicked ()
{
  // ... put code here

  // For example, you could call the "bbbb" function of "my.service" by doing:
  // myService.bbbb(123, "abc");
}

// -----------------------------------------------------
// Handlers for data coming in from server
// -----------------------------------------------------

// This gets called with the results of calls to the server function "bbbb".
function bbbb_Result ( result )
{
  // ... put code here

  // For example, if the result is a RecordSet, you could display it in a ListBox by
doing:
  // myListBox.setDataProvider(result);
}

// -----------------------------------------------------
// Application initialization
// -----------------------------------------------------

if (inited == null)
{
  // do this code only once
  inited = true;

    // set the default gateway URL (this is used only in authoring)
    NetServices.setDefaultGatewayUrl("http://localhost:8100/flashservices/gateway");
```

* Although this template does not show it, it's considered a "best practice" to always var local variables in Flash with a "var" keyword—just as you do in JavaScript or in ColdFusion UDFs.

Example 28-1. Generic template for creating Flash Remoting applications (continued)

```
    // connect to the gateway
    gateway_conn = NetServices.createGatewayConnection( );

    // get a reference to a service
    myService = gateway_conn.getService("my.service", this);
}

stop( );
```

We won't go into every line of code in the template in detail (besides, the comments are actually pretty good), but we will walk through the basic sections.

The first line of code includes an ActionScript file called *NetServices.as*. This file is installed as part of the Flash Remoting Components for Flash MX and contains ActionScript code used for Flash Remoting. The next section of code defines an event handler (similar to a CFC method) that can be called from an event such as a user clicking a button in the Flash movie. The third section consists of a result handler. A result handler is automatically invoked when a call to an event handler returns results. The `_result` portion of the function name tells Flash that the function should be invoked when function "bbbb" returns a result.

The final section of code is used to instantiate a connection to the Flash Remoting gateway. The code is designed to execute a single time and places the instantiated connection in an object called `myService`. This object can be called anywhere it's needed in the ActionScript code (I'll cover this in later examples).

Now that you've seen what an ActionScript template for Flash Remoting looks like, we're going to focus our attention on how you can use it to pass data back and forth between Flash MX and ColdFusion MX via Flash Remoting. On the client side, the ActionScript you write in the Flash MX editor is pretty straightforward. On the opposite end, however, you have several choices for coding the server-side functionality. These choices include ColdFusion pages, ColdFusion Components, server-side ActionScript and Java objects hosted on the ColdFusion MX server. Each of these options is discussed in detail the remaining sections of this chapter.

Interacting with ColdFusion Pages

Prior to Flash Remoting, communication between Flash and ColdFusion was a little awkward. On the Flash end, you wrote ActionScript code that called a ColdFusion page via the Flash `loadVars` object. This object had a method called `load( )` that took the URL of a page (in this case ColdFusion) that output variable names and values in a format that Flash could understand. Interaction using this method was fairly cumbersome, on both the Flash and ColdFusion sides. Additionally, it was difficult to pass complex datatypes, such as query record sets, arrays, and structures, between ColdFusion and Flash. Typically, these complex types had to be broken down into simpler name/value pairs before they could be passed. ColdFusion MX and Flash Remoting change this paradigm completely. Combined, these technologies allow you to pass various ColdFusion and Flash datatypes back and forth between Flash and ColdFusion as if they were native datatypes.

If you refer back to the last section of code in Example 28-1, you'll see that we created a reference to the Flash Remoting gateway by calling the `createGatewayConnection()` method of the `NetServices` object:

```
// connect to the gateway
gateway_conn = NetServices.createGatewayConnection();
```

Once the connection is established, the next step is to get a reference to a service. In Flash MX–speak, a service is the directory path that contains the ColdFusion page you want to connect to via Flash Remoting. As in Java, the actual directory path is referred to using dot notation. Thus, if your CFML pages reside in */webroot/my/service*, you would use code like this:

```
// get a reference to a service
myService = gateway_conn.getService("my.service", this);
```

Once you have a connection to your service (directory) established, you can call individual CFML pages stored in that directory by name as if they were methods. Each individual CFML file represents a single method available to your ActionScript code. For example, if you had a CFML page called *getUsers.cfm*, you would refer to it like this:

```
myService.getUsers();
```

Within your CFML file, a special scope known as the Flash scope is available. The Flash scope contains three predefined variables:

`flash.params`
: Structure containing all arguments passed to ColdFusion from Flash.

`flash.pagesize`
: The number of records returned from ColdFusion to Flash at one time. This variable can be used to return an entire record set to Flash, or it can be used to return a record set in increments.

`flash.result`
: Variable to return to Flash from ColdFusion. Table 28-1 shows the mapping between ColdFusion datatypes and Flash datatypes.

Table 28-1. ColdFusion and Flash datatype mapping

ColdFusion datatype	Flash datatype
String	String
Numeric	Number (primitive)

Table 28-1. ColdFusion and Flash datatype mapping (continued)

ColdFusion datatype	Flash datatype
Date/Time	Date object
Boolean	Boolean (primitive)
Array	Ordered array
Structure	ActionScript object, Named array
Query	RecordSet
XML Document Object	XML object

To get a better idea of how this all fits together, let's create a simple CFML file that gets a list of users from the `EmployeeDirectory` table of our `ProgrammingCF` data source and returns it to a Flash movie that uses the data to populate a list box. Example 28-2 shows the code for the CFML file.

Example 28-2. Returning a record set from a ColdFusion page to a Flash movie

```
<cfquery name="getEmployees" datasource="programmingcf">
  SELECT ID,Name
  FROM employeeDirectory
  ORDER BY Name
</cfquery>

<!--- Number of records going back to the flash movie.  In this case,
      we return all of them at once. --->
<cfset flash.pageSize = getEmployees.recordCount>

<!--- Return result set to Flash movie --->
<cfset flash.result = getEmployees>
```

This example executes a simple `cfquery` to retrieve the `ID` and `Name` of every user in the `EmployeeDirectory` table in our database. It then uses the `flash.pageSize` variable to specify the number of records at a time to return back to the Flash movie. Here, we specify that all records should be sent back at once. It is possible to send records back in increments, too. To do this, though, you need to use the `RecordSet` object in your client-side ActionScript to continue to retrieve additional records beyond the first chunk sent back to the Flash movie. The final line of code sends the complete record set returned by the query back to the Flash movie. Once you have finished entering the code, save the page as *getEmployees.cfm* in */webroot/programmingcf/ch28*.

Creating a Flash front end to call the CFML page in Example 28-2 is almost as easy. Let's walk through the process. First, open Flash MX, select File→New From Template, choose Web from the Category box and Basic from the Category Items box, then click the Select button. This gives us a fresh template with which we can build our movie.

Flash MX comes preinstalled with a set of UI components you can use in your movies. These UI components make it very easy to build consistent user interfaces in your Flash movies. The UI components that make up the Flash UI Components include a checkbox, list box, combo box, and push button. Each UI component has several properties and methods you can use to control its behavior. To see the components, you'll need to choose "Flash UI Components" from the dropdown box in the Components panel. You should see an icon for each UI component type, as shown in Figure 28-3.

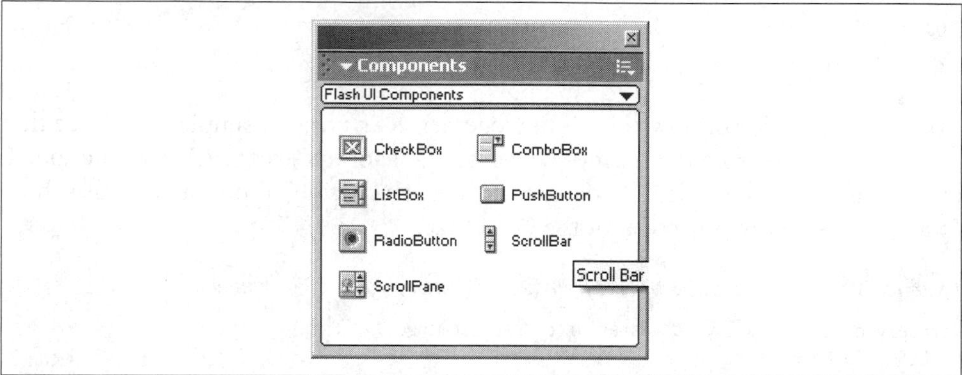

Figure 28-3. Flash UI Components

To place a UI component in your movie, simply drag and drop it from the Components panel onto the stage. When you do this with a ListBox component, your stage should look like that in Figure 28-4.

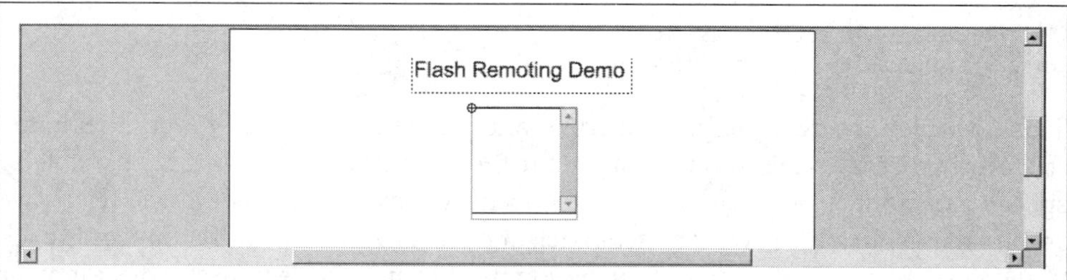

Figure 28-4. Placing a UI component on the stage

Now that we have our ListBox component on the stage, we need to give it a name so that we can tell Flash MX what to bind the data we return from our CFML page to. We're going to name our ListBox component "lb1." To name the ListBox component, enter `lb1` in the text box under the Component label in the Preferences panel shown in Figure 28-5. Note that the component must have focus on the stage in order to do this.

All that's left to do now is write the ActionScript code that connects to the Flash Remoting gateway, calls our CFML page, and binds the result set returned by it to our ListBox component. We're going to modify the ActionScript that was automati-

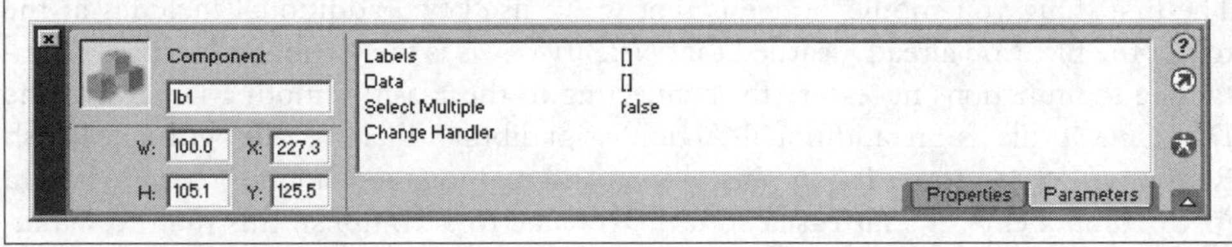

Figure 28-5. Naming a UI component

cally created when we chose to create a new file from a template. To make things easy, let's erase all of the ActionScript that was automatically generated and replace it with the code in Example 28-3.

Example 28-3. Using Flash Remoting to call a ColdFusion page

```
// include the flash remoting library
#include "NetServices.as"
// include AS library for binding data to UI components
#include "DataGlue.as"
// include AS library for debugging Flash Remoting
#include "NetDebug.as"

// -----------------------------------------------------
// Application initialization
// -----------------------------------------------------
if (inited == null) {
  // do this code only once
  var inited = true;
  // set the default gateway URL (this is used only in authoring)
  NetServices.setDefaultGatewayUrl("http://localhost/flashservices/gateway");
  // connect to the gateway
  var gateway_conn = NetServices.createGatewayConnection( );
  // get a reference to a service
  var myService = gateway_conn.getService("programmingcf.ch28", this);
}

// call the getEmployees() "method"
myService.getEmployees();

// -----------------------------------------------------
// Handlers for data coming in from server
// -----------------------------------------------------
// Bind the results to the lb1 list box using data glue
function getEmployees_Result(result) {
  DataGlue.bindFormatStrings(lb1, result, "#Name#", "#ID#");
}
stop( );
```

The organization and content of this code is a little different than what you've seen so far. This makes it easier to explain in a top-down fashion.

The first thing you should notice is that we've used two additional includes at the top of the file. You already learned that *NetServices.as* is the ActionScript library containing the functions necessary for connecting to the Flash Remoting Gateway. The *DataGlue.as* file is an additional ActionScript library that installs with the Flash Remoting Components. It contains objects and methods for binding record set data to UI components. It's far easier to use DataGlue to accomplish this than to manually loop through all the records in the returned record set, adding them one at a time to the UI control. If you want to see all the objects and properties in the DataGlue library, simply click on Remoting → DataGlue in the tree under the Actions panel.

The *NetDebug.as* library contains objects and methods you can use to debug your Flash Remoting operations. Like the DataGlue library, you can see the objects and properties available by clicking on Remoting→NetDebug in the tree under the Actions panel. Including the *NetDebug.as* library is also necessary to use the NetConnection Debugger. This handy tool allows you to watch what is happening with your Flash Remoting application as it happens. To launch the NetConnection Debugger, choose Window→NetConnection Debugger from the toolbar in Flash MX. You'll see how this works when we test our Flash movie.

The next section of code initializes the connection to the Flash Remoting Gateway and creates a reference to the service (in this case, */webroot/programmingcf/ch28*). With the reference to the service established, the `getEmployees()` method (*getEmployees.cfm*) is called. On the ColdFusion end, the `EmployeeDirectory` table is queried, and a record set containing all of the employee names and ids is returned back to the flash movie.

The `getEmployees_Result()` function handles the result set returned by the `getEmployees()` method. It uses the `bindFormatStrings()` method of the `DataGlue` object to bind the result set to our ListBox Component (named `lb1`).

To test the movie, choose Control → Test Movie from the toolbar. If you've entered everything correctly, you should see a ListBox UI Component populated with the names of the employees from the `EmployeeDirectory` table. The results are shown in Figure 28-6.

If you close the movie test (click the "x" in the upper right-hand corner of the screen), you can retest it with the NetConnection Debugger turned on so that you can see exactly what is taking place as the movie plays. The NetConnection Debugger displays tons of useful information that can help you troubleshoot your way out of most connectivity-related issues.

Interacting with ColdFusion Components

While it's fairly easy to use ColdFusion pages and the Flash variable scope to interact with a Flash movie, it can be a bit awkward at times. In some cases, you may not want to deal with a different CFML file for each method that makes up your service.

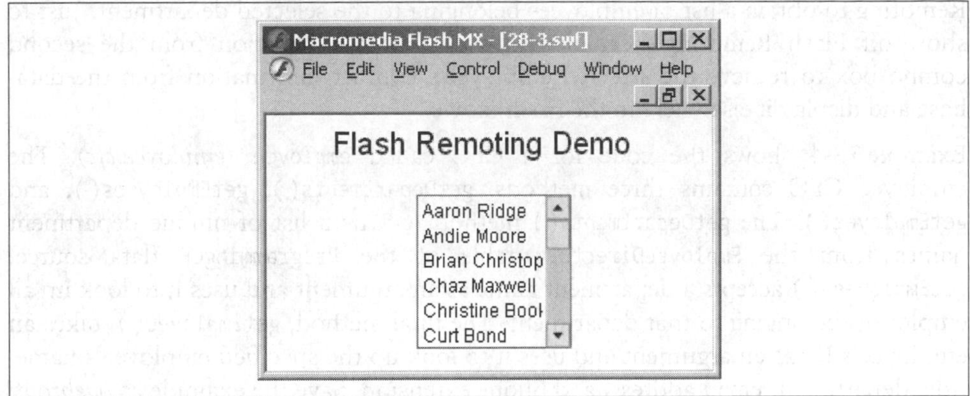

Figure 28-6. Populating a UI control via Flash Remoting

Also, while the Flash scope isn't hard to use, wouldn't it be much nicer if you could just pass various datatypes, such as record sets, arrays, and structures, back and forth between Flash MX and ColdFusion without having to assign them to a special scope or manipulate them in other ways?

This is where CFCs come in. CFCs provide the most natural and integrated way to pass data between Flash MX and ColdFusion MX. Components are nice because you can wrap multiple functions (methods) inside a single file. With pages, each CFML file corresponds to a single function. Also, unlike with ColdFusion pages, you do not need to use the Flash scope when referencing arguments passed to the CFC or return values to be sent back to the Flash MX movie. When a Flash MX movie calls a method of a CFC, any arguments it passes to the CFC are automatically available as named arguments in the CFC's arguments scope. Likewise, to return data from the CFC method to the Flash movie, all you need to do is use the `cfreturn` tag. The Flash Remoting gateway handles everything else for you automatically.

CFCs offer additional advantages over the page approach. Whereas CFML pages tend to be specific to Flash applications (because of the Flash scope), an equivalent CFC can be written once and used to return data to a Flash movie and/or to a ColdFusion program (or other client via web services). Also, components offer built-in roles-based security.

Let's create an example that demonstrates just how simple, elegant, and powerful the combination of Flash MX, Flash Remoting, and ColdFusion MX is. We'll create a Flash movie that contains two related combo (select) boxes. Related combo boxes are a desirable element in many ColdFusion applications. They work by displaying two combo boxes that are linked. When an item in the first combo box is selected, the available choices in the second combo box change, based on the selected value from the first box. In our example, we'll build a set of related combo boxes that display a list of departments (pulled from a query via Flash Remoting) in the first combo box. When a department is selected, we'll run a second query over Flash

Remoting to obtain a list of employees belonging to the selected department. Just to show off Flash Remoting's capabilities, we'll use the selection from the second combo box to retrieve the selected employee's contact information from the database and display it elsewhere in the Flash movie.

Example 28-4 shows the code for a CFC called `employee` (*employee.cfc*). The employee CFC contains three methods: `getDepartments()`, `getEmployees()`, and `getEmployee()`. The `getDepartments()` method returns a list of unique department names from the `EmployeeDirectory` table of the `ProgrammingCF` data source. `getEmployees()` accepts a department name as an argument and uses it to look up all employees belonging to that department. The final method, `getEmployee()`, takes an employee's ID as an argument and uses it to look up the specified employee's name, title, department, email address, and phone extension. Save the example as */webroot/programmingcf/ch28/employee.cfc*.

Example 28-4. employee.cfc used for populating related combo boxes

```
<cfcomponent>
  <cffunction name="getDepartments" access="remote" returntype="query"
            output="no"
            hint="I retrieve a list of distinct department names"
            description="I retrieve a list of distinct department names">
    <cfquery name="getDepartments" datasource="programmingcf">
      select distinct(department)
      from employeeDirectory
      order by department
    </cfquery>

    <cfreturn getDepartments>
  </cffunction>

  <cffunction name="getEmployees" access="remote" returntype="query"
            output="no"
            hint="I retrieve a list of all employees in a given department"
            description="I retrieve a list of all employees in a given department">
    <cfargument name="department" type="string" required="yes">

    <cfquery name="getEmployees" datasource="programmingcf">
      SELECT ID, Name
      FROM employeeDirectory
      WHERE department = '#arguments.department#'
      ORDER BY Name
    </cfquery>

    <cfreturn getEmployees>
  </cffunction>

  <cffunction name="getEmployee" access="remote" returntype="query"
            output="no"
            hint="I retrieve an employee record provided their ID"
            description="I retrieve an employee record provided their ID">
```

Example 28-4. employee.cfc used for populating related combo boxes (continued)

```
    <cfargument name="id" type="numeric" required="yes">

    <cfquery name="getEmployee" datasource="programmingcf">
      SELECT Name, Title, Department, Email, PhoneExt
      FROM employeeDirectory
      WHERE ID = #arguments.id#
    </cfquery>

    <cfreturn getEmployee>
  </cffunction>
</cfcomponent>
```

To make a method of a CFC available to Flash Remoting, just set the access attribute of the `cffunction` tag to `remote`.* As you can see, no references to the Flash scope are used within any of the CFC's methods. This is because arguments passed from Flash MX to the CFC via Flash Remoting are automatically available in the CFC's arguments scope. Likewise, to return data from a CFC method back to a Flash movie, you need only use the `cfreturn` tag.

Now that we've created the CFC, it's time to create the Flash movie and associated ActionScript to tie everything together. Create a new Flash movie from a web template as we've done in our previous examples. Drag two ComboBox Flash UI Components from the Components panel and drop them onto the stage (Figure 28-7). In the Properties panel, name them "cb1" and "cb2," respectively.

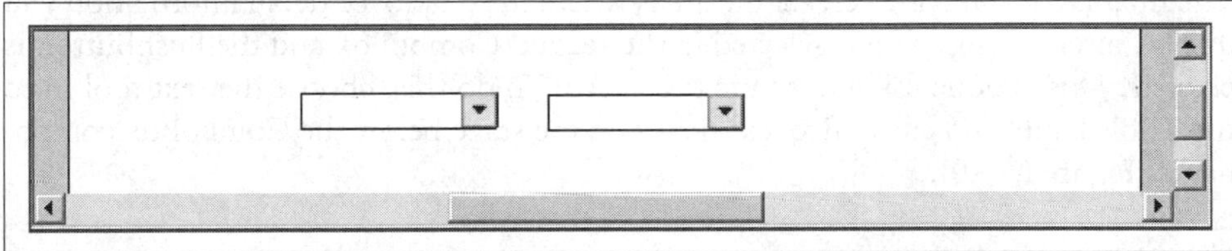

Figure 28-7. Laying out two related combo boxes in Flash MX

Next, grab a PushButton Flash UI Component from the Components panel and drop it on the stage next to the ComboBox components so that it looks similar to Figure 28-8.

* It's also possible to call web services (including ColdFusion-based ones) using Flash Remoting. This allows Flash movies hosted on one server to access CFCs stored on a different server. For more information on invoking web services using Flash Remoting, see the Macromedia whitepaper "Using Flash Remoting MX with ColdFusion MX," available in PDF format from *http://download.macromedia.com/pub/coldfusion/documentation/using_frmx_with_cfmx.pdf* Additionally, as of Updater 3, calling ColdFusion web services from Flash Remoting is disabled by default. For information on this, see Macromedia TechNote 18608 at *http://www.macromedia.com/support/coldfusion/ts/documents/enable_flash_webservices.htm*.

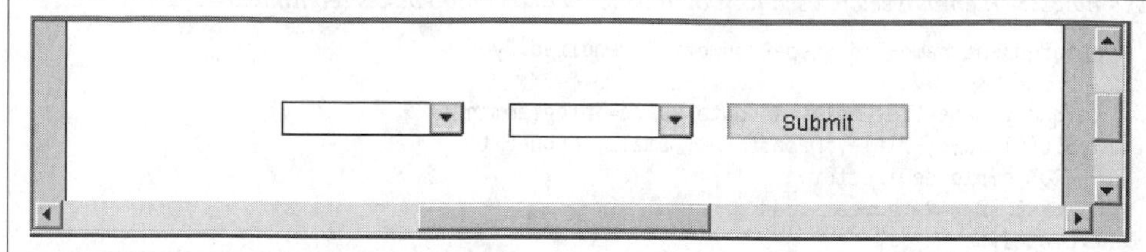

Figure 28-8. Adding a PushButton component to the Flash movie

In the Properties panel, shown in Figure 28-9, name the component "pb_submit." Change the Label property to "Submit". The Label property determines what text to display on top of the PushButton. Next, set the ClickHandler property to "employee-Handler." This tells the Flash movie to call an ActionScript event handler called `employeeHandler` (we'll code this in a minute) when the PushButton is clicked.

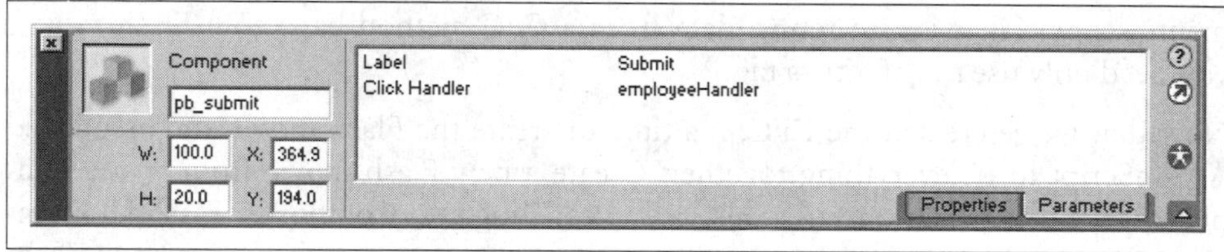

Figure 28-9. Changing the properties of the PushButton component

The final layout step is to create the areas where the employee detail information will display after an employee is selected in the second ComboBox and the PushButton is clicked. This is done using dynamic text areas. To do this, choose the text tool from the Tools panel and create five text boxes on the stage below the ComboBox components (Figure 28-10).

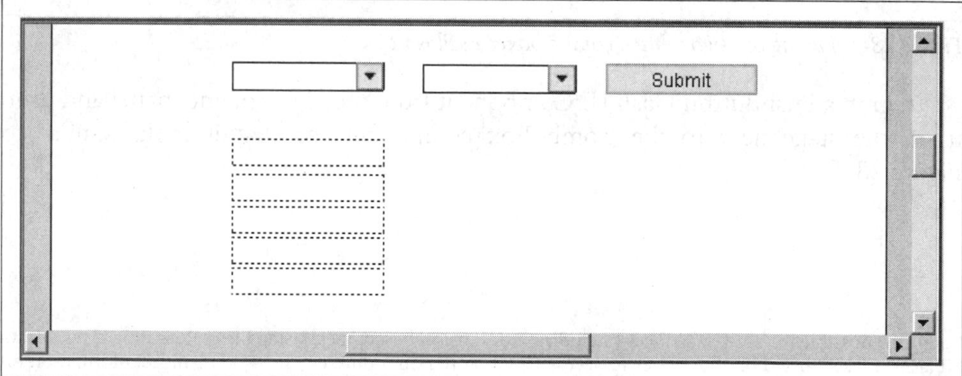

Figure 28-10. Adding dynamic text areas to the Flash movie

In the Properties panel for each text area, choose DynamicText from the combo box. This tells Flash MX that the text to appear in the box will be generated dynamically as opposed to hardcoded. Below the combo box is a text box you can use to specify a name for the dynamic text area. Name the text areas "dName," "dTitle," "dDepartment," "dEmail," and "dPhoneExt," respectively. When you have finished editing all of the text areas, your stage should look similar to the one in Figure 28-10.

Add the ActionScript in Example 28-5 to the Actions layer of your Flash MX movie (you can overwrite any existing ActionScript generated by the template).

Example 28-5. ActionScript for relating two combo boxes via Flash Remoting

```
#include "NetServices.as"
#include "DataGlue.as"
#include "NetDebug.as"

// ---------------------------------------------------
// Application initialization
// ---------------------------------------------------
if (inited == null) {
  // do this code only once
  var inited = true;

  // set the default gateway URL (this is used only in authoring)
  NetServices.setDefaultGatewayUrl("http://localhost/flashservices/gateway");

  // connect to the gateway
  var gateway_conn = NetServices.createGatewayConnection();

  // get a reference to a service
  var myService = gateway_conn.getService("programmingcf.ch28.employee", this);
}

// ---------------------------------------------------
// cb1 combo box
// ---------------------------------------------------
//call the getDepartments() method
myService.getDepartments();

//Bind the results to the cb1 combo box using data glue
function getDepartments_Result (result) {
  DataGlue.bindFormatStrings(cb1, result, "#Department#", "#Department#");
}

// ---------------------------------------------------
// cb2 combo box
// ---------------------------------------------------
// When a selection in the first combo box is made, call showEmployees()
cb1.setChangeHandler("showEmployees");

function showEmployees(component){
```

Example 28-5. ActionScript for relating two combo boxes via Flash Remoting (continued)

```
  cb2.removeAll( );
  myService.getEmployees(cb1.getSelectedItem( ).data);
  cb2.addItem("loading...","");
}

function getEmployees_Result(result) {
  cb2.removeAll();
  for (var i = 0;i < result.items.length;i++) {
    cb2.addItem(result.items[i].Name,result.items[i].ID);
  }
}

// ------------------------------------------------
// Button handler and full record get/display
// ------------------------------------------------
// Retrieve the full employee record based on the employee selected
function employeeHandler(){
  myService.getEmployee(cb2.getSelectedItem( ).data);
}

// Display the full employee record
function getEmployee_Result(result) {
  dName.text = result.items[0].Name;
  dTitle.text = result.items[0].Title;
  dDepartment.text = result.items[0].Department;
  dEmail.text = result.items[0].Email;
  dPhoneExt.text = result.items[0].phoneExt;
}
stop();
```

This code is fairly straightforward. First, the NetServices, DataGlue, and NetDebug ActionScript libraries are included, and a connection to the Flash Remoting Gateway is established. Notice that the name of the CFC file is included as part of the service (path) when a reference to the service is made:

```
// get a reference to a service
  var myService = gateway_conn.getService("programmingcf.ch28.employee", this);
```

This differs from calling a CFML page, where no filename is required. When connecting a Flash movie to a CFC, you must include the CFC's filename as part of the service name.

The next section of code calls the `getDepartments( )` method in the employee CFC and binds the results to the `cb1` ComboBox component using DataGlue. When a selection in the first combo box is made (which happens as soon as the box is loaded with data or a different department is selected), the `showEmployees( )` ActionScript function is called. This function clears the contents of the second ComboBox component (`cb2`) and calls the `getEmployees( )` method in the employee CFC, passing it the department name selected in `cb1` as an argument. While it is waiting for data to be returned from ColdFusion, a "loading..." message is displayed in the second ComboBox component. Once the data arrives from the CFC, a loop is used to iterate over the returned result set, populating `cb2` with the employee names for the selected department. Note that a loop and the `addItem( )` method of the `cb2` object are used in lieu of DataGlue in order to demonstrate yet another way to bind data to a UI control.

The final section of code contains the ActionScript used to retrieve and display the full employee record when an employee is chosen from the second combo box and the submit button is clicked. The `employeeHandler( )` function gets called when the submit button is pushed. It passes the value selected in `cb2` to the `getEmployee( )` method of the `employee` CFC. The CFC then returns the name, title, department, email address, and phone extension for the selected employee as a record set. The results are individually bound to the dynamic text fields we created.

To test all this, choose Control→Test Movie from the Flash MX toolbar. You may want to enable the NetConnection Debugger first to watch each step of the interaction in case there are any problems getting the movie to run. Testing the movie should give you results similar to those shown in Figure 28-11.

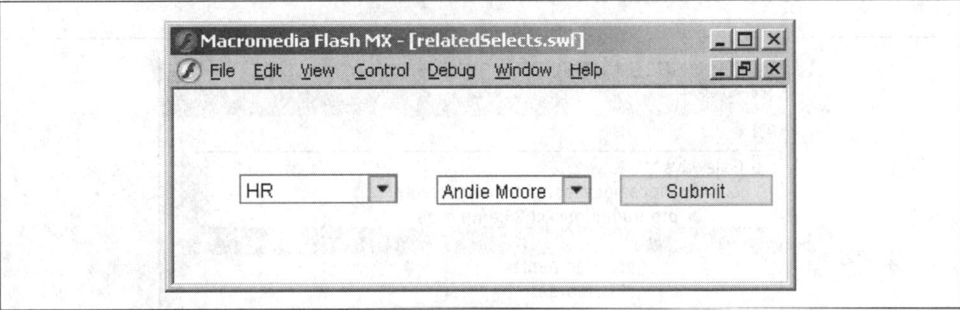

Figure 28-11. Relating two combo boxes using Flash Remoting

Introspecting CFCs in Flash MX

In Chapter 22, we said the `cffunction` and `cfargument` tags differ from most other ColdFusion tags in that you can pass arbitrary attributes to them as user-defined attributes. Although these attributes don't cause the tags to do anything, they are available as metadata when the method is introspected.

Flash MX has a tool called the Service Browser that you can use within the Flash MX authoring environment to introspect component methods and arguments that include an arbitrary argument called `description`. If you take a second look at the `employee` CFC we created in Example 28-4, you'll notice that we included description attributes for all three component methods.

To use the Service Browser, open Flash MX and follow these steps:

1. Choose Window → Service Browser (Figure 28-12).
2. If you don't see your Flash Remoting gateway, which you probably won't, you'll need to add it. Do this by clicking on the blue box with the right-facing arrow and choosing Add Gateway. Enter the URL to your Flash Remoting gateway (e.g., *http://localhost/flashservices/gateway*). Note you may need to append the port to the service if you are using a port other than 80. When you have finished, click Add Gateway.
3. The next step is to add to the gateway any services you want to browse. To add the employee service (*employee.cfc*) to the gateway, highlight the gateway you created and click the blue box with the right-facing triangle again. This time, choose Add Service.
4. Enter the new service address (using dot notation) in the text area and click the Add Service button. To add the `employee` CFC, enter `programmingcf.ch28.employee`.
5. When the service browser refreshes, you should see all three methods of the `employee` CFC in the service browser window. Clicking on the folder of any of the component methods displays a description of the method (if provided) along with any of the arguments the method accepts.

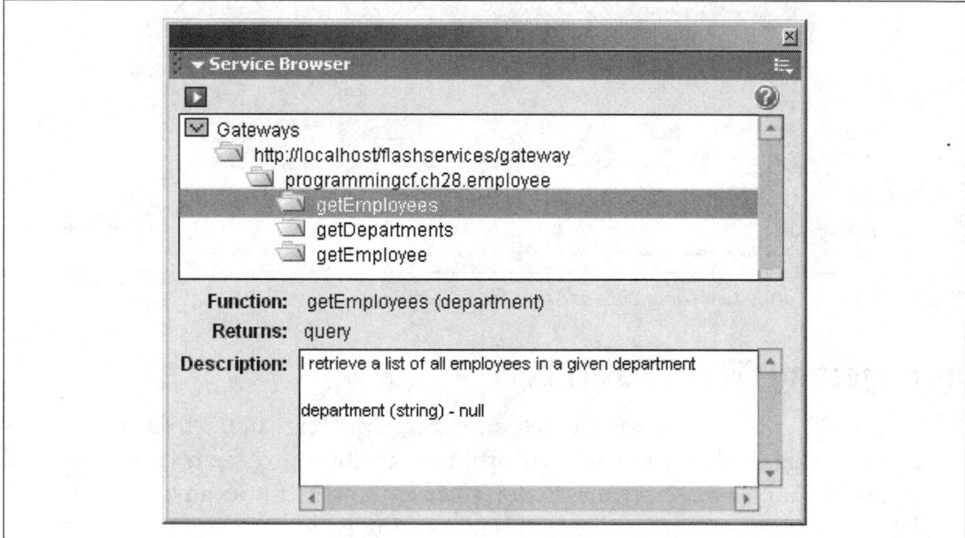

Figure 28-12. The Flash MX Service Browser

Securing Flash Remoting Applications

You can control Flash Remoting access to your CFCs using ColdFusion MX's built-in security framework. This works for Flash Remoting the same way it does for CFCs and web services. You can control access based on assigned roles at the invocation level. To add access control to the *employe.cfc* component we created in Example 28-4, we'll need to add the following attribute to each `cffunction` tag in the component:

```
Roles="administrator"
```

Once you do this, each method in the CFC can be invoked only by clients with a role of "Administrator."

The framework for authenticating a Flash Remoting client is the same as we discussed in Chapters 8 and 24. Using an *Application.cfm* file, we can leverage ColdFusion MX's security framework and ActionScript's `setCredentials()` function to provide a means to authenticate clients before allowing them to access Flash Remoting. Example 28-6 shows one way to do this.

Example 28-6. Authenticating a client

```
<cfapplication name="myFlashRemotingSecurity">

<cflogin idletimeout="600">
  <cfif not isdefined("cflogin")>
    <!--- Send something back to Flash letting it know login failed. --->
    <cfabort>
  <cfelse>
    <cfquery name="validateUser" datasource="programmingcf">
      SELECT Roles, Salt, Password
      FROM Users
      WHERE Username = <cfqueryparam value="#cflogin.name#"
                                     cfsqltype="CF_SQL_VARCHAR"
                                     maxlength="255">
    </cfquery>

    <cfif (validateUser.recordCount eq 1) and
          (validateUser.password is hash(validateUser.salt &
           cflogin.password))>
      <cfset userRoles = valueList(validateUser.roles)>
      <cfloginuser name="#cflogin.name#" password="#cflogin.Password#"
                   roles="#userRoles#">
    <cfelse>
      <!--- Send something back to Flash letting it know login failed. --->
      <cfabort>
    </cfif>
  </cfif>
</cflogin>
```

When a Flash MX movie calls a CFC (or web service), a check is made to see whether there is an *Application.cfm* file that should be run first, just as there is when a CFML file is called from the browser. This lets you use the same mechanisms you are already familiar with to build a security framework for your Flash Remoting applications. When our *Application.cfm* file is called, a number of things happen.

First, a check is made to see whether the cflogin structure exists. If not, a message could be written back to the Flash movie letting it know the login failed. If the cflogin structure does exist, we know that the call to the CFC also included an authorization header containing (hopefully) a username and password. Those values are automatically available inside the cflogin structure as cflogin.name and cflogin.password. A query is made to see if the username exists in the Users table of our example database. If so, the salt value associated with the cflogin.name (from the database query) is concatenated with the password provided by cflogin.password. The resulting string is hashed and then compared to the hashed value stored in the database. If a record was found for the username, and the salted, hashed password matches the value stored in the database, we consider this a valid login. The cflogin tag is then used to log the user in and assign her roles from the database. In this example, when we lookup the username "pmoney", we find she is assigned the roles "Administrator, User".

To pass the username and password from the Flash movie to the Application.cfm file, you'll need to add a line of ActionScript that calls the setCredentials( ) function. You can call the function when you initialize your connection to the Flash Remoting Gateway. You'll need to modify the application initialization section of code from Example 28-5 in order to add in the call to the setCredentials( ) function:*

```
// ---------------------------------------------------
// Application initialization
// ---------------------------------------------------

if (inited == null)
{
  // do this code only once
  var inited = true;

  // set the default gateway URL (this is used only in authoring)
  NetServices.setDefaultGatewayUrl("http://localhost/flashservices/gateway");

  // connect to the gateway
  var gateway_conn = NetServices.createGatewayConnection( );

  // pass username/password to Application.cfm on CF Server-Side
  gateway_conn.setCredentials("pmoney","cat");

  // get a reference to a service
  var myService = gateway_conn.getService("programmingcf.ch28.employee", this);
}
```

* For demonstration purposes, we've hardcoded the username and password in the getcredentials( ) function call. In a real application, you would be passing these values to the function dynamically, such as from a login prompt. Because it's very easy to decompile *.swf* files, you should never hardcode sensitive information such as passwords inside your Flash movies.

If you test the movie using the new code, you should see the two related combo boxes populated with data. If you wait 30 minutes (the time specified in the idletimeout attribute of the cflogin tag) and change the username or password to a different value, then retest the movie, both combo boxes should be blank as you will no longer be authorized to call the CFC methods necessary to populate them with data.

Interacting with Server-Side ActionScript

Every ColdFusion MX server comes with native support for server-side ActionScript. Server-side ActionScript adds the basic functionality of ColdFusion's cfquery and cfhttp tags to ActionScript. As a ColdFusion developer, you may not have much use for server-side ActionScript; you'll most likely find yourself developing CFCs as the back end for Flash Remoting applications. However, like everything else, it's worth understanding how server-side ActionScript works, as you may find yourself in a situation where it's desirable to have a Flash developer write the server-side code for a Flash Remoting application as well. Having server-side ActionScript as an option makes it easier for Flash developers to leverage the power of cfquery and cfhttp without having to learn ColdFusion.

Server-side ActionScript files are written just like any other text-based file, and they can be stored anywhere on your ColdFusion MX server under the web server's root directory. Server-side ActionScript files have a file extension of *.asr*. In your client-side ActionScript, a server-side ActionScript file is instantiated by referring to the file in the gatewayConnection.getService( ) function call. Dot notation is used to point to the server-side ActionScript file's location. For example, to instantiate a server-side ActionScript file called *test.asr* located in *webroot/programmingcf/ch28*, your client-side ActionScript would look like this:

```
var myService = gatewayConnection.getService("programmingcf.ch28.test", this);

// Call the getEmployees funciton
myService.getEmployess();

// Call the getPage function
myService.getPage();
```

The calls to the CF.query( ) and CF.http( ) functions available in server-side ActionScript files are written just like calls to any other native ActionScript functions:

```
function getEmployees(){
  var employees = CF.query({datasource:"programmingcf",
                    sql:"select ID, Name as fullName from employeeDirectory"});
  return employees;
}

function getPage(){
```

```
    var thePage = CF.http({method:"get",
                          url:"http://www.example.com"});
    return thePage.get("Filecontent");
}
```

There isn't enough room here to thoroughly cover the `CF.query()` and `CF.http()` ActionScript functions—besides, we're ColdFusion developers. If you want a detailed description of the ins and outs of server-side ActionScript, the ColdFusion MX documentation does a more than adequate job. That said, let's take a cursory look at what we have here.

Arguments available to the `CF.query()` function are `datasource`, `sql`, `username`, `password`, `maxrows`, and `timeout`. With the exception of `sql`, each of these arguments is identical to the `cfquery` attribute of the same name. The `sql` argument is used to pass the entire SQL statement for the query.

When the `CF.query()` function is called, it returns a `RecordSet` object. This ActionScript class is used by the client-side ActionScript code in your Flash movie to manipulate the record set data returned by the server-side ActionScript file. There are several methods you can call to interact with the `RecordSet` object. These methods are explained in detail in both the ColdFusion MX documentation and the Flash MX documentation.

Arguments available to the `CF.http()` function are a subset of the attributes available to the `cfhttp` tag and include `method`, `url`, `username`, `password`, `resolveurl`, `path`, `file`, and `params`. Since `CF.http()` is a function and not a tag, the `param` argument performs the same duty the `cfhttpparam` tag would. It allows you to pass HTTP parameters as an array of objects to the function.

When the `CF.http()` function is called, it returns an object containing a set of properties that can be referenced to provide access to information like the HTTP header, file content, MIME type, character set, etc. These properties are fully detailed in the ColdFusion MX documentation on server-side ActionScript.

For more information on server-side ActionScript, see the *Using Server-Side ActionScript in ColdFusion MX* book on the Macromedia LiveDocs site, available at *http://livedocs.macromedia.com/cfmxdocs/Using_Server-Side_ActionScript_in_ColdFusion_MX/contents.htm*.

Flash Remoting with Java Objects Hosted on the ColdFusion MX Server

In Chapter 27, we talked about ColdFusion MX and Java interaction. We covered several ways in which you can leverage Java in your ColdFusion MX applications, including using the ColdFusion MX server to host Java objects. One of the additional benefits of Flash Remoting's integration with ColdFusion MX is the ability to have Flash MX communicate directly with these Java objects. To take advantage of this feature, you first need to make sure that the directory where your Java object(s) are stored is registered in the Class Path field under the Java and JVM section of the ColdFusion Administrator. After registering, you'll need to restart the ColdFusion server for the changes to take effect.

Once the class path is set, any public methods in the Java object are available as methods to your Flash MX movie.* If you have a Java object called *employee.class* in *com/example/utils*, you could reference a public method called `getEmployee( )` from within your Flash movie like this:

```
#include "NetServices.as"

// Call the getEmployee() method on the service specified below
myService.getEmployee();


function getEmployee_Result(result) {
  // ActionScript for handling results returned by the Java object
}

if (inited = = null){
  // do this code only once
  var inited = true;

  NetServices.setDefaultGatewayUrl("http://localhost/flashservices/gateway");

  var gatewayConnection = NetServices.createGatewayConnection( );

  // Note getService() includes the filename of the Java object as part of
  // the service name.
  var myService = gatewayConnection.getService("com.example.utils.employee",
      this);
}
stop( );
```

A connection is made to the Java object by specifying the path to the class file as the service name in the ActionScript code. A public method of the Java object called `getEmployee( )` is referenced as if it were a method of a native ActionScript object.

* Flash Remoting does not support calling alternate constructors in Java objects. If you invoke a Java object within your Flash movie, you must use the default constructor.

APPENDIX A
Tag Reference

ColdFusion tags are the core components of the CFML language. They take what would otherwise be considered low-level programming tasks, such as making an ODBC/JDBC or SMTP connection, and abstract them, providing a simple way to program complex functionality. ColdFusion contains over 90 tags that allow you to perform all sorts of tasks, from querying databases to sending and receiving email. This appendix contains reference material on all ColdFusion tags through ColdFusion MX.

Tags by Type

The following sections group the CFML tags by their functionality.

Custom Tag Tags

`cfassociate`	`cfexit`	`cfimport`
`cfmodule`		

Database Tags

`cfinsert`	`cfprocparam`	`cfprocresult`
`cfquery`	`cfqueryparam`	`cfstoredproc`
`cftransaction`	`cfupdate`	

Error, Exception-Handling, and Debugging Tags

`cfabort`	`cfcatch`	`cfdump`
`cferror`	`cflog`	`cfthrow`
`cftrace`	`cftry`	`cfrethrow`

Extensibility Tags

cfchart	cfchartdata	cfchartseries
cfgraph	cfgraphdata	cfimport
cfinclude	cfinvoke	cfinvokeargument
cfmodule	cfobject	cfservlet
cfservletparam	cfwddx	cfxml

Filesystem Tags

cfdirectory	cffile

Flow Control Tags

cfabort	cfbreak	cfcase
cfdefaultcase	cfelse	cfelseif
cfexit	cfif	cfimport
cfinclude	cfinvoke	cfinvokeargument
cflocation	cfloop	cfmodule
cfswitch		

Form Tags

cfapplet	cfform	cfgrid
cfgridcolumn	cfgridrow	cfgridupdate
cfinput	cfselect	cfslider
cftextinput	cftree	cftreeitem

Miscellaneous Tags

cfapplication	cfcache	cflock
cfschedule	cfscript	

Output Tags

cfcol	cfcontent	cfdump
cfflush	cfheader	cfhtmlhead
cfoutput	cfprocessingdirective	cfreport
cfsavecontent	cfsetting	cfsilent
cftable	cftrace	

Protocol Tags

cfftp
cfhttp
cfhttpparam
cfldap
cfmail
cfmailparam
cfpop
cfmailpart

Security Tags

cfadminsecurity
cfauthenticate
cfimpersonate
cflogin
cfloginuser
cflogout
cfnewinternaladminsecurity

System Tags

cfexecute
cfnewinternalregistry
cfregistry

UDFs/CFCs/Web Services Tags

cfargument
cfcomponent
cffunction
cfimport
cfinvoke
cfinvokeargument
cfobject
cfproperty
cfreturn

Variable Manipulation Tags

cfcookie
cflock
cfparam
cfset

Verity Search Engine Tags

cfcollection
cfindex
cfsearch

Alphabetical List of Tags

This section lists all the CFML tags alphabetically, with detailed descriptions of their attributes and proper syntax. Version information is included for many tags; if no version information is listed, the tag is available in ColdFusion 4.5 and later.

cfabort

```
<cfabort>
```

Halts processing of the CFML template at the tag position.

Attributes

showerror="*text_message*"
: A message to display when the cfabort tag is executed. Optional. If this attribute is used in conjunction with a cferror tag, ColdFusion passes the error message to the template specified in the cferror tag. Otherwise, it is output directly to the browser.

---

cfadminsecurity

Enhanced in ColdFusion 5.0; no longer supported in ColdFusion MX

```
<cfadminsecurity>
<cfnewinternaladminsecurity>
```

This undocumented tag handles administrative tasks related to ColdFusion's Advanced Security services. Because of the complexity of this tag and the fact that no documentation exists on its usage, the following information provided may be incomplete.

Attributes

action="*action*"
: Specifies the action the tag should perform. Possible actions include the following: AddHost, AddPolicy, AddRule, AddRuleToPolicy, AddSecurityContext, AddSecurityRealm, AddUserDirectory, AddUserDirectoryToContext, AddUserToPolicy, CreateODBCQueryScheme, DeleteHost, DeleteODBCQueryScheme, DeletePolicy, DeleteRule, DeleteSecurityContext, DeleteSecurityRealm, DeleteUserDirectory, FlushCache, GenerateRule, GetHost, GetODBCQueryScheme, GetPolicy, GetResourceInfo, GetRule, GetRuleForPolicy, GetSecurityContext, GetSecurityRealm, GetUserDirectory, GetUserDirectoryForContext, GetUserPolicy, GetUserForUserDirectory, RemoveRuleFromPolicy, RemoveUserDirectoryFromContext, and RemoveUserFromPolicy.

authtype="Basic|X509"
: The authentication protocol to use. The default value is Basic. This attribute is optional and used only when action is set to AddSecurityRealm.

cachetype="Basic|X509"
: The type of security cache to flush. Required when action is FlushCache. New as of ColdFusion 5.0.

description="*text*"
: A description for the object being referenced.

directory="*directory_name*"
: The name of the security context being referenced.

IP="*IP_address*"
: The IP address of the ColdFusion Application Server. Used when action is AddHost. Currently, this attribute must be set to 127.0.0.1.

name="*name*"
: The name of the object being referenced.

output="*variable_name*"
: The name of a ColdFusion variable that holds the results when action is GenerateRule or GetResourceInfo. The data is returned as a ColdFusion structure.

policy="*policy_name*"
: The name of the security policy being referenced.

protectall="Yes|No"
: Whether or not to protect all resources for a given security context. This attribute is optional and used only when action is set to AddSecurityRealm. The default is No.

query="*query_name*"
: The name to use for the query object returned when action is set to GetODBC-QueryScheme, GetHost, GetPolicy, GetRule, GetRuleForPolicy, GetSecurityContext, GetSecurityRealm, GetUserDirectory, GetUserDirectoryForContext, GetUserPolicy, or GetUserForUserDirectory. Required for the aforementioned action values.

resource="*resource_name*"
: The name of the resource when adding or generating a rule.

resourceaction="*resource_action*"
: The action to associate with a resource when action is set to AddRule or GenerateRule.

response=""
: Optional; is available only when action is set to AddRuleToPolicy. response should be set to "".

results="*integer*"
: The maximum number of results to return when searching an LDAP directory. Optional; used only when action is set to AddUserDirectory.

root="*search_root*"
: The search root for the LDAP server when adding a user directory. Usually, the search root is set to "organization" (o) or "organizational unit" (ou). Optional; used only when action is set to AddUserDirectory.

scope="*search_scope*"
: The scope for the LDAP search. Possible entries are One Level or Subtree. Optional; used only when action is set to AddUserDirectory.

searchend="*search_end*"
: The value to use when constructing the uid (uid=) part of the dn string for an LDAP query. Optional; used only when action is set to AddUserDirectory.

searchstart="*search_start*"
: The value to use when constructing the rest of the dn string (after the UID) for an LDAP query. Optional; used only when action is set to AddUserDirectory.

secret="*string*"
: A string to be used in generating the encryption key used by advanced security services. Used only when action is set to AddHost.

server="CFSM"
: The name of the ColdFusion security server. The default server used by ColdFusion is CFSM. You shouldn't use a value other than CFSM unless you manually modify the Site Minder security database. Used only when action is set to AddSecurityRealm or AddUserDirectory.

sqlauthuser="*SQL_statement*"
: Specifies the SQL statement to use for the Authenticate User field when using an ODBC data source to store security profile tables. Required when action is CreateODBCQueryScheme. New as of ColdFusion 5.0.

sqlenum="*SQL_statement*"
: Specifies the SQL statement to use for the Enumerate field when using an ODBC data source to store security profile tables. Required when action is CreateODBCQueryScheme. New as of ColdFusion 5.0.

sqlgetgroupprop="*SQL_statement*"
: Specifies the SQL statement to use for the Get Group Property field when using an ODBC data source to store security profile tables. Required when action is CreateODBCQueryScheme. New as of ColdFusion 5.0.

sqlgetgroupprops="*SQL_statement*"
: Specifies the SQL statement to use for the Get Group Properties field when using an ODBC data source to store security profile tables. Required when action is CreateODBCQueryScheme. New as of ColdFusion 5.0.

sqlgetgroups="*SQL_statement*"
: Specifies the SQL statement to use for the Get Groups field when using an ODBC data source to store security profile tables. Required when action is CreateODBCQueryScheme. New as of ColdFusion 5.0.

sqlgetobjinfo="*SQL_statement*"
: Specifies the SQL statement to use for the Get User/Group Info field when using an ODBC data source to store security profile tables. Required when action is CreateODBCQueryScheme. New as of ColdFusion 5.0.

sqlgetuserprop="*SQL_statement*"
: Specifies the SQL statement to use for the Get User Property field when using an ODBC data source to store security profile tables. Required when action is CreateODBCQueryScheme. New as of ColdFusion 5.0.

sqlgetuserprops="*SQL_statement*"
: Specifies the SQL statement to use for the Get User Properties field when using an ODBC data source to store security profile tables. Required when action is CreateODBCQueryScheme. New as of ColdFusion 5.0.

sqlinituser="*SQL_statement*"
: Specifies the SQL statement to use for the Init User field when using an ODBC data source to store security profile tables. Required when action is CreateODBCQueryScheme. New as of ColdFusion 5.0.

sqlisgroupmember="*SQL_statement*"
: Specifies the SQL statement to use for the Is Group Member field when using an ODBC data source to store security profile tables. Required when action is CreateODBCQueryScheme. New as of ColdFusion 5.0.

sqllookup="*SQL_statement*"
: Specifies the SQL statement to use for the Lookup field when using an ODBC data source to store security profile tables. Required when action is CreateODBCQueryScheme. New as of ColdFusion 5.0.

sqllookupgroup="*SQL_statement*"

Specifies the SQL statement to use for the Lookup Groups field when using an ODBC data source to store security profile tables. Required when action is CreateODBCQueryScheme. New as of ColdFusion 5.0.

sqllookupuser="*SQL_statement*"

Specifies the SQL statement to use for the Lookup Users field when using an ODBC data source to store security profile tables. Required when action is CreateODBCQueryScheme. New as of ColdFusion 5.0.

sqlsetgroupprop="*SQL_statement*"

Specifies the SQL statement to use for the Set Group Property field when using an ODBC data source to store security profile tables. Required when action is CreateODBCQueryScheme. New as of ColdFusion 5.0.

sqlsetuserprop="*SQL_statement*"

Specifies the SQL statement to use for the Set Group Properties field when using an ODBC data source to store security profile tables. Required when action is CreateODBCQueryScheme. New as of ColdFusion 5.0.

timeout="*seconds*"

The time in seconds that ColdFusion should wait before timing out an LDAP directory search. Optional; used only when action is set to AddUserDirectory.

type="*object_type_or_namespace*"

The object type to be protected within a given security context when action is Addrule, DeleteRule, or GenerateRule. Possible entries are Application, CFML, Collection, Component, Custom Tag, Data Source, File, Function, UserObject, and User. When action is set to AddSecurityContext, the type attribute specifies the namespace for the user directory, either Windows NT, LDAP, or ODBC.

update="Yes|No"

Whether or not the data being written to the security database should be added (No) or updated (Yes). Optional. The default value is No.

user="*user*"

The name of a user within a valid user directory. Used only when action is set to AddUserToPolicy, GetUserPolicy, and RemoveUserFromPolicy.

usercredentials="Yes|No"

Whether or not to pass login credentials to the LDAP server. Should be set to Yes only when used in conjunction with a username. Used only when action is set to AddUserDirectory.

username="*username*"

A username to use if required by the domain, LDAP directory, or database. You can leave this attribute blank if ColdFusion is running as Administrator. Used only when action is set to AddUserDirectory.

userpwd="*password*"

A password to use if required by the domain, LDAP directory, or database. You can leave this attribute blank if ColdFusion is running as Administrator. Used only when action is set to AddUserDirectory.

usersecureconnect=Yes|No"
: Whether or not to encrypt authentication information during transmission between the ColdFusion server and an LDAP server. This attribute must be enabled when connecting to an LDAP server using SSL. Optional; used only when `action` is set to `AddUserDirectory`. The default is `No`.

cfapplet

Enhanced in ColdFusion MX

`<cfapplet>`

References a custom Java applet that has been registered with the ColdFusion Administrator. Applet registration is handled via the ColdFusion Administrator. As of ColdFusion MX, you no longer need to use the `cfapplet` tag within a `cfform` tag.

Attributes

appletsource="*registered_applet_name*"
: The actual name of the Java applet. Required.

name="*form_field_name*"
: What to call the Java applet within the context of `cfform`. Required.

align="*alignment*"
: Alignment of the applet. Optional. Valid entries are `Left`, `Right`, `Top`, `TextTop`, `Bottom`, `AbsBottom`, `Middle`, `AbsMiddle`, and `Baseline`.

height="*height_in_pixels*"
: Height of the applet in pixels. Optional.

hspace="*horizontal_spacing_in_pixels*"
: Horizontal space in pixels along each side of the applet. Optional.

paramn="*parameter_value*"
: Additional user-defined parameters to pass to the applet. Optional.

notsupported="*text_messsage*"
: Text to appear if Java isn't supported by the user's browser. Optional.

vspace="*vertical_spacing_in_pixels*"
: Vertical space in pixels along the top and bottom of the applet. Optional.

width="*width_in_pixels*"
: Width of the applet in pixels. Optional.

cfapplication

Enhanced in ColdFusion MX 6.1

`<cfapplication>`

Names a ColdFusion application and controls various application settings, such as the availability of client, session, and application variables, and length of various timeouts.

Attributes

name="*application_name*"
: The name of the ColdFusion application. May contain up to 64 characters. Required if enabling session or application variables.

applicationtimeout="#CreateTimeSpan(*days, hours, minutes, seconds*)#"
: The timeout value for application variables. Specified as an interval using the CreateTimeSpan( ) function. Optional. The default value is specified in the Memory Variables section of the ColdFusion Administrator.

clientmanagement="Yes|No"
: Enables client management for the application. Optional. Default is No.

clientstorage="*Datasource*|Registry|Cookie"
: The client storage type for the application. Valid entries are *Datasource* (enter the data source name), Registry, and Cookie. Optional. Default is Registry.

loginstorage="cookie|session"
: Specifies whether login information associated with the cflogin scope should be stored in a cookie or session variable. If set to session, a login is tied directly to a user's ColdFusion session and the login remains active for as long as the session exists. Optional. The default is cookie. This attribute is new in ColdFusion MX 6.1.

sessionmanagement="Yes|No"
: Enables session management for the application. Optional. Default is No.

sessiontimeout="#CreateTimeSpan(*days, hours, minutes, seconds*)#"
: The timeout value for session variables in the application. Specified as an interval using the CreateTimeSpan( ) function. Optional. The default value is specified in the Memory Variables section of the ColdFusion Administrator.

setclientcookies="Yes|No"
: Enables client cookies. If cookies are disabled, the values for CFID and CFToken must be passed manually from template to template in the URL. Optional. The default is Yes.

setdomaincookies="Yes|No"
: Indicates whether or not to set client cookies at the domain level, which is useful when you need to share client variables in a clustered environment. If set to Yes, ColdFusion creates a new variable at the domain level called CFMagic. CFMagic tells ColdFusion that cookies have been set at the domain level and contains the values of the CFID and CFToken cookies. Existing host-level cookies are compared automatically to the values stored in CFMagic and migrated to domain-level cookies if the values don't match. Optional. The default is No.

cfargument

New in ColdFusion MX

```
<cffunction>
  [<cfargument>]
  ...
</cffunction>
```

Defines one or more arguments for a user-defined function (UDF). Acts as a subtag of cffunction. If used within the context of a ColdFusion Component (CFC), cfargument defines an argument for the method defined in the cffunction tag. cfargument tags must be placed immediately after the cffunction tag, before any other CFML tags are used. Arguments passed into a function/method can be referenced using the argument's name

(#*ArgumentName*#), the argument's scoped name (#arguments.*ArgumentName*#), or by the argument's index within the arguments array (#arguments[*i*]#).

Besides the named attributes listed below, you can pass any additional desired attributes to the cfargument tag as user-defined attributes. Although these attributes don't do anything, they are available as metadata when the component containing the method with the cfargument tag is introspected using the GetMetaData( ) function. You may use any attribute names you wish with the exception of those reserved by cfargument: name, displayname, hint, type, required, and default.

Attributes

name="*ArgumentName*"
: Name of the argument. Required.

default="*Value*"
: Value to assign the argument if required="No" or if required is not specified and no argument is passed to the function when it is called.

displayname="*display_name*"
: Used to display a descriptive name for the argument in ColdFusion MX's Component Browser. Optional.

hint="*text*"
: Used to display a hint describing what the argument is for in ColdFusion MX's Component Browser. Optional.

required="Yes|No"
: Indicates whether the argument must be supplied in the function call for the request to be processed. Default is No.

type="*ArgumentType*"
: Type of argument. Valid options are Any, Array, Binary, Boolean, Date, GUID, Numeric, Query, String, Struct, UUID, VariableName, and *ComponentName*. Optional. The default is Any. For information on how GUID differs from UUID, see the CreateUUID( ) function in Appendix B.

cfassociate

<cfassociate>

Associate a subtag with a base tag (child tag with a parent tag) by saving all the subtag's attributes to a special structure that is available to the base tag. This tag is for use only within custom tags.

Attributes

basetag="*tag_name*"
: The name of the base tag. Required.

datacollection="*collection_name*"
: The name of the structure that contains subtag data. Optional. By default, ColdFusion saves all subtag attributes in a structure called AssocAttribs.

cfauthenticate

No longer supported in ColdFusion MX; see cflogin for more information.

```
<cfauthenticate>
```

Authenticates a user within a given security context.

Attributes

securitycontext="*security_context*"
: The name of the security context to authenticate the user within. Required. Security contexts are defined in the ColdFusion Administrator.

username="*username*"
: The name of the user being authenticated. Required.

password="*password*"
: The password of the user being authenticated. Required.

authtype="Basic|x509"
: The authentication type to use. Basic specifies a username/password while x509 specifies an x509 client certificate passed via SSL. Optional. The default is Basic.

setcookie="Yes|No"
: If set to Yes, ColdFusion sets an encrypted cookie on the user's browser that contains the username, security context, browser's remote address, and HTTP user agent. Optional. The default is Yes.

throwonfailure="Yes|No"
: Determines if ColdFusion should throw an exception if authentication fails. Optional. The default is Yes.

cfbreak

```
<cfbreak>
```

Breaks out of a cfloop. The cfbreak tag has no additional attributes.

Example

```
<cfloop index="i" from="10" to="100" step="10">
  <cfif i eq 50>
    <cfbreak>
  </cfif>
</cfloop>
```

cfcache

Updated in ColdFusion MX

```
<cfcache>
```

Caches a ColdFusion page for faster access by writing a temporary static HTML version of the page to disk (either server-side or in the client's browser cache, or both). To cache a ColdFusion template, just add the cfcache tag to the top of the page.

When the cfcache tag caches a page, two files are actually written to the server. First, a temporary file (with a *.tmp* extension) is created that contains the HTML necessary to generate the static version of the page. A mapping file contains the mapping to the temp file, as well as a timestamp that determines when to expire the cached file. The name for the mapping file is determined by appending the hash of the current URL (see `Hash( )` in Appendix B) to *cfcache_*. This results in filenames like this: *cfcache_D6BF3A60769FD03FE598BB2E8490CB11.tmp*. When using the `cfcache` tag, there are a few additional points that should be considered:

- Templates that generate errors don't get cached.
- Pages generating personalized content should be cached on the client only (`action="ClientCache"`) to avoid serving the cached content to people who are not intended to see it.
- By default, the `cfcache` tag suppresses all debugging information for a ColdFusion template. To use debugging within a cached page, you must explicitly turn it on for the template using the `cfsetting` tag.
- Simultaneous Requests in the ColdFusion Administrator must be set to a minimum of 2 for the `cfcache` tag to work.
- In ColdFusion MX, it's now possible to cache pages that maintain state. Additionally, pages secured using the new `cflogin` security framework can also be cached.

Attributes

`action="Cache|ClientCache|ServerCache|Flush|Optimal"`
: The action to be performed by the `cfcache` tag. `Cache` is used to cache the page on both the client and the server. This is new in ColdFusion MX. In previous versions, `Cache` only cached the file on the server. `ClientCache` caches the page in the client's browser, `ServerCache` caches the page on the server only (Macromedia recommends against this option), `Flush` refreshes the cached page, and `Optimal` caches the page using both server-side and browser caching (this is the recommended action in most cases). Optional. The default is `Cache` (note that `Cache` and `Optimal` are interchangeable in ColdFusion MX).

`cachedirectory="`*`directory_name`*`"`
: Obsolete in ColdFusion MX. The full path of a directory where the page should be cached. By default, pages are cached in the directory of the currently executing template. Optional.

`directory="`*`directory_name`*`"`
: The full path of the directory containing the *.tmp* file used by the `cfcache` tag. Optional. The default cache directory is */cfroot/cache*.

`expireurl="`*`wildcarded_URL`*`"`
: A wildcarded URL reference used by ColdFusion to match mappings in the cache directory when `action="Flush"`; ignored otherwise. Optional. The default flushes all mappings.

`password="`*`password`*`"`
: A password to use if required by the page being cached. Optional.

`port="`*`port_number`*`"`
: Port number on the web server where the file being cached resides. Optional. The default is the port of the current page.

protocol="*protocol_name*"
: The protocol to use when creating the pages from the cache. Options are *HTTP://* and *HTTPS://*. Optional. The default is the protocol of the current page.

timeout="*timeout*"
: Obsolete in ColdFusion MX. A date/time value that specifies the oldest acceptable page to pull from the cache. If the cached page is older than the timeout value, ColdFusion refreshes the cached page. Optional.

timespan="*decimal_num_of_days*|#CreateTimeSpan(*days, hours, minutes, seconds*)#"
: Amount of time ColdFusion should use the cached version of the template before flushing the cache and fetching a fresh copy. The amount of time can be specified as a decimal number representing the number of days (1.5 is a day and a half). If you prefer, a time span can be provided instead by using the `CreateTimeSpan()` function. Optional. The default is not to flush the page until the `cfcache` tag is called with `action="Flush"`.

username="*username*"
: A username to use if required by the page being cached. Optional.

cfcase

See `cfswitch`.

cfcatch

See `cftry`.

cfchart

New in ColdFusion MX; enhanced in ColdFusion MX 6.1; replaces the cfgraph tag from ColdFusion 5.0.

```
<cfchart>
  <cfchartseries>
    [<cfchartdata>]
    ...
  </cfchartseries>
  ...
</cfchart>
```

Container tag for rendering graphs and charts in ColdFusion MX. `cfchart` is used in conjunction with `cfchartseries` and, optionally, `cfchartdata` to draw several chart types including `Area`, `Bar` (vertical and horizontal), `Cone`, `Curve`, `Cylinder`, `Line`, `Pie`, `Pyramid`, `Scatter`, and `Step`. Both 2D and 3D versions of most types can be rendered.

Attributes

backgroundcolor="*Hex*|*Web_Color_Name*"
: Color for the background area behind the chart. Colors are specified using the same rules as the `foregroundcolor` attribute. Optional. The default is `White`.

chartheight="*Height_in_Pixels*"
: Height in pixels for the chart. Optional. The default is 240.

chartwidth="*Height_in_Pixels*"
: Width in pixels for the chart. Optional. The default is 320.

databackgroundcolor="*Hex|Web_Color_Name*"
: Background color for the chart's data area. Colors are specified using the same rules as the foregroundcolor attribute. Optional. The default is White.

foregroundcolor="*Hex|Web_Color_Name*"
: Color for text, gridlines, and labels. Colors may be specified by using one of the 16 available web color names: Aqua (##00FFFF), Black (##000000), Blue (##0000FF), Fuchsia (##FF00FF), Gray (##808080), Green (##008000), Lime (##00FF00), Maroon (##800000), Navy (##000080), Olive (##808000), Purple (##800080), Red (##FF0000), Silver (##C0C0C0), Teal (##008080), White (##FFFFFF), Yellow (##FFFF00); or hex code in the form ##FFFFCC. The double pound signs are necessary to keep ColdFusion from throwing an error. Optional. The default is Black.

font="Arial|Courier|Times|arialunicodeMS"
: Font name to use for displayed text on the chart. Optional. Default is Arial. You must use arialcodeMS if you are trying to display double-byte characters on a Unix or Linux server, or if you are trying to display double-byte characters on a Windows server in Flash format.

fontbold="Yes|No"
: Indicates whether to make all display text boldface. Optional. Default is No.

fontitalic="Yes|No"
: Indicates whether to italicize all display text. Optional. Default is No.

fontsize="*Integer*"
: Font size in pixels for displayed text. Optional. The default is 11.

format="Flash|JPG|PNG"
: The file type to use when displaying the graph. Options are Flash (*.swf*), JPG (*.jpg*), and PNG (*.png*). Optional. The default is Flash.

gridlines="*Integer*"
: Number of grid lines, including the axis, to display on the axis containing the charted values when the appropriate attribute (showxgridlines or showygridlines) is set to Yes. Setting gridlines="0" should suppress grid line display but does not in the current release of ColdFusion MX due to a bug. To suppress grid line display, set showxgridlines and/or showygridlines to No. Optional.

labelformat="Number|Currency|Percent|Date"
: Specifies a format type for y-axis labels. Optional. Default is Number.

labelmask="*mask*"
: This attribute is currently undocumented in the ColdFusion MX documentation and appears to be disabled. It's supposed to allow you to apply a mask to the values shown in the y-axis label. Optional.

markersize="*Integer*"
: Marker size in pixels if showmarkers="Yes". Optional. The default size is automatically determined.

`name="Var_Name"`
: Specifies a variable name to hold ISO-8859-1 encoded binary data representing the chart. No chart is displayed in the browser. This attribute is generally used to make charts created with `cfchart` available to Flash Remoting users. Optional.

`pieslicestyle="Solid|Sliced"`
: Specifies how to display pie slices if a `cfchartseries` tag is used with `type="Pie"`. `Solid` displays a solid pie chart; `Sliced` draws each slice segmented. Optional. The default is `Sliced`.

`rotated="Yes|No"`
: Specifying `Yes` rotates the chart 90 degrees clockwise. This attribute is generally used to create a horizontal bar chart. Optional. The default is `No`.

`scalefrom="Integer"`
: The minimum value to place on the y-axis of the chart. Optional. The default is dependent on (but not necessarily equal to) the minimum value in the set of data points.

`scaleto="Integer"`
: The maximum value to place on the y-axis of the chart. Optional. The default is the maximum value in the set of data points.

`showborder="Yes|No"`
: Indicates whether to display a border around the chart. Optional. The default is `No`.

`showxgridlines="Yes|No"`
: Indicates whether to display gridlines along the x-axis. Optional. The default is `No`.

`showygridlines="Yes|No"`
: Indicates whether to display gridlines along the y-axis. Optional. The default is `Yes`.

`seriesplacement="Default, Cluster, Stacked, Percent"`
: Specifies the relative positioning of one data series to another for charts of the same type with more than one data series. Options are `Default` (ColdFusion determines the best placement based on the chart type), `Cluster`, `Stacked`, and `Percent`. Optional. The default is `Default`.

`show3D="Yes|No"`
: Whether to display a 3D version of the chart. Optional. The default is `No`.

`showlegend="Yes|No"`
: `Yes` displays a legend if more than one data series is charted. Optional. Default is `Yes`.

`showmarkers="Yes|No"`
: Specifying `Yes` displays markers for data points when the `type` attribute in any `cfchartseries` tags is `Curve`, `Line`, or `Scatter`, and the chart is rendered in 2D. Optional. The default is `Yes`.

`sortxaxis="Yes|No"`
: Indicates whether to sort column labels alphabetically along the x-axis. Ignored if `xaxistype="scale"`. Optional. The default is `No`.

`tipbgcolor="Hex|Web_Color_Name"`
: Specifies a background color for tip popup windows when `format="Flash"`. Colors are specified using the same rules as the `foregroundcolor` attribute. Optional. The default is `White`.

`tipstyle="MouseDown|MouseOver|None"`
: Specifies how the tip popup window that displays information about graph elements is called. `MouseDown` displays the popup when the mouse pointer is placed over a chart element and the mouse button is pressed and held (when `format="Flash"` only). `MouseOver` displays the popup when the mouse pointer moves over a chart element. `None` disables tip popup windows and works for all `format` types. Optional. The default is `MouseOver`.

`URL="`*`Url|JavaScript`*`"`
: A URL to link to or a JavaScript function to call when a data point on the chart is clicked. Additionally, the following variables are available and can be used anywhere in the URL: `$value$` (value of the data point selected), `$itemlabel$` (item label associated with the selected data point), and `$serieslabel$` (series label associated with the selected data point). Optional. Here's an example showing both a standard URL with additional parameters and a call to a JavaScript function:

```
URL="MyDrillDown.cfm?val=$value$&item=$item$&series=$series$"
URL="javascript:MyFunct('$value$','$itemlabel$','$serieslabel$');"
```

`xaxistitle="`*`Title_Text`*`"`
: Title for x-axis. Optional.

`xaxistype="category|scale"`
: Treatment of x-axis values. `category` specifies that the x-axis values should be displayed in the order in which they are coded, while `scale` tells the charting engine to display the values according to their numeric order. If `scale` is used, all x-axis values must be numeric, otherwise ColdFusion throws an error. Optional. The default is `category`. This attribute is new in ColdFusion MX 6.1.

`xoffset="`*`-1_to_1`*`"`
: Number between –1 and 1 specifying the number of units the graph should be rotated on the horizontal axis when `show3D="Yes"`. `-1` is 90 degrees left, `0` is no rotation, and `1` is 90 degrees right. Optional. The default is `.1`.

`yaxistitle="`*`Title_Text`*`"`
: Title for y-axis. Optional.

`yaxistype="category|scale"`
: Treatment of y-axis values. This attribute is currently ignored as all y-axis values must be numeric. Optional. The default is `scale`. This attribute is new in ColdFusion MX 6.1.

`yoffset="`*`-1_to_1`*`"`
: Number between –1 and 1 specifying the number of units the graph should be rotated on the vertical axis when `show3D="Yes"`. `-1` is 90 degrees left, `0` is no rotation, and `1` is 90 degrees right. Optional. The default is `.1`.

cfchartdata

New in ColdFusion MX

```
<cfchart>
  <cfchartseries>
    [<cfchartdata>]
    ...
  </cfchartseries>
  ...
</cfchart>
```

Specifies individual data points for use in a `cfchartseries`. May be used alone or in conjunction with a chart generated with query data.

Attributes

`item="text"`
: Label for the data point to be graphed. Optional. If no label is specified, the value is displayed in its place.

`value="value"`
: The data point value to be graphed. Required.

cfchartseries

New in ColdFusion MX

```
<cfchart>
  <cfchartseries>
    [<cfchartdata>]
    ...
  </cfchartseries>
  ...
</cfchart>
```

Used as a child tag of `cfchart` to specify the type of chart to draw and to define a series of data points to graph. Multiple `cfchartdata` tags may be used within a `cfchart` container to chart multiple series of data and/or to overlay multiple chart types.

Attributes

`type="chart_type"`
: Type of chart to render. Options are `Area`, `Bar`, `Cone`, `Curve`, `Cylinder`, `Line`, `Pie`, `Pyramid`, `Step`, and `Scatter`. Required.

`colorlist="color"`
: A comma-delimited list of colors to use for the data points in `Pie` charts. Color names follow the same rules as those for the `seriescolor` attribute. If there are more data points than colors specified in `colorlist`, the list is simply reused once all the options have been exhausted. Optional. If no `colorlist` is specified, ColdFusion uses a default list of colors.

`itemcolumn="query_column"`
: Name of the query column containing the label text for individual data points in the chart. Required if a value is provided for `query`.

`markerstyle="style"`
: Style for data point markers in 2D charts. Options are `Circle`, `Diamond`, `Letterx`, `Mcross`, `Rcross`, `Rectangle`, `Snow`, and `Triangle`. Optional. The default is `Rectangle`.

`paintstyle="plain|raise|shade|light"`
: Paint style to use for the series. Options are `Plain` (solid color fill), `Raise` (beveled appearance), `Shade` (gradient filling darker toward the edges), and `Light` (gradient filled lighter shade of color). Optional. The default is `Plain`.

`query="query_name"`
: Name of the query object containing data you want to chart. Optional.

seriescolor="*Hex|Web_Color_Name*"
: Color for the chart elements or the first pie slice in a pie chart. Colors may be specified by using one of the 16 available web color names: Aqua (##00FFFF), Black (##000000), Blue (##0000FF), Fuchsia (##FF00FF), Gray (##808080), Green (##008000), Lime (##00FF00), Maroon (##800000), Navy (##000080), Olive (##808000), Purple (##800080), Red (##FF0000), Silver (##C0C0C0), Teal (##008080), White (##FFFFFF), Yellow (##FFFF00); or hex code in the form ##FFFFCC. The double pound signs are necessary to keep ColdFusion from throwing an error. Optional.

serieslabel="*text*"
: Text for the series label. Optional.

valuecolumn="*query_column*"
: Name of the query column containing the values for individual data points in the chart. Required if a value is provided for query.

cfcol

```
<cftable>
  [<cfcol>]
  [<cfcol>]
  ...
</cftable>
```

Used within a cftable block to define the column header, including alignment, width, and text.

Attributes

text="*text*"
: The text to display in the column. The text attribute can contain plain text, HTML, and CFML variables. Required.

align="Left|Right|Center"
: The alignment for the header text. Valid entries are Left, Right, and Center.

header="*header_text*"
: The text to use for the column's header. Required if the cftable colheaders attribute is used.

width="*width_in_characters*"
: The width in characters for the column; a longer heading is truncated. The default width is 20 characters.

cfcollection

Updated in ColdFusion MX

```
<cfcollection>
```

Creates and manages Verity collections. The cfcollection tag provides a programmatic interface to many of the administrative functions of the ColdFusion Administrator.

Attributes

action="*action*"
: The action to perform on the specified Verity collection. Valid entries are `List` (new in ColdFusion MX), `Create`, `Repair`, `Delete`, `Optimize`, and `Map`. `Map` is no longer necessary in ColdFusion MX as the server is now capable of automatically determining whether a collection is internal or not. The `Optimize` action from previous versions of ColdFusion is no longer supported in ColdFusion MX. If `action="List"`, ColdFusion returns a query object (specified in `name`) containing the names of all of the Verity collections (both VDK and K2 Server) registered on the server. Required.

collection="*collection_name*"
: The name of the Verity collection to perform the specified `action` on. As of ColdFusion MX, collection names may contain spaces. Required.

language="*language*"
: The language to be used when creating the collection. To specify a language other than U.S. English (the default), you must download and install the appropriate Verity Language Pack for ColdFusion MX, available at *http://www.macromedia.com/go/verity/*. Optional.

name="*query_name*"
: The name to assign the query object containing the collection information when `action` is `List`. Required for this action; ignored otherwise.

path="*directory*"
: The path to a Verity collection. Required when `action` is `Create` or `Map`.

Returned Query Columns

The following values are returned when `action` is `List`:

queryname.Name
: If the collection is a registered VDK collection, returns the name of the collection registered with the ColdFusion Administrator. For K2 collections, returns the collection alias set in the *k2server.ini* file.

queryname.Path
: The absolute path to the Verity collection. If the collection is mapped or is a registered K2 server collection, returns the absolute path, including the collection name.

queryname.Language
: The locale setting used by the collection. This column is blank for K2 server collections.

queryname.External
: Returns `Yes` if the collection is external, `No` if it is not, and `Not Found` if the collection is registered but is not available at the specified path.

queryname.Mapped
: Returns `Yes` if the collection is mapped, `No` if it is not. This column is blank for K2 server collections.

queryname.Online
: Returns `Yes` if the collection is online and available for searching, `No` if it is not or if *queryname*`.External` returns `Not Found`.

queryname.Registered

Returns CF if the collection is registered with the ColdFusion Administrator or K2 if it is registered with the K2 server.

cfcomponent

New in ColdFusion MX

```
<cfcomponent>
  CFML...
  [<cfproperty>]
  ...
  [<cffunction>
  ...
  </cffunction>]
  ...
</cfcomponent>
```

Acts as a container for a ColdFusion Component (CFC). Any CFML code outside a cfproperty or cffunction container is considered a constructor and is automatically executed when the component is instantiated. Any variables set are automatically available to all methods in the component.

Besides the named attributes listed below, you can pass any additional desired attributes to the cfcomponent tag as user-defined attributes. Although these attributes don't do anything, they are available as metadata when the component is introspected using the GetMetaData( ) function. You may use any attribute names you wish with the exception of those reserved by cfcomponent: name, displayname, hint, output, path, properties, and functions.

Attributes

displayname="*display_name*"

Used to display a descriptive name for the component in ColdFusion MX's Component Browser. Optional.

extends="*component_name*"

Name of a parent component from which the component should inherit methods and properties. Optional.

hint="*text*"

Used to display a hint describing what the component does in ColdFusion MX's Component Browser. Optional.

output="Yes|No"

Indicates whether the component allows output within the "constructor" area (the area outside any cffunction tags). If Yes, expressions surrounded with pound signs are automatically evaluated without the need for cfoutput tags, and output is permitted. If No, ColdFusion suppresses any output within the constructor area of the component. Optional. If output is not specified, ColdFusion allows output within the constructor area, but all expressions must be within cfoutput tags.

cfcontent

Updated in ColdFusion MX

<cfcontent>

Sends content of the specified media type to the browser. Content may be dynamically generated by ColdFusion or come from a file. The `cfcontent` tag is often used to send files stored above the web root directory to the browser or to generate non-HTML content for other clients, such as wireless devices (cell phones, PDAs, etc.).

Attributes

`type="`*`MIME_type_and_or_charset`*`"`
: The MIME type and/or character set for the content to be sent to the browser. *`charset`* lets you specify a Java character set to use for the encoding. The most common character sets are `UTF-8` (the default), `UTF-16`, `UTF-16BE`, `UTF-16LE`, `US-ASCII`, and `ISO-8859-1`. You may use any character set supported by your JRE. If you want to specify a MIME type and a character set, delimit them with a space or a semicolon: `type="text/html; charset=utf-8"`. Required unless `file` or `reset` is specified.

`deletefile="Yes|No"`
: Whether or not to delete the file after it has been sent to the browser. Valid only if a file was specified in the `file` attribute. Optional. The default is `No`.

`file="`*`filename`*`"`
: The name of the file being sent to the browser. Required unless `type` or `reset` is specified.

`reset="Yes|No"`
: Whether or not to suppress any output preceding the call to the `cfcontent` tag. The `reset` attribute is ignored if a value is specified for `file` or `type`. The default is `Yes`.

cfcookie

Updated in ColdFusion MX 6.1

<cfcookie>

Writes a cookie to the user's browser. Due to the way ColdFusion assembles dynamic pages, you shouldn't attempt to use the `cflocation` tag within a template after a cookie variable has been set. In versions of ColdFusion prior to MX, setting a cookie variable and using `cflocation` afterward resulted in the cookie not being set. This is no longer the case in ColdFusion MX.

Attributes

`name="`*`cookie_name`*`"`
: Name of the cookie to write. Cookie names can consist of any printable ASCII characters with the exception of commas, semicolons, and whitespace characters. Required.

`value="`*`value_of_cookie`*`"`
: The value to assign the cookie. Required.

`domain="`*`domains`*`"`
: The domain for which the cookie can be read and written. Entries must always start with a dot. For example, `domain=".oreilly.com"` is a valid entry. Multiple entries may be separated by semicolons. Optional.

`expires="time_period"`
: The cookie's expiration date. May be specified as a date, number of days, `Now`, or `Never`. Optional. If no value is provided for `expires`, the cookie is set as an in-memory-session-only cookie. This means that the cookie is never written to the user's hard drive and automatically expires when the browser is closed.

`path="URLs"`
: The URLs in `domain` that the cookie applies to. Multiple entries can be separated by semicolons. Optional.

`secure="Yes|No"`
: Whether the cookie must be transmitted securely via SSL. Optional. The default is `No`.

cfdefaultcase

See `cfswitch`.

cfdirectory

Updated in ColdFusion MX

`<cfdirectory>`

The `cfdirectory` tag lists directory contents, as well as creates, renames, and deletes directories on the ColdFusion application server.

Attributes

`action="action"`
: The action to perform on the specified `directory`. Valid options are `Create`, `Delete`, `List`, and `Rename`. Required. The default value is `List`.

`directory="directory_name"`
: The name of the directory to perform the `action` on. Required.

`filter="file_extension"`
: A file extension to filter the results returned when `action` is `List`. Optional for this action; ignored otherwise. Only one file extension can be used with the `filter` attribute.

`mode="permissions"`
: Allows you to set permissions the way you would with the Unix *chmod* command. For example, setting `mode="777"` assigns read, write, and execute permissions to the directory for everyone. Optional when `action` is `Create`; ignored otherwise.

`name="query_name"`
: The name to assign the query object containing the directory listing when `action` is `List`. Required for this action; ignored otherwise.

`newdirectory="new_directory_name"`
: The name of the new directory to be created when `action` is `Rename`. Required when `action` is `Rename`; ignored otherwise.

`sort="sort_criteria"`
: How to sort each query column returned when `action` is `List`. Optional for this action; ignored otherwise. The `sort` attribute can take a single query column or a comma-

separated list. The actual direction for the sort is specified as `Asc` for ascending and `Desc` for descending.

Returned Query Columns

The following values are returned when `action` is `List`:

`queryname``.Attributes`
: The attributes, if any, for the given object.

`queryname``.DateLastModified`
: The time/date stamp that the object was last modified.

`queryname``.Mode`
: This column applies only to the Unix versions of ColdFusion and specifies the permissions set for the file or directory. The `Mode` is the same as the permissions set by the Unix *chmod* command.

`queryname``.Name`
: The name of the directory or file.

`queryname``.RecordCount`
: The total number of files and/or directories. In ColdFusion MX, `cfdirectory` no longer returns the current directory and parent directory, (`.`) and (`..`) respectively. These two directories were always present in any listing returned by the `cfdirectory` tag. Because of this, *`queryname`*`.RecordCount` would return 2 for an empty directory.

`queryname``.Size`
: The size in bytes of the directory or file.

`queryname``.Type`
: `Dir` if the object is a directory or `File` if it is a file.

---

cfdump

New as of ColdFusion 5.0; updated in ColdFusion MX and MX 6.1

`<cfdump>`

Displays the value of a variable in a color-coded DHTML-formatted table. `cfdump` is useful in debugging situations where you need to display a variable's contents, especially for arrays and structures. The `cfdump` tag can output the contents of most datatypes.

Attributes

`var="#`*`variable_name`*`#"`
: The name of the variable you want to display the value(s) for. `cfdump` is capable of recognizing simple datatypes as well as arrays, binary data, CFCs, COM objects (new in ColdFusion MX 6.1), Java objects, query objects, structures, UDFs, WDDX, and XML document objects. Note that it is necessary to surround the variable name with pound signs.

`expand="Yes|No"`
: Indicates whether to expand DHTML table views (works in most modern browsers). Optional. Default is `Yes`.

`label="`*`Label_Text`*`"`
: Specifies a header for the table created by the dump. Optional.

cfelse

See `cfif`.

cfelseif

See `cfif`.

cferror

Updated in ColdFusion MX

```
<cferror>
```

Displays a custom error page when an error occurs in a ColdFusion application. The `cferror` tag is most often included within an application's *Application.cfm* template.

Attributes

`type="Request|Exception|Validation"`
: Specifies the error type to watch for. Required. The default is `Request`, which handles all errors that occur during a page request. `Exception` handles exceptions, and `Validation` handles form validation errors that occur when a form is submitted (useful only in an *Application.cfm* template). In previous versions of ColdFusion, `cferror` supported another type, `Monitor`, which could be used to set up an exception monitor.

`template="`*`path`*`"`
: The relative path to the custom error template. Required.

  When `type` is `Exception`, any ColdFusion tags can be used in the exception-handling template. Exception handling templates may also be invoked by specifying a Site-wide Error Handler within the Server Settings section of the ColdFusion Administrator.

  When `type` is `Request`, a number of variables are available in the error-handling template (listed in "Return Variables"), but no other CFML tags can be used. These variables are also available when `type` is `Exception`.

  When `type` is `Validation`, a number of variables are available to the validation error-handling template (listed next in "Return Variables"), but no other CFML tags may be used in the template.

`exception="`*`exception_type`*`"`
: The type of exception to watch for. Required when `type` is `Exception`. Possible values are `Any` (the default), `Application`, *`CustomType`*, `Database`, `Expression`, `Lock`, `MissingInclude`, `Object`, `SearchEngine`, `Security`, and `Template`. For more details on these types, see `cftry`. ColdFusion also supports a number of additional structured exception types, as listed under `cftry`.

`mailto="`*`email_address`*`"`
: The email address of the person who should be notified if an error occurs. Optional.

Returned Variables

When type is Exception or Request, the following variables are made available to the template specified in the template attribute and can be referenced within a cfoutput block:*

error.Browser
: The browser in use when the error occurred

error.DateTime
: The date and time when the error occurred

error.Diagnostics
: A detailed error message provided by the ColdFusion server

Error.GeneratedContent
: The content generated by the template up to the point of the error

error.HTTPReferer
: The page containing the link to the template where the error occurred

error.MailTo
: The email address specified in the mailto attribute of the cferror tag

error.RemoteAddress
: Specifies the IP address of the remote client

error.QueryString
: The URL query string, if any, from the client's request

error.Template
: The page that was in the process of executing when the error occurred

If type is set to Exception, you can use the following additional variables:

error.Message
: Abbreviated error message thrown by the ColdFusion server. The detailed message is available in error.Diagnostics.

error.RootCause
: Returns a Java object containing the Java servlet exception generated by the JVM as the exception's root cause. This variable is new in ColdFusion MX.

error.TagContext
: The name and position of each tag in the tag stack as well as the full pathnames of the files containing the tags as an array of structures. Each structure in the TagContext array contains the following elements:

  type
  : Type of page generating the exception. type always returns "CFML". This key is new in ColdFusion MX.

  ID
  : The name of the tag within the stack where the exception occurred. If the exception occurs within cfscript tags, ID returns "??".

* You can use the cferror prefix instead of the error prefix if you have type set to Exception, as in cferror.Browser or cferror.Template. The cferror prefix is preferred as it matches the cferror tag name and makes identifying variable names and scopes easier. Just like error, cferror can also be referenced as a structure.

`template`
: The full path to the template containing the tag.

`line`
: The line number within the template where the tag was found.

`column`
: No longer supported in ColdFusion MX. This key is still available for backward compatibility with previous versions of ColdFusion, but it always returns 0. In previous versions of ColdFusion, `column` returned the column number within the template where the tag was found.

`raw_trace`

The raw Java stack trace for the exception. This key is new in ColdFusion MX. In versions of ColdFusion prior to MX, CFML Stack Trace must be enabled in the Debugging section of the ColdFusion Administrator in order to populate this variable. If this option isn't enabled, ColdFusion returns a zero-length array for `error.TagContext`.

`error.Type`
: The exception type thrown by the server

Additionally, you can use any `cfcatch` return variables available to the exception specified in the `exception` attribute of the `cferror` tag. These can be referenced within the `error.RootCause` object. For example, if a `Database` exception is trapped, you can reference the data source name (`cfcatch.Datasource`) as `error.RootCause.Datasource`. The `cfcatch` variables are listed under `cftry`.

When `type` is `Validation`, the following variables are available:

`error.ValidationHeader`
: Header text for the validation error page

`error.InvalidFields`
: An HTML unordered (`<ul>`) list of validation errors

`error.ValidationFooter`
: Footer text for the validation error page

`error.MailTo`
: In versions of ColdFusion prior to MX, the email address specified in the `mailto` attribute of the `cferror` tag

cfexecute

Updated in ColdFusion MX 6.1

```
<cfexecute> ... </cfexecute>
```

Executes a command-line program on the server. No HTML or CFML should appear between the start and end of the `cfexecute` tags, and `cfexecute` tags can't be nested. If for some reason an exception is thrown while attempting to execute the `cfexecute` tag, the following rules apply:

- If the application specified in the name attribute can't be found, an "Application File Not Found" exception is thrown.
- If the ColdFusion user executing the application doesn't have permission to do so, a security exception is thrown.

- If a value is specified for `outputfile`, and the file can't be opened, an "Output File Cannot Be Opened" exception is thrown.

Attributes

`name="`*`command`*`"`
: The full path to the program you want to execute. Required.

`arguments="`*`argument_string`*`"`
: Arguments to pass to the external program being called. Optional. Arguments can be either strings or arrays. On Windows platforms, a string is passed to the Windows process control subsystem for processing. On Unix and Linux systems, a string is tokenized into an array of strings, delimited by spaces. If spaces occur in the array elements, they are escaped by double quotes. On Windows platforms, the elements of an array are concatenated into a space-delimited string of tokens, which is then passed to the Windows process control subsystem for processing. On Unix and Linux systems, the elements of an array are copied into an array of `exec()` arguments.

`outputfile="`*`output_file`*`"`
: The path to an output file where any text output by the external program is written. Relative path names are relative to the ColdFusion temp directory. If `outputfile` is specified, you may not use the `variable` attribute. If both `outputfile` and `variable` are omitted, the output is returned to the browser. Optional.

`timeout="`*`seconds`*`"`
: The time in seconds that ColdFusion should wait before timing out the call to the external program. Setting the `timeout` attribute to `0` equates to a nonblocking execution mode. This causes ColdFusion to spawn a thread for the process and immediately return without waiting for the process to end. By contrast, setting the `timeout` attribute to an arbitrarily high value equates to a blocking execution mode. Optional. The default timeout is `0`.

`variable="`*`variable_name`*`"`
: Variable name used to store any output generated by the executed program. If `variable` is used, you may not use the `outputfile` attribute. If neither `variable` nor `outputfile` are specified, any output is written directly to the browser. Optional. This attribute is new in ColdFusion MX 6.1.

---

cfexit

`<cfexit>`

Aborts processing of a custom tag and returns control to the calling template or parent custom tag (in the case of nested tags). The `cfexit` tag is similar in functionality to the `cfabort` tag, except it is intended for use within custom tags. If the `cfexit` tag is used outside of a custom tag, it acts exactly like the `cfabort` tag.

Attribute

`method="`*`method`*`"`
: The method used to exit the custom tag. Each method produces different results, depending on the location of `cfexit` within the custom tag.

The default method is ExitTag, which simply halts processing of the custom tag and returns control to the calling template. If placed within a block of code where ThisTag.ExecutionMode is Start or End, processing continues after the end tag.

ExitTemplate halts processing and returns control to the calling template. If placed within a block of code where ThisTag.ExecutionMode is Start, processing continues from the first child tag of the calling tag. If ThisTag.ExecutionMode is End, processing continues after the end tag.

Loop reexecutes a block of code in the currently executing custom tag (emulating a cfloop). This method can be used only when ThisTag.ExecutionMode is End. Using it in any other location results in an error.

cffile

Updated in ColdFusion MX and MX 6.1

<cffile>

Operates on files on the ColdFusion server. The action taken depends on the action attribute. Append appends additional text to the end of a file. Copy copies a file from one location to another. Delete deletes a file from the server. Move moves a file from one location to another. Read reads a text file and stores the contents in a variable. ReadBinary reads a binary file and stores the data as a byte-array, allowing both string and array functions to be used to manipulate the data. Rename renames a file on the server. Upload uploads a file from a form submission. Write writes a text or binary file to the server.

Attributes

action="*action*"

The action to be performed by the cffile tag. Required. Possible actions are Append, Copy, Delete, Move, Read, ReadBinary, Rename, Upload, and Write.

accept="*MIME_types*"

A comma-separated list of MIME types that the ColdFusion server should be allowed to accept for upload. Optional for Upload; ignored otherwise. The default is to accept all MIME types.

addnewline="Yes|No"

If set to Yes, a newline character is added to the end of the file. Optional for Append and Write; ignored otherwise. The default is Yes.

attributes="*attributes*"

Single attribute for Windows, or comma-delimited list of attributes for other operating systems, to be applied to the file. In ColdFusion MX, valid choices are Hidden, Normal, and ReadOnly. Previous versions supported the additional attributes Archive, System, and Temporary. Optional. If no value is specified, the file's original attributes are maintained. If ReadOnly is specified along with other attributes, they are ignored.

charset="*charset*"

New in ColdFusion MX. charset lets you specify a character set for the contents of the file and can be used when the action attribute is set to Move, Read, Write or Append. The most common character sets are UTF-8 (the default), UTF-16, UTF-16BE, UTF-16LE, US-ASCII, and ISO-8859-1. You may use any character set supported by your JRE. When a text file is read using cffile, a check is performed to determine whether the first character is a byte order marker (BOM). If so, ColdFusion uses this to automatically determine the character encoding for the file. If the file contains a BOM, and a value is also specified for the `charset` attribute, ColdFusion throws an error.

`destination="`*`filename`*`"`
: The full path to the new location of the file. If a relative path is used, the location is relative to the ColdFusion temp directory. Required for `Copy`, `Move`, `Rename`, and `Upload`. On Windows servers, use the backslash (\) to denote directories. On Unix servers, use the forward slash (/).

`file="`*`filename`*`"`
: The full path to the file to be operated on. If a relative path is used, the location is relative to the ColdFusion *temp* directory. Required for `Append`, `Delete`, `Read`, `ReadBinary`, and `Write`.

`filefield="`*`form_field`*`"`
: The name of the submitted form field (without pound signs) that contains the selected file. Required for `Upload`.

`mode="`*`mode`*`"`
: Allows you to set permissions the way you would with the Unix *chmod* command. For example, setting `mode="777"` assigns read, write, and execute permissions to the directory for everyone. Optional for `Upload` and `Write`; ignored otherwise.

`nameconflict="error|makeunique|overwrite"`
: How ColdFusion should behave if the file being uploaded has the same name as a file already existing in the destination directory. Optional for `Upload`; ignored otherwise. The default is `Error`, which means that the file isn't saved to the server, and ColdFusion halts processing with an error. `MakeUnique` assigns the file a unique name and saves it to the server, `Overwrite` overwrites the existing file, and `Skip` aborts uploading of the file and returns control to the ColdFusion application without throwing an error.

`output="`*`content`*`"`
: The text to be appended to the file for `Append` or the content to store in the file for `Write`. Required for these two actions.

`source="`*`filename`*`"`
: The full path to the current location of the file. If a relative path is used, the location is relative to the ColdFusion *temp* directory. Required for `Copy`, `Move`, and `Rename`.

`variable="`*`variable_name`*`"`
: Variable where the file contents is stored. Required for `Read` and `ReadBinary`.

Returned Values

With an `Upload` action, once the `cffile` tag has executed, a number of ColdFusion variables are created to hold information about the transaction. These variables are read-only and can be referenced using the file scope, as in `cffile.`*`VariableName`*.* The following list describes all the variables available within the file scope:

* In versions prior to MX, ColdFusion supported the `file` prefix instead of `cffile`. `file` was deprecated in ColdFusion 5 and is no longer supported in ColdFusion MX. The `cffile` prefix should be used instead.

`cffile.AttemptedServerFile`
: The filename that ColdFusion first attempted to save the uploaded file as.

`cffile.ClientDirectory`
: The directory location on the client's machine where the uploaded file came from.

`cffile.ClientFile`
: The name of the file uploaded from the client's machine.

`cffile.ClientFileExt`
: The file extension of the file uploaded from the client's machine (without an initial period).

`cffile.ClientFileName`
: The filename without the extension of the file uploaded from the client's machine.

`cffile.ContentSubType`
: The media subtype of the uploaded file.

`cffile.ContentType`
: The media type of the uploaded file.

`cffile.DateLastAccessed`
: The time and date that the uploaded file was last accessed.

`cffile.FileExisted`
: `Yes` or `No` depending upon whether the uploaded file already existed.

`cffile.FileSize`
: The file size of the uploaded file.

`cffile.FileWasAppended`
: `Yes` or `No` depending upon whether the uploaded file was appended to a file already existing on the server.

`cffile.FileWasOverwritten`
: `Yes` or `No` depending upon whether a file already on the server was overwritten by the uploaded file.

`cffile.FileWasRenamed`
: `Yes` or `No` depending upon whether the uploaded file was renamed to resolve a name conflict.

`cffile.FileWasSaved`
: `Yes` or `No` depending upon whether the uploaded file was saved to the server.

`cffile.OldFileSize`
: If a file on the server was overwritten, the file size of the file that was overwritten.

`cffile.ServerDirectory`
: The directory on the server that contains the newly saved file.

`cffile.ServerFile`
: The filename (filename and extension) of the file saved on the server.

`cffile.ServerFileExt`
: The file extension (without the initial period) of the file saved on the server.

`cffile.ServerFileName`
: The filename (without the extension) of the file saved on the server.

cffile.TimeCreated
: The time the uploaded file was created.

cffile.TimeLastModified
: The time and date the uploaded file was last modified.

cfflush

New as of ColdFusion 5.0

<cfflush>

Flushes all currently available content to the client. cfflush is typically used within loops or output queries to send results back to the client in incremental chunks. The first time a cfflush tag is encountered on a page, it sends all the HTTP headers for the request along with any generated content up to the position in the template where the tag is encountered. Successive cfflush tags return any content generated since the previous flush. Once a cfflush tag has been used in a template, you can't use any other CFML tags that write to the HTTP header; doing so causes ColdFusion to throw an error because the header has already been sent to the browser. These tags include cfcontent, cfcookie, cfform, cfheader, cfhtmlhead, and cflocation. In addition, attempting to set a variable in the cookie scope with the cfset tag results in an error because cookies are passed from the server to the browser in the HTTP header.

Attribute

interval="*integer*"
: The minimum number of bytes that should be returned by the server before the output buffer is flushed. Optional.

cfform

Enhanced in ColdFusion 5.0 and ColdFusion MX

<cfform> ... </cfform>

Creates a form capable of using controls, including HTML input types such as input boxes, drop-down boxes, and radio buttons, as well as a number of specialized Java applets, such as tree, grid, and slider controls.

New in ColdFusion MX, the preservedata attribute now works with radio button and checkbox types provided the value of the control matches the value of the posted data.

Attributes

action="*form_action*"
: Location (page) where the form should be submitted upon completion. Optional.

archive="*URL*"
: Specifies the URL to a downloadable Java archive file containing Java-based cfform controls. Optional. The default URL is */CFIDE/classes/cfapplets.jar*.

class="*style_name*"
: Name of a CSS (Cascading Style Sheet) style to apply to the HTML form tag generated by cfform. Optional.

codebase="*URL*"
: Specifies the URL to a downloadable JRE plugin for MS Internet Explorer. Optional. The default URL is */CFIDE/classes/cf-j2re-win.cab*.

enablecab="Yes|No"
: No longer supported in ColdFusion MX or ColdFusion 5. Whether or not Java controls associated with other `cfform` elements should be made available to Microsoft Internet Explorer users as Microsoft cabinet files. Optional.

enablejar="Yes|No"
: Not currently supported (in the initial MX release). Optional.

enctype="*MIME_type*"
: The MIME type for data being submitted via the Post method. Optional. The default is `application/x-www-form-urlencoded`. If, however, you plan to allow file uploads via your form, you must specify `multipart/form-data`.

ID="*name*"
: Specifies a unique identifier for the form. Corresponds to the attribute of the same name in the generated HTML `form` tag. Optional.

method="Post"
: Specifies the method for sending information submitted by the form. Corresponds to the attribute of the same name in the generated HTML `form` tag. Optional. The default (and only value currently allowed) is `Post`.

name="*name*"
: A name for the form. You should specify a value for `name` if you plan to reference the form later in your application. Optional. The default is `cfform_1`.

onload="Yes|No"
: Not currently supported (in the initial MX release). Optional. The default is `No`.

onreset="*javascript_function*"
: JavaScript function to execute if a reset button is present and clicked by the user. Corresponds to the attribute of the same name in the generated HTML `form` tag. Optional.

onsubmit="*javascript_function*"
: A JavaScript function that should be executed after validation occurs but before the form is submitted. Optional.

passthrough="*HTML_attributes*"
: Any additional HTML attributes you want to specify that aren't directly supported by the `cfform` tag. Optional.

preservedata="Yes|No"
: Whether or not to retain and display data submitted from a `cfinput`, `cftextinput`, `cfslider`, or `cftree` control when a form is submitted to itself or to another page with like-named `cfform` controls. This allows you to display the data entered by the user for `cfinput` and `cftextinput` controls without any additional coding. For `cfslider` controls, the slider is set automatically to the position from the previous form post. For `cftree` controls, the tree expands automatically to the previously selected item. For `preservedata` to work with a tree control, the `completepath` attribute of the `cftree` tag must be set to `Yes`. Optional. The default is `No`.

target="*window_name*"
: The name of a frame or window where the target template specified in the action attribute should be opened. Optional.

scriptsrc="*path*"
: New in ColdFusion MX. The path to the JavaScript source file used by cfform if you store it in a location other than */wwwroot/cfide/scripts/cfform.js*. Optional.

style="*style_code*"
: Inline CSS markup to apply to the HTML form tag generated by cfform. Corresponds to the attribute of the same name in the generated HTML form tag. Optional.

---

cfftp

Updated in ColdFusion MX and MX 6.1

```
<cfftp>
```

Allows a ColdFusion program to communicate with an FTP server. The action taken depends on the action attribute. Open opens an FTP connection between the ColdFusion server and a remote FTP server, while Close closes a connection to an FTP server. The rest of the actions perform various file and directory operations. Note that file and directory names are case sensitive.

Attributes

action="*action*"
: The action to be performed by the cfftp tag. Required. Possible actions are Close, ChangeDir, CreateDir, Exists, ExistsDir, ExistsFile, GetCurrentDir, GetCurrentURL, GetFile, ListDir, Open, PutFile, Remove, RemoveDir, and Rename.

agentname="*agent_name*"
: A name for the application or entity making the FTP connection. Optional. This attribute is no longer supported in ColdFusion MX.

asciitextextensionlist="*extensions*"
: A semicolon-delimited list of file extensions that force the transfer mode to ASCII when the transfermode attribute is set to Auto. Optional. The default extension list is txt;htm;html;cfm;cfml;shtm;shtml;css;asp;asa.

attributes="*file_attributes*"
: A comma-delimited list of attributes to be applied to the file being downloaded when action is set to GetFile. Valid choices are Archive, Compressed, Directory, Hidden, Normal, ReadOnly, System, and Temporary. Optional. The default value is Normal. File attributes vary depending on the operating systems involved in the file transfer. This attribute is no longer supported in ColdFusion MX.

connection="*connection_name*"
: For Open, the name to assign a cached FTP connection so that batch operations can be performed without having to reestablish a new connection for each task. For file and directory operations, can be used to refer to an existing cached FTP session. For Close, the name of the FTP connection to close. If session variables are used to cache the connection, it is important to make sure that you lock access to the session variables during read/write via the cflock tag. Optional.

`directory="`*`directory_name`*`"`
: The directory on which to perform an FTP operation. Required when `action` is `ChangeDir`, `CreateDir`, `ExistsDir`, `ListDir`, or `RemoveDir`.

`existing="`*`file_or_directory_name`*`"`
: The current name of the file or directory being renamed on the FTP server. Required when `action` is `Rename`.

`failifexists="Yes|No"`
: Whether or not a `GetFile` action fails if a local file with the same name as the downloaded file already exists. Optional. The default is `Yes`.

`item="`*`file_or_directory_name`*`"`
: The file, directory, or object to act on when `action` is `Exists` or `Remove`. Required for these actions.

`localfile="`*`filename`*`"`
: The name of the file on the local system. Required when `action` is `GetFile` or `PutFile`.

`name="`*`query_name`*`"`
: The name of a query to hold the directory listing when `action` is `ListDir`. Required for this action.

`new="`*`file_or_directory_name`*`"`
: The new name for the file or directory being renamed on the FTP server. Required when `action` is `Rename`.

`passive="Yes|No"`
: Whether or not to use passive transfer mode. Optional. The default is `No`.

`password="`*`password`*`"`
: Password to send to the FTP server in conjunction with `username`. If none is required, convention dictates that you pass the email address of the user as the password. Required for `Open`. Also required for all file and directory operations unless using a cached connection.

`port="`*`port_number`*`"`
: Port on the FTP server that listens for incoming FTP requests. Optional. The default FTP port is 21.

`proxybypass="`*`proxy_bypass`*`"`
: A list of IP addresses or hostnames that don't need to be routed through the proxy server. Optional.

`proxyserver="`*`proxy_server`*`"`
: The IP address or hostname of a proxy server or servers if required. If this attribute is omitted, ColdFusion attempts to obtain proxy server information from the JVM startup arguments (configurable from the ColdFusion Administrator). In versions prior to MX, the registry was used in place of JVM startup arguments.

`remotefile="`*`filename`*`"`
: The name of the file on the remote FTP server. Required when `action` is `ExistsFile`, `GetFile`, or `PutFile`.

`retrycount="`*`number`*`"`
: The number of times the FTP operation should be attempted before an error is reported. Optional. The default number of retries is 1.

server="*FTP_server*"
: Hostname or IP address of the FTP server you want to connect to. Required for Open. Also required for all file and directory operations unless using a cached connection.

stoponerror="Yes|No"
: If set to Yes, ColdFusion throws an exception and halts processing if an error occurs. Optional. The default is No, which allows ColdFusion to continue processing the page after an error has occurred.

timeout="*seconds*"
: The length in seconds that an operation has to execute before the request is timed out. Optional. The default is 30.

transfermode="ASCII|Binary|Auto"
: The FTP transfer mode to use when uploading and downloading files. Possible options are ASCII, Binary, and Auto. Optional. The default value is Auto.

username="*username*"
: The username to send to the FTP server. If none is required, convention dictates that you pass "anonymous" as the username. Required for Open. Also required for all file and directory operations unless using a cached connection.

Returned Variables

When stoponerror is set to No, the cfftp tag returns three variables that contain information related to the error:

cfftp.Succeeded
: Yes if the FTP connection was closed successfully and No if it was not.

cfftp.ErrorCode
: An error number corresponding to a value in cfftp.ErrorText. If no error occurred, returns 0.

cfftp.ErrorText
: A text message describing the error.

Several of the file and directory operations performed by the cfftp tag also return a variable called cfftp.ReturnValue. The following table lists the actions that return this variable as well as a description of the returned value:

Action value	Returned value
GetCurrentDir	Current directory
GetCurrentURL	Current URL
Exists	Yes or No
ExistsDir	Yes or No
ExistsFile	Yes or No

Returned Query Columns

Query objects created by the cfftp tag when action is ListDir contain the following query columns:

queryname.Attributes
: The attributes, if any, for the given object. As of ColdFusion MX, operating system–specific attributes such as ReadOnly are no longer returned. Instead, *queryname*.Attributes returns Directory or Normal.

queryname.IsDirectory
: true if the object is a directory, false if it isn't.

queryname.LastModified
: The date that the file or directory was last modified.

queryname.Length
: The length in bytes of the file or directory.

queryname.Mode
: This column applies only to the Unix and Linux versions of ColdFusion and specifies the permissions set for the file or directory. The Mode is the same as the permissions set by the Unix *chmod* command.

queryname.Name
: The name of the file or directory.

queryname.Path
: The path without drive letter designation to the file or directory.

queryname.URL
: The URL for the file or directory.

cffunction

New in ColdFusion MX

```
[<cfcomponent>]
  <cffunction>
    [<cfargument>]
    ...
  ...
  </cffunction>
  ...
[<cfcomponent>]
```

Creates a tag-based user-defined function (UDF) or a component method for a ColdFusion Component (CFC). The terms "function" and "method" are used interchangeably.

Besides the named attributes listed in the "Attributes" section, you can pass any additional desired attributes to the cffunction tag as user-defined attributes. Although these attributes don't do anything, they are available as metadata when the component containing the method is introspected using the GetMetaData() function. You may use any attribute names you wish with the exception of those reserved by cffunction: name, displayname, hint, returntype, roles, access, output, and arguments.

Attributes

name="*Name*"
: Name for the function. Function names follow the same naming rules as ColdFusion variables. They must begin with a letter, underscore, or Unicode currency symbol ($) and can contain only letters, numbers, underscores, and Unicode currency symbols.

Compound variable names such as My.Function are not allowed. Function names also may not begin with cf, cf_, coldfusion, or coldfusion_. Additionally, you may not give a function the same name as a built-in ColdFusion function. Required.

access="Private|Package|Public|Remote"
: Used only when function is used as a component method. Specifies the context within which the component method can be accessed. Options are:

  Private
  : Method only available to the component that declares it.

  Package
  : Method available to the component that declares it as well as any other component in the same package.

  Public
  : Method available to a locally executing page or other component on the server.

  Remote
  : Method available to locally executing pages, to other components on the server, via URL invocation, via form post invocation, via Flash Remoting, or as a web service. This access type is required in order to publish the method as a web service. Optional.The default is Public.

displayname="*display_name*"
: Used to display a descriptive name for the method in ColdFusion MX's Component Browser. Optional.

hint="*text*"
: Used to display a hint describing what the method is for in ColdFusion MX's Component Browser. Optional.

output="Yes|No"
: If Yes, contents of the method body are processed as if surrounded by cfoutput tags. If No, method body is processed as if surrounded by cfsilent tags. Optional. If output is omitted, contents of the method body are processed as regular CFML. This attribute is generally used only when the function is called as a component method.

returntype="*Return_Type*"
: The datatype for the data returned by the function/method. Options are Any, Array, Binary, Boolean, Date, GUID, Numeric, Query, String, Struct, UUID, VariableName, Void (doesn't return a value), and *ComponentName* (for a custom return type). Required when component method is callable as a web service; optional otherwise.

roles="*Roles*"
: Used only when function is used as a component method. Comma-delimited list of roles defined in the ColdFusion security framework that is authorized to invoke the component method. Optional. If roles is not specified, the method is accessible by anyone.

cfgraph

New as of ColdFusion 5.0; deprecated in ColdFusion MX; see cfchart

```
<cfgraph>
  [<cfgraphdata>]
  ...
</cfgraph>
```

Draws a bar, horizontal bar, line, or pie chart from query and/or static data. The `cfgraph` tag uses Macromedia Generator and JRun, both installed when you install ColdFusion, to handle the graphing. Because the `cfgraph` tag can graph only numeric data, you must convert any date, time, and formatted numeric data to integers or real numbers. The `cfgraph` tag can render graphs in Flash, PNG, and JPEG formats. Although you can adjust the size of the graph, the `cfgraph` tag currently maintains a height/width aspect ratio of 3: 4. Changing one aspect without changing the other accordingly can result in an excess border around your graph. It should be noted that the `cfgraph` tag isn't supported when running ColdFusion on Windows 95/98. This tag has been replaced by `cfchart`, `cfchartseries`, and `cfchartdata` in ColdFusion MX. It is still functional for backward compatibility; however, it may not function exactly as it did in ColdFusion 5. It is recommended you port your `cfgraph/cfgraphdata` code to `cfchart`.

Attributes

`type="Bar|HorizontalBar|Line|Pie"`
: The type of graph to create. Required.

`backgroundcolor="`*`color`*`"`
: Background color for the graph. Colors may be specified by name or hex code in the form `bgcolor="##FFFFCC"`. The double pound signs are necessary to keep ColdFusion from throwing an error. Optional. The default is `White`.

`barspacing="`*`spacing_in_pixels`*`"`
: Spacing in pixels between bars in a `Bar` or `HorizontalBar` chart. Optional. The default is `0` (no spacing).

`bordercolor="`*`color`*`"`
: Color for the border if a border is present. Colors are specified using the same rules as the `backgroundcolor` attribute. Optional. The default color is `Black`.

`borderwidth="`*`width_in_pixels`*`"`
: Thickness of the border in pixels. To specify no border, use `0`; the default is `1`. Optional.

`colorlist="`*`color`*`"`
: A comma-delimited list of colors to use for the data points in `Bar`, `HorizontalBar`, and `Pie` charts. Color names follow the same rules as in the `backgroundcolor` attribute. If there are more data points than colors specified in `colorlist`, the list is simply reused once all the options have been exhausted. Optional. If no `colorlist` is specified, ColdFusion uses a default list of colors.

`depth="`*`depth_in_pixels`*`"`
: Depth of the graph in pixels. Specifying a depth gives the graph a three-dimensional look. Optional. The default is `0` (i.e., not three-dimensional).

`fileformat="Flash|PNG|JPG"`
: The file type to use when displaying the graph. Optional. The default is `Flash`.

`fill="Yes|No"`
: Whether or not to fill the area below the line in a `Line` graph with the same color used for the line, effectively creating an area graph. Optional. The default is `No`.

`graphheight="`*`height_in_pixels`*`"`
: Height in pixels for the graph. Optional. The default is `240`.

graphwidth="*width_in_pixels*"
: Width in pixels for the graph. Optional. The default is 320.

gridlines="*integer*"
: Number of grid lines to display between the top and bottom lines on a Bar, HorizontalBar, or Line chart. When grid lines are displayed, a corresponding value is displayed alongside the line. Optional. The default is 0.

itemcolumn="*query_column*"
: The name of a query column containing item labels that correspond to the data points from the query column specified in valuecolumn. For Bar and Line charts, item labels are displayed on the horizontal axis. For HorizontalBar charts, the labels appear on the vertical axis. Pie charts display item labels in an optional legend. Optional.

itemlabelfont="Arial|Courier|Times"
: The font to use for the item labels on Bar, HorizontalBar, and Line charts. Optional. The default is Arial.

itemlabelorientation="Horizontal|Vertical"
: Whether item labels should be displayed horizontally or vertically. Valid only if item labels are displayed. Optional. For Bar and Line charts, the default is Vertical. For HorizontalBar charts, the default is Horizontal.

itemlabelsize="*integer*"
: The font size to use for the item labels for Bar, HorizontalBar, and Pie charts. Optional. The default is 12.

legendfont="Arial|Courier|Times"
: The font to use for items displayed in the legend. Optional. The default is Arial.

linecolor="*color*"
: Color used to draw the line in a Line graph. Colors are specified using the same rules as the backgroundcolor attribute. Optional. The default color is Blue.

linewidth="*width_in_pixels*"
: The width in pixels of the line in a Line graph. Optional. The default is 1.

query="*query_name*"
: The name of an available query containing the data you want to graph. Required if no cfgraphdata tags are specified.

scalefrom="*integer*"
: The minimum value to place on the value axis of the graph (vertical axis for Bar and Line charts, horizontal axis for HorizontalBar charts). Optional. The default is 0.

scaleto="*integer*"
: The maximum value to place on the value axis of the graph (vertical axis for Bar and Line charts, horizontal axis for HorizontalBar charts). Optional. The default is the maximum value in the set of data points.

showitemlabel="Yes|No"
: Whether or not to display item labels on Bar, HorizontalBar, and Line charts. For Line and Bar charts, the item labels are displayed along the horizontal axis. For HorizontalBar charts, they are displayed along the vertical axis. Optional. The default is Yes.

`showlegend="Above|Below|Left|Right|None"`
: The position of the legend associated with a `Pie` chart. Choices are `Above` (horizontal layout centered above the chart), `Below` (horizontal layout centered below the chart), `Left` (vertical layout to the left of the chart), `Right` (vertical layout to the right of the chart), and `None`. Optional. The default is `Left`.

`showvaluelabel="Yes|No|Rollover"`
: Whether or not to display the value associated with each data point for `Bar`, `HorizontalBar`, and `Pie` charts. `Rollover` works only when `fileformat` is `Flash` and indicates that the value be displayed when the user moves her mouse over the data point. Optional. The default it `No`.

`title="`*`text`*`"`
: The title to display for the graph. The title is displayed centered above the graph unless a legend is present above the graph, in which case the title is displayed centered and below the graph. Optional.

`titlefont="Arial|Courier|Times"`
: The font to use for the graph title. Optional. The default is `Arial`.

`URL="`*`URL`*`"`
: A URL to link to when a data point on the chart is clicked. `URL` is valid only for `Bar`, `HorizonatalBar`, and `Pie` charts, and only when `fileformat` is `Flash`. `URL` is typically used in conjunction with the `urlcolumn` attribute, to pass a value associated with a data point to another page for processing. For example, a typical value for `URL` might look like one of the following:

```
URL="MyPage.cfm?MyVar="
URL="http://www.example.com/graph.cfm?MyVar="
```

The actual value assigned to the URL variable you create is populated by the `urlcolumn` attribute. Optional.

`urlcolumn="`*`query_column`*`"`
: Query column containing a value to append to the URL specified in `URL`. The `urlcolumn` attribute lets you build dynamic drill-down capabilities into your graphs by providing a way to pass a value associated with a particular data point as a URL parameter to another template for processing. Query columns whose values contain spaces and other special characters are automatically URL-encoded before being appended to the URL string. `urlcolumn` is valid only when `fileformat` is set to `Flash`. Optional.

`valuecolumn="`*`query_column`*`"`
: The name of the query column containing the data you want to graph. `cfgraph` can be used only to graph numeric data. Required if no `cfgraphdata` tags are specified.

`valuelabelfont="Arial|Courier|Times"`
: The font to use for the value labels for `Bar`, `HorizontalBar`, and `Pie` charts. Optional. The default is `Arial`.

`valuelabelsize="`*`integer`*`"`
: The font size to use for the value labels for `Bar`, `HorizontalBar`, and `Pie` charts. Optional. The default is `12`.

valuelocation="OnBar|OverBar|Inside|Outside"

Indicates where values should be placed on a Bar, HorizontalBar, and Pie chart. For a Bar or HorizontalBar chart, options are OnBar (the default), indicating that values should be displayed on the bar itself, or OverBar, indicating that values should be displayed over the bar. For Pie charts, options are Inside (the default), indicating that values display inside each segment of the pie chart, or Outside, indicating that they display outside the slice of the pie. Optional.

cfgraphdata

New as of ColdFusion 5.0; deprecated in ColdFusion MX; see cfchart, cfchartseries, and cfchartdata

```
<cfgraph>
  [<cfgraphdata>]
  ...
</cfgraph>
```

Used as a child tag of cfgraph to define a single data point to graph. cfgraphdata tags may be used alone within a cfgraph tag block or in combination with data from a query. This tag has been replaced by cfchart, cfchartseries, and cfchartdata in ColdFusion MX. It is still functional for backward compatibility; however, it may not function exactly as it did in ColdFusion 5. It is recommended you port your cfgraph/cfgraphdata code to cfchart.

Attributes

value="*data_point_value*"

The data point value to be graphed. Required.

color="*color*"

Color associated with the data point. Colors may be specified by name or hex code in the form color="##FFFFCC". The double pound signs keep ColdFusion from throwing an error. Optional. By default, the cfgraphdata tag takes the color for the data point from the colorlist attribute specified in the cfgraph tag. If no colorlist is present, cfgraphdata uses a color from ColdFusion's default list of colors.

item="*data_point_label*"

Label for the data point to be graphed. Optional.

URL="*URL*"

A URL (including any relevant URL parameters) to link to when a data point on the chart is clicked. URL is valid only for Bar, HorizonatalBar, and Pie charts, and only when the fileformat attribute of the cfgraph tag is Flash. Optional.

cfgrid

Updated in ColdFusion MX

```
<cfform>
  <cfgrid>
    [<cfgridcolumn>]
    [<cfgridrow>]
    ...
  </cfgrid>
  ...
</cfform>
```

Provides a Java-based grid control for displaying and editing tabular data. Used within a cfform block.

Attributes

name="*name*"
: The form-field name for the grid control. Required.

align="*alignment*"
: Alignment for the grid control. Valid entries are Left, Right, Top, TextTop, Bottom, AbsBottom, Baseline, Middle, and AbsMiddle. Optional.

appendkey="Yes|No"
: Whether or not to pass the cfgridkey variable along with the value of the selected grid item in the URL to the template specified in the cfform tag. Optional. The default is Yes.

autowidth="Yes|No"
: Whether or not the grid should adjust the width of each column automatically so that all columns appear within the grid without having to scroll horizontally. Optional. The default is No. New as of ColdFusion 5.0.

bgcolor="*color*"
: Background color for the grid control. For color choices, see the textcolor attribute. Optional. The default is White.

bold="Yes|No"
: If Yes, displays all grid data in bold. Optional. The default is No.

colheaders="Yes|No"
: Whether or not to display column headers on the grid. Optional. The default is Yes.

colheaderalign="*alignment*"
: Alignment for the column headers. Valid entries are Left, Right, and Center. Optional. The default is Left.

colheaderbold="Yes|No"
: Whether or not to display the column header text in bold. Optional. The default is No.

colheaderfont="*font_name*"
: The font to use for the column headers. Optional.

colheaderfontsize="*integer*"
: The font size to use for the column headers. Optional.

colheaderitalic="Yes|No"
: Whether or not to display the column header text in italic. Optional. The default is No.

colheadertextcolor="*color*"
: The text color for column headers in the grid. For color choices, see the textcolor attribute. Optional. The default is Black. New as of ColdFusion 5.0.

colheaderwidth="*width_in_pixels*"
: The width in pixels of the column header. Optional.

delete="Yes|No"
: Whether or not to allow users to delete data from the grid. Optional. The default is No.

deletebutton="*text*"
: The text to use on the delete button. Optional. The default is Delete.

`font="font_name"`
: The font name used for all data in the grid. Optional.

`fontsize="integer"`
: The font size for all data in the grid. Optional.

`griddataalign="alignment"`
: Alignment for the grid data. Valid entries are `Left`, `Right`, and `Center`. Optional. The default is `Left`.

`gridlines="Yes|No"`
: Whether or not to add row and column lines to the grid. Optional. The default is `Yes`.

`height="height_in_pixels"`
: Height in pixels for the grid's display area. Optional.

`highlighthref="Yes|No"`
: Whether or not to highlight links associated with the grid control and defined within the `href` attribute. Optional. The default is `Yes`.

`href="URL"`
: A URL to associate with the grid item or the name of a query column containing `href` values. The URL may be relative or absolute. Optional.

`hrefkey="column_name"`
: The name of a query column to use as the `Key` when a query is used to populate the grid. Optional.

`hspace="horizontal_spacing_in_pixels"`
: Width in pixels for the padding to the left and right of the grid. Optional.

`insert="Yes|No"`
: Whether or not to allow users to insert new data into the grid. Optional. The default is `No`.

`insertbutton="text"`
: The text to use on the insert button. Optional. The default is `Insert`.

`italic="Yes|No"`
: If `Yes`, displays all grid data in italic. Optional. The default is `No`.

`onerror="function_name"`
: The name of a JavaScript function that should be executed if validation fails for any reason. Optional.

`onvalidate="javascript_function"`
: A JavaScript validation function that should be executed before the form is submitted. Optional.

`maxrows="integer"`
: Maximum number of rows to display in the grid. Optional.

`notsupported="text_message"`
: A text message to display if the user's browser doesn't support Java or Java is disabled. Optional. If no message is specified, ColdFusion displays a default message.

`picturebar="Yes|No"`
: `Yes` displays images for the `Insert`, `Delete`, and `Sort` buttons, while `No` displays text buttons. Optional. The default is `No`.

`query="query_name"`
: The name of a query to associate with the grid control. Optional.

`rowheaderbold="Yes|No"`
: Whether or not to display the row header text in bold. Optional. The default is `No`.

`rowheaderalign="alignment"`
: Alignment for the row headers. Valid entries are `Left`, `Right`, and `Center`. Optional. The default is `Left`.

`rowheaderfont="font_name"`
: The font to use for the row headers. Optional.

`rowheaderfontsize="integer"`
: The font size to use for the row headers. Optional.

`rowheaderitalic="Yes|No"`
: Whether or not to display the row header text in italic. Optional. The default is `No`.

`rowheadertextcolor="color"`
: The text color for row headers in the grid. For color choices, see the `textcolor` attribute. Optional. The default is `Black`. New as of ColdFusion Version 5.0.

`rowheaders="Yes|No"`
: Whether or not to display row headers on the grid. Optional. The default is `Yes`.

`rowheaderwidth="width_in_pixels"`
: The width in pixels of the row header. Optional. This attribute is ignored in ColdFusion MX.

`rowheight="height_in_pixels"`
: The number of pixels for the minimum row height of the grid control. Optional.

`selectcolor="color"`
: The background color for an item that has been selected. For color choices, see the `bgcolor` attribute. Optional.

`selectmode="mode"`
: The selection mode to use for items in the grid. Optional. The default value is `Browse`, which allows browsing of data only. `Edit` allows editing of data, `Single` confines selections to a single cell, `Column` causes a selection to automatically include the entire column, and `Row` causes a selection to automatically include the entire row.

`sort="Yes|No"`
: Whether or not to allow users to sort data in the grid using a simple text sort. Optional. The default is `No`.

`sortascendingbutton="text"`
: The text to use on the ascending sort button. Optional. The default is "A → Z".

`sortdescendingbutton="text"`
: The text to use on the descending sort button. Optional. The default is "Z → A".

`target="URL_target"`
: The name of a frame or window that the template specified in the `href` attribute should be opened in. Optional.

`textcolor="color|expression"`
: The text color for all data in the grid. Colors may be specified by name (`Black`, `Blue`, `Cyan`, `Darkgray`, `Gray`, `Lightgray`, `Magenta`, `Orange`, `Pink`, `Red`, `White`, `Yellow`) or hex code

in the form `textcolor="##FFFFCC"`. The double pound signs are necessary to keep ColdFusion from throwing a syntax error, or you may omit the pound signs altogether. By using the appropriate hex code, you may specify colors that can't be specified by name. Optional. The default is `Black`. New as of ColdFusion 5.0.

`vspace="`*`vertical_spacing_in_pixels`*`"`
: Height in pixels for the padding above and below the grid control. Optional.

`width="`*`width_in_pixels`*`"`
: Width in pixels for the grid's display area. Optional.

Returned Variables

Depending on the value of `selectmode`, the `cfgrid` tag returns several variables on submission. For `Browse`, no variables are returned. When `selectmode` is `Edit`, three one-dimensional arrays are returned containing information about the changes to the data:

`form.`*`gridname.columnname[RowIndex]`*
: The new value of an edited grid cell

`form.`*`gridname`*`.original.`*`columnname[RowIndex]`*
: The original value of the edited grid cell

`form.`*`gridname.RowStatus.Action[RowIndex]`*
: The type of edit made to the grid cell: `I` for insert, `U` for update, and `D` for delete

When `selectmode` is `Single`, there is one variable:

`form.`*`gridname.selectedname`*
: The value of the selected cell from the grid

When `selectmode` is `Column`, grid data is returned as a comma-delimited list of values for the selected column.

When `selectmode` is `Row`, there is one variable:

`form.`*`gridname.columnname`*
: The column data for the selected row

cfgridcolumn

Updated in ColdFusion MX

```
<cfgrid>
  [<cfgridcolumn>]
  [<cfgridrow>]
  ...
</cfgrid>
```

Specifies individual column data and formatting information within a `cfgrid`. Values specified for a `cfgridcolumn` override any attributes set in the `cfgrid` tag.

Attributes

`name="`*`column_name`*`"`
: A name for the grid column. If the grid column is populated by a query, `name` must be the name of an available query column. Required.

`bgcolor="color|expression"`
: A background color for all the cells in the column or an expression that returns a color based on its evaluation. For color choices, see the `textcolor` attribute. `bgcolor` also supports the expression syntax listed for `textcolor`. Optional. The default is `White`. New as of ColdFusion 5.0.

`bold="Yes|No"`
: Whether or not to display the column data in bold. Optional. The default is `No`.

`dataalign="alignment"`
: Alignment for the column data. Valid entries are `Left`, `Right`, and `Center`. Optional. The default is `Left`.

`display="Yes|No"`
: Whether or not to display the column in the grid. Optional. The default is `Yes`.

`font="font_name"`
: The font name for the data in the column. Optional.

`fontsize="integer"`
: The font size for the data in the column. Optional.

`header="header"`
: The text to use for the column's header. Optional. If no value for `header` is specified, ColdFusion uses the same value as `name`.

`headeralign="alignment"`
: Alignment for the column headers. Valid entries are `Left`, `Right`, and `Center`. Optional. The default is `Left`.

`headerbold="Yes|No"`
: Whether or not to display the column header text in bold. Optional. The default is `No`.

`headerfont="font_name"`
: The font to use for the column headers. Optional.

`headerfontsize="integer"`
: The font size to use for the column headers. Optional.

`headeritalic="Yes|No"`
: Whether or not to display the column header text in italic. Optional. The default is `No`.

`headertextcolor="color"`
: Specifies the text color for the column header. For color choices, see the `textcolor` attribute. The default is `Black`.

`href="URL"`
: A URL to associate with the grid item. The URL may be relative or absolute. Optional.

`hrefkey="column_name"`
: The name of a query column to use as the `Key` when a query is used to populate the grid. Optional.

`italic="Yes|No"`
: Whether or not to display the column data in italic. Optional. The default is `No`.

`numberformat="format"`
: A mask to use for formatting numeric column data. For valid options, see the `NumberFormat()` function in the Appendix B. Optional.

select="Yes|No"

Whether or not to allow users to select column data to be edited. select is ignored when the selectmode attribute of the cfgrid tag is set to Row or Browse. Optional. The default is Yes. New in ColdFusion MX, if select is No, the cell cannot be edited, regardless of the value specified for cfgrid selectmode.

target="*URL_target*"

The name of a frame or window that the template specified in the href attribute should be opened in. Optional.

textcolor="*color|expression*"

The text color for all data in the grid. Colors may be specified by name (Black, Blue, Cyan, Darkgray, Gray, Lightgray, Magenta, Orange, Pink, Red, White, Yellow) or hex code in the form textcolor="##FFFFCC". The double pound signs are necessary to keep ColdFusion from throwing a syntax error, or you may omit the pound signs altogether. By using the appropriate hex code, you may specify colors that can't be specified by name. Optional. The default is Black. New as of ColdFusion 5.0.

You can dynamically specify the text color for a cell based on its value or that of another column in the same row using a special expression as the value of textcolor. The expression uses the following format:

```
( CX|Cn gt|lt|eq string ? color_true : color_false )
```

CX represents the current column, while C*n* specifies a specific column where *n* is the index position of the column (only displayed columns are available). The operator can be gt, lt, or eq for both string and numeric comparisons. The ? separates the expression from the values you wish to return. *color_true* is the color to return in the event the expression evaluates true, while *color_false* is the color to return if the expression evaluates false. Colors are specified using a color name or hex code (without the pound signs). The two return values are separated with a colon. Note that whitespace is ignored within the expression except for within *string*.

For example, to specify that text in a certain column of data be blue if the value of the data is greater than 21 and black if it isn't, you can use the following code:

```
textcolor="(CX gt 21 ? blue : black)"
```

Likewise, if the first column of data in your grid contains department names, and you want to highlight the names of employees (in gray) in another column who are part of the marketing department, you can code it like this:

```
textcolor="(C1 eq Marketing ? C0C0C0 : 000000)"
```

type="*type*"

The type of column data to display. Valid entries are Image, Numeric, String_ NoCase, and Boolean. Optional.

Image

Specifies an image corresponding to the column value to display. You may specify a path to your own image or use one of the images supplied with ColdFusion by referencing the image name. Valid options are CD, Computer, Document, Element, Folder, Floppy, Fixed, and Remote. If the image is larger than the cell it is being displayed in, the image is automatically cropped to fit within the cell.

Numeric

Allows data in the grid to be sorted by the user as numeric data rather than as text.

`String_NoCase`
: Allows data in the grid to be sorted by the user as case-insensitive text rather than the case-sensitive default.

`Boolean`
: Places a checkbox in the grid column. Useful in situations where you want to represent Boolean data in a grid column. If the grid column containing the checkbox is editable, the checkbox may be checked and unchecked; otherwise it is read-only. New as of ColdFusion 5.0.

`values="`*`list|range`*`|Off"`
: Creates a drop-down box of values for each cell in the grid column. You may specify a delimited list of values, a range of numeric values, or `Off`. For a delimited list of values, the default delimiter is the comma. To specify a range of numeric values, use the format *`n-m`* where *`n`* is the minimum value in the range, and *`m`* is the maximum value. Optional. The default is `Off`. New as of ColdFusion 5.0.

`valuesdelimiter="`*`delimiter`*`"`
: An optional delimiter that separates items in the `values` and `valuesdisplay` attributes. Optional. The default is the comma (,). New as of ColdFusion 5.0.

`valuesdisplay="`*`list|range`*`|Off"`
: Used in conjunction with the `values` attribute. `valuesdisplay` allows you to provide a delimited list or range of values to display in lieu of the values in the `values` attribute. This works like the HTML `select` control in that it allows you to display one set of values in the drop-down box while associating them with different values behind the scenes. Optional. The default is `Off`. New as of ColdFusion 5.0.

`width="`*`width_in_pixels`*`"`
: The width of the column in pixels. Optional. The default column width is determined by the longest column value.

cfgridrow

```
<cfgrid>
  [<cfgridcolumn>]
  [<cfgridrow>]
  ...
</cfgrid>
```

Populates a `cfgrid` row with data when a query is not used to populate the grid.

Attribute

`data="`*`col1, col2, ... coln`*`"`
: A comma-delimited list of column values. Required.

cfgridupdate

Updated in ColdFusion MX

```
<cfgridupdate>
```

Updates records in a database using values passed from a `cfgrid` control.

Attributes

grid="*grid_name*"

Name of the grid control containing the data to be updated. Required.

datasource="*data_source_name*"

The name of the data source to connect to when performing the update. Required.

connectstring="*connection_string*"

Passes additional connection information to an ODBC data source that can't be passed via the ColdFusion Administrator. `connectstring` can also override connection information set for a data source already registered in the ColdFusion Administrator. When making a dynamic data source connection (when `dbtype` is `Dynamic`), `connectstring` specifies all the information required to connect to the data source. For specific connection-string options, you should consult the documentation for your particular database. New as of ColdFusion 5.0. This attribute is no longer supported in ColdFusion MX.

dbname="*database_name*"

The database name. For the Sybase System 11 native driver and SQLOLEDB provider only. Optional. Overrides any value set for `datasource`. This attribute is no longer supported in ColdFusion MX.

dbserver="*database_server*"

The name of the database server to connect to when using native drivers. Specifying a `dbserver` overrides any value set for `datasource`. Optional. This attribute is no longer supported in ColdFusion MX.

dbtype="*database_type*"

The type of database driver to use. Optional. This attribute is no longer supported in ColdFusion MX. Possible choices are:

`ODBC` *(the default)*

Connect to the data source using an ODBC driver.

`OLEDB`

Make the connection using an OLEDB driver.

`Oracle73`

Connect using the Oracle 7.3 native driver. This requires the 7.3.4.0.0 or later client libraries be installed on the ColdFusion server.

`Oracle80`

Connect using the Oracle 8 native driver. This requires the 8.0 or later client libraries be installed on the ColdFusion server.

`Sybase11`

Connect using the Sybase 11 native driver. This requires the 11.1.1 or later client libraries be installed on the ColdFusion server.

`DB2`

Connect using the DB2 5.2 native driver.

`Informix73`

Connect using the Informix 7.3 native driver. This requires the Informix SDK 2.5 or later or Informix-Connect 2.5 (or later) for Windows.

`Dynamic`

Allows ColdFusion to make an ODBC connection to a data source without having to have the data source registered in the ColdFusion Administrator. When making a dynamic connection, all information normally provided in the ColdFusion Administrator for the connection must be specified in the `connectstring` attribute. New as of ColdFusion 5.0.

`keyonly=Yes|No"`
: If `Yes`, the `WHERE` clause of the SQL update contains only the key values. If `No`, the `WHERE` clause contains the original values of any changed grid cells as well as the key values. Optional. The default is `Yes`.

`password="`*`password`*`"`
: Password associated with `username`. Optional. If a password is specified, it overrides the value set in the ColdFusion Administrator.

`provider="`*`COM_provider`*`"`
: COM provider for OLE DB connections. Optional. This attribute is no longer supported in ColdFusion MX.

`providerdsn="`*`data_source`*`"`
: COM provider's data-source name for OLE DB. Optional. This attribute is no longer supported in ColdFusion MX.

`tablename="`*`table_name`*`"`
: The name of the table to insert the data into. Required. Note that Oracle database drivers require the table name to be in all uppercase. In addition, Sybase database drivers use a case-sensitive table name.

`tableowner="`*`table_owner`*`"`
: The name of the table owner for databases that support this feature (e.g., Oracle, SQL Server, and SQL Anywhere). Optional.

`tablequalifier="`*`qualifier`*`"`
: The table qualifier for databases that support the feature (e.g., Oracle and SQL Server). Optional.

`username="`*`username`*`"`
: Username to pass to the data source if one is required. Optional. If a username is specified, it overrides the value set in the ColdFusion Administrator.

cfheader

Updated in ColdFusion MX 6.1

`<cfheader>`

Generates a custom HTTP header that contains either a custom name/value pair or an HTTP status code and optional text message. Only one name/value pair or status code can be specified per `cfheader` tag. Name/value attributes can't be mixed with status code attributes within the same `cfheader` tag. Multiple `cfheader` tags can be used to set multiple header values as long as they are declared separately. Note that `cfheader` can't be used on the same page as the `cfflush` tag.

Attributes

name="*header_name*"

The name of the header element. Required when using the cfheader tag to pass a name/value pair. If name="Content-Disposition", the header's value is encoded using the default file encoding. This allows the name of the file to contain characters encoded using the same character encoding as the file.

statuscode="*status_code*"

The HTTP status code to pass in the HTTP header. Required when using the cfheader tag to pass status code information.

statustext="*status_text*"

A text message to accompany an HTTP status code. The statustext attribute can be used only in conjunction with the statuscode attribute. Optional.

value="*header_value*"

The value of the header element. Required when using the cfheader tag to pass a name/value pair.

cfhtmlhead

```
<cfhtmlhead>
```

Writes output within the head section of a dynamically generated HTML page. cfhtmlhead is useful for dynamically including JavaScript and other code within the head tags at runtime.

Attribute

text="*text*"

The text to add inside of the HTML <head>...</head> tags. Required.

cfhttp

Updated in ColdFusion MX and MX 6.1

```
<cfhttp>
  [<cfhttpparam>]
  ...
</cfhttp>
```

Makes an HTTP or HTTPS request and manages any resulting server response.

Attributes

method="*http_method*"

Specifies the method for the HTTP operation. Required. The default is Get. Options are:

Delete

Requests that the target server delete the resource specified in the URL attribute. This option is new in ColdFusion MX 6.1.

Get

Retrieves the information from the target server specified in the URL attribute.

`Head`
: `Head` is identical to `Get` except that no message body is sent in the response from the server. This method is often used to test the validity of hyperlinks. This option is new in ColdFusion MX 6.1.

`Options`
: Sends a request for information about the communication options available to the server specified in `URL` without requiring additional action from the server. This option is new in ColdFusion MX 6.1.

`Post`
: Sends information to the target server identified in the `URL` attribute. Information to be sent is set using one or more `cfhttpparam` tags.

`Put`
: Sends information to the target server identified in the `URL` attribute for storage. The `Put` method is most often used to send files to the server. `Put` differs from `Post` in that put specifies a location where data should be stored whereas `Post` specifies a resource that should handle posted data. This option is new in ColdFusion MX 6.1.

`Trace`
: Useful for testing HTTP operations, `Trace` instructs the server specified in the `URL` attribute to loop-back (echo) the original request header back to the server that made the request. `Trace` requests may not contain a message body. This option is new in ColdFusion MX 6.1.

`URL="`*`URL`*`"`
: The full URL of the remote web page to Get or Post to. If you are trying to resolve a URL that doesn't end in a filename (such as *http://www.myserver.com*), and you set the `resolveurl` attribute to `Yes`, you need to supply a trailing forward slash (*http://www.myserver.com/*) for this attribute in order for certain URLs (such as those in IMG tags) to resolve properly. Additionally, a port number may be appended to the URL. (*http://www.myserver.com:8080/*). If a port number is appended to the URL, it overrides any value set with the `port` attribute. Required.

`charset="`*`character_set`*`"`
: A Java character set for the file or URL the `cfhttp` tag is getting or posting. The most common character sets are `UTF-8` , `UTF-16`, `UTF-16BE`, `UTF-16LE`, `US-ASCII`, and `ISO-8859-1`. You may use any character set supported by your JRE. Optional. The default is `UTF-8`. This attribute is new in ColdFusion MX.

`columns="`*`query_columns`*`"`
: A comma-delimited list of column names if they are different from the column names listed in the first row of data from the retrieved file.

`delimiter="`*`delimiter`*`"`
: The delimiter to use when using `cfhttp` to create a query. Valid entries are a comma (`,`) or a tab. Required if creating a query. The default delimiter is a comma.

`file="`*`filename`*`"`
: The filename to use when saving the retrieved file. Required when `method="Post"` if `path` is specified. Defaults to the filename in the URL when `method="Get"`.

`firstrowasheaders="Yes|No"`

Specifies how ColdFusion should treat the first row of data when `method` is set to `Get` and `cfhttp` is used to retrieve a text file containing delimited data. If set to `Yes`, and `columns` is not specified, the first row of data is treated as column headers. If set to `Yes`, and `columns` is specified, this attribute is ignored. If `No`, and `columns` is not specified, the first row of the text file is treated as data, and column names are automatically generated using the convention `column_1`, `column_2`, ..., `column_n`.* If `No`, and `columns` is specified, ColdFusion uses the values specified in `columns` as the column headers and treats the first row in the text file as data. Optional. The default is `Yes`.

`getasbinary="Yes|No|Auto"`

Indicates whether to convert the response body returned by a `cfhttp` operation to the ColdFusion binary data type. If `Yes`, ColdFusion converts the response body to the binary data type. If `No`, a response body not recognized by ColdFusion as text is automatically converted to a ColdFusion object. If `Auto`, a response body not recognized as text is automatically converted to the binary data type. ColdFusion recognizes any response body as text that meets one or more of the following criteria: the header doesn't specify a content type, the content type starts with "text" or "message", or the content type is set as "application/octet-stream". Optional. The default is `No`.

`multipart="Yes|No"`

If `Yes`, ColdFusion sends all form field data (set using the `cfhttpparam` tag) as non-URL-encoded multipart form data (`Content-Type=multipart/form-data`). Additionally, the request's charset is sent along in each Content-Type description, and each form field must be encoded using the same `charset`. If `No`, form field data is sent as `Content-Type=application/x-www-form-urlencoded` unless file type data is also included, in which case all parts are sent using `Content-Type=multipart/form-data`. Optional. The default is `No`.

`name="`*`query_name`*`"`

Name of the query to be returned if one is created from a retrieved file. Optional.

`password="`*`password`*`"`

A password when one is required by the remote server. Optional.

`path="`*`path`*`"`

The path to a directory where the retrieved file should be saved. Optional.

`port="`*`port_number`*`"`

Port number on the remote server where the file being retrieved resides. If used in conjunction with the `resolveurl` attribute, the port number is automatically appended to all resolved URLs. The `port` attribute is ignored if a port is specified in the `URL` attribute. Optional. The default is `80`.

`proxypassword="`*`password`*`"`

A password, if any, required by the proxy server. Optional. This attribute is new in ColdFusion MX 6.1.

* Due to a bug in the initial release of ColdFusion MX, specifying `firstrowasheaders="No"` and omitting the `columns` attribute causes ColdFusion to treat the first row of data in the text file as column headers (just as if the attribute was set to `Yes`). This issue has been fixed in ColdFusion MX 6.1.

proxyport="*port_number*"
: A port number on the proxy server. Optional. The default is 80.

proxyserver="proxy_server"
: The hostname or IP address of a proxy server that cfhttp must pass through. Optional.

proxyuser="*username*"
: A username, if any, required by the proxy server. Optional. This attribute is new in ColdFusion MX 6.1.

redirect="Yes|No"
: Whether or not to allow a cfhttp request to be automatically redirected. If set to No, the cfhttp request fails upon encountering a redirect. If the throwonerror attribute is set to Yes, an error code and message are written to the cfhttp.Status_Code return variable. You can see where a request would have been redirected by referencing the location key in the cfhttp.ResponseHeader structure. The cfhttp tag can follow up to four (five in versions of ColdFusion prior to MX) redirections per request. If the limit is exceeded, ColdFusion treats the next redirect as if the redirect attribute is set to No. Optional. The default is Yes.

resolveurl="Yes|No"
: Yes causes any partial or relative URLs embedded in the retrieved document to be fully resolved, so that all links in the document remain valid. Optional. The default is No.

textqualifier="*character*"
: The character used to mark the beginning and end of a column. Optional. The default is the double quotation mark (escaped equivalent is textqualifier="""").

throwonerror="Yes|No"
: Whether or not to throw an exception that can be caught using a cftry/cfcatch block if an error occurs. Optional. The default is No.

timeout="*seconds*"
: A timeout in seconds for the cfhttp operation. If a timeout parameter is set using the cfsetting tag in conjunction with the template employing the cfhttp tag, and the timeout attribute of the cfhttp tag is used, ColdFusion uses the lesser of the two values. If, however, no cfsetting timeout value is used, the timeout attribute isn't used, and no default timeout value is set in the ColdFusion Administrator, ColdFusion will wait indefinitely for the cfhttp tag to process. This can have serious performance consequences, as each instance of the cfhttp tag being processed requires a thread of its own. Depending on your server and ColdFusion configuration, the potential to hang the server exists if the cfhttp tag utilizes all available threads on the system. Optional. In ColdFusion MX, the timeout attribute is not functional with versions of the SUN JDK prior to version 1.4.0.

useragent="*user_agent*"
: The user agent to pass in the HTTP request header when cfhttp makes a request to a remote web server. The default user agent is determined by the underlying JRE. For example, the Sun JDK 1.3.1_03, reports "Java1.3.1_03" as the user agent. In versions of ColdFusion prior to MX, the default user agent is "ColdFusion." Optional.

username="*username*"
: A username when one is required by the remote server. Optional.

Returned Variables

All cfhttp operations return a structure called cfhttp that contains information returned by the target server. Depending on the HTTP operation performed (as defined by the method attribute) as well as the response returned by the target server, the cfhttp structure may or may not contain values for the following keys:

cfhttp.charset
: Character encoding specified by the response Content-Type header.

cfhttp.errorDetail
: In the event of a connection failure, contains details related to the failure. If no failure occurs, this key contains an empty string.

cfhttp.FileContent
: Contains the response body resulting from an HTTP operation. If the response is saved as a file, cfhttp.fileContent is blank.

cfhttp.header
: A string that contains the complete HTTP header in raw form. Contains the same information as cfhttp.responseHeader.

cfhttp.mimeType
: MIME type of the response as specified by the Content-Type header.

cfhttp.responseHeader
: A ColdFusion structure that contains the names and values from the HTTP response header. If a particular key appears only once in the header, it is stored as a simple value within the structure. If a key appears more than once, it is stored as an array within the structure. In ColdFusion MX 6.0, keys that appeared more than once in the response header were stored as a structure within the cfhttp.responseHeader structure. This is important to note for backward compatibility.

cfhttp.statusCode
: Returns the HTTP status code and associated message relating to the status of the HTTP operation.

cfhttp.text
: Boolean indicating whether the response body Content-Type is text. For a list of the rules used to determine whether the response body is text, see the getasbinary attribute.

If the throwonerror attribute is set to Yes, ColdFusion returns a variable that contains status information about the cfhttp operation:

cfhttp.Status_Code
: Returns the HTTP status code and associated message relating to the status of the cfhttp operation.

cfhttpparam

Updated in ColdFusion MX and MX 6.1

```
<cfhttp>
  [<cfhttpparam>]
  ...
</cfhttp>
```

Used as a child tag of the cfhttp tag to send data with an HTTP request. Multiple cfhttpparam tags may be used to send multiple values in most cases. At least one cfhttpparam tag is required when method is Post. The cfhttpparam tag is optional for all other HTTP operations.

Attributes

name="*name*"
: The name of the parameter to pass. Required when type is CGI, Cookie, Formfield, Header, and URL. Ignored when type is Body or XML. When type is File, name specifies the filename to be sent in the request.

type="*type*"
: The parameter type to pass. Options are:

  Body
  : Body of an HTTP request. Only one cfhttpparam tag with type="Body" can be used per cfhttp request. Additionally, no other cfhttpparam tags with a type of File, Formfield, or XML may be used in the same request when type="Body". Body cannot be used when the method attribute of cfhttp is set to Trace. This option is new in ColdFusion MX 6.1.

  CGI
  : Sends a variable as a URL encoded HTTP header.

  Cookie
  : Cookie data to send as an HTTP header. The value is automatically URL encoded.

  File
  : Sends the contents of the specified file without URL encoding. File may only be used when the cfhttp method attribute is set to Post or Put.

  Formfield
  : Form field to send. By default, ColdFusion URL encodes the form field value. Formfield is only used when the method attribute of cfhttp is set to Get or Post.

  Header
  : Sends a non-URL-encoded HTTP header. This option is new in ColdFusion MX 6.1.

  URL
  : Appends a URL parameter to the query string on the URL specified in the URL attribute of the cfhttp tag. The query string is URL encoded.

  XML
  : Sets a Content-Type header of "text/xml" for the request. Automatically sets the body of the request to the XML specified in the value attribute. The XML data is not URL encoded. Only one cfhttpparam tag with type="XML" can be used per cfhttp request. Additionally, no other cfhttpparam tags with a type of Body, File, or Formfield may be used in the same request when type="XML". XML cannot be used when the method attribute of cfhttp is set to Trace. This option is new in ColdFusion MX.

file="*filename*"
: The name (including path) of the file to post. Required when type is File.

value="*value*"

The value being sent. Required for all value of type except File. Passed values must be strings or convertible to strings by ColdFusion for all types except Body. Body type data may be either string or binary data.

encoded="Yes|No"

Indicates whether to URL encode form field and/or header data. Optional when type="Formfield" or type="File", ignored otherwise. The default is Yes.

mimetype="*MIME_type[and_charset]*"

Applies only when type="File". The MIME type, and optionally, character set for the file. charset lets you specify a character set to use for the encoding. The most common character sets are UTF-8, UTF-16, UTF-16BE, UTF-16LE, US-ASCII, and ISO-8859-1. You may use any character set supported by your JRE. If you want to specify a MIME type and a character set, delimit them with a space or a semicolon: (e.g., type="text/html; charset=utf-8"). Optional when type="File", ignored otherwise.

cfif

```
<cfif expression>
   HTML and CFML
[<cfelseif expression>]
   HTML and CFML
[<cfelse>]
   HTML and CFML
</cfif>
```

Performs if-then-else processing of expressions. cfif/cfelseif/cfelse statements can be nested, and multiple cfelseif statements may be used within a single cfif block. cfif statements can contain more than one expression to evaluate, as in:

```
<cfif IsDefined('MyVar') and MyVar is "a">
```

Compound cfif statements that contain multiple expressions separated by operators, such as and and or, are processed using short-circuit Boolean evaluation. This means that ColdFusion stops processing the cfif statement once an expression evaluates to true. Consider using cfswitch when you have many cases, as it is generally faster than cfif.

cfimpersonate

No longer supported in ColdFusion MX

```
<cfimpersonate> ... </cfimpersonate>
```

Allows you to impersonate a user within a security context previously set up within the ColdFusion Administrator.

Attributes

securitycontext="*security_context*"

The name of the security context to authenticate the user within. Required. Security contexts are defined in the ColdFusion Administrator.

username="*username*"

The name of the user you want to impersonate for authentication. Required.

`password="password"`
: The password of the user you want to impersonate. Required.

`type="CF|OS"`
: The type of impersonation to use. `CF` specifies impersonation at the application level; `OS` specifies impersonation at the operating system, where the user specified is a valid user on the system. OS is available only with the Windows NT version of ColdFusion. The operating system user being impersonated must be assigned the user right to "Logon as a Batch Job". While `OS` impersonation processes faster than `CF` impersonation, it is limited in the types of resources the operating system can grant or deny access to. Required.

cfimport

New in ColdFusion MX

`<cfimport>`

Imports custom tags, adaptive custom tags, and JSP tag libraries for use in a template.

Attributes

`taglib="taglib_location"`
: For JSP tag libraries, the URL to the JAR file containing the tags or to the tag library descriptor file (*.tld*) if it is not already included in the JAR file. For custom and adaptive custom tags, the path to the directory containing the tags. Required.

`prefix="namespace"`
: Prefix to use for referring to imported tags. You refer to an imported tag using the syntax *<prefix:tagname>*. If a blank prefix ("") is specified or the `prefix` attribute is omitted altogether, the tag is referred to using only its name *<tagname>*. This allows you to perform server-side preprocessing, creating what are known as adaptive tags that replace existing HTML tags with custom functionality. Optional.

cfinclude

`<cfinclude>`

Embeds a reference to another template within the current ColdFusion template.

Attributes

`template="template_name"`
: Path to the template to be included. The path must be relative to the current directory or mapped in the ColdFusion Administrator. Required.

cfindex

Updated in ColdFusion MX

`<cfindex>`

Creates an index to use with ColdFusion's embedded Verity search engine.

Attributes

`action="`*`action`*`"`

Specifies the action for the `cfindex` tag to take. Optional. The default value is `Update`, which updates the index of the specified collection and adds the key if it doesn't already exist. `Delete` deletes the key from the specified collection, Purge purges the specified collection of data and leaves it ready to be repopulated with new data, and `Refresh` clears the specified collection of all data and then repopulates it with new data. `Optimize` optimizes the specified collection. Optimize is no longer supported by `cfindex` in ColdFusion MX. Use the `cfcollection` tag instead to optimize a collection.

`body="`*`body`*`"`

The actual text to index or a comma-delimited list of query column names containing text to index. Required when `type` is `Custom`; Ignored otherwise.

`collection="`*`collection_name`*`"`

The name of the Verity collection to perform the action on. If the collection being indexed is external, you must specify the full path to the collection. In ColdFusion MX, collection names can now contain spaces. Required.

`custom1="`*`custom_value`*`"`

Custom field that can store additional data for the collection. Optional.

`custom2="`*`custom_value`*`"`

Custom field that can store additional data for the collection. Optional.

`extensions="`*`file_extensions`*`"`

A comma-delimited list of file extensions to use when `type` is set to `Path`. The default is `"HTM, HTML, CFM, CFML, DBM, DBML"`. An asterisk (*) may be used as a wildcard such that `extensions="*."` returns all files with no extensions. Optional.

`external="Yes|No"`

Whether or not the Verity collection specified in `collection` was created with a version of Verity other than the one bundled with ColdFusion. Optional. The default is `No`. This option is no longer used in ColdFusion MX as ColdFusion is now capable of automatically detecting whether a collection is internal or external.

`key="`*`ID`*`"`

A unique identifier for each record in the index. Optional. An entry for `key` should specify one of the following: the document filename when `type` is `File`, the full path when `type` is `Path`, or a unique identifier such as the table's primary key column when `type` is `Custom`.

`language="`*`language`*`"`

The language to be used when indexing the collection. To specify a language other than U.S. English (the default), you must download and install the appropriate Verity Language Pack for ColdFusion MX, available at *http://www.macromedia.com/go/verity/*. Optional.

`query="`*`query_name`*`"`

The name of the query object containing the data being indexed. Optional.

`recurse="Yes|No"`

Whether or not the directories below the path specified in `key` should be included in the indexing process. Optional when `type` is `Path`; ignored otherwise.

title="*title*"
: The column name containing the title for each individual record being indexed. Required when type is Custom.

type="*type*"
: The type of index to create. Optional. Custom indexes the contents of a ColdFusion query, File indexes a specific file, and Path indexes all files in the specified path with extensions specified in extensions.

urlpath="*URL*"
: The base URL path to be used when type is File or Directory. The value specified in urlpath is automatically prepended to the URL variable returned by a cfsearch operation. Optional.

---

cfinput

Enhanced in ColdFusion 5.0; updated in ColdFusion MX and MX 6.1

```
<cfform>
  <cfinput>
  ...
</cfform>
```

Creates text and password input controls, as well as checkboxes and radio buttons, within a cfform.

New in ColdFusion MX, if the preservedata attribute of the cfform tag is set to Yes, radio button and checkbox types are checked provided the value of the control matches the value of the posted data.

Attributes

name="*name*"
: The form-field name for the input control. Required.

checked="Yes|No"
: Whether or not a checkbox or radio button input control should be checked. Optional. The default is No.

maxlength="*integer*"
: The maximum number of characters to accept for a Password or Text input control. Optional.

message="*validation_message*"
: Text to appear if validation fails. Optional.

onerror="*function_name*"
: The name of a JavaScript function that should be executed if validation fails for any reason. Optional.

onvalidate="*javascript_function*"
: A JavaScript validation function that should be executed before the form is submitted. Specifying a value for onvalidate overrides any values set in the validate attribute. Optional.

passthrough="*HTML_attribute*"
: Any additional HTML attributes you need to pass that aren't directly supported by the cfinput tag. Optional.

`pattern="javascript_regular_expression"`
: JavaScript regular expression that matches form input when `validate` is `Regular_Expression`. `pattern` may contain ColdFusion variables and expressions as they are evaluated prior to the execution of the regular expression. Optional. New as of ColdFusion 5.0.

`range="min_value, max_value"`
: A range of acceptable numeric values for the form-field. Optional.

`required="Yes|No"`
: Whether or not the input control requires a value before being submitted. Optional. The default is `No`.

`size="integer"`
: The size of the input control. Optional. Ignored when `type` is Checkbox or `Radio`.

`type="type"`
: Type of input control to create. Valid entries are `Checkbox`, `Password`, `Radio`, and `Text`. Optional. The default value is `Text`.

`validate="data_type"`
: Validates the contents of the form-field before it is submitted, using one of the following criteria:

  `CreditCard`
  : Validates the form-field data using the mod10 algorithm. A credit-card number can be entered as a single value or with dashes or spaces and must be between 12 and 16 digits in length. ColdFusion automatically strips dashes and spaces before validating.

  `Date`
  : Requires the form-field value to be in the U.S. date format, *mm/dd/yyyy*.

  `EuroDate`
  : Requires the form-field value to be in the European date format, *dd/mm/yyyy*.

  `Float`
  : Requires the form-field value to be a floating-point number.

  `Integer`
  : Requires the form-field value to be an integer.

  `Social_Security_Number`
  : Requires the form-field value to be a U.S. social-security number in the format *xxx-xx-xxxx* or *xxx xx xxxx*.

  `Telephone`
  : Requires the form-field value to be a U.S. telephone number formatted either *xxx-xxx-xxxx* or *xxx xxx xxxx*. The area code and exchange are required to begin with a number in the range 1–9.

  `Time`
  : Requires that the form-field value be entered as a valid time using the format *hh:mm:ss*.

  `ZipCode`
  : Requires that the form-field value be entered as either a five- or nine-digit U.S. ZIP code number using the format *xxxxx*, *xxxxx-xxxx*, or *xxxxx xxxx*.

`Regular_Expression`
: Validates the form-field data against a JavaScript regular expression specified in the `pattern` attribute.

`value="`*`initial_value`*`"`
: The initial value for the input control. Optional.

cfinsert

Updated in ColdFusion MX

```
<cfinsert>
```

Inserts new records into a data source. The `cfinsert` tag provides a way to insert data into a data source without having to wrap the SQL in a `cfquery`.

Attributes

`datasource="`*`datasource_name`*`"`
: The name of the data source to connect to when performing the insert. Required.

`connectstring="`*`connection_string`*`"`
: Passes additional connection information to an ODBC data source that can't be passed via the ColdFusion Administrator. `connectstring` can also be used to override connection information set for a data source already registered in the ColdFusion Administrator. When making a dynamic data source connection (when `dbtype` is `Dynamic`), `connectstring` specifies all the information required to connect to the data source. For specific connection string options, you should consult the documentation for your particular database. New as of ColdFusion 5.0. This attribute is no longer supported in ColdFusion MX.

`dbname="`*`database_name`*`"`
: The database name. For the Sybase System 11 native driver and SQLOLEDB provider only. Optional. Overrides any value set for `datasource`. This attribute is no longer supported in ColdFusion MX.

`dbserver="`*`database_server`*`"`
: The name of the database server to connect to when using native drivers. Specifying a `dbserver` overrides any value set for `datasource`. Optional. This attribute is no longer supported in ColdFusion MX.

`dbtype="`*`database_type`*`"`
: The type of database driver to use. Optional. This attribute is no longer supported in ColdFusion MX. Possible choices are:

  `ODBC` *(the default)*
  : Connect to the data source using an ODBC driver.

  `OLEDB`
  : Connect using an OLEDB driver.

  `Oracle73`
  : Connect using the Oracle 7.3 native driver. This requires the 7.3.4.0.0 or later client libraries be installed on the ColdFusion server.

  `Oracle80`
  : Connect using the Oracle 8 native driver. This requires the 8.0 or later client libraries be installed on the ColdFusion server.

`Sybase11`
: Connect using the Sybase 11 native driver. This requires the 11.1.1 or later client libraries be installed on the ColdFusion server.

`DB2`
: Connect using the DB2 5.2 native driver.

`Informix73`
: Connect using the Informix 7.3 native driver. This requires the Informix SDK 2.5 or later or Informix-Connect 2.5 (or later) for Windows.

`Dynamic`
: Allows ColdFusion to make an ODBC connection to a data source without having to have the data source registered in the ColdFusion Administrator. When making a dynamic connection, all information normally provided in the ColdFusion Administrator for the connection must be specified in the `connectstring` attribute. New as of ColdFusion 5.0.

`formfields="`*`formfield1, formfield2, ...`*`"`
: A comma-delimited list of form fields to insert. Optional. If no form fields are supplied, ColdFusion uses all the form fields passed from the form.

`password="`*`password`*`"`
: Password associated with `username`. Optional. If a password is specified, it overrides the value set in the ColdFusion Administrator.

`provider="`*`COM_provider`*`"`
: COM provider for OLE DB connections. Optional. This attribute is no longer supported in ColdFusion MX.

`providerdsn="`*`provider_datasource`*`"`
: COM provider's data source name for OLE DB. Optional. This attribute is no longer supported in ColdFusion MX.

`tablename="`*`table_name`*`"`
: The name of the table to insert the data into. Required. Note that Oracle database drivers require the table name to be in all uppercase. In addition, Sybase database drivers use a case-sensitive table name.

`tableowner="`*`table_owner`*`"`
: The name of the table owner for databases that support this feature (e.g., Oracle, SQL Server, and SQL Anywhere). Optional.

`tablequalifier="`*`table_qualifier`*`"`
: The table qualifier for databases that support the feature (e.g., Oracle and SQL Server). Optional.

`username="`*`username`*`"`
: Username to pass to the data source if one is required. Optional. If a username is specified, it overrides the value set in the ColdFusion Administrator.

cfinternaldebug

No longer supported as of ColdFusion MX

```
<cfinternaldebug>
```

This undocumented tag is used by the product development group at Macromedia for internal debugging purposes. The tag can also compile ColdFusion templates without executing them. The CFML Syntax Checker that comes with ColdFusion 4.x uses this tag.

Attributes

`action="action"`
: Specifies the action for the tag to take. Optional. The default action is Break, which forces a break-point exception in the execution of a template. Leak causes the ColdFusion server to leak memory. The amount of memory to be leaked is specified in the `leaksize` attribute. These two actions are used by the Macromedia product development group for internal debugging. PCode compiles the ColdFusion template specified in `templatepath` into p-code without executing it.

`leaksize="integer"`
: The amount of memory to leak. Must be a value greater than 1. Required when `action` is `Leak`.

`outvar="variable"`
: The name of the variable that holds any error messages generated when compiling a template. If no errors are generated, an empty string is saved to the variable. Required when `action` is `PCode`.

`templatepath="path"`
: Full path including filename of the ColdFusion template you want to compile. Required when `action` is `PCode`.

cfinvoke

New in ColdFusion MX; updated in ColdFusion MX 6.1

```
<cfinvoke>
  [<cfinvokeargument>]
  ...
</cfinvoke>
```

Instantiates a ColdFusion Component (CFC) or SOAP-based web service, and/or invokes a method on an instantiated CFC or web service. Arguments can be passed to a component or web service's invoked method via the `attributecollection` attribute, `cfinvokeargument` tag, or as an attribute of the `cfinvoke` tag. If more than one passed argument has the same name, ColdFusion uses the aforementioned order of precedence.

Attributes

`component="component_name"`
: Name of the component (CFC) to instantiate or invoke a component method on. Required when invoking a component method on a CFC.

`webservice="url_to_wsdl|registered_name"`
: Absolute URL to the web services WSDL file or the name of the web service as registered in the ColdFusion Administrator. Required when invoking a method on a web service.

`method="method_name"`
: Name of the method in the CFC or web service you want to invoke. Required.

argumentcollection="*structure*"
: The name of a ColdFusion structure containing argument names as keys and their associated values. Optional. If an argument is passed to the cfinvoke tag using more than one technique, the order of precedence is cfinvokeargument, cfinvoke (inline), and finally argumentcollection.

password="*password*"
: Password for accessing the web service specified in the webservice attribute. Overrides the value (if any) set in the ColdFusion Administrator under the web services section. Optional.

proxypassword="*password*"
: A password, if any, required by the proxy server. Optional. This attribute is new in ColdFusion MX 6.1.

proxyport="*port*"
: A port number on the proxy server specified in the proxyserver attribute. Optional. This attribute is new in ColdFusion MX 6.1.

proxyserver="*proxy_server*"
: The IP address or hostname of a proxy server or servers if required for connecting to a web service. If this attribute is omitted, ColdFusion attempts to obtain proxy server information from the JVM startup arguments (configurable from the ColdFusion Administrator). This attribute is new in ColdFusion MX 6.1.

proxyuser="*username*"
: A username, if any, required by the proxy server. Optional. This attribute is new in ColdFusion MX 6.1.

returnvariable="*var_name*"
: Variable name to hold the results of the method call to the CFC or web service invocation. Optional.

timeout="*seconds*"
: Amount of time in seconds ColdFusion should wait for a web service request to complete. Optional. This attribute is new in ColdFusion MX 6.1.

username="*username*"
: Username for accessing the web service specified in the webservice attribute. Overrides the value (if any) set in the ColdFusion Administrator under the web services section. Optional.

cfinvokeargument

New in ColdFusion MX

```
<cfinvoke>
  [<cfinvokeargument>]
  ...
</cfinvoke>
```

Passes a name/value pair as an argument to a ColdFusion Component (CFC) method or web service. Used as a child tag of cfinvoke.

Attributes

`name="argument_name"`
: Name of the argument to pass. Required.

`value="argument_value"`
: Value of the argument. Required.

cfldap

Updated in ColdFusion MX

<cfldap>

Provides ColdFusion with an interface to Lightweight Directory Access Protocol (LDAP) servers.

Attributes

`server="ldap_server"`
: The server name or IP address of the LDAP server you want to connect to. Required.

`action="action"`
: Specifies the LDAP action to perform. Optional. The default value is `Query`, which returns entry information from the LDAP server and requires the `attributes`, `name`, and `start` attributes. `Add` adds entries to the LDAP server and requires the `attributes` attribute. `Delete` deletes entries from the LDAP server and requires the `dn` attribute. `Modify` modifies entries on the LDAP server except for the distinguished name and requires the `attributes` and `dn` attributes. `ModifyDN` modifies distinguished name entries on the LDAP server and requires the `attributes` and `dn` attributes.

`attributes="attribute1, attribute2, ..."`
: When `action` is `Query`, specifies a comma-delimited list of attributes to be returned by the query. Specifying a wildcard (*) returns all attributes associated with a query. When `action` is `Add`, specifies the list of update columns to be used when adding an entry. When `action` is `Modify`, specifies the list of update columns to be used when modifying an entry. When `action` is `ModifyDN`, specifies a comma-delimited list of attributes to be passed to the LDAP server without any syntax checking. In all cases, multiple attributes should be separated with a semicolon (;). Required for all these actions.

`delimiter="delimiter"`
: The delimiter to use when separating more than one name/value attribute pair when multiple attributes are specified in `attributes`. `delimiter` can be used when the `action` attribute is set to `Query`, `Add`, or `Modify`. Optional. The default is the semicolon (;).

`dn="distinguished_name"`
: The distinguished name to use for updates to the LDAP server. Required when `action` is `Add`, `Delete`, `Modify`, or `ModifyDN`.

`filter="filter"`
: The search criteria to use when `action` is set to `Query`. `filter` entries are referenced as (*attribute operator value*) as in (`c=US`). Optional. The default is (`objectclass=*`). ColdFusion supports the following operators within the `filter` attribute: `=`, `~=` (approximately equals), `<=`, `>=`, `*` (wildcard), `&` (and), `|` (or), and `!` (NOT).

`filterfile="filename, stanza"`
: The name of a valid LDAP filter file and the stanza tag within that filter file that contains an LDAP filter string. The `filterfile` attribute accepts either the full path to the filter file or simply the filename provided it resides in the default ColdFusion LDAP directory (*c:\cfusion\ldap*). No longer supported in ColdFusion MX.

`maxrows="integer"`
: The maximum number of results to be returned for an LDAP query. Optional.

`modifytype="Add|Replace|Delete"`
: Whether to add, replace, or delete an attribute or set of attributes within a multivalue list of attributes. Optional. The default is `Replace`.

`name="query_name"`
: The name to assign to the LDAP query. Required when `action` is `Query`. ColdFusion MX validates the name provided for the query.

`password="password"`
: Password to accompany `username`. Optional.

`port="port_number"`
: The port that the LDAP server listens for requests on. Optional. The default LDAP port is 389.

`rebind="Yes|No"`
: Whether or not to attempt to rebind the referral callback and reissue the query using the original credentials. If `No`, referrals bindings are anonymous. Optional. The default is `No`.

`referral="number"`
: The maximum number of hops allowed in a referral. Any positive integer may be used. If `referral` is set to `0`, no data is returned for entries that are referrals. Optional.

`scope="scope"`
: The scope of the search in relation to the value specified in `start`. Optional when `action` is `Query`. The default value is `OneLevel`, which searches one level below the entry specified in the `start` attribute. `Base` searches just the entry specified in `start`, and `Subtree` searches the entry specified in `start` and all the entries below it.

`secure="cf_security_type_ID[, additional_fields]"`
: The type of security to use when authenticating with the LDAP server. Possible options are `cfssl_basic` and `cfssl_client_auth`. Both options require additional parameters as follows:

  `cfssl_basic`
  : Uses V2 SSL to provide encryption and server authentication. The `username` and `password` attributes are required when using `cfssl_basic` security. Setting this attribute tells ColdFusion to make a secure LDAP connection via SSL v2 using JSSE (Java Secure Socket Extension). In versions of ColdFusion prior to MX, a second attribute called *`certificate_database`* was used to pass the full path, including the filename of the certificate database file to use. For more information on configuring your server to take advantage of this feature, see the ColdFusion documentation that came with your server.

`cfssl_client_auth`
: Uses V3 SSL to provide encryption, server authentication, and certificate-based client authentication. No `username` and `password` attributes are required as authentication is handled via client certificates. The correct syntax for using `cfssl_client_auth` is:

  secure="cfssl_client_auth, *certificate_database, certificate_ name, key_database, key_password*"

  certificate_database is the full path, including the filename of the certificate database file to use. *certificate_name* specifies the name of the client certificate to use. *key_database* specifies the keyword database file that holds the public/private key pair. *key_password* is the password used by the keyword database.

separator="*separator*"
: The delimiter to use when separating attribute values in multivalue attributes. The `separator` is used when the `action` attribute is set to `Query`, `Add`, or `Modify`, as well as for outputting multivalue attributes. Optional. The default is the comma (,).

sort="*attributes*"
: The attribute or comma-delimited list of attributes to use when sorting query results. Optional.

sortcontrol="Nocase|asc|desc"
: Specifies how results should be sorted. If you wish to perform a case-insensitive sort, `sortcontrol` should be set to `Nocase`. Additionally, sort order may be specified as `Asc` (ascending, the default) or `Desc` (descending). Case sensitivity and sort order may be combined as in `sortcontrol="Nocase, Asc"`. Optional. Sorting is case-sensitive by default.

start="*distinguished_name*"
: The distinguished name to use as the start of a search. Required when `action` is `Query`.

startrow="*row_number*"
: The row to begin outputting LDAP entries from. Optional.

timeout="*seconds*"
: The maximum amount of time in seconds ColdFusion should wait when processing an LDAP action. Optional. The default is `60`.

username="*username*"
: Username required for the LDAP connection. Optional. If no username is specified, the LDAP connection is anonymous.

Returned Variables

If the `action` attribute is set to `Query`, the `cfldap` tag returns the following variables:

queryname.ColumnList
: Comma-delimited list of the query column names from the database

queryname.CurrentRow
: The current row of the query that is being processed by `cfoutput`

queryname.RecordCount
: The total number of records returned by the query

cflocation

<cflocation>

Redirects the user's browser to a new location. Due to the way ColdFusion assembles dynamic pages, you shouldn't attempt to use the `cflocation` tag within a template after a cookie variable has been set. Setting a cookie variable and using `cflocation` afterward results in the cookie not being set. If you need to redirect to a different template after setting a cookie, consider using the `cfheader` tag instead, as in:

```
<cfcookie name="MyCookie" value="Hey, look at me!">
<cfheader name="Refresh" value="0; URL=http://www.example.com/mytemplate.cfm">
```

Or:

```
<cfheader name="Location" value="mytemplate.cfm">
<cfheader statuscode="302" statustext="Document Moved">
```

Attributes

`URL="`*`URL`*`"`
: The URL to redirect the user's browser to. Required.

`addtoken="Yes|No"`
: Whether or not to append client variable information to the end of the URL specified in the `URL` attribute. In order to use the `addtoken` attribute, `clientmanagement` must be turned on in the *Application.cfm* file. Optional. The default is `Yes`.

cflock

Updated in ColdFusion MX

```
<cflock>
  CFML and HTML to be locked
</cflock>
```

Provides single-threaded access to code within the `<cflock>...</cflock>` tags. `cflock` should be used when reading and writing persistent variables (application, session, and server variables) within your ColdFusion applications, to eliminate the potential for unintentionally overwriting or sharing data. `cflock` can also lock access to non thread-safe CFX tags and to file-manipulation operations that can result in multiple threads attempting to access an already open file.

In ColdFusion 5.0, additional locking options are available via the ColdFusion Administrator under the Server section. They are, however, no longer available in ColdFusion MX. These options allow you to determine how ColdFusion treats locking for all applications across the server. Performance can be significantly affected depending on the options you choose. The following choices are available:

Single-Threaded Sessions (Session Scope)
: ColdFusion single-threads access to each session by session ID for the duration of a request. While this eliminates all potential variable corruption and conflict within a session, it can have a dramatic effect on performance.

No Automatic Checking or Locking (Session, Application, and Server Scope)
: ColdFusion performs no automatic checking or locking of persistent variables. All variables must be locked explicitly using the `cflock` tag. No exceptions are thrown

when nonlocked variables are encountered. This method is how ColdFusion handled locking prior to Version 4.5. This option offers the best overall performance.

Full Checking (Session, Application, and Server Scope)
: ColdFusion checks to make sure locks are placed around all reads/writes of the variable type specified. If an unlocked variable is encountered, an exception is thrown. This option is useful in debug mode for locating unlocked persistent variables and should be used with care as it can have a negative impact on performance.

Automatic Read Checking (Session, Application, and Server Scope)
: If this option is checked, ColdFusion automatically locks reading of the variable scope specified. All writes to the variable scope must be explicitly locked using `cflock`. If a write occurs to an unlocked variable, an exception is thrown. This option should also be used with careful planning as it can have a negative impact on performance.

Attributes

`name="`*`lock_name`*`"`
: The name to associate with a particular instance of `cflock`. If no `name` is specified, ColdFusion assigns a random name to the lock. In order to ensure synchronization across sessions and applications using locks, `session.SessionID` and `application.ApplicationName` should be used for the `name` attribute when locking access to session and application variables, respectively. If a value is supplied for the `scope` attribute, `name` can't be used. Optional.

`scope="Application|Server|Session"`
: The scope of the variable you are attempting to lock access to. If a value is supplied for the `name` attribute, `scope` can't be used. Optional.

`throwontimeout="Yes|No"`
: How ColdFusion should behave in the event that a `cflock` request times out. If set to `Yes`, and a timeout occurs, ColdFusion throws an error that can be caught with `cftry/CATCH`. If `No`, the template continues execution after skipping the code within the `cflock` tag. Optional. The default is `Yes`.

`timeout="seconds"`
: The time in seconds that ColdFusion should wait when attempting to obtain an exclusive lock before timing out. Required.

`type="ReadOnly|Exclusive"`
: The type of lock to employ. Optional. The default value is `Exclusive`, which allows only one request at a time to access the block of code within the `cflock` tag. This option should be used when writing data to persistent variables. `ReadOnly` allows more than one request at a time to access the block of code within the `cflock` tag. This option should be used when reading persistent variables. This is the faster of the two options.

cflog

New as of ColdFusion 5.0; updated in ColdFusion MX

`<cflog>`

Logs messages to the *Application.log* file, the *Scheduler.log* file, or to a custom log file. The log files generated by `cflog` follow a standard format. The first line of each log file contains a comma-delimited list of column headers qualified with double quotes that looks like this:

```
"Severity","ThreadID","Date","Time","Application","Message"
```

When an entry is made to the log file, the values that are written to each column are also qualified with double quotes and delimited with commas.

Attributes

`text="`*`message`*`"`
: Text you want to appear in the log entry. Required.

`application="Yes|No"`
: Whether or not to include the application name if one is specified in a `cfapplication` tag for the application. Optional. The default is `Yes`.

`date="Yes|No"`
: Whether or not to include the system date in the log entry. Optional. The default is `Yes`. This attribute is deprecated in ColdFusion MX. The system date is now included in all log entries.

`file="`*`filename`*`"`
: The name of the log file to write the log entry to. You must specify the name of a file with a *.log* extension. When specifying the filename, leave off the extension. If the file doesn't exist, ColdFusion automatically creates it in the default log file directory specified in the ColdFusion Administrator. Optional. If you specify a value for `file`, you must omit the `log` attribute.

`log="`*`log_type`*`"`
: The standard ColdFusion log file to write the entry to. Valid options are:

  `Application`
  : The entry is written to the *Application.log* file. This file is automatically created by ColdFusion and logs application-specific messages.

  `Scheduler`
  : The entry is written to the *Scheduler.log* file. This file is used by ColdFusion to log execution information concerning scheduled tasks.

  If you wish to write to a custom log file, omit the `log` attribute and use `file` instead. Optional.

`thread="Yes|No"`
: Whether or not to include the ID of the service thread responsible for logging the message in the log entry. Service threads typically handle a particular page request from request through completion before moving to the next queued request. Logging thread IDs can be useful (especially to Macromedia technical support) for identifying server activity patterns. Optional. The default is `Yes`. This attribute is deprecated in ColdFusion MX. The thread ID is now included in all log entries.

`time="Yes|No"`
: Whether or not to include the system time in the log entry. Optional. The default is `Yes`. This attribute is deprecated in ColdFusion MX. The system time is now included in all log entries.

`type="severity"`
: The severity you wish to assign to the log entry. Possible entries are `Information` (the default), `Warning`, `Error`, and `Fatal`.

cflogin

New in ColdFusion MX; updated in ColdFusion MX 6.1

```
<cflogin>
...
  [<cfloginuser>]
...
</cflogin>
```

Acts as a container for ColdFusion MX's built-in security framework. The `cflogin` tag provides a facility for authenticating users against a database, LDAP directory, or other authentication store. The body of the tag gets executed only if the user is not logged in. Code to authenticate the user, such as a database or `cfldap` query, is executed within the `cflogin` tags. A `cfloginuser` tag is used to establish the user's identity and any roles she might have. The `cflogin` tag is usually used within an *Application.cfm* page.

Attributes

`applicationtoken="unique_application_identifier"`
: Specifies a unique identifier for the application to which the security framework should apply. Optional. The default is the application name as specified in the `name` attribute of the `cfapplication` tag. In practice, there is rarely an instance where you would use this attribute.

`cookiedomain="domain"`
: The domain for which the security framework cookie can be read and written. Entries must always start with a dot. For example, `cookiedomain=".oreilly.com"` is a valid entry. Multiple entries may be separated by semicolons. Optional. The default is no domain restrictions.

`idletimeout="seconds"`
: Number of seconds of idle time (no page interactivity) ColdFusion should wait before logging the user off. Optional. The default is `1800` (30 minutes). When the `cflogin` tag is used in conjunction with the `cfloginuser` tag, and the `loginstorage` attribute of the `cfapplication` tag is set to `cookie`, an in-memory cookie identifying the security session is set. When the user closes his browser, this cookie is automatically destroyed, effectively logging the user out within the context of the ColdFusion MX security framework. If `loginstorage` is set to `session`, the lesser of the `idletimeout` value set in `cfloginuser` or the session timeout period set in the `cfapplication` tag (or ColdFusion Administrator) is used to determine the timeout value for the session. This behavior is new in ColdFusion MX 6.1; in ColdFusion MX 6.0, the `cflogin` scope could only be tied to a cookie and not to the session scope.

Returned Variables

If HTTP Basic Authentication, HTTP Digest, or NTLM Authentication is used, or if form or URL variables named `j_username` and `j_password` are used to pass a username and password, respectively, to the `cflogin` tag, a special scope structure named `cflogin` is available that contains the following key/value pairs:

`cflogin.Username`
: The username passed via HTTP Basic, HTTP Digest, or NTLM Authentication or a `j_username` form or URL variable.

`cflogin.Password`
: The password passed via HTTP Basic Authentication or a `j_password` form or URL variable. Both HTTP Digest and NTLM Authentication do not usually supply the password. If you use either of these methods, `cflogin.Password` usually contains an empty string.

In order to take advantage of the `cflogin` scope, you must either use HTTP Basic, HTTP Digest, or NTLM authentication or name the username and password fields in your login form `j_username` and `j_password`.

cfloginuser

New in ColdFusion MX

```
<cflogin>
  <cfloginuser>
</cflogin>
```

Identifies a user to the ColdFusion MX security framework and assigns access roles. The `cfloginuser` tag is generally used within a `cflogin` tag block.

Attributes

name="*username*"
: The username of the user. Required.

password="*password*"
: The user's password. Required.

roles="*roles*"
: Comma-delimited list of roles for the user. Required. Be sure that there are no spaces between commas and list elements; otherwise, ColdFusion processes them as part of the list element.

cflogout

New in ColdFusion MX

```
<cflogin>
  <cfloginuser>
</cflogin>

<cflogout>
```

Logs a user out when used with ColdFusion MX's security framework. If a `cflogout` tag is not used, a user is automatically logged out when their session ends as defined by the `idletimeout` attribute in the `cflogin` tag. The `cflogout` tag can only be used after a user has been logged in with the `cflogin` tag. This tag has no attributes.

cfloop

```
[<cfloop index="index_name" from="integer" to="integer" [step="integer"]>]
[<cfloop condition="expression">]
[<cfloop index="index_name" list="list"  [delimiters="delimiters"]>
[<cfloop query="query_name" [startrow="integer"] [endrow="integer"]>]
[<cfloop collection="COM_Object|Structure" item="collection|key">]
  HTML and CFML
</cfloop>
```

A looping construct that can implement different kinds of looping, depending on the attributes specified. ColdFusion has five basic loop types: index, conditional, list, query, and collection.

Attributes

`collection="COM_Object|Structure"`
: The `collection` attribute loops over a COM collection object or a ColdFusion structure. Requires the `item` attribute and can't be used with any other attributes.

`condition="expression"`
: Using the `condition` attribute creates a `while` loop that repeats while a specified expression is `true`. In order to work, the expression being tested must change with each iteration until the condition evaluates to `false`. Can't be used with any other attributes.

`delimiters="delimiters"`
: The characters used to separate items in the list. Optional. The default delimiter is a comma.

`endrow="integer"`
: Row to stop looping. Optional. By default, ColdFusion continues the loop until it reaches the end of the record set.

`from="integer"`
: Number specifying the beginning value for the loop. Required when `index` is used to loop through a range of values.

`index="index_name"`
: Using the `index` attribute creates a `for` loop. This loop either repeats a specified number of times, when used with the `from`, `to`, and `step` attributes, or it loops through a list with the `list` and `delimiters` attributes. `index` specifies a variable that can access the current value of the index loop. When used with the `from`, `to`, and `step` attributes, the `index` value is set to the `from` value (required) and incremented by the `step` value (optional) for each iteration of the loop until the `TO` value (required) is reached. When used with the `list` (required) and `delimiters` (optional) attributes, `index` is a placeholder for the current list item. Can't be used with any other attributes.

`item="collection|key"`
: The variable name for the collection (COM object) or key (structure) referenced in a `collection` loop. Required with `collection`.

`list="list"`
: Delimited list of items or variable containing a delimited list of items. Required when `index` is used to loop through a list.

query="*query_name*"
: Using the query attribute creates a loop over the contents of a query object. query specifies the name of the query to loop over. Can be used with the startrow and endrow attributes, but no others.

startrow="*integer*"
: Row number to begin looping from. Optional. By default, ColdFusion begins the loop with the first row of the query.

step="*integer*"
: The value by which the index loop is incremented or decremented after each iteration. To decrement values, specify a negative vale for step. Optional. The default is 1.

to="*integer*"
: Number specifying the ending value for the loop. Required when index is used to loop through a range of values.

---

cfmail

Updated in ColdFusion MX and MX 6.1

```
<cfmail>
  [<cfmailparam>]

  [<cfmailpart>
  message body
  </cfmailpart>]
  ...
</cfmail>
```

Generates an email message and sends it through a designated SMTP server. New in ColdFusion MX, email addresses that contain spaces cause the cfmail tag to throw an exception. In prior versions, ColdFusion would still generate the mail spool file, even though it contained an invalid email address. Email address may be specified using any of the following formats:

pmoney@example.com
<pmoney@example.com>
pmoney@example.com (Pere Money)
"Pere Money" <pmoney@example.com>
Pere Money <pmoney@example.com>

Attributes

from="*sender*"
: The sender of the message. May be an email address or other arbitrary string. Required.

to="*recipient*"
: Recipient's email address. Separate multiple recipients with commas. Required.

subject="*subject*"
: The subject of the email. Required.

bcc="*blind_copy_to*"
: A list of recipients to send blind copies of the email. bcc recipients aren't shown in the email header. Separate multiple recipients with commas. Optional.

`charset="charset"`
: Specifies the character set to use in encoding the message. The most common character sets are `UTF-8`, `UTF-16`, `UTF-16BE`, `UTF-16LE`, `US-ASCII`, and `ISO-8859-1`. You may use any character set supported by your JRE. Optional. The default is the character encoding specified in the Mail section of the Server Settings area in the ColdFusion Administrator. By default, this is set to `UTF-8`. This attribute is new in ColdFusion MX 6.1.

`cc="copy_to"`
: A list of recipients to send copies of the email. Separate multiple recipients with commas. Optional.

`failto="address"`
: Specifies an email address where mail servers should send delivery failure messages. Optional. This attribute is new in ColdFusion MX 6.1.

`group="query_column"`
: The query column that should be used to group data. Grouping data results in the elimination of duplicate output. Grouping is case-sensitive unless the `groupcasesensitive` attribute is set to `No`. Optional.

`groupcasesensitive="Yes|No"`
: Whether grouping should be case-insensitive or case-insensitive. Optional. The default is `Yes`. This attribute works only if the record set has already been grouped appropriately. `cfmail` can't reorder or resort the record set on its own.

`mailerid="header_ID"`
: A mailer ID to pass along in the X-Mailer SMTP header. The X-Mailer header identifies the program generating the SMTP message. Optional. The default is "ColdFusion MX Application Server".

`maxrows="integer"`
: The maximum number of emails to send from a query-based mailing. Optional.

`mimeattach="attachment_path"`
: The full path to a file to be MIME-encoded and attached to the email message. `mimeattach` performs the same function as the `cfmailparam` tag but allows only a single file to be attached to the mail message. Using the `cfmailparam` tag is the preferred method for attaching files to your email messages. Optional.

`password="password"`
: Password required by an SMTP server for authentication. If specified, a `username` must also be provided. Optional. This attribute is new in ColdFusion MX 6.1.

`port="port_number"`
: The port used by the mail server to listen for SMTP requests. The default SMTP port is `25`. Specifying a value here overrides any values set in the ColdFusion Administrator. Optional.

`query="query_name"`
: The name of a query to use for pulling data to populate messages or to send messages to multiple recipients. Optional.

`replyto="address"`
: Specifies an email address or comma delimited list of email addresses where mail clients should send replies to the message. Optional. This attribute is new in ColdFusion MX 6.1.

`server="address_or_list_of_addresses"`
: Server address or comma-delimited list of server addresses (ColdFusion MX 6.1 Enterprise only) ColdFusion should use to send SMTP mail. If more than one address is specified, ColdFusion attempts to connect to the first mail server in the list. If that fails, it attempts to connect to the second server, etc. ColdFusion will not attempt to connect to a mail server if it was previously unavailable within the previous 60 seconds. This behavior is new in the Enterprise version of ColdFusion MX 6.1. If you specify multiple server addresses in ColdFusion MX 6.1 Standard, only the first server address is tried. Specifying a value for server overrides any values set in the ColdFusion Administrator. Additionally, you may prepend a username and password and/or append a port number to the server address (*username:password@servername:port*) if desired. If you specify a port number in this way, it overrides any value set in the ColdFusion Administrator. You must set a server value either in the ColdFusion Administrator or the `cfmail` tag; otherwise, ColdFusion throws an error. Optional.

`spoolenable="Yes|No"`
: `Yes` tells ColdFusion to save a copy of the message to disk until it can be sent. `No` causes the messages to queue in memory until they can be sent. Although queuing in memory may be faster than writing the messages to disk, it is not fault-tolerant, meaning, if the ColdFusion server goes down before the messages can be sent, they are lost. Optional. The default is `Yes`.

`startrow="row_number"`
: The query row to begin emailing from. Optional. The default is 1.

`timeout="seconds"`
: The number of seconds the ColdFusion server should wait before timing out the connection to the SMTP server. A value set here overrides a timeout value set in the ColdFusion Administrator. Optional.

`type="text|plain|html|mime_type"`
: MIME type of the message. You can specify `text` (text/plain), `plain` (text/plain), `html` (text/html), or any valid MIME type you wish. Optional. The default is text/plain.

`username="username"`
: Username required by an SMTP server for authentication. If specified, a `password` must also be provided. Optional. This attribute is new in ColdFusion MX 6.1.

`wraptext="number_of_characters"`
: Specifies the maximum number of characters to allow per line in the message. If a line is longer than the specified number of characters, an attempt is made to break the line by inserting a line break at the nearest whitespace character (space, tab, etc.) before the character limit. If the line contains no whitespace characters before the maximum number of characters per line, a line break is inserted at the maximum line length. Optional. The default is no text wrapping. This attribute is new in ColdFusion MX 6.1.

cfmailparam

Updated in ColdFusion MX 6.1

```
<cfmail>
  [<cfmailparam>]
  ...
message body
</cfmail>
```

Used within a cfmail block to send file attachments and custom header information. Multiple cfmailparam tags may be nested within a cfmail block. Only one file attachment or custom header can be specified per cfmailparam tag.

Attributes

file="*filename*"
: The full path to the file you wish to attach to your email message. Multiple cfmailparam tags may be used to attach more than one file. Files are MIME encoded before they are sent. Cannot be used with any other attribute besides type. You should note that ColdFusion does not make a copy of any file attachments before sending. If you attach a file to a mail message, you must wait until after the message is sent before deleting the file. If ColdFusion tries to send a message with an attachment and it cannot find the attachment, an exception is raised, and the message is not sent. Required when attaching a file.

type="text|plain|html|*mime_type*"
: MIME type of the file attachment. You can specify text (text/plain), plain (text/plain), html (text/html), or any valid MIME type you wish. Optional. The default is text/plain. This attribute is new in ColdFusion MX 6.1.

name="*name*"
: The name of the header entry to write. Multiple header entries may be written using a cfmailparam tag for each entry. Can be used only with the value attribute. Required when including custom header information.

value="*value*"
: The value to be written for the header entry. Can be used only with the name attribute. Required when including custom header information.

cfmailpart

New as of ColdFusion MX 6.1

```
<cfmail>
  [<cfmailparam>]

  [<cfmailpart>
  message body
  </cfmailpart>]
  ...
</cfmail>
```

Used within a cfmail block to specify a part of a multi-part message. Multi-part messages are typically used to send multiple versions of the same message. For example, it may be desirable to send both a plain text and an HTML version of a message. To specify multiple parts, use one cfmailpart tag pair for each part. If you send a multi-part message using cfmailpart, all message contents must appear within cfmailpart tags. Any content outside the tag body is ignored.

Attributes

charset="*charset*"

Specifies the character set to use in encoding the message part. The most common character sets are UTF-8, UTF-16, UTF-16BE, UTF-16LE, US-ASCII, and ISO-8859-1. You may use any character set supported by your JRE. Optional. The default is the character encoding specified in the cfmail tag.

type="text|plain|html|*mime_type*"

MIME type of the message part. You can specify text (text/plain), plain (text/plain), html (text/html), or any valid MIME type you wish. Optional.

wraptext="*number_of_characters*"

Specifies the maximum number of characters to allow per line of the message part. If a line is longer than the specified number of characters, an attempt is made to break the line by inserting a line break at the nearest whitespace character (space, tab, etc) before the character limit. If the line contains no whitespace characters before the maximum number of characters per line, a line break is inserted at the maximum line length. Optional. The default is no text wrapping.

cfmodule

```
<cfmodule>
  [<cfmodule />]
  ...
[</cfmodule>]
```

Provides an alternative method for calling CFML custom tags. Multiple cfmodule tags may be nested, provided each nested tag is closed using the syntax <cfmodule />.

Attributes

attributecollection="*attribute_structure*"

The name of a ColdFusion structure containing attribute names and their associated values. Optional. If an attribute contained in the structure passed by attributecollection has the same name as an attribute passed in to the tag as a parameter, the one passed via attributecollection is used.

attribute*n*="*value*"

Additional attributes and their associated values as required by the custom tag. Optional.

name="*name*"

The name of the custom tag you want to use. The default location for custom-tag storage is *\cfroot\customtags*. Custom tags residing in this location may be referenced with dotted notation. For example, a custom tag called MyCustomTag *(MyCustomTag.cfm)* residing in the default custom tags directory is referenced as MyCustomTag. The same tag residing under a subdirectory of the *\customtags* directory called *\SpecialTags* is referenced as SpecialTags.MyCustomTag. This dotted notation can reference custom tags residing in or any number of levels below the default *customtags* directory. Optional. If a value is specified for name, the template attribute isn't used.

template="*template_path*"

The path to the ColdFusion template to use as a custom tag. Relative paths are automatically expanded from the current page, while absolute paths are expanded using the mappings defined in the ColdFusion Administrator. Optional. If a value is specified for `template`, the `name` attribute isn't used.

cfnewinternaladminsecurity

This tag is the same as the `cfadminsecurity` tag, except it functions even if the `cfadminsecurity` tag is disabled in the Basic Security area of the ColdFusion Administrator. For syntax and attributes, see `cfadminsecurity`.

cfnewinternalregistry

This tag is the same as the `cfregistry` tag, except it functions even if the `cfregistry` tag is disabled in the Basic Security area of the ColdFusion Administrator. For syntax and attributes, see `cfregistry`. This tag is deprecated and nonfunctional as of ColdFusion 4.5.

cfobject

Updated in ColdFusion MX

```
<cfobject>
```

Allows ColdFusion to connect to various objects, including COM objects, CORBA objects, Java objects and EJBs, ColdFusion Components (CFCs), and SOAP-based web services. COM objects aren't currently supported for Unix versions of ColdFusion. The `cfobject` tag can be disabled in the Security Sandbox section of the ColdFusion Administrator (ColdFusion Enterprise and ColdFusion for J2EE only).

Using the `cfobject` tag to call a Java object loads the class but doesn't create an instance of the object. Constructors can be explicitly called using the `init()` method:

```
<cfset MyVar=MyObject.init(argument1, argument2)>
```

Calling a public method within an object without first calling the `init()` method results in an implicit call to the default constructor. Arguments and return values may be of any valid Java datatype. ColdFusion handles the conversion of strings automatically when they are passed as arguments or as return values. In addition, methods may be overloaded as long as the number of arguments used differs. The `JavaCast()` function may be used to cast a ColdFusion variable before it is passed to an overloaded method.

When the `cfobject` tag is used to call a web service, it instantiates a proxy object for the service.

Attributes

type="COM|CORBA|Java"

The type of object to create. Required when connecting to a COM, CORBA, or Java object.

`name="name"`
: A name for the object to be used by your application when referencing the object's attributes and methods. Required.

`class="object_class"`
: For a COM object, the component program ID for the object to be invoked. For a CORBA object, if `context` is `IOR`, `class` specifies the name of a file that contains the stringified version of the IOR. If `context` is `NameService`, `class` specifies a forward slash-delimited naming context for the naming service. Note that previous versions of ColdFusion used a period-delimited naming context For a Java object, the Java class. Required.

`action="Create|Connect"`
: With a COM object, `Create` instantiates the object (usually a *.dll*), while `Connect` connects to a COM object (usually an *.exe*) that is already running on the server. With a Java object, `Create` is the only valid action. Required for these objects; ignored otherwise.

`component="component_name"`
: Name of the component (CFC) to instantiate. Required when instantiating a CFC.

`context="context"`
: For a COM object, valid entries are `InProc`, `Local`, or `Remote`, and the attribute is optional. `InProc` specifies an in-process server object (usually a *.dll*) running in the same process space as the ColdFusion server. `Local` specifies an out-of-process server object (usually a *.exe*) that's running on the same server as ColdFusion, but not in the same process space. `Remote` specifies an out-of-process server object (usually an *.exe*) that's running on another machine. If `Remote` is specified, the `server` attribute is required. When no value is specified, ColdFusion uses the registry setting for the object.

  For a CORBA object, valid entries are `IOR`, which causes ColdFusion to use the Interoperable Object Reference to access the object, and `NameService`, which causes ColdFusion to use the naming service to access the object. Required for CORBA objects.

  Not used with Java objects, CFCs, or web services.

`locale="-type_value_pair1, -type_value_pair2, ..."`
: For CORBA objects, type/value pairs of arguments to pass to `init_orb( )`. This feature is specific to VisiBroker orbs and has been tested to work with the 3.2 C++ version only. Note that all type/value pairs must begin with a minus sign (-).

`server="server_name"`
: With COM objects, a valid server name using Universal Naming Convention (UNC) or Domain Name Server (DNS) conventions. Required when `context` is `Remote`; ignored otherwise.

`webservice="url_to_wsdl|registered_name"`
: Absolute URL to the web services WSDL file or the name of the web service as registered in the ColdFusion Administrator. Required when instantiating a web service.

cfobjectcache

New as of ColdFusion 5.0

```
<cfobjectcache>
```

Clears the ColdFusion query cache. This tag was previously an undocumented ColdFusion tag.

Attribute

action="Clear"
: Specifies the action to be taken by the cfobjectcache tag. The only action currently supported is Clear. Required.

cfoutput

```
<cfoutput>
HTML and CFML
</cfoutput>
```

Displays the results of a query or other ColdFusion operation.

Attributes

group="*parameter*"
: The column name that should be used to group data. Grouping data results in the elimination of duplicate output. Optional.

groupcasesensitive="Yes|No"
: Whether grouping should be case-sensitive. Optional. The default is Yes. This attribute works only if the record set has already been grouped appropriately. cfoutput can't reorder or resort the record set on its own.

maxrows="*integer*"
: The maximum number of rows to output. Optional.

query="*query_name*"
: The name of the query from which to pull the data to be output. Optional.

startrow="*row_number*"
: The query row to begin outputting from. Optional.

cfparam

Updated in ColdFusion MX

```
<cfparam>
```

Defines a parameter and sets a default value. Can also be used to test for the existence of a parameter and its datatype.

Attributes

name="*parameter_name*"
: Name of the parameter to create. Required.

default="*value*"
: Default value to assign to the variable if it doesn't exist or has no value already assigned.

type="*data_type*"

The required parameter type. Valid entries are Any, Array, Binary (new in ColdFusion MX), Boolean, Date, GUID (new in ColdFusion MX), Numeric, Query, String, Struct, UUID, and VariableName (checks to make sure the variable you are checking contains a value that is a valid variable name). Optional. The default is Any. For more information on the difference between a GUID and a UUID, see the entry for CreateUUID( ) in Appendix B.

cfpop

Updated in ColdFusion MX 6.1

```
<cfpop>
```

Retrieves email, including multi-part mail messages containing HTML and text as well as file attachments, from a POP server.

Attributes

server="*POP_server*"

Hostname or IP address of the POP server you want to retrieve mail from. Required.

action="*action*"

Specifies the action for the cfpop tag to take. Optional. The default value is GetHeaderOnly, which returns the message header only. GetAll returns the message header and message body, plus file attachments if a value is specified for attachmentpath. Delete deletes messages from the server.

attachmentpath="*path*"

The full path to use to store file attachments when action is GetAll. Optional.

generateuniquefilenames="Yes|No"

Whether or not to automatically generate unique filenames for file attachments so that name conflicts can be avoided. Generated names are guaranteed to be unique within the specified directory. Optional. The default is No.

maxrows="*integer*"

The maximum number of messages to be retrieved for the query. Optional. This attribute is ignored if a value is given for messagenumber.

messagenumber="*message_number*"

The message number or comma-delimited list of message numbers to perform the specified action on. Optional.

name="*query_name*"

The name to assign the query object created when action is Get or GetAll. Optional.

password="*password*"

A password to use in order to log into the POP server. Optional.

port="*port_number*"

Port on the POP server to use. Optional. The default is 110.

startrow="*row_number*"

The starting row for the message query. Optional. The default is 1. This attribute is ignored if a value is given for messagenumber.

timeout="*seconds*"
: The maximum amount of time in seconds that ColdFusion should wait while performing a mail operation before timing out. Optional. The default is 60.

username="*username*"
: A username to use when logging into the POP server. Optional. If no username is specified, the tag defaults to anonymous access.

UID="*UID*"
: The unique identifier (UID) assigned to a mail message or comma-delimited list of UIDs, to perform the specified action on. UID may be used in place of the messagenumber attribute in cases where the specified POP server doesn't support message numbers (as in the case of the Mercury POP server). Optional.

Returned Variables

The cfpop tag returns several variables depending on the value of the action attribute. When action is GetHeaderOnly or GetAll, cfpop returns the following variables:

queryname.ColumnList
: A comma-delimited list of the query column names.

queryname.CurrentRow
: The current row of the query being processed.

queryname.RecordCount
: The total number of messages returned by the query.

queryname.Date
: Date and time the message was sent. POP dates can be converted to GMT (Greenwich Mean Time) using the ParseDateTime( ) function.

queryname.MessageNumber
: The message number of the current message.

queryname.UID
: The UID of the current message.

queryname.From
: The email address of the sender of the message.

queryname.To
: The email address or comma-delimited email addresses of the message recipient(s).

queryname.CC
: Email address or comma-delimited list of email addresses that received copies of the message.

queryname.BCC
: Email address or comma-delimited list of email addresses that received blind copies of the message.

queryname.ReplyTo
: Email address specified as the reply-to address.

queryname.Subject
: The subject of the message.

queryname.Header
: Returns the complete SMTP message header.

When action is GetAll, there is an additional variable:

queryname.Body
: The content of the message body.

If action is set to GetAll and the attachmentpath attribute is set, ColdFusion returns two additional variables containing information about any file attachments included with the message:

queryname.Attachments
: A tab-delimited list of the original filenames of all attached files.

queryname.AttachmentFiles
: A tab-delimited list of the names of the attachment files as they were written to the directory specified in attachmentpath.

cfprocessingdirective

Updated in ColdFusion MX

```
<cfprocessingdirective>
CFML
[</cfprocessingdirective>]
```

Specifies a compiler processing option to suppress all whitespace produced by ColdFusion within the cfprocessingdirective tag pairs. In ColdFusion MX, a new attribute called pageencoding was added, allowing you to specify a character encoding to use to read the page. cfprocessingdirective tags must occur in matched pairs (i.e., have an end tag) when used to suppress whitespace (this is not necessary if you are only setting the page encoding) and may also be nested. cfprocessingdirective settings don't apply to templates called via cfimport, cfobject, cfinvoke, cfinclude, or cfmodule or as custom tags. Macromedia recommends using either the suppresswhitespace attribute or the pageencoding attribute within a single cfprocessingdirective tag, but not both at the same time.

Attribute

pageencoding="*character_set*"
: New in ColdFusion MX. Specifies a Java character set for ColdFusion to use when reading the contents of the page. The most common character sets are UTF-8 (the default), UTF-16, UTF-16BE, UTF-16LE, US-ASCII, and ISO-8859-1. You may use any character set supported by your JRE. Optional. If the pageencoding attribute is used, the following guidelines apply:

- The cfprocessingdirective tag can not be used within a conditional statement (cfif or cfcase) because it's evaluated when ColdFusion compiles the page, not at runtime.
- If there are multiple cfprocessingdirective tags within a page that use the pageencoding attribute, they must all have the same value; otherwise ColdFusion throws an exception.
- When pageencoding is used, the cfprocessingdirective tag must appear within the first 4096 bytes on the page.

suppresswhitespace="Yes|No"

Whether ColdFusion should suppress all whitespace between cfprocessingdirective tag pairs. Optional.

cfprocparam

Updated in ColdFusion MX

```
<cfstoredproc>
  [<cfprocparam>]
  [<cfprocresult>]
  ...
</cfstoredproc>
```

Specifies parameter information to send to a stored procedure. cfprocparam tags are nested within a cfstoredproc tag.

Attributes

cfsqltype="*parameter_data_type*"

The SQL type of the parameter being passed to the stored procedure. Required. The default is cf_sql_char. Possible values are cf_sql_bigint, cf_sql_bit, cf_sql_blob, cf_sql_char, cf_sql_clob, cf_sql_date, cf_sql_decimal, cf_sql_double, cf_sql_float, cf_sql_idstamp, cf_sql_integer, cf_sql_longvarchar, cf_sql_money, cf_sql_money4, cf_sql_numeric, cf_sql_real, cf_sql_refcursor (Oracle only), cf_sql_smallint, cf_sql_time, cf_sql_timestamp, cf_sql_tinyint, and cf_sql_varchar.

dbvarname="*database_variable_name*"

The name of the parameter within the stored procedure. Required if named notation is used. Named notation is not supported in ColdFusion MX (and has never worked correctly in previous versions). This attribute is deprecated and ignored by MX if used.

maxlength="*length*"

The maximum length of the parameter. Optional.

null="Yes|No"

Whether or not to pass the parameter as NULL. If Yes, ColdFusion ignores the value attribute and passes NULL. Optional. The default it No.

scale="*decimal_places*"

The number of decimal places for the parameter. Optional.

type="In|Out|InOut"

Whether the variable being passed is an input, output, or input/output variable. Optional. Default is In.

value="*parameter_value*"

The value to pass to the stored procedure. Required when type is In or InOut.

variable="*variable_name*"

The name of the ColdFusion variable that references the value returned by the output parameter after the stored procedure is called. Required when type is Out or InOut.

cfprocresult

```
<cfstoredproc>
  [<cfprocparam>]
```

```
    ...
    [<cfprocresult>]
    ...
</cfstoredproc>
```

Specifies the name for a result set returned by the cfstoredproc tag. This allows other ColdFusion tags to reference the result set. One or more cfprocresult tags may be nested within the cfstoredproc tag.

Attributes

name="*query_name*"
: A name for the query result set returned by the stored procedure. Required.

maxrows="*row_number*"
: The maximum number of rows to return with the result set. Optional. By default, maxrows is set to -1, resulting in all rows returned.

resultset="*integer*"
: The result set to use if the stored procedure returns more than one result set. You must have one cfprocresult tag for each result set returned by the stored procedure. Optional. The default value is 1.

cfproperty

New in ColdFusion MX

```
<cfcomponent>
  <cfproperty>
  ...
</cfcomponent>
```

Defines a component as a complex datatype for use in publishing web services. Multiple cfproperty tags can be used within a single cfcomponent tag to define the complex datatype. The complex datatype can then be called from a CFC published as a web service by using the name of the component containing the complex datatype definition in the type attribute of the CFC's cfargument tag. cfproperty tags must be positioned as the first code in a cfcomponent container. If they are not, ColdFusion throws an exception

Although cfproperty is designed for use with web-services authoring, it can also be used to expose additional metadata about a CFC. Besides the named attributes listed in the "Attributes" section, you can pass any additional desired attributes to the cfproperty tag as user-defined attributes. Although these attributes don't do anything, they are available as metadata when the component is introspected using the GetMetaData() function. You may use any attribute names you wish with the exception of those reserved by cfproperty: name, displayname, hint, and type.

Attributes

name="*property_name*"
: The name of the property. name must be a static value. Required.

displayname="*display_name*"
: Used to display a descriptive name for the property in ColdFusion MX's Component Browser. Optional.

hint="*text*"
: Used to display a hint describing what the property is for in ColdFusion MX's Component Browser. Optional.

type="*data_type*"
: Type of property. Valid options are Any, Array, Binary, Boolean, Date, GUID, Numeric, Query, String, Struct, UUID, VariableName, *ComponentName*. Optional. The default is Any. For information on how GUID differs from UUID, see the CreateUUID( ) function in Appendix B.

---

cfquery

Updated in ColdFusion MX

```
<cfquery>
  [<cfqueryparam>]
SQL statements
</cfquery>
```

Performs SQL operations against a data source or existing query object. In ColdFusion MX, SQL reserved words can no longer be used as column or query names. When building dynamic queries from form or URL parameters, Macromedia recommends always binding the parameters with cfqueryparam tags.

Attributes

name="*query_name*"
: Name to assign to the query. Valid query names must begin with a letter, underscore, or Unicode currency symbol ($) and can contain only letters, numbers, underscores, and Unicode currency symbols. Required when passing an SQL select statement; optional for all other SQL operations. Although the name attribute is required only for SQL select statements, you may wish to use it in all your queries. It makes debugging easier, especially for templates that contain multiple queries, because it allows you to identify each query by name in the debugging output.

datasource="*datasource_name*"
: The name of the data source to connect to when executing the query. Required except when dbtype is Query or Dynamic.

blockfactor="*block_size*"
: The maximum number of rows to retrieve from the server at a time. Optional. The range is from 1 to 100; 1 is the default. Note that some drivers may reduce the block factor automatically.

cachedafter="*date*"
: A date for using cached query data. Cached query data is used only if the date of the original query is after the date specified in CACHEDAFTER. To use cached query data, this feature must be enabled in the ColdFusion Administrator. Optional.

cachedwithin="*time_span*"
: A time span (created using the CreateTimeSpan( ) function) for using cached query data. To use cached query data, this feature must be enabled in the ColdFusion Administrator. Optional.

`connectstring="`*`connection_string`*`"`
: Passes additional connection information to an ODBC data source that can't be passed via the ColdFusion Administrator. `connectstring` can also override connection information set for a data source already registered in the ColdFusion Administrator. When making a dynamic data-source connection (when `dbtype` is Dynamic), `connectstring` specifies all the information required to connect to the data source. For specific connection string options, you should consult the documentation for your particular database. New as of ColdFusion 5.0. This attribute is no longer supported in ColdFusion MX.

`dbname="`*`database_name`*`"`
: Specifies the database name. For the Sybase System 11 native driver and SQLOLEDB provider only. Optional. Overrides any value set for `datasource`.

`dbserver="`*`database_server`*`"`
: The name of the database server to connect to when using native drivers. Specifying a `dbserver` overrides any value set for `datasource`. Optional.

`dbtype="`*`database_type`*`"`
: The type of database driver to use. Optional. This attribute no longer supports options other than `Query` in ColdFusion MX. Possible choices are:

  `ODBC` *(the default)*
  : Connect to the data source using an ODBC driver. No longer supported in ColdFusion MX.

  `OLEDB`
  : Connect using an OLEDB driver. No longer supported in ColdFusion MX.

  `Oracle73`
  : Connect using the Oracle 7.3 native driver. This requires the 7.3.4.0.0 or later client libraries be installed on the ColdFusion server. No longer supported in ColdFusion MX.

  `Oracle80`
  : Connect using the Oracle 8 native driver. This requires the 8.0 or later client libraries be installed on the ColdFusion server. No longer supported in ColdFusion MX.

  `Sybase11`
  : Connect using the Sybase 11 native driver. This requires the 11.1.1 or later client libraries be installed on the ColdFusion server. No longer supported in ColdFusion MX.

  `DB2`
  : Connect using the DB2 5.2 native driver. No longer supported in ColdFusion MX.

  `Informix73`
  : Connect using the Informix 7.3 native driver. This requires the Informix SDK 2.5 or later or Informix-Connect 2.5 (or later) for Windows. No longer supported in ColdFusion MX.

  `Query`
  : Specifies that the query should use an already existing query as the data source. If this option is used, you don't need to specify a value for `datasource`. New as of ColdFusion 5.0.

`Dynamic`
: Allows ColdFusion to make an ODBC connection to a data source without having to have the data source registered in the ColdFusion Administrator. When making a dynamic connection, all information normally provided in the ColdFusion Administrator for the connection must be specified in the `connectstring` attribute. New as of ColdFusion 5.0. No longer supported in ColdFusion MX.

`debug[="Yes|No"]`
: Specifying `debug` results in the output of debugging information, which includes the actual SQL passed to the data source as well as the number of records returned by the query. Optional.

`maxrows="`*`row_number`*`"`
: Maximum number of rows to return in a record set. Optional. The default is `-1` (all rows).

`password="`*`password`*`"`
: Password associated with `username`. Optional. If a password is specified, it overrides the value set in the ColdFusion Administrator.

`provider="`*`COM_provider`*`"`
: COM provider for OLE DB connections. Optional. This attribute is no longer supported in ColdFusion MX.

`providerdsn="`*`datasource`*`"`
: COM provider's data-source name for OLE DB. Optional. This attribute is no longer supported in ColdFusion MX.

`username="`*`username`*`"`
: Username to pass to the data source if one is required. Optional. If a username is specified, it overrides the value set in the ColdFusion Administrator.

`timeout="`*`seconds`*`"`
: Number of seconds to allow each action of the query to execute before timing out. Note that the total time to execute a query may exceed the `timeout` value. Support for this attribute varies by driver. Optional.

Returned Variables

When the `cfquery` tag selects records from a data source, four variables are returned:

`cfquery.ExecutionTime`
: The amount of time in milliseconds it took the query to execute; note the `cfquery` prefix

`queryname``.ColumnList`
: A comma-delimited list of the query column names from the database

`queryname``.CurrentRow`
: The current row of the query being processed

`queryname``.RecordCount`
: The total number of records returned by the query

cfqueryparam

```
<cfquery>
SQL statements
  [<cfqueryparam>]
</cfquery>
```

Checks the datatype and optionally validates a query parameter within the SQL statement of a cfquery tag. Multiple cfqueryparam tags may be used with a single cfquery tag.

The SQL that is generated by the cfqueryparam tag is dependent on the database used. If the database being used doesn't support bind parameters, validation is still performed with the validated parameter being written back to the string. If for any reason validation fails, ColdFusion throws an exception. The following rules determine the validation performed:

- cf_sql_smallint, cf_sql_integer, cf_sql_real, cf_sql_float, cf_sql_double, cf_sql_tinyint, cf_sql_money, cf_sql_money4, cf_sql_decimal, cf_sql_numeric, and cf_sql_bigint can be converted to numbers.
- cf_sql_date, cf_sql_time and cf_sql_timestamp can be converted to a valid date format.

In versions of ColdFusion prior to MX, Sybase 11 native drivers don't support the binding of SQL parameters. This is not an issue in MX as native drivers are no longer supported.

If the maxlength attribute is used, the length of the value for the specified parameter can't exceed the specified length; otherwise an error is thrown.

Attributes

value="*parameter_value*"
: The value that ColdFusion should pass to the right of the comparison operator in the WHERE clause. Required.

cfsqltype="*parameter_data_type*"
: The SQL type that the parameter is bound to. Required. The default is cf_sql_char. Possible values are cf_sql_bigint, cf_sql_bit, cf_sql_blob, cf_sql_char, cf_sql_clob, cf_sql_date, cf_sql_decimal, cf_sql_double, cf_sql_float, cf_sql_idstamp, cf_sql_integer, cf_sql_longvarchar, cf_sql_money, cf_sql_money4, cf_sql_numeric, cf_sql_refcursor (Oracle only), cf_sql_real, cf_sql_smallint, cf_sql_time, cf_sql_timestamp, cf_sql_tinyint, and cf_sql_varchar.

list="Yes|No"
: Whether or not the value attribute of the cfqueryparam tag should be treated as a list of values separated by the character specified in the separator attribute. If set to Yes, an SQL parameter is generated for each value in the list. Each list item is validated separately. If a value is specified for the maxlength attribute, the maxlength applies to each item in the list as opposed to the list as a whole. If the value passed is NULL, it is treated as a single NULL value. Optional. The default is No.

maxlength="*length*"
: The maximum length of the parameter. Optional.

null="Yes|No"
: Whether or not to pass a NULL for the value. If Yes, ColdFusion ignores the value attribute. Optional. The default it No.

separator="*separator_character*"
: The character that delimits the list of values when list attribute is Yes. Optional. The default is the comma (,).

scale="*decimal_places*"
: The number of decimal places of the parameter. Optional.

cfregistry

Updated in ColdFusion MX; no longer supported in Unix versions of ColdFusion

```
<cfregistry>
```

Performs an operation on the Windows registry, based on the value of the action attribute. In ColdFusion MX, configuration information is stored in XML configuration files, not the system registry.

Attributes

action="*action*"
: The action for the cfregistry tag to take. Required. Get retrieves a value from the registry and stores it in a variable. GetAll retrieves all the registry keys and values for a specified registry branch and stores them in a query object. Delete deletes a key or value from the registry. Set adds or updates a registry key or value.

branch="*branch*"
: For Get, GetAll, and Set, the name of the registry branch containing the value to be accessed or set. For Delete, specifies either the name of the registry key to be deleted (don't specify an entry) or the name of the registry branch that contains the value to be deleted (specify a value for entry). Required.

entry="*key_or_value*"
: The value in the registry to be operated on. Required for all actions except GetAll and certain Delete operations.

maxrows="*integer*"
: The maximum number of rows to retrieve when action is GetAll and type is Key. Optional. The default is to retrieve all remaining rows. This attribute is new in ColdFusion MX.

name="*query_name*"
: The name of a query object to hold the keys and values returned by cfregistry. Required for GetAll; ignored otherwise.

sort="*sort_criteria*"
: The sort order for the result set obtained by the cfregistry action. Results may be ordered by Entry, Type, and Value. Multiple sort criteria can be entered as a comma-delimited list. In addition, the sort type may be specified after each column name as either Asc (ascending) or Desc (descending). Optional for GetAll; ignored otherwise.

startrow="*row_number*"
: The query row to begin retrieving from when action is GetAll and type is Key. Optional. The default is 1 (the first row). This attribute is new in ColdFusion MX.

type="*type*"
: The type of registry data to be operated on. Valid entries are Key, DWord, and String (the default). Optional.

value="*string_or_value*"

The value you want to set. Optional for Set; ignored otherwise. If no value is specified, ColdFusion automatically sets a default value based on type. If type is DWord, value is set to zero. If type is String, value is set to an empty string ("").

variable="*variable*"

The name of a ColdFusion variable to hold the data returned by cfregistry. Required for Get; ignored otherwise.

Returned Variables

The following query columns are returned when action is GetAll. The name of the query object is set in the name attribute:

queryname.Entry

The name of the registry entry

queryname.Type

The type of registry entry returned

queryname.Value

The value of the registry entry if type is set to String or DWord

cfreport

Updated in ColdFusion MX

<cfreport> ... </cfreport>

Executes a predefined Crystal Reports report and populates it with data from a ColdFusion template. This feature is only available on the Windows version of ColdFusion. In order to use this tag, you must have Crystal Reports installed on your ColdFusion server. In ColdFusion MX, ColdFusion no longer handles data source connectivity for the Crystal Report.

Attributes

report="*report_path*"

The full path to the Crystal Report file to be executed. Required.

datasource="*datasource_name*"

The name of the ODBC data source to obtain data for the report from. If no datasource is provided, the data source specified when the report was created is used. datasource is a previously undocumented attribute of the cfreport tag. Optional.

formula="*formula*"

One or more named formulas within the report. Separate formula parameters with semicolons. If the formula contains a semicolon, it should be escaped by doubling it up. Optional.

orderby="*result_order*"

Orders results according to your specifications. Optional.

password="*password*"

Password associated with username. Optional. If a password is specified, it overrides the value set in the ColdFusion Administrator.

timeout="*seconds*"
: Time in seconds ColdFusion should wait before timing out a connection to the Crystal Reports engine. Optional.

type="*report_type*"
: The type of HTML that should be used to generate the report. Options are `Standard`, `Netscape`, and `Microsoft`; they refer to the web browser the report is destined for. This attribute can be dynamically set by first determining the browser in use with the CGI variable `CGI.http_user_agent`. When using the `cfreport` tag in versions of ColdFusion prior to 5.0 to generate a report in Crystal Reports 8.x, you must set the `type` attribute to `Netscape` or `Microsoft`. Optional. The default value is `Standard` (don't use the default if using Crystal Reports 8.x). This issue has been fixed in ColdFusion 5.0. As of ColdFusion 5.0, you no longer need to use the `type` attribute to avoid an error.

username="*username*"
: A username for the database providing data for the report. Optional. If a username is specified, it overrides the value set in the ColdFusion Administrator.

cfrethrow

```
<cftry>
  CFML
<cfcatch type="exception_type">
  HTML and CFML
  <cftry>
    CFML
    <cfcatch type="exception_type">
      HTML and CFML
      <cfrethrow>
    </cfcatch>
</cfcatch>
<cfcatch type="Any">
HTML and CFML
</cfcatch>
</cftry>
```

Used within a `cfcatch` block to rethrow the active exception while preserving the `cfcatch.Type` and `cfcatch.TagContext` return variables. This tag takes no additional attributes.

cfreturn

New in ColdFusion MX

```
[<cfcomponent>]
  <cffunction>
  ...
  <cfreturn>
  </cffunction>
[<cfcomponent>]
```

Returns an evaluated expression or variable from a tag-based user-defined function or ColdFusion Component (CFC) method. This tag provides the same functionality as the `Return` statement in CFScript-based UDFs. Only one `cfreturn` tag may be used per function.

Attribute

`expression`

Expression to evaluate and return. Any valid ColdFusion expression may be used (evaluated expression, variable name, string or numeric literal, etc.). Required.

cfsavecontent

New as of ColdFusion 5.0

```
<cfsavecontent>
HTML and CFML
</cfsavecontent>
```

Saves all generated content between tag pairs in a variable. `cfsavecontent` is useful in situations where you want to reuse the content generated by a specific block of code.

Attribute

`variable="`*`variable_name`*`"`

A variable name for storing the content generated by code between the `cfsavecontent` tag pairs.

cfschedule

```
<cfschedule>
```

Creates, updates, deletes, and kicks off the execution of a URL on a scheduled basis. Depending on your underlying JRE, you may or may not be able to use `cfschedule` to call an `https` (SSL-enabled) URL.

Attributes

`action="`*`action`*`"`

Action you want the scheduler to perform. Valid entries are `Delete`, `Run`, and `Update`. Required.

`task="`*`task_name`*`"`

The name of the task to delete, run, or update. Required.

`enddate="`*`date`*`"`

End date for the scheduled task. Optional.

`endtime="`*`time`*`"`

End time for the scheduled task. Optional.

`file="`*`filename`*`"`

Filename to use for the static file being published. Required when `publish` is `Yes`.

`interval="`*`seconds`*`"`

The interval the scheduler should use when scheduling tasks for execution. Intervals can be set in seconds or as `Once`, `Daily`, `Weekly`, or `Monthly`. Required when `action` is `Update`. The default interval is one hour. The minimum interval allowed is 60 seconds.

`operation="`*`HTTPRequest`*`"`

The operation the scheduler should perform. Required when `action` is `Update`. The only `OPERATION` currently supported is `HTTPRequest`.

password="*password*"
: Specifies the password to use for protected URLs. Optional.

path="*path*"
: The path to the location where the static file should be written. Required when publish is Yes.

port="*port_number*"
: Port number on the server where the template being executed resides. Optional. The default is 80.

proxyport="*port_number*"
: Specifies a port number on the proxy server where the template is being executed. Used in conjunction with the resolveurl attribute, proxyport allows you to preserve links within a template that resolve to a port other than 80. Optional. The default is 80.

proxyserver="*proxy_server*"
: Hostname or IP address of your proxy server. Optional.

publish="Yes|No"
: Whether or not the output of the scheduled task should be saved as a static file. Optional. The default is No.

requesttimeout="*seconds*"
: Extends the time allowed for execution beyond the default set in the ColdFusion Administrator. Optional.

resolveurl="Yes|No"
: Whether or not to resolve relative links in the retrieved template to absolute URLs. Optional. The default is No.

startdate="*date*"
: Start date for the scheduled task. Required when action is Update.

starttime="*time*"
: Start time for the scheduled task. Required when action is Update.

URL="*URL*"
: Absolute URL to the template to be executed when the scheduled task runs. Required when action is Update.

username="*username*"
: Specifies the username to use for protected URLs. Optional.

cfscript

Updated in ColdFusion MX

```
<cfscript>
script code
</cfscript>
```

Tells ColdFusion to process the content between <cfscript></cfscript> as CFScript code. CFScript can also be used to create user-defined functions (UDFs).

cfsearch

Updated in ColdFusion MX

<cfsearch>

Performs search operations on data contained in Verity collections.

Attributes

name="*search_name*"
: Name for the query containing the search results. Required.

collection="*collection_name|collection_path*"
: The name of the collection you wish to search, or in the case of externally generated collections, the full path to the collection directory. Multiple collections may be searched provided the collection names or paths are separated by commas. When specifying multiple collections, you can't mix internal and external collections, nor can you have VDK and K2 collections in the same search operation. New in ColdFusion MX, collection names can now contain spaces. Required.

criteria="search_criteria"
: The criteria for the search. All-uppercase or all-lowercase text is treated as case insensitive. Mixed case text is treated as case-sensitive. Optional.

external="Yes|No"
: Whether or not the Verity collection being searched was created with a version of Verity other than the one bundled with ColdFusion. Optional. The default is `No`. This option is no longer used in ColdFusion MX as ColdFusion is now capable of automatically detecting whether a collection is internal or external.

language="*language*"
: The language to be used when searching the collection. To specify a language other than U.S. English (the default), you must download and install the appropriate Verity Language Pack for ColdFusion MX, available at *http://www.macromedia.com/go/verity/*. Optional.

maxrows="*integer*"
: Maximum number of records to return for a given search. Optional. The default is all rows.

startrow="*row_number*"
: The first record number in the query results from which to retrieve data. Optional. The default is `1`.

type="Simple|Explicit"
: Type of search to be performed. Optional. The default is `Simple`, which allows you to use single words, comma-delimited lists of words, and phrases as the `criteria` for a search. Simple searches treat the comma as a Boolean `or`. Phrases can also be used as the `criteria` by surrounding them in quotation marks. By default, `Simple` searches employ the `stem` operator and the `many` modifier. `Explicit` searches treat each search term as a literal, so operators must be used explicitly.

Returned Variables

queryname.ColumnList
: Comma-delimited list of the query column names from the search result set.

queryname.CurrentRow
: The current row of the query that is being processed by cfoutput.

queryname.Custom1 *and queryname*.Custom2
: Whatever values were placed in the custom fields during the cfindex process.

queryname.Key
: The value placed in the key attribute during the cfindex operation.

queryname.RecordCount
: The number of records in the Verity collection that match the search criteria provided.

queryname.RecordsSearched
: Returns the total number of records from the collection searched by Verity.

queryname.Score
: A measure of how relevant a particular record in the Verity collection is in relation to the search criteria provided.

queryname.Summary
: The contents of the summary that the Verity engine automatically creates for each record in the collection. The summary is made up of the top three sentences from each record and has a 500-character limit.

queryname.Title
: The value placed in the title attribute during the cfindex operation. For collections containing HTML files, the value inside the <title> </title> tags is returned. For PDF and Microsoft Office documents, the title assigned by the application is returned.

queryname.URL
: The value specified in the urlpath during the cfindex operation. This variable is always empty when the type attribute is set to Custom during the cfindex operation.

cfselect

```
<cfform>
  <cfselect>
  ...
</cfform>
```

Creates a Java select box control to use in a cfform block.

Attributes

name="*name*"
: The form-field name for the select box control. Required.

display="*text*"
: An alternate field from the query (other than value) to display in the select box. Optional. The default is value.

message="*text*"
: Text to appear if validation fails. Optional.

multiple="Yes|No"
: Whether or not multiple item selections should be allowed. Optional. The default is No.

onerror="*function_name*"
: The name of a JavaScript function that should be executed if validation fails for any reason. Optional.

passthrough="*HTML_attributes*"
: Any additional HTML attributes you want to pass that aren't directly supported by the cfselect tag. Optional.

query="*query_name*"
: A query to use for populating the drop-down box. Optional.

required="Yes|No"
: Whether or not the select box control requires a value before being submitted. Optional. The default is No.

selected="*column_value*"
: A value that matches at least one value that is automatically selected when the template is called. Optional.

size="*integer*"
: The size of the drop-down box in terms of number of entries. Optional.

value="*text*"
: The field from query to use to fill in the option values of the select box. Optional.

cfservlet

Deprecated in ColdFusion MX; use the GetPageContext( ) function instead

```
<cfservlet>
  [<cfservletparam>]
  ...
</cfservlet>
```

Invokes a Java servlet from a ColdFusion template. The cfservlet tag requires Macromedia's JRun software in order to work. Attributes and parameters may be passed to the Java servlet by nesting cfservletparam tags within the cfservlet tag. This tag has been deprecated in ColdFusion MX. Servlets and JSP pages can now be called using the GetPageContext().include() and GetPageContext().forward() functions. Additionally, servlets can be hosted by J2EE servers other than JRun. See Chapter 23 and Appendix B for more information.

Attributes

code="*servlet_name*"
: The name of the Java servlet that you want to execute. Required.

debug="Yes|No"
: Whether or not to write additional information about the JRun connection status and other activity to the JRun error log file. For JRun 2.3.3, the error log is located in *jrun-homedir/jsm-default/logs/stderr.log*. For JRun 3.0, the error log is found in *jrunhomedir/logs/jrunservername_event.log*. Note that *jrunservername* can be specified as default, admin, or the name of another JRun server that you are running.

jrunproxy="*server:port*"
: The hostname or IP address and the port where the JRun engine is located. Required when connecting to a JRun 3.x server. Optional when connecting to a JRun 2.3.3

server, as the JRun engine is assumed to be on the same machine as the ColdFusion application server and listening on port 8081.

timeout="*seconds*"
: The number of seconds ColdFusion waits while processing a cfservlet request before timing out the operation. Optional. The default is 60.

writeoutput="Yes|No"
: Whether to write output from the servlet as inline text or to store in a variable. If Yes, ColdFusion outputs the text to the screen. If No, ColdFusion writes the text to the variable cfservlet.output. Optional. The default is Yes.

Returned Variables

The cfservlet tag can return two output variables depending on how the tag is called:

cfservlet.Output
: Returns the text output by the cfservlet tag. This variable is returned only if the WRITEOUTPUT attribute is set to No.

cfservlet.ServletResponseHeader
: If any response headers are returned by the servlet, they are available in a special structure called cfservlet. Each response header is accessed by specifying its name as a key in the cfservlet structure.

---

cfservletparam

Deprecated in ColdFusion MX

```
<cfservlet>
  [<cfservletparam>]
  ...
</cfservlet>
```

Used as a child tag of the cfservlet tag to pass parameters and attributes to a Java servlet. Multiple cfservletparam tags may pass multiple parameters/attributes. Both simple and complex datatypes such as arrays, queries, and structures can be passed to servlets via cfservletparam tags.

Data can be passed to a servlet in two ways: by value and by reference. To pass data by value (as a parameter), use the name and value attributes. Data passed by value is modified only within the servlet. To pass data by reference (as an attribute), use the name, variable, and optionally the type attribute. If the servlet modifies data passed by reference, the data in the corresponding ColdFusion variable is also changed.

This tag has been deprecated in ColdFusion MX. See cfservlet for more information.

Attributes

name="*parameter_name*"
: The name of the parameter to pass to the cfservlet tag when value is also specified. If variable is used in lieu of value, specifies the name of the Java attribute to associate with the ColdFusion variable specified in variable. Required.

type="Bool|Date|Int|Real|String"
: The datatype of the ColdFusion variable being passed to the servlet. Options are Bool, Date, Int, Real, and String. Optional. The default is String. To see how various ColdFusion datatypes map to Java equivalents, see Table A-1.

Table A-1. ColdFusion datatypes and Java equivalents

ColdFusion datatype	type attribute	Java equivalent
Boolean	Bool	java.lang.Bool
Date	Date	java.util.Date
Numeric (integer)	Int	java.lang.Integer
Numeric (real)	Real	java.lang.Double
String	String	java.lang.String
Array	N/A, omit type	java.util.Vector
Structure	N/A, omit type	java.util.Hashtable
Query	N/A, omit type	com.allaire.util.RecordSet

value="*parameter_value*"
: The value of the parameter to pass to the cfservlet tag. Required when name is a parameter.

variable="*CF_variable_name*"
: The name (not the value) of the ColdFusion variable to pass to the cfservlet tag. Required when name is an attribute. Using the variable attribute allows you to pass complex ColdFusion datatypes, such as arrays, queries, and structures to Java servlets. To see how various ColdFusion datatypes map to Java datatypes, see Table A-1.

cfset

Updated in ColdFusion MX

```
<cfset scope.varname=expression>
<cffunction>
  [<cfset Var scope.varname=expression>]
  ...
</cffunction>
```

Sets the value of a ColdFusion variable. As of ColdFusion MX, the cfset tag can be used within a cffunction container to create variables local to the function.

cfsetting

Updated in ColdFusion MX and MX 6.1

```
<cfsetting enablecfoutputonly="Yes|No"
           showdebugoutput="Yes|No">
           catchexceptionsbypattern="Yes|No"
           requesttimeout="seconds">
CFML
[<cfsetting enablecfoutputonly="Yes|No"
            showdebugoutput="Yes|No">
            catchexceptionsbypattern="Yes|No">]
```

Controls whitespace, debugging output, exception handling, and request timeout parameters within ColdFusion templates.

When the `enablecfoutputonly` attribute is used, `cfsetting` tags must occur in matched pairs where both a `<cfsetting enablecfoutputonly="Yes">` and a `<cfsetting enablecfoutputonly="No">` are present. `cfsetting` tags may be nested any number of levels as long as there are always matching tag pairs. You don't need to use paired `cfsetting` tags with the `showdebugoutput`, `catchexceptionsbypattern`, or `requesttimeout` attribute unless it is used in combination with an `enablecfoutputonly` attribute. Note that if you provide an end tag (`</cfsetting>`) for `cfsetting`, ColdFusion essentially ignores it as it neither functions nor throws an error.

Attributes

`catchexceptionsbypattern="Yes|No"`
: Whether or not to override structured exception handling. Optional. The default is `No`. This attribute is no longer available in ColdFusion MX.

`enablecfoutputonly="Yes|No"`
: Specifying `Yes` results in the suppression of all HTML output (including whitespace) between `cfsetting` tags. Optional. The default is `No`.

`requesttimeout="seconds"`
: New in ColdFusion MX. Specifies the number of seconds ColdFusion should wait for the page to process before marking the thread as unresponsive and timing out the request. This attribute is designed to replace the method in previous versions of ColdFusion whereby `RequestTimeout=x` was passed as part of the query string to a ColdFusion template in order to specify how long the page should run before timing out. If the `requesttimeout` attribute is used, it overrides the value set in the ColdFusion Administrator. If you have older code that uses the URL parameter `RequestTimeOut`, you can avoid having to recode all of your templates by placing the following code at the beginning of your *Application.cfm* template:

```
<cfif IsDefined('URL.RequestTimeOut')>
    <cfsetting requesttimeout = "#URL.RequestTimeout#">
</cfif>
```

This code checks to see if a `URL.RequestTimeOut` exists, and if it does, its value is assigned to the `requesttimeout` attribute of the `cfsetting` tag.

`showdebugoutput="Yes|No"`
: Whether or not to suppress debugging information normally output to ColdFusion templates when debugging is turned on in the ColdFusion Administrator. Optional. The default is `Yes`.

cfsilent

```
<cfsilent> ... </cfsilent>
```

Suppresses all output produced between the `cfsilent` tags. `cfsilent` partially supersedes the `cfsetting` tag by using a more structured format. `cfsilent` can suppress generated whitespace in instances where your template does a lot of looping but doesn't produce any output.

cfslider

Enhanced in ColdFusion 5.0; updated in ColdFusion MX

```
<cfform>
  <cfslider>
  ...
</cfform>
```

Creates a Java slider control for use within a `cfform` block.

Attributes

`name="name"`
: The form-field name for the slider control. Required.

`align="alignment"`
: Alignment for the slider control. Valid entries are `Left`, `Right`, `Top`, `TextTop`, `Bottom`, `AbsBottom`, `Baseline`, `Middle`, and `AbsMiddle`. Optional.

`bgcolor="color"`
: Background color for the slider control. Follows the same rules as `GROOVECOLOR`. Optional.

`bold="Yes|No"`
: Whether or not to display the `label` text in bold. Optional. The default is `No`.

`font="font_name"`
: A font name for the `label` text. Optional.

`fontsize-"integer"`
: A font size for the `label` text. Optional.

`groovecolor="color"`
: The text color for all data in the grid. Colors may be specified by name (`Black`, `Blue`, `Cyan`, `Darkgray`, `Gray`, `Lightgray`, `Magenta`, `Orange`, `Pink`, `Red`, `White`, `Yellow`) or hex code in the form `textcolor="##FFFFCC"`. The double pound signs are necessary to keep ColdFusion from throwing a syntax error, or you may omit the pound signs altogether. By using the appropriate hex code, you can specify colors that can't be specified by name. Optional. The default is `White`. This attribute is deprecated and no longer functional as of ColdFusion 5.0.

`height="height_in_pixels"`
: Height in pixels for the slider. Optional. The default is `40`.

`hspace="horizonal_spacing_in_pixels"`
: Width in pixels for the padding to the left and right of the slider control. Optional.

`img="filename"`
: The filename of an image to appear in the slider groove. Optional. This attribute is deprecated and no longer functional as of ColdFusion MX.

`imgstyle="style"`
: The style to use for the image provided in `img`. Valid entries are `Centered`, `Tiled`, and `Scaled`. Optional. The default is `Scaled`. This attribute is deprecated and no longer functional as of ColdFusion 5.0.

`italic="Yes|No"`
: Whether or not to display the `label` text in italic. Optional. The default is `No`.

`label="text"`
: Text to appear with the slider control. Additionally, `%value%` may be used within the label text to insert the current slider value. If `%value%` is omitted, the current slider value is output to the right of the label text. Optional.

`lookandfeel="Windows|Motif|Metal"`
: Specifies a theme governing the look and feel of the slider control. Options are `Windows`, `Motif`, and `Metal`. If no value is specified, ColdFusion first tries `Windows`, then uses the platform default. New as of ColdFusion 5.0.

`message="text"`
: Text to appear if validation fails. Optional.

`notsupported="text"`
: A text message to display if the user's browser doesn't support Java or Java is disabled Optional. If no message is specified, ColdFusion displays a default message.

`onerror="function_name"`
: The name of a JavaScript function that should be executed if validation fails for any reason. Optional.

`onvalidate="javascript_function"`
: A JavaScript validation function that should be executed before the form is submitted. Optional.

`range="min_value, max_value"`
: The beginning and ending values (numeric only) for the slider control. Optional. The default is `0,100`.

`refreshlabel="Yes|No"`
: Whether or not the label should be refreshed when the slider moves. Default is `Yes`.

`scale="integer"`
: The incremental value to use between the values provided by `range`. Optional. The default is `1`.

`textcolor="color"`
: Color to use for the `label` text. Follows the same rules as `groovecolor`. Optional.

`tickmarkimages="URL"`
: A URL or comma-delimited list of URLs (relative or absolute) to images you wish to use as tick marks for the slider control. The default is no images. New as of ColdFusion 5.0.

`tickmarklabels="Yes|No|String"`
: Whether or not to display labels next to each major tick mark. If `Yes`, the numeric value corresponding to the tick mark is displayed. Instead of numeric values, you may choose to display string values instead, by specifying a string or comma-delimited list of string values, one for each major tick mark between the minimum value and the maximum value for the slider. If you don't provide enough tick mark strings, the `cfslider` control repeats the last value until enough have been displayed. Optional. The default is `No`. New as of ColdFusion 5.0.

`tickmarkmajor="Yes|No"`
: Whether or not to display tick marks at every increment value along the axis of the slider control. For example, if the range for the slider is between 0 and 100 with an

increment of 10, a major tick mark is displayed every 10 values, at 0, 10, 20, etc. The default is `No`. New as of ColdFusion 5.0.

`tickmarkminor="Yes|No"`
: Whether or not to display tick marks between every increment value along the axis of the slider control. For example, if the range for the slider is between 0 and 100 with an increment of 10, a minor tick mark is displayed every 10 values, between the major tick marks, at 5, 15, 25, etc. The default is `No`. New as of ColdFusion 5.0.

`value="`*`integer`*`"`
: The default slider value. Optional. The default is the bottom number in `range`.

`vertical="Yes|No"`
: Indicates whether the slider control should be vertical, with the slider moving up and down. The default is `No`. New as of ColdFusion 5.0.

`vspace="`*`vertical_spacing_in_pixels`*`"`
: Height in pixels for the padding above and below the slider control. Optional.

`width="`*`width_in_pixels`*`"`
: Width in pixels for the slider. Optional.

cfstoredproc

```
<cfstoredproc>
 [<cfprocparam>]
 [<cfprocresult>]
 ...
</cfstoredproc>
```

Executes a stored procedure on a data source.

Attributes

`procedure="`*`procedure_name`*`"`
: The name of the stored procedure on the database server that you want to call. Required.

`datasource="`*`datasource_name`*`"`
: The data source that contains the stored procedure. Required.

`blockfactor="`*`block_size`*`"`
: The maximum number of rows to retrieve from the server at a time. Optional. The range is from `1` to `100`. `1` is the default. Note that some drivers may reduce the block factor automatically.

`connectstring="`*`connection_string`*`"`
: Passes additional connection information to an ODBC data source that can't be passed via the ColdFusion Administrator. `connectstring` can also override connection information set for a data source already registered in the ColdFusion Administrator. When making a dynamic data-source connection (when `dbtype` is Dynamic), `connectstring` specifies all the information required to connect to the data source. For specific connection-string options, you should consult the documentation for your particular database. New as of ColdFusion 5.0. This attribute is no longer supported in ColdFusion MX.

dbname="*database_name*"
: Specifies the database name. For the Sybase System 11 native driver and SQLOLEDB provider only. Optional. Overrides any value set for `datasource`. This attribute is no longer supported in ColdFusion MX.

dbtype="*database_type*"
: The type of database driver to use. Optional. This attribute is no longer supported in ColdFusion MX. Possible choices are:

    `ODBC` *(the default)*
    : Connect to the data source using an ODBC driver.

    `OLEDB`
    : Connect using an OLEDB driver.

    `Oracle73`
    : Connect using the Oracle 7.3 native driver. This requires the 7.3.4.0.0 or later client libraries be installed on the ColdFusion server.

    `Oracle80`
    : Connect using the Oracle 8 native driver. This requires the 8.0 or later client libraries be installed on the ColdFusion server.

    `Sybase11`
    : Connect using the Sybase 11 native driver. This requires the 11.1.1 or later client libraries be installed on the ColdFusion server.

    `DB2`
    : Connect using the DB2 5.2 native driver.

    `Informix73`
    : Connect using the Informix 7.3 native driver. This requires the Informix SDK 2.5 or later or Informix-Connect 2.5 (or later) for Windows.

    `Dynamic`
    : Allows ColdFusion to make an ODBC connection to a data source without having to have the data source registered in the ColdFusion Administrator. When making a dynamic connection, all information normally provided in the ColdFusion Administrator for the connection must be specified in the `connectstring` attribute. New as of ColdFusion 5.0.

dbserver="*database_server*"
: The name of the database server to connect to when using native drivers. Specifying a `dbserver` overrides any value set for `datasource`. Optional. This attribute is no longer supported in ColdFusion MX.

debug="Yes|No"
: Whether or not debugging information is to be output. Optional. The default is `No`.

password="*password*"
: Password associated with `username`. Optional. If a password is specified, it overrides the value set in the ColdFusion Administrator.

provider="*COM_provider*"
: COM provider for OLE DB connections. Optional. This attribute is no longer supported in ColdFusion MX.

providerdsn="*datasource*"
: COM provider's data-source name for OLE DB. Optional. This attribute is no longer supported in ColdFusion MX.

returncode="Yes|No"
: If set to Yes, populates cfstoredproc.StatusCode with the status code returned by the stored procedure. Optional. The default is No.

username="*username*"
: Username to pass to the data source if one is required. Optional. If a username is specified, it overrides the value set in the ColdFusion Administrator.

Returned Variables

cfstoredproc.StatusCode
: Returned when returncode is set to Yes. Contains the status code returned by the stored procedure.

cfstoredproc.ExecutionTime
: The number of milliseconds it takes the stored procedure to execute.

---

cfswitch

Updated in ColdFusion MX

```
<cfswitch expression="expression">
  <cfcase value="value" delimiters="delimiter">
  HTML and CFML
  </cfcase>
  <cfcase value="value" delimiters="delimiter">
  HTML and CFML
  </cfcase>
  ...
  [<cfdefaultcase>
  HTML and CFML
  </cfdefaultcase>]
</cfswitch>
```

Evaluates an expression against multiple values until a match is made. Once a match has been made, cfswitch passes control to the appropriate cfcase tag where additional action can take place. If no value matches expression, the code between the cfdefaultcase tags is executed. As of ColdFusion MX, the cfdefaultcase tag no longer has to be coded as the last statement in a cfswitch block, although it is considered good style to do so.

cfswitch/cfcase/cfdefaultcase is similar in function to cfif/cfelseif/cfelse. cfswitch/cfcase/cfdefaultcase is usually faster than using multiple cfif statements and is generally easier to read.

Attributes

expression="*expression*"
: Any ColdFusion expression that evaluates to a simple value (string, number, Boolean, date/time). Required.

value="*value*"
: A value or delimited list of values `cfswitch` uses to perform a case-insensitive comparison against the specified `expression`. If a value listed in `value` matches `expression`, the code between the `cfcase` tags is executed. Required.

delimiters="*delimiter*"
: Specifies the character that separates multiple entries in the `value` attribute. Optional. The default is a comma.

cftable

Builds an HTML table from a query result set.

```
<cftable>
  [<cfcol>]
  [<cfcol>]
  ...
</cftable>
```

Attributes

query="*query_name*"
: The name of the query from which to pull the data used to populate the table. Required.

border
: Used in conjunction with the `htmltable` attribute. Adds a border to the table. Optional.

colheaders="*integer*"
: Displays the header for each column as specified in the `header` attribute of the `cfcol` tag. Optional.

colspacing="*integer*"
: The number of spaces to insert between columns in the table. Optional. The default is 2.

headerlines="*integer*"
: Displays headers for each column as specified in the `cfcol` tag. Optional.

htmltable
: Creates the table as an HTML 3.0 table. Optional.

maxrows="*integer*"
: The maximum number of rows to output. Optional.

startrow="*row_number*"
: The query row to begin outputting from. Optional.

cftextinput

Updated in ColdFusion MX 6.1

```
<cfform>
  <cftextinput>
  ...
</cfform>
```

Creates a Java-based text input control for use within a `cfform`. Provides data validation as well as customizable display characteristics.

Attributes

name="*name*"
: The form-field name for the text input control. Required.

align="*alignment*"
: Alignment of the text input control. Optional. Valid entries are Left, Right, Top, TextTop, Bottom, AbsBottom, Middle, AbsMiddle, and Baseline.

bgcolor="*color*"
: Background color for the text input control. Colors may be specified by name (Black, Blue, Cyan, Darkgray, Gray, LightGray, Magenta, Orange, Pink, Red, White, Yellow) or hex code in the form bgcolor="##FFFFCC". The double pound signs are necessary to keep ColdFusion from throwing a syntax error, or you may omit the pound signs altogether. Optional.

bold="Yes|No"
: If Yes, displays text in bold. Optional. The default is No.

font="*font_name*"
: The font face to use for text displayed in the text input control.

fontsize="*integer*"
: The font size for text displayed in the text input control.

height="*height_in_pixels*"
: Height of the text input control in pixels. Optional.

hspace="*horizontal_spacing_in_pixels*"
: Width in pixels for the padding to the left and right of the text input control. Optional.

italic="Yes|No"
: If Yes, displays text in italic. Optional. The default is No.

message="*text*"
: Text to appear if validation fails. Optional.

maxlength="*integer*"
: The maximum number of characters to accept in the text input control. Optional.

notsupported="*text*"
: A text message to display if the user's browser doesn't support Java or Java is disabled Optional. If no message is specified, ColdFusion displays a default message.

onerror="*function_name*"
: The name of a JavaScript function that should be executed if validation fails for any reason. Optional.

onvalidate="*javascript_function*"
: A JavaScript validation function that should be executed before the form is submitted. Specifying a value for onvalidate overrides any values set in the validate attribute. Optional.

pattern="*javascript_regular_expression*"
: JavaScript regular expression used to match form input when validate is Regular_Expression. pattern may contain ColdFusion variables and expressions as they are evaluated prior to the execution of the regular expression. Optional. New as of ColdFusion 5.0.

range="*min_value, max_value*"
: A range of acceptable numeric values for the form-field. Optional.

required="Yes|No"
: Whether or not the text input control requires a value before being submitted. Optional. The default is No.

size="*integer*"
: The number of characters to display before a horizontal scroll bar appears. Optional.

textcolor="*color*"
: Color to use for text entered in the text input control. Follows the same rules as bgcolor. Optional.

validate="*validation_type*"
: Validates the contents of the form-field before they are submitted using one of the following criteria; optional:

  CreditCard
  : Validates the form-field data using the mod10 algorithm. A credit-card number can be entered as a single value or with dashes or spaces and must be between 12 and 16 digits in length. ColdFusion automatically strips dashes and spaces before validating.

  Date
  : Requires the form-field value to be in the U.S. date format, *mm/dd/yyyy*.

  EuroDate
  : Requires the form-field value to be in the European date format, *dd/mm/yyyy*.

  Float
  : Requires the form-field value to be a floating-point number.

  Integer
  : Requires the form-field value to be an integer.

  Social_Security_Number
  : Requires the form-field value to be a U.S. Social Security number in the format *xxx-xx-xxxx* or *xxx xx xxxx*.

  Telephone
  : Requires the form-field value to be a U.S. telephone number formatted either *xxx-xxx-xxxx* or *xxx xxx xxxx*. The area code and exchange are required to begin with a number in the range of 1–9.

  Time
  : Requires that the form-field value be entered as a valid time using the format *hh:mm:ss*.

  ZipCode
  : Requires that the form-field value be entered as either a five- or nine-digit U.S. ZIP code number using the format *xxxxx*, *xxxxx-xxxx*, or *xxxxx xxxx*.

  Regular_Expression
  : Validates the form-field data against a JavaScript regular expression specified in the pattern attribute.

value="*text*"
: The initial value for the text input control. Optional.

`vspace="vertical_spacing_in_pixels"`
: Height in pixels for the padding above and below the text input control. Optional.

`width="width_in_pixels"`
: Width of the text input control in pixels. Optional.

cfthrow

Updated in ColdFusion MX

```
<cfthrow>
```

Creates a custom exception type that can be caught by the `cftry/cfcatch` tags when the `type` attribute of the `cfcatch` tag is set to `Application`, `Any`, or the custom type you specify in the `cfthrow` tag.

You can name custom exception types in a hierarchical manner so that you can reference groups of custom exception types with a single `cfcatch` tag. Consider the following `cfthrow` tag:

```
<cfthrow type="MyApp.RequiredParameters.MyVar">
```

Any of the three following `cfcatch` tags can be used to catch the exception:

```
<cfcatch type="MyApp.RequiredParameters.MyVar ">
<cfcatch type="MyApp.RequiredParameters">
<cfcatch type="MyApp">
```

Attributes

`detail="event_description"`
: Additional information to append to the detailed error information supplied by ColdFusion. Optional.

`errorcode="error_code"`
: A custom error code you want to make available. Optional.

`extendedinfo="extended_information"`
: Additional information regarding the error that you want to make available. Optional.

`message="error_message"`
: Message describing the event that triggered the exception. Optional.

`object="name"`
: Used to throw a Java exception from a CFML page. *Name* specifies the name of the object throwing the exception. This must be the same as the `name` attribute of the `cfobject` tag. Optional. If the `OBJECT` attribute is used, all other attributes are ignored.

`type="exception_type"`
: A name for the exception type. You may give the exception type a custom name or use the predefined types `Application` or `Any`. Optional. The default is `Application`.

Returned Variables

When `cfthrow` is used in conjunction with the `cftry` and `cfcatch` tags, the following variables are available when an exception is thrown:

`cfcatch.Type`
: The exception type specified in the `type` attribute of the `cfcatch` tag.

`cfcatch.Message`
: The error message generated by the exception, if any.

`cfcatch.Detail`
: A detailed error message generated by the CFML interpreter.

`cfcatch.TagContext`
: The name and position of each tag in the tag stack as well as the full pathnames of the files containing the tags. In versions of ColdFusion prior to MX, CFML Stack Trace had to be enabled in the Debugging section of the ColdFusion Administrator in order to populate this variable. This is no longer true in ColdFusion MX.

`cfcatch.ErrorCode`
: The contents of the `ErrorCode` attribute, if any, from the `cfthrow` tag.

`cfcatch.ExtendedInfo`
: The contents of the `ExtendedInfo` attribute, if any, from the `cfthrow` tag.

---

cftrace

New in ColdFusion MX

```
<cftrace>
```

Traces execution of a ColdFusion page. Logs and optionally displays customizable debugging information about the trace. Trace information is automatically written to a log file named *cftrace.log*, stored in *\cfmxroot\logs*. The log entry is made using the `cflog` tag behind the scenes. Debugging must be enabled in the ColdFusion Administrator in order to use `cftrace`.

The log file generated by `cftrace` follows a standard format. The first line of each log file contains a comma-delimited list of column headers, qualified with double quotes, that looks like this:

```
"Severity","ThreadID","Date","Time","Application","Message"
```

When an entry is made to the log file, the values that are written to each column are also qualified with double quotes and delimited with commas. The values written to the log file are:

`Severity`
: The severity of the trace point as defined by the `type` attribute of the `cftrace` tag.

`ThreadID`
: The ID of the thread that serviced the page request.

`Date`
: Date the trace took place.

`Time`
: Time the trace took place.

`Application`
: Name of the application as defined in the application's `cfapplication` tag. If no `cfapplication` tag exists for the page being traced, a blank entry is made in the log file.

`Message`
: Contains information about the trace point, including execution time up until the trace point occurred, the full path to the template containing the trace, the line number where the trace occurred, user-defined category for the trace, the name of the

variable (if any) specified in the var attribute of the cftrace tag and its value if it contains a simple value, and any user-defined message text specified in the text attribute of the cftrace tag. The log entry for the Message field follows this format:

```
"[execution_time] [template_path @ line_num] - [category] [variable] message text"
```

In addition to the log file, trace information can also be displayed in the browser by setting the inline attribute to Yes. If debugging is turned on and Tracing Information is checked in the Debugging section of the CF Administrator, tracing summary information is also displayed in the debug output section generated with the page request.

Attributes

abort="Yes|No"
: If Yes, automatically calls the cfabort tag after the cftrace tag has executed. Optional. The default is No.

category="*category_name*"
: Specifies a user-defined category name for grouping trace data. The category is displayed to the browser if inline is Yes, and it is always written to the *cftrace.log* file. Optional.

inline ="Yes|No"
: If Yes, displays trace code in the browser. Optional. The default is No.

text="*text*"
: Text to write to the *cftrace.log* file, and optionally to output to the browser if inline is Yes. Corresponds to the cflog tag's text attribute. You may include variables (enclosed in pound signs) containing simple datatypes in this attribute; they will be evaluated at runtime. Optional.

type="*severity*"
: The severity you wish to assign to the trace. If the trace output is inline (to the browser), a graphic icon representing the severity is displayed. Possible entries are Information, Warning, Error, and Fatal. These values correspond to the types available in the cflog tag's type attribute. Optional. The default is Information.

var="*variable_name*"
: Name of a variable you want display in the browser. The variable can be simple (such as a string) or complex (such as an array). If inline is Yes, this attribute causes the cftrace tag to output the value of the variable in a nicely formatted table, just like the cfdump tag. In fact, cftrace uses cfdump behind the scenes to generate the output. Unlike cfdump, the value you specify for var need only be the variable name and should not be surrounded by pound signs. Optional.

cftransaction

```
<cftransaction>
CFML code
</cftransaction>
```

Treats all query operations between <cftransaction>...</cftransaction> tags as a single transaction. Changes to the database aren't committed until all queries in the transaction have executed successfully. In the event that a query within the transaction fails, all previous queries are automatically rolled back.

cftransaction tags may be nested to allow portions of the transaction to be committed or rolled back within the main cftransaction block. More than one database may be written to within a single cftransaction block if each transaction is committed or rolled back prior to writing a query to the next database. Exception handling using cftry/cfcatch gives you full control over how queries are committed and rolled back within cftransaction blocks.

Attributes

action="begin|commit|rollback"
: The action to take. Optional. The default value is Begin, which specifies the beginning of a block of code to execute as a transaction. Commit commits a pending transaction, and Rollback rolls back a pending transaction.

isolation="*ODBC_lock_type*"
: The ODBC lock type to use for the transaction. The following ODBC lock types are supported: Read_Uncommitted, Read_Committed, Repeatable_Read, and Serializable.

---

cftree

Enhanced in ColdFusion 5.0

```
<cfform>
  <cftree>
    [<cftreeitem>]
    ...
  </cftree>
  ...
</cfform>
```

Creates a Java tree control within a cfform block.

Attributes

name="*name*"
: The form-field name for the tree control. Required.

align="*alignment*"
: Alignment for the tree control. Valid entries are Left, Right, Top, TextTop, Bottom, AbsBottom, Baseline, Middle, and AbsMiddle. Optional.

appendkey="Yes|No"
: Whether or not to append the cftreeitemkey variable to the end of the value of a selected cftreeitem. Optional. The default is Yes.

bold="Yes|No"
: If Yes, displays text in bold. Optional. The default is No.

border="Yes|No"
: Whether or not to add a border around the tree control. Optional. The default is No.

completepath="Yes|No"
: Whether or not to pass the root level of the Path form variable (form.*TreeName*.Path) when the cfform containing the cftree is submitted. If No, the root level of the form isn't passed. Optional. The default is No.

delimiter="*delimiter*"
: The delimiter to use to separate the segments of returned in the Path form variable (form.*TreeName*.Path). Optional. The default is the backslash (\).

font="*font_name*"
: Font face to use for text appearing in the tree control. Optional.

fontsize="*integer*"
: Font size to use for text appearing in the tree control. Optional.

height="*height_in_pixels*"
: Height in pixels for the tree control's display area. Optional.

highlighthref="Yes|No"
: Whether or not to highlight links specified in the href attribute of associated cftreeitem tags. Optional. The default is Yes.

hscroll="Yes|No"
: Whether or not to allow horizontal scrolling. Optional. The default is Yes.

hspace="*horizontal_spacing_in_pixels*"
: Width in pixels for the padding to the left and right of the tree control. Optional.

italic="Yes|No"
: If Yes, displays text in italic. Optional. The default is No.

lookandfeel="Windows|Motif|Metal"
: Specifies a theme governing the look and feel of the tree control. Optional. If no value is specified, ColdFusion first tries Windows, then uses the platform default. New as of ColdFusion 5.0.

message="*text*"
: Text to appear if validation fails. Optional.

notsupported="*text*"
: A text message to display if the user's browser doesn't support Java or Java is disabled Optional. If no message is specified, ColdFusion displays a default message.

onerror="*function_name*"
: The name of a JavaScript function that should be executed if validation fails for any reason. Optional.

onvalidate="*javascript_function*"
: A JavaScript validation function that should be executed before the form is submitted. Optional.

required="Yes|No"
: Whether or not the tree control requires a value before being submitted. Optional. The default is No.

vscroll="Yes|No"
: Whether or not to allow vertical scrolling. Optional. The default is Yes.

vspace="*vertical_spacing_in_pixels*"
: Height in pixels for the padding above and below the tree control. Optional.

width="*width_in_pixels*"
: Width in pixels for the tree control's display area. Optional.

Returned Variables

When you submit a `cfform` containing a `cftree` control, two form variables are made available to the template being posted to:

`form.`*`TreeName`*`.Node`
: The node selected by the user from the tree.

`form.`*`TreeName`*`.Path`
: If the `completepath` attribute is set to `Yes`, `form.`*`TreeName`*`.Path` returns the user's selection specified as *`root\node1\noden\value`*. Otherwise, `form.`*`TreeName`*`.Path` returns the path from the first node. The delimiter can be changed by specifying a value for the `delimiter` attribute.

---

cftreeitem

```
<cftree>
  [<cftreeitem>]
  ...
</cftree>
```

Used in conjunction with `cftree` to populate a Java tree control.

Attributes

`value="`*`text`*`"`
: The value to pass when submitting the `cfform`. If populating the tree from a query, multiple column names should be specified in a comma-delimited list. Required.

`display="`*`text`*`"`
: The label to use for the tree item. Label names are specified in a comma-delimited list when populating a tree from a query. Optional. The default is `value`.

`expand="Yes|No"`
: Whether or not a given branch should be expanded to show its children branches by default. Optional. The default is `Yes`. Although undocumented, the `expand` attribute can accept a comma-delimited list of `Yes|No` values indicating whether or not to expand additional sublevels in the tree.

`href="`*`URL`*`"`
: A URL to associate with the tree item or the name of a query column (from a query used to populate the tree) containing `href` values. If the tree is being populated from a query, `href` URLs can be specified in a comma-delimited list. The URLs may be relative or absolute. Optional.

`img="`*`filename`*`"`
: The image to use with the tree item. You may specify a path to your own image or use one of the images supplied with ColdFusion by referencing the image name. Multiple images may be assigned to recursive levels of the tree by entering them in a comma-separated list. Valid options for `img` are `CD`, `Computer`, `Document`, `Element`, `Folder`, `Floppy`, `Fixed`, and `Remote`. Optional. The default image is `Folder`. If you choose to use your own image, you should try to limit the size to 20 pixels by 20 pixels.

imgopen="*filename*"
: Image to display when a tree branch is opened. You may use the same images as the IMG tag or supply your own. Optional.

parent="*parent_name*"
: The value of the tree item's parent. Optional.

query="*query_name*"
: Name of the query that generates data for the tree control. Optional.

queryasroot="Yes|No|*string*"
: Defines the specified query as the root level of the tree control. This prevents having to code an additional parent cftreeitem for the root level. Optional. The default is No. Besides Yes|No, queryasroot also allows you to specify an arbitrary string to use as the query root.

target="*URL_target*"
: The name of a frame or window that the template specified in the href attribute should be opened in. Optional.

---

cftry

Updated in ColdFusion MX

```
<cftry>
CFML
<cfcatch type="exception_type">
HTML and CFML
</cfcatch>

<cfcatch type="exception_type">
HTML and CFML
</cfcatch>
...
</cftry>
```

Traps and processes predefined and developer-specified exceptions within ColdFusion templates. The cftry/cfcatch tags allow you to handle exceptions in your templates gracefully, without having to abort processing. Exceptions occurring within cfcatch blocks can't be handled by the same cftry block governing the cfcatch block. At least one cfcatch block must be nested within a cftry block. cfcatch tags are processed in the order in which they are coded within a template.

Attributes

type="*exception_type*"
: Specifies the type of exception to trap. Valid entries are:

Application
: Catches application-level exceptions defined using the Application type in the cfthrow tag.

Any *(default)*
: Catches unexpected exceptions. In versions of ColdFusion prior to MX, it was recommended that this exception type be coded as the last cfcatch within a cftry block. This is no longer the case in ColdFusion MX.

CustomType
: Catches developer-specified exceptions as defined with the `cfthrow` tag.

`Database`
: Catches exceptions raised when interacting with data sources.

`Expression`
: Catches exceptions that occur when an expression's evaluation results in an error.

`Lock`
: Catches exceptions associated with the `cflock` tag, such as timeouts, etc.

`MissingInclude`
: Catches exceptions that occur when an included template isn't found. This exception type covers exceptions thrown by the `cfinclude`, `cfmodule`, and `cferror` tags.

`Object`
: Catches exceptions associated with external objects such as COM/DCOM, CORBA, and Java.

`SearchEngine`
: Catches exceptions associated with the `cfcollection`, `cfindex`, and `cfsearch` tags. New in ColdFusion MX.

`Security`
: Catches exceptions that result when authentication fails within the ColdFusion security framework.

`Template`
: Catches general application errors associated with ColdFusion templates.

Besides the values already listed for the type attribute, ColdFusion also supports a number of additional structured exception types. These exception types are generated by very specific conditions such as request timeouts or by exceptions encountered as the result of a call to various ColdFusion tags. These exception types are as follows:

```
COM.Allaire.ColdFusion.HTTPConnectionTimeout
COM.Allaire.ColdFusion.HTTPFailure
COM.Allaire.ColdFusion.HTTPAuthFailure
COM.Allaire.ColdFusion.HTTPFileNotFound
COM.Allaire.ColdFusion.HTTPFileNotPassed
COM.Allaire.ColdFusion.HTTPUrlValueNotPassed
COM.Allaire.ColdFusion.HTTPCGIValueNotPassed
COM.Allaire.ColdFusion.HTTPCookieValueNotPassed
COM.Allaire.ColdFusion.HTTPFileNotRenderable
COM.Allaire.ColdFusion.HTTPFileInvalidPath
COM.Allaire.ColdFusion.HTTPContinue
COM.Allaire.ColdFusion.HTTPSwitchingProtocols
COM.Allaire.ColdFusion.HTTPCreated
COM.Allaire.ColdFusion.HTTPAccepted
COM.Allaire.ColdFusion.HTTPNonAuthoritativeInfo
COM.Allaire.ColdFusion.HTTPNoContent
COM.Allaire.ColdFusion.HTTPResetContent
COM.Allaire.ColdFusion.HTTPPartialContent
COM.Allaire.ColdFusion.HTTPMultipleChoices
COM.Allaire.ColdFusion.HTTPMovedPermanently
COM.Allaire.ColdFusion.HTTPMovedTemporarily
COM.Allaire.ColdFusion.HTTPSeeOther
```

```
COM.Allaire.ColdFusion.HTTPNotModified
COM.Allaire.ColdFusion.HTTPUseProxy
COM.Allaire.ColdFusion.HTTPBadRequest
COM.Allaire.ColdFusion.HTTPPaymentRequired
COM.Allaire.ColdFusion.HTTPForbidden
COM.Allaire.ColdFusion.HTTPNotFound
COM.Allaire.ColdFusion.HTTPMethodNotAllowed
COM.Allaire.ColdFusion.HTTPNotAcceptable
COM.Allaire.ColdFusion.HTTPProxyAuthenticationRequired
COM.Allaire.ColdFusion.HTTPConflict
COM.Allaire.ColdFusion.HTTPGone
COM.Allaire.ColdFusion.HTTPContentLengthRequired
COM.Allaire.ColdFusion.HTTPPreconditionFailed
COM.Allaire.ColdFusion.HTTPCFHTTPRequestEntityTooLarge
COM.Allaire.ColdFusion.HTTPRequestURLTooLarge
COM.Allaire.ColdFusion.HTTPUnsupportedMediaType
COM.Allaire.ColdFusion.HTTPServerError
COM.Allaire.ColdFusion.HTTPNotImplemented
COM.Allaire.ColdFusion.HTTPBadGateway
COM.Allaire.ColdFusion.HTTPServiceUnavailable
COM.Allaire.ColdFusion.HTTPGatewayTimeout
COM.Allaire.ColdFusion.HTTPVersionNotSupported
COM.Allaire.ColdFusion.POPConnectionFailure
COM.Allaire.ColdFusion.POPAuthFailure
COM.Allaire.ColdFusion.POPDeleteError
COM.Allaire.ColdFusion.SERVLETJRunError
COM.Allaire.ColdFusion.Request.Timeout
COM.Allaire.ColdFusion.cfexecute.Timeout
COM.Allaire.ColdFusion.cfexecute.OutputError
COM.Allaire.ColdFusion.FileException
```

Additionally, as of ColdFusion MX, you can now specify Java exception classes in the `type` attribute. This gives you even more granular control over error handling as every exception thrown by ColdFusion belongs to one of these classes. An exception's class can be viewed by turning debugging on in the ColdFusion Administrator and looking at the first line in the stack trace of the error output. Another benefit of this type of exception handling is you can use it to handle exceptions thrown by non CFML Java objects.

Returned Variables

The following variables are available regardless of the exception type raised. Note that `cfcatch` variables without values do not appear in the output generated by the `cfdump` tag:

`cfcatch.Type`
: The exception type specified in the `type` attribute of the `cfcatch` tag.

`cfcatch.Message`
: The error message generated by the exception, if any.

`cfcatch.Detail`
: A detailed error message generated by the CFML interpreter.

`cfcatch.RootCause`
: Returns a Java object containing the Java servlet exception generated by the JVM as the exception's root cause. This variable is new in ColdFusion MX.

`cfcatch.TagContext`
: The name and position of each tag in the tag stack as well as the full pathnames of the files containing the tags as an array of structures. Each structure in the `TagContext` array contains the following elements:

  `type`
  : Type of page generating the exception. `type` always returns "CFML". This key is new in ColdFusion MX.

  `ID`
  : The name of the tag within the stack where the exception occurred. If the exception occurs within `cfscript` tags, `ID` returns "??".

  `template`
  : The full path to the template containing the tag.

  `line`
  : The line number within the template where the tag was found.

`column`
: No longer supported in ColdFusion MX. This key is still available for backward compatibility with previous versions of ColdFusion, but it always returns 0. In previous versions of ColdFusion, `column` returned the column number within the template where the tag was found.

`raw_trace`
: The raw Java stack trace for the exception. This key is new in ColdFusion MX. In versions of ColdFusion prior to MX, CFML Stack Trace must be enabled in the Debugging section of the ColdFusion Administrator in order to populate this variable. If this option isn't enabled, ColdFusion returns a zero-length array for `cfcatch.TagContext`.

`cfcatch.ErrorCode`
: The contents of the `ErrorCode` attribute, if any, as passed from the `cfthrow` tag when `type` is `Application` or `Custom`. Returns the same value as `SQLState` when `type` is `Database`. Returns an empty string for all other `type` values.

The remaining variables are all specific to the exception type specified in the `type` attribute of the `cfcatch` tag:

`cfcatch.DataSource` *(type is* `Database`*)*
: The name of the data source where the exception occurred. This variable is new in ColdFusion MX.

`cfcatch.NativeErrorCode` *(type is* `Database`*)*
: The native error code supplied by the database driver for the particular exception. If no error code is provided, ColdFusion returns a value of –1. If the database driver used for the data source is a type 1 JDBC driver, the value returned is the same as would be returned in ColdFusion 5. Type 4 drivers may return different values.

`cfcatch.SQLState` *(type is* `Database`*)*
: The `SQLState` supplied by the database driver for the particular exception. If no `SQLState` is returned, ColdFusion returns a value of –1.

cfcatch.Where *(type is* Database*)*
: Only available if a cfqueryparam tag was used with the query throwing the error. Returns name/value pairs representing the attributes of the cfqueryparam tag and their associated values. This variable is new in ColdFusion MX.

cfcatch.QueryError
: Error message returned by the database driver.

cfcatch.SQL
: SQL contained in the query that generated the exception. This variable is new in ColdFusion MX.

cfcatch.ErrNumber *(type is* Expression*)*
: An internal error number associated with the expression.

cfcatch.LockName *(type is* Lock*)*
: The name of the lock affected by the exception. If the lock is unnamed, returns anonymous.

cfcatch.LockOperation *(type is* Lock*)*
: The operation that caused the exception. Valid return values are Timeout, MuteEx, and Unknown.

cfcatch.MissingFileName *(type is* MissingInclude*)*
: The name of the missing include file.

cfcatch.ExtendedInfo *(type is* Application *or* Custom*)*
: The contents of the ExtendedInfo attribute, if any, from the cfthrow tag.

cfupdate

Updated in ColdFusion MX

<cfupdate>

Updates records in a database. The cfupdate tag provides a way to update database records without having to wrap the SQL in a cfquery.

Attributes

datasource="*datasource_name*"
: The name of the data source to connect to when performing the update. Required.

connectstring="*connection_string*"
: Passes additional connection information to an ODBC data source that can't be passed via the ColdFusion Administrator. connectstring can also override connection information set for a data source already registered in the ColdFusion Administrator. When making a dynamic data source connection (when dbtype is Dynamic), connectstring specifies all the information required to connect to the data source. For specific connection-string options, you should consult the documentation for your particular database. New as of ColdFusion 5.0. This attribute is no longer supported in ColdFusion MX.

dbname="*database_name*"
: The database name. For the Sybase System 11 native driver and SQLOLEDB provider only. Optional. Overrides any value set for datasource. This attribute is no longer supported in ColdFusion MX.

`dbtype="`*`database_type`*`"`

The type of database driver to use. Optional. This attribute is no longer supported in ColdFusion MX. Possible choices are:

`ODBC` *(the default)*

Connect to the data source using an ODBC driver.

`OLEDB`

Connect using an OLEDB driver.

`Oracle73`

Connect using the Oracle 7.3 native driver. This requires the 7.3.4.0.0 or later client libraries be installed on the ColdFusion server.

`Oracle80`

Connect using the Oracle 8 native driver. This requires the 8.0 or later client libraries be installed on the ColdFusion server.

`Sybase11`

Connect using the Sybase 11 native driver. This requires the 11.1.1 or later client libraries be installed on the ColdFusion server.

`DB2`

Connect using the DB2 5.2 native driver.

`Informix73`

Connect using the Informix 7.3 native driver. This requires the Informix SDK 2.5 or later or Informix-Connect 2.5 (or later) for Windows.

`Dynamic`

Allows ColdFusion to make an ODBC connection to a data source without having to have the data source registered in the ColdFusion Administrator. When making a dynamic connection, all information normally provided in the ColdFusion Administrator for the connection must be specified in the `connectstring` attribute. New as of ColdFusion 5.0.

`dbserver="`*`database_server`*`"`

The name of the database server to connect to when using native drivers. Specifying a `dbserver` overrides any value set for `datasource`. Optional. This attribute is no longer supported in ColdFusion MX.

`formfields="`*`field_names`*`"`

A comma-delimited list of form fields to update. Optional. If no form fields are supplied, ColdFusion attempts to update the database using all the form fields passed from the form.

`password="`*`password`*`"`

Password associated with `username`. Optional. If a password is specified, it overrides the value set in the ColdFusion Administrator.

`provider="`*`COM_provider`*`"`

COM provider for OLE DB connections. Optional. This attribute is no longer supported in ColdFusion MX.

`providerdsn="`*`datasource`*`"`

COM provider's data-source name for OLE DB. Optional. This attribute is no longer supported in ColdFusion MX.

`tablename="table_name"`
: The name of the table to perform the update on. Required. Note that Oracle database drivers require the table name to be in all uppercase. In addition, Sybase database drivers use a case-sensitive table name.

`tableowner="table_owner"`
: The name of the table owner for databases that support this feature (e.g., Oracle, SQL Server, and SQL Anywhere). Optional.

`tablequalifier="qualifier"`
: The table qualifier for databases that support the feature (e.g., Oracle and SQL Server). Optional.

`username="username"`
: Username to pass to the data source if one is required. Optional. If a username is specified, it overrides the value set in the ColdFusion Administrator.

---

cfwddx

`<cfwddx>`

Serializes and deserializes data according to the WDDX XML DTD. The `cfwddx` tag can also create JavaScript statements that instantiate equivalent JavaScript objects. The `cfwddx` tag can serialize/deserialize binary data. Binary data is automatically base64-encoded before being serialized. This capability allows you to send binary files in WDDX packets. More information on WDDX can be found at *http://www.openwddx.org*.

Attributes

`action="action"`
: The action to be performed by the `cfwddx` tag. Required. Possible actions are `CFML2WDDX`, which serializes CFML to WDDX; `WDDX2CFML`, which deserializes WDDX to CFML; `CFML2JS`, which serializes CFML to JavaScript; and `WDDX2JS`, which deserializes WDDX to JavaScript.

`input="data"`
: The data to be serialized/deserialized. Required.

`output="variable_name"`
: A variable to hold the data after it has been serialized/deserialized. Required when `action` is `WDDX2CFML`. For all other actions, if no value is specified for `output`, the processing results are outputted in the HTML stream.

`toplevelvariable="variable_name"`
: The name of the top-level JavaScript object created when deserialization occurs. Required when `action` is set to `CFML2JS` or `WDDX2JS`.

`usetimezoneinfo="Yes|No"`
: Whether or not to use time-zone information when serializing CFML to WDDX. If this attribute is set to `Yes`, ColdFusion calculates the hour/minute offset for all date/time objects in the WDDX packet. If set to `No`, local time is used for all date/time objects. Optional. The default is `Yes`.

validate="Yes|No"
: Whether or not to use a validating XML parser with the WDDX DTD to determine whether the value specified in `input` is a well-formed WDDX packet when `action` is `WDDX2CFML` or `WDDDX2JS`. If the value is a well-formed WDDX packet, deserialization takes place. If the value isn't well-formed WDDX, an exception is thrown. The `validate` parameter performs the same job as the `IsWDDX()` function.

---

cfxml

New in ColdFusion MX

```
<cfxml>
  XML and CFML
</cfxml>
```

Creates a ColdFusion XML document object from the XML and CFML code between `<cfxml></cfxml>` tags. CFML code is executed and the results assigned to appropriate elements in the XML document object.

Attributes

`variable="`*`variable_name`*`"`
: Variable name for holding the resulting XML document object. Required.

`casesensitive="Yes|No"`
: If `Yes`, ColdFusion maintains the case of XML document elements and attributes. Optional. The default is `No`.

APPENDIX B

Function Reference

ColdFusion functions are an integral part of the CFML coding environment. ColdFusion contains over 265 functions that allow you to manipulate data and format it to suit your specific requirements. Functions can be used for everything from performing mathematical calculations to formatting time and date values. This appendix contains reference material on all the ColdFusion functions through ColdFusion MX, along with proper syntax, a detailed description, and a working example where possible.

Functions by Category

The following sections group ColdFusion's built-in functions according to functionality.

Array Functions

`ArrayAppend`	`ArrayAvg( )`
`ArrayClear( )`	`ArrayDeleteAt( )`
`ArrayInsertAt( )`	`ArrayIsEmpty( )`
`ArrayLen( )`	`ArrayMax( )`
`ArrayMin( )`	`ArrayNew( )`
`ArrayPrepend( )`	`ArrayResize( )`
`ArraySet( )`	`ArraySort( )`
`ArraySum( )`	`ArraySwap( )`
`ArrayToList( )`	`Duplicate( )`
`IsArray( )`	`ListToArray( )`

Date/Time Functions

CreateDate()	CreateDateTime()
CreateODBCDate()	CreateODBCDateTime()
CreateODBCTime()	CreateTime()
CreateTimeSpan()	DateAdd()
DateCompare()	DateConvert()
DateDiff()	DateFormat()
DatePart()	Day()
DayOfWeek()	DayOfWeekAsString()
DayOfYear()	DaysInMonth()
DaysInYear()	FirstDayOfMonth()
GetHTTPTimeString()	GetNumericDate()
GetTickCount()	GetTimeZoneInfo()
Hour()	IsDate()
IsLeapYear()	IsNumericDate()
LSDateFormat()	LSParseDateTime()
Minute()	Month()
MonthAsString()	Now()
ParseDateTime()	Quarter()
Second()	TimeFormat()
Week()	Year()

Decision/Evaluation Functions

CF_IsColdFusionDataSource()	DE()
DirectoryExists()	Evaluate()
FileExists()	IIf()
IsArray()	IsAthenticated()
IsAuthorized()	IsBinary()
IsBoolean()	IsCustomFunction()
IsDate()	IsDebugMode()
IsDefined()	IsK2ServerABroker()
IsK2ServerDocCountExceeded()	IsK2ServerOnline()
IsLeapYear()	IsNotMap()
IsNumeric()	IsNumericDate()
IsObject()	IsProtected()
IsQuery()	IsSimpleValue()
IsStruct()	IsUserInRole()
IsWDDX()	IsXmlDoc()
IsXmlElem()	IsXmlRoot()

LSIsCurrency( )
LSIsDate( )
LSIsNumeric( )
SetVariable( )

Encoding/Encryption Functions

CFusion_Decrypt( )
CFusion_Encrypt( )
Decrypt( )
Encrypt( )
Hash( )
SetEncoding( )
ToBase64( )
ToBinary( )
ToString( )
URLDecode( )
URLEncodedFormat( )

File/Directory Functions

DirectoryExists( )
ExpandPath( )
FileExists( )
GetBaseTemplatePath( )
GetCurrentTemplatePath( )
GetDirectoryFromPath( )
GetFileFromPath( )
GetTempDirectory( )
GetTempFile( )

Formatting Functions

DateFormat( )
DecimalFormat( )
DollarFormat( )
FormatBaseN( )
HTMLCodeFormat( )
HTMLEditFormat( )
JSStringFormat( )
Lcase( )
LSCurrencyFormat( )
LSDateFormat( )
LSEuroCurrencyFormat( )
LSNumberFormat( )
LSTimeFormat( )
NumberFormat( )
ParagraphFormat( )
TimeFormat( )
Ucase( )
Wrap( )
XMLFormat( )
YesNoFormat( )

Internationalization/Localization Functions

GetLocale( )
LSCurrencyFormat( )
LSDateFormat( )
LSEuroCurrencyFormat( )
LSIsCurrency( )
LSIsDate( )
LSIsNumeric( )
LSNumberFormat( )
LSParseCurrency( )
LSParseDateTime( )

LSParseEuroCurrency( )	LSParseNumber( )
LSTimeFormat( )	SetEncoding( )
SetLocale( )	

List Functions

ArrayToList( )	ListAppend( )
ListChangeDelims( )	ListContains( )
ListContainsNoCase( )	ListDeleteAt( )
ListFind( )	ListFindNoCase( )
ListFirst( )	ListGetAt( )
ListInsertAt( )	ListLast( )
ListLen( )	ListPrepend( )
ListQualify( )	ListRest( )
ListSetAt( )	ListSort( )
ListToArray( )	ListValueCount( )
ListValueCountNoCase( )	QuotedValueList( )
ReplaceList( )	ValueList( )

Mathematical Functions

Abs( )	ACos( )
ASin( )	ATan( )
BitAnd( )	BitMaskClear( )
BitMaskRead( )	BitMaskSet( )
BitNot( )	BitOr( )
BitSHLN( )	BitSHRN( )
BitXor( )	Ceiling( )
Cos( )	DecrementValue( )
Exp( )	Fix( )
IncrementValue( )	InputBaseN( )
Int( )	Log( )
Log10( )	Max( )
Min( )	Pi( )
Rand( )	Randomize( )
RandRange( )	Round( )
Sgn( )	Sin( )
Sqr( )	Tan( )

Miscellaneous Functions

CreateObject( )	CreateUUID( )
DeleteClientVariable( )	GetBaseTagData( )
GetBaseTagList( )	GetClientVariablesList( )
GetException( )	GetFunctionList( )
GetHTTPRequestData( )	GetMetaData( )
GetMetricData( )	GetPageContext( )
GetProfileSections( )	GetProfileString( )
JavaCast( )	ReleaseCOMObject( )
SetProfileString( )	WriteOutput( )

Query Functions

Duplicate( )	IsQuery( )
PreserveSingleQuotes( )	QueryAddColumn( )
QueryAddRow( )	QueryNew( )
QuerySetCell( )	QuotedValueList( )
ValueList( )	

Security Functions

AuthenticatedContext( )	AuthenticatedUser( )
IsAuthenticated( )	IsAuthorized( )
IsProtected( )	

String Functions

Asc( )	Chr( )
CJustify( )	Compare( )
CompareNoCase( )	Find( )
FindNoCase( )	FindOneOf( )
FormatBaseN( )	GetToken( )
Insert( )	Lcase( )
Left( )	Len( )
LJustify( )	LTrim( )
Mid( )	REFind( )
REFindNoCase( )	RemoveChars( )
RepeatString( )	Replace( )
ReplaceList( )	ReplaceNoCase( )

```
REReplace()                    REReplaceNoCase()
Reverse()                      Right()
RJustify()                     RTrim()
SpanExcluding()                SpanIncluding()
StripCR()                      ToBase64()
Trim()                         Ucase()
Val()
```

Structure Functions

```
Duplicate()                    IsStruct()
StructAppend()                 StructClear()
StructCopy()                   StructCount()
StructDelete()                 StructFind()
StructFindKey()                StructFindValue()
StructGet()                    StructInsert()
StructIsEmpty()                StructKeyArray()
StructKeyExists()              StructKeyList()
StructNew()                    StructSort()
StructUpdate()
```

Undocumented Functions

```
CF_GetDataSourceUserName()          CF_IsColdFusionDataSource()
CF_SetDataSourcePassword()          CF_SetDataSourceUserName()
CFusion_DBConnections_Flush()       CFusion_Decrypt()
CFusion_Disable_DBConnections()     CFusion_Encrypt()
CFusion_GetODBCDSN()                CFusion_GetODBCINI()
CFusion_SetODBCINI()                CFusion_Settings_Refresh()
CFusion_VerifyMail()                IsNotMap()
```

Verity Functions

```
GetK2ServerCollections()            GetK2ServerDocCount()
GetK2ServerDocCountLimit()          IsK2ServerABroker()
IsK2ServerDocCountExceeded()        IsK2ServerOnline()
```

XML Functions

```
IsXmlDoc()                     IsXmlElem()
IsXmlRoot()                    XmlChildPos()
```

XmlElemNew( )	XmlFormat( )
XmlNew( )	XmlParse( )
XmlSearch( )	XmlTransform( )

Alphabetical List of Functions

This section lists all the ColdFusion functions alphabetically, with proper syntax, a detailed description, and a working example where possible. Version information is included for many of the functions; if no version information is listed, the function is available in ColdFusion 4.5 and later.

Abs

`Abs(number)`

Returns the absolute value of a number. Example:

```
The absolute value of -33 is <cfoutput>#Abs(-33)#</cfoutput>
```

ACos

`ACos(number)`

Returns the arccosine of a number expressed in radians. The value of *number* must be between –1 and 1. Example:

```
The arccosine of -1 is <cfoutput>#ACos(-1)#</cfoutput>
```

ArrayAppend

`ArrayAppend(array, value)`

Appends an element to the end of an array. Upon successful completion, `ArrayAppend( )` returns a value of `true`. Here's an example of appending a new element to a one-dimensional array:

```
<cfset Grades = ArrayNew(1)>
<cfset Grades[1] = 95>
<cfset Grades[2] = 93>
<cfset Grades[3] = 87>
<cfset Grades[4] = 100>
<cfset Grades[5] = 74>

<b>Original Array:</b><br>
<cfdump var="#Grades#">

<p>Append the value 66 to the array:<br>
<cfset ArrayAppend(Grades, "66")>

<p><b>New Array:</b><br>
<cfdump var="#Grades#">
```

ArrayAvg

`ArrayAvg(array)`

Returns the average (mean) of the values in the array. The following example returns the average of the values contained in the one-dimensional array Grades:

```
<cfset Grades = ArrayNew(1)>
<cfset Grades[1] = 95>
<cfset Grades[2] = 93>
<cfset Grades[3] = 87>
<cfset Grades[4] = 100>
<cfset Grades[5] = 74>

<cfdump var="#Grades#">

<p><cfoutput>The average grade is #ArrayAvg(Grades)#%</cfoutput>
```

ArrayClear

`ArrayClear(array)`

Removes all data from the specified array. Upon successful completion, ArrayClear( ) returns a value of true. Here's an example of clearing all the data from the array Grades:

```
<cfset Grades = ArrayNew(1)>
<cfset Grades[1] = 95>
<cfset Grades[2] = 93>
<cfset Grades[3] = 87>
<cfset Grades[4] = 100>
<cfset Grades[5] = 74>

<cfif ArrayIsEmpty(Grades)>
  The array <b>Grades</b> is empty.
<cfelse>
  The array <b>Grades</b> contains data.
</cfif>

<p>Clearing the array...
<cfset ArrayClear(Grades)>

<p><cfif ArrayIsEmpty(Grades)>
  The array <b>Grades</b> is empty.
<cfelse>
  The array <b>Grades</b> contains data.
</cfif>
```

ArrayDeleteAt

`ArrayDeleteAt(array, position)`

Deletes data from the designated array at the specified position. Returns a value of true upon successful completion. The following example deletes the third element from the one-dimensional array Grades:

```
<cfset Grades = ArrayNew(1)>
<cfset Grades[1] = 95>
<cfset Grades[2] = 93>
<cfset Grades[3] = 87>
<cfset Grades[4] = 100>
<cfset Grades[5] = 74>
<b>Original Array:</b><br>
<cfdump var="#Grades#">

<p>Delete Element 4:
<cfset ArrayDeleteAt(Grades, 4)>

<p><b>New Array</b><br>
<cfdump var="#Grades#">
```

ArrayInsertAt

`ArrayInsertAt(`*`array, value, position`*`)`

Inserts *value* into the designated *array* at the specified *position*. Values having an index position greater than the inserted data are shifted right by one. Using `ArrayInsertAt()` increases the size of the array by 1 and returns a value of `true` upon successful completion. Here's an example of inserting an element into the third position of a one-dimensional array called `Grades`:

```
<cfset Grades = ArrayNew(1)>
<cfset Grades[1] = 95>
<cfset Grades[2] = 93>
<cfset Grades[3] = 87>
<cfset Grades[4] = 100>
<cfset Grades[5] = 74>

<b>Original Array:</b><br>
<cfdump var="#Grades#">

<p>Insert 65 into Element 3:
<cfset ArrayInsertAt(Grades, 3, 65)>

<p><b>New Array</b><br>
<cfdump var="#Grades#">
```

ArrayIsEmpty

`ArrayIsEmpty(`*`array`*`)`

Returns `true` if the specified array contains no data or `false` if it does contain data. Example:

```
<cfif ArrayIsEmpty(Scores)>
     There are no scores available for this game!
<cfelse>
     There are scores available for this game!
</cfif>
```

ArrayLen

```
ArrayLen(array)
```

Determines the length of the specified array. The following example returns the number of elements in the one-dimensional array Grades:

```
<cfset Grades = ArrayNew(1)>
<cfset Grades[1] = 95>
<cfset Grades[2] = 93>
<cfset Grades[3] = 87>
<cfset Grades[4] = 100>
<cfset Grades[5] = 74>

<cfoutput>The array <b>Grades</b> contains #ArrayLen(Grades)# elements.</cfoutput>
```

ArrayMax

```
ArrayMax(array)
```

Returns the largest numeric value contained in the array. Useful only for arrays containing numeric values. Here's an example that returns the highest grade in the array Grades:

```
<cfset Grades = ArrayNew(1)>
<cfset Grades[1] = 95>
<cfset Grades[2] = 93>
<cfset Grades[3] = 87>
<cfset Grades[4] = 100>
<cfset Grades[5] = 74>

<cfoutput>The highest grade is #ArrayMax(Grades)#%.</cfoutput>
```

ArrayMin

```
ArrayMin(array)
```

Returns the smallest numeric value contained in the array. Useful only for arrays containing numeric values. Here's an example that returns the lowest grade in the array Grades:

```
<cfset Grades = ArrayNew(1)>
<cfset Grades[1] = 95>
<cfset Grades[2] = 93>
<cfset Grades[3] = 87>
<cfset Grades[4] = 100>
<cfset Grades[5] = 74>

<cfoutput>The lowest grade is #ArrayMin(Grades)#%.</cfoutput>
```

ArrayNew

```
ArrayNew(dimension)
```

Creates an array of between 1 and 3 dimensions where the value of *dimension* is an integer between 1 and 3. Examples:

```
<cfset PartNumbers = ArrayNew(1)>
<cfset Samples = ArrayNew(2)>
<cfset Colors = ArrayNew(3)>
```

ArrayPrepend

```
ArrayPrepend(array, value)
```

Adds a value to the beginning of an array. A value of true is returned upon successful completion. The following example adds an element to the beginning of an array:

```
<cfset Grades = ArrayNew(1)>
<cfset Grades[1] = 95>
<cfset Grades[2] = 93>
<cfset Grades[3] = 87>
<cfset Grades[4] = 100>
<cfset Grades[5] = 74>

<b>Original Array:</b><br>
<cfdump var="#Grades#">

<p>Prepend the value 80 to the array:<br>
<cfset ArrayPrepend(Grades, "80")>

<p><b>New Array:</b><br>
<cfdump var="#Grades#">
```

ArrayResize

```
ArrayResize(array, size)
```

Resizes the designated array to a size as specified by the size parameter. For performance gains, this function is usually used immediately after creating an array with the ArrayNew() function to resize the array to its estimated size. Upon successful completion, ArrayResize() returns a value of true. Here's an example that creates an array called Grades and then resizes it to 50 elements:

```
<cfset Grades = ArrayNew(1)>

<cfoutput>Grades contains #ArrayLen(Grades)# elements.</cfoutput>
<p>Resize the array...<br>
<cfset ArrayResize(Grades, 50)>

<p><cfoutput>Grades now contains #ArrayLen(Grades)# elements.</cfoutput>
```

ArraySet

```
ArraySet(array, start, end, value)
```

Initializes one or more elements in a one-dimensional array, where *start* is the starting position, *end* is the ending position, and *value* is the value to use. The following example creates a one-dimensional array and populates the first five elements with the string "Place holder":

```
<cfset MyArray = ArrayNew(1)>
<cfset ArraySet(MyArray, 1, 5, "Place holder")>

<cfdump var="#MyArray#">
```

ArraySort

```
ArraySort(array, type [, order])
```

Sorts an array based on the sort *type* (`numeric`, `text`, or `textnocase`) and optionally, the sort *order* (asc, the default, or desc). Here's an example that sorts the values in an array called `Grades` from highest grade to lowest grade in descending order:

```
<cfset Grades = ArrayNew(1)>
<cfset Grades[1] = "95">
<cfset Grades[2] = "93">
<cfset Grades[3] = "87">
<cfset Grades[4] = "100">
<cfset Grades[5] = "74">

<b>Original Array:</b><br>
<cfdump var="#Grades#">

<p>Sort Array...
<cfset ArraySort(Grades, "Numeric", "desc")>

<p><b>Sorted Array:</b><br>
<cfdump var="#Grades#">
```

ArraySum

```
ArraySum(array)
```

Calculates the sum of the values in the specified array. The following example calculates the sum of all the values contained in an array called `Grades`:

```
<cfset Grades = ArrayNew(1)>
<cfset Grades[1] = "95">
<cfset Grades[2] = "93">
<cfset Grades[3] = "87">
<cfset Grades[4] = "100">
<cfset Grades[5] = "74">

<b>Original Array</b><br>
<cfdump var="#Grades#">

<p><cfoutput>The sum of all of the grades is #ArraySum(Grades)#.</cfoutput>
```

ArraySwap

```
ArraySwap(array, position1, position2)
```

Swaps the values stored in the positions specified in *`position1`* and *`position2`*. Here's an example that takes an array and swaps the values contained in elements 5 and 2:

```
<cfset Grades = ArrayNew(1)>
<cfset Grades[1] = 95>
<cfset Grades[2] = 93>
<cfset Grades[3] = 87>
<cfset Grades[4] = 100>
<cfset Grades[5] = 74>

<b>Original Array</b><br>
<cfdump var="#Grades#">

<p>Swap 5th and 2nd array elements...
<cfset ArraySwap(Grades, 5, 2)>

<p><b>Array after ArraySwap</b><br>
<cfdump var="#Grades#">
```

ArrayToList

`ArrayToList(`*`array`*` [, `*`delimiter`*`])`

Converts the specified one-dimensional array to a ColdFusion list. An optional ***delimiter*** may be specified (a comma is the default delimiter). The following example converts an array to a comma-delimited list:

```
<cfset Grades = ArrayNew(1)>
<cfset Grades[1] = 95>
<cfset Grades[2] = 93>
<cfset Grades[3] = 87>
<cfset Grades[4] = 100>
<cfset Grades[5] = 74>

<b>Original Array</b><br>
<cfdump var="#Grades#">

<p>Convert Array to List...
<cfset GradeList = ArrayToList(Grades)>

<p><b>New List</b><br>
<cfoutput>GradeList = #GradeList#</cfoutput>
```

Asc

`Asc(`*`character`*`)`

Returns the ASCII character code (number) for a given character. Here's an example that generates a chart of the printable ASCII character codes:

```
<table border="1">
  <tr><th>Character</th><th>ASCII Code</th></tr>

<cfloop index="Character" from="33" to="255">
  <cfoutput>
    <tr><td>#Chr(Character)#</td><td>#Asc(Chr(Character))#</td></tr>
```

```
    </cfoutput>
  </cfloop>
  </table>
```

Asin

```
ASin(number)
```

Returns the arcsine of a number expressed in radians. The value of *number* must be between –1 and 1. Example:

```
The arcsine of -1 is <cfoutput>#ASin(-1)#</cfoutput>
```

Atn

```
Atn(number)
```

Returns the arctangent of a number expressed in radians. Example:

```
The arctangent of 1 is <cfoutput>#Atn(1)#</cfoutput>
```

AuthenticatedContext

Not supported in ColdFusion MX

```
AuthenticatedContext( )
```

Returns the name of the security context for a given application when used with ColdFusion's Advanced Security. Example:

```
The current security context is <cfoutput>#AuthenticatedContext( )#</cfoutput>.
```

AuthenticatedUser

Not supported in ColdFusion MX

```
AuthenticatedUser( )
```

Returns the name of the authenticated user within an application when used with ColdFusion's Advanced Security. Example:

```
The authenticated user is <cfoutput>#AuthenticatedUser( )#</cfoutput>.
```

BitAnd

```
BitAnd(number1, number2)
```

Returns the bitwise AND of two 32-bit integers. Examples:

```
<cfoutput>
BitAnd(1,1): #BitAnd(1,1)#<br>
BitAnd(2,10): #BitAnd(2,10)#<br>
BitAnd(3,45): #BitAnd(3,45)#<br>
BitAnd(128,256): #BitAnd(128,256)#<br>
BitAnd(1024,32): #BitAnd(1024,32)#
</cfoutput>
```

BitMaskClear

```
BitMaskClear(number, startbit, length)
```

Returns *number* bitwise cleared with *length* bits beginning at the bit specified by *startbit*. Both *startbit* and *length* must be integers between 0 and 31. Examples:

```
<cfoutput>
BitMaskClear(127,0,1): #BitMaskClear(127,0,1)#<br>
BitMaskClear(255,3,3): #BitMaskClear(255,3,3)#<br>
BitMaskClear(511,2,4): #BitMaskClear(511,2,4)#<br>
BitMaskClear(1023,4,25): #BitMaskClear(1023,4,25)#<br>
BitMaskClear(2047,7,4): #BitMaskClear(2047,7,4)#
</cfoutput>
```

BitMaskRead

```
BitMaskRead(number, startbit, length)
```

Returns the integer from *length* bits of *number* beginning from the bit specified by *startbit*. Examples:

```
<cfoutput>
BitMaskRead(127,0,1): #BitMaskRead(127,0,1)#<br>
BitMaskRead(255,3,3): #BitMaskRead(255,3,3)#<br>
BitMaskRead(511,2,4): #BitMaskRead(511,2,4)#<br>
BitMaskRead(1023,4,25): #BitMaskRead(1023,4,25)#<br>
BitMaskRead(2047,7,4): #BitMaskRead(2047,7,4)#
</cfoutput>
```

BitMaskSet

```
BitMaskSet(number, mask, startbit, length)
```

Returns *number* bitwise masked with *length* bits of *mask* beginning at the bit specified by *startbit*. Examples:

```
<cfoutput>
BitMaskSet(127,12,0,1): #BitMaskSet(127,12,0,1)#<br>
BitMaskSet(255,3,3,3): #BitMaskSet(255,3,3,3)#<br>
BitMaskSet(511,4,2,4): #BitMaskSet(511,4,2,4)#<br>
BitMaskSet(1023,0,4,25): #BitMaskSet(1023,0,4,25)#<br>
BitMaskSet(2047,247,7,4): #BitMaskSet(2047,247,7,4)#
</cfoutput>
```

BitNot

```
BitNot(number)
```

Returns the bitwise NOT of a 32-bit integer. Examples:

```
<cfoutput>
BitNot(0): #BitNot(0)#<br>
BitNot(1): #BitNot(1)#<br>
BitNot(10): #BitNot(10)#<br>
```

```
BitNot(128): #BitNot(128)#<br>
BitNot(1024): #BitNot(1024)#
</cfoutput>
```

BitOr

```
BitOr(number1, number2)
```

Returns the bitwise OR of two 32-bit integers. Examples:

```
<cfoutput>
BitOr(1,1): #BitOr(1,1)#<br>
BitOr(2,10): #BitOr(2,10)#<br>
BitOr(3,45): #BitOr(3,45)#<br>
BitOr(128,256): #BitOr(128,256)#<br>
BitOr(1024,32): #BitOr(1024,32)#
</cfoutput>
```

BitSHLN

```
BitSHLN(number, count)
```

Bitwise shifts *number* to the left (without rotation) *count* bits where *count* is an integer between 0 and 31. Examples:

```
<cfoutput>
BitSHLN(0,1): #BitSHLN(0,1)#<br>
BitSHLN(1,5): #BitSHLN(1,5)#<br>
BitSHLN(10,9): #BitSHLN(10,9)#<br>
BitSHLN(128,23): #BitSHLN(128,23)#<br>
BitSHLN(1024, 31): #BitSHLN(1024,31)#
</cfoutput>
```

BitSHRN

```
BitSHRN(number, count)
```

Bitwise shifts *number* to the right (without rotation) *count* bits where *count* is an integer between 0 and 31. Examples:

```
<cfoutput>
BitSHRN(0,1): #BitSHRN(0,1)#<br>
BitSHRN(90000,5): #BitSHRN(90000,5)#<br>
BitSHRN(256,3): #BitSHRN(256,3)#<br>
BitSHRN(128,1): #BitSHRN(128,1)#<br>
BitSHRN(1024, 2): #BitSHRN(1024,2)#
</cfoutput>
```

BitXor

```
BitXor(number1, number2)
```

Returns the bitwise XOR of two 32-bit integers. Examples:

```
<cfoutput>
BitXor(1,1): #BitXor(1,1)#<br>
BitXor(2,10): #BitXor(2,10)#<br>
BitXor(3,45): #BitXor(3,45)#<br>
BitXor(128,256): #BitXor(128,256)#<br>
BitXor(1024,32): #BitXor(1024,32)#
</cfoutput>
```

Ceiling

```
Ceiling(number)
```

Returns the closest integer greater than the number specified. Examples:

```
<cfoutput>
-2.5: #Ceiling(-2.5)#<br>
-1: #Ceiling(-1)#<br>
-1.123: #Ceiling(-1.123)#<br>
-0.123: #Ceiling(-0.123)#<br>
0: #Ceiling(0)#<br>
0.123: #Ceiling(0.123)#<br>
1: #Ceiling(1)#<br>
1.123: #Ceiling(1.123)#<br>
2.5: #Ceiling(2.5)#
</cfoutput>
```

CFusion_DBConnections_Flush

Not supported in ColdFusion MX

```
CFusion_DBConnections_Flush( )
```

Drops any existing connections (including database locks) with ColdFusion data sources. This is an undocumented function used by the ColdFusion Administrator. Example:

```
<cfset CFusion_DBConnections_Flush( )>
All ColdFusion database connections have been dropped...
```

CFusion_Decrypt

```
CFusion_Decrypt(encryptedstring, key)
```

Decrypts *encryptedstring* using *key*. This is an undocumented function used by the ColdFusion Administrator; it was introduce in the 3.x version of ColdFusion. `CFusion_Decrypt( )` is similar to the `Decrypt( )` function except it works only with strings encrypted using the `CFusion_Encrypt( )` function. Example:

```
<cfset x=CFusion_Encrypt("this is a message", 12345)>
<cfset ux=CFusion_Decrypt(x, 12345)>

<cfoutput>
Original String: this is a message<br>
Encrypted:  #x#<br>
Decrypted:  #ux#
</cfoutput>
```

CFusion_Disable_DBConnections

Not supported in ColdFusion MX

```
CFusion_Disable_DBConnections(datasource, Yes|No)
```

If set to Yes, *datasource* is disabled as a ColdFusion data source. Specifying No enables a previously disabled data source. This is an undocumented function used by the ColdFusion Administrator. Example:

```
<cfset CFusion_Disable_DBConnections('CFExamples', 'Yes')>
The ColdFusion examples database has been disabled...
```

CFusion_Encrypt

```
CFusion_Encrypt(string, key)
```

Encrypts *string* using *key*. This is an undocumented function used by the ColdFusion Administrator; it was introduced in the 3.x version of ColdFusion. Cfusion_Encrypt( ) is similar to the Encrypt( ) function but results in a 32-character hexadecimal string, making it more useful than the CFEncrypt( ) function. Example:

```
<cfset x=CFusion_Encrypt("this is a message", 12345)>
<cfset ux=CFusion_Decrypt(x, 12345)>

<cfoutput>
Original String: this is a message<br>
Encrypted:  #x#<br>
Decrypted:  #ux#
</cfoutput>
```

CFusion_GetODBCDSN

Not supported in ColdFusion MX

```
CFusion_GetODBCDSN( )
```

Used in place of the cfregistry tag on Unix-based ColdFusion servers to return the names of ODBC data sources stored in the "registry." This is an undocumented function used by the ColdFusion Administrator. Example:

```
<cfset TheDataSourceNames = CFusion_GetODBCDSN( )>

<table>
  <tr><th>Name</th><th>Description</th><tr>
  <cfoutput query="TheDataSourceNames">
  <tr><td>#Name#</td><td>#Description#</td></tr>
  </cfoutput>
</table>
```

CFusion_GetODBCINI

Not supported in ColdFusion MX

```
CFusion_GetODBCINI("ODBC Data Sources"|datasource_name, entry, value)
```

Used in place of the cfregistry tag on Unix-based ColdFusion servers to return ODBC data-source information stored in *odbc.ini*. This is an undocumented function used by the ColdFusion Administrator. Example:

```
<cfset WorkstationID = CFusion_GetODBCIni("ProgrammingCF", "WorkstationID", "")>

<cfoutput>Output: #WorkstationID#</cfoutput>
```

CFusion_SetODBCINI

Not supported in ColdFusion MX

CFusion_SetODBCINI("ODBC Data Sources"_*or_datasource_name, entry, value*)

Used in place of the cfregistry tag on Unix-based ColdFusion servers to write ODBC data-source information to *odbc.ini*. This is an undocumented function used by the ColdFusion Administrator. Example:

```
<cfset CFusion_SetODBCINI("Employees", "Description",
  "This is the employee master database")>
```

CFusion_Settings_Refresh

Not supported in ColdFusion MX

CFusion_Settings_Refresh( )

Refreshes ColdFusion server settings that don't require a server restart in order to take effect. This is an undocumented function used by the ColdFusion Administrator. Example:

```
<cfset CFusion_Settings_Refresh( )>
ColdFusion Administrator settings not requiring a server restart have been
refreshed...
```

CFusion_VerifyMail

Not supported in ColdFusion MX

CFusion_VerifyMail(*server, port, timeout*)

Verifies that a connection can be made to the SMTP mail server specified in *server*. *port* specifies the port that the SMTP server is using. The default SMTP port is 25. *timeout* specifies an amount of time in seconds ColdFusion should wait before timing out the verification attempt. If a connection can't be made, a diagnostic error message is returned. This is an undocumented function used by the ColdFusion Administrator. Example:

```
<cfset Verify = Cfusion_VerifyMail('127.0.0.1',25,60)>

<cfif Verify is not "">
  <cfoutput>#Verify#</cfoutput>
<cfelse>
  Connection verified!
</cfif>
```

CF_GetDataSourceUserName

Not supported in ColdFusion MX

CF_GetDataSourceUserName(*datasource*)

Returns the username registered under *datasource* within the ColdFusion Administrator. This is an undocumented function used by the ColdFusion Administrator. Example:

```
<cfoutput>
The username regstered with the CFExamples datasource is:
#CF_GetDataSourceUserName('cfexamples')#
</cfoutput>
```

CF_IsColdFusionDataSource

Not supported in ColdFusion MX

```
CF_IsColdFusionDataSource(datasource)
```

Returns true if *datasource* is a valid ColdFusion data source or `false` if it isn't. This is an undocumented function used by the ColdFusion Administrator. Example:

```
<cfoutput>
CFExamples: #CF_IsColdFusionDataSource('cfexamples')#<br>
CFSnippets: #CF_IsColdFusionDataSource('cfsnippets')#<br>
Cheese: #CF_IsColdFusionDataSource('cheese')#<br>
</cfoutput>
```

CF_SetDataSourcePassword

Not supported in ColdFusion MX

```
CF_SetDataSourcePassword(datasource, password)
```

Sets the ColdFusion login password for the data source specified in *datasource*. This is an undocumented function used by the ColdFusion Administrator. Example:

```
<cfset CF_SetDataSourcePassword('CFExamples', 'admin')>
The CFExamples data source password has been changed...
```

CF_SetDataSourceUserName

Not supported in ColdFusion MX

```
CF_SetDataSourceUserName(datasource, username)
```

Sets the ColdFusion login username for the data source specified in *datasource*. This is an undocumented function used by the ColdFusion Administrator. Example:

```
<cfset CF_SetDataSourceUserName('CFExamples', 'admin')>
The CFExamples data source username has been changed...
```

Chr

```
Chr(number)
```

Returns the character equivalent of the ASCII character code. The following example generates a chart of all the printable ASCII characters:

```
<table border="1">
  <tr><th>Character</th><th>ASCII Code</th>/tr>
<cfloop index="Character" from="33" to="255">
  <cfoutput>
    <tr><td>#Chr(Character)#</td><td>#Asc(Chr(Character))#</td></tr>
  </cfoutput>
</cfloop>
</table>
```

CJustify

```
CJustify(string, length)
```

Center-justifies `string` within a field of `length` characters. Example:

```
<cfset OriginalString = "ColdFusion">

<cfoutput>
<b>Original String (quoted):</b> "#OriginalString#"<br>
<b>Center-justified String (quoted):</b> "#CJustify("ColdFusion", 20)#"
</cfoutput>
```

Compare

```
Compare(string1, string2)
```

Performs a case-sensitive comparison of two strings based on their ASCII values. If *string1* is less than *string2*, returns –1. If *string1* and *string2* are equal, returns 0. If *string1* is greater than *string2*, returns 1. Examples:

```
<cfoutput>
Compare('Apples', 'apples'): #Compare('Apples', 'apples')#<br>
Compare('oranges', 'oranges'): #Compare('oranges', 'oranges')#<br>
Compare('apples', 'Oranges'): #Compare('apples', 'Oranges')#<br>
Compare('oranges', 'Apples'): #Compare('oranges', 'Apples')#<br>
</cfoutput>
```

CompareNoCase

```
CompareNoCase(string1, string2)
```

Performs a case-insensitive comparison of two strings based on their ASCII values. If *string1* is less than *string2*, returns -1. If *string1* and *string2* are equal, returns 0. If *string1* is greater than *string2*, returns 1. Examples:

```
<cfoutput>
CompareNoCase('Apples', 'apples'): #CompareNoCase('Apples', 'apples')#<br>
CompareNoCase('oranges', 'oranges'): #CompareNoCase('oranges', 'oranges')#<br>
CompareNoCase('apples', 'Oranges'): #CompareNoCase('apples', 'Oranges')#<br>
CompareNoCase('oranges', 'Apples'): #CompareNoCase('oranges', 'Apples')#<br>
</cfoutput>
```

Cos

```
Cos(number)
```

Returns the cosine of an angle expressed in radians. Example:

```
The cosine of 45 is <cfoutput>#Cos(45)#</cfoutput>
```

CreateDate

```
CreateDate(year, month, day)
```

Returns a date/time object for the given date. The time value is set to `00:00:00`. For the *year* parameter of the function, ColdFusion MX accepts years in the range AD 100–9999. ColdFusion MX uses the underlying JRE as well as the current locale to determine how to process two-digit years. For most locales, two-digit years are processed relative to the current century. Based on this, two-digit years are interpreted to within 80 years before the current date and 20 years after. There are a few exceptions to this. The following locales interpret two-digit years to within 72 years before the current date and 28 years after: English (Australian), English (New Zealand), German (Austrian), German (Standard), German (Swiss), Portuguese (Brazilian), Portuguese (Standard), Swedish. Example:

```
April 15, 2003 looks like:
<cfoutput>
Four digit year: #CreateDate(2003, 04, 15)#<br>
Two digit year#CreateDate(03, 04, 15)#
</cfoutput>
```

CreateDateTime

```
CreateDateTime(year, month, day, hour, minute, second)
```

Returns a date/time object for the given date and time. For the *year* parameter of the function, ColdFusion MX accepts years in the range AD 100–9999. For information on how ColdFusion MX handles two-digit years, see `CreateDate( )`. Example:

```
7 p.m. on April 15, 2003 looks like
<cfoutput>#CreateDateTime(2003, 04, 15, 19, 0, 0)#</cfoutput>
as a date/time object.
```

CreateObject

Updated in ColdFusion MX

```
CreateObject("COM", class, context, server)
CreateObject("CORBA", class, context, [locale])
CreateObject("Java", class)
CreateObject("Component", component_name)
CreateObject("Webservice", wsdl_url)
```

Allows ColdFusion to call different kinds of objects from within `cfscript` blocks. This function has the same functionality as the `cfobject` tag.

When the first argument is `"COM"`, the function supports instantiating and using COM objects on local and remote machines. COM objects aren't currently supported for Unix versions of ColdFusion. In this case, *`class`* specifies the program ID for the object, and *`context`* specifies the context the object is running in (`InProc`, `Local`, or `Remote`). *`server`* is required when context is `Remote`; it specifies a valid server name using Universal Naming Convention (UNC) or Domain Name Server (DNS) conventions. Example:

```
<cfscript>
  MyWord = CreateObject("COM","Word.Application","Local");
</cfscript>
```

When the first argument is `"CORBA"`, the function supports calling methods in CORBA objects from within `cfscript` blocks. In this case, *`context`* specifies the context for accessing the CORBA object (`IOR` or `NameService`). If *`context`* is `IOR`, *`class`* specifies the name of a file that contains the stringified version of the Interoperable Object Reference (IOR). If *`context`* is `NameService`, *`class`* specifies a period-delimited naming context for the naming service. *`locale`* specifies type/value pairs of arguments (which must begin with a minus sign) to pass to init_orb( ) (which is specific to VisiBroker orbs and has been tested to work with the 3.2 C++ version only). Example:

```
<cfscript>
  MyCORBAObject = CreateObject("CORBA","C:\myobject.ior","IOR");
</cfscript>
```

When the first argument is "Java", the function supports calling Java objects and Enterprise JavaBeans (EJBs) from within a cfscript block. In this case, *class* refers to the Java class to call. Any Java class listed in the class path area of the Java section within the ColdFusion Administrator may be specified. Example:

```
<cfscript>
  MyObject = CreateObject("Java","HelloWorld");
</cfscript>
```

When the first argument is "Component", the function supports instantiating a ColdFusion Component (CFC) from within cfscript. Here, all you need to specify, in addition to "Component" as the type, is the name of the CFC you want to invoke. Methods within the component are called by treating the method as if it were a normal function. Example:

```
<cfscript>
  stats=CreateObject("component" "components.stats");
  totalPackages= stats.qryTotalPackages( );
  totalCFCs=stats.qryTotalCFCs( );
</cfscript>
```

When the first argument is "WebService", the function can invoke a SOAP-based web service by passing the URL to the web service's WSDL file in the *wsdl_url* parameter of the function. Additional arguments are passed to the web service by calling the desired method using dot notation. For example, if you want to pass parameters to a method called SetEmployee, in a web service named Employee, and have any results written to a variable called ReturnVar, you would code something like this:

```
<cfscript>
  Employee=CreateObject("WebService", "http://www.example.com/employee.cfc?wsdl");
  ReturnVar=Employee.SetEmployee(Name="Pere Money", Title="President");
</cfscript>
```

CreateODBCDate

CreateODBCDate(*date*)

Returns the date in ODBC date format. For information on how ColdFusion MX handles two-digit years, see CreateDate( ). Example:

```
04/15/2003 looks like
<cfoutput>#CreateODBCDate('04/15/2003')#</cfoutput>
in ODBC date format.
```

CreateODBCDateTime

CreateODBCDateTime(*date*)

Returns the date and time in ODBC format. For information on how ColdFusion MX handles two-digit years, see CreateDate( ). Example:

```
7pm on 04/15/2003 looks like
<cfoutput>#CreateODBCDateTime('04/15/2003 19:00:00')#</cfoutput>
in ODBC timestamp format.
```

CreateODBCTime

`CreateODBCTime(date)`

Returns the time in ODBC time format. Example:

```
7:00pm looks like
<cfoutput>#CreateODBCTime('19:00:00')#</cfoutput>
in ODBC time format.
```

CreateTime

`CreateTime(hour, minute, second)`

Returns a date/time object for the given time. The date value is set to December 30, 1899. Example:

```
7:00pm looks like
<cfoutput>#CreateTime(19,00,00)#</cfoutput>
as a date/time object.
```

CreateTimeSpan

`CreateTimeSpan(days, hours, minutes, seconds)`

Creates a date/time object for adding to and subtracting from other date/time objects. The *days* parameter accepts an integer number of days in the range 0–32768. Here's an example that creates a date/time object for one hour and thirty minutes and adds it to the current time:

```
<cfset CurrentTime = Now( )>
<cfset TimeToAdd = CreateTimeSpan(0,1,30,0)>
<cfset NewTime = CurrentTime + TimeToAdd>

<cfoutput>
Current Time: #TimeFormat(CurrentTime, 'hh:mm tt')#<br>
Time Span:  #TimeFormat(TimeToAdd, 'hh:mm')#<br>
Current Time + Time Span: #TimeFormat(NewTime, 'hh:mm tt')#
</cfoutput>
```

CreateUUID

`CreateUUID( )`

Creates a universally unique identifier (UUID). UUIDs are 35-character representations of 128-bit strings, where each character is a hexadecimal value in the range 0–9 and A–F. UUIDs are used when you need to create a unique identifier (such as a user ID or primary key value). UUIDs are guaranteed to be unique and are assigned randomly on most operating systems. Note that the format that ColdFusion uses for UUIDs is not the same format used by Microsoft and DCE. ColdFusion UUIDs follow the format xxxxxxxx-xxxx-xxxx-xxxxxxxxxxxxxxxx whereas Microsoft/DCE UUIDs are formatted as xxxxxxxx-xxxx-xxxx-xxxxxx-xxxxxxxxxx. If you need a UUID that follows the Microsoft/DCE format, see the CreateGUID( ) UDF available at *http://www.cflib.org*. Example:

```
Here is your UUID:  <cfoutput>#CreateUUID( )#</cfoutput>.
```

DateAdd

Updated in ColdFusion MX 6.1

DateAdd(*datepart, number, date*)

Adds *number* to the *datepart* of the specified *date*. Dates must be in the range AD 100-9999. To subtract, make *number* negative. Valid entries for *datepart* are l (millisecond), s (second), n (minute), h (hour), ww (week), w (weekday), d (day), y (day of year), m (month), q (quarter), and yyyy (year). For information on how ColdFusion MX handles two-digit years, see CreateDate( ). Examples:

```
<cfset MyDateTime = Now( )>

<cfoutput>The original time and date is
#TimeFormat(MyDateTime,'hh:mm:ss tt')#, #DateFormat(MyDateTime,'mmmm dd, yyyy')#

<p><b>Add 30 Seconds:</b>
#TimeFormat(DateAdd('s', 30, MyDateTime),'hh:mm:ss tt')#
<br><b>Subtract 10 minutes:</b>
#TimeFormat(DateAdd('n', -10, MyDateTime),'hh:mm:ss tt')#
<br><b>Add 2 hours:</b>
#TimeFormat(DateAdd('h', 2, MyDateTime),'hh:mm:ss tt')#
<br><b>Add 9 weeks:</b>
#DateFormat(DateAdd('ww', 9, MyDateTime),'mmmm dd, yyyy')#
<br><b>Add 3 weekdays:</b>
#DateFormat(DateAdd('w', 3, MyDateTime),'mmmm dd, yyyy')#
<br><b>Subtract 67 days:</b>
#DateFormat(DateAdd('d', -67, MyDateTime),'mmmm dd, yyyy')#
<br><b>Add 45 days of the year:</b>
#DateFormat(DateAdd('y', 45, MyDateTime),'mmmm dd, yyyy')#
<br><b>Add 7 months:</b>
#DateFormat(DateAdd('m', 7, MyDateTime),'mmmm dd, yyyy')#
<br><b>Add 2 quarters:</b>
#DateFormat(DateAdd('q', 2, MyDateTime),'mmmm dd, yyyy')#
<br><b>Add 5 years:</b>
#DateFormat(DateAdd('yyyy', 5, MyDateTime),'mmmm dd, yyyy')#
</cfoutput>
```

DateCompare

DateCompare(*date1, date2* [, *datepart*])

Compares two date/time objects. Returns –1 if *date1* is less than *date2*, 0 if both date/time objects are equal, or 1 if *date1* is greater than *date2*. Dates must be in the range AD 100–9999. The precision of the comparison may be limited to a specific part of the date/time object by specifying a value for the optional *datepart* parameter. Valid attributes for *datepart* are s (second), n (minute), h (hour), d (day), m (month), and yyyy (year). For information on how ColdFusion MX handles two–digit years, see CreateDate( ). Examples:

```
<cfoutput>
Compare 04/15/03 and 04/15/03: #DateCompare('04/15/03', '04/15/03')#<br>
Compare 04/15/03 and 04/15/2003: #DateCompare('04/15/03', '04/15/2003')#<br>
Compare 15 Apr 2003 and 4/15/03: #DateCompare('15 Apr 2003', '4/15/03')#<br>
Compare August 15, 2003 and July 4, 2002:
#DateCompare('August 15, 2003', 'July 4, 2002')#<br>
Compare 19:00:00 and 7pm: #DateCompare('19:00:00', '7pm')#<br>
Compare 6:00 and 7:00: #DateCompare('6:00', '7:00')#<br>
Compare 4/15/2003 and Jan 3, 2003 by year:
#DateCompare('4/15/2003', 'Jan 3, 2003', 'yyyy')#<br>
Compare 6:59 and 7:38 by minute: #DateCompare('6:59', '7:38', 'n')#
</cfoutput>
```

DateConvert

DateConvert(*type, date*)

Converts *date* to Universal Coordinated Time (UTC) or UTC to local time based on *type* (local2UTC or UTC2Local). Conversions for daylight savings time are automatically applied if enabled on the server running ColdFusion. For information on how ColdFusion MX handles two–digit years, see CreateDate( ). The following example converts local time to UTC time:

```
<cfset TheTimeDate = Now( )>
<cfset UCT = DateConvert('local2UTC', TheTimeDate)>

<cfoutput>
<b>Current time/date:</b> #TimeFormat(TheTimeDate,'hh:mm:ss tt')#,
#DateFormat(TheTimeDate,'mmmm dd, yyyy')#
<p><b>UCT:</b> #UCT#
</cfoutput>
```

DateDiff

DateDiff(*datepart, date1, date2*)

Returns the interval in *datepart* units by which *date2* is greater than *date1*. Dates must be in the range AD 100–9999. Valid entries for *datepart* are s (second), n (minute), h (hour), ww (week), w (weekday), d (day), y (day of year), m (month), q (quarter), and yyyy (year). If *date1* is greater than *date2*, a negative number is returned. For information on how ColdFusion MX handles two-digit years, see CreateDate( ). Examples:

```
<cfset FirstDate = DateFormat(Now( ),'mm/dd/yyyy')>
<cfset SecondDate = "01/01/2000">

<cfoutput>
FirstDate: #FirstDate#<br>
SecondDate: #SecondDate#
<p>
There are #DateDiff("s", FirstDate, SecondDate)# seconds between
#FirstDate# and #SecondDate#.<br>
There are #DateDiff("n", FirstDate, SecondDate)# minutes between
```

```
#FirstDate# and #SecondDate#.<br>
There are #DateDiff("h", FirstDate, SecondDate)# hours between
#FirstDate# and #SecondDate#.<br>
There are #DateDiff("d", FirstDate, SecondDate)# days between
#FirstDate# and #SecondDate#.<br>
There are #DateDiff("ww", FirstDate, SecondDate)# weeks between
#FirstDate# and #SecondDate#.<br>
There are #DateDiff("m", FirstDate, SecondDate)# months between
#FirstDate# and #SecondDate#.<br>
There are #DateDiff("yyyy", FirstDate, SecondDate)# years between
#FirstDate# and #SecondDate#.<br>
</cfoutput>
```

DateFormat

Updated in ColdFusion MX

`DateFormat(`*`date`*` [, mask])`

Returns *date* formatted according to *mask*. Dates must be in the range AD 100–9999. If no value is specified for *mask*, `DateFormat()` uses the default `dd-mmm-yy`. Valid entries for *mask* are:

Mask	Description
d	Day of the month as a number with no leading zero for single-digit days
dd	Day of the month as a number with a leading zero for single-digit days
ddd	Three-letter abbreviation for day of the week
dddd	Full name of the day of the week
m	Month as a number with no leading zero for single-digit months
mm	Month as a number with a leading zero for single-digit months
mmm	Three-letter abbreviation for the month
mmmm	Full name of the month
y	Last two digits of year with no leading zero for years less than 10
yy	Last two digits of year with a leading zero for years less than 10
yyyy	Four-digit year
gg	Period/era
short	Java short date format
medium	Java medium date format
long	Java long date format
full	Java full date format

Dates passed as literals must be enclosed in quotes. Otherwise, ColdFusion interprets the date as a numeric date. If an invalid mask is passed to the function, ColdFusion outputs the invalid characters. Note that `DateFormat()` supports U.S. date formats only. To use locale-specific date formats, see the `LSDateFormat()` function. For information on how ColdFusion MX handles two-digit years, see `CreateDate()`. Examples:

```
<cfset TheDate = Now()>

<cfoutput>
```

```
TheDate = #DateFormat(TheDate, 'mm/dd/yyyy')#
<p>
m/d/yy: #DateFormat(TheDate, 'm/d/yy')#<br>
mm/dd/yy: #DateFormat(TheDate, 'mm/dd/yy')#<br>
mm/dd/yyyy: #DateFormat(TheDate, 'mm/dd/yyyy')#<br>
dd/mm/yyyy gg: #DateFormat(TheDate, 'dd/mm/yyyy gg')#<br>
dd mmm yy: #DateFormat(TheDate, 'dd mmm yy')#<br>
dddd mmmm dd, yyyy: #DateFormat(TheDate, 'dddd mmmm dd, yyyy')#<br>
<p>
And these formats are new in ColdFusion MX:<br>
short: #DateFormat(TheDate, 'short')#<br>
medium: #DateFormat(TheDate, 'medium')#<br>
long: #DateFormat(TheDate, 'long')#<br>
full: #DateFormat(TheDate, 'full')#<br>
time mask included: #DateFormat(TheDate, 'mm/dd/yyyy hh:mm:ss')#<br>
</cfoutput>
```

DatePart

Updated in ColdFusion MX 6.1

`DatePart(`*datepart, date*`)`

Returns the specified part of a valid date/time object. The value supplied for *date* must be in the range AD 100–9999. Valid values for the *datepart* parameter are `l` (millisecond), `s` (second), `n` (minute), `h` (hour), `ww` (week), `w` (weekday), `d` (day), `y` (day of year), `m` (month), `q` (quarter), and `yyyy` (year). For information on how ColdFusion MX handles two-digit years, see `CreateDate( )`. Examples:

```
<cfoutput>
The current time and date  is
#TimeFormat(Now( ),'hh:mm:ss tt')#, #DateFormat(Now( ),'mmmm dd, yyyy')#
<p>

<b>Second:</b> #DatePart('s', Now( ))#<br>
<b>Minute:</b> #DatePart('n', Now( ))#<br>
<b>Hour:</b> #DatePart('h', Now( ))#<br>
<b>Week:</b> #DatePart('ww', Now( ))#<br>
<b>Weekday:</b> #DatePart('w', Now( ))#<br>
<b>Day:</b> #DatePart('d', Now( ))#<br>
<b>Day of year:</b> #DatePart('y', Now( ))#<br>
<b>Month:</b> #DatePart('m', Now( ))#<br>
<b>Quarter:</b> #DatePart('q', Now( ))#<br>
<b>Year:</b> #DatePart('yyyy', Now( ))#
</cfoutput>
```

Day

`Day(`*date*`)`

Returns the day of the month for a given *date* as a number between 1 and 31. The value supplied for *date* must be in the range AD 100–9999. For information on how ColdFusion MX handles two-digit years, see `CreateDate( )`. Example:

```
<cfoutput>#Day(Now( ))#</cfoutput>
```

DayOfWeek

```
DayOfWeek(date)
```

Returns the day of the week for a given *date* as a number between 1 (Sunday) and 7 (Saturday). Note that ColdFusion uses Sunday as the first day of the week while ISO uses Monday. The value supplied for *date* must be in the range AD 100–9999. For information on how ColdFusion MX handles two-digit years, see `CreateDate( )`. Example:

```
<cfoutput>#DayOfWeek(Now( ))#</cfoutput>
```

DayOfWeekAsString

```
DayOfWeekAsString(number)
```

Returns the name of the day of the week for a given day's *number* between 1 (Sunday) and 7 (Saturday). Note that ColdFusion uses Sunday as the first day of the week while ISO uses Monday. Example:

```
Today is <cfoutput>#DayOfWeekAsString(DayOfWeek(Now( )))#</cfoutput>.
```

DayOfYear

```
DayOfYear(date)
```

Returns the day of the year as a number between 1 and 365 (366 for leap years). The value supplied for *date* must be in the range AD 100–9999. For information on how ColdFusion MX handles two-digit years, see `CreateDate( )`. Example:

```
<cfoutput>#DayOfYear(Now( ))#</cfoutput>
```

DaysInMonth

```
DaysInMonth(date)
```

Returns the number of days in the given month. The value supplied for *date* must be in the range AD 100–9999. Example:

```
There are <cfoutput>#DaysInMonth(Now( ))#</cfoutput> days in the current month.
```

DaysInYear

```
DaysInYear(date)
```

Returns the number of days in the specified year. The value supplied for *date* must be in the range AD 100–9999. For information on how ColdFusion MX handles two-digit years, see `CreateDate( )`. Example:

```
There are <cfoutput>#DaysInYear(Now( ))#</cfoutput> days this year.
```

DE

```
DE(string)
```

DE( ) (for delay evaluation) is used with the Evaluate( ) and IIF( ) functions to allow you to pass a string without having it evaluated. DE( ) returns *string* enclosed within double quotation marks. The following example shows the DE( ) function used in conjunction with the Evaluate( ) function:

```
<cfset MyVar = "3 * 3">

<cfoutput>
MyVar = #MyVar#
<p>
DE(MyVar): #DE(MyVar)#<br>
Evaluate(MyVar): #Evaluate(MyVar)#<br>
Evaluate(DE(MyVar)): #Evaluate(DE(MyVar))#
<p>
All together:<br>
#Evaluate(DE(MyVar))# is #Evaluate(MyVar)#
</cfoutput>
```

DecimalFormat

```
DecimalFormat(number)
```

Returns *number* as a string formatted to two decimal places with thousands separators. Examples:

```
<cfoutput>
1:  #DecimalFormat(1)#<br>
10: #DecimalFormat(10)#<br>
100: #DecimalFormat(100)#<br>
1000: #DecimalFormat(1000)#<br>
10000: #DecimalFormat(10000)#<br>
100000: #DecimalFormat(100000)#<br>
1000000: #DecimalFormat(1000000)#<br>
</cfoutput>
```

DecrementValue

```
DecrementValue(number)
```

Decrements the integer part of a given number by 1. Examples:

```
<cfoutput>
-1: #DecrementValue(-1)#<br>
-1.123: #DecrementValue(-1.123)#<br>
-0.123: #DecrementValue(-0.123)#<br>
0: #DecrementValue(0)#<br>
0.123: #DecrementValue(0.123)#<br>
1: #DecrementValue(1)#<br>
1.123: #DecrementValue(1.123)#
</cfoutput>
```

Decrypt

```
Decrypt(encryptedstring, key)
```

Decrypts *encryptedstring* using *key*. This function is designed to decrypt strings encrypted with the Encrypt( ) function. The following example takes an encrypted string and decrypts it:

```
<cfset MyString = "This is the secret message.">
<cfset MyKey = "1a2">
<cfset EncryptedString = Encrypt(MyString, MyKey)>
<cfset DecryptedString = Decrypt(EncryptedString, MyKey)>

<cfoutput>
<b>Original String:</b> #MyString#<br>
<b>Key:</b> #MyKey#
<p><b>Encrypted String:</b> #EncryptedString#<br>
<b>Decrypted String:</b> #DecryptedString#
</cfoutput>
```

DeleteClientVariable

```
DeleteClientVariable("variable")
```

Deletes the specified client variable (where the variable name is in double quotes). Returns true if successful. The following example creates a client variable, attempts to delete it, and reports whether it was successful (the example assumes you have client variables turned on in the ColdFusion Administrator and that a valid *Application.cfm* file exists in the directory containing the example):

```
<cfset Client.MyVar="This is a client variable">

<cfoutput>#Client.MyVar#</cfoutput><p>

<cfset DeleteClientVariable("MyVar")>

<cfif IsDefined('Client.MyVar')>
Couldn't delete the client variable.
<cfelse>
Client variable deleted.
</cfif>
```

DirectoryExists

```
DirectoryExists(path)
```

Returns Yes if the specified directory exists or No if it doesn't. The absolute path to the directory being evaluated must be provided. Example:

```
<cfif DirectoryExists('c:\CfusionMX')>
  Directory exists!
<cfelse>
  Directory doesn't exist!
</cfif>
```

DollarFormat

```
DollarFormat(number)
```

Returns *number* as a string formatted to two decimal places with a dollar sign and thousands separators. If *number* is negative, it is returned in parentheses. Examples:

```
<cfoutput>
-1000: #DollarFormat(-1000)#<br>
-100: #DollarFormat(-100)#<br>
-10: #DollarFormat(-10)#<br>
-1: #DollarFormat(-1)#<br>
1:  #DollarFormat(1)#<br>
10: #DollarFormat(10)#<br>
100: #DollarFormat(100)#<br>
1000: #DollarFormat(1000)#<br>
10000: #DollarFormat(10000)#<br>
100000: #DollarFormat(100000)#<br>
1000000: #DollarFormat(1000000)#<br>
</cfoutput>
```

Duplicate

```
Duplicate(variable)
```

Creates a duplicate copy of *variable* without any references to the original. *variable* can be any ColdFusion datatype with the exception of component objects (COM, CORBA, and Java). `Duplicate( )` overcomes problems associated with copying structures and queries. Generally, when copying a structure or query, any future change to the original object results in a change to the copy. `Duplicate( )` eliminates this by making an independent copy of the original object. The duplicate copy isn't affected by changes to the original. The `Duplicate( )` function is especially useful for copying nested structures and XML objects, and should be used in place of the `StructCopy( )` function. The following example illustrates the difference between copying and duplicating query objects:

```
<!--- create a query object --->
<cfset Products = QueryNew("ProductName, Color")>
<cfset NewRows  = QueryAddRow(Products, 1)>
<cfset QuerySetCell(Products, "ProductName", "Widget", 1)>
<cfset QuerySetCell(Products, "Color", "Silver", 1)>

<!--- create a copy and a duplicate of the query --->
<cfset CopyProducts = Products>
<cfset DuplicateProducts = Duplicate(Products)>

<cfoutput>
<b>Original:</b> You selected a #Products.Color# #Products.ProductName#.<br>
<cfset QuerySetCell(Products, "Color", "Black", 1)>
<b>Copy:</b> You selected a #CopyProducts.Color# #CopyProducts.ProductName#.<br>
<b>Duplicate:</b> You selected a #DuplicateProducts.Color#
#DuplicateProducts.ProductName#.
</cfoutput>
```

And here's an example with nested structures:

```
<!--- Create a nested structure --->
<cfset Company=StructNew( )>
<cfset Company.Employee=StructNew( )>
<cfset Company.Employee.Name="Pere Money">
<cfset Company.Employee.Title="President">
<cfset Company.Employee.Department="Executive Management">
<cfset Company.Employee.Email="pmoney@example.com">
<cfset Company.Employee.PhoneExt="1234">

<!--- Create a copy and a duplicate of the structure --->
<cfset CompanyCopy = StructCopy(Company)>
<cfset CompanyDuplicate = Duplicate(Company)>

<cfoutput>
<b>Name:</b> #Company.Employee.Name#<br>
<b>Original Title:</b> #Company.Employee.Title#<br>
<cfset Company.Employee.Title = "CEO">
<b>Copied Title:</b> #CompanyCopy.Employee.Title#<br>
<b>Duplicate Title:</b> #CompanyDuplicate.Employee.Title#
</cfoutput>
```

Encrypt

Encrypt(*string, key*)

Encrypts *string* using the specified *key*. Encrypt( ) uses the value of *key* as a seed to generate a random 32-bit key for use in an XOR-based encryption algorithm. The resulting string is then uuencoded and may be as much as three times the size of the original string. The following example takes a string and encrypts it:

```
<cfset MyString = "This is the secret message.">
<cfset MyKey = "1a2">
<cfset EncryptedString = Encrypt(MyString, MyKey)>
<cfset DecryptedString = Decrypt(EncryptedString, MyKey)>

<cfoutput>
<b>Original String:</b> #MyString#<br>
<b>Key:</b> #MyKey#
<p><b>Encrypted String:</b> #EncryptedString#<br>
<b>Decrypted String:</b> #DecryptedString#
</cfoutput>
```

Evaluate

Evaluate(*string1* [,*string2*] [,*stringN*])

Evaluates string expressions from left to right and returns the result from the rightmost expression. Evaluate( ) is useful when you need to evaluate multiple expressions at one time. Examples:

```
<cfset x=1>
<cfset y=2>
<cfset z=3>
<cfset Form.Name="Jim">
```

```
x=1<br>
y=2<br>
z=3<br>
Form.Name=Jim
<p><cfoutput>
Evaluate(1+1): #Evaluate(1+1)#<br>
Evaluate(3 MOD 2): #Evaluate(3 MOD 2)#<br>
Evaluate(x*y*z): #Evaluate(x*y*z)#<br>
Evaluate(sin(1)): #Evaluate(sin(1))#<br>
Evaluate((x+y+z)/3): #Evaluate((x+y+z)/3)#<br>
Evaluate('Form.Name'): #Evaluate('Form.Name')#<br>
Evaluate(7+2, 3+5): #Evaluate(7+2, 3+5)#<br>
Evaluate(7+2, 3+5, 1/4): #Evaluate(7+2, 3+5, 1/4)#<br>
</cfoutput>
```

Exp

`Exp(number)`

Returns *e* to the power of `number`. The constant *e* is the base of the natural logarithm and is equal to 2.71828182845904. Example:

```
<cfoutput>10 to the E power is #Exp(10)#.</cfoutput>
```

ExpandPath

`ExpandPath(relativepath)`

Returns the platform-appropriate absolute path for the specified `relativepath`. Example:

```
<cfoutput>#ExpandPath('*.*')#</cfoutput>
```

FileExists

`FileExists(path)`

Returns `Yes` if the specified file exists or `No` if it doesn't. The absolute path to the file being evaluated must be provided. Example:

```
<cfif FileExists('c:\boot.ini')>
  File exists!
<cfelse>
  File doesn't exist!
</cfif>
```

Find

`Find(substring, string [, startpos])`

Returns the position of the first occurrence of `substring` in `string`. If `substring` isn't found, `Find()` returns 0. An optional starting position for the search can be specified by the `startpos` parameter. `Find()` performs a case-sensitive search. Example:

```
<cfset MyString="This is a case-sensitive example of using the Find function to
find a substring within a string.">
```

```
<cfset MySubString="find">

<cfoutput>
<b>String:</b> #MyString#<br>
<b>Substring:</b> #MySubstring#
<p>The first occurrence of <b>#MySubstring#</b> is at position
#Find(MySubstring, MyString)#.
</cfoutput>
```

FindNoCase

```
FindNoCase(substring, string [, startpos])
```

Returns the position of the first occurrence of *substring* in *string*. If *substring* isn't found, FindNoCase( ) returns 0. An optional starting position for the search can be specifies by the *startpos* parameter. FindNoCase( ) performs a case-insensitive search. Example:

```
<cfset MyString="This is a case-insensitive example of using the FindNoCase
function to find a substring within a string.">
<cfset MySubString="find">

<cfoutput>
<b>String:</b> #MyString#<br>
<b>Substring:</b> #MySubstring#
<p>The first occurrence of <b>#MySubstring#</b> is at position
#FindNoCase(MySubstring, MyString)#.
</cfoutput>
```

FindOneOf

```
FindOneOf(set, string [, startpos])
```

Returns the position of the first occurrence of any character from *set* in *string*. If no characters from *set* are found, FindOneOf( ) returns 0. An optional starting position for the search can be specified by the *startpos* parameter. FindOneOf( ) performs a case-sensitive search. Example:

```
<cfset MyString="This is a case-sensitive example of using the FindOneOf function
to find a character from a set of charcters within a string.">
<cfset MySet="zFx">

<cfoutput>
<b>String:</b> #MyString#<br>
<b>Set:</b> #MySet#
<p>The first occurrence of any character from the set <b>#MySet#</b>
is at position #FindOneOf(MySet, MyString)#.
</cfoutput>
```

FirstDayOfMonth

```
FirstDayOfMonth(date)
```

Returns the day of the year for the first day in the specified month. Example:

```
<cfoutput>
The first day of this month is day #FirstDayOfMonth(Now( ))# of this year.
</cfoutput>
```

Fix

```
Fix(number)
```

Returns the closest integer less than the specified number if the number is greater than 0. If the specified number is less than 0, the closest integer greater than the number is returned. Examples:

```
<cfoutput>
-2.5: #Fix(-2.5)#<br>
-1: #Fix(-1)#<br>
-1.123: #Fix(-1.123)#<br>
-0.123: #Fix(-0.123)#<br>
0: #Fix(0)#<br>
0.123: #Fix(0.123)#<br>
#Fix(1)#<br>
1.123: #Fix(1.123)#<br>
2.5: #Fix(2.5)#
</cfoutput>
```

FormatBaseN

```
FormatBaseN(number, radix)
```

Converts *number* to a string in the base specified by *radix*. Valid values for *radix* are integers in the range of 2 to 36. Examples:

```
<cfoutput>
FormatBaseN(1,2): #FormatBaseN(1,2)#<br>
FormatBaseN(10,2): #FormatBaseN(10,2)#<br>
FormatBaseN(100,2): #FormatBaseN(100,2)#<br>
FormatBaseN(1,6): #FormatBaseN(1,6)#<br>
FormatBaseN(10,6): #FormatBaseN(10,6)#<br>
FormatBaseN(100,6): #FormatBaseN(100,6)#<br>
</cfoutput>
```

GetAuthUser

New in ColdFusion MX

```
GetAuthUser( )
```

Returns the name of an authenticated user when used in conjunction with ColdFusion MX's built-in security. Example:

```
<cflogin>
  <cfquery name="AuthenticateUser" datasource="ProgrammingCF">
    SELECT *
    FROM Users
    WHERE Username='pmoney'
    AND Password='#Hash("cat")#'
  </cfquery>
```

```
  <cfloginuser
    name="pmoney"
    password="#Hash("CAT")#"
    roles="editor,user">
</cflogin>

<cfoutput>
Who is the current authenticated user? #GetAuthUser()#
</cfoutput>
```

GetBaseTagData

```
GetBaseTagData(tag [, instance])
```

Returns an object containing data from the specified ancestor *tag*. An optional *instance* number may be set to specify the number of ancestor tag levels to skip through before returning data. The default value for *instance* is 1. Example:

```
<cfset BaseTagData = GetBaseTagData("CF_MyCustomTag")>
```

GetBaseTagList

```
GetBaseTagList()
```

Returns a comma-delimited list (in uppercase) of ancestor tag names. `GetBaseTagList()` is meant for use in custom CFML tags for intertag data exchange. The first element in the returned list of ancestor tags is always the parent tag. Example:

```
<cfoutput>
The parent tag is: #ListFirst(GetBaseTagList())#
<p>The entire list of ancestor tas: #GetBaseTagList()#
</cfoutput>
```

GetBaseTemplatePath

```
GetBaseTemplatePath()
```

Returns the full path to the top-level ColdFusion template calling the function. Example:

```
<cfoutput>The base template path is:  #GetBaseTemplatePath()#</cfoutput>
```

GetClientVariablesList

```
GetClientVariablesList()
```

Returns a list of nonread-only client variables available to the ColdFusion application. In order to use this function, client variables must be turned on in the application's *Application.cfm* file. The following example returns the list of client variables available to the application (it assumes an *Application.cfm* file exists in the application's root directory and that client variables are enabled):

```
<cfset Client.Name="Jen">
<cfset Client.ID=123456>
```

```
<cfoutput>
Client Variables available to this application: #GetClientVariablesList()#
</cfoutput>
```

GetCurrentTemplatePath

```
GetCurrentTemplatePath(path)
```

Returns the full path to the ColdFusion template that calls the function. This function differs from `GetBaseTemplatePath()` in that it returns the path to an included template if called from a directory other than the parent template. Example:

```
<cfoutput>The full path to the template is: #GetCurrentTemplatePath()#</cfoutput>
```

GetDirectoryFromPath

```
GetDirectoryFromPath(path)
```

Returns the directory from a full path. The following example returns the directory in which the current template resides:

```
<cfoutput>This directory is: #GetDirectoryFromPath(GetBaseTemplatePath())#</cfoutput>
```

GetException

New as of ColdFusion 5.0

```
GetException(object_name)
```

Used in conjunction with try/catch code, `GetException()` returns a Java exception object thrown by the specified object. The following example shows how to use `GetException()` with an imaginary Java object called `MyObject`:

```
<cfobject type="Java" action="Create" class="MyClass" name="MyObject">

<cfset Test = MyObject.init()>
<cftry>
<cfset Test = MyObject.CauseError()>

<cfcatch type="Any">
   <cfset MyException = GetException(MyObject)>
   <!--- call the GetErrCode and GerErrMsg methods within the exception
         object --->
   <cfset ErrorCode = MyException.GetErrCode()
   <cfset ErrorMessage = MyException.GetErrMsg()>

   <cfoutput>
     Error Code: #ErrorCode#<br>
     Error Message: #ErrorMessage#
   </cfoutput>
</cfcatch>
</cftry>
```

GetFileFromPath

```
GetFileFromPath(path)
```

Returns the filename from a full path. The following example returns the filename of the current ColdFusion template:

```
<cfoutput>This file is: #GetFileFromPath(GetBaseTemplatePath( ))#</cfoutput>
```

GetFunctionList

```
GetFunctionList( )
```

Returns a ColdFusion structure containing the names of the functions available to ColdFusion. Example:

```
<cfoutput>
There are #StructCount(GetFunctionList( ))# functions available in this version of
ColdFusion for #Server.OS.Name#.
</cfoutput>
<cfdump var="#GetFunctionList( )#">
```

GetHTTPRequestData

New as of ColdFusion 5.0

```
GetHTTPRequestData( )
```

Returns a structure containing the HTTP request headers and body available to the current page. This function is especially useful for parsing Simple Object Access Protocol (SOAP) requests, which are often passed in the HTTP header. The structure returned by `GetHTTPRequestData( )` contains the following keys:

`Headers`
: Structure containing all the HTTP request headers as key/value pairs.

`Content`
: If the current page is accessed via a form post, `Content` contains the raw content (string or binary) of the form post; otherwise it is blank. In order to be considered string content, the value of the `content_type` request header must be "application/x-www-form-urlencoded" or must begin with "text/". All other content types are automatically stored as binary objects. Because of this, you should first use the `IsBinary( )` function when evaluating `Content`. You may also consider using the `ToString( )` function to convert binary data stored in `Content` to a string value that can then be displayed.

`Method`
: The value contained in the `Request_Method` CGI variable.

`Protocol`
: The value contained in the `Server_Protocol` CGI variable.

The following example demonstrates the use of the `GetHTTPRequestData( )` function (try calling the template directly and via a form post to see how the `Content` key is populated differently):

```
<cfset RequestHeader = GetHttpRequestData( )>
<cfdump var = "#RequestHeader#">
```

GetHTTPTimeString

```
GetHTTPTimeString([date_time_object])
```

Returns *date_time_object* formatted according to the HTTP protocol put forth in RFC1123. If no parameter is specified, `GetHTTPTimeString( )` returns the current date/time (on the ColdFusion server). Times are output as GMT time. Example:

```
<cfset x = GetHTTPTimeString( )>

<cfoutput>
The current date/time (formatted according to RFC 1123) is: #x#
</cfoutput>
```

GetK2ServerCollections

New as of ColdFusion 5.0; not supported in ColdFusion MX

```
GetK2ServerCollections( )
```

Returns a comma-delimited list of collection aliases for collections used by the K2 server. The K2 server engine must be started in order for this function to return any results. The following example loops through the list of available K2 server collections, displaying the collection aliases:

```
<h3>K2 server collections:</h3>
<cfloop list="#GetK2ServerCollections( )#" index="CollectionName">
   <cfoutput>#CollectionName#</cfoutput><br>
</cfloop>
```

GetK2ServerDocCount

New as of ColdFusion 5.0

```
GetK2ServerDocCount( )
```

Returns the total number of documents in all collections accessible by the Verity K2 engine. The following example displays the total number of documents in all collections available to the K2 server:

```
<cfoutput>
There are currently #GetK2ServerDocCount( )# documents available for
searching by the K2 server.
</cfoutput>
```

GetK2ServerDocCountLimit

New as of ColdFusion 5.0

```
GetK2ServerDocCountLimit( )
```

Returns the maximum number of documents searchable by the Verity K2 server. For ColdFusion Professional, the document limit is 125,000. ColdFusion Enterprise has a 250,000-document limit. Sites running Macromedia Spectra have a limit of 750,000 documents. The following example outputs the K2 server document limit for your ColdFusion server:

```
<cfoutput>
The K2 server can search a maximum of #GetK2ServerDocCountLimit( )#
documents on
this ColdFusion server.
</cfoutput>
```

GetLocale

```
GetLocale()
```

Returns the current locale for your server. The server's locale determines display and formatting options for currency, date, number, and time values and is determined by the server's operating system. At startup, ColdFusion sets a variable, `Server.ColdFusion.SupportedLocales`, that contains a comma-separated list containing all supported locales for your ColdFusion server. The following example lists all supported locales for your server, with the current locale in bold:

```
Supported Locales with Current Locale in <b>Bold</b>:
<p><cfloop index="Locale" list="#Server.ColdFusion.SupportedLocales#">
  <cfoutput>
    <cfif Locale is GetLocale()>
      <b>#Locale#</b><br>
    <cfelse>
      #Locale#<br>
    </cfif>
  </cfoutput>
</cfloop>
```

GetMetaData

New in ColdFusion MX

```
GetMetaData(object)
GetMetaData(THIS)
```

Returns metadata such as properties, methods, and parameters for the specified ColdFusion Component (CFC) when used within a CFML page. When used within a CFC, pass `GetMetaData()` the `THIS` scope, and it will return all of the metadata for the component. Metadata is returned as a structure containing various key/value pairs depending on the contents of the CFC. Values in the metadata structure may contain additional nested structure. The following outlines the minimum keys available for the various pieces of a CFC:

Component metadata

`Name`
: The name of the component

`Path`
: Absolute path to the component

`Extends`
: Structure containing ancestor component metadata

`Functions`
: Array of structures containing metadata about each function (method) in the component

Function (method) metadata

`Name`
: Name of the function

`Parameters`
: Array of structures containing metadata about each argument

Argument metadata

`Name`
: Name of the argument

Property metadata

`Name`
: Name of the property

Additional keys may be available depending on how the CFC is coded. For example, Function metadata may also contain keys for `Hint`, `ReturnType`, `Output`, and `Access`. The best way to understand what metadata is available for a particular object is to retrieve the metadata for it and output the results to your browser with cfdump. Here's an example that does just that for the CFC Explorer component that ships with ColdFusion MX:

```
<cfscript>
  myObj = createObject("component", "cfide.componentutils.cfcexplorer");
  Metadata = GetMetaData(myObj);
</cfscript>

<h2>Metadata for the CFC Explorer</h2>
<cfdump var="#Metadata#">
```

GetMetricData

`GetMetricData(`*`mode`*`)`

Depending on *`mode`*, returns data representing information about the performance of the ColdFusion server. The following modes may be used by `GetMetricData()`:

`Perf_Monitor`
: Returns a ColdFusion structure containing Performance Monitor data (Windows NT) or CFSTAT data (on Unix/Linux). For this mode to work on Windows NT systems, the Enable Performance Monitoring option must be checked in the Debugging section of the ColdFusion Administrator.

`Simple_Load`
: Returns a number representing the load on the server. This number is produced by an internal algorithm based on ColdFusion queue depths.

`Prev_Req_Time`
: Returns a number representing the previous request time in milliseconds. This metric can calculate server load using the formula:

  Load (as a percentage) = Prev_Req_Time / Max_Allowable_Response_Time_In_Milliseconds * 100

`Avg_Req_Time`
: Returns a number representing the average request time in milliseconds. This metric can calculate load using the formula:

  Load (as a percentage) = Avg_Req_Time / Max_Allowable_Response_Time_In_Milliseconds * 100

If mode is set to `Perf_Monitor`, `GetMetricData()` returns a structure containing the following key/value pairs:

`AvgDBTime`
: Length of time in milliseconds averaged over the current and previous request that ColdFusion took to process queries.

`AvgQueueTime`
: Length of time in milliseconds (averaged over the current and previous request), that the request spent in the staging queue.

`AvgReqTime`
: Length of time in milliseconds averaged over the current and previous request that it took ColdFusion to process the request.

`BytesIn`
: Total number of bytes in HTTP requests to the ColdFusion server since last restart.

`BytesOut`
: Total number of bytes in HTTP requests served by the ColdFusion server since last restart.

`CachePops`
: Deprecated in ColdFusion MX. Always returns –1.

`DBHits`
: Total number of database requests from the ColdFusion server since last restart.

`InstanceName`
: Name of the ColdFusion server. By default, this is `cfserver`.

`PageHits`
: Total number of page requests received by the ColdFusion server since last restart.

`ReqQueued`
: Current number of HTTP requests sitting in the staging queue waiting to be processed.

`ReqRunning`
: Current number of HTTP requests being processed by the ColdFusion server.

`ReqTimedOut`
: Total number of HTTP requests that timed out while in the staging queue or being executed by the ColdFusion server.

The following example demonstrates the four modes available to the `GetMetricData()` function:

```
<cfset PerformanceMonitoring = GetMetricData("Perf_monitor")>
<cfset Load = GetMetricData("Simple_Load")>
<cfset PreviousRequestTime = GetMetricData("Prev_Req_Time")>
<cfset AverageRequestTime = GetMetricData("Avg_Req_Time")>

<cfoutput>
Load: #Load#<br>
Previous Request Time: #PreviousRequestTime#<br>
Average Request Time: #AverageRequestTime#<br>
</cfoutput>

<h2>Performance Monitoring</h2>
<cfdump var="#PerformanceMonitoring#">
```

GetNumericDate

New in ColdFusion MX

```
GetNumericDate(date)
```

Returns the specified date/time as a real number. Storing dates in this manner allows ColdFusion to quickly and efficiently store and manipulate dates and times. The date is stored as the integer part of the number, and the time is stored as the fractional part. 0 represents 12:00 AM on 12/30/1899. The following example returns the numeric date representing 12/31/2002 at 7:00 PM:

```
<cfoutput>#GetNumericDate('12/31/2002 19:00:00')#</cfoutput>
```

7:00 PM on 12/31/2002 would be 37621.7916667. The whole part of the number represents 37621 days since 12/30/1899; 0.7916667, or 7:00 PM is obtained by dividing the hour (19) by the total number of hours in a day (24).

GetPageContext

New in ColdFusion MX

Acts as a wrapper for the Java `PageContext` object. This function returns an object containing the attributes, methods, and other configuration information available to the current page. Using this object, it is possible to look up various information concerning the current page, such as scope and variable values. This function can also be useful for integrating ColdFusion with J2EE applications as it provides access to request and response objects. Additionally, include and forward methods are exposed, making it possible to communicate with JSP pages using the equivalent of `jsp:forward` and `jsp:include`. To see the contents of the object for the current page, simply dump it using the `cfdump` tag:

```
<cfdump var="#GetPageContext()#">
```

Method objects can be viewed by dumping them as well:

```
<cfdump var="#GetPageContext().getRequest()">
```

This retrieves the server name from the `getRequest` method:

```
<cfdump var="#GetPageContext().getRequest().getServerName()#">
```

The following example includes a JSP page named *hello.jsp* in your ColdFusion page while passing it a URL parameter:

```
<cfoutput>
#GetPageContext().include("hello.jsp?name=Joe")#<br>
</cfoutput>
```

GetProfileSections

New in ColdFusion MX

```
GetProfileSections(path_to_iniFile)
```

Returns a structure containing all the sections from the specified *.ini* file. Initialization files are used to set operating system and application-specific variables during system boot or application launch. Initialization files can be identified by their *.ini* file extension. Each section name of the *.ini* file is returned as a structure key. The entries for each section are returned as a value for the associated key. The following example gets the sections from an *.ini* file named *odbc.ini*, located in *c:\winnt* on Windows machines, and dumps the contents using the `cfdump` tag:

```
<cfset MyIni = GetProfileSections('c:\winnt\odbc.ini')>

<cfdump var="#MyIni#">
```

GetProfileString

`GetProfileString(inipath, section, entry)`

Returns *entry* from *section* of the initialization file specified in *inipath*. Initialization files are used to set operating system and application-specific variables during system boot or application launch. Initialization files can be identified by their *.ini* file extension. Here's an example that returns a profile string from one of ColdFusion's initialization files:

```
<cfset MyPath = "c:\winnt\odbc.ini">
<cfset MySection = "cfsnippets">
<cfset MyEntry = "driver32">

<cfoutput>
<b>Path:</b> #MyPath#<br>
<b>Section:</b> #MySection#<br>
<b>Entry:</b> #MyEntry#<br>
<p><b>Profile String:</b> #GetProfileString(MyPath, MySection, MyEntry)#
</cfoutput>
```

GetTempDirectory

`GetTempDirectory( )`

Returns the absolute path, including trailing backslash, of the temporary directory used by ColdFusion. Example:

```
<cfoutput>
The temporary directory being used by ColdFusion is: #GetTempDirectory( )#
</cfoutput>
```

GetTempFile

`GetTempFile(directory, filenameprefix)`

Returns the full path to a uniquely named temporary file that ColdFusion creates and saves in *directory*. The filename is assigned by taking up to the first three characters of *filenameprefix*, appending a unique string to them, and tacking on a *.tmp* extension. The following example creates a temporary file that begins with "tmp_" and saves it to the current directory:

```
<cfset MyTempFile = GetTempFile(GetDirectoryFromPath(GetBaseTemplatePath( )), "tmp_")>

<cfoutput>
<b>Temporary file:</b> #GetFileFromPath(MyTempFile)#<br>
<b>Path:</b> #GetDirectoryFromPath(MyTempFile)#
</cfoutput>
```

GetTickCount

Updated in ColdFusion MX 6.1

```
GetTickCount( )
```

Returns a counter representing the elapsed time in milliseconds from the Unix epoch (January 1, 1970, 00:00 GMT). `GetTickCount( )` is useful for reporting the amount of time it takes to process specific parts of CFML code. The following example counts the time (in milliseconds) it takes to process a loop with 10,000 iterations:

```
<cfset Start = GetTickCount( )>

<cfoutput><b>Start TickCount:</b> #Start#</cfoutput>

<p>Looping from 1 to 10000

<cfset Timer="0">
<cfloop index="counter" from="1" to="10000">
  <cfset Timer=Timer+1>
</cfloop>
<cfset End = GetTickCount( )>

<p>
<cfoutput><b>End TickCount:</b> #End#</cfoutput>

<cfset TotalTime = (Evaluate(End - Start))>
<p>
<cfoutput><b>Total processing time:</b> #TotalTime# milliseconds</cfoutput>
```

GetTimeZoneInfo

```
GetTimeZoneInfo( )
```

Returns a structure containing time-zone information for the host server calling the function. The following structure keys are returned by calling `GetTimeZoneInfo( )`:

`UTCTotalOffset`
: Returns the local offset time in minutes from Universal Coordinated Time (UTC). UTC is coordinated on the prime meridian (running through Greenwich, U.K.). Positive offset values represent time zones west of the prime meridian, while negative offsets represent time zones east of the prime meridian.

`UTCHourOffset`
: Returns the local offset time from UTC in hours.

`UTCMinuteOffset`
: Returns the local offset time in minutes after `UTCHourOffset` is applied. The value for `UTCHourOffset` can range from 0 to 60 depending on where a particular time zone falls in relation to the nearest hour offset. All North American time zones return 0 for `UTCMinuteOffset`.

`IsDSTOn`
: Returns true if daylight savings time (DST) is turned on for the host machine and `false` if it isn't.

Example:

```
<cfset MyTimeZoneInfo = GetTimeZoneInfo( )>

<cfoutput>
Local time is offset #MyTimeZoneInfo.utcTotalOffset# minutes from UTC.<br>
Local time is offset #MyTimeZoneInfo.utcHourOffset# hours and
#MyTimeZoneInfo.utcMinuteOffset# minutes from UTC.<br>
Daylight Saving Time is <cfif #MyTimeZoneInfo.isDSTOn#><b>on</b>
<cfelse><b>off</b></cfif> for the host.
</cfoutput>
```

GetToken

`GetToken(`*`string, index`* `[,` *`delimiters`* `])`

Returns the token from *string* occupying the specified *index* position. An optional set of *delimiters* may be specified. If no *delimiters* are specified, ColdFusion uses the default of spaces, tabs, and newline characters. If *index* is greater than the total number of tokens in *string*, `GetToken( )` returns an empty string. `GetToken( )` is similar in function to the `ListGetAt( )` function but is more versatile because it uses multiple sets of *delimiters*. Note that the `GetToken( )` function currently treats successive instances of the same delimiter as a single delimiter. Here's an example of this function:

```
<cfset MyString="999-99-9999">

<cfoutput>
<b>String:</b> #MyString#
<p>GetToken(MyString, 3, "-"): #GetToken(MyString, 3, "-")#
</cfoutput>
```

Hash

`Hash(`*`string`*`)`

One-way encrypts *string* using the MD5 hash algorithm. The resulting string is a 32-character hexadecimal representation of the original string. Because the MD5 algorithm is a one-way hash, there is no way to decrypt the encrypted string. The `Hash( )` function is often used to hash passwords before storing them in a database. This allows you to store passwords in a database without being able to see the actual password. When building an application that uses hashed passwords for authentication, the password entered by the user should be hashed, then compared to the hashed value stored in the database. If they match, you know the user entered a valid password. Here's an example using the `Hash( )` function:

```
<cfoutput># Hash('This is a test')#</cfoutput>
```

Hour

`Hour(`*`date`*`)`

Returns the hour portion of a time/date object as a number between 0 and 23. Example:

```
The current hour is<cfoutput>#Hour(Now( ))#</cfoutput>.
```

HTMLCodeFormat

```
HTMLCodeFormat(string [, htmlversion])
```

Returns *string* enclosed in <pre> and </pre> tags with all carriage returns removed and special characters (<, >, ", and &) escaped. The HTML version to use for character-escape sequences can be specified using the optional *htmlversion* parameter. Valid entries are `-1` (current HTML version), `2.0` (HTML 2.0, default), and `3.2` (HTML 3.0). Example:

```
<cfset MyString="<h3>This is an example of the HTMLCodeFormat function.</h3>
View the source of this document to see the escaping of the HTML characters.">

<cfoutput>#HTMLCodeFormat(MyString)#</cfoutput>
```

HTMLEditFormat

```
HTMLEditFormat(string [, htmlversion])
```

Returns *string* with all carriage returns removed and special characters (<, >, ", and &) escaped. The HTML version to use for character-escape sequences can be specified using the optional *htmlversion* parameter. Valid entries are: `-1` (current HTML version), `2.0` (HTML 2.0, default), and `3.2` (HTML 3.0). Example:

```
<cfset MyString="<h3>This is an example of the HTMLEditFormat function.</h3>
View the source of this document to see the escaping of the HTML characters.">

<cfoutput>#HTMLEditFormat(MyString)#</cfoutput>
```

IIf

```
IIf(condition, expression1, expression2)
```

Evaluates *condition* as Boolean. If *condition* is `true`, `IIf( )` then evaluates *expression1*. If *condition* is `false`, `IIf( )` evaluates *expression2*. Examples:

```
<cfoutput>
<b>IIF(1+2 is 3, DE("Yes"), DE("No")):</b><br>
#IIF(1+2 is 3, DE("Yes"), DE("No"))#
<p><b>IIF(DayOfWeek(Now( )) is 4, DE("Today is <b>Wednesday</b>!"),
DE("Today is #DayOfWeekAsString(DayOfWeek(Now( )))#")):</b><br>
#IIF(DayOfWeek(Now( )) is 4, DE("Today is <b>Wednesday</b>!"),
DE("Today is #DayOfWeekAsString(DayOfWeek(Now( )))#"))#
</cfoutput>
```

IncrementValue

```
IncrementValue(number)
```

Increments the integer part of a given number by 1. Examples:

```
<cfoutput>
-1: #IncrementValue(-1)#<br>
-1.123: #IncrementValue(-1.123)#<br>
-0.123: #IncrementValue(-0.123)#<br>
0: #IncrementValue(0)#<br>
```

```
0.123: #IncrementValue(0.123)#<br>
1: #IncrementValue(1)#<br>
1.123: #IncrementValue(1.123)#
</cfoutput>
```

InputBaseN

```
InputBaseN(string, radix)
```

Converts *string* to the base specified by *radix*. *radix* must be an integer between 2 and 36. Example:

```
<cfloop index="Radix" from="2" to="36">
  <cfoutput>InputBaseN(10, #Radix#): #InputBaseN(10, Radix)#<br></cfoutput>
</cfloop>
```

Insert

```
Insert(substring, string, position)
```

Inserts *substring* into *string* after *position*. Example:

```
<cfset MyString="This is how the cookie crumbles.">

<cfoutput>#Insert("chocolate chip ", MyString, 16)#</cfoutput>
```

Int

```
Int(number)
```

Returns the closest integer smaller than the given number. Examples:

```
<cfoutput>
-1: #Int(-1)#<br>
-1.123: #Int(-1.123)#<br>
-0.123: #Int(-0.123)#<br>
0: #Int(0)#<br>
0.123: #Int(0.123)#<br>
1: #Int(1)#<br>
1.123: #Int(1.123)#
</cfoutput>
```

IsArray

```
IsArray(value [, dimension])
```

Returns true if the *value* specified is an array. In addition, `IsArray( )` can check to see if the array is a specified *dimension* (1, 2, or 3). Examples:

```
<cfset Form.MyFormVar = "This is a form variable">
<cfset URL.MyURLVar = "This is a URL variable">
<cfset Grades = ArrayNew(1)>
<cfset Grades[1] = 95>
<cfset Grades[2] = 93>
<cfset Grades[3] = 87>
```

```
<cfset Grades[4] = 100>
<cfset Grades[5] = 74>

<cfif IsArray(Form.MyFormVar)>
  Form.MyFormVar is an array!
<cfelseif IsArray(URL.MyURLVar)>
  URL.MyURLVar is an array!
<cfelseif IsArray(Grades)>
  Grades is an array!
<cfelse>
  No variables are arrays!
</cfif>
```

IsAuthenticated

No longer supported in ColdFusion MX

IsAuthenticated([*securitycontext*])

Returns true if the user has been authenticated for the given *securitycontext* using cfauthenticate. ColdFusion returns true if the user has been authenticated or false if they haven't. If no *securitycontext* is given, ColdFusion returns true if the user has been authenticated for any security context. The IsAuthenticated( ) function is commonly used within an *Application.cfm* file. In order to use the IsAuthenticated( ) function, Advanced Security needs to be enabled within the ColdFusion Administrator, and a valid security context must already be defined. The following example uses IsAuthenticated( ) to determine if a user is authenticated for a security context called Administrator:

```
<cfif not IsAuthenticated("Administrator")>
  <cfauthenticate securitycontext="Administrator"
                  username="#Form.username#"  password="#Form.password#">
</cfif>
```

IsAuthorized

No longer supported in ColdFusion MX

IsAuthorized(*resourcetype*, *resourcename* [, *action*])

Returns true if the user is authorized to perform the *action* specified against a particular ColdFusion resource. The parameter *resourcetype* specifies the type of resource to check, while *resourcename* specifies the actual name of the resource. Possible resource types include Application, CFML, Collection, Component, CustomTag, Datasource, File, Function, User, and UserObject. *action* is required for all resource types except Component, CustomTag, Function, and User and specifies the action to check authorization for. The following table lists each resource type with possible values for *action*:

Resource type	Possible values for action
Application	All, UseClientVariables
CFML	Any valid action of the CFML tag specified in *resourcetype*
Collection	Delete, Optimize, Purge, Search, Update
Component	N/A
CustomTag	N/A

Resource type	Possible values for action
`Datasource`	`All`, `Connect`, `Delete`, `Insert`, `Select`, `SP` (stored procedure), `Update`
`File`	`Read`, `Write`
`Function`	N/A
`User`	N/A
`UserObject`	*`action`* as specified in the ColdFusion Administrator

To use the `IsAuthorized()` function, Advanced Security needs to be enabled within the ColdFusion Administrator, and a valid security context must already be defined. The following example uses the `IsAuthorized()` function to determine if a user is authorized to use the `cffile` tag to perform a file upload:

```
<cfif IsAuthorized('CFML', 'cffile', 'Upload')>
  perform file upload...
<cfelse>
  You are not authorized to upload files!
</cfif>
```

IsBinary

New as of ColdFusion 4.5

`IsBinary(`*`value`*`)`

Returns true if the specified value is binary or `false` if it isn't. Examples:

```
<cfset GifImage=ToBinary("R0lGODlhAQABAPcAAAAAAAAAAAAAAAAAAAAAAAAAAAAAAAAAAAAAAAAAAA
AAAAAAAAAAAAAAAAAAAAAAAAAAAAAAAAAAAAAAAAAAAAAAAAAAAAAAAAAAAAAAAAAAAAAAAAAAAAAAAAA
AAAAAAAAAAAAAAAAAAAAAAAAAAAAAAAAAAAAAAAAAAAAAAAAAAAAAAAAAAAAAAAAAAAAAAAAAAAAAAAAA
AAAAAAAAAAAAAAAAAAAAAAAAAAAAAAAAAAAAAAAAAAAAAAAAAAAAAAAAAAAAAAAAAAAAAAAAAAAAAAAAA
AAAAAAAAAAAAAAAAAAAAAAAAAAAAAAAAAAAAAAAAAAAAAAAAAAAAAAAAAAAAAAAAAAAAAAAAAAAAAAAAA
AAAAAAAAAAAAAAAAAAAAAAAAAAAAAAAAAAAAAAAAAAAAAAAAAAAAAAAAAAAAAAAAAAAAAAAAAAAAAAAAA
AAAAAAAAAAAAAAAAAAAAAAAAAAAAAAAAAAAAAAAAAAAAAAAAAAAAAAAAAAAAAAAAAAAAAAAAAAAAAAAAA
AAAAAAAAAAAAAAAAAAAAAAAAAAAAAAAAAAAAAAAAAAAAAAAAAAAAAAAAAAAAAAAAAAAAAAAAAAAAAAAAA
AAAAAAAAAAAAAAAAAAAAAAAAAAAAAAAAAAAAAAAAAAAAAAAAAAAAAAAAAAAAAAAAAAAAAAAAAAAAAAAAA
AAAAAAAAAAAAAAAAAAAAAAAAAAAAAAAAAAAAAAAAAAAAAAAAAAAAAAAAAAAAAAAAAAAAAAAAAAAAAAAAA
AAAAAAAAAAAAAAAAAAAAAAAAAAAAAAAAAAAAAAAAAAAAAAAAAAAAAAAAAAAAAAAAAAAAAAAAAAAAAAAAA
AAAAAAAAAAAAAAAAAAAAAAAAAAAAAAAAAAAAAAAAAAAAAAAAAAAAAAAAAAAAAAAAAAAAAAAAAAAAAAAAA
AAAAAAAAAAAAAAAAAAAAAAAAAAAAAAAAAAAAAAAAAAAAAAAAAAAAAAAAAAAAAAAAAAAAAAAAAAAAAAAAA
AAAAAAAAAAAAAACwAAAAAAQABAAAIBAABBAQAOw==")>

<cfoutput>
12:  #IsBinary(12)#<br>
abc:  #IsBinary("abc")#<br>
GifImage:  #IsBinary(GifImage)#<br>
</cfoutput>
```

IsBoolean

`IsBoolean(`*`value`*`)`

Returns true if the specified value can be converted to a Boolean or `false` if it can't. Examples:

```
<cfoutput>
-1: #IsBoolean(-1)#<br>
0: #IsBoolean(0)#<br>
1234: #IsBoolean(1234)#<br>
abcdef: #IsBoolean('abcdef')#<br>
true: #IsBoolean(true)#<br>
false: #IsBoolean(false)#<br>
yes: #IsBoolean('yes')#<br>
no: #IsBoolean('no')#<br>
as45sd-1: #IsBoolean('as45sd')#<br>
!@$%^: #IsBoolean('!@$%^')#
</cfoutput>
```

IsCustomFunction

New as of ColdFusion 5.0

```
IsCustomFunction( )
```

Returns true if the specified `Name` is that of a user-defined function.

The following example uses `IsCustomFunction( )` to determine whether `Mean` is a user-defined function. The `IsDefined( )` function makes sure the name exists before testing it with `IsCustomFunction( )`. If you attempt to evaluate a name that doesn't exist with `IsCustomFunction( )`, ColdFusion throws an error.

```
<cfscript>
if(IsDefined('Mean') and IsCustomFunction(Mean)){
   WriteOutput("Mean is a custom function!");
   }
else{
   WriteOutput("Mean is not a custom function!");
   }
</cfscript>
```

IsDate

```
IsDate(string)
```

Returns true if the specified string can be converted to a valid date/time object or `false` if it can't. Valid dates must be in the range AD 100–9999. For information on how ColdFusion MX handles two-digit years, see `CreateDate( )`. Examples:

```
<cfoutput>
Now( ): #IsDate(Now( ))#<br>
04/15/2003: #IsDate('04/15/2003')#<br>
15/04/2003: #IsDate('15/04/2003')#<br>
13/13/2003: #IsDate('13/13/2003')#<br>
August 15, 2003: #IsDate('August 15, 2003')#<br>
15 Apr 2003: #IsDate('15 Apr 2003')#<br>
August fifteenth, nineteen hundred ninety eight : #IsDate('August fifteenth,
nineteen hundred ninety eight')#<br>
7 p.m.: #IsDate('7 p.m.')#<br>
7pm: #IsDate('7pm')#<br>
19:00: #IsDate('19:00')#<br>
six thirty: #IsDate('six thirty')#
</cfoutput>
```

IsDebugMode

```
IsDebugMode( )
```

Returns true if debugging mode is turned on in the ColdFusion Administrator or false if it is turned off. Example:

```
Debugging is currently <cfif IsDebugMode( )><b>on</b><cfelse><b>off</b></cfif>
for your ColdFusion server.
```

IsDefined

```
IsDefined('variable_name')
```

Determines if the specified variable exists. Returns true if the specified variable exists or false if it doesn't. Note that IsDefined( ) replaces the deprecated ParameterExists( ) function. Examples:

```
<cfset MyVar="Variable">
<cfset Form.MyFormVar="Form Variable">

<cfoutput>
<cfif IsDefined('MyVar')>
  Variable MyVar exists:<br> MyVar = #MyVar#
<cfelse>
  No variable called MyVar exists.
</cfif>
<p><cfif IsDefined('MyFormVar')>
  Variable MyFormVar exists:<br> MyFormVar = #MyFormVar#
<cfelse>
  No variable called MyFormVar exists.
</cfif>
<p><cfif IsDefined('Queryname.field')>
  Variable Queryname.Field exists:<br> QueryName.Field = #Queryname.Field#
<cfelse>
  No variable called Queryname.Field exists.
</cfif>
</cfoutput>
```

IsK2ServerABroker

New in ColdFusion MX

```
IsK2ServerABroker( )
```

Returns true if the Verity K2 server installation is running as a broker. For this feature to be enabled, you must license the full version of the K2 Server from Verity. Example:

```
<cfoutput>
Is the local version of the K2 server a broker?  #IsK2ServerABroker( )#
</cfoutput>
```

IsK2ServerDocCountExceeded

New as of ColdFusion 5.0

```
IsK2ServerDocCountExceeded( )
```

Returns true if the number of documents contained in collections accessible by the K2 server exceeds the document limit for the server or false if it doesn't. For more information on the document limit, see the GetK2ServerDocCountLimit( ) function. The following example determines whether the K2 server document limit is exceeded:

```
Is the K2 server document limit exceeded?
<cfoutput>#IsK2ServerDocCountExceeded( )#</cfoutput>
```

IsK2ServerOnline

New in ColdFusion MX

```
IsK2ServerOnline( )
```

Returns true if the K2 server is configured and available for use. ColdFusion MX is bundled with an OEM version of the Verity K2 Server release K2.2.0. Example:

```
Is the K2 server online? <cfoutput>#IsK2ServerOnline#</cfoutput>
```

IsLeapYear

IsLeapYear(*year*)

Returns true if the specified year is a leap year or false if it isn't. It is important to note that IsLeapYear( ) expects a year (e.g., 2000) as opposed to a date. Example:

```
<cfoutput>
#Year(Now( ))# <cfif IsLeapYear(Year(Now( )))><b>is</b><cfelse><b>isn't</b></cfif>
a leap year.
</cfoutput>
```

IsNotMap

New in ColdFusion MX

IsNotMap(*variable_name*)

Returns true if the specified variable does not map to an object of type Structure, Query, XML Document Object, COM, CORBA, Java, ColdFusion Component, or web service. This is an undocumented function in ColdFusion MX. Here's an example that attempts to evaluate both a simple value and an object:

```
<cfset x=1>
<cfobject type="Java" action="Create" name="FileReader" class="java.io.FileReader">

<cfoutput>
Does x not map to an object? #IsNotMap(x)#<br>
Does FileReader not map to an object? #IsNotMap(FileReader)#
</cfoutput>
```

IsNumeric

IsNumeric(*string*)

Returns true if the specified string can be converted to a number or false if it can't. Examples:

```
<cfoutput>
-1: #IsNumeric(-1)#<br>
```

```
0: #IsNumeric(0)#<br>
1234: #IsNumeric(1234)#<br>
1,234,567,890: #IsNumeric('1,234,567,890')#<br>
$1234.99: #IsNumeric('$1234.99')#<br>
04/15/2003: #IsNumeric('04/15/2003')#<br>
7pm: #IsNumeric('7pm')#<br>
abcdef: #IsNumeric('abcdef')#<br>
true: #IsNumeric(true)#<br>
false: #IsNumeric(false)#<br>
yes: #IsNumeric('yes')#<br>
no: #IsNumeric('no')#<br>
as45sd-1: #IsNumeric('as45sd')#<br>
!@$%^: #IsNumeric('!@$%^')#<br>
1234abcd: #IsNumeric('1234abcd')#
</cfoutput>
```

IsNumericDate

```
IsNumericDate(realnumber)
```

Returns Yes if *realnumber* can be converted to a numeric date and No if it can't. Examples:

```
<cfoutput>
IsNumericDate(Now( )): #IsNumericDate(Now( ))#<br>
IsNumericDate('2003-04-15 19:00:00'): #IsNumericDate('2003-04-15 19:00:00')#<br>
</cfoutput>
```

IsObject

New in ColdFusion MX

```
IsObject(value)
```

Returns true if *value* is an object of type COM, CORBA, Java, ColdFusion Component, or web service. Example:

```
<cfset x=1>
<cfobject type="Java" action="Create" name="FileReader" class="java.io.FileReader">

<cfoutput>
Is x an object? #IsObject(x)#<br>
Is FileReader an object? #IsObject(FileReader)#
</cfoutput>
```

IsProtected

No longer supported in ColdFusion MX

```
IsProtected(resourcetype, resourcename [, action])
```

Returns true if the specified resource is protected by a rule within the security context of the currently authenticated user. The parameter *resourcetype* specifies the type of resource to check while *resourcename* specifies the actual name of the resource. Possible resource types include Application, CFML, Collection, Component, CustomTag, Datasource, File, Function, User, and UserObject. *action* is required for all resource types except Component, CustomTag, Function, and User and specifies the action of the resource to check. The following table lists each resource type along with possible values for *action*:

Resource type	Possible values for action
Application	All, UseClientVariables
CFML	Any valid action of the CFML tag specified in *resourcetype*
Collection	Delete, Optimize, Purge, Search, Update
Component	N/A
CustomTag	N/A
Datasource	All, Connect, Delete, Insert, Select, SP (stored procedure), Update
File	Read, Write
Function	N/A
User	N/A
UserObject	*action* as specified in the ColdFusion Administrator

In order to use the `IsProtected()` function, Advanced Security needs to be enabled within the ColdFusion Administrator, and a valid security context must already be defined. The following example uses the `IsProtected()` function to determine if file uploading via `cffile` is a protected resource:

```
<cfif IsProtected('CFML', 'cffile', 'Upload')>
  File uploading using cffile is a protected resource!
<cfelse>
  File uploading using cffile isn't a protected resource!
</cfif>
```

IsQuery

```
IsQuery(value)
```

Returns `true` if the specified value is a valid ColdFusion query or `false` if it isn't. Examples:

```
<cfset Form.MyFormVar = "This is a form variable">
<cfset URL.MyURLVar = "This is a URL variable">
<cfset Grades = ArrayNew(1)>
<cfset Grades[1] = 95>
<cfset Grades[2] = 93>
<cfset Grades[3] = 87>
<cfset Grades[4] = 100>
<cfset Grades[5] = 74>

<cfif IsQuery(Form.MyFormVar)>
  Form.MyFormVar is a query!
<cfelseif IsQuery(URL.MyURLVar)>
  URL.MyURLVar is a query!
<cfelseif IsQuery(Grades)>
  Grades is a query!
<cfelse>
  No variables are queries!
</cfif>
```

IsSimpleValue

```
IsSimpleValue(value)
```

Returns true if the specified value is a number, string, Boolean, or date/time object or false if it isn't. Examples:

```
<cfset MyArray = ArrayNew(1)>
<cfset MyArray[1]="George">
<cfset MyArray[2]="Jeff">

<cfoutput>
IsSimpleValue(123): #IsSimpleValue(123)#<br>
IsSimpleValue('abc'): #IsSimpleValue('abc')#<br>
IsSimpleValue('123,abc,456,def'): #IsSimpleValue('123,abc,456,def')#<br>
IsSimpleValue(MyArray): #IsSimpleValue(MyArray)#<br>
IsSimpleValue(true): #IsSimpleValue(true)#<br>
IsSimpleValue(11/11/02): #IsSimpleValue(11/11/02)#<br>
</cfoutput>
```

IsStruct

```
IsStruct(variable)
```

Returns true if the specified variable is a ColdFusion structure or false if it isn't. Examples:

```
<cfset Employee=StructNew( )>
<cfset Employee.Name="Pere Money">
<cfset Employee.Title="President">
<cfset Employee.Department="Executive Management">
<cfset Employee.Email="pmoney@example.com">
<cfset Employee.PhoneExt="1234">

Is Employee a structure? <cfoutput>#IsStruct(Employee)#</cfoutput>
```

IsUserInRole

New in ColdFusion MX

```
IsUserInRole("role")
```

Returns true if the current authenticated user belongs in the specified *role*. `IsUserInRole( )` is used in conjunction with ColdFusion MX's built-in security. Example:

```
<cflogin>
  <cfquery name="AuthenticateUser" datasource="ProgrammingCF">
    SELECT *
    FROM Users
    WHERE Username='pmoney'
    AND   Password='#Hash("cat")#'
  </cfquery>

  <cfloginuser
    name="pmoney"
    password="#Hash("cat")#"
    roles="editor,user">
</cflogin>
```

```
<cfoutput>
Is #GetAuthUser()# an editor? #IsUserInRole("editor")#
</cfoutput>
```

IsWDDX

`IsWDDX(value)`

Uses a validating XML parser with the WDDX DTD to determine whether a specified value is a well-formed WDDX packet. Returns true if the specified value is a well-formed WDDX packet or false if it isn't. The following example shows how to use the IsWDDX( ) function to detect if a value is a well-formed WDDX packet:

```
<!--- Serialize a string into a WDDX packet --->
<cfwddx action="CFML2WDDX" input="I am a string!" output="MyWDDXPacket1">

<cfset MyWDDXPacket2 = "I am a string too!">

<cfoutput>#HTMLEditFormat(MyWDDXPacket1)#<br></cfoutput><p>

<!--- Check if MyWDDXPacket1 contains a well-formed WDDX packet --->
<cfif IsWDDX(MyWDDXPacket1)>
  <b>Is</b> a well-formed WDDX packet!
<cfelse>
  <b>Is not</b> a well-formed WDDX packet!
</cfif>

<cfoutput>#HTMLEditFormat(MyWDDXPacket2)#<br></cfoutput><p>

<!--- Check if MyWDDXPacket2 contains a well-formed WDDX packet --->
<cfif IsWDDX(MyWDDXPacket2)>
  <b>Is</b> a well-formed WDDX packet!
<cfelse>
  <b>Is not</b> a well-formed WDDX packet!
</cfif>
```

IsXmlDoc

New in ColdFusion MX

`IsXmlDoc(value)`

Returns true if *value* is a ColdFusion XML document object. XML document objects are created using the XmlParse( ) function or the cfxml tag. The following example grabs an XML news feed from *macromedia.com*, uses XmlParse( ), then reports whether the result is an XML document object:

```
<cfhttp URL="http://www.macromedia.com/devnet/resources/macromedia_resources.xml"
        method="Get">

<cfset DesDev = XmlParse(cfhttp.FileContent)>

Is the feed from Macromedia.com an XML document object?
<cfoutput>#IsXMLDoc(DesDev)#</cfoutput>
```

To see the structure of the XML document object, use the cfdump tag.

IsXmlElem

New in ColdFusion MX

```
IsXmlElem(value)
```

Returns true if *value* is an element of a ColdFusion XML document object. Example:

```
<cfhttp URL="http://www.macromedia.com/devnet/resources/macromedia_resources.xml"
        method="Get">

<cfset DesDev = XmlParse(cfhttp.FileContent)>

<cfoutput>
Is DesDev.macromedia_resources.resource.title an XML Element?
#IsXmlElem(DesDev.macromedia_resources.resource.title)#
</cfoutput>
```

To see the structure of the XML document object, use the `cfdump` tag.

IsXmlRoot

New in ColdFusion MX

```
IsXmlRoot(value)
```

Returns true if *value* is the root element of an XML document object. Example:

```
<cfhttp URL="http://www.macromedia.com/devnet/resources/macromedia_resources.xml"
        method="Get">

<cfset DesDev = XmlParse(cfhttp.FileContent)>

<cfoutput>
Is DesDev.macromedia_resources.resource.title the XML root?
#IsXmlRoot(DesDev.macromedia_resources.resource.title)#
</cfoutput>
```

To see the structure of the XML document object, use the `cfdump` tag.

JavaCast

```
JavaCast(type, variable)
```

Casts a ColdFusion variable before being passed to an overloaded Java method. Possible entries for *type* include `boolean`, `int`, `long`, `double`, or `string`. The `JavaCast()` function can't cast complex objects, such as query objects, arrays, and structures, nor can it cast to a super-class. The following example demonstrates how to explicitly cast a ColdFusion variable before passing it to an overloaded method within a Java object:

```
<cfobject type="Java" action="Create" class="MyClass" name="MyObject">

<cfset x=10>

<!--- Cast x to a string --->
<cfset MyString = JavaCast("string",x)>
<cfset void = MyMethod(MyString)>

<!--- Cast x to an integer --->
<cfset MyInteger = JavaCast("int",x)>
<cfset void = MyMethod(MyInteger)>
```

JSStringFormat

```
JSStringFormat(string)
```

Returns *string* with special characters escaped so that it is safe to use in JavaScript statements. Example:

```
<cfset MyString="""Escape double quotes"".  Escape the \ character. 'Escape
single quotes'">

<cfset SafeString=JSStringFormat(MyString)>

<cfoutput>
<b>Original String:</b> #MyString#<br>
<b>JavaScript Safe String:</b> #SafeString#
</cfoutput>
```

Lcase

```
Lcase(string)
```

Converts *string* to lowercase. Example:

```
<cfset MyString="I WANT THIS STRING TO APPEAR IN ALL LOWERCASE.">

<cfoutput>#Lcase(MyString)#</cfoutput>
```

Left

```
Left(string, count)
```

Returns the number of characters specified by *count*, beginning at the leftmost position of *string*. The following example returns the 13 leftmost characters of a string:

```
<cfset MyString="(555)555-5555 x5555">
<cfset BasePhoneNumber = Left(MyString, 13)>

<cfoutput>
<b>String:</b> #MyString#<br>
<b>Base Phone Number:</b> #BasePhoneNumber#
</cfoutput>
```

Len

```
Len(string)
```

Returns the length of a string as a number. If *string* is binary, `Len()` returns the length of the binary buffer. Example:

```
<cfset MyString="This is my string.">

<cfoutput>
String:  #MyString#<br>
MyString is #Len(MyString)# characters long.
</cfoutput>
```

ListAppend

```
ListAppend(list, element [, delimiters])
```

Appends *element* to the end of *list*. An optional delimiter can be specified if the list is delimited with a character other than the comma (the default). Here's an example that appends an element to the end of a list:

```
<cfset MyList = "Monday,Tuesday,Wednesday,Thursday,Friday,Saturday">
<cfset MyAppendedList = ListAppend(MyList, 'Sunday')>

<cfoutput>
<b>List:</b>  #MyList#<br>
<b>Appended List:</b> #MyAppendedList#
</cfoutput>
```

ListChangeDelims

```
ListChangeDelims(list, new_delimiter [, delimiters])
```

Changes the delimiters used in the list to the specified new delimiters. The following example changes the delimiters in the list from commas to pipes (|):

```
<cfset MyList = "Monday,Tuesday,Wednesday,Thursday,Friday,Saturday,Sunday">
<cfset NewList = ListChangeDelims(MyList, '|', ',')>

<cfoutput>
<b>Old Delimiters:</b> #MyList#<br>
<b>New Delimiters:</b> #NewList#
</cfoutput>
```

ListContains

```
ListContains(list, substring [, delimiters])
```

Returns the index of the first element in the list that contains the specified substring as part of the element. If the substring isn't found, 0 is returned. The search is case-sensitive. An optional delimiter can be specified if the list is delimited with a character other than the comma (the default). Here's an example that returns the index of the first element in a list that contains `wed`:

```
<cfset MyList = "Monday,Tuesday,Wednesday,Thursday,Friday,Saturday,Sunday">
<cfset TheSubstring = "wed">
<cfset TheIndex = ListContains(MyList, TheSubstring)>

<cfoutput>
<b>List:</b> #MyList#
<p><cfif TheIndex is 0>
  The substring (#TheSubstring#) could not be found in the list!
<cfelse>
  The substring (#TheSubstring#) was found in element
  #TheIndex# (#ListGetAt(MyList, TheIndex)#).
</cfif>
</cfoutput>
```

ListContainsNoCase

```
ListContainsNoCase(list, substring [, delimiters])
```

Returns the index of the first element in the list that contains the specified substring as part of the element. If the substring isn't found, 0 is returned. The search is case-insensitive. An optional delimiter can be specified if the list is delimited with a character other than the comma (the default). The following example returns the index of the first element in a list that contains `wed`:

```
<cfset MyList = "Monday,Tuesday,Wednesday,Thursday,Friday,Saturday,Sunday">
<cfset TheSubstring = "wed">
<cfset TheIndex = ListContainsNoCase(MyList, TheSubstring)>

<cfoutput>
<b>List:</b> #MyList#
<p><cfif TheIndex is 0>
  The substring (#TheSubstring#) could not be found in the list!
<cfelse>
  The substring (#TheSubstring#) was found in element #TheIndex#
  (#ListGetAt(MyList, TheIndex)#).
</cfif>
</cfoutput>
```

ListDeleteAt

```
ListDeleteAt(list, position [, delimiters ])
```

Deletes an element from a list occupying the specified *position*. An optional delimiter can be specified if the list is delimited with a character other than the comma (the default). Here's an example that deletes the list element occupying the fifth position in the list:

```
<cfset MyList = "Monday,Tuesday,Wednesday,Thursday,Friday,Saturday,Sunday">
<cfset NewList = ListDeleteAt(MyList, 5)>

<cfoutput>
<b>Original List:</b> #MyList#<br>
<b>New List:</b> #NewList#
</cfoutput>
```

ListFind

```
ListFind(list, value [, delimiters])
```

Returns the index of the first occurrence of value in the specified list. The search is case-sensitive. If no matches are found, 0 is returned. An optional delimiter can be specified if the list is delimited with a character other than the comma (the default). The following example returns the index of the first element in a list that matches `saturday`:

```
<cfset MyList = "Monday,Tuesday,Wednesday,Thursday,Friday,Saturday,Sunday">
<cfset TheValue = "saturday">
<cfset TheIndex = ListFind(MyList, TheValue)>

<cfoutput>
```

```
<b>List:</b> #MyList#
<p><cfif TheIndex is 0>
  The value (#TheValue#) could not be found in the list!
<cfelse>
  The Value (#TheValue#) was found in element #TheIndex#
  (#ListGetAt(MyList, TheIndex)#).
</cfif>
</cfoutput>
```

ListFindNoCase

`ListFindNoCase(`*`list, value`* `[, `*`delimiters`*`])`

Returns the index of the first occurrence of value in the specified list. The search is case-insensitive. If no matches are found, 0 is returned. An optional delimiter can be specified if the list is delimited with a character other than the comma (the default). Here's an example that returns the index of the first element in a list that matches `saturday`:

```
<cfset MyList = "Monday,Tuesday,Wednesday,Thursday,Friday,Saturday,Sunday">
<cfset TheValue = "saturday">
<cfset TheIndex = ListFindNoCase(MyList, TheValue)>

<cfoutput>
<b>List:</b> #MyList#
<p><cfif TheIndex is 0>
  The value (#TheValue#) could not be found in the list!
<cfelse>
  The Value (#TheValue#) was found in element #TheIndex#
  (#ListGetAt(MyList, TheIndex)#).
</cfif>
</cfoutput>
```

ListFirst

`ListFirst(`*`list`* `[, `*`delimiters`*`])`

Returns the first element in the specified list. An optional delimiter can be specified if the list is delimited with a character other than the comma (the default). Example:

```
<cfset MyList = "Monday,Tuesday,Wednesday,Thursday,Friday,Saturday,Sunday">

<cfoutput>
<b>List:</b> #MyList#<br>
<b>First Element:</b> #ListFirst(MyList)#
</cfoutput>
```

ListGetAt

`ListGetAt(`*`list, position`* `[, `*`delimiters`*`])`

Returns the list element specified by *`position`*. An optional delimiter can be specified if the list is delimited with a character other than the comma (the default). Note that the

`ListGetAt()` function currently treats successive instances of the same delimiter as a single delimiter. Here's an example that retrieves the third element of the list:

```
<cfset MyList = "Monday,Tuesday,Wednesday,Thursday,Friday,Saturday,Sunday">

<cfoutput>
<b>List:</b> #MyList#<br>
<b>Third Element:</b> #ListGetAt(MyList, 3)#
</cfoutput>
```

ListInsertAt

```
ListInsertAt(list, position, value [, delimiters])
```

Inserts *value* into list at the specified position. An optional delimiter can be specified if the list is delimited with a character other than the comma (the default). The following example inserts a value into a list:

```
<cfset MyList = "Monday,Tuesday,Thursday,Friday,Saturday,Sunday">
<cfset MyNewList = ListInsertAt(MyList, 3, "Wednesday")>

<cfoutput>
<b>Original List:</b> #MyList#<br>
<b>New List:</b> #MyNewList#
</cfoutput>
```

ListLast

```
ListLast(list [, delimiters])
```

Returns the last element in the specified list. An optional delimiter can be specified if the list is delimited with a character other than the comma (the default). Example:

```
<cfset MyList = "Monday,Tuesday,Wednesday,Thursday,Friday,Saturday,Sunday">

<cfoutput>
<b>List:</b> #MyList#<br>
<b>Last Element:</b> #ListLast(MyList)#
</cfoutput>
```

ListLen

```
ListLen(list [, delimiters])
```

Returns the number of elements in the specified list. An optional delimiter can be specified if the list is delimited with a character other than the comma (the default). Example:

```
<cfset MyList = "Monday,Tuesday,Wednesday,Thursday,Friday,Saturday,Sunday">

<cfoutput>
<b>List:</b> #MyList#<br>
<b>Number of elements:</b> #ListLen(MyList)#
</cfoutput>
```

ListPrepend

```
ListPrepend(list, element [, delimiters])
```

Prepends *element* to the beginning of *list*. An optional delimiter can be specified if the list is delimited with a character other than the comma (the default). The following example appends an element to the beginning of a list:

```
<cfset MyList = "Tuesday,Wednesday,Thursday,Friday,Saturday,Sunday">
<cfset MyprependedList = ListPrepend(MyList, 'Monday')>

<cfoutput>
<b>List:</b>  #MyList#<br>
<b>Prepended List:</b> #MyPrependedList#
</cfoutput>
```

ListQualify

```
ListQualify(list, qualifier [, delimiters] [, elements])
```

Places qualifiers (such as single or double quotes) around elements of *list*. An optional delimiter can be specified if the list is delimited with a character other than the comma (the default). Elements accepts `All` or `Char` and specifies whether the function qualifies all elements in the list (the default) or only list items made up of alphabetic characters. Examples:

```
<cfset MyAlphaList = "Monday,Tuesday,Wednesday,Thursday,Friday,Saturday,Sunday">
<cfset MyAlphaNumericList =
"1,Monday,2,Tuesday,3,Wednesday,4,Thursday,5,Friday,6,Saturday,7,Sunday">

<cfset MyQualifiedAlphaList = ListQualify(MyAlphaList, """")>
<cfset MyQualifiedAlphaNumericList =
  ListQualify(MyAlphaNumericList, """", ',', 'CHAR')>
<cfoutput>
<b>Original Alpha List:</b> #MyAlphaList#<br>
<b>Original AlphaNumeric List:</b> #MyAlphaNumericList#<br>
<p><b>Qualified Alpha List:</b> #MyQualifiedAlphaList#<br>
<b>Qualified AlphaNumeric List:</b> #MyQualifiedAlphaNumericList#<br>
</cfoutput>
```

ListRest

```
ListRest(list [, delimiters])
```

Returns all the elements in the specified list excluding the first element. An optional delimiter can be specified if the list is delimited with a character other than the comma (the default). The following example returns all the elements in the list except for the first element:

```
<cfset MyList = "Monday,Tuesday,Wednesday,Thursday,Friday,Saturday,Sunday">

<cfoutput>
<b>List:</b> #MyList#<br>
<b>All Elements Excluding First:</b> #ListRest(MyList)#
</cfoutput>
```

ListSetAt

```
ListSetAt(list, position, value [, delimiters])
```

Sets *value* at specified *position*, overwriting the element already occupying that space. An optional delimiter can be specified if the list is delimited with a character other than the comma (the default). Here's an example that replaces the value in the third element of the list with a new value:

```
<cfset MyList = "Monday,Tuesday,Wednesday,Thursday,Friday,Saturday,Sunday">
<cfset MyNewList = ListSetAt(MyList, 3, "Humpday")>

<cfoutput>
<b>Original List:</b> #MyList#<br>
<b>New List:</b> #MyNewList#
</cfoutput>
```

ListSort

```
ListSort(list, sort_type [, order] [, delimiters])
```

Sorts a list based on the *sort_type* (numeric, text, or textnocase) and optionally, the sort *order* (asc, the default, or desc). An optional delimiter can be specified if the list is delimited with a character other than the comma (the default). The following example sorts a list by alphabetical order:

```
<cfset MyList = "Monday,Tuesday,Wednesday,Thursday,Friday,Saturday,Sunday">

<cfoutput>
<b>List:</b> #MyList#<br>
<b>Sorted by Alphabetical Order:</b> #ListSort(MyList, 'text')#
</cfoutput>
```

ListToArray

```
ListToArray(list [, delimiters])
```

Converts a ColdFusion list to a one-dimensional array. An optional delimiter can be specified if the list is delimited with a character other than the comma (the default). Here's an example that converts a list containing the days of the week to a one-dimensional array:

```
<cfset MyList = "Monday,Tuesday,Wednesday,Thursday,Friday,Saturday,Sunday">
<cfset MyArray = ListToArray(MyList)>

<cfdump var="#MyArray#">
```

ListValueCount

```
ListValueCount(list, value [, delimiters])
```

Counts the number of times *value* appears in the specified list. The search performed is case-sensitive. An optional delimiter can be specified if the list is delimited with a character other than the comma (the default). The following example counts the number of times each unique value appears in the list and outputs the results for each item:

```
<cfset MyList = "Apple,orange,apple,Orange,Peach,pear,apple,pear,peach,Pear,
Apple,Peach,orange,apple">
<cfset UniqueList = "">

<cfloop index="Element" list="#MyList#">
  <cfif ListFind(UniqueList, Element) is "No">
    <cfset UniqueList = ListAppend(UniqueList, Element)>
  </cfif>
</cfloop>

<cfoutput><b>Original List:</b> #MyList#</cfoutput>
<p><cfloop index="Element" list="#UniqueList#">
  <cfoutput>
    #Element# appears: #ListValueCount(MyList, Element)# times.<br>
  </cfoutput>
</cfloop>
```

ListValueCountNoCase

`ListValueCountNoCase(`*`list, value`*` [, `*`delimiters`*`])`

Counts the number of times *value* appears in the specified list. The search performed is case-insensitive. An optional delimiter can be specified if the list is delimited with a character other than the comma (the default). Here's an example that counts the number of times each unique value appears in the list and outputs the results for each item:

```
<cfset MyList = "Apple,orange,apple,Orange,Peach,pear,apple,pear,peach,Pear,
Apple,Peach,orange,apple">
<cfset UniqueList = "">

<cfloop index="Element" list="#MyList#">
  <cfif ListFindNoCase(UniqueList, Element) is "No">
    <cfset UniqueList = ListAppend(UniqueList, Element)>
  </cfif>
</cfloop>

<cfoutput><b>Original List:</b> #MyList#</cfoutput>
<p><cfloop index="Element" list="#UniqueList#">
  <cfoutput>
    #Element# appears: #ListValueCountNoCase(MyList, Element)# times
    regardless of case.<br>
  </cfoutput>
</cfloop>
```

LJustify

`LJustify(`*`string, length`*`)`

Left-justifies *`string`* within a field of *`length`* characters. Example:

```
<cfset OriginalString = "ColdFusion">

<cfoutput>
<b>Original String (quoted):</b> "#OriginalString#"<br>
<b>Left-justified String (quoted):</b> "#LJustify("ColdFusion", 20)#"
</cfoutput>
```

Log

```
Log(number)
```

Returns the natural logarithm of a number. *number* must be a positive number greater than zero. Examples:

```
<cfoutput>
Log(0.01) = #Log(0.01)#<br>
Log(1) = #Log(1)#<br>
Log(10) = #Log(10)#<br>
Log(100) = #Log(100)#<br>
Log(1000) = #Log(1000)#<br>
Log(1000.234) = #Log(1000.234)#
</cfoutput>
```

Log10

```
Log10(number)
```

Returns the base-10 logarithm of a number. Examples:

```
<cfoutput>
Log10(0.01) = #Log10(0.01)#<br>
Log10(1) = #Log10(1)#<br>
Log10(10) = #Log10(10)#<br>
Log10(100) = #Log10(100)#<br>
Log10(1000) = #Log10(1000)#<br>
Log10(1000.234) = #Log10(1000.234)#
</cfoutput>
```

LSCurrencyFormat

```
LSCurrencyFormat(number [, type])
```

Returns a JRE-dependent, locale-specific currency format where *number* is the currency amount, and *type* is the locale-specific convention. Valid entries for *type* are `None` (the amount), `Local` (the amount with locale-specific currency formatting; the default), and `International` (the amount with its corresponding three-letter international currency prefix). Note that for JDK 1.3, Euro Zone countries use the currency symbol of their locale. For JDK 1.4, Euro Zone countries use the euro. For this reason, it is suggested you use the `LSEuroCurrencyFormat( )` function if you need to deal with the euro. The following example displays currency formats for each locale:

```
<cfloop index="locale" list="#Server.Coldfusion.SupportedLocales#">
  <cfset SetLocale(locale)>
  <cfoutput>
    <p><b>#locale#</b><br>
    None: #LSCurrencyFormat(1000000.99, "None")#<br>
    Local: #LSCurrencyFormat(1000000.99, "Local")#<br>
    International: #LSCurrencyFormat(1000000.99, "International")#<br>
  </cfoutput>
</cfloop>
```

LSDateFormat

```
LSDateFormat(date [, mask])
```

Returns a locale-specific date format according to *mask*. Dates must be in the range AD 100–9999. If no value is specified for *mask*, `LSDateFormat( )` uses the locale-specific default. For valid mask entries, see the `DateFormat( )` function. Dates passed as literals must be enclosed in quotes. Otherwise, ColdFusion interprets the date as a numeric date. If an invalid mask is passed to the function, ColdFusion outputs the invalid characters. For information on how ColdFusion MX handles two-digit years, see the entry for `CreateDate( )`. The following example applies the `LSDateFormat( )` function to each locale:

```
<cfloop index="locale" list="#Server.Coldfusion.SupportedLocales#">
  <cfset SetLocale(locale)>
  <cfoutput>
    <p><b>#locale#</b><br>
    #LSDateFormat(Now( ))#<br>
    #LSDateFormat(Now( ), "d/m/yy")#<br>
    #LSDateFormat(Now( ), "d-mmm-yyyy")#<br>
    #LSDateFormat(Now( ), 'dd mmm yy')#<br>
    #LSDateFormat(Now( ), 'dddd, mmmm dd, yyyy')#<br>
    #LSDateFormat(Now( ), "mm/dd/yyyy")#<br>
    #LSDateFormat(Now( ), "mmmm d, yyyy")#<br>
    #LSDateFormat(Now( ), "mmm-dd-yyyy")#<br>
    short: #LSDateFormat(Now( ), 'short')#<br>
    medium: #LSDateFormat(Now( ), 'medium')#<br>
    long: #LSDateFormat(Now( ), 'long')#<br>
    full: #LSDateFormat(Now( ), 'full')#<br>
  </cfoutput>
</cfloop>
```

LSEuroCurrencyFormat

```
LSEuroCurrencyFormat(amount [, type])
```

Returns a locale-specific currency format with the euro as the symbol where *number* is the currency amount and *type* is the locale-specific convention. Valid entries for *type* are `None` (the amount), `Local` (the amount with locale-specific currency formatting; the default), and `International` (the amount with its corresponding three-letter international currency prefix). In ColdFusion MX, if the current locale is not part of the Euro Zone, the currency format specific to the locale is used instead of the euro. The following example displays euro currency formats for each locale:

```
<cfloop index="locale" list="#Server.Coldfusion.SupportedLocales#">
  <cfset SetLocale(locale)>
  <cfoutput>
    <p>
    <b>#locale#</b><br>
    None: #LSEuroCurrencyFormat(1000000.99, "None")#<br>
    Local: #LSEuroCurrencyFormat(1000000.99, "Local")#<br>
    International: #LSEuroCurrencyFormat(1000000.99, "International")#<br>
  </cfoutput>
</cfloop>
```

LSIsCurrency

```
LSIsCurrency(string)
```

Returns true if *string* is a locale-specific currency string and false if it isn't. Here's an example that determines whether the given strings are locale-specific currency values for each locale:

```
<cfloop index="locale" list="#Server.Coldfusion.SupportedLocales#">
  <cfset SetLocale(locale)>
  <cfoutput>
    <p><b>#locale#</b><br>
    99.99: #LSIsCurrency('99.99')#<br>
    $1234: #LSIsCurrency('$1234')#<br>
    $1,234,567,890: #LSIsCurrency('$1,234,567,890')#<br>
    $1234.99: #LSIsCurrency('$1234.99')#<br>
  </cfoutput>
</cfloop>
```

LSIsDate

```
LSIsDate(date)
```

Functions identically to the IsDate( ) function within the context of the current locale. Returns true if *date* can be converted to a date/time object in the current locale or false if it can't. In ColdFusion MX, the hyphen is only a valid date delimiter in the Dutch (Standard) and Portuguese (Standard) locales. Additionally, if you have the Sun JRE 1.3.1 running in the English (UK) locale, the month and day portion of a date string must have a leading zero for single-digit months/days. The following example determines whether the supplied values are valid date/time objects for each locale:

```
<cfloop index="locale" list="#Server.Coldfusion.SupportedLocales#">
  <cfset SetLocale(locale)>
  <cfoutput>
    <p><b>#locale#</b><br>
    04/15/2002: #LSIsDate('04/15/2002')#<br>
    15-04-2002: #LSIsDate('15-04-2002')#<br>
    15/04/2002: #LSIsDate('15/04/2002')#<br>
    13/13/2002: #LSIsDate('13/13/2002')#<br>
    August 15, 2002: #LSIsDate('August 15, 2002')#<br>
    15 Apr 2002: #LSIsDate('15 Apr 2002')#<br>
    7 p.m.: #LSIsDate('7 p.m.')#<br>
    7pm: #LSIsDate('7pm')#<br>
    19:00: #LSIsDate('19:00')#<br>
    six thirty: #LSIsDate('six thirty')#
  </cfoutput>
</cfloop>
```

LSIsNumeric

```
LSIsNumeric(string)
```

Functions identically to the IsNumeric( ) function within the context of the current locale. Returns true if *string* can be converted to a number in the current locale or false if it can't. Here's an example that determines whether the supplied values are valid numbers for each locale:

```
<cfloop index="locale" list="#Server.Coldfusion.SupportedLocales#">
  <cfset SetLocale(locale)>
  <cfoutput>
    <p><b>#locale#</b><br>
    -1: #LSIsNumeric(-1)#<br>
    0: #LSIsNumeric(0)#<br>
    1234: #LSIsNumeric(1234)#<br>
    1,234,567,890: #LSIsNumeric('1,234,567,890')#<br>
    $1234.99: #LSIsNumeric('$1234.99')#<br>
    04/15/2003: #LSIsNumeric('04/15/2003')#<br>
    7pm: #LSIsNumeric('7pm')#<br>
    abcdef: #LSIsNumeric('abcdef')#<br>
    true: #LSIsNumeric(true)#<br>
    false: #LSIsNumeric(false)#<br>
    yes: #LSIsNumeric('yes')#<br>
    no: #LSIsNumeric('no')#<br>
  </cfoutput>
</cfloop>
```

LSNumberFormat

```
LSNumberFormat(number [, mask])
```

Returns *number* formatted according to *mask* using the locale convention. If no value is specified for *mask*, `LSNumberFormat()` returns *number* rounded to the nearest integer. Valid entries for *mask* are the same as for `NumberFormat()`. The following example applies the function to various numbers for each locale:

```
<cfloop index="locale" list="#Server.Coldfusion.SupportedLocales#">
  <cfset SetLocale(locale)>
  <cfoutput>
    <p><b>#locale#</b><br>
    LSNumberFormat(1000.99): #LSNumberFormat(1000.99)#<br>
    LSNumberFormat(1000.99, '____'): #LSNumberFormat(1000.99, '____')#<br>
    LSNumberFormat(1000.99, '9999.99'): #LSNumberFormat(1000.99, '9999.99')#<br>
    LSNumberFormat(1000.99, '09999.9900'):
      #LSNumberFormat(1000.99, '09999.9900')#<br>
    LSNumberFormat(-1000.99, '(9999.99)'):
      #LSNumberFormat(-1000.99, '(9999.99)')#<br>
    LSNumberFormat(1000.99, '+9999.99'):
      #LSNumberFormat(1000.99, '+9999.99')#<br>
    LSNumberFormat(-1000.99, '+9999.99'):
      #LSNumberFormat(-1000.99, '+9999.99')#<br>
    LSNumberFormat(1000.99, '-9999.99'):
      #LSNumberFormat(1000.99, '-9999.99')#<br>
    LSNumberFormat(-1000.99, '-9999.99'):
      #LSNumberFormat(-1000.99, '-9999.99')#<br>
    LSNumberFormat(1000.99, '$9,999.99'):
      #LSNumberFormat(1000.99, '$9,999.99')#<br>
    LSNumberFormat(1000.99, 'L999,999.99'):
      #LSNumberFormat(1000.99, 'L999,999.99')#<br>
```

```
    LSNumberFormat(1000.99, 'C999,999.99'):
      #LSNumberFormat(1000.99, 'C999,999.99')#<br>
    LSNumberFormat(1000.99, 'C_____(^___)'):
      #LSNumberFormat(1000.99, 'C_____(^___)')#<br>
  </cfoutput>
</cfloop>
```

LSParseCurrency

`LSParseCurrency(string)`

Returns the numeric value of *string* where *string* is a locale-specific currency amount from a non–Euro Zone locale. LSParseCurrency( ) can be converted from any of the locale-specific currency formats (None, Local, International). For euro currency formats, see the LSParseEuroCurrency( ) function. The following example demonstrates for each locale:

```
<cfloop index="locale" list="#Server.Coldfusion.SupportedLocales#">
  <cfset SetLocale(locale)>
  <cfoutput>
    <p><b>#locale#</b><br>
    Local: #LSCurrencyFormat(1000000.99, "local")#<br>
    LSParseCurrency: #LSParseCurrency(LSCurrencyFormat(1000000.99, "local"))#<br>
  </cfoutput>
</cfloop>
```

LSParseDateTime

`LSParseDateTime(datestring)`

Returns a locale-specific ColdFusion date/time object from *datestring*. LSParseDateTime( ) is similar to the ParseDateTime( ) function except it doesn't handle POP dates. If the supplied *datestring* contains a time zone, and it is different than the time zone of the ColdFusion server, the *datestring* is converted to the time zone of the ColdFusion server. Example:

```
<cfloop index="locale" list="#Server.Coldfusion.SupportedLocales#">
  <cfset SetLocale(locale)>
  <cfoutput>
    <p><b>#locale#</b><br>
    #LSParseDateTime("#LSDateFormat(Now())# #LSTimeFormat(Now())#")#<br>
  </cfoutput>
</cfloop>
```

LSParseEuroCurrency

`LSParseEuroCurrency(string)`

Returns the numeric value of *string* where *string* is a locale-specific currency amount that contains the euro symbol. LSParseEuroCurrency( ) can be converted from any of the locale-specific euro currency formats (None, Local, International). The following example demonstrates for each locale:

```
<cfloop index="locale" list="#Server.Coldfusion.SupportedLocales#">
  <cfset SetLocale(locale)>
```

```
    <cfoutput>
      <p><b>#locale#</b><br>
      Local: #LSEuroCurrencyFormat(1000000.99, "local")#<br>
      LSParseEuroCurrency: #LSParseEuroCurrency(LSEuroCurrencyFormat(1000000.99,
      "local"))#<br>
    </cfoutput>
  </cfloop>
```

LSParseNumber

`LSParseNumber(string)`

Converts *string* to a locale-specific numeric value. Here's an example that applies the function to each locale:

```
<cfloop index="locale" list="#Server.Coldfusion.SupportedLocales#">
  <cfset SetLocale(locale)>
  <cfoutput>
    <p><b>#locale#</b><br>
    Local: #LSNumberFormat(1000000.99)#<br>
    LSParseNumber: #LSParseNumber(LSNumberFormat(1000000.99))#<br>
  </cfoutput>
</cfloop>
```

LSTimeFormat

`LSTimeFormat(time [, mask])`

Returns locale-specific *time* formatted according to *mask*. If no value is specified for *mask*, `LSTimeFormat()` uses the default locale's format. Valid entries for *mask* are the same as for `TimeFormat()`. If an invalid mask is passed to the function, ColdFusion outputs the invalid characters. The following example demonstrates for each locale:

```
<cfset TheTime = Now()>

<cfloop index="locale" list="#Server.Coldfusion.SupportedLocales#">
  <cfset SetLocale(locale)>
  <cfoutput>
    <p><b>#locale#</b><br>
    TheTime = #LSTimeFormat(TheTime)#<br>
    LSTimeFormat(TheTime, 'h:m:s'): #LSTimeFormat(TheTime, 'h:m:s')#<br>
    LSTimeFormat(TheTime, 'h:m:s t'): #LSTimeFormat(TheTime, 'h:m:s t')#<br>
    LSTimeFormat(TheTime, 'hh:mm:ss'): #LSTimeFormat(TheTime, 'hh:mm:ss')#<br>
    LSTimeFormat(TheTime, 'hh:mm:ss tt'):
      #LSTimeFormat(TheTime, 'hh:mm:ss tt')#<br>
    LSTimeFormat(TheTime, 'H:M:ss'): #LSTimeFormat(TheTime, 'H:M:s')#<br>
    LSTimeFormat(TheTime, 'HH:MM:ss'): #LSTimeFormat(TheTime, 'HH:MM:ss')#<br>
    <p>
    And these formats are new in ColdFusion MX:<br>
    short: #LSTimeFormat(TheTime, 'short')#<br>
    medium: #LSTimeFormat(TheTime, 'medium')#<br>
    long: #LSTimeFormat(TheTime, 'long')#<br>
    full: #LSTimeFormat(TheTime, 'full')#<br>
  </cfoutput>
</cfloop>
```

LTrim

```
LTrim(string)
```

Removes leading spaces from the specified string. Example:

```
<cfset OriginalString = "         ColdFusion">

<cfoutput>
<b>Original String (quoted):</b> "#OriginalString#"<br>
<b>Left-trimmed String (quoted):</b> "#LTrim(OriginalString)#"
</cfoutput>
```

Max

```
Max(number1, number2)
```

Returns the greater value of two specified numbers. Example:

```
<cfset x=10>
<cfset y=20>

<cfoutput>#Max(x,y)# is a larger number than #Min(x,y)#.</cfoutput>
```

Mid

```
Mid(string, startpos, count)
```

Returns *count* number of characters from the *string* beginning at the position specified by *startpos*. Example:

```
<cfset MyString="(555)555-5555 x5555">
<cfset AreaCode = Mid(MyString, 2, 3)>

<cfoutput>
<b>String:</b> #MyString#<br>
<b>Area Code:</b> #AreaCode#
</cfoutput>
```

Min

```
Min(number1, number2)
```

Returns the lesser value of two specified numbers. Example:

```
<cfset x=10>
<cfset y=20>

<cfoutput>#Min(x,y)# is a smaller number than #Max(x,y)#.</cfoutput>
```

Minute

```
Minute(date)
```

Returns the minute for a valid date/time object as a number between 1 and 59. Example:

```
It is currently <cfoutput>#Minute(Now( ))#</cfoutput> minute(s) past the hour.
```

Month

```
Month(date)
```

Returns the month of the year for a given date as a number between 1 and 12. Example:

```
The current month is month <cfoutput>#Month(Now( ))#</cfoutput>.
```

MonthAsString

```
MonthAsString(number)
```

Returns the name of the month for a given month's number between 1 and 12. Example:

```
The current month is <cfoutput>#MonthAsString(Month(Now( )))#</cfoutput>.
```

Now

```
Now( )
```

Returns the current server time and date as a time/date object in the format `{ts 'yyyy-mm-dd HH:MM:SS'}`. Example:

```
<cfoutput>
Today is #DateFormat(Now( ),'dddd mmmm dd, yyyy')#.<br>
It is currently #TimeFormat(Now( ),'hh:mm tt')#.
</cfoutput>
```

NumberFormat

```
NumberFormat(number [, mask])
```

Returns *number* formatted according to *mask*. If no value is specified for *mask*, `NumberFormat` returns *number* as an integer formatted with thousands separators. Valid entries for *mask* are:

Mask	Description
_	Optional digit placeholder
9	Optional digit placeholder; same as _ but better for showing decimal places
.	Decimal-point location
	Forces padding with zeros
( )	Surrounds negative numbers in parentheses
+	Places a plus sign in front of positive numbers and a minus sign in front of negative numbers
-	Places a space in front of positive numbers and a minus sign in front of negative numbers
,	Separates thousands with commas
L	Left-justifies the number within the width of the mask
C	Centers the number within the width of the mask
$	Places a dollar sign in front of the number
^	Separates left from right formatting

Examples:

```
<cfset MyNumber = 1000.99>

<cfoutput>
<b>MyNumber = #MyNumber#</b>
<p>
NumberFormat(MyNumber, '____'): #NumberFormat(MyNumber, '____')#<br>
NumberFormat(MyNumber, '9999.99'): #NumberFormat(MyNumber, '9999.99')#<br>
NumberFormat(MyNumber, '09999.9900'): #NumberFormat(MyNumber, '09999.9900')#<br>
NumberFormat(-MyNumber, '(9999.99)'): #NumberFormat(-MyNumber, '(9999.99)')#<br>
NumberFormat(MyNumber, '+9999.99'): #NumberFormat(MyNumber, '+9999.99')#<br>
NumberFormat(-MyNumber, '+9999.99'): #NumberFormat(-MyNumber, '+9999.99')#<br>
NumberFormat(MyNumber, '-9999.99'): #NumberFormat(MyNumber, '-9999.99')#<br>
NumberFormat(-MyNumber, '-9999.99'): #NumberFormat(-MyNumber, '-9999.99')#<br>
NumberFormat(MyNumber, '$9,999.99'): #NumberFormat(MyNumber, '$9,999.99')#<br>
NumberFormat(MyNumber, 'L999,999.99'): #NumberFormat(MyNumber, 'L999,999.99')#<br>
NumberFormat(MyNumber, 'C999,999.99'): #NumberFormat(MyNumber, 'C999,999.99')#<br>
NumberFormat(MyNumber, 'C_____(^___)'):
  #NumberFormat(MyNumber, 'C_____(^___)')#<br>
</cfoutput>
```

ParagraphFormat

`ParagraphFormat(`*`string`*`)`

Returns *string* formatted so that single newline characters are replaced with a space character, and double newline characters are replaced with HTML <p> tags. `ParagraphFormat( )` is most often used to format text that has been entered in a `Textarea` HTML form field. Example:

```
<cfset MyText="This is my block of text.
It has both single newline characters in it like this paragraph, and
double newline characters like in the next paragraph.

This is the paragraph with the double newline characters.">

<form action="" method="Post">
  <cfoutput>
   <textarea cols=50 rows=10 name="TheText"
             wrap="virtual">#ParagraphFormat(MyText)#</textarea>
  </cfoutput>
</form>
```

ParseDateTime

`ParseDateTime(`*`datestring`*` [, `*`conversiontype`*`])`

Returns a valid ColdFusion date/time object from an English (US) locale *datestring*. An optional *conversiontype* may be specified. Valid entries for *conversiontype* are `POP` and `Standard` (the default). If `POP` is specified, *datestring* is converted to GMT (Greenwich Mean Time) using the English (US) locale. If `Standard` is specified, no conversion is performed. For conversion between different time zones, see DateConvert( ). For information on how ColdFusion MX handles two-digit years, see CreateDate( ). Examples:

```
<cfoutput>
<b>ParseDateTime("4/15/2003 19:00:00"):</b>
#ParseDateTime("4/15/2003 19:00:00")#<br>
<b>ParseDateTime("Tue, 15 Apr 2003 19:00:00 +0400 (EDT):</b>
#ParseDateTime("Tue, 15 Apr 2003 19:00:00 +0400 (EDT)", "Standard")#<br>
<b>ParseDateTime("Tue, 15 Apr 2003 19:00:00 +0400", "POP"):</b>
#ParseDateTime("Tue, 15 Apr 2003 19:00:00 +0400", "POP")#<br>
<b>ParseDateTime("Tue, 15 Apr 2003 19:00:00 +0400 (EDT)", "POP"):</b>
#ParseDateTime("Tue, 15 Apr 2003 19:00:00 +0400 (EDT)", "POP")#<br>
</cfoutput>
```

Pi

```
Pi()
```

Returns the value of Pi accurate to 15 decimal places (3.14159265358979). Note that without applying a NumberFormat( ) mask, Pi( ) will only actually display 11 decimal places. The following example uses Pi( ) to calculate the circumference of a circle with a radius of 12 inches:

```
<cfset r=12>
<cfset Circumference = 2*Pi()*r>

<cfoutput>
The circumference of a circle with a radius of 12 inches is
#Circumference# inches.
</cfoutput>
```

PreserveSingleQuotes

PreserveSingleQuotes(*variable*)

Returns *variable* without escaping single quotation marks. PreserveSingleQuotes( ) keeps ColdFusion from automatically escaping single quotation marks within dynamically set variables. The PreserveSingleQuotes( ) function is most often used with SQL statements when it is necessary to pass dynamically generated values. Example:

```
<cfset Names = "'Pere Money','Mark Edward','Marcel Haney'">

<cfquery name="GetRecords" datasource="ProgrammingCF">
        SELECT * FROM EmployeeDirectory
        WHERE Name IN (#PreserveSingleQuotes(Names)#)
</cfquery>

<cfoutput>#GetRecords.RecordCount# record(s) found.</cfoutput>
```

Quarter

Quarter(*date*)

Returns the quarter as a number for the given date. Example:

```
<cfoutput>The current quarter is: #Quarter(Now())#</cfoutput>
```

QueryAddColumn

`QueryAddColumn(`*`query, columnname, arrayname`*`)`

Adds a new column called *columnname* to *query* and populates its rows with data from a one-dimensional array specified by *arrayname*. If an invalid column name (one that violates variable naming rules) is passed, ColdFusion throws an error. The following example adds a new column to a query and populates it with data from an array:

```
<cfset Products = QueryNew("ProductName, Color, Price, Qty")>
<cfset NewRows = QueryAddRow(Products, 3)>

<cfset QuerySetCell(Products, "ProductName", "Widget", 1)>
<cfset QuerySetCell(Products, "Color", "Silver", 1)>
<cfset QuerySetCell(Products, "Price", "19.99", 1)>
<cfset QuerySetCell(Products, "Qty", "46", 1)>

<cfset QuerySetCell(Products, "ProductName", "Thingy", 2)>
<cfset QuerySetCell(Products, "Color", "Red", 2)>
<cfset QuerySetCell(Products, "Price", "34.99", 2)>
<cfset QuerySetCell(Products, "Qty", "12", 2)>

<cfset QuerySetCell(Products, "ProductName", "Sprocket", 3)>
<cfset QuerySetCell(Products, "Color", "Blue", 3)>
<cfset QuerySetCell(Products, "Price", "1.50", 3)>
<cfset QuerySetCell(Products, "Qty", "460", 3)>

<cfset ShippingArray = ArrayNew(1)>
<cfset ShippingArray[1] = "1.99">
<cfset ShippingArray[2] = "3.48">
<cfset ShippingArray[3] = "5.00">

<cfset MyNewColumn = QueryAddColumn(Products, "Shipping", ShippingArray)>

<cfdump var="#Products#">
```

QueryAddRow

`QueryAddRow(`*`query`*` [, `*`number`*`])`

Adds *number* empty rows to *query*. If *number* is omitted, a single blank row is added. Here's an example that creates a blank query and adds three empty rows to it:

```
<cfset Products = QueryNew("ProductName, Color, Price, Qty")>
<cfset NewRows = QueryAddRow(Products, 3)>

<cfoutput>
There are now #NewRows# rows in the query named Products.
</cfoutput>
```

QueryNew

```
QueryNew(columnlist)
```

Creates an empty ColdFusion query object with column names as specified by *`columnlist`*. *`columnlist`* can be a comma-delimited list of column names or a blank string ("") so you can use the `QueryAddColumn( )` function to populate the rows with the contents of a one-dimensional array. The following example creates a query called `Products` with four column names:

```
<cfset Products = QueryNew("ProductName, Color, Price, Qty")>
<cfdump var="#Products#">
```

QuerySetCell

```
QuerySetCell(query, columnname, value [, row])
```

Sets the cell in *columnname* to *value* for the specified *query*. An optional *row* number may be set, specifying the row for the cell to be set in. If no *row* number is specified, the cell in the last row of the query is set. `QuerySetCell( )` returns `true` upon successful completion. Here's an example that adds data to an empty query:

```
<cfset Products = QueryNew("ProductName, Color, Price, Qty")>
<cfset NewRows  = QueryAddRow(Products, 3)>

<cfset QuerySetCell(Products, "ProductName", "Widget", 1)>
<cfset QuerySetCell(Products, "Color", "Silver", 1)>
<cfset QuerySetCell(Products, "Price", "19.99", 1)>
<cfset QuerySetCell(Products, "Qty", "46", 1)>

<cfset QuerySetCell(Products, "ProductName", "Thingy", 2)>
<cfset QuerySetCell(Products, "Color", "Red", 2)>
<cfset QuerySetCell(Products, "Price", "34.99", 2)>
<cfset QuerySetCell(Products, "Qty", "12", 2)>

<cfset QuerySetCell(Products, "ProductName", "Sprocket", 3)>
<cfset QuerySetCell(Products, "Color", "Blue", 3)>
<cfset QuerySetCell(Products, "Price", "1.50", 3)>
<cfset QuerySetCell(Products, "Qty", "460", 3)>

<cfdump var="#Products#">
```

QuotedValueList

```
QuotedValueList(queryname.column [,delimiter])
```

Returns a comma-separated list of values for the previously executed query column specified in *`queryname.column`*. Each element in the list is qualified with a single quote character. An optional delimiter can be specified if the list is to be delimited with a character other than the comma (the default). The following example creates a quoted value list from a ColdFusion query:

```
<cfquery name="MyQuery" datasource="ProgrammingCF">
  SELECT * FROM EmployeeDirectory
```

```
</cfquery>

<cfoutput>
<b>The query column Name contains the following values:</b>
#QuotedValueList(MyQuery.Name)#
</cfoutput>
```

Rand

```
Rand( )
```

Returns a random number between 0 and 1. Here's an example that returns a random number between 0 and 100:

```
<cfoutput>The random number is: #int(100*Rand( ))#</cfoutput>
```

Randomize

`Randomize(`*`number`*`)`

Seeds ColdFusion's random number generator with the integer part of *number*. This allows the `Rand( )` function to generate numbers with a higher degree of randomness. Note that the number returned by the `Randomize( )` function isn't random. The following example uses the `Randomize( )` function to seed ColdFusion's random number generator before creating random numbers with the `Rand( )` function:

```
<cfset Randomize(GetTickCount( ))>

Here are 10 random numbers:<p>
<cfloop index="counter" from="1" to="10">
  <cfoutput>#Rand( )#<br></cfoutput>
</cfloop>
```

RandRange

`RandRange(`*`number1, number2`*`)`

Generates a random integer in the range between two numbers, where *number1* and *number2* are integers less that 100,000,000. Here's an example that generates a random integer between 1 and 100:

```
<cfoutput>
The following random number should be between 1 and 100: #RandRange(1,100)#
</cfoutput>
```

REFind

`REFind(`*`regex, string`*` [, `*`startpos`*`] [, `*`returnsubexpressions`*`])`

Performs a case-sensitive search. Returns the position of the first occurrence of *regex* in *string*. *regex* can be any valid ColdFusion regular expression. An optional starting position for the search can be specified by *startpos*. If *returnsubexpressions* is set to `true` (`false` is the default), `REFind( )` returns a CFML structure containing two arrays, pos and len that represents the position and length, respectively, of the matched regular expression. If the regular expression contains parenthesized subexpressions, the first index of the array returns the len and pos of the first occurrence of the match for the entire regular expression. Each subsequent array index in the returned structure contains the len and pos for the first occurrence of each parenthesized subexpression in the matched regular expression. If REFind( ) is unable to find a match for the regular expression, 0 is returned. REFind( ) performs a case-sensitive search. The following example demonstrates the use of the REFind( ) function with the *returnsubexpressions* parameter set to true:

```
<cfset MyString="The ratio of good to bad apples is 4:1.">
<cfset matches= REFind("([0-9]+):([0-9]+)", MyString, 1, "true")>

<cfoutput>
<b>String:</b>  #MyString#<br>
<b>Regex:</b>  REFind(&quot;([0-9]+):([0-9]+)&quot;, MyString, 1,
&quot;true&quot;)<br>
<b>Position:</b> #matches.pos[1]#<br>
<b>Length:</b> #matches.len[1]#
</cfoutput>
<p>
Dump:
<cfdump var="#matches#">
```

REFindNoCase

```
REFindNoCase(regex, string [, startpos] [, returnsubexpressions])
```

Performs a case-insensitive search. Returns the position of the first occurrence of *regex* in *string*. *regex* can be any valid ColdFusion regular expression. An optional starting position for the search can be specified by *startpos*. If *returnsubexpressions* is set to true (false is the default), REFindNoCase( ) returns a CFML structure containing two arrays, pos and len that represents the position and length, respectively, of the matched regular expression. If the regular expression contains parenthesized subexpressions, the first index of the array returns the len and pos of the first occurrence of the match for the entire regular expression. Each subsequent array index in the returned structure contains the len and pos for the first occurrence of each parenthesized subexpression in the matched regular expression. If REFindNoCase( ) is unable to find a match for the regular expression, 0 is returned. Here's an example that demonstrates the use of the REFindNoCase( ) function with the *returnsubexpressions* parameter set to true:

```
<cfset MyString="The name of the bank robber is Rob.">
<cfset Matches= ReFindNoCase("(Rob)", MyString, 1, "true")>

<cfoutput>
<b>String:</b>  #MyString#<br>
<b>Regex:</b>  RefindNoCase(&quot;catRob&quot;, MyString, 1, &quot;true&quot;)<br>
<b>Position:</b> #Matches.pos[1]#<br>
<b>Length:</b> #Matches.len[1]#
</cfoutput>

<cfdump var="#Matches#">
```

ReleaseCOMObject

New in ColdFusion MX 6.1

```
ReleaseCOMObject(object)
```

Terminates any connections to the specified COM object and returns any resources (such as RAM) to the server. `ReleaseComObject()` should only be used once you have finished with the COM object. Many COM objects have a method you can call to explicitly close the connection to the object, typically `close()` or `quit()`. While this method explicitly tells ColdFusion to terminate the connection to the COM object, it does not immediately release the resources it was consuming. It still has to wait for the garbage collection to occur. `ReleaseCOMObject()` is designed to get around this. If you call the function while the COM object is still in use, ColdFusion throws an exception. Example:

```
<cfset ReleaseComObject(myObject)>
```

Or:

```
<cfscript>
ReleaseComObject(myObject);
</cfscript>
```

RemoveChars

```
RemoveChars(string, startpos, count)
```

Removes *count* characters from *string* beginning at the position specified by *startpos*. If no characters are removed, 0 is returned. Example:

```
<cfset MyString="cosdafol">

<cfoutput>
<b>Original String:</b> #MyString#<br>
<b>RemoveChars(MyString, 3, 4):</b> #RemoveChars(MyString, 3, 4)#
</cfoutput>
```

RepeatString

```
RepeatString(string, count)
```

Returns a string consisting of *string* repeated *count* times. Example:

```
<cfset MyString="I love ColdFusion!<br>">

<cfoutput>#RepeatString(MyString, 10)#</cfoutput>
```

Replace

```
Replace(string, substring1, substring2 [, scope])
```

Returns *string* with *substring1* replaced by *substring2* according to *scope*. *scope* may be set as either `One` or `All`, where `One` results in the replacement of the first occurrence of *substring1*, and `All` results in the replacement of all occurrences of *substring1*. The default *scope* is `One`. `Replace()` performs a case-sensitive search. The following example demonstrates this function:

```
<cfset MyString="This is a case-sensitive example of using the Replace
function to replace a substring within a string.">
<cfset MySubstring1="Replace">
<cfset MySubstring2="<b>Replace</b>">

<cfoutput>
<b>String:</b> #MyString#<br>
<b>Replace:</b> #MySubstring1# with #MySubstring2#
<p>#Replace(MyString, MySubstring1, MySubstring2)#
</cfoutput>
```

ReplaceList

`ReplaceList(string, list1, list2)`

Returns *string* with all the elements from *list1* replaced by the corresponding elements from *list2*. ReplaceList( ) performs a case-sensitive search. Here's an example that shows how to use this function:

```
<cfset MyString="This is my string.">
<cfset List1=" is,my,string">
<cfset List2=" function,is,cool">

<cfoutput>
<b>Original String:</b> #MyString#<br>
<b>List1:</b> #List1#<br>
<b>List2:</b> #List2#<p>
<b>ReplaceList(MyString, List1, List2):</b> #ReplaceList(MyString, List1, List2)#
</cfoutput>
```

ReplaceNoCase

`ReplaceNoCase(string, substring1, substring2 [, scope])`

Returns *string* with *substring1* replaced by *substring2* according to *scope*. *scope* may be set as either One or All, where One results in the replacement of the first occurrence of *substring1*, and All results in the replacement of all occurrences of *substring1*. The default *scope* is One. ReplaceNoCase( ) performs a case-insensitive search. The following example demonstrates the use of this function:

```
<cfset MyString="This is a case-insensitive example of using the ReplaceNoCase
function to replace a substring within a string.">
<cfset MySubstring1="Replace">
<cfset MySubstring2="<b>Replace</b>">

<cfoutput>
<b>String:</b> #MyString#<br>
<b>Replace:</b> #MySubstring1# with #MySubstring2#
<p>#ReplaceNoCase(MyString, MySubstring1, MySubstring2, "All")#
</cfoutput>
```

REReplace

```
REReplace(string, regex, substring [, scope])
```

Returns *string* with *regex* replaced by *substring* for the specified *scope*. *regex* can be any valid ColdFusion regular expression. *scope* may be set as either `One` or `All`, where `One` results in the replacement of the first occurrence of the regular expression, and `All` results in the replacement of all occurrences of the regular expression. The default *scope* is `One`. `REReplace( )` performs a case-sensitive search. Here's an example that demonstrates the use of this function:

```
<cfset OriginalString="T8h3i53s 1i2s3 8a3 t3e2s9t.">
<cfset NewString = REReplace(OriginalString, "[[:digit:]]", "", "ALL")>

<cfoutput>
Original String:  #OriginalString#<br>
New String:  #NewString#
</cfoutput>
```

REReplaceNoCase

```
REReplaceNoCase(string, regex, substring [, scope])
```

Returns *string* with *regex* replaced by *substring* for the specified *scope*. *regex* can be any valid ColdFusion regular expression. *scope* may be set as either `One` or `All`, where `One` results in the replacement of the first occurrence of the regular expression, and `All` results in the replacement of all occurrences of the regular expression. The default *scope* is `One`. `REReplaceNoCase( )` performs a case-insensitive search. The following example uses the `REReplaceNoCase( )` function to remove doubled words from a string:

```
<cfset MyString = "I want to go to to the park.">
<cfset NewString = ReReplaceNoCase(MyString, "\b([A-Z]+)[ ]+\1", "\1", "All")>

<cfoutput>
<b>Original String:</b> #MyString#
<p>
<b>New String:</b> #NewString#
</cfoutput>
```

Reverse

```
Reverse(string)
```

Returns *string* with all the characters in reverse order. Example:

```
<cfset MyString="0123456789">

<cfoutput>
<b>String:</b> #MyString#<br>
<b>Reversed:</b> #Reverse(MyString)#
</cfoutput>
```

Right

```
Right(string, count)
```

Returns the number of characters specified by *count*, beginning at the rightmost position of *string*. The following example returns the five rightmost characters of a string:

```
<cfset MyString="(555)555-5555 x5555">
<cfset Extension = Right(MyString, 5)>
<cfoutput>
<b>String:</b> #MyString#<br>
<b>Extension:</b> #Extension#
</cfoutput>
```

RJustify

```
RJustify(string, length)
```

Right-justifies *string* within a field of *length* characters. Example:

```
<cfset OriginalString = "ColdFusion">

<cfoutput>
<b>Original String (quoted):</b> "#OriginalString#"<br>
<b>Right-justified String (quoted):</b> "#RJustify("ColdFusion", 20)#"
</cfoutput>
```

Round

```
Round(number)
```

Rounds off a number to the nearest integer. Examples:

```
<cfoutput>
-2.5: #Round(-2.5)#<br>
-1: #Round(-1)#<br>
-1.123: #Round(-1.123)#<br>
-0.123: #Round(-0.123)#<br>
0: #Round(0)#<br>
0.123: #Round(0.123)#<br>
1: #Round(1)#<br>
1.123: #Round(1.123)#<br>
2.5: #Round(2.5)#
</cfoutput>
```

RTrim

```
RTrim(string)
```

Removes trailing spaces from the specified string. Example:

```
<cfset OriginalString = "ColdFusion     ">

<cfoutput>
<b>Original String (quoted):</b> "#OriginalString#"<br>
<b>Right-trimmed String (quoted):</b> "#RTrim(OriginalString)#"
</cfoutput>
```

Second

```
Second(date)
```

Returns the seconds for a valid date/time object as a number between 0 and 59. Example:

```
<cfoutput>
It is currently #Minute(Now( ))# minute(s) and #Second(Now( ))# second(s) past the
hour.
</cfoutput>
```

SetEncoding

New in ColdFusion MX

```
SetEncoding("Form|Url", charset)
```

Sets the character encoding for `form` or `URL` variables to `charset` when the submitted form or URL data is not in Latin-1 encoding. *charset* lets you specify a Java character set to use for the encoding. The most common character sets are `UTF-8` (the default), `UTF-16`, `UTF-16BE`, `UTF-16LE`, `US-ASCII`, and `ISO-8859-1`. You may use any character set supported by your JRE. The following example assumes the page is receiving a form post with form field data that is not Latin-1 encoded. Is simply sets the encoding to `UTF-8` and dumps the `form` scope to the browser:

```
<cfset SetEncoding("form", "UTF-8")>

<cfdump var="#form#">
```

SetLocale

Updated in ColdFusion MX

```
SetLocale(newlocale)
```

Changes the current locale used by ColdFusion to *newlocale* for the duration of the current page request. The server's locale determines how ColdFusion treats and displays numeric, currency, date, and time values. Returns the old locale so that it can be used again if necessary. Valid entries for *newlocale* are determined by the underlying JRE and operating system of your ColdFusion server. For a complete list of locales available on your server, output the variable `server.Coldfusion.SupportedLocales`. In general, ColdFusion supports the following locales. They may be referenced with their ColdFusion locale name, or their equivalent Java locale name where appropriate.

ColdFusion Locale	Java locale
Chinese (China)	N/A
Chinese (Hong Kong)	N/A
Chinese (Taiwan)	N/A
Dutch (Belgian)	nl_be
Dutch (Standard)	nl_NL
English (Australian)	en_AU
English (Canadian)	en_CA
English (New Zealand)	en_NZ

ColdFusion Locale	Java locale
English (UK)	en_GB
English (US)	en_US
French (Belgian)	fr_BE
French (Canadian)	fr_CA
French (Standard)	fr_FR
French (Swiss)	fr_CH
German (Austrian)	de_AT
German (Standard)	de_DE
German (Swiss)	de_CH
Italian (Standard)	it_IT
Italian (Swiss)	it_CH
Japanese	ja_JP
Korean	ko_KR
Norwegian (Bokmal)	no_NO
Norwegian (Nynorsk)	no_NO_nynorsk
Portuguese (Brazilian)	pt_br
Portuguese (Standard)	pt_PT
Spanish (Modern)	es_ES
Spanish (Standard)	es_ES
Swedish	sv_SE

In ColdFusion MX, the locale Spanish (Mexican) is no longer supported. It has been replaced by Spanish (Modern). Additionally, Spanish (Modern) now maps to Spanish (Standard).

The following example changes the current locale to Swedish for the duration of the current page request:

```
<cfoutput>
Default Locale: #GetLocale( )#

<p>Changing locale to Swedish...
<cfset OldLocale = SetLocale("Swedish")>

<p>New Locale: #GetLocale( )#<br>
Old Locale: #OldLocale#
</cfoutput>
```

SetProfileString

```
SetProfileString(inipath, section, entry, value)
```

Sets the *value* of a profile string *entry* in *section* of the initialization file specified by *inipath*. If *section* does not exist, ColdFusion creates it first. If the operation is successful, an empty string is returned. If not, an exception is thrown. Here's an example that changes the number of threads used by the Verity K2 server in the *k2server.ini* file:

```
<cfset MyPath = "c:\cfusionmx\lib\k2server.ini">
<cfset MySection = "Server">
<cfset MyEntry = "numThreads">
<cfset MyValue = "6">

<cfset MyProfileString = SetProfileString(MyPath, MySection, MyEntry, MyValue)>
<cfoutput>
<b>Path:</b> #MyPath#<br>
<b>Section:</b> #MySection#<br>
<b>Entry:</b> #MyEntry#<br>
<p><b>Profile String:</b> #MyValue#
</cfoutput>
```

SetVariable

```
SetVariable(variablename, value)
```

Assigns `value` to `variablename` where `value` is any passed value. `SetVariable( )` is useful when you want to create dynamically named variables. The following example uses `SetVariable( )` to assign values to several dynamically created variables:

```
<cfloop index="index" from="1" to="10">
  <cfset ValueOfVariable = SetVariable("MyVar#index#", #Index#)>
</cfloop>

<cfloop index="pos" from="1" to="10">
  <cfoutput>MyVar#pos# = #Evaluate("MyVar"&"#pos#")#<br></cfoutput>
</cfloop>
```

Sgn

```
Sgn(number)
```

Returns 1 if the specified number is positive, 0 if the specified number is 0, or –1 if the number is negative. Examples:

```
<cfoutput>
-1: #Sgn(-1)#<br>
-1.123: #Sgn(-1.123)#<br>
-0.123: #Sgn(-0.123)#<br>
0: #Sgn(0)#<br>
0.123: #Sgn(0.123)#<br>
1: #Sgn(1)#<br>
1.123: #Sgn(1.123)#
</cfoutput>
```

Sin

```
Sin(number)
```

Returns the sine of an angle expressed in radians. Example:

```
The sine of 45 is <cfoutput>#Sin(45)#</cfoutput>
```

SpanExcluding

`SpanExcluding(string, set)`

Returns all the characters contained in *string* until any character from *set* is encountered. `SpanExcluding( )` performs a case-sensitive search. Example:

```
<cfset MyString="I like ColdFusion alot">

<cfoutput>
<b>Original String:</b>  #MyString#
<p><b>SpanExcluding(MyString, "ab"):</b> #SpanExcluding(MyString, "ab")#
</cfoutput>
```

SpanIncluding

`SpanIncluding(string, set)`

Returns all the characters contained in *string* until any character not in *set* is encountered. `SpanIncluding( )` performs a case-sensitive search. Example:

```
<cfset MyString="I like ColdFusion alot">

<cfoutput>
<b>Original String:</b>  #MyString#
<p><b>SpanIncluding(MyString, "I like"):</b> #SpanIncluding(MyString, "I like")#
</cfoutput>
```

Sqr

`Sqr(number)`

Returns the positive square root of a number. Examples:

```
<cfoutput>
0: #Sqr(0)#<br>
1: #Sqr(1)#<br>
10: #Sqr(10)#<br>
100: #Sqr(100)#
</cfoutput>
```

StripCR

`StripCR(string)`

Returns *string* with all carriage returns removed. Example:

```
<cfset MyString="This is a paragraph of text with carriage returns hardcoded.
#Chr(10)##Chr(13)#As you can see, this is a new line.
#Chr(10)##Chr(13)#This is a new line too.">

<cfoutput>
<b>Original String with Carriage Returns:</b><br>
<pre>
#MyString#
</pre>
```

```
<p>
<b>String with Carriage Returns Removed:</b><br>
<pre>
#StripCR(MyString)#
</pre>
</cfoutput>
```

StructAppend

```
StructAppend(structure1, structure2 [, overwrite])
```

Appends the contents of *structure2* to *structure1*. After completion, *structure1* contains the newly appended structure while *structure2* remains unchanged. Setting the optional *overwrite* parameter to Yes allows overwriting of existing keys/values within the appended structure. The default value for *overwrite* is Yes. The following example demonstrates the StructAppend( ) function:

```
<cfset Employee=StructNew( )>
<cfset Employee.Name="Pere Money">
<cfset Employee.Title="President">
<cfset Employee.Department="Executive Management">

<cfset ContactInfo=StructNew( )>
<cfset ContactInfo.Email="pmoney@example.com">
<cfset ContactInfo.PhoneExt="1234">

<h2>Employee Struct</h2>
<cfdump var="#Employee#">

<h2>ContactInfo Struct</h2>
<cfdump var="#ContactInfo#">

<cfset StructAppend(Employee, ContactInfo, "No")>

<h2>Appended Employee Struct</h2>
<cfdump var="#Employee#">
```

StructClear

```
StructClear(structure)
```

Removes all data from the specified structure. Here's an example that removes all data from a structure, then tests to see whether the structure is empty:

```
<cfset Employee=StructNew( )>
<cfset Employee.Name="Pere Money">
<cfset Employee.Title="President">
<cfset Employee.Department="Executive Management">
<cfset Employee.Email="pmoney@example.com">
<cfset Employee.PhoneExt="1234">

<cfset StructClear(Employee)>

<h2>Employee Struct</h2>
<cfdump var="#Employee#">
```

StructCopy

```
StructCopy(structure)
```

Makes an exact copy of the specified structure. This copy isn't by reference, meaning that any changes made to the original structure aren't reflected in the copy. You should note that the `StructCopy( )` function shouldn't be used to copy deeply nested structures. If you need to copy nested structures, use the `Duplicate( )` function instead. The following example demonstrates the use of the `StructCopy( )` function:

```
<cfset Employee=StructNew( )>
<cfset Employee.Name="Pere Money">
<cfset Employee.Title="President">
<cfset Employee.Department="Executive Management">
<cfset Employee.Email="pmoney@example.com">
<cfset Employee.PhoneExt="1234">

<cfset EmployeeCopy = StructCopy(Employee)>

<h2>EmployeeCopy Struct</h2>
<cfdump var="#EmployeeCopy#">
```

StructCount

```
StructCount(structure)
```

Returns a count for the number of key/value pairs contained in the specified structure. Here's an example that returns the number of name/value pairs contained in the structure `Employee`:

```
<cfset Employee=StructNew( )>
<cfset Employee.Name="Pere Money">
<cfset Employee.Title="President">
<cfset Employee.Department="Executive Management">
<cfset Employee.Email="pmoney@example.com">
<cfset Employee.PhoneExt="1234">

<cfoutput>
There are #StructCount(Employee)# key/value pairs in the structure.
</cfoutput>
```

StructDelete

```
StructDelete(structure, key [, indicatenotexisting])
```

Deletes *key* (and its value) from *`structure`*. Returns true regardless of success or failure unless the optional *`indicatenotexisting`* parameter is set to true. The following example deletes several keys from a structure named `Employee`:

```
<cfset Employee=StructNew( )>
<cfset Employee.Name="Pere Money">
<cfset Employee.Title="President">
<cfset Employee.Department="Executive Management">
<cfset Employee.Email="pmoney@example.com">
<cfset Employee.PhoneExt="1234">
```

```
<cfset StructDelete(Employee, "Email")>
<cfset StructDelete(Employee, "PhoneExt")>

<cfdump var="#Employee#">
```

StructFind

```
StructFind(structure, key)
```

Searches structure and returns the value for the specified key. Here's an example that searches the structure `Employee` for various keys:

```
<cfset Employee=StructNew( )>
<cfset Employee.Name="Pere Money">
<cfset Employee.Title="President">
<cfset Employee.Department="Executive Management">
<cfset Employee.Email="pmoney@example.com">
<cfset Employee.PhoneExt="1234">

<cfoutput>
Find the value of the key <b>Name</b>: #StructFind(Employee, "Name")#<br>
Find the value of the key <b>Email</b>: #StructFind(Employee, "Email")#<br>
</cfoutput>
```

StructFindKey

```
StructFindKey(top, key [, scope])
```

Searches complex structures for keys matching the *key* parameter. *top* specifies the starting point to begin the search. *key* specifies the key you want to perform the search for. *scope* is optional and may be set as either `One` or `All`, specifying the number of matching keys that should be returned. The default *scope* is `One`. `StructFindKey( )` returns an array that contains one structure for each key matched by the search. Each structure contains the following keys:

`Value`
: The value held by the found key

`Path`
: A string that can be used with other functions to reference the found key

`Owner`
: The parent object containing the found key

The following example demonstrates the use of this function on a structure containing an array of nested structures:

```
<!--- Create a structure of nested arrays containing nested structures. --->
<cfset Stock.Company = "Example.com">
<cfset Stock.Ticker = "EXAMP">

<cfset Temp = StructGet("Stock.TradeInfo[1]")>
<cfset Temp.Price = 60>
<cfset Temp.TradeDate = "6/11/02">
<cfset Temp.Volume = 750000>
```

```
<cfset Temp.Day.High = 62>
<cfset Temp.Day.Low = 59>

<cfset Temp = StructGet("Stock.TradeInfo[2]")>
<cfset Temp.Price = 63>
<cfset Temp.TradeDate = "6/12/02">
<cfset Temp.Volume = 737000>
<cfset Temp.Day.High = 66>
<cfset Temp.Day.Low = 60>

<cfset Temp = StructGet("Stock.TradeInfo[3]")>
<cfset Temp.Price = 67>
<cfset Temp.TradeDate = "6/13/02">
<cfset Temp.Volume = 1220000>
<cfset Temp.Day.High = 67>
<cfset Temp.Day.Low = 66>

<!--- change the value of KeyToFind to see how different values work --->
<cfset KeyToFind = "Price">
<cfset FindTheKey = StructFindKey(Stock, KeyToFind, "All")>

<cfoutput>
There are  #ArrayLen(FindTheKey)# keys (returned as structures) matching your
key search for &quot;<b>#KeyTofind#</b>&quot;:<p>
<!--- Loop over the array of structures returned by the search --->
<cfloop index="i" from="1" to="#ArrayLen(FindTheKey)#">
    <cfset TheStructures = FindTheKey[#i#]>
    <b>Structure #i# has the following key/value pairs:</b><br>
    <!---- Display all of the key/value pairs from each structure in array --->
    <table border="1">
    <cfloop collection="#TheStructures#" item="key" >
        <cfset Value = StructFind(TheStructures, #key#)>
        <tr><td>#key#:</td>
          <cfif IsSimpleValue(Value)><td>#Value#</td>
          <cfelseif IsStruct(Value)><td>This key's owner is a  structure</td>
          <cfelseif IsArray(Value)><td>This key's owner is an array</td>
          <cfelse><td>This key's owner is of an undetermined data type</td><br>
          </cfif>
        </tr>
    </cfloop>
    </table>
<p></cfloop>
</cfoutput>

Here's a dump of the struct:
<cfdump var="#Stock#">
```

StructFindValue

`StructFindValue(`*top*`,` *value* `[,` *scope*`])`

Searches complex structures for values matching the *value* parameter. *top* specifies the starting point to begin the search. *value* specifies the actual value you want to search for.

scope is optional and may be set as either `One` or `All`, specifying the number of matches that should be returned. The default *scope* is `One`. `StructFindValue()` returns an array containing one structure for each value matched by the search. Each structure contains the following keys:

`Key`
: The key holding the found value

`Path`
: A string that can be used with other functions to reference the found value

`Owner`
: The parent object containing the found value

Here's an example that demonstrates this function:

```
<!--- Create a structure of nested arrays containing nested structures. --->
<cfset Stock.Company = "Example.com">
<cfset Stock.Ticker = "EXAMP">

<cfset Temp = StructGet("Stock.TradeInfo[1]")>
<cfset Temp.Price = 60>
<cfset Temp.TradeDate = "6/11/02">
<cfset Temp.Volume = 750000>
<cfset Temp.Day.High = 62>
<cfset Temp.Day.Low = 59>

<cfset Temp = StructGet("Stock.TradeInfo[2]")>
<cfset Temp.Price = 63>
<cfset Temp.TradeDate = "6/12/02">
<cfset Temp.Volume = 737000>
<cfset Temp.Day.High = 66>
<cfset Temp.Day.Low = 60>

<cfset Temp = StructGet("Stock.TradeInfo[3]")>
<cfset Temp.Price = 67>
<cfset Temp.TradeDate = "6/13/02">
<cfset Temp.Volume = 1220000>
<cfset Temp.Day.High = 67>
<cfset Temp.Day.Low = 66>

<!--- Change the value of ValueToFind to see how different values work --->
<cfset ValueToFind = 60>
<cfset FindTheValue = StructFindValue(Stock, ValueToFind, "All")>

<cfoutput>
There are  #ArrayLen(FindTheValue)# keys (returned as structures) matching your
key search for &quot;<b>#ValueTofind#</b>&quot;:
<p>
<!--- Loop over the array of structures returned by the search --->
<cfloop index="i" from="1" to="#ArrayLen(FindTheValue)#">
    <cfset TheStructures = FindTheValue[#i#]>
    <b>Structure #i# has the following key/value pairs:</b><br>
    <!---- Display all of the key/value pairs from each structures in array --->
    <table border="1">
    <cfloop collection="#TheStructures#" item="key" >
        <cfset Value = StructFind(TheStructures, #key#)>
```

```
        <tr><td>#key#:</td>
          <cfif IsSimpleValue(Value)><td>#Value#</td>
          <cfelseif IsStruct(Value)><td>This key's owner is a  structure</td>
          <cfelseif IsArray(Value)><td>This key's owner is an array</td>
          <cfelse><td>This key's owner is of an undetermined data type</td><br>
          </cfif>
        </tr>
    </cfloop>
    </table>
<p></cfloop>
</cfoutput>
```

StructGet

```
StructGet("path")
```

Returns a structure (flat or nested) from the specified *path*. Allows you to create nested structures without the need for multiple `StructNew( )` calls. `StructGet( )` takes a single argument, *path*, that specifies the path to the nested structure (including XML document objects) you want to return. `StructGet( )` returns a pointer to the substructure specified as the last element in *path*. The `StructGet( )` function automatically creates all the necessary structures and substructures specified in *path* if they do not exist. The `StructGet( )` function can also be used to create nested one-dimensional arrays. The following example demonstrates the use of this function for creating a nested structure:

```
<!--- Create the Grades.Mary structure --->
<cfset temp1 = StructGet("Grades.Mary")>
<cfset temp1.Test1 = 98>
<cfset temp1.Test2 = 92>
<cfset temp1.Test3 = 100>
<cfset temp1.Test4 = 90>

<!--- Create the Grades.Tom structure --->
<cfset temp2 = StructGet("Grades.Tom")>
<cfset temp2.Test1 = 96>
<cfset temp2.Test2 = 88>
<cfset temp2.Test3 = 94>
<cfset temp2.Test4 = 90>

<cfdump var="#Grades#">
```

You can also use `StructGet( )` to return the structures from an XML document object as this example demonstrates:

```
<cfset MyEmployees = QueryNew("Name,Title")>
<cfset QueryAddRow(MyEmployees, 3)>
<cfset QuerySetCell(MyEmployees, "Name",  "Pere Money", 1)>
<cfset QuerySetCell(MyEmployees, "Title", "President", 1)>
<cfset QuerySetCell(MyEmployees, "Name",  "Aaron Ridge", 2)>
<cfset QuerySetCell(MyEmployees, "Title", "Analyst", 2)>
<cfset QuerySetCell(MyEmployees, "Name",  "Martin Grant", 3)>
<cfset QuerySetCell(MyEmployees, "Title", "Manager", 3)>

<cfset EmployeeXml = XMLNew('no')>
```

```
<cfset EmployeeXml.XmlRoot = XmlElemNew(EmployeeXml,"company")>

<cfloop index="i" from="1" to="#MyEmployees.RecordCount#">
  <cfset EmployeeXml.XmlRoot.XmlChildren[i] = XmlElemNew(EmployeeXml, "employee")>
  <cfset EmployeeXml.XmlRoot.XmlChildren[i].Name = XmlElemNew(EmployeeXml, "name")>
  <cfset EmployeeXml.XmlRoot.XmlChildren[i].Name.XmlText = MyEmployees.name[i]>
  <cfset EmployeeXml.XmlRoot.XmlChildren[i].Title = XmlElemNew(EmployeeXml, "title")>
  <cfset EmployeeXml.XmlRoot.XmlChildren[i].Title.XmlText = MyEmployees.title[i]>
</cfloop>

<cfset x=StructGet("EmployeeXml.XmlRoot.XmlChildren")>

<cfdump var="#x#">
```

StructInsert

`StructInsert(`*`structure, key, value`*` [, `*`allowoverwrite`*`])`

Inserts *key* and *value* into *structure*. Returns `Yes` if the operation is successful and `No` if it isn't. Setting the optional *allowoverwrite* parameter to `true` allows overwriting of existing keys. The default is `false`. Here's an example that inserts key/value pairs into a structure called `Employee`:

```
<cfset Employee=StructNew( )>
<cfset StructInsert(Employee, "Name", "Pere Money")>
<cfset StructInsert(Employee, "Title", "President")>
<cfset StructInsert(Employee, "Department", "Executive Management")>
<cfset StructInsert(Employee, "Email", "pmoney@example.com")>
<cfset StructInsert(Employee, "PhoneExt", "1234")>

<cfdump var="#Employee#">
```

StructIsEmpty

`StructIsEmpty(`*`structure`*`)`

Returns `true` if the specified structure contains no data or `false` if it contains data. `StructIsEmpty( )` throws an error if the specified structure does not exist, so it's generally a good idea to test for the existence of the structure first using `IsDefined( )`, before checking whether it is empty. The following example checks to see if the structure `Employee` is empty:

```
<cfset Employee=StructNew( )>
<cfset Employee.Name="Pere Money">
<cfset Employee.Title="President">
<cfset Employee.Department="Executive Management">
<cfset Employee.Email="pmoney@example.com">
<cfset Employee.PhoneExt="1234">

<cfif IsDefined('Employee')>
  <cfif StructIsEmpty(Employee)>
    The structure <b>Employee</b> is empty!
  <cfelse>
    The structure <b>Employee</b> is not empty.
  </cfif>
</cfif>
```

StructKeyArray

```
StructKeyArray(structure)
```

Returns an array containing all the keys in *structure*. StructKeyArray( ) throws an error if the specified structure does not exist, so it's generally a good idea to test for the existence of the structure first using IsDefined( ). Here's an example that lists all the keys contained in a structure called Employee:

```
<cfset Employee=StructNew( )>
<cfset Employee.Name="Pere Money">
<cfset Employee.Title="President">
<cfset Employee.Department="Executive Management">
<cfset Employee.Email="pmoney@example.com">
<cfset Employee.PhoneExt="1234">

<cfset MyKeyArray = StructKeyArray(Employee)>

<table>
  <tr><th>Key</th><th>Value</th></tr>
<cfloop index="i" from="1" to="#ArrayLen(MyKeyArray)#">
<cfoutput>
  <tr><td>#MyKeyArray[i]#</td>
    <td>#Employee[MyKeyArray[i]]#</td></tr>
</cfoutput>
</cfloop>
</table>
```

StructKeyExists

```
StructKeyExists(structure, key)
```

Checks for the existence of *key* in the specified structure. Returns true if the key exists or false if it doesn't. StructKeyExists( ) throws an error if the specified structure does not exist, so it's generally a good idea to test for the existence of the structure first using IsDefined( ). The following example checks for the existence of different keys in a structure called Employee:

```
<cfset Employee=StructNew( )>
<cfset Employee.Name="Pere Money">
<cfset Employee.Title="President">
<cfset Employee.Department="Executive Management">
<cfset Employee.Email="pmoney@example.com">
<cfset Employee.PhoneExt="1234">

<cfif StructKeyExists(Employee, "Name")>
  The key <b>Name</b> exists in the <b>Employee</b> structure.
<cfelse>
  The key <b>Name</b> doesn't exist in the <b>Employee</b> structure.
</cfif>
```

StructKeyList

`StructKeyList(structure)`

Returns a comma-delimited list containing the names of all the keys contained in *structure*. The key names are returned in all uppercase. `StructKeyList()` throws an error if the specified structure does not exist, so it's generally a good idea to test for the existence of the structure first using `IsDefined()`. Here's an example that returns a list containing the names of the keys in a structure called `Employee`:

```
<cfset Employee=StructNew( )>
<cfset Employee.Name="Pere Money">
<cfset Employee.Title="President">
<cfset Employee.Department="Executive Management">
<cfset Employee.Email="pmoney@example.com">
<cfset Employee.PhoneExt="1234">

The following keys are in the <b>Employee</b> structure:
<cfoutput>#StructKeyList(Employee)#</cfoutput>
```

StructNew

`StructNew()`

Creates a new structure. The following example creates a new structure called `Employee`:

```
<cfset Employee = StructNew( )>
```

StructSort

`StructSort(base [,sorttype, sortorder, pathtosubelement])`

Returns an array of structures with the top-level key names sorted by the subelement specified by *pathtosubelement*. *base* is a required parameter and specifies the name of the top-level structure containing the element you want to sort. *sorttype* is an optional parameter and specifies the type of sort to perform (`numeric`, `text`, or `textnocase`). *sortorder* is also optional and specifies the sort order for the operation (asc, for ascending (the default), or desc, for descending). *pathtosubelement* is optional and specifies the path (using dot notation) from the *base* to the subelement you wish to sort on. Leaving *pathtosubelement* blank results in the sort being performed on the top-level structure specified in *base*. Only substructures of structures may be specified in *pathtosubelement*. Here's an example that demonstrates the use of this function:

```
<cfset Quotes = StructNew( )>
<cfset Stocks = StructNew( )>
<!--- Populate both structures --->
<cfloop index="i" from="1" to="5">
  <cfset Price = NumberFormat((rand( )*100),'99.99')>
  <cfset Quotes["Stock#i#"] = Price>
  <cfset Stock = StructNew( )>
  <cfset Stock.Price = Price>
  <cfset Stocks["Stock#i#"] = Stock>
</cfloop>
```

```
<cfoutput>
<h2>Quote Structure</h2>
Sort Stock Name by Price (No parameters): #ArrayToList(StructSort(Quotes))#<br>
Sort Stock Name by Price (Text, desc):
  #ArrayToList(StructSort(Quotes, "Text", "desc"))#<p>
Sort Stock Name by Price(Numeric, asc):
  #ArrayToList(StructSort(Quotes, "Numeric", "asc"))#

<h2>Stocks Structure</h2>
Sort Stock Name by Price (numeric, desc, Price):
  #ArrayToList(StructSort(Stocks, "Numeric", "desc", "Price"))#<br>
</cfoutput>
```

StructUpdate

```
StructUpdate(structure, key, value)
```

Updates the specified *key* in *structure* by overwriting the existing data with *value*. The following example uses this function to update a key/value in a structure:

```
<cfset Employee=StructNew( )>
<cfset Employee.Name="Pere">
<cfset Employee.Title="President">
<cfset Employee.Department="Executive Management">
<cfset Employee.Email="pmoney@example.com">
<cfset Employee.PhoneExt="1234">

<cfset StructUpdate(Employee, "Name", "Pere Money")>

<cfdump var="#Employee#">
```

Tan

```
Tan(number)
```

Returns the tangent of an angle expressed in radians. Example:

```
The tangent of 45 is <cfoutput>#Tan(45)#</cfoutput>
```

TimeFormat

Updated in ColdFusion MX 6.1

```
TimeFormat(time [, mask])
```

Returns *time* formatted according to *mask*. If no value is specified for *mask*, `TimeFormat( )` uses the default `hh:mm tt`. Valid entries for *mask* are:

Mask	Description
h	Hours based on a 12-hour clock with no leading zeros for single-digit hours
hh	Hours based on a 12-hour clock with leading zeros for single-digit hours
H	Hours based on a 24-hour clock with no leading zeros for single-digit hours
HH	Hours based on a 24-hour clock with leading zeros for single-digit hours
m	Minutes with no leading zero for single-digit minutes

Mask	Description
mm	Minutes with a leading zero for single-digit minutes
s	Seconds with no leading zero for single-digit seconds
ss	Seconds with a leading zero for single-digit seconds
l	Milliseconds with no leading zeros for single or double-digit milliseconds
t	Single-character meridian, either A or p
tt	Multicharacter meridian, either AM or PM
short	Java short time format
medium	Java medium time format
long	Java long time format
full	Java full date format:

If an invalid mask is passed to the function, ColdFusion outputs the invalid characters. Examples:

```
<cfset TheTime = Now()>

<cfoutput>
TheTime = #TimeFormat(TheTime,'hh:mm:ss tt')#<p>

TimeFormat(TheTime, 'h:m:s'): #TimeFormat(TheTime, 'h:m:s')#<br>
TimeFormat(TheTime, 'h:m:s t'): #TimeFormat(TheTime, 'h:m:s t')#<br>
TimeFormat(TheTime, 'hh:mm:ss'): #TimeFormat(TheTime, 'hh:mm:ss')#<br>
TimeFormat(TheTime, 'hh:mm:ss tt'): #TimeFormat(TheTime, 'hh:mm:ss tt')#<br>
TimeFormat(TheTime, 'H:M:ss'): #TimeFormat(TheTime, 'H:M:s')#<br>
TimeFormat(TheTime, 'HH:MM:ss'): #TimeFormat(TheTime, 'HH:MM:ss')#<br>
<p>
And these formats are new in ColdFusion MX:<br>
short: #TimeFormat(TheTime, 'short')#<br>
medium: #TimeFormat(TheTime, 'medium')#<br>
long: #TimeFormat(TheTime, 'long')#<br>
full: #TimeFormat(TheTime,'full')#<br>
</cfoutput>
```

ToBase64

```
ToBase64(value)
```

Base64 encodes a binary object or string. Base64 is an encoding scheme that uses printable characters to represent binary data. Base64 is typically used to encode binary data before it is sent via email or stored in a database. Here's an example that reads in a binary file using `cffile` and encodes it using `ToBase64()`:

```
<cffile action="ReadBinary" FILE="D:/mydir/myfile.gif" VARIABLE="MyBinaryFile">

<cfset MyBase64 = ToBase64(MyBinaryFile)>

<cfoutput>Base64: #MyBase64#</cfoutput>
```

ToBinary

```
ToBinary(value)
```

Converts a base64-encoded string to its binary form. The following example take a base64-encoded string (in this case a GIF image of the letter R), converts it to a binary object using `ToBinary( )`, writes the object out to a file, and then displays it using `cfcontent`:

```
<cfset MyBase64="R0lGODlhGQAZAPcAAP////v7+/Pz8+7u7uLi4t3d3dnZ2dXV1cTExLe3t6qqqp6e
npGRkYmJiYiIiH9/f3t7e25ubmZmZllZWVZWVlFRUURERDw8PDQ0NC8vLyIiIhUVFREREQwMDAQEBAAAA
AAAAAAAAAAAAAAAAAAAAAAAAAAAAAAAAAAAAAAAAAAAAAAAAAAAAAAAAAAAAAAAAAAAAAAAAAAAAAAAAA
AAAAAAAAAAAAAAAAAAAAAAAAAAAAAAAAAAAAAAAAAAAAAAAAAAAAAAAAAAAAAAAAAAAAAAAAAAAAAAAAA
AAAAAAAAAAAAAAAAAAAAAAAAAAAAAAAAAAAAAAAAAAAAAAAAAAAAAAAAAAAAAAAAAAAAAAAAAAAAAAAAA
AAAAAAAAAAAAAAAAAAAAAAAAAAAAAAAAAAAAAAAAAAAAAAAAAAAAAAAAAAAAAAAAAAAAAAAAAAAAAAAAA
AAAAAAAAAAAAAAAAAAAAAAAAAAAAAAAAAAAAAAAAAAAAAAAAAAAAAAAAAAAAAAAAAAAAAAAAAAAAAAAAA
AAAAAAAAAAAAAAAAAAAAAAAAAAAAAAAAAAAAAAAAAAAAAAAAAAAAAAAAAAAAAAAAAAAAAAAAAAAAAAAAA
AAAAAAAAAAAAAAAAAAAAAAAAAAAAAAAAAAAAAAAAAAAAAAAAAAAAAAAAAAAAAAAAAAAAAAAAAAAAAAAAA
AAAAAAAAAAAAAAAAAAAAAAAAAAAAAAAAAAAAAAAAAAAAAAAAAAAAAAAAAAAAAAAAAAAAAAAAAAAAAAAAA
AAAAAAAAAAAAAAAAAAAAAAAAAAAAAAAAAAAAAAAAAAAAAAAAAAAAAAAAAAAAAAAAAAAAAAAAAAAAAAAAA
AAAAAAAAAAAAAAAAAAAAAAAAAAAAAAAAAAAAAAAAAAAAAAAAAAAAAAAAAAAAAAAAAAAAAAAAAAAAAAAAA
AAAAAAAAAAAAAAAAAAAAAAAAAAAAAAAAAAAAAAAAAAAAAAAAAAAAAAAAAAAAAAAAAAAAAAAAAAAAAAAAA
AAAAACwAAAAAGQAZAEcIiwABCBxIsKDBgwQffPigAIHDBh4+YEBoUOGHAgMlLHRAsaPHjyApWlxI8sMEA
SFTqlwpkIGGlzAxUECQ0iLGgRc+cAhpE4CBDR86HKi58KbABQsrsFzKtKlTkCNLfvCQgGdRghUWWv0Q4c
EDCBYWRthaoQKHoFWJXhSYYGGGAFuNDgDagcDTu3gpBgQA0w= =">

<cfset MyBinary=ToBinary(MyBase64)>

<cffile action="write" file="c:\inetpub\wwwroot\mybinary.gif" output=#MyBinary#>

<cfcontent type="image/gif" file="c:\inetpub\wwwroot\mybinary.gif"
          deletefile="Yes">
```

ToString

```
ToString( )
```

Converts any datatype, including binary, to a string. If *value* can't be converted, an exception is thrown. Example:

```
<cfset MyString="Have a nice day!">
<cfset Base64String = ToBase64(MyString)>
<cfset BinaryString = ToBinary(Base64String)>
<cfset BackToString = ToString(BinaryString)>
<cfoutput>
MyString: #MyString#<br>
Base64String: #Base64String#<br>
BackToString: #BackToString#<br>
</cfoutput>
```

Trim

```
Trim(string)
```

Removes all leading and trailing spaces from a string. Example:

```
<cfset OriginalString = "      ColdFusion      ">

<cfoutput>
<b>Original String (quoted):</b> "#OriginalString#"<br>
<b>Trimmed String (quoted):</b> "#Trim(OriginalString)#"
</cfoutput>
```

Ucase

```
Ucase(string)
```

Converts a string to uppercase. Example:

```
<cfset MyString="i want this string to appear in all uppercase.">

<cfoutput>#Ucase(MyString)#</cfoutput>
```

URLDecode

Updated in ColdFusion MX 6.1

```
URLDecode(URLEncodedString [, CharacterSet])
```

Decodes a URL-encoded string. An optional Java character set for the encoded string may be specified. Depending on your JRE, options typically include `UTF-8`, `UTF-16`, `UTF-16BE`, `UTF-16LE`, `US-ASCII`, and `ISO-8859-1`. If no character set is specified, ColdFusion defaults to the character encoding of the URL scope. URL-encoded strings have all nonalphanumeric characters replaced with their equivalent hexadecimal escape sequences. Both `%20` and the plus sign (+) are treated as spaces. Here's an example that takes a URL-encoded string and decodes it:

```
<cfset MyString="Why is the sky blue?">
<cfset EncodedString=URLEncodedFormat(MyString)>
<cfset DecodedString=URLDecode(EncodedString)>

<cfoutput>
Original String: #MyString#<br>
URL Encoded: #EncodedString#<br>
Decoded: #DecodedString#
</cfoutput>
```

URLEncodedFormat

Updated in ColdFusion MX 6.1

```
URLEncodedFormat(string [, CharacterSet])
```

Encodes strings that otherwise cause errors when passed as URLs. Optionally, a Java character set for the string to be encoded can be specified. Depending on the server's JRE, options typically include `UTF-8`, `UTF-16`, `UTF-16BE`, `UTF-16LE`, `US-ASCII`, and `ISO-8859-1`. If no character set is specified, ColdFusion defaults to the response character encoding. `URLEncodedFormat()` replaces nonalphanumeric characters with their equivalent hexadecimal escape sequences. ColdFusion automatically decodes any URL-escaped strings it encounters. The following example creates a URL-encoded hyperlink from a string containing spaces and nonalphanumeric characters:

```
<cfset TheDate = "04/15/2003">
<cfset ItemID = "123456">
```

```
<cfset Customer = "Caroline Smith">

Click on the link below to check-out:<br>
<p><cfoutput>
<a href="http://www.myserver.com/index.cfm?TheDate=#UrlEncodedFormat(TheDate)#&
ItemID=#UrlEncodedFormat(ItemID)#&Customer=#UrlEncodedFormat(Customer)#">Check-out
</a>
</cfoutput>
```

URLSessionFormat

New in ColdFusion MX

```
URLSessionFormat(url)
```

If the client does not accept cookies, `URLSessionFormat()` appends appropriate client identification parameters (`CFID`, `CFToken`, `jsessionid`) to the end of the specified URL. Otherwise, the URL is returned as is. This function provides similar functionality to the `addtoken` attribute of the `cflocation` tag. However, `URLSessionFormat()` is more powerful and versatile in that it only appends identification information in the event a client does not support cookies. Additionally, `URLSessionFormat()` can be used anywhere a URL is coded, whereas `cflocation` is only used to redirect a user to another location. Here's an example that uses `URLSessionFormat()` to create a link that passes identification parameters only if your browser doesn't support cookies:

```
<cfoutput>
<a href="#URLSessionFormat("checkout.cfm")#">Check Out</a>
</cfoutput>
```

Val

```
Val(string)
```

Returns a number that the beginning of the specified string can be converted to. If conversion isn't possible, returns 0. Examples:

```
<cfoutput>
Val(123): #Val(123)#<br>
Val('abc'): #Val('abc')#<br>
Val('1a2b3c'): #Val('1a2b3c')#<br>
Val(true): #Val(true)#<br>
Val(11/11/02): #Val(11/11/02)#<br>
</cfoutput>
```

ValueList

```
ValueList(queryname.column [,delimiter])
```

Returns a comma-separated list of values for the previously executed query column specified in `queryname.column`. An optional delimiter can be specified if the list is to be delimited with a character other than the comma (the default). The following example creates a value list from a ColdFusion query:

```
<cfquery name="MyQuery" datasource="ProgrammingCF">
  SELECT * FROM EmployeeDirectory
```

```
</cfquery>

<cfoutput>
<b>The query column Name contains the following values:</b>
#ValueList(MyQuery.Name)#
</cfoutput>
```

Week

```
Week(date)
```

Returns the week of the year for a given date as a number between 1 and 53. Example:

```
The current week is week <cfoutput>#Week(Now( ))#</cfoutput>.
```

Wrap

New in ColdFusion MX 6.1

```
Wrap(string, limit [,strip])
```

Specifies the maximum number of characters to allow per line in *string*. If a line is longer than the specified number of characters, an attempt is made to break the line by inserting a line break at the nearest whitespace character (space, tab, etc) before the character limit. If *string* contains no whitespace characters before the maximum number of characters per line, a line break is inserted at the maximum line length. `Wrap()` uses operating system specific line breaks. On Windows, it's a carriage return and newline character. On Unix/Linux, it's a newline. Optionally, you can specify a third Boolean argument to indicate whether to remove all existing carriage line breaks before wrapping the string. The default for this argument is false.

```
<cfset myString="This is a string that is so long, I probably would like to break
 it up.  What do you think about that?  Is it a good idea?">

<cfoutput>
<pre>#Wrap(myString, 80, False)#</pre>
</cfoutput>
```

WriteOutput

```
WriteOutput(string)
```

Writes text to the page output stream. `WriteOutput( )` is meant to be used inside `cfscript` blocks but can also be used inside `cfoutput` sections. Examples:

```
<cfscript>
WriteOutput('The WriteOutput function works best inside cfscript blocks<br>');
</cfscript>

<cfoutput>
#WriteOutput('Although you can use it in cfoutput spaces, why would you?')#
</cfoutput>
```

XmlChildPos

New in ColdFusion MX

`XmlChildPos(element, childName, N)`

Returns the index position of the Nth occurrence of *childName* within an XmlChildren array in an XML document object. If no *childName* is found in the specified position, –1 is returned. The following example parses an XML feed from *macromedia.com* into an XML document object, then returns the index position of the fifth occurrence of the "resource" child:

```
<cfhttp URL="http://www.macromedia.com/devnet/resources/macromedia_resources.xml"
        method="Get">

<cfset DesDev = XmlParse(cfhttp.FileContent)>

<cfset x = XmlChildPos(DesDev.Macromedia_Resources, "resource", 5)>

<cfoutput>
#x#
</cfoutput>
```

XmlElemNew

New in ColdFusion MX

`XmlElemNew(XmlDocObj, ChildName)`

Creates an empty child element in the specified XML document object. The following example creates a new element named `Company` in an XML document object called `EmployeeXML`. The XML document object is then output to the browser using `cfdump`:

```
<cfset EmployeeXml = XMLNew('no')>
<cfset EmployeeXml.XmlRoot = XmlElemNew(EmployeeXml,"company")>

<cfdump var="#EmployeeXml#">
```

XmlFormat

New in ColdFusion 4.5

`XMLFormat(string)`

Returns *string* in a format that is safe to use with XML by escaping the following special characters: ampersands (&), double quotes ("), greater-than signs (>), less-than signs (<), and single quotes ('). Example:

```
<cfset MyString="Here is an example of the XMLFormat function: 5+5<20">

<cfoutput>#XMLFormat(MyString)#</cfoutput>

<p><I>View the page source to see the escaped text.</I>
```

XmlNew

New in ColdFusion MX

`XmlNew([case_sensitive])`

Creates an empty XML document object. An optional `Yes`/`No` parameter lets you specify whether XML document elements should maintain their case. The default is `No`. The following example creates an XML document object and populates it with the contents of a query object:

```
<cfset MyEmployees = QueryNew("Name,Title")>
<cfset QueryAddRow(MyEmployees, 3)>
<cfset QuerySetCell(MyEmployees, "Name",  "Pere Money", 1)>
<cfset QuerySetCell(MyEmployees, "Title", "President", 1)>
<cfset QuerySetCell(MyEmployees, "Name",  "Aaron Ridge", 2)>
<cfset QuerySetCell(MyEmployees, "Title", "Analyst", 2)>
<cfset QuerySetCell(MyEmployees, "Name",  "Martin Grant", 3)>
<cfset QuerySetCell(MyEmployees, "Title", "Manager", 3)>

<cfset EmployeeXml = XMLNew('no')>
<cfset EmployeeXml.XmlRoot = XmlElemNew(EmployeeXml,"company")>

<cfloop index="i" from="1" to="#MyEmployees.RecordCount#">
  <cfset EmployeeXml.XmlRoot.XmlChildren[i] = XmlElemNew(EmployeeXml, "employee")>
  <cfset EmployeeXml.XmlRoot.XmlChildren[i].Name = XmlElemNew(EmployeeXml, "name")>
  <cfset EmployeeXml.XmlRoot.XmlChildren[i].Name.XmlText = MyEmployees.name[i]>
  <cfset EmployeeXml.XmlRoot.XmlChildren[i].Title = XmlElemNew(EmployeeXml, "title")>
  <cfset EmployeeXml.XmlRoot.XmlChildren[i].Title.XmlText = MyEmployees.title[i]>
</cfloop>

<cfdump var="#EmployeeXml#">
```

XmlParse

New in ColdFusion MX

```
XmlParse(XML_string [, case_sensitive])
```

Converts an XML string to a ColdFusion XML document object. Setting the optional *case_sensitive* parameter to Yes causes ColdFusion to maintain the original case of the XML document elements and attributes. The default value for *case_sensitive* is No. The following example retrieves an XML file from the Macromedia web site and parses it into a ColdFusion XML document object:

```
<cfhttp URL="http://www.macromedia.com/devnet/resources/macromedia_resources.xml"
        method="Get">

<cfset DesDev = XmlParse(cfhttp.FileContent)>

<cfdump var="#devnet#">
```

Note that XML encoded in character sets other than ASCII or Latin-1 must have the character set explicitly defined to ColdFusion. If you are using the cffile tag to read an XML file, the character set can be defined using the charset parameter of the cffile tag. If the XML file is retrieved via another method, it may be necessary to first change the encoding.

XmlSearch

New in ColdFusion MX

```
XmlSearch(XmlDocObj, XPath_exp)
```

Searches the specified ColdFusion XML document object using an XPath expression. If a successful match is made, the function returns an array of XML document object nodes that match the search criteria. The following example reads in an XML news feed from *macromedia.com*, parses it into an XML document object, uses XPath to return only the XML nodes containing tutorials, and outputs the results to the browser:

```
<cfhttp URL="http://www.macromedia.com/devnet/resources/macromedia_resources.xml"
        method="Get">

<cfset DesDev = XmlParse(cfhttp.FileContent)>
<cfset SearchResults = XmlSearch(DesDev, "/macromedia_resources/resource[attribute::
type='Tutorial']")>

<h2>Available Tutorials</h2>
<cfloop index="i" from="1" to="#ArrayLen(SearchResults)#">
  <cfoutput>
  <a href="#SearchResults[i].URL.XmlText#">#SearchResults[i].Title.XmlText#</a><br>
  </cfoutput>
</cfloop>
```

For more information on XPath, see *http://www.w3.org/TR/xpath/* or *XML in a Nutshell*, 2nd Ed. by Elliotte Rusty Harold and W. Scott Means (O'Reilly).

XmlTransform

New in ColdFusion MX

```
XmlTransform(XmlString|XmlDocObj, XslString)
```

Performs an XSLT (eXtensible Stylesheet Language Transformation) on an XML string or document object using an XSL (eXtensible Style Language) string. The results are returned as a string. The following example reads in an XML document containing employee names and titles:

```
<?xml version='1.0' standalone='yes'?>
<company>
  <employee>
    <name>Pere Money</name>
    <title>President</title>
  </employee>
  <employee>
    <name>Aaron Ridge</name>
    <title>Analyst</title>
  </employee>
  <employee>
    <name>Martin Grant</name>
    <title>Manager</title>
  </employee>
</company>
```

The example then reads in a simple XSL file for formatting the XML as HTML:

```
<xsl:stylesheet
  xmlns:xsl="http://www.w3.org/1999/XSL/Transform"
  version="1.0">
  <xsl:output method="html"/>

  <xsl:template match="/company">
    <html>
      <head>
```

```
        <title>Employees</title>
      </head>
      <body>
      <table border="1">
        <tr>
          <th>Name</th>
          <th>Title</th>
        </tr>
      <xsl:apply-templates select="employee"/>
      </table>
      </body>
    </html>
  </xsl:template>

  <xsl:template match="employee">
    <tr>
      <td><xsl:value-of select="name"/></td>
      <td><xsl:value-of select="title"/></td>
    </tr>
  </xsl:template>
</xsl:stylesheet>
```

Finally, the XML is transformed using XmlTransform( ), and the resulting HTML table is output to the browser:

```
<cffile action="read" file="d:\cfusionmx\wwwroot\programmingcf\b\employee.xml"
        variable="MyXml">

<cffile action="read" file="d:\cfusionmx\wwwroot\programmingcf\b\employee.xsl"
        variable="MyXsl">

<cfset Transformed = XmlTransform(MyXml, MyXsl)>

<cfoutput>
#Transformed#
</cfoutput>
```

For more information on XSLT and XSL, see *http://www.w3.org/TR/xslt/* and *http://www.w3.org/TR/xsl/* respectively, or *XSLT* by Doug Tidwell (O'Reilly).

Year

```
Year(date)
```

Returns the year as a number for the given date. Example:

```
The current year is <cfoutput>#Year(Now( ))#</cfoutput>.
```

YesNoFormat

```
YesNoFormat(value)
```

Returns all nonzero values as Yes and zero values as No. Also returns a Boolean true as Yes and a Boolean false as No.

```
<cfoutput>
-1: #YesNoFormat(-1)#<br>
```

```
-1.123: #YesNoFormat(-1.123)#<br>
-0.123: #YesNoFormat(-0.123)#<br>
0: #YesNoFormat(0)#<br>
0.123: #YesNoFormat(0.123)#<br>
1: #YesNoFormat(1)#<br>
1.123: #YesNoFormat(1.123)#<br>
true: #YesNoFormat(true)#<br>
false: #YesNoFormat(false)#
</cfoutput>
```

APPENDIX C

Example Database Tables

The examples used throughout this book reference several database tables. The schemas and data for these tables are listed in this appendix. Because of its low cost, wide availability, and ease of use, all tables were designed using Microsoft Access. Because Access is a desktop database, I don't recommend using it in production environments, especially where many concurrent users are expected to use the database. Access isn't designed for heavy concurrent use and may experience scalability and performance issues if placed under load. Additionally, there are limits on the amount of data that can reliably be stored in an Access database.

For production applications, I recommend you use an enterprise-level database, such as Microsoft SQL Server, Oracle, DB2, Informix, Sybase, MySQL, or PostgreSQL. These databases provide advanced features and functionality, such as stored procedures and triggers, and are specially tuned for handling multiple concurrent requests and massive amounts of data.

Table C-1 lists the schema for the `EmployeeDirectory` table that is used throughout the book, while Table C-2 lists the actual data.

Table C-1. EmployeeDirectory table schema

Field name	Field type	Max length
ID (primary key)	AutoNumber	N/A
Name	Text	255
Title	Text	255
Department	Memo	N/A
Email	Date/Time	N/A
PhoneExt	Number (long int)	N/A
Salary	Number (double, two decimal places)	N/A
Picture	Memo	N/A

Table C-2. EmployeeDirectory table data

ID	Name	Title	Department	Email	Phone Ext	Salary
1	Pere Money	President	Executive Mgmt	*pere@example.com*	1234	400,000
2	Greg Corcoran	Director	Marketing	*greg@example.com*	1237	96,000
3	Mark Edward	VP	Sales	*mark@example.com*	1208	155,000
4	Marcel Haney	Engineer I	Product Engineering	*marcel@example.com*	1296	86,000
5	Brian Christopher	Junior Accountant	Finance	*brian@example.com*	1211	40,000
6	Nick Gosnell	Risk Mgmt Analyst	Finance	*nick@example.com*	1223	54,000
7	Hugo Keane	Sr. Account Manager	Sales	*hugo@example.com*	1214	100,000
8	Chaz Maxwell	Engineer II	Product Engineering	*chaz@example.com*	1287	78,000
9	Kris Moritz	Network Manager	IT	*kris@example.com*	1254	65,000
10	Aaron Ridge	Analyst	IT	*aaron@example.com*	1233	68,000
11	Tareq Varga	Sr. Analyst	IT	*tareq@example.com*	1278	76,000
12	Jeff Shields	Marcom Manager	Marketing	*jeff@example.com*	1282	63,000
13	Martin Grant	Manager	Business Develop	*martin@example.com*	1215	57,000
14	Curt Bond	VP	Investor Relations	*curt@example.com*	1256	125,000
15	Ray Roy	Instructor	Training	*ray@example.com*	1276	42,000
16	Rob Tyler	Manager	Training	*rob@example.com*	1290	70,000
17	Andie Moore	Director	HR	*andie@example.com*	1241	84,000
18	Jen Newton	Benefits Coordinator	HR	*jen@example.com*	1283	41,000
19	David Holmes	Market Analyst	Investor Relations	*david@example.com*	1225	76,000
20	Christine Booker	Account Manager	Sales	*christine@example.com*	1262	80,000

Table C-3 lists the schema for the `IncentiveAwards` table that is used in Chapter 11, while Table C-4 lists the actual data.

Table C-3. IncentiveAwards table schema

Field name	Field type	Maxlength
ID (foreign key)	Number (long int)	N/A
DateAwarded	Date	N/A
Category	Text	255
Amount	Number (double, two decimal places)	N/A

Table C-4. IncentiveAwards table data

ID	Date awarded	Category	Amount ($)
1	2/15/01	Referral	5000
2	7/12/01	Referral	5000
3	4/3/01	Sales goal	3000
3	7/12/01	Sales goal	3000
3	10/3/01	Sales goal	3000
4	6/23/01	Patent award	8000
4	2/4/02	Referral	5000
5	3/17/01	Referral	5000
5	1/10/02	Perfect attendance	500
6	9/14/01	Referral	5000
7	12/19/01	Account growth	4000
8	4/29/01	Leadership achievement	500
8	1/5/02	Patent award	8000
9	8/1/01	Employee contest	500
10	11/4/01	Anniversary	200
11	3/29/02	Referral	5000
12	5/7/03	Anniversary	200
13	2/4/03	Account growth	2000
14	7/8/02	Referral	5000
15	11/17/02	Leadership achievement	500
16	1/10/03	Perfect attendance	500
24	2/15/03	Sales Goal	2000
24	5/1/03	Referral	5000
25	7/23/03	Anniversary	200

Table C-5 lists the schema for the `Links` table that is used in Chapter 10, while Table C-6 lists the actual data.

Table C-5. Links table schema

Field name	Field type	Max length
ItemID (primary key)	AutoNumber	N/A
ParentItemID	Numeric	N/A
ItemName	Text	255
LinkURL	Text	255

Table C-6. Links table data

ItemID	ParentItemID	ItemName	LinkURL
1	0	Financial	
2	1	Brokers	
3	2	E*Trade	*http://www.etrade.com*
4	2	Ameritrade	*http://www.ameritrade.com*
5	1	Banks	
6	5	PNC Bank	*http://www.pncbank.com*
7	5	Wilmington Trust Bank	*http://www.wilmingtontrust.com*
8	0	Computers	
9	8	Software	
10	8	Hardware	
11	9	Macromedia	*http://www.macromedia.com*
12	9	Microsoft	*http://www.microsoft.com*
13	9	IBM	*http://www.ibm.com*
14	9	Sun Microsystems	*http://www.sun.com*
15	10	Cisco	*http://www.cisco.com*
16	10	Intel	*http://www.intel.com*
17	10	HP	*http://www.hp.com*

ColdFusion Resources

This appendix lists sources of additional information about ColdFusion. One of the great things about ColdFusion is the wide variety of available information, from official Macromedia resources to community-related material. The majority of resources listed in this appendix are available free of charge and were created by developers for developers.

Official Macromedia Resources

The following table lists the ColdFusion web sites that are maintained by Macromedia. These sites should be among your first stops when searching for information on ColdFusion.

Beta site	*http://mmbeta.macromedia.com*
Certification program	*http://www.macromedia.com/support/training/certified_professional_program/*
Macromedia DevNet	*http://www.macromedia.com/devnet/*
Product Updaters	*http://www.macromedia.com/support/coldfusion/downloads_updates.html*
Hot Fixes	*http://www.macromedia.com/support/coldfusion/ts/documents/tn17883.htm*
ColdFusion MX Documentation Additions	*http://www.macromedia.com/support/coldfusion/ts/documents/tn18228.htm*
ColdFusion MX Documentation Updates	*http://www.macromedia.com/support/coldfusion/ts/documents/tn18196.htm*
ColdFusion MX LiveDocs	*http://livedocs.macromedia.com/cfmxdocs/*
ColdFusion MX Release Notes	*http://www.macromedia.com/support/coldfusion/releasenotes/mx/releasenotes_mx.html*
ColdFusion Support Center	*http://www.macromedia.com/support/coldfusion/*
ColdFusion Support Forums	*http://webforums.macromedia.com/coldfusion/*
ColdFusion Exchange	*http://www.macromedia.com/cfusion/exchange/index.cfm?view=sn130*
Events	*http://www.macromedia.com/v1/company/events/*
FAQ	*http://www.macromedia.com/software/coldfusion/productinfo/faq/*
Macromedia Web Site	*http://www.macromedia.com/*

TechNote Index	*http://www.macromedia.com/support/coldfusion/technotes.html*
Tutorial & Article Index	*http://www.macromedia.com/support/coldfusion/tutorial_index.html*

Magazines

Several quality magazines dedicated to ColdFusion, both online and print, have popped up over the last few years. The following table lists the more popular.

CF Advisor	*http://www.cfadvisor.com/*
ColdFusion Developer's Journal	*http://www.sys-con.com/coldfusion/*
ColdFusion Monthly	*http://www.coldfusionmonthly.com/*
Defusion	*http://www.defusion.com/*
The Fusion Authority	*http://www.fusionauthority.com/*

Mailing Lists

Several popular email lists exist for the discussion of ColdFusion and related topics. By far the most popular list is the House of Fusion's CF-Talk list. In fact, House of Fusion hosts over a dozen ColdFusion related mailing lists. The following table lists several of the more popular mailing lists along with links to subscription information. Many additional ColdFusion User Groups have mailing lists which may not be mentioned here.

CF-Talk, CF-RegEx, CF-Community, CF-Jobs-Talk, Spectra-Talk, Fusebox-Co-Op, CF-Partners, CF-Server, CF-Linux, CF-Jobs, CF-XML, SQL, CF-OpenSource, Fusebox, FB-Community, CF-Stock, Studio, and more...	*http://www.houseoffusion.com/cf_lists/*
CFCDev	*http://www.cfczone.org/listserv.cfm*
CFDJList	*http://www.sys-con.com/coldfusion/list.cfm*
ColdFusion-HowTo	*http://groups.yahoo.com/group/coldfusion-howto/*
AZCFUG	*http://www.azcfug.org/*
BACFUG-L	*http://www.bacfug.org/*
CFUGCNY	*http://www.cfugcny.org/news/?storyID=99*
L-CFUG-SC	*http://www.cfug-sc.org/resources.cfm*
PACFUG	*http://www.pacfug.org/listserv.cfm*
RICFUG	*http://www.ricfug.com/www/news2.cfm?recid=19*
NCFUG	*http://www.ncfug.org/index.cfm?method=mailinglist*

Blogs

As blogging continues to grow, a decent number of high quality ColdFusion related blogs are popping up all over the place. Rather than list them individually here and risk leaving someone out, I suggest checking out the two most popular ColdFusion related blog aggregators. For those of you unfamiliar with blog aggregators, they are a place you can go that displays the contents of multiple blogs in a single interface. The two most popular are Full As A Goog, run by Geoff Bowers and available at *http://www.fullasagoog.com*, and MXNA, run by Macromedia and available at *http://www.markme.com/mxna/index.cfm*.

Community Resources

The sites listed in the following table contain a vast array of ColdFusion-related resources. Many sites provide free code samples, custom tags, tips and tricks, and newsletters. Most resources are free and supported by ColdFusion developers.

BlackBox	*http://www.black-box.org/*
CF Comet	*http://www.cfcomet.com/*
CFConf.org	*http://www.cfconf.org/*
CFCZone.org	*http://www.cfczone.org/*
CFDev.com	*http://www.cfdev.com/*
CFDevX.com	*http://www.cfdevx.com/*
CFFaq	*http://www.cffaq.com*
CFHub.com	*http://www.coldfusionhub.com/*
CFM!Central.com	*http://www.cfmcentral.com/*
CFMentor (Italian)	*http://www.cfmentor.com/*
CFnewbie?com	*http://www.cfnewbie.com/*
CFXtras	*http://www.cfxtras.com/*
CFM-Resources	*http://www.cfm-resources.com/*
CFNewbie	*http://www.cfnewbie.com/*
cfObjects	*http://www.cfobjects.com/*
CFTipsPlus.com	*http://www.cftipsplus.com/*
CFVault.com	*http://www.cfvault.com/*
CFXchange	*http://www.cfxchange.com/*
CodeBits	*http://www.codebits.com/*
ColdCuts	*http://www.teratech.com/coldcuts/*
ColdFusion FAQ	*http://www.thenetprofits.co.uk/coldfusion/faq/*
ColdFusion Tips-N-Tricks	*http://209.236.1.64/CF_tipsNtricks/*
CoolFusion	*http://www.coolfusion.com/*

Common Function Library Project	*http://www.cflib.org/*
FlashCFM.com	*http://www.flashcfm.com/*
Forta.com	*http://www.forta.com/*
Four-Runner.com	*http://www.four-runners.com/*
Fusebox	*http://www.fusebox.org/*
Fusion Directa (Spain)	*http://www.fusiondirecta.com.ar/*
HalHelms.com	*http://www.halhelms.com/*
House of Fusion	*http://www.houseoffusion.com/*
Intrafoundation Software	*http://www.intrafoundation.com/freeware.html*
MaxFusion	*http://www.maxfusion.co.uk/*
OBJECT-fuse	*http://www.it-fuse.com*
OpenWDDX.org	*http://www.openwddx.org/*
OraFusion.com	*http://www.orafusion.com/*
Situs Pengguna (Indonesia)	*http://www.coldfusion.web.id/*
SysteManage	*http://www.systemanage.com/*
WebTricks	*http://www.webtricks.com/*

User Groups

ColdFusion user groups (CFUGs) and Macromedia user groups (MMUGs) are a great way to learn more about ColdFusion and other Macromedia products and to share your experiences with other developers. CFUGs and MMUGs are officially sanctioned by Macromedia and provide a forum for learning about the latest ColdFusion and Macromedia-related technologies and techniques. New CFUGs and MMUGs are forming all the time, and as of this writing, there are over 200 worldwide. For the most up-to-date information on CFUGs and MMUGs, see Macromedia's web site at *http://www.macromedia.com/v1/usergroups/*.

Index

Symbols

A

We'd like to hear your suggestions for improving our indexes. Send email to *index@oreilly.com*.

B

C

D

E

F

G

H

I

J

K

L

M

N

O

Q

R

S

T

U

V

W

X

Y

About the Author

Rob Brooks-Bilson is a freelance writer and a senior technology manager at Amkor Technology, where he has worked since 1996. Rob's involvement with ColdFusion goes all the way back to version 1.5 and includes several large-scale projects, the creation of numerous open source custom tags, and, more recently, CFLib.org and CFCzone.org where along with Raymond Camden, he coordinates several libraries of freely available functions and CFCs. He has written several articles on ColdFusion for Macromedia, *Intranet Design Magazine*, CFAdvisor, O'Reilly, and CNET's Builder.com. Rob is a frequent speaker at ColdFusion user groups and conferences and is also a Team Macromedia member as well as a Macromedia Certified Advanced ColdFusion Developer.

Although he still considers himself a Delawarean, Rob recently relocated to Phoenix, Arizona, where he lives with his lovely and talented wife. Rob can be reached at *rbils@amkor.com*.

Colophon

Our look is the result of reader comments, our own experimentation, and feedback from distribution channels. Distinctive covers complement our distinctive approach to technical topics, breathing personality and life into potentially dry subjects.

The animal on the cover of *Programming ColdFusion MX*, Second Edition is an Arctic tern. Arctic terns (*Sterna paradisaea*) are small birds, about 12 to 15 inches long, that make the longest migration of any avian on Earth. They breed in the Arctic tundra but fly to the edge of the Antarctic ice pack during the winter. An Arctic tern flies over 21,750 miles each year; it spends most of its life, about 20 years, flying.

The Arctic tern has webbed feet. The tail is long and forked, the legs are short and red, and the head is rounded and white with a black cap and a bright orange beak. Research has shown that Arctic terns don't swim well and will do everything possible to stay out of the water. Even though their feet are webbed, they are small, so the birds swoop down, catch a fish, and eat it while flying.

During breeding or courtship time, male terns fly a "fish flight." A male takes a small fish in its bill and passes as low as it can over a female on the ground. If she notices, she'll join him in the fish flight, and they soon mate.

In Arctic breeding grounds, females lay one or two cream-colored eggs with brown speckles (1.6 inches long). The eggs are laid in a grassy area for protection from their predators and because there are no trees in the Arctic. Both parents care for the eggs and feed the hatchlings.

Local inhabitants watch to see where Arctic terns are feeding. By monitoring where the terns hunt, they can find large schools of fish and increase their catch.

Darren Kelly was the production editor, and Leanne Soylemez was the copyeditor for *Programming ColdFusion MX*, Second Edition. Mary Brady, Derek Di Matteo, and Claire Cloutier provided quality control. Nancy Crumpton wrote the index. Jamie Peppard, Matt Hutchinson, and Reg Aubry provided production assistance.

Hanna Dyer designed the cover of this book, based on a series design by Edie Freedman. The cover image is an original illustration created by Lorrie LeJeune. Emma Colby produced the cover layout with QuarkXPress 4.1 using Adobe's ITC Garamond font.

David Futato designed the interior layout. This book was converted by Joe Wizda to FrameMaker 5.5.6 with a format conversion tool created by Erik Ray, Jason McIntosh, Neil Walls, and Mike Sierra that uses Perl and XML technologies. The text font is Linotype Birka; the heading font is Adobe Myriad Condensed; and the code font is LucasFont's TheSans Mono Condensed. The illustrations that appear in the book were produced by Robert Romano and Jessamyn Read using Macromedia FreeHand 9 and Adobe Photoshop 6. This colophon was written by Mary Anne Weeks Mayo.